Foreigners in European Prisons

Foreigners in European Prisons

Edited by:

A.M. van Kalmthout,
F.B.A.M. Hofstee-van der Meulen &
F. Dünkel

Foreigners in European prisons, *A.M. van Kalmthout, F.B.A.M.Hofstee-van der Meulen & F. Dünkel (eds.).*
ISBN: 978-90-5850-975-8 (reprint in one volume, 2013)
Published by Wolf Legal Publishers (WLP) 2007

This study was funded by the European Commission

ISBN: 978-90-5850-275-9 (1st edition, 2 volume set)

Published by:
Wolf Legal Publishers (WLP)
P.O. Box 31051
6503 CB Nijmegen
The Netherlands

Tel: +31 24 355 19 04
Fax: + 31 24 355 48 27

E-Mail: info@wolfpublishers.nl
Http://www.wolfpublishers.nl

Contents

Volume 1

Chapter 1 Comparative overview, Conclusions and Recommendations
Anton van Kalmthout/Femke Hofstee-van der Meulen/Frieder Dünkel

Chapter 2   Austria
Arno Pilgram/Veronika Hofinger

Chapter 3 Belgium
Sonja Snacken

Chapter 4 Cyprus
Andreas Ellinas

Chapter 5   Czech Republic
Petr Škvain

Chapter 6   Denmark

Anette Storgaard

Chapter 7   Estonia
Piret Liba

Chapter 8   Finland
Tapio Lappi-Seppälä

Chapter 9   France
Pascal Décarpes

Chapter 10   Germany

Frieder Dünkel/Andrea Gensing/Christine Morgenstern

Chapter 11   Greece

M. Akritidou/A. Antonopoulou/A. Pitsela

Chapter 12   Hungary

Tímea Szabó/Balázs Tóth/Gábor Győző/András Kádár

Chapter 13   Ireland
Mary Moore

Chapter 14   Italy
Paola Balbo

Chapter 15 Latvia
Leine Zeibote

Volume 2

Chapter 16   Lithuania
Sonata Malisauskaite – Simanaitiene

Chapter 17 Luxembourg
Stefan Braum

Chapter 18 Malta
Tonio Cachia/Mark F. Montebello

Chapter 19   Netherlands

Anton van Kalmthout/Femke Hofstee – van der Meulen

Chapter 20 Poland
Barbara Stando-Kawecka

Chapter 21 Portugal
Rui Abrunhosa Gonçalves

Chapter 22   Slovakia
Martin Skamla

Chapter 23   Slovenia
Dragan Petrovec

Chapter 24   Spain

José Luis de la Cuesta

Chapter 25   Sweden

Agneta K. Johnson

Chapter 26   United Kingdom
Nick Hammond

Chapter 27   Aire Centre
Nuala Mole

Chapter 28   Conférence Permanente Européenne de la Probation (CEP)
Leo Tigges

Chapter 29   Foreign Liaison Office of the Dutch Probation Service

Rolf Streng/Raymond Swennenhuis/Hans van Kooten

Chapter 30   International Centre for Prison Studies (ICPS)

Andrew Coyle

Chapter 31   Jesuit Refugee Service Europe (JRS-Europe)

Cornelia Bührle RSCJ

Chapter 32 Prisoners Abroad

Stephen Nash

Foreword

by Dr Silvia Casale
President of the SPT (United Nations Subcommittee on Prevention of Torture and Other Cruel, Inhuman or Degrading Treatment or Punishment) and former President of the CPT (European Committee for the Prevention of Torture and inhuman or degrading treatment or punishment).

The phenomenon of migration of people across and to Europe presents both opportunities and challenges for the states of the European Union. The cultures and skills of foreign nationals in Europe enrich the region, when states are open to experiencing diversity positively. At the same time a variety of situations arise in which foreign nationals come into contact with the legal system. In practice the responses of each country differ to foreign nationals of different legal status. The increased incidence of mobility and the co-ordinated measures to combat cross-border crimes have led to a sharp increase in the number of foreign prisoners held worldwide and this holds true for Europe also.

The studies in this compilation examine the size of the custodial population of foreign nationals in each of the states of the European Union, including over-representation in the custodial population on remand and on sentence relative to representation in the community at large, and provide insights into the treatment of and the provisions for foreign nationals under the authority of the different ministries responsible for their custody in the different jurisdictions. Both high and low numbers (in percentage and absolute terms) give rise to particular problems for foreign nationals in custody. States with a low percentage of foreign prisoners or a low number in absolute terms, often lack policies and programmes to take account of the special needs of foreign nationals, whereas states with a large population of foreign prisoners may have difficulty in coping adequately with the procedures applying to them, in particular as regards transfer or status under immigration legislation.

The detention of foreign nationals and their marginalisation within the custodial population are issues of growing concern all over Europe. Foreign prisoners may experience additional hardships above and beyond that generally faced by prison population - the inevitable distress engendered by the deprivation of liberty. All prisoners, including those of foreign nationality, retain all rights not necessarily taken away by the fact of imprisonment. It is, however, a recurring risk that foreign prisoners may not be able to exercise their rights effectively, including their fundamental human rights.

For 60 years a body of international legal instruments and mechanisms has been developing reflecting the will to create a community of states governed by the rule of law. Many of the treaties at the global and regional level affirm the fundamental prohibition of discrimination on the grounds of "race, colour, sex, language, religion, political or other opinion, national or social origin, property, birth or other status" (Universal Declaration of Human Rights, 1948). The prohibition applies to all persons, whether at liberty or in custody. A critical test of a state's commitment to the rule of law lies in the way it deals with those in custody, which, in the context of the European Union, is the state's most extreme legal measure, since the abolition of capital punishment.

1

The studies compiled in this report of the Social Exclusion Project on Foreign Prisoners provide an important body of information about the situation of foreign prisoners in the European Union. Although the report cannot provide exhaustive detail on all aspects of custody, it does constitute an important resource for increasing awareness and knowledge of the practical and human rights dimensions of the phenomenon. The recommendations contained in the comparative overview should inform and guide policy makers at the national and EU level. Thus it is to be hoped that the report will serve as a tool for identifying those areas in which policy and practice need to be improved in order to eliminate or reduce to a minimum the disadvantages experienced by foreign nationals in prison.

Silvia Casale,
April 2007.

Acknowledgement

In early 2005 Tilburg University was granted approval by the European Commission (DG Employment, Social Affairs and Equal Opportunities) to start a one-year project addressing the issue of social exclusion of prisoners who are detained in the EU outside their country of origin. This project was carried out together with the Liaison Office of the Dutch Probation Service, Greifswald University in Germany, Jesuit Refugee Service-Europe (JRS-Europe), the Hungarian Helsinki Committee (HHC) and the Conférence Permanente Européenne de la Probation (CEP).

This publication is the result of the studies that have been conducted by national experts from each EU country. Based on a common questionnaire these experts described and analysed the sentencing and prison system in their country, the treatment of foreign prisoners, the situation of foreigners in administrative detention and of foreign nationals detained abroad. Furthermore, this publication includes five contributions from involved organisations and a comparative overview with conclusions and recommendations.

The first results of the studies have been presented in the European Parliament in Brussels on 13 September 2006. The conference was hosted by Jules Maaten, Member of the European Parliament and Chairman of the working group *Prisoners Abroad*, and was attended by parliamentarians, representatives from European Prison Services, Consulates, Ministries of Foreign Affairs, Ministries of Justice, NGO's, academics and press.

There are many persons and organisations who have contributed to this project. We are greatly indebted to them. First of all we would like to thank our partners for their early commitment and support during the project. Secondly we thank the European Commission 'DG Employment, Social Affairs and Equal Opportunities' for acknowledging the necessity of addressing the issue of foreign prisoners and for their generous co-financing.

We are especially grateful to all national experts and other authors for their commitment and for conducting such a 'pioneering' research.

Furthermore, we are grateful to all ministries, diplomatic missions, prison services and individual penitentiary institutions for providing information and opening their 'doors'. We also want to extend our gratitude to those foreign prisoners who were interviewed for this project and gave insight into their situation.

The task of editing and revising the various contributions was not an easy one. Therefore, we are very thankful to Zarif Bahtiyar, Philip Horsfield, Carla de Jongh and Lulu van der Meer for their support and indispensable contribution.

It is our fervent hope that this volume and the continuation of this project on the topic of the detention of foreign prisoners via the website www.foreignersinprison.eu will make policy makers, prison authorities and scholars in the European Union more aware of the vulnerable position and situation of foreign prisoners and can contribute to improve their socially excluded position.

Anton van Kalmthout
Femke Hofstee-van der Meulen
Frieder Dünkel

Tilburg, Greifswald March 2007

Chapter 1

Comparative overview, Conclusions and Recommendations

1 INTRODUCTION

1 General introduction

Over the last few decades, prison populations in European countries have grown and their profiles have changed. Whereas prison populations used to be rather homogeneous, nowadays they have been transformed into more diverse populations. The portion of foreign prisoners, those without citizenship of the state in which they are detained, has increased rapidly – both in absolute and relative terms. At this moment there are more than 100.000 foreign prisoners in European countries. Their numbers vary greatly per country, but the average percentage of foreigners in the total European prison population is over 20%, which is an over-representation.

Why are foreigners over-represented in European prison populations? Who are they and on what grounds are they held in detention? Are foreign prisoners more vulnerable due to language difficulties, cultural differences and their distance from relatives? Are they being socially excluded? And how are national prison systems and other authorities addressing this issue? These are all questions to which up till now little attention has been paid to. This also explains why there has been hardly any data or information available on this issue. One could say that foreign prisoners are in general a 'forgotten group'.

In this study, the terms 'prisoners' and 'prisons' are used in a broader sense than usual. In this way, the term 'prisoners does not only include 'persons who have been remanded in custody by a judicial authority or who have been deprived of their liberty following conviction' as stated in the European Prison Rules, but also persons detained under administrative law such as: (rejected) asylum seekers or irregular migrants deprived of their liberty in preparation of their departure, expulsion or deportation. The term prison is likewise not restricted to penitentiary institutions for remand and sentenced offenders, but entails all places were people can be deprived of their liberty (such as re-trial institutions, open or closed prisons, detention centres for irregular migrants, airport reception or holding centres and police cells). With 'foreign prisoner' is meant all persons without citizenship of the state in which they are detained. It encompasses short term visitors, migrant workers, long-term residents, second generation migrants, (rejected) asylum seekers, irregular migrants and stateless people. As far as it seems to be relevant, a distinction is made between three categories of foreign prisoners: 1) those prisoners who are detained under criminal law and who after release will remain in the country of detention or 2) will be deported or expelled to their home country or a third country and 3) foreign nationals who are detained under administrative (immigration) law.

There are good grounds to adduce for the question why this study on 'foreigners in European prisons' also includes the group of foreign nationals who are administratively detained. In some countries the issue of foreign prisoners either as foreign nationals with residence in the host country or as foreigners who want to get access to stay in the host country (asylum seekers, refugees, irregular migrants etc.) increasingly have been of major concern in public and political debates. However, this does not seem to be the case in all countries. Middle and Eastern European countries are less exposed to migration and foreign immigration. On the other hand particularly the "rich" countries of Western Europe have been facing waves of legal and illegal immigration since the Second World War and particularly in the 1980's and 1990's.

If we can characterize foreign prisoners as a 'forgotten group', then this counts for certain for foreign nationals who are detained on the basis of immigration laws. The holding centres and other institutions where they are kept, awaiting their removal are officially not prisons and often not under the responsibility of the Ministry of Justice. Other Ministries, such as the Ministry of Interior, the Police Department and/or the Ministry of Defence or the Ministry for Refugees, Immigrants and Integration are responsible for administrative detention. This is why these foreigners are usually not recorded in the prison statistics and as far as they are not detained in ordinary prisons, the European Prison Rules are not applicable on them. Although administrative detainees are not allowed to be considered as criminals nor to be treated as one, the practice shows a difference. An actual look at the detention conditions of these foreigners shows quite some similarities with ordinary prisons. Certain countries apply the same penitentiary legislation on remand or sentenced prisoners, as well as on administrative detainees. In other countries, their legal position is even weaker, as they are provided with fewer safeguards. Practically, it can be said that in a substantive sense, there is no difference between criminal and administrative detainees regarding their deprivation of liberty. Furthermore, the line between the two groups is even more vague when it comes to foreigners who are detained on a criminal basis and lost their right to residence as a consequence of the committed crime, and have to leave the country after their detention, either forced or voluntarily. The regime during criminal detention has often the same restrictions which are applied on administrative detainees, as regarding to leave, conditional release and integration programmes. When a foreigner can not be immediately removed after the end of his/her detention, it is possible in a number of countries to continue the detention, whether in the same penitentiary institution or not, which then is based on the immigration laws. It is for these reasons, why administratively detained foreigners are a target group of the Council of Europe's Committee for the Prevention of Torture and Inhuman and Degrading Treatment and also a part of our research.

The following paragraphs in this chapter will summarize the main results of the European comparative project within the European Union 'Social Exclusion'-scheme which has been conducted from September 2005 until September 2006. Hereby, it is taken into account, as much as possible, the structure and order of the country reports. In the following subparagraphs of paragraph 1, an overview will be given on the sanctions and prison systems in the European countries, involvement of consulates/embassies/ probation services of home countries/NGO's, trends and the relevant national and European legislation. Paragraph 2 contains an overview regarding the treatment of foreign prisoners in the various countries with the focus on the following topics; general situation, living conditions and facilities, reception and admission, work-education-training-sports-recreation, food-religion-personal hygiene-medical care, consular help and legal aid, contact with the outside world, re-integration activities and prison leave, release and expulsion, aftercare and probation, staff and projects. In Paragraph 3 attention will be paid on the administrative detention of foreign prisoners, in which there will be dealt with the various institutions that are in use and their capacity, the responsible Ministries and legislation, length of stay, decision and appeal, data and the non-expelled foreigners, detention irregulars under criminal law and minors. Paragraph 4 will give an overview on EU foreign nationals detained abroad. The numbers and composition, countries of detention, reasons for detention and sentencing, authorities and organisations involved, release and reception home country, aftercare and the public opinion and media are the issues discussed in this part. In conclusion of this chapter, the recommendations will be presented in paragraph 5.

1.1 Overview penalties and measures

The countries involved in the foreign prisoners' project all dispose of a criminal law system as well as administrative laws by which foreigners can be dealt with.

The penal law systems differ with respect of the sanctions provided and the practice of prosecutors and courts. Foreigners in theory should not be sanctioned differently from native offenders. However, numerous examples are given in the present volume that in practice foreigners or members of ethnic minorities are discriminated insofar that they do not profit from alternative sanctions and diversion measures in the same way as non-foreigners in fact do. This is the case, for example, in the Netherlands and – although empirical evidence is not easy to acquire – also in Germany. In the Netherlands it is not Penal Law that formally discriminates foreigners, but the prosecutorial guidelines which influence the courts' sentencing practice. These guidelines provide that particular groups of foreigners like irregular migrants, foreigners who are expected to lose their residence permit because of the crime committed, etc. are excluded from alternative sanctions such as the so-called task penalty (including community service), electronic monitoring, hospital orders etc.

The average length of custodial penalties is longer in the Middle and Eastern European countries compared to continental Europe and particularly Scandinavia. This is the result of a range of custodial penalties which sometimes covers 20 or 30 years as maximum and life sentences with possibilities for conditional release only after having served 25 years (e. g. Czech Republic, Poland). In many European countries law reforms have been passed that increased minimum or maximum penalties for sexual and violent offences in the last 20 years. It is also claimed that the sentencing practice in general has become more severe. There is, however, no empirical evidence that these changes have led to a further discrimination against foreign offenders. On the other hand, at least in some countries statistical analyses show that foreigners have a higher risk of being held in pre-trial detention than national suspects (see e. g. Denmark, Malta).

Administrative detention everywhere is seen as a last resort for the execution of an expulsion order, but the practice shows a different view. It is regularly restricted to a shorter period of confinement, like for instance 40 days in Spain or six months in Germany (for more details see paragraph 3.4).

1.2 Overview of the prison system

Prison systems in nearly all European countries are administered by the Ministry of Justice. The conditions vary considerably when looking at daily life and human rights issues. Large dormitories in the Middle and Eastern European countries (with up to 70 or more persons housed in one dormitory) compared to the single cell accommodation in Scandinavia and larger parts of the prison systems in the Netherlands or Germany demonstrate that imprisonment even in the enlarged Europe of the European Union does mean very different conditions of prison life. Foreigners in all countries are accommodated in the regular prisons and not separated from national prisoners. In some prisons there are, however, departments where foreigners are overrepresented (see e.g. England and

Wales). This is more frequently the case in closed units than in open prisons. Sometimes prison authorities concentrate foreigners of the same nationality in specific departments or cells in order to make communication between prisoners easier (see e.g. Hungary). National prison law or administrative rules often provide that foreigners do not qualify for being transferred to open prisons. This is especially the case when extradition is possible or even likely to take place (see e.g. Germany).

Administrative detention of asylum seekers, refugees etc. is in most of the countries organised by the Ministry of the Interior. In some countries or regions asylum seekers who shall be expelled are held in special departments of regular prisons. According to the Council of Europe's Annual Penal Statistics SPACE I, Survey 2005, this is the case in Belgium, Hungary, Luxembourg, the Netherlands, Sweden, Switzerland and Northern Ireland.[1] According to the report on Germany in some parts of the country asylum seekers are also accommodated in prisons. Regularly – and in the vast majority of countries exclusively (30 in the SPACE survey) – administrative detention for foreigners is executed in special units of the Ministry of Interior.

1.3 Overview involvement Consulates, Embassies, Ministries Home Country, Probation Service Home Country, NGO's, etc.

Most national reports have no good data base on this issue. With the exception of the Dutch probation service that takes care of Dutch nationals incarcerated abroad, almost no systematic care from the home countries exists. On the other hand there can be found a lot of NGO's which take care of foreign prisoners in the host countries like 'Prisoners Abroad' in the United Kingdom, the *Jesuite Refugee Center* in Germany or other Christian or laic initiatives.

1.4 Overview of trends (foreign prisoners, administrative detention etc.)

The number of foreign prisoners varies considerably in the European countries. According to the SPACE I survey of 2005 the proportion is from 0,4% in Latvia up to 71.4% in Luxembourg. A very high proportion can also be seen in Belgium (41.2%), Greece (41.6%) and Cyprus (45.6%). The high rate of 40.4% in Estonia is mainly due to the fact that inmates of Russian origin are defined as foreigners as long as they have not applied for Estonian nationality, even if they have lived in Estonia for many years or were even born there. Most of the Middle and Eastern European countries quantitatively have only small minorities of foreign prisoners of regularly less than 10%, or even less than 5% of the total prison population (e.g. Hungary: 3.8%; Lithuania: 0.8%).

The following table in addition shows that large proportions of foreign prisoners are pre-trial detainees. This proves that foreigners are highly overrepresented in pre-trial detention (see e. g. Belgium, Czech Republic, Denmark, Germany, Hungary, Italy, Luxembourg, the Netherlands, Poland, Spain, and the United Kingdom). The living conditions there are often far poorer than the ones for sentenced prisoners, as can be seen in

---

[1] See Aebi, M., Stadnic, N. (2007): SPACE I. Council of Europe Annual Penal Statistics. Survey 2005. Internet-publication www.coe.int. The statistics regarding the total numbers of prisoners are not complete as certain countries have not included the category of administrative detainees in these.

many of the reports in this volume as well as in the reports of the CPT and in the literature.[2]

Table 1: Number of foreign prisoners in Europe, 2005

Foreign prisoners				
	Number of foreign prisoners (including pre-trial detainees)	% of foreign prisoners (including pre-trial detainees)	Of which: Number of foreign pre-trial detainees	% of foreign prisoners who are pre-trial detainees
Austria	3,979	45.4	1,199	30.1
Belgium	3,860	41.2	1,670	43.3
Cyprus	241	45.6	57	23.7
Czech Republic	1,652	8.7	721	43.6
Denmark	754	18.2	363	48.1
Estonia[3]	1,780	40.4	466	26.2
Finland	286	7.5	114	39.9
France	11,820	20.5	No inf.	-
Germany	22,095	28.0	6,954	31.5
Greece	3990	41.6	No inf.	-
Hungary	631	3.8	No inf.	-
Ireland	3,080	9	277	
Italy	19,656	33.0	9,655	49.1
Latvia	26	0.4	No inf.	-
Lithuania	67	0.8	14	20.9
Luxembourg	495	71.4	273	55.2
Malta	91	30.5	35	38.5
Netherlands	5,818	32.9	1,666	28.6
Poland	750	0.9	408	54.4
Portugal	2,386	18.5	1,005	42.1
Slovakia	220	2.4	147	66.8
Slovenia	144	12.7	69	47.9
Spain	18,436	30.1	7,285	39.5
Sweden	1475	20.9	No inf.	-
UK: England and Wales	9,650	12.7	2,271	23.5
UK: Northern Ireland	38	2.8	15	39.5
UK: Scotland	71	1.0	15	21.1

---

[2] See e. g. *Dünkel, J., Vagg, J.* (1994): Waiting for Trial. International Perspectives on the Use of Pre-Trial Detention and the Rights and Living Conditions of Prisoners Waiting for Trial. Vol. 1 and 2. Freiburg i. Br.: Max-Planck-Institut für ausländisches und internationals Strafrecht.

[3] The numbers of "foreigners" apparently comprise Russians with no Estonian passport who, how-ever, in most cases have been born and grown up in Estonia.

While the numbers of foreign prisoners have generally increased during the last 20 years (see e. g. Luxembourg with a more than doubled foreign prison population only between 2002 and 2006, or Spain), this trend is not uniform. In Germany and other continental European countries during the 1990's many asylum seekers and illegal immigrants arrived, creating problems of overcrowding in prisons or refugee centres. Since the mid-nineties the trend has been reversed or at least a "levelling off" of the increase of foreign prisoners' rates can be observed (e.g. Germany, Poland, and Slovakia). In Poland the number of foreigners suspected of having committed a crime as well as of foreign prisoners since 2001 dropped by more than half. In Hungary the number of convicted foreigners has increased during the last ten years, whereas the numbers of foreigners sentenced to imprisonment has been stable or lately even decreasing. Similar tendencies can be observed in countries that traditionally have been emigration instead of immigration countries like Ireland. The increase of foreigners there is not comparable to the problems with foreign prisoners in France, England, Germany, the Netherlands or Spain. Other Eastern European countries like Latvia or Lithuania do not really have a problem with foreign prisoners (the very low numbers are even decreasing), but with minorities that have no passport at all (mostly Russians refusing nationalization) or that are of Russian nationality who have been living in the country for a long time.

The foreign prison population often can be characterised by certain crimes that are overrepresented compared to the national prison population: in England and Wales, Germany or the Netherlands foreigners are overrepresented with respect to drug offences, in England also concerning fraud and forgery, whereas violent offenders are overrepresented by UK-nationals. In Germany certain groups of foreigners like Turkish and former Yugoslavian citizens are overrepresented in the field of violent crimes. Foreign drug dealers are a specific problem in the larger cities where airports with connections to Latin America etc. are situated. Therefore, foreigners are sometimes concentrated in prisons in the neighbourhoods of Amsterdam, Madrid, London Heathrow or Frankfurt/Main.

1.5 Overview of national legislation

National *penal legislation* in many countries has been amended with respect to more severe sanctions for foreign offenders (expulsion) as well as to more strict *immigration laws* that aim to prevent asylum seekers and other migrants from permanent residence in the host countries (see e.g. Germany, the Netherlands). Some countries have extended the possibilities for expulsion of foreigners under anti-terrorism legislation (see e.g. Italy). On the other hand nationalization has been made easier in some countries as well (e.g. Belgium, Finland, and Germany). Thus one has to realise that a considerable part of the "national" prison population consists of persons with a migrant background (e.g. in Germany the immigrants from states or regions of the former Soviet Union who are by definition "Germans"). A remarkable step of a legislation that wants to prevent undue discrimination is the Finish Equality Act of 2004 which among others introduced an Ombudsman for Minorities.

Prison legislation has also been changed in many countries, particularly in the Middle and Eastern European countries entering the Council of Europe and/or the European Union. Guiding principle in these countries was the adoption of human rights standards and the observation of the rule of law. Prison legislation in general does not provide specific rules or regimes for foreigners. However, foreigners can be discriminated because they are less eligible for a transfer to open prisons or relaxations of the prison regime (prison leaves etc., see e. g. Germany, Slovenia and the Netherlands).

1.6 Overview of European legislation

There are International and Regional treaties, conventions, guidelines and rules available addressing detention of foreigners. These instruments state for example procedural guarantees that have to be afforded to persons facing restrictions on their freedom of liberty, but also the conditions of detention. It is beyond the scope of this work to deal with the International legislation regarding detention in complete, as this requires an extensive study.[4] This is why the research is restricted to European legislation, in particular to the regulations of the two relevant bodies in Europe: the Council of Europe and the EU.

1.6.1 Council of Europe

The Council of Europe is the oldest political organization in Europe, founded in 1949, which groups together 46 countries. The Council was set up to, *inter alia*, defend human rights, parliamentary democracy, the rule of law and to develop continent-wide agreements to standardize member countries' social and legal practices. Among the efforts to achieve the last mentioned goal, many binding and non-binding instruments have been developed by the Council. Within the context of detention, the following can be mentioned:

- European Convention for the Protection of Human Rights and Fundamental Freedoms (ECHR).[5] According to article 1 ECHR, 'everyone' within the jurisdiction of a contracting party benefits from the rights and freedoms enumerated in the ECHR. Thus, the rights and freedoms recognized by the ECHR, are in theory at least, universally available to all individuals, including aliens, be they nationals (e.g. immigrants or refugees) or non-nationals (e.g. stateless) of a foreign state. Considerations of nationality, residence or domicile are irrelevant to a determination of a claim of a violation of the ECHR. All that needs to be shown is some physical presence in the territory of the (alleged) violator contracting party, and some exercise of control by that state over the individual and over the protection of the ECHR's rights secured within the territory of the state.[6] For the enforcement of the ECHR and its several Protocols[7], the Convention established the European Court of Human Rights (hereinafter the Court). The Court has played a crucial role in the enforcement of the rights and still is. The decisions of the Court are legally binding and since the entry

---

[4] For an extensive overview of the legislation see: Undocumented Migrants Have Rights! An overview of the International Human Rights Framework, Brussels PICUM March 2007.

[5] Date entry into force is 3 September 1953.

[6] H. Lambert, *The position of aliens in relation to the European Convention on Human Rights*, Strasbourg: Council of Europe Publishing 2006, p. 8.

[7] As of May 2006, 14 Protocols to the ECHR have been opened for signature. These can be divided into two main groups: those changing the machinery of the Convention, and those adding additional rights to those protected by the Convention. The former require unanimous ratification before coming into force, while the latter are optional Protocols which only come into force between ratifying member states.

into force of Protocol no. 11 on 1 November 1998, also individuals have gained direct access to the Court. Though, the Convention provides individuals such a high degree of protection, it may only deal with the matter after all domestic remedies have been exhausted (article 35 ECHR). A useful tool in refoulement cases in which a person is facing departure, is that the Court can take interim measures.[8] This way the State can be stopped, until the final decision is made by the Court. The supervision of the execution of judgments is done by the Committee of Ministers (article 46 ECHR).

- European Convention for the Prevention of Torture and Inhuman or Degrading Treatment or Punishment.[9] Article 1 of this Convention provided for the creation of a committee (CPT) to visit places of detention (including immigration detention centres) to ensure compliance with its provisions. The CPT has unlimited access and can organize 'ad hoc' visits as necessary. Access to persons deprived of their liberty includes free communication in private with detainees and with any person whom the CPT believes may be able to provide it with relevant information. There is also a general duty upon states to make available whatever other information the CPT requires to discharge its tasks. After completing a visit, the CPT provides information concerning its concerns confidentially to the government to begin a dialogue with the ultimate objective being improvement of the situation. Member states are expected to provide an interim report within six months of receipt of the report containing details of steps already taken and how it is intended to implement any remaining recommendations, and to furnish within twelve months a follow-up report providing a full account of action taken. According to the treaty, visits to places of detention, information received and recommendations and reports to states are confidential, but this is subject to three exceptions: according to article 11 (2) a state may request publication of the report and any comments it may have on the report; article 10 (2) states that if a state refuses to co-operate or to improve matters in light of CPT recommendations, a public statement may be issued and the committee's General reports made to the Committee of Ministers, now provide sufficient detail to provide some impressions of the care of detainees in particular states.[10] In several of its General reports, the CPT has described some of the substantive issues it addresses during its visits to places of detention. The CPT Standards[11] represent updated substantive sections of those reports providing guidance to countries on issues dealing with, *inter alia*, foreign nationals detained under aliens legislation.

- Twenty Guidelines on forced return.[12] The Guidelines constitute an international instrument in which all the stages of the procedure of forced return are covered, from the moment of the adoption of a removal order until the effective return. It is the first time that states have agreed on dealing with every aspect of this issue in a single instrument. The Guidelines on forced return serve as a practical guide to be used both

---

[8] Rule 39 of the Rules of the European Court of Human Rights (interim measures).

[9] The date of entry into force of this Convention is 1 February 1989.

[10] J. Murdoch, *The treatment of prisoners. European Standards*, Strasbourg: Council of Europe Publishing 2006, p. 42-44.

[11] Council of Europe, October 2001, CPT/Inf/E (2002).

[12] Adopted on May 2005, on the 925th meeting of the Ministers' Deputies, the Committee of Ministers of the Council of Europe.

by government officials and by all those directly or indirectly involved in return operations in Europe.

- European Prison Rules.[13] The European Prison Rules apply only to remand or sentenced prisoners and to persons detained in prisons "for any other reason", see Rules No. 10.1 and 10.3. Foreigners in administrative detention therefore are only protected if they are held in prisons.
- Committee of Ministers, Recommendation No. R (84) 12 concerning Foreign Prisoners.[14] The principles in the Recommendation are designed to apply to foreign prisoners, that is to say to prisoners of different nationality who on account of such factors as language, customs, cultural background or religion may face specific problems. Attention is paid on, *inter alia*, treatment in prison, assistance by consular authorities, training and use of prison staff and expulsion and repatriation.
- Parliamentary Assembly Resolution 1509 (2006) on the Human Rights of Irregular Migrants.[15] With this resolution, the Parliamentary Assembly stated that: "(...) international human rights instruments are applicable to all persons regardless of their nationality or status. Irregular migrants, as they are often in a vulnerable situation, have a particular need for the protection of their human rights, including basic civil, political, economic and social rights."

1.6.2 EU

The entry into force of the 1997 Amsterdam Treaty on the EU in 1999 provided for the establishment of an 'Area of Freedom, Security and Justice' and the creation of a Directorate-General for Justice and Home Affairs. In the same year with the Treaty of Amsterdam coming into effect, the European Council held a special meeting in Tampere and placed this objective at the head of the EU's political agenda. The EU Council agreed, *inter alia*, to create a common EU policy with regard to immigration and asylum as well as setting out a political strategy and putting forward a 5 year programme. In 2004, the Brussels European Council adopted the Hague Programme which set the objectives to be implemented to 'strengthen Freedom, Security and Justice in the EU'.[16] The Programme that is drawn up for the period 2005-2010 can be seen as the successor of the Tampere programme. On EU level the following documents are relevant regarding detention:

- Charter of Fundamental Rights of the EU. As it stands, the Charter is not a treaty, constitutional, or legal document and has the ambiguous value of a 'solemn proclamation' by the European Parliament, the Council of the EU and the European Commission in December 2000. Part II of the proposed European Constitution, which was signed in October 2004 but failed to be ratified after referendum defeats in France and the Netherlands, contained a version of the Charter. The intention was to enable the EU to accede to the ECHR, thus enabling the European Court of Justice to rule on the basis of this Charter.

---

[13] Recommendation Rec (2006) 2, adopted by the Committee of Ministers on 11 January 2006, on the 952nd meeting of the Ministers' Deputies.
[14] Adopted on 21 June 1984.
[15] Adopted on 27 June 2006.
[16] Council of EU, Brussels 13 December 2004, 16054/04.

- Commission Proposal for a Directive of the European Parliament and the Council on common standards and procedures in Member States for returning illegally staying third-country nationals (Commission Proposal Returns Directive), COM (2005) 391 final.
- Proposal for a Council Framework Decision on the European supervision order in pre-trial procedures between Member States of the EU, COM (2006) 468 final.
- Proposal for a Council Framework Decision on the recognition and supervision of suspended sentences and alternative sanctions (Home Office), 5325/07 COPEN 7.

In conclusion of this part, regarding to the European legal framework, it can be said that the available European legislation is mainly soft law as they are not binding on states and thus not enforceable. This is different for the ECHR and the decisions of the Court. The case law of the Court and also the work of the CPT are important tools for the protection of detainees. It is not difficult to notice that the Council of Europe has a much more developed system than the EU does, as at EU level there is neither a common EU institution exercising responsible authority on the system nor an EU institution periodically and publicly reporting about detention centres in the EU or an EU monitoring mechanism.

Conclusions
- The portion of foreign prisoners, those without citizenship of the state in which they are detained, has been increasing rapidly – both in absolute and relative terms.
- In 2006 there were more than 100.000 foreign prisoners in European countries and although their numbers vary greatly per country the average percentage of foreigners in the total European prison population is over 20%.
- The percentage of foreign prisoners varies from less than one percent in Latvia to 75% in Luxembourg.
- Foreigners are in general an over-represented group in penitentiary institutions, in comparison with the percentage of foreign nationals residing in EU countries.
- Reasons for the over-representation of foreigners in European penitentiary institutions are the higher probability of detection and apprehension of foreigners by legal systems, the exclusion from alternatives to pre-trial detention and exclusion from non-custodial sanctions.
- Further, foreign prisoners tend not to fulfil requirements for conditional release (risk of escape, no secure home address), transfer of foreign prisoners is rarely applied, difficulties in enforcing expulsion orders and the increase of prison sentences for violation of Immigration Laws.
- European legislation regarding detention is mainly soft law.

2 TREATMENT OF FOREIGN PRISONERS

This paragraph looks into the treatment of foreign prisoners in the different EU countries. Treatment of this particular group of prisoners has hardly been studied in the past and as a result there is only very limited information, data or literature available[17]. In order to cast more light on the situation of foreign prisoners, several experts in this study have been carrying out interviews with foreign prisoners in order to get a better picture of

---

17   The Prison Service of England and Wales is an exemption to this.

their actual situation. Besides individual prisoners prison staff has also been interviewed, like staff with mainly a guarding role to specialised staff like social workers, psychiatrists, psychologists, religious representatives and probation workers and also representatives from prison services and ministries of Justice. In some cases advocates, visitors and representatives of civil society organisation were also included in the research.

This paragraph will look into the situation for foreign prisoners in the following twelve topics; general treatment, living conditions and facilities, reception and admission, work/education/ training/sports and recreation, food/religion/personal hygiene and medical care, consular and legal help, contact with the outside world, reintegration activities and prison leave, release and expulsion, aftercare and probation, staff and projects.

2.1 General situation

Penal codes and regulations are in principle equally applicable to all prisoners. Prisoners should receive similar legal guarantees for just, fair and humane treatment. According to prison regulations no discrimination is allowed based on the grounds of religion or belief, race, colour, language, nationality etc. As a result all prisoners should in practice receive equal treatment. Although this concept of non-discrimination is used as a starting point in prisons in practice it is not always the case. The difficulties that foreign prisoners experience in every day life are numerous and they are often not able to exercise their formally equal rights. Very often prison authorities do not impose these disadvantages deliberately.

In order to compensate these disadvantages countries like Austria and Czech Republic have special paragraphs in their penal legislations that prescribe special treatment. It seems that the implementation of this form of 'positive discrimination' in order to meet the special needs of foreign prisoners works well but that it depends heavily on the commitment of the director and staff of individual penitentiary institutions. Even when there is attention in prisons for the special needs of foreign prisoners there are a few threats that often result in additional problems for prisoners and staff. One of them is overcrowding which can result in multiple cell sharing, lack of space and lack of attention of staff, long time behind the door, less opportunities for work, education, vocational training and re-integration activities. Another hampering fact is that most prison populations represent more than 50 different nationalities and as a result there is a large diversity of languages, religions and cultures. Racism, religious intolerance and prejudice, especially in times of fear for terrorism, are not uncommon.

The most common and significant problem faced by foreign prisoners is the lack of knowledge of the national language. As a result verbal and written communication is severely hampered and that causes feelings of social isolation, uncertainty and helplessness. The less they are in number, the more isolated they tend to become. Daily interactions between foreign prisoners and staff are crucial and it often depends on the goodwill of prison staff and fellow-prisoners and the availability of an interpreter. Linguistic barriers are often the main source of other problems that foreign prisoners are facing in penitentiary institutions.

Treatment of prisoners often depends on the kind of regime (maximum security, closed, half-open, open, conditional freedom) they are placed in. Those that are placed in (semi-) open regimes receive a more relaxed treatment with more entitlements and more opportunities to prepare for resettlement into society after release. In general, foreign prisoners are excluded from the right to be placed in (semi-) open institutions even when their sentence length is relatively short or when they have nearly finished their sentence. This is especially the case for those that will leave or will be expelled afterwards to their country of origin. The fear of escape is mainly used as argument for this discriminatory practice because many foreigners have no secure home address in the country of detention.

Prison rules in general do not contain special rules for foreign prisoners on living conditions, reception and admission, work, education, training, food, religion or any other aspect described in this book. However, the lack of special regulations sometimes generates unequal opportunities for foreign prisoners taking into account the distance from relatives, differences in culture, religion and above all communication barriers. In the following sections the differences between foreign prisoners and national prisoners are being highlighted in more detail per topic.

Conclusions
- Penal codes and regulations are in principle equally applicable to all prisoners and discrimination is not allowed on the grounds of religion or belief, race, colour, language, nationality etc. As a result all prisoners should receive equal treatment.
- Foreign prisoners experience difficulties in daily life that are connected to their foreign status and as a result they are not able to exercise the same rights as national prisoners.
- Even when there is attention for the special needs of foreign prisoners, this can be easily threatened by common struggles of daily prison life such as: overcrowding, limited number of staff, limited opportunities for work and education, large diversity of nationalities etc.
- Racism, religious intolerance and prejudice, especially in times of fear for terrorism, are not uncommon.
- The most common and significant problem faced by foreign prisoners is the lack of knowledge of the national language. Linguistic barriers are often the main source of other problems and causes feelings of social isolation, uncertainty and loneliness.
- Foreign prisoners are in general excluded from placement in (semi) open penitentiary institutions with a more relaxed regime and (more) opportunities for work, education, re-integration programmes and contact with the outside world. Main reasons for this discriminatory practice are the fear of escape and the lack of a secure home address.

2.2 Living conditions and facilities

Foreigners who are suspected of or sentenced for a criminal offence are held in the same penitentiary institutions as national prisoners in the European Union. Only foreigners under administrative detention are held in separate centres (see under paragraph 3). Foreign prisoners have access to the same living conditions and facilities as other prisoners. The kind of living conditions and facilities vary per country, per region and according to the type of prison regime (closed, semi-open and open).

2.2.1 Allocation

According to Rule 17 of the European Prison Rules prisoners should be 'allocated, as much as possible, to prisons close to their homes or places of social rehabilitation'. For foreign prisoners this is difficult. The allocation of prisoners to penitentiary institutions depends generally speaking on the decision of the court. Prisoners that have not been convicted go to pre-trial detention and convicted prisoners are allocated to prisons according to the type and length of their sentence. In principle pre-trial prisoners are not accommodated with sentenced prisoners, young offenders are separated from adults, men are separated from women, healthy prisoners from sick prisoners and smokers from non-smokers. Selection based on 'nationality' seems not to be included under the criteria that govern the allocation of prisoners.

In allocating foreign prisoners to cells many prison authorities tend to make attempts to put people of the same language/culture/religion or nationality together. Individual wishes are often taken into consideration but due to overcrowding or security risks this is not always possible. It is very important that allocation is carefully applied because it can also become the source of further segregation. In many countries, like the United Kingdom and the Netherlands this selection is done by a Selection Officer who reviews each prisoner individually before allocation is doing process for each prisoner. 'Mixing' of nationalities among prison populations can be seen as a good practice in order to prevent the creation of subcultures within prisons but on the other hand it can increase the feeling of social exclusion among foreigners. Accommodation of prisoners with the same nationality, religion or cultural background in one cell or on a particular wing can elevate this feeling of isolation but on the other hand it can also can create tensions and undesirable hierarchical or violent subcultures, for example between nationals of recently partitioned new states.

In Finish prisons, attention is given to those prisoners who felt threatened by fellow prisoners. In 2004 a specific section was established for these 'fearing' prisoners and among those 142 prisoners 25 had an ethnic background and 18 were gypsies. In the Irish 'Cloverhill' pre-trial prison in Dublin, a separate wing is used to house non-Irish nationals. In France of the total foreign prison population are accommodated in the three big Parisian prisons; 'Fleury-Mérogis', 'La Santé', and 'Fresnes'. In the pre-trial prison 'La Santé' the proportion of foreign prisoners is 55% and there is a representation of 86 different nationalities. Foreign prisoners are placed in 4 units: Unit A hosts the 'Europeans', Unit B the 'Africans', Unit C the 'North Africans' and Unit D the 'rest of the world'. The head of the prison to limit conflicts and to create more group 'affinity' is justifying this structure. In practice a Christian English prisoner can be placed in the same cell with a Muslim from African origin with a German passport. The Austrian prison service tends to send foreign prisoners, mainly from African countries, to remote prisons like 'Suben' because they are less likely to receive visitors. In Poland nationals from Eastern European countries are placed in prisons situated close to the east border to facilitate visits from families. Most foreign prisoners in Portugal are sent to 'Funchal' prison in the Island of Madeira, one of the newest prisons built (1994) and with more places available.

Although 'nationality' is not a ground for not allowing prisoners to move to a more relaxed open regime, most foreign prisoners are in reality often excluded from this entitlement. In (semi-) open institutions prisoners have more freedom to walk around on the premises, are permitted to go outside for work or training related activities in society and spend only time behind a closed door during the night.

2.2.2 Cells

Foreign prisoners, mainly from outside the EU, prefer commonly shared rooms to solitary cells. However, most European penitentiary institutions were designed for single cell accommodation. Due to overcrowding many cells have been reconstructed for multi occupancy. Penitentiary institutions from relatively new EU member states have more dormitories for 2-6 persons or even more. Foreign prisoners are accommodated in the same cells as national prisoners.

Most cells and dormitories are equipped with a bed, table, chair, wardrobe and some cells have washing facilities and a separate toilet. The size of single cells varies among countries and there is no agreed universal standard. The Council of Europe's Committee for the Prevention of Torture (CPT) recommended that cells should be not less than 4 square metres per person[18]. Material conditions and the level of hygiene differ greatly per country but overall prisoners are required to keep their cells clean and in good condition. Most cells have central heating, lighting and ventilation. In many institutions prisoners are allowed to rent a television, a refrigerator and a radio. In Dutch prisons prisoners can keep a bird in a cage or a fish in a bowl. Danish prisons are run by the principle 'normalization' which aims at creating conditions and facilities as similar as possible to normal life in society. To carry this out prisoners are requested to take care of their own needs during the day and this implies shopping, cooking, cleaning, washing clothes etc. For this reason each prison is equipped with appropriate facilities.

Overcrowding is a common phenomenon in European prisons and has a devastating effect on living conditions and facilities for prisoners and staff. Besides a lack of space prisoners are also confronted with longer hours behind a closed door because staff has to divide their time over more prisoners. In Poland this has led to remarks from the Council of Europe's Committee for the Prevention of Torture (CPT) in 2004 to redouble their efforts to combat prison overcrowding.

Conclusions

- Besides special detention centres for foreigners who are detained for administrative reasons there are no special penitentiary facilities for foreign prisoners.
- It is not uncommon that prison authorities allocate prisoners with the same nationality, language, culture or religion together in one cell or wing. Individual wishes are sometimes taken into account.

2.3 Reception and admission

2.3.1 Reception

Reception is one of the most delicate phases of imprisonment; it is the point where citizens surrender their freedom. It can be experienced as intimidating and dehumanising. It is therefore essential that prisoners have a proper understanding of what is actually hap-

---

[18] CPT Report on visit to Poland in 1996 (1998), recommendation 70, page 32.

pening. Prison authorities should acknowledge that in this situation foreign prisoners are even more vulnerable and therefore special provisions should be made. In practice many penitentiary institutions are ill prepared to receive non-national prisoners. Language barriers and lack of information about the prison, prison rules and the legal process are the main reasons for this.

2.3.2 Admission

According to Rule 15.1 of the European Prison Rules prison authorities should 'record upon admission the following details of each prisoner: identity, reasons for commitment and the authority for it, the day and hour of admission, inventory of the personal property, any visible injuries and complaints about prior ill-treatment and information about the prisoners' physical and mental well-being'. Other personal data that is normally recorded is marital status, religion, offence of which the prisoner is suspected of or convicted for, court decision and date of discharge. Further it is not uncommon that a picture is taken and a fingerprint. In case a prisoner is transferred to another penal institution the personal file will be forwarded. In most countries this information is kept in an electronic register or database but in Cyprus a register is used with numbered pages. Upon admission all prisoners are subjected to a thorough body search and search of their luggage and personal belongings. Normally a prison officer of the same sex as the prisoner performs this.

Admission procedures are in general similar for all prisoners. The main disadvantage for foreign prisoners is that staff available in reception areas does not speak normally more than one language. As a result newly arrived foreign prisoners feel even more isolated and lost.

2.3.3 Information for prisoners

Upon admission prisoners are informed about the prison regulations, prison 'house rules', aspects of daily prison life, disciplinary sanctions, visits scheme, transfer procedures, opportunities for legal assistance and above all their rights and duties inside the institution. Especially for foreign prisoners it is essential that this information is available in a language that they can understand. In practice this is often not the case and foreign prisoners have to depend on the willingness and cooperation of staff and other prisoners to be informed. As a result foreign prisoners have a very bad start and they are ill prepared for their time in prison because they are not made properly aware of prison regulations and regime.

In several countries, like Belgium and The Netherlands, prison authorities claim that information is provided in a number of languages. However in practice it seems that the availability of information in multi languages depends on individual penitentiary institutions and that in general prison authorities do not prescribe this provision. Even in Austria where there is information available in 13 languages some prisoners complained in 2004 to the Council of Europe's Committee for the Prevention of Torture (CPT) about a lack of information. As a result the Ministry of Justice is regularly reminding penal institutions about their duty to hand out these regulations. Also in the Czech Republic there is a discrepancy. Although instructions of rights and duties are translated into 25 foreign languages most interviewed foreign prisoners indicated that they were not made aware of that. In some Belgian prisons initiative has been taken to translate the house rules in other languages, usually including English and Arabic or a video is showed. However, with over 100 different nationalities, it remains difficult to cover all possible languages. In Estonia, France, Greece and Ireland prisoners are seen on the first or second day of their arrival by the director (or his/her appointee). During this meeting their rights and duties are explained. For foreign prisoners in Estonia this information is translated into Russian and English.

Spanish penitentiary institutions are obliged by law to provide informative booklets about the prison regime and system in the most 'popular' languages. In case there are no booklets in a language the prisoners can understand, an oral translation is provided by a staff member, a fellow prisoner or the help from consular services are requested. The fact that there are no interpreters is seen as a severe omission. Also in some Hungarian penitentiary institutions there are information brochures for prisoners that are developed by non-governmental organizations. Some of these brochures are translated in foreign languages. In case a foreign prisoner is unable to understand this, an interpreter will be used. Each prisoner in Hungary, including foreigners, has to sign a declaration that they have been informed properly about their rights and obligations. In the Irish Mountjoy Prison a short video message about how the prison system works and what services are available to prisoners, is shown in the reception area. It is the intention to make this video available in different languages. In another Irish prison, in Cork, information is put in strategic locations in different languages by the Education Department. Also in Latvia the extracts of the 'Regulations on the Internal Order in Prisons' are made available in Latvian and Russian on the walls in the living area of prisons.

Some local prisons in England and Wales that are close to air and seaports receive a significant proportion of foreign prisoners. Prison staffs often seek assistance of 'Foreign National Prisoner Orderlies'; these are prisoners with certain language skills that are trained in informing newcomers and to reduce their isolation. The initiative to carefully recruit and train 'Foreign National Prisoner Orderlies' came from a large local London prison called HMP Wandsworth. This practice has been praised, also in prison inspections, and adopted by other prisons.

Another good practice that can be found in England and Wales is the 'Foreign National Prisoners Information Pack' that is handed out to foreign prisoners upon admission. The Pack, available in 20 languages, contains information about the rules, prisoners' rights and duties, how to make a complaint, how to contact embassies, how to apply for repatriation etc. The Prison Service Headquarters and the Prison Reform Trust produced the first edition of the Pack in 1994. Besides a section for foreign prisoners there is also a training and education package for staff. The latest edition, which was made in co-operation with the London Probation, dates from December 2004.

2.3.4 Medical check

Rule 16 of the European Prison Rules prescribes that 'as soon as possible after admission prisoners should receive a medical examination'. In penitentiary institutions it is common that a doctor sees newly arriving prisoners for a physical examination as soon as possible but normally within two days. Besides a physical examination prisoners are also seen by the psychosocial service for a mental diagnosis. Medication is arranged if necessary. Information about the physical and mental health is recorded in their personal record.

2.3.5 Contact diplomatic mission

Prisoners are entitled to contact a representative of their diplomatic mission upon admission in a penitentiary institution. In practice prisoners are often not made aware of this right or have personal reasons not to do so. On the other hand many foreign prisoners do not want their embassy to know about their criminal situation, especially those awaiting removal or expulsion. In Hungary penitentiary institutions are obliged to immediately notify the competent embassy or consulate once a foreign prisoner is admitted. According to Article 222 of the Hungarian penitentiary regulation institutions can only refrain from this if the prisoners requests so in writing.

2.3.6 Contact with family

At reception prisoners are in principle entitled to call their families to inform them about their detention. In practice not all penitentiary institutions facilitate this or do not provide financial means to make a short phone call. In practice many prisoners, including foreign prisoners, do not have financial means to make this contact.

In France prison staff refuses conversations in any language other than French. In the Irish Cloverhill pre-trial prison special consideration is being given to foreign prisoners to contact their family at appropriate times for their families. For this reason clocks with various international time zones are placed in the main circle area of the prison. In the Netherlands prisoners are given upon admission a telephone card to make a call. In practice the amount on these cards is not sufficient to make long distance calls.

Conclusions
- Individual penitentiary institutions are in general unprepared to receive prisoners that are unable to understand the national language.
- At reception there is normally no multi-language information available about prison rules, prison procedures, disciplinary sanctions, visits scheme, transfer agreements etc.
- Prison staff in the reception area does not often speak more than one language and are not specifically trained in receiving visitors from abroad.
- In practice not all penitentiary institutions provide facilities and/or (enough) financial means for foreign prisoners to contact their family.

2.4 Work - Education - Training - Sports - Recreation

2.4.1 Work

The European Prison Rules state in Rule 26 that prison authorities should strive to provide sufficient work of a useful nature and prisoners shall receive 'equitable' remuneration for it. Work should never be a punishment and discrimination on the basis of gender is not allowed. Pre-trial prisoners are, unlike sentenced prisoners, in general not obliged to work. In principle no differentiation is made in prison regulations between nationals and foreigners regarding the allocation of work. Normally other criteria are set by prison authorities like; prisoners' skills, knowledge, experience, state of health, age, duration of the sentence, behaviour as well as preferences. But in practice most types of work require sufficient knowledge of the national language and as a result foreign prisoners are often excluded and end upon the bottom of waiting lists. Besides this, work available in penitentiary institutions tends to be limited. Shortage of labour results in long waiting lists and the phenomena that work is not seen as a legal obligation for sentenced prisoners but as a privilege. Lack of work affects both national and foreign prisoners. However, the combination of scarce work and language barriers leads to the fact that foreign prisoners are often excluded from work provisions inside European penitentiary institutions.

Being engaged in useful and paid work is essential for prisoners. Work is one of the most important activities in prison. Many prisoners and in particular foreigners depend on the small income they receive from work, especially when they have no other forms of income to buy telephone cards, rent a TV, buy additional food and items to maintain their personal hygiene or to send money back to their families. Being involved in work can mitigate the detrimental psychological effects of detention and it can teach prisoners a skill that they can use to earn a living after release. Sometimes prisoners are offered to take a vocational training in relation to the work they are doing. Further it is common that employment in prison entitles prisoners to certain privileges like more freedom of movement and more time out of cell. Prisoners are often divided into units for 'workers' and for 'non-workers', with the 'workers' having a much more relaxed regime with a good balance between work, other activities and time inside the cell. In many pre-trial prisons where no work is available prisoners spend often more than 20 hours behind closed doors. Being involved in work can also have a positive effect on the decision of a court when considering a sentence or for conditional release.

Work is generally divided into three types: maintenance work of the penitentiary institution, in-house production and work outside the prison walls. The majority of prisoners allocated to work are involved with in-house production. Normally only a limited number of prisoners are selected for maintenance work inside the institution, like cleaning the corridors, common rooms and helping in the kitchen and those who are trusted to work in the community. In general work is facilitated by the prison authorities and can be organised in collaboration or directly with external entities or firms. Prisoners working conditions should be healthy and safe and prison authorities should ensure that the conditions comply with the requirements as set by labour protection laws. Prisoners may be required to work overtime, on their day's off and on public holidays but only with the consent of the prisoners.

In Austria there is a small enterprise in Vienna's court prison where only juveniles and young adults from Africa work. Despite efforts to provide all prisoners with work it is striking that statistics of the Austrian penitentiary system show that foreigners are less often employed than nationals and as a result Austrian national prisoners earn in average twice as much as foreigners. This difference can also be explained because foreigners are more frequently in pre-trial detention where they are not obliged to work. In Portugal and Spain in some cases foreigners tend to have more access to work activities than national prisoners due to their lack of other forms of income. The most demanding and therefore well-paid prison jobs in the United Kingdom tend to have a high proportion of foreign nationals. This is due to the fact that foreign nationals often are motivated to support their dependants abroad. So-called 'Work Boards' in prison in the United Kingdom are responsible to ensure that prison jobs are distributed fairly and equitably. Maintenance work is often allocated to national prisoners because close cooperation and good communication with prison staff is required. In Hungary maintenance work is not being paid but in the Netherlands it is remunerated in the same way as other work in prison. In Austria prisoners who have worked inside the prison receive unemployment benefits after release. In Slovenia prisoners who are involved in full-time work receive all rights that arise from employment including holiday from 18 tot 30 days per year. Ordinary basic payment for prison work is in Denmark € 1. (8 Danish Kronen) per hour and for extraordinary good or demanding work it can go up to € 1.5 per hour in 2005. In The Netherlands the hourly rate is €0.64 and prisoners can earn a maximum salary of €12.80 (20 hours) per week. When there is no work or not enough work available prisoners receive 80% of their wages. Misbehaviour during work or malingering can lead to disciplinary punishment. Those Dutch open penitentiary institutions that offer work outside the institution are obliged by law to pay all prisoners, also those engaged in education, a salary of 40% of the gross minimum salary, which is approximately € 120.00 per week. In order to increase the availability of work in Estonian penitentiary institutions and to decrease the expenses of prisons a state company called 'PLC Estonian Prison Industries' (AS Eesti Vanglatöös- tus) was established in 2001. In case due to their fault, prisoners deliver unsatisfactory work, the prison director can reduce their remuneration by up to 60%. In Germany it is unlawful for prison authorities to reduce the remuneration for any reason.

It is remarkable to note that in many European countries foreigners are not allowed to work without a work-permit. In practice this seems to be not an obstacle for foreign pris- oners to be involved in work activities inside a penitentiary institution. For example ac- cording to labour laws in the Netherlands and Slovakia the fact that condemned foreign- ers are working inside a penitentiary institution does not constitute a working relationship and therefore a work-permit is not obligatory.

2.4.2 Education and training

According to Rule 28 of the European Prison Rules each 'prison should seek to provide all prisoners with access to educational programmes which are as comprehensive as pos- sible and which meet their individual needs while taking into account their aspirations. Particular attention should be paid to the education of young prisoners and those with special needs'.

Sentenced prisoners are in principle entitled to follow educational and vocational training courses. In practice the availability of educational and training courses varies a lot from country to country and from prison to prison but in general these courses are limited or hardly available. Although foreign prisoners are by law not excluded from par- ticipation in classes, in practice they are often not able to attend due to the selection crite- ria or tests that they cannot meet. Poor understanding of the national language is the main obstacle. Provisions for education are often not available in pre-trial detention and since many foreigners are held in remand they cannot attend educational classes. In Sweden a case was taken up by the Justice Ombudsman in 1995 when a local prison re- fused a foreign prisoner, who was due to be expelled, to participate in educational course. The Justice Ombudsman decided that the practice of excluding a certain sub-group of prisoners from educational activities was not in accordance with the Swedish Prison Treatment Act. Educational classes range from basic education to secondary education and in some cases prisoners are permitted to study at educational institutions or voca- tional training institutes located outside penitentiary institutions. In Slovenia foreigners are in practice not able to follow classes outside the prison. Since a considerable group of prisoners are illiterate or have not finished primary school the majority of educational courses are on elementary or secondary level. In Portugal, data shows that foreign prisoners from European countries and female prisoners from South American countries possess, in average, higher degrees of formal education than nationals. No information is available about the level of educational background of foreigners in other countries.

Some European penitentiary institutions offer language courses to foreigners to become more acquainted with the national language or English. These classes are in the interest of 'both sides' because it is also beneficial for staff when they can better communicate with foreign prisoners. In most institutions demand for this type of courses is greater than the supply. Besides these language courses there are in general no educational courses especially developed for foreigners. Although the CPT judged the situation in Austrian prisons as 'far from satisfactory' in 2005, prison authorities provide courses for juveniles and 'young adults' in order to obtain a compulsory school certificate and many young foreigners are participating in this. The CPT also emphasized in a report of 2002 that the Polish authorities should strive to provide young adult prisoners with a full programme of educational, recreational and other purposeful activities adapted to their specific needs. In Ireland the 'Education Service Computer Class' in Mountjoy prison accommodates juveniles of which at least half the participants are foreigners. It is remarkable to note that in various countries like Ireland and the United Kingdom, foreign prisoners tend to be in general more motivated to attend courses. The types of vocational and professional trainings offered by prison authories varies greatly but they are mainly focussed on jobs for constructions and building, painting, mechanics, electricity and computers and for women more often in the field of personal care like hairdressing. The costs related to the educational and training provisions are assumed by the prison authorities or financed from the state budget allocated for national education. Besides these costs, prison authorities are entitled to give financial remuneration to those prisoners who are participating in educational courses. According to the European Prison Rules education should have 'no less status than work within the prison regime and prisoners shall not be disadvantaged financially or otherwise by taking part in education.' In practice not all prisoners that follow educational classes or training receive a financial remuneration equal to prison work. Distance learning courses organised for foreigners by their diplomatic missions and consulates are rare.

2.4.3 Sports and recreation

Most prisoners are spending the majority of their time inside a penal institution and often behind cell doors. In these circumstances it is essential for their physical and mental health that they are given an adequate amount of time each day in the open air and are allowed participate in sports and recreational activities. Rule 27 of the European Prison Rules states that all prisoners should be able to spend 'at least one hour of exercise every day in the open air' and 'adequate exercise' and 'recreational opportunities' should form an integral part of the prison regime. Recreational activities include sport, games, cultural activities, hobbies and other leisure pursuits. Penal institutions should organise activities and provide facilities and equipment. Unlike older prisons, more recently built prisons are normally equipped with a gym hall, a fitness room and an outdoor sporting field. Specially trained prison staff supervises prisoners during sport activities like fitness, team games and contests.

In general foreign prisoners are not excluded from participating in sports or recreational activities. However, in Austria foreign prisoners are not allowed to participate in jogging-teams that make trips outside the institution because of the presumed higher risk of escape.

Foreign prisoners participate in sports and recreational activities as much as other prisoners. Although there are still communication difficulties, foreign prisoners tend to manage with non-verbal communication. Especially the recreation hours are important for foreign prisoners because they can seek assistance from other prisoners or staff for a better understanding about how the institution and its procedures function. Furthermore, foreign prisoners tend to have less visitors and for them this is a way to socialise.

The use of prison library is open to all prisoners. In most libraries in European penitentiary institutions books are also available in a limited number of foreign languages. In Belgium and Greece prison libraries often work together with local libraries in order to enlarge the selection of books. When the Greek Penitentiary Code was discussed in the Greek Parliament on 1 December 1999 it became clear that the budget for books for prisoners for the year 2000 was only □ 3.000 annually. In some countries prison libraries receive foreign national magazines and newspapers from diplomatic missions and in Austria prisons receive regularly international magazines from special foreigners 'advisors' (so called 'Ausländerreferents'). Books can often be read inside the cell.

Recreational activities and facilities can vary per country and per penitentiary institution but often prisoners can meet in a communal area on their wing where they can sit together to watch television and video movies, play table tennis, chess or darts. Sometimes art classes are offered where prisoners can watch performances like dance and drama. In some countries external welfare organisations are invited to organise cultural events. In Cyprus, prisoners can be involved in expressive art classes such as design, copper work and iconography but also in theatre. There is a team of prisoners that gives theatre performances in and outside the prison. In Austria quarterly 'instructive, artistic or amusing' events are organised like concerts, cabaret, slideshows, drum groups and even belly dancing performances. The Austrian Code of Imprisonment explicitly refers to foreign prisoners and that their special needs should be taken into account. In Greece a pay TV channel can be placed for sports events and films upon request of prisoners. The prisoners themselves cover the costs.

Conclusions

-   Although foreign prisoners are in principle not excluded to participate in work they are often not able to join because it often requires a sufficient knowledge of the national language.
-   Work is in general only limited available. As a result there are often long waiting lists and it is seen as a privilege.
-   In practice foreign prisoners are less often engaged in work than national prisoners.
-   Also educational and training programmes are limited available in European penitentiary institutions and foreign prisoners are often unable to participate due to language barriers.
-   Foreign prisoners are especially over-represented in pre-trial detention and in these settings education and training programmes are often not available at all.
-   Some penitentiary institutions provide national language classes for foreign prisoners. These classes are very popular and therefore there are often long waiting lists.

- Participation of foreign prisoners in sport and recreational activities seems to be no problem.

2.5 Food – Religion – Personal Hygiene – Medical Care

2.5.1 Food

Prison authorities are obliged to provide prisoners with sufficient and healthy food of reasonable variety in accordance with dietary principles and hygiene. Prison authorities are required to take into consideration religious and cultural requirements like not eating any meat, not eating particular meat (Halal), only eating food prepared under specific hygienic conditions (Kosher or according to the Cheriáa) etc. In practice this means that penitentiary institutions have to prepare several different meals on a daily basis. Although by far not all penitentiary institutions do so, especially when the number of prisoners with dietary requirements is small, often certain group preferences are being respected like serving rice for prisoners from Africa, non-pork food for Muslims etc. More common is that prison authorities respect religious holidays of religions that are well represented by groups of prisoners. In France for example Jewish prisoners receive specially prepared kosher food for Easter, New Year's Eve (Rosh-ha-Shana) and Yom Kippur. Muslim prisoners are enabled to celebrate Ramadan (Aid El Fitr) and Ail El Kebir with the appropriate food.

In Cyprus and Estonia the diet is set by the Director of the prison after consultation with the Prison's medical officer who takes into consideration age, health, work and as much as possible the religious beliefs of prisoners. Foreign prisoners in the Czech Republic can choose between nationally prepared food or non-pork food and in case they will or cannot eat that they can request 'additional' food at their own expenses. In Denmark, prisoners receive a daily sum to buy ingredients in the prison shop to prepare their own meal. A common heard complaint is that the food supply in the prison shop is too expensive, too monotonous and not fresh. Prison shops in Finland are provided also with ethnic food. French prison shops tend to have only French and European products and the prices are between 10%-50% higher than in normal supermarkets. In Latvia and Portugal no special diets are provided and therefore, especially foreign prisoners have to purchase products in the prison store. The Portuguese prison authorities accept also specially prepared food by prisoners' families. Upon admission in a Dutch penitentiary institution prisoners are being asked about their dietary requirements for medical, religious or cultural reasons. Although there is not much variation in the menu each institution prepares at least specially prepared food for Muslims, Jews and vegetarians. Due to budgetary restrictions most prisoners in Dutch prisons receive their food in a plastic box that they have to heat in a microwave. As a result the quality of the food is rather low and especially foreign prisoners regret the fact that they cannot cook their own meals. Also in the United Kingdom, where the range of food available to prisoners increased in recent years, there is criticism especially among foreign prisoners about the bland taste of the food. Penitentiary institutions in the United Kingdom provide Halal meat, kosher, vegetarian and vegan options.

2.5.2 Religion

All prisoners have the right to freedom of thought, conscience and religious belief. Prison authorities should create, as far as possible, opportunities in the prison programme to allow prisoners to observe their religion, to pray, to attend services and to read religious text. Facilities should be provided for prisoners who wish to practice their religion and qualified religious representatives should have the right to visit prisoners on a regular basis. Some religions have specific practices which have to be observed and they may include; praying at set times and under certain conditions; dietary restrictions, dress requirements and prescriptions about the length of hair. Freedom of religion also entails the right to be free from religious influence and coercion. Therefore, no prisoner can be forced to participate in any religious meeting or to receive the visit of a representative. Prisoners can choose freely if and which religion or philosophy they want to turn to and can change course during their detention. Normally upon admission prisoners can inform prison staff about their religion.

It is interesting to note that foreign prisoners in interviews for this study indicated that practicing their personal religion was an important element in their lives and in that in some cases there religious feelings became more apparent during detention. Attending religious services or private conversations with religious representatives are also seen as a way to escape daily prison routine and boredom.

Although all penitentiary institutions enable prisoners to practice their religion, not all institutions are willing or equipped to meet the religious needs of all prisoners, including foreigners. This is especially difficult for foreign prisoners because they tend not to practice the same religion as the main national religion of the country in which they are detained. As a result many foreigners are not or hardly able to practice their own religion and to observe praying, dietary and dress requirements.

European prison authorities are dealing with the rather recent development that a considerable part of their prison population consists of prisoners from various religious beliefs. As a result many prisons are struggling to meet the needs of well-represented groups of prisoners with a certain religion. In practice prisons come with creative solutions like providing a multi-faith room for the use of prisoners and for recruiting religious representatives from the community. All prisons give access to qualified religious representatives in order to organise religious services or to meet prisoners on an individual basis. These representatives are often paid by the Prison authorities or by local churches or by religious organisations. In practice it turns out to be difficult to obtain (enough) religious representatives in order to meet the needs. Further the language barrier makes it sometimes difficult for foreign prisoners to attend religious services in a language that they can understand. Contrary to the other staff members the religious staff practises professional secrecy. In many prisons religious events and holy days are respected and special food or access to religious services is provided. In some cases practicing a religion is being misused by prisoners to obtain power. In some countries prisoners who are held in isolation are not permitted to attend religious services with other prisoners. Some religious practices can cause conflicts between prisoners, especially when prisoners are sharing one cell. For example when one prisoner likes to watch television and the other one needs to pray. In many penitentiary institutions efforts are made, upon request of prisoners, to place prisoners of the same nationality and or religion together in one cell so that they can speak their own language and share their religious beliefs.

In Austria the 'Vienna-Josefstadt' prison houses a synagogue, a Catholic church, a Protestant chapel and recently also a mosque. Other prisons in Austria have fewer facilities for prisoners and most religious services are held in the refectory. In Portugal, being a Catholic country, penitentiary institutions in general only house chapels.

In Belgium religion was an important aspect of prison life until after the Second World War. Catholic chaplains were part of the prison staff and catholic nuns ran units for female prisoners until the 1980's. However, the right to freedom of religion was, together with the right of access to a lawyer, the only formally recognized prisoners' rights under the General Prison Regulation of 1965. This right has been confirmed by the new Prison Act of 12 January 2005. The following religions are officially recognized in Belgian prisons: Catholicism, Protestantism, Orthodox faith, Judaism, Islam and non-confessional moral philosophy. Representatives of these recognized religions or philosophies are attached to each prison and they can visit individual prisoners, organise meetings and receive uncensored letters from prisoners. Although the role of Imams are seen as very important for the large group of Muslim prisoners, the Belgium prison authorities could only find two Imams who have to visit 34 prisons.

The Czech Republic Prison Service has 29 prison chaplains employed from 10 state-registered churches that are active in 22 penitentiary institutions. Further there are the Prison Religious Care (PRC) associations that provide voluntary broad ecumenical services in prisons. Muslim prisoners indicated that their religious rights are not observed in Czech prisons because they are not allowed to wear their habit and to wash themselves before every prayer. The Finnish Prison Service has arrangements with the Orthodox Church to take care of the Russian prisoners and part-time orthodox clerks who hold services visit prisons. In French penitentiary institutions there were in 2003 in total 918 religious representatives working in prison of whom 323 were paid. Of this group 513 were Catholics, 267 Protestants, 69 Muslims, 64 Jewish, 3 Orthodox and 2 Buddhists. Despite the considerable number of Muslim religious representatives working for the French prison service, 'Fresnes' a big prison with 637 foreign prisoners could not find an Imam in 2004. In Greek penitentiary institutions prisoners who do not belong to the Eastern Orthodox Christian Church or Roman Catholic Church have very limited opportunities to perform their religious duties. All registered churches in Hungary, over one hundred, are allowed access to prisons and to organise religious services. In practice only relationships with the Catholic Church, Lutherans, Calvinists and the Jewish denomination have been institutionalised. In Ireland there are 20 full-time and 3 part-time chaplains working in penitentiary institutions. In 2003 the Irish chaplains came in the news when they opposed the inappropriate use of prisons as detention centres for expulsion. They recommended that this practice should stop and that a less severe but secure environment should be provided for those foreigners waiting expulsion. In Latvia the prison chaplains play an important role in organising religious services but also in social life. In case a prisoner wants to meet a religious representative, it is the prison chaplain who communicates this and sets up a meeting for the prisoner. In the United Kingdom there is a special 'Chaplain General' at the Prison Service headquarters that ensures that the religious needs of prisoners are met. In Lithuania foreign embassies sometimes help to set up religious meetings in order to meet the religious needs for foreigners. In Malta, as in several other European countries, the Imam plays an important role for Muslim foreign prisoners, especially because there is a large Arab prison community. Also in The Netherlands there are many Muslim prisoners and there is often a lack of Imams. In order to fill this gap the Minister of Justice organised a special Imam training. During Ramadan, the holiest month on the lunar Islamic calendar, Muslim prisoners are allowed to fast from sunrise to sunset and traditional Muslim food is provided between sunset and sunrise. Prisoners who are under any form of segregation or punishment can have access to services but are separated from other prisoners. Although foreign prisoners in Dutch penitentiary institutions indicated in interviews that they were satisfied with the opportunities to practice their religion, the language barriers remained. The Swedish Prison and Probation Service have a network of representatives of different nominations who visit foreign prisoners. This network, called the Council for Spiritual Welfare, consists of around 130 persons.

2.5.3 Personal hygiene

Penitentiary institutions should be properly maintained and kept clean and equipped with adequate sanitary installations. Each prisoner should receive from the prison authorities clean and adequate clothing and bedding together with products to maintain personal hygiene. The accommodation provided for prisoners should respect human dignity, and as far as possible privacy and meet the requirements of health and hygiene.

Hygienic standards may differ per person but also per culture. This can lead to tensions especially when prisoners have to share cells. In many penitentiary institutions prisoners are entitled to wear their own clothes. Newcomers that have no clean or suitable clothing are normally provided with a set of clothing by the prison authorities. Also toiletries for personal hygiene are normally given to prisoners upon admission. In some penitentiary institutions prisoners are not allowed to wear their own clothing nor footwear and for some prisoners this is problematic because it can conflict with their religious dress requirements. In other prisons people are allowed to wear their own clothes as long as they pose no security risk and are correct. In the United Kingdom prisoners are allowed to wear religious headdress such as turbans for Sikhs and headscarves for Muslim women. Normally all prisoners are able to take a shower or bath once or twice a week and upon admission. In Finland prisoners can shower as often as they wish and in Estonia they can also make use of a sauna. Further prisoners' hair can be cut on a regular basis. In case prisoners fail to take care of their own personal hygiene and when this can impose a health risk for him or herself of for other prisoners the director may impose coercion to ensure compliance with hygiene requirements. Prisoners are requested not only to observe their personal hygiene but also their clothing, beddings, cells, shower facilities and communal living facilities should be kept clean at all times.

2.5.4 Medical care

Access to healthcare is a basic right that applies to all human beings. Prison authorities are requested to provide medical care to sustain or improve the physical and mental state of health of prisoners. Medical care and treatment in penal institutions should be equal to that provided in the community and preferably there should be a close link between the public health service and the prison health service. Normally each prisoner receives a health check within 24 hours after admission. Until recently this was the case in Danish prisons but for economical reasons prisoners are now offered to have a health check.

In general foreign prisoners receive the same kind of medical treatment as national prisoners. The main obstacle is the language difficulty. Requesting interpreter assistance from non-medical staff or fellow prisoners can be practical but is not desired because of medial confidentiality and the quality of translation of medical terminology. A Danish prison report on ethnic minorities recommended that interpreters should also have a deep knowledge of the cultural background of foreign prisoners. Professional interpreters are hardly ever used. In the United Kingdom medical staff can use an interpreter-telephone service.

Two large Austrian prisons 'Wien-Josefstad't and 'Stein' have special medical departments where information sheets on medical issues are available in different languages and also medical staff has foreign language competences. In case prisoners can not be treated inside the prisons they are transferred to local hospitals or specialised prison hospitals. Statistical data from Austrian penitentiary institutions shows that foreigners are less often transferred to local hospitals compared to national prisoners. In the Netherlands if medical surgery for foreign prisoners is not strictly urgent they are normally not carried out. This decision also depends on the duration of detention and if follow-up treatment and aftercare can be given in the country of return. Prisoners in Dutch and Spanish penitentiary institutions can, at their own expenses, consult medical doctors of their own choice. With the growing number of prisoners from Central and Eastern European countries, 'new' illnesses are appearing in Belgium prisons like open TB.

Penitentiary institutions in the Czech Republic provide medical care free of charge to national prisoners but foreign prisoners without a health insurance have to pay except in emergency cases. All prisoners, including foreign prisoners, in French prisons are automatically part of the social security system. For irregular foreign nationals this affiliation is only during their time in detention and for foreigners with a legal residence it is valid up to three years after release. Health care in Malta is free for Maltese citizens but not for foreigners except when they are in prison. However, in case particular health requisites are not provided efficiently by the prison health service, foreign prisoners can purchase these on their own expenses. Drug treatment units in Danish prisons tend to have a smaller portion of foreign prisoners compared to the percentage of foreigners in the total prison population. This might have to do with communication and cultural barriers but also with the fact that treatment places are limited and expensive and that many foreigners are being expelled after release. In the United Kingdom there are special health care issues for foreign prisoners that particularly focus on mental health due to the separation from families abroad and isolation due to cultural and language differences.

Conclusions
- Many penitentiary institutions take into consideration the religious and cultural dietary requirements of foreign prisoners.
- Although prisoners are entitled to practice their religion, not all penitentiary institutions are willing and equipped to meet the religious needs of all prisoners.
- Hygienic standards may differ per person but also per culture. This may create tension.
- Foreign prisoners receive in principle similar medical care but in practice they receive less treatment (e.g. drugs) and are less often transferred to local hospitals.

2.6 Consular help and Legal aid

2.6.1 Consular help

Rule 37.1 of the European Prison Rules states that 'prisoners who are foreign nationals shall be informed, without delay, of their right to request contact and be allowed reasonable facilities to communicate with the diplomatic or consular representative of their state'. In case their country has no representation in the country they are allowed to communicate with the representative of the state that takes care of their interest. Prison authorities are requested to co-operate fully with diplomatic representatives of foreign prisoners with special needs.

In practice not all foreign prisoners are willing to contact their embassies and not all embassies and consulates are interested in their detained countrymen. The attitude of embassies varies from pro-active, helpful and caring to indifference and unwillingness to provide any assistance. As a result foreign prisoners have different opinions about the consular assistance they receive, it ranges from very positive to negative. The assistance that may be provided by consular authorities can include: personal visits, providing information on legal proceedings and advice on legal and medical assistance, sending parcels (newspapers, magazines, toiletries etc), sending money and staying in contact with relatives and state authorities in the home country. Diplomatic missions are also involved in the attainment of legal status and documentation for foreign prisoners for release or transfer. It is not uncommon that foreign prisoners are forced to stay longer in detention because their diplomatic mission does not issue travel documents on time.

In most European countries foreign prisoners are entitled upon admission to one free phone call to their diplomatic mission. In Hungary when foreign prisoners indicate that they do not want to contact their embassy they have to do this in writing. In the United Kingdom it can happen that diplomatic missions are informed of the detention of their countrymen by the prison regardless of the personal consent of the prisoner. In Belgium a delay of maximum 3 days is allowed for foreign prisoners who are on remand and who have been restricted by the investigating judge to have contact with the outside world. Article 36 of the Vienna Convention on Consular Relations (1963) requires that foreign nationals who are arrested or detained be given notice 'without delay' of their right to have their embassy or consulate notified of their arrest. In interviews with foreign prisoners in Dutch penitentiary institutions it became clear that not all foreign prisoners were made aware by prison staff about their right to contact their diplomatic mission. The reason for foreign prisoners not to inform their embassies was because they were either embarrassed or afraid of the consequences for their relatives or upon return to their home country or pessimistic about the kind of assistance they could expect from their embassies.

Correspondence with diplomatic missions is in principle confidential and cannot be controlled or censured. In Hungary foreign prisoners are entitled to keep contact with the representative of their diplomatic mission in writing or verbally (by phone or visits) without restriction and supervision but once convicted only written correspondence is exempt from supervision. In Latvia costs for correspondence with diplomatic missions are covered by the prison service and in some prisons regular consultation hours with consular representatives are organised. Also in the United Kingdom there are biannual meetings hosted by the Prison Service Headquarters and London Probation for diplomatic missions. These meetings are organised to inform consulate staff about prison regimes to enable

33

them to provide a knowledgeable and professional service to their imprisoned nationals. These well-attended meetings have been organised since 1992. In the Netherlands the 'Foreign Liaison Office' of the Dutch Probation Service plays an important role in the care of Dutch nationals detained abroad. The 'Foreign Liaison Office' coordinates the visits of 275 volunteers who are Dutch nationals who live and work abroad and who pay social visits to Dutch nationals in detention every four to six weeks in close cooperation with diplomatic missions around the world.

2.6.2 Legal aid

According to Rule 23.1 of the European Prison Rules 'all prisoners are entitled to legal advice, and the prison authorities shall provide them with reasonable facilities for gaining access to such advice'. Prisoners may consult on any legal matter with a legal adviser of their own choice and at their own expense. Visits by lawyers are confidential and shall not be attended by prison staff or others. In case free legal aid is available, prison authorities shall bring this to the attention of all prisoners. Communication and correspondence about legal matters between prisoners and their legal advisers are in principle confidential. Prisoners are allowed to keep documents related to their legal proceedings in own possession.

In many European legal systems if accused persons cannot afford a lawyer, the court assigns at their own costs a lawyer. In case the accused person does not understand the language of the court an interpreter is being used and paid by the court. In practice some countries encountered difficulties to find suitable interpreters. Especially during the pre-trial period, information from the court is of crucial importance to prisoners. Foreign prisoners are severely disadvantaged when they are unable to understand the information and legal proceedings.

Foreign prisoners tend to be dissatisfied with the legal support they receive. Very often the lawyers do not spend any or very little time on their case, only show up (if they show up) in court, provide very little information about court proceedings and outcome of case. This is aggravated by the fact that the lawyers often do not speak the language of clients and are often not trained and familiar with legal aspects of foreign prisoners' cases.

In order to provide more insight in legal proceedings some Belgian prisons organise for lawyers 'foreign prisoners' information sessions'. Prisoners in Cyprus who cannot afford a lawyer can request free legal aid but once the person is convicted the free legal assistance stops. In the Czech Republic, the Czech Helsinki Committee provides free legal help to foreign prisoners. Also in Hungary and Malta non-governmental organisations provide assistance. In Greece if a prisoner is financially unable to pay for legal assistance a complex procedure needs to be followed. The prisoner is requested to fill out an application with supporting documents like tax return papers, statement of income by the revenue office, certificate of financial need or granting of a welfare allowance, certificate of unemployment subsidy by the Manpower Employment Organisation, records of proceedings of judicial authorities or other documents. It seems to be difficult for foreigners to provide these documents.

Legal assistance to foreign prisoners in connection with disciplinary proceedings is also unsatisfactorily organised. In Spain there is a legal procedure that states that assistance should be given by a member of the prison staff or by another prisoner. This is seen as unacceptable and therefore the assurance of permanent access to competent interpreters in order to be heard and to understand what is being said in disciplinary proceedings should be recognized as a right for foreign prisoners.

Conclusions
- Although foreign prisoners are entitled to contact their diplomatic missions in practice they do not often make use of this right. Sometimes because they are afraid or ashamed to inform them but more often because they are not made aware of this.
- The position of diplomatic missions varies from pro-active, helpful and caring to indifferent and unwilling to provide any assistance.
- Foreign prisoners are in desperate need of legal assistance since they are often unable to understand legal proceedings and as a result of that they even do not understand their own legal case.
- Very often foreign prisoners do not know if they will be expelled after release or not. This creates severe tensions and aggravates the feeling of desperation.
- Foreign prisoners tend to be dissatisfied with the (free) legal aid they receive. Lawyers do often not speak the language of their clients and are often not trained or familiar with the legal aspects of foreign prisoners' cases.

2.7 Contact with the outside world

Prisoners retain, despite being deprived of their liberty, the right to maintain contact with family, friends and the outside world. The right to interact and communicate with the outside world is of vital importance to the socialization in prison and also in the facilitation of a successful return into society after release. Foreign prisoners are hampered by the fact that they are far away from home and that maintaining contact is more difficult. The language barrier proves to be a difficult hurdle also in relation to contact with the outside world. As a result many foreign prisoners are socially isolated. According to article 24 of the European Prison Rules prison authorities are requested to provide facilities and opportunities for prisoners to maintain contact with the outside world by letter and telephone and to receive visits. Communication and visits may be subject to restrictions and monitoring when necessary for the maintenance of good order, safety and security. Contact with lawyers, diplomatic missions, Ombudsman and international organisations are in principle confidential and may not be censored by prison authorities. In many countries the rules to maintain contact with the outside world depend on the legal status of prisoners. Prisoners serving a sentence are subjected to different regulations than unconvicted prisoners in pre-trial detention. In pre-trial detention the decision over the level of contact a prisoner is allowed is also depending on the decision of the judicial authority.

The most important instruments for prisoners to maintain contact are visits, communication via telephone and letters and access to news via newspapers, magazine, television and radio.

2.7.1 Visits

Although foreign prisoners are entitled to as many visits as national visitors in practice they receive far less visitors than national prisoners and sometimes even none. Only a limited number of penitentiary institutions agreed on working with a more flexible visiting scheme in order to alleviate the social exclusion of foreign prisoners. In some special cases, like when relatives have to travel long journeys, the length of visits can be extended. In Austria, Germany, Ireland, Malta and Sweden the visiting hours are dealt with generously and foreign prisoners may receive up to a whole day of visit, or divided over some days in a row in case a visitor comes from abroad. In Hungary visits from relatives from abroad may last up to two hours but in The Netherlands no exemptions are made to the visiting rule of one hour per week.

Normally visits last about one hour and are supervised by prison staff. In some countries prisoners are also entitled to unsupervised visits. In Estonia these 'long-term' visits may last up to three days in designated rooms inside the prison without constant supervision. In Poland there are officially no conjugal (or intimate) visits but the frequency as well as conditions of visits can be modified by means of rewards granted to prisoners for good behaviour. The rewards are: the permission to receive an additional or longer visit, the permission to receive an unsupervised visit in a common room and the permission to receive an unsupervised visit in a separate room. In Spanish prisons, for those who cannot obtain permissions of leave are authorized to have a conjugal visit or family visit once a month from one to three hours.

Visiting hours granted to prisoners are often depending on their legal status. In Hungary pre-trial prisoners are, apart from the lawyer or representative of the diplomatic mission, not allowed to receive visitors without the prior authorization by the prosecutor or, in the trial stage, the court. In Austria pre-trial prisoners have in principle the right to a 15-minute visit of at least twice a week and sentenced prisoners are entitled to receive longer visits. In Belgium pre-trial prisoners are entitled to daily visits while sentenced prisoners may receive up to 3 visits. In the Czech Republic foreign prisoners are allowed to receive visits with a total time of 3 hours per month but some persons, like lawyers, representatives of diplomatic missions or NGO's may pay visits without any limitation.

In principle foreign prisoners can be visited by anyone but in most cases the visitors are direct family, partners, legal representatives, representatives from diplomatic missions, religious persons and representatives from NGO's. In some countries there are community organisations that pay social visits to prisoners, including foreigners. Sometimes family members may be unwilling to visit because of their illegal status in the country. In Belgium visitors other than direct family must request first permission from the prison director. Visitors of prisoners in French penitentiary institutions are obliged by law to speak in French but fortunately for visitors from foreign origin this rule is not strictly applied. Further, prisoners under French regime are allowed to attend family events and receive prison leave for weddings, death or in cases of illness as long as it is inside the country. Some Irish prisons have special 'Visitors Centres' that are run by prison staff for families with children that are visiting their relatives in prison. The centre provides tea and coffee facilities in a hospitable atmosphere with a child care area for children and in special cases they try to liaise on behalf of the prisoners and their families with the prison on certain issues. The number of families of foreign prisoners has been on the increase. In the Swedish Kumla Prison provisions are made for visitors from abroad to stay overnight in a local church for around □ 10 per night.

2.7.2 Telephone and correspondence

In practice written correspondence can be problematic because a considerable percentage of prisoners, including foreign prisoners, are unable to write and sometimes read. The fact that foreign prisoners write in a foreign language makes it difficult for prison authorities to censor it when there are security reasons for doing so. In German prisons the regulation that prisoners are not allowed, 'without compelling reason', to write letters in a foreign language, usually excludes letters written by foreigners. In Malta prisoners' correspondence is systematically read and therefore the CPT recommended the Maltese prison authorities in 1995 and in 2001 that 'it would be preferable to provide that, save in exceptional cases, letters may only be examined (rather than read) by prison staff.' In the United Kingdom unconvicted prisoners may send out two free letters per week and convicted prisoners one in order to maintain contact with their relatives.

International calls are expensive and penitentiary institutions often do not take into consideration the different time zones when granting prisoners permission to make a phone call. Many foreign prisoners, especially when they are not involved in work, have insufficient means to call their family abroad. Some penitentiary institutions introduced for this reason free phone cards, an international calling card or created the possibility to make 'collect calls', a system where the person who receives the call is paying. In Belgian prisons this system was recently abolished. Making a phone call is a lengthy process for prisoners in Austrian pre-trial prisons because they have to apply first for a permit to the investigating judge. Calls are only allowed during business hours and there are often not enough telephones available. In Cyprus national prisoners are allowed one telephone call per week whereas foreign prisoners are allowed telephone calls twice a week in order to compensate the fact that they receive fewer visitors. Those who are financially not able to afford a telephone card receive one from the prison authorities.

In Irish penitentiary institutions all prisoners are allowed to make a daily six-minute telephone call free of charge. In Latvia prisoners are only allowed to make 1 to 3 phone calls per month and in Lithuania in principle only 6 to 12 calls a year. In Slovakia and Spain phone calls by prisoners are made in the presence of a prison official. In Sweden listening in to any prisoner's telephone conversation may only occur with the prisoner's knowledge and calls with lawyers may never be monitored. Prisoners in Swedish closed prison settings must apply in writing for approval of each telephone number they wish to call. Before consent is being given first criminal record checks are being conducted. Those persons using a cash card where no physical person is registered are not likely to be approved. Especially for foreign prisoners with family in countries where such cash cards are used this poses a difficulty and also when security checks cannot be conducted on persons living abroad.

Prisoners in Spain cannot receive telephone calls but are allowed to make 5 calls per week of not more than five minutes per call. In Spain there are certain non-governmental organisations that provide not only financial support to foreign prisoners for stamps and telephone calls but also provide mediation between the prisoner and their families. Also in the United Kingdom there are NGO's such as the New Bridge organisation that provides support to foreign prisoners.

2.7.3 Access to news

Prisoners are allowed to keep themselves informed about public affairs by subscribing to and reading newspapers, magazines and by listening to radio and watching television.

Prisoners in Belgian penitentiary institutions are allowed to purchase all newspapers and publications that are legally available. In Cyprus, prisoners receive local newspapers daily on their wing. Foreign prisoners in Czech Republican prisons may receive by mail books, daily press and magazines without any restriction. Each penitentiary institution in Estonia has at least one daily newspaper in Estonian and one in Russian available. Also in Lithuania sentenced prisoners are in theory allowed to spend their money on buying an unlimited number of books and subscribing to newspapers and magazines as long as the publications are not propagating violence and cruelty or contain pornographic publications. In practice however most prisoners have no financial means for this and are depending on their relatives to send parcels with literature. Most Lithuanian institutions are subscribed to some foreign periodicals in Russian and Polish.

In several countries, like Belgium, Lithuania, The Netherlands, prisoners can rent a television that offers many channels, including many foreign languages. In Cyprus and in France only national channels can be watched on television. Libraries in European penitentiary institutions can provide prisoners access to news. Some prison libraries have newspapers and magazines available and sometimes embassies assist in providing foreign periodicals. Although newspapers, books and magazines in foreign languages are officially allowed inside Portuguese prisons, they are hardly available because prison directors often do not authorize them because they are in languages that are not understandable for the officers whose job is to screen them. Libraries in Swedish penitentiary institutions offer a few foreign newsmagazines and 'easy Swedish' papers for those who are learning Swedish. Further are Swedish librarians so kind to print for foreign prisoners the covers of their national newspapers.

Conclusions
- Due to language difficulties and distance from family and relatives many foreign prisoners are disconnected from the outside world and feel socially isolated.
- Prison authorities do not set up normally a more flexible visiting scheme for foreign visitors.
- In Germany prisoners are in principle not allowed to write in a foreign language and in France prisoners are not allowed to speak on the telephone in a language that prison staff can not understand. In Malta prisoners' correspondence is systematically being read by the prison authorities.
- In several penitentiary institutions, prisoners are allowed to watch television with various foreign channels.

2.8 Re-integration activities and Prison leave

Reintegration of prisoners into society is seen in the European Prison Rules as a fundamental focus of penitentiary intervention. European Prison Rule 6 states that 'detention shall be managed so as to facilitate the reintegration into free society of persons who have been deprived of their liberty'. Prison leave offers a natural way in which prisoners can gradually get used to the outside world again and start rebuilding their personal and professional lives. Reintegration activities and prison leaves are for foreign prisoners as important as for other prisoners even if they will be returning to another country.

2.8.1 Re-integration

According to Rule 33.3 of the European Prison Rules 'all prisoners should have the benefit of arrangements designed to assist them in returning to free society after release' and this should be done through a programme of positive care and assistance. In various countries prison authorities work in partnership with community organizations and authorized organizations like Probation in order to facilitate reintegration activities and facilities. In general there are no agencies or authorities specifically concerned with the foreign prisoners after they leave prison.

Educational and vocational training, especially when the training can be continued after release, can be regarded as a reintegration measure. The same applies to work, as long as it maintains or increases prisoners' ability to earn a living after release. In practice however, the lack of education and work in penitentiary institutions make these measures less effective, especially for foreign prisoners who are often not able to participate because of the language barrier. Although foreign prisoners are in principle eligible for placement in reintegration activities in practice they tend to be excluded. The main reasons for this exclusion are that reintegration activities are usually available only on a limited scale and as there are not sufficient places for all prisoners, foreign prisoners are given less priority because they might not return to society in the country of detention. Lastly as these courses tend to be given in semi-open prison settings where less foreign prisoners are allocated. Foreigner prisoners who will be expelled after release are in principle excluded from reintegration activities.

Open penitentiary institutions in Germany specialise in preparing prisoners for release by offering training programmes. In a German study (2002) it became clear that only 10% of all foreign prisoners were placed in such open institutions compared to 28% of all national prisoners. In the Czech Republic there is a similar situation. Although in principle all prisoners should be prepared for resettlement at least three months before release in practice foreign prisoners are often excluded. In Latvia a probation officer visits prisoners six month before release in order to plan and organize their return into society or stay in a halfway house. The State Probation Service started supervision of offenders in society since 2006 and assistance is granted to both national and foreign prisoners. Most probation officers also speak English. In Lithuania 46% of all prisoners participated in resocialisation programmes in 2005 against 23% of the foreign prison population. In order to stimulate the smooth transition from prison to society the Dutch prison service introduced the 'Penitentiary programme'. Motivated prisoners that have served at least five sixths of a sentence of at least 6 months are eligible to participate in this programme and are allowed to work or follow educational classes outside the institution and stay home overnight and during weekends. An additional condition for participation is that the remaining sentence amounts to a minimum of 4 weeks and a maximum of a year. Foreign prisoners are excluded from participation and there are further no reintegration programmes or facilities available.

2.8.2 Prison leave

The system of prison leave is an integral part of the overall regime for sentenced prisoners. According to European Prison Rule 24.7, 'whenever circumstances allow, the prisoner should be authorised to leave prison either under escort or alone in order to visit a sick relative, attend a funeral or for other humanitarian reasons'. Prison leave is also granted in order to facilitate re-integration by for example maintaining family ties, preparing for work or training, arranging legal matters etc.

Foreign prisoners are rarely allowed to leave prison for a certain time, especially when they will be expelled after release. The situation is slightly better for foreigners who are integrated in the country and who have a resident permit. One of the main reasons for this is that prison authorities consider a high risk of escape, especially when foreign prisoners want to avoid expulsion at the termination of their sentence.

During imprisonment prison authorities often do not know whether a prisoner will be expelled or not afterwards. In practice this means that prison authorities and individual prison directors deal with this problem differently. Some prison authorities and prison directors refuse categorically every prison leave in case of uncertainties about expulsion after custody while others let foreigners leave prison even when the immigration authority has not taken its decision yet. A precondition is that foreign prisoners have a secure home or contact address in the country. If the aim of prison leave is not re-integration and if the prisoner has no social contacts in the country, it will hardly be granted.

In Austria, prison leave exists for so-called 'Ausgang', for a maximum of 5 days to organise personal, economic, educational or legal affairs, or 'Freigang' for those prisoners working without surveillance outside the prison. Two-thirds of the national prisoners serving a sentence were granted 'Ausgang' compared to 11% of foreign prisoners. National prisoners are allowed to leave prison on average 3.4 days per 100 days compared to 0.5 days for foreign prisoners. From this group of foreign prisoners EU citizens are granted the lowest number of prison leave days, namely 0.3 per 100 days. Under 'Freigang' only 4% of the foreign prison population left prison for work compared to 31% national prisoners. On average national prisoners worked 10 per 100 days outside prison compared to 1 per 100 days for foreigners.

In Belgium, foreign prisoners who are not registered in the Foreigners' Register in the Population Register or in the EU Register are excluded from systematic prison leave. For those who are registered, the decision will depend on their administrative status. In case of expulsion, only in exceptional cases is prison leave granted but never in the case of extradition. In practice, prison leave is hardly granted to foreign prisoners since around two-thirds of them have no legal permit to stay. Swedish prisons have so-called 'Breathing space leaves' for prisoners serving sentences of two years or more, a category that often includes foreign prisoners. These leaves allow prisoners an annual leave for up to four hours to take part in an activity outside prison, like watching a football match, shopping etc. On these visits prison officials accompany prisoners.

Foreign prisoners in Cyprus, Denmark and Germany may be granted prison leave in case they will not be expelled after release. An exception is made in Germany if prison officials accompany foreign prisoners. A German research study (2002) revealed that 58% of national prisoners compared to 18% of foreign prisoners were granted prison leave. Foreign prisoners with a secure (home) address in the country of detention have a chance in Estonia, Greece, Italy, Malta and The Netherlands to obtain prison leave. The Greek

Ombudsman refers to this severe disadvantage for foreign prisoners in its annual report of 2005. Prison leave in Poland is only granted to foreign prisoners under escort by prison officials, in Lithuania no prison leave was granted to foreigners in 2005 and in Spain only in exceptional cases. Spanish NGO's like 'Horizontes Abiertos' and 'Caritas' are addressing these disadvantages for foreign prisoners by providing secure shelters and dormitories to make prison leave possible. In nearly all penitentiary institutions in Europe foreign prisoners who are awaiting expulsion are not eligible for prison leave.

Conclusions

- Foreign prisoners tend to be excluded from re-integration activities because prison authorities do not want to invest in people that might not return to their own society.
- Foreign prisoners are rarely allowed prison leave, especially when they will be expelled after release.

2.9 Release - Expulsion

Prison authorities are required by the European Prison Rules to prepare prisoners for a successful return into society and to provide them upon release with appropriate documents, financial means and adequate clothing. Prisoners that served their sentence are entitled to be released or granted conditional release (parole) when they have served a part of their sentence. Expulsion from a country can be the result of a criminal penalty or an administrative measure under the Immigration Law. Information on expulsion of foreign prisoners that are solely detained to safeguard their administrative removal can be found in chapter 3.

Foreign prisoners are in theory not exempt from conditional release provisions but in most countries parole is granted less often in comparison to national prisoners. All European countries have legal provisions to expel foreigners that have breached the (immigration) law and this provision is frequently used. The combination of complex and frequently changing criminal and administrative procedures leads to a difficult situation for foreign prisoners, full of uncertainty and anxiety.

2.9.1 (Conditional) Release

On release, the items, documents and personal clothing deposited in the prison will be returned to the prisoner. If the prisoner has no personal clothing or if the prisoner's personal clothing is not suitable for the season, the prison will provide the prisoner to be released with adequate clothing without charge. On release, the deposited savings fund accrued from the funds deposited on the personal account of the prisoner will be handed over to the prisoner. In order to prepare prisoners for release many prison authorities provide leaflets with practical information about housing, work, social insurances, social welfare allowances etc.

In Austria, all prisoners are in theory entitled to parole but in practice prisoners without Austrian citizenship are released on parole slightly less often than nationals. Nationals with a sentence of up to six months are conditionally released twice as often as foreigners whereas nationals and foreign prisoners serving a sentence six to twelve months there are no noteworthy differences. In the case of long sentences, one to three years, foreigners are more often released conditionally. In Belgium, with regards to conditional release there is officially no distinction between national and foreign prisoners but in practice there is. The system that prisoners, serving between one and three years of imprisonment, are provisionally released after serving one third of their sentence is not applicable to foreign prisoners without a legal residence permit.

In Cyprus it is not possible to apply for parole. In Denmark the decision to grant parole is based on the risk assessment of committing a new crime and conditions like appropriate housing and occupation and for example treatment for alcoholism. Foreign prisoners are not excluded from conditional release as long as they have a permanent home address. In Finland, foreign prisoners like national prisoners are granted parole after half or two-thirds of the sentence has been served. In France only 2% of the foreign prison population were granted conditional release in 1998. In Latvia, parole is granted to persons regardless of their citizenship. The application for parole is reviewed by the 'Administrative Commission' that consists of representatives from prison, probation and prosecutors office and by the judge. Although in Lithuania and in Slovakia foreigners are also eligible for parole in practice it is rarely applied. Foreign prisoners that are not subject to a removal order in Malta are treated like national prisoners and can be granted conditional release. In the Netherlands there is no parole or conditional release, it was abolished in 1986 and replaced by early release. Foreign prisoners with valid papers and a permission to stay in the Netherlands are given upon release money to travel to the location where they were arrested. In Poland, foreign prisoners, even those who are to be expelled after serving their sentences, could be released on parole according to general rules. Since the implementation of the Criminal Justice Act 2003 in England and Wales release arrangements for foreign prisoners changed considerably. It is in the majority of cases up to the prison governor to make parole decisions in respect of the 'Early Removal Scheme' (ERS). The ERS, implemented in April 2004, allows eligible foreign prisoners to be removed up to 4 ½ months before their half way release date. Foreign prisoners who appealed against expulsion or who have an outstanding asylum claim cannot be considered under the ERS.

2.9.2 Expulsion

A decision to expel or remove a foreigner after imprisonment varies per country but general criteria are based on: legal status, time spent in the country of detention before conviction, number of offences and the length of the sentence. If the person is seen as a 'danger to public interest', which is usually assumed after a 'considerable' prison sentence, the person will be expelled. Also incorrect information given to the national authorities, lack of financial means, illegal work and other (administrative) offences can lead to a ban on residence.

An expulsion order is in some countries connected to a (long) prison sentence and in some countries it can be imposed as an additional penalty to imprisonment. Foreign prisoners see the imposed expulsion order often as an additional punishment. Execution of the expulsion order has to take place after the basic penalty has been served. Foreign prisoners are entitled to appeal against the removal decision. Expulsion criteria tend to be less restrictive in case a foreigner has been living for a long time in the country of detention and when the person has strong family bonds and is well integrated. The decision of expulsion or removal is normally taken by courts and national immigration authorities and carried out in cooperation with police and border control authorities. Courts and penitentiary institutions provide information on convictions of foreigners and on the end date of the sentence. It is often up to the immigration police to determine whether the prisoner will be detained in special custody for the purpose of removal or not.

Very often expulsion cannot be enforced. Most common reasons for that are; unsafe conditions in country of return, refusal of the country of origin to take back a certain person, the expulsion decision is being legally challenged or an application is made for asylum. Legal remedies against expulsion decisions have normally a suspensive effect. In case execution of the expulsion order cannot be effectuated directly after release from prison, foreign prisoners are normally transferred to detention centres to await their removal. In some countries, like in Ireland, it is possible for foreign prisoners to apply for voluntarily return to the country of origin. The fact that the decision of expulsion or removal is often taken at the end of the detention period is very stressful for foreign prisoners. The uncertainty about what might happen after release aggravates detention.

In Belgium, foreign prisoners with a sentence of at least six months can be expelled after serving their sentence. Re-entry is prohibited for a period of ten years. The decision for expulsion is made by a 'Bureau D', the 'D' stands for detainees in the Office for Foreigners' Affairs (OFA) of the Ministry of Interior. In case foreign prisoners have requested asylum status or regularisation of their irregular status the process of reviewing is being postponed and prisoners can get 'released with a view on expulsion'. The many changes in the already complex expulsion procedures in Belgium over the last years led to dramatic situations were foreign prisoners went on hunger strikes and attempted suicides.

In the Czech Republic, the police execute the penalty of expulsion and can provide the necessary travel documents. Half of all foreign nationals that were sentenced received a penalty of expulsion in 2004. In Denmark, foreign prisoners that will be expelled have to pay for their transport themselves in case they have sufficient means. Expulsion takes place after serving 7/12 of the sentence. This '7/12' rule can be explained by the fact that foreigners who will be expelled are not given temporary prison leave and therefore receive an equivalent reduction in their sentence. In Lithuania, foreigners have to pay for the expenses of removal. In Estonia, foreign prisoners without a residence permit will be expelled upon release. If immediate expulsion from Estonia is not possible, the foreigner will be placed in an expulsion centre upon release. Before Finnish national authorities make a decision of expulsion particular attention is paid to the best interests of children and the protection of family life. Foreign prisoners that are approved asylum seekers or who have a legal residence permit are in principle protected against removal in Germany. In the majority of the German 'Länder' the expulsion is considered after the enforcement of half of the sentence and in some cases two thirds. Greek courts may order expulsion once a foreigner receives a prison sentence of at least one year. Those expelled foreigners may return to Greece three years after their expulsion once they receive permissions from the Minister of Justice. The vast majority of foreigners convicted by the criminal court in Hungary will be expelled. The expulsion order is seen, like in Latvia, as an additional penalty to imprisonment that can be with terminal effect or for a definite period between one and ten years. Besides the criminal court, the alien policing authority also has the right to order expulsion, for example when foreigners breach the provisions of immigration law. In Italy, the 'Penitentiary Police' is charged to transfer foreign prisoners who have a removal order. In Malta, a foreign prisoner that will be expelled is taken to the embassy pending the return to the home country.

Foreign prisoners in Dutch penitentiary institutions that cannot be expelled directly after release from prison are brought to the Aliens Police and put in detention centres until the Dutch Immigration and Naturalisation Service will execute the removal. There is no limit for the duration of the stay. In Slovakia, citizens from the European Economic Area (EEA) can only be expelled if they constitute a threat to the security of the country, public order, or public health. Appealing a decision of expulsion does not always suspend the execution. In Slovenia around 65% of foreign prisoners are expelled. The most common penal sentence imposed on a foreigner in Spain is expulsion. The expulsion order, that prohibits re-entry into Spain for 10 years, has to be applied without delay and within 30 days. In practice the execution of expulsion is complicated and takes much more time. Foreign prisoners that are going to be expelled in Sweden receive 10% of their own savings in cash that were held on a separate account. European Union citizens in the United Kingdom with a prison sentence of over two years, and non-EU nationals receiving a sentence of over one year are usually considered for expulsion. The changes in the parole scheme and the introduction of the ERS in England and Wales (see above) resulted in a higher proportion of foreign nationals being expelled.

Conclusions
- In practice foreign prisoners are granted less often conditional release than national prisoners.
- The decision of expulsion is normally taken by courts and national immigration authorities and carried out in cooperation with police and custom authorities. The decision is often taken at the end of the detention period which creates extra tension for foreign prisoners.
- Very often expulsion can not be enforced because of the unsafe conditions in countries of return, refusal from countries to take back people, or the expulsion decision is legally challenged or an application is made for asylum.

2.10 Aftercare - Probation

In many European countries prisoners who have been released or who will be released shortly receive aftercare support from social welfare organisations, community based organisations and non-governmental organisations. Besides aftercare services most European countries have Probation Services that provide nationwide rehabilitative assistance to (ex-) offenders. Many foreign prisoners cannot make use of this because they have to return upon release immediately to their country of origin or because probation services are not investing in foreign (ex-) offenders. Arranging good aftercare for those that return is difficult. Contacts with social welfare agencies and probation services are often difficult because of language barriers and the fact that there are, besides the 'Conférence Permanente Européenne de la Probation' (CEP), hardly any established links or networks between involved organisations.

Foreign prisoners that remain in the country of detention are in some countries entitled to make use of probation service as long as they have a residence permit and are not under a removal or expulsion order. Although these 'new clients' led to adjustments in the traditional work of some probation services, most probation services are not providing specific programmes for foreigners. Traditional activities of probation services are supervision during conditional release and providing assistance in finding a suitable house, a job training, applying for legal papers, applying for social welfare allowance, helping to re-establish family relations, mediation between victim and offender, etc. The effectiveness of aftercare and probation depends heavily on the language skills of the ex-offender.

2.10.1 Aftercare

Danish juvenile institutions have a 'mentor programme' where an adult from the outside community provides support to young foreign prisoners just before and just after release. In Estonia there are no specific aftercare facilities for foreign ex-offenders. In Finland there are special drugs and alcohol programmes developed for ex-offenders from Russia and Estonia.

In Lithuania provisions are made that foreign ex-offenders with a residence permit can apply for a single social welfare allowance from the municipality upon release. In Portugal the 'Instituto de Reinserção Social' and other social welfare services support the re-integration process of foreign ex-offenders with a residence permit. In the United Kingdom there are several non-governmental organisations, funded through charitable sources and increasingly through contracts with individual prisons that provide specific services to foreigners before and after release. These organisations are; 'Vamos Juntos', assisting Spanish, Portuguese and Latin American prisoners, 'Detention Advice Service', providing specialist immigration advice, 'New Bridge' providing general befriending support and casework and 'Hibiscus', working with Afro-Caribbean and Latin American Women.

2.10.2 Probation

In Belgium, foreign prisoners with a residence permit are entitled to the same support as national citizens but this did not led to specific programmes. The Danish Probation Service has one consultant specialised in the re-integration of ethnic minorities into society. In Estonia there are no specific probation activities for foreigners. There is no probation service for adults in Greece and the public prosecutor of the court that ordered conditional release exercises supervision. In Ireland there is no statutory aftercare for persons completing a sentence, except for prisoners who are granted temporary release with a condition of supervision by the Probation Service. The Linkage Programme, a re-integration initiative, which is supported and funded by the Probation Service has no breakdown of referrals by nationality. In Latvia ex-offenders can stay in one of the eight halfway houses financed by the Probation Service. This facility is open to foreigners but until now no foreign ex-offenders have made use of it. In the plans for the new structure of the Dutch Prison Service there are no special aftercare facilities for foreign prisoners and also the Dutch Probation Service is not able to intervene because local community authorities are responsible for providing aftercare for ex-offenders in their community. Since January 2006 the Swedish Probation Service has been given more responsibilities for providing aftercare. In the United Kingdom, an 'Offender Manager' of the local Probation Service in the area of their home address supervises foreign prisoners that have been released.

Conclusions
- Foreign prisoners that remain in the country of detention after release can make use of aftercare service if they have a residence permit and are not under an expulsion order.
- Probation services do not provide specific programmes for foreigners.

2.11 Staff

Prison authorities should recognise that dealing with prisoners in a professional, humane and personal manner requires effective management and great interpersonal and technical skills from prison staff. Prison staff carries out an important public service and they should be carefully selected, properly trained, paid as professional workers and receive a respected status in society. Prison staff should work under adequate conditions that enable them to maintain high standards in their care of prisoners. Every penal institution should have a proper management structure and sufficient range of specialist staff like psychiatrists, psychologists, doctors, nurses, social workers, pastoral workers, librarians, teachers, sport-instructors, placement officers etc. Over the last decades and especially over the last few years, the increasing presence of foreigners has changed daily prison life. In some prisons more than a quarter of the prisoners are foreigners from various countries around the world. This meant new challenges for prison staff and prison authorities have been responding to this in various ways.

Rule 81.3 of the European Prison Rules states that 'staff who are to work with specific groups of prisoners, such as foreign nationals, women, juveniles or mentally ill prisoners, etc., shall be given specific training for their specialised work. In many countries providing special training for prison staff working with foreign prisoners has not been given priority. One of the most important trainings should be language as good communication between prison staff and foreign prisoners is essential. It is therefore striking that in the recruitment process, a foreign language competence is hardly a required competence. Furthermore prison authorities should acknowledge that cultural characteristics influence persons' interactions in prison and that some staff members might have difficulties in working with persons from different cultures or are prejudiced against foreigners. It would therefore be beneficial if prison authorities provide special courses about the background of certain cultures, cultural habits, religions and also courses like 'how to handle certain situations' etc. For example how to deal with prisoners from more patriarchal cultures that refuse to accept the authority of female prison staff. Or how to assess if prisoners are justifying their behaviour by referring to their religion while infringing the rules.

2.11.1 Training

In Austria, special information about foreign cultures (16 hours) and an English course (32 hours, including technical terminology) are parts of the basic training for new prison staff since 2004. There is also a voluntary and well attended follow-up training that includes courses on migration, globalisation, foreign prisoners, 'Slav Culture' and English language. In Denmark it takes a person three years to become a trained prison official. The biggest part of the education period is practical and takes place in prison and half a year is theory and includes knowledge of society, psychology and conflict solution. The

Dutch Training Institute for prison staff offers a 42days basic training that includes one course on cultural diversity.

In Estonia and Finland there are, besides a language course, no other special trainings to deal with foreign prisoners. In Greece, Hungary, Latvia, Lithuania, Malta and Poland, there are no special language courses for prison staff. In France, Probation staffs receive a nine-hour course on 'foreign nationals' among other specific groups like women, juveniles and elderly people. The last years Portuguese prison authorities have been investing in the security side of prison and did not focus on specific programs and interventions directed to acquiring social competences and dealing with emotional problems. Although there is no legal basis for training in Slovakia, foreign languages and cultural diversity courses are included in the educational programme. In Spain special training courses, particularly for jurists and social workers, are organised by the Prison Service on an annual and voluntary basis. In order to deal with language barriers, special training in different languages is organised in connection with the Spanish Open University (UNED).

The mandatory training for prison staff in Sweden helps staff to acquire skills but also helps the Prison Service to identify individuals that demonstrate undesirable attitudes that conflict with the value system of treating all persons in a humanitarian and non-discriminatory manner. Swedish prison staffs working directly with foreign prisoners participate in a university level course on 'intercultural understanding' and training in 'Diversity and Dialogue'. Although in the United Kingdom prison staff does not receive in their initial training specific programmes for working with foreign prisoners, local or regional training events can be arranged and delivered by non-governmental organisations and others involved in this area of work.

It is remarkable to see that several prison authorities, including countries where staff has often no foreign language competence, do not provide language skills training programmes for their staff.

2.11.2 Diversity

In Belgium, prison staff of foreign origin indicated that the prison administration institutionalised racism by hiring only Belgian citizens and appointing only native Belgian citizens to important functions. Despite the positive influence on foreign prisoners, Belgian prison staff from foreign origin felt that they are not only easily accepted by their colleagues but also were seen as 'traitors' by prisoners from their country of origin. In Denmark only 1% of the prison staff has a foreign background compared to 15% of the prison population. Efforts are being made by the Danish Prison Service to recruit prison staff from various ethnic backgrounds and a pre-school for foreign aspirants was opened in 2006. In German prisons in Hamburg, with a foreign prison population of 40%, so called 'Ausländerberate' or foreigners aides are employed to assist prison staff. In Sweden a study on ethnicity in prisons in 2003 revealed that s staff speaking in a foreign language with prisoners could arouse suspicions amongst other staff since the latter are unable to be sure that the former is not being exploited or manipulated by the prisoner. In order to avoid a sense of insecurity within the work force it is crucial that prison management creates forums for open discussion to prevent that staff loses confidence in each other.

2.11.3 Treatment

In Belgium, foreign prisoners, especially the young ones, refer to the lack of respect by prison officials and that they were seldom granted positions of trust. And although a survey amongst prison directors by the 'Centre against racism and xenophobia' concluded that racism is not very prominent in Belgium prisons, prison staff indicated that there is racism based on nationality amongst prisoners.

Foreign prisoners in Czech prisons indicated that prison staff treated them similar to national prisoners and that sometimes efforts were made to speak in another language than Czech. In Ireland a 'National Action Plan Against Racism' was published in 2005 to mainstream the intercultural strategy within the prison service. The existence of Race Relations Liaison Officers (RRLO), a Race Relations Management Team and a Prisoner Diversity Representative has resulted in good practice in prisons in England and Wales. However, a prison survey in 2005 discovered that black and minority ethnic prisoners 'have worse perceptions of their treatment than white prisoners across many key areas of prison life'. In interviews held in Dutch penitentiary institutions, foreign prisoners indicated that staff in general was qualified, helpful and respectful and the fact that communication was sometimes difficult was accepted as a fact that could not be changed easily. The situation in some Dutch detention centres and detention boats for irregular migrants is less positive because staff are often hired from private security companies and are less qualified and skilled.

Conclusions
- In most European penitentiary institutions staff is not specially trained to work with foreign prisoners.
- Although prison staff is working with foreign prisoners on a daily basis and communication is an important asset of keeping order and safety in prisons, a foreign language skill is not a required competence in the recruitment process of prison staff.
- Some prison authorities, like in Denmark, are recruiting prison staff from various ethnic backgrounds.

2.12 Projects

Prison authorities have seen over the last decades a sharp increase in the number of foreign prisoners in their institutions. Besides prison authorities, individual penitentiary institutions and prison staff also universities, community based organisations, churches and non-governmental organisations have been anticipating and responding to this trend. This section will give an overview of various projects that have been developed and implemented in the various European countries in order to address the special needs of foreign prisoners.

In Austria, a special department for foreigners called the 'Ausländerreferat' was founded in 1989. The aim of this department, with one part-time staff member, is to support and advise foreign prisoners with regard to their special needs concerning language problems and cultural differences. In practice the activities are focused on managing contacts between prisons and diplomatic missions. In Austrian penitentiary institutions there are several projects implemented for foreign prisoners that are organised by individual staff members. The director of the court prison in Linz for example developed with an expert group of representatives of human rights organisations ('SOS-Menschenrechte' and 'Neustart') a '10-point-programme' to address the specific needs of foreign prisoners.

In Belgium the King Boudewijn Foundation financed a research by Professor Sonja Snacken into the situation of foreign prisoners in Belgium. Based on this research several initiatives were taken like solving the delay for foreign prisoners in receiving early release, introducing 'migration counsellors' in prisons and translating information about the new Prison Act.

In the Czech Republic the Institute of Criminology and Social Prevention in Prague carried out a study about foreign prisoners in 2002-2003.

In Danish prisons a mentor programme for young foreign prisoners was introduced in 2000. The mentor is an adult who is not part of the prison system and whose task is to support the released person just before and just after release. This programme received the 'International Community Justice Award' in 2004. In the State Prison of Ringe an evening study was introduced with an Imam and researcher for prisoners with a Muslim background. The Danish Probation Service has one consultant specialised in the re-integration of ethnic minorities into society.

In autumn 2005 the Finnish Prison Service established a working group to study whether ethnic minorities (mainly foreigners and gypsies) in prison, around 12% of the prison population, receive equal treatment.

The French prison administration announced in May 2006 that it would financially support a comprehensive 20 months research into the situation of foreign prisoners.

The University of Bielefeld in Germany recently conducted a study into the problems of foreigners and members of ethnic minorities in prisons. Researchers questioned experts of the federal state ministries and revealed the lack of appropriate programmes.

In Ireland the Irish Commission for Prisoners Overseas (ICPO) together with a commission of the Irish Bishops Conference undertook an evaluation of their family support service for families of prisoners serving sentences overseas. Financial difficulties, lack of clear information, legal support and release assistance were seen as the most significant problems faced by families of prisoners detained abroad. In 2002 the Irish Probation Service at Mountjoy Prison introduced in collaboration with the Education Unit, an inter-agency programme to address the specific needs of foreign prisoners. In 2002 an 'Evaluation of Research and Training Project for Intercultural Awareness' was conducted to determine the nature of intercultural awareness, communication and racial equality within a prison in Dublin. Further there are anti-racism trainings for both staff and prisoners on this topic and it is currently being considered for the main prison in Dublin.

The high percentage of prisoners from Arabic countries led to the appointment of an Egyptian assistant manager in the Maltese Prison Service in order to understand the needs of foreign inmates better.

In 2005 the Dutch Prison Service carried out a 'Foreign Prisoners' survey into the perception of detention by individual prisoners. Although the survey has been completed, it has not been made public yet. In 2002 Dr. Miranda Boone from the Willem Pompe Institute in Utrecht published the study 'Dutch Probation Service & Cultural Diversity'.

Based on good experiences in Wandsworth Prison in the United Kingdom, the Prison Service introduced Foreign National Orderlies to support the work of the Foreign Nationals Co-ordinator and staff in penitentiary institutions. These Orderlies are prisoners that are entrusted to provide support to foreign prisoners. They visit foreign prisoners systematically, provide them with practical information and other support, represent their views to staff, keep a list of prisoners willing to interpret and help to identify foreign prisoners in need of particular help. Since 1992 the Prison Service hosts biannual meetings with embassies to provide them with the latest information on prison regimes and procedures.

The non- governmental organisation 'Hibiscus' is working over 20 years with female foreign prisoners in various institutions to alleviate the disadvantages they face. 'Hibiscus' has also offices in Jamaica to support the families of Jamaican prisoners and to assist with their resettlement and expulsion. In 'Morton Hall', a prison with the largest proportion of female foreign prisoners, there are two full-time Foreign National Officers and a Foreign Nationals Co-ordinator that have built an extensive international network to ensure the best resettlement provisions. The Prison Service headquarters promotes good practice by sharing initiatives amongst prisons through the provision of a quarterly Foreign Nationals Bulletin and by organising in 2004 a National Foreign National Prisoners Conference.

Besides national language courses there are no specific projects for foreign prisoners in Estonia, Finland, Greece, Hungary, Latvia, Lithuania, Poland, Portugal, Slovenia and Sweden.

Conclusions
-   Over the last years, various initiatives have been taken by prison authorities, individual penitentiary institutions, universities, welfare organizations, churches and non-governmental organisations.

3 ADMINISTRATIVE DETENTION OF FOREIGN PRISONERS

Administrative detention, which can be stated as detention of non-citizens for migration related issues, is a common practice in the European countries nowadays. The detention of foreign nationals is an administrative measure and, consequently, not a measure of the penal system. Among the persons who can be subject to detention are asylum seekers regarding their asylum procedure and irregular migrants who are awaiting their removal.[19] The notion of 'irregular migrants' of the last mentioned category is in this text used in reference to the terminology of the EU and the Council of Europe. It is a comprehensive definition for foreigners who are residing in a country without a residence permit. This group includes, *inter alia*, rejected asylum seekers, 'economic refugees', tourists with expired visa dates, victims of human trafficking or - smuggling, foreigners whom residence permits are reversed or not renewed and labour migrants without a work permit. The term 'irregular migrants' is not an unambiguous one, as the terminology in use among European countries differs. While some countries also use the term 'irregular migrants', others speak about 'clandestine' or 'undeclared migrants'.[20]

Relying on only the amount of more then 650.000 removal orders that are being issued in the EU on a yearly basis makes it already presumable that the numbers of aliens

---

[19] Some countries such as the UK do not use the legal term of forced 'removal' of irregular migrants, but instead they talk about 'deportation'. On the European continent the term deportation is often avoided because of the negative associations it brings along and a preference is given to the less emotionally charged term of removal or sometimes expulsion. In this text the term removal will be used following on the Council of Europe and the European Union.

[20] For more on the terminology that is in use in Europe see S. de Tapia, *New patterns of irregular migration in Europe*, Strasbourg: Council of Europe Publishing 2003, chapter I p. 13-22.

residing temporarily or permanently in the EU without a valid residence permit are several millions. The tables 2 & 3 below show the number of removal orders that have been issued by the EU countries and also the numbers of the actual removals by the EU countries.[21]

Table 2: The number of return decisions

	2002	2003	2004	Totals
Austria	23.750	22.641	15.511	61.902
Belgium	53.215	52.169	50.000	155.384
Denmark	8.000	8.000	8.000	24.000
Finland	3.526	3.456	3.800	10.782
France	49.124	55.938	50.000	155.062
Germany	143.000	143.000	143.000	429.000
Greece	29.602	29.542	29.776	88.920
Ireland	2.465	2.425	2.866	7.756
Italy	94.995	70.147	70.320	235.462
Luxemburg	1.000	1.000	1.000	3.000
Netherlands	62.000	62.000	62.000	186.000
Portugal	2.000	2.000	2.000	6.000
Spain	56.130	69.773	66.419	192.322
Sweden	18.497	22.656	27.876	69.029
United Kingdom	70.000	70.000	70.000	210.000
Cyprus	1.300	1.300	1.400	4.000
Czech Republic	25.496	29.366	25.317	80.179
Estonia	1.000	1.000	1.000	3.000
Hungary	7.233	7.878	6.911	22.022
Latvia	362	709	286	1.357
Lithuania	556	823	775	1.357
Malta	1.949	970	1.319	4.238
Poland	5.796	5.531	4.275	15.062
Slovenia	6.256	3.917	3.110	13.283
Slovak Republic	1.245	1.591	2.849	5.685
EU-25	668.497.494	667.832	649.810	1.986.139

Source: Member States.
1. *Where no data were provided by the Member States, the Commission has made estimates. Some data may have been amended to take into account other statistical information (for instance the number of persons receiving a negative asylum decision).*
2. *To date no definition of a return decision exists in Community law. Data have been collected on the basis of existing information and data collections.*

---

[21] European Commission, Common standards on return, Memo/05/288, Brussels 1 September 2005, Annexe p. 2 & 4.

Table 3: Number of removed aliens during the period 2002-2004

	Absolute number			Indexed (2004 = 100)		
	2002	**2003**	**2004**	**2002**	**2003**	**2004**
Belgium	10.352	9.996	9.647	107	104	100
Denmark	1.627	3.100	3.093	53	100	100
Germany	31.311	30.176	26.807	117	113	100
Greece	45.299	40.930	35.942	126	114	100
Spain	26.257	26.757	27.364	96	98	100
France	10.015	11.692	15.672	64	75	100
Ireland	:	:	:	:	:	:
Italy	33.289	31.013	27.402	121	113	100
Luxembourg	:	:	41	:	:	100
Netherlands	22.579	23.206	5.564	406	417	100
Austria	9.858	11.070	9.408	105	118	100
Portugal	1.991	2.798	3.507	57	80	100
Finland	2.223	2.773	2.775	80	100	100
Sweden	6.854	7.355	11.714	59	63	100
United Kingdom	15.100	21.380	:	:	:	:
EU15	216.755	222.246	178.936			
Czech Republic	4.873	2.602	1.528	319	170	100
Estonia	255	171	101	252	169	100
Cyprus	2.932	3.307	2.982	98	111	100
Latvia	197	375	234	84	160	100
Lithuania	487	846	306	159	276	100
Hungary	3.602	4.804	3.980	91	121	100
Malta	952	847	680	140	125	100
Poland	6.847	5.879	6.042	113	97	100
Slovenia	4.268	3.209	2.632	162	122	100
Slovakia	1.069	1.293	2.528	42	51	100
EU10	25.482	23.333	21.013			
EU25	242.237	245.579	199.949			
Bulgaria	722	814	1.271	57	64	100
Romania	333	500	650	51	77	100
Missing data for the period 2003 - 2004						
M5: Ireland, Luxembourg, The Netherlands, United Kingdom						

Traditionally the treatment of aliens has been regulated by the law of state responsibility. This is why the policies regarding administrative detention of irregular migrants vary strongly between European countries. There is currently no common legislation available in Europe, concerning the forcible return of irregular migrants. However, as more recently, the treatment of aliens has come to be measured against international standards to be found in human rights law, *all* human beings have become subjects of modern international law to the extent that human rights treaties grant rights to individuals that they may enforce directly before an international body, without a link of nationality.[22]

---

[22] H. Lambert, *The position of aliens in relation to the European Convention on Human Rights*, Strasbourg: Council of Europe Publishing 2006, p. 7.

This paragraph will present a comparative overview with respect to administrative detention policies in 25 EU countries.[23] The focus will be on the following topics; institutions and capacity, the responsible Ministry and legislation, length of stay, the decision procedure, appeal and review, irregular stay, data and the non-expelled foreigners, detention irregulars under criminal law and minors which will be hold to the light of relevant European legislation relating to the topic that is being discussed.

3.1 and 3.3 Institutions and capacity

Foreigners who are caught for their irregular stay are taken to places where they are detained, awaiting their removal. The most important reason for detention is 'deterrence' as it is considered to prevent people coming to European countries by irregular channels. In all of the EU countries these places are guarded institutions on which various terms are in use by European bodies. Among these terms are detention facilities, detention -, holding, - reception, - expulsion, and removal centres. Notions in national legislation are very different, too. For example, in Germany, a 'detention centre' is called '*Abschiebungshaftanstalt*', i.e. an 'institution of 'imprisonment pending deportation'. In Italy a 'detention centre' is called '*Centro di Permanenza Temporanea e Assistenza*', i.e. 'Centre of Temporary Permanence and Assistance. In the UK and in France they are named 'immigration removal centres' and '*centres de rétention*'.[24] Though there are countries with special detention centres for these foreigners, others accommodate them in police stations, penitentiary institutions, transit zones or in prisons. A combination of the various institutions does also occur in several countries.

EU countries with special detention centres for foreigners are, *inter alia*, Italy, Slovenia, the Czech Republic, Slovakia and Poland.
In Slovenia detained illegal residents are accommodated in so-called Illegal Residents Centres of which there are two in the country, with a total capacity of 160 places. The detention measures used for illegal residents differ by the degree of security applied and the restrictions placed on the freedom of movement. Besides the Illegal Residents Centres, they can also be placed in a social care facility or in the rigorous police supervision division within the Illegal Residents Centre. The Czech Republic has four administrative detention facilities for foreigners. With regard to Slovakia, it can be said that there are two special detention facilities for foreign administrative detainees which can accommodate up to 500 foreigners at one time in total. Poland holds administrative detainees in guarded centres for foreigners or detention centres for the purpose of expulsion. Exceptionally, if there are obstacles that make it impossible to escort or admit a foreigner to the guarded centre or to the detention centre for the purpose of expulsion, he or she may be temporarily placed in the separate facilities for detainees of the police or the border guard. In practice there is one guarded centre for foreigners which has a capacity of 131 persons (further guarded centres for foreigners are planned to be taken into operation in the near future) and over 20 expulsion-detention centres (with each a capacity between the 20 and 50 persons).

---

[23] Bulgaria and Romania, which joined the EU in January 2007, have not been part of the research.

[24] Observation and Position Document: *Detention in Europe. Administrative detention of asylum seekers and irregular migrants*, Jesuit Refugee Service Europe 2004 p. 32-35.

Luxembourg, Finland and Northern Ireland which do not face large numbers of irregular migrants, have all created one unit for administrative aliens detention. The unit in Finland has a capacity of ca. 40 detainees, as this number is 11 for Northern Ireland. Greece has only a small number of special centres for foreigners, which results in that every police station detention room – all over the country – constitutes *de facto* an institution of administrative detention for foreign nationals. Neighbouring Cyprus has detention cells in all districts, of which some are specially designated for the detention of foreigners and others hold foreigners together with penal offenders. This last mentioned practice also happens in Ireland, as it is the only country which does not have a separate location for aliens detention. Administrative detainees are placed in two prisons in Dublin where they have access to the same facilities as the prisoners.

Among the countries, which make use of the last mentioned category, which is a combination of several institutions are the Netherlands, Germany and the UK.

The Netherlands detains yearly over 20.000 irregular migrants on the basis of the Immigration Law. This is done in police stations, penitentiary institutions, detention boats and detention centres. The enforcement of the detention is similar as of criminal detention based on the Penitentiary Principles Act. The total capacity of aliens detention in 2007 will be over 3000 divided over ten institutions, five of these are boats with a capacity of 1732 in total. Germany has three different models for the accommodation of detainees pending expulsion: allocation to special establishments for the administrative detention of illegal residents; in regular penitentiary institutions ('Justizvollzugsanstalt', JVA) or in special departments of such a JVA. In Germany, roughly 2250 foreign detainees awaiting removal can be accommodated. In the UK detainees can be held in Immigration Removal Centres (of which there are ten), prisons, police stations, short term holding centres at ports, screening units and appealing hearing centres. The Detention Centre Rules 2001 provide a comprehensive set of rules and procedures covering the treatment of those held under detention. It should also be noted that in the UK it is possible for detainees to apply for bail and that the Home Office may agree to temporary release from removal, subject to a restriction order which will include the requirement to live at a specified address and report to the authorities at specified intervals.

There are two countries which also provide for accommodation in special open units for those awaiting their removal. These are Sweden and Austria. In Sweden, detainees who are not escape prone can be placed in these units, in which activities are designed to prepare foreigners for their departure from Sweden and reintegration into their home country. As it considers Austria, it can be said that the revised law of 1 January 2006 has explicitly introduced these units for the first time and that it is not a binding rule yet.

As shown in this subparagraph, all of the countries use detention as the only measure for foreigners who are awaiting their removal. There is no question of the use of alternative non-custodial measures by the countries, with the exception of a few. These alternatives are promoted by article 14 (1) of the Commission Proposal Returns Directive as well as by Guideline 6 (1) of the Twenty Guidelines on forced return (hereinafter Guidelines). According to the first mentioned article, temporary custody shall be only used when there are serious grounds to believe that there is a risk of absconding and where it would not be sufficient to apply less coercive measures such as regular reporting to the authorities, deposit of a financial guarantee, handing over documents, an obligation to stay at a designated place or other measures to prevent that risk.[25]

The types of institutions in which the foreigners are kept differ among the countries, but most of the countries have created special detention centres for foreigners who are awaiting their removal. The CPT has pointed out in its Standards what its expectations are from these centres:

'Obviously, such centres should provide accommodation which is adequately furnished clean and in a good state of repair, and which offers sufficient living space for the numbers involved. Further, care should be taken in the design and layout of the premises to avoid as much as possible any impression of a carceral environment. As regards regime activities, they should include outdoor exercise, access to day room and to radio/television and newspapers/magazines, as well as other appropriate means of recreation (e.g. board games, table tennis). The longer the period for which persons are detained, the more developed should be the activities which are offered to them'.[26]

The reports of the CPT on EU countries are mainly critical about the conditions under which foreigners are detained. Points of critique are mainly on the lack of medical care, overcrowding, access to legal aid and activities. In some countries, such as the Netherlands, Malta and France, the treatment of irregular migrants who are administratively detained is worse than that of prisoners who are detained on a criminal basis. Holding detainees in police stations and prisons as done by certain countries is in contravention of the CPT Standards. These state that:

'Prolonged deprivation of liberty in police stations in mediocre material conditions and without activity is entirely inappropriate. Nor is it acceptable to hold immigration detainees in prisons, even when actual conditions of detention are adequate. This is a fundamentally flawed approach as a prison is by definition not a suitable place in which to detain someone who is neither convicted nor suspected of a criminal offence'.[27]

Conclusions

- Foreigners are detained in guarded institutions on which various terms are in use by European bodies and countries.
- The majority of countries accommodate detainees in special detention centers, but police stations, prisons, penitentiary institutions and transit zones are in use as well.
- Treatment of irregular migrants who are administratively detained is often worse than that of ordinary prisoners.
- Overcrowding, lack of medical care/legal aid, unqualified staff are widespread and religious-cultural requirements are not always respected.
- Alternative non-custodial measures are not in use, except by a few countries such as the UK, Sweden and Austria.

---

[25] For the notion 'detention of illegally staying third-country nationals', the EU Commission is referring to 'temporary custody of a third-country national'.

[26] CPT Standards, Chapter IV Foreign nationals detained under aliens legislation, under point 29. Guideline 10 (2) corresponds with this point.

[27] Ibid under points 27 & 28.

3.2 The responsible Ministry and legislation

As administrative detention is not a measure of the penal system, it is in general not based on the Criminal Laws of the countries. All of the countries have specific legislation relating to the grounds, procedure and regime of the detention of foreigners.

Among the EU countries, the Ministry of Interior is often the responsible Ministry for the administrative detention of foreigners. This goes for the following EU countries:

- Hungary: Alien Policing Act, Alien Policing Detention Decree;
- Austria: Police Detention Order, Decrees on Police Detention, § 4 AnhO , Law of 1 January 2006;
- Belgium: Law of 15 December 1980 on Foreigners (which is modified and enhanced by the Laws of 6 May 1993/15 July 1996 and 29 April 1999), Royal Decree of 8 October 1981 on Foreigners and the Royal Decree of 2 August 2002 which lays down the operational rules of detention centres;
- The UK: Immigration Act 1971 schedule 2 & 3 and the Immigration and Asylum Act 1999 section 10;
- Slovakia: Foreigners Act;
- Portugal: Law 60/93 of 3 March 1993;
- Slovenia: Illegal Residents Act of 1999, amended in 2005, Regulations on the implementation of the Illegal Residents Act 1991, Regulations on special conditions for the accommodation and movement of illegal residents in the Illegal Residents Centre, and on grounds and the procedure for the use of lenient measures 2000;
- Poland: 2003 Act on Illegal Residents;
- Czech Republic: Act No. 326 of 30 November 1999 on Residence of Foreigners and Amendment to Some Acts (Aliens Act);
- Estonia: Foreigners Act, Obligation to Leave and Prohibition on Entry Act;
- Lithuania: Law on the Legal Status of Aliens;
- France: CESEDA, Book V, Title V, Decree N° 2004-1215 from 17 November 2004, Decree N° 2005-617 from May 2005;
- Germany: Immigration Law of 2005 *(Zuwanderungsgesetz)*, of which the Residence Act *(Aufenhaltsgesetz)* is a part of. It is completed by a number of further laws, which are either Federal or Regional Law *(Landesrecht)*;
- Italy: Immigration Law 1998 *(Decreto legislative n. 286/1998)* to which the 2002 Immigration and Asylum Bill *(or Bossi-Fini Law)* brought about further changes.

Regarding the three islands Ireland, Malta and Cyprus can be said that in Ireland the Ministry of Justice, Equality and Law Reform is responsible for the administrative detention of foreign prisoners and the rules are laid down in the Immigration Act 1999. Malta has a co-responsibility between the army and the police (army - Office of Prime Minister, police -Ministry of Justice and Home Affairs). To overcome this inter-ministerial responsibility, it was deemed more appropriate to have a single authority headed by an army colonel administering the closed centres. The law that covers the detention is the Immigration Act of 1970. In Cyprus the police detention cells are under the supervision of the chief of the police department which in turn is supervised by the Ministry of Justice and Public Order.

Aliens detention in the Netherlands is enforced by the Ministry of Justice (the Immigration and Naturalization Service) based on the Immigration Law. The ways for enforcement are determined by the Penitentiary Principles Act.[28] In Luxembourg detention is based on the Law on the entry and stay of foreigners, the medical control of foreigners and foreign labour.

With respect to the Scandinavian EU countries the following is the case: in Denmark the competent superior authority is the Ministry for Refugees, Immigrants and Integration, which is often simply called the Ministry of Integration. When a foreigner is confined by force he/she is under the authority of the Department of Prisons and Probation. The legal possibilities of depriving a foreigner of his liberty are mentioned in the Code on Foreigners. In Sweden, the Migration Board, subordinate to the Ministry of Foreign Affairs has the responsibility and is the detention based on the Aliens Act and Regulations of the Migration Board specific to its fields of operations. In neigbouring country Finland the Custody Unit, subordinate to the Ministry of Labour is the responsible institute. The relevant legislation is the Aliens Act (301/2004), Act on the Treatment of Aliens in Custody and on a Custody Unit (116/2002).

For the three last EU countries Greece, Spain and Latvia, the following Ministries have respectively the responsibility; the Ministry of Public Order (Foreigners Act, 3386/2005), the General Direction of Police (Foreigners Act, partly introduced by OA14/2003 - and Regulation, Royal Decree 2392/2004), since 2002 the State Border Guard and Office of Citizenship and Migration Affairs (Immigration Law 2003).

As shown above, all of the countries have separate laws regarding foreigners, which for example state the grounds for detention. The availability of the specific laws is relevant as according to article 5 (1) ECHR detention is permitted 'in accordance with a procedure prescribed by law' and for the exclusive purposes enumerated therein. With regard to administrative detention, article 5 (1)f ECHR is relevant as it permits the lawful arrest or detention of a person to prevent his effecting an unauthorized entry into the country or of a person against whom action is being taken with a view to deportation and extradition. The Court has ruled that a procedure prescribed by law implies the notion of a fair and proper procedure which means a procedure conducted by an appropriate authority and free from arbitrariness.[29] In the *Amuur*[30] judgment the Court has interpreted this requirement to mean that the domestic law authorising the deprivation of liberty "must be sufficiently accessible and precise, in order to avoid all risk of arbitrariness". It must also be of "sufficient quality ', i.e. it must offer possibilities for judicial review, provisions setting time limits and access to legal assistance, humanitarian and social assistance.[31] In 2002, the Court has recalled these principles and cited that: 'where the lawfulness of the detention is in issue, including the question whether a procedure prescribed

---

[28] In 2002, a new function of Minister for Immigration and Integration was established. The Minister had not an own Office, but was a part of the Ministry of Justice. Under the new government that is formed in 2007, the function of Minister for Immigration and Integration is cancelled and the immigration policy placed under the responsibility of the State Secretary of Justice.

[29] A.M. Gallagher, H. Ireland, N. Muchopa, *Handbook for visitors and workers in Detention Centres*, Brussels: Jesuit Refugee Service Europe 2006, p. 64. *Winterwerp v. the Netherlands*, judgment of 24 October 1979, para. 45.

[30] *Amuur v. France*, judgment of 25 June 1996, para. 53.

[31] H. Lambert, *The position of aliens in relation to the European Convention on Human Rights*, Strasbourg: Council of Europe Publishing 2006, p. 19.

by law has been followed, the ECHR refers essentially to the obligation to conform to the substantive and procedural rules of national law, but it requires in addition, that any deprivation of liberty should be in keeping with the purpose of article 5, namely to protect the individuals from arbitrariness'.[32]

Other legislation which state the principle of legality are the Guidelines 2 & 6 which are based on article 5 (1) ECHR and also article 14 European Prison Rules.

Conclusions

- Ministry of Interior is often the responsible one for administrative detention.
- Administrative detention is in general not based on the Criminal Laws of the countries.
- All countries have specific regulations relating to administrative detention of foreigners.
- European legislation prescribes the principle of legality of the detention of which the main purpose is to protect the individuals from arbitrariness.

3.4 Length of stay

The length of stay in administrative detention varies among EU countries, with some countries setting a low time limit and others not even having a fixed duration. The table below provides an idea of the maximum period under which migrants are held in administrative detention under the national laws of EU member states.[33]

---

[32] *Conka v. Belgium*, judgment of 5 February 2002, para. 39.

[33] The source for the table is A.M. Gallagher, H. Ireland, N. Muchopa, *Handbook for visitors and workers in Detention Centres*, Brussels: Jesuit Refugee Service Europe 2006, p. 30. The last two countries in the rows; Estonia and Cyprus were not mentioned in the 'Handbook' and are added according to the information from the country reports. For some countries the information from the Handbook does not correspond with what is discussed in the country reports. These deviations are placed in the third column.

Table 4

Country	Length of stay	Deviations according to the country reports
Denmark	72 hours	-
Finland	4 days (in police stations); 8 days (aliens centre)	No fixed duration of time, in practice the limit is 3 months
Sweden	10 days	Up to 2 months when an expulsion decision is taken and the person is believed to be a risk
Hungary	1 month	Depending on the type of detention, the maximum can be extended up to 12 months
France	32 days	-
Spain	40 days	-
Portugal	60 days	-
Austria	60 days	-
Italy	60 days	-
Ireland	8 weeks (for those facing removal)	
Greece	3 months	
Luxembourg	3 months	
Slovenia	6 months (migrants)	
Belgium	5 months	When necessary detention can be prolonged to the absolute maximum of 8 months
Lithuania	180 days	No fixed duration of time, average term is 63 days, but there are many cases of persons who spend 1 or 2 years in detention
Slovakia	180 days	-
Czech Republic	180 days	-
Poland	1 year	-
Germany	18 months	-
Malta	18 months	-
Latvia	20 months	-
UK	Indefinite (no maximum prescribed by law)	-
Netherlands	Indefinite (no maximum prescribed by law)	-
Estonia	-	4 months
Cyprus	-	No information available

As shown in table 4, there are quite some countries which have time limits that can lead to a long period of detention. When a foreigner can be easily send out of the country, there is no need for such a long period of detention. However, it is often the case that certain conditions are not fulfilled which lead to difficulties and makes the removal of the foreigner impossible. Among these difficulties are that the foreigner does not have a passport or another document which can be used to leave the country, is hiding his/her nationality and that there is no embassy or consulate residing of the country of origin from which documents can be obtained.[34] In these situations foreigners are detained for long periods of time, while the prospect of removal is actually unrealistic. The result of such hopeless cases is that the foreigners are eventually being released from detention. This does not mean they are safe outside, as they face the risk of being caught again for their irregular stay in the country.

The ECHR makes no specific mention of time limits for administrative detention. However, the Court developed case law regarding the just mentioned practice in countries. The Court has recalled in the *Chacal*[35] judgment that any deprivation of liberty under article 5 para. 1(f) will be justified only for as long as deportation proceedings are in progress. If such proceedings are not prosecuted with due diligence, the detention will cease to be permissible under article 5 para. 1(f). It is thus necessary to determine whether the duration of the deportation proceedings was excessive.[36] Guidelines 7 & 8 are laid down following the case law of the Court on article 5 para. 1(f). Contrary to the ECHR and the Guidelines, the Commission Proposal Returns Directive does set a time limit, as it states in article 14 (4) that 'temporary custody may be extended by judicial authorities to a maximum of six months'.

Conclusions
- Various time limits in countries, with some setting a low limit and others not even having a fixed duration.
- Uncertainty about length of stay.
- Uncertainty about the future, especially when removal can not be realized.
- The ECHR has no specific time limit, but the Court stated that has to be determined whether the duration is excessive.
- The Commission Proposal Returns Directive sets a limit of six months.

3.5 The decision procedure

As the EU countries have specific legislation relating to the grounds and procedure of administrative detention, they also differ with regard to the question on who is responsible for taking the decision on detention. On this ground, a classification in 3 categories can be made. Under the first category can be placed, the countries where the administrative authorities decide on detention, which are usually the foreigners or border police, and no judicial check takes place within a few days. The second category of countries is the one in which the administrative authorities also decide on detention, but where a con-

---

[34] There is also the principle of non-refoulement that has to be respected by countries, see above footnote 16.

[35] *Chacal v. The United Kingdom*, judgment of 15 November 1996, para. 113.

[36] See also *Shamsa v. Poland*, judgment of 27 November 2003, in which case the Polish authorities continued to try to enforce the deportation order without any legal basis even though the statutory time-limit had expired. The Court noted that there was no domestic decision or provision which laid down the conditions for such detention. Accordingly, Polish legislation did not fulfill the requirement of "foreseeability" for the purposes of Article 5 (1) ECHR.

trol within a short time does take place by the judiciary. The last category consists of countries which detain foreigners by court order.

Slovakia, Slovenia, the Netherlands, the UK, Ireland and Greece, Belgium, Malta are among the countries which belong to the first category. Under the second category there are, *inter alia*, Lithuania, Finland, Denmark and France.

In Lithuania a foreigner may be detained for a period of over 48 hours on court order on the delegation of the officer of the law enforcement institution. In Finland the police and border guards take the decision for detention after which the District Court decides on further detention. The assessment of the justification and necessity of detention is performed by the District Court at the latest within 4 days from the apprehension under section 124 of the Aliens Act. Also in Denmark the police are the responsible authority for the execution of all expulsions and at the same time the competent authority to decide whether or not a foreigner should be detained. Detention for the purpose of ensuring a person's presence for the time when an expulsion is to be executed (pursuant to article 36 of the Code on Foreigners) must be brought before a local court within 72 hours from the moment when the person is locked up. In France, administrative detention is been decided on by the préfet, who within the first 48 hours must request from the 'judge of liberties and detention' ("juge des libertés et de la détention" – JLD) the authorisation for the prolongation of detention by 15 more days. Once the 17 days have expired, the préfet may request a new extension of up to 15 days. Regarding the 'Waiting Zones' in France, it can be said that the stay is evaluated after 72 hours by a judge who will decide on its prolongation.

Portugal, Spain, Germany and Estonia belong to the last category. In these countries foreigners have to appear before a judge who may decide to place them in detention.

The States' power to detain foreigners is not unlimited. According to article 5 (1) ECHR, detention is permitted when it is 'in accordance with a procedure prescribed by law' and for the exclusive purposed enumerated therein (article 5 para. 1 (f) ECHR for administrative detention). What is meant with this article is already discussed in § 3.2 and is also relevant within the context of the decision procedure. In addition is to be mentioned the *Shamsa*[37] judgment, in which the Court pointed out that detention for several days which has not been ordered by a court or judge or any other person authorized to exercise judicial power can not be regarded as "lawful" within the meaning of article 5 (1) of the ECHR. Also article 14 (2) of the Commission Proposal Returns Directive underlines the importance of the judiciary regarding detention as it states that:

> *'Temporary custody orders shall be issued by judicial authorities and that in urgent cases they may be issued by administrative authorities, in which case the order shall be confirmed by judicial authorities within 72 hours from the beginning of the temporary custody'*

The practice in use by most of the countries, by which in general the administrative authorities issue the detention order, is not in accordance with the case law of the Court nor with article 14 (2) of the Commission Proposal Returns Directive.

Conclusions

- General practice is that administrative authorities decide on administrative detention.
- In certain countries there is no judicial check within a few days.

---

[37] See footnote 36.

- In Portugal, Spain, Germany, Estonia foreigners have to appear before a judge who may decide on detention.
- The case law of the Court and the Commission Proposal Returns Directive underline the importance of the judiciary regarding detention.

3.6 Appeal and review

Regarding the right of the foreigner to challenge the decision for detention, it can be said that the greater part of the EU countries provide appeal procedures through courts. That the case can be appealed does not mean in certain countries that foreigners are always enabled to make fully use of their right. This has, *inter alia*, to do with a short period of time that is given for appealing, which makes preparing the case very difficult. Examples are Poland and Cyprus, where an appeal against the decision for detention can be filed, respectively before the Regional Court and Supreme Court, within seven days of said decision. Lithuania provides ten days for appealing to the Supreme Administrative Court. In France, the appeal against the decision of the JLD to prolong the length of detention ("appel 35bis") is to be filed before the "cour d'appel - CA". To contest the legality of the removal decision, in most of the cases, it deals with a "préfectoral arrêté" against which an appeal before the administrative court (TA) ("recours 22bis") is possible within 48 hours.

In Slovenia, Denmark and Malta the administrative agencies decide upon appeal. In the first two countries the appeal does not have a suspensive effect and thus the execution of the order to remove the foreigner can be enforced immediately, which renders the right of appeal meaningless. In Slovenia it is the Ministry of Interior that takes the decision upon appeal. The illegal resident can file a lawsuit against this decision which is then decided on by the Administrative Court (Illegal Residents Act, Art. 58). In Denmark an appeal can be lodged with the Ministry of Integration. Just like Slovenia and Denmark, also in Slovakia an appeal does not have suspensive effect. Hereby, the country has no time limit for a court to decide on the appeal. The Maltese Immigration Act provides for an Immigration Appeals Board to rule on excessive length of detention. Since February 2005 the Board has been able to grant release from custody, but the Immigration Act severely restricts the cases where the Board can authorize release.

Until 2006, Sweden also belonged to the countries where appeals are made to administrative agencies. From 31 March 2006 on, three Migration Courts and a Migration Court of Appeal replaced the Aliens Appeal Board. In Finland it is not possible for the foreigner to appeal the decision of the District Court, which assesses the detention within four days from the apprehension on.

Interrelated with the right to appeal a case, is the right to have access to legal assistance. Even though foreigner can appeal a decision, this right has not much of meaning for them without access to legal aid. Detained foreigners are vulnerable and can not be expected to know how to exercise their rights. It is essential that they obtain effective legal assistance and are advised about their position. Most of the countries guarantee providing legal aid, but in practice this is not always the case. The detainees are mainly dependent on the assistance they get from international organizations and NGO's, who are active in this field.

Article 5 (4) ECHR states that:

> *Everyone who is deprived of his liberty by arrest or detention shall be entitled to take proceedings by which the lawfulness of his detention shall be decided speedily by a court and his release ordered if the detention is not lawful*[38]

This right applies to all forms of deprivation of liberty, including administrative detention. The crucial elements of the obligation in this provision are that:[39]

- The legality of the detention must be determined by a court which is independent and impartial.[40] Appeals to executive bodies do not constitute a sufficient remedy for the purposes of challenging the lawfulness of deprivations of liberty, as in the case of Slovenia, Denmark and Malta;
- The court must have the power to review both the procedural and substantive grounds for the deprivation of liberty and be empowered to make a binding order for release of the detained person in the event that his or her deprivation of liberty is unlawful;
- Every person deprived of his/her liberty is entitled to have the lawfulness of the continued detention subjected to periodic reviews for the purpose of testing whether the reasons for the deprivation of liberty remain valid. Article 14 (2) of the Commission Proposal Returns Directive is conform to this point as it states that 'temporary custody orders shall be subject to review by judicial authorities at least once a month;
- The detained person must be allowed access to legal assistance which goes beyond the preparation of a claim and entails representation in the court proceedings. [41] This right also implies that the detainee must have access to all relevant information concerning his/her case (equality of arms). The general practice is that the countries do not provide for legal assistance where the detainees are entitled to. As mentioned above, the detainees are mainly dependent on the assistance they get from international organizations and NGO's, who are active in this field. The short time of period for appealing that some countries prescribe does not allow the detainee to have a fair opportunity for preparing his/her case;
- The court must act without delay/speedily. What is considered to be 'without delay' or 'speedily' depends on the circumstances of each case.[42] A delay must not be unreasonable and a lack of resources or vacation periods are not acceptable justifications for delay. The situation in Slovakia, where there is no time limit for a court to decide on the appeal, and the practice is two or three months, is not acceptable within the context of article 5 (4) ECHR.

---

[38]   Guideline 9 (1) corresponds with article 5 (4) ECHR and follows from the case law of the Court relating to this article.

[39]   M. Macovei, *The right to liberty and security of the person. A guide to the implementation of Article 5 of the European Convention on Human Rights*, Strasbourg: Council of Europe Publishing 2002, p. 60-66. Chapter 5 Human Rights and Arrest, Pre-Trial and Administrative Detention in *Human Rights in the Administration of Justice: A Manual on Human Rights for Judges, Prosecutors and Lawyers*.

[40]   See Eur. Ct. *Al Nashif v. Bulgaria*, judgment of 20 June 2002.

[41]   Eur. Ct. *Woukam Moudefo v. France*, judgment of 11 October 1988 and Eur. Ct. *Megyeri v. Germany*, judgment of 12 may 1992.

[42]   See Eur. Ct. *Ilowiecki v. Poland*, judgment of 4 October 2001.

Other relevant articles within the context of judicial remedies are article 12 of the Commission Proposal Returns Directive and also Guideline 5. Both of them mention, *inter alia*, that an effective remedy should be offered to the detainee which has a suspensive effect. This is currently not the case in Slovenia and Denmark.

Conclusions
- Most of the countries provide appeal procedures through courts.
- Inadequate possibilities for judicial review by, *inter alia*, given a short period of time for appealing as is the case in Poland, Cyprus and France.
- In Slovenia, Denmark and Malta the administrative agencies decide upon appeal, which is according to the Court not a sufficient remedy for the purposes of challenging the lawfulness of the detention.
- An appeal does not have suspensive effect in Slovenia, Denmark and Slovakia.
- Legal aid is guaranteed by the states, but in practice the detainees are mainly dependent on assistance from international organizations and NGO's.

3.7 Irregular stay

With regard to the question if an irregular stay is a criminal offence, it can be said that for the greater part of the EU countries the illegal/irregular stay itself is not a crime. This means that the foreigner cannot be detained on a criminal basis for staying in the country without having the required valid documents (these countries are Portugal, Slovenia, Malta, Sweden, Hungary, Denmark, Poland, the Netherlands, Lithuania and Greece). Though an irregular stay is not a criminal offence, this does not mean that acts related to the irregular stay, such as producing false documents, illegal entry and not leaving the country while declared a 'persona non grata' (the Netherlands, 197 Penal Code) are not punishable in these countries. Also in Slovakia the illegal stay itself is not a criminal offence, but if someone has been issued with a decision on expulsion and he/she does not leave the country despite of this fact, he/she can be charged of a criminal offence for not respecting an official decision. This is different in Denmark where not leaving the country as ordered by the court is not seen as a crime and may be executed by the police.

In Germany, Finland, Ireland, France and Cyprus an irregular stay does constitute a criminal offence. Finland criminalized an illegal stay in the country as an intentional crime which makes its punishable with fines. Under the Immigration Act 2004, illegal/irregular stay in Ireland is a criminal offence on 2 grounds and the maximum penalty is 12 months imprisonment (Section 4 (2) and Section 6 (1) of the Immigration Act 2004). In addition persons can be detained on remand for immigration related reasons under the Criminal Justice Act 2001. Not having a permanent or temporary residence permit, refusal to board a plane during removal, use of false identities, refusal to give identity or nationality to oppose removal, false weddings, etc. are criminal offences in France. More than 200 immigration related offences lead to removal. An irregular migrant - illegal entry or stay - can be handed a prison sentence of up to one year. According to Cypriot law illegal residence can be punished with up to 2 years in prison. As it considers Estonia, it can be noted that § 260 of the Penal Code of the country states that a foreigner who is detected in the country at least twice within a year without having a legal basis for his/her stay shall be punished by a pecuniary punishment or up to one year of imprisonment.

Currently, there is no one who is being punished in prisons or the expulsion centre according to this paragraph.

Conclusions

- Irregular stay itself is not a criminal offence for the majority of the EU countries, though the criminalization of 'illegal immigration', particularly to create offences punishable by prison sentences, is problematic.
- In Germany, Finland, Ireland, France and Cyprus an irregular stay does constitute a criminal offence.

3.8 - 3.10 Data and the non-expelled foreigners

The number of arrivals of irregular migrants on Europe's Southern shores has increased immensely in 2006. Countries such as Spain, Italy, Malta and Greece are at the front and bear the brunt, however all European countries are facing the problems, in particular due to secondary movements of these arrivals.[43] As a consequence of the large number of arrivals also the detention of foreigners, who are awaiting their removal, is increased. This appears not only from the facilities in several EU countries which are overcrowded and unsuitable, but also from the expansion of detention capacity in some countries. Currently, there are no exact data available about the number of detainees in Europe, because of the fact that not all of the countries register them. Yet on the grounds of data, which are partially available, the number of detainees in Europe may be in the 100.000 persons per year.[44]

As there are no exact data available about the number of detainees, this also counts for the foreigners who are actually being removed after being in administrative detention. There are many countries which do not have statistics available, while others give mainly estimates on the numbers. From a comparison between the data on removals and on return decisions for the period 2002-2004 (which are given in tables 2 & 3), the European Commission concludes that only one third of the return decisions are effectively implemented and result in removal.[45] Then the question rises, what happens with the rest?

The general practice of the European countries with regard to foreigners who are not removed from the country is that they are released, either by court order or after the end of the maximum period of time for detention in the concerning country, and ordered to leave the country on their own account. This goes for; *inter alia*, Greece, Italy, Spain, the Netherlands, Germany, Slovakia, Finland and Austria. However, for many foreigners returning to the country of origin is not an option.[46] What remains is staying in the concerning country, where he/she faces the risk of being detected again by the police and subsequently detained, or travelling to other EU countries, which are among the foreign-

---

[43] Parliamentary Assembly Council of Europe, Mass arrival of irregular migrants on Europe's Southern shores, Doc. 11053, 3 October 2006.

[44] Observation and Position Document: *Detention in Europe. Administrative detention of asylum seekers and irregular migrants,* Jesuit Refugee Service Europe 2004.

[45] European Commission, Common standards on return, Memo/05/288, Brussels 1 September 2005, p. 5.

[46] The International Organization for Migration (IOM) has programmes for assisting migrants in voluntary return to their country of origin. For more see www.iom.int.

ers known as countries where it is easy to get documents and work, where occasionally large numbers of irregular migrants are being regularized and where illegal residence - and labour are checked to a limited extent. Within this context, countries as France, Spain, Italy and Belgium, are being mentioned.[47] Moving to another EU country, is in many occasions not a solution as again the risk of detention and removal exists. This way many foreigners move in and out of detention over again and again. The way to get out of the vicious circle where the irregular migrants find themselves in is very difficult.

Conclusions

- There are no exact data available about the number of detainees in Europe, because of the fact that not all of the countries register them.
- On the grounds of data, which are partially available, the number of administrative detainees may be in the 100.000 persons per year.
- No exact data on the actual removals after administrative detention, but the European Commission concludes that one third of the return decisions are effectively implemented and result in removal.
- Non-expelled foreigners are released and maintain their irregular stay in the concerning country or travel to another EU country, by risking detention again.

3.11 Detention irregulars under criminal law

As stated earlier, administrative detention of foreigners is not a measure of the penal system, thus the foreigners are not detained because they are convicted or suspected of a criminal offence, but solely on the ground of residing in a country without a valid residence permit. For this reason, administrative detainees should not be seen as criminals nor to be treated as one.[48] Attention has been paid in 3.1 and 3.3 on the institutions in which foreigners are kept in the EU countries. Though, the practice in Europe is that administratively detained foreigners are kept separate from criminal prisoners in special detention centres, an actual look at the detention conditions of these foreigners shows quite some similarities with ordinary prisons. In countries where administratively detainees are placed in police stations or prisons, it even occurs that they are kept together with criminal offenders. This is for example the case in Ireland where there is no difference between administrative and criminal prisoners, they are detained together in prisons. In Cyprus there are specially designated detention cells for foreigners, but also detention cells which hold foreigners together with penal offenders exist.

Portugal, France, Germany and Finland have created separate detention places for foreigners, however this does not exclude the possibility in these countries, for detaining them together with criminal prisoners. Regarding Lithuania it can be said that before the foreigners can be and are accommodated in the Foreigner's Registration Centre, they are placed together with persons who have committed criminal offences, in the police custody facilities (maximum 48 hours). If there is a possibility, the foreigners awaiting transfer to the centre are accommodated separately.

---

[47] Spain has had recent regularization programmes in 2003; 800.000 and 2005; 600.000 irregular migrants, respectively. Italy has regularized in 2003 a group of 705.000 irregular migrants.
[48] See R. Cholewinski, *Irregular migrants: access to minimum social rights*, Strasbourg: Council of Europe Publishing 2005, p.8-9.

If we take a particular look at criminal prisoners who will be removed to their country of origin (category two prisoners), it can be said that the majority of the countries have the same policy on the question; how this category relates to the one of administrative detention? Just like common criminal prisoners, they are detained in general prisons and kept separate from administrative detainees. An example is the Netherlands where category 2 foreigners first serve their term of sentence in prison, after which they are transferred to a detention centre for waiting out the time for removal. Despite the fact that in the Netherlands the detention takes place in different locations, the administrative detainees are subject to the same penitentiary rules and regulations as category 2 prisoners.

The CPT's statement on this issue is that administrative detainees have to be held separately from prisoners, whether on remand or convicted.[49] Also article 15 (2) of the Commission Proposal Returns Directive and Guideline 10 (4) call for holding foreigners, who are detained pending their removal, separate from ordinary prisoners. Countries where criminal and administrative detainees are placed together act counter to these rules.

Conclusions
- Administrative detainees are not criminals and should not be treated as one.
- The legislation calls for detention separate from criminal offenders.
- The practice is that administrative detainees are kept separate from criminal prisoners, yet there are exceptions with countries such as Portugal, France, Germany and Finland, which make it possible to detain them together.
- Criminal prisoners who will be removed to their country of origin are detained in general prisons and kept separate from administrative detainees.

3.12 Minors

Children make up a large proportion of international migration flows to Europe. This group that is in need of special care and protection includes asylum and refugee seeking children, children forced or voluntarily migrating for work, children being abandoned when their parents migrate, as well as children trafficked for various exploitative purposes. The growing number of minors who are staying in an irregular way in European countries, face similar to adults, the risk of detention awaiting their removal to their country of origin. The policies regarding detention of children in EU countries differ for unaccompanied children and children who are in the concerning country together with their family.

With the exception of a few countries, such as Ireland (which prohibits the detention of persons under the age of 18 years) and the Czech Republic (where children under the age of 15 years may not be detained), the general practice in EU countries is that they allow the detention of irregular migrant children who are accompanying their family. In this way, Belgian law does not prohibit the detention of minors and provides explicitly that families may be detained. In the Netherlands, the detention of minors younger than 16 years has to be restricted as far as possible. The removal has to take place as soon as possible, so that the detention will be restricted. The fact that the foreigner has a departure duty (article 5 Aliens Act 2000) does not change this. Greece and the UK do not

---

[49] CPT Standards, Chapter IV Foreign nationals detained under aliens legislation, under point 28.

have an upper or lower age for detention, which results in that minors can be detained and removed under the same conditions and regulations as adult detainees. The majority of the countries which detain minors have separate units for accompanying the minors. This goes for; *inter alia*, Slovenia, Slovakia, Austria, Lithuania, France, Spain, Germany and Portugal. However, in practice it occurs that children with parents stay together in for example detention centres, prisons, penitentiary institutions, which are not equipped for the stay of children.

In the case of unaccompanied minors in general the help of Juvenile Welfare Agencies are called in by the authorities and a guardian is appointed. In Italy and France, these minors can not be removed nor detained. In Greece, children who are not yet 13 years old and who have no relatives in Greece can not be detained and must be accommodated in special hostels or institutions while the Greek authorities attempt to locate their family. British law allows their detention only in "exceptional circumstances and then only overnight, with appropriate care, whilst alternative arrangements for their safety are made". However, the fact that this provision is not binding can raise problems. The Dutch law makes the detention of unaccompanied minors between the ages of 12 to 16 years possible, but only when the child is not later than 4 days after the deprivation of liberty, placed in a juvenile institution.[50] Poland and Hungary exclude the removal of unaccompanied minors if the unification with the family or appropriate institutional care is not guaranteed in the country of origin.

Before dealing with the relevant European legislation related to children, there is an important International instrument that deserves attention. The Convention on the Rights of the Child is the first legally binding instrument which is setting out the civil, cultural, economic, political and social rights of children.[51] The Convention is child-centric and deals with the child-specific needs and rights. It requires that states act in the best interests of the child as stated in article 3 (1) and is monitored by the Committee of the rights of the Child, which is composed of members from countries around the world.

Article 37 of the Convention regards the detention of children. Under *b*. it is prescribed that:

> *'No child shall be deprived of his or her liberty unlawfully or arbitrarily. The arrest, detention or imprisonment of a child shall be in conformity with the law and shall be used only as a measure of last resort and for the shortest appropriate period of time'*[52]

Furthermore, under *c*. it is stated that children who are deprived of their liberty have to be separated from adults unless it is considered in the child's best interest not to do so.[53]

The general practice with regard to the detention of minors in Europe is not compatible with the Convention. Detention is certainly not a measure of last resort and children are also detained together with adults. Certain countries such as Malta and the Netherlands do not even have separate accommodation places for minors. The Commissioner for Human Rights has often noted in its reports that detention or holding centres where

---

[50] Part A, chapter 6 article 1.5 (c) Aliens Circular 2000.
[51] Date entry into force 2 September 1990.
[52] Guideline 11 (1) is inspired by article 37 b. of the Convention and is in conformity with it.
[53] See also article 35.4 European Prison Rules.

minors or families are housed are absolutely unsuitable for the needs of minors: they lack of appropriate facilities, foodstuffs and supplies. A play area, for instance, is never provided for these children, who spend their whole day locked in with their parents.[54]

The Commission Proposal Returns Directive has paid attention on minors in the articles 5, 8 (2c) and 15 (3). Article 8 (2c) states that:

> *'Member States shall postpone the execution of a removal order when there is a lack of assurance that unaccompanied minors can be handed over at the point of departure or upon arrival to a family member, an equivalent representative, a guardian of the minor or a competent official of the country of return, following an assessment of the conditions to which the minor will be returned'*

Within the context of article 8 (2c), I want to mention the Kaniki Mitunga[55] case of the Court which considers the detention and removal of an unaccompanied minor from the perspective of the ECHR. A five year old child arrived at Brussels airport on her own without having the necessary documents for entering Belgium. Before her removal, she was detained for almost two months in a centre that had initially been intended for adults, even though she was unaccompanied by her parents and no one had been assigned to look after her. No measures had been taken to ensure that she received proper counselling and educational assistance from a qualified person specially assigned to her. The conditions were not adapted to the position of extreme vulnerability in which she found herself as a result of her status as an unaccompanied alien minor. When the child was removed to the Democratic Republic of Congo, she was accompanied by a social worker who placed her in the care of the police at the airport. On board the aircraft she was looked after by an air hostess who had been specifically assigned to that task by the chief executive of the airline. She travelled with three Congolese adults who were also being deported. No members of her family were waiting for her when she arrived in the Democratic Republic of Congo. The Court therefore held that on the account of the detention and the removal to the country of origin, there had been violations of articles 3 and 8 ECHR to the child and her mother and a violation of article 5 ECHR in relation to the child.

Conclusions

- Growing number of minors who are staying in an irregular way in Europe face detention, awaiting their removal.
- Children, accompanied by their parents are detained together in places which are not equipped for the stay of children.
- Unaccompanied minors are in general taken care of by Juvenile Welfare Agencies and a guardian is appointed.
- The Convention on the Rights of the Child states detention of children as a measure of last resort, but in European countries it is daily practice.

---

[54] Speech by the Deputy Secretary General, Council of Europe. *European Conference on the respect of the rights of foreign minors in Europe and against their detention and forced removal*, Strasbourg, 14 March 2007.

[55] Judgment of 12 October 2006.

4 NATIONALS DETAINED ABROAD

This paragraph looks into nationals from EU countries that are being detained in countries other than their country of citizenship, either within or outside Europe. Not all research experts were able to obtain up-to-date information from official bodies regarding their nationals detained abroad. One of the reasons behind it is that in some countries there is no official information or data collection on this. The countries that could not provide information are Cyprus, Czech Republic, Greece, Latvia and Luxembourg. Information on Estonian and Finish nationals detained abroad is included in this overview but official numbers are missing because they are not being recorded.

4.1 Numbers and composition

From the 18 countries[56] that provided information the majority of their nationals were detained within the European Union. Only Portugal, Slovakia, Spain, Sweden and the United Kingdom have more nationals detained outside the European Union. The total number of nationals of 18 EU countries detained abroad is nearly 23.000. This total number is based on officially recorded statistics but is likely to be considerably higher. In practice some EU citizens detained abroad do not want to inform their diplomatic mission about their detention for various reasons. It is also not uncommon that foreign nationals are not made aware by prison authorities that they are entitled to inform their diplomatic representatives about their detention. Also European citizens who are detained in another country for administrative reasons are not always included in the official prison statistics. As a result these three groups are not represented in this total number. Neither are the data of seven EU countries that could not provide information on numbers of their nationals detained abroad.

---

[56] Austria, Belgium, Denmark, France, Germany, Greece, Hungary, Ireland, Italy, Lithuania, Malta, Netherlands, Poland, Slovakia, Slovenia, Spain, Sweden and the United Kingdom.

Figure 1

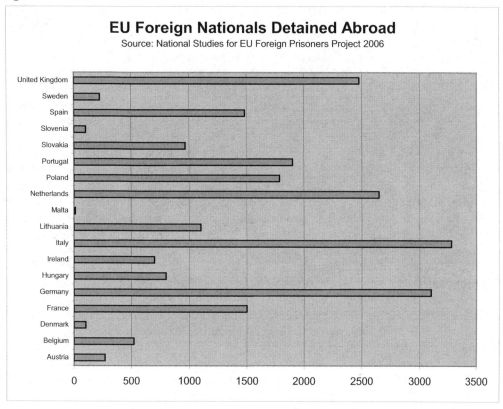

EU Foreign Nationals Detained Abroad
Source: National Studies for EU Foreign Prisoners Project 2006

Half of the group of 23.000 are detainees with citizenship from Italy, Germany, Netherlands or the United Kingdom. The total number of Dutch nationals detained abroad, around 2.645, is remarkably high, especially in relation to the small size of the country.

Table 5: Number of Nationals Detained Abroad

Country	Number	Country	Number	Country	Number
Austria	270	Greece	-	Poland	1.787
Belgium	523	Hungary	800	Portugal	1.900
Cyprus	-	Ireland	700	Slovakia	965
Czech Republic	-	Italy	3.279	Slovenia	103
Denmark	103	Latvia	-	Spain	1.485
Estonia	-	Lithuania	1.100	Sweden	225[57]
Finland	-	Luxembourg	-	United Kingdom	2.476
France	1.500	Malta	12		
Germany	3.100	Netherlands	2.645	Total	22.973

Source: National Studies for EU Foreign Prisoners Project 2006

---

[57] The number of nationals detained in other Nordic countries (Denmark, Finland and Norway) is not included.

Many EU countries indicate that the number of their nationals detained abroad is drastically on the rise in recent years. For example in Germany there has been an increase from 2.435 nationals in 2004 to 3.100 in 2005, an increase of 27% in only one year. There has also been a sharp increase in the Netherlands, in 1992 the number was around 1.000 and in 10 years time it has more than doubled to 2.330.

According to the Council of Europe *Convention on Mutual Assistance in Criminal Matters* (1959) each contracting party (all EU Member States) shall according to article 22 'inform others about all criminal convictions and subsequent measures in respect of nationals of the latter party. Ministries of Justice shall communicate such information to one another at least once a year'. It is therefore disappointing that even within the EU not all countries inform each other about the number of EU nationals in detention.

In Finland, for example, the Criminal Records Act reconfirms that information from the criminal records shall be delivered to a State Party of the European Convention on Mutual Assistance in criminal matters and that provisions on the delivery of data from the criminal records to another Nordic country shall be issued by Decree. However, according to the officials of the Legal Register Centre the procedure of receiving data from abroad is not realised in practise (except for data exchange between the Nordic countries). As a result there is no valid information available on the volume of the Finnish prison population detained abroad. This lack of information should be addressed.

In most countries the composition based on ethnic origin of the group EU nationals detained abroad is not being recorded. Exceptions are the United Kingdom where data is collected by Prisoners Abroad and The Netherlands where the Foreign Liaison Office of the Dutch Probation collects data. According to the Foreign Liaison Office a majority of the Dutch prisoners do not originally come from the Netherlands; many of them are born in Surinam, Netherlands Antilles/Aruba, Morocco, Turkey or the Dominican Republic. A quarter of the Dutch prisoners do not or barely speak Dutch, about 60% do not have a vocational education or diploma, and 60% do not have a job, income or allowance prior to detention. A large majority of nationals detained abroad is male; this percentage is 90% for British nationals and 84% for Dutch nationals. Information on ethnic origin is also kept by Prisoners Abroad: 76% of British citizens detained overseas are white and 17% are black or black British, 3.1% are Mixed, 2.3% are Asian or Asian British and 1.4% are Chinese or from another ethnic group. Two thirds of all Britons detained abroad are under 44 years.

4.2 Countries of detention

In nearly all EU countries a majority of nationals detained abroad are detained within the European Union and mostly in one of the neighbouring countries. In June 2006, 523 Belgian nationals were detained abroad of which 83% in Western European countries and only 1.7% in Eastern European countries. In Poland about 80% of Polish citizens arrested abroad in 2004 were detained within the EU. From the 12 Maltese citizens detained abroad 5 were held in Italy. Hungarian citizens detained abroad are mainly located in Austria, Germany and Italy. A total of 79 out of 103 Danes in prison abroad are detained in the EU. Estonians are mainly detained in Finland, Sweden, Germany, Austria and Spain.

A relatively high number of EU citizens are detained in the USA. One tenth of all German, Spanish and Swedish nationals detained abroad are locked up in the USA, for

French and Dutch nationals this is 5% and 26% for British citizens. The fact that so many British are detained in the USA, by far the country where most British nationals are detained, has a few reasons. Firstly the imprisonment rate in the USA is far higher than other countries, the USA is a popular destination for those emigrating from the UK and many of these people have not been naturalised. A majority of the Irish citizens detained abroad, around 64%, are detained in the UK (England and Wales, excluding Northern Ireland). Although Dutch prisoners are scattered around the world over 81 countries, around 60% are detained in EU member states. From this group 75% are detained in seven European countries, namely Germany (479), France (232), Spain (213), United Kingdom (155), Italy (133) and Belgium (93). Nearly half of all Slovenian foreign nationals are detained in Germany.

4.3 Reasons for detention and sentencing

In most European countries foreigners are arrested and held in detention for crimes related to smuggling, trafficking and possession of drugs. In most countries drug crimes are punished severely and offenders receive long sentences. Portuguese and Dutch nationals detained abroad are held in 80% of all cases for possession or smuggling of (mainly hard) drugs and for Spanish nationals this number is 72%. In Austria, Germany and the United Kingdom this number is 50% and in Belgium 57%. Other common reasons for arrest and detention are minor (traffic) offences, irregular stay, violence, property crimes, robbery, sex-crimes and homicide. Nearly all EU citizens that are held abroad are detained under criminal law, rather than being held under administrative or immigration law.

In France those foreign nationals that are awaiting death sentences abroad are being transferred back to France. In total there are 9 French prisoners detained abroad for political reasons. Sex tourism is a growing cause of imprisonment, but French prisoners tend to be ashamed of their crime and therefore do not contact the French authorities. Four German nationals are on death row in the USA and a further six in Kenya, Lebanon, Thailand, Taiwan and Philippines. At the moment German embassies in Tunisia, Egypt and Syria are looking into cases in which Germans were possibly tortured during their detention. In Brazil a German national is said to have died as a result of having been tortured to death. Most Hungarian nationals are detained for offences related to breaching working and staying regulations. The most frequent reason for detention for Irish citizens is homicide and for Slovak citizens property offences. Nearly half of all sentences served by Dutch nationals detained abroad are longer than one year. As a result the turnover rate is very high; in 2005 1.241 Dutch nationals were arrested abroad and 1.135 released. In 2004 a vast majority of Polish nationals were serving abroad short prison sentences imposed for misdemeanours and petty offences. In some countries, like the USA, foreign prisoners are transferred to immigration detention at the end of their criminal sentence, prior to being expelled back to their country of origin. For British nationals detained in the USA this is typically for a short period of time like a few weeks to a few months.

4.4 Authorities and organisations involved

In most countries there is more than one ministry responsible for the care of nationals detained abroad. In general these are the Ministry of Foreign Affairs and the Ministry of Justice (in some cases Ministry of Interior) that in cooperation with consulates and embassies supports national detained abroad. European citizens in need of consular help in a country without diplomatic or consular representation of their own country may turn to any consular or diplomatic mission of another EU Member State. According to Article 20 of the *Treaty establishing the European Community* and article 46 of the *Charter of Fundamental Rights of the European Union* should EU citizens 'be entitled to protection by the diplomatic or consular authorities of any Member State, on the same conditions as the nationals of that State'. The Ministry of Justice cooperates often closely with the Ministry of Foreign Affairs in transfer procedures of foreign nationals.

Consular help varies according to the individual situation in a country but in principle national authorities visit their nationals in detention, stay in contact with them and keep their relatives informed, monitor the human circumstances of detention (living conditions, food, medical care), provide magazines and newspapers, check the fairness and speed of the trial in accordance with local legislation, help to obtain a lawyer, provide information about the Council of Europe's *Convention on the Transfer of Sentenced Persons* (1983) or bi-lateral transfer agreements and help to prepare transfers. It is not unusual for EU consulates to provide small amounts of money to support nationals who do not have other sources in purchasing additional food, telephone cards and tobacco. In some cases consulates pay for the ticket back to the country of origin. Sometimes consulates facilitate money transfers from families to prisoners. Prisoners detained in developing countries may not be provided with basic essentials such as food, clothing or toiletries. British nationals can apply for grants to purchase these vital necessities, varying between □20 and □40 per prisoner per month (depending on the country). In 2005 more than □ 10.000 was provided to British prisoners for a wide variety of health issues; operations, asthma inhalers, consultations with specialists, glasses and dental treatment. In Spain nationals detained abroad can receive up to □100 per month to buy food, clothes and medicines when prison authorities provide nothing.   Most common problems experienced by prisoners detained abroad are the poor living conditions, uncertainty about their situation, complex and bureaucratic legal procedures and limited contact with relatives and the outside world.

In Austria 60% of the Austrian nationals detained in the EU are supported by the Ministry of Foreign Affairs, and 80% of their nationals detained outside the EU. Some Ministries of Foreign Affairs, like in Belgium, Germany and The Netherlands, have published a booklet with information for nationals detained abroad. For example the leaflet from the Belgium department of International Judicial Cooperation of the Ministry of Foreign Affairs published a leaflet 'Help and guidance for Belgians in foreign prisons'.

In the Netherlands the 'Foreign Liaison Office' of the Dutch Probation Service plays an important role in the care of Dutch nationals detained abroad. It has been established 30 years ago and with its nine regional coordinators it coordinates the work of 275 visiting volunteers and 15 corresponding volunteers. The visiting volunteers are Dutch nationals who live and work abroad and who pay a social visit to Dutch nationals in detention every four to six weeks. These visits are carried out in close cooperation with the Consular Department of the Ministry of Foreign Affairs and the various Dutch consulates and embassies around the world. The Liaison Office receives financial assistance from both the Ministry of Foreign Affairs and the Ministry of Justice and besides friendly visits it offers study facilities through a separate foundation, the Foundation Education behind Bars.

In the United Kingdom the non-governmental organisation 'Prisoners Abroad' works with British citizens detained abroad. It is an independent organisation, formed in 1978 and funded through voluntary donations, that provides support on a voluntary basis during detention and also upon return in the UK after a period of imprisonment. Prisoners Abroad employs 16 staff, all based in their office in north London. Prisoners Abroad sends, on request, newspapers and magazines to British citizens in prison all over the world, produces a thrice-yearly newsletter, a series of leaflets and handbooks for prisoners and a pen pal scheme.

Besides authorities like ministries, consulates and embassies in some countries there are also non-governmental organisations or religious groups that provide support to nationals detained abroad. In France there was an organisation called 'FIL' (*Français incarcérés au loin / Far off imprisoned French*) but unfortunately their activities are reduced due to a lack of volunteers. The Hungarian Ministry of Foreign Affairs supports assistance from civilian organizations and volunteers that stay in contact with detained Hungarians. These visits are made on a voluntary basis and without any payment. Irish organisations involved with Irish prisoners overseas are, besides the Department of Foreign Affairs and the Department of Justice, 'Equality and Law Reform' and the 'Irish Commission for Prisoners Overseas' (ICPO).

The Epafras Foundation in the Netherlands, initiated by Reverend Joop Spoor in 1984, provides pastoral and material assistance for Dutch nationals detained abroad. Epafras is incorporated in the associated churches of the Netherlands and receives funding from the Dutch Ministry of Foreign Affairs and Ministry of Justice. Four times a year Epafras issues a special magazine 'Gezant van Nederland ('Ambassador from the Netherlands', that is send to all Dutch citizens detained abroad. In Sweden, the non-governmental organisation 'Bridges to Abroad' supports Swedish citizens imprisoned abroad. Their representatives had experienced imprisonment abroad themselves.

4.5 Release and reception home country

In principle there are no European countries that provide nationals that have been detained abroad any kind of support once they are released and return to their home country. In case things are arranged it is being done on an individual basis by the relatives or in some countries by non-governmental organisations. In Austria there is an organisation called 'Neustart' that provides probation and help on release. In Ireland the Probation Service provides a voluntary advice and referral service to prisoners returning to Ireland and the 'Irish Commission for Prisoners Overseas' (ICPO) can send a booklet 'What Now?' with information on social welfare service in the ex-prisoners home area.

In case nationals are transferred back to their home country in order to continue their sentence they will be taken under the care of their national prison authority. In the Netherlands only 6% of the Dutch nationals detained abroad are being transferred back on an annual basis. The fact that the Netherlands has a relatively mild sentencing regime towards drug crimes makes other countries more hesitant to agree to a transfer. Once a Dutch national is released and/or transferred back to the Netherlands the contact with the consulate will stop. In practice only the Liaison office of the Dutch Probation remains in contact in case aftercare is facilitated upon return to the Netherlands. Aftercare is limited to offering advice and referral to other professional social workers.

British prisoners returning to the UK after serving their sentence overseas cannot expect any support from the UK Probation Service because they are under no obligation to provide any form of practical assistance. In many cases, without the help of Prisoners Abroad, the ability of returning prisoners to access welfare systems and obtain emergency accommodation would be severely limited. When prisoners return to the UK after the completion of their sentence, they usually arrive at one of the main London airports. At Heathrow airport they can be met by a small British charity called 'Heathrow Travel Care' and at Gatwick airport by a similar, but unrelated charity called 'Gatwick Travel Care'. These organisations provide ex-prisoners if necessary with clean clothes, they can make free phone calls, take a shower and receive instructions on how to find the Prisoners Abroad office. Prisoners Abroad can only offer financial assistance for the first four weeks after arrival back in the UK. Lithuanian citizens detained abroad often do not want to be transferred back to their home country because of the relatively harsh conditions in their national prisons.

In case a foreign national is being expelled, the expelling state takes charge of the expulsion. When a foreign national is being released in the foreign state, the person has to pay personally for his/her return to the home country. Some consulates may cover the transportation expenses, sometimes under the condition of later reimbursement.

4.6 Aftercare

In most EU countries there is no special aftercare for nationals that have been detained abroad. However, in general they are not excluded from social welfare support. However, for many former detainees who after many years come back to their home country it is very difficult to find their way to the social welfare institutions. During their detention abroad none or too little attention is paid to the difficulties and obstacles that foreigner prisoners have to cope with after their return in the home country. In Belgium if an ex-prisoner has no family ties left in Belgium and insufficient financial means, the department of International Judicial Cooperation may ask the Red Cross to support the prisoner upon his arrival and look for housing through the welfare services of his last place of residence. In Ireland the 'Homeless Persons Service Unit' of the Health Service Executive provides information and accommodation for those who have been detained abroad. In Lithuania those nationals that have served a sentence abroad are not excluded from social support but they have to apply within two months and to provide documents to confirm their citizenship, permit of residence and proof of previous conviction. Swedish nationals detained abroad that were interviewed for this study after their return to Sweden expressed a need, especially those who experienced a long and traumatic detention period, for mental and physical support. Although the Swedish social welfare system is well established, this service is not available.

4.7 Public opinion and media

Media attention for the situation of nationals detained abroad is generally low apart from certain exceptional cases that receive special attention. In most European countries, despite the rising numbers of nationals detained abroad, the issue is not a hot topic for the general public. In Lithuania a rather negative opinion prevails about citizens that committed crimes abroad.

However, some individual cases receive a lot of media attention. In these cases the main concern is the well being of the prisoner in severe conditions and extreme long sentences. Cases where French nationals were sentenced for sex-crimes (sexual relations with minors) produced moral condemnation and public exclusion. In principle national authorities like the Ministry of Foreign Affairs and consulates are reserved in putting a prisoners' case in the public light. But very often families and lawyers do while expecting or hoping that public pressure might influence the local justice or politicians. It practice this is often counter-productive and even negative for the prisoner, because local justice or politicians are not willing to be seen as weak under international or diplomatic pressure.

Conclusions
- Not all European countries keep official data on the number of nationals detained abroad.
- Although EU countries shall, according to article 22 of the Council of Europe 'Convention on Mutual Assistance in Criminal Matters', inform other Member States about the number of EU nationals in detention, this is not always applied in practice.
- The total number of nationals of 18 EU countries detained abroad is nearly 23.000 and their number is drastically on the rise. A majority of them are detained within the EU.
- A large majority of the EU nationals detained abroad is male with no or limited educational background and often without an official job.
- In most EU countries foreigners are arrested and held in detention for crimes related to smuggling, trafficking and possession of drugs.
- Nearly all EU citizens that are held abroad are detained under criminal law and not under administrative or immigration law.
- In most European countries there is more than one ministry responsible for the care of nationals detained abroad. In most cases these are the Ministry of Foreign Affairs and the Ministry of Justice in cooperation with diplomatic missions.
- Consular help to foreign prisoners varies per country and per individual case. From hardly no visits to frequent visits and legal / social / and financial support.
- There are limited non-govermental organisations that provide social / pastoral and or practical support to their nationals detained abroad. Some of these organisations are partially of fully financed by the government.
- Despite the existence of bi-lateral and European transfer agreements only a limited number of nationals are enabled to serve the remainder of their sentence in their home country.
- Once nationals are released and return to their home country there are in principle no aftercare or probation facilities available.
- Despite the rising number of foreign nationals detained abroad there is, except for exceptional cases, low media attention.

5 RECOMMENDATIONS

5.1.1 Recommendations with respect to paragraphs 1.1 - 1.6

Recommendation (1)
Foreign sentenced prisoners should either be transferred to their home country in order to properly provide rehabilitative measures and preparation for release in their home country or the host country has to develop special training and vocational programmes that help the integration in the future home country. In cases where the foreigner does not speak the language of the country where he/she will be expelled to, specific language courses could be provided.

Recommendation (2)
Rehabilitation/re-integration is a principal aim for all prisoners. The necessity to provide rehabilitative programmes is laid down in the European Prison Rules which provide rehabilitation as the sole aim of deprivation of liberty for sentenced prisoners (see No. 102.1 European Prison Rules)

Recommendation (3)
At least for those detainees who will stay in the host country alternatives to pre-trial detention and to imprisonment should be further developed. The discrimination and disadvantages of foreigners (often excluded from such community sanctions or alternatives) must be of serious concern. The same is true for conditional (early) release.

Recommendation (4)
Foreign prisoners should get a decision on whether to be expelled or not in the first stage of serving any prison sentence. This will allow planning concrete rehabilitative programmes and the preparation for release in either the host or the future home country.

Recommendation (5)
Foreign prisoners often do not receive sufficient (written) information about their legal rights and duties in a language they understand. Staff in prisons and immigration detention centres should be particularly educated to address the specific needs and language deficits of foreign detainees.
In many countries racism amongst prisoners is a concrete problems that should get more concern by the prison and detention authorities.

Recommendation (6)
Overcrowding is a severe problem in many prisons but also administrative detention centres.
It increases the "normal" problems of foreigners and therefore should be prevented.

5.1.2 Recommendations with respect to the EU - level

Recommendation (7)
From a criminal justice perspective, there are initiatives, which should be developed on a European front that would both meet some of the needs of the humanitarian/welfare agenda and from that of protecting the public and reducing the risk of re-offending, they are not mutually exclusive. These require co-ordination and co-operation between or-ganisations and agencies in the EU.

Recommendation (8)
Meeting the needs of justice and public protection, there should be protocols established amongst EU countries so that previous convictions and other relevant information can be obtained for sentencing. Such information will also be important during the prison sen-tence to work on offending behaviour, rehabilitation and resettlement issues. The repa-triation of EU prisoners to serve their sentence in their own country does have advan-tages in areas of education, training and general rehabilitation needs.

Recommendation (9)
The number of EU prisoners who voluntarily return to serve their sentence in their coun-try is low and while, in the UK context, only about 20% of FNPs are from EU countries, serving their sentence in their own country has distinct advantages. Depending on EU countries prisoner release arrangements, it might also mean that prisoners are released under supervision as opposed to being released with no requirements.

Recommendation (10)
EU national prisoners, who complete their sentences in the UK (or any other EU coun-try) and are then deported, are not under any form of supervision on release. Protocols should be established between EU member countries to facilitate the transfer of supervi-sion licences on deported prisoners to supervise resettlement and better protect their pub-lic against re-offending.

Recommendation (11)
The ability for community penalties and conditional release to be transferred, managed and enforced between EU countries, could also provide courts with sentencing alterna-tives to imprisonment and thereby reduce the FNP population" (see the recommendation of the UK national report). Social exclusion is likely to have negative impact on successful reintegration into society after release.

5.2 Recommendations with respect to the treatment of foreign offenders

5.2.1 General Recommendation (12)
Prison authorities should acknowledge the vulnerable position of foreign prisoners and should be committed to address their special needs. For this reason prison authorities should introduce special sections in prison regulations and implement special pro-grammes in order to compensate for the disadvantages that foreigners experience in daily prison life.

5.2.2 Living conditions & facilities

Recommendation (13)
Prison authorities should be aware that allocating prisoners of the same national/cultural/religious background can be seen as a 'good practice' as it can elevate the feeling of isolation, it can also create undesirable hierarchical or violent subcultures.

Recommendation (14)
Foreign prisoners should be allowed to penitentiary institutions where they have better chances for successful resettlement, even if they do not stay in the country of detention after release.

Recommendation (15)
Foreign prisoners should be lodged in penitentiary institutions located in the capital city in order to facilitate regular contact with diplomatic missions and relatively easy transportation from the airport when relatives from abroad pay a visit.

5.2.3 Reception and admission

Recommendation (16)
Admission to penitentiary institutions can be seen as an intimidating and dehumanising experience. It is therefore essential that prisoners have a proper understanding of what is actually happening and prison authorities should therefore have information available in various languages. Further prison authorities should at least translate prison rules and house rules in several most common foreign languages and should ensure that they are presented to foreign prisoners upon admission. A good practice can be found in England and Wales where foreign prisoners receive a 'Foreign National Prisoners Information Pack' upon admission. This pack contains information in 20 languages about the rules, prisoners' rights and duties, complaint procedures, how to contact the embassy, how to apply for a transfer etc.

Recommendation (17)
Staff at reception should receive special language training and learn about cultural diversity.

Recommendation (18)
Prison authorities should take into consideration that foreign prisoners often have to make long distance calls and sometimes at odd hours, due to different time zones, in order to notify their families about their detention.

Recommendation (19)
A good practice can be found in England and Wales where 'Foreign National Orderlies' are used to inform new foreign prisoners about prison life, how to find their way and how to reduce their isolation. These Orderlies are foreign prisoners themselves who that have multi language skills and who received a special training.

5.2.4 Work – Education – Training – Sports – Recreation

Recommendation (20)
Being engaged in useful and paid work is essential for prisoners and especially for foreign prisoners because they often do not receive financial support from outside the institution. Prison authorities should ensure that foreign prisoners have equal access to work, education and training programmes. Providing classes for foreigners to become more acquainted with the national language or English could be beneficial for both prisoners and staff.

Recommendation (21)
Prison authorities could seek support from local libraries and diplomatic missions to create a prison library collection of books, magazines and newspapers in various foreign languages.

5.2.5. Food – Religion – Personal hygiene – Medical care

Recommendation (22)
Prison authorities should stock prison shops with cultural specific ingredients or products.

Recommendation (23)
Prison authorities should create a multi-faith room for the use of prisoners of various religious backgrounds.

Recommendation (24)
Prison authorities should make sure that representatives of the most common religions have regular access to foreign prisoners for individual meetings and to hold religious meetings. A good practice can be found in Sweden where the Swedish Prison Service created a network of representatives of different nominations that visit foreign prisoners. This 'Council for Spiritual Welfare' network consists of around 130 persons.

Recommendation (25)
All prisoners should be allowed to wear their own clothing, hair and head dress. Turbans for Sikhs and head scarves for Muslim women should be accepted like in the United Kingdom.

Recommendation (26)
Prison authorities should provide medical care free of charge to all prisoners, so also to foreign prisoners that might not have health insurance.

Recommendation (27)
Requesting interpreter assistance from non-medical staff or other prisoners seems practical but is not desired because of medical confidentiality and the quality of the translation of medical terminology.

5.2.6 Consular help and Legal aid

Recommendation (28)
In order to avoid that foreign prisoners are not made aware of their right to contact their diplomatic mission, prison staff should be informed that foreign prisoners can only refrain from this right if the prisoners requests so in writing.

Recommendation (29)
Diplomatic missions should acknowledge the important role they play or could play for foreign prisoners. In many cases diplomatic mission are their only 'life-line'. The practice of the Prison Service in England and Wales that organises biannual meetings for diplomatic missions to inform consular staff about prison regimes and how to provide a professional service to their imprisoned nationals is worth following.

Recommendation (30)
Another good practice can be found in The Netherlands. The 'Foreign Liaison Office' of the Dutch Probation Service coordinates the visits of 275 Dutch volunteers who live and work abroad in 80 countries and who pay social visits to Dutch nationals in foreign detention. These visits take place every four to six weeks and are organised in close cooperation with Dutch diplomatic missions.

Recommendation (31)
Prison authorities should provide (free) legal assistance to foreign prisoners. Some Belgium penitentiary institutions organise 'Foreign Prisoners' Information Sessions' for lawyers in order to give them more insight in specific foreign prisoners' legal proceedings. In countries like the Czech Republic, Hungary and Malta non-governmental organisations, provide free legal help to foreign prisoners.

Recommendation (32)
Foreign prisoners should be made aware about their status as soon as possible. Are they eligible to remain in the country of detention or will they be expelled after release?

5.2.7 Contact with the outside world

Recommendation (33)
Prison authorities should allow foreign prisoners more flexible visiting schemes in order to allow family and relatives to make the long trip worthwhile. Further prison authorities should allow foreign prisoners to make telephone calls at different hours in relation to different time zones.

Recommendation (34)
Community welfare organisations should be encouraged to pay social visits to foreign prisoners in order to reduce their social isolation. Visits to Dutch citizens detained abroad by volunteers of the 'Foreign Liaison Office' of the Dutch Probation Service can be seen as a good practice. Another example that is worth following are the Spanish non-governmental organisations that provide free stamps and telephone cards to foreign prisoners but also mediation between the prisoner and their families.

5.2.8 Re-integration activities – Prison leave

Recommendation (35)
Prison authorities should acknowledge that re-integration activities and prison leave for foreign prisoners are as important as for other prisoners. Social welfare organisations can play a role in the resettlement of foreign prisoners. An example is Spain where some non-governmental organisations provide secure shelters and dormitories in order to make prison leave possible for foreign prisoners.

5.2.9 Release – Expulsion

Recommendation (36)
The decision of expulsion of foreign prisoners should be made as early as possible (see also recommendation 32) and foreign prisoners should preferably not be put in administrative detention while waiting to be expelled.

5.2.10 Aftercare – Probation

Recommendation (37)
It is advisable that also social welfare services provide assistance to foreign ex-offenders in their re-integration process, like in Portugal and England and Wales.

5.2.11 Staff

Recommendation (38)
Prison authorities should recognise that dealing with prisoners, and foreign prisoners in particular, in a professional, human and personal way requires effective management and great human and technical skills from prison staff. Prison staff should be carefully selected, properly trained, paid as professionals, work under adequate conditions and receive a respected status in society.

Recommendation (39)
Staff working with foreign prisoners should receive special training in language but also on the background of certain cultures, religion etc. A good example is the Swedish prison staff that work directly with foreign prisoners participate in a university level training on 'Intercultural Understanding' and 'Diversity and Dialogue'.

5.3 Recommendations with respect to foreigners in administrative detention

5.3.1 and 5.3.3 Institutions and capacity

Recommendation (40)
Detention of irregular migrants should never be used as a deterrent to put off possible future arrivals.

Recommendation (41)

Detention of foreigners in order to secure their removal or the prevention of unauthorised entry, is only acceptable if it can be shown conclusively that these measures are necessary in order to protect essential public interests and that no other less restrictive methods of achieving these aims are likely to be effective.

Recommendation (42)

Alternative, non-custodial measures which are available to the European states, such as reporting requirements, supervision systems, placement in open centres and the deposit of a financial guarantee should always be considered before detention.

Recommendation (43)

The place and conditions of detention as well as the detention regime should reflect the basic difference that exists between the sanctions and measures of detention that are applied within the criminal justice system and the system of administrative detention that is applied to irregular migrants. Irregular migrants should not be transferred to prisons as a punitive measure unless they are suspect or have been convicted of a criminal offence. As far as possible, an 'open regime' should be maintained within the institution.

Recommendation (44)

All staff in detention centres for irregular migrants should be qualified and trained for the specific needs of irregular migrants, who are detained pending the removal procedure.

5.3.2 The responsible Ministry and legislation

Recommendation (45)

Detention must not be imposed arbitrarily and never purely for the convenience of the authorities. It must be lawful, in accordance with a procedure and based on grounds prescribed by law, reasonably predictable, necessary and applied without discrimination.

Recommendation (46)

The law must define in a clear and concrete way the requirements which have to be satisfied, before detention may be authorised.

Recommendation (47)

The grounds for their detention and their rights while in detention should be communicated to the detainees.

5.3.4 Length of stay

Recommendation (48)

Detention of irregular migrants should be for the minimum period necessary. An absolute maximum duration for any such detention should be specified in national law, which should provide that, as a rule, the detention may not exceed three months. A prolongation should only be allowed if the detainee has not co-operated in facilitating his removal. In no case should the detention exceed six months as stated in the Commission Proposal Returns Directive.

Recommendation (49)

Detention is only justified as a temporary measure. If the aims for which it is used can not be achieved within a reasonable period that is defined by law, it should be terminated.

Recommendation (50)

Foreigners should not be detained for prolonged periods for reasons beyond the detainee's own control, such as states failing to cooperate in the removal process.

5.3.5 The decision procedure

Recommendation (51)

The decision for administrative detention should be issued by judicial authorities. In urgent cases they may be issued by administrative authorities, in which case the order shall be confirmed by judicial authorities within 72 hours from the beginning of the administrative detention as prescribed in the Commission Proposal Returns Directive.

Recommendation (52)

The decision of the judge should always contain clear reasons why other non-custodial measures would be inadequate for the purpose and, in the light of existing alternative measures, there should be clear proportionality between the detention and the end to be achieved. It should be communicated to the detainee in a language and in terms that he understands together with reasons for the decision. They. There should be a presumption in favour of release.

5.3.6 Appeal and review

Recommendation (53)

Administrative detainees should have the right to appeal against the first instance and the review decisions and should be provided with the means, through legal assistance to exercise this right. They must have access to independent and competent legal advice and assistance from the beginning of the detention, irrespective of his ability to pay and they should have the right to attend any appeal hearing and to present their case.

Recommendation (54)

Periodical judicial reviews should be guaranteed by statute in the event of continuing detention. In order to assess the proportionality of the detention, the judge should take into account the conditions of detention. When they are found to be seriously deficient, the judge should have the power to order the release of the detainee on the ground that detention in such circumstances is not proportional, having regard to the aims for which it is being used.

Recommendation (55)

Any review institution should be independent from the detaining authorities. The periodic reviews should take place regardless of whether the detainee has exercised his right to appeal. Detainees and their legal representatives should have the right to attend any review hearings and to present their case. The reviews should include an opportunity for the detainee to refute any assertions made by the detaining authorities.

Recommendation (56)
An effective complaints procedure should be provided relating to the treatment of detainees within the institution, so that problems may be speedily investigated and appropriate remedies provided, in cases where they are warranted. Depending on the different legal traditions and institutional arrangements to be found within each of the countries concerned, such complaints might either be directed to a judge or some other institution such as an Ombudsman or Board of Visitors.

5.3.7 Irregular stay (57)

Illegal entry to the territory of a European state or irregular stay in such a state should in itself not be considered to be a crime punishable with imprisonment.

5.3.8 – 5.3.10 Data and the non-expelled foreigners

Recommendation (58)
National authorities should provide detailed information on relevant statistics, regarding the total number of foreigners in administrative detention, in order to ensure transparency.

Recommendation (59)
Prior to and during detention highest priority should be given to encourage voluntary return through intensive and individualised counselling. Furthermore, the involvement of the International Organization for Migration and other national and international organisations should be stimulated, so they can contribute effectively to the process of voluntary return.

Recommendation (60)
In the case of foreign nationals who can not (or no longer) be lawfully detained, but who have not been granted rights of residence, the law should regularize their status in order to minimise the risks associated with 'social exclusion'.

Recommendation (61)
Persons who are unable to return to their home countries due to the situation in these countries and/or the risk of being 'subjected to torture or to inhuman or degrading treatment or punishment' should not be detained while the host state waits for a change of situation which would allow return.

5.3.11 Detention irregulars under criminal law

Recommendation (62)
Restriction to which criminal offenders are subjected should be applied to irregular migrants as few as possible, especially with respect to restrictions of the right to make phone calls, visits, correspondence, possession of personal goods, disciplinary sanctions, library, free movement inside the holding or detention centre. Therefore, irregular migrants should not be considered and treated as criminals.

Recommendation (63)
Administrative detainees should not be detained together with remand or sentenced prisoners. To accommodate such detainees in an institution which is otherwise integrated into the criminal justice system is acceptable only in exceptional circumstances. Even then, however, administrative detainees should not be in the same building as are used for ordinary criminal prisoners, nor subject to the same restrictions. There should be no co-mingling of the two groups.

5.3.12 Minors

Recommendation (64)
Unaccompanied persons who are under the age of 18 should never be detained and should be released into the care of family members who already have residency within the certain country. Where this is not possible, alternative care arrangements should be made by the competent child care authorities for unaccompanied minors to receive adequate accommodation and appropriate supervision. Residential homes or foster care placements may provide the necessary facilities to ensure their proper development. A legal guardian or adviser should be appointed.

Recommendation (65)
All appropriate alternatives to detention should be considered in the case of children accompanying their parents. Children and their primary care-givers should not be detained, unless this is the only means of maintaining family unity. Such detention should occur only in the most exceptional cases and in the least restrictive conditions. Nursing mothers and women in the later stages of pregnancy should not be detained.

5.4 Recommendations with respect to paragraphs 4.1 - 4.7

Recommendation (66)
Collection of data on nationals detained abroad should be done on a national and European level.

Recommendation (67)
More cooperation between national states and involved authorities is beneficial.

Recommendation (68)
There is an urgent need for the Introduction of minimum standards in consular care for nationals detained within the EU. These standards should contain provisions for social/legal/financial support, assistance to families at home and help with transfer agreements.

Recommendation (69)
Social visits made by volunteers of the 'Liaison Office' of the Dutch Probation Service to Dutch nationals detained abroad can be regarded as a good practice. As are the activities of the non-governmental organisations like the British 'Prisoners Abroad', the 'Irish Commission for Prisoners Overseas' and the Swedish 'Bridges to Abroad'.

Recommendation (70)

Transfer agreements between European countries could be more effective when the procedures are simplified and quicker. The transfer of EU prisoners to their home countries does have advantages for their social, educational and rehabilitation needs. As a result it will better protect the public against re-offending.

Recommendation (71)

The ability for community penalties and conditional release to be transferred, managed and enforced between EU countries, could also provide courts with sentencing alternatives to imprisonment and thereby reduce the EU foreign national prisoners population.

Recommendation (72)

Prison authorities should develop special training and vocational programmes which help the integration of foreign prisoners' into their home country.

Recommendation (73)

Nationals that have been detained abroad should receive access to national aftercare and probation provisions upon return in the home country. Providing practical assistance to nationals detained abroad directly after return, like how to obtain official documents, how to apply for housing, a job, social benefits etc is essential to combat recidivism.

Chapter 2

Austria

Arno Pilgram
Veronika Hofinger

1 INTRODUCTION

1.1 Overview Penalties and Measures

The following types of detention are legally admissible in Austria:
- *police detention (Verwahrungshaft)* (up to 48 hours) to bring someone who is strongly suspected of a criminal offence before the investigating judge (§§ 175-179 StPO);
- *pre-trial detention (Untersuchungshaft)* (up to a maximum of 2 years under special preconditions), proposed by the public prosecutor and decided by a judge (§§ 179-181 StPO);
- *custodial sentence (Strafhaft)* (from 1 day to 20 years, or lifelong, § 18 StGB), after conviction by penal court or after commutation of an irrecoverable fine into a substitute prison sentence (§ 19 para. 3 StGB);
- placement in *preventive custody (Unterbringung)* (in some cases for an indefinite time span) based on penal court's decision against 'mentally abnormal offenders', 'addicted offenders' or 'dangerous recidivists' (§§ 21-23 StGB).
- *administrative penal servitude (Verwaltungsstrafhaft)* (from 12 hours to 6 weeks, § 11 VStG), after sentence by an administrative authority or after commutation of an irrecoverable administrative fine into a substitute penal servitude (§ 16 VStG);
- *police arrest (Polizeihaft)* (up to 24 hours) to ensure an administrative penal procedure (§§ 35, 36 para. 1 VStG);
- *administrative detention of irregular migrants (Fremdenpolizeiliche Haft)* (up to 48 hours) to bring somebody before the immigration authorities (§ 39 FPG);
- *detention pending expulsion (Schubhaft)* (10 months within 2 years at maximum) to ensure administrative procedure to enforce ban of residence and removal (§§ 76 and 80 FPG).[1]

1.2 Overview of the Prison System

Detention can be executed in different institutions:
- *police detention* in cells and detention centres of the police;
- *pre-trial detention* (with some exceptions) in prisons at the location of the courts of first instance. In these court prisons there are separate departments for juvenile and female prisoners;
- *custodial sentences* up to 18 months generally in court prisons, with longer sentences in penitentiaries;
- *preventive custody* in special institutions provided for by the justice administration, but partly also in penitentiaries. Preventive detention of certified insane offenders due to § 21 para.1 StGB to a great extent takes place in general psychiatric hospitals.
- *administrative penal servitude* in police detention centres, in single cases (if following a custodial sentence) also in penitentiaries;

---

[1] Constraints of freedom are also admissible in connection with less severe means: If ban on residence or removal is deferred a directive is possible not to leave a certain area (§ 68, para.2 (1) FPG) or to reside in a place which is designated by the immigration authority (§ 77 para.3 FPG). The strongest restriction can be made according to § 77 para.5 FPG. To ensure the expulsion, forcible return or transition of immigrants they can be demanded not to leave a designated room for at most 72 hours.

- *administrative arrest of irregular migrants* in the police detention centres like police detention of criminal offenders;
- *detention pending expulsion* in the same institutions as administrative penal servitude or police detention of suspected criminal offenders whereas these different detainees are kept in separate cells or departments (following a custodial sentence this custody in some cases can also take place in penitentiaries).

The relevance of these penalties and measures may be assessed by the size of the prison population (daily average): While about 6,000 persons are serving a custodial sentence and 2,500 are kept in pre-trial detention, preventive custody and detention pending expulsion are affecting about 600 persons each and administrative penal servitude another 200. These figures (daily average prison population) correspond to the aggregate number of years of detention imposed.

Institutions under the responsibility of the Ministry of Justice
(*Justizanstalten, JA*): There are 28 JA with 16 small dependent outposts. Of these are:
- 16 court prisons (these are institutions for pre-trial detention and custodial sentences up to 18 months, housing between 50 [*Steyr*] and 1,300 [*Vienna*] prisoners, with separate departments for juveniles and women);
- 9 penitentiaries (for longer custodial sentences and a size between about 120 [youth prison in *Gerasdorf*] and 870 inmates [*Stein*]). One of these penitentiaries is designated for juveniles, another one for women[2];
- Besides these institutions the Ministry of Justice runs three institutions of rather small size for the execution of preventive custody, two of which are designated for mentally ill offenders, one for drug addicts;
- Persons subjected to preventive custody acc. to § 21 (1) StGB are legally under the authority of prisons (one of which is a specialised clinic, *Göllersdorf,*) but most of them are actually placed in psychiatric hospitals. At present there are nine hospitals in eight federal states hosting inmates of this category, partly on closed forensic departments, partly in open sections.[3]

The capacity of justice prisons is 8,068 places (1 Dec 2005). In February 2005 3,630 employees worked there. From this number 2,970 are especially trained guards. Furthermore there are about 300 staff members for special services, about one-third are social workers, another one-third are qualified nurses and the rest are psychologists, physicians or teachers. In 2005 the total budget for these prisons (without building costs) was 255.2 Mio €, of which 133.8 was spent for personnel. These prisons are directly managed and inspected/controlled by the Ministry of Justice.

---

[2] These penitentiaries are all closed prisons that partly contain high security departments, partly (semi-) open departments for the imprisonment of first offenders.

[3] On 1 Dec 2005 246 mentally ill offenders have been placed acc. to § 21 para. 1 StGB in psychiatric hospitals (or psychiatric departments of general hospitals). There is no information available about the percentage of foreigners in this population.
The hospitals and the health administration of the federal states are responsible for the treatment of these offenders, yet the time of release falls into the responsibility of penal courts that consult psychiatric experts.

Prisoners may address their complaints to the director of the prison (§ 11 StVG); if the complaint is directed against the prison management they may address their complaints to a special chamber of the regional court of appeal (§ 11a StVG) or to the Ministry of Justice as a last resort (§ 121 StVG). In the latter case the prisoner has no entitlement to reply (§ 122 StVG). Prison monitoring committees (*Vollzugskommissionen*) at each regional court exercise some extra supervision over prisons. These committees consist of seven members of the local community appointed by the minister of justice after nomination by the head of the local government and by ministers of some other resorts (§ 18 StVG).[4] The *Volksanwaltschaft* (the national ombudsman-institution) may control the administration of justice, including the management of prisons. It may act on its own initiative (e.g. because of media reporting) or react to citizens' complaints, and make an annual report to the House of Parliament.[5] The *Committee for the Prevention of Torture and Inhumane or Degrading Treatment or Punishment (CPT)* has visited Austria four times since 1990, the last time in 2004.

Institutions under the responsibility of the Ministry of the Interior (*Polizeianhaltezentren, PAZ*): Cells in police stations are for temporary police detention (before admission to police detention centres or to court prisons) and 16 police detention centres are for administrative penal servitude and detention pending expulsion. There are no special centres for juveniles and women, yet care should be taken for their spatial separation according to the law (§ 4 AnhO).

The capacity of police detention centres (PAZ) is 1,118 places, of which 717 are designated for detention pending expulsion and 305 for administrative penal servitude.[6] The smallest institution is located at the Vienna airport in *Schwechat* with 8 places; the largest is also in Vienna the *PAZ Hernalser-Gürtel* with 304 places. There are no figures available on budget and employees, because these institutions use personnel from different local police departments.[7]

---

[4]   Since the reports of the committees and their recommendations are not published, their impact – if there is any – stays invisible. A draft law from 2000 intended to substitute the committees by advisory boards for each prison. They should also include members of human rights groups and spokesperson for inmates. At the end of the 21st legislative period no more agreement on the bill could be reached.

[5]   In the 2000-2004 reports a decreasing number of prisoners' complaints is mentioned. The majority of these complaints refer to judicial decrees that are outside the competence of the *Volksanwalt*. There is no evidence from the reports that foreign prisoners complain more frequently, on the contrary. Because of five cases of prisoners' death the *Volksanwaltschaft* in 2001 specifically investigated the penitentiary in Stein. The annual report denies shortcomings and generally acquits the guards stating the growing congestion of the facilities by a 'dramatic change' in the prison population. Apart from a growing readiness to escape, from increasing drug and mental health problems the high number of foreigners among prisoners is seen as a stress factor: 'An additional strain for the personnel results from the high portion of foreign prisoners who do not speak German (presently 30% of prisoners coming from 60 different nations)' (Annual Report of the Austrian Ombudsman Board 2001, p. 13).

[6]   Information obtained from the Ministry of the Interior (Abt. II/3).

[7]   After a key date (10 Jan 2001) assessment by the *Human Rights Advisory Council* 458 officials have been busy in police detention centres, thereof 51 women. Social care workers only care for prisoners in detention pending expulsion. According to contracts between the Ministry of the Interior and private organisations there should be two to three care workers for each detention centre with office hours on every working day.

An important control function is exercised by the *Human Rights Advisory Council* (*Menschenrechtsbeirat, MRB*) that resorts under the Ministry of the Interior but is free from its directives. This council has been established through an amendment to the Security Police Act 1999 (introducing §§ 15a/b/c SPG) in compliance with a *CPT recommendation* in 1990, that living conditions in police detention centres should be controlled by an independent body. The real trigger for the establishment of the broad competence of the MRB was the death of a Nigerian citizen during forced removal in 1 May 1999. Besides its annual activity report the council periodically publishes progress-reports on the implementation of its numerous recommendations.[8] The *Volksanwaltschaft* can also be appealed to in matters of police detention and it regularly reports its observations to the House of Parliament.[9]

In principle none of the different types of prisons is reserved for foreigners. In practice, pending expulsion foreigners are detained in police detention centres segregated from the other categories of detainees. There is only one PAZ (in *Eisenstadt*) that exclusively houses detainees pending expulsion. The mean share of foreigners is highest in PAZ (about 75%) and is higher in court prisons (with mainly pre-trial detainees, 50%) than in penitentiaries (40%). The lowest portion of foreigners can be found in institutions (prisons or hospitals) for preventive detention (13%). The regional differences are substantial. The maximum share of foreigners in a prison under justice administration is 70% (*JA Suben*). Compared with their 9.3 %-rate in the whole population[10] foreigners are strongly over-represented in prisons, except in preventive detention measures, yet compared with their rate in the offender population (29% in total, 46% with felony offenders, in 2004) foreigners are only over-represented in pre-trial detention and not in penitentiaries.

There is no department with special responsibilities for foreigners, neither in prisons under justice nor under police administration, except in the largest Austrian court prison in Vienna. There is a foreigners' advisor (*Ausländerreferent*) who may be consulted by prisoners and guards from other prisons and who organizes trainings for officers working with foreign prisoners. Within the new curriculum for the basic training for wardens (enacted in 2004) an extended course 'foreign cultures' is mandatory, but there is also considerable demand for similar courses in further education programmes. The situation is similar in police basic and advanced training courses.

---

[8] *CPT* is demanding an even greater independence of the *MRB* with regard to budget and selection of members and also an extension of its competence to prisons under justice administration (*CTP* 2005, p. 15).

[9] In fact only very few complaints against police relate to forcible action or detention measures, even less to actions taken against foreigners. The bulk of complaints refer to police service, respectively to omission of service.

[10] In the age group >15-64 the foreigners' rate in 2004 was 10.6% (*Statistisches Jahrbuch Österreichs* 2006, p.191). In addition population statistics are fairly incomplete with respect to non-residents. If we consider a daily average of about 320,000 tourists in the country, the growing number of statistically neglected seasonal workers and the illegally present – estimated at about 80,000 (*Futo/Jandl* 2005, *National Contact Point* 2005) – the rate of foreigners in the population might come up to at least 15%.

Table 1: Prisoners in Austria on 1 December 2005

	total	Austrians	Foreigners	% Foreigners
Court prisons (CP)				
total CP	4918	2406	2512	51.1%
Penitentiaries (P)				
Penitentiaries (men)	3354	2039	1315	39.2%
Gerasdorf (juveniles)	126	60	66	52.4%
Schwarzau (women)	165	105	60	36.4%
total P	3645	2204	1441	39.5%
Facilities for preventive custody (PC)				
total PC	403	350	53	13.2%
total (justice prisons)	8966	4960	4006	44.7%
Police Prisons, by date 23 Nov 2005				
	total	Austrians	Foreigners	% Foreigners
Administrative penalcustody	178	148	30	16.9%
Police detention	14	6	8	57.1%
Detention pending xpulsion	424		424	100.0%
total (police prisons)	616	154	462	75.0%
all prisons	9582	5114	4468	46.6%

Source: IVV-Data (based on prisoners' electronic files), provided by Ministry of Justice, February 2006; Personal communication from Ministry of the Interior, Dep. II/3; own calculations

1.3 Overview Involvement Consulates, Embassies, Ministries Home Country, Probation Service Home Country, NGO's etc

See 2.6

1.4 Overview of Trends

At present the number of prisoners in Austria has reached the highest level since the early 1980s. The marked rise since 2000 is the result of increasing prison input (offenders detected by the police) and inadequate political counter-measures. Such measures have been repeatedly taken between 1987 und 1998, namely a series of penal code and penal procedure law reforms (ranging from the penal law amendment in 1987 to the juvenile court law in 1988 and the so called diversion law in 1998; see: Pilgram 2004).

Even a first crime wave caused by foreigners after the opening of the Eastern borders in the early 1990s was at the time still responded to by liberal reforms (e.g. Penal Procedure Law amendment 1993 and Code of Imprisonment 1993). These could not completely prevent rising numbers of prisoners. Notably the Austrian citizens profited from this policy to avoid pre-trial detention and prison sentences, whereas the growth of the prison population (daily average in justice institutions) from about 5,900 to 7,200 between 1989 and 1993 and from about 6,900 to 8,400 after 2000 is exclusively due to rising numbers of foreigners imprisoned. Criminal policy today, however, propagates imprisonment and prison construction. Criminal policy shows itself as security policy in the face of perceived crime threats originating abroad, and is no longer primarily guided by principles of compensation and re-integration. The increase of foreigners in prisons at the beginning of the 1990s was first effectuated by new 'tourist groups' from the neighbouring countries (Czechoslovakia, Hungary, but also from Poland), second by migrants from the disintegrating Yugoslavia (by people fleeing civil war). Labour migrants to Austria typically originate from these regions (Pilgram 2003a). These groups committed primarily property crimes (occasionally even on a commercial scale).

The increase in the number of foreign prisoners after 2000 can be traced back almost exclusively to citizens from more distant Eastern European regions (e.g. Rumania, Bulgaria, former Soviet Republics) on one hand and to persons from Western African states on the other hand (Pilgram 2003b). They usually only have a provisional residence status as asylum seeker or stay illegally in the country. Almost half of the 20%-increase of the average prison population between 2001 and 2004 (from 7,059 to 8,443) originates from citizens of Eastern European states (n=655, 47%), more than a third (n=508; 37%) of Western African states. Those in the first group invariably get arrested because of recurrent property crimes those in second group because of street drug dealing. While the number in prison of Austrian citizens is falling and that of citizens of states traditionally providing for labour migrants (Yugoslavia, Turkey) remains the same, the portion of prisoners from distant Eastern Europe states rises from 3.9 to 10.3% (maximum 2004) and that of prisoners from Western Africa from 4.0 to 9.1% (2005). (See figures 1-7)

Figure 1 Austrian and Foreign Citizens in Austrian Prisons 1981 – 2005

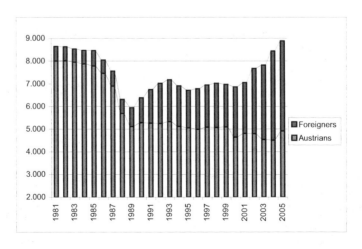

Source: Annual 'Statistische Übersicht über den Strafvollzug'; Bundesministerium für Justiz (1996): Unterlagen zur Budgetdebatte 1997, own calculations; data 2000-2004: personal communication Mag. Gneist (Ministry of Justice); 2005: IVV-Daten, provided by Federal Computing Centre of Austria, March 2006: Mean number of Austrian prisoners; foreign prisoners on key date Sep. 1st (since 2001: Dec. 1st).

Figure 2 Prisoners by Nationality (all prisons)

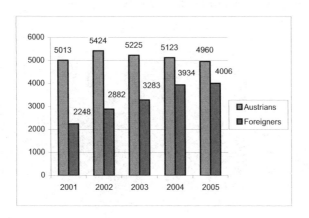

Figure 3 Prisoners in Court Prisons (upper court-district Vienna)

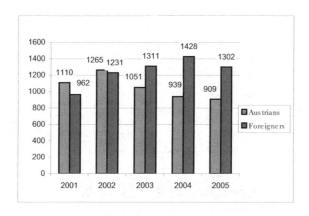

Figure 4 Prisoners in Court Prisons (other upper court districts)

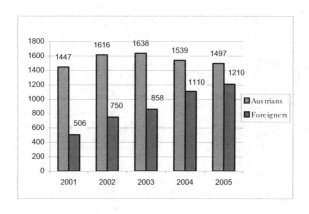

Figure 5 Prisoners in Penitentiaries (for adult males)

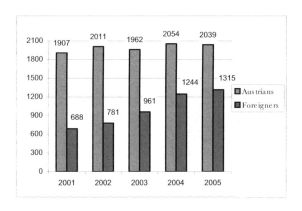

Figure 6 Prisoners in Special Institutions (for juveniles, females, mentally ill)

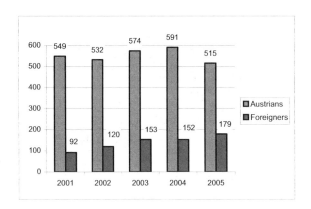

Figure 7a Prison Population● in Austria by Nationality (%) 2001

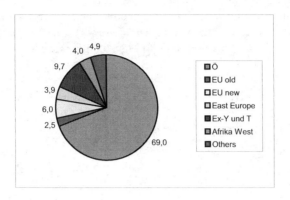

Figure 7b Prison Population● in Austria by Nationality (%) 2005

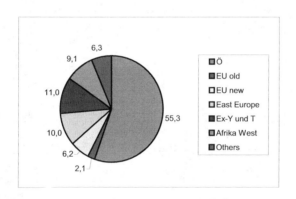

*) Population in prisons under justice administration.
Source: Figure 2 to 7b: IVV-Data (based on prisoners' electronic files, not including police prisons), provided by Ministry of Justice, February 2006
Nationality:
EU-new: Estonia, Latvia, Lithuania, Malta, Poland, Slovakia, Czech Republic, Hungary, and Cyprus
East Europe: Albania, Armenia, Azerbaijan, Bulgaria, Georgia, Kazakhstan, Bishkek, Moldova, Romania, Russia, Ukraine, Uzbekistan, Tajikistan, Belarus
Ex-Y and T: Bosnia and Herzegovina, Yugoslavia, Croatia, Macedonia, Serbia, Turkey
Africa West: Angola, Equatorial Guinea, Benin, Burkina Faso, Cote d'Ivoire, Gabon, Gambia, Ghana, Guinea, Guinea Bissau, Cameroon, Congo, Liberia, Mali, Mauritania, the Niger, Nigeria, Senegal, Sierra Leone, Togo, Chad, Central African Republic

Though in the long range a diminishing number of people are sentenced (namely native born and naturalized persons, but even foreigners integrated into the labour market) prison sentences become more frequent – in particular against certain groups of foreigners. They endure more frequently pre-trial detention and short-term prison sentences. Austrians, however, a priori do not experience pre-trial detention and imprisonment as often, but if they do their sentences are longer and more often combined with preventive detention. Criminal policy shows a kind of polarization along the line Austrian – foreign offenders. A slightly growing proportion of juveniles and women among prisoners in recent times is a consequence of the increasing rate of foreigners in prisons. Alternatives to prison sentences are less often used with foreign offenders. (Pilgram 2002; see: Table 2 and 3)

Table 2 Prison Population by Status of Detention and Citizenship

by date 01.12	Austrian					other EU-citizenship					third state citizenship*				
	pre trial detention	penal servitude	preventive custody	others	total	pre trial detention	penal servitude	preventive custody	others	total	pre trial detention	penal servitude	preventive custody	others	total
2001	769	3603	532	94	4998	252	337	6	22	617	555	1000	32	45	1632
2002	859	3862	554	75	5350	231	372	8	14	625	872	1159	42	52	2125
2003	815	3708	605	76	5204	262	312	4	15	593	1074	1506	48	57	2685
2004	834	3578	642	52	5106	326	441	8	16	791	1127	1909	56	45	3137
2005	703	3570	657	35	4965	268	443	16	14	741	935	2213	59	41	3248
percentage															
2001	15.4	72.1	10.6	1.9	100	40.8	54.6	1.0	3.6	100	34.0	61.3	2.0	2.8	100
2002	16.1	72.2	10.4	1.4	100	37.0	59.5	1.3	2.2	100	41.0	54.5	2.0	2.4	100
2003	15.7	71.3	11.6	1.5	100	44.2	52.6	0.7	2.5	100	40.0	56.1	1.8	2.1	100
2004	16.3	70.1	12.6	1.0	100	41.2	55.8	1.0	2.0	100	35.9	60.9	1.8	1.4	100
2005	14.2	71.9	13.2	0.7	100	36.2	59.8	2.2	1.9	100	28.8	68.1	1.8	1.3	100

*Source: Source: IVV-Data (based on prisoners' electronic files, not including police prisons). Provided by Federal Computing Centre of Austria, March 2006, own calculations. *Including stateless persons*

Table 3: Released Prisoners, by Citizenship and Length of Detention, 2005

	citizenship				
	Austrian	other EU	third state	foreign state total	total
Released prisoners	6620	1741	5940	7681	14301
after days (mean) of					
pre-trial detention	44	63	60	122	53
penal custody	202	82	110	192	149
total (pre-trial d./penal cust.)	246	145	169	314	202
percentage penal custody	82.2	56.8	64.7	61.1	73.9

Figure 8 Released Prisoners 2005, Citizenship and Length of Detention (days)

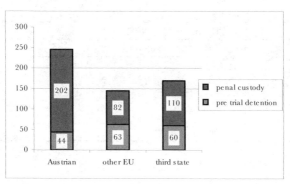

Source: IVV-Data (based on prisoners' electronic files, not including police prisons). Provided by Federal Computing Centre of Austria, April 2006, own calculations

With respect to police detention centres statements of trends cannot be made, because there is no steady data reporting by the Ministry of the Interior. The administration only offered very limited statistics, the total number of detentions in 2003 and 2004 (accession data), and the stock of detainees at two key dates (special inquiry at the turn of 2005/2006). From these sources it can be concluded that more persons are passed through PAZ than through prisons under justice administration, while the average time of detention is rather low there: 14 hours with police detention, 11 days with administrative penal custody and 16 days with detention pending expulsion.

Table 4: Entrances to Police Prisons in 2003 and 2004

	2003	2004	Population in police prisons by		mean stay (days)*
			23 Nov 2005	23 Jan 2006	
total	26,263	25,889	616	790	9.8
thereof foreigners	18,184	17,807	462	652	11.3
% foreigners	69.2	68.8	75.0	82.5	
thereof % women	13.7	14.2	7.6	14.3	
thereof % juveniles	6.7	6.7	3.0	1.5	
administrative penal custody	5,932	6,212	178	198	11.3
thereof foreigners	1,255	1,307	30	56	12.3
% foreigners	21.2	21.0	16.9	28.3	
thereof % women	7.6	6.8	0.0	21.4	
thereof % juveniles	1.3	2.4	6.7	0.0	
police detention	8,028	8,740	14	13	0.6
thereof foreigners	4,626	5,563	8	4	0.4
% foreigners	57.6	63.6	57.1	30.8	
thereof % women	9.8	7.6	0.0	0.0	
thereof % juveniles	15.8	13.8	0.0	0.0	
detention for the purpose of removal	12,303	10,937	424	592	16.0
% foreigners	100.0	100.0	100.0	100.0	
thereof % women	15.7	18.4	8.3	13.7	
thereof % juveniles	3.8	3.6	2.8	1.7	

Source: Personal communication from Ministry of the Interior, Dept. II/3; own calculations
Comment: Data not including administrative detention facility in Bludenz
* Mean of entrance and population data used for calculation of mean stay.

Forecasting future trends is quite difficult and risky. Since the last year there are some hints that after 2000 the wave of offences committed by foreigners already might have transgressed its peak. Prison populations might even decrease due to factors like the expansion of the EU and the intensified co-operation in police and justice matters, migration policy agreements within the EU and with accession countries and, last but not least, bi-lateral conventions with third countries. Yet in principle more restrictive regulations concerning residence, occupation, settlement and naturalisation for not privileged nationals, respectively for citizens lacking full citizen status in Austria and migration control by means of criminal law[11] will lead to illegalising of parts of the foreign population. Two

---

[11] The effects of the Immigration Police Law from 2005 on the numbers of detainees pending expulsion slowly become apparent now according to a press release from the Association for Human rights Austria on 29.01.2006 a doubling of the numbers can be expected in 2006 as compared with the year before.

classes of foreigners with respect to sentencing practice and implementation of prison sentences towards them are a quite presumable scenario for the future.

1.5 Overview of National Legislation

The legal grounds for deprivation of freedom can be:
- Security Police Law (*Sicherheitspolizeigesetz*, SPG) and Penal Procedure Law (*Strafprozessordnung*, StPO) – regulating arrest, police detention and pre-trial detention;
- Penal Law (*Strafgesetzbuch*, StGB) – including principles of sentencing, later modification of sentences and release;
- Code of Imprisonment (*Strafvollzugsgesetz*, StVG) – determining the exertion of prison sentences and of preventive measures;
- Imprisonment Decree (*Vollzugsordnung*) – instructions by the Ministry of Justice for the administration of the code of imprisonment;
- Several administrative state laws or province laws imposing administrative penal custody sanctions on norm violations, or allowing for commutation of irrecoverable fines into penal custody;
- Administrative Penal Law (*Verwaltungsstrafgesetz*, VStG) – determining the imposition and exertion of administrative penal sanctions;
- Police Detention Order (*Anhalteordnung*, AnhO) – instructions by the Ministry of the Interior for the administration of detention in police cells and police detention centres;

All these laws are applicable to Austrians and foreigners. Penal Procedure Law, Code of Imprisonment, and Imprisonment Decree in some articles consider particular requirements for foreigners, therefore the law formally rather entitles than discriminates them. Exclusion from certain rights and benefits usually takes place without reference to nationality, but with reference to rather undefined risk criteria. Actually risk attributions – like inclination to escape or similar assumptions – are more frequently made towards foreigners. While the Administrative Penal Law (VStG) only marginally considers foreign detainees the Police Detention Order (AnhO) acknowledges the situation of foreigners in a similar way as the Code of Imprisonment does. Before an amendment to the Decree of Police Detention which came into force on 1 Jan 2006 detainees pending expulsion in principle, were not treated differently from other police detainees or from persons in administrative penal custody.

- The Immigration Police Law (*Fremdenpolizeigesetz*, FPG) is a law primarily affecting foreigners and it is a significant part of the so-called Immigration Law Package (Fremdenrechtspaket) 2005). It allows arrest of foreigners to bring them before the immigration authority and defines the preconditions for putting somebody into detention pending expulsion.
- Illegal entering and stay in the country are no criminal offence, though an extended range of supporting acts are.

Detention pending expulsion can be applied to assure the administrative procedure for interdiction of residence or removal till enforceability, or to assure rejection, passage in transit or expulsion (§ 76 para.1 FPG). Foreigners can also be detained if the authorities determine that they are not eligible for asylum in Austria, since they have travelled through a so called safe third country (§ 76 para.2 FPG). The use of more lenient instruments can be bound to conditions (adherence to residence and notification obligations) whose violation may also lead to detention pending expulsion (§ 77 para.4 and 5 FPG). Though, in principle, the duration of detention pending expulsion should not exceed two months there are some exceptions. If a procedure is pending whether removal is admissible at all, the custody may take up to six months (§ 80 para.2 FPG), if the detainee is responsible for non-deportability (for instance, because of covering his identity or resisting police force) the custody may be extended to ten months within a period of two years (§ 80 para.4 FPG).[12] Complaints against detention pending expulsion can be brought before the Independent Administrative Senate and have to be decided within one week (§ 83f FPG). Minors in custody have to be separately accommodated, if their parents are also detained, they might be detained with them, except when their well-being demands separate accommodation (§ 79 para.3 FPG).

- The devolution of execution of prison sentences imposed on foreigners by Austrian courts, the take over of the execution of sentences against Austrians imposed by courts abroad and the assistance in law enforcement in general, including extradition[13], is subject matter of the Extradition and Legal Assistance Law (ARHG).

In principle this law under strict conditions also allows the transfer of sentenced persons outside the frame of European conventions and bilateral agreements. Practically this leeway is irrelevant. The large majority of transfers are done on the ground of multilateral and bilateral agreements. The most important legal basis for prisoners' transfer is the European Convention on the Transfer of Sentenced Persons from 1983 (accomplished in a Council of Europe framework and ratified in Austria in 1986). Austria belongs to the states that also ratified the Additional Protocol to the European Convention from 1997 in 2001 which first legalized the transfer without consent of sentenced persons if they had evaded penal execution by escape or got a final and executable ban of residence. While at present no requests for taking over the execution of sentences are made to Georgia or Ukraine, though they already have ratified the Additional Protocol, a memorandum of understanding between Austria and Romania was signed in 2004 to enforce the transfer of sentenced persons by speeding up the procedure through recognizing sentences as a matter of principle.

Further bilateral agreements exist between Austria and Thailand and Cuba. These agreements are of minor relevance and primarily are to ease the execution at home of prison sentences imposed in these countries against Austrians. With substantial groups of convicts in Austrian prisons from Nigeria and other Black-African states, formal interstate agreements with such countries and the prerequisites for transfer requests are inadequate. In 2005 the Austrian Ministry of Justice made 230 requests to foreign states to take over the execution of prison sentences imposed by Austrian courts on their citizens - two to three times more frequent than in the years before - in 76 cases requests were agreed

---

[12] Regarding the potential consequences see fn. 11.

[13] The documentation of extradition is deficient in Austria. We know about the number of extradition requests from Austria on foreign states and vice versa. On an average 94 requests were made on Austria in the period 2000-2004 (with 215 in 2004). Yet how many persons have been put into custody on request of extradition from abroad, and how many actually have been extradited is still unknown.

to.[14] This corresponds to only about 2% of those foreigners who had been unconditionally sentenced to a prison term of one year or more; with Romanians the transfer rate is 5 out of 43 such cases.

2 TREATMENT OF FOREIGN PRISONERS

The following report on the situation of foreigners in Austrian prisons is based on 14 interviews with experts in selected penitentiary institutions.[15] Managing officials, social workers, a psychiatrist, a psychologist, a pastor, an expert in the field of aftercare and probation as well as an advocate and officials from the Ministry of Justice gave information about the situation of foreigners in Austrian prisons.[16] Whenever possible the qualitative interviews are backed up by quantitative data for the whole of Austria by referring to the statistics of the Austrian penitentiary system, based on electronic prisoners' files, the *IVV (Integrierte Vollzugsverwaltung)*. Unfortunately there are no research projects about the situation of foreign prisoners in Austria. While the *Human Rights Advisory Council (Menschenrechtsbeirat)* of the Ministry of the Interior reports on police detention, no regular public reports exist for the penitentiary system. Information from the *CPT*, the *European Committee for the Prevention of Torture and Inhuman or Degrading Treatment or Punishment* could partly be used for this chapter.[17]

2.1 General

The Penal Procedure Code, the Code of Imprisonment and the Imprisonment Decree are, in general, equally applicable to foreigners and Austrians. Individual paragraphs prescribe special treatment for foreigners intending to compensate disadvantages.[18] In the treatment of foreigners, the wording of the laws in question does not discriminate between those with or without residence permits or whether foreigners are expelled after their detention or not. What does this legal equality or even this form of 'positive discrimination' mean in practice? The interviews showed a typical attitude on the part of

---

[14] On top are requests addressing Romania (n=52), followed by Poland (n=36), Hungary and the Netherlands (n=20, each) and to German federal states (n=17, aggregate). The reasons for not making requests or for their failure cannot be figured out statistically. According to expert opinion the main reasons are the duration of the procedure as compared to the length of sentences, the missing consent or undecided residence status of the prisoner (no legally effective ban). From 2000 to 2005 662 requests to foreign states to take over the execution of prison sentences imposed by Austrian courts on their citizens have been made in all. In this period 315 requests (48%) have been agreed to. No accurate figures exist about prisoners having actually been transferred to their home countries. In at least 41 documented cases the transfer did not take place because of the prisoners having already served their sentence or having been paroled in the meantime, or because of revocation of their consent.

[15] The interviews were conducted at the largest court prison (*Wien-Josefstadt*), at the largest penitentiary (*Stein*), at the penitentiary with the highest share of foreigners (*Suben*, 70% on 1 Dec 2005) as well as in two other court prisons and one other penitentiary.

[16] In the scope of this study it was not possible to hold interviews with foreign prisoners themselves.

[17] The CPT has visited several Austrian penitentiaries since 1990. The report cited in this chapter refers to the 2004 visit to *Wien-Josefstadt*, *Linz* and *Wien-Mittersteig*. For the CPT reports as well as the Austrian government's response see http://www.cpt.coe.int/en/states/aut.htm.

[18] See also s. 1.5

employees and officials in Austrian penitentiary institutions that can be summarised as follows: 'We do not discriminate; we treat Austrians and foreigners the same way!' It was admitted that there may be a (small) part of the staff with prejudices against foreigners – but basically there *could* actually be no different treatment because of the high share of prisoners of foreign origin.

On a daily basis, however, foreign detainees are disadvantaged in many ways. Often they do not or hardly speak German, they do not have relatives nearby, they are confronted with prejudice, and in addition to their sentencing, they have to face the decisions of the immigration authorities. Even though nationality is no grounds for exclusion from semi-open places, better equipped facilities, courses, work and so on, foreigner status has negative consequences, such as, for example, the assumption that non-integrated foreigners are more likely to attempt escape. Language barriers often lead to information deficits and reduce the chances that individual wishes and needs are respected. Therefore the question arises: *Shouldn't* foreigners be treated *differently* in order to meet their special needs?

In some spheres (as for example religious practice, food, equipping of libraries, or German lessons) concrete steps were taken to fulfil the special needs of foreigners and to compensate disadvantages to a certain degree. When different penitentiary institutions are compared, however, it seems that the implementation of these and other compensating measures depends to a great extent on the atmosphere in the institution, its director, and on the commitment of individuals.

Communication ought to be improved. The language problem is more serious in court prisons than in penitentiary institutions where foreign prisoners usually arrive after having spent some time in the penal system. Particularly with people from former Soviet Republics and Eastern Europe, a common language is often lacking. This leads to mistrust, fear and incomprehension. Some officials scarcely differentiate and refer to Moldavians, Chechens, Georgians, Armenians, Ukrainians simply as 'the Russians', a group that is attributed various bad attitudes and characteristics. Professional translators are not used in daily prison life – too costly and too much effort. Other prisoners or the staffs do most translations. Even at disciplinary procedures professional translators are the exception.[19]

2.2 Living Conditions and Facilities

Pre-trial detainees are held in the prison of the court in charge of the case.[20] Sentenced prisoners are classified by the Ministry of Justice (§ 134 StVG) and assigned a place in a penitentiary somewhere in Austria. There are no special penitentiary institutions for foreign prisoners. The share of foreign prisoners varies according to the type of regime and

---

[19] The CPT also criticised this fact after its visit (*Report to the Austrian Government on the visit to Austria carried out by the European Committee for the Prevention of Torture and Inhuman or Degrading Treatment or Punishment (CPT) from 14 to 23 April 2004*, Strasbourg July 2005, s.103, p.46). The Republic of Austria's response refers to a draft decree of the Ministry of Justice: The head of the prison will have to document the approval of the prisoner if another prisoner is translating at a disciplinary procedure (*Response of the Austrian Government to the report of the European Committee for the Prevention of Torture and Inhuman or Degrading Treatment or Punishment (CPT) on its visit to Austria from 14 to 23 April 2004*, Strasbourg July 2005, s.103, p. 43).

[20] If necessary the Ministry of Justice may impose detention in another court prison (§ 185 StPO).

differs regionally. The prison in *Suben* is a special case with its high share of foreigners (70 % on 1 Dec 2005). Foreigners (particularly Africans) are sent to this remote prison,[21] since it is presumed that they do not have relatives in Austria and therefore no long journeys for visitors would be necessary (as they receive no visits at all).

Legal regulations for accommodating detainees *in* prisons follow criteria that are not based on nationality. They direct for example that those sentenced for intentionally committed offences are to be accommodated separately from those who had committed offences of negligence; first offenders not together with repeat offenders; pre-trial detainees without prior sentences not together with sentenced prisoners; young offenders separated from adults, men from women, and smokers from non-smokers. Sexual offenders are accommodated separately in some prisons; preventive custody is also spatially separated.

In none of the penitentiaries under investigation were there special sections for foreigners. Allocation depends on the type of regime or the prisoner's workplace. When allocating prisoners to cells, attempts are made to put people of the same provenance and/or the same language together.[22] If possible the prisoners' wishes are considered, but massive overcrowding minimizes the opportunities and makes even legally prescribed separations (such as first offender-repeat offender) sometimes impossible. In practice it comes down to cells with for example only Africans or only Georgians, a fact that is judged differently by the interviewees. While some don't see it as a problem and refuse any kind of 'mixing' as generating further conflicts, others warn against the creation of subcultures. The opinion was occasionally expressed that certain groups of foreigners (e.g. Africans) would actually like to be in cells accommodating eight to ten people, and that they would not mind overcrowded conditions. One interviewee notes that solitary cells – a highly appreciated option in a prison – were inhabited more by Austrians than by foreigners.

2.3 Reception and Admission

The Imprisonment Decree prescribes that prison social services should talk to prisoners with communication problems and 'provenance based adaptation problems' when they are admitted. It is also the role of prison social services to help to establish contact with families or consulates and embassies.

On admission prisoners receive information sheets in different languages – statements on the number of languages available vary from nine (EU) languages up to 'in all languages'. The Austrian government's response to the *CPT* report states that house regulations are available in 13 languages and that the Ministry of Justice regularly reminds the institutions' directors of their duty to hand out these regulations. The *CPT* had reported earlier that prisoners they had talked to on their visits had complained about lack of information.[23]

---

[21] *Suben* is a village in Upper Austria. Some years ago the closure of the prison had been discussed.

[22] Only in *Stein*, the largest Austrian penitentiary did an interviewee regret that it was no longer possible to separate ethnic groups because of recent overcrowding. It was said that there were still 'mixed' cells.

[23] *Report to the Austrian Government on the visit to Austria carried out by the European Committee for the Prevention of Torture and Inhuman or Degrading Treatment or Punishment (CPT) from 14 to 23 April 2004*, Strasbourg July 2005, s.108, p.49.

During pre-trial detention information from the court is of crucial importance, and the question arises whether official notifications and application forms are written in a language the prisoner understands. The current situation has been partly criticised in interviews. While information on court procedures exists in many languages, official notifications are said to be usually only in German (at least as far as Vienna is concerned).

Some prisons have further information materials. The prisons *Wien-Josefstadt* and *Stein* contain special medical departments (so called *Sonderkrankenanstalten*) and in both institutions information sheets on medical issues are available in different languages.[24] A director of a court prison reported on his initiative to provide prisoners with information brochures in 20 languages and with application forms (e.g. for conditional release or for the permission to go out) in languages used in prison.

2.4 Work – Education – Training – Sports – Recreation

The wording of the law concerning allocation of work does not differentiate between nationals and foreigners, but names criteria such as the prisoner's state of health, age, knowledge, duration of the sentence and behaviour in prison as well as preferences and advancement after release (§ 47 StVG). Pre-trial detainees are, unlike sentenced prisoners, not obliged to work. Participation in courses is not bound to the Austrian citizenship either, but for programmes that are conducted in cooperation with the Austrian Public Employment Service (AMS) preferably those detainees are chosen who have permission to work in Austria after release. Austrian prisons are overcrowded[25] which makes work and training positions in prison scarce. The CPT judges the situation as 'far from satisfactory' in the visited prisons and apparently throughout the Austrian prison system.[26] Apart from overcrowding, several prisons and their workshops suffer from lack of orders. Another problem evolves because prisoners often do not have the necessary qualifications. The situation varies greatly in the different prisons, the lowest employment rate is found in court prisons.[27]

Employment in prison is very important for prisoners. Sentenced prisoners who are not able to work receive a small amount of money. Many detainees, and especially foreigners, depend on what they earn in prison, because many of them don't receive money from outside. Employment in prison also entitles a prisoner to unemployment benefit after release. Furthermore many privileges in prison are connected to employment.

It can be said from the interviews that the prisoner's skills and qualifications are the most important criteria for the allocation of work, i.e. a sentenced prisoner with useful qualifications usually gets work in a penitentiary. Prisoners who don't speak German have more difficulties in getting work. One prison director states: 'If I have 200 detainees and only 100 places for work, then the Russian or Georgian prisoners will be the last to get the job.' On the other hand, efforts to give work to all prisoners are made in several institutions. Some groups of foreigners enjoy the reputation that they work hard and do it well. There is a small enterprise in Vienna's court prison where only juveniles and 'young adults' from Africa work. In the prison at *Suben* we were told that only newcomers or

---

[24] See also 2.5 medical care.
[25] At a capacity of 8,068 places, an average of 8,885 persons were imprisoned in 2005. In March 2006 more than 9,000 prisoners were reported (*die Presse*, 22 March 2006).
[26] Ibidem, s.70, p.35.
[27] In Vienna's court prison only about 30% of the prisoners can be occupied.

people not willing to work were unemployed; after three to six months everyone who wanted to work found employment – regardless of their nationality.

The statistics of the Austrian penitentiary system show that foreigners are altogether less often employed than nationals. Austrians earn in average more than twice as much as foreigners per day in prison. The main reason for this difference is that foreigners are more frequently in pre-trial detention.[28] Another index for measuring the difference is obtained when one does not compare the average income earned during the whole period in prison but when income is set in relation to a detainee's time in prison after being sentenced: Austrian sentenced prisoners earn only 1.3 as much as foreign sentenced prisoners.

With regard to training and courses two types have to be distinguished: courses especially for foreigners, i.e. German classes, and courses open to everyone who fulfils certain selection criteria. Nationality is again no reason for exclusion and even when a detainee is expelled from Austria following his release, he is formally not excluded from courses. There are different tests and selection mechanisms, whereof the lack of language competence is a substantial disadvantage. All juveniles and 'young adults' can complete a course of study for a school leaving certificate – a chance taken by foreign young prisoners too. Furthermore computer classes, first aid courses, 'fork-lift truck driving' courses and training in the form of apprenticeships are offered. The supply of training and courses varies a lot from prison to prison; there are no nationwide minimum standards. 'German as foreign language' is offered almost everywhere; English classes for prisoners are provided in some places. Some prisoners are able to study German by themselves on a computer. German classes are in the interest of both sides: not only foreigners but also staff benefit when prisoners speak at least a little German. In most institutions demand is greater than supply.[29] This results mainly from financial problems and shortage of space caused by overcrowding. Some interviewees complained that there were no German courses designed for foreigners from former Soviet Republics.

All prisoners are entitled and obliged to 'exercise' outdoors for one hour a day (juveniles two hours). Gym halls and fitness rooms are mainly for the use of those prisoners who are employed. In many institutions – especially in older penitentiaries – there is a shortage of such facilities. The situation in some prisons is equally bad for all detainees. One disadvantage for foreigners that was mentioned is that jogging-groups organised outside a prison with insufficient facilities are not open to foreigners because of the presumed higher risk of escape.[30]

'Instructive, artistic or amusing' events have to be held once quarterly (§ 65 StVG). In this section the Code of Imprisonment explicitly refers to foreign language prisoners: when organising events and activities their special needs should be taken into account (§ 65a StVG). Examples include concerts, cabaret, slideshows, drum groups, and even belly dancing performances. The penitentiaries under investigation have large libraries (e.g. 16,000 books in *Wien-Josefstadt* or 13,000 books in *Stein*) containing a lot of foreign lan-

---

[28] The share of foreigners of all pre-trial detainees was 63% in 2005. 89% of all foreigners, who have only been in pre-trial detention, did not work one day in prison. Within the larger group of sentenced prisoners the share of Austrians is higher (57% in 2005).

[29] Even in the largest penitentiary (*Stein*), the demand is estimated to be higher than supply despite German lessons four times a week.

[30] See also 2.8 re-integration activities – prison leave.

guage literature.[31] Furthermore the foreigners' advisor (*'Ausländerreferent'*) sends international magazines to prisons all over Austria.[32] Reading has become less important with the distribution of television.[33]

2.5 Food – Religion – Personal Hygiene – Medical Care

The Code of Imprisonment (§ 38 StVG) regulates that religious guidelines concerning nutrition have to be respected. In all institutions where interviews were conducted, the daily preparation of several different meals was practised (ritual food, diets, vegetarian meals, etc.). The interviewees also reported that certain group preferences were respected (e.g. to serve white bread or rice for Africans). The impression gained from the interviews is that there are relatively few problems in this aspect of daily prison life.

The Code of Imprisonment also regulates the sphere of religious practice within prison walls. § 85 StVG entitles prisoners to take part in religious services and to address themselves to a spiritual advisor. If there is no such contact person sharing someone's religion in a particular prison, the head of the prison may allow the visit of a spiritual advisor. An official of the Ministry of Justice states that supply was generally adequate: On the one hand, there are still a few employed catholic pastors, on the other hand there is an increasing number of spiritual advisors from Austria's recognised religious communities[34] that work in the prisons on a contract basis with the state. A Muslim spiritual advisor visits the two largest Austrian prisons (*Wien-Josefstadt* and *Stein*) once every two weeks. Interviewees in Vienna reported that this was not enough to satisfy demand. Jewish prisoners from all over Austria are brought to Vienna's court prison twice a year to celebrate their highest holidays. The prison houses a synagogue, a Catholic church, a Protestant chapel and for the last few years a mosque. In Stein, there is also a Catholic church and a mosque. This is not the case in all prisons. In one prison visited, religious services are held in the refectory and not all religious groups are attended to. It is argued that there was no demand or that requests to the religious communities to send someone remained unanswered. A widespread attitude is one of not having anything against religious activities per se but it is seen as the churches' and communities' duty to take the initiative. Language barriers play a role in the religious sphere too: there is a demand for religious services in a language the prisoners understand.

For the interviewees there was no doubt that all prisoners would get the same medical treatment. Language difficulties are met in different ways. The institutions partly employ medical staff with foreign language competence. But also other members of the staff or other prisoners translate – a practice that is not without problems, not only because of the lack of medical confidentiality but also because of the quality of the translation (special medical terms). A professional interpreter is hardly ever used. An information sheet in several languages on medical issues exists in the special medical departments (in *Wien-Josefstadt* and *Stein*).

Statistical data (based on the IVV) contains information on the number of transfers to hospitals, to special medical departments of other prisons, and information on the consul-

---

[31] § 65a StVG prescribes those foreign prisoners have to be considered when equipping libraries.

[32] More about the foreigners' advisor see 2.12 projects.

[33] More about television see 2.7 contact with the outside world.

[34] At the moment, 13 religious communities are officially recognised in Austria, among them the Muslim and the Jewish community.

tation of a medical specialist or a doctor other than the prison doctor. Analysing this data shows that foreigners are less often taken out (76% of all foreigners are never referred externally in comparison with 68% of all Austrians).

Psychological and psychiatric care is barely possible when the professional does not speak the prisoner's language (or at least a language a prisoner understands). It happens now and then that psychiatrists or psychologists speak (even unusual) languages, but this is more the result of coincidence than of systematic recruitment. The practise of drug substitution seems to vary extensively between the different prisons and depends to a considerable extent on the attitude of the attending physician.

2.6 Consular and Legal Help

The Penal Procedure Law prescribes that prisoners on remand must have a defence lawyer in court (cases of mandatory defence, § 41 StPO). If the accused person cannot afford a lawyer, the court assigns a lawyer to the prisoner on remand (as to all persons who do not understand the language of the court). A lawyer assists nationals and foreigners when it comes to hearings concerning pre-trial detention. In all these cases there has to be an interpreter if the prisoner is not able to speak the language of the court. The interpreter is paid by the court (§ 38a para.2 StPO). In Austria's largest court prison in Vienna we were told that the assignment of a lawyer for foreigners by the court did not usually cause any problems. But again and again some lawyers would come to meet prisoners without an interpreter or too late (right before the trial).

Prisoners can get in contact with the representations of their country if necessary with the support of prison social services. Not everyone wants this contact and not all consulates and embassies are interested in the fate of their fellow countrymen. The extent of co-operation between the detention centres and the representations varies: many interviewees pointed to the good relationships with Western European representatives (esp. the Netherlands, Germany and Britain), with the Turkish embassy and partly with the Romanian. They would come regularly, bring movies and magazines and would 'collaborate'. Little to no contact at all existed with the former Yugoslavian states, the former USSR or with African representations.

2.7 Contact with the Outside World

Prisoners on remand and prisoners serving a sentence are subjected to different regulations with regard to contact with the outside world. In pre-trial detention, the decision over whom a prisoner is allowed to stay in contact with depends on the investigating judge. In the following section we consider contact with the outside world through visits, phone calls, and through TV information.

Prisoners on remand have the right to a 15-minute visit at least twice a week (§ 187 StPO) unless it endangers the aim of detention. Prisoners serving sentences do not need authorisation from a judge. They are entitled to receive longer visits and in the case of relatives having to make long journeys to the prison, the length of visits has to be extended (§ 93 StVG). As expected foreigners receive fewer visits than nationals and many of them none at all. In most of the prisons, visiting hours are extended when relatives come from far away. In the largest court prison we were told that even when the visitor had to make a long trip to the prison, visiting hours were seldom accumulated (to half an hour a week). In the largest penitentiary visiting hours are dealt with generously (prisoners can get up to a whole day of visit). In *Suben*, a prison away from the urban areas, the proportion of foreigners who never receive visits was estimated at 50%. Apart from friends and relatives there are visiting services, partly from organisations specialised in the care for foreigners.

Prisoners on remand who want to make a telephone call have to apply for a permit to the investigating judge (something that according to an interviewee not all foreigners know). Approval is a lengthy process. Difficulties arise because there is not enough telephone boxes in many prisons (especially in the old ones). Mobile phones are forbidden. Calls are only allowed during business hours. Besides that many foreign prisoners (esp. on remand) do not have enough money to make phone calls.

Depending on the prison the number of TV channels differ. Sometimes it varies among the different parts of a single prison. In all detention centres where no foreign language programmes are available at the moment, it is intended to rectify this deficiency.

2.8 Re-integration Activities - Prison Leave

If educational and vocational training measures and incorporation into the working process is seen as re-integration activity, then foreigners and nationals are basically equal, at least in theory. The situation is different when activities are related to leaving prison for a certain time. The wording of the relevant laws does not mention nationality but it is a fact that foreign prisoners are rarely allowed to leave prison (on '*Ausgang*' or '*Freigang*' i.e. to regulate important affairs, to work outside the prison, etc.) especially when they will be expelled from Austria after custody.[35] Foreigners integrated in Austria have better chances of leaving prison for a certain time than foreigners without residence permits or asylum-seekers. During imprisonment the authorities often do not know whether a prisoner will be expelled from Austria afterwards. The interviews revealed that prison directors[36] dealt with this problem differently: while some refused categorically every prison leave in case of uncertainties about expulsion after custody, other prison directors let foreigners leave prison even when the immigration authority has not taken its decision yet. Another precondition for leaving prison for a certain period of time is that prisoners can name specific reasons why they need to go out (e.g. arranging important affairs) as well as a contact address (if they want to stay overnight). If the aim of prison leave is not re-integration and if the prisoner has no social contacts in the country, it will hardly ever be granted.

Statistical information is available about how often a prisoner leaves the prison and for what purpose. A distinction is made between 'Ausgang' (prison leave to regulate important personal, economic or legal affairs, for educational training, etc.; single days, not more than five days) and 'Freigang' (the prisoner works regularly outside prison). 89% of

---

[35] A decision of the Austrian Supreme Administrative Court stated that only concrete indications that the inmate might misuse prison leave to escape justify the refusal of an application for permission to leave prison (Supreme Administrative Court 19 February 2004, decision 2003/20/0502). A blanket refusal of all applications from foreigners is not permitted.

[36] The prison director allows prison leave.

all foreigners who have been serving sentence[37] did not get a single day of 'Ausgang' – in comparison to only 36% of nationals in this category. The situation is especially bad for some groups of foreigners: Hardly anybody from the former Soviet Republics left an Austrian prison on 'Ausgang' (1% of all sentenced Georgians, Russians, Moldavians; Ukrainians). Austrians are allowed to leave prison on an average of 3.4 per 100 days while prison leave for foreigners only amounts to 5 per 1,000 days.

Table 5a: Prison Leave ('*Ausgang*')

		no prison leave	prison leave	total
Austrians	number	1,654	2,983	4,637
	%	35.7	64.3	100
EU citizens	number	951	60	1,011
	%	94.1	6.0	100
non EU citizens	number	2,988	445	3,433
	%	87.0	13.0	100
all foreigners	number	3,939	505	4,444
	%	88.6	11.4	100
total	number	5,593	3,488	9,081
	%	61.6	38.4	100

Table 5b: Average Number of Prison Leaves ('*Ausgang*')

	number of persons	mean per 100 days in prison*
Austrians	4,637	3.4
EU citizens	1,011	0.3
Non EU- citizens	3,433	0.5
foreigners	4,444	0.5
total	9,081	2.0

* Per day in prison after being sentenced
Source: IVV-Data, provided by the Austrian Federal Computing Centre, April 2006, own calculations

'Freigang' means that a prisoner works outside prison in a factory, a company, etc. without surveillance. 96% of all foreign prisoners (who were not only on remand but have been sentenced) did not work one single day outside prison while 31% of all nationals did leave the penitentiary for work. On average Austrians work outside prison 10 per 100 days but foreigners only 1 per 100 days. There are special departments or even houses

---

[37] Prisoners who were only on remand were not considered in the calculation because prison leave during pre-trial detention is something very atypical.

(the so called '*Freigängerhaus*') for those who work outside the prison – in these semi-open places few foreigners can be found.

Table 6a: Prison Leave to Work outside Prison ('*Freigang*')

		no prison leave	*prison leave*	*total*
Austrians	number	3,199	1,438	4,637
	%	69.0	31.0	100
EU citizens	number	991	20	1,011
	%	98.0	2.0	100
non EU citizens	number	3,276	157	3,433
	%	95.4	4.6	100
all foreigners	number	4,267	177	4,444
	%	96.0	4.0	100
total	number	7,466	1,615	9,081
	%	82.2	17.8	100

Table 6b: Average Number of Prison Leaves to Work outside Prison (*Freigang*')

	number of persons	*mean per 100 days in prison**
Austrians	4,637	9.7
EU citizens	1,011	0.5
Non EU- citizens	3,433	1.1
foreigners	4,444	1.0
total	9,081	5.4

* Per day in prison after being sentenced
Source: IVV-Data, provided by the Austrian Federal Computing Centre, April 2006, own calculations

All prisoners have the right to parole. Comparing the frequencies of conditional release between nationals and foreigners show that – on a nationwide level and for all duration of sentences – prisoners without Austrian citizenship are released on parole slightly less often than nationals (Pilgram 2005). But there are regional differences and differences depending on the length of a sentence. Nationals with short-term sentences (three to six month) are conditionally released twice as often as foreigners. One reason for this is that Austrians do serve short sentences whereas foreigners often do their time on remand. When medium-length sentences (six to twelve months) are considered there are no noteworthy differences concerning conditional release between nationals and foreigners. Foreigners are more often released conditionally from long sentences (one to three years) than nationals.[38]

2.9 Release - Expulsion

On the occasion of release social workers speak to nationals as well as to foreigners. Prisoners get information sheets with contact addresses. The mission of social workers changes when advising foreigners who are not allowed to live and work legally in Austria. They then have to give legal advice in the field of immigration law, and clarification of what happens after release. Help upon release in the sense of helping to find a flat or a job is not possible in these cases. Social workers get the necessary knowledge in training sessions (at the '*Strafvollzugsakademie*', the Austrian prison staff academy, or at *Neustart*).

Courts and prisons have to inform the immigration police on convictions of foreigners and at the start/end of a sentence. At the latest when the prisoner is released, there ought to be a decision by the immigration police on whether the prisoner will be detained in custody for the purpose of removal or not. Several interviewees pointed to the fact that this decision is not always taken until the end of custody and that there was a lot of insecurity during detention about what might happen after release. The decision to expel or remove a foreigner after imprisonment depends on his or her legal status, the time he or she had spent in Austria before conviction, and on the length of the sentence. The immigration authorities make this decision. In any case the removal to the country of origin must be possible. Even if removal is not possible, a ban on residence can be declared. A foreigner will be expelled (and removed) if he or she is seen as a 'danger to public interest' that is usually assumed after a prison sentence of more than three months or a (semi-) conditional sentence of six months. But also incorrect information given to the Austrian authorities, lack of means of sustenance, illicit work and other (administrative) offences can lead to a ban on residence (§ 60 FPG 2005). For foreigners who have spent much of their lives in Austria the expulsion criteria are less restrictive depending on the extent of integration and on the intensity of family relations. For asylum seekers special regulations are valid (AsylG 2005).

In practice, it very often happens that removal (especially to countries outside Europe) is not possible - people are not removed but at the same time they don't have the right to stay and work legally in Austria. One reason for the rejection of a removal is the existence of a concrete danger in the country of origin, or that the country refuses to 'take back' the person. After release from prison, ex-offenders are often detained in custody for the purpose of removal for a certain time[39] and released after that time because they cannot be removed to their country of origin. The expulsion-decision can be challenged. Legal remedies against expulsion decisions basically have a suspending effect.

---

[38] One reason for this inverted ratio might be that Austrians with long sentences usually have more prior convictions.

[39] The upper time limit has been extended to a maximum of 10-month custody for the purpose of removal as of 1 Jan 2006.

2.10 Aftercare - Probation

In Austria help upon release as well as probation services are provided nationwide by the association *Neustart*. When the proportion of foreigners increased in Austrian prisons the proportion of foreigners also increased in aftercare facilities. This caused difficulties: Apart from increasing numbers of clients the classic social work concepts designed for ex-offenders were no longer appropriate. *Neustart*'s reaction was a minimum programme for foreigners without legal status, which meant no intensive, long-term support and no legal remedies in cases with no chances of obtaining legal status (permission of residence, asylum, etc.). Since a system of basic support for asylum seekers (the so called '*Bundesbetreuung*') was established by the Austrian government, tensions eased and demand was distributed all over Austria. But still the staffs working in aftercare facilities face the difficult situation that they should 'integrate' people into Austrian society who are actually excluded from it, because every legal status is denied to them.

Probation after custody for foreigners is rare. It is difficult in general for social workers to find jobs or flats for foreign ex-offenders (again language barriers, prejudices against ex-offenders and against foreigners, etc). If a foreigner with insecure legal status is put on probation, it is an even more difficult task: How can a social worker find a job for someone who is not allowed to work? How to find a residence for someone without permit to stay?

2.11 Staff

When staff is recruited foreign language competence is not a required criteria. There are very few prison officers with a background in migration. Language competence or migration experience can be an advantage when applying for a job in prison but it remains within the prison director's discretion and is not actively encouraged as criteria. Since 2004, prisons officers-in-training are informed about 'foreign cultures' (16 hours during basic training) and they are taught English (32 hours, technical terminology). As voluntary further training, prison staff can attend courses on migration, globalisation, foreigners in Austrian prisons, a special course on the 'Slav cultural area' and English classes. Many employees attend these seminars.

Over the last few years the increasing presence of foreigners has changed daily prison life. In some prisons more than half the detainees are foreigners from over 100 countries. This meant new challenges for the staff. Information from the interviews points to the presumption that after a period of change and conversion, adaptation to the new situation was achieved. It is admitted that some staff members were prejudiced against foreigners (similar prejudices existed in the rest of the population). But apart from these elements, the treatment of foreigners and relations with them are described as relatively unproblematic. Problems were admitted only in the treatment of people from the former Soviet Republics

2.12 Projects

In 1989 a special department for foreigners (the so called '*Ausländerreferat*') was founded.[40] The project started with a headquarters in Vienna's court prison *Wien-Josefstadt* and there were contact persons in the other Federal States. Today there is only one contact person outside Vienna left and the responsible social worker in Vienna has to divide his time between his work in the court prison (in a section of the prison) and his responsibility for all foreigners in penitentiary institutions in Austria. His aim is to inform people in the justice system on issues concerning foreigners. The last remaining contact person (in *Stein*) sees his duty in managing contacts between the prison and the consulates and embassies of foreign countries.

Special projects for foreigners exist in different prisons to a varying extent. Usually these projects are based on the initiatives of individuals. For example an 'integration group' was mentioned where Austrian and foreign women met once a week to exchange experiences or an information evening about the situation of refugees from the Caucasian region. Repeatedly it was reported that the so called 'group counselling' was successfully held with groups of foreigners. Language courses and cultural events have already been mentioned above.[41] After the CPT had criticised the treatment of foreign prisoners by some staff members and the situation of foreigners in the court prison in Linz in general, the new prison director founded an expert group with representatives from a human rights association (*SOS-Menschenrechte*) and from *Neustart*. They developed a '10-point-programme' listing for example language training for prison officers, TV in foreign languages, and information sheets in a sufficient number of languages. This programme can be seen as an example of how attempts were made to improve the situation of foreigners in the wake of a critical report from an independent committee.

3 ADMINISTRATIVE DETENTION OF FOREIGN PRISONERS

Statistical and administrative reporting on police detention is extremely deficient in Austria.[42] This paper is based on very limited information given by the Ministry of the Interior (Dept. II/3); this information in turn is based on unpublished annual reports from the Security Directorates of the provinces and on two special surveys on two key-days. However, the most profitable data source for this chapter on police detention stems from the *Human Rights Advisory Council* (*Menschenrechtsbeirat*, *MRB*) because of its proactive and systematic control activities (differing from the singular instance and reactive control by the state ombudsman/*Volksanwalt*). Since its foundation the *MRB* delivered 13-targeted

---

[40] The department was founded by a decree by the Ministry of Justice in 1989. The Imprisonment Decree (1995) describes its function as supporting and advising foreign prisoners with regard to their special needs concerning language problems and cultural differences. They are to be supplied with reading and audiovisual material; special events should be organised for them.

[41] See 2.4 Work, Education, Training, Sports, Recreation

[42] The annual Governmental Report on Internal Security surprisingly lacks a chapter on police detention centres and a particular one on detention pending expulsion. Correspondingly there is lacking scientific and media attention paid to the issue.

reports, five of which directly focus on matters of police detention.[43] These reports regularly integrate observations made by *CPT*. Moreover, since 1999 annual activity reports of the *MRB* are published. The reports always contain clear recommendations to the minister of the interior. The implementation of the recommendations is periodically evaluated by workgroups of the council.[44] The following *MRB*-reports are directly touching matters of detention. The reports on:

-   The problem of minors in custody pending detention (2000)
-   Human rights questions in connection with detention of women through police agents (2001)
-   The problem of information of detainees (2002)
-   Medical care for detainees (2002)
-   Conditions of detention and police facilities (2005).

3.1 General

In principle all different categories of detainees in police detention centres are to be treated equally according to the Police Detention Order (AnhO), whereby for detainees pending expulsion a better standard ought to be realized. Even though their separated accommodation from other detainees (in administrative penal custody or in police detention for criminal reasons) has already been demanded by former Decrees on Police Detention (§ 4 AnhO), the revised law of 1 Jan 2006 explicitly introduces for the first time 'custody in open sections' of detainees for the purpose of removal provided there are no objections related to safety such as infectious diseases, aggressiveness, escape attempts, etc. This regulation at least partly takes into account recommendation No. 274 of the *MRB* from Oct 2004. While the administration of detention in open sectors is still legally bound to sufficient spatial facilities and personnel capacities of detention centres the administration of 'custody with temporary open cells' (§ 5a para.4 AnhO) is not yet a binding rule and is not yet realized in each centre.[45] Apart from that only the supervision of phone calls and visits is more generously regulated for detainees pending expulsion than for other inmates. This is also problematic insofar as it actually prevents the common accommodation of spouses and relatives (in particular of children of opposite sex) during detention pending expulsion. This unnecessarily violates the right to have a protected private and family life (that means: recommendation No. 130 of the *MRB* from March 2002 is not yet implemented for lack of spatial and other provisions). While administrative penal custody of juveniles under age 16 is ruled out (§ 7 para.5 AnhO), detention pending expulsion is admissible even with minors of lower age if accommodation and care according to age can be warranted (§ 4 para.4 AnhO). Although the *MRB* from July

---

43 Further general reports of the *MRB* refer to the linguistic usage of police officers, to the use of force by police, or to police training and further education. More significant for this paper are some priority reports of the *MRB* concerning single detention facilities or the report on 'problem-removals' which not at least may result from inadequate preparation and administration of detention pending expulsion. See: http://www.menschenrechtsbeirat.at

44 In particular the last interim report of the *MRB* evaluation-working group (dating from quarter 4/2004) on the recommendations for detention pending expulsion is a very informative one. See: http://www.menschenrechtsbeirat.at/de/index_evaluierung.html

45 This fact was heavily criticised by several NGOs (e.g. refugee service of *Diakonie* and *Caritas*) when they rendered an expert opinion on the draft of the current Police Detention Order.

2000 on (see recommendations no. 33-37) repeatedly denies the existence of appropriate police detention facilities for minors, the numerous invocations of the advisory council to abolish detention pending expulsion with minors under age 14, to restrict it to elder minors, to stipulate the administration of lenient measures, to reduce the maximum time to 2 months and to advance juvenile welfare measures remained without response. The detention of minors and juveniles in detention pending expulsion has been markedly reduced throughout the last years as the co-operation between police and juvenile welfare agencies improved.

A particular problem is identified by the *MRB* when it comes to the joint accommodation of detainees pending expulsion and of criminal prisoners taking place in institutions under justice administration. Though at present no use is made of the rule that detainees in detention pending expulsion may be kept in court prisons or penitentiaries if police detention centres are overcrowded (§ 78 para.1 FPG), detention for the purpose of removal following prison sentences is still practised in general prisons. Detainees are subjected to general prison rules (to the Code of Imprisonment) without relief and have no access to specialized social services like in police detention centres. Because of lacking coordination between immigration authorities and justice administration, measures to end residence and stay in the country sometimes cannot be put into effect immediately after the prison sentence.

3.2 Living Conditions and Facilities

The Decree of Police Detention (§ 4 para.1a) requires detention facilities 'worthy of human beings'. Nevertheless the *MRB* in his report on 'Conditions of detention a police facilities' points to the problem of detention in 'historically grown prisons' for the sake of nothing else than to ensure the administrative procedure before immigration authorities (*MRB*, 2005, 8). Though the facilities are not essentially below national and international standards and though there is only sporadic critique by the *MRB* concerning the location, size, occupancy, ventilation, lightening or the sanitary installations (and usually remedying construction measures have been prompted by the critiques) the advisory council recommends better standards in particular for detainees in detention pending expulsion. As non-offenders they would deserve more privacy (e.g. lockable boxes, access to lavatories, washing machines and dryers) as well as more freedom of movement. Detainees pending expulsion appear unreasonably burdened by the living conditions in prisons under police administration. Yet it cannot be decided on the basis of available data, whether foreigners in police detentions centres are discriminated in other ways as well.

3.3 Reception and Admission

In his report 'The problem of information of detainees' (2002) the *MRB* recommends the translation (in additional languages) and availability of more comprehensive and complete information sheets (and as alternative of sound carriers) for detainees in general and those in detention pending expulsion in particular (recommendation no. 131-162). Similar improvements are demanded regarding information policies on the Decree of Police Detention, the house rules, and the social service for detainees pending expulsion (*Schubhaftbetreuung*). Since detainees pending removal are under severe stress the *MRB* has suggested improving the flow of information on matters concerning expulsion. Deportees should be informed in due time and social services should be more easily available to them to prevent situations of crisis and problematic removals. Only a few of these recommendations have been implemented so far.

3.4 Work – Education – Training – Sports – Recreation

Inactivity is a greater problem in pre-trial detention and penal custody in prisons under justice administration compared to relatively short-term detentions in police prisons. Yet also short periods of detention do not justify the denial of meaningful activities. *CPT* complains about inadequate access to recreation areas, books, and games and also to useful domestic work or paid work in Austrian police detention centres. The committee misses an activity regime that is structuring the daytime. Open cells and access to TV alone are not accepted as substitute (*MRB* 2005, 44ff).

3.5 Food – Religion – Personal Hygiene – Medical Care

In 2005 *CPT* recommends to assure free direct access to drinking water for everybody in police custody. The *MRB* urges uniform regulations regarding mealtimes and a general directive for the quality of nutrition, further on the provision of complete cutlery and a more generous absorption of costs for board by the institution. Detainees should have the opportunity to prepare their own meals. The *MRB* also repeatedly concerns about the lack of sufficient clothing for detainees and of clothing that reduces suicide risks. Effective local remedy measures must not belie the defects in central management. This is also true in case of suicide prevention and medical care in PAZ (recommendations 163-222 from May 2002; *MRB*-AG Evaluierung, III. Quartal 2004). On different occasions the lack of sensibility and of special training of the personnel (including police officers and physicians) is pointed out, in particular the lack of regular supervision of and communication (enabled by proper interpreters) with persons at risk and the avoidance of solitary confinement.

With respect to medical care the lacking differentiation between administrative, official expert and medical duties of police doctors is criticised. The same holds true for paramedics. For police detainees the contact with independent medical examiners is complicated. Discrete medical examination and treatment out of sound and visual range of fellow detainees and comprehensible mother tongue clarification as well as medical after care of the released are still not generally granted. Verified by *MRB*, progress has been made in informing about the dangers related to hygiene by the personnel handling hunger striking detainees (communication through social care workers instead of restrictions and punishment) (*MRB*-AG Evaluierung, III. Quartal 2003).

3.6 Consular and Legal Help

Although the right to free access to lawyers also applies to police detainees the practice evidently does not fully comply with the norm. The confidential consultation with a lawyer, the presence of a lawyer in interrogations, the legal assistance free of charge for the destitute, the calling in of a trusted person or lawyer in juvenile cases are not granted without any exception (*MRB* 2005, 70ff). According to *MRB* the social care for detainees pending expulsion is no full surrogate for free of charge legal advice throughout the administrative procedure before the immigration authority (*MRB* 2005, 75f).[46] *CPT* on the occasion of its 2004 visit also argued that the information given to foreign prisoners about the procedure could be substantially improved and that the obligation of external agents (diplomatic missions) to give support does not exempt the state from information duties.

3.7 Contact with the Outside World

According to the Police Detention Order written correspondence is not subject to restrictions (even if some controls are admissible, except with advocates, national administrative and representative bodies of the home country and international organisations for the protection of human rights) and must be made available also for destitute persons. Rights regarding phone calls are at the discretion of the authorities. These rights have to be granted, unless the effort would be disproportionate. The *MRB* (2005, 82ff) argues for the permanent (and not only during a call) availability of mobile phones to detainees pending expulsion, respectively for enabling passive reception of phone calls, particularly because destitute prisoners only may have the first call to relatives free of charge. At least one half hour visiting time per week has to be permitted according to law, detainees pending expulsion should be allowed more visits without supervision as a rule to maintain family and other social relations, however organisational resources and constraints should be considered. (A special recommendation of *MRB* refers to visiting rights of prisoners in hunger strike. These rights should not be restricted even in sickrooms.)

3.8 Re-integration Activities - Prison Leave

Preparation for release is confined to an absolute minimum in police detention centres. According to the new § 25 AnhO released prisoners are at least entitled to an attestation of detention time and documents on medical evidence and treatment. At present the law only provides for some minimum social care through employees of private organisations for detainees pending expulsion. The Ministry of the Interior has been accused of contracting preferably with such organisations that pose advice for returning before counselling in right of asylum and support during asylum procedure. Help for returnees include advice in bureaucratic matters and financial support.

3.9 Release - Expulsion

There are no precise data available and no research has been conducted on measures taken by the immigration police after release from police detention centres or prisons. In 2003 and 2004 11,173 resp. 9,041 imposed custodies compare to 8,073 resp. 5,811 removals carried out (Sicherheitsbericht der Bundesregierung, 2005, p. 331). Since there are no statistics on the reasons for release from detention pending expulsion this difference can hardly be interpreted. We do not know whether the release was because of bad physical condition, so the person could no longer be kept in prison, or whether a transgression of maximum time of detention has occurred, or whether successful legal claims, or postponement of expulsion (§ 46 para.3 FPG), or impracticality or inadmissibility of

---

[46] This is also stated by the UN High Commissioner for Refugees in his written comment on the Police Detention Order (AnhO) 2005.

removal (§ 50 FPG) provide the reason for release. Therefore information about the legal status after release, whether it is a regular, precarious or irregular one, remains unclear too.

3.10 Aftercare - Probation

see 3.8

3.11 Staff

Questions regarding qualification of staff in PAZ have been raised in different contexts. For a long time the *MRB* has been concerned about detention of women (*MRB* 2001). One impact of this concern is the ruling of the now amended Police Detention Order (§ 3 AnhO) that supervision in principle ought to be done by staff of the same sex. In view of insufficient space and staffing in smaller police detention centres the *MRB* recommends to avoid accommodation of females there and to employ more women in the police administration (recommendations no. 93-116, July 2001). Facing the disproportionate high share of women among detainees pending expulsion (18%) foreigners are particularly affected by these deficiencies. According to the latest evaluation (*MRB* Evaluierung I/2004) only 9 out of 16 PAZ have sufficient rooms and personnel to properly accommodate females in separate sections. In particular at small facilities (e.g. border control posts) shortcomings still have to be conceded. The *MRB* several times also recommended training measures, especially for officers enforcing removal and wardens in PAZ, who deal with minors. The improvement of language capabilities and of capacities for intercultural communication through further education courses, the improvement of communication between police officers, social care workers and medical personnel and improved training of the paramedics to recognize mental abnormities and illness were up to now widely neglected recommendations of the *MRB* (Evaluierung I/2004).

3.12 Projects

In nearly every domain concerning spatial arrangements, social and medical care in general and for women in particular, legal aid, and co-operation between professionals and authorities, the committees of the *Human Rights Advisory Council* discovered local models of 'good practise', yet they also see too little exchange, centrally binding standards and quality management.

4 NATIONALS DETAINED ABROAD

By 30 Jan 2006, 151 Austrians had been detained abroad on long-term prison sentences. Furthermore 119 Austrians were imprisoned in short-term detention in 2005.[47] The statistics only contain cases that are reported to the Austrian Federal Ministry for Foreign Affairs. If a national detained abroad does not want contact to be established, the Minis-

---

[47] The Austrian Foreign Ministry (section IV.1) differentiates in its statistics between long-term and short-term detention in relation to custody of under 12 months or more than 12 months.

try is unaware of the detention. Most Austrian detainees are imprisoned within the European Union.

Table 8: Nationals Detained Abroad[48]

	actual number of long-term detainees *	short-term detentions 2005
EU- Europe	92	76
Central and South America	22	4
Asia	15	17
Non EU-Europe	11	7
North America	9	11
Australia and Oceania	2	2
Africa	0	2
total	151	119

Source: Austrian Federal Ministry for Foreign Affairs
* by 30 Jan 2006

The main reasons for imprisonment are offences related to drugs (smuggling, trafficking and possession). Offences related to drugs account for about 50% of all long-term detentions.

Different ministries support nationals detained abroad: The Ministry of the Interior establishes contact with the prisoners' family; the Ministry of Justice organises transfers to Austria. The Ministry for Foreign Affairs supports the offender in cooperation with the consulates and embassies on-site, coordinates help, stays in contact with the relatives, manages the so called *Depot-Verkehr (*e.g. money transfers from relatives to nationals detained in foreign countries) and the *Red Cross Campaign* (sending presents or money to detainees abroad at Christmas). 60 percent of (officially reported) Austrian detainees are supported by consulates and embassies on-site. Outside the European Union the share of supported prisoners is higher (80 percent). If someone is not cared for, it is usually because he or she does not want any support from the Austrian representations (which often happens when someone is detained in another European country). If support is not possible because there is no Austrian representation in a particular country, the Austrian Foreign Ministry asks embassies or consulates from other (European) countries, or (Christian) NGOs to take care of the prisoner.

The organisation *Neustart* is the nation-wide provider for probation and help on release. They do not support nationals detained abroad unless a detainees themselves get in contact with them (e.g. to inform himself about aftercare facilities or because he or she wants to serve the rest of a sentence in Austria). Back in Austria all aftercare facilities are open to them. There are no bi- or multilateral agreements concerning probation services.

---

[48] The number of long-term detentions is available as *stock (prevalence)* data (number of detainees on January 30th 2006) while the number of short-term detentions refers to incoming *flow (incidents)* of short-term detainees in the year 2005. The two statistics therefore must not be merged. For both groups of detainees no statistical information on age, gender or social background is available.

5 EVALUATION AND RECOMMENDATIONS

There is no manifest legal discrimination against non-Austrians with respect to entitlements and living conditions in police or justice prisons. The law on the contrary demands to take into account the particular situation and needs of imprisoned foreigners. As a matter of fact religiously founded claims thereby seem to get more easily accepted while rights to legal information in particular and information in general are less readily respected. Yet general social marginality and the attribution of risks to foreigners become effective in the prison context too and lead to social exclusion. The lack of language competence, non-existing social networks and prospects for social integration also affect social opportunities in prison. Whether it comes to alternatives to detention (in particular to pre-trial detention with its less favourable conditions) or to participation in prison labour, related income and consumption opportunities, leisure time activities, relaxation of prison conditions and preparation for release, the accumulating deficiencies of non-Austrian prisoners operate against them. There are no mandatory standards regarding the institutional duties to compensate for disadvantages of foreigners. It is largely up to the single institution how much it effectively cares about foreigners. There are occasional informal attempts to improve living conditions of foreigners in prison, but no state wide official policy is implemented in this regard.

The growing number of foreigners in severely overcrowded prisons has some contrasting consequences. On the one hand it shows a clearly preserving function. The closing down of old, remote and ill-equipped institutions and departments is interrupted, it becomes more difficult to stop and overcome an un-communicative locking away of prisoners and to simply leave them to the rule of prison subcultures. On the other hand the rising number of foreigners causes a new routine and normality in relations among foreign and native inmates and between foreign inmates and staff, everyday racism is mitigated. Certain challenges through the new prison population also lead to innovations (for instance in the field of medical and social care for prisoners, language education, cable television etc.) and certain groups are even appraised as a 'gain' for the prison system. However, at the same time new unwanted 'problem groups' are identified, with whom communication and co-operation is said to fail – not only because of language barriers. Top ranking among these problem groups are the prisoners from former Soviet Republics. Arguments for a harsher prison regime are explained with this new groups of prisoners.

Bearing the Austrian situation in mind strict separation of administrative detention for the purpose of removal of irregular migrants from other kinds of detention of suspected or sentenced criminals has to be postulated. Detention pending expulsion should be the ultimate resort to enforce the ban on residence and removal, it should be reserved for special risk groups (previously convicted, with disposition to escape or to behave violently) and should exclude minors and traumatised persons. If special institutions for detention pending expulsion are established, their regime should not resemble that of traditional prisons. Open sections and common residence for family members, free access to means of communication with the outside world should be the rule. With every kind of detention of foreigners due information about legal procedures and their respective status has to be granted. The fact of imprisonment should speed up decision making on the residence status of the detainee to reduce uncertainty and psychic stress, to minimize denial of freedom and to prevent critical situations (e.g. in case of unprepared removal). Advice for removal must not curtail legal information and legal aid in asylum and other procedures before the immigration authorities. The transfer of offenders for the execution of sentences to their home country (against the will of the person, according to the Additional Protocol from 1997 to the European Convention on the Transfer of Sentenced Persons from 1983) must not ignore the real social integration in Austria.

The handicaps of many non-Austrian prisoners concerning language and other cultural skills should not be underrated. These handicaps prevent recourse to social, psychological and medical care and to legal grants and they cause social dependencies and disproportional private costs. Multi-lingual information, enhanced language skills of police and justice prison staff (as employment criterion), contracting with private organisations with multilingual personnel for visiting, educational and medical services should be the order of the day.

Considering the low articulation and the conflict potential of foreign prisoners the opening of prisons for independent pro-active control agencies furnished with substantial legal power of audit and resources turns out to be very important. By comparing the activities of the *Human Rights Advisory Council* (competent for police detention centres) and of the Prison Monitoring Committees (for prisons under justice administration) the significance of public presentation of findings and the transparency of administrative reactions to criticisms and recommendations can be demonstrated. Control boards reporting in closed sessions exclusively to the state administration are not a proper solution of the problem. Though the *Human Rights Advisory Council* at the Ministry of the Interior regularly issues focal reports there is a total lack of statistical and political routine reporting by the state administration on the execution of police detention and only fragmentary reporting on justice prisons. The annual Government Report on Internal Security offers a lengthy crime report but pays little attention to institutional detention and penal practise. The current study, anyhow, contributed to cause a redesign of statistical reporting on prisons under Ministry of Justice administration. For the future the data will enable to identify groups of prisoners that are discriminated with respect to access to work, education and training, and to social and medical care. However, the residence status of detained and released prisoners and the administrative measures taken by the immigration police against them still remain undocumented and unreported by the Austrian police and justice administration.

Chapter 3

Belgium

Sonja Snacken

1 INTRODUCTION

Belgium has a positive immigration balance, which means that more foreigners immigrate to Belgium than Belgians emigrate to other countries (+ 12.137 in 2000). The largest groups of immigrants are, in decreasing order, French, German, Moroccan and Turkish nationals. Around 900.000 foreigners live in Belgium legally, i.e. 8.8% of the population. 60% of these are citizens from other EU Member States, in decreasing order from Italy, France, the Netherlands and Germany. The other large groups of foreigners are from Morocco and Turkey. Asylum seekers since 1995 are mainly coming from former Yugoslavia, Russia, Albania and Iran[1]. The largest ethnic minority group in Belgium, the Moroccans, often live in poor neighbourhoods in vulnerable socio-economic circumstances, characterised by high unemployment, and suffer different forms of social exclusion. With the political changes in Central and Eastern European countries in the 1990's and the recent EU enlargement, the presence of immigrants from these countries has also become very visible. Since the topic of "immigration and criminality" gave electoral success in 1991 to an extremist right wing party, these themes have become hot political issues.

In 2004 foreign prisoners represented 44% of the prison population in Belgium. The large proportion of foreign prisoners and the ensuing problems during their detention and upon their release was the subject of a research we carried out for the King Boudewijn Foundation (Koning Boudewijn Stichting) between 1 November 2003 and 31 January 2004, to which we will often refer here[2].

1.1 Overview of penalties and measures

The police under supervision of the public prosecution perform investigation. Only an investigating judge can impose restrictions on fundamental freedoms, such as remand custody. Although provided for in legislation, monetary bail is seldom applied, as it is considered a form of class-justice that discriminates against the poor. In 1990, a new alternative to remand custody was introduced: freedom or release on conditions. Freedom on conditions refers to the decision taken by an investigating judge, within 24 hours of the arrest of a suspect, not to remand the suspect in custody under certain conditions. Release on conditions refers to a similar decision taken, either by the investigating judge or the investigating court, after the suspect has been remanded in custody. Remand custody can only be imposed in case of absolute necessity for the public security and for offences that can be punished with at least 1-year imprisonment. If the punishment for the alleged offence does not exceed 15 years imprisonment, remand custody can only be imposed in case of a risk of recidivism, absconding, collusion or meddling with evidence. Freedom or release under conditions can only be imposed in cases where remand custody is possible.

---

[1] Overlegcentrum Integratie Vluchtelingen, Migrants in Europe – Survey Belgium, European Reintegration Networking, www.reintegration.net/belgium/index.htm

[2] This research was carried out with two researchers, Jan Keulen and Leentje Winkelmans. This lead to the publication of a report in Dutch and French: S. Snacken, J.Keulen & L. Winkelmans, *Buitenlanders in de Belgische gevangenissen: knelpunten en mogelijke oplossingen (Détenus étrangers dans les prisons belges: problèmes et solutions possibles)* Brussel 2004 (Bruxelles 2004), Koning Boudewijn Stichting (Fondation Roi Baudoin).

At the level of sentencing, the Belgian judge has a variety of penal options: a conditional or unconditional fine (to be accompanied by a substitute imprisonment in case of non-payment), a suspended sentence with or without probation (a declaration of guilt without a formal conviction, which is suspended for a period of one to five years; this decision is not mentioned on the criminal record), conditional imprisonment with or without probation (here a sentence of imprisonment up to five years is imposed, but its implementation is suspended for a period of one to five years; this decision is registered on the criminal record), community service (an autonomous penalty since 2002), imprisonment (from one day to life imprisonment), internment of mentally ill offenders and preventive detention of repeat offenders and sexual offenders. The application of suspended sentences, conditional imprisonment and probation are limited by law to offences punishable by up to five years imprisonment and to offenders whose criminal record does not exceed prison sentences of more than two months for a suspended sentence (brought to six months in 1999) and 12 months for a conditional imprisonment. In case of failure to abide by the conditions of probation or in case of recidivism, the suspended sentence and conditional imprisonment may lead to imprisonment.

1.2 Overview of the prison system

1.2.1. Organisational structure

In the federal state of Belgium, the Prison Administration is a department of the Ministry of Justice, which is a federal ministry. The Prison Administration consists of a central administration, 33 prisons and one institution for "social defence" (i.e., for mentally ill offenders). There are two separate institutions for psychiatric patients and mentally ill offenders, which fall under the joint administration of the federal Ministry of Justice and the regional Ministry of Public Health.

Prisons in Belgium are divided into remand prisons (in each major city), open, half-open and closed prisons for the execution of sentences. Remand prisons have a closed, cellular regime, and are used for pre-trial detention. All major remand prisons have a psychiatric unit for mentally ill offenders and a unit for female prisoners. Most remand prisons are also used for execution of sentences, either by design (subdivisions inside the prison) or due to prison overcrowding (resulting in sentenced prisoners waiting for their transfer).

The division between open, half-open and closed prisons is based on the level of security inside the prison. Open prisons have a dormitory system and prisoners are expected to voluntarily accept prison discipline, while half-open prisons have an open regime during the day and a closed regime at night. Open and half-open prisons are located in more remote areas, where prisoners are deemed unlikely to escape, can work on the surrounding land, or receive educational or vocational training[3]. Since the 1990s, part of the open capacity has been transformed into closed capacity (now totalling 80%), due to a changing prison population and the overcrowding in remand and closed prisons, increasing the need for closed capacity.

---

[3] The term "open" therefore does not refer - as in some other countries - to the fact that prisoners are allowed to leave the prison to work in outside society: this possibility exists in Belgium as "semi-detention", but is organized from closed prisons.

The Prison Administration designed a classification of prisoners in 1971, based on legal and administrative criteria such as length of sentence, criminal history, gender, age, and language. In the '80s, attempts to foster the detention of prisoners as close as possible to their homes and social relations (principle of "regionalization") were hampered by the increasing overcrowding issue[4].

Mentally ill offenders remain in the prison system or can be placed in a private psychiatric institution. The decision lies with the "commission of social defence", an administrative commission composed of a psychiatrist and a barrister and headed by a judge. With only three penitentiary institutions specialised in the treatment of mentally ill offenders, all situated in the French speaking part of the country, many of the mentally ill offenders who can not be placed in a private institution find themselves in the psychiatric unit of a remand prison or on normal location, without adequate treatment. This has been severely criticised by both the European Court for Human Rights and CPT[5].

The Belgian juvenile justice system is a combination of a welfare approach towards "children in danger" and a sanctioning approach towards "juvenile delinquents", with possible interactions and transfers between the two categories. Juvenile delinquents can be admonished, receive a community sanction or placed in an open or a closed institution. While the juvenile justice system is part of the federal Ministry of Justice, the juvenile institutions fall under the competence of the regional Departments of Welfare, with the exception of one remand prison for juveniles in Brussels. By Act of 15 May 2006, juveniles between 16 and 18 years old who have committed a serious offence can be brought before a special chamber of three juvenile judges or before an adult court, which can sentence them to a maximum of 30 years imprisonment. A "closed federal centre for juveniles" will have to be built for the implementation of these sentences.

A prison governor and one or several deputies supervise each prison. A majority of them have a university degree in criminology[6]. The majority (85%) of the prison staff consists of prison guards, who – once they are nominated - have the status of public servants. Guard-prisoner ratio in Belgium is 1:2. This figure however does not take into account the fact that staff works in eight hours shifts nor that staff absenteeism ranks high in some institutions. Over the last ten years, financial efforts have been made to ensure that each prison has a "psycho-social team" - at least one full-time social worker, a part-time psychologist and a part-time psychiatrist. Due to the reform of the parole system in 1998, following the Dutroux case, which was highly publicised, these teams are increasingly pressured into a predominantly diagnostic function. Custodial staff was traditionally gender-based (men for male prisoners, women for female prisoners), but the introduction of mixed staff (with a minimum and maximum of 20% "other sex") was decided in 1997 and is now implemented in all prisons. Despite efforts made to improve training of custodial staff, this is still hampered by the prison overcrowding, as staff can hardly be missed in the prisons.

Following the institutional reforms of the Belgian state in 1980 and 1988, all aspects relating to "forensic welfare" (i.e., social aid to offenders, victims and their families) are

---

4   S. Snacken, K. Beyens & H. Tubex, Adult corrections in Belgium. In: *Adult Corrections: International Systems & Perspectives*, edited by John Winterdyk, Monsely, NY 2004: Criminal Justice Press: 21-61

5   ECHR, Aerts v Belgium, Judgement 30 July 1998; CPT reports on Belgium CPT/Inf (94)15, (98)11, (2002)25, (2006)15.

6   Until recently, only criminologists (which is a separate degree in Belgian universities) or professionals already working in a prison could participate in selection examinations for prison governor.

the exclusive responsibility of the regional authorities that are distinguished according to their language base. This has led to "Cooperation agreements" between the Ministry of Justice and the regional authorities, and to the introduction of mixed "welfare teams" in prisons in which internal social workers and external services define their respective tasks[7]. Participation of the community at large in prisons however remains modest and develops unequally between regions.

Internal and external inspection bodies exercise control over the prisons. The two "regional directors" of the central prison administration, who visit the prisons regularly, perform internal inspections. A "Central supervision council" and several local "Supervision committees" perform the external inspection. The central council and the local committees are composed of a minimum of six members, of which at least one acting judge, one medical doctor and one barrister (art. 20-31 Prison Act 2005).

1.2.2. Foreign prisoners

"Foreign" prisoners in Belgium are defined as all prisoners not having the Belgian nationality. They represent around 40% of the prison population since the 1990s, and 44% on 15 January 2004. This definition however covers different categories. As a rule, only foreigners who are suspected of having committed an offence or have been convicted will be placed in a prison. 76% of these have no legal permit of residence, 21% are second or third generation immigrants who did not acquire Belgian nationality and 10% come from neighbouring countries. Recent legislation has made it easier for members of ethnic minorities who are born in Belgium to get the Belgian nationality. This means that on top of the 44% already mentioned, there is a group of prisoners who, although having the Belgian nationality, are of foreign origin. Their problems in prison will be partly similar, partly different from the other categories of "foreign" prisoners (below). Illegal aliens who have not committed an offence and asylum seekers who have been refused refugee status will normally not be placed in prisons but in institutions under the Ministry of Interior. In case of serious disciplinary problems in closed centres an illegal alien may be transferred to a prison. Due to the prison overcrowding, this number has steadily dwindled to a few people.

1.3 Overview of involvement of Consulates and Embassies

See II.1.6.

1.4 Overview of trends

1.4.1. Sentencing trends

Crime statistics in Belgium are hampered by the lack of continuity in registration, due to the partly overlapping competences of the three major police forces (national, judicial, local police) until 1998 and the ensuing police reform (1998-2001). However, the most reli-

---

[7] S. Snacken, Belgium. In : *Imprisonment today and tomorrow. International perspectives on prisoners' rights ans prison conditions (second edition)*, edited by Dirk van Zyl Smit and Frieder Dünkel, Den Haag, London, Boston 2001: Kluwer Law International: 32-81

able figures show that in 1999 46% of crimes registered by the police related to theft and extortion, 11% to destruction and arson, 8% to physical integrity and 5% to drugs[8]. These statistics do not differentiate between nationalities of the suspect.

The number of decisions by investigating judges to remand people in custody fluctuated around 9 000 between 1993 and 2001 (index 108 in 1997, 96 in 1998), but has increased since to around 10 500 (index 115 in 2004)[9]. From research we conducted from 1996 to 2001 on the use of remand custody and its alternatives, it appeared that in most cases remand custody is requested from the investigating judge by public prosecutors (92%). In the majority of cases, the investigating judge followed the request of the public prosecutor: 63 % were dealt with by remand custody, 30 % by a simple release and only 8 % by freedom under conditions. Since then, the limited available data for the whole country and for all offences show a very slow positive evolution in the use of alternatives, but remand custody remains by far the most applied measure[10]. The prison statistics however show a much more important increase in the number and proportion of remand prisoners in Belgian prisons. While incarcerations decreased, the average prison population on remand increased (table 2: index 149 in 2004 compared to 1993, and 248 compared to 1980), indicating an important increase in the length of the remand custodies. The population on remand now represents around 40% of the total average prison population.

At the level of sentencing, the majority of criminal cases are dealt with by the police courts, competent for all petty offences and some misdemeanours (79 % in 2003). The correctional courts, competent for most misdemeanours and for cases of felonies in which mitigating circumstances have been accepted, represented 18.5 % in 2003. Only the most serious felonies are dealt with by the Courts of Assizes, these cases represented only 0.05 % of all judgments in 2003.

Fines are the most applied sanction in Belgium, being imposed in 83 % of petty offences and misdemeanours. Conditional imprisonment is applied in 20 % of misdemeanours and probation in only 4 %[11]. Suspended sentences represent only 4 to 5 % of the decisions, internments of mentally ill offenders only 0.2 %. Preventive detention is used sparingly, but its application has increased after its introduction in the new parole legislation in 1998 for sex offenders[12].

At the level of the correctional courts, sentences to short terms of imprisonment (< six months) decrease while sentences to long terms of imprisonment (> five years) increase. Despite these increases, prison sentences remain predominantly below the one-year limit. In 2003, 82.5 % of prison sentences remain below one year, 97.3 % below three years and only 0.4 % above five years.

The total number of sentences for serious felonies at the level of the Courts of Assizes remains rather low (87 in 1994, 55 in 2001, 75 in 2003). Life sentences fluctuate from

---

8   Algemene Politiesteundienst, Afdeling Politiebeleidsondersteuning, Brussels 2000, Ministry of Interior.

9   Justitie in cijfers (Justice in numbers), Ministry of Justice 2005, p.14.

10 A. Raes & S. Snacken, The application of remand custody and its alternatives in Belgium, *The Howard Journal of Criminal Justice*, 2005 Vol. 43, n°5, December 2004: 506-517.

11 S. Snacken & K. Beyens Alternatieven voor de vrijheidsberoving: hoop voor de toekomst? In: *Strafrechtelijk beleid in beweging*, edited by Sonja Snacken, Brussel 2002: VUBPress, Criminologische Studies: 271-316.

12 Chamber of Representatives 2005: 24 cases in 2003, of which 11 are sexual offenders.

28.7 % in 1994 over 13.6 % in 1999 and back to 32 % in 2003. The other categories, however, indicate a trend towards longer prison sentences. Sentences to more than ten years imprisonment represent 73.5 % of the cases of serious felonies in 1994, sentences to more than 15 years 51.7 %. In 2003, these proportions have increased to 90.6 % for the sentences to more than 10 years and 74.6 % for those to more than 15 years[13].

1.4.2. Characteristics of the (foreign) prison population

While incarcerations decreased between 1980 and 2004 from around 20 000 to 15 500 a year (table 1: index 79), the average daily population increased from 5 700 to 9 300 (index 163), indicating an increase in the average length of detentions.

Table 1 Average daily prison population and annual number of incarcerations (1980-2004)

Year	Average daily population	Index	Incarcerations	Index
1980	5677	100	19719	100
1981	5784	102	20153	102
1982	6112	108	20802	105
1983	6450	114	22274	113
1984	6728	119	22166	112
1985	6454	114	19879	101
1986	6695	115	20102	102
1987	6497	118	18437	93
1988	6688	114	17308	88
1989	6549	118	18202	92
1990	6549	115	17406	88
1991	6194	109	18221	92
1992	6869	121	19058	97
1993	7489	132	18261	93
1994	7489	132	16976	86
1995	7693	136	15853	80
1996	7935	140	15660	79
1997	8522	150	14688	74
1998	8707	153	14127	72
1999	8143	143	14434	73
2000	8543	150	14960	76
2001	8536	150	14443	73
2002	8804	155	15695	80
1/3/2003	9308	164	15402	78
1/3/2004	9250	163	15545	79

---

[13] W. De Pauw, c.a De Belgische veroordelingsstatistiek, in: E. Devroe, K. Beyens & E. Enhus (eds.) Criminografie, VUBPress, .2006 forthcoming Criminologische studies.

Source: Prison Administration; Snacken, Beyens & Tubex (2004); Tubex & Strypstein (2006 forthcoming)

During this period, the proportion of foreigners in the prisons however rose from 25% in 1980 to 45% in 1991, and their proportion in the average prison population doubled from 21% in 1980 to 44% in 2004 (index 319 compared to 117 for Belgian nationals)[14]. While the pace of the increase of foreign prisoners in Belgian prisons is fairly steady over these years (index 191 in 1991), we see an even sharper increase since 1998[15]. Since non-Belgian nationals constitute only 9 to 10 % of the registered total population in Belgium, it would seem that they are strongly over-represented in the prison population. We have to remember though that 76% of these foreign prisoners have no legal permit of residence, and only 21% are second or third generation immigrants who did not acquire Belgian nationality.

As far as nationalities are concerned, Belgian prisons were facing not less than 104 different nationalities in 2003, covering all the world continents. The profile of the foreign population has changed however since 1998. Moroccans, who constitute the largest ethnic minority group in Belgium, traditionally represented the largest group within the population of non-Belgians in prison, 38% in 1992, compared to 30% of Western and Southern European foreign prisoners (including 12% from neighbouring countries, 8.6% Italian and 6% Turkish prisoners, the other important minority groups in Belgium) and 10% of Eastern European prisoners. The opening-up of the borders between Western and Eastern Europe has however altered the mix of foreign nationalities in prison. Since the beginning of the 1990s, the number of prisoners with a former Soviet nationality (i.e. Central and Eastern Europe, Russia and Community of Independent States) has steadily increased, and quite sharply so since 1998. In March 2003, both groups represented 28% of the foreign prison population (N= 1.030 Eastern Europeans and 1.043 Moroccans), while the number of prisoners with a Western and Southern European nationality stabilized around 22% (N= 830 prisoners)[16]. The age and gender structure of the foreign prison population is however very similar to the Belgian prison population: in 2003, 65% of foreign prisoners were between 18 and 35 years old, while female prisoners represented only 4%[17].

When we compare Belgian and foreign prisoners with regard to the categories of prison sentences and measures, we see an overrepresentation of foreign prisoners under remand: on 1 March 2003, 48% of the foreign prisoners versus 32% of the Belgian prisoners are imprisoned under remand. Foreigners are underrepresented though in the sentences of more than five years or life for felonies (2% versus 4% for sentences > 5 years, 1% versus 4% for life sentences) and in internment of mentally ill offenders (2% versus 10%) (tables 2 and 3).

---

[14] K. Beyens, S. Snacken, C. Eliaerts, C. *Barstende muren. Overbevolkte gevangenissen : omvang, oorzaken en mogelijke oplossingen*, Antwerpen-Arnhem 1993: Kluwer-Gouda, Interuniversitaire Reeks Criminologie en Strafwetenschappen nr. 26; Snacken, Keulen & Winkelmans , ibidem.

[15] Snacken, Keulen & Winkelmans, ibidem.: figure 2.

[16] For a more detailed overview of the nationalities, see Snacken, Keulen & Winkelmans ibidem.: table 3.

[17] Snacken, Keulen & Winkelmans ibidem: tables 4 and 5.

Table 2 Remand prisoners and sentenced prisoners (1980 – 2004)

Year	Remand			Sentenced prisoners		
	Average daily population –	Index	Proportion of the total population	Average daily population –	Index	Proportion of the total population
1980	1458	100	26%	2377	100	42%
1985	2004	137	31%	2726	115	42%
1990	1821	125	28%	3236	136	49%
1991	1722	118	28%	2910	122	47%
1992	2191	150	32%	3080	130	45%
1993	2431	167	32%	3723	157	50%
1994	2614	179	35%	3616	152	48%
1995	2546	175	33%	3953	166	51%
1996	2497	171	31%	4344	183	55%
1997	2469	169	29%	4922	207	58%
1/03/	2773*	190	32%	4615*	194	53%
1/03/	2554*	175	31%	4580*	193	56%
1/03/	3023*	207	35%	4900*	206	57%
1/03/	2951*	202	35%	4776*	201	56%
1/03/	3238*	222	37%	4497*	189	51%
1/03/	3680*	252	40%	4807*	202	52%
1/03/	3614*	248	39%			

* Population on March 1st
Source: Prison Administration; Snacken, Beyens & Tubex (2004); Tubex & Strypstein (2006 forthcoming)

Table 3: Foreign and Belgian prisoners: categories of sentences and measures (1 March 2003)

	Foreign prisoners	Belgium prisoners
remand custody	48%	32%
1-3y	10%	13%
3-5y	16%	16%
>5y (misdemeanours)	22%	22%
>5y (felonies)	2%	4%
life imprisonment	1%	4%
internment	2%	10%
total	100%	100%

Source: Prison Administration; Snacken, Keulen & Winkelmans (2004)

This overrepresentation of foreign prisoners under remand is a constant feature of the last 15 years[18]. Researchers that explain this overrepresentation have found several mechanisms[19]. A first element is the absence of legal residence for part of these foreign prisoners, which is seen by many investigating judges as enhancing both the risk of absconding and the risk of recidivism; two criteria that allow them to impose remand custody. As this situation usually does not change during the detention, remand custody for this category is also confirmed every month until the person appears before the court. A second element is the poor socio-economic and financial situation of many foreign or ethnic minority offenders, which is again seen as enhancing the risk of recidivism. A third element concerns more particularly offenders belonging to the Moroccan ethnic minority, who were found to be at a higher risk than Belgian or other foreign offenders to find themselves under remand custody or sentenced to imprisonment, due to their "negative" attitude during the procedure. Judges referred more particularly to their sustained denial even in the face of evident proof and their poor use of "earlier offered opportunities for treatment" in case of drug use. Intercultural misunderstandings seem to play a role here. While the denial by Moroccans can be explained in the framework of a more collective culture of shame, in which it allows to save the family's honour, Belgian judges evaluate this attitude within the western framework of individual guilt and responsibility as a lack of insight into the wrongfulness of their behaviour and therefore proof of a higher social danger. It also led some judges to stereotypical thinking of this group as "liars"[20]. On the other hand, judges often assume that drug use is part of the Moroccan culture and accepted by the Islam and therefore see this group again as representing a higher risk of criminality, both because of their assumed acceptance of drug use in itself and because their poor financial situation will lead to other forms of criminality in order to sustain this use[21].

1.5 Overview of national legislation[22]

1.5.1. The legal status of foreign nationals under Belgian law

The administrative legal status of foreign nationals is mainly regulated by the Act of 15 December 1980 on the entry into the country, the stay, settlement and expulsion of foreigners[23], the Geneva Convention of 28 July 1951 on the status of refugees[24] and the Act of 22 December 1999 on the regularization of the administrative situation of certain categories of foreigners[25]. National sovereignty in these matters is of course also dependent on

---

[18] Beyens, Snacken & Eliaerts ibidem: table 25; Snacken, Keulen & Winkelmans ibidem: table 6.

[19] Snacken & Raes ibidem; W. De Pauw, *De afhandeling van drugzaken in Brussel in 1993 en 1994*, BRES, Brussel 1996: IRIS; W. De Pauw, *Migranten in de balans*. Brusse 2001: VUB Press. Criminologische Studies.

[20] S. Snacken, S. Deltenre, A. Raes, Ch. Vanneste and Paul Verhaeghe, *Kwalitatief onderzoek naar de toepassing van de voorlopige hechtenis en de vrijheid onder voorwaarden*, Onderzoeksrapport VUB/NICC, Brussel 1999.

[21] De Pauw (1996, 2000, 2006 forthcoming), ibidem.

[22] Snacken, Keulen & Winkelmans ibidem, 29-49.

[23] B.S. (Belgisch Staatsblad) 31 december 1980, repeatedly altered since.

[24] Act of 26 June 1953, B.S. 4 October 1953; Protocol 31 january 1967 on the status of refugees, New York, act 27 february 1969, B.S. 3 May 1969.

[25] B.S. 10 January 2000.

international (cf. European) bilateral and multilateral conventions. The competence over immigration policy was transferred from the Ministry of Justice to the Ministry of Interior in the 1990s (1992-1994).

According to the Act of 1980, entry into the country is dependent upon possession of legal documents. The stay is normally limited to a maximum period of three months. In certain cases, foreigners with legal documents can be refused entry (e.g. when signalled in the Schengen Information System, when seen as a possible threat to public order or national security) or can be ordered to leave the country by Ministerial Decree (e.g. when seen as a threat to public order or national security, in case of insufficient means of subsistence and inability to obtain such means legally). Foreign residents can be expelled by Royal Decree in case of breach of public order or national security, following recommendation by a multidisciplinary "Advisory commission for Foreigners". Orders to leave or decrees of expulsion prohibit re-entry into the country for a period of ten years. In 2000, 50 such Ministerial Decrees and 6 Royal Decrees were issued[26]. Foreign prisoners who have been sentenced to at least six months imprisonment can be expelled after serving their sentence. A special Bureau "D" ("detainees") in the Office for Foreigners' Affairs evaluates the opportunity of expulsion of foreign prisoners on the basis of their situation of residence and the seriousness of the crimes committed.

Foreigners can be recognised as refugees on the basis of a reasonable fear of prosecution for reasons of race, religion, nationality, social group or political conviction (Convention of Geneva 28 July 1951). Asylum seekers who fail to be recognised as refugees can lodge an administrative appeal with the *Conseil d'Etat*.

The Act of 22 December 1999 provided for the regularization of the administrative situation of certain categories of foreigners on the basis of four criteria: asylum seekers submitted to a disproportionate long procedure, foreigners for whom return to the country of origin is impossible, seriously ill foreigners, and finally humanitarian reasons and long lasting social bonds. A more permanent procedure of regularization is based on art.9.3 of the Act of 1980, which allows foreigners "in exceptional circumstances" to request permission of residence from the mayor of the local community, who will send the request to the Minister of Interior[27].

Table 4 shows the administrative situation of the foreign prisoners in Belgian prisons from 1993 to 2003. We can see that in a majority of cases, the Office for Foreigners has not yet taken a decision towards the future legal situation of the foreign prisoners: that was true for 98% of foreign prisoners in 1993, and is still true for 65% of this population in 2003. This has vast implications for their early release (see below II.1.9).

1.5.2. Legal framework for the detention of foreign nationals

a. Administrative detention. In principle, an illegal alien is expected to leave the country on his own initiative. He can acquire help from the International Organisation for Migration, which provides assistance in gathering travel documents, pays a flight ticket and other travel expenses. In case of failure to leave, an illegal alien may be detained for the time strictly necessary for the organisation of the forced repatriation. Such administrative

---

[26] Office for Foreigners Affairs, Annual report, Ministry of Interior, Brussels 2000.

[27] J. Keulen, Operatie regularisatie, dissertation in criminology, Brussels, Vrije Universiteit Brussel 2003; Snacken, Keulen & Winkelmans, ibidem.

detention normally takes place in a closed centre of the Ministry of Interior. Administrative detention is normally imposed for a maximum of two months, but can be extended to five months. Only when necessary for the protection of public order or national security can it be further prolonged to the absolute maximum of eight months. Appeal against the administrative detention can be lodged with the investigation chamber of the correctional court.

b. Penal la. Belgian penal law is applicable to all crimes committed in Belgium, independent of the nationality of the offender. The fact that a certain deed would not be punishable under the lex personae of the foreigner does not exclude his prosecution and punishment. Remand custody can be imposed in accordance with the Act of 20 July 1990. When the alleged crime is punishable with a maximum of 15 years of imprisonment, remand custody can only be imposed in case of risk of recidivism, absconding, collusion or tampering with evidence. The Directorate General implements sentences of imprisonment for the Implementation of Penalties and Measures. The Bureau "D" of the office for Foreigners' Affairs is responsible for the administrative follow up of foreigners imprisoned for criminal acts, i.e. with regard to their administrative status upon release (permission to stay, order to leave, expulsion.).

c. Prison law. Prison life used to be regulated by the General Prison Regulation, a Royal Decree of 1965 setting only a general framework for the implementation of sanctions and measures involving deprivation of liberty, numerous ministerial circular letters and the house rules of the different prisons. These regulations did not offer substantial or formal rights to prisoners. Although efforts were made since the 1970s to develop prison regimes and open up the prisons to the outside world, most elements of prison regimes remained privileges, which could be withdrawn or refused, with the exception of the right of access to a lawyer and the right to freedom of religion. There was no formal complaint procedure, disciplinary breaches and sanctions were not enumerated and decisions could not be appealed. As a result, situations and regimes differed greatly between prisons and prisoners were uncertain about their rights and duties[28]. After many years of a "hands off policy" by courts towards decisions taken by the Prison Administration, and in accordance with the case law of the European Court of Human Rights, Belgian courts increasingly recognized that prisoners maintain their fundamental rights and that curtailment of these rights must be legitimate and proportionate.

On 12 January 2005, the first Prison Act for Belgium was issued (B.S. 1 February 2005), enumerating for the first time the basic principles that must lead the implementation of sanctions and measures implying deprivation of liberty:

- to guarantee psychosocial, physical and material circumstances of detention which respect human dignity, which allow the prisoner to retain or improve his self respect and which appeal to his individual and social responsibility (art.5.1),
- to safeguard order and security in the prison (art.5.2), through dynamic interactions between prison staff and prisoners ("dynamic security") and a good balance between technical instruments of security and a constructive prison regime (art.105.1),
- no limitations to the political, civil, social, economical and cultural rights of the prisoner will be imposed other than those resulting from the imposed sanction or measure, the inherent consequences of the deprivation of liberty or the law (art.6.1),

---

[28] CPT reports on Belgium CPT/Inf (94)15, (98)11, (2002)25, (2006)15.

- detrimental effects of the deprivation of liberty must be avoided as much as possible (art.6.2),
- prisons must strive for a climate of consultation with prisoners (art.7.1),
- the implementation of prison sentences aims at reparation of the harm caused to the victims, the rehabilitation of the offender and the individual preparation of his social reintegration (art.9.2), through the elaboration of an individual sentence plan in collaboration with the prisoner (art.9.3),
- prisons are subjected to independent inspection bodies: a central counsel for central decisions and local supervision committees for decisions taken by the director of the prison (art.20),
- complaint procedures are introduced within these inspection bodies (art. 147-166),
- the disciplinary breaches and sanctions are enumerated in the act; the disciplinary procedure is thoroughly reformed (art.122-146).

Several working groups within the Prison Administration are currently preparing the implementation of this new Act.

d. International conventions. Several international conventions are applicable to foreign prisoners, but are seldom applied in practice.

a) Convention of Strasbourg of 21 March 1983 on transfer of sentenced prisoners (Act of 23 May 1990). Sentenced prisoners can be transferred to their country of origin if certain conditions are fulfilled: the sentence must be definitive, the offence is incriminated in both countries, the prisoner must agree with the transfer, there is no request for extradition and no pending case, the prisoner has at least another six months to serve or has received an indeterminate sentence. The transfer is a favour that will be granted by the Minister of Justice after careful balance of all interests involved and should be decided as soon as possible after the final verdict. Possible counter-indications based on the interests of society are: the request for transfer aims at or will result in a reduction of punishment, e.g. because the country will adapt the sentence to its own maximum punishment or because release can be granted earlier; the prisoner attempts to escape payment of judicial costs or fines or the transfer will hamper such payment. Possible counter-indications based on the victims' interests are: the transfer aims at or will result in hampering payment of civil compensation; the compensation represents an important amount for the victim. These counter-indications will be evaluated on the basis of the efforts made by the prisoner to fulfil his financial obligations, taking into account his personal situation. Transfer can be granted under the condition that (part of) the judicial costs, fines or compensation will be paid; if all these obligations are still open, compensation of individual victims will be prioritised.

The Council of Europe issued an additional Protocol to this Convention on 18 December 1997, in which the agreement of the prisoner for his transfer is no longer obligatory. This Protocol has been signed by Belgium, but not ratified yet. Bilateral Agreements have also been reached with countries outside the Council of Europe, i.e. with Morocco (Agreement of 7 July 1997 on assistance to detained persons and transfer of sentenced prisoners).

b) Convention of Strasbourg of 21 May 1972 on transfer of criminal procedures. This Convention has been signed, but not ratified by Belgium.

c) Convention of Strasbourg of 30 November 1964 on supervision of conditionally sentenced or conditionally released offenders (Act of 15 July 1970). The Belgian state can request the State in which an offender is normally residing to carry out supervision over the offender only, or to carry out supervision and if necessary to enforce the sentence (e.g. in case of revoking an early release), or to assume entire responsibility for applying the sentence (as if it had been imposed by its own court). In complying with a request for supervision, the requested State shall, if necessary, adapt the prescribed supervisory measures in accordance with its own laws. In no case however may this result in more severe measures than those prescribed by the requesting State.

2 TREATMENT OF FOREIGN PRISONERS[29]

2.1 General situation

Imprisonment raises many personal and social problems for all prisoners. On top of this, Belgian prisons face severe overcrowding, especially in remand prisons. This results in additional quantitative and qualitative problems for prisoners and staff: sharing cells designed for one person intensifies feelings of insecurity and possible tensions or conflicts, lack of space hampers normal family visits or prison labour, too many prisoners hinder the possibilities of developing a dynamic security with staff and an adequate preparation of the social reintegration[30]. Being a foreigner can further exacerbate particular difficulties. This will vary however: we mentioned that prisoners in Belgium represent more than 100 different nationalities, which implies a large diversity in language, culture and religion, but also in social isolation and exclusion, depending on the family and social ties of the prisoner in Belgium. Not all foreign prisoners will therefore face the same problems: second or third generation immigrants (mainly Moroccans) will speak the local language and have all their family ties in Belgium, but may still face racism or religious intolerance, while the more recently immigrated Eastern Europeans may not speak any of the languages and find themselves totally isolated.

Language and communication are important in any system, but even more so in prison. Daily interactions between prisoners and staff are seriously hampered if a prisoner does not speak any of the common languages (Dutch, French, and English). Attempts to find a solution will often depend on the goodwill of both partners in the interaction, or the involvement of a fellow prisoner as interpreter. This latter solution may be difficult in more delicate situations (disciplinary procedure, personal information) and will hamper the establishment of a relation of trust with staff (cf. dynamic security). Moreover, many aspects of daily prison life or prison regimes must be asked for in written form (participation in activities, request to see the director or the psychosocial service, etc.). On top of being unable to formulate such requests in one of the local languages, some of the foreign prisoners are also illiterate in their own language. In practice, involving a fellow prisoner or a guard again usually solves this. However, two major risks are mentioned as a result of communication problems: insufficient awareness of the house rules or misunderstand-

---

[29] These results of the research carried out for the Koning Boudewijn Foundation are based on interviews with prisoners and prison staff in six prisons, interviews with members of the central prison administration, a parole commission, an external welfare service, the Office for Foreigners Affairs of the Ministry of Interior, and focus groups with officials of the Ministries of Justice and Interior.

[30] K. Beyens, S. Snacken & C. Eliaerts, Barstende muren. *Overbevolkte gevangenissen: omvang, oorzaken en mogelijke oplossingen*, Antwerpen 1993, Kluwer Rechtswetenschappen.

ings may lead to more disciplinary sanctions for certain foreign prisoners, while others will retreat in isolation and become "invisible".

2.2 Living conditions and facilities

Foreign prisoners are detained in the same institutions as nationals and have in principle access to the same living conditions and facilities as other prisoners. They are not separated from other prisoners, but some nationalities may sometimes be allocated to the same unit to solve language problems.

Belgian prisons, both for remand custody and for implementation of sentences, are in principle designed for single cell accommodation, with only some cells designed for two, three or four prisoners[31]. However, due to the prison overcrowding of the last 20 years, especially in remand prisons, single cells often have to be shared by two or three prisoners, and multi occupancy cells see their real capacity doubled. In such cases, prison directors may try to allocate foreign prisoners from the same nationality, culture or language to the shared cells, especially when they have serious communication problems. This may facilitate their adaptation to prison rules and internal order, but has on occasion led to external security problems (escape). Criteria applied by the prison directors are however not always in accordance with the individual appreciation by the prisoners. Accommodation on the basis of language or religion has sometimes led to other conflicts, for example between nationals of recently partitioned new states. Other criteria are also taken into account, for example smoking, possession of a TV set. Individual prisoners can request accommodation in a particular cell or with a particular fellow prisoner, which will be granted as much as possible, taking into consideration the overcrowding and security concerns.

The presence of larger cultural subgroups in a prison, such as "North African" (mainly Moroccan) and "Eastern European", is said to increase the development of a group feeling and the risk of group conflicts. Some Central and Eastern European prison systems have large dormitories, in which prisoners' subcultures often develop more easily than in cellular systems. Prisoners from these countries may then import their (sometimes more hierarchical and violent) subculture into the Belgian prisons.

2.3 Reception and admission

Foreign prisoners are submitted to similar procedures on reception and admission as national prisoners. Language problems may arise again here concerning written documents and/or oral interactions. All legal documents in Belgium, including juridical and prison documents, must be written in one of the official languages (Dutch, French or German. Problems may arise at the moment of registration in the prison registry on admission or when explaining the house rules of the prison for foreign prisoners who do not understand these languages. The house rules of the prison inform prisoners about most aspects of daily prison life: discipline, visits, prison labour, activities, use of TV and canteen, etc. Some prisons have taken the initiative to translate the house rules into other languages, usually including English and Arabic, or to show a video, but even these may be insuffi-

---

[31] Some of the open and half open prisons have limited dormitory systems.

cient: with 100 different nationalities in Belgian prisons it remains difficult to cover all possible languages.

All incoming prisoners are seen by a prison director and should be seen by the psychosocial service upon admission. The latter however are heavily involved in the preparation/advice on prison leaves or early release, and do not always succeed to see all incoming prisoners. This problem exists for all prisoners, independent of their nationality.

2.4 Work – education – training – sports - recreation

The availability of work and activities varies in different prisons. This is linked to both architectural and policy differences. Most prisons in Belgium were built in the nineteenth or first half of the twentieth century following the so-called "Belgian design", based on the idea of individual isolation and cellular segregation, religion and education. Prison labour was limited to in-cell work. The typical star-shaped prisons had small individual cells and a chapel, but no workplaces or rooms for communal activities. When penological ideas changed, the possibilities for architectural transformations and extensions to existing prisons especially remand prisons that were very often built in town centres were limited. More recently built prisons provide more room for communal activities and specialized forms of prison labour. Policy differences are linked to the division of competences between the regional authorities: the Flemish Community has elaborated a "Strategic Plan for assistance and services to prisoners", offering several educational and socio-cultural activities to prisoners in Flemish prisons, while the provision of services by the other Communities is not systematic yet. On top of this, different priorities may be developed by the local prison directors in collaboration with local NGO's or associations: some will emphasize prison labour, others education or social-cultural activities.

In general though, Belgian prisons face a shortage of labour, resulting in waiting lists, and turning the theoretically legal obligation for sentenced prisoners to work into a de facto privilege. Most prisons are divided in units for "workers" and for "non-workers", with the "workers" having a much better regime combining work, activities and more freedom of movement inside the unit. In remand prisons, large parts of the prison population will remain in their (often overcrowded) cell for 22 or 23 hours a day, with one or two hours of exercise in the open air as only activity. Prison directors will normally not differentiate between foreign and national prisoners when allocating work, but some types of work may require language skills or sufficient knowledge of one of the Belgian languages. Central and Eastern European prisoners are said to be good and hard workers, but will often find themselves in the less demanding manual work because of communication problems. Many foreign prisoners see prison labour as very important, especially if they have no other forms of income to rent a TV, use the telephone, buy goods in the canteen, or if they want to send money home to their families.

Activities such as theatre or movies may be a source of language problems. Some prisons have multicultural music groups or make efforts to provide books in different languages, often in collaboration with the local library. Most prisons also provide forms of vocational training such as language courses or programmes for tackling illiteracy, but usually only to a limited number of prisoners.

2.5 Food – religion – personal hygiene – medical care

As mentioned above, religion was an important feature of the cellular prison regime in Belgium, which lasted from the independence of the country in 1830 to after the Second World War. Catholic chaplains were attached to each prison and were subsidized as part of the prison staff. Units for female prisoners were even staffed by catholic nuns until as late as the 1980s. On the other hand, freedom of religion is an important constitutional right in Belgium, which has lead to some political struggles against the influence of religion and religious groups on Belgian society. As a result, this right to freedom of religion was, with the right of access to a lawyer, the only formally recognized prisoner's right under the General Prison Regulation of 1965. This right has been confirmed by the new Prison Act of 12 January 2005 (art.71 PA), which states that each prisoner has the right to profess his religion or philosophy individually and in community with others, with respect for the rights of others, and has the right to receive religious, spiritual or moral support from representatives of his religion or philosophy attached or admitted to the prison.

Several religions are officially recognized in Belgium, including in Belgian prisons: Catholicism, Protestantism, Orthodox faith, Judaism, Islam and the non-confessional moral philosophy. Representatives of these recognized religions or philosophies are attached to each prison, can visit individual prisoners, can receive uncensored letters and can organize religious/philosophical meetings. Representatives of non-recognized religions can also be admitted to the prison (art.72 PA). Nutritional or other consequences of these officially recognized religions would also be applicable in Belgian prisons: Jewish prisoners are allowed to receive kosher meals; Islamic prisoners can observe Ramadan, etc. On the other hand, freedom of religion also entails the right to be free from religious influence. Therefore, no prisoner can be forced to participate in any religious meeting or to receive the visit of a representative, prisoners can choose freely if and which religion or philosophy they want to turn to and can change course during their detention (art.74 PA).

In practice, not all religions are equally represented in Belgian prisons. Subsidized representatives such as the catholic chaplains and the non-confessional moral advisers are present in all prisons and fulfil an important task of support and guidance. Representatives of the other denominations however are volunteers, and their presence may vary according to regional circumstances. The Imam is generally considered to be very important for the large group of Islamic prisoners, because of his high moral standing and influence. However, as only one or two Imams are currently willing to visit prisoners, they have to cover all 34 prisons over the whole country, resulting in a lower accessibility.

Some religious practices may cause conflicts between prisoners (e.g. a shared cell where one prisoner wants to watch TV while the other is praying) or small forms of disorder (e.g. call for prayer for Islamic prisoners through the whole prison). During the interviews, prisoners were said to be rather intolerant towards other religions.

Personal hygiene or medical care are provided for by the Prison Service independently of nationality or language, but may raise cultural problems. Art. 44 PA states that the prison director must guarantee that prisoners can take care of their personal hygiene on a daily basis. However, hygienic standards may differ personally and culturally, which may raise tensions when cells have to be shared, as is the case in the overcrowded remand prisons. The Central medical Service organizes medical care. It must be of similar (high) quality as outside the prison and adapted to the individual situation of the prisoner (art.88

PA). In reality, psychiatric care is insufficiently provided for in Belgian prisons generally, and for mentally ill offenders more specifically (see above 2). Physical and mental health also has cultural connotations, which will usually not be familiar to the general practitioners and psychiatrists visiting the prisoners. Language problems may also hamper adequate communication in these areas, which may result in some prisoners and their problems becoming "invisible" to medical and other prison staff (e.g. suicide prevention). With the growing presence of prisoners from Central and Eastern European countries, new phenomena such as open TB are also appearing in Belgian prisons.

2.6 Consular and legal help

Foreign prisoners are entitled to contact their consular agency upon admission to prison (one free phone call), with the exception of those remand prisoners whose contacts with the outside world have been restricted by the investigating judge for three days at most (atr.64§2 PA). Correspondence with the consular agencies is confidential and cannot be controlled or censured (art.69 PA). The attitude of consulates or embassies towards their imprisoned citizens varies however: while some will provide help and information, others will remain indifferent and unwilling to provide support.

Prisoners are entitled to all legal help available in society at large, including free legal aid for those who cannot afford to pay for a lawyer (art.104.1 PA). In practice, most foreign prisoners have free legal aid. Many are dissatisfied though, claiming they see their lawyer only in court and receive little information about the procedures ruling their administrative status as a foreigner. Language may again be a problem here. But it is also generally recognized that few lawyers are sufficiently trained in or familiar with the legal aspects of residence permits, asylum seeking and regulations concerning illegal aliens. Some prisons organize information sessions where prisoners can ask questions to a lawyer. However, more and better legal aid was one of the recurrent requests heard during the research.

2.7 Contact with the outside world

Art 58 PA stipulates that, unless otherwise imposed by law, remand prisoners are entitled to daily visits, while sentenced prisoners are entitled to three visits a week. Visits should last at least one hour. Prisoners are also entitled to unsupervised visits once a month, in accordance with conditions determined by Royal Decree. Direct family members (parents, children, siblings, aunts and uncles), and married or cohabiting partners are entitled to visit the prisoner in principle, on proof of their identity, unless specific and individual circumstances endanger the order and security of the prison and cannot take place in a different way, for example through visits behind glass. Other visitors must request permission to visit a prisoner from the prison director (art.59 PA).

Foreign prisoners who have no family or friends in Belgium may find themselves in a situation of serious social isolation. The lack of external support and knowledge of the Belgian system may increase tensions and even aggressiveness. It may also be difficult to ascertain the identity and family relationship of certain visitors. On the other hand, some family members may be unwilling to visit because of their illegal status in the country. Regular transfers of prisoners, for example because of overcrowding, may also hamper the organization of visits. When visitors from abroad have travelled specifically to visit the prisoner, the prison director may adapt visit arrangements accordingly.

Other forms of contact with the outside world may depend on the individual financial situation. All prisoners (unless legal exceptions) are entitled to use the telephone daily, but have to pay for this expense (art.64§1 PA). As the system of "collect calls" was recently abolished in prisons, foreign prisoners may have insufficient financial means to call their family abroad. Similarly, the prisoner can purchase all newspapers or publications legally available in outside society, and radio and television programmes can be listened to and watched in accordance with the house rules (art.77 PA). A television can be rented on a monthly basis, offering access to more than twenty networks, including many foreign programmes (English, Italian, Spanish, Turkish, etc.). Access to the prison library is free though, and many prisons try to diversify the languages available, often in cooperation with outside libraries. Again, this may not cover the whole range of the more than 100 nationalities present in the Belgian prisons.

2.8 Reintegration activities – prison leave

Modalities for prison leave vary with the administrative status of the foreign prisoner. Systematic prison leave, decided by the Prison Administration, allows certain prisoners to leave the prison every month (or three months) for one day (or three days) in order to maintain family and social ties, prepare for social reintegration or in view of a conditional release. A ministerial circular letter of 10 June 1986 regulates the possibilities of prison leave for foreign prisoners:

- Foreign prisoners who are not registered in the Foreigners' Register, in the Population Register or in the Immatriculation (EU) Register cannot be granted prison leave.
- For foreign prisoners who are registered, the decision will depend on their administrative status:
    - If the Office for Foreigners' Affairs has not yet decided on their status, they will be treated like Belgian prisoners.
    - If a proposal to leave the country or be deported has been submitted by the Office to the Advisory Commission, but the latter has advised against expulsion, or has not decided yet and the prisoner has close family ties in the country who are willing to house him, prison leave may still be granted.
    - If the Advisory Commission favours expulsion, the prison administration waits for the definite decision on expulsion.
    - If the prisoner does not appeal against the decision, or if the administrative court does not grant temporary suspension of the decision, no prison leave can be granted.
    - If the prisoner has appealed the decision or the administrative court grants suspension of the decision, prison leave may be granted in case of close family ties in the country.
    - Exceptionally prison leave may be granted in spite of a decision for expulsion, when a combination of conditions are fulfilled: the prisoner serves his term in an open or half open prison, earlier prison leaves were successful, there are no counter indications, the prisoner had a legal permit at the time of incarceration, a certain period is imposed in which to leave to country.
    - If extradition of the prisoner is requested, no prison leave can be granted.

We can conclude that when deciding on prison leave, the Prison Administration takes into account both the legal and the social situation of the foreign prisoner. However, as 76% of foreign prisoners in 2004 had no legal permit to stay, we can assume that a large proportion of foreign prisoners in Belgian prisons will not be granted prison leave.

As far as other forms of prison leave are concerned, only Belgian prisoners or foreign prisoners who have permission to reside in Belgium can be granted incidental prison leave (return the same day), release from prison under electronic monitoring or semi detention (employment, training or therapy outside the prison during daytime, return to prison every night).

2.9 Early release - expulsion

This area is fraught with difficulties for foreign prisoners in Belgium, more particularly due to the combination of criminal and administrative procedures. Criminal procedures of importance here are conditional release, provisional release and provisional release in view of expulsion.

The Act of 5 March 1998 on conditional release does not distinguish between Belgian and foreign prisoners. In practice, conditional release is applied to prisoners serving sentences totalling more than three years. Prisoners are admissible for conditional release after serving 1/3 and minimum three months of their sentences (2/3 and minimum six months for legal recidivists), life sentence prisoners after serving ten years (14 years for legal recidivists). The decision is taken by a "Commission for Conditional Release", a multidisciplinary commission of three members: a specialist in social reintegration, one in prison matters and a judge as president. A commission in the prison where the prisoner serves his sentence, composed of the prison director, members of the psychosocial staff and a senior guard, must discuss all eligible prisoners, including foreign prisoners, except those against whom an order to leave the country or a decree of expulsion has been issued. The latter fall under the system of provisional release in view of expulsion. Prisoners serving between one and three years of imprisonment are provisionally released after serving 1/3 of their sentence[32]. The director of the prison where the sentence is served takes the decision. In case of counter-indications and insufficient prospects for social reintegration, this provisional release can be coupled to specific conditions. If specific conditions are deemed insufficient, the procedure for conditional release will be applied. This form of release is not applicable to foreign prisoners without legal permit of residence. Foreign prisoners, who, due to their administrative situation cannot be released under either of the two previous forms, can be provisionally released in view of expulsion. The minimum terms to be served are the same as for the other forms of early release, depending on whether the total terms exceed three years imprisonment or not.

A first, major problem results from the interaction of these criminal procedures with the administrative procedure of expulsion or order to leave the country. As mentioned above, foreign residents can only be expelled by Royal Decree in case of breach of public order or national security, following recommendation by a multidisciplinary "Advisory commission for Foreigners". Orders to leave or decrees of expulsion prohibit re-entry into the country for a period of ten years. In 2000, 50 such Ministerial Decrees and 6 Royal

---

[32] Prisoners serving less than one year are released after an even shorter term. This system has been introduced in order to cope with the severe overcrowding of certain prisons in Belgium.

Decrees were issued[33]. Foreign non-resident prisoners who have been sentenced to at least six months imprisonment can be expelled after serving their sentence. A special Bureau "D" ("detainees") in the Office for Foreigners' Affairs (OFA) of the Ministry of Interior appreciates the opportunity of expulsion of foreign prisoners on the basis of their situation of residence and the seriousness of the crimes committed. Many non-resident foreign prisoners however have requested asylum status or regularisation of their illegal status. As long as the administrative status of the prisoner as foreigner is uncertain, it is also unclear which procedure for early release must be applied. We have seen that this was the case for 98% of foreign prisoners in 1993, and was still the case for 65% of them in 2003 (table 4).

The Ministry of Justice issued several circular letters to tackle this situation. In a first such letter of 20 May 1981, it was decided that prisoners who had a permit of residence when they were apprehended should be treated like Belgian citizens: i.e. through the normal procedure of conditional or provisional release depending on the length of the sentence. Those who did not possess a permit of residence upon apprehension should be provisionally released with a view on expulsion[34]. The Office for Foreigners' Affairs (OFA) was immediately informed of the start of such procedures, in order to take a decision as to the future administrative position of the prisoner. In case of absence of such a decision at the moment of release, the prisoner was released anyway. In the opposite case, the decision of the OFA was applied accordingly.

One of the consequences of this system is that the procedure for conditional release is sometimes started but can not be finalised in the absence of a decision by the OFA, which means that the prisoner serves more than the minimum of 1/3 or 2/3 imposed by law. Sometimes conditional release is granted by the Commission, but is then followed by a negative decision by the OFA, refusing residence. Transfer of supervision to another country is not always possible, and reintegration or treatment in the country of origin may be difficult to assess. This may hamper granting a conditional release. The same problem arises with mentally ill offenders who can only be released under the condition of adequate psychiatric treatment in their country of origin.

Foreign prisoners without legal permit of residence face serious problems at the time of their apprehension. Pressed by prison overcrowding, the Ministry of Justice issued a circular letter nr. 71 of 20 June 2002, in which prison directors were requested to release prisoners without permit of residence, against whom no decision for repatriation, expulsion or transfer to a closed centre had been taken by the OFA, 15 days after the decision on provisional release in view of expulsion had been reached. The OFA was to be informed of the date of the provisional release as soon as the decision was reached. If a measure of expulsion or repatriation was decided by the OFA within these 15 days, the prisoner could not be held in a prison for more than an additional 15 days on administrative grounds. The total period of additional administrative detention could therefore not exceed 30 days. This policy was revoked however by circular letter of 17 December 2003, following refusals by police forces to be further involved in the transfer or expulsion of foreigners. This was the result of a trial in which police forces were held responsible for

---

[33] Office for Foreigners Affairs, Annual report, Ministry of Interior, Brussels 2000.

[34] By circular letter of 28 July 1989, a third category was added, i.e. prisoners against whom a procedure for expulsion has been started and who are awaiting the advice of the Commission for Advice concerning Foreigners.

the death by asphyxiation of a Nigerian woman who was forcefully expelled. According to this latter circular letter, foreign prisoners without permit of residence who could not be transferred to a closed centre for illegal aliens were not to be released anymore. This meant that although these prisoners had served the required proportion of their prison sentence for the Ministry of Justice, they could be further detained in the prison on administrative grounds. It appeared from our research that, in practice, the OFA did not really take into account the possibility of provisional early release after serving 1/3 of the sentence, as this is not a formal right to which prisoners are entitled. The OFA assumed it was sufficient to reach a decision about the administrative status of the foreigner by the end of the prison sentence. As a result, it happened on several occasions that a prisoner was about to leave the prison on provisional release but was held back by a last-minute fax by the OFA requesting his further detention for administrative reasons. This mixture of procedures was sometimes hard to understand for the prisoners involved, and often resulted in dramatic consequences such as hunger strikes, suicide attempts or aggressive behaviour. As a consequence of this research finding, a new cooperation agreement was reached between the Ministries of Justice and Interior, through which the OFA now decides more quickly on the administrative status of the foreign prisoner Circular letter nr. 84 of December 2004 reintroduced the original maximum period of 30 additional days in case of provisional release in view of expulsion. Since September 2005, nine "migration counsellors" (formerly "return agents") from the OFA work inside the prisons in order to hasten the administrative procedure and decision. An information leaflet on the administrative procedures has been developed and is now handed over to all foreign prisoners upon admission to the prison.

That doesn't mean that all problems have been solved. Illegal aliens who will be released provisionally with a view on expulsion, must agree with the expulsion as a condition of release. However, many of them have lived in Belgium for many years and may have a procedure pending on regularisation of their illegal status, sometimes they have no social or family ties left in the country of origin. If they return to Belgium after expulsion and are caught again, they will have to serve the remainder of their prison sentence, without having committed a new criminal offence. This is true even if they come back to Belgium with a legal document, e.g. a tourist visa.

A second problem results from the fact that all these forms of early release require some preparation by the psychosocial service of the prison. Although the number of psychologists in prison has been vastly increased since the Act of 1998 on conditional release, many psychosocial services still find themselves overburdened. This results sometimes in long waiting lists to see prisoners and to answer their queries. This may in its turn postpone the preparation and organisation of the early release and result in longer prison stays. Language problems may arise because of the complexity of the different procedures. But specific cultural problems are also mentioned here. Following the Act of 5 march 1998 on conditional release, the psychosocial service of the prison where a sentence is served must evaluate the possibilities for and efforts towards social reintegration of the prisoner, his behaviour inside the prison, his attitude towards the victims, the risks of relapse into recidivism. For sexual offenders, any form of early release must be coupled to a specialised advice by a psychosocial service and the acceptance of specialised treatment upon release (Act November 2000). Cultural problems may arise due to a different attitude towards certain forms of delinquency, for example linked to matters of honour or to help provided to fellow illegal aliens. The emphasis in the Belgian conditional release system on individual responsibility, guilt and reparation towards the victims of crime may be foreign to more collectivistic cultures, or to foreign prisoners who commit offences to survive. Psychological tests also raise cultural problems: standard tests are based on Western thinking, leading to interpretation problems towards other cultures, and psychologists working in the prisons are trained in Western psychology, with often very little knowledge of ethno psychiatry or –psychology. These cultural problems may subsist even when the pure language problem can be solved.

2.10 Aftercare – Probation

Foreign prisoners who on the basis of their residence permit when apprehended are released under conditional release are entitled to the same guidance and aftercare as national citizens. There are no specific programmes for these prisoners.

2.11 Staff

Prison staff has no special training to deal with foreign prisoners. As mentioned above (II.1.1.) language and communication are very important in prison, where many aspects of prison regime must be asked for, verbally or in written form. Where none of the common languages can help (Dutch, French, English), language problems are solved through the use of fellow prisoners, which may raise other problems.

Staff also mentions cultural problems during the interviews and focus groups. Cultural characteristics are said to influence personal interactions in prison, both between prisoners and staff and amongst prisoners. More patriarchal cultures may lead to refusal by male prisoners to accept the authority of female guards, to talk about personal matters with a female psychologist or to be treated by a female nurse or doctor. Some groups are seen as presenting a more disrespectful, insubordinate and oppositional behaviour, without however resorting to physical violence (e.g. North Africans), while other groups seem rather quiet and well adapted to prison life but become easily violent in case of conflicts (e.g. Eastern Europeans). In some cultures, violent private resolution of conflicts is seen as the norm, with both conflicting parties refusing any interference by prison staff (e.g. Albanians). Some prisoners may also justify their behaviour by referring to their religion, which according to prison staff makes it more difficult for them to assess an infringement on the rules.

Both prisoners and staff mention racism. Prison guards of foreign origin mention institutional racism by the prison administration, as only Belgian citizens can become staff members, and important functions are said to be reserved for native Belgian citizens. The prison environment is described as a very closed field, in which other staff members, despite their positive influence on foreign prisoners, do not accept guards of foreign origin. Expectations are much higher towards guards of foreign origin, and any mistake or fault is said to lead to more extreme reactions by their colleagues. They may also suffer from an additional stigma by foreign visitors of the same origin, who consider them as "traitors".

Foreign prisoners refer to the lack of respect by prison guards, especially the younger ones, and to discrimination in the application of disciplinary reports and sanctions. The more privileged jobs and positions of trust inside the prison are also said to be always granted to Belgian prisoners. Some prisoners assume this is due to the higher level of communication necessary for these jobs, while others mention that foreign prisoners without a permit of residence are automatically seen as presenting a higher risk of escape, and are therefore never granted these positions of trust.

Prison staff also mentions racism amongst prisoners based on nationality. According to a survey of prison directors performed by the "Centre against racism and xenophobia", racism is not very prominent in the prisons though and certainly not a priority problem[35].

2.12 Projects

As a result of this research financed by the King Boudewijn Foundation, the Foundation took several initiatives. At general policy level, a meeting was organised with senior officials of the Ministries of Justice and Interior in order to solve the problems relating to the interaction between criminal and administrative procedures and the ensuing delays in early release of foreign prisoners. This resulted in the above mentioned new cooperation agreement and the introduction of "migration counsellors" working in the prisons in order to fasten the administrative decision-making. The Foundation also financed the translation of a new information leaflet with the rights and duties of the prisoners resulting from the new Prison Act of 2005.

Table 4: administrative status of foreign prisoners – absolute numbers (14 November 1993-2003)

		Uncertain residence	Residence	No residence	Residence
Year	Total	Not mentioned	Unknown to OF	Expulsion decided	Residence granted
1993	3122	33	3012	19	58
1994	3031	40	2916	22	53
1995	3131	44	3020	20	47
1996	3164	45	3053	17	49
1997	3208	212	2850	54	92
1998	2951	471	2066	88	326
1999	3209	498	2054	82	498
2000	3606	542	2231	96	737
2001	3514	715	1977	89	733
2002	3936	1511	1105	403	917
2003	3917	1411	1115	447	944

Source: Snacken, Keulen & Winkelmans (2004):

[1]. We prefer to use average daily data, but these are not available for the last years. The use of data on a certain date can give a misleading picture since they only refer to the situation on that moment. Calculations are based on the average daily prison population.

---

[35] Mentioned by Patrick Charlier of the "Centre against racism and xenophobia" during the focus group on 26 January 2004.

3 ADMINISTRATIVE DETENTION OF FOREIGN PRISONERS

Asylum seekers who have been refused asylum and illegal aliens who have not been granted residence or have not been regularised must leave the country. In case of failure to leave, they may be detained for the time strictly necessary for the organisation of the forced repatriation. Such administrative detention normally takes place in a closed centre of the Ministry of Interior. Administrative detention is normally imposed for a maximum of two months, but can be extended to five months. Only when necessary for the protection of public order or national security can it be further prolonged to the absolute maximum of eight months. Appeal against the administrative detention can be lodged with the investigation chamber of the correctional court.

There are now five closed centres: three for illegal aliens (Merksplas, Brugge, Vottem; the first two are former prisons, capacity around 160 places), one Centre for Repatriation ("127bis", located at Steenokkerzeel, capacity 192 places) and one Transit Centre for asylum seekers arriving at the National Airport ("127", located in the Transit zone of the National Airport, capacity 100 places). To these must be added the "INAD" Centre ("inadmissables"), also located inside the airport zone, taking in persons arriving at the airport without legal documents and who are refused entry into the country (capacity 30 places).

According to the Annual Report 2004 of the OFA[36], 7.622 persons have been detained in the closed centres during 2004. The average number of detainees during 2004 was 513. The different centres had an average population of 105 for Brugge, 145 for Merksplas, 106 for Vottem and 98 for the 127bis. The Transit centres 127 and INAD had an average of 49 and 10 detainees. The average length of stay in these centres was resp. 56, 51, 44, 19, 9 and 2 days. In 2004, 5.612 detainees were expelled, mainly through repatriation (4.065), while 1.866 were released.

The regime and functioning of the closed centres are regulated by a Royal Decree of 2 August 2002 and monitored by the "General Coordination and Control Department" of the OFA. The Royal Decree shows similarities with the Prison Act of 2005, as it was broadly based on an earlier version of the Draft Prison Act. Some examples: right to unlimited correspondence (art.19), daily telephone (art.24), right to and freedom of religion (art.16, 46-50), right to legal aid (art.62).

There are however some notable differences, through which the inmates of the closed centres are entitled to more or broader rights than prisoners: the inmates must receive a leaflet with the house rules, which must be explained to them by a staff member in a language they can understand, if necessary through the assistance of an interpreter (art.17), they can request help with reading or writing of letters (art.22), they are entitled to free writing paper and if necessary stamps (art.23), they must be able to talk undisturbed with their visitors (art.29), they have the right to receive visits by diplomatic or consular agents every day from 8.00 to 22.00 (art.32), they have the right to receive daily visits of minimum one hour from their close family (art.34, except in the Transit Centre 127, located inside the airport), they may call their lawyer every day for free from 8.00 to 22.00 (art.63). The director of the centre must foster the general development of the inmates (art.69) by organising recreational, cultural and sports activities (art.70), every centre must have a library (art.71) and all inmates must have access to the media (art.72). Activities

---

[36] Annual Report of the Office for Foreigners' Affairs, Ministry of Interior, 2004.

can be organised by NGO's if authorised by the Ministry of Interior (art.73). A complaint committee has been established as of 9 September 2003. On the other hand, no work is provided for these detainees.

A remarkable feature concerning staff: nothing is said about the duties and responsibilities of staff (no reference to "dynamic security" as in the Prison Act, nothing about language or communication problems), but religious counsellors and external services or NGO's must have "a neutral attitude towards" or "not act against" the legislation on the closed centres and the legislation on entry and residence of foreigners (art.51, 79). Similarly, the social and medical services must offer counselling to the inmates during their stay in the centre, "prepare them for a possible repatriation" and "guide them into acceptance of the decision concerning their administrative status" (art.68). Many efforts are made by the OFA to improve relations with diplomatic and consular services, in order to foster swifter identification and repatriation of the foreigners and with the International Organisation for Migration in order to stimulate voluntary return to the country of origin[37].

Not surprisingly, life inside the closed centres is rather strained. Frustrations of the inmates run high when their expectations are disappointed (failed appeal against refusal of asylum or regularisation), the communal regime limits individual privacy, despite regulations to the contrary (art.83), and foreigners who have not been involved in criminal activities resent being detained together with former prisoners awaiting their expulsion. Recurrent complaints by staff about verbal and physical aggressions and subjective feelings of insecurity have led to the establishment of a working group on "violence control". Proposals formulated by this working group relate mainly to a better training of staff to cope with aggression and the improvement of some regime aspects for the inmates, thus improving their responsibilities and self-esteem[38]. Several collective protests erupted in the closed centre of Merksplas in 2004, often requiring police intervention, of which one followed a suicide of an inmate of the centre. In the closed centre of Vottem, a few inmates committed arson, thus reducing the capacity of the centre with 1/3. During each of its visits to Belgium, CPT inspected several of these centres:

- the former Repatriation Centre of Walem and the Transit Centre 127 at the airport in 1993 (there were no closed centres for illegal aliens at that time yet),
- the INAD, the Transit Centre 127, the Repatriation Centre 127bis and the closed centre of Merksplas in 1997,
- the forced expulsions of foreigners in 2001 and 2005,
- and finally a follow up visit to the INAD, the Transit Centre 127 and the Repatriation Centre 127bis in 2005.

CPT criticisms were most severe for:
- the Repatriation Centre of Walem in 1993, where material conditions and regime were considered unacceptable and where staff was composed of military conscripts; the centre was closed in 1994;
- the transit zone of the airport in 1993, where material conditions were considered unacceptable;

---

[37] Annual Report of the Office for Foreigners' Affairs, Ministry of Justice, ibidem p.78-79.
[38] Ibidem, p. 76-77.

- the INAD and Transit Centre 127 in 1997 and 2005, for their lack of possibilities for visits by family and even by lawyers and the lack of regime;
- the lack of juridical information offered to illegal aliens generally in 1997, and more particularly at the INAD in 2005, concerning the different administrative procedures relating to entry and residence;
- the violence and the techniques used by police forces in 1993, 1997 and 2001 to ensure forced expulsion of foreigners resisting their departure; this had improved by 2005.

Positive aspects were mentioned in 1997 concerning the material circumstances, the regime of activities and the improved staff training in the closed centre of Merksplas, the Transit Centre 127 and the Repatriation Centre 127bis.

Unaccompanied minors (UAM): Belgium has the third largest number of UAM in Europe (1.050 in 2002)[39]. The Act of 1980 on the entry and residence of foreigners does not distinguish between adults and minors. By Act of 24 December 2002, a guardianship service has been established for UAM, defined as "persons younger than 18y, unaccompanied by a person who exercises parental authority or guardianship according to the national legislation of the minor, who is citizen of a country outside the European Economic Area, and who has either requested refugee status or does not meet the conditions for entry or residence inside the country". The guardianship service must identify the UAM, assess their age (if necessary through a medical test), trace their family and coordinate the stay of the UAM in Belgium with the asylum authorities and the reception centres. Guardians are not required to have a specific background, but are trained on the job in several issues concerning children.

The open reception centres are under the competence of the Ministry of Social Integration through the agency Fedasil. According to a policy paper of 21 March 2004 by this Ministry, reception of UAM should follow a dual model. In a first phase, taking 14 days at most, the UAM is brought to a safe place with access to psychological, social, administrative and juridical assistance for observation and orientation. In a second phase, the UAM is transferred to a reception centre of Fedasil or the Red Cross, is placed in a specific centre for UAM created in 2002 or placed in a foster family or in a flat with the help of the children welfare system. The specific centres have multidisciplinary staff and cooperate with other NGO's involved in children's' rights. In reality, many UAM are caught when entering the country at the airport and will be placed in the INAD or the Transit centre 127, or will be placed in an open or closed centre for asylum seekers, which do not always have adequate facilities for children. The disappearance of a number of UAM from these centres illustrates the problem of their vulnerability to organised sexual exploitation.

UAM have the same rights as other children to medical assistance and education. Special classes have been created to help UAM to quickly learn one of the national languages, and all children are entitled to go to school, notwithstanding their illegal status. UAM are entitled to legal assistance free of charge as soon as they arrive at the border. This may however not always be the case in practice, especially during the first stage of the reception. The procedure for asylum seeking is the same for adults or minors, there

---

[39] European Union 2002, Migration and asylum in Europe: the largest numbers are found in the UK (6.200) and the Netherlands (3.232).

are no specific considerations for their status as UAM and immigration services are not trained to deal with minors[40].

4 NATIONALS DETAINED ABROAD

On the 13 June 2006, 523 Belgian nationals were detained abroad, of which 83% were detained in other Western European countries. The top countries are Spain (27%), France (22%), Germany (12%) and Great Britain (7.5%). Only 1.7% are held in Eastern European prisons. Morocco scores highest within the non-European countries (4.6%), followed by the USA (2.3%). The main reason for detention is drugs (57%), followed by violence (6.3%), theft (4%), sexual offences (3.4%) and murder (2.9%). 3.6% are held in custody in view of extradition[41]. There is no statistical information on the length of the sentences or the personal characteristics of the detainees.

The department of International Judicial Cooperation of the Ministry of Foreign Affairs is responsible for the consular help and advice to these nationals detained abroad. No other organisations are involved. A pamphlet "Help and guidance for Belgians in foreign prisons", with information concerning the possibilities and restrictions for consular help, is issued by the department, can be found on its Website[42] and is distributed by the Belgian embassies and consulates to Belgian prisoners abroad. It explains that foreign authorities do not have an obligation to inform the embassy or consulate of every prisoner, so the prisoner should formally request the local authority to do so on the basis of the Convention of Vienna concerning consular help (1963). If no Belgian embassy or consulate is present in the country of detention, the embassy or consulate of another European Union member state can be informed, within the framework of the Agreement on European Consular Help.

Consular help will vary according to the individual situation and the country. Examples given in the pamphlet are: to inform family and friends of the detention, to help the prisoner to establish and keep contacts with family or with the consular services, to monitor the humane circumstances of the detention (in particular food and medical and dental care) and the absence of discriminatory treatment, to check on the fairness and the speed of the trial in accordance with local legislation and procedures, to inform family on the justice and prison system of the country of detention, the average length of trials, the case law and conditions for early release. Consular help does not include financial help, but can mediate in order to foster the possibilities for the prisoner to buy food or to provide for other basic needs.

Information is also provided concerning the Convention for the transfer of sentenced prisoners of 1983, ratified by Belgium in 1990 (see above I. 5.2.4.). It lists the countries that are party to the Convention and the conditions for its application. The bilateral agreement with Morocco is also mentioned.

No special after care is provided upon return to Belgium, there is no difference with other prisoners released in Belgium. If a prisoner has no family ties left in Belgium and

---

[40] C. Joppart, *Separated children in Europe. Questionnaire for country assessment: Belgium*, Brussels 2003, Defence for Children International Belgium.

[41] Information provided by the department for International Judicial Cooperation of the Ministry of Foreign Affairs on 13 June 2006.

[42] http://www.diplomatie.be/nl/services/prisondetail.asp?textID=659

has insufficient financial means to survive, the department of International Judicial Cooperation may ask the Red Cross to support the prisoner upon his arrival and look for housing, e.g. through the welfare services of his last place of residence. Occasionally, the department advances money to pay the return flight ticket.

Attention to the situation of nationals detained abroad in Belgian media and public opinion is generally low, apart from certain exceptional cases (cf. media attention and public sympathy for a Belgian bus driver imprisoned in Russia for a traffic accident, or another driver supposedly framed for drug trafficking and held for many years in a prison in Tanger, which lead to the recent movie "The hell of Tanger").

5 EVALUATIONS AND RECOMMENDATIONS

Social exclusion is present at different stages and in different forms for foreign prisoners. First, some ethnic minority groups, such as Moroccans, and many illegal aliens live in poor neighbourhoods in bad socio-economic circumstances. Second, this lack of social integration is often seen by actors of the criminal justice system to enhance the risk of criminality or recidivism, resulting in a higher application of deprivation of liberty, at the level of both remand custody and sentencing. Third, foreigners or ethnic minorities face different problems during detention, ranging from severe language and communication problems to religious or cultural conflicts or racism. Fourth, prisoners who have no legal permit of residence will be excluded from some regime aspects such as prison leave or electronic monitoring. Fifth, the combination of criminal and administrative procedures hampers the preparation and swift application of early release procedures. Sixth, when expelled to their country of origin, foreign prisoners may find themselves isolated from their real family and social ties, which may still be in Belgium.

Belgium has a large proportion of foreign prisoners (44% in 2004) and prisons have to cope with more than 100 different nationalities. The King Boudewijn Foundation commissioned the research on which this paper is partly based in 2004, bringing to the fore the difficult situation of foreign prisoners in Belgian prisons. Problems inside the prisons and concerning the procedures of early release were listed and discussed with the relevant authorities. Some of the problems have been tackled since, but many remain. Pressed by prison overcrowding, administrative detention of foreigners who have not committed an offence is now seldom implemented in a prison, and detention in a closed centre of the Ministry of Interior is the norm. These closed centres however also face severe tensions and conflicts. Regime and activities should be further improved for prisoners and detainees, and staff of prisons and centres alike should receive more training enabling them to cope with the multicultural and stressful environment in which they have to work. Transfer of sentenced prisoners to their country of origin for the implementation of the sentences could offer a solution for those prisoners whose social ties are still there. This would however also require sufficient guarantees that living conditions in all prisons and centres respect human dignity.

Chapter 4

Cyprus

Andreas Ellinas

1 INTRODUCTION

Cyprus is a small island in the eastern Mediterranean Sea and it is the closest European country to the Middle East and Asia. It joined the EU as a full member in 2005. Cyprus currently applies the Anglo-Saxon legal system due to the fact that the island was a British colony until 1960. There is only one penitentiary institution in Cyprus (Central Prison Nicosia) which operates under a new comprehensive legislative and regulatory framework that was put in place in 1996 and 1997. This legislation incorporates the European Prison Rules and conforms to the standards contained in the relevant instruments of the Council of Europe.

1.1 Overview of Penalties and Measures

A person can only be deprived of his or her liberty after having been convicted by a court for committing an offence, or when reasons are evident that require a person to be detained while awaiting trial. The penalties that are imposed by the courts in Cyprus depend upon the seriousness of the offence and the likelihood of the offender committing further offences. As far as discipline, security, punishment and penalties are concerned, the Disciplinary Code is applied equally to everyone. According to the law, all prisoners are equal and foreigners have the right to request legal aid if they cannot afford legal representation themselves. In case either Cypriot or foreign prisoners do not have financial means the state shall provide legal aid and - in addition to this - foreigners have the right to an interpreter during police interviewing and through the course of their trial. The Prison Law and regulations are applicable to all prisoners. However, in some cases security issues can make it difficult for foreigners to receive the full benefits of the law, which also include home leaves. In exchange, they receive additional rights to more visits and telephone calls.

1.2 Overview of the Prison System

The issue of foreign prisoners is considered to be of major concern for the Prison Department because of their large number in comparison to Cypriot prisoners. The key factor that influences the proportion of the foreign population in prison is the fact that a greater proportion of foreigners are involved in criminal activity, for a number of reasons:

-   The large numbers of tourists, who are unaware of Cypriot law
-   Foreign workers (legal and illegal)
-   Illegal entries into the country from unauthorised ports
-   Foreign residents
-   Foreigners taking advantage of the geographical and political setting of Cyprus (financial services etc)

Due to the geographical position of Cyprus, immigrants come in search of a better life. An explanation for the flow of illegal immigrants to Cyprus is the fact that Asian and African countries are very close to the island and migrants can come easily by boat. Based on several sources of information, today there are around 40,000 illegal foreigners (coming predominantly from Pakistan, Sri-Lanka and Bangladesh) in Cyprus, who initially enter the country as students or seasonal workers and then fail to conform to the conditions of their visas. It is often the case that many apply for asylum when their visa is cancelled or expires. In Cyprus, foreign workers are employed as manual or unskilled workers, (for instance in agriculture, farming etc), but also as house servants and in the nursing of elderly people. Many illegal immigrants come from the Turkish occupied areas of Cyprus in which the Cypriot authorities are unable to enforce the law. The Turkish occupied areas are linked with Turkey and do not comply fully with illegal immigration rules, thus allowing movement from the northern part of Cyprus. Furthermore, because of the fact that many illegals have no proof of their personal details, their Embassies often refuse to issue them new travel documents and - as a consequence - they are detained in police custody until their identity has been verified. European citizens are usually convicted for crimes such as drug dealing and possession, assault, burglary and theft. European citizens tend to have fewer problems in organizing new travel documents and as soon as they have completed their sentence the immigration service decides whether they can stay or are to be expelled. The 2006 budget for the Prison Department was approx. 32.000.000 Euros. The Prison Administration includes:

- One Prison Director,
- Two Senior Superintendents
- Four Superintendents
- Eight Inspectors,
- Forty non-commission officers
- Two hundred and sixty one wardens
- Two trainers who are responsible for the prisoners' education program

The wings of the prison have a residential capacity of about 340, and currently hold 577 prisoners. The prison population on 17.4.2006 was 499 convicted prisoners and 78 unconvicted, of whom 340 were foreign prisoners.

1.2.1 Organisational Structure

The central penitentiary institution consists of eight closed prison wings, seven for male offenders and one for female offenders, as well as one wing for pre-trial prisoners. In addition to the above, there are blocks for the accommodation of young offenders, a top security block, an isolation centre (which is used to separate prisoners from the remaining prison population), one open section and one 'Centre for the Guidance and Extra-institutional Employment of Prisoners'. In addition to the central prison in Cyprus, there are detention cells in the police stations in all districts. These are the responsibility of the police and are used to detain suspects of crimes under the courts warrants or any other legal authority, including foreigners who have been arrested for illegal entry or under the order of the immigration official according to the authorization given by the Law on Immigration.

1.2.2 Foreign Prisoners

According to the philosophy of the above law relating to the imprisonment of offenders as a judicial sentence, deprivation of liberty has the purpose not only to keep them in secure conditions, but also to apply various programs in the correctional institution to reform, re-educate and rehabilitate prisoners in order for them to become useful members of society. The Department of Central Prisons is under the administration of the Ministry of Justice and Public Order. Nicosia Central Prison receives all categories of convicted and pre-trial prisoners of both genders and all age groups. No person shall be admitted into the prison as a prisoner unless under a judicial warrant. The prison system places paramount importance in the understanding of different cultures and origins of detainees. There are strict rules and regulations concerning any form of discrimination, whether it is due to racial origin, colour, language, as well as religious, political or other beliefs concerning ethnic or social background. Discrimination is strictly prohibited and severe disciplinary measures are to be imposed if these rules are broken or not adhered to.

1.3 Overview of the Involvement of Consulates, Embassies, Cypriot Ministries and Probation Service, NGO's etc

The prison living conditions, catering, administration practices and everything concerning the prison system are supervised by the Prison Board, the Commissioner of Law and the Ombudsman, who have the right to initiate investigations for wrong practices. In addition to the above, the prison is also subject to frequent visits by the C.P.T., advising for further possibilities of improvement. In order to facilitate communication between prisoners with the above mentioned authorities, the prison administration has installed mailing boxes in various areas of the prison where the prisoners can communicate freely in writing without any censorship.

1.4 Overview of Trends

1.4.2 Characteristics of the Foreign Prison Population

According to prison statistics, in the year 2005 there were 1,187 detainees:
-   650 (54.75%) were foreigners,
-   459 (70.61%) of whom were imprisoned for less than six months
-   37 foreign offenders on drug charges
-   54 foreign offenders for offences against the person
-   nine foreign offenders for sexual crimes
-   150 foreign offenders for offences related to property
-   4 foreign offenders for malicious injuries to property / criminal damage
-   31 foreign offenders on forgery charges,
-   365 foreign offenders on other charges, like guns and ammunitions, illegal entry & stay, fines.

Table 1: Foreign prisoners by age (2005).

Age	Male	Female	Total
16-20 years old	46	4	50
21-24 years old	132	7	139
25-29 years old	180	12	192
30-39 years old	172	18	190
40-49 years old	53	9	62
50+ years old	15	2	17
Total	598	52	650

According to the above table the majority of foreign offenders are 25-39 years old.

2 TREATMENT OF FOREIGN PRISONERS

2.1 General Information

According to the constitution, no form of discrimination is allowed against any person. Discriminations on the grounds of ethnicity, language, country of origin, and religion are prohibited and all people are to be treated equally in relation to the law. Therefore, foreign prisoners have the same benefits and same rights as the Cypriot prisoners provided no security issues give reason for differentiated treatment.

The legislator takes into consideration what the Constitution states in respect for Human Rights and the equal treatment of prisoners. The Prison Law and regulations include measures which forbid discriminations of any kind (for example race, colour, language, religion); concurrently, it includes disciplinary penalties for the staff and for the prisoners in cases of non-adherence. Despite the provision in law sometimes there are cases of minor discriminations, which certainly are not deliberate, but rather are subject to special circumstances such as:

- The foreign prisoners do not have six visits per month as is the case for Cypriots because their families live abroad. But, in the event of their families being in Cyprus, special arrangements are made to allow visits every day during their stay in Cyprus. If the foreign prisoners have local friends and acquaintances that can offer them psychological support and help during their imprisonment, they are permitted to visit the prisoners.

- Prisoners from countries that have a bilateral agreement with the Republic of Cyprus for the transfer of convicted prisoners, or which have signed the European Arrest Warrant, are moved to the open prison which is the last stage before their reintroduction into society, provided they meet the necessary requirements.

- All prisoners receive wages according to the work assigned to them and according to the effort and industry they show during their imprisonment, but sometimes this is not enough. Often foreigners apply to the Welfare Committee for financial support. This is examined and assistance is provided based upon the needs of the offender.

- Foreign detainees are permitted to make home visits like Cypriots do, so long as their normal residence or their families are in Cyprus. Such home visits can be both supervised and unsupervised.

2.2 Living Conditions and Facilities

There is the aim of accommodating sentenced and non-sentenced prisoners separately from each in different wings. However, due to overcrowding in the prison this cannot always be fully achieved. The Evaluation Committee, after gathering the relevant information, places the prisoner in a wing and then assigns him/her to working activities. There is no special approach of separation for the placement of foreigners to the wings, and great effort is given to increase socialization and communication among foreigners. In these cases, arrangements are made in order for the foreigner to be placed in a cell with a prisoner of his/her own nationality, so that he/she can communicate and have company.

2.3 Reception and Admission

A general register is kept for every prisoner admitted into the prison, with numbered pages in which personal data are kept such as for instance marital status, the offence of which he/she has been convicted, the courts decision, as well as the date and time of admission and discharge. In addition to the registration information, each prisoner has to go through physical and mental examinations in order to diagnose his/her physical and mental state and to determine whether the person is substance dependent or has a disturbed personality. The results of the examinations are collected and stored in a prisoner's personal record.

On reception, all prisoners - including foreigners - are subjected to a body search and a search of their luggage and belongings. They are then directed to the Admission and Release Office, where each prisoner has to give his/her personal details in order to create a comprehensive database and to further ascertain the needs and requirements of each individual. Foreign prisoners are also informed that they are allowed to be repatriated or to be transferred to their home country to serve their sentence, so long as their country is signatory to the convention for the repatriation of prisoners. They also have the right to apply for political asylum. In such a case assistance is provided for the completion of the application forms.

2.4 Work - Education – Training – Sports - Recreation

The prison administration is bound by law to provide education and training (improving skills) to all prisoners who wish to further their education All prisoners sentenced to imprisonment of more than one month and who wish to benefit from the programs granted by the Prison Law as well as to receive work allowance are in work (classified by the Classification Committee). If they cannot be employed for health reasons due to a recommendation by the Medical Officer or for other reasons after a decision by the director they are excluded from work or sports. The organisation and the methods of the work are as similar as possible to those of free society in order to prepare the prisoners for the conditions of work that they will encounter after release. Detainees awaiting trial are not bound to work. However, they can apply to the Classification Committee and work will be offered to them. They are entitled to receive the appropriate wages once they have been issued a working schedule. This is great assistance to the foreign prisoners who have nobody to look after them.

Prison officers and prison educational staff, in association with departmental psychologists, psychiatrists, general practitioners, nursing staff, and social workers deliver lectures and awareness programs to prisoners. According to law, participation in academic education is voluntary. The overall curriculum is organized by the education staff and other professionals, and it is their responsibility to make the curriculum attractive and interesting, according to the prisoners needs. The prisoners may also borrow books (books are available in foreign languages) from the prison library. Presently, the prisoners' school offers:

- Adult basic education, including literature and maths
- Computer education, (access to the internet is not allowed)
- Expressive arts such as painting, design, copper work, iconography, dance and drama. (The prisoners' theatre team performs both in and outside of the prison. Membership to the group is open to foreigners as well)
- Languages such as Greek (for foreigners), and English
- Traditional education such as history and geography
- Psychology
- Drug and alcohol education
- Health education such as sexually transmitted diseases and other
- First aid
- Cooking, gardening, plumbing
- Chess

Each prisoner has the right to participate in any of the physical exercise programs. Specially trained personnel supervise the prisoners for physical fitness, instrumental gymnastics, team games and contests, both in and outside of prison (a specialized prison officer and a gymnast from the Cyprus Organization of Athletics train a football team). The sporting activities are also available to foreign prisoners.

2.5 Food – Religion – Personal hygiene – Medical care

The food provided to the prisoners is healthy, nutritious, suitably prepared, of reasonable variety, satisfactory in terms of quantity and quality and adjusted in accordance to dietary principles and modern hygiene. The diet is set by the director with close reference to recommendations from the medical officer of the prison, who takes into consideration the age, health, work and – as far as possible - the religious beliefs of the inmates. Every detainee has the right to perform his/her religious duties. Religious representatives are allowed to visit the prisoners in order to offer them guidance. Yet the conversion of a prisoner by another prisoner or by any representative of any religion or doctrine is prohibited. There are both a mosque and a Christian church within the prison. Every Friday - or whenever the case arises - the Muslim prisoners pray in the mosque and the Christians every Sunday in church. They all have the right to celebrate their religious events, religious festivals are observed, and special diets are available to them.

Every effort is made to place prisoners in accommodation where they can be with their fellow countrymen, so that they can speak their own language and share their religious beliefs (if this is what they want). The guards make sure that the prisoners follow the generally accepted code of rules of personal hygiene. These include the cleanliness of communal areas of the prison, of their personal cells and of the public utility rooms. (The department provides all the items that are required for cleaning the prison).

Prisoners have the right to wear their own clothes (in order to reduce stigmatisation, uniforms are abolished). The prison provides every newcomer with a set of clothing as well as toiletries for personal hygiene, and continues to provide them until they are able to buy the items themselves.

Health checks are conducted as soon as possible after admission. They include a full examination, blood tests (non compulsory), registration of the medical history of the family, etc. A general practitioner, qualified nursing personnel, a psychiatrist with assistants, two psychologists, and a work therapist offer their services in the prison on a daily basis. A part time dentist provides his services to the prison. All medical requirements are offered through the medical services of the Republic.

2.6 Consular and Legal Help

Immediately after being admitted to the prison every prisoner is entitled to appoint a legal advisor or to apply to the court for free legal aid. Foreigners have the right to ask for a person who contributes to the amelioration of the special problems that are caused by them being in custody, and especially a person that speaks their own language.

Representatives from the Embassies and the Consulates are notified by the prison administration and are permitted to visit a prisoner at any time as long as they arrange an appointment through the department for suitable hours.

Legal aid is approved for all prisoners in pre-trial detention in court if they are not financially capable to appoint a lawyer. If the court approves a prisoner's request for legal aid, then it will appoint a legal representative. However, after his/her conviction, he/she is not entitled to any form of legal help.

2.7 Contact with the Outside World

The prisoners' communication with the outside world is of vital importance, both to the socialization in prison as well as to the gradual reintegration into the conditions of free society. When a prisoner enters the prison the department is responsible for setting up all the necessary procedures for informing the prisoner's family that their relative has been imprisoned. As far as foreign prisoners are concerned, the prison department informs the Embassy or Consulate.

Telephone communication with the outside world is allowed for all prisoners. Cypriot prisoners are allowed four telephone calls per month, whereas foreign prisoners are entitled to eight, because they cannot receive frequent visits from their families. If required, the department provides free telephone cards to those who can not afford to buy them.

All prisoners are allowed up to six visits per month. There are special procedures for the foreign prisoners regarding family visitors. Also, the monthly number of visits to which they are entitled can be increased to eight, depending on the discretion of the director. This adjustment can be made because the Cypriot prisoners have the advantage of home leaves so long as the Classification Committee approves them – as well as the possibility of being placed in the open prison.

Every day, each wing is provided with local and foreign newspapers (Daily Press) and magazines. Additionally, all cells in the new wings of blocks "five" and "eight" have televisions that receive all of the local television channels. In blocks "one" and "two" prisoners can watch TV in the communal rooms except for offenders who have been sentenced to more than four years imprisonment, who are permitted to have there own television sets in theirs cells. A decision has been made to allow all prisoners, including foreigners to have their own TV in their cell. All prisoners can borrow books and magazines in many languages.

2.8 Re-integration Activities - Prison Leave

The purpose of detention in prisons - besides securing the prisoners - is to attempt to change their behaviour so that they can become capable and respectable members of society. This is to be achieved through social training, work, and support from their families. Foreign prisoners who are granted temporary exit permission or a home leave are divided into three categories:
-    Those who will remain in Cyprus after their release,
-    Those whose country has signed a statement of intent with the Republic of Cyprus for the transfer of convicted people, and
-    Those whose families are permanent residents in Cyprus.

For prisoners who have a criminal or disciplinary offence pending against them, and those who for safety reasons are not permitted to exit the prison, the Classification Committee only decides for a supervised exit permit. The open prison is the last stage before a detainee is discharged. It operates in the outer walls, and prisoners stay, work and move under low security conditions, yet still in accordance with the same principles of conduct, discipline and order that apply to the rest of the prisoners. The privileges of the open prison include free visitations, no locking up during the night and the permission for temporary leave. There is also the guidance centre, which is the last stage before their release, and operates close to the prison. Prisoners who are sent to the centre serve the rest of their sentence in conditions of restricted and controlled freedom with the purpose of their gradual reintegration into free society. Foreign prisoners have the right to be in the centre under the condition that they will remain in Cyprus after their release. There is no parole system currently in place in Cyprus.

2.9 Release - Expulsion

After a foreigner has been convicted, the migration office is responsible for whether or not he is to be expelled. Even European citizens who have committed a serious offence such as murder, drugs offences, robbery or burglary come under the same rule. If the decision of the migration office is for the offender to be expelled from Cyprus, then the offender has the right to appeal before the Supreme Court. In this event the offender remains in custody until the court has made its final decision.

2.10 Aftercare – Probation

Before their release, all prisoners who have been sentenced to more than six months – including foreigners – can request financial assistance before the Rehabilitation Committee. If the latter decides in their favour, they receive a small amount of money as well as a set of clothes to wear on the day of their release. The committee informs those who shall remain in Cyprus about the services and authorities that can assist them in finding employment and in filing applications for financial support, thus helping to gradually reintegrate them into free society.

3 ADMINISTRATIVE DETENTION OF FOREIGN PRISONERS

3.1 Institutions for Administrative Detention

Foreigners who are arrested for offences related to illegal entrance and/or residence in Cyprus, working without permission, or who have applied for political asylum, are kept in prison for the duration of the sentence. If an application for asylum is rejected then they are kept in police detention cells until their removal has been arranged and executed.

3.2 Ministry Responsible and Relevant Legislation

The police detention cells are under the supervision of the chief of the police department which in turn is supervised by the Ministry of Justice and Public Order.

3.3 Capacity of Institutions

The police operate detention cells in all districts. In Nicosia there are two detention cells specially designated for the detention foreigners: one operates inside the prison centre (wing 10) with a capacity for 65 persons, and one is in the district police station of Lakatamia in Nicosia, which is designed to hold up to five female detainees. Unfortunately, in Larnaka, Limasol and Paphos there are no specified cells for foreigners; instead they are held together with criminal offenders. The cells in Larnaka are designed to hold 11 male and three female detainees, while the facilities in Limassol can hold up to 43 male and 12 female prisoners. The cells in Paphos can hold up to nine males and four females.

3.4 Length of stay

Unfortunately, delays occur due to the fact that sometimes Embassies are slow in issuing travel documents and - as a result - the foreigners may be kept in custody for a long time while awaiting their expulsion.

3.6 Appeal Procedure

Foreigners have the right to appeal against the detention order before the Supreme Court within seven days and request their immediate release on the grounds of being illegally held in custody. According to Cypriot law, illegal entrance, residence and work without permission are criminal offences and can be punished with up to two years in prison. Currently, the penalties range from fifteen days to six months for first time offenders, but in cases in which the offender has had previous convictions, the penalty can be up to a year in length.

5 EVALUATION AND RECOMMENDATIONS

The state provides free education especially for those whose native language is not Greek so that they can be in a position to communicate with Cypriots. The government of Cyprus puts great effort into assimilating the foreigners into wider society while attempting to retain their national identity. Schools provide a special curriculum for foreign children in order to assist integration, and the welfare office provides assistance for a fresh start in life.

The Embassies should be more sensitive towards their citizens, and protect and advise them about local laws and customs. More cooperation is necessary when a foreigner is facing expulsion and his travelling papers need to be arranged quickly, in order to avoid unnecessary trouble and worry. Moreover, the government of Cyprus needs to conduct a study to evaluate the living conditions of the foreign prison population.

Foreigners must demand to be treated equally by the local population, but at the same time respect local values, customs and sensitivities. The relevant authorities must increase awareness in the general population concerning cohabitation with foreigners. Last but not least, it is very important to inform all foreigners who want to travel to the island about the penal and penitentiary laws that are in place in Cyprus. Before coming to the island, they must be aware of the laws and legislation, their rights and their obligations in order to avoid committing offences that can result in their imprisonment.

Chapter 5

Czech Republic

Petr Škvain

1 INTRODUCTION[1]

After the fall of the totalitarian regime in former Czechoslovakia at the end of 1989, fundamental social, political and economic changes occurred that subsequently influenced the structure of criminality. In the following years new types of crime emerged and the number of offending foreign nationals rapidly changed. Nowadays, criminality by foreign nationals is considered to be a very contemporary issue of security policy in the Czech Republic.[2]

The issue of how foreign nationals are treated in Czech penitentiary institutions became a priority for the Prison Service after the prison riots in January 2000. On the basis of cooperation with various parties, the basic theses and the most problematic moments in the treatment of foreign prisoners were named in May 2000.[3] Hunger strike, attempted uprising and escape of 'Russian speaking' prisoners accentuated the urgency of this task in November 2001 as well as hunger strike of 'former Soviet Union' prisoners in Praha-Pankrác remand prison in August 2002. Upon the assignment of the Prison Service of the Czech Republic, the Institute of Criminology and Social Prevention in Prague conducted research concerning foreign nationals in Czech penitentiary institutions in 2002-2003. Its main objective was to characterize the prison population, to determine the main problems concerning the treatment of foreign prisoners, and, on the basis of all information, to state specific recommendations.[4] The main objective of the Czech national study within the frame of the EU 'social exclusion' project on foreign prisoners in European penitentiary institutions is to provide information on the situation and the position of foreign prisoners in the Czech Republic and to state specific recommendations. The outcome of the national study will be used not only for the purpose of this project, but will be also submitted to other involved parties (the Institute of Criminology and Social Prevention in Prague, The Prison Service and Department of Criminal Law at the University of West Bohemia in Pilsen etc.).

1.1 Overview of Penalties and Measures

The penal sanctions provided in the Czech Criminal Code (law no. 140/1961 Coll.) are classified into penalties (punishments) and protective measures. According to Article 39 of The Charter of Fundamental Rights and Freedoms (law no. 2/1993 Coll.)[5], sanctions may be imposed only in accordance with the law. The penalties are exhaustively listed in Article 27 of the Czech Criminal Code (hereinafter the Criminal Code) and include imprisonment, community service, deprivation of titles, honours and awards, loss of a mili-

---

[1] Petr Škvain works with the Department of Criminal Law at the Faculty of Law, University of West Bohemia in Pilsen, The Czech Republic.

[2] Government of the Czech Republic (2005), Resolution of the Government of the Czech Republic, *The Report on Public Order and Internal Security in the Czech Republic in 2004 (compared with 2003)*, No. 827 of 29 June 2005, Government of the Czech Republic, Prague.

[3] Dočekal, M.(2001), *'Koncepce zacházení s vězněnými cizinci'* (*'Conception of treatment of foreign prisoners'*), České vězeňství (Journal of the Czech Prison Service), 1-2, pp. 48-50;.

[4] Scheinost, M. at al. (2004), *Výzkum cizích státních příslušníků v českých věznicích (Research on foreign nationals in the Czech penitentiary institutions)*, Institut pro kriminologii a sociální prevenci (The Institute of Criminology and Social Prevention), Praha (Prague).

[5] Charter of Fundamental Rights and Freedoms (law no. 2/1993 Coll.) is the part of the Czech Constitutional order.

171

tary rank, prohibition to participate in certain activities, forfeiture of property, fines, forfeiture of good or other property value, expulsion, and the prohibition of residence. The protective measures are listed in Article 71 of the Criminal Code and include protective treatment, seizure of goods or other property value, and protective rehabilitation that may be imposed only upon a juvenile. The objectives of these measures are mainly therapeutic, educational and preventive.[6] Protective measures are imposed irrespectively of the criminal responsibility of an offender, either as a separate sanction or in addition to penalties. In other words, the Criminal Code provides for a bifurcated system of sanctions. In the case of juvenile offenders, the sanctions may be imposed only according to *lex specialis* – The Juvenile Justice Act (law no. 218/2003 Coll.) – and include educational, protective and punitive measures.[7]

There are also cases in which penalties can be replaced by a prison sentence. According to Article 54 para.3 of the Criminal Code and Article 344 para.2 of the Criminal Procedural Code, a court can impose a substitute sentence of imprisonment for up to two years in cases of non-payment of fines. Also, should an offender who has been sentenced to community service not comply with his or her sentence, the court can convert the original sanction into a prison term, the length of which depends on the period of community service that had been originally adjudicated. In this context, two un-served hours of community service equal one day of imprisonment[8].

1.2 Overview of the Prison System

1.2.1 Organisational Structure

The Prison Service of the Czech Republic (hereinafter referred to as the Prison Service) was established according to the law no. 555/1992 Coll. on the 'prison guard' and the 'judicial guard' of the Czech Republic. It is state-financed, is allocated its own budget and is therefore an entity that is responsible for managing and accounting its own funds. The main purpose of the Prison Service is to provide administration and surveillance of both remand and regular prisons. It is responsible for observing the rules and conditions in pre-trial detention and regular imprisonment; for supporting prisoners by means of treatment programmes in detention in order to support their reintegration after release; for conducting research in the field of penology and using scientific findings within the framework of pre-trial detention and imprisonment; for establishing working conditions for prisoners, and providing them with health care etc.[9] The Prison Service consists of the prison guard, the judicial guard and the administrative service.[10] The prison guard patrols, transports and escorts prisoners and provides surveillance for both remand and regular prisons. The judicial guard provides security in courthouses, at public prosecutors' offices and at the Ministry of Justice. The administrative service makes administrative decisions and provides organizational, economical, educational and other

---

[6] Šámal, P., Král, V., Púry, F. (2004), *Trestní zákon – komentář (Commentary on the Criminal Code)*, C. H. Beck, Praha (Prague)

[7] Šámal, P., Válková H., Sotolář, A., Hrušáková M. (2004), *Zákon o soudnictví ve věcech mládeže – komentář (Commentary on the Juvenile Justice Act)*, C. H. Beck , Praha (Prague).

[8] art. 45a para 4 of the Criminal Code and art. 340b of the Criminal Procedural Code.

[9] See: Art. 2 of the law no. 555/1992 Coll., on prison and judicial guard of the Czech Republic.

[10] The prison and judicial guards have status of armed corps.

professional activities as well as health care. [11] The organizational structure of the Prison Service comprises The General Directorate, remand institutions, prisons and the Institute of Education. The Minister of Justice appoints and dismisses the Director General as head of the Prison Service who is responsible for all of its activities. Governors of both remand and regular prisons are appointed and dismissed by the Director General. At present, the Prison Service administers 35 prison facilities - 11 remand prisons and 24 regular prisons. At the end of 2005, the actual maximum capacity of the prison system was 18.784 places, each providing four square meters of space. 3,258 of these places were in remand institutions, while the remaining 15,526 were in regular prisons. The problem of prison overcrowding was registered particularly in some specific prisons (for example: Heřmanice – overcrowding 20,76 %, Kuřim 27,68 %, Odolov 15,08 %, Oráčov 16,56 %, Teplice 64,71 %, Valtice 24,53 %, Znojmo 35,44 %) and in the remand prisons of Brno (16, 98 %) and Ostrov (38, 55 %). As of 31 December 2005, as many as 10.474 persons were working for the Prison Service, of whom 6.431 were prison guards and judicial guards. A breakdown of the structure of employees reveals that 11,1% were working in educational programs, 58,1 % were active in security and surveillance and 13,7 % were working in administration. At the end of December 2005, 24% of all employees were women.[12]

Penitentiary institutions are classified into four basic categories according to the levels of surveillance and security: minimum security, medium security, high security and maximum security. Additionally, there are special prisons for juveniles, women and mothers with children. Different types of departments can also be located within the same institution so long as the purpose of imprisonment is not endangered.[13] According to the law on the state budget, the budget of the Prison Service for 2005 consisted of income indicators CZK 1,011,080,000 and expenditure indicators CZK 7,507,952,000. During the year 2005 the budget was cut and it was necessary to utilize finances from the reserve fund in order to be able to effectively carry out all tasks and activities. The Prison Service also faced increased expenditures due to increases in the price of materials, medicines and energies as well as a growth of the prison population. The total cost per prisoner per day was CZK 860 (+ CZK 11) in 2005.[14] In comparison to 2004 the prison population of 2005 slightly increased to 18.937 persons.[15] In 2005 the new concept for the development of the Czech prison system up to the year 2015 was introduced.[16]

---

[11] See: Art. 3 of the law no. 555/1992 Coll., on prison and judicial guard of the Czech Republic.

[12] The General Directorate (2006), Yearbook of the Prison Service 2005, The General Directorate of the Prison Service of the Czech Republic, Prague.

[13] The General Directorate (2006), Czech Prisons, The General Directorate of the Prison Service of the Czech Republic, Prague.

[14] The General Directorate (2006), Annual Report of the Activities of the Prison Service of the Czech Republic for 2005, The General Directorate of the Prison Service of the Czech Republic, Prague;

[15] As of 31 December 2005 (18 343 as of 31 December 2004).

[16] The Prison Service of the Czech Republic (2005), The Concept for the Development of the Czech Prison System up to 2015, The Prison Service of the Czech Republic, Prague.

1.2.2 Foreign nationals in the Czech Republic

In 2004 the total population of the Czech Republic was 10,206,923 to an area of 78,866 km². The population density was 129 persons per km². In 2004, the average unemployment rate was 8.3 %.[17] The Czech Republic is administratively divided into 14 self-governing regions. The largest ethnic groups are Ukrainians, Slovaks, Vietnamese, Poles, Russians and Germans.

Table no. 1 – Foreigners by category of residence, sex and citizenship in 2005

Country of citizenship	Total	incl.: Females*	% of females	Residence permits, total	Permanent residence	Asylum	Temporary EU/ Long-term residence	90-days-and-over visa
Total	**280 111**	**112481**	**40**	**258 306**	**110 598**	**1 799**	**145 909**	**21805**
EU 25 total	**87 143**	**34 019**	**39**	**87 089**	**42 202**	**1**	**44 886**	**54**
Belgium	299	67	22	299	144	-	155	-
Denmark	205	50	24	205	83	-	122	-
Estonia	41	20	49	41	23	-	18	-
Finland	127	55	43	127	50	-	77	-
France	1 551	488	31	1 551	603	-	948	-
Ireland	230	49	21	230	91	-	139	-
Italy	1 761	285	16	1 761	1 079	-	682	-
Cyprus	42	5	12	42	31	1	10	-
Lithuania	223	126	57	223	101	-	122	-
Latvia	84	57	68	84	54	-	30	-
Luxembourg	15	4	27	15	6	-	9	-
Hungary	512	190	37	510	386	-	124	2
Malta	17	8	47	17	6	-	11	-
Germany	7 187	1 978	28	7 182	3 957	-	3 225	5
Netherlands	1 260	350	28	1 260	489	-	771	-
Poland	17 810	8 721	49	17 798	11 384	-	6 414	12
Portugal	59	16	27	59	27	-	32	-
Austria	2 368	505	21	2 365	1 161	-	1 204	3
Greece	805	258	32	804	752	-	52	1
Slovakia	49 446	20 026	41	49 418	20 227	-	29 191	28
Slovenia	184	66	36	184	150	-	34	-
United Kingdom	2 234	457	20	2 231	986	-	1 245	3
Spain	282	100	35	282	162	-	120	-
Sweden	401	138	34	401	250	-	151	-

---

[17] See the Czech Statistical Office – www.czso.cz

Country of citizenship	Total	incl.: Females*	% of females	Residence permits, total	Permanent residence	Asylum	Temporary EU/ Long-term residence	90-days-and-over visa
Other countries total	**192 968**	**78 462**	**_41_**	**171 217**	**68 396**	**1 798**	**101 023**	**21 751**
Other European countries								
Albania	194	74	_38_	175	74	14	87	19
Belarus	3 191	1 758	_55_	2 924	951	171	1 802	267
Bosnia and Herzegovina	1 697	648	_38_	1 656	1 349	13	294	41
Bulgaria	4 586	1 631	_36_	4 153	2 337	35	1 781	433
Croatia	2 143	711	_33_	2 075	1 524	3	548	68
Iceland	14	5	_36_	14	6	-	8	-
Liechtenstein	3	1	_33_	3	1	-	2	-
Macedonia	1 218	254	_21_	1 116	561	3	552	102
Moldova	4 682	1 741	_37_	3 563	678	8	2 877	1 119
Norway	95	26	_27_	95	39	-	56	-
Romania	2 864	1 035	_36_	2 634	1 962	163	509	230
Russian Federation	16 627	8 597	_52_	15 004	6 012	354	8 638	1 623
San Marino	1	-	_0_	1	-	-	1	-
Serbia and Montenegro	3 633	1 119	_31_	3 469	2 306	74	1 089	164
Switzerland	399	122	_31_	399	252	-	147	-
Ukraine	87 834	34 003	_39_	75 663	15 334	45	60 284	12 171
Africa								
Algeria	461	36	_8_	458	369	1	88	3
Angola	194	29	_15_	185	137	22	26	9
Egypt	228	19	_8_	207	159	-	48	21
South Africa	119	55	_46_	114	74	4	36	5
Libya	352	118	_34_	324	61	1	262	28
Morocco	158	17	_11_	150	124	1	25	8
Nigeria	225	24	_11_	220	140	19	61	5
Tunisia	274	23	_8_	272	247	1	24	2
other	794	167	_21_	705	387	96	222	70
Asia								
Afghanistan	359	33	_9_	356	75	241	40	3
Armenia	1 351	583	_43_	1 294	906	83	305	57
Azerbaijan	195	80	_41_	169	52	26	91	26
China	3 587	1 553	_43_	3 331	1 471	7	1 853	256
Georgia	398	167	_42_	360	192	23	145	38

Country of citizenship	Total	incl.: Females*	% of females	Residence permits, total	Permanent residence	Asylum	Temporary EU/ Long-term residence	90-days-and-over visa
India	543	149	27	436	153	2	281	107
Iraq	269	62	23	255	132	86	37	14
Iran	159	27	17	148	55	35	58	11
Israel	614	198	32	529	183	-	346	85
Japan	1 235	543	44	927	105	-	822	308
Yemen	169	45	27	161	95	-	66	8
Jordan	185	19	10	174	120	1	53	11
Kazakhstan	2 289	1 278	56	2 149	1 313	42	794	140
Korea, Republic of	275	150	55	179	38	-	141	96
Korea, Democratic People's Republic of	333	309	93	273	-	-	273	60
Kyrgyzstan	305	168	55	289	65	12	212	16
Lebanon	233	33	14	223	161	1	61	10
Mongolia	2 435	1 583	65	1 965	309	-	1 656	470
Pakistan	251	47	19	247	162	8	77	4
Palestinian Territory	108	13	12	102	42	1	59	6
Syrian Arab Republic	377	84	22	366	285	13	68	11
Thailand	215	189	88	130	42	-	88	85
Tchaj-wan	131	66	50	61	8	-	53	70
Turkey	655	147	22	548	229	20	299	107
Uzbekistan	384	161	42	278	50	21	207	106
Viet Nam	36 902	15 911	43	34 735	23 235	70	11 430	2 167
other	564	215	38	496	172	27	297	68
North America								
Canada	590	247	42	487	310	-	177	103
Cuba	230	56	24	225	175	27	23	5
United States	3 952	1 497	38	3 198	2 051	-	1 147	754
other	184	66	36	144	89	-	55	40
South America								
Brazil	120	60	50	94	64	-	30	26
Colombia	102	53	52	88	48	-	40	14
Peru	108	33	31	101	67	-	34	7
other	293	112	38	256	147	-	109	37
Australia/New Zealand								
Australia	336	137	41	316	238	-	78	20

Country of citizenship	Total	incl.: Females*	% of females	Residence permits, total	Permanent residence	Asylum	Temporary EU/ Long-term residence	90-days-and-over visa
other	85	25	_29_	75	41	-	34	10
Stateless, not identified	461	150	_33_	459	419	24	16	2

Source: *The Czech Statistic Office – www.czso.cz*

At the end of 2005, as many as 258,306 foreign nationals officially held residence permits in the Czech Republic, 110,598 of whom had permanent residence permits, and 167,714 were foreigners with long-term residence permits. Since 1 May 2004 the category of long-term residence has covered persons residing in the Czech Republic by virtue of a visa for more than 90 days, long-term residence permits and temporary residence for citizens of the EU Member States and their family members.[18] Dealing with the problem of integration of foreigners into Czech society, the government has adopted a resolution governing the fundamental principles of migration.[19] Nowadays, the trend is to support legal migration, because the long-term perspectives appear worthwhile and it restricts illegal migration in accordance with international and EU standards.

1.3 Overview Involvement of Consulates, Embassies, Ministry of the Czech Republic, Probation Service, Ngo's etc.

It is obvious that the involvement of 'third parties' is considered to be very important, especially for foreign national prisoners. The involvement of Consulates and Embassies is significant for foreign national prisoners especially in situations in which they have to overcome language barriers. In reality, activity of a diplomatic mission/consulate may also significantly influence the duration of expulsive custody, where a foreign prisoner has to remain while waiting for his/her passport to be issued in order to be expelled. Regarding the role of NGO's, the Czech Helsinki Committee monitors human rights issues in criminal proceedings. The extensive project covered not only the monitoring of conditions in Czech prisons and the cases of individual prisoners, but also training and interactive seminars for prison staff, probation officers and mediators, as well as other activities.[20] The European Committee for the Prevention of Torture and Inhuman or Degrading Treatment or Punishment (hereinafter CPT) adopted the report following its visit to the Czech Republic from 21 to 30 April 2002 and requested that the Czech authorities provide a response setting out the measures that had been taken following its visit report. The report refers to the facts found in police establishments, detention facilities for foreign nationals detained under legislation on illegal residents, in prisons and psychiatric establishments, and states specific actions. The government of the Czech Re-

---

[18] ibidem, p. 17.
[19] Government of the Czech Republic (2003), Resolution of the Government of the Czech Republic, Fundamental Principles on the field of Migration of Foreigners, No. 55 of 13 January 2003, Government of the Czech Republic, Prague.
[20] See www.helcom.cz

public provided the response to the CPT in 2003 as well as a report on the measures that had been taken following the visit report of the CPT in 2005.[21] Up to the 1 January 2006, there was no authority responsible for executing systematic, preventive and independent supervision and control over all places in which persons are deprived of their personal liberty in the Czech Republic. In accordance to the Optional Protocol to the UN Convention against Torture (OPCAT) it falls under the competence of the Ombudsman (Veřejný ochránce práv). In July 2006, the Office of the Ombudsman released a report on the situation in detention facilities for foreign nationals. It refers to the facts that were found during visits to facilities and states specific recommendations.[22]

1.4 Overview of Trends

1.4.1. Crime and Sentencing Trends

The Czech police statistics of 2005 indicate that the number of police registered crimes has slightly decreased (-2, 2 %) in comparison to 2004. From a long-term perspective, it should be noted that the number of police registered crimes has decreased, while the figure for 2005 was the lowest since 1993, with a total number of 344,060.[23]

---

[21] See: Vláda České republiky (2006), Zpráva o plnění doporučení Evropského výboru pro zabránění mučení a nelidskému či ponižujícímu zacházení nebo trestnátní (CPT) v roce 2005, vyplývající z návštěvy tohoto výboru v České republice v roce 2002, Vláda České republiky, Praha *(The Government of the Czech Republic (2006), Report of the Czech Government on measures taken upon CPT visit in 2002 for 2005, The Government of the Czech Republic, Prague)*.

[22] Veřejný ochránce práv (2006), Zpráva z návštěv zařízení pro zajištění cizinců, Úřad Veřejného ochránce práv, Brno *(The Ombudsmann (2006), Report on Visits in Facilities of Detained Foreign Nationals, The Office of the Ombudsman, Brno)*.

[23] Ministerstvo vnitra ČR (2006), Informace o zjištěné trestné činnosti v České republice v roce 2005 ve srovnání s rokem 2004, Ministerstvo Vnitra ČR, Odbor bezpečnostní politiky, Praha. *(The Ministry of the Interior (2006), Information on Crimes detected in the Czech Republic in 2005 in comparison with 2004, The Ministry of the Interior, The Department of Security Policy, Prague)*.

Figure 1 – The development of crime in the Czech Republic 1989 - 2005

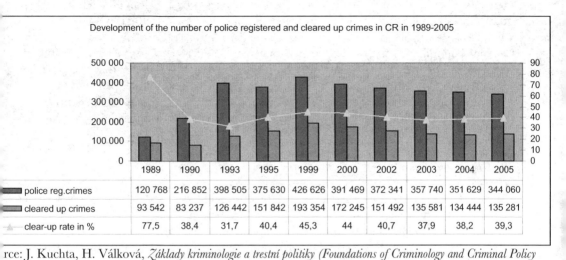

Development of the number of police registered and cleared up crimes in CR in 1989-2005

	1989	1990	1993	1995	1999	2000	2002	2003	2004	2005
police reg.crimes	120 768	216 852	398 505	375 630	426 626	391 469	372 341	357 740	351 629	344 060
cleared up crimes	93 542	83 237	126 442	151 842	193 354	172 245	151 492	135 581	134 444	135 281
clear-up rate in %	77,5	38,4	31,7	40,4	45,3	44	40,7	37,9	38,2	39,3

rce: J. Kuchta, H. Válková, *Základy kriminologie a trestní politiky (Foundations of Criminology and Criminal Policy*

The following should be mentioned regarding developments in crime compared to 2004:

- the share of property crime has decreased to 66,6 % (-2,7 %). On the other hand, the proportion of economic crimes increased to 12,8 % (+3,2 %). Violent crimes made up 6,3 % of all registered offences, a very minor decrease of 0,4 %. Robbery still remains a problem. The share of crimes against human dignity stagnated at 0,5 %;[24]
- the number of cleared up crimes increased to 135,281 (+0,6 %), i. e. the clear-up rate reached 39,3 % However, in the capital city of Prague it was only 21 %;
- the sequence of the regions has not markedly changed; the largest number of crimes were committed in the capital city of Prague (share 27,8 %), followed by the Central Bohemian Region (10,8 %), the Moravian-Silesian Region (10 %) and the Ústí Region (9,5 %), followed by the regions of South Bohemia, Plzeň, Liberec, Olomouc and Hradec Králové. The lowest crime rates (up to three percent) were recorded in the Vysočina, Karlovy Vary, Pardubice and Zlín Regions;[25]
- the total number of prosecuted and investigated persons stagnated between 2004 and 2005 (121,511 persons). The age structure of offenders was dominated by the 20 – 30 year olds (34 %) and 30- 60 year olds (49,7 %), while the overall numbers of offenders among children (under 15 years of age) and juveniles groups declined . The proportion of recidivists stagnated (45,97 %), however the figure for 2005 was the highest since 1993;[26]

---

[24]   ibidem, p.23.

[25]   ibidem, p.23.

[26]   It is necessary to mention that according to the police statistics a recidivist is a person who has already been sentenced for another intentional crime, while interpretation of this term differs in the court and prison statistics.

'The passing of a sentence on an offender is probably the most public face of the criminal justice process.'[27] The Criminal Code provides certain general provisions regarding sentencing, most importantly Article 31., which is governed by two fundamental principles: the principle of legality of sentencing, and the principle of individualization of the penalty. Article 31 provides that in sentencing, the court must consider the seriousness of the offence committed, the prospects of whether the offender can be reformed, and the offender's personality. In particular, the court must examine the damage that resulted from the offence, the nature and type of offence, all circumstances of time, place and method of commission and the degree of *mens rea* of the offender.[28] Furthermore, the court has to determine a prognosis on the offender's future behaviour and finally examine his/her personal background.[29]

According to the court statistics, Czech courts lawfully sentenced 67,561 persons for 87,578 crimes in 2005. Compared to previous years, the composition of sentencing showed no major fluctuations. The suspended prison sentence was imposed upon 36,006 offenders (i.e. 53.3%), and was thus the most frequently passed sentence, followed by community service, which was the case for 11, 990 offenders (i.e. 17, 8 %). 2,663 offenders were fined (3,9%), and 10,082 received unconditional prison sentences (14,9%).[30] Regarding the length of the imposed unconditional sentences to imprisonment in 2005, the majority (6,315 offenders; 62.6%) received sentences for up to one year. A further 31,8% (3,210 offenders) received prison terms for between one and up to five years. 539 offenders received unconditional prison sentences for between 5 and 15 years (5,4%), while extraordinary sentences – 15 to 25 years, and life imprisonment - were imposed upon 14 and four offenders respectively.[31]

1.4.2 Crime, Sentencing Trends and Characteristics of the Foreign Prison Population

There are no special prisons or remand prisons for foreign prisoners. The question of specialized institutions for foreigners was also the subject of the research conducted by the Institute of Criminology and Social Prevention in 2002-2003 and is still being discussed. In reality foreign prisoners are usually overrepresented. The most foreign prisoners are imprisoned in the prison of Valtice, Plzeň and Horní Slavkov, while on remand in Praha – Pankrác and Praha – Ruzyně. There are no special controlling mechanisms for foreign prisoners within the Czech prison system (see 1.3 and 2.1.1).

The total number of prosecuted and investigated foreign nationals in 2005 declined (i. e. -3,1 %) to 6, 994 persons compared to the 2004 figures. From a long term perspective, since 1994 the number of prosecuted and investigated foreign nationals has not markedly

---

[27] Maguire, M. et al (2002) , The Oxford Handbook of Criminology, Oxford University Press, Oxford, pp. 718.

[28] See Art. 3 para. 4 of the Criminal Code.

[29] See: Šámal, P., Král, V., Púry, F. (2004), *Trestní zákon – komentář (Commentary on Criminal Code)*, C. H. Beck, Praha (Prague).

[30] Ministerstvo spravedlnosti ČR (2005), Statistická ročenka kriminality za rok 2005, Odbor informatiky a statistiky Ministerstva spravedlnosti ČR, Ministerstvo spravedlnosti ČR, Praha; *(Ministry of Justice of the Czech Republic (2005), Statistical Yearbook of Criminality 2005, Department of statistic, Ministry of Justice of the Czech Republic, Prague.*

[31] ibidem, p. 30.

changed, averaging roughly 6 % of all prosecuted and investigated persons. In 2005, foreign nationals committed 8,353 crimes (down by 7, 5% in comparison to the previous year).[32] The following should be mentioned regarding the structure of crimes committed by foreign nationals in 2005:

- the most frequently committed crimes were crimes against property in 2,307 cases (i. e. 5 % of the total number of this type of crime), followed by economic crimes in 1, 766 cases (i. e. 7 %), violent crimes in 1,088 cases, i.e. 6,8 % (including 24 murders, i. e. 15 %; intentional injury 302, i.e. 5, 6 %; 291 robberies, i.e. 12,6 %) and crimes against human dignity in 129 cases, i.e. 8, 3 %;[33]
- the highest share of offending foreign nationals is found in the capital city of Prague with a share of 15,1 % of all offenders, followed by the Plzeň Region. The capital is considered to be, from a long-term perspective, the most vulnerable area in the Czech Republic;
- Concerning nationality, citizens of Slovakia are the most frequently prosecuted foreign nationals (34, 5 %), followed by Ukrainians (21, 6 %), citizens of Vietnam, Poland and Russia;
- The offence types with the highest shares of prosecuted foreigners were obstructions of the execution of an official decision (14,5 %), pick pocketing (14,4 %), murders (15,5 %) and robberies (9,6 %);
- there is a link between selected serious crimes committed by foreign nationals and organized crime[34].

According to court statistics, 4,223 foreign nationals were sentenced in 2005 (i. e. 6, 3 % of all convicts); the majority of all sentenced foreign nationals were sentenced by the Courts in the capital of Prague (1, 685), followed by West Bohemian (581) and North Moravian Courts (530).[35] The nationalities that were most strongly represented among sentenced foreign nationals were Slovaks (1, 239) and Ukrainians (1, 129).

---

[32] Ministerstvo vnitra ČR (2006), Zpráva o situaci v oblasti veřejného pořádku a vnitřní bezpečnosti na území České republiky v roce 2005 ve srovnání s rokem 2004, Ministerstvo Vnitra ČR, Praha. *(The Ministry of the Interior (2006), Report on Public Order and Internal Security in the Czech Republic in 2005 compared with 2004, The Ministry of the Interior, Prague.*

[33] ibidem, p. 32.

[34] Ministerstvo vnitra ČR (2005), Zpráva o situaci v oblasti veřejného pořádku a vnitřní bezpečnosti na území České republiky v roce 2004 ve srovnání s rokem 2003, Ministerstvo Vnitra ČR, Praha. *(The Ministry of the Interior (2005),Report on Public Order and Internal Security in the Czech Republic in 2004 compared with 2003, The Ministry of the Interior, Prague.*

[35] It has to be noted that the court districts differ from the administrative regions of the Czech Republic.

Table. 2 – Foreign national offenders, by nationality

Prosecuted, accused and convicted persons by nationality in 2004

	Prosecuted	Accused	Simplified proceedings	Moved for punishment in simplified proceedings	Convicted
Total	**89 288**	**75 861**	**18 773**	**18 569**	**68 443**
European countries, total	**88 513**	**75 206**	**18 493**	**18 292**	**67 756**
EU 25, total	**87 605**	**74 416**	**17 392**	**17 239**	**66 133**
Belgium	5	3	-	-	1
Czech Republic	85 760	72 894	16 648	16 508	64 344
Denmark	2	1	4	3	3
Estonia	-	-	3	3	1
France	25	22	10	7	10
Ireland	4	3	3	3	9
Italy	24	17	10	10	10
Lithuania	54	48	49	49	77
Latvia	3	2	3	3	4
Hungary	9	6	3	3	3
Germany	92	76	10	10	69
Netherlands	18	14	-	-	5
Poland	187	127	71	71	183
Austria	31	25	1	1	21
Greece	9	8	-	-	8
Slovakia	1 160	971	448	439	1 132
Slovenia	4	1	1	1	1
United Kingdom	20	17	4	4	12
Spain	3	2	1	1	3
Sweden	2	1	4	4	4
Other European countries, total	**908**	**790**	**1 101**	**1 053**	**1 623**
Russian Federation	111	87	54	52	111
Ukraine	526	469	858	821	1 164
Other	271	234	189	180	348
Asian countries, total	**634**	**534**	**193**	**190**	**544**
Viet Nam	427	360	109	107	368
other	207	174	84	83	176
African countries, total	**82**	**75**	**53**	**53**	**103**
American countries, total	**35**	**27**	**8**	**8**	**29**
Czech and other citizenship	21	16	21	21	3

Citizens of more states	-	-	-	-	4
Stateless	1	1	2	2	3
Not identified	2	2	3	3	1

Source: The Czech Statistic Office – www.czso.cz

The penalty of expulsion was imposed on 2,068 foreign nationals in 2004. Other numbers and the structure of the penalties to which foreign nationals were sentenced are not available at the moment.[36] In 2005, the total prison population slightly increased to 18,937 prisoners (+ 594 prisoners, i.e. + 3,2 %) compared to 2004. From a long term perspective, the total prison population has rapidly decreased since the fall of the totalitarian regime in 1989, which was directly affected by the amnesty of the president of former Czechoslovakia in 1989 and 1990. This drop has to be exemplified by the data. At the end of 1989 there were 22,365 prisoners in former Czechoslovakia prisons, whilst at the end of 1990 there were 'only' 8,231. In the following years the prison population was on the permanent increase until 1999 (23,060 prisoners), while 2002 showed the lowest (16,213 prisoners) figures. In 2003 the prison population began to increase again, however not to a profound degree.

Table 3 – Development of the Prison Population

Development of the Prison Population in 1989 - 2005										
Situation on 31.12. of respective year										
	1989	1990	1991	1993	1995	1999	2002	2003	2004	2005
on remand	2 537	4 172	5 373	7 810	8 000	6 934	3 384	3 409	3 269	2 860
in imprisonment	19 828	4 059	7 357	8 757	11 508	16 126	12 829	13 868	15 074	16 077
Total	22 365	8 231	12 730	16 567	19 508	23 060	16 213	17 277	18 343	18 937

Source: The Prison Service of the Czech Republic

The total prison population of foreign nationals decreased to 1,578 prisoners (- 134 prisoners, i.e. 8,5 %) in 2005 compared to 2004. If one looks at long-term trends, the total number of foreign prisoners was on the increase in the early 1990's, primarily the number of foreigners on remand. On the other hand, it has to be noted that the low number of foreign prisoner might have also been affected by the amnesty of the president of former Czechoslovakia in 1989 and 1990. The major increase of foreign prisoners is apparent in 1994, because former Czechoslovakia was split into two independent states – the Czech Republic and the Slovak Republic - on 1 January 1993, and consequentially from that time onwards imprisoned citizens of Slovakia were registered as foreign prisoners.

---

[36]   It has to be mentioned that foreigners are not a separate category in the available judicial statistics.

Table 4 – The Prison Population of Foreign Nationals

	Foreign prisoners on remand/in imprisonment in 1989 - 2005									
	Situation on 31.12. of respective year									
	1989	*1990*	*1991*	*1994*	*1997*	*1999*	*2000*	*2002*	*2004*	*2005*
on remand	60	69	159	1301	1594	1656	1405	757	792	663
in imprisonment	129	34	75	1406	1730	1309	1129	917	920	915
Total	189	103	234	2707	3324	2965	2534	1674	1712	1578

Source: The Prison Service of the Czech Republic

Up to 1996 the number of foreign nationals in Czech prisons had been on the increase. From 1997 onwards it continuously and steadily decreased, and between 2000 and 2003 it comprised about 7 % of the total prison population. In 2005, this share dropped to 5, 7 %.[37] The number of foreign prisoners on remand was on the increase until 1999[38], but in the following years it started to continuously decline. The current population of foreign prisoners detained on remand is the lowest since 1994. On the other hand, it has to be noted that the relative share of foreign prisoners on remand has not rapidly changed in total number of prisoners on remand and ranged between 23 %. The reason for the drop in the foreign prison population could also be attributed to legislative changes in 2000 and 2004 concerning the residence of foreigners as well as to fundamental changes of remand conditions in the Criminal Procedural Code. Concerning the composition of the foreign prisoner population in 2005 it has to be noted that the most represented nationalities were citizens of Ukraine (412 persons, i.e. 26, 1 %) followed by citizens of Slovakia (330, i.e. 20, 9 %), Vietnam (159, i. e. 10 %), Serbia and Monte Negro (79, i.e. 5 %) and Russia (62, i.e. 3, 9 %).

---

[37] See: Kuchta, J., Válková, H. (2005), *Základy kriminologie a trestní politiky (Foundation of Criminology and Criminal Policy)*, C. H. Beck , Praha (Prague).

[38] Except 1998, when the number was probably affected by the amnesty of the President.

Table 5 – Prisoners on remand/in imprisonment: by citizenship, 31 December 2005

Prisoners on remand/in imprisonment: by citizenship; 31 December 2005

Citizenship	Total	Accused			Convicted		
	Total	Total	Males	Females	Total	Males	Females
Total	**18 937**	**2 860**	**2 697**	**163**	**16 077**	**15 336**	**741**
Czech Republic	17 122	2 116	1 990	126	15 006	14 305	701
Outstanding[1]	237	81	75	6	156	142	14
Foreigners, total	1 578	663	632	31	915	889	26
EU 25, total	**469**	**169**	**158**	**11**	**300**	**282**	**18**
Belgium	2	1	1	0	1	1	0
Estonia	2	2	2	0	0	0	0
France	1	1	1	0	0	0	0
Italy	5	3	3	0	2	2	0
Lithuania	49	21	20	1	28	27	1
Latvia	1	0	0	0	1	1	0
Hungary	2	0	0	0	2	2	0
Germany	21	17	14	3	4	4	0
Netherlands	3	3	3	0	0	0	0
Poland	42	10	10	0	32	30	2
Austria	6	4	4	0	2	2	0
Greece	2	0	0	0	2	2	0
Slovakia	330	104	97	7	226	211	15
United Kingdom	1	1	1	0	0	0	0
Sweden	2	2	2	0	0	0	0
Other countries	**1 109**	**494**	**474**	**20**	**615**	**607**	**8**
Other European countries							
Belarus	32	11	11	0	21	21	0
Bosnia and Herzegovina	6	3	3	0	3	3	0
Bulgaria	42	18	18	0	24	23	1
Romania	58	24	18	6	34	34	0
Russian Federation	62	32	32	0	30	29	1
Serbia and Monte Negro	79	39	39	0	40	40	0
Ukraine	412	152	146	6	260	258	2
Macedonia	26	16	16	0	10	10	0
Moldova	39	13	10	3	26	26	0
other	6	3	3	0	3	3	0
Africa							
Algeria	18	5	5	0	13	13	0
Tunisia	18	5	5	0	13	13	0
other	24	14	13	1	10	10	0

Asia							
Armenia	11	3	3	0	8	8	0
China	41	27	25	2	14	14	0
Georgia	17	8	8	0	9	9	0
Viet Nam	159	91	89	2	68	65	3
other	48	25	25	0	23	23	0
North America, total	3	0	0	0	3	3	0
South America, total	2	2	2	0	0	0	0
Australia, total	1	1	1	0	0	0	0
Stateless	5	2	2	0	3	2	1

1) Refers to persons whose citizenship (Czech or Slovak) is not evident from available documents

Source: The Prison Service of the Czech Republic

A very peculiar and particular problem has arisen concerning the issue of nationality within the prison population of the Czech Republic. There are still 237 prisoners who are ex – nationals of the Czechoslovak Federation for whom the available documents do not clearly indicate whether they are in fact Czech or Slovak nationals. Taking this issue into consideration, the overall prison population in the Czech Republic can be divided into the following groups:[39]
- Czech nationals
- Ukrainians
- Slovaks
- Vietnamese
- Nationals of the ex – Soviet Union excluding Ukrainians
- Nationals of the Balkan states Albania, Bosnia and Herzegovina, Bulgaria, Croatia, Serbia and Monte Negro, Macedonia
- Nationals of the Islamic states Afghanistan, Algeria, Bahrain, Egypt, Iraq, Iran, Jordan, Kuwait, Libya, Morocco, Pakistan, Palestine, Syria, Tunis
- Other foreign nationals
- Stateless
- Ex – nationals of the Czechoslovak Federation for whom available documents do not clearly indicate whether they are Czech or Slovak nationals

1.5 Overview of National Legislation

1.5.1 Criminal Law and Criminal Procedure, Penitentiary Legislation

Criminal law in the Czech Republic is predominantly codified into the Criminal Code (law no. 140/1961 Coll.), the Criminal Procedural Code (law no. 141/1961 Coll.) and

---

[39] See: Scheinost, M. at al. (2004), *Výzkum cizích státních příslušníků v českých věznicích* (*Research on Foreign Nationals in the Czech Penitentiary Institutions*), Institut pro kriminologii a sociální prevenci (The Institute of Criminology and Social Prevention), Praha (Prague).

the Juvenile Justice Act (law no. 218/2003 Coll.). The recodification of Czech criminal law began over 14 years ago; the Criminal Code (law no. 140/1961 Coll.) was originally adopted in 1961 and provides the basis of criminal law in the Czech Republic. It has, of course, been amended many times in the course of its existence, but due to fundamental economic, political and social changes that since the fall of the totalitarian regime in 1989, it is necessary to adopt a new Criminal Code that will provide society with better protection against criminality.[40]

The proposal for a new Criminal Code was introduced in the Parliament of the Czech Republic in July 2004. It was discussed for more than one and half years and finally passed in the Lower House; however, it was rejected by the Upper House and subsequently rejected by the Lower House as well.[41] Although the new Criminal Code has not been adopted yet, progress was made when the so called "great amendment" (law no. 265/2001 Coll.) of the Criminal Procedural Code and the Juvenile Justice Act (law no. 218/2003 Coll.) were adopted in 2001 and 2003 respectively.[42] The Council Framework Decision on the European Arrest Warrant and the Surrender Procedures between the Member States (2002/584/JHA) were finally implemented into the Criminal Code and the Criminal Procedural Code by the laws no. 537/2004 Coll. and no.539/2004 Coll. and came into effect on 1 November 2004. There is no code on the execution of sanctions, while detention in remand prisons is governed by the law no. 293/1993 Coll. and specified by the Ordinance of the Minister of Justice no. 109/1994 Coll. Imprisonment is governed by the law no. 169/1999 Coll. and specified by the Ordinance of the Minister of Justice no. 345/1999 Coll. The execution of other sanctions is regulated in the Criminal Procedural Code.

1.5.2. Criminal Law, Criminal Procedure, Penitentiary Legislation & Foreigners

Regarding the special sections in national legislation that apply to foreigners, the following should be noted:

- According to Article 57 of the Criminal Code the court expel foreign nationals or stateless persons - except those who bear the legal status of a refugee - but only in cases where it is necessary for public safety or other public interest. Expulsion may be imposed for a period of one up to ten years or *ad infinitum*,[43] either as a separate sanction or in addition to penalties. The court may not impose an expulsion in cases in which the nationality of an offender is unknown, the offender has been granted asylum, the offender is staying in the Czech Republic on a long-term residence permit, has a social and working background and the imposition of such a penalty will be inconsistent with the interest of family integrity[44]. Also, a person may not be expelled when an offender

---

[40] See: e. g. Šámal, P. (2002), *'K úvodním ustanovením připravované rekodifikace trestního zákona'* (*'Commentary to the front provisions of prepared codification of Criminal Code'*), Trestněprávní revue (Criminal Law Revue), 12, pp. 349 ff.

[41] See: Škvain, P. (2004), *'Nad probíhající kodifikací trestního práva hmotného'* (*'Codification of substantion criminal law in motion'*), Trestněprávní revue (Criminal Law Revue*)*, 10, pp. 304 ff.

[42] For more detailed information about the national legislation see: e. g. Z. Karabec et al. (2002), The Criminal Justice System in the Czech Republic, Institut pro kriminologii a sociální prevenci, Praha;

[43] See Art. 26 para. 3 of the Juvenile Justice Act (maximum for five years).

[44] See Convention on the Rights of The Child.

faces persecution in the country he/she will expelled to on grounds of his/her race, nationality, ethnic origin, affiliation with a certain social group, political opinion, religion, or will be exposed to torture or inhuman and/or degrading treatment or punishment.

- According to Article 350c of the Criminal Procedural Code the court may decide to place a convict in expulsive custody when there is a danger that he/she will abscond or in any way obstruct the imposed expulsion and when there are no grounds to replace such a decision by a guarantee / promise of a convict or by bail.[45]
- There are special sections dealing with the foreign prisoners in remand prisons within the law no. 293/1993 Coll., Articles 27, 28 as well as in the Ordinance of the Minister of Justice no. 109/1994 Coll., Articles 79, 79a, 80.[46]
- There are special sections dealing with the foreign prisoners in imprisonment in the law no. 169/1999 Coll., Article 72 as well as in the Ordinance of the Minister of Justice no. 345/1999 Coll., Article 98 [47]
- Article 375 and following of the Criminal Procedural Code on the process of liaison with other states governs in particular the procedure of extradition and the European Arrest Warrant.
- The administrative detention of foreign nationals is governed by Articles 124-149 of the law no. 326/1999 Coll. on residence of foreigners in the Czech Republic.

It is necessary to mention that the Czech Republic is a signatory of many bilateral treaties with European and non-European states that were ratified before 1989 but are still in power. Multilateral international treaties ratified by the former Czechoslovakia were also succeeded by the Czech Republic. There is no information available on the actual application of these international agreements. However, it remains to be mentioned that a very characteristic phenomenon within the foreign prison population is the lack of interest in serving their prison sentences in their home countries.

2 TREATMENT OF FOREIGN PRISONERS

Introduction: Facts about the Research on Social Exclusion of Foreign Prisoners realized in Plzeň (Pilsen) Prison in March 2006.

The objective of this project is to address the issue of social exclusion of prisoners detained in European penitentiary institutions outside their country of national origin. Although the problem of social exclusion was not the objective of the research realized by the Institute of Criminology and Social Prevention, a very important step has been made in that foreign prisoners have become the subject of the first relevant study in the Czech Republic. [48] The objective of the Czech national study - to provide information on the situation and position of foreign prisoners in the Czech Republic - may not be realized properly without awareness of the foreign prisoner's opinion. In order to know more facts about the 'real' treatment of foreign prisoners, the research was conducted in Plzeň (Pilsen) prison. It was executed via questionnaires that were distributed to both foreign pris-

---

[45] Compare Art. 350c and Art. 67, Art. 73 and 73a of the Criminal Procedural Code.
[46] See chapter 2.1 on General Facts about Treatment of Foreign Prisoners.
[47] ibid., p. 46.
[48] See Introduction.

oners as well as members of prison staff. The Tilburg University in the Netherlands provided the foundations of both questionnaires. The questionnaires were edited and finalized at the end of February 2006 and then submitted to the Prison Service. Both questionnaires were structured into sections, while some of the questions were intentionally repeated within different sections in order to validate previous answers. The Research was executed at the beginning of March 2006 and at the end of April 2006 in the prison in Plzeň (Pilsen)[49]; the first questionnaire was submitted to convicted foreign prisoners while the other was handed to employees of the Prison Service working with foreign prisoners. Their willingness to cooperate was one of the most important factors for the successful completion of this task. The Prison Service selected voluntary foreign prisoners while taking the structure of the current prison population into consideration. For safety reasons my personal presence was not permitted, but both foreign prisoners and the employees of the Prison service working with these prisoners were free to answer all of the questions of the submitted questionnaires without interference from others.

Regarding the evaluation of the research, a total of 32 questionnaires were returned. One can say that the vast majority of respondents generally understood the questions, and some of them were able to illustrate and elaborate their answers. All 22 questioned foreign prisoners were male citizens of either Ukraine, Algeria, Afghanistan, Bahrain, Tunisia, Kazakhstan, Moldavia, Russia, Macedonia, Serbia and Monte Negro, Rumania, Slovakia, Mexico or were stateless; 77 % of them were sentenced to expulsion. The prison of Plzeň was targeted for various reasons. Firstly it has the fourth largest population of foreign prisoners within Czech penitentiary institutions. Furthermore, the research could be accomplished within one month not least due to the helpful and professional approach of Mr. Šefl, the Governor of Plzeň prison.

---

[49] For more detailed information about Prison Plzeň, see www.vscr.cz

Table 6 – Local Prison Population in the prison of Plzeň (Pilsen)

Local prison population in the Prison Plzeň on 5 May 2006	
Citizenship	**Prisoners**
Afghanistan	1
Algeria	6
Austria	1
Bahrain	1
Serbia and Monte Negro	3
Bulgaria	3
Belarus	4
China	2
Croatia	1
Czech Republic	911
Germany	1
Iraq	1
Kazakhstan	1
Lithuania	5
Mexico	1
Moldova	5
Morocco	1
Nigeria	1
Poland	3
Romania	8
Russian Federation	4
Slovakia	15
Viet Nam	8
Tunisia	4
Turkey	2
Ukraine	40
Former Republic of Yugoslavia	6
Macedonia	3
ČSFR (ex - Czechoslovakia nationals)	5
Total	**1047**

Source: The Prison Service of the Czech Republic

At the end of February 2006 there were 23 foreign prisoners on remand, 146 prisoners in imprisonment and eight persons in custody awaiting expulsion in the prison of Plzeň. Given the facts about the structure of the prison population in the Czech Republic, the responding foreign prisoners were categorized into the following groups:
- Ukrainians (seven prisoners);
- Nationals of the former Soviet Union except Ukrainians: (three prisoners) Russia, Kazakhstan, Moldavia;

- Nationals of Islamic states: (five prisoners) Afghanistan, Algeria, Bahrain, Morocco, Tunisia;
- Nationals of Balkan states: (two prisoners) Serbia and Monte Negro, Macedonia;
- Slovaks:(two prisoners);
- Other foreign nationals: (two prisoners) Rumania, Mexico;
- Stateless: (one prisoner) ethnic origin Albanian.

The following is a breakdown of the data on the foreign prisoners who responded in our research according to the categories of nationality listed above:

Ad a) Ukrainians (seven prisoners):
- serious crimes were committed by the respondents in six cases (rape, murder, attempted murder, robbery);
- average age of the respondents is 32, 9 years;
- average term of the imposed prison sentence is 10 years;
- penalty of expulsion imposed upon all seven respondents.

Ad b) Nationals of the former Soviet Union, except Ukrainians (three prisoners)
- Two of the respondents in this group were imprisoned for violent offences (robbery), one for embezzlement;
- the average age of the respondents is 30,6 years;
- the average term of the imposed prison sentence is six years;
- penalty of expulsion imposed upon all three respondents.

Ad c) Nationals of Islamic states (five prisoners)
- three respondents of this group were sentenced for drug trafficking, and one each for fraud and theft;
- the average age of the respondents is 37,8 years;
- the average term of imprisonment is 5,7 years;
- two of the respondents are to be expelled.

Ad d) Nationals of Balkan states (two prisoners)
- one respondent was imprisoned for violent crime (murder), the other for theft and blackmail;
- the average age of the respondents is 33 years;
- the respondents were sentenced to 10 and two and a half (2, 5) years of imprisonment respectively;
- penalty of expulsion imposed upon both respondents.

Ad e) Slovaks (two prisoners)
- One prisoner was sentenced for obstructing the execution of an official decision together with endangering under the influence of an addictive substance, the other for grievous bodily harm;
- the respondents were 22 and 32 years old;
- sentenced to 16 months and five years of imprisonment;
- one respondent of this group is to be expelled.

Ad f) Other foreign nationals (two prisoners) Rumania, Mexico
- One prisoner was sentenced for drug trafficking, the other for fraud and forgery ;
- respondents were 31 and 35 year old;
- both respondents sentenced to five and half years of imprisonment;
- penalty of expulsion imposed upon one respondent.

Ad g) Stateless (one prisoner) ethnic origin Albanian
- sentenced to prison for murder;
- respondent is 60 year old;
- sentenced to 13 years of imprisonment;
- penalty of expulsion was imposed.

Concerning the second group of respondents - the employees of the Prison Service working with foreign prisoners- they are all Czech nationals working for the Prison Service in the prison of Plzeň. Seven of them are men and three are women, with an overall average age of 45,8 years. Three of the responding employees have a university degree and one of them is working with foreign prisoners on remand.
They are active in the following professions:
- Psychologist
- Pedagogue
- Educationist and therapist
- Prison guard
- Inspector of prison guards
- Educationist
- Social worker

2.1 General Facts about the treatment of Foreign Prisoners

2.1.1 Theoretical situation

There are special sections dealing with foreign prisoners in remand prisons in the law no. 293/1993 Coll., Articles 27, 28 as well as in the Ordinance of the Minister of Justice no. 109/1994 Coll., Articles 79, 79a, and 80. These provisions mainly concern a different reception and admission procedure; in other issues foreign prisoners on remand are subject to the same rights and obligations as Czech prisoners. There are special sections dealing with foreign prisoners in regular imprisonment in the law no. 169/1999 Coll., Article 72 as well as in the Ordinance of the Minister of Justice no. 345/1999 Coll., Article 98. These provisions mainly provide for special procedures of reception, admission and for the accommodation of foreigners with fellow foreign prisoners. In other issues foreign prisoners serving prison sentences are subject to the same rights and obligations as Czech prisoners. It is necessary to emphasize that Article 98 para. 2 of the Ordinance of the Minister of Justice no. 345/1999 Coll., states that it should be taken into consideration whether the penalty of expulsion has been imposed while drawing up a sentence plan for foreign prisoners.
There are no special controlling mechanisms for foreign prisoners. The public prosecutor regularly inspects the places of remand and imprisonment. He/she is entitled to visit all locations where prison sentences are being served at any time, to access prison

documents, to speak with prisoners without the presence of other persons and to request relevant explanations from the Prison Service. He/she has the power to order the release of a person who has been illegally remanded or imprisoned. The supervision of the public prosecutor does not override the obligation of the Prison Service to perform its own control activities. The Ministry of Justice, through the minister's general inspectorate, is also directly involved in control and supervision activities.[50]

2.1.2 Actual situation

2.1.2.1 Generally, the majority of the responding foreign prisoners perceived no differences in their treatment compared to Czech prisoners. However, some respondents highlighted the problems of healthcare delivery and language barriers as the most significant. Two foreign prisoners felt that they are treated differently by some of the prison guards, while three felt to be treated differently by doctors in medical care. Three foreign prisoners believed that the reason for these differences in treatment may well lie in their nationality and in language barriers; one foreign prisoner was unable to pinpoint any reason. Two prisoners think that they are being socially excluded because of the difficulties in language. The most frequent/common problems in the everyday life of foreign prisoners were found in health care delivery, an unprofessional approach of prison staff (lack of respect), health problems and other prisoners. To overcome language barriers, some of them can speak Czech, while others rely on help from their fellow prisoners, study the Czech language, use dictionaries etc.[51] Six foreign prisoners gave information that referred to their stay in other Czech penitentiary institutions.

2.1.2.2 The vast majority of responding prison staff spoke of potential differences in the treatment of foreign prisoners compared to national prisoners due to language barriers. One respondent illustrated his answer as follows: 'Knowledge of language plays the key role; otherwise a prisoner does not have the opportunity to communicate with others and it will be easier to end up in social isolation. Such a prisoner is not able to understand what his/her obligations are in prison and he/she is treated differently not only by prison staff, but by his/her fellow prisoners too.' Because all responding staff members work with imprisoned foreigners, it is very important to show their awareness of the most frequent/usual problems that foreign prisoners face. Nine respondents answered positively, while language barriers are considered to be the most frequent/usual problem as well as differences in mentality, culture and religious environment. In order to overcome language barriers, some of them can speak foreign languages, while the others rely on help from their colleagues and from other foreign prisoners.

---

[50] See law no. 293/1993 Coll., Art. 29; law. no. 169/1999 Coll., Art. 78.
[51] It has to be noted that for Slovak prisoners the problem of language barriers practically does not exist, because the Czech and Slovak languages are very similar.

2.2 Living Conditions and Facilities

2.2.1 Theoretical situation

According to the law, foreign prisoners on remand have access to the same living conditions and facilities as Czech prisoners. Foreign prisoners on remand who speak the same language are to be placed together. Foreign prisoners in custody awaiting expulsion are placed in a section with a more relaxed regime, together with other eligible prisoners on remand. According to the law, foreign prisoners in imprisonment have access to the same living conditions and facilities as national prisoners. Foreign prisoners are not placed separately; those with the same nationality or who speak the same language are placed together.

2.2.2 Actual situation

2.2.2.1 The majority of the foreign prisoners within the sample feel that they have access to the same living conditions and facilities as Czech prisoners. Foreign prisoners are not placed separately and they usually share cells with other foreign nationals, however some also reported to be accommodated with Czech prisoners. This in turn did not, however, result in any complaints. It was ascertained that nearly all respondents have the opportunity to meet and speak with other foreign prisoners of the same nationality.[52] Some of the foreign prisoners are allowed to spend approximately 16 hours a day outside their prison cells.[53]

2.2.2.2 The view that foreign prisoners have access to the same living conditions and facilities as Czech prisoners was confirmed by all of the prison staff in the study. They stated that foreign prisoners are usually placed together with prisoners of the same or different nationality. Prisoners of the same nationality or those who speak the same language have the opportunity to meet regularly in the course of their activities (e. g. club of the Russian culture, sport, watching TV, work etc.).

2.3 Reception and Admission

2.3.1 Theoretical situation

According to the law, foreign prisoners on remand/in imprisonment have to be appropriately instructed upon arrival about their rights and duties in their native language or in a language that they understand. Foreign prisoners have to be especially instructed about their right to contact the diplomatic mission or consulate of their home country. Instructions of rights and duties are currently available in 25 foreign languages.

---

[52] Other citizens of Mexico are not placed in The Prison Plzeň.
[53] Depending on the level of security.

2.3.2 Actual situation

2.3.2.1 Nearly all responded foreign prisoners are not aware of different reception pro-cedures for foreigners. Four prisoners were instructed in languages they did not under-stand. The vast majority of prisoners were instructed in the Czech language that they supposedly understand, and some of them in Russian. Five respondents had no opportu-nity to contact the diplomatic mission or consulate of their native country; nor could they call their family members upon arrival in the institution. This inability *could* be due to the fact that the use of the telephones was often problematic (see also section 2.7.1).

2.3.2.2 The vast majority of responding prison staff assumes that there is no special re-ception procedure for foreigners; some of them find the instruction of a foreign prisoner to be most problematic due to language barriers. All of the respondents answered that foreign prisoners are instructed upon arrival about their rights and duties in their native language or in a language that they understand, and that they have the opportunity to call to their family members. All foreign prisoners have the opportunity to contact the diplomatic mission or consulate of their native country as well.

2.4 Work – Education – Training – Recreation

2.4.1 Theoretical situation

A prisoner may be employed while he/she applies for a work and the prison may provide with a suitable work. According to the law, foreign prisoners are allowed to have access to books written in their native/understandable language. Depending on the period of im-prisonment the Prison Service shall provide suitable conditions for Czech language les-sons.

2.4.2 Actual situation

2.4.2.1 According to the research, 16 prisoners are physically able to work (for instance in terms of their state of health), while eight of them are in fact currently working and are paid (gross salary varies according to the occupation from CZK 4, 500 to 6, 750).[54] One prisoner stated that foreign prisoners are not entitled to work. All responding foreign prisoners reported to be participating in educational and vocational training classes; only one respondent mentioned his participation in the Czech language course for foreigners. Four prisoners claimed to have no access to books in an understandable language, while pointing out that the selection of these books is very limited. Foreign prisoners participate in the following recreational activities: PC, TV, video club, relaxation, painting club, ta-ble tennis, chess, body building or darts.

2.4.2.2 The second group of respondents - prison staff - assumes that foreign prisoners utilise the possibility to participate in educational and vocational training classes, have access to the books in a language they understand and are entitled to participate in all recreational activities.

---

[54] approx. 150 – 225 Euros.

2.5   Food – Religion - Personal Hygiene - Medical Care

2.5.1 Theoretical situation

The Prison Service provides regular food for all prisoners and takes their cultural and religious traditions into consideration. A prisoner may refuse the provided food on the
grounds of his/her dietary habits. In such cases 'additional' food is provided at his/her
own expense.[55] The Prison Service provides freedom of religion according to the law.[56]
'The prison religious service is currently composed of 29 prison chaplains (persons in an
employment relationship with the Czech Prison Service) from 10 state-registered
churches with authorisation to execute special rights (in accordance with Act no. 3/2002
Coll.); they are active in 22 prisons and remand prisons in the Czech Republic. Their activities are primarily directed towards the ensuring of religious services in individual facilities and co-operation with clerics, who travel to prisons as part of the activities of the
Prison Religious Care (PRC) civic association and voluntary activities of the churches and
religious associations.'[57] 'Prison Religious Care (PRC) is a non-governmental organisation
providing broad ecumenical services, traditionally sharing in activities with charged and
convicted persons. In its existence and in practice it is a guarantee of the constitutional
right to practise one's religious faith.'[58] The Prison Service shall provide for penniless
prisoners basic hygiene requirements. The delivery of health care is regulated in the law
no. 20/1966 Coll. However, it should be noted that foreign national prisoners without
health insurance have to pay for medical care except in cases of emergency.[59]

2.5.2 Actual situation

2.5.2.1 The issue of religion as well as medical care is considered to be the most problematic for foreign prisoners. For example, foreign prisoners from Ukraine (Orthodox
Catholics) find that freedom of religion as well as cultural requirements are equally respected inside the prison, while some of the foreign prisoners of another religion, for example Muslims, feel that they are hindered because of prescribed dress (wearing a habit is
not allowed), personal hygiene (the need for everyday hygiene before prayer) and food
(Muslim food is not prepared properly according to the rules of *Cheriáa*). Meeting with
qualified religious representatives is very important for many prisoners, yet only some of
them actually have that possibility. Concerning medical care, 14 respondents think that
foreign prisoners are treated differently compared to Czech prisoners, because they do
not have health insurance. Therefore, they are apparently not entitled to receive any

---

[55]   In the Prison of Plzeň so called "Muslim food" is provided as basic food free of charge.
[56]   Law no. 3/2002 Coll., on churches and religious associations.
[57]   Generální ředitelství Vězeňské služby ČR (2006), Výroční zpráva Vězeňské služby České republiky
       za rok 2005, Generální ředitelství Vězeňské služby ČR, Praha , pp. 103-104. *(The General Directorate of
       the Prison Service of the Czech Republic (2006), Annual Report of the Activities of the Prison Service of the Czech Re-
       public for 2005, The General Directorate of the Prison Service of the Czech Republic, Prague, pp. 103-104), bilin-
       gual version;*
[58]   ibidem, p. 57.
[59]   See: The Council of Europe (2004), *Report to the Czech Government on the visit to the Czech Republic carried
       out by the European Committee for the Prevention of Torture and Inhuman and Degrading Treatment or Punishment
       (CPT) from 21 to 30 April 2002*, The Council of Europe - CPT/Inf 4, Strasbourg.

treatment or medicine. However, some responses from working prisoners indicate the contrary.

2.5.2.2 Awareness of religion and cultural requirements may be essential to prison staff working with foreign prisoners. The vast majority of the prison staff believes that freedoms of religion as well as other cultural requirements are well respected in the prison. Only two respondents are aware of the problem with prescribed dress for Muslims.[60] Concerning health care delivery, only two respondents highlighted the problem with health insurance mentioned above.

2.6 Consular and Legal Help

2.6.1 Theoretical situation

Foreign prisoners have to be especially instructed about their right to contact the diplomatic mission or consulate of their native country upon their arrival or to admit a visit of a representative of the respective diplomatic mission or consulate. The Prison Service has the legal obligation to inform the respective diplomatic mission/consulate when a foreign prisoner has been transferred. The Czech Helsinki Committee also provides free legal aid to foreign prisoners within the bounds of observance of human rights in the Czech Republic.[61]

2.6.2 Actual situation

2.6.2.1 The vast majority of foreign prisoners stated that they have the opportunity to communicate with officials of the diplomatic mission or consulate of their native country, while two foreign prisoners (a citizen of Macedonia and a stateless person) claimed that this had not been possible. Only five foreign prisoners were visited by a lawyer, embassy or consular official of their country of origin. The vast majority of foreign prisoners have had access to (free) legal aid. However, it has to be noted that some of them claimed to have experience with *ex offo* lawyers in criminal proceedings, whose service is basically not for free. Good cooperation with an embassy or consulate is especially necessary when a foreign prisoner has to stay in expulsive custody while waiting for his/her travel documents. I am personally aware of a case, when a citizen of Serbia was forced to spend more time in custody awaiting expulsion than necessary, because the Embassy failed to issue his travel documents.

2.6.2.2 The vast majority of prison staff respondents claim that foreign prisoners stay in touch with officials of their diplomatic mission or consulate and that they have access to (free) legal help.

---

[60] See: B. Spalek, 'Muslims in British Prisons' / www.hmprisonservice.gov.uk
[61] See: www.helcom.cz

2.7 Contact with the Outside World

2.7.1 Theoretical situation

According to the law, foreign prisoners are allowed to receive and to send correspondence without any restriction at their own expense.[62] However, correspondence is subject to inspection of its contents. The inspection of mail is inadmissible in a number of cases enumerated in law, for example written correspondence from a defence attorney. Foreign prisoners (except those in 'collusive' remand) are entitled to call to their close relatives should they have a legitimate reason for doing so. Should very important reasons arise, access to the telephone may be allowed for communication with persons other than close relatives. A foreign prisoner is obliged to cover the costs for the calls that he/she makes. The Prison Service is allowed to listen in to and record calls except those with enumerative bodies and persons. Foreign prisoners on remand have the right to one 90-minute visit (no more than four persons) once every 14 days. They may also use a radio or TV set under prescribed conditions and purchase (foreign) daily press and magazines so long as it is generally distributed and available in the Czech Republic. Foreign prisoners in regular imprisonment are entitled to visits that amount to three hours per calendar month. Some persons (e.g. barristers, clerics, representatives of embassies/consulates, NGOs etc.) may visit foreign prisoners without any limitation or upon agreement with the Prison Service. Books, daily press and magazines may be sent to foreign prisoners by mail without any restriction. A TV set or radio may be owned only upon the decision of the Governor of the prison.

2.7.2 Actual situation

Nearly all foreign prisoners claim that they are enabled to stay in contact with their relatives. The vast majority of the foreign prisoners we questioned stated that they have received visits from their relatives, friends and other persons, whilst seven prisoners have not been visited yet. Only a few prisoners made any statement on the frequency with which they received visitors. For example, a stateless 60 year old man with a total sentence of 13 years imprisonment received roughly ten visits in a period of eight years. Regarding means of communication, all prisoners use written correspondence as the most frequent connection with the outside world, followed by visits and phone calls. Only one foreign prisoner stressed the problem of not having the financial means to use the telephone, but we can assume that more foreign prisoners in fact face this problem. One foreign prisoner stated that his source of information about the outside world is TV and radio broadcasting.

---

[62] The costs of correspondence with a barrister are covered by the Prison Service when a foreign prisoner is insolvent.

2.8 Re-integration activities, Prison leave

2.8.1 Theoretical situation

According to the law, a prisoner's sentence plan is prepared on the basis of all available information about a foreign prisoner with respect to the total term to be served, the offender's personality as well as the circumstances of and the reasons for committing the crimes. While following the plan, suitable conditions for resettlement into society after release shall be established for all prisoners at least three months before their release. The Governor may decide (on the basis of recommendation of qualified prison staff) to transfer a prisoner to a 'release' department within the same prison. This usually occurs six months before release. It is necessary to emphasize that Article 98 para. 2 of the Ordinance of the Minister of Justice no. 345/1999 Coll. states that it should be taken into consideration whether the penalty of expulsion was imposed while drawing up a sentence plan for foreign prisoners.

2.8.2 Actual situation

2.8.2.1 All 22 foreign prisoners are familiar with their right to apply for parole; six respondents applied for parole, five applications were refused, one has not yet been decided on. None of the foreign prisoners were placed to another prison department to prepare them for resettlement into society after release, and nobody was eligible according to the law.[63] However, it has to be noted that one Ukrainian prisoner who had been sentenced to six years of imprisonment and expulsion, claimed that he had not yet been subjected to any 'preparation' for release six months before his release. In general, the preparation for release is usually implemented in a special section of a prison called 'výstupní oddělení' ('release department') and is primarily focused on prisoners who have been imprisoned for three years or more. The conditions in the release department differ from prison to prison, but its main objective is to prepare prisoners for activities of every day life, such as for instance cooking, laundry, applying for a job and social support.

2.8.2.2 Somewhat miscellaneous answers were registered when the responding prison staff answered the question on whether foreign prisoners are transferred to other prison departments in order to prepare them for resettlement into society. Five respondents stated that such transfers in fact take place, while two members of staff answered to the contrary. One respondent stated that such a placement is only possible if a foreign prisoner requests it. Respondents were not able to illustrate their answers about differences in 'release' departments (e.g. conditions, regimes, programs etc.).

---

[63] See: Chapter 2.8.1.

2.9 Release, Expulsion

2.9.1 Theoretical situation

The Criminal Procedural Code regulates the execution of expulsion.[64] Respective prisons shall be notified by the Court that the penalty of expulsion that has been imposed upon a foreign prisoner is to be executed following his/her release. The police of the Czech Republic (hereinafter the police) are responsible for the ensuring that an expulsion is in fact carried out. Where necessary, the Court can also require of the police to provide a foreign prisoner with the necessary travel documents (usually a passport) so that expulsion can be executed immediately after his/her release. The Court can also annul the expulsion of a foreign prisoner should new consequences/circumstances arise. The Court shall decide about releasing a foreign prisoner from serving the penalty of expulsion if new circumstances / consequences are present and, should this be the case, the penalty of expulsion may not be imposed.[65] Regarding the general procedures of release from penitentiary establishments in the Czech Republic, the same provisions apply to foreigners as to Czech inmates.

2.9.2 Actual situation

According to the court statistics, 4,097 foreign nationals were sentenced in 2004. Also, in the same year the penalty of expulsion was imposed upon 2,068 foreign nationals.[66] Of the foreign prisoners who participated in our study, 17 were to be expelled from the Czech Republic after their release from prison (77%). Foreign prisoners - including all citizens of Ukraine who responded to the questionnaire - were sentenced to both imprisonment and expulsion when serious and violent crimes were committed. This is in line with the established judicial practice that is in adherence to the purpose and aims of punishment (individual and general prevention) which make it necessary to impose the penalty of expulsion alongside imprisonment when a foreign national has committed a serious crime of violent nature or against property *(R 42/1994-II)*.[67] Some foreign prisoners try to 'prevent' being expelled by applying for asylum. According to the Highest Court of the Czech Republic, an asylum applicant can be expelled, and the responsible court need not await the decision on the application for asylum. Also, it can decide that an expulsion is not possible due to legal obstacles that can also lie in issues of internationally recognized human rights *(Tpjn 310/2001 from 17 April 2003)*.

2.10 Aftercare – Probation

'In co-operation with the Probation and Mediation Service of the Czech Republic, concrete steps were initiated [in 2005] towards the implementation of the Parole project, which utilises European Union funds; continuing to work towards tools for prisoner assessment. Training was subsequently carried out by workers at remand prisons and pris-

---

64   See: Law no. 141/1961 Coll., the Criminal Procedural Code, art. 350b and following.
65   See: Chapter 1.5.2 Criminal Law, Criminal Procedure, Penitentiary Legislation & Foreigners.
66   See: Chapter 1.4.2 Crime, Sentencing Trends and Characteristics Foreign Prison Population.
67   Of course other legal requirements also have to be fulfilled – ibid., p. 65.

ons and centres of the Probation and Mediation Service, which resulted in the creation of several working groups for the purpose of preparing and launching a pilot cognitive-behavioural program for prisoners before and after their conditional release. Based on the analysis of current experience, work continued on the Risk and Need Assessment project, which, apart from the requirement for individualisation of treatment, will lead to a better prediction of results of re-socialisation activities. A methodological paper was published as part of the gradual implementation of the concept of risk and needs assessment into the methodology of the handling of imprisoned persons. This paper updates the content and structure of comprehensive reports in an effort to seek possibilities for the formulation of treatment programs so that they logically relate to the risk and need assessment system.'[68] It has to be noted that nowadays the role of mediation within imprisonment is being increasingly discussed, when successful mediation helps to remedy the relationship between the convict and victim.[69]

2.11 Staff

2.11.1 Theoretical situation

'Lifelong learning remained an integral part of the fulfilment of the main objectives of personnel work. Through it, the Prison Service endeavours improved development of its employees in their professions, or the possibility of their occupying managerial positions, and last but not least the enhancing of their responsibilities and performance.'[70] This enhancement is to be achieved through special courses that the Prison Service organizes.[71]

2.11.2 Actual situation

Nearly all responded prisoners have positive or neutral relationship with prison guards and other prison staff; twenty foreign prisoners claim that prison guards and other prison staff do not treat them differently compared to Czech prisoners.[72] All respondents answered that prison staff communicates with them in Czech language, and that the prisoners try to speak Czech as well.[73]

One member of prison staff who participated in the study assumes that prison guards treat foreign prisoners differently, which can however be predominantly attributed to communication difficulties. All ten respondents claim that prison guards speak only in Czech with foreign prisoners. Somewhat miscellaneous answers were registered in comparison with foreign prisoners, while six respondents supposedly speak with foreign pris-

---

[68] Generální ředitelství Vězeňské služby ČR (2006), Výroční zpráva Vězeňské služby České republiky za rok 2005, Generální ředitelství Vězeňské služby ČR, Praha pp. 19. *(The General Directorate of the Prison Service of the Czech Republic (2006), Annual Report of the Activities of the Prison Service of the Czech Republic for 2005, The General Directorate of the Prison Service of the Czech Republic, Prague, pp. 19), bilingual version;*

[69] Bernard, J. et al (2005), '*Mediace v rámci výkonu trestu odnětí svobody*', ('*Mediation within Imprisonment*'), Příloha časopisu České vězeňství (Supplement of the Journal of the Czech Prison Service), 1, p.p. 5-14.

[70] ibid p. 68, pp. 26 ff.

[71] See: www.ivvs.cz/vzdelani/kurzy *(Czech version only)*.

[72] See: Chapter 2.1.

[73] See: Chapter 2.1 – solving the problem of language barriers.

oners in foreign languages.[74] Merely one respondent participated in the special course – Treatment of Foreign Prisoners – that is organized by the Prison Service, and only one respondent took part in the special language course that aims to improve communication with Russian speaking prisoners.

2.12 Projects

As mentioned above under section two the Institute of Criminology and Social Prevention in Prague conducted the research concerning foreign nationals in Czech penitentiary institutions in 2002-2003. Its main objective was to characterize the prison population, to name the main problems concerning treatment of foreign prisoners and to state specific recommendations on the basis of all information.[75] The Czech Helsinki Committee realized the project focused on the Czech Prison Service in 2003-2005. The research also includes the monitoring of Czech prisons and case agenda.[76] This project is not primarily focused on foreign prisoners. Nowadays a three year project 'Šance' ('Chance') is being realized. The project focuses on the reintegration of prisoners after their release. The prison in Plzeň (Pilsen) provides a special Czech language course for foreign prisoners.

3 ADMINISTRATIVE DETENTION OF FOREIGN PRISONERS

Illegal migration is considered to be a serious problem in the Czech Republic. The term 'illegal migration' comprises two basic categories:

- Illegal migration across the national border into the territory of the Czech Republic
- Breach of residency rules

In 2004 a total of 9,433 persons illegally crossed the Czech national border (7,555 foreign nationals were obliged to have a visa when entering the Czech Republic), which was a decrease of 19% compared to the previous year.. Most illegal migrants came from the Russian Federation (3,725 persons), China (1,009), Ukraine (878), Georgia (564), Moldova (294) and Vietnam (237).[77] The number of asylum-applicants declined after the EU accessions of May 2004. In that year, 2,728 asylum-applicants were registered, the most of whom were citizens of Ukraine (29,3 %), the Russian Federation (27,4 %), Vietnam (7,1 %), China (5,9 %) and Belarus (4,1 %). 142 foreigners were in fact granted asylum (i.e. 2,6 %). According to the report the trend of illegal migrants abusing asylum procedures continues, while 417 persons were transferred from detention facilities for foreigners to asylum facilities.[78] The total number of persons breaching the residency rules in the Czech Republic dropped to 16,696 persons (-21, 8 %) in 2004. Illegal residence of

---

[74] ibid., p. 73.

[75] See Introduction.

[76] See www.helcom.cz

[77] Ministerstvo vnitra ČR (2005), Zpráva o situaci v oblasti veřejného pořádku a vnitřní bezpečnosti na území České republiky v roce 2004 ve srovnání s rokem 2003, Ministerstvo Vnitra ČR, Praha; *(The Ministry of the Interior (2005), Report on Public Order and Internal Security in the Czech Republic in 2004 compared with 2003, The Ministry of the Interior, Prague).*

[78] ibidem, p. 77.

foreign nationals usually goes hand in hand with other illegal activities such as work without permission, obstruction of the execution of an official decision (which is a criminal offence)[79], pick pocketing or thefts. According to the law, an administrative decision of expulsion was imposed upon 15,194 foreigners, predominantly concerning citizens of Ukraine (66,9 %), China (7 %) and the Russian Federation (5 %).

The conditions of detention facilities for foreign nationals were subject to repeated critique from the CPT and the Ombudsman among others.[80] In concordance with recommendations, the law no. 326/1999 Coll. on the residence of foreigners in the Czech Republic was amended in order to establish appropriate regimes in such facilities. Since 1 January 2006 the issue of administrative detention has fallen within the competence of The Administration of Refugee Facilities (Správa uprachlických zařízení) within the Ministry of the Interior. The conditions for administrative detention of a foreign national are regulated in Articles 124-149 of the Law on Residence of Foreigners. A detained foreign national has the right to a judicial review of the administrative decision. The maximum duration of such administrative detention may not exceed 180 days (90 days for minors). The police are legally obliged to inform a respective diplomatic mission/consulate as well as a relative should the individual in question request this. Currently, 305 persons (249 men, 56 women, 11 minors) are detained in four administrative detention facilities in the Czech Republic - Poštorná, Frýdek-Místek, Velké Přílepy and Bělá-Jezová. [81]

The asylum issue has been a matter for the Ministry of the Interior since 1990. Nowadays, the issue more specifically lies in the competence of the Department of Asylum and Migrant Policy and is directed by the first deputy of the Minister of the Interior. The Administration of the Refugee Facilities (Správa uprchlických zařízení) was established in 1996 as a structural unit of the Ministry of the Interior. The main objective is to provide accommodation, food, health care, social and other services for asylum-applicants.[82] According to the law we recognize three types of asylum facilities: entrance, stay and integrative facilities.[83]

The objective of entrance facilities is to provide new asylum-applicants with accommodation and basic surroundings until the entrance procedure has been completed. This procedure involves the identification of a person, complex medical examinations and the initiation of administrative proceedings. All asylum-applicants must undergo such a procedure in a closed facility. It is necessary to emphasize that applicants are not allowed to leave such a facility, because they could pose 'health hazards' to the general population. There are two main entrance facilities in Vyšní Lhota with a capacity of 580 places and a transit area in airport Praha- Ruzyně with a capacity of 16 places. There is also a reserve capacity of 167 places in the asylum stay facility in Červený Újezd. After the entrance procedure has been completed, the asylum-applicant has the right to arrange his/her

---

[79] See: Art. 171 of the Criminal Code, e. g. Failure to leave the Czech Republic after administrative expulsion decision was imposed.

[80] See: The Council of Europe (2004), *Response of the Czech Government to the Report of European Committee for the Prevention of Torture and Inhuman and Degrading Treatment or Punishment (CPT) on its visit to the Czech Republic from 21 to 30 April 2002*, The Council of Europe - CPT/Inf 5, Strasbourg.

[81] Veřejný ochránce práv (2006), Zpráva z návštěv zařízení pro zajištění cizinců, Úřad Veřejného ochránce práv, Brno; *(The Ombudsman (2006) , Report on Visits in Facilities of Detained Foreign Nationals, The Office of the Ombudsman, Brno).*

[82] For more detailed information see www.suz.cz *(Czech version only).*

[83] See law no. 325/1999 Coll., o azylu.

own accommodation, or will be placed in a facility of stay. Basic surroundings as well as other services are provided for 'waiting' asylum-applicants, too. Such asylum facilities are open, so asylum applicants are able to move outside of the facility, however their movement is still regulated by the law, for example applicants have a right to leave the facility for a maximum period of ten days per calendar month. Any leave longer than 24 hours has to be notified in writing to the Ministry of the Interior. Furthermore, leaves or three days or longer have to be notified to the Ministry 24 hours in advance..[84] It is also necessary to mention that such facilities are internally divided into first and second round sections. The first round sections are for asylum-applicants who are awaiting a decision from the Ministry of the Interior about their application, while the second-round sections accommodate those applicants who have lodged an appeal to the court because their application for asylum has been turned down. There are ten facilities of stay in the Czech Republic – Bělá pod Bezdězem, Červený Újezd, Zastávka u Brna, Kostelec nad Orlicí, Havířov, Bruntál, Kašava, Stráž pod Ralskem, Seč and Zbýšov.

Facilities of integration serve as temporary accommodation for persons who have been granted asylum. People whose applications for asylum have been accepted have the same legal position as Czech nationals in the labour market and in the social security and health-care systems. Their accommodation is regulated by lease, and rent has to be paid until a person has acquired permanent accommodation from the state integrative program or private accommodation. There are four facilities of integration in the Czech Republic – Předlice, Hošťka, Jaroměř a Zastávka u Brna. The Administration of the Refugee Facilities *(Správa uprchlických zařízení)* cooperates with a number of international and national organizations (e. g. UNHCR Prague, IOM Prague, Hessisches Sozialministerium, Office for Repatriation and Illegal Residents etc.)[85]

4 NATIONALS DETAINED ABROAD

The Ministry of Justice is not able to provide any information on Czech nationals detained abroad. In case that there is no international treaty on assistance in criminal matters Czech nationals might be imprisoned without awareness of the Czech authorities. Some cases of Czech nationals who have been imprisoned abroad have been highlighted by the media (for instance Emil Novotný and Radek Hanykovics case of drug smuggling in Thailand) while other cases remain unknown both to the public and to the Czech authorities. It has to be noted that those cases of Czech nationals who have been imprisoned abroad that the Czech authorities are aware of usually seek to serve their sentences in their home country, because of inhuman imprisonment conditions in some countries.

---

[84] art. 82 of the law no. 325/1999 Coll., o azylu.
[85] http://www.unhcr.cz; www.iom.cz; www.sozialministerium.hessen.de; www.uric.gov.pl, www.minv.sk/mumvsr/; www.fedasil.be; www.asylum.redcross.dk; www.justice.ie; www.coa.nl; www.hero.no; www.migrationsverket.se; www.bmbah.hu

5 EVALUATION AND RECOMMENDATIONS

Information obtained through this research is necessarily evaluated as preliminary, because it is the first time that the specific issue of social exclusion of foreign prisoners in Czech prisons has been debated. It is obvious and it should be recognized that foreign national prisoners have different needs than Czech prisoners do. The research, even though it was conducted within two months and with a limited scope, objectively revealed that some groups of foreign prisoners are socially excluded. One of the findings of the research is that medical care is considered to be the most problematic issue for foreign prisoners. The vast majority of responding prisoners claim that they are treated differently, because they do not have health insurance. Accordingly, they are allegedly not entitled to receive any or proper treatment or medicine. The situation is based on the legislation that is in force, which indicates that only necessary and urgent medical care is provided 'free of charge' for foreign prisoners on remand/in imprisonment without health insurance. It shall be noted that the Prison Service has to cover all costs of such provided medical care with its own budget. Difficulties with the freedom of religion have also been highlighted. Some Muslim prisoners claim that they feel to be disadvantaged because of the prescribed prison dress (wearing *habits* is not allowed), personal hygiene and food (dietary needs in concordance with *halal* are not properly adhered to). Foreign Muslim prisoners have no access to qualified religious representative (*Imam*), although this is very important to many of them.

I would like to propose to the Prison Service that a Muslim adviser be appointed whose work would involve the preparation of a directory and guide on religious practices to enable prison staff to know more about religious needs of foreign prisoners. Such a book should provide information about the Muslim religion as well as the corresponding diet, dress, the role of personal hygiene and families etc. Members of other religious groups have the same right to practise their religion (e.g. Christian prisoners), so it is also necessary for the Prison Service to provide access to a qualified Muslim religious representative (*Imam*) for all Muslim prisoners.

Other findings of the Research are that although progress has been made, the Prison Service is still heading to its objectives with overcoming language barriers. It will be worthwhile to prepare special booklets (not only a translation of the laws on execution of remand/imprisonment) designed for foreign prisoners in the most common foreign languages. These booklets should contain information on his/her rights and duties and contacts to embassies /consulates. Furthermore, it should deal with issues of asylum, prison regimes etc. It would also be appropriate to provide brief information for visitors (e.g. family members of foreign prisoners) in most common foreign languages. More things have to be changed, for instance regarding the professional training of prison staff who works with foreign prisoners. Without any doubt it is absolutely necessary that prison staff undergo a special course as well as foreign language courses that are currently provided by the Prison Service.[86] Another finding has to be necessarily mentioned. The procedure of access to the telephone shall be regulated as more transparent, while the term 'legitimate' reason may be interpreted different ways.

In conclusion I would like to mention that evaluation as well as other relevant information stemming from this research should be submitted to all involved and relevant par-

---

[86] See: Chapter 2.11 Prison staff.

ties in order to address the issue of social exclusion of foreign prisoners within Czech penitentiary institutions.[87]

---

[87] E.g. The Prison Service, The Institute of Criminology and Social Prevention in Prague, University of West Bohemia /Faculty of Law/ Department of Criminal Law, The Czech Helsinki Committee etc.

Chapter 6

Denmark

Anette Storgaard

1 INTRODUCTION

Article 71 of the Danish Constitution of 1953 requires the legality of any deprivation of liberty. Subsections 1-5 regulate criminal procedure while subsections 6-7 are concerned with administrative detention. Detailed rules are given in different, more specific legal sources. In this context the Penal Code, the Code on Legal Procedure and the Code on Foreigners are the most relevant to mention. Deprivation of liberty is never the one and only legal solution. An individual may only be deprived of his/her liberty when it is provided for in law and, firstly, if no less intrusive mean is sufficient in order to reach the aim and, secondly, if the the principle of proportionality applies.[1]

The following article focuses primarily on Danish rules, practices and procedures. International and European conventions shall only occasionally be mentioned. Focus is also concentrated on the deprivation of liberty, which means that other forms of legal interference, like for instance taking fingerprints or orders to stay in contact with the police, are not regarded here. Furthermore, other issues that are of relevance to foreigners in Denmark are not elaborated on here, such as for example residence and permits, citizenship and so on.

An attempt to describe and discuss the issue of nationality in relation to the criminal system cannot be based on one single statistical source or piece of research. One consequence of the fact that experiences must be collected from a number of different sources is that – when observed together – the individual pieces do not form a homogeneous and coherent picture of the actual situation.

There is no difference between foreigners and Danish citizens in terms of legal definitions and the legal framework of charge, offence and imprisonment. According to the Danish Ministry of Justice and to Statistics Denmark, 84,7 % of all charges[2] and 89,9 % of all criminal dispositions in the year 2004 were against Danish citizens.[3]

1.1 Overview of penalties and measures

According to section 31 of the Penal Code fines and imprisonment are the two ordinary sanctions. Although both fines and prison sentences can technically be ordered in both a suspended as well as an unsuspended form, in practice only sentences to imprisonment are in fact suspended. Imprisonment as a response to a criminal offence may only be imposed by the court. Fines may be imposed by the courts or agreed upon between the respective person and the police. Furthermore, according to section 722 of the Code on Legal Procedure, the decision on whether a charge is to be withdrawn (in specific cases, for example for young offenders who come to the attention of the police for the first time) lies in the hands of the police and is consequently confirmed by the court.

In the period from 2001 to 2004, between 100.000 and 150.000 fines (which shall not be further discussed in this article) were imposed annually, if one includes all fines without making any distinction between which rules were violated and which authority – either the police or the court – imposed the fine.

---

[1] Foreign Right, p. 782-783.
[2] Sigtelser 2004 fordelt efter indvandrerbaggrund og oprindelsesland. www.jm.dk
[3] Criminal Statistics 2004, p 27.

Beside a number of possible conditions for suspended sentences that are regulated in section 57 of the Penal Code, two interventions are stated as alternatives to imprisonment. Firstly, the Community Service Order (CSO) has been gradually introduced into and implemented in the Danish sanctioning system since 1982. Initially, CSOs were introduced in specific geographical regions, but from 1984 onwards they were introduced at the national level. In 1992[4] the status of the CSO was changed from being an experiment to an ordinary penalty that is regulated in sections 62-67 of the Penal Code. The CSO is described as an alternative to imprisonment but is imposed by the courts as a condition of a suspended sentence. Secondly, in 2005 electronic monitoring[5] with „bracelets" or „tags" ("serving sentences at home"; "home curfew") was introduced as an alternative to imprisonment for cases of drunk driving, in sections 78A-78F of the CEP. In April 2006, the scope of application for electronic monitoring is to be extended to cases of juveniles (aged 15-17) who have committed less serious offences.

Section 74a of the Penal Code provides for the so-called Youth Sanction as a specific intervention for juveniles. The Youth Sanction is a two-year measure that incorporates both institutional as well as social training. It may be applied when juveniles are convicted of a crime for which the most appropriate sanction is imprisonment of at least three months.

Both the CSO and the Youth Sanction can only be imposed by the court, while electronic tagging is an administrative measure. These alternatives are viewed as ordinary elements of the sanctioning system. The criteria for their application are general, like for instance age and the crime committed, while nationality is not a formal criterion.

1.2 Overview of the Prison System

1.2.1 Organisational Structure

With only few exceptions[6], any detention that stands in connection with (the suspicion of) crime in Denmark takes place in institutions that are governed, controlled and supervised by the Department of Prisons and Probation. There are two main categories of penal institutions in Denmark. Firstly, there are pre-trial-prisons, which are located in the close vicinity of the court-buildings. They are designed to house persons awaiting trial as well as sentenced persons either serving a relatively short sentence (six months or less) or awaiting placement in a prison. The latter category is "prisons", which solely accommodate convicted offenders serving a sentence.

The decision on whether a person is to be placed in pre-trial detention or in prison mainly depends on the degree of suspicion and on the sentence that is to be served. Neither gender nor national background is explicitly taken into account in the legal framework, neither in formal law nor in administrative instructions. But if a suspect or

---

[4] Supplement to the Penal Code, no. 6 of 3 January 1992.
[5] Supplement to Code on Execution of Penalties, no. 367 of 24 May 2005 and Parliamentary instruction no 506 of 17 June 2005.
[6] The exceptions where a punishable person may be detained in an institution that is governed and controlled by other authorities or services are mainly when persons suffering from a mental disease before or after conviction are placed in a secure hospital for the mentally ill; and juveniles, who should be placed in institutions for juveniles under the Social Services in stead of in pre-trial detention centres or prisons. These groups, however, are not central to this article.

sentenced person is aged between 15 and 18, the authorities are obliged to make an effort to find an alternative institution[7]. After having been sentenced the prisoner is allocated to either a closed or an open institution. The majority of the closed prisons are located in the cities whereas open prisons are predominantly based in the countryside. The pre-trial-detention facilities and the closed prisons have the same levels of security. They all have perimeter walls supplied with video cameras and separated wards. An open prison is more like a campus in which the prisoners can move relatively freely during the daytime.

In the mid 1990s a number of open prisons established semi-open departments. The Department of Prisons and Probation justified this decision by pointing to a lower utilization rate in the open prisons than in the closed institutions, which was said to be due to the fact that a smaller proportion of the convicted persons were suitable for open prisons. In other words an upcoming proportional imbalance between the number of prisoners and the capacity of the prisons was foreseen. An inmate may only be placed in a semi-open ward if he or she is "qualified" for closed prison but need not necessarily be transferred to such an institution.[8] While the courts decide on the length of the sentence, the type and location of the prison is determined by the Department of Prisons and Probation.

Ultimo 2005 the total capacity of the Danish prisons system was 4.316. Though the borderline between closed and open prisons is becoming unclear because of the semi-open and semi-closed units it is still meaningful to describe the capacity as follows: closed capacity: 939 places distributed in five closed prisons and two closed units in open prisons, and 1.659 places distributed in 12 open prisons. The rest of the capacity is distributed in about 40 pre-trial prisons, which in terms of security are to be compared with closed prisons.

As is mentioned below (section 1.4) the prison capacity is and has been under pressure for several years. In order to ease the pressure, defeat drugs among prisoners and decrease absence owing to sickness among staff the budget of the penalty sector was increased as a result of a political agreement in 2004. According to this political agreement the budget of the sector was increased with totally 1.556 million Dkr over the years 2004-2007. This brings the annual budget up to a little more than 2 billion Dkr.[9]

There is, however, another category of persons who are detained in institutions under the Department of Prisons and Probation without in fact having committed a crime (or being under the suspicion of having done so). This group comprises foreigners who are seeking asylum and who may be detained according to one of the reasons listed in the Code on Foreigners[10] while awaiting a decision on their case.

1.2.2 Foreign Prisoners

Foreign prisoners who are to be expelled after having served their sentence are always placed in closed prisons (see section 2.9 below). But foreigners are not placed in separate units or wards in the closed prisons. The placing of foreign prisoners is administered like

---

[7]   It happens, though only once in a while, that a 15-17 year old person is placed in prison.
[8]   Department of Prisons and Probation, Yearly Reports 1999 and 2000.
[9]   Year 2007: 2.066 billion Dkr. (1 Euro = 7,50 Dkr). Kriminalforsorgen, marts 2004.
[10]   Code on Foreigners, no 826 of 24 August 2005.

the placing of prisoners in general, which implicates that normally prisoners serve their sentence as close to important relatives as possible.

On 4 November, in 2005 there were 12.906 prisoners and other clients in the Danish criminal system out of whom 2 % were foreigners, 82 % were Danish and the rest were immigrants (13%) or descendants (3%).[11] The proportions are equivalent to the proportions in May 2004. However, the groups are not evenly dispersed in the different subgroups. All foreigners are either to be found in the closed prisons, or the pre-trial prisons. In the closed prisons Danish prisoners form 68 %, immigrants 20 %, descendants 4 % and foreigners 8 %, whereas there are no foreigners among the clients under supervision by the probation service, a group in which the Danish clients form 85 %.

A little less than half of all immigrant prisoners (309 out of 760) come from Asia (mainly Lebanon and Iraq), whereas among the imprisoned descendants in 2005 94 out of 177 came from Europe (mainly Turkey).

In the decade 1995-2005 the average yearly number of imprisoned asylum seekers were between 72,4 and 107,7. Averagely throughout the year 2005 74,4 asylum seekers were imprisoned.[12]

1.3 Overview over the involvement of Consulates, embassies, Ministries of the home country, Probation Service of the home country, NGO's etc.

It is not possible to describe the concrete involvement of different consulates and embassies. Neither the media nor reports from the Ombudsman, NGOs or the like indicate major problems in relation to prisoner's rights to meet embassy representatives (described below).

The most important NGOs in Denmark in the field of foreigners are the Red Cross and the Danish Refugee Council. Their efforts are mainly concentrated on general issues, for instance the situation of children in asylum centres. The NGOs do not focus much on individual cases.

The Danish Red Cross offers visits to lonely people in general. Among others the organisation offers visits in prisons. This service as well as the efforts to support children of prisoners, however, is not in any way dedicated to foreigners.

The Red Cross offers translation services in more than 20 languages. The price is 400 Dkr per hour no matter if the interpretation is oral or written. The court-language is Danish but persons who do not understand Danish have the right to have everything, including documents, interpreted. Interpretation is needed (and prescribed in the Procedural Code section 149) in all criminal cases involving foreigners. If the the accused is found guilty, he is also obliged to refund all costs to the state, including defence, interpretation etc. This is one of the very important explanations why prisoners are often deeply in debt. Foreign prisoners are no exception in this question, except for the additional costs that arise from the necessary translations.

Normally interpretation is only in use during the investigation and in court. Afterwards when a person is in prison interpretation is no daily or regular occurrence. It may even happen that a prisoner is transferred from one prison to another without being pro-

---

[11] Department of Prisons and Probation, Yearly Report, 2005, page 32.

[12] Department of Prisons and Probation, Yearly Report, 2005, page 37.

vided with any understandable explanation. Such a transfer can take place for different reasons, among others in order to use the total prison capacity as well as possible.

1.4 Overview of trends

1.4.1. Sentencing trends

The number of criminal dispositions has not been developing continuously over the years. However, the general impression when comparing dispositions according to the Penal Code and the Traffic Code is that the share of the former is declining while the latter share is on the increase. This trend goes on as for 2005 where 62 % of all criminal dispositions were related to the Traffic Code and 25 % were related to violations of the Penal Code.[13] Furthermore, the proportion of sentences to unsuspended imprisonment appears to be declining slightly while the imposition of suspended sentences and fines tends to be slightly increasing. The proportions between males, females and companies are almost stagnant. See tables 1.A, 1.B and 1.C below. [14]

Table 1.A Penal dispositions by violated code

	1994	1995	2000	2001	2002	2003	2004
Absolute number of criminal dispositions	172.946	165.566	165.487	164.872	148.903	161.714	194.926
Type of Code (%)	100	100	100	100	100	100	100
Penal Code	37	37	32	32	36	33	29
Traffic Code	51	51	58	58	54	55	59
Other spec. Codes	12	13	10	10	10	12	12

Table 1.B Penal disposition by type of disposition in %

	1994	1995	2000	2001	2002	2003	2004
Type of disposition	100	100	100	100	100	100	100
Unsusp.imprisonment	9	8	7	6	7	7	6
Susp. Imprisonment	5	5	6	8	8	8	7
Fine	74	75	76	74	71	71	76
Other[15]	12	12	12	12	14	14	11

---

[13] Criminal Statistics, Yearly Report 2005, page 21.
[14] Concerning tables 1.A-1.C: Criminal Statistics Yearly Report 2004, page 19.
[15] Withdrawal of charge, neglect of charge and verdict of not guilty.

213

Table 1.C Penal disposition by gender

	1994	1995	2000	2001	2002	2003	2004
Gender	100	100[16]	100	100	100	100	100
Male	84	84	82	83	84	84	82
Female	15	15	16	15	14	14	16
Companies	1	2	2	2	2	2	2

Table 1.D below shows an increasing number of inmates in all the main categories of imprisonment. This is the case for males as well as for females.

Table 1.D Average number of inmates per day[17] - main[18] categories

	Custody/pre-trial Male/Female	Closed imprisonment Male/Female	Open imprisonment Male/Female	Secure imprisonment Male/Female
2001	805 / 44	1047 / 44	963 / 53*	24 / 0
2002	956 / 46	1119 / 55	1097 / 54*	23 / 0
2003	1005 / 55	1170 / 51	1191 / 53	23 / 0
2004	1028 / 61	1220 / 51	1254 / 58	26 / 0

* a special type of imprisonment, "lenient imprisonment", was phased out at the beginning of this decade. In 2001 the average number of male and female inmates in lenient imprisonment was 96 and four respectively. In 2002 the figures were 16 and two. As lenient imprisonment was almost comparable to open prisons the number of "leniently imprisoned" people should be added to the number of inmates in open prisons to complete the information.

Table 1.E shows that as the number of convicted persons admitted to prisons mainly seems to have been declining, the number of unsuspended sentences more severe than fines appears to have been increasing. The majority of all unsuspended sentences to imprisonment are shorter than six months.

---

16 The counting error is copied from the source.
17 Criminal Statistics Yearly Reports 2001, p. 124, 2002, p. 122, 2003, p. 122 and 2004, p. 122.
18 The categories which are not included are unpaid fines, imprisonment for breaches of the Code on Foreigners, to which we will return below, and for 2001 and 2002 also lenient imprisonment.

Table 1.E Admission to prison, unsuspended sentences and their length[19]

	Convicted persons admitted to prison		Unsuspended sentences greater than fine		Sentenced to 6 months or less
	Abs	Pr. 100.000	abs.	Average length	
1985	15007	360	6306	7,0	4582 (72%)
1990	13878	325	7432	6,4	5729 (77%)
1995	17746	410	8074	5,8	6607 (81%)
2000	11700	269	7561	7,4	5821 (76%)
2004	9602	219	10722	6,1	8643 (80%)

From 2004 to 2005 the average length of all unsuspended sentences declined from 6,1 months to 5,7 months. Unsuspended sentences for violations of the Traffic Code declined from 1,5 months to 1,4 months on average, whereas the average concerning violation of the Penal Code declined from 7,3 months to 6,8 months. The only crime for which the average length increased was minor violence for which the average length of the unsuspended part of the sentences increased from 2,7 to 2,9 months.[20]

If we focus on the share of criminal dispositions and the share of sentences to imprisonment and compare 1995 with 2005 it becomes obvious that there are less convictions for violations of the Penal Code (1995: 1.405/100.000 and 2005: 1.284/100.000) but more prison sentences (1995: 388/100.000 and 2005: 410/100.000). The trend is almost opposite regarding violations of the Traffic Code (1995:1.908/100.000 and 2005: 3.089/100.000) and the share of resulting prison sentences (1995: 99/100.000 and 2005: 100/100.000).[21]

Each year on a random day in December the Department of Prisons and Probation creates an overview of the crimes for which the prisoners are serving their sentences. Table 1 F below shows a few of the crimes which changed by 1,0% or more from 2001 to 2005.

Table 1.F Crime committed[22]

	27th Dec 01	20th Dec 02	2nd Dec 03	27th Dec 04	27th Dec 05
Prisoners[23]	2.146	2.440	2.709	2.567	2.994
Murder %	8,8 %	6,9 %	6,3 %	6,6 %	5,7 %
Violence %	20,2 %	20,3 %	22,4 %	24,0 %	23,7 %
Drugs %	16,0 %	15,7 %	15,0 %	17,8 %	17,3 %
Theft %	13,8 %	13,8 %	13,8 %	12,8 %	15,6 %

---

19 Criminal Statistics Yearly Reports; 1985, p 56 and 58, 1990, p. 62 and 65, 1995, p. 59 and 64, 2000, p. 65 and 67, 2004, p. 45, 73 and 74.
20 Criminal Statistics, Yearly Report 2005, page 23.
21 Criminal Statistics Yearly Report, 2005, page 22-23.
22 Department of Prisons and Probation, Yearly Report, 2005, page 26.
23 The number of prisoners is the total number of convicted prisoners on that random day, whereas the information about each crime shows how many % of the total number of prisoners were convicted for this specific crime.

Since 1994, the average utilization of the prison-capacity has increased almost every year, from 91.3 % in 1994[24] to over 97 % in 2005. The Department of Prisons and Probation finds a utilization of averagely 92 % normal in relation to manpower and physical facilities within the prisons.[25] A Danish prison director describes occupation and leisure-facilities as insufficient when occupancy levels are so high. One of his points is that marginal clients (by which he may mean women or foreigners) can not possibly be occupied, and that relevant considerations in matching the right prison for the right person can not be properly taken into account.[26]

Overcrowding in prisons has self-evident negative consequences. Especially in the closed prisons even a small conflict could escalate if there is no empty cell to which a prisoner can be transferred. Since the total numbers of employees as well as technical equipment are intended and provided for lower occupancy levels, there is less time and less energy per inmate in relation to prison-life and in relation to their preparation for release, for instance organising future accommodation or employment. Furthermore, as release on parole cannot take place if the inmate does not have adequate housing, overcrowding may result in a person being in prison for a longer period of time than is in fact necessary.

In the periods of high utilization another tendency has been dominant in the Danish prison system. That is a tendency of developing different types of special units, like family-units, treatment-units for drug addicts respectively alcoholics, semi-closed units in open prisons and others. Today every prison has at least one – and more often several – special units. From an adminstrative and efficiency oriented point of view, these two tendencies do not combine with each other very well.

Recently, the Department of Prisons and Probation announced that due to an increased institutional capacity and to the introduction of electronic monitoring the backlog of persons waiting to serve a prison sentence will have nearly disappeared at the beginning of 2006.

1.4.2 Characteristics of the Foreign Prison Population

In combination, overcrowding and specialization result in prisons with less resource for prisoners, who are not immediately motivated, and who do not need or who are not taken in to one of the special units. For instance foreigners will be at risk of being "dumped" into the prison-places without receiving any special or specific attention.

In the year 2005 the Department of Prisons and Probation published a report on ethnic minorities within the prison population.[27]

It appears that foreigners account for 23 % of the imprisoned population and they are mainly placed in the ordinary units, which house about two thirds of all prisoners. Additionally, interviewed staff members have stressed that inmates belonging to ethnic minorities often band together and to a certain degree form groups which seem to be powerful in a problematic way.

---

24 Department of Prisons and Probation, Yearly Report, 2004, page 23.
25 Department of Prisons and Probation, Nyt fra Kriminalforsorgen, no. 6, 2005, page 5.
26 Engbo, Hans Jørgen in WWW.helsinki-komiteen.dk
27 http://www.kriminalforsorgen.dk (publikationer/rapporter og undersøgelser/Undersøgelse og anbefalinger vedrørende etniske minoriteter i kriminalforsorgen 2005).

In the light of this background, the publishers of the report recommends that foreigners should be spread out across more units in more prisons in order to avoid the development of problematic groups and to promote their integration (those who are not expelled after having served the prison sentence) into Danish society. Furthermore, the report stresses that a better distribution requires that (more) foreigners be placed in the treatment units which again challenges both the motivation of the prisoners as well as the capacity of treatment places in the prisons.

Apart from the recommendation of including more foreigners in the treatment units, the report stresses the importance of a successful mentoring concept (also mentioned below under 2.8). Further still, reference is made to inspiring experiences from using consultants from ethnic minorities, and it recommends more common prison-activities where Danish as well as foreign prisoners and staff members are active together, for instance team sports or the like. More organised contacts between the foreign prisoners and the "external" employment service, educational establishments and, for instance, relatives and former teachers are also recommended.

The authors of the departmental report were not the first to suggest that more foreigners should be admitted to the treatment units. Earlier evaluations had already indicated a very low proportion of foreigners in these units, as is elaborated under section 2.8 below.

In spite of the fact that – in principle – there are no legal differences between foreigners and Danes, two Danish researchers, Holmberg and Kyvsgaard, find it relevant to raise the question: "Are immigrants and their descendants discriminated against in the Danish criminal justice system?"[28]

Part of the background for their question is an overrepresentation of foreigners in the penal system which can be illustrated through one of the statistics from Statistics Denmark that is not published on a regular basis. Every now and then statistics on the registration of crime for national groups compared to their respective share in the overall population are published. The latest publication covers the period from 1995 to 2002.[29] The proportion of penal sentences for male foreigners increased from 1995 to 2000 but it was stable from 2000 to 2002. In 1995 the proportion of sentences was 24 % higher for foreign men than for men in general, and in 2000 and 2002 it was even 38 % higher. The increase is markedly higher for foreign descendents than for immigrants. In 1995, male descendents had 64 % more sentences for crimes and in 2002 they had 98 % more sentences than all men sentenced in Danish courts. For immigrants the sentences were 21 % and 30 % above the general level in 1995 and 2002 respectively, including a modest decrease from 2000 to 2002. Descendents form 10 % of the foreign men between 15 and 64 years olds, so the difference is much more significant when observed in relative terms rather than in absolute numbers. The same can be observed for women, however at a much lower level. Women found guilty of at least one crime form 1 % of the population

---

[28] L. Holmberg and B. Kyvsgaard, *"Are Immigrants and Their Descendants Discriminated against in the Danish Criminal Justice System?"* Journal of Scandinavian Studies in Criminology and Crime Prevention, 2003 vol. 4, no. 2., pp. 125-142.

[29] New statistical information is expected for May 2006. Unless stated otherwise, the statistics refer to the male population between 15 and 64 years. The minimum age of criminal responsibility in Denmark is 15.

but 1,8 % of the female descendant population and 1,4 % of the female immigrant population.[30]

It is a general experience that criminal activity varies considerably by age, urbanization and other social and economic conditions, such as for instance their affiliation with the labour market. Since the conditions of immigrants differ from those of the general population, these differences may account for some of their overrepresentation in the statistics.

1.G Overrepresentation of male immigrants and descendents with a penal disposition, corrected for different conditions.[31]

	Overrepresentation in percent
Not corrected	+ 49 %
Controlling for differences in age	+ 38 %
Controlling for differences in age and urbanization	+ 35 %
Corrected for differences in age and income	+ 19 %
Corrected for differences in age and socio-economic background	+ 8 %

Holmberg and Kyvsgaard consider that this could very well not solely explain the overrepresentation of foreigners. Rather, they could also tend to have a higher probability of being detected and apprehended. According to the authors this assumption corresponds with research experiences from other countries.

Beginning with charges in combination with arrests (a charge is sometimes, but not always, combined with an arrest) and subsequently convictions, Holmberg and Kyvsgaard find a clear trend: "for immigrants, the event of an arrest not leading to a conviction is 39% more frequent than for persons with a Danish background. For descendants, the difference is even greater (73%). For all persons with a foreign background the difference is 45%."[32]

Out of a total number of 2,690 custody cases not resulting in a subsequent conviction, 2,115 involved persons with a Danish background, while the remaining 575 were against foreigners. The 2,115 of these cases against Danes constituted four percent of all custody cases against Danish citizens. The 575 cases against foreigners formed eight percent of all custody cases against foreigners.[33]

Turning their attention to all penal dispositions, Holmberg and Kyvsgaard[34] indicate that while 3,3 % of the population with a Danish background have had a penal disposition passed against them the same goes for 5,0 % of the population with a foreign background (4,7% of immigrants and 7,9% of their descendants).

30 www.dst.dk/ Nyt fra Danmarks Statistik, nr. 235, 27 May 2004.
31 L Holmberg and B. Kyvsgaard, 2003, pp. 127. The authors use information from Statistics Denmark but regret that the figures are not corrected simultaneously for all the differences, namely age, urbanization, income and socio-economic background. Further recent data (published June 2004) show an overrepresentation at 50 % with no correction and at 4 % with correction for age and socio-economic background, http://www.jm.dk/image.asp?page=image&objno=72137
32 Holmberg, L. and Kyvsgaard, B. 2003 p. 129.
33 Holmberg, L. and Kyvsgaard, B. 2003, p. 132.
34 Holmberg, L. and Kyvsgaard, B. 2003, p. 127.

The authors conclude that: "Persons with a foreign background are, in fact, more likely to be arrested and remanded in custody without a subsequent conviction than are persons with a Danish background, even when their age, gender and crimes are readily comparable."[35] But they do not claim to have found the explanation for it. Rather, they stick to what they can tell from their own research, which besides the statistics also contains their observations from taking part in police patrols: "[A]ll previous studies on Danish police work regarding minorities agree that persons with a foreign background will often attract a disproportionate amount of police attention. They also agree that confrontations between the police and members of such groups are not entirely uncommon." And further: "Based as it is on group probability rates, this kind of police practice is self-reinforcing: the more control, the more illegal acts will be discovered. Police targeting on certain groups will yield evidence that can only reinforce the notion that these groups are worthy of special attention-and will contribute to their overrepresentation in the criminal justice system. This problem seems impossible to solve; it is inherent in proactive policing, and it does not only concern ethnic minorities."

The major part of the overrepresentation of foreigners within the penal system relates to violations of the Penal Code, mainly theft (178 %), whereas in the cases of rape (110 %) and violence (130 %) – which attract more media attention – the degree of overrepresentation is lower. Two thirds of all penal dispositions are reactions to breaches of the Traffic Code. Here the overrepresentation of foreigners is 8 %.[36]

1.5 Overview of national legislation

1.5.1 Penitentiary Legislation

Being locked up in prison results in lonesomeness, but it also implies a lack of or weak access to public services, information, debate, and so on. Consequently it is of common interest for both the prisoners and the prisons to be well aware of prisoners' legal rights. For the people in prison, legal rights are essential in order to prevent arbitrariness in the fulfilment of the sentence, while for the prisons adhering to and providing legal rights is extremely important in order to obtain respect from and generate confidence among the population.

The penalties are regulated in the Penal Code[37] as is the extent to which they should be imposed. In the year 2000, the first Danish Code on the Execution of Penalties[38] (CEP) was passed. Prior to this legislation all matters of prison life had been regulated administratively through circulars and instructions given by administrative authorities at different levels. Such circulars and instructions are still used complementary to the Code. Further, the European Prison Rules[39] as well as the UN Standard Minimum Rules are viewed as components of the legal basis of the Danish prison system.

---

[35] Holmberg, L. and Kyvsgaard, B. 2003, p. 137.

[36] www.jm.dk. Notat vedrørende Kriminalitet og national oprindelse. 2002.

[37] Penal Code, no 126 of 15 April 1930. Latest revised edition Consolidate Act no 909 of 27 September 2005.

[38] Code on the Execution of Penalties, no 432 of 31 May 2000. Latest revised edition Consolidate Act no 207 of 18 March 2005.

[39] Rec(2006)2.

Within the framework of the CEP the Department of Prisons and Probation is responsible for the running of the prison system. Circulars and instructions are given by the Minister of Justice or the Department or by a lower authority under direction from the Minister or the Department.

Up until the CEP was passed, prisoners had no possibilities for bringing any decisions made by the prison authority before a court. Conflicts had to be solved administratively in the prisons (before the director) or by the Department of Prisons and Probation. Very few kinds of conflicts might (and may still) be brought before the Ombudsman. Complaints are now regulated in chapter 22, sections 111-123 of the CEP, according to which conflicts must firstly be stated before the prison director and subsequently before the Department of Prisons and Probation. When a decision is final it may in a limited number of cases - which are explicitly listed in section 112 CEP - be challenged before the courts. Practically the only question which has been brought before the courts since the introduction of this rule is when release on parole has been denied, and the court has to date always confirmed such refusals of parole.

The European Convention on Human Rights was incorporated into Danish law in 1992.[40] This provides the possibility to file claims of infringements of the Convention before the European Human Rights Courts.

Finally the Programme of Principles (Principprogram) for the Department of Prisons and Probation should be mentioned. The Programme was published in 1993 and was the very first official definition of principles and functions for the prison sector. The programme lays down that the main task is the execution of penalties and that this task consists of two parallel components: first, to exercise the control necessary for executing the penalty, and secondly to support and motivate the sentenced person to lead a life without crime by supporting his social and personal development through work and education. This programme can be seen as the beginning of an increased focus on education and social/cognitive training in prisons. Additionally, the societal trend of 'decentralisation' implies that in the following years the prisons developed different concepts for supporting and motivating their prisoners.

1.5.2 Penitentiary Legislation & Foreigners

As has already been mentioned above there are no formal differentiations between Danish and foreign prisoners in institutions for convicted persons. Consequently, an introduction to foreigners in Danish prisons is more or less an introduction to imprisoned people in Danish prisons in general.

There are cases, however, in which foreigners are mentioned explicitly in the law. These are situations in which it is evident that by simply applying the same rules and practices to both Danes and to foreigners the latter would be treated unequally. When foreigners are mentioned explicitly in the legal sources the intention is not to create or maintain different conditions for foreigners and Danes but - on the contrary - to prevent unequal conditions from arising; in other words, to place individuals in unequal positions on an equal footing. It may, however, be worth some extra thought to enlighten some

---

[40] No 285 of 29 April 1992, revised in no 750 of 19 October 1998 and in Governmental Order no 749 of the same date, CEP with comments, page 247.

further aspects of everyday life in prison in order to secure a higher degree of actual (not just formal) equality.

2005 Denmark codified the European Warrant of Arrest[41], which implicates broader extradition possibilities/duties than before, of Danes as well as foreigners from within Europe. Also, there are a number of bilateral agreements between Denmark and the Nordic countries, USA and a few others. Traditionally the Nordic Countries including Denmark do cooperate very much in the protection of citizens but until now it is not possible to tell to which degree the European Arrest Warrant is going to influence the practices of extradition. The fact is that Denmark often tries to make a Dane who has been convicted abroad serve his sentence in Denmark, whereas foreigners convicted in Denmark do not always want to go to their home country in order to serve the sentence there.

2 TREATMENT OF FOREIGN PRISONERS

Originally there were no general restrictions for foreigners who wanted to stay in Denmark so long as they did not cause problems in relation to public order or demanded help from the social security system. In 1926 a legal demand for residence and work permits for foreigners who wanted to stay in Denmark for more that 3 months was implemented. The approach witnessed a shift from individual control of foreigners geared towards keeping problematic individuals out to a general form of control directed at everybody who is not a Danish citizen. Consequently, everybody now requires their own personal residence and work permits. Thus, permission – not prohibition – must be concrete and individual.

Since the 1970ies there have been two overall tendencies in the developments: some groups - mainly citizens from the Nordic countries and EU-citizens - are privileged, while the possibilities for others are restricted. Unemployment and more recently terrorism are the main arguments for strengthening the control and practice of issuing permits.[42]

2.1 General

A prisoner has the right to be informed of his rights, duties and the prison conditions as soon as possible. It is a general main rule that imprisonment is served in open prisons, unless the sentence is of five years or more. A prison sentence over five years in length, however, can also be served in an open institution insofar as it is considered unproblematic to do so. On the other hand, if – in spite of a sentence being shorter than five years – the sentenced person is a foreigner who is to be expelled after release, the term will always be served in a closed prison (see more under 2.9 below).

Furthermore, a person may always be placed in a closed prison instead of in an open institution for security reasons if the prisoner is classed as being dangerous to himself or to others. More than 90 % of all persons, who are imprisoned, are allocated to an open prison.[43]

---

[41] Code no 833 of 25th of August 2005, revised in Code no 538 and 542 of 8th of June 2006.
[42] Foreign Right, pp. 3-5.
[43] CEP with comments, p. 65.

In general, the open prisons have better possibilities to vary and develop both work-facilities and treatment programmes due to the space available and the different category of inmates that they house in comparison to those that are located in the closed prisons. But overall funding is a major problem. Different practical skills such as painting, brick-laying, farming, driving licenses and carpentry to name but a few are taught within the prison system as a whole. Besides basic school each prison has individual occupation and treatment programmes for the prisoners.

In the prisons - both open and closed - a ward typically comprises eight to 12 cells. Should the institution also house women there will be wards in which the sexes are separated and other wards where they are mixed. Each ward has a kitchen and toilets as well as shower and washing facilities that are adequate for the respective number of persons.

Taking into account factors such as housing, guarding, occupation and so on, a cell in an open prison costs about half as much as a cell in a closed prison. The daily costs for a cell in an open prison are 727 Dkr , while the daily expenses that arise from a cell in a closed prison lie at 1.576 Dkr.[44]

2.2 Living conditions and facilities

In general, it is intended that all prisoners have a cell of their own. But several prisons also retain the possibility of using cells for up to five or six persons in case of a temporary lack of places. Apart from one totally new prison the prisons in Denmark are relatively old and - due to a lack of funds - many prison buildings are in need renovation. A indication of this is given in a new study on imprisoned women[45] where 41% of the respondents state that the temperature in their cells is not appropriate, which obviously implies that the cells tend to be too warm in the summer and too cold in winter.

A very fundamental principle in the management of prisons is *normalization*. This principle contains the ambition to create general prison conditions and facilities that resemble life and conditions in wider society as closely as possible. Normalization is not – which some might believe – a question of "normalizing" the prisoners but of "normalizing" life in prison. A logical consequence of this principle is that because deprivation of liberty is not normal it should never take place to a larger degree than is required due to security reasons.

The principle of normalization consists of at least two core elements, namely the principles of *self management* and *supplying oneself with provisions*, as laid out in section 43 of the CEP. The idea is a kind of de-institutionalization of the prisons which means that even if the prisoners confined they are neither sick nor unable to take care of their own needs in the course of an ordinary day. In other words, individual daily routines, such as for instance cooking, cleaning, washing clothes, beddings etc, are to be carried out by every single person. Consequently, every prison houses a drug-store where prisoners at specific times can buy what they require to cover their daily needs. The above mentioned new research on imprisoned women (of all nationalities) showed a great deal of frustration

---

[44] 1 Euro=7,50 Dkr. Department of Prisons and Probation, Yearly Report, 2003.

[45] The report is coordinated by the Department of Criminology at the University of Greifswald, Germany, and the information regarding Danish prisons can be ordered from the author. The report is not published as a whole.

among the respondents about the stores which were described as being too expensive, selling old goods and offering a very "limited" assortment.

In the pre-trial prisons or the prisons there are sets of "Guidelines for detainees & remand prisoners" in several languages as for instance: Arabic, Czech, Estonian, Farsi, Finnish, French, German, Greenlandic, Italian, Latvian, Lithuanian, Polish, Russian, Serbian, Spanish, Turkish and Urdu [46]. The guidelines are not very detailed but do contain information on rights of defence, duty to work and of course means for contacting the relevant embassy.

2.3 Reception and admission

Once a person has been convicted he/she will either be taken (back) into custody to await information on which prison he shall be serving his sentence in, or he/she returns home to await this information. Practice is mainly dependent on the crime committed and on whether he/she was held in pre-trial detention or not.

As soon as possible after being admitted to prison an action plan [47] for the person's stay in prison and for the initial time period after release must be elaborated. The plan must be made and revised on the basis of dialog and cooperation between the prison and the prisoner. The demand for the elaboration of such an action plan is common for all prisoners [48] except for prison sentences of 60 days or less. An action plan must also be elaborated for the short-term convicted if a Danish prisoner is 18 years old or younger or a foreigner is 26 years old or younger.

2.4 Work – Education – Training – Sports – Recreation

Every prisoner under any kind of deprivation of liberty has the right and the obligation to take part in *work, training/treatment or school* every day (section38, subsection 1 CEP). Before the CEP was confirmed and implemented, the question was only about actual work, but now more forms of constructive occupation are accepted – sometimes even recommended – and consequently remunerated like work. The standard rate of pay for prison work is 8 Dkr per hour, while extraordinarily good or demanding work can be remunerated with an increased salary of up to 12 Dkr per hour (2005). [49]

If a prisoner participates in an education programme or has to interrupt his/her daily work routine in order to attend a cognitive skills programme, the time for which he/she is absent is not deducted from the basic salary. However, on the other hand no bonuses can be achieved. Similarly, full time school education - either in the prison school or in educational institutions outside the prison in some cases - or full time participation in a structured treatment programme are financially rewarded at the same rate as for ordinary prison work. Also, more individual activities can also be financially rewarded, for instance if a prisoner is working as a spokesperson for the prison.

---

[46] The Guidelines may be downloaded from http://www.kriminalforsorgen.dk/

[47] This is solely a plan on developing social skills. Newcomers are not regularly taken to medical and dental checks (see section 2.5 below).

[48] Section 31 CEP, CEP with comments p 82, Instruction no 367 of 17 May 2001, circular no 166 of 29 June 2001 and instruction no 155 of 29 June 2001.

[49] Engbo, p. 211.

It is stressed in a report by the Department of Prisons and Probation on ethnic minorities in the prison and probation system, that more attention should be given to prepare (not least the young) prisoners for the labour-market, that the needs and wishes of ethnic minorities should be taken into account and that external partners should be increasingly included. "External partners" refers to professional as well as non-professional partners like for instance local job-consultants or mentors.[50] In the report on imprisoned women mentioned under section 2.2 above the need for relevant and constructive occupation is also stressed.

Regarding education and training - like for instance cognitive skills - it is stressed in the report on ethnic minorities that the prisons need to know more about the levels of basic education and knowledge of the foreigners in prison. In order to develop adequate programmes the foreign prisoners' knowledge of Danish society, behaviour and the language should be more enhanced. Also, the development of specific cognitive programmes should take cultural, societal and linguistic differences into account.[51]

In relation to foreigners in the prisons the departmental report[52] highlights the following issues as being the most important: information, communication and ensuring that decisions by the prison staff or director have been understood by the prisoners. In order to assist in addressing these issues the authors of the report suggest that persons from the prisoners' network outside the prison be consulted, for example former teachers, parents or social workers.

The fact that there is no proper contact between foreign prisoners and the staff is stressed in interviews with foreign prisoners, referred to in the report. The departmental report points out the importance of common spare time activities as a remedy for the integration of foreign prisoners with Danish prisoners and staff members.

In order to meet the very remarkable and expressed common message from all the prisoners that education is needed the state prison of Ringe piloted the approach of admitting an imam[53] to the institution. In general the foreign prisoners are not experienced by the prison system as being open-minded towards the Danish treatment system for drug addicts, but they are always interested in conversing with the imam.[54]

According to the Code on Execution of Penalties, section 58, prisoners must be able to read newspapers, listen to radio and see TV to some (yet not defined) degree. Further they must be given the possibility to borrow books etc in the public libraries –also to a not defined degree. Finally, the section states that foreign prisoners should – as far as possible – be given the opportunity to read papers, magazines and books in their own languages. The comments to this subsection state, however: "The term "as far as possible" means that there are not only practical but also economical limitations of the prisons duty to make this possible[55].

---

[50] www.kriminalforsorgen.dk/publikationer/rapporterogundersøgelser/Undersøgelse og anbefalinger vedrørende etniske minoriteter i kriminalforsorgen 2005, page 5.

[51] www.kriminalforsorgen.dk/publikationer/rapporterogundersøgelser/Undersøgelse og anbefalinger vedrørende etniske minoriteter i kriminalforsorgen 2005, page 4.

[52] www.kriminalforsorgen.dk/publikationer/rapporterogundersøgelser/Undersøgelse og anbefalinger vedrørende etniske minoriteter i kriminalforsorgen 2005, page 6.

[53] See more under section 2.12 below.

[54] Nyt fra Kriminalforsorgen , December 2005, p 18-19. (News from the Prison and Probation Service, December 2005, p 18-19).

[55] CEP wih comments, page 137.

2.5 Food – Religion – Personal Hygiene – Medical care

It follows from the principles of self management and providing for oneself (CEP section 43) (see above section 2.2) that every prisoner takes care of cooking, personal hygiene and so on. All necessities must be bought in the prison store - including food, soap, toothpaste and whatever else might be needed except for clothes. All prisoners receive 51 Dkr per day (about 7 Euro) (2005) – if they are working or not – to cover their personal needs in this respect (section 42, subsection 2, CEP).[56]

The report on imprisoned women (see section 2.2 above) is very convincing in relation to food at least regarding female prisoners. They are all satisfied with both the quality and quantity of the food provided.

Food-supplies in the stores, however, are not satisfactory. The stores (which obviously have a monopoly in the prison) are expensive and offer products which are not fresh, very one-sided and monotonous. According to the prisoners the special offers that are available in the main department of the same store in the local city never reach the prison store. When a prisoner is out – either on leave, or in order to frequent a job or school– he/she can see the special offers in the local store. However, due to various limitations stemming from the rules – and maybe also due to the prisoner's own financial limitations– it is not possible to bring an unlimited supply of goods from the local store into the prison.

Section 35 CEP states the right to freedom of religion. This implies that prisoners have the right to practice their religion in relation to - for instance - attending services, praying and living in accordance with other religious customs that are important to each individual, like food or work.

This is, however, a rule that was formulated before the number of foreigners and the focus on foreigners reached level that they are at today. Originally, this rule was intended for Christians, but now almost one fourth of the prisoners belong to another religion, and 15-20 % of the prisoners are Muslims. This fact presents new – and still more perceptible - challenges for the principle of religious liberty. Most prisons offer facilities organised for use as churches and staff include full time or part time priests. Also, prison staff also includes an imam in a number of prisons.

Newly published research on the practice of religion in prison concludes that Danish prisons are open to and tolerant of religion. The researching sociologist assumes that an important motive for prisons to be highly aware of religion is that the presence of religion has a positive influence in the prisons. Not least the priests' or the imams' role as a spiritual adviser to all the prisoners who desire it is a very important factor. Contrary to the other staff members, members of religious staff adhere to professional secrecy.[57]

A newspaper article that referred to a PhD on the sociology of religion by Lene Kühle pointed out that the prison staff needs to be better and more frequently instructed on how to handle Muslim prisoners. It is the experience of the author that some prisoners are tending to overemphasize the meaning of their religion in order to obtain power. For instance, food may be an issue in this respect. It is well known that Muslims do not eat

---

[56] Engbo, p. 154.

[57] Kristeligt Dagblad (Christian Daily) 16 of May 2006, Karitte Lind Bejer is the journalist who interviews Lene Kühle about the anthology "Straffens menneskelige Ansigt?" ("The human face of the penalty") and her PhD on the role of religion in the Danish Prisons.

pork. The author refers to an example where Muslim prisoners have attempted to deny Danish prisoners access to the prison kitchens because Muslim food could not be prepared in the same kitchen where pork had been prepared. The same article also states that a new set of treatment guidelines and instructions are on the way.

The existing guidelines for prisoners on serving custodial sentences state the following on religion: "Church services are held in penal institutions and some local prisons. You have the right to speak to the penal institution's/local prison's priest, who belongs to the Danish Lutheran Church. The priest can also arrange for contact with a priest from another faith."

If a prisoner belongs to a recognised faith which forbids him to be working on certain days, he is to be exempted. Concerning food (for a religious perspective): "If you are a vegetarian or belong to a recognised religious faith, special requirements regarding food can be followed. Ask the section's staff or the priest." However, the interviewed foreign prisoners[58] are not satisfied with the limited assortment and the prices in the prison stores, just like the interviewed female prisoners in the above (section 2.2) mentioned report on imprisoned women.

With this background in mind, and according to my personal experience with prison-life, it is reasonable to conclude that the formal rights of the prisoners are modest and in terms of practising religion as well as other essential questions the conditions in reality are often better than the minimum rights that are prescribed in the sources prescribe. This may have different reasons. One reason may be the wish to generate a better atmosphere in the prison (like Lene Kühle suggests). Another may be that each prison has a professional interest in doing a good job by fulfilling legal needs and legal rights to the highest possible degree.

A doctor is associated to every prison and upon reception to the institution a prisoner will always have the opportunity to speak with the doctor or a nurse. Until recently, it was common practice that every prisoner saw the doctor at least once after reception to the institution, but for economical reasons practice has been adapted so that this formerly compulsory visit to the doctor is now only offered.. Also, a prisoner can always ask to be seen by a doctor or nurse and the doctor decides if treatment is required. Should treatment be deemed necessary, it is performed in the prison or in a hospital. Prisoners do not have the right to choose their own doctor or to administer their own medicine as is the case for regular citizens.

An administrative instruction on health care[59] states that if a female prisoner is pregnant the staff must inform the doctor and make it possible for the prisoner to see him/her as soon as possible. Furthermore, if the woman is still in the prison three months or less prior to the expected date of delivery, it has to be agreed in which hospital the child is to be born. It is to be ensured (as far as possible) that children are not born within the prison (sections 10 and 11). There are no special or supplementary provisions for foreigners in this respect.

Each year a number of persons who are guilty of a crime but are suffering from a mental illness are acquitted and sentenced to treatment. Foreigners form 23,5 % of those sentenced to psychiatric treatment after having been found guilty of a crime, compared to

---

[58] www.kriminalforsorgen.dk/publikationer/rapporterogundersøgelser/Undersøgelse og anbefalinger vedrørende etniske minoriteter i kriminalforsorgen 2005, page 39.

[59] No 374 of 17 May 2001.

the 23 % of the prison population for which they account (see part A2 above). This takes place in accordance with sections 16 and 68 or 69 of the Criminal Code. On average, 330 persons were sentenced to treatment per year in the period of 2001 to 2004.[60]

Prisoners (both male and female) who are suffering from psychiatric and mental illnesses, but nonetheless are sentenced to imprisonment, will – if they are not (temporarily) placed in a hospital - be allocated to the closed state prison of Hersted Vester. This prison houses mentally ill prisoners as well as serious sex-offenders, those sentenced to secure (time unlimited) imprisonment (forvaring) and the Greenlanders, who are sentenced in Greenland but in accordance with the Greenlandic criminal law have to serve their sentence in Denmark. Hersted Vester is the only penal institution where psychiatrists belong to the basic staff and where the prisoners can receive continuous psychiatric treatment while serving their prison sentences. From 2002 to 2004 the number of prisoners who were waiting for a cell in Hersted Vester increased from 10 to over 20. The former peak in the number of imprisoned persons waiting for a place there was 18 in 2000. [61]

It is certainly stressed in the report from the Department of Prisons and Probation on ethnic minorities, which has been mentioned several times above, that cooperation between the psychiatric system and the prisons regarding diagnostics and treatment should be expanded and improved. In the same context, it is explicitly suggested to ensure that the interpreters, who are assisting the communication between the foreigner and the prison system, doctors etc, have deep knowledge of both the language as well as the cultural background of the foreign prisoners.[62]

Psychiatric treatment as well as imprisonment may both involve a certain legal restraint towards the patient respectively the prisoner. The psychiatric system and the prison system have different sets of rules on restraint and the choice of rules depends on the institution in which the person is staying at the moment where restraint is necessary. This implies for instance that a prisoner can not be forced to stay in the hospital unless medical indicators prescribe this. However, as long as the prisoner is serving a sentence of imprisonment, he/she returns to prison if he/she does not stay in hospital.

For years, drugs have been an issue of great attention in the Danish criminal system. In 1994 the state prison of Ringe opened the very first drug treatment unit in a Danish prison, the so-called contract-unit. An evaluation of this special unit was conducted in 1998, and revealed that 7,1 % of the prisoners who were treated in there were foreigners, while at the same time foreigners accounted for 49 % of the total population of the institution.[63] A further treatment unit was opened in the state prison in Vridsløselille in 1997. A report on this unit covering the first five years of its operation showed that of the 193 prisoners who had been treated in the examined period, only 13 (6,7 %) were foreigners. [64]

---

[60] Psychiatric diseases and crime (Psykisk sygdom og kriminalitet), p 76. 2006. The Ministry of Social Affairs, The Ministry of Justice and The Home Office.

[61] Psychiatric diseases and crime (Psykisk sygdom og kriminalitet), p 102.

[62] www.kriminalforsorgen.dk/publikationer/rapporterogundersøgelser/Undersøgelse og anbefalinger vedrørende etniske minoriteter i kriminalforsorgen 2005, page 8.

[63] Anette Storgaard: The contract in the State Prison of Ringe, p. 32. Centre for Alcohol and Drug Research, University of Aarhus, Denmark. 1998.

[64] Anette Storgaard: The Import model in the State Prison of Vridsløselille, Appendix 1, p. 2. The Department of Prisons and Probation. 2003.

It must certainly be stressed that neither all Danish nor all foreign prisoners are necessarily in need of treatment for a drug or substance addiction. However, the situation remains that foreigners only account for a very small proportion of those prisoners who receive drug-treatment in the prisons compared to their share of the total prison population. The new and more widespread report published by the Department of Prisons and Probation which is mentioned above[65] concludes that the foreign prisoners are still more frequently placed in ordinary (non-treatment) units than Danish prisoners. Furthermore, the report encourages efforts to determine how foreigners can be more efficiently motivated to participate in drug treatment during their time in prison. Although interviews have shown that Danish prisoners more frequently suffered from addiction problems than their foreign counterparts, still roughly one third of the foreign inmates are assumed to be (ab)users of drugs.

What the drug treatment report might have stressed more clearly is that there may be structural and cultural barriers in the organisation of the programmes (for instance language, methods, approach etc.) that could very well make the concept seem less inviting and relevant to foreigners.. Furthermore, there may be the issue of motivating the prison staff to better motivate the foreign prisoners as firstly: foreigners are often expelled after having served their sentence. Since treatment in prison is more expensive and requires more resources than imprisonment without treatment the staff may find it more plausible to offer one of the few treatment-places to a Dane. Secondly, treatment units are very often funded through short-term financial grants. Such grants are more likely to be extended if it can be proven that the provided treatment is successful. Since the treatment programme was developed in Denmark with Danes in mind, the degree of its success may appear to be greater if predominantly Danish persons are admitted to it.

In July 2006 the Danish Ministry of Justice published a draft proposal for a change of the CEP which intends to guarantee access to treatment for drug addiction for more prisoners and in more prisons than is the case today.[66]

2.6 Consular and legal help

Visits in the prisons as such may among others be paid by The Ombudsman, the Standing Committee on Legal Matters of the Parliament (Folketinget) and the European Committee for the Prevention of Torture and inhuman or degrading Treatment or Punishment (CPT). The prison authorities are obliged to respond to any questions or queries that they may have, and their comments and questions as well as the responses from the prison authorities are published. The Ombudsman provides the Parliament with annual reports on the prison situation. He can take up issues of all kinds, general as well as specific, legal as well as procedural. Traditionally, the Ombudsman is very much aware of prison conditions and his statements are taken very seriously. However, neither the Ombudsman nor the other two mentioned bodies can give orders or prescriptions in relation to prison life.

It occasionally occurs that other groups or bodies arrange visits to the prisons, for example the Danish Institute for Human Rights or groups of lawyers, law students, judges

---

[65] http://www.kriminalforsorgen.dk (publikationer/rapporter og undersøgelser/Undersøgelse og anbefalinger vedrørende etniske minoriteter i kriminalforsorgen 2005).

[66] www.jm.dk

and others with a special or professional interest in the prison system. Though these last mentioned visits do ensure some public contact to the world behind the bars they cannot be categorized as parts of the formal control.

Apart from this and without a defined limitation of duration, every prisoner has the right to receive unsupervised visits from his defence lawyer. Furthermore, foreign prisoners have the right to receive visits from consulates and embassies of their home country.[67] Such visits may – as is the case for all of the previously stated visits with the exception of visits from defence lawyers – be attended by members of staff for security reasons.[68]

According to section 56 CEP all prisoners (national and foreign) have the right to continued correspondence with different national and international organisations and authorities, which all intend to exercise legal and legality control as for instance the Ministry of Justice, the Department of Prisons and Probation, the Ombudsman, Members of Parliament (Folketinget), The European Human Rights Court, the CPT and the defence lawyer of the prisoner.

Foreign prisoners have the right to correspond in unlimited secrecy with diplomats and consulates from their home country.[69] Letters between a foreign prisoner and a diplomat or consular representative may not be opened, damaged or retained. If there are reasons to believe that a letter from one of the mentioned senders contains illegal substances (drugs) it may be screened. Also, if there are reasons to believe that the intended sender is not the actual sender of a letter, the prison may either contact the authority in question (the intended sender) to ensure that they did in fact send the letter, or return the letter asking the authority to confirm that it was sent from there.

2.7 Contact with the outside world[70]

It is a most fundamental principle in section CEP that during the execution of the penalty restrictions cannot be imposed apart from those laid out in the law or resulting as a direct consequence of the penalty.

Nevertheless, prison life is definitely lonesome irrespective both of which country the prison is located in and of the nationality of the prisoner. In practice, imprisonment intervenes in customary access to persons and authorities outside of the penal institutions. Consequently, prisoners are provided with a set of minimum rights to enable them to remain in "contact with the outside world" through, for instance, visits and written correspondence.

These rights are - to some extent -adequately extended for foreign prisoners. The CEP confers to prisoners the right to one visit of at least one hour – and as far as possible two hours – every week.[71] As a main rule prisoners receive visits without the presence of members of the prison staff. But it may be decided by the Ministry of Justice or the prison

---

[67]　Section 51 CEP which is related to art. 36 of the Vienna Convention where it is laid down that consulate representatives have the right – though not if it is against the wish of the prisoner – to see prisoners from their country.

[68]　CEP section 53 and CEP with comments p 128.

[69]　Instruction on letters no. 377 of 17 May 2001.

[70]　The following strictly applies to convicted prisoners but rules and conditions are to a very large extent the same for prisoners in pre-trial prison so long as they are not in solitary confinement.

[71]　CEP section 51.

director (upon authorization from the Ministry of Justice) that a staff member must be present during the visit.

In closed prisons visits take place in cells, which are located side by side and connected by a corridor. If a visitor needs to visit the WC during the visit he or she must pass the other cells. The women from the state prison of Hersted Vester, who were interviewed in relation to the report on imprisoned women (see section 2.2 above) felt that this was problematic when for instance children or grandchildren might glimpse a "famous" sex-offender or murderer.

As the open prisons are predominantly located in the countryside, their accessibility by public transport may be an issue of relevance. Some of the respondents in the above mentioned research on imprisoned women (see section 2.2 above) expressed much frustration over the fact that public busses do not pass the prison. This means that relatives coming to the nearest train station must travel several kilometres by taxi. In spite of a flexible practice on behalf of the prison regarding the planning and duration of visits, this complicates the efforts to maintain good contact with children and other close relatives.

In relation to visits it should finally be mentioned that the general protection of individuals' protection of homes[72] is in force in prisons as well as in private homes. That means that investigative monitoring of a cell in which a visit takes place requires permission to do so from the court and must be in accordance with the conditions in sections 780 and 781 of the Law of Procedure. On the other hand, it is the prison that is informed about monitoring having taken place, not to the prisoner whose visit was in fact monitored. The reason for monitoring is typically that the prisoner is under the suspicion of having committed a new offence.

The right of prisoners to send and receive letters is another aspect of the issue of securing the possibility of "contact with the outside world" as it is prescribed in Article 24 of the European Prison Rules.

A basic right to correspondence does exist for foreign as well as Danish prisoners. The reasons for the limitations that are laid down in sections 55 and 56 CEP are justified mainly in terms of the security of the prison and the security of the victim of the crime for which the prisoner is serving a sentence. The ways of legally breaching the secrecy of correspondence in accordance with the mentioned sections also concern letters sent to the prison that are addressed to the prisoners as well as letters sent to the prisoners' private address that are subsequently forwarded to the prison. The CEP defines different degrees of breaching the secrecy of correspondence. The less radical intervention is the opening and closing of mail with the prisoner present. This takes place when there is the suspicion that the letter may contain drugs. It is by far more intrusive when a staff member actually reads a letter. This is only justifiable if there is a fear that the security of the institution or the victim of the offence are in jeopardy. The decision to read a letter/letters may be made specifically for one letter or for all letters that are sent to a prisoner. The prisoner must be informed when a letter has been read but such a notification may be given up to four weeks after the letter has been read by the prison staff. The most radical intrusion into secrecy is when a letter is retained and not handed over to a prisoner. In this case it must normally be returned to the sender. But for the reasons of security mentioned above, a letter may also not be returned but simply retained by the prison. In such cases the sender must be informed within four weeks.

---

[72] Section 72 of The Danish Constitution.

Section 56 CEP mentions a number of authorities the secrecy of whose written correspondence with a prisoner – both national and foreign – cannot legally be breached. That is for instance the Ministry of Justice, the Department of Prisons and Probation, the Ombudsman, Members of the Parliament (Folketinget), The European Human Rights Court, the CPT, the solicitor of the prisoner and other public and international authorities.

The Administrative Instruction no. 377 of 17 May 2001 on letters states that foreign prisoners have the right to correspond in unlimited secrecy with diplomats and consulates from their home country. In these cases the letters may be neither opened nor broken nor kept back (see above). If there are reasons to suspect that a letter from one of the mentioned senders bears illegal contents (for instance drugs) it may be screened. Also, if there are reasons to suspect that the apparent sender is not the original sender the prison may either contact the authority in question (the apparent sender) to secure that they did in fact send the letter or return the letter asking the authority to confirm it was sent from there.

Another way to stay in contact with "the outside world" is by telephone. However, prisoners are not allowed to be in possession of mobile phones and the possibilities of using telephones in the prisons depend on "practical conditions". On the one hand it is not impossible and not illegal for prisoners to make phone calls while on the other hand they can not stay in telephone contact with the outside world to an unlimited extent. "Practical conditions" concerns the availability of staff who need to be present during the phone call or who listen to a taped conversation afterwards. The possibility of using telephones may be denied for the same reasons that also justify a breach of the secrecy of correspondence as mentioned above. In general prisoners in open prisons have better telephone facilities than prisoners in closed prisons. An aspect that is of specific relevance for foreigners is that the staff may demand that the conversation be held in an understandable language.[73] The prison can only deny a prisoner the right to call one of the persons or authorities with whom he is granted uncontrolled correspondence by the CEP or the administrative instruction in exceptional circumstances.

The possibilities of sending or receiving emails and faxes are extremely limited as prisoners have no explicit rights to posses or demand access to computers or fax machines. The only exception from this is that in a few cases the prison-schools in open prisons allow prisoners to use email. This is seen as a privilege rather than a right.[74]

Finally, it should be mentioned that prisoners have the right to access literature from public libraries and to read newspapers, listen to the radio and watch television. In order to comply with this prisoners have the right to bring their own televisions with them or to rent one from within the prison. In section 58 subsection 3 CEP it is laid down that as far as possible foreign prisoners should have access to newspapers and other written media in their own language.

Another aspect of having access to the media is the right of prisoners to participate in interviews with media representatives, according to section 59 CEP. Prisons may only deny this for concrete security reasons. A lack of staff resources may have the consequence that interviews must be held in special parts of the prison or at a time when it is

---

[73] CEP article 57 and Instruction on the use of telephone no. 378 of 17 May 2001.
[74] Instruction on articles no. 208 of 18 March 2005.

possible and convenient for the staff. It is not legal to make photos of other persons than the prisoner who has agreed to it.

2.8 Re-integration activities – Prison leave

In principle all training and educational programmes as well as occupations and activities in the prisons all fall within the category of preparation for release. The same must be said for efforts to stay in good contact with relatives outside the prisons, i.e. visits in the prisons and temporary leaves for the prisoners. The latter is not possible for prisoners who are to be expelled after their prison sentence. However, the majority of the other prisoners do have a systematic possibility to have temporary leaves from the institution every three weeks.

In each individual action-plan release must be prepared as well as possible, which includes the provision of housing, occupation and so on prior to release. Release on parole can be postponed until these issues have been resolved. But when the whole sentence has been served the prisoner must be released whether there is housing and occupation for him or not. The probation service can only supervise a released prisoner if he/she has been released on parole. Supervision is not possible when the full sentence has been served (see below section 2.9).

2.9 Release - Expulsion

Release must be prepared in accordance with the prisoner-specific action plan that is continuously revised in the course of the stay in prison and according to section 38 (section 41 for life sentences) of the Criminal Code. Prisoners are normally released on parole when 2/3 of the custodial sentence has been served. This only applies, however, if the sentence is for a total period of at least three months. In exceptional cases a prisoner can be released after having served between 1/2 and 2/3 of the sentence. Either the prison or the Ministry of Justice (Department of Prisons and Probation) decides whether a prisoner is to be released on parole. Parole can be denied if it is judged that there is a risk of reoffending. Furthermore, it can only be granted under the condition that the prisoner has been provided with appropriate housing and occupation.[75]

Upon release on parole a probationary period will be set. If a crime is committed during this period of probation, the remainder of the previous sentence will normally be added to the new custodial sentence resulting from the new offence. In some cases parole can be supplemented with the condition of being under the supervision of the probation and after-care system. In addition, there can be special supplementary conditions, for example treatment for alcoholism. If the conditions are breached the Ministry of Justice (Department of Prisons and Probation) may decide that the released prisoner must return to prison in order to serve the rest or part of the rest of the sentence. The rules described above are supplemented with more specific details on release requirements and procedures – including special provisions for foreigners – which are contained in the "Guidelines on serving custodial sentences".

The issue of expulsion is of pivotal importance for some foreigners, and the guidelines state the following: "If the court has decided that you are to be expelled upon your re-

---

[75] Criminal Code section 38, subsection 5.

lease, you must normally serve your sentence in a closed prison. If you are to be expelled, you have the possibility of being released on parole when 7/12 of your custodial sentence has been served. Even if you do not want release on parole, for example because you are trying to have a sentence of expulsion changed, you will be released after 2/3 of the punishment. You can seek advice from the staff or your defence lawyer. The police decide how you are to be expelled. If you have the money, you must pay for the transport home yourself. Ask the staff if you are in doubt about anything concerning expulsion."

The rule on release after 7/12 is explained by the fact that foreigners who are to be expelled are not granted temporary prison leave (normally every three weeks). 7/12 of a sentence without any interruption is estimated as being equivalent to 2/3 of a sentence when ordinary leaves are included.

Regarding the possibility for foreigners to be transferred to their home country the guidelines state the following: "In certain cases it is possible for you to serve your custodial sentence in your home country. Ask the staff". It is never an obligation for any authority – courts or others – to expel a foreigner – on the contrary. The expulsion of a foreign national who is legally residing in Denmark requires a legal basis, for example a criminal conviction.

* A refugee, who has obtained a residence permit as well as a foreigner who has legally been staying in Denmark for seven years or more may be expelled:[76]
- if he/she is sentenced to unsuspended imprisonment for four years or more (for one crime as a first conviction),
- if he/she is sentenced to unsuspended imprisonment for two years or more (for several crimes sentenced at the same time but as a first conviction),
- if he/she is sentenced to unsuspended imprisonment for two years or more (for one crime but he/she has been sentenced to imprisonment before),
- if he/she is sentenced to unsuspended imprisonment for an attack on the security of the State, drugs offences, trafficking in human beings, forcing somebody else to marry against his/her own will or for certain crimes which are deemed more serious and (possibly) more severely punishable in the Criminal Code, for instance sexual offences, arson, robbery and murder.

* A foreigner who has legally been staying in Denmark for three years or more may be expelled in the following cases:[77]
- for the same reasons as mentioned above
- if he/she is sentenced to unsuspended imprisonment for two years or more (for one crime as a first conviction)
- if he/she is sentenced to unsuspended imprisonment for one year or more (for several crimes sentenced at the same time as a first conviction),
- if he/she is sentenced to unsuspended imprisonment for one year or more (for one crime but he/she has been sentenced to imprisonment before).

* Other foreigners may be expelled:[78]

---

[76] Code on Foreigners, section 22 and Foreign Right, p 660 ff.
[77] Code on Foreigners, section 23.
[78] Code on Foreigners, section 24.

- for the reasons mentioned above,
- if he/she is sentenced to suspended or unsuspended imprisonment.

If a person is sentenced to reside in a psychiatric institution, he/she may also be sentenced to expulsion alongside the rules described above about prison sentences.

The question of expulsion must be raised in court by the prosecutor simultaneously with the accusation for the committed crime. Consequently the accused has a defence lawyer; he/she has the right to appeal and the right to a fair trial. It is up to the courts to decide whether or not the foreigner is to be expelled and if so, for what period of time. Expulsion is to be considered in the light of issues of the enforcement of law (whether the crime so grave that we want the person out of the country) and of legal protection (considerations of the necessity to protect wider society against future offending by the person in question). [79]

Further, the courts have to balance the arguments for expulsion against arguments drawing in the opposite direction. Section 26 of the Code on Foreigners mentions the arguments that are to be considered; the degree to which the foreigner is involved with somebody or something in Denmark, age, state of health, consequences of possible expulsion for relatives, involvement in the home-country and possible safety risks in home-country.

Even if the courts are free to decide within the legal framework, an indication whether or not to expel someone is given in section 26 subsections 2. Here it is stated that if the crime committed is related to drugs, trafficking, national security or another of the serious crimes mentioned above, the reasons *not* to expel a person should be very strong. It has not been possible to find authoritative statistics on how many foreigners are expelled when convicted for a crime. But it is possible to attain an impression of practice in the Supreme Court.[80]

According to the 2003-2004 annual report by the public prosecution service, the Supreme Court had 94 cases – involving 107 persons - in which expulsion was an issue from 1 January 1997 to the end of June 2005. It must, however, be stressed that Supreme Court practice does not provide statistical proof. Mentioning them here merely serves the purpose of illustrating judicial prejudices.

Out of these 107 persons 76 were expelled. In turn, of the 76 persons who were expelled two were expelled for a period of five years and one for ten years, while the remainders were expelled indefinitely.

This part shall be concluded by referring to a few examples of Supreme Court decisions in which expulsion was an issue. The intention behind the examples that I have chosen does not lie in proving homogeneity but rather to illustrate how difficult it is to foresee whether a case will result in the issuance of an expulsion or not.

U99.1394 H. Drugs offence. 3rd conviction. Imprisonment for four months. Had been living in Denmark for 23 years. All relatives in Denmark. Not expelled.

---

[79] Foreign Right, p 641 ff.
[80] Annual Report 2003-2004 from the Director of Public Prosecutions (Rigsadvokatens årsberetning), pp. 193-216.

<u>U2003.56 H</u>. Serious violence. 1st conviction. Imprisonment for four months. Had been living in Denmark a little less than 7 years. Job but no relatives in Denmark. Expelled for five years.

<u>U2000.546 H</u>. Drugs offence. Previously sentenced to six years imprisonment in 1985. Imprisonment for five months. Had been living in Denmark for 21 years. Divorced. Was living with his mother in Denmark. Expelled for five years.

<u>U2004.2772 H</u>. Serious violence. 1st conviction. Imprisonment for five months. Had been living in Denmark a little less than 8 years. Some relatives in Denmark. Not expelled.

2.10 Aftercare – and Probation

The general release and after care procedure is common for everybody who is released from prison and is described above (section 2.9). Furthermore, a few additional projects for the reintegration of foreigners have been implemented in the last few years. They are mentioned in section 2.12 below.

2.11 Staff

Roughly 70 % of the budget of the Department of Prisons and Probation is spent on wages.[81] Including housing, security, occupation and so on, a cell in an open prison costs about half as much as a cell in a closed prison. The daily costs of a cell in an open prison lies at roughly 820 Dkr, while a cell in a closed institution is 1.640 Dkr. The prison guards undoubtedly constitute the largest group of staff and employees in the prisons and prison administration – 2.950 of the 4.400 prison staff members are prison guards. 650 to 700 people are engaged in management and administration. The remaining roughly 1000 persons are social workers, teachers, nurses or other specialists such as for instance psychiatrists, priests, imams or the like.[82] It takes a person three years to become a trained prison guard. The largest share of the training period is practical and takes place within the prisons. Theoretical education is concentrated in a period of 26 weeks, where knowledge of society, psychology, conflict resolution and self defence are trained.

It is a fact that the proportions of foreigners among prisoners and prison staff are unequal. Altogether 15 % of the clients in the prison and probation services (23 % of the imprisoned clients, 12 % of the clients in the probation service) are of foreign background, whereas in the third quarter of 2004 1% of the staff in the prison and probation service had a foreign background. But as it is a part of the official policy to try to secure a broad representation in terms of age, gender and ethnic background among prison staff efforts have been made to recruit more guards with a background other than Danish. Firstly, special courses for foreigners aspiring to start the ordinary education for prison guards have been offered from 2000 to 2004. Out of 38 pupils in these courses 32 went through the total program, 16 passed the tests successfully and in April 2005 six of them were still appointed to the prison system. Secondly, a preparatory school (introductory

---

[81] http://www.kriminalforsorgen.dk. 1 Euro=7,5 Dkr.
[82] http://www.kriminalforsorgen.dk

course) for foreign aspirants was opened in 2006. The first group of ten persons who passed the preparatory school consisted of one woman and nine men from Pakistan, Turkey, Serbia and Lebanon.[83] Furthermore, a small number of special days and five-day courses are arranged in the ordinary education for prison staff. This applies both to ordinary basic training as well as to senior training. It is not explicitly described what the aim and content of these courses are. In the light of their extension the ambition cannot be to teach languages to the staff but rather to present some basic cultural and maybe religious background.

The trainees receive a modest salary during the education period. The average yearly wages that a skilled prison guard receives is equivalent to that of "other guards", for example car park attendants, and lies at about 270.000 Dkr, but is lower than the average salary of for instance police officers, who earn about 356.000 Dkr per year.[84]

2.12 Projects[85]

In the year 2000 a mentor programme was introduced for released young foreign prisoners. A mentor is an external adult who is not part of the authoritative system but who does cooperate with it and whose task it is to support the released person during the final stages of the prison sentence and the initial period of time after having been release. The programme has been evaluated by a Danish University and in 2004 it was the winner of the "International Community Justice Award" in the category of the "Social Inclusion Award". The prize is given by the English National Probation Service.

The state prison of Ringe (which accommodates female prisoners and young male prisoners) introduced a possibility for foreign prisoners with a Muslim background to spend evenings of study and debate with an Imam and a researcher. The experiment shows that in spite of coming from different home countries many ethnic prisoners share common experiences about being born into the culture and lifestyle of another country. Starting with a sentence from the Koran the group discusses both religious and practical everyday issues.[86]

The Probation Service has one consultant for the reintegration of ethnic minorities into the society. The tasks of this person are to try to establish contact between labour-market representatives and foreigners being released as well as to assist the education of the staff.

During 2006 and 2007 the state prisons in Nyborg and Horsens plan to establish special units for foreigners who were gang members. The inmates in these units shall attend more intensive education on Danish culture and the unit staff shall receive support from a representative of the department.[87]

---

[83] www.kriminalforsorgen.dk/publikationer/rapporterogundersøgelser/Undersøgelse og anbefalinger vedrørende etniske minoriteter i kriminalforsorgen 2005.

[84] http://www.oes-cs.dk/PUBLIKATIONER/LSTATISTIK/2005/

[85] On projects for staff see section 2.11 above.

[86] Nyt fra Kriminalforsorgen , December 2005, p 18-19. (News from the Prison and Probation Service, December 2005, pp. 18-19).

[87] Information received from a prison director personally.

3 ADMINISTRATIVE DETENTION OF FOREIGN PRISONERS

3.1 Institution

As mentioned in the introduction any deprivation of liberty needs to be explicitly legalised. Further, the deprivation of a person's liberty is never an obligatory mean. The principles of proportionality between mean and aim must be kept in mind both by the courts and the administrative decision makers.

3.2 Ministry Responsible & Legislation

The competent superior authority in relation to the asylum centres is the Ministry for Refugees, Immigrants and Integration, which is often simply called the Ministry of Integration. According to the specialization within the Ministry a Foreigners' Service is taking care of most of the questions in relation to the asylum centres and the asylum seekers. When a foreigner is confined by force he/she is under the authority of the Department of Prisons and Probation.

The legal possibilities of depriving a foreigner of his liberty are mentioned exhaustively in section 36 of the Code on Foreigners.[88] But of course the police (the responsible authority) are left with a wide scope of discretion. The largest share of this group are asylum seekers who have no address in Denmark and who are in a situation where the police find it necessary to detain them in order to be able to lead them out of the country as soon as all necessary formalities have been achieved.. See more about the legality and legal control in section 3.5 below.

3.3 Capacity Institutions

In February 2006 there were a total number of ten asylum centres, eight of which are run by the Danish Red Cross. The other two institutions are run by local municipalities. At the same time, 2.479 individuals were located in the centres. The biggest and most famous asylum centre in Sandholm houses not only persons seeking asylum but also constantly about 70-100 foreign persons (mainly asylum seekers) who are confined on the basis of an administrative (police) decision (see section 3.2 above and section 3.5 below).

3.4 Length of Stay

The average time that a person spends in an asylum centre is 1000 days. This has increased from 300 to 1000 within a short time. The situation in the centres is described as very tense by politicians, the media and the director of the Red Cross. Among experts it is a wide spread opinion that the longer a stay in a centre is the more traumatic the experience. Not least the children are suffering from the lack of normal socialisation, and first and foremost from the lack of proper possibilities to frequent schools. An illustration of the tension is the number of (attempted) suicides which has been increasing the latest

---

[88] Code on Foreigners, no 826 of 24 August 2005.

years. In the year 2001 seven attempts were registered per 1000 residents over the age of 17. Four years later in 2005 the figure had increased to 15 per 1000.[89]

3.5 Decisions procedure

Under certain circumstances, foreigners may be denied entry to Denmark at the border by the police (section 48, Code on Foreigners). If the foreigner claims to be seeking asylum the competence is transferred to the Ministry mentioned above in section 3.2. It is common that persons who are seeking asylum or residence permits and are waiting for a decision to be made stay in one of the ten asylum centres.[90] If the person has another place to stay (for instance with relatives) – and there is no legal justification to detain him/her – he/she may stay there.

Detention for the purpose of ensuring a person's presence for the time when an expulsion is to be executed (pursuant to article 36) must be brought before a local court within 72 hours from the moment when the person is locked up. If the court accepts the legality of the deprivation of liberty a time limit must be fixed. This time limit may be extended as many times as the court deems necessary for up to four weeks each time. The foreigner must be provided with a defence counsel. The police are obliged to inform the foreigner about his rights, including the right to unlimited contact with diplomatic representatives of his home country. [91]

All of the legal reasons for the administrative detention of a foreigner are related to the actual execution of the expulsion, refusal of admission, transfer or other means of removing the person from Denmark. The main idea of the rules is that a foreigner can be detained if he/she does not cooperate with the authorities who are treating his/her case and if other restrictions of his/her behaviour do not fulfil the need. The legal definition of not cooperating with the authorities consists for instance of withholding information, not appearing when the authorities summon him/her for interviews etc. Furthermore, a released prisoner, who is sentenced to be expelled, will most typically be detained in the closed unit in Sandholm until his/her expulsion can be executed.[92] According to section 36 subsection 1 of the Code on Foreigners, a foreigner who has a permanent address in Denmark may only be detained if he/she poses a threat to national security. As mentioned above, a foreigner who is under the suspicion of or who is convicted for having committed a crime is treated in accordance with the general rules of criminal investigation and procedure. But as a supplement to these rules the Code on Foreigners stipulates more possibilities for taking a foreign suspect into custody. The intention behind section 35 is to secure the possibility of retaining a foreigner until his conviction is final if there is a possibility that the conviction will include expulsion, the foreigner has no permanent address and there are firm reasons to believe that he/she might abscond before the expulsion can be executed.

---

[89]   http://nyhederne.tv2.dk

[90]   http://www.udlst.dk/asyl

[91]   Code on Foreigners section 37.

[92]   This information is given via telephone by the Department of Prisons and Probation and seems to be part of a not all that clear rule in the Code on Foreigners section 25b.

3.6 Appeal Procedure

Decisions on refusal of entry to Denmark or expulsion may be executed immediately. If the foreigner/asylum seeker wishes to contest the decision, an appeal may be lodged with the Minister of Integration. However, such an appeal has no delaying effects on an expulsion order and does not make it possible for the foreigner to enter the country again. Up to now it has not happened that an appealed expulsion was changed in favour of the foreigner/asylum seeker.[93]

3.7 Irregular stay

Without a valid visa or residence permit, in principle a foreigner has no right to stay in the country and should leave. However, he/she may be granted so-called procedural residence as long as his/her case is being addressed by the authorities, in which case his stay is not illegal or irregular. If the application is turned down the foreigner has to leave the country within a fixed time-limit whereafter his residence in the country is illegal and he may be expelled by the use of police force. Under certain circumstances, namely most typically if the foreigner is in danger of being victimised in the country to which he/she is to be expelled, he may stay in Denmark in accordance with section 31 of the Code on Foreigners. The foreigner's residence in Denmark is then tolerated so long as this danger exists.[94] In accordance with section 59 of the Foreign Code and section 125a of the Penal Code it is seen as a crime to cross the border illegally as well as organising illegal border crossing (trafficking). But the fact that a person does not leave the country though ordered to do so by the court is not seen as a crime and may be executed by the help of the relevant authority, in this case the police.

3.8 Numbers

In February 2006 the total number of individuals in the ten Danish asylum centres was 2.479. The number of rejected asylum seekers who do not want or who are unable to leave Denmark is increasing (see section 3.7 above on tolerated residence). In October 2005 this was the case for 1.620 persons, and by April 2006 the number of foreigners who had been refused residence permits but who were still not leaving had increased to 1.940[95]. In reality, this group is not allowed to reside anywhere else but in the asylum centres. If they cooperate with the authorities they can stay in one of the open units and when not, they may be locked up[96]. This of course makes the problems of capacity in the centres even worse. Especially the children are suffering socially, educationally and emotionally from this situation.

---

[93] Foreign Right, pp. 111-112.
[94] Foreign Right, pp. 14-15.
[95] http://www.dr.dk/P1
[96] Code on Foreigners sections 34, subsection 3, 36, subsection 7 and 42a, subsection 8.

3.9 Expulsion

According to section 36 of the Code on Foreigners there is a close connection between the execution of decisions of expulsion and administrative detention. The Danish police are the responsible authority for the execution of all expulsions and at the same time the police are the competent authority to decide whether or not a foreigner should be detained.

In May 2003 the Danish government decided to be more effective in the execution of expulsion once it was formally decided. In other words it was the wish to reduce the number of persons staying in the country after a legal and final decision on expulsion.

According to the police there has been a systematic decrease in the number of asylum seekers who were formally in a position of leaving the country but remained in Denmark nonetheless. From January 2005 to December 2005 the number decreased from 1.928 to 1.468 and by ultimo September 2006 there were 1.252 asylum seekers who were ordered to leave Denmark but who were still present.

In the whole period from January 2005 to September 2006 between 500 and 600 individuals out of the total number of asylum seekers, who were ordered to leave Denmark, were from Iraq. The group from Kosovo is also numerous but it has steadily decreased over the 21 months from 400 in January 2005 to 184 in September 2006. From Afghanistan there were 161 in January 2005 and 20 persons in September 2006. It has not been possible to reduce the number of asylum seekers from Somalia with a final order to leave Denmark. In January 2005 there were 63 individuals in that position and in September 2006 the number had increased to 77. [97]

3.10 Not-expelled prisoners

In principle, a foreign prisoner who is convicted of a crime but who is not expelled serves his/her sentence in accordance with the same rules and practices as everybody else. Decisions on release on parole also occur within the same legal framework. Foreigners can be detained while their application for asylum is being dealt with. If the application is turned down the person in question has to leave Denmark and will most typically be expelled very quickly, if necessary by force (see section 3.7 above). Should asylum be granted the person is released from the closed unit in Sandholm (see section 3.5 above) and transferred to an open section until he can be situated normally.

3.11 Detention irregulars under criminal law

Under certain circumstances irregulars may be taken into custody without being encompassed by the rules on custody in the Code on Legal Procedure. This is a consequence of section 35 of the Code on Foreigners which lays down the following main conditions: custody should be a necessity to secure the person's presence while his case or his appeal is treated or until a conviction to expulsion can be enforced; the foreigner is suspected of having committed an offence which may result in an expulsion; the foreigner is already expelled and has entered the country regardless. The general rules on duration and the

---

[97] Rigspolitiet, oktober 2006.

prolongation of custody are in force when foreigners are taken into custody under section 35 of the Code on Foreigners.

3.12 Minors

In November 2005, 1.060 children were living in Danish asylum centres. They were either waiting for their family's application for asylum to be approved, for a decision on their appeal against the refusal of asylum, or they were simply waiting for the Danish police to come and take them to the airport. There are examples of children who have been living under this pressure for ten years and more[98]. This situation is very much criticised by different experts, among others a child psychiatrist who claims that Denmark is breaching the UN Convention on Children's Rights by treating children in the asylum centres worse than Danish children in general, who would have been taken into foster homes if they had been living under similar conditions[99]. In 2005 the Danish Red Cross reported to Danish city authorities (councils) about 52 children in the asylum camps who did not thrive well - mentally and/or physically. An extra appropriation of 37 million Dkr to improve living conditions in the asylum centres – mainly those of children – in May 2006 was immediately followed by a reduction in the budget of the same amount[100].

4 NATIONALS DETAINED ABROAD[101]

4.1 Numbers and composition group

In February 2006, 97 Danes – including immigrants to Denmark who have been granted Danish citizenship – were imprisoned abroad. The length of the sentences varied very much from a few months to life sentences.[102]

4.2 Detention countries

Only 23 of the 97 persons, who were imprisoned abroad primo February 2006, were imprisoned in a non-European country. Also, 28 of the 97 Danes, who were imprisoned abroad, were detained in a German Prison. [103]

Further the Foreign Ministry website informed in April 2006 that eight Danes were in penal institutions in America and a small part was distributed around the world, with seven in Asian prisons, four in Africa, and three in the Middle East and finally two in South America.

---

[98] In Norway a new rule gave asylum to everybody who had been waiting for the administrative procedure for more than 3 years.

[99] http://programmer.tv2.dk/article.php?id=3164437

[100] Newsletter from Danish Refugee Council 03/2006.

[101] http://www.dr.dk/nyheder

[102] Information via telephone from the Foreign Ministry on the 5th of February 2007.

[103] Information via telephone from the Foreign Ministry on the 5th of February 2007.

4.3 Reasons for detention & sentencing

More than half the Danes in foreign prisons are detained for drugs offences and they are serving sentences that range from a few months up to life sentences. This also goes for those imprisoned in Germany, which can be seen as the southern entrance to Denmark and with similar restrictions on drugs as Denmark has.

4.4 Involved organisations

The Danish Foreign Ministry states[104] that everybody who is imprisoned in a foreign country has the right to see a representative of the embassy. The latter will offer assistance in finding a defence solicitor as well as in establishing contact with relatives in Denmark. However, Danish embassies do not offer assistance if the imprisoned person is both a citizen of Denmark as well as of the country in which he/she is being detained. The Danish Foreign Ministry is not able to cover the costs of defence, travel or the like for the prisoner or his/her relatives. All forms of financing , for instance of living costs if a person is retained by foreign authorities, must be covered and organised by the person in question. However, support in communication and transfer costs are usually covered by the respective Embassies. This practice applies for criminal cases as well as civil cases.

4.5 Release and reception home country

If a Dane arrives in Denmark after having served the full sentence abroad he/she will normally be free. The only exception is if the crime committed was threatening to the national security of Denmark[105]. If he/she is transferred due to either a convention, a bilateral agreement or a concrete agreement before the time of release, the sentence is to be fulfilled in a Danish prison and in that case in accordance with Danish rules and routines.

4.6 Aftercare

It depends on concrete agreements between the country where the person was imprisoned and Denmark if there will be a period of probation if the prison sentence is served abroad. But if the prisoner is transferred to a Danish prison during the period of imprisonment, he will be released on similar conditions to Danish prisoners.

4.7 Public opinion and media

Danes in foreign prisons is not a very hot issue in the media. It is a wide spread impression that the conditions in foreign prisons are tougher than in the Danish prisons.

---

[104] http://www.um.dk/CMS
[105] Criminal Code section 6-12.

5 EVALUATION AND RECOMMENDATIONS

Being a minority excluded from societal existence individuals deprived of their liberty are undoubtedly in a vulnerable position. This is the case for Danes as well as foreigners in (foreign and Danish) prisons. The presentation above raises the question whether detention has the same meaning and implications for all who experience it. Basic principles of equality as well as section 4 of the CEP presuppose, however, that prisoners are mainly equally vulnerable. Contrary to this some sections in the CEP define special rules for foreign prisoners (for instance access to embassies). This legislation can only be a token of realisation of the extra vulnerability of foreigners being imprisoned abroad.

The legal differences between national and foreign prisoners are founded on international human rights conventions or basic principles of equality. It may be questioned if equality is achieved to a sufficient degree within the CEP. The practice of religious liberty may be discussed. The right to see a Lutheran priest is obviously of different relevance for Christians, Catholics and Muslims. Resources, traditions as well as capacity of room and staff surely cause limitations for practising religion. Historically there has been no reason to consider religious matters in relation to the prison budgets. Today the choice is between a (relatively) high budget for one religion, or common low budgets for several or all religions of relevance. It is a "hot issue" in the political arena that foreigners do commit crime and do go to prison. But it has not become an issue of similar interest how to offer foreign prisoners religious services.

Apart from those serving in the state prison of Hersted Vester there are no authoritative statistics on prisoners suffering from psychiatric diseases and of course also not on foreign prisoners in need of psychiatric or psychologist assistance. But a report on the occupation of prisoners from the Department of Prisons and Probation which was published 2002[106] states: "A relatively large share of the prisoners has acute or permanent psychiatric problems, which often are expressed in huge problems of behaviour or self-destruction [...] there is a massive need of psychologist treatment in the institutions." There is no reason to believe that foreign prisoners should not be (at least proportionally) represented among those in need of treatment and it should be considered whether problems of language and culture come more into the foreground than in connection with somatic health problems.

Alcoholism and drug-addiction are multifactoral occurrences which demand consideration in the light of somatic and psychiatric/psychological health as well as language, culture, tradition and other "soft" aspects. According to Danish experiences the capacity of and access to alcohol and drug treatment while serving a prison sentence requires much awareness while discussing prisoner equality.

Occupation (work, education, and training/treatment) as well as daily routines like cooking and spare time in the prisons are organised on the basis of the national way of organising daily life, education and production. It is taken for granted that the prisoners are familiar with (or rather an integrated part of) the Danish society and the perspective is to (re)integrate the prisoners into Danish society.[107] The conditions are equal for everybody though everybody is not equally familiar with them nor are they equally motivated

---

[106] Beskæftigelse af indsatte, Kriminalforsorgen, 2002, p. 92. (Occupation of prisoners). My translation.
[107] Beskæftigelse af indsatte, Kriminalforsorgen, 2002, p. 94. (Occupation of prisoners). My translation.

to adapt to the Danish way of working, learning and living because their chances of being released into the Danish society are not equal.

There is no possibility in the prisons to prepare for a future in another country. Foreigners may have their duty to work modified for religious reasons but apart from that the prisons do not offer any program or job that has been created specifically for foreigners. The committee behind the Report on Occupation recommended firstly to find out how many foreign prisoners are going to be expelled after their sentence and secondly to study the experiences from a Swedish prison that runs a special program for prisoners who are to be expelled. The prisoners who are to be expelled do often have long sentences.

Release is seen as the ultimate aim for prisoners but it is also the ultimate challenge for many of them. Prisoners who have to leave the country do often not know what awaits them, and prisoners – foreigners as well as Danes – who are released in Denmark are familiar with some places and people outside the prison but not necessarily the most desirable ones.

In relation to release (on parole) the Criminal Law and the CEP leaves the impression of uniformity but instructions beyond the law in the judicial hierarchy put other perspectives forward. In order to prevent the prisoner from re-offending it is a general requirement for release on parole that the prisoner will have appropriate occupation and housing.[108] There is no exception from this, neither in the law itself nor in the comments or the remarks on it. Nevertheless the instruction on release[109] says in section 39 that when a foreigner who is to be expelled is being released on parole the only condition is a probationary period. Though if the prisoner is from another Nordic country there is a possibility, due to specific Nordic agreements, of asking the Probation Service of his home country to take over the supervision. And the instruction says that if a Nordic prisoner denies co-operating with the Probation Service of his home country, he should not be released on parole.

To put it short: a Danish prisoner, who most typically wants to get out of prison, must be considered for release on parole after 2/3 of the sentence but may be forced to serve it in full for some (more or less well) defined reasons. Whereas a foreigner who has to leave the country permanently (and more typically even prefers to stay in prison), will be forced to the leave the prison and the country after at least 7/12 and no later than 2/3 of the prison term have passed. Since 2003 foreign prisoners who are to be expelled indefinitely may be (forcedly) released after ½ of the time. This decision was part of authoritative efforts to use the prison places more efficiently.[110] About release and expulsion it is even more contradictory that after having been forcedly released from prison the person may be forced to spend some time in one of the overcrowded asylum centres or in some cases even in custody until the expulsion can be executed. Expulsion is decided by the courts – not the prisons. Supreme Court practice does not raise doubt about the formal legality of the expulsions. However, nobody will deny that official and popular attitudes towards foreigners in Denmark has become more negative in recent years, and many experts and engaged professionals claim that not only the tone but also practice have become harsher.

---

[108] Criminal Law section 38, subsection 5.

[109] Instruction no 29 of 19 April 2006.

[110] Engbo, p. 358. The Ministry of Justice estimated that this change would free 10-15 prison places per year.

Overrepresentation of foreigners in the penal system may prove that foreigners tend to commit more crimes than Danes. But criminologist experience shows that some social factors do correspond with the crime level and if the figures on foreigners are corrected for some of the well known factors the degree of overrepresentation tends to decrease. Without correction the overrepresentation is 49 % but corrected for age and socio-economic background it falls to 8 %. The major part of the overrepresentation of foreigners within the penal system relates to violations of the Penal Code, mainly theft (178 % overrepresentation), whereas rape (110 %) and violence (130 %) – which attract more media attention – both have a lower degree of overrepresentation. Two thirds of all penal dispositions are related to breaches of the Traffic Code. Here the overrepresentation of foreigners is 8 %. The description above may leave an impression of an intolerant police, intolerant prisons or even an intolerant society, but conclusions should not be drawn too early.

In some prisons great efforts are made to create humane and tolerable conditions. A few examples are the newly published research on practising religion in the prisons, which concludes that Danish prisons are open and tolerant towards religion; one prison has introduced visits by an imam and a researcher with the intention to study and debate issues on specific importance for Muslims; the Department of Prisons and Probation has introduced a mentor programme for young foreign prisoners who are released. The impression is far from unambiguous: on the one hand attempts are made to secure humanity and equality while on the other hand equal rules do not automatically secure equal living conditions or even equal chances for everybody.

It is documented in this article that in important issues like preparation for the labour market and drug-addiction-treatment equality between Danish and foreign prisoners has not yet been established. Attention is also paid to pre-time release from prison. It is argued that from an equality point of view there are evident discrepancies between foreigners who are expelled and Danish prisoners. Danes cannot obtain pre-time release without housing and adequate occupation whereas expelled foreigners cannot avoid pre-time release after 2/3 time (often already after ½ of their sentence). These rules are laid down in the law and cannot be changed by the prisons.

Finally we must conclude that while the borders are opened for some of the inhabitants of the world other inhabitants are not welcomed warmly. The problem is not (always) that they have ever hurt the Danish society but that they started the travel from the wrong place and very often were in a situation where they could hardly afford the ticket. The debate on foreigners is strong in Denmark and divides the population markedly. It is worthwhile to remark that while the government and its supporting party stick to a restrictive course, large shares of the population as well as local politicians find that the enough is enough.

Chapter 7

Estonia

Piret Liba

1. INTRODUCTION

1.1 Overview of penalties and measures

According to the Estonian Penal Code, offences are categorized into criminal offences and misdemeanours.[1] A misdemeanour is an offence for which the principal punishment prescribes a fine or detention. For a misdemeanour, a court may impose detention for a term of up to thirty days. An imposed fine could also be substituted by detention, if an offender fails to pay it. Ten fine units (600 EEK/ 40 EUR) correspond to one day of detention. In the case of substitution of a fine by detention, the minimum term of detention shall be one day. A criminal offence is an offence for which the principal punishment prescribes a pecuniary punishment or imprisonment in the case of natural persons and a pecuniary punishment or compulsory dissolution in the case of legal persons. A criminal offence in the first degree is an offence for which the maximum punishment is prescribed which is imprisonment for a term of more than five years, life imprisonment or compulsory dissolution. A criminal offence in the second degree is an offence for which imprisonment for a term of up to five years or a pecuniary punishment can be imposed. For a criminal offence, the court may impose imprisonment for a term of thirty days to twenty years, or life imprisonment. Imprisonment for a term of more than ten years or life imprisonment will not be imposed on a person who, at the time of commission of the criminal offence, is less than 18 years of age.

If a convicted offender fails to pay the amount of the pecuniary punishment imposed on him or her, the court shall substitute the punishment by imprisonment or, with the consent of the convicted offender, by community service. Three daily rates (not less than 150 EEK/ 10 EUR) of a pecuniary punishment correspond to one day of imprisonment. In the case of substitution of a pecuniary punishment by imprisonment, the minimum term of the imprisonment shall be ten days.

One principal punishment and one or several supplementary punishments may be imposed for one offence. Supplementary punishments for criminal offences imposed on natural persons are:
- occupational ban;
- deprivation of driving privileges;
- deprivation of the right to hold weapons or ammunition;
- deprivation of hunting or fishing rights;
- a fine to the extent of assets;
- expulsion.

If a court convicts a citizen from a foreign state of a criminal offence in the first degree and imposes imprisonment, the court may impose expulsion on the convicted offender with a ten year prohibition of entry as a supplementary punishment. If the spouse or a minor child of the convicted person lives with him or her in the same family in Estonia on a legal basis, the court shall provide in its judgment reasons for an imposition of expulsion. Expulsion shall not be imposed on a convicted citizen of a foreign state who, at the time of commission of the criminal offence, was less than 18 years of age.

---

[1] Penal Code.

According to the Penal Code a punishment can either be substituted by community service or be suspended. If a court imposes imprisonment of up to two years, the court may substitute the imprisonment by community service. One day of imprisonment corresponds to two hours of community service. Imprisonment shall be substituted by community service only with the consent of the convicted offender. The duration of community service shall not exceed eight hours a day. If an offender performs community service during the free time from his or her other work or studies, the duration of community service shall not exceed four hours a day. A convicted offender shall not be remunerated for community service. The term for the performance of the service shall not exceed twenty-four months. If a convicted offender evades community service, fails to comply with supervisory requirements or to perform the obligations imposed on him or her, the court may, on the basis of a report prepared by the probation officer, enforce the imprisonment initially imposed on the convicted offender. In the case of execution of the imprisonment, the sentence shall be deemed to be served to the extent of the community service, whereas two hours of community service correspond to one day of imprisonment.

If a court – taking into consideration the circumstances relating to the commission of a criminal offence and the personality of the offender – finds that service of the imprisonment imposed for a specified term or payment of the amount of the pecuniary punishment by the convicted offender is unreasonable, the court may order suspension of the sentence on probation. In such case, the court shall order that the imprisonment imposed shall not be enforced in full or in part if the convicted offender does not commit a new intentional criminal offence within the period of probation determined by the court and complies with the supervisory requirements and obligations imposed on him or her for the term of supervision of conduct. If the court decides that an imposed imprisonment is partially not enforced, the court shall determine the part of the imprisonment to be borne immediately and such part of the imprisonment which is suspended on probation. Probation shall be ordered for a period of three to five years. In case a convicted offender has been subjected to supervision of conduct, probation shall be imposed for a period of eighteen months to three years.

Besides principal and supplementary punishments there are some other sanctions, for instance confiscation, coercive psychiatric treatment and sanctions applicable to minors. The court shall order coercive psychiatric treatment of the person:
- if at the time of commission of an unlawful act the person lacks capacity or if he or she becomes mentally ill or feeble-minded or suffers from any other severe mental disorder, after the making of the court judgment but before the service of the full sentence;
- if it is established during preliminary investigation or the court hearing of the matter that the person suffers from one of the aforementioned conditions and therefore his or her mental state at the time of commission of the unlawful act cannot be ascertained and he or she poses a danger to himself or herself and to the society due to his or her unlawful act and mental state and is in need of treatment,

The coercive psychiatric treatment shall be provided by a psychiatric institution which is issued with a corresponding licence. Coercive psychiatric treatment will be applied until the person recovers or ceases to pose a threat. Termination of treatment will be ordered by the court. If a punishment is imposed on a person after coercive psychiatric treatment, the period of treatment will be included in the term of the punishment. One day of treatment corresponds to one day of imprisonment.

Taking into account the level of the moral and mental development of a person between 14 and 18 years of age and his or her ability to understand the unlawfulness of his or her act or to act according to such understanding, the court may release the person from punishment and impose the following sanctions on him or her:
- admonition;
- subjection to supervision of conduct;
- placement in a youth home;
- placement in a school for pupils who need special treatment due to behavioural problems.

A person under the age of 18 is placed in a youth home or a school for pupils who need special treatment due to behavioural problems for up to two years, taking into consideration the end of the academic year. The court may extend the term of stay in a youth home or a school for pupils who need special treatment due to behavioural problems by up to one year, taking into consideration the end of the academic year.

Detention can also be a preventive measure which is applied with regard to a suspect or an accused or convicted offender which means deprivation of a person of his or her liberty on the basis of a court ruling. A suspect or accused person may be arrested at the request of a Prosecutor's Office and on the basis of an order of a preliminary investigation judge or on the basis of a court ruling if he or she is likely to abscond from the criminal proceeding or continue to commit criminal offences. In pre-trial procedure, a suspect or accused shall not be kept under detention for more than six months.[2]

Provisional custody will be included in the term of a punishment. One day of provisional custody corresponds to one day of imprisonment or three daily rates of a pecuniary punishment. If a person is held in custody in the course of misdemeanour proceedings, this will be included in the term of a punishment. Twenty-four hours of custody corresponds to one day of detention or to ten fine units.

Detention and up to three months imprisonment is to be served at a house of detention on the location of the court that adjudicated on the matter or in the residence of a detained person.[3] Custody pending trial shall be served in wards prescribed for pre-trial detention in maximum-security prisons or in houses of detention. Imprisonment is applied in maximum-security or open prisons. A maximum-security prison is a prison with a guarded wall or other barrier which enables the constant supervision of prisoners. An open prison is a prison with a territory marked by clearly visible signs. A house of detention is a part of police prefecture within the area of administration of the Ministry of Internal Affairs.[4] A prison is a government agency in the area of government of the Ministry of Justice.

As of 4 April 2006 there were 4,803 detained persons in a house of detention and prisons. There were 4,397 persons held in custody in closed prisons - 3374 convicted prisoners and 1023 pre-trial prisoners – and 55 in open prison departments. In Estonia there is one prison for women with 159 prisoners (04.04.06) and one prison for juveniles

---

[2] Code of Criminal Procedure.

[3] Imprisonment Act.

[4] Police Act.

with 103 prisoners (04.04.06). There are 33 prisoners serving life imprisonment in maximum-security prisons. The coercive psychiatric treatment is provided by a psychiatric institution which has been issued a corresponding licence. There is one hospital (Viljandi Hospital) in Estonia with a special department for coercive psychiatric treatment, with a capacity of 71 places.

In order to complete expulsion, the person to be expelled can be placed in an expulsion centre until his or her expulsion has been executed, but for no longer than two months, this at the request of the governmental authority who is applying and enforcing the expulsion of the foreigner and on the basis of a judgment of an administrative court judge. When a person is to be expelled and is to be placed in an expulsion centre, he or she may be detained in a police detention house for up to thirty days instead of an expulsion centre. The expulsion centre works under the administration of the Ministry of Internal Affairs. In 2005 31 persons were placed in the expulsion centre.

1.2 Overview of the Prison System

1.2.1 Organisational Structure of the Estonian Prison System

A prison is a government agency in the area of government of the Ministry of Justice, its task being the implementation of custodial sentences and pre-trial imprisonment.[5] The Prisons Department is the administrative management unit of the prison system the main task of which is the work arrangement, development and supervision of prisons. The department is managed by the deputy secretary general on prisons of the Ministry of Justice and it is sub-divided into three divisions: sentence implementation, social welfare and a legal and development division. In addition, the staff of the department also includes an advisor-head chaplain, a secretary and an assistant to the deputy secretary general. There are 21 officials working in the prison department of the Ministry of Justice in Estonia.

---

[5] Imprisonment Act.

Management structure of the prison system as of January 1st, 2006

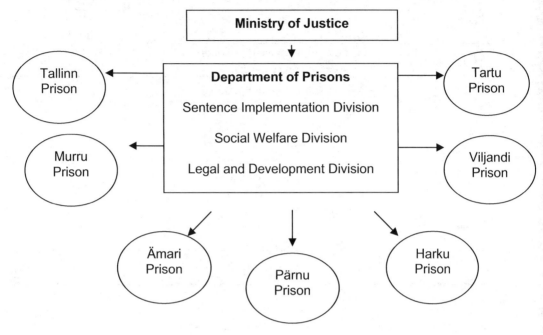

Supervisory control over the prisons is executed by the Minister of Justice. The Minister of Education and Research and the Minister of Social Affairs exercise professional supervision over the performance of duties in the areas of education, social welfare and health care in prisons. Activities of prisons or ministries can also be supervised by the State Audit Office (SAO) as an independent external auditor. The main task of the SAO is to inform Parliament about how money has been spent to achieve any given results. Control can also be performed by the Chancellor of Justice whose main function is to exercise supervision over the constitutionality and legality of legislation passed by the legislative and executive powers and by local governments. The second main function of the Chancellor of Justice is to serve as an ombudsman and to verify whether agencies and officials who perform public functions comply with the constitutional rights and freedoms of persons and the principles of good governance. The agencies whose activities the Chancellor of Justices supervises are the ministries, the boards and inspectorates and their local subordinate bodies, as well as local governments.

The population of Estonia is 1 344 000 (01.01.2006). As of 1 January 2006 there were 4,410 people held in custody in prisons, 3,386 convicted prisoners and 1,024 pre-trial prisoners. There are 328 prisoners per 100 000 inhabitants.

At the moment, there are seven closed prisons and two open prison department in Estonia. Prisons differ in size and groups of persons held in custody:

Prison	Group of persons held in custody	Number of persons
Harku Prison	Female adult and juvenile convicted prisoners	137 (including 1 juvenile)
Murru Prison	Male adult convicted prisoners, in open prison department	1485 34
Pärnu Prison	Male adult convicted prisoners	100
Tallinn Prison	Male adult pre-trial prisoners, female adult pre-trial prisoners and male adult convicted prisoners	605 44 416
Tartu Prison	Male adult pre-trial prisoners, female adult pre-trial prisoners, juvenile pre-trial prisoners and male adult convicted prisoners	295 27 53 563
Viljandi Prison	Male juvenile convicted prisoners in open prison department	103 8
Ämari Prison	Male adult convicted prisoners	540

According to the Internal Rules of the Prison approved by the Minister of Justice there should be at least 2.5 m² per prisoner. Hence the estimated capacity of prisons is 4,499 places: 3,107 places for convicted prisoners and 1,392 places for pre-trial prisoners. Thus the general capacity utilisation of prisons is 99% although facilities for convicted prisoners are overcrowded (with a capacity utilisation of 110%).[6]

In the year 2005 the operation costs of prisons were 20 553 772 euros. Personnel costs constituted the biggest share of the prison budget (66%). The average cost per prisoner per month was 381 euros. To draw a parallel, the average monthly gross wages in the last quarter of 2005 were 555 euros in Estonia.

As of 1 January 2006 there were 2,013 job positions in prisons, of which 1,620 were staffed. Among the prison staff you will find prison officers, public officials and support staff. A public official is a person elected or appointed to the office of the staff of an administrative agency. Support staff are clerical staff employed under employment contracts in support staff positions of the staff of an administrative agency.

According to the Public Service Act, an Estonian citizen who has reached the age of eighteen, who has at least a secondary education and who has an active legal capacity and is proficient in Estonian to the extent provided by or pursuant to law, may be employed in the service of a state or local government official. A citizen of a Member State of the European Union who conforms to the requirements established by law may, on the basis of the law, also be appointed to a position. Only Estonian citizens can be appointed to positions which involve the exercise of public authority and protection of public interest.[7] Prison officers are officials in the prison service who are divided according to the

---

6   Internal Rules of the Prison.
7   Public Service Act.

complexity of duties, the directing function and scope thereof. This is related to positions which correspond to the given official ranks specified in the following descending order:
- chief inspector of prison;
- class 1 prison inspector;
- class 2 prison inspector;
- class 1 guard;
- class 2 guard.

Persons who comply with the requirements stipulated for public officials and who have undergone a preparatory service for prison officers and who have complied with the obligation of military service, may be appointed to office as prison officers. A prison officer who has undergone preparatory service will be appointed to a position in the lowest official rank which corresponds to his or her preparatory service. Persons who fall within any of the following categories are not admitted to the preparatory service for prison officers or appointed to positions as prison officers:
- persons without active legal capacity or with restricted active legal capacity;
- persons convicted of intentionally committed criminal offences;
- persons who have served imprisonment sentences;
- persons who are suspects, accused or accused at trial in criminal matters or
- persons who are divested of the right to work as prison officers by court judgments entered into force.

Preparatory service for prison officers consists of practical and theoretical professional training. The prison officer candidates undergo preparatory service in prison where the candidates participate in practical training and in an institution of applied higher education for public defence. To become a prison guard, one year of training is required of which at least one half is spent in practical training. To become a prison inspector, three years of training are required in the course of which the person acquires applied higher education.

A person undergoing preparatory service for prison officers is referred to as a prison officer candidate. The latter will be admitted to preparatory service by the executive officer of the educational institution carrying the said service out. A prison officer can be appointed to office by the director of a prison or by an official authorised by the director. A director of a prison shall be appointed to office by the Minister of Justice.

Approximately three quarters of the job positions in the prison system are prison officers (imprisonment, also management). Administration (finances, personnel, and correspondence) takes up 15% of all the positions and social welfare (social workers, psychologists, chaplains) and health care accounts for 10 % of all the job positions in prisons (Figure 1).

Figure 1: Breakdown of job positions on 1 January 2006

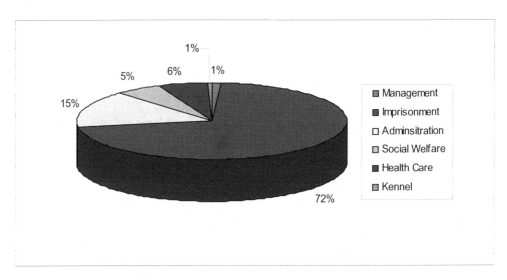

Since the re-establishment of the Estonian prison system (after the Soviet army had left), the number of female prison officers has increased. The former closed military system has become more open and humane. 42 % of all employees are women and 58 % are men. Employees with higher education constitute nearly one-third of the staff. Five percent of employees have a basic education (Figure 2), while more than half of the staff is older than 40 years.

Figure 2. Education of employees on 1 January 2006

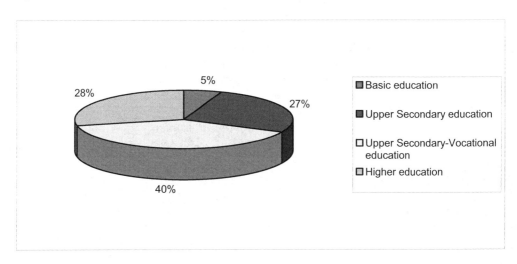

41-50 year-olds constitute the largest age group among employees (31%), followed by 51-60 year-olds (26%) and 31-40 year-olds (21%) (Figure 3).

Figure 3. Age of employees on 1 January 2006

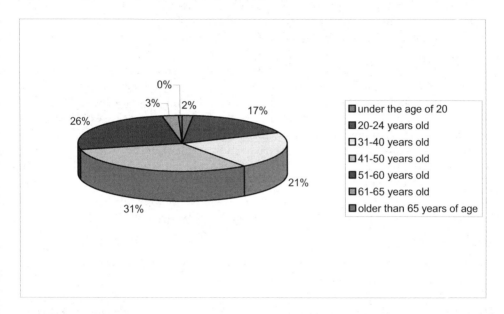

1.2.2 Foreign Prisoners

As of 4 April 2006 there were 1,941 foreigners detained in police houses of detention and prisons, which is 40% of all the detainees held in such institutions. More than half of the prisoners are Russian or other ethnic nationalities from the territory of the former Soviet Union. Thereby most of the Estonian prison population is Russian speaking.

In Estonia foreign prisoners are not kept separately from others. There are no specific institutions for foreign prisoners and no specific section of the prison service is responsible just for foreigners. As a part of preparatory service prison officers are taught about different cultures and their customs, and it is mandatory to learn the Russian and English language.

Most of the foreign prisoners are persons with undefined citizenship, mostly born in Estonia or in Russia or other former Soviet Union countries. According to the Citizenship Act Estonian citizenship is acquired by birth if at least one of the parents of the child holds Estonian citizenship at the time of the birth of the child.[8] Presumptively prisoners with undefined citizenship or their parents hold a citizenship of a country of the former USSR. It is very likely that most of these prisoners with undefined citizenship held in custody in Estonia actually have the right to acquire Russian citizenship by birth.

According to the Citizenship Act of the Russian Federation all citizens of the former Soviet Union who were born in the territory of the Russian Federation since 30 December 1922 and after, had acquired Russian citizenship by birth. According to the order of

---

8   Citizenship Act.

the Constitutional Court of the Russian Federation from 21 April 2005 the same also applies to their children wherever in the territory of the former Soviet Union they were born.

There are several conditions for the acquisition of Estonian citizenship by naturalisation, among others the requirement for knowledge of the Estonian language and knowledge of the Constitution of the Republic of Estonia and the Citizenship Act. This knowledge is assessed by way of examination which can also be prepared and taken while in prison.

On 1 January 2006 the population of Estonia was 1 344 684.[9] According to the Statistical Office of Estonia the number of ethnical Estonians is 921 908, which constitutes 68,6 % of the total population. The proportion of Estonians is lowest among 40 – 60 year olds and highest among 5 – 15 year olds and persons older than 80. [10] In 1992 almost one third of the Estonian population consisted of foreigners with undefined citizenship i.e. persons who had during the past 50 years arrived from the territory of the former Soviet Union and settled in Estonia. According to the Estonian Citizenship and Migration Board 82% of the Estonian population are Estonian citizens, 10% are with undefined citizenship and eight percent are citizens of other countries. [11] The proportion of foreigners among the prison population (40%) is more than twice as high as in the national population (18%).

1.3 Overview of the involvement of Consulates, Embassies, Ministries and the Probation service, NGO's etc

In Estonia, the organisation of international judicial cooperation has been placed within the competence of the Ministry of Justice. The International Judicial Cooperation Division of the Courts Department is responsible.

International judicial cooperation means proceedings of requests for assistance from judicial authorities (courts, prosecutor's offices) by a competent legal authority in the territory of another country. International agreements allow mutual recognition of court judgements and the performance of procedural acts (delivery of documents, collection of evidence, legalisation of documents issued abroad) as well as the resolution of various legal issues with the help of the public authorities of another country. International judicial cooperation includes both civil and criminal matters. The competence of judicial authorities in international communication depends on the laws of the state and on international agreements (conventions, legal assistance agreements, EU legislation). As a rule, in the framework of an international agreement, one authority is assigned to coordinate the provision of legal assistance. Usually, this is the Ministry of Justice, but depending on the judicial system of the state in question, this function may be performed for example by the public prosecutor's office or other judicial authorities.

International legal assistance includes the performance of several procedural acts, including mutual legal assistance in criminal matters, which lies in the exchange of infor-

---

[9]   The main Social and Economic Indicators of Estonia. 12/06. /2006).Statistical Office of Estonia. www.stat.ee

[10]   Tiit, E.-M. (2006). The main indicators of Estonian population in 2005—2006 in the background of Europe. Office of the Minister for Population and Ethnic Affairs, Tartu University, Statistical Office of Estonia.

[11]   Citizenship and Migration Board Yearbook. (2006). Tallinn. www.mig.ee

mation as well as in the extradition and surrender of people in the framework of criminal proceedings.

Estonia ratified the Convention on the Transfer of Sentenced Persons (ETS 112) on 28 April which into force on 1 August 1997. The Additional Protocol to the Convention on the Transfer of Sentenced Persons came into force on 1 June 2000. The transfer of sentenced prisoners is organised according to the conditions and rules of the convention. Although 41% of the prison population and 39% of all convicted prisoners are foreigners, most of them have undefined citizenship. As of 21 February 2006 there were 201 prisoners with the citizenship of a foreign country, including 174 Russian citizens. As Russia has not ratified the European convention and Estonia does not have a bi-lateral transfer agreement with Russia, no Russians have been transferred. During the last few years Estonia has transferred five Latvians to Latvia and one Finn to Finland.

In 1992 the Estonian Migration Foundation was established by the Estonian government. The Migration Foundation consults and, if necessary, supports migrants financially. The foundation also collects and analyses information about migration and migrants, conducts research on migration, integration and asylum, and organizes events where migration topics are discussed. In the year 2005 the Estonian Migration Foundation supported the remigration of 217 foreigners to their ethnic countries of origin with nearly two million croons, mainly to Russia, Byelorussia and Ukraine. Among the supported migrants there were 33 former Soviet military personnel and their family members, 81 retired persons and 47 unemployed persons. The Migration Foundation also supported the return of 12 Estonians to Estonia with nearly 200,000 croons. In comparison, in 2004 such remigration support was given to 235 persons in amount of 2.4 million croons and with about 400,000 croons the return of 36 Estonians to their homeland was supported. In 2005, the Estonian Migration Foundation also assisted with the expulsion of 12 illegal residents from Estonia.

Financial support from the Foundation is also available for foreign prisoners, but there were only a few cases where such support was used. Many foreign prisoners are not motivated to leave Estonia because they prefer applying for Estonian citizenship or a residence permit.

Regarding the involvement of Embassies and Consulates, it can be noted that there has been some cooperation with representatives from the Russian Federation, Latvia and Lithuania. Their involvement has predominantly been in the areas of providing documents and passports in order to enable their citizens to be able to leave Estonia once they have been released.

1.4 Overview of trends

1.4.1 Sentencing Trends

The official statistics on sentencing and committed criminal offences do not make distinctions according to nationality. Since nearly half of the Estonian prison population are foreigners, the following trends and figures basically apply to both foreign and Estonian prisoners. Over the past ten years, the number of prisoners in Estonia has not changed significantly, ranging from 4,200 – 4,800 per year. There were 3,386 convicted prisoners and 1,024 pre-trial prisoners in Estonian prisons in early 2006. The percentage of pre-trial prisoners among persons held in custody in prisons has decreased during the past ten years from 32% in 1997 to 23% in 2006 (Figure 4).

Figure 4: Number of convicted and pre-trial prisoners in prisons

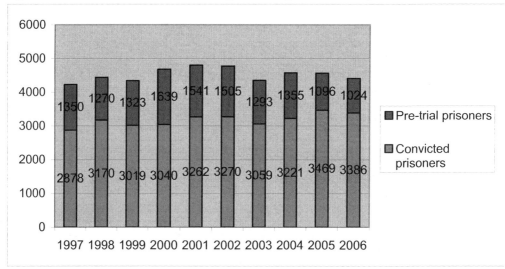

95% of prisoners are adult men, four percent are adult women, and juvenile men account for one percent of all convicted prisoners. Most of the prisoners are relatively young, about half of the convicted prisoners are younger than 30 years, 78% of all convicted prisoners are younger than 40 years. 22 – 29 year olds constitute the most numerous group among prisoners (36%), followed by 30 – 39 year olds (30%) and 40 – 49 year olds (14%) (Figure 5).

Figure 5: Convicted prisoners by age on 1 January 2006

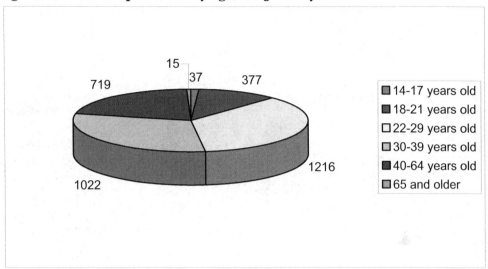

During the period 1991 – 2001 an increase in the percentage of 22 – 30 year olds (42% in 2001) and a decrease in the percentage of 31 – 40 year olds (26% in 2001) could be regarded as the most important change. The age composition of prisoners became somewhat younger in the years 1994 – 2001.[12] During the few last years the percentage of 22 – 29 year olds has decreased and the percentage of 30 – 39 year olds has increased a little but both stayed in the same magnitude during 2004 - 2005.

As of 1 January 2001 persons with a secondary education constituted the largest group among prisoners (43%), followed by persons with a basic education (37%). When looking at the change in the level of education of prisoners during the period 1991 – 2001, we can see a definite decline, a trend that is in fact ongoing. This is particularly evident in the approximate tripling of the number and percentage of persons with the lowest level of education.[13] Still, in 2003 prisoners with secondary education constituted the largest group among the prison population (36%). Currently the largest group are prisoners with basic education (37%), followed by prisoners with secondary education (31%). Approximately one-fifth of the prisoners have primary education or less (19%) (Figure 6). The share of persons in Estonian prisons who have a low level of education is growing.

---

12   Saar, J., Markina, A., Ahven, A. jt. (2002). Crime in Estonia 1991 – 2001. TPÜ Rahvusvaheliste ja Sotsiaaluuringute Instituut; EV Justiitsministeerium.

13   Ibid.

Figure 6. Convicted prisoners by educational background on 1 January 2006

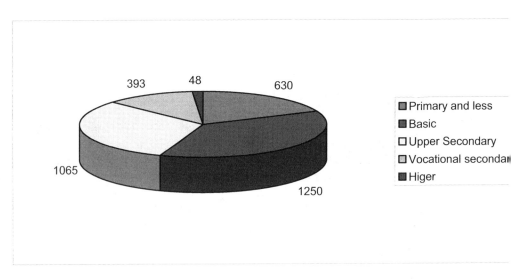

The main type of criminal offences for which prisoners are being punished is property offences (50%). Approximately one-fifth are serving sentences for offences against persons (21%) (Figure 7).

Figure 7: Types of criminal offences for which prisoners are imprisoned 1 January 2006

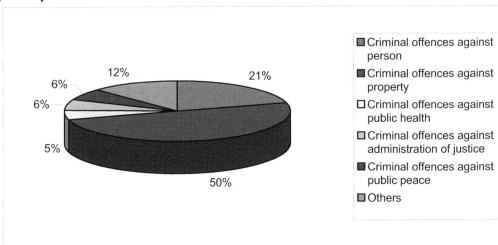

A trend that is apparent in the period from 1991 to 2001 is a decrease of the percentage of offences against property (58% in 1992; 51% in 2001) and an increase in the percentage of offences against persons (23% in 1992; 32% 2001). The percentage of offences against persons was the highest in the mid-1990s (36% in 1994-95).[14] Since 2001 the percentage of such offences has decreased from one-third to one-fifth; at the same time the share of offences against property has stagnated at about half of all offences. Many prisoners serve sentence for both – offence against property and offence against persons. The proportion of prisoners who have committed violent crimes is at 54% (Figure 8).

Figure 8: Breakdown of convicted prisoners by the main offence 1 January 2006

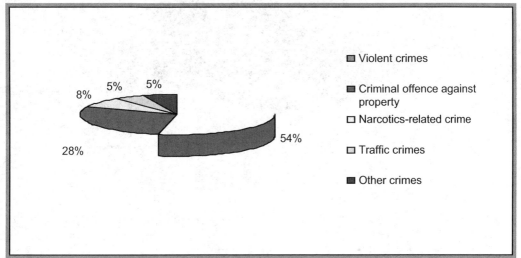

Roughly 50% of the prisoners in Estonia are serving sentences of between one and five years, while approximately one-third have been sentenced to five to ten years in prison. 10% of prisoners have sentences up to one year. There are 33 prisoners serving life sentences, which accounts for roughly one percent of the overall prison population (Figure 9).

---

[14] Ibid.

Figure 9: Convicted prisoners according to length of sentence on 1 January 2006

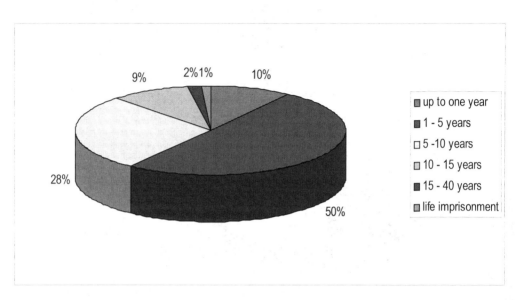

Since 2001 there have been no remarkable changes in the percentage of prisoners who are serving sentences to ten years or more. The share of long term prisoners has been 12% to 14%. From 2001 to 2006, the proportion of prisoners serving short prison terms of up to one year has doubled from five to ten percent. Over the same period, the percentage of prisoners serving sentences with the length one to five years has increased from 43% in 2001 to 50% in 2006. Also, there has been a ten percent decrease in the proportion of prisoners who are to serve five to ten years, from 38% in 2001 to 28% in 2006. These developments are in line with an ongoing trend supported by state criminal policy to shorten the length of sentences.

1.4.2 Characteristics of the Foreign Prison Population

45% of all prisoners are Estonians; more than half of the prisoners are Russian speaking (Russians and other ethnic nationalities from the territory of the former Soviet Union) (Figure 10). Already in 1992 there were fewer Estonians than non-Estonians in prisons and Estonians have been a minority among prisoners throughout the whole period of re-independence.

Figure 10: Breakdown of convicted prisoners according to nationality on 1 January 2006

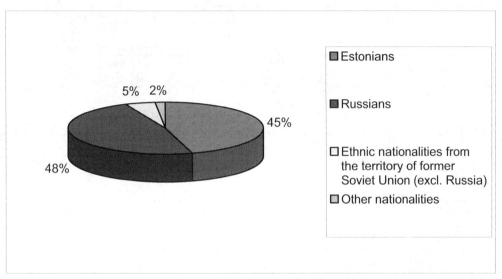

When considering the citizenship of prisoners, until 1999 the percentage of persons without citizenship was the highest (66% in 1999). The number of persons with Estonian citizenship has increased very quickly since then. As of 1 January 2006, Estonian citizens already constituted 61% of the prison population (31% in 1999) (Figure 11).

Figure 11: Convicted prisoners by citizenship

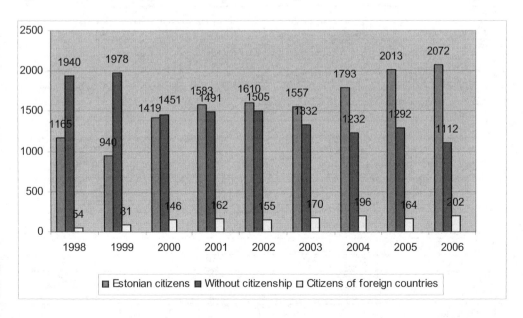

According to the database of persons held in custody as of 21 February 2006 there are 2,624 Estonian citizens (59%) and 1,823 foreign prisoners (41%) in Estonian prisons:

	Pre-trial prisoners (1,057)	Convicted prisoners (3,390)
Estonian citizens	561 (53% of pre-trial prisoners)	2,063 (61% of convicted prisoners)
Foreign prisoners	496 (47% of pre-trial prisoners)	1,327 (39% of convicted prisoners)
Including prisoners with undefined citizenship	417	1,126

Prisoners with undefined citizenship constitute 85% of all foreigners held in custody in prisons:

Citizenship of foreign prisoners	Pre-trial prisoners (496)	Convicted prisoners (1,327)
Azerbaijan	1	1
Dominican Republic	0	1
Israel	2	0
Canada	1	0
Lithuania	1	7
Latvia	6	12
Moldova	0	1
Nigeria	0	1
Peru	1	0
Germany	1	0
Finland	1	0
Turkey	1	0
Ukraine	3	3
Byelorussia	0	1
Russia	57	174
Undefined	417	1,126
No data	4	0

79% of prisoners with undefined citizenship were born in Estonia, 13% in Russia, seven percent in other former Soviet Union countries and one percent in other Baltic States:

Place of birth of prisoners with undefined citizenship	Pre-trial prisoners (417)	Convicted prisoners (1,126)
Armenia	1	1
Azerbaijan	4	6
Estonia	333	883
Georgia	1	1
Kazakhstan	6	6

Place of birth of prisoners with undefined citizenship	Pre-trial prisoners (417)	Convicted prisoners (1,126)
Kyrgyzstan	1	2
Lithuania		2
Latvia	6	11
Moldova	2	1
Mongolia		1
Germany		1
Tajikistan	1	
Czech		1
Turkmenistan		1
Ukraine	8	38
Uzbekistan		4
Byelorussia	6	14
Russia	48	146
No data		7

89% of prisoners with undefined citizenship who are born in Estonia are ethnic Russians; five percent are other ethnics of former Soviet Union; one percent is Finns and a further percent is gypsies. In the future there is the intention to decrease the number of persons with undefined citizenship. It is very likely that most prisoners with undefined citizenship held in custody in Estonia are actually entitled to Russian citizenship by birth.

1.5 Overview of national legislation

1.5.1 Penitentiary Legislation

The Penal Code defines and provides offences and the punishments that can be imposed in response to criminal behaviour. The Code of Criminal Procedure provides the rules and provisions for the pre-trial procedure and court procedure for criminal offences as well as the procedures for the enforcement of decisions made in criminal matters. The procedures for and organisation of the execution of imprisonment, detention and pre-trial custody as well as the definition and conditions of the prison service are provided in the Imprisonment Act.

1.5.2 Penitentiary Legislation relevant to Foreigners

Generally there are no differences between citizens and foreigners in terms of the punishments to which they can be sentenced, but there are two exceptions:
- according to § 54 of the Penal Code, if a court convicts a citizen of a foreign state of a criminal offence in the first degree and imposes imprisonment, the court may impose expulsion with a prohibition to enter Estonia for ten years as a supplementary punishment on the convicted offender;
- according to § 260 of the Penal Code a foreigner who is caught residing in Estonia without a legal basis at least twice within one year shall receive a pecuniary punishment or be sentenced to up to one year of imprisonment.

Currently, there is only one convicted prisoner in prison who has been punished according to § 54, and none according to § 260.

According to § 416 of the Code of Criminal Procedure a judge in charge of execution of court judgments may rule to waive the enforcement of a sentence to imprisonment for a specified term if the convicted offender is extradited to a foreign state or is expelled. Also, the responsible judge may enforce a sentence of imprisonment for a specified term if the convicted offender who has been extradited or expelled returns to Estonia earlier than ten years after his or her extradition or expulsion.

According to § 75 of the Imprisonment Act, a prisoner who is a foreigner and who has no residence permit shall be expelled from Estonia upon release. If immediate expulsion from Estonia is not possible, the foreigner shall be placed in an expulsion centre upon release.

The Citizenship Act provides procedures for the acquisition, resumption and loss of Estonian citizenship. According to § 21, Estonian citizenship shall not be granted to or resumed by a person who among other things:
-   does not observe the constitutional order and Acts of Estonia;
-   has acted against the Estonian state and its security;
-   has committed a criminal offence for which a punishment of imprisonment of more than one year was imposed and whose criminal record has not expired or who has been repeatedly punished under criminal procedure for intentionally committed criminal offences.

The Foreigners Act regulates the entry of foreigners into Estonia, their stay, residence and employment in the country and the bases for legal liability of foreigners. For the purposes of this Act, a foreigner is a person who is not an Estonian citizen. § 5 stipulates rights and duties of foreigners:
-   foreigners staying in Estonia are guaranteed rights and freedoms equal to those of Estonian citizens unless the Constitution, this Act, other Acts or international agreements of Estonia state otherwise;
-   foreigners are guaranteed the rights and freedoms arising from the generally recognised rules of international law and international custom;
-   foreigners staying in Estonia are required to observe the constitutional order and legislation of Estonia.

According to § 12, a residence permit shall not be issued to or extended for a foreigner if among other criteria:
-   he or she does not observe the constitutional order and laws of Estonia;
-   he or she has committed a criminal offence for which he or she has been sentenced to imprisonment for a term of more than one year and his or her criminal record has neither expired nor been expunged, or the information concerning the punishment has not been expunged from the punishment register;
-   he or she has been repeatedly punished pursuant to criminal procedure for an intentionally committed criminal offence;
-   there is information indicating or good reason to believe that he or she belongs to a criminal organisation, that he or she is connected to the illegal trafficking of narcotics, psychotropic substances or persons across the border, that he or she is a member of a

terrorist organisation or has committed an act of terrorism, or that he or she is involved in money laundering.

Exceptionally, temporary residence permits may be issued to foreigners on certain conditions. In practice, temporary residence permits are granted to most foreign prisoners prior to their release.

The Refugees Act regulates the legal status and bases for stay in Estonia for applicants for asylum and refugees, based on the United Nations Convention relating to the Status of Refugees and the Protocol relating to the Status of Refugees of 31 January 1967 (hereinafter the Convention). For the purposes of this Act, a refugee is a foreigner who has been issued a residence permit on the grounds that the foreigner is deemed to be a refugee pursuant to the Convention.

The Obligation to Leave and Prohibition on Entry Act provides the bases and procedure for the application to foreigners of the obligation to leave Estonia as well as the prohibition to enter the country. This act also stipulates conditions for detention in an expulsion centre, which is discussed under section three below.

2 TREATMENT OF FOREIGN PRISONERS

2.1 General Information

In the Estonian prison system only nine citizens from countries other than former Soviet Union or other Baltic States are being held in custody. Thus, the majority of the prison population is Russian speaking and not as multi-cultural as is the case in the prisons of Western European countries. There are no provisions that foreign prisoners are to be treated differently compared to national prisoners.

According to the Penal Code, in imposing a punishment the possibility to influence the offender not to commit further offences in the future shall be taken into consideration. The aim is to develop a flexible and individualised system of punishment. The reasons for behaving in a criminal fashion in each individual case are at the centre of attention of imprisonment. Each prisoner has an individual sentence or action plan, the objective of which is to plan the work that is to be conducted with every prisoner individually, to identify possibilities to reduce his or her risk of re-offending (the need to provide education, opportunity to work, working skills etc.) and to determine a time schedule for the implementation of these measures. Hence, every prisoner is being treated as an individual and thus the treatment of offenders can differ and vary. However, this differential treatment is based rather on individual risks and needs and not on nationality. Generally there are no different rules regarding the implementation of sentences in legislation.

As almost all prisoners and members of prison staff can speak Russian, which in turn reduces the problems that could in fact arise from language barriers in practice. However, when placing prisoners into cells or rooms, the nationality and mother tongue of the prisoners is also to be taken into account. There are also many employees and prisoners who speak English, so communication with those two convicted prisoners who are not from any former Soviet Union country is not a problem (one is from the Dominican Republic and one is from Nigeria; both have been resident in Estonia for a long time and are known as former pop-singers, convicted for drug trafficking). In cases in which there is someone in prison who does not speak Estonian, Russian or English (there have been few cases in practice) an interpreter will be roped in.

2.2 Living conditions and facilities

First of all, it should be pointed out that the same living conditions and facilities as well as access thereto apply to both foreign and Estonian prisoners. The respective relevant provisions make no differentiation according to nationality in this regard.

Regarding accommodation, a maximum-security prison has cells which allow for prisoners to be constantly visually and electronically monitored. Prisoners are permitted to move about freely within the territory of a maximum-security prison at locations that are stated in the internal prison rules, from the time of rising until the time of retiring. During sleeping hours, prisoners are separated in their individual locked cells. Since the majority of Estonian penitentiary institutions are colonies from Soviet times, usually more than one prisoner is allocated to each cell. In some cases, more than ten persons are accommodated together, however usually there are between two and six persons to a cell. In 2002 a new prison was opened in Southern Estonia (Tartu Prison) and a further new institution is planned to be put into operation in Eastern Estonia by the end of 2007.

An open prison has residential buildings with rooms for the accommodation of prisoners. Prisoners are permitted to move about freely within the territory of an open prison from the time of rising until the time of retiring. With the permission of the director of a prison, prisoners are also permitted to move outside of the territory of an open prison in connection with their studies or work. At nighttimes, prisoners are to retire to their individual rooms which can be locked if necessary. With the permission of the director of a prison, prisoners are permitted to stay within or outside of the territory of the open prison in connection with their work from the time of retiring until the time of rising. Currently there are open prison facilities only in Murru prison and Viljandi prison. However, it is planned that there will be open prison facilities in every prison.

Prisoners will be placed to prisons pursuant to the treatment plan, taking into consideration the length of the actual sentence imposed, their age, sex, state of health and personal characteristics. Prisoners are separated according to their age, gender, and whether they are convicted or pre-trial prisoners. Men and women are split, as are minors and adults. Furthermore, there are special accommodation provisions for persons whose previous professional activities could put them at risk of acts of revenge or retaliation.

2.3 Reception and admission of Foreign Prisoners

According to the Code of Criminal Procedure, a preliminary investigation judge or court shall immediately give notification of a person's arrest to a person close to him or her and to his or her place of employment or study. If a foreign citizen is arrested, a copy of the arrest warrant or court judgment shall be sent to the Ministry of Foreign Affairs. If a convicted offender was not held in pre-trial detention during the court proceedings, the county court enforcing the court decision shall send a notice to the convicted offender, setting out by which time and to which prison the convicted offender must appear for the service of the sentence.[15]

A person is received into a prison on the basis of a copy of a court judgment or court ruling entered into force and the identity document or, if the person has no identity document, on the basis of identification documents prepared by the police. Upon arrival in a prison, a prisoner and his or her personal effects are thoroughly searched by a prison officer of the same gender as the prisoner is question, which is followed by a medical examination. Also, arriving inmates are photographed and their fingerprints are taken. No later than on the day following the date of reception into an institution, a prisoner shall meet with the director of the prison or with a prison officer appointed by the director, who then explains the rights and obligations that a prisoner has within the institution. He or she is then provided with written information concerning the Acts and legislation that regulate the application of his or her imprisonment, the internal rules of the prison and the submission of complaints. The largest part of this documentation is available in Estonian, Russian and English. Some regulations that are not available as translated and written information will be interpreted and explained to the prisoner.

Persons sentenced to more than one year of imprisonment are placed in the so called reception ward, where their biographical data is verified, a socio-psychological prognosis is made, and other information is ascertained that is needed in order to prepare an individual action and treatment plan. Prisoners can not stay in a reception ward for longer than three months. A personal file of a prisoner is opened upon his or her reception into a prison. Documents pertaining to the grounds for the detention of a prisoner, disciplinary sanctions imposed on the prisoner and the time and reason for imposition thereof, information on the conduct, studies and work of the prisoner and other information and documents provided for in the internal rules of the prison will be recorded in this personal file. Furthermore, the photographs and fingerprint cards that were taken upon arrival are attached to the personal file. One set of photographs will be forwarded to the pre-trial investigation authority which requested that the person be taken into custody where it shall be annexed to the criminal file and one fingerprint card will be forwarded to the Police. If a prisoner is transferred to another prison, his or her personal file will be forwarded accordingly.

Upon reception into prison, a prisoner will receive counselling with regard to ensuring social security to the people close to him or her, as well as the retention of his or her property. Prisoners shall also be provided with legal assistance. All abovementioned requirements and provisions apply equally to foreigners as well.

2.4 Work - Education – Training – Sports - Recreation

According to the law the objective of providing prisoners with an opportunity to further their education is to ensure that they have adequate knowledge, skills and ethical principles which should allow them to continue their education and work after release.

Education activities in prisons are organised pursuant to the Republic of Estonia Education Act, the Basic Schools and the Upper Secondary Schools Act and the Vocational Educational Institutions Act and legislation issued on the basis thereof. A prison administration will ensure that general premises, classrooms and workshops necessary for the

---

[15] The Code of Criminal Procedure.

acquisition of general education, vocational education and for carrying out vocational training exist, as well as the possibility to receive practical training in the areas of specialisation taught in the prison.

The acquisition of education is organised during working hours. A prison administration will direct and encourage prisoners to acquire an and / or further their education. They have the opportunity to attain (and build on) basic education on the basis of national curricula. This implies that prisoners can attend basic education, and/or further this by attending secondary education should they request to do so. A prisoner will be ensured preliminary vocational training within the framework of elective subjects prescribed by national curricula for basic schools and upper secondary schools and according to the national curricula for preliminary vocational training according to the Vocational Education Institutions Act. Prisoners may, at their request, be permitted to study at educational institutions located outside of prisons.

Educational institutions providing basic and general secondary education as well as secondary vocational education within the premises of a prison are state schools, municipal schools or their structural units operating in the prison. They are funded by the state budget on the bases of and pursuant to the procedures provided by the Basic Schools and Upper Secondary Schools Act and the Vocational Educational Institutions Act respectively. The costs related to and arising from the furnishing, repairs and operation of the premises that educational institutions are allowed to use are covered by the budget of the prison. Additionally, prisoners are provided with the opportunity to acquire secondary vocational education and can participate in vocational training according to their wishes and aptitude. Those areas of vocational specialisation are preferred that are in the highest demand in society, most commonly metal- and woodworks, construction and sewing.

Educational degrees can be achieved both in Estonian and in Russian. The provision of education in prison is arranged by the Ministry of Education and Research. Prisoners who are not proficient in Estonian can – at their request – be provided with the opportunity to study Estonian. With the aim to integrate non-Estonians to the Estonian society, Prisons organise courses in Estonian language and citizenship studies that aim at integrating non-Estonians into Estonian society.

The study work is supported by the prison libraries. There is a social pedagogue in the juvenile prison who offers counselling and support to the juvenile in their studies. Estonian prisons employ so-called education-organisers with the aim of improving the cooperation between the prison and the schools, as well as providing the prisoners with counselling in education related questions.

According the Imprisonment Act, all convicted prisoners under the age of 64, who are not participating in educational courses and who have no medical contraindications, are obliged to work. Working prisoners are categorized into prisoners who are engaged in prison maintenance work – support staff, cleaners, kitchens, laundry etc. – and prisoners who work in production. In 2001 a state company PLC Estonian Prison Industries (AS Eesti Vanglatööstus) was established in order to increase the number of prisoners in employment, improve the competitiveness of production and to decrease prison expenses. Prisoners' working conditions are in compliance with the requirements established by the labour protection law, with the exception of the specifications arising from the Imprisonment Act. A prison administration is required to ensure that prisoners are guaranteed working conditions which are safe to life and health. Prisoners may be required to work overtime, however on their day's off and on public holidays this is only possible with the consent of the prisoners. Prisoners participating in the maintenance of the prison are required to work according to the nature the work at the discretion of the prison administration. On the order of the prison director, prisoners can be required to participate in the prevention of a natural disaster, epidemic, accident, catastrophe or other emergencies, or in the elimination and alleviation of the effects thereof. In such an event, the prison administration will ensure the security and safety of the prisoners. All of these provisions and requirements apply to Estonians as well as to foreigners.

A prisoner – both national and foreign – with regard to whom there is adequate reason to presume that he or she will not re-offend can, with his or her consent, be allowed to work outside a prison without supervision or under supervision if this complies with the objectives of imprisonment and the individual treatment programme of the prisoner.

Provisions of Labour Law – including those concerning entry into employment contracts, remuneration and holidays – apply to the unsupervised work of prisoners outside of a prison. A prisoner's employment contract shall not indicate that he or she is serving a sentence. An employer will transfer an externally employed prisoner's wages to the bank account of the respective prison. Prisoners who work receive remuneration, which also applies to prisoners who are required to participate in the maintenance of a prison. The remuneration of a prisoner will be at least twenty per cent of the minimum wage rate established on the basis of the Wages Act, and is calculated on the basis of the nature of the work and the amount of time that the prisoner has actually worked. The director of a prison may reduce the remuneration of a prisoner working in the prison by up to 60 per cent for unsatisfactory work results for which the prisoner is at fault. The prisoner will be informed in writing of the amount of his or her remuneration.

Prisoners are provided with the opportunity to engage in sports. There are indoor and outdoor sports facilities in every prison. Hobby, educational, cultural and sporting events in prisons are arranged by free-time counsellors. Prisoners are allowed at least one hour of walking in the open air daily. These requirements apply both to foreigners and national prisoners.

2.5 Food – Religion – Personal hygiene – Medical care

The dwellings of prisoners are in conformity with the requirements of construction technology, health and hygiene, and have windows to ensure that the premises are suitably lighted. Prisoners are required to clean their cells and furnishings and keep them tidy. The provision of food for prisoners is organised in conformity with the general dietary habits of the population with a view to meet the food requirements necessary for survival. Food shall be provided for prisoners on a regular basis and it will meet the requirements of food hygiene. The medical officer of a prison supervises the preparation of the prison's menu and the provision of food. As far as possible, prisoners are permitted to observe the dietary habits of their religion. A prison administration will ensure that prisoners are provided with an opportunity to satisfy their religious needs. Prisoners have the unrestricted right to receive visits from representatives of their religion. Such visits are to take place without any interruption or disturbances of any kind.

Prisoners must take care of their own personal hygiene. Prisoners are given the opportunity to have a sauna, bath or shower at least once a week and upon reception into prison. Furthermore, they have access to hairdressing and barber's services. It is permitted to shave a prisoner's head only with a respective prescription of a doctor or at the prisoner's own request. The director of a prison may impose coercion to ensure compliance with hygiene requirements if a prisoner fails to sufficiently tend to his or her personal hygiene and when this has brought about actual danger to his or her health or to the health of other prisoners. However, the imposition of coercion may not pose s danger to the life or health of a prisoner.

Health care in prisons constitutes a part of the national health care system. Health care in prisons is organised pursuant to the Health Care Services Organisation Act. Provision of health services to prisoners is financed from the state budget though the Ministry of Justice. There are no restrictions for foreign prisoners. Members of the prison's medical staff are required, among other duties, to supervise the state of the prisoners' health on a constant basis. They must treat the inmates within the prison to the extent that the facilities and their fields of specialisation allow and, if necessary, refer them to medical care institutions prescribed for the required treatment. The prisoners are guaranteed that emergency care is available to them twenty-four hours a day. Prisoners who are in need of treatment for which the facilities within the prison cannot provide shall be referred to medical care institutions prescribed for the respective purpose. A prison ensures the guard of prisoners during the time when they are in medical treatment. Any time spent in medical treatment is classed as time served in prison.

2.6 Consular and legal help

According to the Imprisonment Act prisoners have the unrestricted right to receive uninterrupted visits from their criminal defence counsel. Any written materials that a legal representative brings to the meeting are not allowed to be reviewed or read. Prisoners who are citizens of foreign states have the unrestricted right to receive visits from consular officers of their countries of nationality. There have been some contacts with Embassies of Russian Federation, Latvia and Lithuania for support in attaining passports and travel documents. Contact to Embassies is usually established by prison employees, either by telephone or in writing. Prisoners also have the possibility to send written correspondence and use a telephone for these purposes. In practice, it has occurred that a prisoner has visited the Embassy of the Russian Federation during prison leave to arrange the documents that are necessary for acquiring passport.

2.7 Contact with the outside world

According to the Imprisonment Act, prison administrations must facilitate the prisoners' contact with the outside world. Primarily, such contact is supposed to facilitate staying in touch with family, relatives and close friends in order to prevent that a prisoner's social links and ties break while he or she is in prison. Prisoners are permitted to receive at least one supervised visit per month from their family members. Visits from other persons are allowed so long as with regard to whose reputation the prison administration has no reasonable doubts regarding their reputation. A short-term visit can last for up to three hours. A prisoner is allowed to receive long-term visits from his or her spouse, father, mother, grandfather, grandmother, child, adoptive parent, adoptive child, brother or sister. A long term visit from a cohabitee is also allowed under the condition they have a common child or a shared household or that they had been cohabiting for at least two years before the prisoner began to serve his or her sentence. Long-term visit means that the prisoner and the visitor are allowed to live together without constant supervision in specially designated prison premises for a period of one up to three days.

Prisoners have the right to written correspondence and the use of a telephone (except mobile phones) if the relevant technical conditions are fulfilled. The prisoner has to bear any costs arising from letters and telephone calls. The director of a prison may restrict these rights if they endanger the security or violate the internal rules of the prison or damage the objectives imprisonment. Such restrictions are not applicable to communication with state agencies, local governments or their officials, or with the prisoner's legal defence counsel. Costs related to a prisoner's correspondence with the Chancellor of Justice; Ministry of Justice, Office of the President, prosecutor, investigator or court will be borne by the prison.

A prison officer can open letters sent by or to a prisoner in the presence of the prisoner – except letters addressed to the persons and agencies mentioned above – and may confiscate any items the possession of which is prohibited by the internal rules of the prison. The contents of a prisoner's correspondence and messages forwarded by telephone may be examined only with the permission of a court and on the basis of and pursuant to the procedures provided for in the Surveillance Act. It is prohibited to examine the contents of prisoners' letters and telephone messages to the legal defence counsel, prosecutor, and court, the Chancellor of Justice or the Ministry of Justice. It is prohibited to refuse to forward a prisoner's letters to state agencies, local governments and the officials thereof, to his or her legal defence counsel and respective consular officers.

Prisoners are provided with the possibility to read national daily newspapers and national periodicals in a prison. In practice there is at least one daily newspaper in Estonian and one in Russian available in every prison. In addition a prisoner is permitted to subscribe to a reasonable number of newspapers, periodicals and other pieces of literature at his or her own expense unless the subscription endangers the objectives of imprisonment, the security of the institution, or violates the internal rules of the prison.

Prisoners are allowed to listen to radio broadcasts and watch television broadcasts in prison. With the permission of the director of a prison, a prisoner is allowed to possess a personal radio, television set, audio tape recorder, video tape recorder or other such leisure time equipment unless the use of such items violates the internal rules of the prison or disturbs other inmates. In practice, those who do not have their own radio or television sets are provided with the opportunity to listen to the radio or watch TV by the prison. In these cases, the channels are changed after every couple of hours to change the language of the broadcasts so that the majority of prisoners can in fact listen to or watch TV in a language that they understand.

2.8 Re-integration activities - Prison leave

The preparation of a prisoner's release includes the organisation of social welfare support, the granting of privileges or a prison leave, or a transfer to an open prison. Furthermore, the prisoner is provided with assistance in resolving issues related to the management of his or her financial affairs and personal life, and in the preparation of documents. A prisoner is informed of the possibility to receive social benefits provided by the general social welfare system.

In preparation of the release of a prisoner, information concerning the prisoner's need for social welfare services after his or her release are forwarded to the rural municipality or city government of the prisoner's residence, and the prisoner's possibilities to receive specific aid will be ascertained. If the residence of a prisoner or his or her family is not known or if a prisoner does not wish to return to his or her former place of residence, information concerning the prisoner will be forwarded to another rural municipality or city government considering, if possible, the prisoner's wishes concerning his or her choice of residence. At the request of a rural municipality or city government, a prison is required provide them with the information and documents necessary for the provision of a released person with social welfare services. When a person is released from prison before having served the full sentence (early release), information concerning the prisoner will be forwarded to the probation supervision department of the residence of the prisoner or his or her family. If the residence of a prisoner or his or her family is not known or if a prisoner does not wish to return to his or her former residence, information concerning the prisoner shall be forwarded to another probation supervision department considering, if possible, the prisoner's wishes concerning his or her choice of residence. At the request of a probation officer appointed by the court, a prison can be required to forward information and documents necessary to initiate and conduct probation.

Prison leave can be granted by the director of a prison under a number of different conditions. In general, such leaves are for an overall length of 21 calendar days per year. Firstly, they are granted to prisoners who are serving their sentence in a maximum security prison and who have already served at least one year of their prison terms. Prisoners who are serving sentences for at least the second time for an intentionally committed crime in the first degree can be granted leave if they have already served at least half of their total sentence. In the case of open institutions, permission to leave the prison for 21 days per year can be granted regardless of the proportion of the total prison term that a prisoner has already served. Whether or not a person is in fact granted prison leave depends on a number of factors. The responsible prison director has to take facts relating to the commission of the criminal offence into consideration, the progress that a prisoner has made in his or her individual treatment and action plan, and whether the granting of leave is compatible with the objectives of imprisonment.

It is also possible for a prisoner to be allowed to go on prison leave for up to seven days should the prisoner's spouse, father, mother, grandfather, grandmother, child, adoptive parent, adoptive child, brother or sister become terminally ill or pass away, or in the case of other family emergencies. The duration of prison leave granted in the case of a family emergency is not subtracted from the total of 21 days to which a prisoner is entitled each year. Prisoners serving a life sentence and prisoners who are likely to abscond are not granted permission for prison leave. Any costs arising from a leave period are carried by the prisoner him/herself. The time spent by a prisoner on prison leave will be included in the duration of the prisoner's total sentence.

If the objectives of imposing imprisonment rule out the possibility of normal prison leave, the director of a prison may grant permission to leave the institution under supervision for up to three days. As is the case with regular prison leave, the arising costs are to be covered by the prisoner in question, and the period of leave is included in the total sentence, and thus counted as days of imprisonment. The decision making procedures and criteria are the same for foreigners and national prisoners. Since during the implementation of a sentence the prisoners are not allowed to leave Estonia – except in cases of transfer – prison leave is not possible if they have no place to go outside the prison, which in turn can have negative implications for the probability of a foreign prisoner actually being granted leave.

2.9 Release - Expulsion

Prisoners are released as early as possible on the last day of their sentence, however, no later than 12 a.m. If the release date of a prisoner falls on a public holiday or a day off, the prisoner will be released on the last working day before the public holiday or day off. When released, prisoners are returned their belongings, documents and personal clothing that had been deposited in the prison. If the prisoner has no personal clothing or if the prisoner's personal clothing is not suitable for the time of year, the prison will provide the prisoner to be released with clothing without charge. Furthermore, the deposited savings fund accrued from the funds deposited in the personal account of the prisoner are handed out. If the amount deposited as a savings fund is less than one month's unemployment benefit, the prisoner will be paid a lump-sum benefit to the extent of the difference between the savings fund and the amount of unemployment benefit.

A prisoner who is a foreigner and who has no residence permit shall be expelled from Estonia upon release. If immediate expulsion from Estonia is not possible, the foreigner will be placed in an expulsion centre upon release. In practice it rarely ever happens that a foreigner prisoner is released without a residence permit; usually this is decided prior to the end of imprisonment. If he has been refused a residence permit, the prison informs the Citizenship and Migration Board. Between 10 March 2003 and 31 March 2006, 24 foreign prisoners were expelled after having served their full sentence. Since 1 January 2007, it has been possible for a foreign prisoner to be released early without supervision of his/her conduct if he/she is to be expelled. However, there has not yet been such a case in practice. According to the Obligation to Leave and Prohibition on Entry Act, expulsion may be contested before the administrative court. Parties and third persons have the right to appeal against a judgment of an administrative court to a circuit court pursuant to appellate procedures. The parties and third persons have the right to appeal against a judgment of a circuit court to the Supreme Court in cassation proceedings.[16]

Pursuant to the Penal Code, prisoners can be released on parole before they have completed their full sentence. An early release proposal is submitted to the court by the prison director together with the personal file of the prisoner in question. The court then considers whether or not to grant early release on the basis of whether a prisoner has successfully completed his or her individual treatment plan, and while taking material characterising the prisoner which is documented in the personal file of the prisoner into account. If a court refuses early release, another such proposal cannot be filed for at least six months. Should a person in fact be released on parole, the prison administration may transfer a part of the prisoner's savings fund to a special account of the probation supervision department of the residence of the prisoner that is then to be paid to the released prisoner in instalments. Parole is also possible for foreigners if they have a place to live in Estonia. Early release cannot be granted without subsequent supervision of conduct.

---

[16] Code of Administrative Court Procedure.

2.10 Aftercare – Probation

According to the Penal Code, if a person has been convicted of a criminal offence in the second degree, or of a criminal offence in the first degree through negligence, the court may release the convicted offender on parole if he or she has actually served at least half but not less than six months of the total term of the imposed punishment. If a person has been convicted for an intentional criminal offence in the first degree, the court may release the person on parole if the convicted person has actually served at least two-thirds of the total sentence. In its decision on whether to release a prisoner on parole, the court shall take the circumstances relating to the commission of the criminal offence, the personality of the convicted offender, his or her previous personal history and his or her conduct in prison into consideration, as well as his or her living conditions and the consequences which release on parole may bring about for the convicted offender. If a person has been sentenced to life imprisonment, the court may release the person on parole if the convicted offender has actually served at least thirty years. Probation shall be ordered for a period of five to ten years. During the period of probation, the person shall be subject to supervision of conduct. This means that a convicted offender is required to comply with the following supervisory requirements:
- he or she has to reside in a permanent place of residence determined by the court, and has to report to the responsible probation supervision department at intervals determined by the probation supervisor;
- he or she has to submit to the supervision of the probation officer, and provide him or her with information relating to the performance of the offender's obligations and means of subsistence;
- he or she has to obtain the permission of the probation officer before leaving the place of residence for longer than fifteen days;
- he or she has to obtain the permission of the probation officer before changing residence, employment or place of study.

Taking into consideration the circumstances relating to the commission of the criminal offence and the personality of the convicted offender, the court may impose the following obligations on the convicted offender for the period of supervision of conduct:
- to remedy the damage caused by the criminal offence within a term determined by the court;
- not to consume alcohol or narcotics;
- not to hold, carry or use weapons;
- to seek employment, acquire general education or a profession within the term determined by the court;
- to undergo the prescribed treatment if the offender has previously consented to such treatment;
- to perform the maintenance obligation;
- not to stay in places determined by the court or communicate with persons determined by the court;
- to participate in social assistance programmes.

In supervising probation, probation officers shall monitor the performance of obligations specified in court orders, assist and advise probationers in the performance of such obligations and provide assistance in their social adjustment. Probationers will receive assistance in finding employment, admission to an educational institution and a place of residence, as well as in the resolution of other personal problems. Probation officers will promote the probationers' ability to cope independently in everyday life. In supervising probation, probation officers will respect the dignity of probationers. After the entry into force of a court order, a probation officer will prepare a plan for the performance of the obligations specified in the court order and for the supervision of probation. Probationers are involved in the preparation of supervision plans. Probation supervisors have the right to amend supervision plans as necessary. There are no specific aftercare facilities or probation activities for foreigners. If they have a residence permit and a place to live, they attend the same programmes as national offenders do.

2.11 Staff

There are no language barriers and no serious cultural difficulties as most foreigners in Estonian prisons are Russian speaking and many officers are Russians as well. However, Russian and English courses are a part of the preparatory service. The staff does not receive any specific training to deal with foreign prisoners.

2.12 Projects

There are several activities related to the rehabilitation of offenders, but no specific project for foreign prisoners. It is possible to attend Estonian language courses, but these are also available for citizens, whose mother tongue is not Estonian and who want to learn it.

Various inmates' rehabilitation programmes are being implemented and developed in Estonia. The aim is to develop them to be more effective and research based. All programmes, which are currently in the test phase, have been developed as a result of a specific need and are directed towards reducing various risk factors. An overview of different programmes is available in compendium "A Selection of Rehabilitation Programmes in Prisons 2005".

3 ADMINISTRATIVE DETENTION OF FOREIGN PRISONERS

3.1 Institutions for Administrative Detention

According to the Obligation to Leave and Prohibition on Entry Act, foreigners are prohibited from staying in Estonia without a legal basis. The legal bases for a foreigner to stay in Estonia are:
- an Estonian residence permit;
- a residence permit issued by a competent agency of a member state of the European Union, a member state of the European Economic Area or the Swiss Confederation, except Estonia;
- an Estonian visa;
- a uniform visa issued by a competent agency of a member state of the European Union, a member state of the European Economic Area or the Swiss Confederation, except Estonia;

- the right to stay in Estonia arising from an international agreement;
- the right to stay in Estonia arising from a resolution of the Government of the Republic to forego the visa requirement;
- the right or obligation to stay in Estonia directly arising from law, a court decision or an administrative act;
- a residence permit or a return visa issued by a competent agency which belongs to the common visa area.

A precept to leave Estonia shall be issued to a foreigner who is staying in Estonia without a basis for stay. A foreigner shall be expelled from Estonia upon expiry of the term for compulsory execution of a precept to leave. If it is not possible to complete expulsion within the term provided for in the Obligation to Leave and Prohibition on Entry Act (described in section 3.4. below), the person to be expelled shall be administratively detained in an expulsion centre until his or her expulsion can be carried out.

Administrative detention is carried out in a so called expulsion centre. Expulsion centres are structural units of the Citizenship and Migration Board. Its function is to enforce the judgments on the detention of persons to be expelled. An expulsion centre is a guarded enclosed territory which is marked by clearly visible signs and which enables the constant supervision of persons who are to be expelled. Officials of an expulsion centre can exercise supervision over persons to be expelled by visual and electronic surveillance. Persons to be expelled can not the centre without supervision and without the permission of the head of the institution.

A person to be expelled is admitted to an expulsion centre on the basis of a transcript of the judgment of an administrative court and an identity document or, in the absence thereof, an identification document. Upon arrival in the centre, administrative detainees and their personal effects are searched by an official of the expulsion centre who is of the same sex. If necessary, a medical examination will be conducted. A person to be expelled who has been placed in an expulsion centre will be photographed and fingerprinted, unless this has been done beforehand in the course of proceedings relating to expulsion. Upon reception into an expulsion centre, a detainee's cash, documents and personal effects – the possession of which is not permitted in the expulsion centre – are deposited with the expulsion centre. As is the case with persons who are admitted to regular penal institution, a personal file of the person to be expelled is be opened which includes the documents and information on which a person's placement in an expulsion centre is based, documents and information transferred to the expulsion centre by the agency which arranged for the detention of the foreigner, photographs, a fingerprint card and other relevant documents and information. Upon arrival in an expulsion centre, a detainee's rights and obligations are explained in a language which he or she understands and, upon request, legal aid and language services can be provided for him or her at his or her own expense. A person to be expelled will be given written information concerning legislation regulating the enforcement of his or her expulsion, the internal rules of the expulsion centre and the submission of complaints.

An expulsion centre has a residential building with rooms for the accommodation of persons to be expelled. Male and female persons to be expelled are accommodated separately and family members are placed together. They could be accommodated in separate rooms if a family member acts violently towards other detainees. Minors are accommodated separately from adults except if this is evidently in conflict with the interests of the minor.

Persons to be expelled are permitted to move about in the residential building of the expulsion centre in the rooms prescribed by the internal rules from the time of rising until the time of retiring. Persons to be expelled may enter other rooms and move about within the territory of the centre in the cases and at times prescribed by the internal rules of the institution. During sleeping hours, administrative detainees are required to stay in their rooms which can be locked if necessary. They can wear their own personal clothing, and if a person to be expelled lacks suitable clothing, the expulsion centre will provide him or her with clothing without charge. There is the obligation for administrative detainees to wear a name tag. Furthermore, they are required to clean, keep in order and regularly change their clothing.

Detainees awaiting expulsion are provided with an opportunity to satisfy their religious needs if the expulsion centre has possibilities therefore and this is not in conflict with the provisions of the internal rules.

The provision of food in expulsion centres is organised in conformity with the general dietary habits of the population of Estonia with a view to meet the food requirement necessary for survival. Food is provided on a regular basis and it will be such as to meet the requirements of food hygiene. The provision of food for minors will be organised taking into consideration the needs resulting from their age. As far as possible, persons to be expelled are permitted to observe the dietary habits of their religion at their own expense. The person who ensures the provision of medical care in an expulsion centre will supervise the preparation of the menu and the provision of food at the expulsion centre.

Administrative detainees awaiting expulsion must take care of their personal hygiene. At least once a week and upon reception into an expulsion centre, persons to be expelled are provided with an opportunity to use a sauna, bath or shower. Once a month, hairdressing and barber's services will be provided. On the command of the head of an expulsion centre, coercion may be imposed to ensure compliance with hygiene requirements if a person to be expelled fails to take care of his or her personal hygiene to a necessary extent and when this has brought about actual danger to his or her health or to the health of other persons in the centre. The imposition may under no circumstances endanger the life or health of a detainee. Toiletries will be provided by the institution if someone does not have these or the funds to purchase them.

Expulsion centres ensure the provision of emergency medical care and have permanent treatment facilities for the supervision of the detainees' state of health. Medical workers are required to constantly supervise the health of persons to be expelled and to place them in treatment in medical care institutions if their medical condition does not allow their detention in the expulsion centre or their expulsion from Estonia. The medical expenses of emergency services and treatment of persons to be expelled are covered by the state budget.

Detainees in expulsion centres can be visited by the following persons:
- consular officers of their country of nationality;
- legal counsels;
- religious representatives with regard to whose reputation the head of the expulsion centre has no reasonable or justifiable doubts.

With the permission of the head of an expulsion centre, an administrative detainee awaiting expulsion is allowed to receive short-term supervised visits of personal, legal or commercial interest in matters that cannot be resolved through third persons, unless such a visit would impede the enforcement of an expulsion. The detainees are permitted to receive visits only from persons with regard to whose reputation and motives the head of the expulsion centre has no reasoned doubts. Officials of an expulsion centre have the right to search visitors and their personal effects. It is, however, prohibited to review the content of the written material brought along by a legal defence counsel. The searches are conducted by an official of the same sex as the visitor. Items the possession of which is prohibited in an expulsion centre shall be temporarily deposited for the duration of the visit, which shall not exceed three hours. Persons to be expelled will be visited in the presence of an official of the expulsion centre. Visits from a legal defence counsel or a religious representative are allowed within sight but not within hearing distance of officials of the expulsion centre.

Persons to be expelled have the right to send and receive written correspondence and to the use of telephone and other public communication channels if the relevant technical conditions exist in the expulsion centre. An official of an expulsion centre will open letters sent to a person to be expelled in the presence of the person to be expelled and confiscate any impermissible items. The actual content of written correspondence and of messages forwarded by telephone or other public communication channels by or to a person to be expelled may be examined only with the permission of a court and on the bases of and pursuant to the procedures provided for in the Surveillance Act. The head of an expulsion centre may restrict the correspondence and use of telephone and other means of communication if it could violate the internal rules of the expulsion centre or impede the enforcement of the expulsion. Written correspondence with state agencies, legal defence counsels, ministers of religion and consular officers will not be restricted. Costs arising from written, telephonic, and other public means of communication will be borne by the detainee. For correspondence with Estonian state agencies, legal defence counsels, ministers of religion and the respective consular officers, a person to be expelled will be provided with stationery and postal charges will be covered if he or she cannot afford them.

Persons to be expelled may, by the mediation of the expulsion centre, purchase food, toiletries and other permitted items, in an amount that is accordance to the procedures and provisions of the internal rules of the expulsion centre. They are also allowed to receive packages. An official of the expulsion centre will examine the content of a package before it is handed over in the presence of the recipient of the package. Parcels are not allowed to contain food and medicinal products. An official of an expulsion centre is required to seize impermissible contents.

3.2 Ministry responsible and relevant legislation

The Citizenship and Migration Board is a government agency within the Ministry of Internal Affairs and its main tasks include:
-    the determination of persons living in Estonia either as Estonian citizens or foreigners and the issuance of identity documents to residents of Estonia;
-    reception and processing of applications for acquiring and restoring Estonian citizenship, as well as for exempting from Estonian citizenship, and preparing the respective

materials for the government of the Republic to make decisions on these applications;

- receiving and processing applications for residence and work permits of foreigners who wish to settle or are living in Estonia, and making decisions on whether to grant or refuse such permits;
- processing of asylum applications and making decisions on whether or not to grant asylum;
- confirming visa invitations and extending the allowed period of stay in Estonia;
- processing of misdemeanours committed by foreigners illegally staying or working in Estonia, issuance of precepts to leave Estonia or to apply for a residence permit in Estonia, organising the expulsion of foreigners from Estonia;
- making decisions on the requests of foreign countries for the readmission of Estonian citizens and foreigners whose habitual residence is in Estonia;
- maintenance of the relevant state registers and databases.

The entry of foreigners into Estonia as well as their stay, residence and employment in the country and the bases for legal liability of foreigners are stipulated in the Foreigners Act. The bases and procedures for the application to foreigners of the obligation to leave Estonia and the prohibition to enter Estonia are provided in the Obligation to Leave and Prohibition on Entry Act. This act also stipulates conditions for detention in an expulsion centre. The internal rules of an expulsion centre are established by the Ministry of Internal Affairs.

3.3 The Capacity of Institutions for Administrative Detention

There is one expulsion centre in Estonia, opened in March 2003. Before that time, persons to be expelled were placed in prison, however in a section separated from criminal offenders.

In the report to the Estonian Government on the visit to Estonia carried out by the European Committee for the Prevention of Torture and Inhuman or Degrading Treatment or Punishment (CPT) from 13 to 23 July 1997 it was stressed that "a prison is not an appropriate place in which to detain someone who is neither suspected nor convicted of a criminal offence. In those cases where it is considered necessary to deprive persons of their liberty for a prolonged period under aliens' legislation, they should be accommodated in centres specifically designed for that purpose, offering material conditions and a regime appropriate to their legal situation and staffed by suitably qualified personnel. Obviously, such centres should provide accommodation which is adequately furnished, clean and in a good state of repair, and which offers sufficient living space for the numbers involved. Further, care should be taken in the design and layout of the premises to avoid as far as possible any impression of a carceral environment. As regards regime activities, they should include outdoor exercise, access to a day room and to radio/television and newspapers/magazines, as well as other appropriate means of recreation (e.g. board games, table tennis). The longer the period for which persons are detained, the more developed should be the activities which are offered to them. The CPT invites the Estonian authorities to review their policy concerning immigration detainees, in the light of the above remarks."[17] The CPT recommended that immediate steps shall be taken:

- to remedy the shortcomings observed in the sanitary facilities used by immigration detainees;
- to offer a wider range of activities to the detainees, in particular to those held for prolonged periods.

Since 2004 there have been 42 places in expulsion centre for persons to be expelled: 16 places for women and families and 26 places for men.

3.4 Length of stay

A precept to leave issued to a foreigner who is staying in Estonia without a basis for stay shall be subject to compulsory execution after the seventh day as of the date of issue of the precept. A precept to leave issued to an illegal resident who is staying in Estonia without a basis for stay, whose residence permit is revoked or whose residence permit has expired shall be subject to compulsory execution of the precept after the sixtieth day as of the date of its issuance.

A foreigner shall be expelled from Estonia upon expiry of the term for compulsory execution of a precept to leave. Expulsion shall be completed within forty-eight hours after the foreigner is detained.

If it is not possible to complete expulsion within the term provided for in the Obligation to Leave and Prohibition on Entry Act, the person to be expelled shall, at the request of the governmental authority which applied for or which is enforcing the expulsion of the foreigner and on the basis of a judgment of an administrative court judge, be placed in an expulsion centre until his or her expulsion, but for not longer than two months. A person to be expelled who is to be placed in an expulsion centre may be detained in a police detention house for up to thirty days instead of an expulsion centre.

Should it not be possible to enforce an expulsion within the term of detention in the expulsion centre, an administrative court can, at the request of a competent official of the Citizenship and Migration Board, extend the term of detention by up to two months at a time until expulsion is enforced or until the foreigner is released.

In practice the average length of stay in the expulsion centre is 129 days, approximately four months.

3.5 Decisions procedure

Foreigners are prohibited from staying in Estonia without a legal basis. A precept to leave Estonia shall be issued to a foreigner who is staying in Estonia without a basis for stay. Precepts shall be issued by the Citizenship and Migration Board.

Judgments concerning the detention of persons to be expelled and extensions of the term of detention shall be made by an administrative court. Placement in the expulsion centre and extension of the term of detention are decided in a court session.

---

[17] CPT/ Inf (2002) 26 Visit 13/07/1997 - 23/07/1997.

3.6 Appeal procedure

A person to be expelled has the right to appeal against a judgment of an administrative court to a circuit court. A written notice of the filing of an appeal shall be submitted to the administrative court which adjudicated the matter within ten days after the court judgment is pronounced or made public. An appeal shall be filed through the administrative court which made the judgment within thirty days after the judgment is pronounced or made public.

3.7 Irregular stay

According to § 260 of the Penal Code a foreigner who is detected in Estonia at least twice within a year without a legal basis shall be punished by a pecuniary punishment or up to one year of imprisonment. Currently, there is no one who is being punished in prisons or the expulsion centre according to this paragraph.

3.8 Numbers

During the period from 10 March 2003 to 31 December 2005 68 persons were administratively detained in the expulsion centre, among them four women and 64 men:

Citizenship of persons placed in the expulsion centre	
Armenia	2
Azerbaijan	7
Bosnia-Herzegovina	1
Estonia	2
Finland	1
Georgia	8
Iraq	1
Latvia	1
Romania	1
Serbia-Montenegro	1
Turkey	1
Ukraine	2
Uzbekistan	1
Russia	25
Undefined	14

In 2003, 23 persons were placed in expulsion centre: two women and 21 men. In 2004 the figure decreased to 14 persons, among which there was only one woman. The year 2005 witnessed an increase in the number of people who were administratively detained, to 31 persons in total. In this year, too, there was only one female detainee. No minors have yet been detained in the centre.

3.9 Expulsion

A person to be expelled shall be expelled to the state from which he or she crossed the Estonian border, to the country of his or her nationality, to his or her country of habitual residence, or to a third state with the consent of the third state. If more than one of these options could in fact apply, the reasoned preference of the person to be expelled shall be the primary consideration, so long as this preference does not significantly impede the enforcement of the expulsion.

A foreigner may not be expelled to a state where he or she could face the consequences specified in Article 3 of the Convention for the Protection of Human Rights and Fundamental Freedoms or Article 3 of the United Nations Convention against Torture and Other Cruel, Inhuman or Degrading Treatment or Punishment, or the application of the death penalty. The expulsion of a foreigner shall comply with Articles 32 and 33 of the United Nations Convention relating to the Status of Refugees.

Once it is possible to actually implement the expulsion of a foreigner who is staying in administrative detention, the person is released from the institution and is expelled at the request of the governmental authority that is responsible for enforcing the expulsion (either the Citizenship and Migration Board or the police). Around 76% of the persons who are placed in the expulsion centre are in fact expelled from Estonia.

3.10 Not-expelled prisoners

An administrative detainee who is not expelled from Estonia is released from the centre if:
- He or she is taken into custody as a suspect or an accused in a criminal matter;
- if a precept is annulled or declared invalid; or
- a decision is made to grant a foreigner the legal basis to stay in the country.

18% of all persons who are placed in the expulsion centre have been released because they have been granted a residence permit. Four percent of the persons to be expelled were taken into custody as a suspect or an accused in a criminal matter, and were consequently released from the expulsion centre on the basis of a ruling to take him or her into custody. Two percent are released because the expulsion proceedings are terminated.

3.11 Detention of Irregulars under Criminal Law

According to § 260 of the Penal Code a foreigner who stays in Estonia without a legal basis at least twice within a year shall be punished by a pecuniary punishment or up to one year of imprisonment. To date there are no known cases of persons being punished in accordance with this legal provision.

As already stated above, administrative detention is performed in expulsion centres, which are structural units of the Citizenship and Migration Board under the Ministry of Internal Affairs. Administrative detainees can not be placed together with criminal convicts who are serving sentences in prisons under the Ministry of Justice.

Minors

According to the Obligation to Leave and Prohibition on Entry Act, if a foreigner to whom a precept is issued is accompanied in Estonia by his or her minor foreign child or ward (hereinafter minor), and if the minor does not have a basis for residing in Estonia, an obligation to organise compliance with the precept with respect to the minor shall be imposed by the precept on the parent, guardian or other person responsible for the minor (hereinafter parent). A precept is issued to a minor staying in Estonia without a parent and compliance therewith shall be organised by a guardianship authority. The expulsion of a minor shall be organised in co-ordination with the competent state agencies of the admitting country and, if necessary, of the transit country and protection of the rights of the minor shall be ensured. However, in practice there have not yet been any minor administrative detainees in the expulsion centre.

4 ESTONIAN NATIONALS DETAINED ABROAD

To date there is no adequate information about Estonian nationals detained abroad, and nobody is known to be collecting such information as official data. Presumably there are quite a few Estonian nationals detained in Finland and Sweden but also in Germany, Austria and Spain. According to the media the main reasons for detention are drug trafficking, robbery and serious theft.

Estonia has ratified the Convention on the Transfer of Sentenced Persons (ETS 112) and its additional Protocol to the Convention on the Transfer of Sentenced Persons. The transfer of nationals detained abroad is also arranged in the framework of this convention and according to the conditions and rules thereof. Additionally there is a bi-lateral agreement between Estonia and Thailand.

Estonians have been transferred back to Estonia from the following countries:
- 12 prisoners in 2003: six from Sweden, one from the Czech Republic and five from Thailand;
- 14 prisoners in 2004: 12 from Sweden and two from Latvia;
- 26 prisoners in 2005: ten from Sweden, 12 from Finland, two from Latvia and two from Germany.

In 2006 at the time of writing, seven Estonians had been transferred home from foreign countries. Three involved prisoners in Austria, while the remaining four came from Sweden. Additionally, there were eight applications for transfers of prisoners back to Estonia, of which seven were to be sent from Sweden and one person had been imprisoned in Finland.

5 EVALUATION AND RECOMMENDATIONS

Foreigners constitute almost half of all people held in custody in police detention houses and prisons (40%). In Estonia, foreign criminal offenders are not kept separately from other prisoners, which can be greatly attributed to the fact that the vast majority of foreigners in Estonian prisons and police detention units speak Russian. Persons to be expelled are kept in the expulsion centre on the basis of administrative law. Compared to

Western European countries the Estonian prison population is not that multi-cultural. More than half of prisoners are Russian or other ethnic nationalities from the territory of former Soviet Union (54%). Thereby most of Estonian prison population is Russian speaking. As many of the prison officers are Russians too, there are no serious cultural or language barriers in communication with foreigners. Even so, as younger people in Estonia are not so fluent in Russian, it is necessary to have Russian language courses in preparatory training. Although the percentage of prisoners with undefined citizenship has decreased, they still constitute the most numerous group among foreigners in prisons (85%). Considering the decision of the Constitution Court of Russian Federation from 21 April 2005 it is very likely that most prisoners with undefined citizenship actually have a right to acquire Russian citizenship by birth. It is one of the main challenges in criminal policy to decrease the number of foreign prisoners (including prisoners with undefined citizenship) in Estonia. There are several possibilities in different stages of detention.

At the beginning of criminal proceedings, these should be increasingly discontinued (or not even initiated). Instead, the provisions of the Penal Code and the Code of Criminal Procedure on the expulsion of foreigners should be more widely applied. Also, expulsion should be more frequently imposed as a supplementary penalty which includes a prohibition to enter Estonia for a fixed period, as provided for in the Penal Code.

Once a foreigner has in fact been admitted to a prison, there should be an improved exchange of information between the involved penal institution and the Citizenship and Migration Board in order to attain a more complete picture of the prisoner's status, which in turn allows for the drafting of a more appropriate individual treatment and action plan. While a foreigner is imprisoned, they should be provided with more information on the possibilities and procedures for acquiring Estonian citizenship or a residence permit. Finally, in preparing foreign prisoners for release, they should receive more and improved support in applying for the necessary documents. Also, correspondence between the prisons and the Citizenship and Migration Board should be improved so that the latter is informed of foreign prisoners who are soon to be released and who do not (yet) hold a permit for legal residence in Estonia.

Chapter 8

Finland

Tapio Lappi-Seppälä

1 INTRODUCTION

Foreigners and immigrants in Finland: historically, Finland has been a country characterized by emigration rather than immigration. A remarkable change in this respect has occurred during the 1990s. Although the amount of immigrants living in Finland is still low
by European standards (ca. 2% of the population are foreign nationals, or circa 100,000
persons of which circa 20,000 are refugees), relative increase of foreign nationals is
among the highest in Europe. The number of foreigners has quadrupled during the last
10 years: from circa 25,000 in 1990 to more than 100,000 in 2003.

Table I Foreigners in the whole population

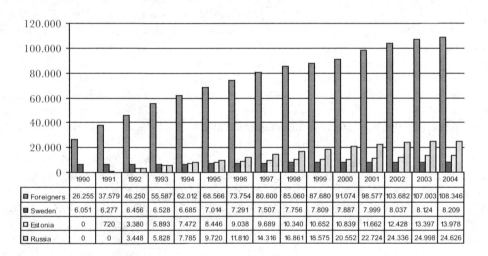

	1990	1991	1992	1993	1994	1995	1996	1997	1998	1999	2000	2001	2002	2003	2004
▣ Foreigners	26.255	37.579	46.250	55.587	62.012	68.566	73.754	80.600	85.060	87.680	91.074	98.577	103.682	107.003	108.346
▣ Sweden	6.051	6.277	6.456	6.528	6.685	7.014	7.291	7.507	7.756	7.809	7.887	7.999	8.037	8.124	8.209
▢ Estonia	0	720	3.380	5.893	7.472	8.446	9.038	9.689	10.340	10.652	10.839	11.662	12.428	13.397	13.978
▣ Russia	0	0	3.448	5.828	7.785	9.720	11.810	14.316	16.861	18.575	20.552	22.724	24.336	24.998	24.626

A little less than 40% of these people are under 30 years old, and 25% are under 21. The
largest groups according to citizenship[1] are Russians (25 000), Estonians (14 000), Swedes
(8 000), and Somali people (5 000). Nearly half of the foreign citizens live in the capital
area (Helsinki, Espoo, Vantaa, and Kauniainen) Even if Finland can be considered a new
country of immigration, the question of cultural diversity is not a new phenomenon:
Finland has a long history of "old national minorities" in particular Sami and Roma people living in Finland. However, the multicultural landscape of Finland has changed substantially during the last 10 years and has been taken up as an important political topic
first in the 1990s – although in a contradictory way. The debate in Finland focused firstly
on concerns about national security and maintaining social order as well as the conditions
under which immigrants could enter and be included in Finnish society. More recently,
this viewpoint has been challenged because of concern over the social integration of im-

---

[1] The concepts of nationality and citizenship are often used interchangeably in the Finnish language.
For example the law regulating citizenship is called a *Nationality Law*. In the Finnish language there is
only a one letter difference between these terms (nationality=kansallisuus, citizenship=kansalaisuus),
which may contribute to the conceptual ambivalence.

migrants. The Finnish debate on immigration has emphasized more demographic changes and the fact that European countries like Finland need more immigrant workers in the future.

Official debate and policy reforms have led to partly new approaches to the management of immigrants. At the same time, Finnish asylum practices are still rather strict. There were 3,221 asylum seekers in 2003 (compared to the number of asylum seekers in Sweden 31,355 or Norway 15,859 in the same year). The Directorate of Immigration (working under the Ministry of the Interior) gave asylum or residence permits to 501 persons; 2,443 persons were rejected (more than 80% of all requests for asylum and residence permits).

Legislative reforms: many reforms related to immigration and non-discriminatory legislation have been made during the last couple of years. The new *Aliens' Act* has been enacted in 2004. The Act formulates the conditions under which permanent residence can be refused, as in the case of a person suspected or convicted of a crime[2]. A new *Nationality Law* was implemented in 2003. Among the reforms, a possibility to grant dual citizenship was launched which can be seen as a welcome reform. Constitutional rights are rights that are granted to all persons living in the country. In a reform of the *Form of Government Act* in 1995, foreigners living in Finland were guaranteed the same constitutional rights as Finnish citizens – with the exception of the right to vote, eligibility for parliament and freedom of movement beyond national borders. A new *Constitution of Finland* was introduced in 2000. The law addresses, among other things, action against discrimination and equal treatment of different groups of persons. According to this law (6 §), everyone is equal before the law. No one shall, without an acceptable reason, be treated differently from other persons on the ground of gender, age, origin, language, religion, conviction (religious belief), opinion, health, disability, or other reasons concerning his or her person. A new *Equality Act* was introduced in 2004. The law can be seen as a signal of more active policy steps within Finnish legislation in the fight against discrimination, partly due to recent changes of immigration and partly due to the pressure from international agreements. To apply the law in practice, new administrative actors (including the Ombudsman for Minorities and Discrimination Board, working in connection with the Ministry of Labour) have been implemented whose role is to give guidance, advice or recommendations to a person who considers her/himself to have been the victim of discrimination

---

[2]   Section 57 – *Obstacles to issuing permanent residence permits*

   (1) A permanent residence permit may be refused if the alien:

     1) is found guilty of an offence punishable by imprisonment;
     2) is suspected of an offence punishable by imprisonment;
     3) is found guilty of two or more offences; or
     4) is suspected of two or more offences.

   (2) The sentence passed for an offence need not be final. When the obstacles to issuing a residence permit are being considered, the nature and seriousness of the criminal act and the length of the alien's residence in Finland shall be taken into account. If an alien has been sentenced to unconditional imprisonment (for the clarification of sentences, see the section 2.1.2), a permanent residence permit may be issued if, on the date of decision on the application, three years have passed since the alien served his or her sentence in full. If the alien has been sentenced to conditional imprisonment, a permanent residence permit may be issued if more than two years have passed since the probation ended. In other cases, a permanent residence permit may be issued if the offence was committed more than two years before the date of decision on the application.

on ethnic grounds, and to participate in societal discussion and concrete discriminatory cases. Thus, the aim for the Ombudsman for Minorities is to improve legal protection related to ethnic minorities. In the course of recent years, public discussion in Finland has moved from focusing solely on "recognition of differences" to more active steps to combat discrimination and inequality on ethnic grounds. At the international level, Finland has taken part in the EUMC (European Monitoring Centre on Racism and Xenophobia) and has been active in the implementation of the European Commission's *Community Action Programme to Combat Discrimination*. Finland is also taking part in implementing Article 13 of the Amsterdam Treaty, which gives the European Union a new competence for combating discrimination based on sex, ethnic origin, religion or belief, disability and age. In addition to this Treaty, there are several international legal instruments directly or indirectly dealing with discrimination, such as the United Nations Convention on the Elimination of all forms of Racial Discrimination, and the European Convention of Human Rights. (Bousetta & Modood 2001).

One of the most dominant judicial and policy steps of the Finnish immigration policy during the 1990s was the *Integration Act* introduced in 1999 concerning persons who have been in Finland for less than 3 years. Immigrants are provided with a three-year integration period during which time they should acquire language skills as well as knowledge of the society necessary for living in the country. Municipalities are responsible for the preparation of integration programmes as well as integration plans for each immigrant person and family living in their area.

Regardless of new legislation and agreements related to immigration policy, there is a gap between the formal level and the practical level. For example, according to an international evaluation in 2002 done by ECRI (the European Commission against Racism and Intolerance), Finnish officials frequently failed to follow new regulations. This may happen in the working place, at schools, etc. In the international evaluation, one central doubt was whether the Finnish police process discrimination cases properly, i.e., whether Finnish anti-discrimination legislation is effective in practice. The ECRI's concern that the Finnish police investigations would discriminate on ethnic or racist grounds is essential from the perspective of this research project as well.

1.1 Overview penalties and measures

Principal punishments in Finland are unconditional and conditional prison sentence, community service, fines and juvenile punishment for young offenders.

Unconditional imprisonment is either for life or fixed term. It is possible to sentence life imprisonment for very few crimes. A fixed-term prison sentence may be 14 days at the shortest and 12 years at the longest. When passing a combined sentence the maximum length is 15 years. When sentences are enforced, the aggregate punishment may be 20 years in maximum.

A prison sentence of two years in maximum can be passed as *conditional*. Besides that a fine can be passed. If conditional sentence is longer than a year, 20-90 hours of community sentence can be passed. A young offender, who has committed his/her crime while being under 21 years of age, may be sentenced to supervision to boost up the conditional prison sentence. The enforcement of conditional imprisonment is postponed for probationary period that is at least one year and at most three years. If the convict commits a new crime during his/her probationary period for which an unconditional imprisonment should be sentenced, the court may decide that the conditional sentence should be executed. The court may also decide that the conditional sentence is enforced only partly, when the sentence remains for other part as conditional with the original probationary period.

Community service can be sentenced instead of an unconditional prison sentence not exceeding eight months, 20 hours in minimum and 200 hours in maximum. Community service is unpaid work carried out under supervision. *The Probation Service* assesses the suitability of the suspect for community service before the sentence is passed and it acquires a service place and supervises the performance of the service.

Fine is sentenced as day fines, the minimum amount of which is one and the maximum 120-day fines. The amount of fines depends on the level of seriousness of the crime. The monetary value of the fine depends on the financial standing of the convict. District court converts unpaid fine in a separate proceedings into imprisonment. Two unpaid fines correspond to one day's imprisonment. Conversion is at least four days and at most 90 days of imprisonment. Petty fine is a fixed currency property fine. It cannot be converted into imprisonment.

Juvenile punishment consists of supervision (4-12 months) and different types of programs. Juvenile punishment may be imposed on a young person who has committed a crime while being under 18 years old, if fine is considered to be too lenient a sanction and no weighty reasons demand unconditional imprisonment. The use of different sentencing alternatives is described in table II.2 below.

1.2 Overview of the Prison System

1.2.1 Organisational Structure

Prisons: sentences of imprisonment are enforced either in closed prisons or in open institutions. Finnish prisons are not formally classified according to their security status, nor are the prisoners classified according to any security grading. However, the intensity of supervision varies to some extent also between closed prisons.

If the sentence of imprisonment is at most two years in length, the sentence may be ordered enforced in an open institution. A further requirement is that the offender is capable of working or participating in training offered at the institution and that he or she presumably will not leave without permission. Open institutions hold about one-fourth of the current prison population. The regime in open institutions is more relaxed. Prisoners receive normal wages for their work. One quarter of their wages is deducted towards their maintenance. Open institutions are in practice prisons without walls: the prisoner is obliged to stay in the prison area, but there are no guards or fences. All open institutions are drug-free institutions in which an inmate is required to controlled commitment not to use any intoxicants.

Prisoners in closed prisons are obliged to work or to take part in vocational training or other activities unless they are relieved from that duty on the grounds of health, studies or for other reasons. Prisoners may also receive permission to pursue other studies either within or outside the institution. Part of the prison sentence may be served also outside the prison in a rehabilitation institution for substance abuse. For those serving sentences in excess of two months, a prison furlough may be granted. A prisoner may be furloughed from prison for a maximum of six days over a four-month period.

Release from prisons. In Finland all prisoners except those few dangerous violent recidivists who serve their sentence in (approximately 20 prisoners at any given day) are released on parole. In practice this means that 99 % of prisoners released every year are released on parole. The director of the prison makes the decision in question. In general, recidivists are always released after they have served two-thirds of their sentence, and first-time prisoners are released after they have served one-half of their sentences. Offenders between 15 to 20 are released either after 1/3 (first offenders) or after ½ (recidivists). In all cases, a further condition is that the prisoner has served at least fourteen days.

The duration of parole reflects the amount of time remaining in the sentence, however, at least three months and at most three years. About one fifth of those released on parole are placed under supervision. The supervisor may be the Probation Service or a private individual appointed by the Service. In principle, the supervision involves both control and support.

The court decides on revocation of parole if the offender commits an offence during the period of his or her parole and on the grounds of a behavioural infraction. In practice all parole revocations are based on new offences, and only such an offence that would normally lead to a prison sentence may serve as a reason to revoke the parole order.

Organization: prison and probation services belong to the administrative field of the Ministry of Justice. *The Prison Service* enforces the prison sentences judged by the courts of justice and detentions and apprehensions connected to trials. The Prison Service has altogether over 30 prisons located in various parts of Finland: 16 closed institutions, 19 open institutions and two hospital units. In 2006 the total budget of the prison service was 166 billion euros. *The Probation Service* is in charge of community sanctions, which include the enforcement of community service, juvenile punishment, the supervision of conditionally sentenced young offenders and conditionally released prisoners (parolees). The Probation Service has 15 district offices and 5 local offices.

Controlling mechanisms; the Ombudsman of the Parliament has a general responsibility to overview also prisons. The ombudsman carries out regular visits to prison-facilities and reports the findings in the annual reports. Another task of the Ombudsman for minorities (since 2001) is to overview the treatment and the conditions of these groups, also of those in detention.

1.2.2   Foreign Prisoners

There are no specific penal institutions for foreigners. Foreign prisoners are mixed with the national prison population. In practice majority of the foreign prisoners are concentrated in the Southern parts of Finland and in the Helsinki region. The Kerava and Helsinki prisons hold half of the 200 foreign prisoners serving a sentence in 1.6.2006. Over half of the 110 remand-prisoners are held in the Vantaa prison (near Helsinki).

In 1.6.2006 the total number of foreign prisoners was 317. Of these 207 were serving a sentence and 110 were on remand. This corresponds some 8 % of the total prison population foreigner are over-represented in the Finnish prison as the share of non-national foreigners is about 2,2 % of the total population. Part of this is explained by the skewed demographic distribution among the foreigners (over-representation of younger age-groups and males).

There is no specific section of the Prison Service responsible for foreigners. However, their affairs are being concentrated in the department of foreign affairs in the Ministry of

Justice. Currently there are no NGO's operating in Finland that are concentrated solely on assisting foreign prisoners. However, the services provided by these organisations are accessible to foreign prisoners as well.

The purpose of the *Probation Foundation Finland* is to support probation service and its development, to foster measures that reduce recidivism and its side effects and to organise and make available services that reinforce the aims of the foundation. The foundation aims to help people who have been convicted of a crime, are in a crisis situation because of a crime or are facing social ostracism. The operation of the Foundation is financed by the income from real estate and stocks owned by the foundation as well as financial aid from the Finland's Slot Machines Association (RAY).

Bridge-Supportorganization produces nationally significant services in the fields of rehabilitation, education and work-life oriented services for people in danger of becoming socially ostracized, such as prison inmates and clients of probation and after-care.

Prison Fellowship Finland is operated by the Finnish Evangelican Lutheran Church and is based on voluntary work. The mission of Prison Fellowship is to mobilise and assist the Christian community in its ministry to prisoners, ex-prisoners, victims, and their families; and in the advancement of restorative justice. The volunteers of the organisation assist needy ex-prisoners with the practical challenges of re-entry into the community. Also the *Finnish Red Cross* trains volunteers to visit those prisoners who have no family of friends to stay in contact with while in prison.

KRIS-Finland and *Support for released prisoners'* target groups are ex criminals and addicts who have decided to start a new life and get back into society. The idea is to help people who are released from prison to stay away from crime and drugs by offering them a new; drug free social network. Vapautuvien Tuki ry also offers help to the families of prisoners during and after the prison sentence.

Back to Life Association does supporting and preventive special youth work among children, young people and young adults who have become alienated or live under the threat of becoming alienated. For example, the "Free...Choice to the future" project aims to prevent repeated offences of young people and by that prevent alienating. With the help of Free Choice project, 17 - 26 year olds who have drug/alcohol problem and lawbreaker backgrounds are supported to return to society. It is carried out by developing e.g. personally co-ordinated activity. The project makes it possible to build "low threshold" services and leisure time activities for specific target groups and tries to develop cooperation between customer service providers and activity networks.

The Guarantee Foundation helps people in difficulties due to huge debts to manage their debts independently. A condition of eligibility for a guarantee is that the amount of the debts is reduced to a sum equal to the clients' ability to pay. The aim is to achieve this reduction through negotiation among the parties concerned if the shortfall problems are beyond the debtor's ability to pay. The Guarantee Foundation was established in 1990 primarily to help people who have been in prison or in a hospital for the mentally ill. Of the guarantees that are made available a total of 50 % are provided for loans made to ex-patients of hospitals for the mentally ill, 13 % for loans made to ex-alcoholics and 9 % for loans made to ex-prisoners. Main financier of the Foundation is the Finland's Slot Machine Association (RAY).

1.3 Overview involvement Consulates, Embassies, Ministries home country, Probation service home country, NGO's etc

See above 1.2.2. and below 2.6. and 3.B.6.

1.4 Overview of trends

1.4.1 Sentencing Trends

a) Foreigners and the criminal justice system

Table II.1. Foreigners (* in the Finnish criminal justice system

	POPULATION (1000)			SUSPECTED OFFENDERS			CONVICTED IN COURTS			PRISONERS		
	Total	For. N	For. %	Total	For. N	For. %	Total	For. N	For %	Total		For. %
1990	4 986	26	0,5	697 918	..		81 716	..		3441	20	0,6
1997	5 138	81	1,6	564 415	..		57 892	2197	3,8	2974	116	3,9
1998	5 154	86	1,7	569 384	..		58 732	2421	4,1	2809	130	4,6
1999	5 166	88	1,7	557 530	13316	2,4	59 651	2738	4,6	2743	138	5,0
2000	5 176	91	1,8	580 266	14273	2,5	64 417	2940	4,6	2855	173	6,1
2001	5 195	99	1,9	580 222	14783	2,5	66 605	3339	5,0	3135	248	7,9
2002	5 206	104	2,0	564 306	15758	2,8	64 791	3511	5,4	3433	293	8,5
2003	5 220	107	2,0	589 179	16621	2,8	64 872	3630	5,6	3578	291	8,1
2004	5 236	108	2,1	633 408	17314	2,7	69 765	3723	5,3	3577	284	7,9
2005	5 256	114	2,2	643 647	19346	3,0	68 856	..	..	3888	282	7,3

*) Foreigners having residence in Finland. Excludes foreign born nationals

In 2005, 19 300 foreigners who had residence in Finland, were suspected of some offence. This rate was 3.0 % out of all persons suspected of offences known to the police in Finland. The number of offences committed by foreigners has increased 79 % since 1996. In 2005, about 114 000 foreigners (2,2 % of the whole population) had residence in Finland. In addition about 16 100 foreigners not having residence in Finland, tourists and other visitors were suspected of offences in 2005.

23 per cent of all foreigners suspected of crimes were Russians, 18 per cent were Estonians, and 8 per cent were Swedes. Foreigners were most typically suspected of traffic offences (45 % in 2005). Forcible rapes and robberies were offences where foreign suspects were most clearly over-represented in 2005 (forcible rapes 21 per cent and robberies 27 per cent of all suspects).

Majority of foreign offenders are suspected of minor offences that lead to summary fines (usually for traffic offences). In 2004 15 441 foreigners received summary fines, while 3635 were sentenced in the courts either to fines or other penalties. The distribution of penalties in 2004 is in table II.2.

Table II.2. Penalties imposed for foreigners 2004

	All		Foreigners	
	N	%	N	%
Summary fines	232 613	77,4	15441	80,9
Courts				
Fines	39420	13,1	2161	11,3
Conditional	16165	5,4	1089	5,7
Community service	3621	1,2	95	0,5
Prison	8530	2,8	290	1,5
Total	300349	100	19077	100

Of all foreigners sentenced to imprisonment in 2005, over one-fourth (27 %) were Estonians, and about one-fifth (21 %) were Russians. The number of foreigners in Finnish prisons has been increasing rapidly in last ten years, from about one per cent to 7–9 per cent of the average daily prison population. Foreigner participation in the growing narcotics markets is a central factor in this development.

b) General trends in prisoner rates 1995-2005

The number prisoners in Finland have – after a long decline –again started to increase. Between 1999 and 2005 the number of prisoners has increased in Finland by 40 %. This change can be analysed in terms of different prisoner groups (for example remand, fine defaulters, foreigners, females, juveniles etc.) and in terms of the principal offence (the trends in prisoner rates is examined in more detail in *Lappi-Seppälä* forthcoming).

Figure 1 Prisoners by **Principal offence 1990-2005**

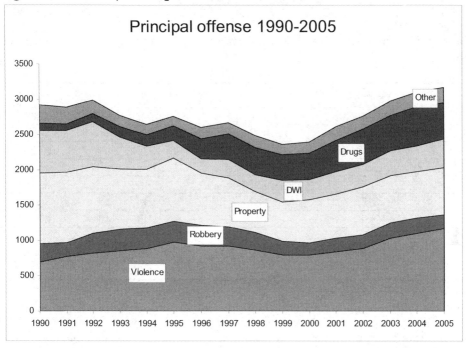

Source: Criminal Justice Agency

Table II.3 Prisoners on 1 May by type of offence in Finland (remand and fine defaulters excluded)

					Change %	
	1.5. 1999	1.5. 2002	1.5. 2005	1.5. 2006	*1999-2005*	*2005-2006*
Property	746	875	864	827	*15,8*	*-4,2*
Violence	794	951	1254	1349	*57,9*	*10,0*
Drunk Driving	312	313	409	386	*31,1*	*-7,3*
Drugs	360	498	512	484	*42,2*	*-5,6*
Other	149	125	134	140	*-10,1*	*4,8*
Total	2361	2762	3173	3186	*34,4*	*0,5*

Property offenses include robberies

Violence crime shows the most rapid increase (58 %) followed by drug offenses (42 %). The number of prison sentences imposed byt the courts for aggravated drug offences have doubled and the sentences have become longer by one third. However, rather than changes in the sentencing traditions, this increase reflects changes in the crime structure (especially in the quantity of the drugs). The good news is that after 2002 the situation seems to have been stabilised and between 2005-2006 the number of drug offenders in prison decreased by 6 %. The bad news is violent offences -- the largest prisoner group – still show an increase of 10 % between 2005 to 2006. This is a result of deliberate overall tightening in the official control of violent offences (in reporting, apprehension and sentencing level).

Table II.4. Prisoner rates according to prisoner groups in Finland 1990–2006

Prisoners serving a sentence by prisoner-group 1990-2005. Annual averages.

	Serving a sentence	*Remand*	*Fine defaulters*	*All*
1998	2421	292	96	2809
1999	2287	354	102	2743
2000	2358	376	121	2855
2001	2529	457	149	3135
2002	2765	478	190	3433
2003	2888	492	198	3578
2004	3023	473	81	3577
2005	3190	519	179	3888
2006	..	..	..	3790

Source: Criminal Justice Agency

The number of remand prisoners has almost doubled in 1998–2005 (but it still modest in the comparative perspective). Fine-defaulters are a specific problem for the Finns. The share of fine defaulters corresponds to some 5 % of the Finnish prison population (while Sweden manages to do without this group altogether). [3]

---

[3] The short-term decline in 2004 is explainable by the fact due to a computer program failure (!) the enforcement of fine-default penalties was interrupted for most part of the year 2004. Unfortunately the programs were fixed, and the number of fine-defaulters rose back to their original level.

Figure 2 The Length of Sentences 1985-1995 (1 October) and 2000-2005 (1 May)

THE LENGTH OF SENTENCE IN 1985-1995 (1 October) AND 2000-2005 (1 May)

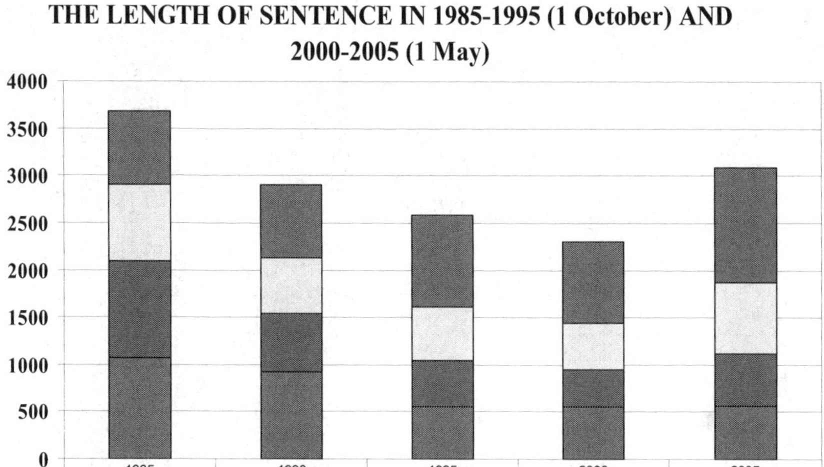

	1985	1990	1995	2000	2005
■ 2 years-	783	775	971	853	1218
□ 1<2 years	816	591	568	503	753
■ 6<12 months	1019	614	494	390	556
■ <6 months	1068	923	551	553	565

■ <6 months ■ 6<12 months □ 1<2 years ■ 2 years-

Source: Criminal Justice Agency

The increase of prisoner rates in Finland in 1998–2004 is a summary effect of five major factors, each affecting in slightly different times: (1) An increase in the number of foreign prisoners (mainly from Russia and the Baltic countries), (2) an increase in drug trafficking (often linked with the former groups), an increase in the number of (3) fine defaulters and (4) prisoners in remand, and (5) an increase in violent offenders (towards the shift 1990/2000).

1.4.2   Characteristics Foreign Prison Population

During the 1990s foreign population living in Finland increased by some 250 % (from 26 000 to 114 000). This change has reflected also in the prisoner rates. The number of foreign prisoners increased from a near zero to a figure that corresponds to about 8 % of the Finnish prisoner rates.

Figure 3 Foreign prisoners rates in Finland 1976-2005

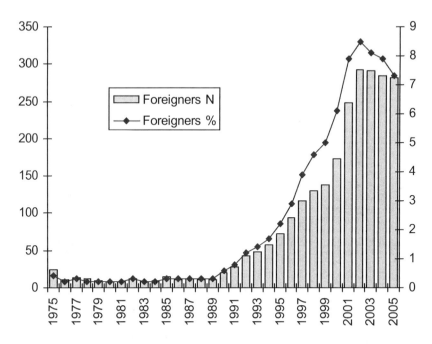

Source: Lappi-Seppälä (forthcoming)

Figure 4 Foreign prisoners by nationality 1995 - 2005

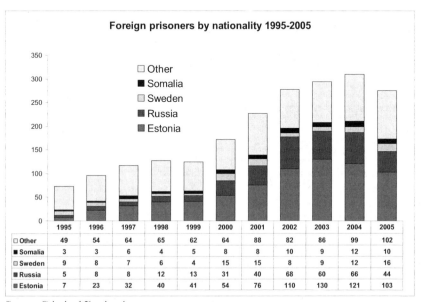

	1995	1996	1997	1998	1999	2000	2001	2002	2003	2004	2005
Other	49	54	64	65	62	64	88	82	86	99	102
Somalia	3	3	6	4	5	8	8	10	9	12	10
Sweden	9	8	7	6	4	15	15	8	9	12	16
Russia	5	8	8	12	13	31	40	68	60	66	44
Estonia	7	23	32	40	41	54	76	110	130	121	103

Source: Criminal Justice Agency

Half of the prisoners are detained for drug offences.

Figure 5

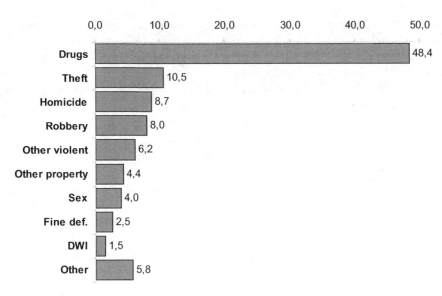

Foreign prisoners by offense 2005 (1.5.)

Source: *Criminal Justice Agency*

About 10 % of FP are women. Half of them are between the ages of 25-39 years.

Figure 6 Foreign prisoners according to their age in 2001-2005 (1 May)

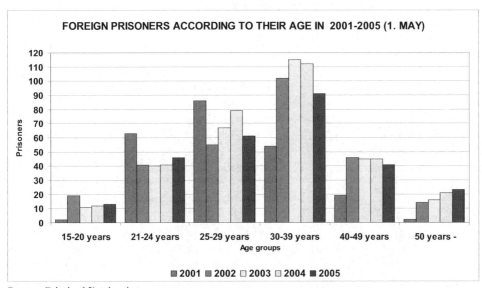

Source: *Criminal Justice Agency*

1.5 Overview of national legislation

1.5.1 Penitentiary Legislation

Provisions related to prisoners and the executions of sanctions are gathered in the new Penitentiary Law in force 2006. New Penitentiary Law gives high priority for the constitutional rights of prisoners. Leading principles in the enforcement include the following starting points (Penitentiary Law sections 2-4):

- "Goal of the enforcement of imprisonment is to increase the ability of a prisoner to a life without crime by promoting the prisoner's potential to cope and his adjustment to society as well as to prevent the committing of offences during the term of sentence."
- "A sentence of imprisonment shall be enforced so that it is safe to society, prison staff and prisoners."
- "The enforcement of imprisonment may not restrict the rights or circumstances of a prisoner in any other manner than that provided in the law or necessary due to the punishment itself."
- "The authorities in charge of the enforcement of imprisonment shall ensure that, during the imprisonment, no person will unjustifiably violate the personal integrity of the prisoner"
- "The conditions in a prison shall be arranged, to the extent possible, so that they correspond to the living conditions prevailing in society" (The principle of normalization)
- "The possibilities of a prisoner to maintain his health and functional ability shall be supported. The goal is to prevent any detriment resulting from the loss of liberty." (The aim of harm-minimization)
- "Prisoners shall be treated with justice and with respect for their human dignity. Prisoners may not, without a justifiable reason, be placed in an unequal position due to race, national or ethnic origin, colour, language, sex, age, family status, sexual orientation, state of health, disability, religion, social opinion, political or professional activity or other reason relating to the person".
- "When enforcing the imprisonment of juveniles, who have committed their offences when under 21 years of age, special attention shall be paid to the needs arising from the age and stage of development of the prisoner."

These principle apply also to foreign prisoners. They have the same legal position as other prisoners and they have the same legal rights and obligations, so the law applies to both groups on similar basis.

Provisions for all types of sanctions as well as crime definitions are in New Penal Code revised in several stages during the 1990s. Foreigners are not excluded from any specific sanctions. However, the use of community service seems to be underrepresented among the foreigners. This may partially result from the fact that to be able to carry out the sentence usually requires some language skills (if not Finnish then at least in Swedish or English). In addition to these provisions there are several special sections in national legislation that are applicable for foreign prisoners and minorities. These have been listed in section A above.

1.5.2 Penitentiary Legislation & Foreigners

Finland has ratified all the main human rights documents that influence the system of sanctions, sentence enforcement, and the treatment of those who are deprived of their liberties. The United Nations International Covenant on Civil and Political Rights entered into force in Finland in 1976 and the European Human Rights Convention (ECHR) in 1990. National courts can apply the provisions of the Convention. All the international agreements that Finland has adopted are part of the Finnish judicial system after having first been incorporated by the decision of the parliament.[4] There is a long lasting tradition of Nordic co-operation in legal matters. This co-operation has produced several legislative acts in each country since the 1960s onwards. In many cases, these Nordic agreements and acts go further than other European instruments. Still, the latter ones are, of course, also applied in relation to other countries. Finland has been active in ratifying agreements drafted within the EU, for instance, the Convention on the Protection of the European Communities' Financial Interests (1995) and the Convention relating to Extradition between the Member States of the EU (1996).

Extradition between the Nordic countries follows simplified rules, as compared to extradition to/from other countries. Between the Nordic countries there is no requirement of double criminality, and also Finnish citizens may be extradited to other Nordic countries. Both are exceptions from those principles that apply currently to other European countries. The Framework decision (11483/02) of the European Union on European arrest warrant and the surrender procedure between Member States will bring changes in both of these aspects (the general demand of double criminality and the obligation to extradite Finnish citizens to other European countries). These extensions are to be included in a bill that will be passed to the parliament in September 2003.

Nordic Agreement on Mutual Assistance between the Nordic states regulates the procedure in situations where a Nordic state needs assistance concerning the service of summons or the collection of evidence. The Agreement involves only certain fairly limited deviations from the European Convention on Mutual Assistance in Criminal Matters and presupposes that the Nordic co-operation shall be governed also by the Convention. In June 2003, the Government passed a bill to the parliament in order to implement the European Convention for Mutual Assistance in Criminal Matters (EYVL C 197, 12.7.2000).

The enforcement of *economic sanctions* follow simplified rules between the Nordic states, and judgements according to which such sanctions (for example fines) are imposed can, on request, be enforced in Finland without further formal conditions. A Nordic judgement on *imprisonment* may be enforced in Finland if the sentenced person, at the time of

---

[4] However, these documents, such as the European Human Rights Convention (ECHR) do not have a general or absolute precedence over other statutory law in Finland. Still, in cases where the provisions of the convention and the contents of national law contradict each other, a doctrine of interpretation known as "human rights friendly interpretation", was adopted in Finland by the Constitutional Committee of the parliament: the interpretation and application of laws shall always aim at obtaining a result that as closely as possible corresponds to the international obligations of Finland in the field of human rights. The same principle has also been declared in the new Finnish Constitution which entered into force in 2000. According to section 22, the public authorities shall guarantee the observance of basic and human rights. As a result, the Finnish courts have more and more often referred to the articles of the convention in their decisions.

enforcement, is a Finnish citizen or is domiciled in Finland. Such a judgement may also be enforced in Finland if the sentenced person is present in Finland and it is considered appropriate that the sentence is enforced here. Consent from the convicted person is, in principle, not needed but his or her opinion is generally respected. Finland can, on request, *supervise offenders sentenced to a suspended (conditional) sentence.* No prerequisites are explicitly stated in the Nordic Act but, in principle, the criteria used with regard to sentences of imprisonment apply (supervision shall be enforced by another state than the one which passed the sentence only when the convicted person resides or plans to reside in the former state). Supervision of persons *conditionally released* in other Nordic states can be executed in Finland. The rules regarding the supervision of conditionally released persons and the rules regarding the supervision of offenders who have received a suspended sentence are very much the same.

These rules, in comparison with those applicable in relation to non-Nordic states, are simpler and contain fewer pre-conditions. However, the Framework decision (10710/01 COPEN 37) of the European Union on the application of the principle of mutual recognition to financial penalties would bring changes in this respect. Under current structure, the financial penalties imposed in other European countries outside the Nordic-region cannot be enforced in Finland. The Finnish government supports this expansion and wishes to extend it also to summary fines. The government also support the proposal for a new Framework decision concerning the enforcement of confiscation order within the EU-countries.

2 TREATMENT OF FOREIGN PRISONERS

2.1   General

Foreign prisoners are treated according to the same principles as national prisoners. However, other prisoners often discriminate those other prisoners, which differ from the Finnish and Europeans by their outlook (race, colour). This discriminated are being placed to sections where the prisoner are not mixed with other prisoners or where also other discriminated prisoners (based on crime or other reasons) are being placed. There are now security classifications but the distinction between open and closed prisons. Low risk prisoners who are capable to work are placed to open prisons (about 23 % of all). About the same percentage (20 %) of foreigners are placed in open prisons.

In autumn 2005 the Finnish prison service nominated a working group to examine whether ethnic minorities (basically foreigners and gypsies) are receiving equal treatment both in legal provisions, administrative guidelines and enforcement practices. In the work two groups of offenders receive the main attention: Foreigners (around 300 prisoners) and gypsies (around 200)n prisoners. These groups cover about 12 % of the daily prison population.

2.2   Living conditions and facilities

Foreign prisoners have access to the same living conditions and facilities as national prisoners. When placing the prisoner within an institution the individual traits of the prisoner, his or her chances to participate the prison activities (work, education etc.) must be taken into account. The prisoners own wishes regarding his or her placement must be considered as well.

Based on the prisoners own request he or she can be isolated from the other inmates if there are reasonable grounds. However, according to the Ombudsman of the Parliament isolating a prisoner must not be exercised as an additional punishment, but the objective can only be either to ensure that the prisoner remains in the facility or to maintain prison safety and security. "Isolation at one's own request" takes place often in cases when prisoner feels to be threatened by fellow prisoners. This group "fearing prisoners" has received attention during the last years in Finland. As it also seems, prisoners of ethnic origin and gypsies are over-represented among this prisoners. In 2004 a specific section was established in Helsinki prison for "fearing prisoners". Among those 142 prisoners who were replaced in that unit, 25 had ethnic background and 18 were gypsies (30 % in contras to overall 12 % see above).

2.3 Reception and admission

Reception procedures are the same for nationals and foreigners. Prison-rules have been translated into English, Russian and Estonian. Prisons have also translated the daily programs into those languages needed. In Helsinki prison additional information is arranged for Russian and Estonian prisoners. Prisoners are entitled to communicate with a representative of their diplomatic mission (consulate). They can also call their families, provided they have money for the telephone. The practical measures regarding phone calls vary in different institutions. The most common procedure is that prisoners can purchase telephones cards to be utilised in the prison telephones during a separately designated time (usually 1-2 hours per week).

There are no separate 'telephone funds' directed to prisoners without money. However, every prisoner is entitled to a prisoner's allowance, which is 0, 20 □/hour both in closed and in open institutions. The prisoner allowance is paid to those prisoners who cannot participate in prison duties (work, education, action programmes). Private telephone calls and other personal expenses are expected to be covered with the allowance. Financial benefit can be received from the social services for official calls such as calls for attorney. If the prisoner is without funds, he or she is also eligible to make a free 'homecoming' phone call when released from prison to a Finnish address he or she is registered (if available).

2.4 Work - Education – Training – Sports - Recreation

Foreign prisoners attend to work and to the educational and vocational training in classes, sports and recreational activities as all other prisoners. However the lack of language skills causes difficulties especially in programs that are based on communication. Russian prisoners have been arranged with outside help health- and service info courses in Kerava. Helsinki and Kerava provide lessons in the Finnish language. The prison libraries have some books in foreign languages. The libraries may order books and videos in other languages if such material is available.

2.5   Food – Religion – Personal hygiene – Medical care

Religion: over 90 % of the Finnish population belong to the Evangelic-Lutheran church. Also the majority of prison priests represent Evangelic-Lutheran church, although every foreign prisoner has a right to a priest of his or her own religion. All prisoners have in principle the right to practice their own religion alone and together with others, provided that this does not breach "the law, good manners and prison order". According to the law, "care must be taken that the prisoners do not have to take part in religious occasions against their own will." The law also obliges the prison to reserve a suitable facility for joint religious ceremonies for those prisoners who form the majority. For other prisoners facilities will be provided "according to practical possibilities". Furthermore, prisoners have the right to discuss privately with a person belong to his/her own religion. Arrangements have been agreed upon with the Orthodox Church to take care of the Russian prisoners (part time orthodox clerks). In Kerava the Muslim prisoners have a prayer-hour once a week.

Diet and food: the Prison Service arranges special diets according to the religions demands. Enforcement appreciates the diet requirements as well as the Ramadan-period. The Cantinas are also provided with ethnic food.

Medical care: medical and the healthcare are organized on similar principles for all prisoner groups. In practice language problems and the lack of interpreters may cause problems. Also personal hygiene requirements are the same for all prisoners. The prisoners are eligible to shower as often as they wish. The inmates may keep their personal clothes.

2.6   Consular and legal help

The prisoners are informed about their choice to take contact with the representatives of their diplomatic mission. They decide themselves, whether they will use this option or not. The income limit to receive free legal aid in Finland is 650 □ per month. Up to the income limit of 1400 □ per month a person is entitled to partially free legal aid. Also non-nationals without legal resident permits are eligible for free legal aid. Interpreters shall be designated for foreign prisoners when needed. In practice difficulties in finding the interpreters have been encountered with prisoner from the African countries.

2.7   Contact with the outside world

Foreign prisoners may stay in contact with their relatives and also receive visits. Telephone is the most frequently used means of communication. Prisoners who cannot read nor write are granted help with their letters and correspondence. Newspapers in different languages (mostly English) are available in some prisons, as well as cable television with various channels. Consulates assist often in providing the reading-materials (newspapers etc).

2.8 Re-integration activities - Prison leave

There are no special programs for foreign prisoners in order to promote the resettlement into society after release. Foreign prisoners are allowed to go on furlough according to individual discretion. Normal rule for parole also apply. Parole is being used on routine-basis after ½ or 2/3 of the sentence has been served.

2.9 Release - Expulsion

Upon release foreign prisoners are being sent to their country of origin depending on the seriousness of their offence and the length of the sentence. The criteria for overall consideration of expulsion are defined in the Aliens Act.

A foreigner who has resided in Finland under a residence permit may be expelled if: 1) he or she resides in Finland without the required residence permit; 2) he or she is found guilty of an offence punishable by imprisonment for a maximum of a year, or if he or she is found guilty of repeated offences; 3) he or she has shown, through his or her activities that he or she is liable to endanger other people's safety; or 4) he or she has been engaged in activities that endanger Finland's national security or relations with a foreign state or on the basis of his or her previous activities and for other reasons, there are grounds to suspect that he or she may engage in such activities. A refugee may be expelled in the cases referred to in 2-4 above. A refugee may not be expelled to his or her home country or country of permanent residence against which he or she still needs international protection. A refugee may only be expelled to a State that agrees to admit him or her.

In the Act it is stated that when considering refusal of entry, expulsion or prohibition of entry and the duration of the prohibition of entry, account shall be taken of the facts on which the decision is based and the facts and circumstances affecting the matter otherwise as a whole. When considering the matter, particular attention should be paid to the best interest of children and the protection of family life. Other facts to be considered include at least the length and purpose of the alien's residence in Finland, the nature of the residence permit issued to him or her and the alien's ties to Finland. Should a refusal of entry be based on any criminal activity of the alien, account shall be taken of the seriousness of the act and the detriment, damage or danger caused to public or private security. This applies mutatis mutandis to IV.9. See below ('Administrative detention of foreign prisoners'). Alien's act is applied to both prisoner groups.

Competentauthorities: police or authorities at the border shall take action to refuse an alien entry or expel an alien who does not meet the requirements for entry into or residence in the country. After that period, police or authorities at the border shall submit a proposal to the Directorate of Immigration to the effect that the alien be refused entry or be expelled, unless the Directorate of Immigration has already taken action to remove the alien from the country.

Police or authorities at the border may order a maximum of two years' prohibition of entry for an alien if he or she is refused entry. Police or authorities at the border shall submit a proposal to the Directorate of Immigration to the effect that the alien be refused entry if they are not competent to refuse entry or if they consider that the alien should be prohibited from entering the country for more than two years.

The Directorate of Immigration decides on refusal of entry upon proposal by the District Police or authorities at the border or on its own initiative. The Directorate of Immigration always decides on refusal of entry if more than three months have passed since the alien's entry into the country, or if the alien has applied for a residence permit on the basis of international or temporary protection. The Directorate of Immigration decides on expulsion upon proposal by the District Police or authorities at the border or on its own initiative. The Directorate of Immigration may prohibit entry of aliens for a fixed term or until further notice. The Directorate of Immigration decides on abolishing a prohibition of entry.

2.10 Aftercare – Probation

In case foreign offenders stay after release in the host country, are they allowed to make use of aftercare facilities and support from the probation service as offered to national ex-offenders. In practice, however, much depends on the language skills of the offender. For Russian and Estonian prisoners special programs related to drugs and alcohol have been arranged.

2.11 Staff

There are some 2700 full time officials working in the Prison Service. More than half of them work in supervising and guarding duties, the majority are on uninterrupted three-shift work. During recent years, the structure of the personnel has been developed and job descriptions broadened for instance by directing the personnel's work input more on various prisoners' activity programmes and close work. The Probation Service employs some 300 civil servants. Most of them are client workers: social workers and instructors whose duty is to enforce community sanctions. Also the assistant directors and a great deal of directors of the district offices carry out client work. At the end of the year 2004 there were 330 private supervisors at the service of the Probation Service. Private supervisors supervise in the direction of the district offices conditionally sentenced young offenders and conditionally released prisoners (parolees). For supervision work a nominal fee is paid. The basic training of the prison staff includes also courses in English. There is no other special training to deal with foreign prisoners.

2.12 Projects

There are no specific projects funded by the Government for foreign prisoners inside or outside penitentiary institutions in Finland. Some of the support services offered by Non-Governmental Organisations have been described in section I. 4 above.

3 ADMINISTRATIVE DETENTION OF FOREIGN PRISONERS

A. General questions
The provisions dealing with the administrative prisoners are in The Aliens Act (301/2004) and the Act on the Treatment of Aliens in Custody and on a Custody Unit (116/2002).

3.1 Institution

Finland has only one custody unit for aliens referred to in the Aliens Act. In 2005 the previous Helsinki Unit was transferred to a new Custody Unit in Metsälä near Helsinki. The new facility has a capacity for ca. 40 detainees.

The detention of an alien is specifically meant to safeguard the clarification of the preconditions of entry of an alien or the enforcement of expulsion in cases where another safety measure, for example the duty to report, cannot be deemed sufficient.

The basic training of the staff is good. Many have degrees from a college, a polytechnic or a vocational institution in the fields of health care, social studies or a corresponding field. In addition, the Custody Unit arranges and acquires additional training for example in safety issues.

The Metsälä Custody Unit also hosts a small reception centre for asylum seekers (46 places) as well as an information/service point for asylum seekers with private accommodation. The aim is for the children and spouse of the detained, where possible, to be accommodated in the premises of the open reception centre. On the other hand, the custody unit can also use the services of the reception centre. The new premises comply with the Finnish standard for institutions, in addition to which the special features and requirements of custody operations have also been observed. In connection with the changes in 2005 the conditions of the customers improved considerably; there is more room for free time activities and hobbies. The outdoor exercise premises will be much more pleasant than at present and there also is a special outdoor area for i.e. smoking, which the customers will have free access to.

A detained alien may exceptionally be placed in police detention premises if the custody unit is full. Another reason for placing a person in police detention premises is that an alien is detained far away from the closest custody unit. In the latter case, the detention may not last more than four days.

3.2 Ministry responsible & legislation

The Custody Unit operates subordinate to the Ministry of Labour. Its operation and the treatment of persons in custody there are governed by the Act on the Treatment of Aliens in Custody and on a Custody Unit (116/2002).

3.3 Capacity institutions

The institution has a capacity of 40 inmates.

3.4 Length of stay

There are no written norms on the maximum length of the stay. The district court decides on the continuation of the detention in two- week intervals. In actual practice the maximum length of stay is, however, 3 months. The average length of stay was in 2005 17 days. The period of detention depends on the progress of the investigation and other authorities. The matters involving a detained person are handled as urgent.

3.5 Decisions procedure

In the first instance the police or border guards take the decision for detention but the district court will decide on further detention. The assessment of the justification and necessity of detention is performed by the District Court at the latest within four days from the apprehension under section 124 of the Aliens Act. Also an asylum seeker who has been given a negative decision can be detained before expulsion.

3.6 Appeal procedure

The decision of the District Court is not subject to appeal.

3.7 Irregular stay

Illegal stay in the country is criminalized as an intentional crime and punishable with fines.

3.8 Numbers

The number of detained irregular foreigners varies from single cases to some 20-30 at any given day.

3.9 Expulsion

No statistics are available on those foreigners that have been expelled after administrative detention. However a rough estimation varies between 70-80 %.

3.10 Not-expelled prisoners

Non-expelled foreigners will be released. In case they receive the status of asylum seeker they are moved under the jurisdiction of asylum seekers centre.

3.11 Detention irregulars under criminal law

Under certain conditions Category 3 prisoners may also be placed in police facilities (see above), which usually hold also prisoners who are detained under criminal law. Minors (under 18 years) may be held in the detention unit. In this case they are immediately appointed a representative to take care of their interests.

The powers of the police to enter the premises of the Metsälä Custody Unit and to impose restrictions on detainees are very limited. In cases involving the safety of the custody unit, the director of the Custody Unit or his deputy contacts the police. These cases involve the safety of the persons in custody and the police act on request of the Custody Unit.

The police have been reserved premises in connection with the Custody Unit, where they can meet with an alien in issues relating to the application of the Aliens Act, such as the reason for entry, travel itinerary and removal from the country. This is done to avoid the transportation of detained aliens and to decrease costs arising from transportation.

It would be contrary to the principle of the least harm and more restrictive of the rights of the detained to transport him separately to police premises solely to hear him if the custody unit has premises where the hearing may take place causing the smallest possible harm to the customer. In some cases, for example to take comparison fingerprints, it is necessary to transport the detainee to the police station for the procedure. In that case, it is also well founded to hear him in the premises of the police.

The hearings are recorded using computer-based forms. Both a pending pre-trial investigation and a police investigation relating to asylum are confidential. In order to ensure data security and the legal protection of both the detained person and the police, no outsider can be allowed access to the premises where the police keep their computers and forms.

Visits of the police to the Custody Unit are agreed upon. The police do not have free access to the premises of the Custody Unit. Nor do the police have authority with regard to the operations and personnel of the Custody Unit.

The independent powers of the police with regard to an alien detained in a custody unit are restricted to the following cases: (1) The police may forbid contacts with an outsider if, for a well-founded reason, the contact is estimated to endanger the clarification of the entry preconditions of an alien taken into custody and his identity or if there is a justifiable reason to assume that the meeting will contribute to a crime. (2) The police make the decision on segregation in a custody unit if segregation is necessary as an exception to safeguard the clarification of the preconditions of entry into the country or identity.

B COMPARISON TO IMPRISONMENT

1. General. Detention units for foreign administrative prisoners are closed social units that differ in many respects from prison. The conditions are often more comfortable and the relationships with the staff and the wards are based on co-operation. The staff consists mainly of tutors, not of guards. Security aspects are not forgotten, but the wards are motivated by the fact that the conditions are more relaxed than in prison and this is also appreciated by the wards themselves. In case of violence and attempted escapes, the ward may temporarily be placed in isolation or in police-premises.

2. Living conditions and facilities. Foreign administrative prisoners have basically access to better and more relaxed living conditions and facilities than normal prisoners (see above).

3. Reception and admission. Upon arrival foreign administrative prisoners receive information on the prison rules in their own language both verbally and, if possible, in writing. They are entitled to communicate with a representative of their diplomatic mission, their family and legal aid instances (e.g. The Refugee Advice Centre). The wards may also keep their own mobile phones, provided that these do not have the camera-facility.

4. Work - Education – Training – Sports – Recreation. There are no educational or vocational training programs available. The wards may participate daily in different kinds of sports and recreational activities. There is a small library with books with foreign languages as well as access to internet and TV.

5. Food – Religion – Personal hygiene – Medical care. Foreign administrative prisoners are able to practice their own religion. For that purpose the unit has a small room for religious duties. However, no visits of qualified religious representatives have been organized. Dietary restrictions based on religious or cultural reasons are appreciated. Issues concerning clothing are not interfered with provided that it is in accordance with the general standards of decency. The Custody Unit has attended to arranging acute dental care. Appropriate treatment and therapy will be acquired for those needing psychological or psychiatric help either by calling in a psychiatrist or a psychologist to the Custody Unit or by transporting the person in need of the help outside the Custody Unit for treatment.

6. Consular and legal help. The unit itself has not established direct contacts with foreign representatives of their diplomatic mission. The foreign prisoners can directly be in contact with consular officials and lawyers and they may meet basically any visitors they wish. Asylum seekers have access to free legal aid.

7. Contact with the outside world. The wards have the right to receive any visitors they prefer and to communicate with the outside world. They may have their own mobile phones, provided that these have no camera-function. They may, further, have access to the Internet, TV and some foreign newspapers. The telephone may be used on condition that the detained alien gives notice of whom he intends to contact. The use of the telephone may be denied if, for a well-founded reason, it may be estimated to endanger the clarification of the preconditions of entry into the country or identity or if there is justifiable reason to assume that the use of the telephone will contribute to a crime. (17 §). The right to be in contact with someone outside the custody unit by using telecommunications, other electronic communications or other such technical connection may be restricted on the grounds provided for in section 17 by confiscating the mobile phone or other means of communication from the alien for the duration of the ban.

8. Re-integration activities - Prison leave. Foreign administrative prisoners are not provided with specific activities that prepare them for resettlement into society after release. Neither are there any intermediate steps, such as furloughs or parole. However, an alien may be granted permission to leave the custody unit in order to visit or bury a seriously ill close relative or other close person or for other similar reasons of special significance.

9. Release – Expulsion.
See above III.9:

4 NATIONALS DETAINED ABROAD

The Legal Register Centre of Finland is the authority responsible for collecting and maintaining statistics regarding sentences imposed abroad on a Finnish national or a foreigner permanently living in Finland. The Criminal Records Act states that information from the criminal records shall be delivered to a State Party of the European Convention on Mutual Assistance in criminal matters. Furthermore, provisions on the delivery of data from the criminal records to another Nordic country shall be issued by Decree. However, according to the officials of the Legal Register Centre the procedure of receiving data from abroad is not realised in practise (except for data exchange between the Nordic countries). This means that there is no valid information available on the numbers and characteristics of the Finnish prison population detained abroad.

Nationals detained abroad are not an issue in Finland. Therefore, there is no media or general public opinion on this particular topic. However, individual cases may receive sometimes quite a lot of media attention. In these cases the main concern is on the well being of the prisoners and then fact that detention times are in many cases much longer in other countries and also usually in much worse conditions.

5 EVALUATION AND RECOMMENDATIONS

Both *legal and material conditions of foreign prisoners* are deemed to be in a fairly satisfying level. The new prison law (in force 1.10.2006) rectifies most of the existing shortcomings in the penitentiary legislation. The problems faced by the foreign prisoners are to large extent similar to those faced by national (minority group) prisoners. *Fear of fellow prisoners* is among those problems (although in international comparison fear in Finnish prisons is relative low. Among those groups suffering most from the pressures and intimidation from fellow prisoners are sexual offenders of "wrong colour". The prison administration faces a serious challenge in order to secure the proper standard of security and safety for foreign prisoners as well as other minority groups.

The CPT carried out in 2003 its third periodic investigation of the Finnish prisons (http://www.cpt.coe.int/documents/fin/2004-20-inf-eng.htm). Foreign *nationals detained under aliens legislation* were among the key topics under consideration. The report was generally positive with relatively few critical remarks. Since the visit of CPT a new custody unit for aliens had been established in order to overcome the earlier shortcomings with the older unit regarding outdoor exercises and medical care. CPT reported also shortcomings regarding the instructions according to which the police and the Frontier Guard establishments should provide detained foreign nationals with a written account of their rights in a language they understand. The Finnish authorities referred to these shortcomings in their report (paragraph 53). Along with the entry into force of the new Aliens Act (301/2004) on 1 May 2004, the procedures have been improved in order to enhance the legal protection of persons under the Act. In all decisions made under the Aliens Act, the person in question is issued a written decision in his case with appeal instructions. All the decision forms of the Frontier Guard relating to alien issues have been renewed and translated into different languages, such as Swedish, Russian, German, Spanish, French and English.

The *accelerated asylum procedures* in Finland have been widely criticized. The legal safeguards are not sufficient considering the interests of asylum seekers. The timeframe of eight days for the execution of the expulsion decision is too short for applicant to prepare the appeal, including appropriate legal and linguistic assistance. Within eight days the Helsinki Administrative Court should process the application and also give the decision. NGOs have presented that the timeframe of eight days should be given up and the expulsion should not be executed before the Administrative Court has dealt with the case. (The Refugee Advice Centre 2006.)

Chapter 9

France

Pascal Décarpes

I INTRODUCTION

Foreign national prisoners have never been high up on the French political agenda[1]. Social and economic difficulties – e.g. a 10% unemployment rate - a persistent and influential xenophobic political minority and a constantly rising prison population partially explain this lack of attention for such a serious issue. In order to observe and analyse the situation of foreign nationals in French prisons, researchers have had quarterly statistics at their disposal since the early 1970's, and the 'individual prisoner file' since 1993 including socio-demographic, penal and release data. The rate of foreign prisoners among the prison population has gone up from 18% in 1975 to 29% in 1995.[2] The absolute growth between 1975 and 1999 was an increase from 4,645 up to 12,164 foreign national inmates. It corresponds to a 162% rise in comparison to 91% for French inmates.

Figure 1: Foreign national prison population in regard to nationalities since 1992 *France-continent and France-overseas*

Year	Total all foreign nationals	Europe	Africa	America	Asia	Oceania	Non-defined nationality
1992	15 044	16,3 %	70,0 %	5,1 %	7,9 %	0,1 %	0,7 %
1998	13 557	23,5 %	62,0 %	5,8 %	8,3 %	0,1 %	0,3 %
2004	13 123	28,5 %	52,3 %	9,1 %	9,6 %	0,1 %	0,4 %

Source: Prison administration statistics, Paris

1.1. Overview of penalties and measures

In total, 82% of all releases (2,859 persons between 1 January 1996 and 30 April 1997) have not benefited either from a conditional release, or from a sentence in the community. In 2004, only 5.8% of released prisoners benefited from conditional release. In this context, foreign prisoners cannot expect much from these rarely applied measures. Moreover, irregular foreign detainees are excluded from measures such as prison leaves, furlough or electronic monitoring. Concerning more specific penal features, 41.7 % of foreign prisoners are pre-trial detainees (vs. 31.3% among the French prison population). About 85% of the foreigners first entered prison through pre-trial detention (69% among French prisoners). 58% of the foreign nationals in pre-trial detention were sent to prison through a 'fast track' procedure (47%), which in turn increases the probability of being sentenced to imprisonment because of the poor trial conditions. 6% of the foreign nationals were imprisoned through a criminal procedure (11%). One fourth was sentenced for drug offences.

---

[1] There is also no mention of foreign nationals in the last CPT-Report (31 March 2004) on French prisons after its visit between the 11 and the 17 June 2003.

[2] All further references and data are, when not mentioned, issued from the Ministry of Justice.

Figure 2: Comparison French / foreign nationals in regard to number of convictions and main sentence

Nature of the main sentence	Total	% Total	Foreign nationals	% Foreign nationals
Imprisonment	258257	54	37188	59.6
(partly)	74783	30	17839	47.9
Partly on probation	24899	9.6	2923	7.8
All on probation	158575	61.4	16426	44.1
Fine	148411	31	17930	28.7
Alternative sentence	49900	10.4	5394	8.6
Other	21367	4.5	1840	2.9

Source: National criminel file 2002, Paris

1.2 Overview of the Prison System

No particular kind of institution is used to detain foreigners - foreign prisoners are allocated to general prisons. Nor is there a specific section of the prison service (or another authority) that is responsible for foreigners. Furthermore, there is no special controlling mechanism for foreign detainees (this also applies to general prisons; most control is performed by judicial bodies).

1.2.1 Organisational structure

Under the authority of the Ministry of Justice, the organisational structure of the prison service is based on a central prison administration (the DAP) which is situated in Paris. There are nine regional administrations and one overseas 'mission' that implement national policies. The responsible authorities are the national head officer, ten regional executives and the local prison directors. There are 188 prisons and one "public facility of national health" (in Fresnes). There are three main types of institutions: 115 pre-trial and short sentence prisons ('maison d'arrêt', hereinafter referred to as MA) and 29 corresponding sections located in other prisons; 24 long[3] sentence prisons ('centre de détention', hereinafter referred to as CD) and 31 corresponding sections; and five prisons for prisoners with very long sentences ('maison centrale') and 8 corresponding sections. There are also 13 semi-liberty centres and four corresponding sections (underused to only 60% of their capacity). Social and judicial care and monitoring are performed by 101 'probation and insertion service' headquarters. The first semi-private prison was opened in the late 1980s, and since then the number of such public-private partnerships has increased to 27. The overall prison budget in 2005 was about 1.654 billion euros, a rise of 3.9% compared to 2004, and accounts for 30.3% of the budget of the Ministry of Justice. On the other hand, the prison staff numbers grew 5.7% in one year, reaching a total of 30,238 employees.

All members of prison staff are public servants. Directors, probation officers, guards, technicians and members of the administration all receive training at the 'National

---

[3] Based on the Recommandation of the Council of Europe Rec(2003)23 on the mamagement by prison administrations of life sentence an other long-term prisoners.

School of the Prison Administration' (ENAP) in Agen. The school budget for 2004 was roughly 26.5 million euros. 238 persons work at the school and each year over 700 non-residents give lectures. In 2005, 5,813 participants - of whom 1,040 were guards - took part in the educational programme.

In July 2006, the prison capacity was 50,332 places. 5,000 new places were created between 2002 and 2006. Four new prisons with 600 places each opened in 2004 and 2005. 13,200 places are planned in the 2002 law, and the first are to be available in 2007. Eight MA - with 700-800 places each - are planned for 2008, three prisons with 400-700 places each for 2009 and 7 prisons for juveniles, with 60 places each, are scheduled from 2007 on. On 1 July 2006, there were 61,413 prisoners (down 1.6% since July 2005), which represents 97.4 prisoners per 100,000 of the resident population. 1,568 prisoners have been supervised with electronic monitoring and 357 have been placed externally without accommodation; consequently, there was a ratio of 118 inmates per 100 places. There were 20,999 pre-trial detainees (34% of the total prison population). On 1 July 2006, in 13 prisons or prison sections the rate of overcrowding was 200% or more. In a further 51 prisons or prison sections, the rate was between 150 and 200%, and between 100 and 150% in yet another 74 prisons or prison sections. The overcrowding is only in pre-trial prisons ('MA'), in which short prison sentences of less than 1 year are served, and of whom most are foreign prisoners.

To sum up, between 1980 and 2006, we can observe a rise from 66 up to 97 prisoners per 100,000 of the resident population. The development of the French prison population rate follows the same trend as all other European countries (with the exception of Finland). As to alternative sanctions, on 1 January 2005, 125,437 persons were under judicial monitoring and supervision in the community. On 1 January 2006, 1,221 were in semi liberty (6,440 measures in 2005), 525 in placement outside (2,310), and 871 were being electronically monitored (4,025). 5,916 benefited from conditional release in 2005 and 16,885 were working for the community on 1 January 2005. At the same time, 108,528 persons were on conditional probation (78% of all measures in the community).

In regard to prison population numbers, on 1 December 2005there were 2,129 women (3.6%) and 744 minors (1.1%) in French prisons. About half of the prison population is under 30 years old. On 1 January 2006, 2,242 prisoners were older than 60 (3.8% of prison population, twice the figure of a decade earlier). 59.5% had received an education, only 44% had a job.

1.2.2 Foreign prisoners

There were 4,645 imprisoned foreign nationals in 1975, 15,507 in 1993 (30.8 %), and most recently 11,125 (20 %) on 1 January 2006. On the one hand, the growth of the foreign prisoners' population between 1982 and 1996 is mainly due to a rise in offences against immigration laws. Concerning other offences, the increase remains equal to the French prisoners' figure[4]. On the other hand, foreign nationals are imprisoned more than French nationals because of a lack of different guarantees or resources[5], such as a home, an income, locally residing family, work, etc. Besides, in 1998, 28.5 % of foreign nationals in prison were detained in relation to immigration offences (illegal residence, refusal of

---

[4]   see *Kensey/Tournier* 2002, p. 24-25.
[5]   see *Mary* 1998.

removal, refusal to give name and citizenship in order to oppose expulsion). Between 2000 and 2003, there was a 32% increase in such sentences to prison, from 2,345 up to 3,085. They were sentenced for immigration- and/or other immigration related offences such as the use of false documents or food theft. A major problem in studying specific groups of inmates is the French citizenship approach of the 'universal citizen'. The prison administration invokes little information on foreign nationals because of the discriminatory aspects of such data. Additionally, there is little information as well as contradictory assertions on ethnic sorting[6]. Moreover, the expulsions and removals should be taken into account within prison population figures. Unfortunately this is seldom the case.

Concerning our studied group, 21.5% are foreign nationals: 29.4% of all foreign prisoners come from Europe, 10.1% from the American continents, 9.6% from Asia, and 50.4% from Africa. Foreign prisoners are clearly over-represented because foreign nationals constitute only around 3.5% of the French population. Among foreign prisoners in 1998, 5.2% were women (4.9% among French prisoners), the average age was 31.1 years (30.3 in the case of French prisoners), 22% were married (11%), 66% had no children (65%), 14% were analphabetic (3%), 50% were unemployed (35%), and 22% were in employment (28%). Among foreign prisoners, 92% of illegal foreign nationals who enter prison come from precarious circumstances vs. 57% of legal foreigners[7].

1.3 Involvement of Embassies, Consulates, NGOs etc.

There is currently no detailed information on the actual involvement of Embassies, Consulates or NGOs in issues relating to foreign prisoners.

1.4 Overview of trends

A key-date concerning the prison population is the abolition of the death penalty in 1981 and its 'replacement' with the life prison sentence. This is one of the reasons for the rise of the average duration of detention between 1982 and 1998 by 54% for French prisoners and 80% for foreign prisoners (around nine months). The penal climate has become harsher. High rates of unemployment, populist and xenophobic discourses, and pressure from the mass media are some reasons for harsher sentences, for instance through tougher drug legislation. The drug law of 31 December 1970 is conservative and punitive as a reaction to the 1968 movement. It has been amended (and strengthened) several times - in 1986, 1987, 1992 and 1996.

In regard to all sentenced offences, French and foreign nationals exhibit the same offending structure. Both groups committed around 0.7% serious offences, 82% misdemeanours, and 17% petty offences (National Criminal File 2002). It indicates that nationality is not a criminogenic characteristic. However, the more an offence is elucidated, the more foreign nationals are among the suspects[8]. This is indicative of the fragility and the visibility of their situation, which in turn facilitate the activities of the police. In 1998, 14% of the convicted and 24% of detainees were foreign nationals[9]. At the same time,

---

[6]   see *Oip* 2005, p. 14.

[7]   see *Lamy* 2004.

[8]   see *Lévy*, R. (1987), Du suspect au coupable, le travail de la police judiciaire, Médecine et Hygiène, Klinsieck, Genève, 53-54.

[9]   "Les condamnations en 1998", Etudes et Statistiques Justice (2000), n° 16, minsitère de la Justice.

15% of foreign nationals were sentenced to prison solely for a drug offence in comparison to 9% for French persons (52% vs. 37% for burglary)[10]. For handling stolen goods as a sole offence, 16% of prison sentences were less than three months in length for foreign nationals vs. 30% for French nationals[11]. Since the 1992 reform of the penal code, more than 200 offences can result in an 'Interdiction from entering French national Territory' (hereinafter referred to as an ITF). In 2004, 8.750 such ITFs were passed: 1,518 as the main sentence, and 7,232 as a complementary sentence. The public prosecutor demands the ITF - almost systematically - when a drug or an immigration offence has been committed. For common offences, it can occur that the judge imposes an ITF, although the public prosecutor did not demand it (for instance in the judicial districts of Rouen and Pontoise)[12]. The ITF is ruled under article 131-30 CP. An immigration offence can lead to a three month prison term with a complementary 3 year ITF sentence. The Rouen court refuses all ITF appeals for drug offences, "even if the person has been living in France for 40 years and has 5 children"[13]. In some cases, public prosecutors were asked by the préfet (local State head officer) to charge illegal foreign nationals with prison sentences in order to have sufficient time to prepare their removal. Many court decisions are in favour of foreign nationals against public authorities' policies in issues such as asylum, removal, expulsion, social security, citizenship and family rights. Still, few foreign nationals are actually aware of their rights. Moreover, the political pressure is permanent. In November 2005, the Minister of the Home Office announced the expulsion of foreign nationals who were arrested during the urban guerrilla in France last spring, even those holding a legal permit of residence.

1.5 Overview of national legislation

Foreign prisoners have about the same legal position as other prisoners as well as the same legal rights and obligations. The main national legislation on foreign nationals is comprised in the 'Code of entry and stay of foreign nationals and of asylum rule' (CE-SEDA), which contains all rules from ordinance n° 45-2658 of 2 November 1945 and law n° 52-893 of 25 July 1952, as well as new codification relevant to Article 92 of the law of 26 November 2003. With regard to foreign prisoners, there is no specific penitentiary law. Prison rules are comprised in the Criminal Code ("Code Pénal", 'CP') in articles 714 to 803-4; and in the Code of criminal procedure ("Code de Procédure Pénale", 'CPP')[14]: Some are in "Rule part-State council" Articles R.55 to R.61-6 but most of them are in "Rule part-simple decrees" within 'Book V procedure of execution, Title I execution of criminal sanctions'.

It is striking that most prison legislation is made of simple decrees in the CPP. Thus, the classical legal hierarchy is adapted since notes, circulars, orders and decrees play a major role in prison rules. For instance, the foreign prisoners' regime is partly documented under the 'Rule Part-Simple Decrees', Title II on detention, Chapter XI on different categories of inmates, Section II on foreign national inmates. Article D.505 (decree

---

[10] Couret, F:, Masson, M.-F., "Français-étrangers : l'écart se resserre", Journal La Croix, 27 December 2000.

[11] see *Mary* 1998.

[12] see *Gisti* 2001, p. 17.

[13] see *Gisti* 2001, p. 19.

[14] Without further mention, all articles mentioned in the text are issued from the CPP.

n° 98-1099 of 8 December 1998) stipulates that "under reserve of particularities relative to conditional release, foreign national inmates are under the same regime as national inmates belonging to their penal category. Particular precautions are required concerning [placement on the outside, semi-liberty and prison leave]". On the other hand, Article D. 506 specifies that "under reserve of application of dispositions of the second clause of Article D. 250-4, redress to an interpreter is valid only in case of absolute necessity, if the inmate can not speak or understand the French language and if there is nobody present who would be able to translate. Visits and correspondence can proceed in their language, under reserve of dispositions of Articles D. 407 and D. 418". Finally, Article D.507 indicates that "inmates detained on an extradition-demand expressed by a foreign government are under the regime of pre-trial detainees. Visit permits and correspondence control are issued and conducted by the public prosecutor".

Additionally, a recent circular (CRIM.06.5/E1 from 21 February 2006) sent to préfets and public prosecutors concerning illegal foreign nationals states that "pragmatism, resoluteness and briskness" shall be the key-words of ITF procedures. Even if an ITF is considered as an "exceptional sentence" and should not be applied to some immigration offences (irregular entry, illegal residence), it will still be required in many cases connected to other offences.

2 TREATMENT OF FOREIGN PRISONERS

Although the difference between a pre-trial detainee (D.50) and a convicted inmate (D.491, D.568 and D.50) is clearly defined, foreign prisoners face the same difficulties being either on remand or sentenced to prison. Still, bad prison conditions in MAs strain the already existing drawbacks of foreign nationals. Furthermore, prison administration does not feel to be responsible for the situation of irregular migrants, since they are detained for immigration offences and will be 'removed' after release. As a matter of fact, foreign prisoners – both with or without a legal residence permit - are often isolated from social and economic resources.

2.1 General situation

Theoretically, foreign prisoners and national prisoners are not to be treated differently. However, prison is per se an unequal structure where the 'strongest' and the 'richest' benefit more from the system than others. As mentioned above, in general foreign prisoners are a burdened population in many issues. To schematise, one could say that they are poor, they are poorly educated, they have no family, relatives or friends nearby and they do not speak French. As a whole, they often have to face discriminations or simply a lack of attention. Prison staff, for instance, is not trained to deal with the cultural and judicial complexity of foreign nationals. Moreover, irregular foreign nationals awaiting expulsion or removal are not seen as 'real' prisoners, but more as 'transit' detainees. Prison staff opinion regarding their situation would rather be "it's none of my business". As far as other prisoners are concerned, communication and common understanding are difficult.

Social exclusion among prisoners may occur during group activities or congregational events. It is often the case that foreign prisoners spend their time either alone or with prisoners from their home country. Large communities of foreign nationals join together in prison and generate a sort of 'home identity'. This natural need for personal acknowledgement is unfortunately perceived by staff and nationals as a refusal of contact and integration. Thus, foreign prisoners do not find much support in or from the general public. There is the wide-spread opinion that foreign criminals broke the trust of France which welcomed them as guests and therefore they should be sent back to their country of origin. Another issue is religion. In times of international terrorism, public opinion and mass media manufacture confusion between Islam believers and Al Qaeda partisans. Tolerance is challenged and foreign prisoners who wish to practice their religion face prejudices and mistrust among European individuals. Unfortunately, we have no data at our disposal concerning racist violence in detention amongst prisoners.

Language is also a key issue. Article D. 407 stipulates that "inmates and visitors must speak in French. When one of them can not speak the language, surveillance must be ensured by a staff member who is able to understand them. Without such a member, visits are only authorised under the condition that the visit permit stipulates clearly that the conversation can be held in a foreign language". Actually, interpreters are rarely consulted in prisons because this is not covered by the budget. Neither interviews between the new prisoner and the members of the prison staff nor interviews with social workers, healthcare staff or psychiatrists are considered as an "absolute necessity". Language is a major problem because prison staff has no translation system at its disposal to communicate with foreign prisoners. Mostly the translations are performed by another inmate. This is obviously problematic concerning the guarantee of medical secrets during a visit to the doctors. Social workers can hardly discuss problems in prison because the inmate could feel pressured through the translation by another inmate. This translation system could also give the interpreter a disproportionate degree of power. Probation officers and inmates may translate, but confidentiality and professional secret must be guaranteed.

2.2 Living conditions and facilities

Foreign prisoners legally and theoretically have access to the same living conditions and facilities as other prisoners. Furthermore, the allocation of a foreign prisoner to a prison establishment should not be effected on the grounds of his nationality alone. However, one fourth of all foreign prisoners are in the three big Parisian prisons (Fleury-Mérogis, La Santé, and Fresnes) and 16 prisons have a proportion of foreign nationals 25% above the national average. One of the reasons for this overrepresentation is the foreign nationals' population density around the capital Paris. In this context, foreign prisoners are placed in these prisons more often and thus more often together. Still, there is criticism concerning the institutionalisation of discrimination in so called 'ethnic units'. Already criticised 30 years ago by the Information Group on Prisons (GIP), this system is in effect for instance in the pre-trial prison "La Santé" in Paris. There, the proportion of foreign inmates is 55 %, with 86 nationalities represented. Inmates are placed in four units: Unit A hosts the "Europeans", Unit B the "Africans", Unit C the "North Africans", and Unit D the "rest of the world". The prison head office justifies this selection as being an aim to limit conflicts and with the reason that inmates wish to be grouped by "affinity" such as common language or religion.

Actually, a Christian English inmate might be placed in the same cell as a Muslim French inmate. French of African origin (often born in France, not knowing the country where his parents or grand-parents are from) are also placed in units B "Africans" and C "North Africans". We also see the problem of citizens from former Yugoslavia being placed together. In Fresnes, an English prisoner spent one week alone in a cell; the prison staff pretended that they did not understand what he said, and asked him to write down his demands[15].

2.3 Reception and admission

All first receptions in a French prison are in MA institutions. Reception procedures are the same for nationals and foreigners. Upon arrival they seldom receive information on the prison rules in a language that they can understand. Theoretically, they are entitled to communicate with a representative of their diplomatic mission. However, they hardly know their rights and prison staff cannot (or do not want to) inform them properly; or they omit to do so. Moreover, because of cultural or legal reasons, many foreign prisoners do not want their embassy to know about their criminal situation, especially those awaiting removal or expulsion. Some problems do arise when it comes to contacting their family: they have no financial means to make a telephone call, the relatives could be irregular migrants and thus not be reached, or prison staff refuses conversations in any language other than French.

Reception is partly regulated by article D.284: arriving prisoners will go to a "waiting cell". But in July 2003, only 75 of the 139 'reception prisons' had 'arriving cells', with a total of 700 places. Foreign prisoners face overcrowding on their very first day. Then, the prison director or his/her representative will meet the detainee either on their day of arrival or the following day. The prisoner will receive a medical examination with the "shortest possible delay", he will meet a probation worker "as soon as possible" and he will be issued information about religious practice. But language barriers are present. For instance, if a Tunisian arrives and receives the house rules in French; it is up to him to seek help from his co-detainees[16]. Prison house rules meet Article D.255 and circular DAP 88-16 G2 of 27 December 1988. They are compiled by the prison director, are often obsolete and sometimes missing. They contain orientations from the CPP (D.247), but are barely binding for the prison administration. House rules are often different from one prison to another, very dense and complicated and not always published. They should be translated into different languages but very few probation agencies offer a complete or even summarized translation.

2.4 Work – Education – Training – Sports – Recreation

Foreign prisoners have the opportunity to work and to participate in educational and vocational training classes, sports and recreational activities (socio-cultural activities are under D.440-D.449-1). However, language and cultural barriers are rarely addressed. There are no data available on the proportion of foreign nationals participating in such programmes. Article D.450 stipulates that "inmates shall acquire or develop necessary knowledge after release in regard to better social adaptation".

---

[15] see *Oip* 2005, p.17.
[16] see *Oip* 2005, p.17.

There are around 1,500 teachers active in prisons. 38,000 inmates took part in school in 2004 and roughly 5,000 took an exam. In article D.452 it is mentioned that special programmes are organised for those who are unable to read or speak French. Still, training courses against illiteracy are overcrowded or rarely offered. On the other hand, 152 prisons provide vocational teaching, in which 18,500 inmates were involved in 2005.

21,500 inmates were paid for work or training in 2005: 6,600 for house work (180 euros per month), 1,200 for a penitentiary workshop (560 euros), and 9,000 for the private market (350-500 euros). House work is often allocated to national prisoners because co-operation and closed relations to prison staff are often required. This is in fact quite an absurd paradox that should be underlined: whereas work outside the prison constitutes an offence for illegally resident foreign nationals, they can work inside the prison

Physical and sporting activities (D.459-1 – D.459-3) are the main opportunity for foreign prisoners to leave their cell and to make contacts, in addition to article D.359 "every inmate shall have the opportunity to walk one hour per day in open air".

Finally, socio-educative intervention done by the probation service (SPIP) must prevent the dissocialising effects of imprisonment (D. 460). This is, however, rarely the case with foreign prisoners.

2.5 Food – Religion – Personal hygiene – Medical care

Foreign prisoners are entitled by law to practice their own religion ("spiritual assistance", D.432-D.439). However, there are not enough special facilities available for prisoners to devote themselves to their religious duties. There is also a lack of qualified religious representatives who have access to foreign prisoners (69 Islam religion officers). On 1 January 2003, there were 918 religion officers working in prison, of which 323 were paid: 513 were Catholics, 267 Protestants, 69 Muslims, 64 Jewish, 3 Orthodox, and 2 Buddhists. To illustrate the problem, a big prison like Fresnes (637 foreign prisons in 2004) could not find an imam[17]. Prison Service deals with dietary restrictions 'as far as possible'. There are no dress requirements.

There are neither special health-care provisions for foreign prisoners nor special care for inmates with mental problems. Since a 1994 law, health care in prison has been under the authority and responsibility of the Ministry of Health. There is a 'Unit of ambulatory consultation and care' (UCSA) in every prison (except in semi-liberty centres) as well as 93 psychiatric sections. Personal hygiene requirements are common to all prisoners (D.348-1 until D.359): "as far as possible, inmates shall be allowed to take a shower three times a week". The inmate may keep his personal clothes (D.61, D.338 and D.348) or ask for a fresh set if so required.

As to alimentation, "the composition of the alimentary regime is done by the prison administration" (D.342). Article D.354 stipulates that "the food shall, as far as possible, take into account inmates' philosophical or religious convictions". The Jewish inmates can receive food for Easter, New Year's Eve (Rosh-ha-Shana) and Yom Kippur. Muslim inmates can celebrate Ramadan (Aid El Fitr) and Ail El Kebir with the appropriate and respective food. Otherwise, food packages are prohibited. Still, article D.343 specifies the possibility to buy food inside the prison but the offer remains centred on French-

---

[17]   Michel Saint-Jean, Head officer of Fresnes Prison, *Journal du dimanche*, 4 April 2004.

European products. Moreover, prices are decided by the prison director (D.344), and are often 10% (sometimes up to 50%) more expensive than in a normal supermarket.

Since a law passed on 18 January 1994, all inmates are affiliated to the social security system. Foreign nationals are also automatically and compulsorily affiliated, for up to three years after release. Their family benefits only under the precondition that they are legal residents. For illegal foreign nationals, the affiliation concerns them only during their time in detention (D.366).

2.6 Consular and legal help

Legal help is regulated by articles 2, 3 and 4 of law n°91-647, passed on 10 July 1991. On 1 January 2004, the income limit in order to receive the complete amount is 830 euros per month, and 1,244 euros for partial help. The request has to be stated before the TGI by the legal help office; the lawyer fees will then be covered. EU citizens and non-EU legal residents in France can benefit from legal help. Exceptionally, some other groups are also eligible when the situation appears worthwhile. Legal help is allowed without conditions for minors as well as persons within the procedure of Articles 18bis, 22bis, 24, 35bis and 35.4 of ordinance from the 2 November 1945 relative to conditions of entry and stay of foreign nationals in France. In 2002, 41,000 admissions for legal help concerned administrative or foreign nationals' cases, which represent only 6% of all admissions[18].

On the other hand, Article 24 of law n° 2000-321 from 12 April 2000 as well as other texts stipulate that an interpreter shall be designated by the prison's chief officer in case of a disciplinary procedure in order to prepare the defence of the prisoner. But the availability of a three hour preparation delay – to be extended by the lawyer – is unknown, too short, or useless for a foreign national. Moreover, the procedure is – predominantly - a written one.

Additionally, the 'offices for legal access' (PAD) can provide prisoners with help. At the end of 2004, 38 PAD were functioning within 52 prisons. In Fleury-Mérogis, the PAD is managed by the association 'ARAPEJ Ile de France'. Among 1,384 consultations in 2004, 44% dealt with foreign national law: 14.95% concerned the stay in France, 18.57% were about administrative procedures and 10% involved penal procedures.

2.7 Contact with the outside world

Foreign prisoners can stay in contact with their relatives and they can receive visitors. The telephone is often used, but is prohibited in pre-trial detention centres where most foreign prisoners are detained. Written correspondence is problematic because many foreign prisoners are analphabetic. Although some can read, many cannot write. Moreover, letters written in a foreign language can be required to be translated in order to be checked (D. 418). As to correspondence (D.413-D.419), no text prohibits sending and receiving letters in a foreign language. Correspondence with diplomatic and consular authorities is subjected to supervision.

Newspapers, magazines and books in a foreign language should be available (D.444), but prison directors are often unwilling to fund media that they can not understand. Few libraries contain books in appropriate foreign languages; most of the books are in English.

---

[18] see *Oip* 2004, pp.69-70.

Newspapers in foreign languages have to be approved and ordered by the prison authorities. Television programs are often kept to a minimum, with only five channels, all of which are in French. Different channels in other languages could be received via cable or satellite television. This is seldom the case, because it is expensive and prison authorities would not be able to control the program content.

Visitors (D.403-D.412) must speak in French, or in another language under certain conditions (D.407). Actually, the rule is not too strictly applied. Still, the soft legal context is a source of discretionary control for the prison services. A problem that remains is that the family members of many foreign nationals are afraid of or mistrustful towards the prison services, especially if they are irregular migrants. On the other hand, 'family relations' (D.420-D.423) implies that they have the right to keep their wedding ring, photos, and to receive money, clothes and books. They can also attend family events and receive prison leave (D.424-D.426) for weddings, death or in cases of illness. However, a foreign prisoner would not be allowed to go abroad within such a measure.

2.8 Re-integration activities - Prison leave

No specific community agency is responsible for the resettlement of foreign prisoners and providing then with aid and support. The foreign nationals participate in the same programmes as all other prisoners do. The law of 26 November 2003 states the possibility for foreign prisoners to benefit from these alternatives during the execution of their prison sentence, yet many inmates believe that such measures give them no benefit[19]. Social workers are not completely informed on foreign prisoners' rights. The prognosis is based on behaviour in prison and prospects of reintegration. Within and during a conditional release, the removal decision is suspended. But during this period the irregular migrant is the titular of a "release card under conditions" and may not work. In this context, semi freedom, placement outside or electronic monitoring may be delivered in order to enable a request for the removal to be revoked. In some regions, judges implement these measures, while others do not. However, there is no possibility for foreign nationals awaiting removal to benefit from such alternatives because the 'judge for the execution of sentences' (JAP) or the probation officer can not provide aftercare and monitoring outside of French territory.

Moreover, according to the 'National consultative commission of human rights' (CNCDH) in its report from 18 November 2004, the JAP tends to estimate a foreign national's chances of obtaining a stay permit in order to allow him to benefit from a sentence arrangement. Since 1 January 2001 (law from 15 June 2000 on the presumption of innocence), the JAP must justify his decisions and a prisoner can file an appeal. A lawyer can assist the inmate in this. In addition, foreign prisoners can apply for a 'composed sentence' in order to ask for the erasure of the removal sentence. The JAP can order a conditional release for a foreign national under a secondary sentence of removal, which will be deleted in the case of no further offence. The CNCDH criticizes the criteria to obtain this composition, since in most of the cases the sentence is only the consequence of the impossibility to regularise his or her administrative situation.

---

[19] see *Trombik* 2005, p.37.

The Court of Cassation decided that a ITF sentence is incompatible with the benefit of a leave permit[20], even if it infringes family relations in regard to Article 8 § 1 ECHR, because the ITF measure is necessary for public safety. It leads to difficulties in the preparation of the removal or - simply - to organise the departure from France. Besides, some local head-offices representing the State (prefecture) refuse to register a demand of regularisation (the allocation of a legal residence permit) before the prisoner's release. Without a legal status, one can not apply for a job or accommodation. In order to exemplify one of many problematic situations, the Oip related the issue to a prisoner living in Belgium, who received no prison leave because - according to the judge - he might have escaped from the French authorities, although his situation abroad was regular. Therefore, he could not prepare his defence before trial[21].

Figure 3: Proportion (%) of conditional release among all releases in regard to the offence: comparison between French and foreign nationals.

Nature of offence	French conditionally released (%)	Foreign national conditionally released (%)
Homicide	36.4	16.7
Violence	11.7	7.7
Sexual offence	16.3	13.3 (only 2 persons)
Drugs	19.1	21.5
Robbery	13.1	5.9
Theft	30.4	10.0
Immigration	16.7 (only 1 person)	6.8

Source: Tournier/Kensey 2000

Foreign nationals have less opportunity to receive a conditional release than nationals. Moreover, more than 92% of persons who serve a sentence in the community are French, and only 7% are foreign nationals[22].

2.9 Release - Expulsion

There are no special requirements and procedures regarding the release of foreign prisoners. Article 729-2 specifies that "when a foreign national, condemned to a prison sentence, is under a measure of expulsion, removal, or ITF, his or her conditional release is dependant on the implementation of the measure. This measure can be executed without his or her agreement. In exception to the precedent clause, the JAP or the TAP can issue a conditional release to a foreign national under ITF. The measure is suspended until the end of the monitoring period. If this has been duly executed, the ITF is automatically revoked. If not, the measure is applicable".

Here is an exemplary situation of a foreign prisoner[23]. A man is married to a French public servant, has held a regular stay permit since 1980 and is the father of one child. He has been sentenced to ten years in prison and three years 'interdiction from the French

---

[20] Cass. Crim, 25 mars 1987, *Gaz. Pal.* 1987, 398, note X.
[21] see *Oip* 2005, p. 17.
[22] see DAP 2000.
[23] see *Oip* 2005,p. 24.

territory' (ITF). He had one year of his term left to serve. His first demand of revocation of the ITF measure was rejected because his "projects of conjugal life do not imply a life in France". Under the law of 26 November 2003, he demanded leave permits. The JAP refused this because the application decrees were not published. The second demand invoked the conservation with family relations. It was rejected because "the ITF can not allow such a demand". After a demand of conditional release, which automatically revokes the ITF once the sentence is duly served, he was again refused because "according to article 78 clause 1 of the law from 26 November 2003, a leave permit can be given to a prisoner under ITF only within the procedure of preparation of revocation of ITF". Also, the prison direction claimed to have "little information about this law".

Another example[24]: a pregnant prisoner wants to give birth while being with her family in a European country. Therefore, she demands a 'conditional release-expulsion'. The expulsion order is signed by the local State service. However, the JAP could not decide because they forgot to ask for psychiatric opinion. Thus, she will have to give birth alone.

A third example deals with a foreign prisoner who arrived in France in 1973 and was condemned to life imprisonment in 1977. He demanded a conditional release four times. The last one was rejected because the préfet signed an expulsion order. He comes from former Yugoslavia, has no more family there but in France instead, and the Serbian government does not recognise his nationality. He feels condemned to spend the rest of his life in prison.

On the other hand, taking into consideration the example of German prisoners, transfer to their native country is not often used[25]. Many expelled foreign prisoners fear spending more time in prison once they are back in their home country.

In 1998, 18,314 foreign prisoners were released (of 72,886 releases, 25.1% of the total). 4,133 thereof involved an immigration offence (22.6%). For an immigration offence only, they served 4.7 months detention (half of foreign nationals' detention length). Regarding releases related to immigration offence, 30% were removed (10% in other cases). Less than 10% of illegal foreign prisoners were released by the judge (20% of legal foreign nationals, 26% of French). Only two percent benefited from conditional release.

A recent text formulates improvements in the coordination between prisons and the Ministry of the Interior in the implementation of the removal and expulsion of foreign nationals (21 January 2004, "AP-2004-02 EMS1/21-01-2004"). Local and regional coordination groups are asked to improve removal measures since these are not statistically satisfying. As soon as a foreign national enters detention, the prison administration has to inform the police services. The prison administration then delivers to the latter all documents concerning the foreign national who is under a measure of removal. All releases and transfers will be immediately communicated. A prison administration circular of 18 April 2003 stipulates that foreign national inmates under a removal measure with less than six months to spend in prison shall only exceptionally be transferred, in order for the police to proceed with their removal. However, it must be taken into account that when an inmate is ill he or she is protected against removal since his or her health status requires treatment that can not be provided should he/she be removed (Article 26-5 of law from 26 November 2003). Finally, a bi-annual conclusion with results and difficulties shall be sent to the central prison administration.

---

[24] see *Oip* 2005, p. 24.
[25] see *Trombik* 2005.

2.10 Aftercare – Probation

In case foreign offenders (can) stay in the host country after release, they are allowed to make use of aftercare facilities and support from the probation service as offered to release French nationals. The two conditions are that they benefit from a stay permit and that they are not under a removal or expulsion measure. Otherwise, there are no special provisions for foreign offenders within the aftercare period. There were no available statistics on this issue.

An irregular migrant can not work, has neither access to social welfare nor benefits from housing and reintegration facilities. Still, a foreign national can benefit from a 'relèvement': removal, as a complementary sentence, might be stopped; the sentence remains but not its effect. The foreign national must wait six months after the sentence is passed; he or she has to be either placed at home or in prison or outside the territory.

2.11 Staff

On 1 January 2005, there were 23,265 guards, 2,322 probation officers, 2,810 administrative employees, 742 technicians, and 426 head officers. 4,000 new jobs have been created since 2002, 700 of which are for probation services. 2,026 new jobs are predicted for 2006.

Prison staff receives little special training to deal with foreign prisoners. All courses are given by the National school of prison administration (ENAP). Language skills are still secondary knowledge and their importance in a prison environment with one fourth 'foreign clientele' is undermined. As to appropriate training among guards, only 'basic guards' are taught about the "problematics of ethnic minorities". There is no specific training for chief guards and supervising guards. Probation staff receives a nine hour course on "foreign nationals" among other specific groups (women, minors, old people) even though foreign prisoners represent a larger population than all other groups together (25% vs. 10%). There is no specific training for chief probation officers. Direction staff also receives some information about "foreign nationals" among other specific groups (women, minors).

Guards have a memento at their disposal, in which legal dispositions concerning foreign prisoners are available[26]. As regards the language issue, the principle is to prohibit communication that guards do not understand. In practice, there are severe discrepancies between individual prisons. From a sociological point of view that takes organisational and work theories into account, a foreign national inmate represents an additional burden of tasks. In this context, some guards are not willing to help foreign nationals who have language difficulties.

Christine Joffre, a social worker in Fresnes prison for ten years, described some difficulties of his job with foreign prisoners[27]. First of all, one shall consider different situations in detention: the stay permit may expire in prison or a person was irregular before sentence or was sentenced to territory ITF. According to Joffre, in such situations, it is "very complicated, almost impossible" to obtain a regular stay permit during detention. Therefore, probation workers need help from specialised associations because they do not know

---

[26] see *DAP* 2005, pp. 108-112.
[27] see *Oip* 2005, p. 22-23.

how to deal with foreign national legal texts. Such training exists, albeit not systematically. Besides, local State services require a release in order to handle the procedure of regularisation. It often means that a pre-detained person with a regular permit may leave prison without a legal status because it was not possible to renew the permit during detention. Joffre concludes by saying that "when we know that regularisation is not possible, we reach the limits of our work". Moreover, some housing and social integration centres ("CHRS") refuse persons with an irregular legal status.

In addition, probation work is mainly based on interviews and discussions with prisoners on their situations and projects. Without a common language, this task can not be fulfilled.

2.12 Projects

There are no significant specific projects for foreign prisoners inside or outside penitentiary institutions. We have little information at our disposal about local activities towards foreign prisoners. For instance, in the MA Fleury-Mérogis it has been encouraged to have prison visitors who speak similar languages as the foreign prisoners.

Interesting information became public in May 2006. The prison administration made a proposal to financially support a study on "foreign prisoners". It will tackle their qualitative and quantitative situations, face their problems, address staff problems associated with this group and analyse answers given by the institution. The research period is 20 months. The time limit for project completion was 31 May 2006. This study would be the first exhaustive research on foreign prisoners in France. It is not excluded that our contemporary European research has played an exemplary role in this decision.

3 ADMINISTRATIVE DETENTION OF FOREIGN PRISONERS

Administrative detention is a deprivation of freedom for the time until the foreign national is removed or expelled. There are 18 administrative detention centres ('CRA') in continental France with between eight and 160 places each. Moreover, there are many smaller local facilities (LRA) on which no information is available. Since 2001, the list of permanent centres has been set by ministerial order. Some are under the control of "regional public security" (SPD), some under the border police and some under the gendarmerie. The logistics are ensured by the prison administration or outsourced to private firms. Administrative detention centres have existed since 1981. They are intended for foreign nationals under administrative measures – removal because of threat to public order, refusal of asylum under judicial decisions – expulsion and/or ITF sentence for an offence as well as illegal residence. All information at our disposal is issued by the CIMADE report. The Cimade is an ecumenical care service and the only association that has access to CRAs (but not LRAs). Created in 1984, it works in cooperation with the State in order to provide social and legal support. The Cimade deplores in its annual report (2004) that not all statistics are available and that there is a possibility of error or impreciseness in the figures.

In 2004, Cimade's employees and volunteers met with 26,000 persons in administrative detention centres. A short and schematised overview of administrative detention leads to one main conclusion: the detention conditions are, in all respects, worse than in prison. Problems are numerous: overcrowding, more and more persons suffering from psychological ailments, violence, self-mutilations, suicide attempts, hunger strikes, no leisure opportunities; etc. The restriction of smoking times (9.00, 11.00, 14.00, 17.00, 21.00) in CRA Coquelles[28] illustrates partially one of the many structural and organisational complexities and absurdities of administrative detention. Moreover, the health situation of administrative detainees is worsening. This statement was issued at the first national congress of medical units for administrative detention centres held on 7 and 8 October 2004. All CRAs have been obliged to provide medical service since 1999. Medical staff does not receive any particular training for the treatment of foreign detainees.

According to the provisional planning of the inter-ministerial committee for immigration control, 1,438 new places are planned for January 2006 (2003: 739 places, 2004: 969 places, 2005: 1,300), 1,718 for June 2006, 2,383 for June 2007, and 2,700 for June 2008. In 2003 and 2004, the Ministry of the Interior compiled instructions setting an amount of removals. A decree from 30 May 2005 foresees that new centres with 140 places shall be built, and that foreign nationals in administrative detention applying for asylum have to pay the interpreter - required for the completion of applications in French - themselves. Asylum application forms have been required to be written in French since August 2004. Furthermore, the creation of centres with family facilities indicates that more and more children are expected. Facilities must be improved but delays are not concretised. A decree from March 2001 proposes to fulfil new material and equipment norms within a three year period. In 2004, the government postponed this obligation for one year. Another decree from 30 May 2005 set the most recent limit to the 31 December 2006.

3.1 Institutions for the Administrative Detention of Foreign Prisoners

There are two types of institutions used for administrative detention: the detention centres (CRA) and detention rooms (LRA).

3.2 Ministry responsible & relevant Legislation

The Ministry of the Interior is responsible for administrative detention facilities. Administrative detention is ruled under dispositions in the CESEDA, Book V "removal measures", Title V "retention of a foreign national in facilities that do not depend upon prison administration". According to Article L.551-2, the administrative authority is responsible for placement decisions. Two more decrees (N° 2004-1215 from 17 November 2004 and N° 2005-617 from 30 May 2005) complete the legal framework.

3.3 Capacity of institutions for Administrative Detention

In 2004, 969 places were distributed across 20 Detention centres (without overseas regions): the largest ones are Paris-Vincennes and Mesnil-Amelot with 140 places each, Paris-dépôt with 96, Coquelles with 79, Lyon with 78, Bobigny with 52 places, and Marseille and Bordeaux with 24 places.

3.4 Length of stay

---

[28] see *Cimade* 2005, p. 126.

A law, passed on 26 November 2003, prolonged the retention delay from 12 to 36 days and somewhat improved the flexibility of the procedure of translation. The average length of stay in administrative detention has almost doubled from 5.3 days in 2003 to 9.9 days in 2004. The time spent varies from 6.7 days in Rivesaltes up to 12.9 days in Paris-Vincennes.

3.5 Decisions procedure

Since a law from 26 November 2003, administrative detention has been decided on by the préfet, who within the first 48 hours must request from the 'judge of liberties and detention' ("juge des libertés et de la détention" – JLD) the authorisation for the prolongation of detention by 15 more days. Once the 17 days have expired, the préfet may request a new extension of up to 15 days. According to Articles L.552-7 and L.552-8 of CE-SEDA, a foreign national can be put in administrative detention "in cases of absolute emergency or particular major threat to public order" or "when diplomatic documents are not available".

3.6 Appeal procedure

The appeal against the decision of the JLD to prolong the length of detention ("appel 35bis") is to be filed before the "cour d'appel - CA". To contest the legality of the removal decision, in most of the cases, it deals with a "préfectoral arrêté" against which an appeal before the administrative court (TA) ("recours 22bis") is possible within 48 hours. In 2004, there were 1,354 appeals (non exhaustive) before the CA against JLD decisions. In 73% of cases, the CA confirmed the JLD decision; and in 15% detention was revoked; in four percent of cases, home placement was ruled until the removal had been executed. On the other hand, in 2004, there were 2,364 appeals (non exhaustive) before the TA against removal decisions. In 65% of cases, the TA confirmed the removal; in 12%, it was revoked; and in one percent, the country of destination was annulled.

3.7 Irregular stay

No permanent or temporary residence permit, refusal to board a plane during removal[29], use of false identities, refusal to give identity or nationality to oppose removal, false weddings, etc are criminal offences. More than 200 immigration related offences lead to expulsion or removal. For example, in Lyon, a foreign national has been sentenced to six months prison and ten years ITF for "drug purchase for personal use", this because of seven grams of cannabis[30]. In 2003, there were 5,606 sentences for immigration offences, of which 3,085 were prison sentences. An irregular migrant – illegal entry or stay - can be handed a prison sentence of up to one year. In 2001, there were 4,295 foreign nationals in prison for immigration offences. In many cases, imprisonment serves as 'second hand administrative detention'. Besides, ITF is often a complementary sentence. On average, there are around 3,000 to 4,000 expulsions per year ("arrêté d'expulsion"), ordered by the préfet or by the Ministry of the Interior because of "threat to public order". There are

---

[29]   average sentence of one up to three months prison and three years ITF, see *Cimade* 2005, p. 141.
[30]   see *Cimade* 2005, p. 136.

around 20,000 removals per year ("arrêté de reconduite à la frontière"), ordered by the préfet for irregular stay.

3.8 Numbers

25,828 persons were detained in 2004. 20,571 foreign nationals were from known nationalities. 4,135 were from Algeria, which represents the biggest group with 20.10% of all administrative detainees. 2,352 were for instance from Morocco (11.43%), 1,814 from Rumania (8.82%), 1,403 from Turkey (6.82%), 1,101 from Tunisia (5.35%), and 901 from Mali (4.38%). In 2003, 1,524 women were detained in administrative centres, accounting for 6.83% of all administrative detainees. In 2004, they were 1,824 (8.87%). 262 female foreign nationals were for instance from Rumania (17.19% of all detained women), 104 from Algeria (6.82%), 101 from China (6.63%), 95 from Morocco (6.23%), and 82 from Ecuador (5.38%).

3.9 Expulsion

The objective for 2005 is 23,000 removals. Previously, removal efficiency rose up from 44% in 2003 up to 55% in 2004, which stands for 10,341 persons (without 'Paris-dépôt', nor 'Paris-Vincennes', nor 'Nantes'). According to statistics covering a ten year period (1992-2002), around 50% of detained foreign nationals are removed. The rate fell from 61% in 1992 to 39.6% in 2002, but the length of detention rose from seven days in 1992 to 12 days in 2002. The average length of detention while awaiting a ruling on the removal or release of a foreign national is four days. 70% of removed or expelled foreign nationals were removed or expelled within the first 12 days, and 23% between the 13th and the 17th day. Concerning the home countries, 67 foreign nationals from Bolivia were removed or expelled, which represents 93.06% of Bolivian detainees in administrative detention centres. The other 7% were released. Among other removed or expelled foreign nationals, there were for instance 382 from Bulgaria (80.76%), 1,259 from Rumania (79.48%), 123 from Ecuador (79.35%), 882 from Turkey (65.97%), 2,237 from Algeria (60.35%), 1,119 from Morocco (54.77%), 425 from Tunisia (44.27%), and 11 from Palestine (9.09%).

3.10 Not-expelled prisoners

8,026 administrative detainees were released in 2004 (statistics without Paris-dépôt, nor Paris-Vincennes, nor Nantes). Among them, 44% remained in detention for more than 12 days. A second prolongation was issued for 13%. Some of them were "déférés", what means that - according to Article L.624.1 CESEDA - they were put before the penal judge because of infringements to the removal procedure. The préfet can demand that the public prosecution take legal action against a released irregular foreign national because of supposed 'refusal of removal'. The foreign national will then be brought before the penal judge and often sent to prison before his or her case is examined before court.

3.11 Detention of Irregulars under Criminal Law

Foreign nationals under measures or procedures of removal or expulsion can be detained with prisoners who are detained under criminal law, thus not in separate sections.

3.12 Minors

Four centres are adequate and qualified for the accommodation of minors. Parents can choose whether to keep their children with them, and they all in fact do so. In 2004, more than 90 foreign nationals in administrative detention declared being minors. Many of them were removed or expelled. In Lyon, 139 children were in administrative detention in 2004. Five other centres are also used for the detention of minors. However, since there is no legal disposition about children, some centres lack adequate facilities or equipment.

3.13 Waiting Zones

Waiting zones ('WZ') were introduced in 1992. They are legally defined as places where "the foreign national arriving in France [...] who is not authorised to enter the French territory or who seeks asylum" will be detained "during the strict necessary time for his leave and, as an asylum seeker, for a check of his demand". The placement of a foreign national is an administrative decision and is evaluated after 72 hours by a judge who will decide on its prolongation. Waiting zones are located near judicial borders – airports, sea-ports/harbours or railway stations. Foreign nationals are only "maintained" and not "detained" because they are free to leave the French national territory. Therefore, the judicial protection is weaker than in other confinement institutions. Foreign nationals can be held in waiting zones for up to 20 days. After this period, if they have not been removed, the boarder authorities must release them, even if they consequentially become irregular migrants. There are more than 100 waiting zone facilities, most of them are small rooms, for instance police stations, hotel rooms, administration offices. The waiting zone Roissy – Charles De Gaulle represents the two international airports in Paris. 95% of the foreign nationals are in the WZ Roissy-CDG. There are 250 beds available; in addition to overcrowded rooms with sometimes more than 200 persons. The law requires "hotel-like conditions", which are not fulfilled. Regular human rights associations have no access to WZs. The association ANAFE ("National Association for Assistance at Borders to Foreign Nationals") is the only one to publish visit reports.

4 NATIONALS DETAINED ABROAD

According to the latest available data, roughly 1,500 French persons are currently being detained abroad[31]. One association has specialised on nationals detained abroad – the so-called FIL ("Français incarcérés au loin" # 'Far off imprisoned French'). Unfortunately,

---

[31]   source: 'European Group for Prisoners Abroad' EGPA.

its activities are reduced at the moment. There have been no more volunteers for the last three years. Therefore, most of our information is from FIL 2001.

4.1 Numbers and Composition of French Nationals detained abroad

In 2001, 1,368 French nationals were prisoners abroad: These figures are probably an underestimation. Some prisoners do not contact the embassies because they fear prosecution by the French authorities upon their return to France. We may assume that figures concerning the rest of the world are more reliable given the need for outside contact due to the distance and the harshness of the imprisonment conditions. There are very little data available on personal and social structures of this group. FIL reported that in Caracas nine out of 18 French prisoners are from the Ivory Coast. This is the case for two out of three in Lima and every second in Rio de Janeiro.

4.2 Countries of Detention

905 nationals were detained in Western Europe; 86 were to be found in North America, 13 in Japan, nine in Australia, 405 in Spain, 169 in Belgium, 85 in Germany, 77 in the USA, 77 in Morocco, 44 in Italy, 25 in Madagascar and 23 in Thailand.

4.3 Sentencing and Reasons for Detention

Half of French prisoners abroad were convicted for misdemeanour or serious drugs-related crimes. This was the case for 307 French nationals detained in Spain, 50 in Morocco, 36 in Belgium, 31 in Great-Britain, 23 in Germany, 22 in Italy, 20 in the United-States, 18 in Venezuela, 13 in Brazil, 12 in Japan and 11 in Thailand.

Three prisoners were sentenced to the death penalty and 14 to life sentences, of whom most were charged with murder. Inmates awaiting death sentences are to be transferred back to France. Nine were imprisoned for political reasons. Some are 'victims' of an argument in which prison is used as a tool of pressure.

Sex tourism is a growing cause of imprisonment, but French prisoners tend to be ashamed of their crime and therefore do not contact the French authorities. Moreover, many countries like Indonesia, Malaysia or Venezuela have hardened their legislation, resulting in longer prison sentences.

4.4 Involved Organisations – Tasks and Activities

The consular protection is based on the 1963 Vienna Convention on consular relations. As soon as a foreign national is arrested or committed to prison, the judicial authorities have to inform him/her of his/her right to contact the embassy/the consulate. Once contact has been established, both prisoner and consular post have the right to converse and correspond, and the consular staff can visit the prisoner. The consular officer informs the prisoner about the local justice system and provides him/her with a list of French speaking lawyers. Consular officers are present at the trial in order to make sure that it is conducted fairly. The consular post deals with money, mail and medicine transfer, which are all sent with the 'diplomatic bag', which has to be prepared and transported. It corresponds also with French local, regional and national authorities concerned by the prisoner's situation.

Nationals detained abroad complain about local prison conditions: lack of food, poor hygiene and health care. Some prisoners feel unsafe and thus pay other detainees to insure their own safety. Some must buy drinkable water. However, in few cases, regarding the rather constraining prison conditions in France, some prisoners prefer to spend their time abroad.

4.5 Release and Reception in France

The reception in France after release is mostly organised on a private and voluntary basis, since the French Justice is not responsible for a foreign sentence. There is no French organisation comparable to 'Prisoners Abroad' in the UK or the 'Liaison Office for Dutch Prisoners Abroad and International Contacts' in the Netherlands.

4.6 Aftercare

When the person being released is expelled, the expelling State takes charge of the expulsion. When the person has been released in the foreign State, he or she has to pay the transportation to France himself or herself. The French State may cover the transportation expenses under the condition of later reimbursement. The consular post informs individuals or associations in France to take care of this person at the airport or train station at which they are arriving.

4.7 Public Opinion and the Media

Nationals detained abroad are not an issue. Therefore, there is no media or general public opinion on this particular topic. The situation of French individuals who have been sentenced abroad for sexual crimes – most of them because of sexual relations with minor prostitutes – may be described from time to time in newspapers or shown on TV. However, the discourse on such cases would rather produce moral condemnation and public exclusion.

The Ministry of Foreign Affairs does not put the prisoner's case on the public scene in opposition to what many families and lawyers do, expecting or hoping that public pressure might influence the local justice or politicians. It is often counter-productive and even negative for the prisoner, because local justice or politicians are not willing to be seen as weak under international or diplomatic pressure. Furthermore, a media campaign let believe that justice abroad might be influenced and partial, whereas French justice is thought to be independent and fair.

To conclude, since FIL stopped its work some years ago, there has been no more systematic legal care and monitoring for French prisoners who are or have been detained abroad.

5 EVALUATION AND RECOMMENDATIONS

Although the proportion of foreign prisoners has been quite stable within the last 25 years (between 20 and 30%), foreign nationals, especially irregular ones, still face disadvantages and discrimination inside French prisons, since their problems have not been addressed consistently. The cultural, social and economic background, in addition to low education, illiteracy and French language deficits, formed a weak individual, to whom prison services can neither offer skills, nor time and provisions in the budget. However, we believe that a positive political attitude towards this issue would enable important improvement.

A first step should officially tackle the problem in order to stop the process of media criminalisation against foreign nationals[32]. Secondly, a proposition of the CNCDH is to abolish prison sentences for immigration offences, or to limit sentences to a maximum of one month. A clearer and fairer procedure shall be implemented in order to simplify and facilitate access to residence permits. Access to asylum right meets similar difficulties, and thus could benefit from similar recommendations. Modalities of expulsion, including administrative detention centres, shall attend further to human care and humanitarian monitoring. Voluntary return shall be facilitated or foreign prisoners shall be allowed to serve their sentence in their home country. More professional interpreters and more language courses shall be hired and offered. The item "absolute necessity" shall be erased from the CPP Unique prison house rules shall help prisoners and reduce translation costs. On the other hand, local councils or centres for legal advice shall be encouraged. 16 projects concerning 23 prisons are planned with a total of 75. One hundred prisons or penitentiary centres are to be "equipped". Finally, prison administration shall hire more foreign staff or migrant nationals in order to facilitate cooperation, communication, and cultural understanding.

---

[32] see *Tsoukala* 2002.

Chapter 10

Germany

Frieder Dünkel
Andrea Gensing
Christine Morgenstern

1 INTRODUCTION

1.1 Overview of penalties and measures

In 1969 the German system of penal sanctions was thoroughly overhauled by the 'great reform of criminal law' of that year. This reform intended to strengthen the preventive purposes of punishment as opposed to its purely retributive aspects, and in this way to reduce the significance of imprisonment, in particular, as a form of punishment. Section 47 of the Penal Code (*Strafgesetzbuch* - StGB), which has since been in force , makes provision for prison sentences of less than six months, but only if the offender's personality or the special circumstances of the offence require such a sanction in order to influence the offender or to protect the legal order. Non-custodial sentences have absolute priority. They range from the dismissal of proceedings combined with the imposition of obligations (for example, compensation or an administrative fine), through pecuniary penalties coupled to a warning that further punishment may be imposed, to the suspension of sentence on probation. Since 1969, the administration of justice has, to a great extent, put these epoch-making changes to the law into practice. Therefore, in comparison with non-custodial measures, the prison sentence currently fulfils only a minor role in the system of sanctions. Only about seven percent of all sentences are unconditional prison terms, whereas fines (80 per cent) and probation coupled with suspended sentences (13 per cent) predominate. The fact that the prison sentence functions as an *ultima ratio* becomes even clearer if one also considers the informal decisions of the public prosecutors who dismiss, perhaps with the imposition of an administrative fine, 52 per cent of all cases[1]. All facts considered, one finds that prison sentences account for a mere three to four percent of all sanctions. Although the official crime rates have increased considerably during the last 30 years and the average length of prison sentences has also increased (*inter alia* because of more violent crime) the incarceration rates have been rather stable until recently. The stability has been achieved by extending the application of fines and suspended sentences, especially for property offenders.

Since the death penalty was abolished constitutionally in 1949 in West Germany by article 102 of the Basic Law (*Grundgesetz* - GG), life imprisonment is the most severe sanction that may be imposed by the state. This sanction still embodies the notion of retribution in its pure form. The Federal Constitutional Court has confirmed that it is constitutional under the condition that persons sentenced to life imprisonment retain the prospect of eventually regaining their liberty.[2] Therefore, where such a sanction is imposed the state has to guarantee an execution of the life sentence that provides for effective forms of rehabilitation (resocialization). As implemented in practice, this type of sanction can be regarded as a prison sentence of an indeterminate duration[3]. In terms of s.57a of the Penal Code, a court may place a prisoner sentenced to life imprisonment on parole once the prisoner has served 15 years, if the prognosis is favourable and the crime was not particularly heinous (for example, parole is not granted easily to repeat murderers or persons

---

[1]   Mostly petty offences, but also cases of economic and environmental crimes, see *Heinz* 2004.

[2]   Decisions of the Federal Constitutional Court, *Bundesverfassungsgerichtliche Entscheidungen* – BVerfGE 45, 187ff.

[3]   see *Kaiser* 1997, p. 423.

convicted of hate crimes). The Federal Constitutional Court has restricted the discretion whether to execute the life sentence for longer than 15 years by demanding that the courts state that the case is particularly heinous at the trial[4]. Annually there are less than 100 persons sentenced to life imprisonment. Approximately 1,800 persons are serving this sentence at any given time (2005). The number of prisoners serving life imprisonment has increased in the last 15 years. The period of time served prior to release averages between 18 and 20 years.

The use of short-term prison sentences is an equally controversial issue. Although it was the stated aim of the 'great reform of criminal law' to abolish the short prison term completely, it is still an essential component of the execution of prison sentences. The reasons for this include: the reduction of the prison sentence by the period of pre-trial detention; the revocation of probation or parole with the result that short, conditionally suspended sentences are brought into operation; imprisonment for failing to pay a fine; and the lack of alternative, non-custodial measures. The annual proportion of persons who serve a prison term of less than six months is much higher than the proportion of such terms actually imposed - it has been estimated to be up to six times higher[5]. In recent debates about penal policy more significance has been attached to short-term imprisonment than at the time of the original legislation, which was heavily influenced by the principle of resocialization.

Recently, however, the debate of the early 1980s about possible penal law reforms in order to shorten the average prison sentences[6] has been replaced by a shift in official crime policy to strengthen penal law. In 1998 two penal law reforms were introduced that increased the penalties for violent and sexual offenders considerably. Furthermore, the possibilities for parole have been restricted. This new penal policy pays more regard to public opinion and pressure for public security more than in the past.

A prison sentence of up to two years may be suspended and an offender placed on probation. Such probation has become an important non-custodial sentence in its own right and is no longer regarded as a type of prison sentence[7]. The law provides that conditions of probation may include both restitution orders and directives prescribing how the probationer should conduct his life. In addition, provision is made for the appointment of a qualified probation officer where this is deemed necessary for the resocialization of the offender (the same rules apply to prisoners released on parole.) About one-third of adult probationers are assigned a probation officer. At present, about 70 per cent of all prison sentences are suspended on probation. This non-custodial sanction therefore clearly outnumbers unconditional prison sentences. The extension of suspended sentences contributed greatly to the fairly stable incarceration rates during the 1970s and 1980s. At the end of 1991, 145,000 probationers were allocated to about 2,100 full-time probation officers. The high ratio of probationers to probation officers (70 : 1) is a considerable problem and the improvement of this ratio is a major concern of penal policy. In spite of these difficulties, the probation service can claim that the recidivism rate of ap-

---

[4]   see BVerfGE 86: 288ff.

[5]   see *Weigend* 1986, p. 261.

[6]   see also the 'memorandum' of a group of academics and practitioners to abolish or reduce long-term imprisonment in 1994, *Jung* and *Müller-Dietz*, 1994.

[7]   See *Jescheck* and *Weigend*, 1996.

proximately 35 per cent, with an average probation period of three years, is much more favourable than the rate of recidivism for those released from prison. Parolees – even when one controls for selection criteria – generally re-offend less often than prisoners released after serving their full sentences[8].

Numerically the fine is the most important penal sanction as it is imposed in about 83 per cent of all cases. The Penal Code has created a day-fine system in which one 'day-fine' corresponds to one day spent in prison. Section 43 of the Penal Code makes provision for a maximum of 360 day-fines and for up to 720 day-fines in exceptional cases, for example for an accumulation of offences. In practice, 96 per cent of all fines do not exceed 90 day-fines. The amount imposed for a day depends on the financial capacity of the offender. Approximately 6 to 7 per cent of the fines are converted into prison sentences because of non-compliance[9]. Since the early 1980s 'free work' (community service) may be imposed as an alternative to imprisonment for failing to pay a fine. Such a substitution may be made by the judicial administration (s. 293 of the Introductory Act to the Criminal Code - *Einführungsgesetz zum Strafgesetzbuch* – EGStGB). Generally, the administration of this alternative is the duty of the social workers who are attached to the courts and who provide for and arrange community service. One day-fine is regarded as the equivalent of six to eight hours of community service[10]. Since the late 1980s the problem of fine defaulters has increased considerably, especially in the new federal states of the former German Democratic Republic[11]. In 1996 about 10 per cent of all adult prisoners served a period of imprisonment in lieu of a fine (*Ersatzfreiheitsstrafe*): 13 per cent in East Germany; in West German federal states seven per cent[12]. The bad economic situation with concomitant high unemployment rates especially in East Germany, is the main reason for this development. Some efforts at reorganizing and intensifying the social services arranging community service have diminished the proportion of fine defaulters in East Germany to 8 per cent of the daily adult prison population in 2004. A special project in Mecklenburg-Western Pomerania had particularly positive effects by reducing the number of fine defaulters serving prison sentences by 50%[13].

1.2   Overview of the prison system

1.2.1 Organisational structure, prisons and numbers of inmates

The German prison system provides a total of 222 prisons with a capacity of 80,000 places. The Federal Prison Act as well as some of the administrative rules (*Verwaltungsvorschriften*) are the same in all federal states. However, as the federal states are responsible for the construction of buildings and the funding of the personnel, great differences between the federal states have emerged. In June 2006 the Federal Parliament (*Bundestag*) – despite heavy criticisms by almost all academics and a large majority of practitioners – decided to transfer the legislation for prisons to the federal states. This was part of a new

---

[8]   see *Dünkel*, 2004; *Dünkel* and *Spiess*, 1992.
[9]   see *Kaiser* 1997, p. 436.
[10]   for details see *Jehle, Feuerhelm*, and *Block* 1990; *Feuerhelm* 1997.
[11]   see *Dünkel* and *Scheel* 2004; 2006.
[12]   see *Dünkel* and *Kunkat* 1997.
[13]   see *Dünkel* and *Scheel* 2006.

distribution of power between the federal states and the central government. Consequentially, in future there could possibly be up to 16 Prison Acts of the "Länder".

Prison administration belongs to the ministry of justice of the federal states. The budgets vary from state to state, as do the numbers of prison staff. The education of regular prison officers in Germany is comparatively good as they are trained for three years in special schools run by the Länder. Privatization is not a major issue in Germany, as privatization would be in contradiction to the Constitutional restriction of coercive power and restriction of freedom only to public services. Therefore, privatization has only been used to build new prisons and to outsource certain services like laundry, transportation of prisoners or medical services. On the other hand the German prison system has proven its openness and readiness for reform by new public management strategies[14].

The prison system provides open and closed facilities. About 20% of the prisoners on a given day are accommodated in open prisons or departments. The proportion varies between more than 30% in some northern states and less than five percent in Bavaria.

Each *Land* provides social-therapeutic treatment for difficult or dangerous offenders, particularly sex offenders (about 2.500 places in total). The treatment programmes include various forms of individual and group therapy in a milieu therapy setting. The results of treatment programmes are encouraging[15].

The controlling mechanisms of individual complaints procedures are well developed in Germany. Extensive jurisdiction on all issues of daily prison life has contributed to extensive publications and commentaries to the Prison Act. The possibility to submit individual complaints to the Constitutional Court (*Bundesverfassungsgericht*) is a further important guarantee to implement the prison system in accordance to the rule of law and principles of human rights (human dignity etc.). The Constitutional Court has issued important decisions on the principle of resocialisation as a constitutional principle (1972, 1973, 1975, 1998 etc.), on the remuneration of prison labour (1998), accommodation in communal cells (2002), preventive detention (2004), and the "unconstitutionality of the present youth prison legislation" (2006). Regular inspections take place only by the ministry of justice itself, not by independent bodies. However, there are parliamentary control mechanisms similar to prison ombudsmen (the Green party and other oppositional parties regularly submit parliamentary inquiries). Furthermore, the so-called "Anstaltsbeiräte" (an independent citizens' board in the neighbourhood of each prison) exercise some control, although they are obliged to work confidentially with the prison directors.

Looking at the prison statistics it can be determined that, after a notable decrease in the 1980s, a serious increase of incarceration rates can be seen from 1989. In 1998 there were 96 prisoners per 100,000 inhabitants, 98 in West and 84 in East Germany. In 2005 East and West-Germany had about the same prison population rates with 97 per 100,000 inhabitants (see *Figure 1.1*). In this respect Germany ranks in the middle of those European countries with the highest imprisonment rates[16]. The comparatively high imprisonment rate, compared to Scandinavian countries, results from the fact that the average period of time served is relatively long. The number of individuals actually sentenced to unconditional prison sentences are not greater than, for example, in the Scandinavian coun-

---

[14] see *Flügge*, *Maelicke* and *Preusker* 2001.

[15] 10-20 percent reduction of serious recidivism, see *Dünkel* and *Drenkhahn* 2001.

[16] see the actual world wide data published by Kings College London under www.prison.org.

tries. The sentencing practice in these countries is, however, characterized by very short prison terms, which result in a lower average daily prison population.

Prison population rates on 31 March 2005 in a comparison of the federal states and changes compared with 1995

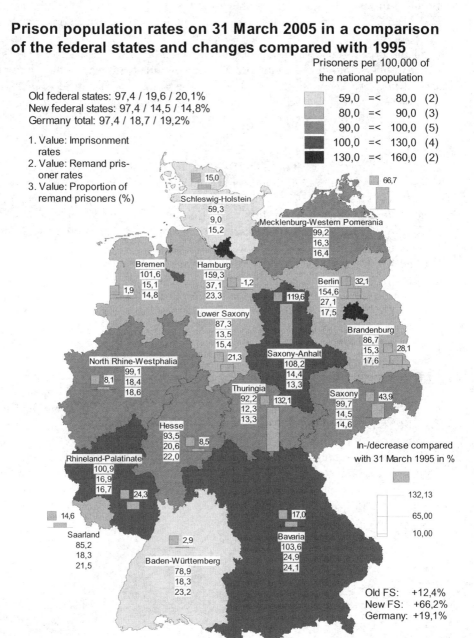

Figure 1.1

The importance of incarceration also varies among the different federal states which is only attributable to a minor extent to different crime rates. The so-called 'city states' of

Berlin, Bremen or Hamburg apparently have higher incarceration rates because of their urban structure and criminality. However, here too, considerable differences can be seen. Bremen, in 2005, had a total prisoner rate of 102 for every 100,000 inhabitants, Berlin had a ratio of 155, and Hamburg a ratio of 159. These remarkable differences are partly the result of a very low pre-trial detention rate in Bremen. Looking at the larger ('mixed' rural and urban) states we find a variation between 59 prisoners per 100,000 of the population in Schleswig-Holstein and 108 in Saxony-Anhalt. In general the southern federal states (with the exception of Baden-Württemberg) have higher incarceration rates than the northern states (see *Figure 1.1*), which seems to be particularly interesting when considering that the official crime rates in general, and those for violent crimes are higher in the northern states. Again we find indications of different policies of incarceration with a more repressive sentencing practice in southern states, like Bavaria or Saxony.

Administrative deprivation of liberty does not exist in Germany. Police custody is restricted to a maximum of 48 hours, after which a judge has to impose pre-trial detention or the person has to be released. The police laws of the different federal states provide for police detention in cases of disturbances of public order, for example, in cases of hooliganism in Bavaria. Up to two weeks are permissible, but - also in these cases - this decision has to be confirmed by a judge within 48 hours.

The prison population rate in West-Germany has been somehow stable, notwithstanding the fact that there have been quite important increases and decreases over time (see Figure 1.2). The first sharp decrease at the end of the 1960ies was the result of a major penal law reform replacing short term imprisonment with fines. The increase in the 1970ies up to the mid 1980ies was partly due to an increase in crime and a more punitive climate influenced by a difficult political situation caused by the Red Army Fraction terrorists. In the early 1980ies a campaign against the extensive use of pre-trial detention was even supported by the federal minister of justice at that time. The result was a decrease in the numbers of pre-trial and sentenced detainees. Other factors were the extension of community sanctions particularly for young offenders under the Juvenile Justice Act (14-21 years old) and of suspended sentences (probation) in the general penal law. Crime rates - including violent crimes - decreased. The opening of the eastern borders and the civil war conflicts in the early 1990ies created a severe burden also for the criminal justice system. Foreigners and migrants from Southern and Eastern Europe contributed to an increase of the prison population rate. But also an increase in violent crimes by young males in general resulted in this development. Since the mid 1990ies the prison population rate remained relatively stable although prison sentences for violent and sexual offenders have been increased due to legislative reforms.

Prison population rates in Germany (old federal states, former FRG)
1962 - 2005

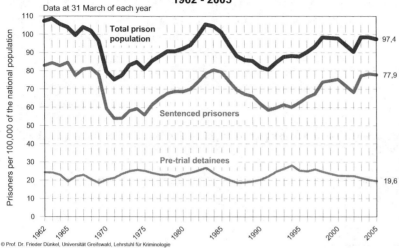

Figure 1.2

1.2.2 Institutions for foreigners and proportion of foreign prisoners

Foreign prisoners in Germany are mixed together with national prisoners. There are no separate wings or prisons as one feels that integration is better achieved by mixing foreigners and Germans. However, the prison administration is aware of the problems of different nationalities and ethnicities. Therefore, Turkish and Kurdish prisoners will not be accommodated in the same cell – and if possible wing – of a prison. The number of foreign prisoners has been stable during the last 20 years (20-25%).

As will be shown below (see 1.4.2), particularly young migrants and members of ethnic minorities have become a major problem and challenge for the prison system. The prison statistics available from the statistical central office at Wiesbaden (*Statistisches Bundesamt*) only show part of the problem, as they only differentiate between persons with and without a German passport. Some "new" groups of immigrants like the so-called Russian Germans (who are naturalised Germans because of the specific German immigration legislation) cause serious crime problems[17] and are also highly over-represented in prisons. Other groups like refugees, citizens of former Yugoslavia as well as asylum seekers (who suffer from particular living conditions as they are not allowed to work and move freely) have influenced the development of prisoner rates. This can be seen when one takes the pre-trial detention rate into account, which increased with the rise of the number of asylum seekers at the beginning of the 1990s by several thousand persons, and decreased after the new immigration legislation in 1993, which reduced the number of asylum seeking immigrants considerably (see below 1.4.2).

The statistical data regarding "foreigners" in German prisons reveal that in the adult prison system the proportion of foreigners is 24%, compared to 19% in youth prisons (2005). The proportion of foreigners has particularly increased in the 1980s and 1990s (from 7% to about 24% in the prisons for adults and from 6% to temporarily over 30% in

---

[17]   see *Kerner* 2001; *Grundies* 2000; *Weitekamp, Reich* and *Bott* 2002; *Reich* 2003 with the explanation for their increased delinquent behaviour by the negative experiences of immigration.

the youth prisons (see *Table 1.1*). Youth prisoners are juveniles (14-17 years) or young adults (18-21years) who are sentenced to a youth prison sentence (six months up to five years, in serious cases or in the case of young adults up to ten years of imprisonment). They can stay in the youth prison until the age of 25. Therefore, almost 90% of the daily youth prison population consists of 18 to 25 year old "adults"[18]. Foreigners are even more over-represented in the age groups of 18-21 years, but also 21-30 year olds in the general prison system and in the very young age group of juveniles in the youth prison system (see *Table 1.2*).

Table 1.1: Proportion of foreign prisoners in Germany in adult and youth prisons 1976-2005

Year	Prisoners in prisons for adults (> 18 y.)	Proportion of foreigners (%)	Youth prisoners (14-25 y.)	Proportion of foreigners (%)
1976	31,592	6.0	5,967	4.8
1980	35,537	7.2	6,490	6,0
1985	41,852	9.7	6,360	9.4
1990	34,799	12,6	4,197	18.5
1995	41,353	21,6	4,980	31.5
2000	53,183	23,7	7,396	21.7
2002	52,988	23,0	7,455	18.6
2005	52,781	24.2	6,913	18.8

Source: Bundesamt für Statistik: Strafvollzugsstatistik 1976-2005, www.destatis.de

Table 1.2: Prisoners of foreign nationality in German prisons according to different age groups (on 31 March 2002)

Sentenced prisoners	n =	% of foreigners
Prisons for adults	52,988	22.3
Age groups		
18-21	214	45.8
21-25	5,619	25.6
25-30	11,292	29.8
30-40	19,697	25.1
40-50	10,801	16.2
50-60	3,979	11.8
60 and more	1,386	7.5
Youth prisons	7,455	18.6
Age groups		
14-18	849	24.0
18-21	3,540	18.4
21 and more	3,066	17.4

Source: Statistisches Bundesamt, Strafvollzugsstatistik 2002.

---

[18] see *Dünkel* 2003a; 2006.

The over-representation of foreigners in German prisons and particularly in youth prisons is considerable (see *Figures 1.3* and *1.4*). Another striking result in this context is that in East Germany, where the foreign population is very small, foreign prisoners are even more over-represented (about six times higher than their proportion of the general population) than in West-Germany (two to three times higher)[19]. These facts raise the question as to which selective practices of the justice system explain the elevated prisoner rates.

Development of German and Non-German youth prisoners in North Rhine-Westphalia, 1980 - 2001

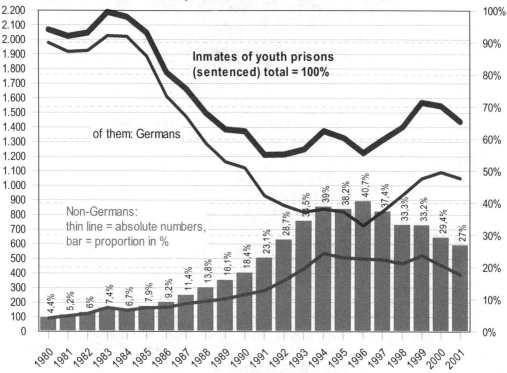

---

[19]   see *Winkler* 2003, 70 ff.; also *Dünkel* and *J. Walter* 2005.

Figure 1.3

Proportion of foreigners in German prisons and overrepresentation according to the population 2002

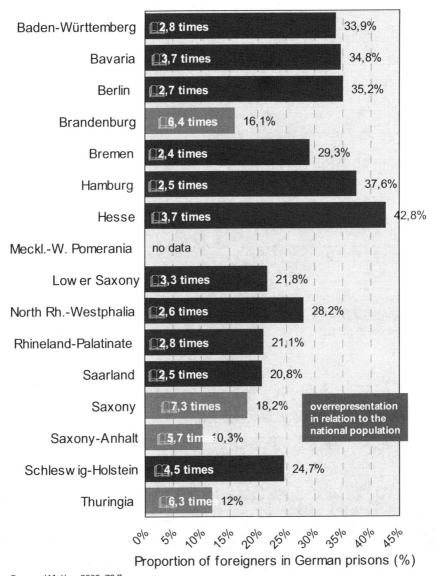

Proportion of foreigners in German prisons (%)

Source: Winkler, 2003, 76 ff.

Figure 1.4

Prison staff has often received no special training for dealing with foreigners, and special controlling mechanisms for foreign prisoners do not exist. The prison administration is making efforts to provide foreign prisoners with the same treatment as Germans (see 2.8. concerning the problems with re-integration activities and prison leaves).

1.3 Overview of the involvement of consulates, embassies, ministries of the home country, NGO's etc.

There is no systematic information about the involvement of foreign consulates and embassies, but in individual cases exchange of information is given, particularly if the extradition is a question of concern. The supervision and care of foreign prisoners is at least one of a number of focal points of various NGOs who campaign for the support of convicts. For example, the protestant pastoral care service in prisons (*Evangelische Gefängnisseelsorge*[20]) has a respective special unit that is in active opposition to the "obligation of removal" in cases of foreign prisoners who are enrooted in Germany. There are also initiatives at the regional level (see for example the *Straffälligen- und Bewährungshilfe Berlin e. V.* which aims to assist foreign prisoners, and has developed a respective information-flyer[21]). The associations of defence attorneys also have sporadic respective initiatives. The creation of a network, as aspired for by the international NGO of the *European Group for Prisoners Abroad*[22] – which bears no permanent German member – is, however, an initiative that is not visible in Germany.

There are more activities that show a greater degree of networking at the federal level when regarding people detained under Foreign Nationals Law, especially for refugees[23]. An important example of such work is the *Jesuite Refugee Service*, based in Berlin[24] that carries our advocacy work for refugees and forcibly displaced persons, e. g. by visiting detainees in the detention centre of Berlin-Köpenick.

1.4 Overview of trends

1.4.1 Trends in sentencing, numbers of prisoners, composition of prison population etc.

The general trend of the German sentencing practice has already been described under 1.1. Fines and suspended prison sentences are the predominant penalties in the German adult penal law system, unconditional prison sentences are considered as a measure of "last resort" ("ultima ratio"). However, there has been a major shift in the composition of the German prison population. There has been an increase of violent and drug offenders, especially of robbery and assault offenders, whereas the proportion of property offenders (theft, larceny) decreased. The extension of community sanctions for property offenders

---

[20]   see online under www.gefaengnisseelsorge.de.
[21]   see online under www.sbh-berlin.de.
[22]   see www.egpa.org for detailed information.
[23]   see for example the initiatives by *Pro Asyl*, www.proasyl.de.
[24]   see www.jesuiten-fluechtlingsdienst.de.

contributed to the above mentioned rather stable prison population even in times where violent crimes were on the increase and resulted in more prison sentences (see *Figure 1.5*).

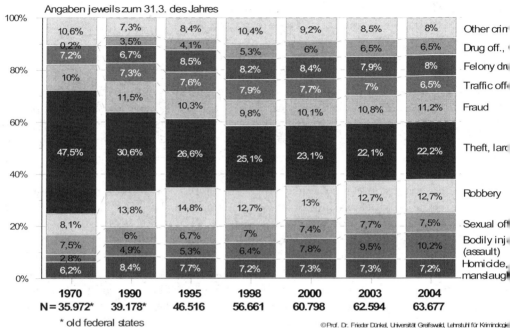

Figure 1.5

Tables 1.3-1.5 demonstrate that the length of prison sentences has also increased, however this is not so much the result of a harsher sentencing practice, but of an increase in the number offenders convicted for more serious crimes like robbery, serious bodily injury and sexual offences. The proportion of sentences of more than two years is still very low (less than 8% of all prison sentences see *Table 1.3*). The increase of sentences of more than one and the decrease of less than one year has been compensated by an extended practice of suspended sentences (probation) also for the longer sentences. In the last years, however, the use of life sentences for homicide has increased considerably. The daily prison population (31 March of the year) for life imprisonment developed as follows:

- 1980   956
- 1985   1.062
- 1990   1.149
- 1995   1.314
- 2000   1.598
- 2003   1.774
- 2004   1.794 (= + 88%)

The number of convictions per year until 1995 was around 70 and then increased to about 110 (2003: 105). The increase of „lifers" in prison is, however, mainly the result of a more restrictive release practice according to § 57a Penal Law (StGB, which in general provides a release after having served at least 15 years of the life sentence).

Table 1.3: Sentenced adult offenders according to the length of prison sentence, 1975-2003 − all crimes

Year	Sentenced adults total	Prison sentence abs.	Pris. sent. % of 2	Pris. sent. % of 3	Suspended p.s. % of 3	PS − 6 m., % of 3	% Sp. 6	− 6 m. susp. p.s. 3	6 m. − 1 J., % Sp.	6 M. − 1 J., susp. p. s., % of 8	1 − 2 y., % of 3	1 − 2 y. susp. p. s. % of 10	2 − 3 y. % of 3	3 − 5 y. % of 3	5 − 10 y. % of 3	10 − 15 y. % of 3	life sentence % of 3
1975	567.606	94.018	16,6	61,6	50,2	73,8	37,9	62,8			7,7	10,1	total 3,5		total 0,7		0,07
1980	599.832	104.850	17,5	65.7	48,0	79,3	39,1	66,9			8,0	18,3	2,4	1,5	0,8	0,11	0,05
1985	600.798	111.876	18,6	66,3	44,0	80,1	40,3	68,5			9,7	35,7	2,9	1,9	1,0	0,14	0,08
1990	615.089	102.454	16,7	68,0	45,8	77,8	37,8	70,5			10,8	54,1	2,8	1,9	0,8	0,11	0,06
1995	683.258	115.767	16,9	69,6	39,8	79,4	39,5	74,7			13,6	62,5	3,4	2,4	1,1	0,15	0,09
2000	638.893	125.305	19,6	67,5	37,1	75,2	41,1	74,0			14,3	64,8	3,7	2,5	1,1	0,16	0,09
2003	634.735	127.511	20,1	69,1	36,5	75,9	40,9	76,1			14,9	68,8	3,6	2,7	1,2	0,13	0,06

Table 1.4: Sentenced adult offenders according to the length of prison sentence, 1975-2003 − serious bodily injury (assault)

Year	Sentenced adults total	Prison sentence abs.	Pris. sent. % of 2	Pris. sent. % of 3	Suspended p.s. % of 3	PS − 6 m., % of 3	% Sp. 6	− 6 m. susp. p.s.	6 m. − 1 J., % Sp.	6 M. − 1 J., susp. p. s., % of 8	1 − 2 y., % of 3	1 − 2 y. susp. p. s. % of 10	2 − 3 y. % of 3	3 − 5 y. % of 3	5 − 10 y. % of 3	10 − 15 y. % of 3	life sentence % of 3
1975	7.085	2.090	29,5	62,3	37,9	72,3	49,9	68,0			8,8	10,4	total 3,1		total 0,3		0,0
1980	8.467	2.720	32,1	67,3	33,0	82,1	52,9	72,7			10,4	17,3	2,7	1,0	0,07	0,0	0,0
1985	8.593	3.099	36,1	66,3	29,5	80,9	54,3	71,1			12,4	31,5	2,7	0,9	0,2	0,0	0,0
1990	8.157	2.844	34,9	68,3	28,3	79,8	56,9	73,3			12,3	46,2	2,9	1,3	0,07	0,0	0,0
1995	9.384	3.616	38,5	73,5	26,2	86,9	53,1	79,1			15,3	57,4	3,7	1,5	0,2	0,0	0,0
2000	10.139	7.176	70,8	78,0	10,8	89,2	69,2	86,5			14,7	60,2	3,3	1,6	0,3	0,0	0,0
2003	11.045	8.370	75,8	79,9	10,0	89,7	70,2	87,5			15,1	64,0	2,9	1,7	0,2	0,01	0,0

Table 1.5: Sentenced adult offenders according to the length of prison sentence, 1975-2003 – drug offences

Year	Sentenced adults total	Prison sentence abs.	Pris. sent. % of 2	Suspended p. s. % of 3	PS – 6 m., % of 3	– 6 m. susp. p. s.	6 m. – 1 y. % Sp. 3	6.M – 1 y. susp. p. s., % of 8	1 – 2 y. % of 3	1 – 2 y. susp. p. s. % of 10	2 – 3 y. % of 3	3 – 5 y. % of 3	5 – 10 y. % of 3	10 – 15 y. % of 3	life sentence % of 3
1980	9.960	6.804	68,3	54,4	13,7	81,6	48,3	76,6	23,2	27,0	6,7	5,5	2,6	0,04	–
1990	17.399	8.777	50,5	60,3	20,5	76,3	38,3	75,9	25,2	61,6	8,6	5,6	1,6	0,2	–
1995	25.748	13.582	52,8	62,0	20,4	77,2	35,2	66,8	25,1	68,8	8,4	5,3	2,0	0,2	–
2000	34.354	16.773	48,8	61,0	20,4	71,3	33,6	77,1	28,2	72,8	9,6	6,0	2,1	0,2	–
2003	35.952	16.378	45,5	61,4	20,2	69,3	30,4	79,4	30,4	76,9	9,7	6,7	2,5	0,1	–

There are no systematic statistical data available for the sentencing practice concerning foreign offenders. However, some individual studies give a somewhat contradictory picture.

Prima vista there is much evidence that some discrimination takes place at the different levels of the criminal justice system[25].

The fact that the police are aware of more than 90% of "classic" crimes is a result of the victim's or witness's reporting behaviour. The rise of crime figures of foreigners in the early 90s according to the lower Saxony study of youth violence is attributed to the fact that foreigners also report violent conflicts to the police more often, as increasingly violent conflicts are not restricted to intra-cultural problems, but also incorporate inter-cultural problems. If Turkish and German youngsters have problems with each other, they are more likely to report than if Turkish or German youngsters have conflicts that are restricted to persons of their national peer group[26] (see 2.3 below). According to several studies in Germany, there seems to be greater risk of being reported to the police for foreigners or those who look like them than for native Germans. I. e. the level of tolerance with regard to deviant behaviour is different[27].

At the police level several research studies show discriminative and sometimes hostile practices, whereas one cannot say that the police in general exhibit xenophobic attitudes. It is, however, the situation of suspecting a person, and sometimes young foreigners at least have the feeling of generally being suspected of having committed crimes. Therefore, their chance of being detected might be greater than for young Germans. Looking from the prosecutor's perspective, an interesting observation can be made: More cases of foreign suspects are dismissed by the public prosecutor than in cases of German suspects (diversion according to §§ 153 ff. Criminal Procedure Act, *StPO*, or §§ 45, 47 Juvenile Justice Act, *JGG*)[28]. This is particularly true for juveniles (14-18 years) and young adults (18-21 years). The result is that the prevalence rates of foreign compared to German offenders are still higher, but not as significantly as the police data would suggest[29]. This means

---

25 see e. g. *Hamburger, Seus* and *Wolter* 1981, p. 168; *Geißler* and *Marißen* 1990; *Walter* and *Pitsela* 1993, p.12; *Mansel* and *G. Albrecht* 2003, p. 679 ff.

26 see *Pfeiffer* and *Wetzels* 2000, p. 107; *Wilmers et al.*, 2002, p. 37.

27 see *Walter* 1993, p. 349; *Schwind* 2003, p. 471 with further references.

28 see in general *Dünkel* 2003.

29 see *Mansel* and *G. Albrecht* 2003, p. 687 ff.

that prosecutors somehow "de-dramatise" (petty) offences of foreigners to a more "realistic" level. *Mansel* and *G. Albrecht* in their comprehensive nation-wide statistical analysis furthermore demonstrate offence related and regional variations and conclude that the considerable differences between federal states can be understood by different strategies of crime control (including different rates of reporting to the police) and not so much by the relevant respective behaviour of foreigners[30].

The research study of *Steffen* in Bavaria revealed, however, that the risk for foreigners of being convicted increased in the 1990s. The proportion of foreigners, particularly those under 21 years of age, measured as a percentage of all (German an Non-German) police suspects resp. all formally sentenced offenders, increased, whereas the proportion of Germans decreased[31], due to an extended application of diversionary procedures (§§ 45, 47 Juvenile, Justice Act, *JGG*). So at least in Bavaria the "de-dramatising" process of earlier years has disappeared. This could be the result of intensive crime policy debates about (illegal) immigrants in the 90s and the strong pressure of public opinion for a tougher policy approach.

The most important stage of discrimination is at the level of pre-trial detention[32] . The legal preconditions are constructed in a way that foreigners – due to the in practice predominant reason "risk to abscond" - a priori run a greater risk of being held in pre-trial detention. This is at least the case for those who do not dispose of a place of permanent residence, like asylum seekers, or other travelling persons. The definition of a risk to abscond and not to stand trial is much greater than for domestic residents. The research evidence is quite clear. *Jehle* (1995) stated in his comprehensive report on pre-trial detention that he found many cases of foreigners being sent to pre-trial detention "who, if they had been Germans, would not have been detained." The negative consequence of this practice is that those having been sent to pre-trial detention run a much greater risk of receiving an unconditional prison sentence than those who stayed outside detention. This might be one of the reasons why foreigners are so over-represented in prisons[33]. On the other hand a *contemporary* empirical study of suspected and sentenced young burglars in Bavaria indicates no negative discrimination of foreign suspects, particularly concerning the sentencing decisions of the courts[34]. The most important factors were confessing to the crime, prior convictions, the value of the stolen good(s) and the fact of being in pre-trial detention. Pre-trial detention in these cases, however, did not correlate with the status of nationality. On the other hand, an indirect effect of "nationality" could be found as foreigners tended more likely to confess to the crime than Germans[35].

Other studies concerning Turkish and Yugoslavian offenders clearly demonstrated that they received harsher punishments than their German counterparts[36]. Foreign recidivists were exposed to more severe punishment, particularly imprisonment[37]. A study was conducted on behalf of the German Association of Probation Workers that concen-

---

[30] see *Mansel* and *G. Albrecht* 2003, p. 713 f..

[31] see *Steffen* 1998, 676 ff.; 2001, 259 ff..

[32] see *Schott* 2004, p. 391; *Pfeiffer* et al. 2005 p. 82 ff.

[33] see *Dünkel* and *J. Walter*, 2005.

[34] see *Dittmann* and *Wernitznig* 2003, 195 ff.

[35] ibid. p. 203.

[36] see *Ludwig-Mayerhofer* and *Niemann* 1997; see also *Mansel* and *G. Albrecht* 2003.

[37] see *Hartmann* 1995.

trated on the typical problems and situations of clients of the probation Service The study stated that although foreigners are overrepresented amongst those convicted (in relation to the population), they are under-represented in the group on probation in most of the Federal States[38].

	Foreigners	Germans
Population	8%	92%
Convicted persons	26%	74%
Probationers	17%	83%

(Source: Engels and Martin 2002)

A reason for this might be the fact that foreign criminals are less often brought under the supervision of the probation service than Germans "because they are either expelled after the conviction or because language problems seem to make successful probation supervision impossible"[39]. A similar under-representation – partly due to specific immigration regulations and pending expulsion – can be found with regard to prison leave and placement in open institutions[40] (see 2.8. below).

Although there are clear indicators for a discrimination of (some groups of) foreigners or at least a more restricted access to non-custodial dispositions of the courts, the database is limited and further research is necessary[41] (). On the other hand there is also evidence that the overrepresentation of foreigners in prisons partly can be explained by a more violent behaviour of certain foreigner groups[42] .

1.4.2 Overview on issues concerning the general population of foreigners and of foreign suspects of crime

Foreigners, migrants and ethnic minorities constitute a heterogeneous phenomenon in Germany which is partly a result of specific regulations of traditional immigration laws. Migrants from the former Soviet countries or other countries who can claim to be of "German" ancestry are legally seen as Germans and have the right to bear a German passport (see Article 116 of the Constitution, *"Grundgesetz"*), whereas third generation Turkish youngsters, although their parents are born in Germany, have until recently been seen as "Foreigners". They often no longer speak the language of their grandparents, whereas the young Russian migrants in many cases have serious problems with the German language.

The problem of defining different groups of ethnic minorities is strongly related to the criminal political debate, as particularly right wing extremist parties, but also the conservative Christian Democratic Party in election campaigns repeatedly run for more restrictive immigration laws in order to fight "imported" criminality of foreigners etc.

---

[38] see *Engels* and *Martin* 2002.
[39] see *Engels* and *Martin* 2002, p. 22.
[40] see *Schott* 2004, p. 385.
[41] see *Suhling* and *Schott* 2001, p. 78, *Walter* and *Trautmann* 2003, 66 f.
[42] see *BMI/BMJ* 2001.

In the political debate populist arguments often emphasise asylum seekers and young male migrants who are prejudiced as being involved more in violent crime than the German residents. In addition, the recent discourse has been greatly influenced by the problems of terrorism and of organised crime where foreigners are over-represented (particularly in drug offences, trafficking young females for prostitution etc.).

As the subject of ethnic minorities and crime is often abused in the political debate for promoting xenophobic attitudes, some go so far to argue that statistics shouldn't even differentiate between Germans and foreigners, a question of political correctness that is emphasised particularly in Sweden. This would, however, result in a loss of knowledge concerning social integration and even disguise discrimination that takes place nonetheless. The differentiation of specific groups of ethnic minorities can support group related integration and therefore crime prevention strategies.

In general, the situation of migrants in Germany has changed considerably since the late 1980s. The absolute numbers of foreigners increased from about 4.5 million foreigners in the 1980s to a stable number of 7.3 million since the mid 1990s (see *Figure 1.6*). A recent calculation of the foreign population revealed, however, that the numbers of foreigners had been overestimated in the past years: There are only about 6.7 million foreigners living in Germany. In addition to foreigners, the number of "German" immigrants from former states of the Soviet Union or empire since the end of the 1980s rose to almost 400,000 annually (in 1990). From 1991 to 1995 the annual numbers were slightly more than 200,000 and then sharply dropped to about 31,000 in 2005 (see *Figure 1.7*). The new Immigration Law from 1999 permits the naturalisation of foreigners who have lived in Germany for longer periods and who are integrated into German society. Moreover, the new Immigration Law changes the concept towards a "ius soli", i. e. "foreign" children born in Germany are by definition "Germans", if the parents have lived in Germany for at least 8 years and have a "right" to live there. The absolute numbers of naturalisation of adult foreigners, however, are unexpectedly low. Only less than 150,000 in 1999 and between 150,000 and 190,000 in the years 2000-2002 were naturalised and consequentially received a German passport, in 2004 the numbers dropped to less than 130,000 (see *Figure 1.8*).

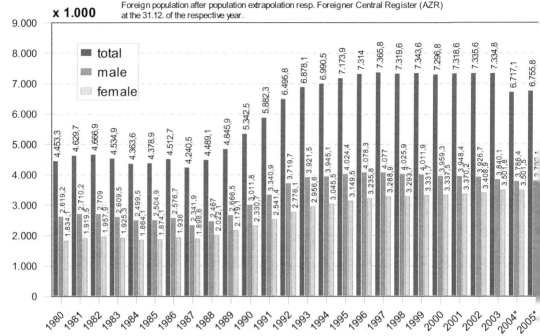

* The data of the population extrapolation for 2005 refer divergently from it to 30.9.2005. The details for the number of the foreigners to the AZR for 2004 and 2005 are not directly comparable with those of the previous years because of the register clearing up carried out in 2004.
Source: Statistisches Bundesamt Deutschland, 2006, http://www.destatis.de

Figure 1.6

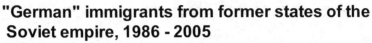

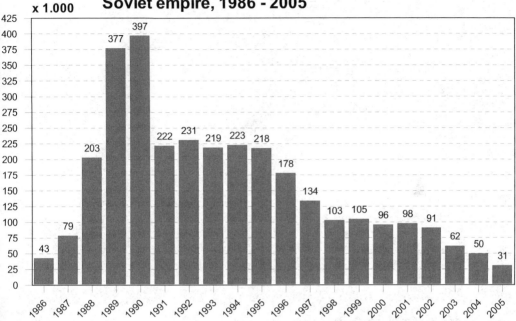

"German" immigrants from former states of the Soviet empire, 1986 - 2005

Source: Statistisches Bundesamt Deutschland, 2006, http://www.destatis.de

Figure 1.7

Naturalization of foreigners in Germany, 1972 - 2004

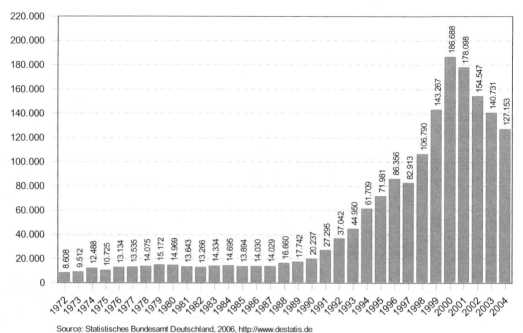

Source: Statistisches Bundesamt Deutschland, 2006, http://www.destatis.de

Figure 1.8

The crime rates of foreigners and ethnic minorities on the basis of registered police data suffer from a number of specific shortcomings. In consequence the police themselves publish the statement that the crime rates per 100.000 are not comparable. The crime rate is at first glimpse about 5 times higher than that for Germans. If we look thoroughly at the shortcomings of the statistical database the picture changes totally.

First we have to consider that certain offences as those against the immigration laws can only be committed by foreigners. The group of foreigners in the population is underestimated as many are not statistically registered (tourists, members of army forces, illegal immigrants). Germans and foreigners differ according to age, gender and social structure. So e. g. almost half of foreigners live in bigger cities against only 29% of the German population.

The risk of being reported to the police and of being prosecuted, sent to pre-trial detention and being sentenced differ considerably (see also 1.4.1 above). A differentiated analysis by the Bavarian police (*Landeskriminalamt*) shows that the relation of 4.9: 1 drops to only 2.7 : 1 if only the registered population of foreigners is taken into account. It further drops to 2.4 if offences that cannot be committed by Germans are deducted. Finally the ratio is 1.9 : 1 if only 14-21 years old male juveniles and young adults are considered. The crucial point is the social structure. No empirical approach so far has successfully eliminated all influential distorting factors. It may well be that the crime rate of really comparable groups will show no difference between foreigners and the domestic national population[43]. The majority of German criminologists claims a real higher crime rate of some groups of foreigners and of the so-called *Spätaussiedler* (Russian immigrants since 1993 with a German passport), which is caused at least in part by more intensive social control by the police and justice system[44].

Whereas the first generation of foreigners, the so-called guest workers of the 50s and 60s, showed no increased crime rates[45], studies in the 70s and 80s already revealed that young foreigners of the second and third generation of immigrants had considerably elevated crime rates (about twice as high as their German counterparts[46]). The hypothesis of cultural conflicts seemed to be somehow plausible. The data of the federal police statistics show that the proportion of foreigners amongst 14-25 years old young offenders is between 17% and 33%, whereas the proportion of foreigners in the total population is between 10% and 16%[47].

A study of the Lower Saxony criminological research institute demonstrated that 83% of the increase of crime rates for the 14-21 years old age group during the period from 1984-97 (in the old federal states) was caused by foreigners[48].

The development until 1993 was also greatly influenced by the increase in the number of asylum seekers and refugees who faced serious discrimination and social control. When the Immigration Law was changed in 1993 the number of asylum seekers dropped considerably (see *Figure 1.9*).

---

[43] see *Geißler* and *Marißen* 1990, p. 633 ff.; *Walter* and *Trautmann* 2003, p. 75 ff., 77.

[44] see *BMI* and *BMJ* 2001, p. 315

[45] see *Schüler-Springorum* 1983; *H.-J. Albrecht*, 1997; perhaps as the social control and pressure to adapt to the new living conditions were felt so strongly.

[46] see *P.-A. Albrecht* and *Pfeiffer* 1979; *Gebauer* 1981; *Villmow* 1983; *Karger* and *Sutterer* 1990; Schöch and *Gebauer* 1991; *Kubink* 1993.

[47] see also *Schwind* 2003, p. 465.

[48] see *Pfeiffer et al.* 1998.

Number of asylum seekers in Germany, 1975 - 2005

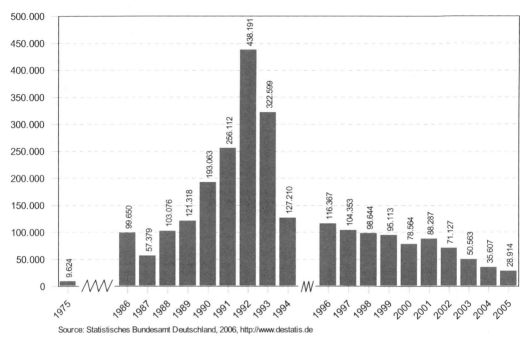

Source: Statistisches Bundesamt Deutschland, 2006, http://www.destatis.de

Figure 1.9

The proportion of foreign suspects of crime with respect to the total number of police recorded suspects of crime dropped from 34% in 1993 to 22.5% in 2005 (if one excludes offences against Immigration Laws, which cannot be committed by Germans, from 27% to 19.5%; see *Figure 1.10*). This development is remarkable as the number of police recorded German suspects continued to rise since 1993. A differentiation of the groups of foreigners involved in police registered crime is given in *Figure 1.11*. It shows that the proportion of so-called guest workers (foreign employees) has decreased from 33% of Non-German suspects in 1984 to around 17-18% in the years 1998-2005. On the other hand, the proportion of asylum seekers (although it has dropped considerably in the late 1990ies) with 10% in 2005 is still higher than in 1984 (8%). A maybe unexpected group are foreign students, who still contribute about 8% to the Non-German group of criminal suspects (in 1984 they even accounted for 15%, see *Figure 1.11*).

Non-German suspects of crime, 1984 - 2005

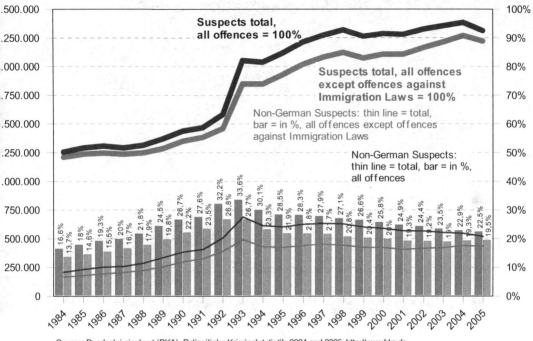

Source: Bundeskriminalamt (BKA), Polizeiliche Kriminalstatistik, 2004 and 2005, http://www.bka.de

Figure 1.10

Non-German suspects of crime according to the reason of stay; 1984 old Federal States, 1998 - 2005 Germany total

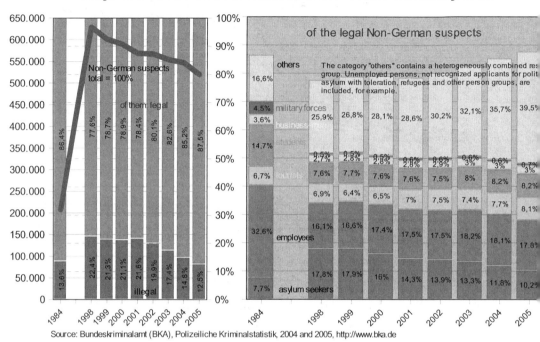

Source: Bundeskriminalamt (BKA), Polizeiliche Kriminalstatistik, 2004 and 2005, http://www.bka.de

Figure 1.11

1.5   Overview of national legislation

1.5.1 Constitution, Penal Code, Criminal Procedure Act

Foreigners are generally protected against discriminatory acts by the basic right of equal treatment before the law (allgemeiner Gleichbehandlungsgrundsatz), Article 3 GG because their cases concern disadvantage by state authorities. The much debated Anti-Discrimination Act (Antidiskriminierungsgesetz) (which has in the meantime been passed as the General Equal Treatment Act (Allgemeines Gleichbehandlungsgesetz (AGG)) which came into force on 18.8.2006) is meant for the protection of minorities within labour law and civil law. It thus has no direct meaning for the protection of foreign criminal prisoners from discrimination. A general anti-discrimination agency – as required by European guidelines - is planned to be founded in the Federal Ministry for Family Affairs, Senior Citizens, Women and Youth. It needs to be stated, however, that there are already active institutions that advocate the rights and interests of foreigners – whether or not specialization is more appropriate in this sense remains to be answered. For example, in their annual reports on the position of foreigners in Germany[49] these delegates often also look into the activities and behaviour of state agencies and can, for example, take sides against the above stated changes to the European Convention on the Transfer of Sentenced Persons.

With the final decision of a court the convict – in principle – knows whether he has to serve a sanction of imprisonment and how long this will be. This is different for foreigners: it is still not clear, when and if the execution of the sanction starts, how long it will continue and whether it will be executed in Germany or not.

As stated earlier, some measures can be taken by the public prosecution agency against foreign suspects or – in its capacity as the enforcement agency (*Vollstreckungsbehörde*) – the foreign convict: § 154b StPO (Criminal Procedure Act) as well as § 456a StPO open up the possibility to refrain from the execution in cases of extradition or expulsion[50]. The conditions for the expulsion are laid out in the new "Residence Act", see below 3., while extradition is regulated by the IRG. It is important to note that the decision to refrain from the execution is at the *agencies discretion*. § 17 of the Code on the Execution of Punishment (*Strafvollstreckungsordnung*) prescribes some criteria that the agency has to consider: No waiver of prosecution /execution is possible when "the personality of the convict or the nature of the crime" do not allow this. Arguments in favour of the waiver are that - as a rule - convicted foreigners are not allowed to leave the prison (Administrative Directives for the Code of Penal Execution; *Verwaltungsvorschriften zum Strafvollzugsgesetz*, Nr.5 and 6 on § 11 Code of Penal Execution) etc. (see 2.8. below), and that family contact is restricted by the external circumstances etc. The German jurisdiction[51] therefore approves the concept of a higher degree of "Strafempfindlichkeit" (*penal sensitivity*) when dealing with foreigners. One aim of these regulations was to return foreign criminals to their home country as soon as possible[52], while also paying regard to an easier reintegration into society. It was also planned to reduce the strain on the prison administrations, given the fact that dealing with foreign inmates is often more difficult. But the implementation of these regulations often bears problems for the persons concerned: § 456a StPO stipulates that in case of the return of this person (legally or illegally) the sentence can be executed later. This is a problem in particular for those who have family members in Germany.

Often foreign nationals see no more perspective of staying in Germany once they have been convicted, so they often have the wish to return to their home country. For some cases the possibility of a "Vollstreckungshilfe" exists in the form of bilateral agreements to execute a sentence of imprisonment. They provide a relatively flexible and quick procedure. In other cases the foreign prisoner can be transferred to his home country on the basis of the European Convention on the Transfer of Sentenced Persons (ETS no. 112, 1983) and its additional protocol (ETS no. 167, 1997). Originally – and this is the case also for Article 71 of the German "Act on International Cooperation in Criminal Matters" (IRG) – this transfer was only possible when the prisoner consented. The 1997 additional protocol gave up the precondition of consent of the prisoner. Rather, the in-

---

[49]   *Beauftragte der Bundesregierung für Migration, Flüchtlinge und Integration* 2005 p. 393 ff.
[50]   see *Tzschaschel* 2002, *Boese* 2003.
[51]   e.g. OLG Celle, *Strafverteidiger* 1981, p. 407 ff.
[52]   for an (older) international comparison see *Plachta* 1993.

strument now sets out the rules applicable to transfer of the execution of sentences, firstly where sentenced persons have absconded from the sentencing state to their state of nationality, and secondly where they are subject to an expulsion or removal order as a consequence of their sentence.

Contemporarily, there is much political debate in Germany on a proposed simplification of the prerequisites for the extradition of foreign prisoners by law enforcement agencies. This direction *was particularly* purposed by conservative groups but was then also included explicitly in the coalition agreement of the new two-party-government. Accordingly, in the near future an amended bill for the implementation of the European Convention on the Transfer of Sentenced Persons and its supplementary protocol shall come into force. The amendments shall effect the removal of the requirement for consent from German Law, while on the other hand aiming to safeguard standards of German Basic Rights by ordering *a judicial review of legitimacy* of the extradition abroad[53]. The verifiability of such extradition rulings *(*which could affect Basic Rights*)* was approved by the Federal Constitutional Court in a landmark decision on 18.6.1997 (BVerfGE 96,100). The German Federal Council (*Bundesrat*) only plans for the retroactive defeasibility of the decision through 23 EGGVG (introductory act to the Penal Code). This safeguard is by far too slack, even if the precondition for the transfer decision by the enforcement agency lies in the fact that the prisoner shall subsequently and definitely be expelled from Germany under Immigration Law. Government's bill plans to provide for an alternative, which is in itself seen as the minimum requirement. This alternative implies an examination according to § 71 IV IRG through which the regional court when dealing with extraditions has to check the foreigner's personal circumstances in their entirety as well as whether or not he/she faces political persecution in the ‚receiving' country. Additionally, a parallel provision must be made to § 80 III IRG, which states that foreigners who are enrooted in Germany may not be extradited to another EU-country against their will. In this context, the legal situation is generally obscure, because these new tendencies do not necessarily suit the direction that has been pursued by, for instance, the German Law on the European Arrest Warrant, which has – as is generally known – been deemed entirely unconstitutional. It did, however, contain the better safeguards in the field of execution for foreigner whose roots lie in Germany.

At this point, reference must also be made to the problems with the trans-national execution of punishment, especially when a foreign detainee who is *transferred* to Germany to serve a sentence has already been remanded to pre-trial custody in another country. Not only does the general rule apply which permits the time served in pre-trial custody abroad to be deducted from the prison sentence. Rather, the ratio need not be 1 to 1, but is at the courts discretion (§ 51 IV StGB). Respective case-law in this context is inconsistent, because evaluation criteria on the conditions in the foreign institution are often missing or are assessed very differently by the courts. Therefore, it can occur that a prisoner, who has spent six months in pre-trial detention in Spain, can have this period deducted from the pending full three year sentence, while another court – taking the conditions of detention in the respective country into consideration – could have deducted one year or even 18 months[54].

---

[53] Source: *Draft Law of the Federal Council, Bundesratsdrucksache* 356/06 of 26.5.2006.
[54] survey of the relevant case-law in München Kommentar-*Franke* § 51 Rn. 24.

1.5.2 Penitentiary law; Legislation for foreign prisoners

The German Prison Act in general does not provide different treatment for foreigners compared to German nationals. However, administrative rules exclude those foreigners from prison leaves and the transfer to open prisons (see the administrative rules to §§ 10, 11 and 13 StVollzG), who are to be or who are in danger of being expelled. On the other hand, the rules for food and religion provide for the peculiarities of foreign prisoners to be taken into consideration. For foreign prisoners as well as for the prison administration the difficulties and specific problems arise more from practical questions than from legal provisions. (see more specifically under 2.5 below).

2 TREATMENT OF FOREIGN PRISONERS

2.1   General

The problems of foreigners and members of ethnic minorities in prisons have recently been the focal point of a study by the University of Bielefeld. This study involved the questioning of experts of the federal state ministries. On the one hand, this revealed the possibility of differentiated structural problems within the prison system as well as its lack of appropriate programmes. Furthermore, problems of the prisoners themselves were also revealed, for example motivational factors and language deficits. A specifically East-German problem seems to be the emergence of the treatment of young neo-nazis and xenophobic offenders as a new challenge for the youth prison system. Another study shows that the main goal of the German *Strafvollzugsgesetz* - the rehabilitation of the of-fender - comes into an unresolvable conflict with the consequences of criminal behaviour in the German immigration laws, i. e. the expulsion of the foreign prisoner[55]. The following table summarises the results of the Bielefeld-study mentioned above.

---

[55]   see *Boese* 2003.

Table 2.1: **Problems of foreign prisoners and members of ethnic minorities and specific treatment programmes and opportunities for these groups** (Questioning of Prof. *Britta Bannenberg*, University of Bielefeld, from September 2002, see *Bannenberg*, 2003; *Winkler*, 2003)

Federal states (Länder)	Problems	Treatment programmes
Baden-Württemberg	• Language problems • Increasing numbers of "German" immigrants from Russia • Problems of the "Russian" subculture	• Language courses for foreigners and "*Aussiedler*" from Russia • Regular school classes in Italian language • working groups and conferences concerning "Russians" in some prisons • Consideration of religious practices (food etc.)
Bavaria	• Language problems complicate individual treatment and care • Increasing numbers of "German" immigrants from Russia • Problems of the "Russian" subculture (resistant to treatment offers, abuse of group activities, specific language problems, etc.)	• Language courses for foreigners and "*Aussiedler*" from Russia • General foreign language courses • Leaflets in foreign languages • Consideration of religious practices (food etc.) • Foreign language courses for staff members • Employment of staff of foreign nationality or with foreign language knowledge (particularly Russian) • Suppression of subculture developments
Berlin	• No information	• Language courses for foreigners and "*Aussiedler*" from Russia • Leaflets in foreign languages
Brandenburg	• Language problems • Proportion of foreigners who participate in work programmes is considerably lower	• Language courses for foreigners and "*Aussiedler*" from Russia • Leaflets in foreign languages
Bremen	• No information	• No specific programmes for foreigners
Hamburg	• No information	• No information
Hesse	• No information	• No information
Mecklenburg-Western Pomerania	• No information	• No information

Federal states (Länder)	Problems	Treatment programmes
Lower Saxony	• Only language problems cause difficulties with foreign prisoners • Instead: sincere difficulties with "German" immigrants from Russia (subculture, extortion of other prisoners, forcing other *Aussiedler* to participate in drug dealing, assaults against other prisoners and prison staff, hunger strikes etc.)	• Language courses for foreigners and "*Aussiedler*" from Russia • Employment of foreigners as staff members • Project "searching social case work", external volunteers contacting foreign prisoners with special need of care • Work-group for problems with *Aussiedler*, developing a treatment and security concept
North Rhine-Westphalia	• Multicultural, multiethnic structure of inmate population causes serious problems with prison subcultures • Language problems • Increasing numbers of "German" immigrants from Russia • Problems of the "Russian" subculture	• In general equal treatment of German and foreign prisoners resp. *Aussiedler* • Consideration of religious practices (food etc.) • Efforts to diminish language barriers and to integrate foreigners into general treatment programmes • Foreign literature in the prison library
Rhineland-Palatinate	• no information	• no information
Saarland	• No specific problems with foreign prisoners • Increasing numbers of "German" immigrants from Russia (subculture problems, hierarchical structure, resistant to treatment offers, strong group cohesion)	• No concrete solutions or programmes
Saxony	• Only few "German" immigrants from Russia, therefore no specific problems	• No information
Saxony-Anhalt	• Language problems with foreign prisoners	• No information
Schleswig-Holstein	• Language problems as a hindrance for integrating foreigners and *Aussiedler* in schooling/vocational training and therapeutic programmes	• Language courses for foreigners and "*Aussiedler*" from Russia • Consideration of religious practices (food etc.) • Counselling and leisure time activities by external foreign volunteers for Turkish, Polish and Russian prisoners

Federal states (Länder)	Problems	Treatment programmes
		• Leaflets in 12 foreign languages • Since 2002: in Neumünster a central office for the work with foreign and *Aussiedler* prisoners was opened (offering language courses for staff members, employment of foreign staff members, further vocational training seminars for staff members
Thuringia	• Proportion of foreign prisoners is very small, therefore no serious problems • In single cases language problems	• Some general measures (not described in detail) to combat language problems

In general we may conclude that the East-German federal states do not face a serious problem with foreigners or members of ethnic minorities in prisons, whereas most West-German states reported language problems in general and the increasing numbers of (young) "German" Russians as a violence-oriented group creating a problematic subculture in prison.

The study by *Winkler*[56] reveals that most federal states offer some language training courses, but besides that have not developed specific treatment programmes for foreign prisoners or members of ethnic minorities (see Table 3 above). Insofar the "German" Russians (*Aussiedler*) are perceived as a particularly problematic group in some West-German states, where they are highly over-represented as indicated before[57].

With respect to the general treatment efforts in prisons in Germany, one can state that particularly in youth prisons young foreigners are integrated into school and vocational training programmes quite well. They are also integrated into anger-management programmes, developed in some institutions for violent offenders in general or in so-called socio-therapeutic units.

An exception must be made in the case of those who are sent back to their country of origin after having served their sentence partially (in general, they are extradited after two thirds of the sentence). They are not granted home leaves or other forms of the relaxation of the prison regime (including the transfer to an open prison).

In some prisons the recruitment of staff with foreign background (e. g. Turkish social workers) has started which simplifies the involvement and commitment of foreign prisoners.

Xenophobic or right-wing extremist offenders have, until recently, not been seen as a specific problem and some prison directors still deny having difficulties with them. In some of the new federal states these (regularly violent) offenders are now a matter of concern as they promote their extremist ideas and by that contribute to the development of a specific subculture which can be as explosive as that of young immigrants from Russia.

---

[56] see *Winkler* 2003.

[57] see *Grundies* 2000; *Reich* 2003.

One experiment which could be interesting in this context is the "just community" project in a department unit of the Adelsheim youth prison in Baden-Württemberg. Its focus lies on developing democratic structures and of educating young prisoners towards tolerance and democratic attitudes[58]. It could be of particular importance for young persons with a social background of former totalitarian systems as well as for young anti-democratic nationalists of the neo-nazi scene. Although an empirical evaluation on its outcome concerning later recidivism has not yet been conducted, there is some evidence that the prison climate has improved and that a culture of democratic conflict resolution can be established even under the particularly difficult situation in youth prisons.

First empirical results have also shown that the level of development of moral judgement[59] of most participants in the pre-post comparison increased significantly, mostly by about half a stage. There is also a visible shift from pre-conventional to conventional levels of development of moral understanding[60]. As negative effects did not occur and as the reported experiences allow confidence, it is now important to integrate the model into the "grey routine" of the total youth prison. At least there is evidence that social and moral learning is possible even under the conditions of the juvenile penal system[61]. The presupposition is therefore that we summon up our courage to dare more democracy, even in prison. The project seems to be of major importance also for the living together of different ethnicities and nationalities in prison. The climate insofar has improved under the rules of the "just community" model, as well.

2.2 Living conditions and facilities

The living conditions of foreign prisoners do not differ from those for Germans as they are not separated from them. Foreign prisoners often prefer to be accommodated in communal cells, if possible with other inmates from their home country. As they are less often in open prisons, their possibilities to freely move around inside prisons are restricted.

2.3 Reception and Admission

Reception and admission procedures are the same as for Germans. In cases of foreigners coming from abroad the prison authorities regularly inform the embassies of the home country.

2.4 Work, education, training, sports, recreation

Foreign sentenced prisoners are obliged to work (see § 41 StVollzG). There is no information available about any form of discrimination towards foreigners if the prison administration cannot provide work for every prisoner. Each prisoner has to save some money during his time in prison (so called "Überbrückungsgeld"). This money can not be seized

---

[58] see *Dünkel* and *Walter* 2004.
[59] in the sense of *Kohlberg's* model of moral development, see *Kohlberg* 1987.
[60] see *Brumlik* and *Sutter* 1996: 46 ff.; see also *Sutter* 1996; *Sutter, Baader* and *Weyers* 1998.
[61] see *Weyers* 2003, p. 106 ff.

for any reason (§ 51 StVollzG). Accordingly, it is not possible for the immigration authorities to use this money to cover the expenses of extradition[62]. Foreign prisoners can take part in all training, sports and recreational activities. The Prison administration is obliged to offer social welfare measures (Soziale Hilfe, § 71 StVollzG) for every prisoner who needs and desires help. Such measures for foreign prisoners can include language classes and special job training.

2.5 Food, religion, personal hygiene, medical care

§§ 53 ff ; 157 StVollzG puts the freedom of worship as laid out in the German constitution (Article 4 GG) into effect. The prison administration is therefore obliged to provide for special dietary and religious food rules (e. g. during Ramadan). Foreign prisoners are allowed to exercise their religion and possess goods to practice their religious duties. It is not always possible for a foreign prisoner to have regular access to a qualified religious representative, e. g. an Imam for Muslim prisoners.

2.6 Consular and legal help

Germany ratified the Vienna Convention on Consular Relations from April 1963. Art. 36 of the Convention requires that foreign nationals who are arrested or detained be given notice "without delay" of their right to have their embassy or consulate notified of that arrest.

2.7 Contacts with the outside world

There are no different regulations for foreign prisoners (the minimum length of visit is one hour per month, see § 24 StVollzG). However, the prison administration may grant long term visits of several hours if a prisoner receives a visit from a relative from abroad. The writing and receiving of letters is in no way restricted at all. Telephone calls can be made subject to supervision by an interpreter. The regulation in § 31 StVollzG that enables the prison administration to seize letters that are written in a foreign language "without compelling reason" usually excludes letters written by foreign prisoners. If nevertheless the prison administration wants to control a letter written in another language, it has to provide for the translation; it must be paid by public means

2.8 Re-integration activities, prison leave

If the foreign prisoner is not to be expelled, he may be granted the same re-integrative activities and prison leave up to the integration into work release programmes. If the foreigner is to be extradited he is generally excluded from prison leaves etc., except those that are accompanied by prison guards. A study by *Tzschaschel*[63] revealed that 58% of all German prisoners but only 18% of all foreign prisoners in the sample were granted the opportunity to leave the prison. Only 10% of all foreign prisoners in the sample were eli-

---

[62] see *Fluhr*, 1989, 103 ff.
[63] see *Tzschaschel* 2002, p. 42 ff.

gible for the placement in an open institution (28% of the German prisoners). On the other hand foreign prisoners may be eligible for internal training programmes preparing for release. In fact, prison administrations tend to exclude foreigners from such rehabilitation programmes when there are not sufficient places for all prisoners.

2.9 The removal of criminal foreign detainees

Detained foreign nationals whose detention functions solely a means for safeguarding their administrative removal in accordance with § 62 AufenthG – as presented under 3. below – are to be held separately from imprisoned foreign nationals who are to be expelled as a response to their perpetrated criminal offences. But there is also the possibility to remove foreigners who have committed crimes or who pose a threat to public order and security. The foreign nationals' department is also responsible for removals in these cases. In cases where grave or repeated premeditated criminal offences specified in § 53 AufenthG (including for example: offences with a conviction to at least three years detention, or deprivation of liberty without probation due to breaches of the German Drugs Act (Betäubungsmittelgesetz, BtMG); for the individual regulations see the appendix) have been committed, a removal is obligatory as stated in § 53 AufenthG. Also, § 54 AufenthG specifies criminal offences (including: leading to sentences of imprisonment without probation; juvenile detention of at least two years for all offences) the perpetration of which normally results in the foreign offender's expulsion from German federal territory. Additionally, certain circumstances are stated in § 55 AufenthG – especially concerning threats for public security and order – under which the decision on removal is a matter of discretion. However, in these cases § 55 III AufenthG requires that the duration of prior legal residence and (other) family ties be taken into account.

Foreigners who are approved asylum seekers or who are otherwise legitimately residing in Germany (e. g. through a settlement permit, *Niederlassungserlaubnis*) are specially protected against removal by § 56 AufenthG. This protection is, however, put into perspective by § 56 I 2, 3 AufenthG when there are profound grounds. This precondition is normally fulfilled in the above mentioned cases of convictions for offences specified in §§ 53, 54 AufenthG. However, a removal order must take into account the restrictions of § 60 AufenthG. This states that persons may not be removed should they be at risk of being tortured in their home country. Also, § 60 V AufenthG forbids that a removal infringe the ECHR, for example Article 8 ECHR (Right to Respect for Private and Family Life).

In addition one needs to consider that, fundamentally, an expulsion lasts indefinitely (§ 11 I 1,2 AufenthG. However, § 11 I 3, 4 AufenthG specifies that a limitation of the removal period can be considered, should the respective application be made. The resulting decision must take the principles of the ECHR into consideration, as has been exemplified by a ruling of the EGMR (www.coe.int/t/d/menschenrechtsgerichtshof/dokumente_auf_deutsch/volltext/urteile/20051027-Keles-U.asp#TopofPage). In fact, in many cases in which the foreign nationals department orders a removal, the person in question is in penal detention.[64]. The course of action regarding the actual departure from Germany has to be determined by the authority responsible for the execution of punishment (Strafvollstreckungsbehörde)

---

[64]   see www.gefachrdetenhilfe.de/download/ 150_abschiebung_aus_untersuchungs_und_strafhaft.pdf.

- in this case the prosecution service,. § 456a StPO allows the latter to decide whether the sentenced foreigner is to be removed immediately, or whether he/she is to serve the sentence in whole or in part in Germany. In any case, the foreign national shall be expelled "out of custody".

In most of the *Länder* the expulsion is considered after the enforcement of half of the sentence (§ 456a StPO), in some cases two thirds of the term of imprisonment are executed before an expulsion. *North hine-Westphalia* even checks the preconditions of an expulsion according to § 456a StPO right at the beginning of the execution of the foreigner´s prison term[65].

2.10 Aftercare, Probation

There are no laws or regulations that provide for a different treatment of foreigners concerning their access to probation or aftercare. As mentioned above, fewer foreigners are supervised and supported by the probation service than Germans. This is party due to the fact that foreign criminals are more often expelled, but it is assumed that another reason lies in the expected difficulties with foreigners as probationers (in particular those who do not speak German).

2.11 Staff

Some West-German prison units recruit prison staff from the most common home countries of foreign prisoners, like Turkish social workers etc. One example is Hamburg, where 40% of all prisoners are not German nationals; they come from 94 different countries. Three prisons employ so called "*Ausländerberater*" (foreigner´s aides). However, given the massive job cuts in prison staff in Hamburg this is probably merely a drop in the ocean.

2.12 Projects

See 2.1 (the just community project in Adelsheim)

3 ADMINISTRATIVE DETENTION OF ILLEGAL RESIDENTS IN GERMANY

Asylum Law and Law concerning Foreign Nationals have been continuously gaining relevance. In this field there have been numerous landmark decisions, and one should also bear the compromise on asylum ('A*sylkompromiß*') in mind. One subject area is the ,removal / expulsion' as well as the 'administrative detention of irregular migrants' ('*Abschiebungshaft*'). Originally, removal/expulsion was regulated in the Foreign Nationals Act (*Ausländergesetz*; AuslG). However, there has been a series of legal amendments especially in the last 15 years. Changes have been made to provisions that concern, for example, the subsequent immigration of dependent family members. However, removal/expulsion was

---

[65] see *Tzschaschel* 2002, p. 11 ff.

also facilitated, penal prescriptions intensified, and § 57 AuslG, which regulated the administrative detention of irregular migrants, was broadened.

On 1st January 2005, the Foreign Nationals Act was replaced by the so called Residence Act (*Aufenthaltsgesetz*; Law on the Residence, Occupation and Integration of Foreigners in the Federal Territory of Germany; AufenthG). Administrative detention of illegal residents is now regulated in § 62 of the Residence Act[66].

3.1 What type of institution is used for this kind of administrative detention?

Expulsion is the enforcement of a foreigner's duty of departure by means of removal from Germany's federal territory[67]. It is a measure of administrative execution in the form of directly exerted compulsion. Such administrative detention acc. to § 62 AufenthG is a measure of liberty-deprival under Civil Law that serves to safeguard the implementation of this compulsive departure[68]. Such detention is neither a sanction for improper conduct nor a means of directly coercing a foreign national to leave the country. Thus, it is not of a punitive nature and merely serves safeguarding purposes[69].

There are three different models for the accommodation of detainees pending expulsion: allocation to special establishments for the administrative detention of illegal residents; in regular penitentiary institutions ('*Justizvollzugsanstalt*', JVA) or in special departments of such a JVA[70]. Special establishments for the administrative detention of irregular migrants can only be found in a select few German Federal States, for example Berlin, Brandenburg and Bremen, and are within the responsibility of the Ministry of the Interior / the administration of justice of the respective Federal States[71]. In Rhineland-Palatinate, the Ministry of the Interior runs special detention establishments for detainees awaiting removal[72]. Accordingly, these states have special ‚Laws on the Execution of Detention pending Removal'. Yet in general the prescriptions of the Law of Prison Administration (*Strafvollzugsgesetz*, StVollzG) are deemed to apply respectively, with the exception of judicial legal protection.

In the other federal states, with the exception of Rhineland-Palatinate, the justice administration assumes responsibility for execution through administrative assistance acc. to § 8 II of the Act on Court Proceedings relating to Deprivation of Liberty, FEVG[73]. In part, for example in Northrhine-Westphalia, there are extra penitentiary establishments that are designed solely and especially to accommodate detainees awaiting expulsion, while on the other hand a proportion of these detainees is also accommodated in regular prisons alongside criminally convicted prisoners or pre-trial detainees. Thus, in these cases the norms of the StVollzG on the execution of liberty-deprivation are applicable, so long as they do not impede the peculiarity and purpose of administrative detention. Thus,

---

[66] For a detailed commentary on the legal regulations on administrative detention for foreigners see *Melchior* 2006.

[67] see *Hailbronner* 2006, p. 197.

[68] see *Beichel-Benedetti* and *Gutmann* 2004, p. 3016.

[69] see *Heinhold* 2004, p. 15.

[70] ibid. 2004, p. 28.

[71] see *Horstkotte* 1999, p. 34; *Heinhold* 2004, p. 94.

[72] see *Heinhold* 2004, p. 236.

[73] see *Horstkotte* 1999, p. 34.

different institutions and establishments - that are associated either to the administration or to the prison system - are used for the detention of illegal residents awaiting removal.

Concerning the quality of living conditions in the respective institutions or units it is important to bear in mind the reports of the Council of Europe's Committee for the Prevention of Torture and Inhuman or Degrading Treatment or Punishment (CPT). The CPT's remark in its report of the visit in the year 2000 is particularly interesting: "For its part, the CPT considers that to hold immigration detainees in prison is a fundamentally flawed approach, even if the actual conditions of detention for the persons concerned in a given prison establishment are adequate. As already emphasised in paragraph 76 of the report on the 1996 visit, a prison is, by definition not an appropriate place in which to detain someone who is neither suspected nor convicted of a criminal offence."

Delegations of the CPT visited Germany five times, and on several occasions special institutions or units for foreigners/immigrants were visited. Some of the visited institutions gave rise to criticism; in particular visits to the unit at the Frankfurt am Main Airport, as well as the institution in Eisenhüttenstadt. The visit to Frankfurt in 1998 was a so-called ad-hoc visit as a response to reports that the CPT had received which were critical of the conditions under which immigration detainees were being held there. Those reports also contained a series of allegations of ill-treatment of such persons; more particularly, allegations were made of the use of excessive force during the enforcement of removal orders. Certain allegations were also made that non-medically qualified staff had administered tranquillizers to the persons concerned. The delegation itself found no evidence of ill-treatment but requested reports on the investigations by the German authorities. The Delegation had several comments on poor ventilation, monotonous food, poor facilities and activities for younger persons and children, on insufficient medical and psychological/psychiatric care and on the need to improve training for those officials dealing with foreign detainees at the airport[74]. Some of these shortcomings had still not been remedied before the follow-up visit by the CPT in the year 2000. During the same visit, the CPT inspected the Eisenhüttenstadt detention centre. Among several rather minor shortcomings, the CPT had strong objections to some of the discipline and security measures employed there, such as the withdrawal of outdoor exercise that was applied occasionally by staff as a disciplinary measure. The delegation found conditions in one of the two security cells totally unacceptable. This cell was fitted with four metal rings anchored to the floor, in order to secure a person's hands and feet while lying prone and spread-eagled. It recommended a completely different approach to agitated detainees than in intimidating security cells.

A delegation of the CPT carried out a visit to Germany from 20 November to 2 December 2005, the CPT's fifth visit to this country. In the course of the visit, the CPT's delegation followed up a number of issues examined during previous visits, in particular the fundamental safeguards against ill-treatment offered to persons deprived of their liberty by the police and the situation of immigration detainees. Three out of the 17 visited institutions or units were designed for foreigners. A report of that visit is not yet available.

---

[74] Ref.: CPT/Inf (99) 10 [EN] (Part 1) - Publication Date: 27 May 1999; all reports are available under www.cpt.coe.int.

Table 3.1: Foreign detainees pending removal in penitentiary establishments 1990-2006

Count on Jan. 1. of the year	1990	1991	1992	1993	1994	1995	1996	1997	1998	1999	2000	2001	2002	2003*	2004	2005	2006
Germany total **	302	430	557	1,242	2,600	2,322	1,690	1,849	2,283	1,938	1,924	2,001	1,824	1,786	1,582	1,302	947
Males total	274	399	503	1,130	2,373	2,135	1,564	1,738	2,034	1,727	1,681	1,758	1,627	1,571	1,346	1,101	820
Females total	28	31	54	112	227	187	126	111	249	211	243	243	197	215	236	201	127
Baden-Württemberg	34	68	37	80	115	220	166	164	174	113	145	164	134	142	136	111	76
Bavaria	104	94	137	205	512	476	333	423	554	465	435	402	388	351	340	314	181
Berlin			9	16	14	18	1	-	15	-	-	1	1	4	3	3	3
Brandenburg				14	9	4	4	4	1	1	-	-	-	1	-	-	-
Bremen	-	-	1	5	14	2	4	3	1	1	-	-	1	-	-	-	-
Hamburg	13	33		33	83	103	54	80	95	79	83	92	93	94	75	55	82
Hesse	14	29	27	35	160	154	84	141	158	188	214	183	206	205	224	137	122
Mecklenburg-Western Pomerania			6	13	33	43	21	24	13	11	14	24	14	19	12	18	10
Lower Saxony	24	58	94	201	283	239	160	177	238	202	206	245	212	188	135	94	55
North Rhine-Westphalia	76	132	160	357	872	696	559	532	705	659	633	676	609	650	513	411	322
Rhineland-Palatinate	18	24	18	67	50	46	22	17	10	1	1	-	6	4	1	-	-
Saarland	8	13	13	23	58	58	43	35	49	40	47	31	1	4	-	1	1
Saxony			30	73	118	71	59	88	56	80	56	109	87	43	63	64	37
Saxony-Anhalt			2	29	94	24	52	42	64	41	39	30	34	30	27	22	20
Schleswig-Holstein	8	8	21	72	140	111	95	83	113	14	8	11	16	32	35	39	26

Count on Jan. 1. of the year	1990	1991	1992	1993	1994	1995	1996	1997	1998	1999	2000	2001	2002	2003*	2004	2005	2006
Thuringia			2	19	45	57	33	36	37	43	43	33	22	19	18	13	12

Source: Statistisches Bundesamt: destatis
* as of 2003 cut-off date on March 31 of the respective year
** as of 1992: All of Germany including the new Federal States

3.2 Which Ministry is responsible and which laws/regulations are applicable to this category?

The regulations that are decisive for expulsion/removal as well as for the administrative detention of illegal residents are contained within the Residence Act. The procedure is regulated in the Act on Court Proceedings relating to Deprivation of Liberty and in the Act on Non-Contentious Proceedings (FGG). Regarding the implementation of detention, the norms of the StVollzG and respective special regulations at the Federal State level apply. Decisions and measures relating to residence issues – which includes removal/expulsion – are matters for the respective local 'Foreign Nationals' Registration Offices' (Ausländerbehörden) (as stated in § 71 I AufenthG). In accordance with § 106 II 1 AufenthG and § 3 S.1 FEVG, these agencies also initiate the procedure of administrative detention pending removal by filing the application for detention. The Foreign Nationals' Registration Offices are directly responsible to the Federal State Ministry of the Interior. Under certain circumstances, such an application for detention can also be filed by customs and excise (§ 71 III Nr.1 AufenthG) as well as by the police forces of the individual Federal States (§ 71 V). Whether or not the application is allowed is decided by the District Court in accordance with § 3 FEVG in the procedure of non-contentious proceedings.

3.3 How many of these institutions exist and what is their capacity?

The number of applicable institutions varies among the Federal States - each State makes use of multiple penitentiary establishments, and the capacities thereof also exhibit a degree of variation. In Germany, roughly 2250 foreign detainees awaiting removal can be accommodated. A detailed listing of the individual Federal States, their institutions and capacities up to the year 2002 can be found in the book „Abschiebungshaft in Deutschland" ("Administrative detention in Germany") by *Heinhold* 2004; see also table 3.2.

Table 3.2: Institutions for the Administrative Detention of Irregular Migrants in the individual Federal States of Germany

	Responsibility	Placement in:	Particularities	Capacity
Baden-Württemberg	JVA in administrative assistance for the Administration of the Interior	JVA Mannheim; JVA Rottenburg	Special section in Mannheim; Accommodation in containers located in yard; surrounded by walls / screened from view	104 places in Mannheim
Bavaria	JVA in admin. Assistance for the Bavarian Ministry of State for the	JVAs	in JVA Nürnberg (and München-Stadelheim) special section	Flexible
Berlin	Ministry for Internal Affairs	Establishment for detainees awaiting expulsion in Köpenick	Police are responsible for custody pending expulsion	340 places, of which 50 for women
Brandenburg	Ministry of the Interior	Establishment for administrative detention in Eisenhüttenstadt		108 places, 30 of them for women
Bremen	Senator for Interior Affairs and Sport	Administrative custody pending removal in the "Vahr76"	In Police Custody; single- and double cells	18 places for men and 10 for women
Hamburg	Ministry of the Interior	Establishment for administrative detention in Glasmoor; JVA Holstenglacis, JVA Suhrenkamp; JVA and Juvenile Detention Centre Hahnöfersand	Containers in Glasmoor	84 places in Glasmoor, 15 for juvenile male detainees in Hahnöfersand, 5 for female and 16 for adult male detainees in pre-trial detention centre
Hesse	Ministry of Justice	Establishment for admin.detention in Offenbach; JVA Fulda, JVA Kassel; JVA Frankfurt/Main for Frauen; JVA Wiesbaden and JVA Rockenberg for male juveniles and young adults		50 places in Offenbach
Mecklenburg-Western Pomerania	Ministry of the Interior	JVA Bützow, men only	special expulsion-department, if overcrowded then transfer to Eisenhüttenstadt;	11 places

	Responsibility	Placement in:	Particularities	Capacity
			Women always to Eisenhüttenstadt or to other Federal States.	
Lower Saxony	Ministry of the interior	JVA Langenhagen; JA Hameln; other JVAs		185-245 places (emergency capacity) in Langenhagen; of which 45 for women
North Rhine-Westphalia	Ministry of the Interior	JVA Büren; Det. Centre Moers; Det. Centre in Neuss; other JVAs		530 places in Büren; 144 for men in Moers, 80 for women in Neuss
Rhineland-Palatinate	Ministry of the Interior and Sports	detention centre for detainees pending expulsion (*Gewahrsamseinrichtungen für Ausreisepflichtige* GfA); Ingelheim; GfA Birkhausen		150 places for men in Ingelheim, 51 for men and 19 for women in Birkhausen
Saarland	Ministry of the Interior and of Sports	GfA Ingelheim a. Zweibrücken/Birkhausen (in Rhineland-Palatinate); JVA Zweibrücken, JVA Ottweiler	GfA for women a. men	GfA has 50 places
Saxony	Ministry of the Interior	JVA Bautzen; JVA Chemnitz; JVA Dresden; JVA Görlitz; JVA Leipzig; JVA Plauen, JVA Stollberg, JVA Zwickau, u.a.	No special penitentiary establishments	Total of 115 places
Saxony-Anhalt	JVA in administrative assistance for the Ministry of the Interior	JVA Volkstedt for men; JA Raßnitz; JVA Halberstadt for women and female juveniles		roughly 50 places
Schleswig-Holstein	Ministry of the Interior; with admin. assistance from the Ministry of Justice	establishment for administrative detention in Rendsburg for men; JVA Lübeck for women	Support from establishment for administrative detention in Eisenhüttenstadt or Glasmoor	56 places in Rendsburg
Thuringia	Ministry of the Interior	JVA Goldlauter for men; JVA Chemnitz for women		45 places in Goldlauter

Source: Heinhold 2004.

3.4 What is the legal length and average length of detention?

Firstly, it should be noted that there are two different forms of administrative detention in Germany. On the one hand, there is so called *preparatory detention* acc. to § 62 I AufenthG., which serves to prepare a removal/ an expulsion according to §§ 53 ff AufenthG. The duration of preparatory detention may not exceed six weeks in accordance with § 62 I 1 AufenthG. An extension shall only be applicable in exceptional cases. On the other hand, there is actual *administrative detention to safeguard removal* which is regulated in § 62 II, III AufenthG. This form of detention serves to secure the successful removal of the detainee from the federal territory (§ 62 II 1 AufenthG). One key precondition for *administrative detention to safeguard removal* is that the detainee's expulsion is beyond any doubt. The maximum period of time for which a person can be detained in this form is six months (§ 62 III 1 AufenthG). In cases in which the foreign national impedes his expulsion, the period of detention can be extended by a further 12 months (§ 62 III 2 AufenthG).

However, § 62 II 4 AufenthG states that, in general, administrative detention while awaiting removal should not exceed three months[75]. If the departure deadline has passed and if it is clear that the detainee's removal can actually be implemented, then the term of *admin. detention to safeguard removal* should not exceed two weeks (§ 62 II 2 AufenthG).

§ 62 III 3 AufenthG stipulates that a period of time spent in preparative administrative detention shall be deducted from the total duration of *administrative detention to safegaurd pending removal*. Additionally, there are two further forms of detention, so called 'Zurückweisungshaft' (when an illegal resident is apprehended upon entry at the border) and 'Zurückschiebungshaft', to which the provisions of § 62 AufenthG also apply (acc. to §§ 15 IV 1, 57 III AufenthG). The average duration of administrative detention is roughly six weeks. However, such a statement could be misleading, not least in the sense that many detainees are only briefly in custody, while others are detained for considerably longer periods[76]. The proportion of detained illegal residents awaiting expulsion who spend more than six months in custody lies at roughly 10 to 20%[77].

3.5 Who makes decisions for administrative detention?

First of all, the local 'Foreign Nationals' Registration Office' has to examine whether the foreign national is to be expelled from Germany or not. Should an expulsion be deemed possible, the office can file an application for administrative detention at the County Court (§ 3 S.1 FEVG), as long as grounds for expulsion/removal in terms of § 62 II 1 AufenthG are affirmed. Article 104 II of the German Constitution stipulates that decisions concerning the deprivation of liberty can be made solely and only by a judge. The County / Civil Court Judge or judge responsible for ordering administrative detention as a sole residing judge then decides whether or not administrative detention is to be ordered in non-contentious proceedings. However, the district judge only reviews whether the application itself is admissible and justified (whether the application was filed by the responsible authority, whether there are grounds for removal, and whether administra-

---

[75] see Heinhold, 2004, p. 304.

[76] see *Hagenmeier* 2000, p. 11.

[77] see *Horstkotte* 1999, p. 36.

tive detention pending expulsion is a proportional measure)[78]. The district judge is not required to examine whether the foreign national is fact obliged to be removed and whether the preconditions for an expulsion are given. An examination of whether the content of the administrative act that justifies the expulsion is proper lies – according to prevailing opinion - only in the competence of the administrative court[79].

The Judge responsible for ordering administrative detention is naturally not limited in his function to being merely the executive body of the Foreign National's Registration Office. Rather, he is also obliged to independently review the individual case (so called "*Amtsermittlungsgrundsatz*"of § 12 FEVG) and to preserve the rights of the affected. In particular, the affected person is to be heard, and the judge is to comprehensively review the foreign person's case file[80].

The right to a hearing as stated in § 5 FEVG also implies the right to an interpreter[81]. Additionally, the right to legal representation also applies. The procedure for administrative detention pending expulsion is not a fast-track procedure. An interim deprivation of liberty (§ 11 FEVG) can only be ordered in exceptional cases. Moreover, one should consider that the judge assumes full responsibility for his decision on administrative detention, and could possibly be held officially liable, because in FGG proceedings the protection of judges from liability for their decisions (so called '*Spruchrichterprivileg*') does not apply[82]. The actual execution of detention is in turn a matter for the Foreign Nationals' Registration Office[83].

3.6 Which body can be appealed to and within how much time?

There is the permission to immediately file an appeal at the Regional Court (acc. to § 7 I FEVG, § 19 FGG) against both general and interim decisions of the County Court. § 22 I FGG sets the time limit for such an appeal at two weeks after the decision has been proclaimed. According to § 27 I FGG, decisions of the Regional Court – being an appellate court – can be immediately appealed against, which falls into the jurisdiction of the Higher Regional Court (§ 28 I FGG). According to a ruling of the German Constitutional Court, an affected detainee awaiting removal has a legally protective right to determine the illegality of his detention even if the measure has already been served (Article 19 IV GG), for being deprived of ones liberty through imprisonment is indicative of a need for redemption[84]. Should immediate execution of administrative detention awaiting removal be ordered in accordance with § 8 I 2 FEVG, then a regular appeal is possible in the terms of § 19 FGG, however, without having a postponing effect[85]. Ordering immediate execution/implementation is – contrary to the intentions of the Law – often the case in practice[86].

---

[78] see *Heinhold* 2004, p. 291, 298 f.; *Beichel-Benedetti* and *Gutmann* 2004, p. 3017.

[79] see *Beichel-Benedetti* and *Gutmann* 2004, p. 3017; *Heinhold* 2004, p. 297.

[80] see *Beichel-Benedetti* and *Gutmann* 2004, p. 3017; *Heinhold* 2004, p. 276.

[81] see Heinhold, 2004, p. 278.

[82] see *Beichel-Benedetti* and *Gutmann* 2004, p. 3016.

[83] see *Laubenthal*, 2003, p. 431.

[84] *BVerfGE*, 2 BvR 2266/00 on 24.07.02. See www.bverfg.de.

[85] see *Heinhold* 2004, p. 286.

[86] ibid. 2004, p. 282 f.

There are possibilities of legal protection during the period of detention depending on the circumstances. One the one hand, should an illegal resident be administratively detained in a JVA on the foundation of administrative assistance, he can file an application as stated in §§ 109 ff. StVollzG. Another means is filing a suit to the Administrative Court (§§ 40 ff. VwGO) if a detainee is being held in an establishment of the Administration of the Interior[87].

3.7 Is illegal/irregular residence a criminal offence? If yes, what is the minimum/maximum penalty?

In many cases, illegal entry and illegal residence in the Federal Territory of Germany constitute a criminal offence (see § 95 I, II AufenthG). The cases stated in § 95 I Nr.1-8 AufenthG are punishable with liberty-deprivation of up to one year or a fine. Breaches of § 95 II Nr.1-2 AufenthG can result in detention for up to three years or a fine. According to § 95 III AufenthG, even the attempt is liable to prosecution. Some cases (see § 98 I – III AufenthG) ‚merely' constitute misdemeanours, which are punishable with an administrative fine of up to 5.000 Euros (§ 98 V AufenthG).

3.8 What is the number of detained irregular foreigners?

There are by all means numerous detainees who were convicted due to breaches of the Residence Act and/or the Asylum Procedure Act. These detainees are, however, predominantly young adults and adults, and only rarely young people sentenced to juvenile imprisonment. One needs to take into consideration that penal detention takes priority over administrative detention pending removal, and that interim pre-trial- or penal detention temporarily suspends administrative detention. For more detailed data see table 3.3.

Table 3.3: Illegal residents in detention

Count on 31. March in Germany	Detainees for breaches of Residence Act provisions	Of those, youth imprisonment	Detained for breach only of § 95 Residence Act	Of those, youth imprisonment	Detained for breach of Law on the Procedure of Asylum	Of those, youth imprisonment
1998	483	5	no data	no data	76	2
1999	639	9	464	9	45	-
2000	674	13	546	12	42	2
2001	683	14	489	6	36	2
2003	605	8	493	7	45	-
2005	440	4	325	3	26	-

Source: Statistisches Bundesamt: www.destatis.de

---

[87] see *Laubenthal* 2003, p. 364.

3.9. What is the percentage that will be expelled after administrative detention?

There is a considerable number of administrative detainees who are in fact not expelled from Germany. The true proportions of expelled or non-expelled foreign detainees cannot be accurately stated due to a lack of respective statistics from the individual Federal States. Estimates assume that roughly 80% of administrative detainees pending removal are actually expelled; figures from other sources are at around 60%[88].

3.10 What happens with non-expelled foreign prisoners?

Those who are ultimately not expelled are released from custody, for which there are several different reasons. Normally, no further supervision or support follows. The released foreigner merely remains in contact with the Foreign Nationals' Registration Office, provided that this is deemed necessary.

3.11 Can Category 3 prisoners also be detained with prisoners who are detained under criminal law? And if so, are they detained in separate sections? What happens with minors (under 18 years)?

In the Federal German States that have no special establishments for foreign detainees awaiting expulsion, they are allocated to regular prisons where they live alongside prisoners convicted of criminal offences as well as pre-trial-detainees. Such practice is criticised especially for its criminalising effect on detainees awaiting removal, who are precisely not deprived of their liberty as a means of punishment but rather in order to safeguard their pending expulsion. When foreign detainees awaiting removal are placed in normal penitentiary establishments, they can in principle be accommodated with other prisoners. Partly there are separate sections within the prison. In cases involving smaller numbers of people, they are usually accommodated together with the other prisoners of the establishment.

The detainees are fundamentally separated according to gender[89]. They are placed predominantly in shared dormitories, sometimes in single cells, and in part there is the problem of overcrowding. The size and facilities of the cells vary from establishment to establishment.

Since the proportion of women among administrative detainees is rather small they are predominantly placed in regular detention facilities[90]. The German Residence Act (§ 80 I AufenthG) states that juveniles aged 16 and above are generally capable of acting and capable of participating in proceedings. Juveniles and minors are, however, especially in need of care and protection and this needs to be taken into consideration throughout the entire process. Accordingly, young people aged 16 and above can still be detained for the purpose of later expulsion[91]. Special establishments for the detention of

---

[88]   see *Heinhold* 2004, p. 59.
[89]   see *Heinhold* 2004, p. 30.
[90]   ibid. 2004, p. 49.
[91]   ibid. 2004, p. 47.

illegal residents pending removal often incorporate special juvenile sections. Should this not apply, however, then the young person is, in general, accommodated in the respective penitentiary establishment. There, he is usually jointly accommodated with prisoners who have been convicted of criminal offences[92].

4 NATIONALS DETAINED ABROAD

4.1 How many German Nationals are detained abroad and what is the composition of this group?

In 2005 there were 3.100 German citizens in foreign penitentiary establishments[93], serving both short-term and long-term periods of detention. In comparison, in 2004 this figure was 2.435. However, estimates also suggest a considerable dark-figure. Overall it is assumed that the number of German nationals detained abroad has increased drastically in recent years. This rise could be accounted for by an increased urge to travel in connection with more criminal offences having been committed. One also needs to assume that these German detainees are predominantly males.

4.2   What are the main countries of detention?

More than half of these German detainees were being held in prisons of the European Union. For example, 657 Germans were detained in Spain, 364 in Great Britain, 246 in France and 150 in Poland[94]. Roughly 301 Germans were in prisons in the United States of America. German nationals can also be found in prisons in Asia, for example in Thailand, where roughly 70 are in prison[95]. Imprisonments are also known to have occurred in Africa.

4.3   What are the main reasons for detention (e.g. drugs) and what sentences do they receive?

Due to a lack of relevant data and information it is difficult to determine which criminal offences were perpetrated. It is, however, evident that drugs-offences play a significant role. Furthermore, it is likely that offences concerning personal injury, property- and sex-crimes are included. It is also probable that there are German nationals in administrative detention awaiting expulsion/removal. Overall, the majority are likely to be in prison due to fines or being sentenced to deprivation of liberty. However, in some countries there is the possibility of being sentenced to death. Contemporarily, there are four Germans on Death Row in the United States, and a further six in Kenya, the Lebanon, Thailand, Taiwan and in the Philippines[96]. The situation becomes increasingly problematic in cases

---

[92]   ibid. 2004, p. 46.
[93]   see http://presseportal.de/story.htx?firmaid=61201.
[94]   see http://presseportal.de/story.htx?firmaid=61201.
[95]   see *Neef* and *Novy* 2004, p. 155.
[96]   see http://presseportal.de/story.htx?firmaid=61201.

of torture. Moreover, the Foreign Offices in Tunisia, in Egypt and in Syria are looking into cases in which Germans were possibly tortured during their period of detention. A detained national in Brazil is said to have died as a result of having been tortured while in detention.

4.4 Which organisations are involved and what are their responsibilities and activities?

The German Embassy is responsible for caring with and supporting German nationals – especially those detained in penitentiary establishments – in the respective countries. § 5 I of the Consular Act (*Konsulargesetz;* KonsularG) stipulates that in the case of emergencies German citizens are entitled to aid and assistance from the German Embassy. § 7 of the Consulate Act states that the responsible consulate officers are to give support – most importantly legal protection - to those German pre-trial- and criminal detainees who request such aid.

In general, the authority responsible for making the arrest should give the suspect the opportunity to contact the German Embassy. A number of countries are even obliged to do so under the Vienna Convention[97]. The primary duties stated in § 7 KonsularG are the provision of an initial legal counselling session and a German-speaking lawyer. It is also often the embassy that informs relatives of an arrest.

It is not a matter of course for an employee of the embassy to observe the proceedings. Such an assignment is however at the discretion of the embassy, and is / should be made in cases in which nationals are facing punishments that – in comparison to our legal understanding – are disproportionately severe. Experience has shown that criminal proceedings are generally conducted more thoroughly when observed by a foreign diplomat[98]. There is also the possibility of financial support, for example by covering the costs of the trip back to Germany. However, financial support from the German State is subsidiary to the detainees / suspect's own financial means[99]. Also, the recipient is obliged to rebate any disembursements as stated in § 5 V KonsularG.

The German Department for Foreign Affairs (*Auswärtiges Amt*) has issued a leaflet with the respective information (also available in the internet). Most prominently, it recommends that German Nationals who are being detained should urge the police that they be allowed to inform the respective German consulate or embassy.

4.5 Who is responsible for the reception in the home country alter release?

Should a German national be extradited prior to having served the full sentence abroad, then he must, in general, serve the sentence in a German penitentiary establishment in accordance with respective existing extradition treaties, thus handing the case over to the court or to the Public Prosecution Office[100].

---

[97] see *Neef* and *Novy* 2004, p. 157.
[98] see *Neef* and *Novy* 2004, p. 157.
[99] Ibid. 2004, p. 159.
[100] see *Neef* and *Novy* 2004, p. 158.

4.6 What kind of aftercare is provided and how is this organised?

Support for nationals who have been held in a foreign prison is generally provided by non-profit organisations, human rights organisations and other similar bodies. The State itself only rarely provides aftercare.

4.7 What is the opinion of the media and general public?

This topic receives relatively sparse interest from the media, thus information is hard to come by. Rather, only dramatic individual cases that involve the possibility of the death penalty or the life imprisonment of a juvenile / young adult tend to attract public and media interest. In this respect it is difficult to determine any predominant opinions and views. The work of the embassies is partly deemed dedicated and good; however there is also room for improvement in certain areas[101].

5 EVALUATION AND RECOMMENDATIONS

In Germany, as in many other European countries, foreigners are overrepresented in prisons. Particular problems emerged in the late 1980s and early 1990s, when the proportion of foreigners increased considerably. Since then the situation has stabilized or even de-escalated by a reduction in the number of foreign prisoners. Their overrepresentation can partly be explained by some groups of younger and more violent foreign offenders compared to the German population. However, empirical research has also revealed that particularly those foreign offenders who have not yet been granted a right of residence according to the German immigration laws are also discriminated by the justice system. Alternative sanctions are less often used than for foreigners with a right of residence and still less than for German residents.

The legal situation of foreigners in prison is not all that different from that of German prisoners. However, they are regularly excluded from relaxations of the prison regime (prison leaves, work release etc.), particularly if they are to be expelled after serving their prison sentence. Some federal states (Länder) provide language courses for foreign prisoners, but the majority of states does not provide specific programmes for foreigners. Foreigners are not disadvantaged regarding internal leisure time and other programmes. The very problems of foreign prisoners result from the more and more restrictive immigration laws, which constitute an obligatory or at least regular expulsion of foreigners if they have committed a crime resulting in an unconditional prison sentence. This is particularly problematic as the traditional German law (until 1999) created severe difficulties for the naturalization of foreign residents, even when they have lived in Germany for years or generations.

The situation of foreign asylum seekers or illegal residents who are detained under administrative law is even more problematic. They are sometimes detained in departments of normal prisons, sometimes in separate detention centres of the ministries of interior. In both cases the protection of human rights and the living conditions in general

---

[101] see Neef/Novy, ZfStrVO 2004, issue 3, p.157; http://presseportal.de/story.htx?firmaid=61201

have to be criticized. The most extreme cases (Frankfurt am Main airport, Eisenhütten-stadt detention centre) have even been a case for the Torture Committee of the Council of Europe. These examples confirm the importance of the work of the CPT, especially when concerning such un-visible groups such as foreigners who are to be expelled for whom subsequently filed appeals are basically pointless. One can suspect that their circumstances would not have improved had the visits and follow-up visits described above not been conducted.

In criminal policy, efforts to enable a quicker transfer of foreign criminal prisoners to their home country without the prisoners' assent are beginning to emerge. This thwarts the notion by which transfers were originally meant just to provide better prospects of rehabilitation. This in itself was the reason why such transfers were subject to the prisoners' consent / application. This, too, exemplifies the problems that foreigners face who actually have their roots in Germany. The soon to be passed law on the creation of the premises for the ratification of the supplementary agreement on the European Convention on the Transfer of Sentenced Persons (currently in the closing stages of legislation, see above) is a real step backwards.

Furthermore, it is lamentable that the courts apparently bear so little knowledge of how to evaluate the harshness of the detention experienced abroad, which can in turn result in non-uniform and possibly unfair rulings.

Chapter 11

Greece

M. Akritidou
A. Antonopoulou
A. Pitsela

1 INTRODUCTION

1.1 Overview of Penalties and Measures

The Greek penal system is based on custodial sanctions. According to the Greek Penal Code (hereinafter: PC), the main penalties are the following categories of deprivation of liberty:

Detention is the deprivation of liberty that involves a minimum duration of one day and a maximum of one month (Article 55 PC). In special cases, the maximum duration of detention can be increased to six months (Article 94 paragraph 1 PC). This type of penalty is provided for contraventions (Article 18 PC). It is rarely served since it is usually suspended or converted into a pecuniary sentence (fine).

Imprisonment is a deprivation of liberty for at least ten days and for a maximum term of five years (Article 53 PC). Any offence punishable by imprisonment is a misdemeanour (Article 18 PC). This penalty, as a rule, is usually suspended or converted into other non-custodial sanctions (pecuniary penalty or community service). In special cases, the maximum duration of imprisonment can be raised to ten years (Article 94 paragraph 1 PC).

Confinement in a penitentiary institution can either be incarceration for life or for a period between five and 20 years (Article 52 PC). This sanction is provided for felonies (Article 18 PC). In special cases, the maximum duration of temporary confinement in a penal institution can be increased to 25 years (Article 94 paragraph 1 PC). According to the penal law about conditional release (Article 105 PC), life confinement actually ranges between 16 and 20 years. Confinement in a penitentiary for an indeterminate period is provided for habitual recidivists (Article 90 and 91 PC). It should be noted, however, that in practice confinement in a penitentiary for an indeterminate period has never been imposed. Confinement in a young offender institution for juveniles between 13 and 18 years of age (Article 54 PC) is a *sui generis* form of imprisonment served in special institutions. Confinement in a psychiatric institution is imposed on (dangerous) offenders with limited imputability (Article 37 et. seq. PC).

Pecuniary sanctions are also central penalties, which exist in two forms: proper pecuniary penalties (150.00-15,000.00 Euros) and fines (29.00-590.00 Euros). They are directly imposed only about 5% of the convicted persons (see Table 7). For some specific offence types, the PC and special penal laws provide that the pecuniary sanctions can also be imposed additionally to the sanctions of deprivation of liberty.

Greek Penal Law provides for a number of non-custodial sanctions that are not main penalties, but which are essentially alternatives to serving custodial sentences. Firstly, custodial sanctions not exceeding one year (detention, imprisonment) can be converted into pecuniary sanctions (Article 82 paragraph 1 PC). As a rule, the court also orders the conversion of imprisonment up to one year but less than two years unless the defendant is a recidivist and the court finds that the sentence must not be converted. Sentences to imprisonment for more than two but less than three years can also be converted if the court adjudges this as appropriate (Article 82 paragraph 2 PC). Community service is legally provided for in two forms and by two different kinds of legislation. Firstly, a sentence to imprisonment for two up to three years can be converted into community service at the stage when the sentence of imprisonment is imposed. In addition – at the same stage - community sentences can be served as a further conversion of imprisonment sentences that have already been converted into pecuniary penalties (Article 82 paragraph 6 PC). Secondly, community service can also be imposed as an alternative measure for prisoners who are already serving a sentence of imprisonment that had initially been converted into a pecuniary sentence, but which was in fact never paid (Article 64 of the Penitentiary Code). Community service is granted on the condition that the person convicted requests or accepts the conversion of his/her sentence. This measure was first instituted at the very beginning of the 1990s and is still applied only very sparingly.

The suspension of a sentence – either with or without supervision (probation) - is also not considered a main sentence according to the PC. Suspension (Article 99 and 100 PC) is imposed on the majority of sentences of up to three years[1] under the condition that the convicted person has not been previously convicted to a sentence longer than six months. Suspension of sentence with supervision is imposed on sentences from three to five years (Article 100A PC). However, due to a lack of technical and human resources (i.e. because probation officers for adults have not been hired as yet), this institution is not enforced. Through the wide application of converting sentences to imprisonment into pecuniary sanctions and the less often applied suspension of sentences, every year only four convicted offenders out of 100 actually serve their sentence in prison[2].

The following supplementary penalties are provided and imposed alongside the main penalties: the deprivation of civil rights (Articles 59-66 PC); The prohibition to exercise a profession that requires special permission from the authority (Article 67 PC); the publication of the sentence (Article 68 PC); the expulsion of a foreigner (Article 74 PC); the confiscation of instruments or products of an offence (Article 76 paragraph 1 PC).

In addition to these supplementary penalties that are provided by the PC and rarely imposed, special penal laws also provide for other supplementary penalties, such as the withdrawal of a driving license (Articles 103 and 106 of Code of Traffic regulations - Law 2696/1999), or the temporary or permanent suspension of a license to operate a business. The PC includes not only penalties but also *security measures* irrespective of the imputability of the defendant in order to protect the public order. Security measures are provided either as substitutes for main penalties for persons who are not criminally responsible, or in addition to penalties for persons who *are* criminally responsible. The security measures consist of:

- *Custody of offenders in a public therapeutic institution.* This measure is applied to convicts who, due to mental illness or deafness/muteness, cannot be punished for a criminal offence that they have committed but who still pose a threat to public safety (Article 69 PC). Its application is rare.

- *Committal of alcoholics and drug addicts to a therapeutic institution* (Article 71 PC). This security measure has never been imposed, primarily because appropriate therapeutic institutions have not yet been established. Since 2002, a pilot program has been running in a therapeutic institution for drugs addicts, not as a security measure but rather as a treatment programme for convicts serving their sentence.

- Offenders whose acts may be attributed to laziness or to a tendency towards vagrancy and irregular life can be *referred to a workhouse* (Article 72 PC). This measure has also never been applied. Furthermore, its character is not in accordance to the Greek

---

[1]   Up to two years the suspension is obligatory. Up to three years, the court has the possibility to suspend the sentence.

[2]   This finding is based on data on the period 1980-1996.

Constitution. According to Article 22 paragraph 4 of the Greek Constitution "any form of compulsory work is prohibited"[3].

- *The prohibition of residence in certain areas* as well as the notification of the place of residence (Article 73 PC).
- *The expulsion of a foreigner* (Article 74 PC).
- *The confiscation of instruments or products of an offence* (Article 76 paragraph 2 PC);
- These two last security measures, mainly expulsion of foreign criminals upon their release from prison, are often imposed.

Pre-trial detention is a measure of penal procedure that is decreed in order to ensure the attendance of the accused person in court. It is provided only for persons accused of having committed a felony (crime punishable by law with confinement in a penitentiary for between five and 20 years or for life), and only under conditions that are restricted by the law (Article 282 Code of Penal Procedure). In practice, this measure is imposed in the majority of felony cases. Pre-trial detention for juveniles (13 to 18 years of age) is provided only for persons accused of having committed a felony punishable by law with confinement in a penal institution for between ten and 20 years or for life.

1.2 Overview of the Prison System

1.2.1 Organisational Structure

According to the provisions of Chapter 14 of the Code of Basic Rules for the Treatment of Prisoners on the prison staff and its duties (Law 1851/1989) - the only chapter which has not been nullified by the Penitentiary Code in force (Law 2776/1999) - the organisation of the prison administration includes a Governor, social work service, health service (including a medical doctor, a dentist, a psychologist, nurses etc.), the administration or secretariat, a number of correctional officers (guards) supervised by a chief correctional officer, and the necessary technicians and other staff (see Article 97). Prison institutions are administrated by Governors who are accountable to the Direction of Crime Prevention and Correctional Treatment of Juveniles and to the Direction of Correctional Treatment of Adults of the Ministry of Justice[4]. The health and social work staff is also accountable to the relevant directions of the Ministry of Justice. Teachers and other educational personnel are provided by the Ministry of Education and accountable to the relevant direction of the Ministry. Certain institutions are staffed with additional specialised personnel, e.g. the psychiatric hospital for inmates with psychiatric staff, the agricultural prisons with specialists in Agriculture.

The Greek Prison System comprises 30 institutions of various kinds that are dispersed all over the country. They are all run by central government, more specifically by the Ministry of Justice. According to Article 19 of the Penitentiary Code, the Greek prison system consists of: a) general institutions of detention b) special institutions and c) therapeutic institutions. The general institutions are categorized into type A institutions for pre-trial detention, people detained for debts and inmates sentenced to short-term im-

---

[3]   for the English text of the Greek Constitution see
www.parliament.gr/english/politeuma/syntagma.pdf.
[4]   Presidential Decree 36/2000, Organisation of the Ministry of Justice.

prisonment, and type B for the remaining inmates (Article 11 of the Penitentiary Code). Women are held in separate sections of male institutions or in the only closed prison for females (Article 13 of the Penitentiary Code) in Korydallos. Special institutions include those for juveniles (Article 12 of the Penitentiary Code) and the semi-open prisons (Article 19 of the Penitentiary Code). The Ministry of Justice, in practice, distinguishes five categories of penitentiary institutions: agricultural prisons, correctional institutions for minors, closed prisons, therapeutic institutions and judicial prisons.

The composition of the prison population in Greece on 16 June 2005 is shown in the tables below.

Table 1: agricultural prisons for adults

Location	Capacity	Number of inmates
Agya	146	231
Kassandra	300	255
Tyrintha	200	255

Table 2: correctional institutions for minors and young adults

Location	Capacity	Number of inmates
Avlona	308	242
Kassavetia (agricultural institution)	250	184
Volos	65	92

Table 3: closed prisons, one of them for females

Location	Capacity	Number of inmates
Alikarnassos	105	251
Kerkyra	160	192
Patra	343	724
Trikala	125	216
Chalkida	120	224
Korydallos for females	270	561

Table 4: therapeutic institutions

Location	Capacity	Number of Inmates
Hospital in Korydallos	60	122
Psychiatric Hospital in Korydallos	160	301
Detoxification in Theben	300	52

Table 5: judicial prisons

Location	Capacity	Number of Inmates
Thessaloniki	370	620
Ioannina	80	264
Komotini	105	239
Korydallos	640	2,194
Kos	45	86
Larissa	363	740
Nafplion	314	463
Neapolis	45	103
Amphissa	100	283
Tripolis	65	132
Chania	67	130
Chios	100	142
Corinth	60	48
Korydallos (semi-open)	38	51
Malandrino	280	269

As of June 2005, 9,598 inmates (adults and juveniles) were detained in the prison system, while there were only 5,584 available places. Thus, it is observed that the occupancy rate in Greek prisons amounts to 172%. As far as the state budget for the prison system is concerned, the estimations - according to the information of the Greek Ministry of Justice - are as follows: 86,127,319.00 € for the year 2003, 96,398,000.00 € for the year 2004, 103,150,000.00 € for the year 2005, 104,460,000.00 € for the year 2006. Two thirds of the estimated funds go to the state employees of the correctional services.

Regarding the prison staff, 3,836 public servants work in Greek prisons today, despite the fact that the Ministry of Justice provides that the total necessary number for covering the needs of the Greek Prison System should be 7,062; thereby, only roughly 54.3% of the necessary posts are covered. It is worth noting that there are only 16 doctors (out of 76 that are deemed necessary), one criminologist (of a recommended 13) and four psychologists (out of 48 that the Ministry considers necessary). The great majority of the prison staff is guards; 2,076 guards for internal supervision and 1,246 guards for external safekeeping, while the recommended numbers given by the Ministry of Justice are 3,024 and 3,040, respectively. Thus, out of the total number of prison staff that is provided as needful by the Ministry, 42.8% should work in internal supervision and 43.0% in external safekeeping. The corresponding percentages of the actual situation, though, are 54.4% and 32.4%, respectively.

All prison personnel have the obligation to attend special educational seminars during the first two years of work in a penal institution. Furthermore, the training needs of the prison staff may be covered by several training programmes provided by the Institute of Durable Education of the National School of Public Administration[5], or by other spe-

---

5   www.ekdd/ESDD/esdd.htm

cial programmes organised by the Ministry of Justice - as long as the respective funds are available[6].

The Greek prison system it is monitored both directly and indirectly, through the Greek Ombudsman or the Body of Inspection and Control of Detention Establishments respectively. The Greek Ombudsman is a constitutionally established Independent Authority that was founded in October 1998 and operates under the provisions of Law 3094/2003. The Ombudsman provides its services to the public free of charge and received more than 41,865 complaints during its first five years in operation (from October 1st 1998 to December 31st 2002). The Greek Ombudsman investigates individual administrative actions or omissions or material actions taken by government departments or public services that infringe upon the personal rights or that violate the legal interests of individual or legal entities. The aim of the Greek Ombudsman is to mediate between public administration and private individuals, in order to protect the citizens' rights, ensuring compliance with the rule of law, observing the rule of law and combating maladministration. In addition, the objectives of the Greek Ombudsman include the protection and promotion of the rights of the child and migrants. The Ombudsman does not have the power to impose sanctions or to annul any illegal actions of public administration. The complaints that citizens submit are investigated in terms of thematic categories, which correspond to five different areas of activity in the institution:
- The Human Rights Department
- The Health and Social Welfare Department
- The Quality of Life Department
- The State-Citizen Relations Department, and
- The Children's Rights Department

Many times prisoners have submitted complaints to the Ombudsman about the conditions and the violation of human rights in Greek prisons. As a result of these complaints, the Ombudsman has visited a number of institutions of detention and has pointed out the declinations of the reality in Greek prisons in comparison to the directions and provisions of the law. The most recent example of such research is described in the Annual Report of the year 2005, where problems with the regular leaves and the social reintegration of prisoners are underlined. Even though the Greek Ombudsman is a relatively new authority, its operation is considered very important and its overall role in the relations between the state and its citizens is estimated as being very positive. It is worth mentioning that a large proportion of the complaints that this authority receives are filed by foreign persons living in the county. For this reason, a special section for the rights of migrants offers its services to foreign nationals in the Human Rights Department.

The Body of Inspection and Control of Penitentiary Institutions (Article 3 Law 3090/2002) acts under the direct supervision of the General Secretary of the Ministry of Justice, and has the following goals: (a) To conduct regular and irregular controls any time of the day in order to confirm the conditions of detention, the maintenance of order, and the observance of safety measures in the penitentiary institution. In addition, the Body inspects the application of the arrangements of the Penitentiary Code and the

---

[6]   As far as it concerns the prison staff, the Direction of Correctional Treatment of Adults of the Greek Ministry of Justice has provided us with the relevant information. For our investigation, the general support of the responsible officers of the Ministry of Justice has been valuable.

proper implementation of the regulations of the penitentiary institution. (b) To research and to hunt down ex *officio any crime* that takes place in penitentiary institutions in the entire country. Furthermore, the Body selects, analyses and exploits the information and elements that document these actions. In every case the results of the investigation are compiled in a written report. Additionally, every year in December a report with observations and recommendations for the improvement of the organisation and the function of the penitentiary institution is submitted to the General Secretary of the Ministry of Justice.

1.2.2 Foreign Prisoners

Before the 1990s, less than 20% of the prison population were not Greek nationals. Nowadays, in the year 2006, more than 40% of the prison population in Greece are foreign prisoners, mostly Albanians, followed - at a great distance - by nationals from the former USSR, Iraq, Rumania, Turkey etc.

Table 6 shows the augmentative trend of their proportion over the last 20 years.

Table 6: Proportion of foreign prisoners in Greek penitentiary institutions in selected years

Year	%
1986	17,7
1990	20,9
1996	35,6
2000	48,4
2005	41,0

Source: Council of Europe. Penological Information Bulletin, No. 10 (1987), 28; No. 12 (1988), 22; Nos. 13 & 14 (1989); No. 15 (1990), 16.; No. 16 (1992), 28; No. 17 (1992) 23, No. 18 (1993), 20; No. 21 (1998), 67; No. 22 (2000), 25, 63; No. 23 & 24 (2002), 72. The data for the year 2005 has been provided by the Direction of Correctional Treatment of Adults of the Greek Ministry of Justice.

This high percentage becomes even more impressive if one considers the fact that foreigners account for only approximately 10% of the general population in Greece as well as of the total number of criminal suspects (excluding traffic offences). Many reasons can be referred to in order to explain this impressive change of the composition of the prison population. The most important reason seems to be the high level of immigration of the 1990s after the geopolitical changes in Europe and the Middle East. Additionally, the age and gender composition of the migrants of the last 15 years have been in line with those most commonly attributed to being liable to and active in criminal activities. The vast majority of them are men between 17 an 50 years of age, and among some nationalities, such as Iraqi, Afghan and Pakistani, there is an impressive absence of women. Furthermore, the social living conditions , concentration in big urban centres, ghettoization, social exclusion, xenophobia of the host society, and prejudice on behalf of the police and criminal justice are some of the factors that contribute not only to the rise of crime attributed to foreigners but also to the punitiveness of the administration of justice. Last, but not least, procedural problems like for example the fact that the migrants do not always have a lawyer or witnesses for their defence make their convictions before criminal courts more often in comparison to Greek offenders. There are no specific establishments for the detention of foreigners; thereby, they are not separated from the other prisoners. Rarely, they are detained in separated wings of the prisons: because of some incidents between Greek and Albanian prisoners in Neapolis, for example, the administration of this prison has decided to keep foreign prisoners in a special wing. The only exception to the unity of penitentiary establishments between Greek and foreign prisoners is the penitentiary institution for young prisoners at Volos, where only young foreigners are detained. The prison staff of this institution is very impressed by the special abilities of young prisoners to quickly learn the Greek language. Theoretically, the prison staff should be afforded with programmes that aim to improve their understanding of the hardships and cultural backgrounds of the prisoners. In practice, however, no special training programme is provided to the prison staff.

1.3 Overview of the Involvement of Consulates, Embassies, Ministries and the Probation Service of Greece, NGOs etc.

Upon their admission into a penal establishment foreign prisoners will be informed of their rights, obligations and of the regulations. They shall be provided with the relevant informative printed matter in a language that they understand (Article 24 paragraph 2 of the Penitentiary Code). They have the right to contact their embassies as well the right to procure information about the possible help that can be provided to them by the competent authorities (Article 52 paragraph 6 of the Penitentiary Code). If a foreign prisoner wishes to seek help from diplomatic or consular representatives, and this help includes procedures concerning social re-integration in case of release, the diplomatic authorities must be informed at once about these requests. An information pamphlet with the address and the phone number of the closest embassy/consulate must be provided to the foreign prisoner upon his/her admission into the penitentiary institution.

Furthermore, the prison authorities in cooperation with NGOs (organisations that are responsible for providing help in the area of rehabilitation) must give their special attention to the foreign prisoners (see Article 52 paragraph 2 of the Penitentiary Code). The latter shall be informed about the help that can be provided to them through the NGOs, and prison authorities have to ensure access to this information as well as making contact with the above organisations. The prison authorities are also obliged to facilitate visits by and correspondence with the NGOs so that the foreign inmate can avail himself/herself of their help, of course so long as the inmate agrees to this. In practice however, members of NGOs often denounce the Greek Prison management's unwillingness and lack of flexibility regarding their intention of visiting penal institutions and prisons in order to communicate with foreign prisoners. The Greek Ombudsman has criticized the Greek Prison System many times for this bad practice [7].

---

[7] For example, the 28 November 2002 letter to the Ministry of Public Order- number of protocol 12393.02.1.

1.4 Overview of trends

1.4.1 Sentencing Trends

The following statistics in table 7 give a general and representative image of the sentences imposed in Greece for the years 1996[8] and 2001:

Table 7: Offenders sanctioned for misdemeanours or felonies according to the type of sanction in Greece for the years 1996 and 2001

Sanctions	1996		2001	
	Convicted persons N	%	Convicted persons N	%
Imprisonment for up to one year (usually suspended or converted)	71,830	82.66	48,043	81.07
Imprisonment 1-5 years	4,673	5.38	3,073	5.19
Pecuniary sentence (imposed as such)	4,648	5.35	3,902	6.58
Temporary confinement in a penitentiary	472	0.55	369	0.62
Confinement for life in a penitentiary	44	0.05	22	0.04
Confinement in a psychiatric institution	17	0.02	31	0.05
Confinement in a young offender institution	164	0.19	88	0.15
Educational/therapeutic measures (only for minors)	5036	5.79	3,555	6.00
Non reported sentence	8	0.01	179	0.30
Total	86,892	100	59,262	100

Source: National Statistical Service of Greece. Statistics of Justice 1996. Table B:19. www.statistics.gr, Table VII:12.

During the 1980s, only a small proportion of offenders were actually admitted to prison which resulted in a general decrease of the prison population in accordance to the general trend of de-institutionalization in Europe. In the decade that followed, despite the introduction of more lenient legislation this proportion increased. Notwithstanding of the wide application of the institutions of suspension of sentence and of conversion of custodial into pecuniary sanctions ("front-door" strategy) as well as conditional release

---

[8]   The year 1996 was the last year in which data on the number of convictions and the type of the sanctions imposed were published by the National Statistical Service of Greece. See the website: www.statistics.gr

("back-door" strategy) that targeted the solution of the prison overcrowding problem, the population in penitentiary institutions remained at a high level. This general increase in the prison population is partly related to the increase in the committal of particular offences. More specifically, while the total number of crimes recorded by the police showed a slight increase, there was a dramatic increase in particular offences, e.g. drug offences and robberies. Drugs, some forms of organised crime, clandestine immigration and the exploitation of women became a social issue after 1990. The augmentative trend in the number of prisoners is furthermore associated with the increasing proportion of foreigners among convicted offenders and pre-trial detainees in the last 15 years, as well as with the increase in the overall number of suspects actually being held in pre-trial detention.

Since the turn of the millennium, despite the fact that the proportion of convicted offenders who are given sentences that can be converted to pecuniary ones is quite high, as well as the ample use of conditional release, the prison population has continued to increase. The detention rate in Greece doubled between 1980 and 2001. In 1980 there were 41 prisoners per 100,000 inhabitants, while in 2001 the figure had increased to 79 prisoners per 100,000.

Table 8: Total number of prisoners in Greek penitentiary institutions in selected years

Year	Prisoners = n
1980	3,419
1986	3,780
1990	4,747
1996	5,304
2000	8,038
2005	9,598

Source: Council of Europe. Penological Information Bulletin, No. 2, 1983, 17, 25; No. 4, 1984, 34; No 5, 1985, 23; No. 6, 1985, 25; No. 8, 1986, 22; No. 15 (1990), 11 ff.; No. 16 (1992), 28 f.; No. 17, 23; No. 18, 18 ff.; No 21, 1998, 64. Data from the Greek Ministry of Justice.

The state's responses to the abrupt social changes and changes in crime patterns since 1990 are ongoing. Personnel and resources of the criminal justice system are constantly increasing. The same is also true with respect to selection, hiring and education of police personnel, members of the judiciary - public prosecutors included - and correctional staff. However, the number of prosecutors and correctional staff that actually work is still low because of the great number of vacant posts.

1.4.2 Characteristics of the Foreign Prison Population

Table 9: Characteristics of the prison population on 16.6.2005:

Prison capacity	5,584
Total number of prisoners	9,598
(Prisoners convicted and untried)	
Untried prisoners	2,725
Foreign prisoners	3,934 (40.98%)
Female prisoners	602
Young prisoners	366
Detained for drug law violations	3,952

Table 10: Convicted prisoners according to the kind and duration of the deprivation of liberty in Greece on 16 of June 2005

penalties of liberty deprivation	*Convicted prisoners = n*	%
Life confinement	620	9.2
Temporary confinement	(3,947)	(58.3)
a) 5-10 years	1,838	27.2
b) 10-15 years	1,170	17.3
c) more than 15 years	939	13.9
Imprisonment	(2,198)	(32.5)
a) up to 6 months	324	4.9
b) 6-12 months	297	4.4
c) 1-2 years	459	6.8
d) 3-5 years	1,118	16.5
Total number	6,765	100

Source: Data of the Ministry of Justice.

Until the 1990s Greece was a homogeneous society: 99% of the population had Greek as a mother tongue and 98% were of the Greek Christian Orthodox religion, 1% were Muslims and 1% were of other religious denominations. After 1990, an influx of refugees and (clandestine) immigrants began, predominantly from countries of Central and Eastern Europe. Thus, Greece developed from a country of emigration to a country of immigration, and was totally unprepared for the reception of immigrants. Neither the relevant legislation nor the required social structure and institutions existed. Hence, the exact figure of illegal immigrants or the total number of non-nationals is unknown.

The Ministry of Labour estimates this number to be roughly 500,000-600,000, while the U.S. Department of State sees it as being closer to 1,000,000. In January 1998 a legislation process for clandestine immigrants was initiated and as of June 1999 approximately 50,000 green cards were granted, while the Greek government planned to issue another 200,000 approximately by the end of 1999. Once again, on 2001 a great number of clandestine immigrants received a green card. During the year 2005, another effort for their regularisation took place, and they were allowed to apply for a green card under some specific conditions named in the new Foreigners Act[9]. The bureaucratic process has not yet been completed. It is estimated that the total number of migrants who shall be issued a green card will not be more than 40,000 to 60,000 (out of more than 100,000 applications). However, due to the geographical position of the county, its enormous coastline, land boundaries and the political situation in the region, there is a continuous influx and outflow of people. The most important nationalities represented among foreigners in Greece are people coming from Russia (although many of them of Greek origin) and Albania, Egypt, Poland, Ukraine, Iraq, Palestine, the Philippines, Nigeria, Pakistan, etc.

1.5 Overview of National Penitentiary Legislation

1.5.1 Penitentiary Legislation

In theory, a shield with various layers of protective legislative provisions covers the body of prisoners in Greek custodial institutions. The first layer compromises provisions of the Greek Constitution (hereinafter: GC) that refer to the human rights of i) Greeks and ii) any person living within the Greek territory. Needless to say, the most fundamental right of every human being is the respect of his/her dignity, even if he/she is deprived of liberty (Article 2 paragraph 1 and Article 5 paragraph 1 of the GC). The second layer of protection is provided by the European Convention of Human Rights (hereinafter: ECHR) and its First, Fourth, Sixth, Seventh and Eighth Protocols that Greece has signed and ratified. According to Article 28 paragraph 1 of the GC all of these ratified international norms constitute an integral part of national law, prevailing over any contrary national legal provisions (other than the GC). The ECHR, like the GC, makes no explicit statement on the rights of prisoners. Yet, the European Court of Human Rights, as already pointed out, guarantees the application of the ECHR to convicted individuals as well. The third and most direct layer protecting persons serving custodial sanctions is constituted by the Greek Penitentiary Code, which replaced the older Code of Basic Rules for the Treatment of Prisoners (except for Chapter 14 on staff duties that still remains). This code, enacted in 1999, contains 14 chapters and 87 Articles and aims at safeguarding the human dignity of detained persons on the one hand, and the orderly function of custodial institutions on the other, by regulating the rights and duties of the prisoners.

Under the prevailing legislative norms, detained persons in Greece, therefore, enjoy three sets of rights stemming from: i) the GC, ii) the ECHR and iii) the Penitentiary Code. Taking a closer look at the human rights protected by the Penitentiary Code, it should be pointed out that functional theorists of Constitutional Law share the widespread opinion that persons deprived of their liberty upon a lawful sanction during the execution of their sentence retain all human rights (Article 4 Penitentiary Code) except

---

[9]   Art. 90 paragraph 11 of Law 3386/2005.

for that of personal liberty (free movement). The basic safeguarded prisoners rights— in accordance to Article 3 about the equal treatment of prisoners and Article 6 about the legal protection of prisoners of the Penitentiary Code - are: the right to make written complaints to the Prison Council first and then to the — never established — Court of Execution of Sentences (in the meantime, however, the Misdemeanours Court Council of the area where the sentence is executed performs this duty); the right to communicate in writing with any public authority and the prison administration has the corresponding duty to expedite the communication without delay and without inspecting its content; the right to satisfy the prisoners' religious needs and customs with no discrimination for of any reason. It should also be added that obligatory/forced work is absolutely forbidden according to the GC (Article 22 paragraph 3 GC), a provision which also encompasses work in prison.

Furthermore, prisoners have the right to be represented by an advocate in disciplinary hearings. In Greek prisons, in principle, there are no prohibitions against receiving books and newspapers (however at the prisoners' own expense). Prisoners may also purchase various goods from the prison shop. Detained persons may also be visited by a physician or a psychiatrist of their choice under certain circumstances. Finally, the GC and the Greek Code of Penal Procedure recognizes a prisoner's right to compensation in case of unlawful detention, a right which is seldom exercised and even more rarely satisfied.

The last and most recent shield of protection lies in the European Convention for the Prevention of Torture and Inhuman and Degrading Treatment or Punishment that Greece ratified in 1991 (Law 1949/1991). Among others, the so-called anti-torture Convention in Article 1 provides for a European Committee that through inspection may prevent or correct breaches of human rights in the context of imprisonment.

1.5.2 Penitentiary Legislation and Foreigners

Foreign prisoners have the same legal position, legal rights and obligations as national prisoners (Article 3 Penitentiary Code). According to the Law 1708/1988[10] it is possible for foreign prisoners to be transferred to their country in order to serve the remainder of their term if:
- the country has signed a convict transfer agreement with Greece or has acceded to the current convict transfer agreement of the European Council;
- they are nationals of the country to which they request to be transferred;
- the sentencing judgement is irrevocable or they have waived all legal remedies (appeals, etc.);
- the sentence they shall continue serving in their country, after their transfer, shall not be greater that the one imposed in Greece;
- the remainder of their term in Greece is not be less than six months, and
- their country consents to such a transfer.

Until recently, foreign prisoners rarely, or never, availed themselves of the possibility of being transferred to a prison in their own country, possibly because living conditions in the prisons of Greece are better than those in their home country. In the meantime,

---

[10] This law ratified the European Convention for the Transfer of Prisoners of 1983.

more and more foreign prisoners – mainly from Albania – have begun to express a desire to serve their penalty in their own country. While inmate relationships are developed among prisoners of the same ethic group, foreign prisoners do not seem to interact either positively or negatively with Greek prisoners. There have of course been some incidents between Greek and Albanian prisoners – like for example in Neapolis, at it mentioned above - that force the administration to keep them separated.

2 TREATMENT OF FOREIGN PRISONERS

2.1 General Information

In responding to section 2 appropriately, for the theoretical part the writers used the Internal Operation Regulation of General Detention Establishments of Type A and B[11] (hereinafter: Internal Regulation), in accordance with the similar Articles of the Penitentiary Code.

It was very difficult to provide answers to the actual situation of foreign prisoners, because information and data on this topic are very limited. The Greek law does not foresee a separation of Greek prisoners from foreign prisoners. For any prisoner, no other right than the right to personal freedom shall be limited. All prisoners may exercise the rights conferred to them by the Constitution and by the special rules of law, in person or by proxy.

2.2 Living Conditions and Facilities

Foreign prisoners have the same access to facilities and they have the same living conditions as Greek prisoners.

Every prisoner may have objects or articles of immediate and daily use that do not exceed in volume the size of a regular suitcase in his cell or in his ward, without metal foils.

2.3 Reception and Admission

The foreign prisoner will be informed upon his/her admission to the establishment by the director of the institution about his/her rights and obligations in a language he/she understands (Article 24 paragraph 2 of Penitentiary Code). If the individual does not understand any commonly known language (i.e. English, French, Spanish, etc) it is foreseen that he/she seek help from a familiar consulate. Under Article 52 paragraph 6 of the Penitentiary Code, the foreign detainee has the right to contact his/her consulate or embassy.

In addition, in case that a foreign prisoner is submitted to a disciplinary procedure because of a disciplinary offence, an interpreter must be provided if the prisoner does not speak the Greek language (Article 71 paragraph 2 of Penitentiary Code and Article 31 No. 37 of Internal Regulation).

---

[11] Ministerial Decision 58819/7.4.2003 by the Ministry of Justice. For this project the formal translation in English by the Ministry of Justice of this regulation was frequently used.

2.4 Work – Education – Training – Sports – Recreation

All prisoners have the right[12] to participate in and co-operate in educational, cultural, sporting, artistic and recreational events and other creative activities during the detention period. They can work in the establishment on their own account. More specifically, the prisoners have the right:

- To exercise under the supervision of guards and coaches for at least one hour daily, on the playing fields of the establishment or on other fields, as long as there are appropriate facilities, as well as in roofed sports facilities located outside the detention areas (Article 17 of Internal Regulation and Article 36 of Penitentiary Code about Sports). The department of social work in co-operation with the Office of Physical Education of the Prefecture Government may organise programs of group exercise for the prisoners by forming athletic teams, as long as suitable facilities exist and the smooth operation of the establishment is not jeopardized. In fact, one of the greatest problems in every detention facility in the whole of Greece is the lack of exercise facilities.

- To be informed by: a) watching television and listening to and radio programs through devices that belong either to them or to the prison service, pursuant to Article 19, paragraphs 2-4 of Internal Regulation, b) reading the daily press and magazines as well as books of their choice, subject to the condition that their content is not indecent, c) lectures and discussions by special scientists and agents, and d) any other convenient way by decision of the Prison Council (Article 18 of Internal Regulation and Article 37 of the Penitentiary Code regarding Information). A lending library shall operate in the establishment, constantly enriched at the initiative of the department of social work and the sociologist. If it is possible, the library of the establishment shall be associated with the library of the Municipality to which the establishment belongs and the operation thereof shall be defined in co-operation with a special librarian. The library shall be open all working days for at least two hours, both in the morning and in the afternoon. All prisoners shall have access thereto, as long as the communication between prisoners from different wings or departments of the establishment is precluded. In fact, there are some books available in foreign languages, yet certainly not enough to cover the needs of all foreign inmates. However, there are neither newspapers nor magazines available in foreign languages.

- To participate, if they wish, in group or individual recreational or artistic events that shall be organised by the Prison Council in a suitable indoor or outdoor part of the establishment (Article 19 of Internal Regulation and Article 38 of the Penitentiary Code on Recreation). In every cell or ward there shall be at least one television set. The operating hours shall be subject to the condition that fellow prisoners are not disturbed and no tensions are created between them. Upon decision of the Prison Council, it is also possible for a pay TV channel to be available for the projection of sports events or films of recreational or cultural content. The interested prisoners have to cover the any expenses that arise. The prisoners may use, upon inspection by the service, a small radio or private television set with earphones, in order to

---

[12] Chapter "Rights and Obligations of the Prisoners", art. 31 "Rights of the prisoners" of the Internal Operation Regulation of the General Detention Establishments of Type A and B.

avoid disturbing their fellow prisoners. The use of computers and games shall be prohibited, unless there are special educational reasons, which depends on the discretion of the Prison Council. In the detention areas the use of computers and games is strictly prohibited. There are some non-governmental organisations, such as AR-SIS[13] (Social Support of Youth), that come into prison and organise recreational activities, for example making mosaics. .

- To attend any education units operating within the detention facilities (primary school; junior high school; second opportunity school) or secondary and tertiary education establishments or vocational training institutions outside the detention facilities through educational leaves (Article 20 of Internal Regulation and Article 35 of the Penitentiary Code concerning Education, Vocational Training and Work of the prisoners). In every establishment, education and vocational training programs for small groups of prisoners shall be organised in co-operation with special training centres, under the supervision of the department of social work, the sociologist and the Educational Council. In any case, at least one guard shall be present to accompany and supervise the prisoners. The Prison Council shall take care of the elaboration of programs: for example a) for illiterates, b) second opportunity school, c) for vocational training, d) foreign languages. The continuation of the prisoners' studies outside the establishment shall take place at recognized and certified educational institutions and schools in which they shall be enrolled. The enrolment and study or apprenticeship at such institutions and in schools of any degree shall be ensured by the granting of educational leaves. Good use of these leaves shall be monitored by the specialized scientific personnel and the public prosecutor-supervisor. The work of the prisoners shall be carried out in various sectors of the operation of the establishment. The posts in which prisoners may work have to be approved by the Ministry of Justice, and their work shall be supervised by the authorised employees, with beneficial counting of sentence days. It is not permitted for a prisoner to be employed in a post different from the one to which he has been officially placed. Article 35 paragraph 4 of the Penitentiary Code provides for the education of the foreign prisoners. According to this article, if it is possible special measures for their training can be taken at any establishment. In practice, however, this task seems to have been left to the few NGOs[14] that are active in the Greek prisons. The overall expenses of education and recreation of the total prison population in Greek prisons are extremely low. It is worth mentioning that during the debates of the Greek Parliament on 1 December 1999 about the Penitentiary Code, it was mentioned that the state budget for books for the prisoners in 1999 and 2000 was not more than 3,000 euro annually. Roughly the same amount was disposed for educational and for athletic material.

2.5 Food – Religion - Personal hygiene - Medical care

According to Article 14 of the Internal Regulation in accordance with Articles 35 and 39 of the Penitentiary Code:
- The state is responsible for the provision of food.

---

[13]   www.arsis.gr
[14]   With the financial support of the European Union.

All prisoners shall be served daily breakfast, lunch and dinner pursuant to the daily operation program of the establishment at the following hours: 07.30, 12.00 noon and half an hour before sunset.

- The menus shall be prepared at the end of each week by the financial department based on known dietetics programs. The content of the weekly menu must provide for dietary diversity and shall be signed by the doctor and members of the Prison Council. The observance of the program and the quality of the food shall be inspected every day by the doctor and the governor of the establishment.

Poorly prisoners shall be issued special diets that are prepared by the doctor of the establishment. If it is not possible to cover all cases that require such special dietary needs, the patients, upon recommendation by the doctor and agreed opinion of the Prison Council, shall obtain at their own expense foodstuffs from the contractual suppliers of the establishment and shall also be provided with food for religious purposes.

- Prisoners are allowed to purchase foodstuffs and other goods at their own expense (a) from the shop/canteen/buffet operating in the establishment, or (b) through the supplier who shall be appointed by tender, or, finally (c) from free trade outside of the establishment, care of the prison service. The provision shall be limited to quantities that are deemed sufficient for the covering a person's needs. Upon decision of the Prison Council, the delivery of meals and foodstuffs that can be checked easily by the personnel of the detention establishment may be permitted up to twice a month during the visits.

- The prisoners are not permitted to receive fruits from visitors.

- The quality of all of the foods (fruits, vegetables, fishes, meat etc.) shall be checked by the competent committee of collection.

- The food that the prisoners obtain and the goods that are brought into the establishment for them shall be subject to examination and search. If prohibited goods are found during such examinations and searches, they shall be retained and the fact shall be immediately reported either to the director of the establishment, to his legal substitute or to the chief guard when the former are hindered or absent.

- On the holidays of New Year, the 25th of March, Easter, the Assumption of Virgin Mary (15th of August), the 28th of October and Christmas, as well as on local national and religious holidays, the prisoners shall be permitted to consume beverages with a low alcoholic content (beer or wine). The shop-canteen or buffet of the establishment shall be paid with chips or coupons or with the use of personal booklets or cards. These chips, coupons and cards are intended to serve as means of limiting the amount of sweets, ice creams and soft drinks that prisoners can purchase. A prisoner may spend no more than 20 euros per week on these goods (Article 13, paragraph 4 of the Internal Regulation). The purchase of goods on credit is not possible.

The detainees shall be entitled to exercise their religious duties and communicate with recognized representatives of their religion and dogma. The exercise of the religious duties shall take place regularly, at the church or another suitable room of the establishment, upon decision of the Prison Council (Article 31, No. 22 of the Internal Regulation). In practice, those prisoners who do not belong to the Eastern Orthodox Christian Church seem to have very limited opportunities to perform their religious duties properly, with the exception of the followers of the Roman Catholic Church.

Article 15 of the Internal Regulation about personal hygiene and cleaning of shared areas states:

- Newly admitted prisoners shall be provided with bedding and the necessary toiletries including, soap, shaving foam, cotton, a disposable razor, toothpaste, a toothbrush and shampoo.
- Soap and toilet paper are provided by the prison service for the entire period of detention, while other toiletries are provided to indigent prisoners through the social service of the establishment.
- The prisoners may purchase personal toiletries from the shop/canteen of the establishment or from the contractual supplier of food and other goods at their own expense.
- Each prisoner is provided with a mattress, a pillow, two pillow-cases, four sheets, two face towels and two bath towels. Such Articles shall be returned to the service by the prisoner on the day of his/ her transfer from the establishment for any reason. Prisoners are allowed to use their own blankets, sheets and towels that may differ in colour from the ones provided by the service, after having previously unsown the hems. In this case the prisoner is obliged to return the relevant linen that he/she no longer requires to the prison service.
- The bedding and linen mentioned above shall be washed by working prisoners, at the laundry of the establishment under the supervision of authorised employees.
- The prisoners shall be obliged to observe the personal hygiene and cleaning conditions and to keep their clothing, blankets and living facilities clean.
- The prisoners shall be provided with hot water in the bathrooms as well as in the laundry on a daily basis. The working hours of such facilities shall be fixed by order of the day by the director of the establishment, upon recommendation of the chief guard.
- The shared areas shall be cleaned every day by the shifts of working detainee cleaners, under the supervision of authorised employees. In addition, the service shall use the appropriate disinfectants in drains and other critical points every day.

Article 16 of the Internal Regulation which concerns Medical Care and Article 44 of the same regulation concerning the duties of sanitary personnel in accordance with Articles 29 and 30 of the Penitentiary Code state the following:

1. Medical personnel, doctors and nurses, as foreseen in Articles 44-49, shall ensure medical and pharmaceutical care for the prisoners at a level corresponding to that of the rest of the population

2. In rendering its services to the prisoners the medical and nursing personnel shall utilize all information available through modern science and their professions, and shall apply the principles of ethics and deontology, relating to the practice of medicine and nursing. In fact, many of the inmates, both Greek and foreign, have complained about considerable delays in seeing a doctor. Due to staff shortages, it is almost impossible to adequately care for all of the prisoners.

2.6 Consular and legal help

According to Article 33 of the Internal Regulation about legal aid, prisoners have the following rights:
-   If the prisoner states that he/she is financially unable to exercise his/her rights to defence, specialised professional personnel of the penal establishment shall be informed, whereupon the detainee shall be requested to file an application with the supporting documents of financial need (tax returns and a statement of income from the revenue office; a certificate of financial need; certificate confirming the granting of a welfare allowance; certificate of unemployment subsidy from the Manpower Employment Organisation; records of proceedings from judicial authorities; documents from which previous appearances without a defence counsellor or ex officio appointment of a counsellor can be concluded; previous failure to comply with pecuniary penalties, etc)
-   Such an application is to be addressed to the public prosecutor-supervisor and the notes of the departments of social work and finances of the detention establishment regarding the probable indigence or financial need of the applicant are to be attached thereto.
-   The application and the relevant supporting documents are checked by the public prosecutor-supervisor (hereinafter: p.p.s.) with assistance from the specialised professional personnel of the establishment with the stipulation that either additional supporting documents (solemn statements, statements of personal accounts, etc.) be presented or, when this does not apply, they be forwarded to the competent judicial authority by the p.p.s. with relevant indication in order to examine the application for ex officio appointment of a counsellor or rendering of legal aid due to financial need. In any case effort shall be made for the application to be forwarded at least fifteen days before the investigation of the judicial act for which the ex officio appointment of a counsellor and the rendering of legal aid in general is requested.
-   The applying prisoner shall be informed of the outcome of his/her application at least fifteen days before the investigation or the date of hearing. Should the application be dismissed, he/she shall be entitled to file an appeal before the immediately higher authority within three days.

2.7 Contact with the outside world

According to Article 21 of the Internal Regulation in accordance with Article 52 of the Penitentiary Code the prisoners have the following rights concerning visits:
-   Sentenced prisoners are entitled to receive visits from spouses and relatives up to the fourth degree at least once a week, with each visit lasting a minimum of 30 minutes. The Prison Council shall set the maximum number of visits and the duration thereof.
-   Prisoners awaiting trial shall be entitled to have visits from spouses and relatives up to the fourth degree at least twice a week, with each visit lasting a minimum of 30 minutes. In exceptional cases, when the harmonious operation and the safety of the establishment as well as the smooth conduct of the investigation justify it, it is possible for restrictions to be imposed through decisions of the public prosecutor-supervisor.

- The chief guard notifies the prisoners of the dates and times of the visits as well as of any possible changes for extraordinary reasons. Notification occurs through notices that are posted in the visiting rooms as well as on the prisoners' notice board.
- Representatives of social agents, members of parliament, and members of scientific societies, cultural, religious or other associations may visit prisoners upon permission of the Prison Council. The Prison Council shall duly inform the Minister of Justice, who then decides within three days whether or not permission is to be granted. If this term expires without any action having been taken, permission is considered to have been approved.
- Foreign prisoners shall be granted the means to communicate with the diplomatic or consular representatives of their home countries. At the discretion of the Prison Council, these means shall also be granted to other persons and agents who contribute to the solution of special problems caused by detention. Such visits by prisoners shall be reported to the Ministry of Justice by the director of the establishment on the following working day, by forwarding the particulars of both the visitor and the detainee who was visited.

Foreign prisoners have the same visitation rights as Greek inmates. The only problem is that foreigners detained in Greek prisons rarely have relatives who live in the country, which in turn results in a lower number of visits actually taking place. One can infer from the CPT report of 2001 that the conditions in which visits are conducted were not satisfactory at that time. For example, the prisoners' entitlement to 30 minutes of visits per week was not always respected. Many prisoners stated (and the prison staff in fact confirmed) that they were allowed only two visits per month lasting a mere 20 minutes each. The facilities revealed shortcomings such as the fact that prisoners and visitors had to shout to make themselves heard, they could hardly see each other, and they were rarely provided with seats.

2.8 Re-integration activities - Prison leave

According to Article 24 of the Internal Regulation in accordance with Articles 54-58 of the Penitentiary Code, regarding leaves prisoners have the following entitlements and rights:
- Prisoners are to be granted regular and educational leaves by the Disciplinary Council. A special log shall be kept registering the date and time when prisoners on leave exit and return to the institution in order to check their return time. The prosecutor-supervisor, pursuant to the provisions of Article 7 paragraph 2 (3) shall grant the special leaves hereof.
- Upon returning from leaves, the prisoners shall be obligatorily searched for any possible contraband in accordance with the provisions of Article 10, paragraph 5.
- In cases of transgression of leaves, the competent judicial and police authorities as well as the Ministry of Justice shall be informed immediately.
- Every month a list containing particulars regarding: a) the submitted applications for leave, b) any form of leaves that have been granted, and c) any possible transgressions of leaves shall be sent to the Ministry of Justice.

No special activities are provided for preparing prisoners for their resettlement into society, neither for foreigners nor for nationals. There is no probation service in Greece.

In order to be granted conditional leave a prisoner must have an address in Greece. This precondition makes it very unlikely that a foreign prisoner shall be granted conditional leave for they rarely have a fixed address within the country. Theoretically, however, these leaves are still allowed. According to Article 54 paragraph 4 of the Penitentiary Code, the right to leaves cannot be annulled only due to the fact that a prisoner is foreign.

The 2005 annual report of the Greek Ombudsman states that foreign prisoners have great difficulties in actually drawing any advantage from this right. According to the report, even though the foreign prisoners theoretically do have the right to apply for leave and no discrimination issue comes up, the necessary requirements –stable residence in Greece, family ties for example - are very rarely fulfilled in their case.

2.9 Release- Expulsion

According to Article 35 of the Internal Regulation that concerns preparation for release, the prisoners have the following rights:
- From their admission into the detention establishment and during the entire period of their stay prisoners are subject to treatment that is orientated towards ensuring a fair hearing of their case if they are awaiting trial, and their adaptation into legal social life if they are convicts.
- Within the frameworks of section 1 of this Article: a) the prisoners awaiting trial shall be assisted in the preparation of their defence before the judicial authorities, b) the prisoners shall collaborate, if they so desire, with the specialised professional personnel in the design of a treatment program (participation in education, work, vocational training, special therapeutic groups, etc), in order to limit further debasement of their actual and legal status and of the position of the persons depending on them.
- The responsible authorities of the detention establishment shall ensure that all prisoners have the opportunity to be incorporated into institutions for service of sentence (participation in education, work, vocational training, therapy etc.) by which the period of detention is creatively exploited and the prisoners' bonds with the wider social environment are strengthened, especially when the time for their final or conditional release approaches.

According to Article 61 of the Internal Regulation in accordance with Articles 78 and 79 of the Penitentiary Code concerning release, the prisoners have the following rights:
- When a period of detention has been completed, the director of the establishment or his/her substitute shall be informed by the head of the administrative department and shall see to the immediate release of the prisoner. If this day coincides with a holiday or any other exceptional occasion, release shall occur on the working day prior to the initially intended day of release.
- Release occurs through the issuance of release papers from the administration department of the establishment. These papers are signed by the secretary and confirmed by the director. The reasons for detention and the duration thereof shall be stated in these release papers and a recent photo of the detainee shall be affixed.
- The prisoner shall receive a copy of the release papers and if he/she so desires, the specialised professional personnel shall inform him/her about the agencies and ser-

vices that offer support after release and he/she shall be referred accordingly. Such information may also take place after release.

Article 74 PC deals with the expulsion of foreigners and provides that if an offender sentenced to confinement in a penitentiary or to imprisonment for not less than one year is a foreigner, the court may order his expulsion from the country after final release from the penitentiary or, in (rare) cases of conditional release, immediately after his release from the penitentiary. The court may also order the expulsion of any foreigner upon whom the security measures under Article 69 PC (custody of offenders in a public therapeutic institution), 71 PC (committal of alcoholics and drug addicts into a therapeutic institution) or 72 PC (referral to a workhouse) have been imposed. In such cases, expulsion may be ordered in lieu of such measures. Foreigners who are expelled under these circumstances may return to the country three years after their expulsion, provided that the Minister of Justice grants them permission to return. If the foreign prisoner has been conditionally released according to Article 105 PC (or Article 129 PC in case that the prisoner is a juvenile), the expulsion imposed according to Article 74 takes place, unless it is infeasible (Article 105 paragraph 4 or Article 129 paragraph 5 PC). In this latter case the released foreign prisoner is not obliged to leave the country, but must only comply to the conditions imposed during his/her early release, as is also the case for released Greek prisoners.

2.10 Aftercare-Probation

There is no probation or after care service for adults in Greece. A probation service for minors has existed since 1954 (Law 2793/1954 especially as amended by Law 378/1976). By contrast, such a service for adults – although provided by Art. 100A PC introduced by Law 1941/1991 – has not been established as yet. Therefore, the law provides that until the creation of a body of probation officers for adults, supervision duties are to be exercised by the public prosecutor of the court that ordered supervised suspension of sentence (Art. 100A paragraph 8 PC).

2.11 Staff

There is no special training for the staff that specialise in the treatment of foreign prisoners. This obviously results in the impossibility to provide prison personnel capable of communicating in a language comprehended by the foreign inmates. Thus, communication of non-Greek speaking foreigners with prison staff and the public prosecutors is rarely direct. Many respondents, however, mention the assistance of informal interpreters i.e. of fellow inmates acting as mediators who facilitate communication. As in many other parts of the prison system (i.e. medical care), empirical knowledge is referred to in order to cover needs due to lack of human agents and resources. According to the prison staff, Albanian prisoners who pose the vast majority of foreign prisoners in Greece seem to have a good knowledge of the Greek language.

2.12 Projects

There are no specific projects in the penitentiary institutions. The only efforts are made by the few NGOs that have access to prison life, and these encompass all prisoners without specifically dealing with the problems of foreign prisoners. Only very few prisons offer Greek language courses.

To sum up, prison overcrowding, a negative psychological climate, pessimism, lack of confidence and difficulties in communication between prisoners and staff are some of the most important problems of prison life. The gap between prison legislation and reality and the lack of social support complete the list of the major problems that have already been stated. The multiple shields of protection offered by the international and national legal norms are not enough to adequately safeguard the fundamental rights of the prisoners. The available domestic and international mechanisms guaranteeing the enforcement of these rights involve complex and bureaucratic procedures to which the average detainee, and especially prisoners from ethnic minorities, has no easy access. As a consequence there is a great discrepancy between the law in writing and the law in action. Furthermore, the provisions of the ECHR do not specifically concern detained individuals, and therefore, these provisions, approached from the angle of prisoners' protection, are vague and set minimum standards only.

3 ADMINISTRATIVE DETENTION OF FOREIGN PRISONERS

3.1 Institutions for Administrative Detention

Any foreign person who has been arrested under an administrative decision of detention and expulsion must be detained in a special institution of detention, according to the Foreigners Act (Law 3386/2005). According to Article 81 of this law, he/she remains detained at the police station of the locality that he/she was initially detained in. Until the proceedings for his/her expulsion have been completed, he/she is to be detained in special institutions that were yet to be established – when the law was passed – by a Ministerial Decision. The same decision will define the terms of operation of these special institutions. The responsibility for these institutions lies with the Greek Police. Until today, no such decision has been made. New special institutions have not yet been added to the already existent[15] special centres for migrants (mentioned below).

3.2 Ministry Responsible and Relevant Legislation

The Ministry responsible for these detention institutions is the Ministry of Public Order and not the Ministry of Justice, as is the case for the rest of the Greek Prison System.

As a result, the Penitentiary Code and all regulations concerning prisoners in Greece do not apply to this category of foreign prisoners. The application of these rules can only be analogical. Generally, the legal status quo of foreigners from third countries[16] is regu-

---

[15] They were established with previous ministerial decisions, under the directions of the previous Foreign Act (Law 2910/2001).

[16] That means non-EU nationals.

lated by the Foreigners Act. At the beginning of the 1990s, after the great migration wave that followed the collapse of the socialist regimes of Eastern Europe, the Greek state was obliged to react by creating a completed Foreigners Act in order to organise its policy towards the massive wave of migration. The Law 1975/1991 was the first legislative reaction to this – at least for Greek society - new phenomenon, with a very restrictive character, corresponding to the general guidelines of intergovernmental agreements of the EU. Ten years later, this law was substituted by a new Foreigners Act (law 2910/2001) in an effort to correct the deficiencies and impasses of the old law. However, this law also failed to correspond, to the expectations of an effective migration policy. One year ago the new Foreigners Act was enacted. The new Law 3386/2005 is based in the same philosophy as the previous one. In general, it is considered more detailed and – in some points - more restrictive. It contains provisions that concern the entrance, stay, expulsion and detention of nationals from outside of the EU.

3.3 Capacity of Institutions for Administrative Detention

The special centres for the detention of illegal migrants are located in the following towns[17]: Chios, Lesbos, Samos, Evros, Athens (Amigdaleza and Ellinikon for women and minors), Piraeus and Thessaloniki. Since only a small number of such special centres of detention exist, every police station detention room - all over the country - constitutes *de facto* an institution of administrative detention for foreign prisoners. In practice, a vast majority of the foreign prisoners under administrative detention is kept at the police establishment of the town near which he/she had been detected and arrested by the police. No published data on the capacity of these two types of institution exist, though. Finally, ad hoc reception centres may be established in different parts of the country (more often on the islands) should a large number of illegal migrants arrive.

3.4 Length of stay

Any foreigner of a third country who has entered the country legally (with a legal visa) can stay in Greece for three months. If he has residence permission, he/she can stay for one year. This permission can be renewed for two years under very specific terms described by the law.

Any foreigner who has violated legal provisions and regulations on legal entrance and the legal stay in Greece can be detained upon an administrative decision. The maximum length of such administrative detention is three months[18]. If the foreign person is not expelled within this period, he/she must be released immediately. However, NGOs in the region state that there are a significant number of cases in which foreign prisoners are being unlawfully held in detention beyond this maximum period of three-months.

3.5 Decisions Procedure

According to the Foreigners Act (Law 3386/2005), any third country national who has violated the rules and the procedures for legal entrance into Greece and who has no

---

[17] According to the Greek Permanent Representation to EU on 18-04-2005.
[18] See art. 76 of Law 3386/2005.

valid (permanent or temporary) residence permit shall be expelled on the order of the commanding police officer authorized to this purpose by the Ministry of Public Order (decision of administrative expulsion). According to the third paragraph of article 76 of the Foreigners Act, the illegal migrant can be detained (decision of administrative detention[19]) until the expulsion has been implemented, especially if the suspect is perceived as likely to abscond or as dangerous for the public order. The Law underlines the obligation of the authorized officers to inform the foreign detainee of the reasons for his/her detention and to facilitate the communication with his/her lawyer.

In general, all registered asylum seekers cannot be arrested and detained as illegal entrants. According to a Ministerial Decision of 1992[20] (the conformity of which has been questioned in relation to the Constitution) as well as the Foreigners Act, asylum seekers who have applied for asylum after having been arrested for illegal stay in Greece, and who have been detained by an order of the police authorities because an expulsion order has been issued against them should remain in detention until a final decision on their application for asylum has been reached or until the period of their detention exceeds the maximum length of three months. If the foreigner lodges an asylum application after the issuance of the expulsion and detention order, his/her expulsion and/or any measure of return will be suspended. However, the foreigner remains in detention. After three months have passed, the asylum seeker must be released from detention if within this detention period a positive decision on his/her asylum application is not reached; if within this detention period a positive decision on his/her asylum application is reached he/she must immediately be released from detention and cannot be deported as a refugee (other than under the cessation and withdrawal grounds provided for by the Geneva Convention).

If an application for asylum is rejected during the three-month period of detention the authorities have to execute the expulsion of the detainee before the three months have expired. Otherwise, as stated above, the detainee is to be released immediately.

3.6 Appeal Procedure

According to the provisions of paragraphs 3 and 4 of Article 78 of the Foreigners Act, an appeal against the decision of administrative detention may be lodged by any detained illegal migrant or asylum seeker before the President of the First Instance Administrative Court in the area of his/her detention. Should the President consider that the detained foreigner is not a threat to public order and that there is no strong likelihood of him/her absconding, he/she is to be immediately released. In practice, only a minority of foreign prisoners - mainly those who have applied for asylum while in detention- has been released through this procedure after having claimed that they do not pose a threat to public order since their only offence was illegal entry, and that there is no strong likelihood of absconding.

---

[19] Also with an order of the Commanding Police Officer authorized to this purpose by the Ministry of Public Order.

[20] Ministerial Decision No 4803/13/7a-1992 by the Ministries of Foreign Affairs, Justice and Public Order.

3.7 Irregular stay

According to Article 83 of the Foreigners Act, any national of a third country who illegitimately crosses or attempts to cross the Greek border is punishable with a penalty of imprisonment of at least three months[21] and a pecuniary penalty of at least 1.500 euros. However, the public prosecutor of the first degree can abstain from the penal prosecution after referring to the public prosecutor of second degree (There is a form of collaboration between the two public prosecutors before the decision to abstain from prosecution is made. The public prosecutor of the first degree needs the approval of the public prosecutor of second degree). In this case, the commanding officer of the police / the coast guard service by which the foreigner had initially been detected is informed of the abandonment of prosecution. Thereupon the commanding officer orders the administrative expulsion of the foreigner. After three months - but not later than one year - if the illegal foreigner has not yet been expelled, the public prosecutor can pursue penal prosecution. The illegal stay of foreigners who have entered the county legally and whose residence permit or visa subsequently expires is not classed as a criminal offence. However, he/she must be expelled with an administrative decision.

3.8 Numbers

The exact number of foreign prisoners being held in administrative detention and awaiting expulsion is very difficult to calculate or even estimate, for a number of reasons. Firstly, the detention facilities of the police stations in which such prisoners are held also accommodate criminal suspects, persons who have been transferred to attend court proceedings or who are in transit to other establishments, as well as persons serving sentences with a total duration of up to 30 days. Secondly, a large number of foreign prisoners are expelled almost immediately within a few days of their arrest. In addition to the great fluctuation of this category of prisoners, the lack of published information on behalf of the Ministry of Public Order makes the determination of exact number of this category even more difficult.

3.9 Expulsion

The vast majority of the foreign persons who have no legal papers and who are detected by the police are detained in order to be expelled back to their countries of origin. The foreign illegal migrants who come from the countries bordering Greece -for example Albania or Bulgaria- are detained for a sort period (for an average of one week), and their expulsion is executed directly as they are transferred without serious delay to the borders by the Greek police officers.

3.10 Not-expelled prisoners

The foreign illegal migrants who come from distant countries - especially Afghanistan, Iran, Iraq, Pakistan and Nigeria in the case of Greece - are usually detained for a period much longer than one week. They either remain in detention for the whole three month

---

[21] As it already has been mentioned above, the maximum length of imprisonment is five years.

period or they are released prior to the expiration thereof, but usually not earlier than one month- as their expulsion is considered infeasible (for example because they have no passport and the country that they claim to come from does not accept them back, or because they have no diplomatic representative in our county, like for instance the case of Afghanistan). In both cases they are released and are ordered to leave the country on their own account within approximately 30 days. If they are still residing illegally in Greece once this period of tolerance has passed, it is possible for them to be detained for another three month period should they be detected again by the police. As a result, many foreign migrants move in and out of detention again and again, a cycle that continues until they apply for asylum and obtain temporary residence permission as asylum seekers.

3.11 Detention of Irregulars under Criminal Law

Detention can also be ordered by a court as a consequence of a decision of expulsion according to criminal law (Article 74 PC). In that case he/she is detained in prison together with other criminal prisoners, and must be expelled not only because he/she has violated the provisions of the Foreigners Act on illegal entrance or stay but also because he/she has committed an act punishable by Greek penal law. Thus, he/she is kept detained in prison together with the other prisoners who have been sentenced under criminal law. According to a Ministerial Decision of 1992[22], if a foreigner is detained after a court (and not the police authorities) has ordered his/her expulsion, there is no precise time limit for the duration of his/her detention. There are general limits, however, provided by the Greek Constitution on lawful conditions for arrest and detention. When the expulsion ordered by a court is impossible or cannot take place in due time for reasons related to 1) international embargos, 2) violations against Article 3 of the European Convention on Human Rights and/or of Article 3 of the UN Convention against Torture etc., or 3) other material obstacles to the expulsion, an appeal against the expulsion order can be submitted before the competent judicial authority.

3.12 Minors

Regarding the general proceedings of expulsion and administrative detention, the Foreigners Act does not distinguish minors as a separate category. Minors can be detained and expelled under the same conditions and regulations as adult illegal foreigners, and they actually are, despite objections of the Greek Ombudsman on this matter. Generally, for the territory of Attica, they are detained in Amigdaleza detention centre for women and minors. If they were detected elsewhere - mainly in northern Greece- and they are older than 13 years, they are detained separately in special rooms of the police establishment. If they are younger than 13 years old and are accompanied by their mothers, the family members are detained together, usually only for a few days. Those minors who are not yet 13 years old and who have no relatives in Greece cannot be detained and must be accommodated in special hostels or institutions while the Greek authorities

---

[22] Ministerial Decision No. 4803/13/7a-1992 by the Ministries of Foreign Affairs, Justice and Public Order.

attempt to locate their family. The treatment of illegal foreign minors poses a significant problem and the role of NGOs is very crucial.

The actual situation of institutions for foreign prisoners under administrative detention in Greece can be characterised presented by the investigations of two international organisations, the NGO Human Rights Watch and the Committee for the Prevention of Torture of the Council of Europe. These two visits took place five and four years ago respectively, yet the general situation has not changed dramatically since then. The prisoners of this category are exposed to worse conditions than the foreign prisoners who are detained under criminal law.

Human Rights Watch conducted research in Greece during a visit in November 2000. With the full co-operation of the Ministry of Public Order, on 18 November 2000 the researchers visited the Attica General Police Directorate on Alexandras Avenue in Athens to monitor the conditions of detention for undocumented migrants held there in a special detention centre for foreigners. The men detained in Alexandras Avenue facility where foreigners detained for entering and/or living in Greece without valid travel documents or residence permits which is in violation of Greece's Foreigners Act. Police authorities insisted that the facility of this establishment was not a prison and that the people were held only temporarily while awaiting expulsion. However, Human Rights Watch interviewed prisoners who stated that they had been detained for five, six, eight and twelve months respectively. Numerous prisoners had been held there for over five months. Those held at the Alexandras Avenue centre and all foreigners held under similar circumstances in police facilities in Greece are in detention as defined by the UN Body of Principles for the Protection of all Persons under Any Form of Detention or Imprisonment (Body of Principles). That is, they are persons deprived of their liberty without a conviction under Greek criminal law. The research team from Human Rights Watch were immediately struck by the degree of overcrowding when they first entered the facility. Dirty mattresses lined the floors of the corridors and large groups of prisoners were seated on them, crammed into individual rooms and milling about in the limited available floor space in hallways. According to police officials, the Alexandras Avenue facility houses approximately 150 men in a space designed for 80 prisoners. There were 19 narrow rooms in two large blocks, each room approximately 12 square meters or 130 square feet and a small cell in which a mentally disturbed detainee was held. According to police officials, each room could sleep four people. Numerous prisoners actually live and sleep on the floors of the inner corridors of the blocks. As many as twelve prisoners shared four single mattresses in the corridor of one section of the centre. The mattresses were thin and narrow and clearly designed for a single person.

Here are a few examples of the conditions that the research team from Human Rights Watch found in the facility: Due to the overcrowding, the average room sleeps between seven and twelve prisoners. Some mattresses were on frames but most of them were on the floor, which left no walking space on the floor for prisoners to move about when other prisoners were lying down. This situation forced the prisoners to walk on each others bedding to get to and from their mattresses during sleeping hours. During the day, the mattresses are piled against the wall in some rooms to allow a passage for walking. Persons living in the hallways routinely tolerate other prisoners walking across their bedding. The corridors in each of the blocks were dimly lit but there were no lights at all in any of the individual rooms. The corridor lights provided minimal lighting in the rooms after sunset, certainly not enough to read. The lights in the corridors and the toilet

/shower rooms were kept on twenty-four hours per day. Prisoners living in the corridors complained that the constant light made it difficult to sleep. There was no natural light at all during the day in the inner corridors where these prisoners stayed. Windows in the outer corridors provided some light in the individual rooms during the day. Despite the best efforts by prisoners, the cells and individual rooms of the detention centre were filthy, and the severe overcrowding in the centre had led to unsanitary conditions that could pose a serious threat to their health.

The centre was roach infested and the researchers even viewed roaches crawling on the walls, on the water fountain and on the prisoners themselves when they were giving the interview. The prisoners also complained of finding them in their bedding both during the daytime and during the night.

Each detainee was responsible for washing his own clothes. Piles of laundry littered the bathroom and lines of drying clothing were hung in the rooms. The prisoners had to purchase soap and toilet paper with their own money and many claimed that police officers selling these products charged them excessive amounts. They even had to provide and launder their own sheets. Prisoners complained of insufficient amounts of food and that the type of food served was nutritionally deficient. The prisoners were not permitted to exercise outdoors or in an indoor facility nor were they granted regular access to fresh air. Despite long periods of detention, they had no access at all to educational programs or social services. One telephone was available for use by all prisoners in both blocks, and consequentially the line to the phone was always extremely long. They could use it at any time but had to purchase their own phone cards. . It was nearly impossible to receive a phone call because the phone was in constant use. Therefore, lawyers and non-governmental organisations working with prisoners were forced to appear in person in order to maintain contact. Although the prisoners could meet with their lawyers at any time, the facilities did not permit privacy.

There is no state supported general legal aid scheme for the indigent in Greece, although asylum seekers can access free legal counsel if they know which organisations offer representation. Prisoners awaiting expulsion at the Alexandras Avenue detention facility had to pay for their own legal counsel. Numerous prisoners complained that they and their families could not afford the high costs that the appointment of legal representation brings with it.

Finally, prisoners at the Alexandras Avenue facility did not, in general, complain about physical abuse by police officers in the course of the daily life at the detention centre. Physical abuse in the process of expulsion, however, was reported to be more common. The substandard conditions of detention in the Alexandras Avenue detention facility detailed above violate many of the requirements of both internationally and regionally recognised, basic, minimum standards for the treatment of prisoners. Moreover, the Standard Minimum Rules is an authoritative set of guidelines for interpreting Article 7 of the International Covenant on Civil and Political Rights (hereinafter: ICCPR) prohibiting cruel, inhuman or degrading treatment or punishment, and ICCPR Article 10 states that "all persons deprived of their liberty shall be treated with humanity and respect for the inherent dignity of the human person".

Prisoners at the Alexandras Avenue detention centre are sometimes held there for many months—even up to a year—and some are held for indefinite periods. The long periods of detention in combination with the conditions endured by prisoners (overcrowding, lack of adequate sleeping accommodations, no access to fresh air or exercise, a dirty, roach-infested environment, questionable access to medical care) raise serious concerns that this situation may amount to cruel, inhuman or degrading treatment.

In pursuance of Article 7 of the European Convention for the Prevention of Torture and Inhuman or Degrading Treatment or Punishment, a delegation of the CPT carried out a visit to Greece in October 2001. The last visit of the Committee that took place was on August of 2005. During this visit, the Committee focused particular attention on detention facilities for foreigners, but until today the respective report has not yet been published.

During the visit in 2001, the visited establishments were: police establishments in the Attica region, Crete, and north-western Greece, as well as coastguard, customs authority, prison and military establishments. Regarding ill-treatment, a considerable number of persons interviewed by the delegation in the course of the visit alleged that they had been ill-treated by law enforcement officials. The allegations concerned mainly the police, however, some of them also related to Coast Guard officials. The alleged ill-treatment consisted mostly of kicks and blows with hands, fists, batons or other objects, often inflicted during questioning. Certain allegations also involved the use of excessive force at the time of arrest or ill-treatment of prisoners during transfers.

Regarding the conditions of the detention establishments, the CPT research team reported the following results: Though the detention facilities in these establishments are designed to hold criminal suspects for short periods, in practise they are frequently used to hold persons for prolonged periods, in particular immigration prisoners. With regard to the establishments designed for detaining persons undergoing ordinary administrative removal procedures (i.e. for a maximum of three months), Amigdaleza Holding Centre, which was designed for women and minors, offered good material conditions. The premises were spacious, clean, had good lighting (including access to natural light) and ventilation, and were adequately albeit sparsely furnished.

The situation at Hellenikon and Piraeus Holding Centres for Foreigners was far less favourable: inmate accommodation was in a poor state of hygiene and devoid of furniture, artificial lightning was insufficient, and there were problems with the water supply, particularly hot water. At Hellenikon, sleeping arrangements consisted of mattresses placed directly on the concrete floor. Furthermore, the Piraeus centre was in need of repair, especially in the toilet and shower areas.

A feature common to all three holding centres was the total absence of organised activities. In addition, inmates were not provided with newspapers, magazines, or books, and could not watch television or listen to the radio. Admittedly, this state of forced idleness was mitigated to some extent by the open door policy practised, and by generous visiting possibilities and access to telephones. However, minors held at the Amigdaleza centre were being offered no outdoor exercise; in addition, no outdoor exercise facilities were available at Piraeus and the exercise yard at Hellenikon was still not open for use. These are particularly serious shortcomings given the possible length of detention in those facilities. Furthermore, the CPT is concerned by the admission of border guard officers to the delegation that they were under no obligation to inform persons subject to immediate readmission procedures (i.e. expedited removal to a neighbouring country) of their rights and more particularly, that such persons did not have the rights of notification of custody and access to a lawyer. It should be noted that the CPT delegation received many complaints from immigration prisoners that very little or no information had been provided to them about their situation and the procedures applied to them.

In their report about Greece "Out of the Spotlight", Amnesty International (2001) writes that they are very concerned about the conditions in the country with regard to immigrants and asylum seekers. Specifically, the organisation is concerned that authorities, especially in border areas, may actively be impeding refugees' access to asylum through the refugee's inability to communicate in Greek. Prisoners interviewed by the organisation's representatives claimed that upon arrival at the detention centres where they were held, police officers asked them to sign papers which they could not read but perceived to be documents relating to legalisation of their status

4 NATIONALS DETAINED ABROAD

The Greek Ministry of Justice provided no information about this category of prisoners and there are no statistics or studies available that are relevant to this part of the project.

5 EVALUATION AND RECOMMENDATION

The most important suggestion is the establishment of probation and after care services, as found in most European countries. A great deal of research regarding the foreign population in Greek prisons needs to be conducted. In particular, matters concerning the foreigners' social backgrounds and families, and their criminal profiles need to be addressed. Furthermore, since there is currently no information available about Greek prisoners abroad, research should be undertaken to fill this gap.

The recommendations of Amnesty International (2005) are as follows:
Conditions of detention for foreigners should conform to international and regional standards, including the *U.N.* "Minimum Rules for the Treatment of Prisoners, U.N. Body of Principles for the Protection of All Persons Under Any Form of Detention, and the European Prison Rules". In particular, at a minimum each detainee should have reasonable sleeping space in an environment conducive to restful sleep, his/her own bed, and adequate toilet/bath facilities and the provision of toiletries; access to reading lights at night and natural light during the day; effective access to medical care and psychological services; adequate means to contact and facilities to meet in confidence with legal counsel; one hour of exercise per day; and access to educational and social service programs.

Asylum seekers, in general, should not be detained. Exceptions to this general principle should be applied on a case-by-case basis only and as a matter of last resort. Asylum seekers must have a prompt and effective opportunity to challenge a detention order before a judicial or administrative body independent of the detaining authorities. Periodic reviews of continuing detention should be conducted and asylum seekers and their representatives should have the right to be present at such reviews.

Undocumented migrants must have a prompt and effective opportunity to challenge the lawfulness of both their detention and expulsion order in a judicial proceeding or before another competent authority. Continued detention should be subjected to periodic review.

Information bulletins detailing the rights of prisoners to minimum standards of treatment and due process guarantees should be made available to every person in a language that he/she can understand. In the case of prisoners who cannot read, this information should be presented orally in a language they can understand. Prisoners should be informed in a language they can understand of their right to seek asylum, the procedure for filing an asylum claim, and the contact numbers of appropriate agencies that provide free legal representation for the asylum procedure;

A complaints procedure regarding conditions of detention should be developed and implemented. All prisoners should be informed of the existence of a complaints procedure in a language he/she understands. Prisoners should have access to a judicial remedy for abuses suffered in detention (e.g. police abuse) that amount to torture or cruel, inhuman or degrading treatment or punishment;

Prisoners should have access to legal counsel. Those who cannot afford counsel should be provided with counsel at no cost. Lawyers should have unhindered access to their clients in detention facilities.

Non-governmental organisations that provide legal assistance and representatives from UNHCR should have unhindered access to all detention facilities for foreigners.

Migrants awaiting expulsion and asylum seekers in detention should be housed in facilities separate from persons in custody for violations of Greek penal law. Furthermore, regarding the Greek prison system, the repletion of vacant staff posts is necessary, mainly within the social services of prisons and other scientific posts. It is also necessary to expand Greek language programs in prisons.

Finally, emphasis must be placed on the training of the staff of the Greek prison system and of the police officers. Existing training programs and any new programs to be introduced should be subject to regular review, to ensure that law enforcement officials are given practical training in how to implement national and international human rights legislation both in their daily duties and in situations of emergency, with particular emphasis on non-violent measures of law enforcement. This training should reinforce measures specifically designed to promote race-awareness and combat racist or xenophobic attitudes amongst police officers and prison staff, in order to prevent the social exclusion trends in the Greek Prison System.

Chapter 12

Hungary

Tímea Szabó
Balázs Tóth
Gábor Győző
András Kádár

1 INTRODUCTION

1.1 Overview of penalties and measures

In the Hungarian legal system are several forms of punishments and measures as a consequence of which someone can be lawfully deprived of his/her freedom. The forms of detention relevant for the purposes of this study can be divided into the main categories of detention for criminal reasons and detention for non-criminal reasons. The most important form of non-criminal detention is alien policing detention. The forms of detention for criminal (or quasi-criminal) reasons are the following:

- *Short-term custody*: the police may take into short-term custody – inter alia - those who are caught in the act of committing an intentional criminal offence; those against whom a warrant of arrest has been issued based on a law or international treaty; those whose custody or pre-trial detention has been ordered; those who escaped during the implementation of custody, pre-trial detention or imprisonment; those who are unable or unwilling to prove their identity; and finally those who are suspected of having committed a criminal offence. Short-term custody is ordered by the police, and may not last longer than 8 (in exceptional cases 12) hours.[1]

- *Custody:* the police, the prosecutor or the court can order the custody of a person in the event that there is a well-founded suspicion that he/she has committed a criminal offence punishable with imprisonment, if the subsequent pre-trial detention of the person is likely to be ordered. Custody may last for no longer than 72 hours (including any form of detention preceding the custody).[2]

- *Pre-trial detention:* in the case of an offence punishable with imprisonment the defendant may be subjected to pre-trial detention if – inter alia – he/she escaped or remains hidden from the court, the prosecutor or the investigative authority; taking into account the risk of his/her escape or any further reason, there are well-founded grounds to presume that his/her presence at the procedure can not be secured in any other way; well-founded grounds justify the presumption that if not taken into pre-trial detention, he/she would frustrate, hinder or threaten the procedure; there are well-founded grounds to presume that if not taken into pre-trial detention, he/she would accomplish the criminal offence he/she attempted or commit another offence punishable with imprisonment. Pre-trial detention – with certain exceptions - may not last longer than three years. It can only be ordered and extended by the court.[3]

- *Imprisonment:* Imprisonment may be imposed on the defendant if he/she is found guilty of a criminal offence for which Act IV of 1978 on the Penal Code ("Penal Code") prescribes this form of punishment as a possible sanction. The minimum length of imprisonment is two months, the maximum duration is fifteen years (in case of cumulative or consolidated sentences twenty years) or a life-sentence.[4] There are three main regimes for the execution of imprisonment: low-security regime, medium-security

---

[1] Art. 33, Act XXXIV of 1994 on the Police ("Police Act")
[2] Art. 126, Act XIX of 1998 on Criminal Procedure ("CCP")
[3] Art. 129, CCP
[4] Art. 39, Penal Code

regime and high-security regime.[5] In the sentence the court defines under which regime the defendant shall serve the prison sentence.

- *Compulsory medical treatment:* "Compulsory medical treatment" is applied with regard to those mentally ill perpetrators who have committed violent crimes against other persons or crimes that have endangered public safety, where there is a danger that they may commit similar crimes in the future, provided that the initial offence would be punished by imprisonment exceeding one year. This treatment is under regular supervision. The first review takes place eight months after the admission, and after that once a year.[6]
- *Reformatory education:* According to the Penal Code, the court may sentence a juvenile offender to serve time in a reformatory institution (reformatory education) if it regards this as necessary for the juvenile offender's development.[7] The minimum length of reformatory education is one year, the maximum time is three years. No parole is possible until one year is served.[8] Reformatory education shall be distinguished from prison sentence served in juvenile penitentiaries (low- or medium security). While these are integrated within the general prison system (under the Ministry of Justice), reformatories are under the Ministry of Youth, Family and Social Affairs and Equality.
- *Forms of detention related to petty offences:* 1. Petty offence arrest: arrest of those presumably having committed a petty offence punishable with petty offence detention. The maximum duration of petty offence arrest is 72 hours. 2. Petty offence detention: an Act of Parliament can prescribe the detention of those having committed a petty offence. The minimum length of petty offence detention is one day; the maximum duration is 60 days.[9]

Detention related to the alien policing procedure may take the following forms:
- detention for refusal (in order to implement the readmission agreements)
- detention in preparation for expulsion
- alien policing detention

Detention for refusal may be ordered by the Border Guards for five days, detention in preparation for expulsion and alien policing detention may be ordered by the Office for Immigration and Nationality (OIN) also for five days. After the initial five days, the court is entitled to prolong the detention. In case of the first two types for a maximum of 30 days, in the case of alien policing detention for a maximum of altogether 12 months. The different forms of the detention shall be summed up, but their total length may not exceed 12 months.

The most frequent of the above is alien policing detention that may be ordered by the OIN with the purpose of securing the subsequent expulsion of a foreigner who hid from the authority or hindered the execution of expulsion in any other way; who refused to leave the country or it is presumable on any other grounds that he/she would hinder or

---

5   Art. 41, Penal Code
6   Art.74, Penal Code and Article 13 of Decree of Minister of Justice 36/2003. (X. 3.) on the Implementation of Forensic Compulsory Treatment, Temporary Forensic Compulsory Treatment and the Tasks and Operation of the Forensic Observation and Psychiatric Institution ("IMEI Regulation")
7   Art. 118, Penal Code
8   Art. 454, Penal Code
9   Art.14, Act LXIX of 1999 on Petty Offences

frustrate the execution of expulsion; who committed a petty offence or a crime during the temporal scope of expulsion; who seriously offended the behavioural rules of the place where he/she is obliged to stay on the basis of the OIN's decision or otherwise hindered the alien procedure; finally if he/she has served a prison sentence imposed for having committed an intentional criminal offence.[10]

There are some other forms of detention applicable in Hungary that will not be mentioned in this study, because they are not applied frequently. The most frequent forms of detention are imprisonment and pre-trial detention (see below). The above-mentioned punishments and measures are executed in penitentiary institutions (imprisonment, pre-trial detention, petty offence detention), the Forensic Observation and Psychiatric Institution (compulsory medical treatment), reformatory institutions (juveniles' pre-trial detention, reformatory education), police jails (criminal custody, pre-trial detention for a maximum of 60 days, petty offence arrest, petty offence detention) and alien police jails (detention related to the alien policing procedure).

1.2 Overview of the Prison System

The different institutions where detention may be implemented are under the scope of authority of different organizations. Below the authors will outline the most important ones, and then go on to deal in more detail with the status and structure of the penitentiary administration.

Institutions under the authority of the Ministry of Justice (and managed directly by the National Penitentiary Administration) include penitentiary institutions (32); the Forensic Observation and Psychiatric Institution (IMEI), where "compulsory medical treatment" is implemented; and the Central Prison Hospital in Tököl, where medical treatment is provided for (not mentally) ill criminal detainees

Institutions under the authority of the Ministry of Interior include police jails (police jails are managed directly by the County Police Headquarters, subordinated to the National Police Headquarters); and alien policing jails, where non-Hungarian citizens can be detained (alien policing jails are managed directly by the Border Guards) (5).

Reformatories for juvenile offenders are under the authority of the Ministry of Youth, Family, Social Affairs and Equality (there are four reformatories – three for male and one for female juveniles).

The status and organization of the Hungarian penitentiary system is set out in Act CVII of 1995 on the Penitentiary System ("Penitentiary Act"). The top unit of the system is the National Headquarters of the Penitentiary System (NHPS), which is financed by the central state under the supervision of the Ministry of Justice since 1963. The basic organisational structure is defined by the Penitentiary Act, but the details are determined by the Minister of Justice who approves the organisational chart and approves of the number of the staff. The NHPS's annual budget is determined by the Parliament in the annual law on the budget, within the budgetary chapter of the Ministry of Justice. Within the framework of the approved budget, the NHPS may autonomously use the resources but it has to comply with the general state budgetary guidelines. The NHPS is a fundamentally military structure headed by the National Commander who directs the penitentiary administration autonomously within the framework created by the laws and

---

[10] Art. 46, Act XXXIX of 2001 on the Enrty and Stay of Foreigners "Alien Policing Act"

regulations in force, as well as the decisions of the Minister of Justice. The Ministry of Justice performs professional supervision through its Department of the Supervision of Penitentiary Matters and the Deputy State Secretary responsible for the penitentiary administration.

The average number of prison population in 2005 was fluctuating between 16,000 and 17,000 (convicted prisoners: around 12,500, pre-trial detainees: 4,000, persons under compulsory medical treatment: 280, persons in petty offence detention: 100). The composition of prisoners on 12 May 2005 was: 15,510 males and 1,011 females. Out of the 16,521 inmates 482 were juveniles and 625 foreigners. The full official capacity of the prison system was 11,253 on 12 May 2005, therefore, the average rate of overcrowding is around 150%, while in certain penitentiaries (especially in ones serving primarily remand purposes) the rate of overcrowding can be as high as 220%. On 12 May 2005, the number of penitentiary personnel was around 8,600 with approximately 6450 uniformed and 2150 non-uniformed staff.[11]

There are three main types of mechanisms controlling detention conditions in Hungary. A specific department of the regional prosecutor's office is regularly supervising the lawfulness of detention in all possible places of detention (including penitentiaries and police jails as well). Prosecutors have access to all kinds of data, may talk to prisoners and other detainees, and may receive written complaints from them as well.[12] The organs implementing detention shall be obliged to comply with any instruction given by the prosecutor. They may challenge the instruction with the prosecutor's superior, this however may not delay the implementation thereof.[13] Another important form of control is the Ombudsman. There is no specific ombudsman for detention matters, but detainees may turn to the General Ombudsman if they think that their fundamental rights have been infringed during detention. While investigating into the complaint, the Ombudsman may request information, a hearing, written explanation, declaration or opinion from the competent official or demand that an inquiry be conducted by a superior. When finding a violation, the Ombudsman issues recommendations, to which the examined authority shall respond within 30 days.[14] The third form of control of detention is civil monitoring carried out by non-governmental organizations. Based on its agreement of cooperation with the NHPS, the Border Guards and the National Police Headquarters, the Hungarian Helsinki Committee has been monitoring detention in penitentiaries, police jails and alien policing jails for years.

Foreigners can be detained in all the institutions listed above. The institution where only foreigners can be detained is the alien policing jail where nationals obviously may not be placed. In terms of Article 223 of Decree 6/1996 (III. 6.) of the Minister of Justice on the Implementation of the Rules of Imprisonment and Pre-trial Detention (hereafter: Penitentiary Regulation), when detaining a foreign prisoner, it should be assured if possible that the detainee be placed in a cell where such other detainees are placed who speak both Hungarian and the language the foreigner speaks and understands. In practice this regulation leads to a situation whereby foreigners from the same country or the same region are placed in the same cells if the rules requiring the separation of

---

11 Data in this section were provided by the Department of Detention Affairs of the NHPS.
12 Art. 11, Act V of 1972 on the Prosecutors of Hungarian Republic ("Prosecutors Act")
13 Art. 12, Prosecutors Act
14 Art. 18, Act LIX of 1993 on the Ombudsman

detainees do not prevent this (e.g. women shall be separated from men, and accomplices from each other in terms of the pertaining legal provisions). Consequently, so called "foreigners' cells" are established in practice. Within the organizational structure of the NHPS there is no special department responsible for foreigners. One reason for this might be that the proportion of foreign detainees in the whole prison population is less than 4%. This might also offer an explanation as to why prison staff does not receive any kind of special training on how to deal with foreigners special problems.

In the experience of the HHC's civilian monitors, the members of the penitentiary personnel usually do not mention problems specially related to foreign detainees, and monitors do not receive significantly more or substantively different complaints from foreign detainees either.[15] The issue of the detention of foreigners is not regarded as one of the central problems within the penitentiary administration. Another reason for the lack of a special unit responsible for foreign prisoners could be that according to the Hungarian legal regulation,[16] foreign detainees can have unrestricted access to the consular authorities of their respective countries. This means that they could in theory receive all the necessary help they need during detention from their country of origin. However, if their own consulate does no provide them with the necessary – or any – help (which does happen in practice) they might face serious problems as shall be seen below.

1.3 Overview involvement Consulates, Embassies, Ministries home country, Probation service home country, NGO's etc

The Penitentiary Regulation[17] prescribes that "foreign prisoners may keep contact with the embassy or consulate of their country of origin in accordance with the rules laid down in the international convention on consular contacts and in international agreements signed by the concerned countries." The penitentiary institution has an obligation to immediately notify the competent embassy or consulate upon the admission of a foreign inmate. The institution may only refrain from this if the inmate requests so in writing.[18] If the foreigner requests that a member of the consulate' personnel visit him/her, or send him/her a parcel or money, this request shall be forwarded to the consulate immediately. The number of visits with or packages sent by the consulate cannot be restricted,[19] whereas with regard to Hungarian nationals there are restrictions in this regard (usually one visit and one parcel per month is allowed). In practice, the actual involvement of consulates in providing detainees with assistance depends on their financial resources and other possibilities. The monitors of the HHC met on a number of occasions with foreigners in police jails or prisons who complained that their respective consulates were not actively supporting them. It also happened occasionally that the HHC turned to a consulate asking for some kind of help but received no reply at all. There are of course positive examples as well. Certain embassies have direct, well-established contacts with the penitentiary institutions where their own citizens are detained. This means that they

---

15 See: IHF Report 2006 on Hungary, Events of 2005 in: *Human Rights of the OSCE Region, International Helsinki Federation for Human Rights* (to be published).
16 Art. 226 of the Penitentiary Regulation.
17 Art. 226, Penitentiary Regulation.
18 Art. 222, Penitentiary Regulation.
19 Art. 226, Penitentiary Regulation

visit them regularly, send them money, parcels and occasionally pay for their lawyers as well.

1.4 Overview of trends[20]

1.4.1 Sentencing Trends

On the basis of the data provided below the overall trends in sentencing can be described as follows. As it can be seen from Table 3, the number of final decisions (i.e. decisions against which no ordinary appeal is possible) ordering imprisonment has been slightly increasing in the past ten years. In the past few years this number has been around 32,000. In about 65% of the cases, the execution of the sentence is suspended. In case of almost all the sentences ordering less six months imprisonment the execution of the punishment will be suspended. There are no official data relating to short term sentences within the meaning of the project's conceptual framework. In Hungary, sentences of less than five years' imprisonment are regarded as short sentences. Most of the offences for which imprisonment is imposed are crimes against property (55%-60%), among which theft is the most frequent (50-66%). The following can be said concerning the social background of the persons sentenced to non-suspended imprisonment. The proportion of recidivists has constantly been around 80% in the past ten years. 95% of perpetrators sentenced to non-suspended imprisonment are adults. Approximately 80% have finished only the primary school, while less than 2% have university or college diplomas.

1.4.2 Characteristics Foreign Prison Population

Concerning the sentences of foreigners, from the comparison of Table 1 and Table 2 it can be established that in the past ten years the number of convicted foreigners has increased with 75%, while the number of non-suspended imprisonment sentences imposed on foreigners has not increased at all. The typical offences committed by foreigners are human trafficking, abuse of drugs and fraud.[21] Around 90% of foreigner convicts are male. Most of the foreign convicts sentenced to imprisonment come from Europe (90%). There are no official data collection with a view to the social background of foreigners.

---

[20] Data in this section were provided by the Department of Informatics and Computer Application of the Chief Public Prosecutor's Office.

[21] Data provided by the NHPS.

Table 1 Data concerning convicted foreigners

Year	Number of convicted foreigners	Male	%	Female	%
1996	2 192	2 000	91,2	192	8,8
1997	2 358	2 130	90,3	228	9,7
1998	2 772	2 477	89,4	295	10,6
1999	2 790	2 482	89,0	308	11,0
2000	2 967	2 611	88,0	356	12,0
2001	3 283	2 835	86,4	448	13,6
2002	3 261	2 878	88,3	383	11,7
2003	3 091	2 617	84,7	474	15,3
2004	3 515	3 071	87,4	444	12,6

Source: Department of Informatics and Computer Application of the Chief Public Prosecutor's Office.

Table 2 Number of foreigners sentenced to imprisonment

		out of which Eurpoean	
Year	Number of foreigners sentenced to imprisonment	number	%
1996	296	282	95,3
1997	546	497	91,0
1998	451	419	92,9
1999	485	437	90,1
2000	421	381	90,5
2001	418	376	90,0
2002	402	370	92,0
2003	336	296	88,1
2004	301	268	89,0

Source: Department of Informatics and Computer Application of the Chief Public Prosecutor's Office.

Table 3

Number of defendants sentenced to imprisonment		out of which				out of not-suspended			
		not-suspended		*suspended*					
Year		= n	%	= n	%	*6 month-3 years*	*3-15 years*	*15-20 years*	*Life sentence*
1996	25 180	9 976	39.6	15 204	60.4	5 673	1 062	5	21
1997	27 592	10 837	39.3	16 755	60.7	6 177	1 223	4	16
1998	30 939	11 710	37.8	19 229	62.2	6 559	1 264	2	9
1999	31 720	12 058	38.0	19 662	62.0	6 978	1 286	5	12
2000	32 373	12 203	37.7	20 170	62.3	7 572	1 498	3	13
2001	32 370	12 600	38.9	19 770	61.1	8 299	1 674	5	9
2002	32 444	12 262	37.8	20 182	62.2	7 711	1 594	6	10
2003	31 626	11 767	37.2	19 859	62.8	7 751	1 669	13	22
2004	30 839	10 608	34.4	20 231	65.6	6 948	1 480	9	22

Source: Department of Informatics and Computer Application of the Chief Public Prosecutor's Office.

1.5 Overview of national legislation

1.5.1 Penitentiary Legislation

The following list contains the most important statutes related to detention with their names as used in this study.
- Act IV of 1978 on the Penal Code – Penal Code
- Act XXXIV of 1994 on the Police – Police Act
- Act CVII of 1995 on the Penitentiary System – Penitentiary Act
- Act XLIII of 1996 on the Service Relationship of the Professional Members of Armed Organ – Armed Organs Act
- Act CXXXIX of 1997 on Asylum – Asylum Act
- Act CLIV of 1997 on Health Care – Health Care Act
- Act XIX of 1998 on the Criminal Procedure – CCP
- Act XXXIX of 2001 on the Entry and Stay of Foreigners – Alien Policing Act
- Decree 19/1995 (XII. 13.) of the Minister of Interior on the Order of Police Jails – Police Jail Regulation
- Decree 6/1996 (III. 6.) of the Minister of Justice on the Implementation of the Rules of
- Imprisonment and Pre-trial Detention – Penitentiary Regulation
- Decree 11/1996 of the Minister of Justice (X. 15.) on the Disciplinary Responsibility of Detainees in Penitentiary Institutions – Disciplinary Decree
- Decree 30/1997 (X. 11.) of the Ministry of Social Welfare – Juvenile Reformatory Regulation
- Decree 5/1998 (VII. 12.) of the Minister of Justice on Health Care Provision for Inmates – Penitentiary Medical Regulation

- Joint Decree 27/2001 of the Minister of Interior and the Minister of Justice (XI. 29.) on the Implementation of Detention Ordered in the Alien Policing Procedure – Alien Policing Detention Decree
- Government Decree 170/2001 (IX. 26.) on the Implementation of the Alien Policing Act (Alien Policing Decree)
- Decree 17/2003 of the Minister of Justice (VI. 24.) on the Activities of the Probation Service (Probation Service Decree)
- Decree 36/2003 of the Minister of Justice (X. 3.) on the Implementation of Forensic Compulsory Treatment, Temporary Forensic Compulsory Treatment and the Tasks and Operation of the Forensic Observation and Psychiatric Institution – IMEI Regulation
- Law Decree 11 of 1979 on the Implementation of Sanctions and Measures – Penitentiary Code.

1.5.2 Penitentiary Legislation & Foreigners

Apart from the statutes pertaining to the alien policing procedure and the different forms of detention related thereto, only the Penitentiary Regulation contains provisions specific to the detention of foreigners. These rules will be discussed below. The reason for the lack of special regulation in the statutes is that with regard to most aspects of detention foreign detainees are not perceived to be different from Hungarian ones: the rights and obligations of foreign detainees are more or less the same as those of Hungarian nationals, while their special needs are acknowledged only to a restricted extent. Foreigners may be subject to any kind of sanction set out in Hungarian laws, while there is one type of sanction that may be applied only in relation to foreigners, namely expulsion. There is however, one particular type of detention that is applied significantly more frequently against foreigners than against nationals, and that is pre-trial detention. The reason for this is that in the case of a foreign suspect or defendant who does not have a permanent – or even temporary – address registered in Hungary, the court tends to accept that there are well-founded grounds to presume that his/her presence throughout the procedure may not be secured in any other way, mostly because the court would not know where to send the summoning orders for the different procedural acts.

2 TREATMENT OF FOREIGN PRISONERS

2.1 General

There are no significant differences in the treatment of foreigners compared to national prisoners. The most important factor that can lead to the social exclusion of foreigners in a penitentiary institution is the lack of knowledge of the Hungarian language. Experience shows that in most cases "newcomers" can survive with the help of detainees who speak their language and have been detained long enough to obtain a relatively good command of Hungarian. However, language can be a really serious barrier for those pre-trial detainees who are detained in places of detention run by the police, where not so many people are held at the same time. In these cases it is highly unlikely that any other detainee in the same facility speaks a language the foreigner understands. All the problems that foreigners have to face in a penitentiary institution are in a certain way connected to the linguistic barriers. The rights and obligations of national and foreign prisoners are basically the same but in practice there are certain differences as to how they can exercise their – formally equal – rights. Therefore the most important rules applying to the detention of all prisoners will be described and the actual differences if any will be pointed out.

2.2 Living conditions and facilities

The number of people to be placed in a cell shall be defined in a way that each inmate have six cubic meters of air space and – in the case of adult male inmates – three square meters of moving space. Minors and women shall be provided with three-and-a-half square meters of moving space. When calculating the moving space, the space covered by equipment and furniture shall not be taken into account.[22] (The required moving space is four square-meters, the required air space is ten cubic meters for pre-trial detainees.)[23] In the cell there must be a washbasin with running water and a separated toilet with proper ventilation. The prison governor regulates when and how cell doors are to be kept open. In the course of detention, the following categories shall be separated from each other: a) women from men; b) pre-trial detainees form convicts; c) accomplices form each other based on the decision of the prosecutor or the court (depending on the phase of the procedure); d) healthy inmates from ill inmates, those suffering from infectious diseases from those with non-infectious diseases, HIV-positives from all other detainees; e) adults from juveniles; f) smokers from non-smokers.[24]

2.3 Reception and admission

There are certain important differences concerning the reception procedure if the detainee is a foreigner. As it was outlined above, the penitentiary institution has an obligation to immediately notify the competent embassy or consulate upon the admission of a foreign inmate. The institution may only refrain from this if the inmate requests so in writing.[25]

Foreigners have a legally prescribed right to receive upon arrival information on the internal rules of the penitentiary institution in a language they can understand. There are information leaflets prepared by NGO's and the NHPS for that purpose. If there are no leaflets translated into a language the foreigner understands, an interpreter shall explain the rules pertaining to detention and the foreigner signs a declaration that he/she has been informed about his/her rights and obligation.[26] Despite the legal provisions, practice shows that written information in foreign languages can rarely be found in

---

[22] Art. 137, Penitentiary Regulation.
[23] Art. 239, Penitentiary Regulation.
[24] Art. 39, Penitentiary Regulation.
[25] Art. 222, Penitentiary Regulation.
[26] Art. 2 and 24, Penitentiary Regulation.

Hungarian places of detention.[27] The foreigner shall also be informed if an international treaty makes it possible that the execution of his/her imprisonment be transferred.[28]

In its report upon its 2005 visit, the European Committee for the Prevention of Torture and Inhuman or Degrading Treatment or Punishment (CPT), also noted this problem.[29] The report declares that that "at most police establishments visited, the delegation did note the presence of the [...] information sheets; however, they were not always available in foreign languages. [...] The CPT welcomes the Hungarian authorities' efforts to improve the provision of written information to persons in police custody. The Committee invites the Hungarian authorities to take further steps to ensure that the information sheet is available in all police establishments in an appropriate range of languages and is systematically given to detained persons."[30] With regard to the general rules, in the beginning of the criminal procedure, the detaining authority (usually the police) has to inform a family member or another person selected by the suspect about his/her whereabouts, therefore the penitentiary is not obliged to notify anyone about the admission. But the detainee is entitled to call his/her family. Due to the absence of general provisions on telephone contacts, the rules of telephoning are specified in the internal rules (house rules) of each penitentiary institution. If a detainee has no money, he/she cannot cover the cost of the call. Hence, it can easily happen that notwithstanding the right to make a phone call the detainee cannot use the phone.

2.4 Work - Education – Training – Sports - Recreation

One of the most sensitive issues concerning the social exclusion of foreigners in detention is their participation in work and education. In theory all the prisoners have the right to request to be given paid work unless there are reasons (e.g. illness, medical examination, other serious reasons) preventing it.[31] (Taking part in basic maintenance tasks, such as cleaning the prison is not considered to be work in this sense, thus one is not entitled to payment for it).[32] Working is one of the most important – if not the most important – activities during detention. The salary detainees receive for work performed in detention enables them to buy essential supplies[33] and save some money for the time of the release, which may have a crucial importance in the case of foreigners, who usually have to cope with the situation without the support of relatives. Furthermore, working is also of key significance from the point of view of mitigating the detrimental psychological effects of detention. Finally, when deciding upon conditional release courts always take into consideration as a relevant factor whether the detainee has been working or not. In spite

---

[27] See for example the mission report of the International Helsinki Federation for Human Rights (IHF) on the IHF's visit to Hungary: http://www.ihf-hr.org/documents/doc_summary.php?sec_id=3&d_id=4218

[28] Art. 222, Penitentiary Regulation.

[29] Report to the Hungarian Government on the visit to Hungary carried out by the European Committee for the Prevention of Torture and Inhuman or Degrading Treatment or Punishment (CPT) from 30 March to 8 April 2005 hereinafter: 2005 CPT Report), see at: http://www.cpt.coe.int/documents/hun/2006-20-inf-eng.htm

[30] 2005 CPT Report, point 25.

[31] Art. 36, Penitentiary Code.

[32] Art. 102, Penitentiary Regulation.

[33] The most essential hygienic articles are provided by the penitentiary administration in terms of the law.

of what is set forth above, our experience is that most of the foreigners are not provided with work in prisons due to the very simple reason that they do not speak Hungarian. Obviously, there are certain kinds of work where speaking Hungarian is not essential, but when prison administration can offer work for only part of the detainees it is natural that those who are the most likely to do their job with the least problems will be selected for such positions.. (The rate of employment among convicted detainees has constantly been around 60 percent.)[34] Another aspect of the issue is that prison work is often preceded by a training period, and the persons providing training only speak Hungarian. Finally, as a result of the general lack of workplaces, many of the foreigners do not have the opportunity to work, consequently they do not earn a salary, cannot access additional articles besides the food and hygienic supplies provided by the penitentiary (unless such articles are sent to them in parcels by relatives or the consulate), and they have less chance to be conditionally released.

Penitentiary institutes provide elementary level education, and – upon a request by the detainee – can also permit participation in secondary and college education, or vocational training. As a rule, the prison service will bear the costs related to participation in elementary education or vocational training.[35] There is no information about education or vocational trainings organized in foreign languages. Therefore many of the foreigners are not in the position to take part in educational activities offered by the prison administration.

Detainees – and therefore foreigners as well - are entitled to do some sports activities. They may use all the facilities provided for this purpose (table tennis, body building room, football etc.) in line with the internal rules. Foreigners are also entitled to recreational activities, e.g. they can use the library. However, in some penitentiaries there are no books in foreign languages. In certain institutions there are not enough Hungarian books either, while in most police jails there are not any books at all. For pre-trial detainees the law does not guarantee the right to participate in education at all.

2.5 Food – Religion – Personal hygiene – Medical care

In theory, foreign prisoners are entitled to practice their religion. The law declares the right to choose, express and practice their religion.[36] This includes the right to take part in communal gatherings (this right is revoked when a person is under solitary confinement, security isolation and detention in special security cell), keeping contact with the cleric without supervision, buying and keeping religious books and items, opining regarding his/her child's religious education, being informed about religious events.[37]

Rights related to religion may be practiced as set forth in the house rules. It is also prescribed that the practice of religious rights may not breach the order and security of the institution (e.g. accomplices must be separated even if they wanted to pray together). It is the duty of the penitentiary to provide adequate place for practicing religion but it is the church that has to provide the sacral necessities. In practice this means that in some

---

[34] See: Double Standard: Prison Conditions in Hungary. Hungarian Helsinki Committee, Budapest, 2002. p. 143.

[35] Art. 73-74, Penitentiary Regulation.

[36] Art. 36 and 118, Penitentiary Code.

[37] Art. 93-99, Penitentiary Regulation.

of the institutions there are rooms appointed for this purpose but due to lack of financial resources there are not enough rooms for all the religions. In certain prisons there is a catholic chapel as well.

There is a difference between the situation of adherents of the four so-called historical denominations and of followers of other religions. The penitentiary system has institutionalized relations with the Catholic, the Lutheran, the Calvinist and the Jewish denominations (based on Decree 13/2000 of the Minister of Justice). Priests and pastors of these religions visit penitentiaries on a regular basis. If an inmate needs another religious representative, then he/she needs to submit a request, and the representative's visit has to be permitted by the penitentiary's warden. The above Decree however claims that based on the needs of the inmates, all registered churches (their number in Hungary is over one hundred) may perform religious activities in the prisons. Muslim detainees claim to sometimes face problems in this respect. The HHC has received complaints that in certain cases the imam was not permitted to enter the penitentiary but this does not appear to be a general problem.

Concerning food and accommodating special religious/dietary needs or requirements the same can be stated as concerning practicing religion. The Penitentiary Regulation provides that the dietary needs based on religious belief shall be taken into consideration. However the Regulation provides at the same time that the existence of this obligation depends upon the possibilities of the given institution.[38] Therefore if in a certain institution there are very few foreign detainees with special dietary needs and it would be too expensive to provide them with proper food then the institution concerned is not obliged to do that. According HHC's experience, in the vast majority of the cases such dietary needs are accommodated, but HHC has heard about shortcomings in this respect as well.

The law does not allow deviation from the general dress code, therefore religious dress requirements cannot be met. Remand prisoners are entitled to wear their own clothes, which in theory should mean that at least in this case religious clothing is allowed, but there is no information about practice in this regard and related complaints have not been heard either. The same goes for personal hygiene requirements, so it is up to the warden's "goodwill" to ensure such possibility within the frame of the house rules.

2.6 Consular and legal help

As a general rule, contacts are regulated in accordance with the International Convention on Consular Relations, and bi-lateral treaties. A foreigner in pre-trial detention has the right to keep contact with the representative of his/her diplomatic mission in writing or verbally (by phone or visits) without restriction and supervision.[39] With regard to convicted inmates, only written correspondence is expressly exempted from supervision. [40] Upon admission to an institution, the respective mission is to be noticed, unless the detainee explicitly asks to refrain from this (in writing). [41] The assistance that may be provided by consular authorities includes: personal visits, sending parcels (the frequency

---

[38] Art.147, Penitentiary Regulation.
[39] Art. 244, Penitentiary Regulation.
[40] Art. 225, Penitentiary Regulation.
[41] Art. 22, Penitentiary Regulation.

is not limited, visits may occur out of the timeframe set out by the house rules, based on prior agreement) or sending money, taking over the costs (duty, postal, other) of receiving packages from abroad, requesting a report on the situation of the detainee. (The detainee's requests to the mission for visits, packages and money are to be forwarded without delay.)[42] No proper information is available to judge whether the assistance provided is adequate or not, but it may be pointed out that it is also up to the given consulate's willingness to be active in this respect, and some countries' missions seem to neglect these tasks.

Defendants whose mother tongue is not Hungarian or do not speak the language of the procedure (which of course includes foreigners in pre-trial detention) are entitled to receive legal assistance from an ex officio appointed lawyer. There are general problems with the work of appointed lawyers (no substantive legal help, failure to keep contact with the client),[43] which is frequently aggravated by the fact that the given appointed lawyer does not speak the language of the client. While interpretation is provided by the authorities during procedural acts (such as interrogations), and on these occasions the authorities usually leave some time for the counsel and the defendant to communicate with the help of the interpreter, consultation with the detained foreigner between procedural acts (e.g. before a court hearing) is impossible for most ex officio counsels, as the fee of the interpreter (which is by the way usually significantly higher than the fee for the ex officio appointed lawyer) should be advanced by the lawyer and can only be reclaimed later in the procedure. If the detainee cannot retain a lawyer of his/her own it is very likely that he/she cannot afford to pay for the interpreter, and it cannot be expected form the lawyer to advance the interpreter's fee either. For all these reasons in most cases the indigent foreigner detainees do not have the possibility to consult their lawyer.

2.7 Contact with the outside world

Basically the general provisions apply for convicted prisoners and pre-trial detainees as well. (For pre-trial detainees, any form of contact with any person – apart from the lawyer or an employee of the consulate – requires prior authorization by the prosecutor or – in the trial stage – the court.) Written correspondence is not limited, for foreigners one letter per month may be sent to a relative at the cost of the institution, provided that the foreigner lacks the necessary financial means (otherwise it is borne by the detainee).[44] At least one occasion per month must be provided for visits, the minimal length is 30 minutes, two adults and two minors may be present at a time.[45] Further details are stipulated in the house rules, so the institution may decide at its own discretion about the scheduling. The internal rules of penitentiaries usually provide that in case of a visitor coming form abroad the time allowed for the visit is two hours. A phone may be used in accordance with the house rules (no minimum or maximum length or frequency is prescribed by the law), at the detainee's cost.[46]

---

[42] Art.226, Penitentiary Regulation.
[43] See: András Kádár: *Presumption of Guilt*, Hugarian Helsinki Committee, Budapest 2004 pp. 21-39.
[44] Art. 225, Penitentiary Regulation.
[45] Art. 89, Penitentiary Regulation.
[46] Art. 92, Penitentiary Regulation.

Institutions are rarely in the position to keep newspapers available at all, so there is no chance for foreign-language newspapers, but it is possible to receive them in packages. Usually there are different channels on television, but there is no information if foreign-language channels are available or not. Other visitors allowed: representatives of monitoring bodies of international organizations, churches, clerics, civil organizations. (Prison cleric missions, churches, civil organizations and foundations may conclude cooperation agreements with one or more institutions, in order to perform various tasks.)

2.8 Re-integration activities - Prison leave

In this respect the general provisions apply to foreigners. Detainees (sentenced to maximum- or medium-security imprisonment) may be placed into a so-called 'transitory group' within the institution two years prior to release (after a minimum of five years served in prison), where some restraints are relaxed: e.g. leave may be permitted for not more than 24 hours, or – as a reward – for not more than 15 days, but this institution is far from being called semi-freedom. [47] From six months prior to release, it is possible to ask for information, or a personal hearing from the probation officer regarding re-integration (employment, housing, education, social welfare, family issues, etc.), and the probation officer can provide assistance in these issues. [48] As a general rule, leaves are provided (and seen) as rewards. Short-term leave may be granted for a maximum of five, ten or fifteen days per year in the maximum-, medium-, and low-security regimes respectively. Short-term leave (for 24 hours) may also be granted as a reward.[49] The provisions for conditional release are as follows. The earliest date is set out by the Penal Code[50] (depending on the crime committed, and the severity of the regime to which the individual is sentenced to), unless the criminal court excludes the possibility of such a measure in its verdict (based on certain legal criteria). Upon the earliest date, the penitentiary judge decides on the conditional release, on the basis of the penitentiary institutions opinion.

2.9 Release – Expulsion

Special procedures depend on whether the detainee will be expelled from the country or not. If expelled by the criminal court after his/her releasethe foreigner is transferred to the alien policing authority which executes the expulsion. In the vast majority of cases foreigners convicted by the criminal court will be expelled. The criminal court may impose expulsion as an additional penalty to imprisonment. (The alien policing authority also has a right to order expulsion for a number of reasons, for instance if a foreigner breaches the provisions of immigration law.)[51] The expulsion may be ordered with terminal effect (in case of certain serious criminal acts, such as trafficking in person, or kidnapping), or for a definite period between one and ten years (the time of the prison sentence is not taken into account when these years are calculated). No recognized refugee may be expelled, while immigrated foreigners may only be expelled if a sentence

---

[47]   Art. 29, Penitententiary Code.
[48]   Art. 196, Penitentiary Regulation.
[49]   Art. 41 and 41/A, Penitentiary Code.
[50]   Art. 47, Criminal Code.
[51]   Art. 61, Criminal Code.

of more than five years may be imposed through the Penal Code, while in case of minors, foreigners having a family, or having a legal status in Hungary this penalty may only be imposed, if the sentence is imprisonment of ten years or more.[52] The alien policing authority reviews if the principle of non-refoulement should be applied (the detainee may request review by the penitentiary judge during the imprisonment as well). Otherwise, the expulsion order can be challenged in the original criminal procedure only. In case of terminal expulsion, exemption may be requested from the criminal court after ten years. The regulation on expulsion has just recently been amended to the form described above, therefore, its overall assessment is not possible yet.

2.10 Aftercare – Probation

In terms of the Penitentiary Code, the penitentiary institution is obliged to get information about where the prisoner wishes to settle after his/her release, and tries to assist him/her in arranging issues related to accommodation and work after release. In doing so, the penitentiary institution may approach the competent probation officer. The probation officer may visit the detainee in the penitentiary institution, may advise him/her and may attempt to assist the detainee in finding a job and/or accommodation. If necessary the probation officer shall assist the prisoner in re-establishing family contacts.[53] In terms of the Probation Service Decree, the probation officer shall also provide these services if a former prisoner requests so after his/her release. There are no specific provisions pertaining to the aftercare of foreigners: the regulation makes no difference between nationals and foreigners in this regard, so – theoretically – these services should be available for foreign prisoners as well. However, according to information provided by the Probation Service of the Justice Office (operating under the Ministry of Justice), foreigners are very rare among the clients of the service.

2.11 Staff

There is no special training for staff on dealing with foreign prisoners. The prison service is trying to solve language barriers by placing together with foreign prisoners detainees who speak both Hungarian and the language spoken by the particular foreigner.

2.12 Projects

There is no information on specific projects concerning foreign prisoners.

3 ADMINISTRATIVE DETENTION OF FOREIGN PRISONERS

3.1 Institutions

Alien policing jails are the institutions most frequently used for the execution of administrative detention. In those cases when the criminal court ordered the

---

[52] Art. 61 (2) – (7), Criminal Code.
[53] Art. 114/A, Penitentiary Code.

imprisonment and the expulsion of the foreigner he/she might temporarily be placed in a penitentiary after the person concerned served his/her sentence.. The number of such placements is extremely low; there were six foreigners placed in penitentiary while in alien policing custody in April 2006.

3.2 Responsible Ministry and legislation

Alien policing jails are under the scope of the Ministry of Interior (and are directly managed by the Border Guards). The main law regulating the forms of administrative detention is the Alien Policing Act, while the implementation of detention is regulated by Alien Policing Detention Decree. The rules were modeled after the rules pertaining to police jails. Article 1 (2) of the Alien Policing Act provides that in alien policing cases, the following authorities are entitled to take measures:
- the Office for Immigration and Nationality (OIN)
- the regional office of the OIN
- the Alien Policing Authority of the Border Guards
- Ministry of Foreign Affairs and Consulates authorized to issue visas

3.3 Capacity of institutions

Altogether there are eight alien policing jails in Hungary. Their official capacities are the following:

Györ	50
Nagykanizsa	56
Kiskunhalas	90
Orosháza	25
Nyírbátor	169
Balassagyarmat	10
Budapest	20
Szombathely	220

3.4 Length of stay

The Alien Policing Act provides a variety of long-duration detention measures aimed at foreigners intercepted by the Border Guards, police or Alien Policing Authority in illegal crossing of borders or illegal stay. These are the following:
a) detention for refusal[54]: in order to implement the readmission agreements;
b) alien policing detention[55];
c) detention in preparation for expulsion[56]: applicable during an alien policing procedure aiming at the identification of the foreigner or the clarification of his/her legal residence.

---

[54] Art. 47, Alien Policing Act.
[55] Art. 46, Alien Policing Act.
[56] Art. 48, Alien Policing Act.

Type a) may be ordered by the Border Guards, while type b) and c) are ordered by the OIN. The administrative authorities may order the detention for five days. The court is entitled to extend the detention type a) and c) for up to 30 days, and type b) for up to 12 months. The different forms of the detention must be summed up, but their total length may not exceed 12 months. Data regarding the average length of stay in such forms of detention was not available.

3.5 Decisions procedure

Detention for refusal can be ordered by the Border Guard. Alien policing detention and detention in preparation for expulsion are ordered by the OIN. Alien policing detention can be ordered only after the OIN decides on the expulsion of the foreigner. During the procedure, the foreigner must be heard by a judge and an interpreter must be provided by the authorities.

The general procedure can be summarized as follows: Article 36 (1) of the Alien Policing Act provides that the alien policing agency of the Border Guard may refuse the entry of the foreigner who crossed or attempted to cross the state border illegally if he/she has been arrested within 30 days from crossing the border and if because of the illegal crossing a readmission agreement is applicable (measure of refusal). Furthermore, Article 47 (1) of the Alien Policing Act makes it possible to place the foreigner in detention whose 'refusal' can be implemented within 30 days from the date of the arrest in order to ensure the implementation of the refusal measure (detention for refusal).

Therefore, in the case of intercepted foreigners, an alien policing procedure is initiated in order to refuse their entry, their 'detention for refusal' is ordered and they are transferred to detention facilities operated by the Border Guard. Alien policing expulsion may be ordered against the foreigner who has violated or attempted to violate the rules of entry and exit (Article 32 (2), Alien Policing Act). However, Article 40 (1) of the Act provides that prior to passing the decision ordering alien policing expulsion, it shall be examined whether the principle of non-refoulement applies[57]. Moreover, Article 39 (2) of the Alien Policing Act excludes the expulsion of unaccompanied minors if the unification with his/her family or appropriate state/other institutional care is not guaranteed for him/her in the state of origin or another admitting state. In practice, if 30 days 'detention for refusal' have elapsed and expulsion was not executed, the Alien Policing Department of the OIN can take a decision on expulsion which then provides the legal basis for further confinement of the foreigner. This type of detention is practically identical with the detention for refusal and is generally implemented in the same detention facility, in the very same cell. Detention pending expulsion is only prohibited by law in the case of unaccompanied minors while asylum seekers with special needs can be detained.

The lengthy detention of asylum seeker asylum seekers in alien policing jails is a particular problem. The question whether an asylum seeker asylum seeker who enters the country (formally) illegally will be detained for a year in an alien policing jail or he/she will be placed in an open reception centre (operated by the OIN) depends on accidental circumstances and on arbitrary decisions of the authorities. If the asylum seeker asylum seeker manages to file an asylum application with the OIN before he/she is caught by the Border Guards, he/she will become an officially recognized asylum seeker who has the

---

[57] Art. 43, Alien Policing Act.

right to legally reside in Hungary until his/her application is adjudicated. If however the asylum seeker (who arrived to Hungary "illegally") is apprehended by the Border Guards before that happens, an alien policing procedure will be initiated against him/her before he/she could possibly submit the asylum application. He/she will be expelled from the country, and although the execution of the expulsion will be suspended as soon as he/she submits an asylum application, the pending expulsion will serve as the basis of the alien policing detention.

Another particular problem to be pointed out is the lack of medical care of foreigners detained in alien police jails. Article 78 (1) of the Alien Policing Decree provides that foreigners placed in an alien police jail are entitled to all necessary medical care free of charge if needed. In practice, in case of medical problems which cannot be dealt with in the jail, they are transferred to a local hospital and are permanently guarded by border guard officers. This places an undue burden on the Border Guard as they have to employ four or five officers to guard a single foreigner and also on the hospital that does not wish to see officers with guns in their wards. In case of mental problems, the patients will be returned after some days of medication to the alien police jail where they usually refuse to take the prescribed medicine and are not under the supervision of a trained psychiatrist; consequently, their mental state deteriorates. As a result foreigners held in alien police jails who did not commit any crime are in this respect in a worse situation than convicted detainees.

In its 2005 report, the CPT pointed out two further problems. The delegation called attention to the fact "that access to a lawyer was not provided in the early stages of deprivation of liberty, i.e. before foreign nationals were transferred to a Border Guard holding facility", and recommended "that the Hungarian authorities take measures to ensure that immigration detainees have an effective right of access to a lawyer/legal representative from the very outset of their deprivation of liberty (i.e. from the moment when the persons concerned are obliged to remain with a law enforcement agency)".[58]

The delegation also noted "that foreign detainees were not systematically provided with written information about their rights in a language they understood, in particular at Border Guard stations at points of entry", and recommended "that steps be taken to ensure that foreign nationals detained under the aliens' legislation and asylum seekers are systematically issued at the very outset of their deprivation of liberty with a form setting out in a straightforward manner their rights and the procedure applicable to them; the form should be available in an appropriate range of languages".[59]

3.6 Appeal

It is not allowed to lodge an administrative appeal against the decision imposing detention.[60] However, it is possible to file an application to the court within five days to review the lawfulness of the imposition of the detention order pending expulsion.

Built-in review exists with regard to detention for refusal and detention in preparation of expulsion. The rules are as follows. The detention may be ordered by alien policing

---

[58] 2005 CPT Report, point 28.
[59] Ibid.
[60] Art. 49 (1), Alien Policing Act.

authorities for five days. After five days, the local court may extend the detention until the individual leaves the country.[61] In most cases an extension is given for 30 days.

After six months, the judicial review is shifted from local courts to county courts. The maximum duration of detention is 12 months[62]. Furthermore, Article 53 (1) of the Alien Policing Act provides that the combined period of the alien policing detention, detention for refusal and detention in preparation for expulsion applied against the foreigner shall not exceed 12 months. Detention shall be terminated immediately when the reason for ordering it has ceased. In principle, the court shall consider the legality of the detention. Detention is frequently prolonged to the maximum duration of 12 months. Some courts do not review adequately the lawfulness of the expulsion or whether it is enforceable, while others conduct a thorough assessment.

3.7 Irregular stay

Illegal/irregular stay 'eo ipso' does not constitute a crime. Article 22 (1) of the Government Decree 218/1999. (XII. 28) on Petty Offences provides that those who enter Hungary illegally may be fined for up to HUF 100,000. Article 22 (2) provides that those who break the law regulating travel documents may be fined for up to HUF 50,000. The Penal Code provides that those foreigners who have been expelled from the country or are banned from entering and staying in the country, but nevertheless stay or enter without a permission, do commit a crime and may be punished with up to one-year imprisonment. In practice the typical sentence is suspended imprisonment and expulsion but pending procedure foreigners are frequently taken into pre-trial detention.

3.8 Numbers

Data on numbers of detained irregular foreigners was not available.

3.9 Expulsion

Data on the percentage that will be expelled after administrative detention was not available.

3.10 Not-expelled prisoners

Article 56 (1) b) of the Alien Policing Act provides that – when the maximum period of detention (12 months) has expired but the reason of ordering the detention still exists and when the expulsion or readmission may not be ordered due to an obligation incumbent upon Hungary on the basis of international treaty – the regional alien policing authority may order the foreigner to stay in a designated place, restricting personal freedom. The mandatory place of stay may be designated in a community shelter when the foreigner is unable to support himself/herself, i.e., does not have appropriate accommodation and financial income. It can also be the private estate of a person who had invited him/her under the obligation to support him/her. The operative part of the resolution shall

---

[61] Art. 47(4) and Article 48(3), Alien Policing Act.
[62] Art. 46, Alien Policing Act.

determine the place of mandatory stay. The costs incurred in relation to staying at a community shelter are borne by the foreigner. If 18 months have passed since ordering mandatory stay at a community shelter but the circumstances due to which it has been ordered continue existing for reasons beyond the control of the foreigner, another place of stay is designated for the foreigner. In certain cases the authorities, upon the request of the foreigner, permit him/her to continue staying at the community shelter for humanitarian reasons.

3.11 Detention irregulars under criminal law

According to Article 54 (2) of the Alien Policing Act, in the course of implementing detention in a penitentiary institution, the detained foreigner shall be separated from those who are in custody, or in preliminary arrest as well from convicts. In practice, foreigners are placed only in alien policing jails. Only those foreigners are accommodated in the Nagyfa Penitentiary Institution who have committed a crime and the court ordered their expulsion. In this institution expelled foreigners are placed separately from Hungarian citizens.

3.12 Minors

Minors shall not be put in detention. Article 52 of the Alien Policing Decree provides that in alien policing procedures, the alien policing authority examines whether the application of rules determined by the Act and the decree pertaining to unaccompanied minors apply to the minor foreigner staying unlawfully in the country. In the course of this examination, it is examined whether the foreigner is a minor and if yes, whether there is any person obliged by virtue of legal rule to be guardian of the foreign minor. If the alien policing authority had ordered detention of the foreigner and it is revealed in the course of the procedure that the rules pertaining to unaccompanied minors are applicable, detention is terminated and a designated place of stay is ordered for the unaccompanied minor.

4 NATIONALS ABROAD[63]

4.1 Numbers and composition group

The Ministry of Foreign Affairs is informed about a couple of hundreds of cases of Hungarian nationals detained abroad per year, including all forms of detention (from short term custody to prison sentences). In 2005, close to 800 Hungarian nationals were incarcreated for shorter or longer periods of time.

---

[63] Information in this section was provided by László Takács, Head of Department of Consular Affairs at the Ministry of Foreign Affairs.

4.2 Detention countries

The countries where on average most Hungarian nationals are detained are Austria, Germany and Italy.

4.3 Reasons for detention & sentencing

According to information provided by the Ministry of Foreign Affairs, minor traffic offences and offences related to breaching the rules of staying and working in the particular foreign country constitute the majority of offences for which Hungarian citizens are detained abroad. According to the Ministry's estimation, between 50 and 75 percent of the offences are of this nature. Minor offences against property also constitute a relatively significant portion of the offences committed by Hungarian nationals in foreign countries.

4.4 Involved organisations – tasks and activities

Most tasks related to Hungarian nationals detained abroad (visits, packages, and so on) are performed by the 98 official foreign representations of the Republic of Hungary. In countries where no such representations function (and also in areas which are geographically difficult to access for official Hungarian consular authorities), these tasks are fulfilled by honorary consuls (their number is about 200).

The Ministry of Foreign Affairs also tries to establish contacts with civilian organizations in order to make sure that detained Hungarians do not remain without any contacts. On an occasional basis, the Ministry approaches Hungarian organizations or Hungarian citizens in the particular foreign country, and asks them to pay visits to Hungarian detainees. This is done on a voluntary basis, without any payment.

4.5 Release and reception home country

No institution has been established with the purpose of providing assistance after release and in connection with reception in Hungary.

4.6 Aftercare

No institution has been established with the purpose of providing aftercare for Hungarians previously detaineed abroad.

4.7 Public opinion and media

The issue of Hungarians in foreign prisons is usually not in the focus of public debates and media coverages. One exception was the story of four young Hungarian men, who were imprisoned in Ecuador for acting as drug couriers. The young men were arrested one by one between December 2004 and the April 2005. The public opinion took notice of their stories after an article was published about them and the horrible conditions in South American prisons in August 2005. For a while, the issue was in the center of attention, but after late 2005, the discussions died away.

5 EVALUATION AND RECOMMENDATIONS

On the basis of the above description it can be concluded that the following are the main reasons for the social exclusion of foreign prisoners:

- Most foreigners cannot participate in work activities, education and vocational training. The ultimate reason for that is the existence of language barriers. The solution for this problem is unclear as due to budgetary constraints the government cannot allocate financial sources for this purpose.
- It is not an unconditional obligation of the penitentiary to provide meals that meet the religious requirements of foreign (or national) detainees. The solution could be to impose unconditional obligation upon the penitentiaries to respect the religious requirements in all aspects.
- Foreigners with special dressing requirements due to religious belief are not allowed to wear clothes other than the prison uniform. The solution might be the same as for the previous shortcoming.
- The actual willingness of consulates to help foreign prisoners is not always satisfactory. In case of prisoners coming from those countries the lack of any external support might result in extreme separation from the outside world.
- Indigent foreign detainees frequently do not receive adequate legal assistance as they cannot pay for the interpreter's fee and the government does not advance that cost. The government should advance a lump sum in each case for covering the cost of interpreters.
- The medical treatment of foreigners detained in alien police jails and suffering from long lasting somatic or mental illness cannot be dealt with. A solution to this anomaly could be terminating the alien policing detention in case of a seriously ill detainee and to place him/her, depending on his/her health condition, either in a civilian hospital or in a reception centre for asylum seekers where appropriate medical care is accessible and available.
- The law does not exclude the possibility of placing someone in alien policing detention who has applied for asylum. Detention rules are often arbitrarily applied and detaining asylum seekers is still the rule rather than the exception. This breaches international law and sometimes national law standards. Asylum seekers should not be detained except when they refuse cooperation with the asylum authority or severely violate the order of a reception centre.
- Alien policing detention should not be treated as a form of punishment. It is a measure used to keep people available for the execution of the expulsion (expulsion) order, therefore the rules pertaining to foreigners in such detention should be much less severe than the ones concerning criminal suspects or convicts.
- The maximum duration of alien policing detention should be further reduced to six months.

Chapter 13

Ireland

Mary Moore

1 INTRODUCTION[1]

1.1 Overview of penalties and measures

There are insufficient sentencing statistics available in Ireland to explore if there has been a bias in sentencing at Court towards custody.[2] However the relatively high use of custody, especially outside of Dublin can be seen from Court Services Report.[3] In Dublin, Probation supervision was generally used more frequently than immediate imprisonment, in Limerick immediate imprisonment was more common than Probation Supervision and Community Service combined. A high use of suspended prison sentences and low use of Community service characterized both areas[4]. O'Donnell notes another trend as the decline in the number of admissions[5] to prison[6] under sentence. There were 6866 in 1994, and 5160 in 2001. The Court Service Report[7] shows a fall of 10% in the number of prison sentences imposed by the District Court 2001-2002 while the average daily population of prisoners is now relatively stable

The length of sentences imposed and the time spent in custody on sentence appears to be increasing. The average length of time for a life sentence prisoner to serve prior to consideration for release on license has increased to 13 years between 1996 and 2001 from less than eight years in 1978 to 1980. In 2003 and since the Minister for Justice, Equality and Law Reform has made a number of statements making it clear that prisoners serving life sentences will expect to serve very substantial sentences.[8] The Minister has indicated that temporary release in the community should be considered only after 15 years of a life sentence except in the most extraordinary circumstances.

1.2 Overview of the Prison System

1.2.1 Organizational Structure

The Irish Prison Service is under the aegis of the Department of Justice, Equality and Law Reform. The financial allocation for the Irish Prison Service in 2004 was €305.8 million.[9] The Irish Prison Service comprises fourteen prisons of which eleven are medium

---

[1] This report was compiled with assistance from the multi-disciplinary team in Mountjoy Prison, comprising the Governors, Chief Officers, Librarian, Chaplain, Psychologist and Head Teacher; the Chaplaincy Service and the Managers of the Visitors' Centres in Mountjoy and Cloverhill Prisons; the Irish Commission for Prisoners Overseas, particularly Grainne Prior; and the Irish Prison Service. Special thanks to Gerry McNally, APPO and my colleagues in the Probation Service who advised me on various aspects of their work in this area. I am also grateful to Eileen Farrell, PO whose dissertation on working with foreign nationals detained in Irish prisons was an invaluable starting point.

[2] O'Donnell, 'Imprisonment and Penal Policy in Ireland', *Howard Journal of Criminal Justice*, 2004, 43 (3), pp. 253-256.

[3] Court Services, *Court Services Report*, Dublin 2003, pp. 105 - 108.

[4] O'Donnell, ibidem, p. 258.

[5] The term 'admission to prison' is used instead of 'committal to prison' throughout this document.

[6] O'Donnell, ibidem, p.258.

[7] Court Services, *Court Services Report*, Dublin 2003, p.100.

[8] Dáil Éireann 25 February 2003, Seanad Éireann, 3 April 2003.

[9] Department of Justice, Equality and Law Reform, *Irish Prison Service Annual Report*, 2004, p. 5.

security, with one high security and two open prisons.

The prisons mentioned below are all closed medium security prisons. Portlaoise is a high security prison and Loughan House and Shelton Abbey are open prisons. The information is taken from the Irish Prison Service Annual Report Daily Average Number of Prisoners (2004: 16)

Table 1 Daily Average Number of Prisoners 2004

	Institution	*Average Number in Custody*
Dublin	Arbour Hill Prison	138
	Cloverhill Remand Prison	392
	Dochas Centre Mountjoy	84
	Mountjoy Prison	485
	St Patrick's Institution	198
	Training Unit	87
	Wheatfield Prison	374
Outside Dublin	Castlerea Prison	210
	Cork Prison	274
	Limerick Prison	260
	Loughan House(open centre)	72
	The Midlands Prison	439
	Portlaoise Prison	123
	Shelton Abbey (open centre)	49

The average cost of keeping a prisoner for one year was €83, 800.00 in 2003.[10] According to the report of the Prison Service Cost Review Group (1997:19) in 1996 it cost €69,327.70 to keep one person in prison for a year in Ireland in comparison to €50,027.68 in the Netherlands, €40,250.70 in England and Wales and €32,251.35 in Canada. On 21 March 2006 the Minister for Justice, Equality and Law Reform responded to a parliamentary question on the cost of keeping an offender in prison. His response is included below:[11]

Minister for Justice, Equality and Law Reform (Mr. McDowell): The key performance indicator identifying the cost and efficiency for the prison service is the cost of keeping an offender in prison. This has fallen over the last three years from €84,750 in 2002 to €83,800 in 2004 as set out below. The reduction in cost is due to the strict budget management, and in particular overtime management. In this regard, I am pleased to inform the Deputy that I have reversed the unacceptable trend of spiralling overtime costs that has been a feature of our prisons operations for many years. As a result of my determination to tackle this unsustainable dependence on overtime to run our prisons there was a reduction in the overtime bill of some €13.4 million in 2004 compared to 2003.

---

[10] Ibidem, p. 7.

[11] Parliamentary question, Dáil Debates, Vol 688 [10855/06], 21 March 2006.

Table 2 Cost of keeping an offender in prison.

Prison/Place of Detention	2002	2003	2004
Arbour Hill	71,550	73,600	70,400
Castlerea	72,100	75,250	70,000
Cork	71,050	72,350	75,000
Cloverhill	72,400	83,300	76,100
Curragh	72,400	70,100	Prison closed
Fort Mitchell	100,100	96,050	Prison closed
Dóchas	Included in Mountjoy	Included in Mountjoy	82,800
Limerick	86,450	90,200	73,000
Loughan House	62,850	67,700	63,900
Midlands	72,850	77,300	75,900
Mountjoy	95,900	97,900	91,800
Portlaoise	206,700	232,100	225,200
Shanganagh Castle	169,450	Prison closed	Prison closed
Shelton Abbey	84,850	80,100	82,000
St Patrick's	85,550	82,300	79,800
Training Unit	63,600	71,800	72,300
Wheatfield	72,350	75,800	71,300
Overall	84,750	87,950	83,800

In 2005 the Irish Prison Service staff establishment comprised 2925.5 posts with 17 positions at Governor Level 1, 11, 111, 12 positions at Deputy Governor Level and 19 positions at Assistant Governor Level.[12]

Inspections: Inspection bodies include the Inspector of Prisons and Places of Detention, Mr. Justice Dermot Kinlan, appointed on a statutory basis with effect from April 2002. One of the terms of reference of this post is to inspect and report on prisons and other places of detention managed on behalf of the Department of Justice, Equality and Law Reform by the Irish Prison Service. The Inspector submits a written report at the end of each year. The first Annual Report of the Inspector of Prisons and Places of Detention was published on 2 July 2003. One of the recommendations in this report was asylum seekers should not be held in prison while awaiting a decision regarding Irish citizenship- those applicants should be detained elsewhere.[13]

Visiting Committees visit prisons on a regular basis and report on various aspects of prison life e.g. the prison buildings, the management of the prison, conditions and treatment of prisoners, including food, health, medical care, education and preparation for release. Visiting Committees hears requests and complaints that persons in custody make to it. The members are free to visit every part of the prison. The committee reports on these matters at least once a year to the Minister for Justice, Equality and Law Reform. In the Mountjoy Prison Visiting Committees Annual Report attention was drawn to 'slopping

---

[12] Department of Justice, Equality and Law Reform, *Irish Prison Service Draft Annual Report*, 2005.
[13] Department of Justice, Equality and Law Reform, *Irish Prison Service Annual Report*, 2003, p. 113.

out' in the prison and in the interests of health and safety and welfare to both staff and prisoners the Report urges the Minister for Justice to address this situation without delay [14] The Irish Prison Services has plans for the development of new prison complexes in Dublin and Cork to replace older institutions and to meet best standards in prison accommodation.

Ireland ratified the Council of Europe Convention for the Prevention of Torture and Inhuman or Degrading Treatment or Punishment in 1988. Under this Convention, the Committee for the Prevention of Torture (CPT) has a right to visit and report on places of detention. Ireland's first visit from the Committee was in 1993 and there have been two further visits in 1998 and 2002. The CPT has written a report after each visit and areas of concern have been highlighted. An inspection visit by the CPT to Ireland is planned during 2006 as part of the CPT's published programme.

The CPT's report on its 2002 visit was published on 18 September 2003 in conjunction with the government's response. In the CPT's opinion prison is not a suitable place to hold persons who are subject to an expulsion order and who have not been convicted of a criminal offence. In those cases where it is necessary to deprive a person of his/her liberty for an extended period then specially designated detention centres would be more suitable.[15]

1.2.2 Foreign Prisoners

The increase in the numbers of foreign nationals in the general population in Ireland has been dramatic in the last ten years and particularly since the enlargement of the EU in 2004 with the inclusion of ten new States. The Statistical Yearbook of Ireland (2005) indicates that foreign nationals made up 5.8% of the population in 2004. For the first time, the census on 23 April 2006 will be available in 11 foreign languages (Arabic, Czech, Chinese, French, Latvian, Lithuanian, Polish, Portuguese, Romanian, Russian and Spanish. Additional information in the above languages and also Estonian, Slovak, Turkish and Yoruba is available on the Central Statistics office website).[16]

An overview of the statistics for 2004 show that 8820 persons were sent to prison, 5064 of those admitted under sentence. 946 foreign nationals were detained under immigration laws, a reduction of nearly 50% on the 2003 figure.[17] A total of 1804 persons (20.4%) sent to prison in 2004 indicated that they were foreign nationals. This compares with 25.6% in 2003 and reflects the reduction in the number of persons detained on immigration matters. According to the Annual Report of the Irish Prison Service the reduction reflected the sizable reduction in the number of asylum applications received in the state that year.[18] 90% of foreign national prisoners are detained on administrative detention in the Pre–Trial Cloverhill Prison[19] and in the Dochas Centre (Mountjoy Women's Prison). Sentenced foreign national prisoners are scattered among the other prisons. There are currently 226 foreign national prisoners serving sentences for a range of of-

---

[14] Mountjoy Prison Visiting Committee, *Annual Report*, 2004, p. 1.
[15] *CPT Report*, 2003, par 69.
[16] *Irish Times*, 30 March 2006.
[17] Department of Justice, Equality and Law Reform, *Irish Prison Service Annual Report*, 2004, p. 7.
[18] Ibidem, pp. 10-11.
[19] The term 'Pre-trial' will be used instead of 'Remand' throughout this document.

fences coming from 44 different countries. This figure includes 109 non-EU nationals.[20] Up to 2003 a breakdown of figures for non-national prisoners was not deemed necessary, as nearly all prisoners were Irish. To illustrate this O'Donnell refers to a survey of prisoners carried out in 1996. Only three of the 108 male prisoners interviewed at that time had current addresses outside of Ireland.[21]

In response to a Parliamentary Question on 11 October 2005 the Minister for Justice, Equality and Law Reform states the number of foreign nationals serving a prison sentence and their States of origin. Out of the total number of sentenced persons of 2520 on that date, there were 172 foreign nationals. The number of non- EU nationals totalled 86 or 3.4% of the sentenced population. The number of non-Irish EU nationals amounted to 91 and corresponded to 3.6% of those serving sentences. A total of 93% of sentenced prisoners were of Irish nationality. The highest number of non-Irish prisoners was British (64) that can be explained by close geographical and economic ties. In descending order there were 17 South Africans, 14 Chinese, eight Lithuanian, seven Romanian, seven Nigerian and five Polish.[22]

Under the Transfer of Sentenced Prisoners Act 1995 & 1997 seven prisoners transferred into the State (five from the UK, one from Panama and one from the United States) and four prisoners transferred out of the State in 2004 (all to the UK). In total, one hundred and seven prisoners have now transferred here from abroad and sixty prisoners here transferred out since the Act came into operation on 1 November 1995.[23]

1.3 Overview involvement Consulates, Embassies, Ministries home country, Probation service home country, NGO's etc

Based on feedback from Probation Officers in prisons countrywide it appears that there is generally little contact with Probation Services outside of Ireland. Contact is usually in relation to repatriation applications with the United Kingdom. In these instances contact is maintained through phone calls and letters/reports. In Ireland admission procedures are called committal procedures. For the purpose of this report the term admission is being used rather than committal. At admission prisoners should be informed that they might request the governor to inform a consular representative of the country of which the prisoner is a citizen of his/her detention. At the moment there is no obligation to do this in writing. Prisoners have access to free telephone calls to nominated persons whether that is a solicitor or consular representative or family member. Consular representative is notified promptly if a prisoner dies in custody.

The experience of the Probation Officers in the prison is that many foreign nationals have few visitors and receive few visits. Prisons around the country facilitate visits by charitable and religious denominations for foreign national prisoners but it would appear to be done on an ad hoc basis. Prison officers, chaplains, Probation staff have identified isolation and lack of any contact with others as a major issue. The following are an ex-

---

20 Parliamentary question. *Dail Debates*, No.448, 3 May 2006.
21 P. O'Mahoney, 'Mountjoy Prisoners: A Sociological and Criminological Profile,' Dublin 1997, pp. 39, Stationary Office.
22 Parliamentary question. *Dáil Debates*, Vol. 607, No. 2, 11 October 2005.
23 Department of Justice, Equality and Law Reform, *Annual Report* by the Minister for Justice to the Government on the operation of The Transfer of Sentenced Persons Act, 1995 & 1997 for the period 1 January 2004 - 31 December 2004, 2005.

ample of the types of organization or non-governmental bodies that visit the prison:

- Befrienders Organization visits the Dochas Centre (Mountjoy Women's Prison).
- Individual religious (Catholic nuns and priests/ representatives of other religious denominations) visit particular prisoners sometimes over long periods of time.
- Open *heart* House (This project challenges the isolation of HIV through peer support & provides a range of services and facilities. The centre caters for cultural diversity and the outreach worker visits the prison to maintain the contact established with individuals in the community that includes foreign national prisoners.).
- The Guild of St Philip of Neri (a branch of the St Vincent de Paul which is the longest established charitable organization visiting prisoners in Ireland). A French speaker sometimes accompanies the members of the St Vincent de Paul in order to include visits to foreign national prisoners that are of benefit in particular to the West and North African prisoners who they visit.
- Doras Luimni (Limerick) is an organization specifically for asylum applications and foreign nationals who have difficulties about issues of expulsion who the prison may contact if a prisoner needs assistance.
- Integrating Ireland is an independent network of community and voluntary groups who work to promote the full integration in Irish Society of asylum seekers, refugees and immigrants. It has not been possible to get a comprehensive list of those organizations that visit prisoners but some do intermittently including SARI (Sport Against Racism visit the young people who were involved with them originally in the community while in custody) Many are awaiting decisions on expulsion orders and who sometimes end up in custody prior to being removed from the country.
- The Dun Laoghaire Refugee Project and the Irish Refugee Council Dublin also visit on an intermittent basis.

1.4 Overview of trends

1.4.1 Sentencing Trends

The average daily population in Irish Prisons has continued to rise over the past ten years while in recent years the numbers of persons committed under sentence has fallen. [24]O'Donnell refers to the falling number of prison sentences imposed by the District Court between 2001-2002. He also refers to the increasing number of foreign prisoners entering the Irish Criminal Justice System. While the average daily population of prisoners in the Republic of Ireland has grown significantly since the mid 1990s, recorded crime statistics have fallen. O Donnell attributes these trends to a number of factors including the 'politicalisation of the debate about crime, build up of long term prisoners, an expansion of the remand population and a reduction of the use of early release to ease overcrowding'.[25]

1.4.2 Characteristics Foreign Prison Population

Prison accommodation in the Republic of Ireland is used to hold a proportion of failed

---

[24]   O'Donnell, ibidem, p. 259.
[25]   ibidem, p. 253.

asylum seekers, pending expulsion.[26] O'Donnell argues that it is also inevitable that the prison population will change as minority groups appear before the Courts on criminal charges. He reports that in 2002, in eight out of the 59 homicides that took place, the victim was a foreign national (four Chinese, one Welsh, one Lithuanian, one Latvian, and one Portuguese).[27] Ireland has changed from being a homogeneous society with high unemployment in the 1980s to a more culturally diverse country with low unemployment and a thriving Celtic Tiger economy that has attracted many foreigners to its shores.

Garret FitzGerald noted that in the 1970s Ireland was the European country with the highest net emigration rate while in the last decade it has experienced net immigration.[28]. It is not unexpected then that those persons entering the prison system will reflect this change and will come from a variety of different national and ethnic backgrounds. However as trends in other countries show minority and marginalized groups can be over represented in the prison population. According to O'Donnell[29] it is not clear to what extent 'the sudden change in the complexion of admissions to Irish prisons reflects targeting by the police, differentiated patterns of offending or sentencing, or the changing composition of the resident population'. As Tonry [30] suggests, 'members of minority groups are over represented among crime victims, arrestees, pre-trial detainees, convicted offenders, and prisoners in every Western country.'[31]

Statistics from the Irish Prison Service Annual Report on the composition of the prison population in 2004 reflect what is common in prison populations elsewhere:
- Many more men (89%) than women (11%);
- more than two thirds of men and three quarters of women are between 21 -40 years;
- nearly half the population came from addresses in Dublin;
- of the admissions to prison three fifths were serving six month sentence or less;
- Four fifths of admissions under sentences of one year.

Reports on the profile of prisoners suggest that there is a disproportionately higher level of mental illness among people admitted to Irish prisons than in the general population that is similar to trends in other countries.[32] While there has not been any study of the particular mental health needs of foreign nationals in Irish prisons the National Health Service UK identified the following factors in the UK as increasing the likelihood of mental disorders particularly depression developing; isolation, worry about the fate of families, reduction in hope due to long sentences and concern about what will happen on release. Poor literacy has also been identified as an important issue [33] and deprivation and

---

[26] The word 'expulsion' is used instead of ' deportation' throughout this document.
[27] O'Donnell, ibidem, p. 262.
[28] *Irish Times*, 1 April 2006.
[29] O'Donnell, ibidem, p. 263.
[30] M. Tonry, (ed.) 'Ethnicity, Crime and Immigration: Comparative and cross national perspectives', *Crime and Justice, A Review of Research*, Vol. 21. Chicago, University of Chicago Press, 1997, p. viii.
[31] O'Donnell, ibidem, p. 265.
[32] Department of Justice, Equality and Law Reform, 'Mental Illness in Irish Prisoners: Psychiatric Morbidity in Sentenced, Remanded and Newly Committed Prisoners'. H.G. Kennedy, S. Monks, K. Curtin, B. Wright, S. Linehan, D. Duffy,, C. Teljeur, and A. Kelly, National Forensic Mental Health Service, 2005, p. 89.
[33] Irish Prison Service, M. Morgan – M. Kett 'The Prison Adult Literacy Survey: Results and implications', Dublin 2003.

disadvantage can lead to problems whatever a person's nationality.[34]

1.5 Overview of national legislation

The main legislative provisions are to be found in a number of Acts of the Oireachtas and in secondary legislation including:
- Irish Nationality and Citizenship Act 1935. (defines Irish citizenship)
- The Aliens Act 1935 [an alien or non national as defined by this act]
- The Criminal Justice Act 1960
- The Prisons Act 1970 (primary piece of legislation relating to prisons)
- The Transfer of Sentenced Persons Act 1995 &1997(prisoner repatriation)
- The Refugee Act 1996 (Places and Conditions of Detention) Regulations 2000
- The Immigration Act 1999 (Expulsion) Regulations 2005
- The Equal Status Act 2000
- The Criminal Justice (Theft and Fraud Offences) Act 2001 (sections 26 and 29 relate to offences which include false passports or forgeries of official documents)
- The Illegal Immigrants (Trafficking) Act 2000
- The Immigration Act 2003 (Removal Places of detention) Regulations 2005.
- The Immigration Act 2004.
- Prison Rules 1947
- The United Nations Convention of Human Rights [ratified by Ireland in 1956]
- The Geneva Convention [signed by Ireland in 1951]
- United Nations International Convention on the Elimination of All Forms of Racial Discrimination [adopted and ratified by Ireland 2001]
- European Convention for the Prevention of Torture and Inhumane or Degrading Treatment or Punishment Strasbourg, 26.XI.1987
- Convention determining the State responsible for examining applications for Asylum lodged in one of the Member States of the European Communities. Dublin Convention EC Official Journal C 254, 19 August 1997.
- Council of Europe Convention for the Protection of Human Rights and Fundamental Freedoms as amended by Protocol No. 11,Rome, 4.XI.1950

The Irish Citizen Child Scheme was introduced in 2005 and a new Immigration and Residence Bill is to be introduced in 2006.

---

[34] O'Mahony Mountjoy Prisoners: A Sociological and Criminological Profile, Dublin 1997, Stationary Office.

2 TREATMENT OF FOREIGN PRISONERS

2.1 General

Emigration has always been a feature of Irish life. Immigration is a recent phenomenon. Economic necessity forced many Irish people to travel across the Irish Sea to Britain and across the Atlantic to America. Irish expulsion to Australia was initially as a form of punishment for crimes committed in Ireland in the 19th century. Emigration to Australia has since been a choice destination. As a country we are used to saying goodbye to people. While we are renowned for being a welcoming people this was in the context of tourism. Our ability to assimilate and integrate other nationalities on a permanent basis has not been tested up until the 1990s. There is a view that as a country Ireland was unprepared for the demands posed by large-scale immigration.

Ireland has attracted an influx of foreign nationals drawn to it by the prosperity of the Irish economy. The National Action Plan against Racism[35] says that the 2002 Census of Population provides the most comprehensive breakdown of national diversity in Ireland to date and identifies five main regions of origin for foreign nationals living in Ireland. These are UK and other EU nationals (3.4% of the total population), Asian (0.5%), African (0.5%) non-EU European nationals (0.5%) and the United States (0.3%). With 9% of the workforce and 10% of population foreign born according to Central Statistics Office we have reached levels of immigration that other European countries took decades to achieve. [36]There have been 750,000 newcomers from 211 countries since 2000.

Ireland in the 21st century has low unemployment. Industries have been sourcing workers from other countries to keep the Irish economy booming. Recent debates concerning foreign nationals taking Irish jobs have featured in the national media. Media views have challenged this and at a recent seminar in Dublin in March 2006 it was stated that there was no evidence of displacement of Irish workers since the accession of the ten new states in 2004. However there was concern raised about the lack of integration measures e.g. in schools and about the exploitation of migrant workers.[37]

A small proportion of the foreign national population in Ireland are asylum seekers fleeing from countries where war and torture are the norm. There was a noticeable increase in the numbers of applicants seeking asylum during the 1990s that has been attributed, in some quarters, to the limited immigration legislation in operation up to 2003. The number of applications rose from 39 in 1992 to 7724 in 1999.[38] The figures increased to 11,630 in 2002 and decreased to 4304 in 2005.[39] The drop in numbers seeking asylum in Ireland was, at least in part as a result of a change in legislation.

The Irish response to asylum seekers is well documented in a report 'Beyond the Pale' on asylum seeking children and social exclusion in Ireland.[40] This report considers the implications of direct provision (hostel accommodation plus €15 per week per adult) that

---

[35] National Action Plan Against Racism, 2005, p.50.
[36] *Irish Times*, 10 March 2006.
[37] *Irish Times*, 10 March 2006.
[38] S. Mullally, *Manifestly Unjust: A Report on the Fairness and Sustainability of Accelerated Procedures for Asylum Determinations*, Irish Refugee Council, 2000, p.15.
[39] *Sunday Tribune*, 26 March 2006.
[40] B. Fanning, A.Veale, D.O'Connor, *Beyond the Pale: Asylum-seeking children and Social Exclusion in Ireland*, Irish Refugee Council Dublin 2001.

was introduced in 2000 that meant that asylum seekers were not entitled to full rates of supplementary assistance.

Some foreign nationals come into contact with the criminal justice system and the next section focuses on conditions for foreign nationals in a prison setting.

2.2 Living conditions and facilities

Living conditions and facilities for foreign nationals in Irish Prisons are in general, the same as for Irish prisoners and tend to vary depending on whether the prison is old or new, but there tends not to be any separation. Cork prison is the main committal prison for the Munster area and it houses approx 265 prisoners. There is no separate area for pre-trial prisoners. Few foreign national administrative detainees awaiting removal are held in this prison.

In Cloverhill Pre-Trial Prison (Dublin) a separate wing is used to house non-Irish nationals. Staff in this prison says that in the early days there had been limited knowledge and experience in working with other nationalities and assumptions were occasionally made about who might get on with whom. In recent times there is an increasing awareness of the sensitivities of different cultures. The facilities on this wing are the same as on other wings of the prison with the exception that there are three beds to a cell rather than two. In the report prepared by Kelly[41] on administrative detention this was remarked on and while it was suggested that the burden of overcrowding fell on the foreign prisoners the Irish Prison Service has indicated that any overcrowding was and is borne equally among all prisoners irrespective of origin. In the Dochas Centre, (Mountjoy Women's Prison) there is no separation policy. In practice most foreign nationals are in the two drug free houses which have both a mixture of Irish and non-Irish foreign nationals. On the 27 January 2006 there were nine Irish women and nine foreign national women in each of the two drug free houses.

2.3 Reception and admission

The reception procedures for foreign prisoners are the same as for national prisoners. When a prisoner arrives at a prison there are a number of procedures that are gone through which are common to all prisons. On being committed to prison each prisoner on reception sees a medical officer, medication is arranged if necessary and personal details are taken. Admissions are required to see the Governor, this usually happens the following morning when an interview is conducted.

In Mountjoy Prison, there is a questionnaire for new admissions that has been translated into fourteen different languages. In practice the questionnaire is not always useful: a prisoner might be able to write down the answers on this form in his/her language but the person issuing the questionnaire would not understand the replies. As there is no on call interpreter service; the prison management occasionally requests other prisoners to translate where necessary. After the admissions interview with the Governor it is decided where each prisoner will be assigned in the prison. This decision can be based on factors

---

[41] M. Kelly, *Immigration – Related Detention in Ireland.* A research report for the Irish Refugee Council, Irish Penal Reform Trust and Immigrant Council of Ireland. Human Rights Consultants, Dublin 2005.

such as a person's previous history, whether they are first time offenders, whether they have health or mental health problems, whether they are drug users and what their behaviour has been like during previous sentences.

The Department of Justice, Equality and Law Reform and the Irish Prison Service are committed to updating the current Prisons Rules published in 1947. A new information booklet to be issued will be based on the New Prison Rules that are due to be approved by the Minister for Justice, Equality and Law Reform. It is intended that the booklet will be available in a number of languages for the benefit of foreign prisoners. In the meantime prisons provide locally prepared information booklets in English to prisoners on regimes and services.[42]

Foreign prisoners are advised on admission about their entitlements to communicate with a representative of their diplomatic mission and asked if they wish to avail of this. Prisoners are also entitled to call a family member at this stage. Special consideration is given in the Cloverhill Pre-Trial Prison to prisoners being able to contact their families at appropriate times for the families. Clocks with the different international time zones are placed in the main circle area of the prison to facilitate prisoners contacting family at the right time. Such clocks are not available elsewhere but assistance is given to foreign nationals to contact family as required.

In Mountjoy Prison efforts are being made to create a five to ten minute video programme for television in the reception area. This will show how the prison system works and what services are available to prisoners. It is intended that it will be available in different languages. In Cork Prison notices about Prison services are put in strategic locations in the prison in different languages by the Education Department.

2.4 Work-Education-Training-Sports-Recreation

There are no separate provisions for foreign prisoners with regard to work or education. The majority of foreign nationals are either on remand where there is no obligation to engage in education, work or training or are short sentence prisoners who often do not engage in these activities. Many foreign nationals serving longer sentences in Mountjoy Prison work in the kitchen areas (this is hard work but would be considered a good job with privileges not enjoyed by other prisoners e.g. longer time unlocked from cell, access to preferred food). Others participate in training and working in the computer area.

The Education Service Computer Class that accommodates six pupils is always full and at least half the participants are non-nationals. The Art class takes place twice a week and it too is well attended by non-nationals. There are currently two non-national students studying for their Leaving Certificate English. There is an ESOL (English for Speakers of other languages) Course on offer twice a week and it is very well attended. At time of writing (April 2006) there were five to six Moldavian, two Lithuanian, one Algerian and two Chinese prisoners attending these classes. The teachers have commented on the enthusiasm of foreign nationals for education that is evidenced by the fact that they arrive first each morning. Some staff have expressed a concern that this group could be the subject of harassment as they avail of the services that Irish prisoners may find it hard to commit to and might resent others obtaining.

Senior prison staff in both Mountjoy Male and Female Prison commented that for-

---

[42]   Department of Justice, Equality and Law Reform, *Irish Prison Service Annual Report*, 2004, p. 82.

eign women serving long sentences were keen to avail of education. They consistently attend educational classes and avail of work opportunities which allows them to send money home to families.

2.5 Food-Religion- Personal hygiene-Medical Care

There are at present 20 full time and three part time chaplains working in the Irish Prison Service. The Chaplaincy provides spiritual and pastoral care to the prison community.[43] The Chaplaincy caters for everyone and they can also bring in representatives from different religions. The prison chaplains have recommended that the inappropriate use of prisons being used as detention centres for expulsion should cease and that a less severe but secure environment be provided where access to the latest information regarding their legal status and entitlements.[44]

Until recently the vast majority of prisoners have been Roman Catholics. In Mountjoy Prison there is Mass every Sunday at 9.30 am which takes place in the Church and a Protestant Service led by the Minister for the Church of Ireland which takes place in a room on D Wing. Many of the non-Catholic prisoners attend this service. The chaplains in Mountjoy also facilitate other denominations coming into the prison at the request of prisoners. The Greek Orthodox Church representative visited a number of times and left information for prisoners with the chaplains. These visits are facilitated in the professional box visiting area where the representative can meet with the prisoner on a one to one basis. Visits by spiritual advisors perhaps for cultural reasons appear to be infrequent to Muslim prisoners.

A Medical Officer sees all prisoners as soon as possible after admission. The medical officer is a doctor appointed to the prison who attends daily and as required. A person in custody may be examined by a Psychiatrist as a result of a Court Order, a Court Recommendation or on the referral of the Prison Doctor. Other disciplines in the prison make referrals on behalf of a prisoner to the psychiatric services. If a prisoner requires inpatient psychiatric care arrangements are made for the prisoner to be transferred to the Central Mental Hospital in Dundrum.

A recent report on mental illness in Irish prisons confirmed that specialist psychiatric care is provided in all the main prisons on an outpatient sessional basis, increasingly delivered by modern multi-disciplinary 'in-reach' teams, at least in the prisons within reach of Dublin. [45]The findings of this report indicate that a higher proportion of people in the Irish Prison system than in the community are diagnosed with severe mental illnesses. This level exceeds international averages for men on remand.[46]

---

[43] *National Prison Chaplains Annual report,* 2003, p. 1.

[44] Ibidem, p. 5.

[45] Department of Justice, Equality and Law Reform, H.G. Kennedy, S. Monks, K. Curtin,B. Wright, S. Linehan, D. Duffy, C. Teljeur and M. Kelly, *Mental Illness in Irish Prisoners: Psychiatric Morbidity in Sentenced, Remanded and Newly Committed Prisoners,* 2005, p. 106.

[46] Ibidem, p. 2.

2.6 Consular and legal help

The draft Prison Rules to be approved by the Minister for Justice, Equality and Law Reform include the following provisions regarding consular access:

17.
1. a foreign national shall be provided with the means to contact a consul and, in addition, an   asylum applicant shall be provided with the means to contact:
- The United Nations High Commissioner for Refugees or the Representative in Ireland of the High Commissioner, and
- subject to such limitation as to numbers as the governor may reasonably impose, national or international authorities and organizations whose principal object is to serve the interests of refugees or stateless person or to protect the civil and human rights of such persons.
2. A person to whom paragraph (1) applies shall be informed in particular of his or her entitlements under Rule 40 (Visit by legal adviser or relating to court appearance).

41.
1. A foreign national shall be entitled to receive a visit from his or her consul at any reasonable time or where he or she is a stateless person the consul of a state of his or her choosing who is willing to visit him or her.
2. An asylum applicant shall be entitled to receive a visit at any reasonable time from-
- such national or international authorities or organizations, as may be designated by the Minister, whose principal object is to serve the interests of the refugee or stateless person, and
- a consul of a state of his or her own choosing[47]

2.7 Contact with Outside World

Foreign prisoners have the same visiting entitlements as national prisoners. The prison rules provide one visit per week of 30 minutes for sentenced prisoners. One additional special visit per week can be requested at the discretion of the Governor. Pre-trial (remand) prisoners are permitted one short visit each day. In both the Male and Female Mountjoy Prisons in Dublin there is flexibility about visits for foreign nationals. Family members who have travelled from abroad to see their family member are granted at the discretion of the Governor, visits on the days that they are in the country during both morning and afternoon (for example if a family visit for a long weekend then they would be able to visit Friday morning and afternoon, Saturday morning and afternoon and Monday morning and afternoon).

Special arrangements at the discretion of the Governor can also be made for a prisoner for one of the visits to be in a less clinical visiting facility (family members may stay for lunch in the Dochas Centre if desired) but this is dependant on availability of prison staff because such visits require one prison officer to supervise one prisoner. The prisoner needs to request extra visits if his /her family is coming. In Mountjoy Male Prison the visiting system requires that prisoners put six named visitors on their visitors list. If this has

---

[47]   This can be referenced to the 2005 publications prisons page at www.justice.ie.

not been done a visitor may not be allowed to see a prisoner. If the prisoner has not re-quested visits the family may not be allowed to visit. In practice prisoners with limited English may be at greater risk of confusion arising around visitor arrangements though prison managements do seek to actively remedy such visiting problems where they do oc-cur.

Each prisoner is granted a six-minute phone call every day for no charge. The num-ber of letters a prisoner can send out of prison is two per week and the number of letters in, is unlimited. All letters may be censored except to legal advisors and any legal docu-mentation. Television in the cell is available in virtually all prisons - programmes are in English.

Visitor Centre: The Visitors Centre at Mountjoy Prison is a well-staffed, comfortable and pleasant environment for families who come to visit with children. There are similar centres at Cloverhill Prison and at the Midlands Prison. The Visitors Centre provides tea and coffee facilities in a hospitable atmosphere with a child care area for children. The Centre also links up with the prison on behalf of prisoners and their families in certain in-stances. The Visitor Centres have noticed the increase in the foreign nationals' families using the centres.

2.8 Re-integration activities – Prison leave

The Probation Service in the prisons work towards the re-integration of prisoners back into their communities. The Probation Officer will seek to address the factors that re-sulted in a person coming to prison in the first place and attempt to help to put in place measures which would help to reduce recidivism and support resettlement in the com-munity in partnership with relevant statutory and voluntary services.

2.9 Release – Expulsion

There is no provision in Irish Law for the automatic expulsion of a foreign national who has committed a criminal offence. For the year 2005 to April 2006 seven non-EU nation-als convicted of offences, and who served a prison sentence for same, had been issued with Expulsion Orders. Of those, four had been deported and a further four had applied to return voluntarily to their countries of origin. [48]

Arrangements for foreign national prisoners released in Ireland are as for Irish prison-ers. The Irish Economic and Social Forum Report on Re-Integration of Prisoners[49] found that release from prison 'can be a very traumatic experience' particularly for those who have been in prison for a long time, have unmet needs about accommodation, train-ing or employment, dependence on drugs or alcohol or family difficulties. The report recommends pre and post release strategies for positive sentence management. At present the Irish Prison Service is developing an integrated sentence management system that seeks to provide a seamless transition from custody back into the community with the support of services in prisons and in the community.

---

[48]   Parliamentary question. *Dail Debates.* No. 190, 4 May 2006.
[49]   National Economic and Social Forum Report No 22, Re-*Integration of Prisoners*, 2002 p. 83.

2.10 Aftercare – Probation

Apart from those being repatriated, there is very little contact with probation services in other countries in relation to foreign nationals. Probation staffs in prisons report that their experience is that foreign nationals can be socially quite isolated. At times they do not seem to have much information about their legal rights and they are often anxious as to what is going to happen to them on their release from prison. On occasion they are distrustful of authorities and do not readily disclose links or family contacts in their reported country of origin. Many fear being expelled from the country.

There is no statutory aftercare for persons completing a sentence except for prisoners who are granted temporary release with a condition of supervision by the Probation Service by the Minister for Justice Equality and Law Reform, those convicted of offences under the Sexual Offenders Act 2001 or those who may have a period of post release supervision imposed by the Circuit or other Court. (The Judge imposes a prison sentence to be followed by a condition of supervision by the Probation Service for a specified period with particular conditions).

Many of those subject to Court directed post release supervision in the Dublin area are referred to the Bridge project, an intensive community based probation supervision initiative which is one example of a re-integration initiative which is staffed largely by the Probation Service and the City of Dublin Vocational Education Committee. To date there have been no foreign nationals subject to the Bridge programme.

The Linkage Programme is a re-integration initiative that is supported and funded by the Probation Service. Training and Employment Officers prepare, plan and implement training/or employment placements for offenders referred to them by the Probation Service. There were a total of 272 referrals from prisons and places of detention in 2004 but there is no breakdown as yet of referrals by nationality.

2.11 Staff

It is evident that there are increasing numbers of foreign nationals in our prisons that reflects the changes in Irish Society in the last ten years. A National Action Plan Against Racism was published in 2005 '*Planning for Diversity*- the National Action Plan Against Racism'. Mainstreaming an intercultural strategy within the prison service' is one of the objectives in this plan.[50] The Irish Prison Service initiated independent research on racial and cultural awareness in Irish prisons that was published in 2003. Training and information on human rights is provided to all prison staff at induction. The Irish Prison Service is currently reviewing its internal procedures for staff training and processing of prisoner complaints.[51]

In England and Wales the HM Inspectorate of Prisons report ' *Parallel Worlds*' found that there was no shared understanding of race issues within prisons and that the variety of viewpoints of prison management, staff (white staff and visible minority staff) and prisoners highlights the difference in perceptions. The existence of Race Relations Liaison Officers (RRLO), a Race Relations Management Team and a Prisoner Diversity Repre-

---

[50] Department of Justice, Equality and Law Reform, *Planning for Diversity - the National Action Plan Against Racism*, 2005 par. 7.1, p. 34.

[51] Department of Justice, Equality and Law Reform, Irish *Prison Service Annual Report*, 2003, p. 87.

sentative has resulted in good practice in those prisons in England and Wales. However prison surveys regularly found that black and minority ethnic prisoners 'have worse perceptions of their treatment than white prisoners across many key areas of prison life'.[52] The report highlights the key areas that need to be developed and concludes that leadership and training are 'critical elements in breaking down the different perceptions and experiences.'[53] This is an area currently undergoing particular development in the Irish Prison Service.

2.12 Projects

Below are just three examples of projects that reflect the range of initiatives taking place:

Special Projects outside of the prison setting. The Irish Commission for Prisoners Overseas (ICPO) requested the Council for Research and Development, a commission of the Irish Bishops Conference, to undertake an evaluation of their family support service for families of prisoners serving sentences overseas. The main findings of this evaluation highlighted the financial difficulties of families who had to finance a visit to support their relative or to meet the cost of basic prison supplies such as clothing, food, stamps and phone cards. The lack of clear information and legal support services emerged as a significant problem for families struggling with a foreign legal and prison system. Families were particularly concerned about the lack of any statutory or formal post release support for their relatives on release from prison. This interesting project focuses attention on those who have emigrated from Ireland. While emigration has decreased in the past decade the CSO figures in 2005 show 16,600 people had emigrated with 50% of those in the 15-24 age group. The experience of the Irish Commission for Prisoners Overseas is that many of those who emigrate are vulnerable and more likely than most to end up in need of services.[54] Similar issues arise for non-Irish prisoners in custody in Ireland. One of the main recommendations of the Report was that the Department of Foreign Affairs should provide an allowance to Irish citizens in prison overseas and that a visitation allowance be provided to all families of prisoners overseas, in order to ease the financial burden of imprisonment on families. Other recommendations included the suggestion that fact sheets on the prison and legal system in different countries should be prepared to support families by providing them with practical advice and information.[55] The overall aim of the research was "to evaluate the needs of families of Irish prisoners overseas, in relation to the service provided by the ICPO and support services in general".[56] The findings of this evaluation are helpful when we turn our attention to the families of foreign national prisoners in custody in Ireland. It is clear that many of the same issues would arise for them.

2.12.1 Special projects within the prison

In 2002 the Probation Service at Mountjoy Prison, in collaboration with the Education

---

[52] HM Inspectorate of Prisons, Parallel *Worlds - A Thematic Review of Race Relations in Prisons*, 2005, p.1.
[53] Ibidem, p.3.
[54] Submission by Irish Commission for Prisoners Overseas (ICPO) to Joint Committee on Foreign Affairs Sub-Committee on Human Rights, 16 June 2005.
[55] Separated Families: Reviewing the needs of Families of Irish Prisoners Overseas, 2005, pp. 26 - 27.
[56] Ibidem, p. 1.

Unit, recognized the special circumstances of the increasing number on foreign prisoners and successfully introduced an inter agency programme to address the specific needs of and provide information and support to foreign prisoners.[57] A Probation Officer at Mountjoy Prison completed a dissertation on the subject of working with foreign prisoners detained in Irish Prisons.[58] In conjunction with the team of Probation Officers working in Mountjoy Prison she helped to identify the main issues arising in relation to working with foreign prisoners. Concerns were also raised about prisoners repatriated from England to Ireland and their misunderstandings about the Irish Criminal Justice System. Some prisoners coming back to Ireland to complete their sentence encounter difficulty adjusting because of structural and operational differences in the two prison systems. The Probation Service in Mountjoy Prison identified significant issues such as the absence of information and advice about what was available in the prison and on statutory rights and entitlements of foreign national prisoners. In response it was decided to consult with the prisoners themselves and to see what the needs were and how they might be addressed. The Prison Governors supported the International Group Mountjoy and there was an input from all the disciplines within the prison. (Prison staff, governor and chief officer, librarian, chaplain, and psychologist). The group ran from Easter to Summer (2002) one morning a week for 10-12 sessions and it took place in the school. There were 10-12 participants with nine different nationalities including French, Belgian, Chinese, Russian, Lithuanian, Scottish, Nigerian, Libyan, and Algerian. A number of the referrals came from D wing where there were a number of Lithuanians whose needs had to be addressed. However other referrals came from all areas of prison. This initiative proved very useful.

Making a Difference. The inter agency programme developed a picture of the specific needs and requirements of the group. While all prisoners may experience stress and fear in a prison setting this group of international prisoners expressed a strong sense of isolation through lack of communication. While there were televisions, for many these were of limited use as their English was poor and all the channels were in English. The group identified in particular feelings of anxiety related to isolation. Some of the suggestions and specific requests made by the group were acted upon by Prison Staff. These included:

- *Newspapers:* Librarians spoke to prisoners and on their request ordered Chinese and French newspapers once a week. Since then, depending on where the foreign national prisoners are from, newspapers are bought on an ad hoc basis by both the library and the school.
- *Learning English:* Linked to school and provided dictionaries in the relevant language to those in the group. This service has developed and notices about English Classes have been translated into 14 different languages.
- *Visits*: Prison Governors approved flexibility for visits for foreign nationals. However the prisoner must go to the Governor in advance of the visit and apply for special visiting arrangements.
- Letters (prison regulations allow two letters a week out of the prison). The prisoners requested more flexibility with this, as some wanted to write as often as they wished as many of the group received no visits. The Governors facilitated this request for the for-

---

57   Department of Justice, Equality and Law Reform, *Irish Prison Service Annual Report*, 2004, p. 84.
58   E. Farrell Working with Non-Nationals detained in Irish Prisons. Unpublished dissertation. University College Dublin 2003.

eign national prisoners in this group.
- *Food:* The home economics teacher in school encouraged making dishes of ethnic nature in class.

In some cases the foreign nationals did not want their family to know that they were in prison. They refused any help with getting in touch with their consular representatives, as they did not want to increase the likelihood of family finding out where they were. One of the teachers involved in the multi-national group provided an illustration of this when she related the story of two Chinese prisoners who were having photographs taken in the group. They requested that the photos be taken in front of a blackboard to suggest to their families that they were indeed studying as their families believed them to be.

Special Projects within the Prison Setting.

The Annual Report of the Inspector of Prisons and Places of Detention 2002-2003 identified the existence of racism in the prison system.[59] The Irish Prison Service had already, at that time, initiated independent research on racial and cultural awareness in Irish prisons having recognized the changing profile and ethnic diversity in the community and prison populations. The 'Evaluation of Research and Training Project for Intercultural Awareness' was conducted in Wheatfield prison in 2002 was published in February 2003. The purpose of the project was to determine the nature of intercultural awareness, communication and racial equality within a prison in Dublin with a view to subsequently informing policy.[60] The Irish Prison Service continues to review its internal procedures for staff training and processing of prisoner complaints.[61]At local level prisons have responded to these new demands. Two handbooks were published in 2003 one for staff and one for prisoners entitled 'Inappropriate Behaviour'. These were produced by the Irish Prison Service for Cloverhill Pre-Trial Prison as a policy statement on racism, harassment and bullying. There has been anti-racism training for both staff and prisoners on this and it is currently being considered for the main committal prison in Dublin.

3 ADMINISTRATIVE DETENTION OF FOREIGN PRISONERS

Foreign prisoners in Ireland who are held in custody not because of a criminal offence but because they have no permanent or temporary resident permit for Ireland are considered in this part of the report. The treatment of foreign nationals held under administrative detention in Ireland will be considered in this part and comparisons made with the treatment of foreign prisoners imprisoned under Criminal law in Ireland which were dealt with in the above section. This type of detention is based on migration or administrative law not criminal law. Detention for immigration purposes is referred to as administrative detention in this paper. A recent research report 'Immigration –Related Detention in Ireland' is the first of its kind in this area of law and is referred to throughout this section. This independent report recommends that the practice of holding immigration detainees in prisons in Ireland be brought to an end as prisons are identified in

---

[59] *First Annual Report of the Inspector of Prisons and Places of Detention* 2002-2003, pp. 65-66.
[60] Fitzpatrick Associates, *Evaluation of Research and Training Project for Intercultural Awareness.* Wheatfield prison, Dublin 2003, p.1.
[61] Department of Justice, Equality and Law Reform, *Irish Prison Service Annual Report*, 2003, p. 87.

the report as inappropriate places in which to hold immigration detainees.[62] The report defines the term 'prisoner' as including all four categories of immigration related detainees namely (1) persons refused permission to land, (2) those detained during the asylum process, (3) people detained pending expulsion and (4) those remanded in custody for immigration-related reasons (awaiting trial).[63]

The European Committee for the Prevention of Torture (CPT) in the report on its visit to Ireland in May 2002 made clear that "a prison is by definition not a suitable place in which to detain someone who is neither convicted nor suspected of a criminal offence. In those cases where it is deemed necessary to deprive persons of their liberty for an extended period under Aliens legislation, they should be accommodated in centres specifically designed for that purpose, offering material conditions and a regime appropriate to their legal situation and staffed by suitably qualified personnel".[64]

3.1 Institution

Ireland uses existing prisons to place this group of people whereas some European countries have created special detention centres

3.2 Ministry responsible and legislation

The Department of Justice, Equality and Law Reform is responsible for the administrative detention of foreign prisoners in Ireland with the overall responsibility lying with the Minister for Justice, Equality and Law Reform. The laws that apply to this group are complex and the growing body of legislation in recent years is evidence of the legal complexity of the issues involved.

3.3 Capacity institutions

The Committee for the prevention of Torture (CPT) 2002 recommended that the holding of administrative detainees in prisons should be reviewed. Nearly all administrative detainees are housed in two prisons in Dublin where they have access to the same facilities as other prisoners.

3.4 Length of stay

Under section 5(6)(a) of the Immigration Act 1999, the period of detention may not exceed eight weeks in total. Most persons, however, are detained for periods less than eight weeks because the sole purpose of detention is to ensure that the person will co-operate in making arrangements, such as securing travel documents. The Supreme Court has considered the constitutionality of certain amendments of the Immigration Act 1999. The Supreme Court judgement of 28 August 2000 held, with regard to detention on foot of

---

[62] M. Kelly, ibidem, p. 2.

[63] Ibidem, p. 48.

[64] Report to the Government of Ireland on the visit to Ireland carried out by the European Committee for the Prevention of Torture and Inhuman or Degrading Treatment or Punishment (CPT) from 20 to 28 May 2002, CPT 2003, 36, par. 69.

an expulsion order, that "in all circumstances the safeguards which do in fact exist and which will be further outlined in this judgement are perfectly adequate to meet the requirements of the constitution".

3.5 Decisions procedure

The Department of Justice, Equality and Law Reform is responsible for the administrative detention of foreign prisoners in Ireland.

3.6 Appeal Procedure

The safeguards to which the Supreme Court judgement cited above referred include the right to challenge, by judicial review, the validity of the expulsion order. The court also held that the extended grounds for detention would not contravene Article 5 of the European Convention on Human Rights and Fundamental Freedom. (Parliamentary Question 43, Dáil Éireann 27 April 2006) Administrative detention can be appealed through the District Court and to the High Court on a *habeas corpus*, judicial review or other legal application.

3.7 Irregular stay

Under the Immigration Act 2004, illegal /irregular stay in Ireland is a criminal offence on two grounds and the maximum penalty is 12 months imprisonment. (Section 4 (2) Immigration Act 2004 and Section 6 (1) Immigration Act 2004.[65]) In addition persons can be detained pre-trial for immigration related reasons under the Criminal Justice (Theft and Fraud Offences) Act 2001. Sections 26 and 29 relate to offences that include false passports or forgeries of official documents. These criminal offences are punishable by fines or imprisonment of 5-10 years.[66]

3.8 Numbers

The number of people detained for immigration related reasons in 2004 was 946, which was a significant reduction form 1852 the previous year.[67] However those held under the Immigration Act (1999) in 2004 were imprisoned for longer: 619 persons were imprisoned for over 51 days in comparison to 367 for the same period in 2003. While the numbers of those detained fell the length of time for those held in prison increased.[68] These figures do not reflect the total number of people detained for immigration–related reasons during this time as persons refused permission to land in Ireland are another category. Few would be taken to prison before being returned to their point of origin.[69]

---

[65] Ibidem, p. 19.
[66] Ibidem, p. 45.
[67] Department of Justice, Equality and Law Reform, Irish *Prison Service Annual Report* 2004, p. 11.
[68] M. Kelly, ibidem, pp.15-16.
[69] Ibidem, p. 16.

3.9 Expulsion

No up to date figures available. There is no preparation for release/expulsion for administrative detainees apart from the work of the chaplaincy in this area. It appears that when persons detained under administrative law are being deported neither the person himself or herself or their families are informed in advance of their expulsion from the country. As this can often happen at any given time it is less likely that families will know or be informed. On occasion 10-15 foreign nationals can be brought up to the prison for expulsion at any one time. The authorities arrange transport arrangements, usually flights.

3.10 Not expelled prisoners

No information

3.11 Detention irregulars under criminal law

Administrative prisoners are detained with prisoners who are detained under criminal law.

3.12 Minors

No up to date figures available.

3.13 Reception and Admission

Admission procedures are the same for administrative detainees as for sentenced prisoners and detainees. Information booklets are given to all prisoners on admission to Cloverhill Prison but only in English at the moment. While admission interview questions have been translated into nine languages in both of the above prisons, staffs say that they can be less than helpful for instance if one is trying to find out if a woman is unwell. Kelly has suggested in his report that immigration related detainees bear the burden of the overcrowding in the prison system in both of these institutions. The Irish Prison Service has indicated that overcrowding, where it occurs bears equally on Irish and non-Irish prisoners and detainees. It is only in Cloverhill (Pre-Trial) Prison that there have been instances of three foreign prisoners or administrative detainees to a cell. Female immigration detainees at the Dochas Centre, Mountjoy Prison will often be detained in one of two houses the first of which should accommodate two but occasionally has more women. Female immigration detainees will often be held in one of two houses that have a fairly stable population of drug free, sentenced and long-term prisoners.[70]

In October 2005, new procedures were put in place that removed responsibility from prison management to either inform the prisoner about making an application for asylum or to process asylum applications. This applies for persons detained under the Immigration Act for refusal of leave to land. Instead the Governor should inform the detainee that she/he could make contact with the Garda National Immigration Bureau (GNIB) who

---

[70] Ibidem, p. 50.

on receipt of a faxed copy of a form of notification from the prison will visit within 24 hours. In the event that a detainee indicates that s/he wishes to apply for asylum, the Immigration Officer will conduct an initial interview with the detainee and will forward the process from there.

3.14 Work-Education-Training –Sport-Recreation

There is no work, training, or educational services at present in Cloverhill Pre-Trial Prison where most administrative detainees are housed. Inmates are out of their cells for six and a half hours each day. There are plans for the development of work and training facilities. The building has been completed and is due to open in the near future. The daily routine is the same as for all other pre-trial prisoners where the use of the recreational yard is available in the morning and use of indoor recreational facilities (including snooker and table tennis) is available in the afternoon. At the Dochas Centre (Mountjoy prison) women are unlocked from the cells for around 12 hours per day (7am -7pm) during which time they are free to avail of the various activities and facilities. The prison library in Cloverhill has a multicultural collection of books, talking books and a limited selection of music CDs, in the following languages: Russian, Arabic, Chinese, Serbian, Romanian, Polish, Portuguese, French, Spanish, Albanian and Croatian. In addiction some foreign language and cultural interest magazines are held e.g. *Jeune Afrique Intelligent, New African, Argumenty y Fakty* (Russian newspaper*)* and *African Geographic.*

3.15 Food-Religion-Personal Hygiene-Medical care

The Prison Service has responded well in relation to food, to the diversity of nationalities and special dietary requirements are provided for in both these institutions (No complaints received in the study mentioned above which considered this issue among others.) All religions are facilitated through the chaplaincy in both institutions. Consideration is given in Cloverhill (Pre-Trial) Prison to the special needs of Muslim prisoners and efforts are made to allow them to do their customary religious rituals. Special food is ordered in, prepared by a Muslim cook and ordered from recognized Muslin traders. Advice was sought by the prison authorities from the Muslim Community about these issues. In the Dochas Centre, Mountjoy Prison, the female prison, all dietary requirements are taken into account and the chef prepares what is requested. Consideration is also given to clothing and the type of material used. For instance Muslim prisoners will not wear the white nylon shirts as the material is like silk and offends the men.

The mental health needs of immigration detainees are well illustrated in CVS Consultants and Migrant and Refugee Communities Forum.[71] The NHS (National Health Service) have done studies of refuge communities in England and Wales which show a high prevalence of mental health problems on two levels, problems of adjustment and those experiencing problems of post traumatic stress relating to incident in country of origin. Isolation, fear about the future and bereavement and loss of station in new country all feature as identifiable factors in a person's mental health. There are few studies done on the mental health of immigration or asylum seeking detainees.

---

[71] CVS Consultants and Migrant and Refugee Communities Forum, A *Shattered World: The Mental Health Needs of Refugees and Newly Arrived Communities,* 1999.

3.16 Contact with the Outside World

Immigration detainees at both Cloverhill Prison and the Dochas Centre Women's Prison are granted the same visiting entitlements as pre-trial prisoners, one 15-minute visit every day, Monday-Saturday and free telephone calls of up to six minutes every day. In the recent report by Kelly [72] it was recommended that time spent speaking to a solicitor by telephone should not be counted as part of time for telephone calls. There is a television in every cell but stations are only in the English language.

Visitor Centre: The Visitors Centre attached to Cloverhill Prison has many foreign national visitors. Communication difficulties and the need for leaflets and literature in other languages have been identified as issues to be addressed. Another area of difficulty is families unwilling to talk about their home lives. They are sometimes suspicious of staff at the centre as they are not sure whether they are prison or police personnel or independent. Visitors may not be aware that this is a confidential service and may be reluctant to ask for information or advice.

3.17 Re-integration activities- Prison leave

There is no prison leave or local settlement programme for this category of administrative detainee.

3.18 After-care- Probation

Probation personnel in the pre-trial prison have limited engagement with administrative detainees. In other prisons there is some limited involvement.

3.19 Staff

Training in cultural awareness and diversity is ongoing for all services working in prisons. As mentioned before, training and information on human rights and diversity is provided to all prison staff at induction and further initiatives are being developed and implemented on an ongoing basis.

4 IRISH NATIONALS DETAINED ABROAD

4.1 Numbers and composition group

There are reported to be approximately 700 Irish Prisoners in England and Wales of whom approximately 50 are women according to the ICPO.

---

[72] M. Kelly, ibidem, p. 54.

Table 3 Number of Prisoners in contact with Irish Commission for Prisoners Overseas (ICPO) on 28 March 2006. (ICPO database)

MALE	FEMALE	TOTAL
497	26	523

AGE	NO OF PRISONERS
Under twenty	3
Between 20 and 35	170
Between 35 and 50	62
Over 50	136

4.2 Detention Countries.

The main countries of detention for those in contact are England and Wales followed by the USA. 448 are detained in the UK (England and Wales, not including Northern Ireland), 29 in USA, and 14 in Spain, 7 in France and smaller numbers in other countries. The Irish Commission for Prisoners Overseas says many prisoners may not know of their organisation or choose not to have contact with them. Some people do not put themselves down as Irish in the UK prisons. The official figures are probably an underestimate. Only very recently have the number of Jamaican prisoners and Nigerian prisoners overtaken the Irish prisoners in the UK prison population. The ICPO does not have contact with all prisoners but their newsletter is distributed widely.

Table 4: The main reasons for detention where known of Irish Prisoners Overseas. (ICPO database)

REASON FOR DETENTION	NUMBER
Homicide	36
Robbery	19
Assaults	11
Sexual offences	9
Drugs	5
Larcenies	5

TERMS OF SENTENCE	
1-3 years	18
4-6 years	91
7-10 years	82
11-15 years	53
over 15 years	34
life	72

4.3 Involved organisations – tasks and activities

The organisations involved with Irish prisoners overseas are the Department of Foreign Affairs, Department of Justice, Equality and Law Reform, local Irish Embassies, Irish Commission for Prisoners Overseas (ICPO), HM Prison Service in the UK, Probation Service UK, Chaplains in the UK prisons.

4.4 Release and reception home country

There is no single organisation responsible for ex prisoner emigrants returning to Ireland. The Probation Service provides a voluntary advice and referral service to prisoners returning to Ireland who contact the Service and call into any Service office. Where the ICPO have prior information and they do in many cases they send on information such as the 'What Now' information booklet published for people leaving prisons by the Department of Social Welfare and Family Affairs in advance of their return and the names of services in the prisoners' home area.

4.5 Aftercare

If the person is homeless they are referred to the Homeless Persons Service Unit of the Health Service Executive. The Homeless Persons Service Unit also provides information and support to those people who may be coming home from prison overseas to families. In some cases the ICPO arrange for ex prisoners to be met at Dublin airport and brought to their accommodation.

4.6 Public opinion and media

With some notable exceptions, the return of Irish prisoners is not and has not been a major issue for the media and general public.

5 EVALUATION AND RECOMMENDATIONS

In order to redress the social exclusion of foreign prisoners it is necessary to look at a variety of solutions.
- *Legal Rights and Entitlements.* There is a lack of easily accessible information in the language of users about legal rights and entitlements. Information booklets, prison rules, handouts on how to apply for a telephone card need to be provided in a variety of languages, text and recorded. [73] Translation, translators and accessible information are needed. The report on Immigration –related detention in Ireland recommends that all newly admitted detainees be provided with an information booklet including details about prison life and about the legal rights and entitlements of immigration detainees. There is an urgent need for translation of basic information to be undertaken.
- *Isolation.* Isolation and lack of communication is a matter of particular concern and

---

[73]   M. Kelly, ibidem.

importance for non-national prisoners. Few visits or no visits, no contact with the outside, lack of reading material in own language all contribute to a sense of isolation. The absence of family contact and significant others can contribute to anxiety and depression. There is a need to develop community based support links, personal and emotional and cultural understanding, access to information and communication for foreign prisoners in recognition of their particular circumstances and needs. This might be done through a non-Government community based initiative.

- *Staffing.* Recruitment of staff from minority groups is important resource in addressing minority and cultural issues. This has been actively pursued and initiated in the Garda Siochana. The Irish Prison Service and other criminal justice agencies would also benefit from this approach. In addition to supporting engagement with the community it is also an important signal of inclusion and recognition.
- Training on cultural diversity needs to be further developed as a core part of basic and ongoing training and practice development. Such training is currently underway in the Irish Prison Service. Farrell (2002) advocates more resources and training in working with minority groups. She also advises that we should look at Britain as a country with a rich experience with ethnic and cultural minorities for models of improving practice and learning from that experience.
- The development, implementation and monitoring of clearly stated and managed diversity policies, practices and structures in all areas of the criminal justice system would underpin and support the current commitments. For example, the UK (England and Wales) has a race relations policy statement, race relations committees, a language line and embassy training days all of which would be welcome here. In the report Parallel Worlds[74], leadership and training are considered critical to breaking down different perceptions and experiences. It stresses that the training needs to be specific to race awareness and that it needs to be mandatory.
- A standard protocol and practice guidelines for the management of prisoners who are not Irish citizens that recognizes their status as non-Irish citizens and addresses their special needs should be developed and implemented. See [See Corrections Department NZ accessed 20-10-05]
- *Communication with Consular Services and Other Agencies.* Improved co-ordination and co-operation between Consulates, Embassies, and Ministries, Probation Services and Non Government Organisations is an important and achievable priority that would enhance current services, alleviate distress and improve information and communication channels. There is also a need for more information for families and one point of contact.
- There is a need for further development of documented anti-discriminatory and anti-oppressive practices for services and service providers in the community and in places of detention.

---

[74] HM Inspectorate of Prisons, Parallel Worlds - A Thematic Review of Race Relations in Prisons, 2005.

Chapter 14

Italy

Paola Balbo

1 INTRODUCTION

1.1 Overview of penalites and measures

In Italy, prisons and the wings inside are organised in maximum, medium and low security regimes according to the seriousness of the crimes committed. Kind of sentence, length of it and way of serving are decided by court again according to the offence, the possible length of sanction provided by law and the dangerousness of the person. When law admits it (because the minimum fixed by law has been served and the convict – both foreign and national, EU or non-EU – has adhered to behaviour-requirements), the tribunale di sorveglianza decides on the admission to the requested measure. Alternative measures can be affidamento in prova (similar to probation), affidamento in prova for drug addicts, home detention, semi-liberty and conditional release. Foreign prisoners account for nearly 40% of the total prison population. They come from a wide array of countries, and each region of Italy and each individual penitentiary institution within each region may have different provisions and opportunities for work and re-integration, according to national directives and local conditions. Thus, it is very difficult to determine one valid state of affairs for the entire national territory of Italy.

1.2 Overview of the Prison System

The institutions of the Italian Prison System can be categorized as follows:
- 162 pre-trial detention institutions: Case mandamentali (local prisons) and Case circondariali (district prisons);
- 37 institutions for serving sentences: Case di reclusione (anche presso case di custodia circondariali) (confinement/reclusion prisons, even at district prisons) and Case di arresto (anche presso case di custodia mandamentali o circondariali) (arrest prisons, even at local or district prisons);
- eight institutions for serving safety measures: Colonie agricole (agricultural camps), Case di lavoro (camp of work), Ospedali psichiatrici giudiziari (judicial psychiatric hospitals);
- Observation centres.

The following table shows the national prison population according to gender and type of institution on 30 June 2006 according to the National Department of Prisons:

37 reclusion prisons

	women	*men*	*total*
Convicts	210	8,256	8,466
Accused	49	744	793
Totals	259	9,000	9,259

162 district prisons

	women	men	total
Convicts	1,481	28,141	29,622
Accused	1,098	19,882	20,980
Totals	2,579	48,023	50,602

Eight institutions for the execution of safety measures

	women	men	total
Convicts	80	1,276	1,356
Accused	5	42	47
Totals	85	1,318	1,403

Total

Sum	2,923	58,341	61,264
of which foreigners	1,342	18,879	20,221

2 TREATMENT OF FOREIGN PRISONERS

2.1 Generale

According to the Italian Penitentiary Law of 25 July 1975, n. 354, there are no differences between Italian and foreign prisoners and detainees, neither concerning their stay in prison nor in the serving of sentences in general and in the possibilities of re-insertion. The availability of work and training as well as the forms and contents thereof depend on what each Region of Italy and each prison administration has organised in each geographic area. The basic principle is stated in Article 1 of the Penitentiary Law: "Penitentiary treatment must suit to humanity and must guarantee the respect of dignity of the individual. Treatment is marked by an absolute impartiality, without discriminations because of nationality, race, economic and social conditions, political and religious opinions"[1].

The principle of non-discrimination has been interpreted in the sense that the more foreigners enter prisons to serve a sentence or pre-trial detention, the more the prison directors feel the necessity to reorganise aspects of common life such as religion, food, and the organisation of cells and wings in order to respect those cultural differences the change of which cannot be demanded.

2.2 Living conditions and facilities

Convicts and detainees are assigned to institutions and prison wings with regard to the possibility of common re-educative treatment and to the opportunity of avoiding mutual prejudicial influences (Article 14, law n. 354/1975) and, of course, to the crimes committed.

---

[1] P. BALBO (2005), *Diritto penitenziario internazionale comparato. Esecuzione penale in carcere e in area esterna*, *Laurus Robuffo*, Roma.

2.3 Reception and admission

If treatment within penitentiary institutions and procedures of admission to measures that are alternatives to prison should be the same for all prisoners regardless of any possible discriminatory characteristics, practice shows us that this is in fact not always the case.

It is true that admission to affidamento in prova (similar to probation with supervision), to home detention, to semi-liberty or just to licences is applicable to every convict who fulfils the legally prescribed requisites. However, it is just as accurate that the court of surveillance cannot in fact apply such alternative measures if there are no reference points, centres or structures outside of prison where a foreigner can stay and be under supervision as required by law.

It is the same reason for which judges and courts prefer to pass a prison sentence even when an alternative measure should be indicated better by law because of the length of the sentence. However, some more recent decisions pronounced by the Court of Cassazione go in the other direction. In 2005 it was confirmed that imprisoned foreign citizens without a visa or regular residential permission also have the right to benefit from measures that are alternatives to prison, in the respect of the principle of equal dignity to Italian citizens. This is due to the aim of re-education and social re-integration that the punishment has (and has to have), in accordance with this principle and to the principle of non-discrimination between Italian citizens and foreigners, regardless of whether they have entered the country regularly or illegally (Cass. Sez. I crim., sent. 8 May 2005, n. 22161, rel. Silvestri). Before, the Court of Cassazione has had the opportunity to clear that a petition for *affidamento in prova* of a foreign prisoner who has to be expelled can not be declared inadmissible *de plano* and this because this measure simply defers but does not stop his/her serving sentence. In fact, should he/she return to Italy again, serving of the sentence must recommence (Cass. Pen., sez. I, 24 Oct. 1995, n. 4752, Padilla Chaves).

2.4 Work – education – training – sports – recreation

Article 35 of the same DPR n. 230/2000 prescribes that linguistic and cultural differences of foreign citizens serving custodial sentences have to be taken into account. Moreover, improvements need to be made in providing cultural mediators, even through agreements with local public administrations or voluntary organisations.

Working opportunities have to be improved inside prisons as well as possibilities to participate in training courses. Convicts as well as persons under safety measures are obliged to work, which is performed in agricultural houses or in working houses.

2.5 Food – religion – personal hygiene – medical care

Inmates and detainees are free to profess their religion, learn it and practice it.

Regarding health assistance, foreign prisoners and foreign interned persons, stateless persons and persons without fixed residence are provided with health assistance from the public health service of the region/locality in which the prison is located (Article 18 sec. 2, Regulation, Decreto del Presidente della Repubblica (D.P.R.) 30 June 2000, n. 230).

Prisoners and detainees have the right and the freedom to profess their religion and to be assisted by ministers of their faith[2].

2.6 Consular and legal help

In 1987 it was reminded to governors of prisons and their staff that they are to advise each foreign prisoner or detainee immediately after his/her entry into a prison establishment that he/she has the right to communicate with Consular Representation of his/her State, as well as to receive visits from their representatives, as guaranteed by the Convention of Vienna[3].

2.7 Contact with the outside world

According to Article 18 of Law n. 354 of 1975 prisoners and detainees are permitted to communicate (35 r.e.) and have correspondence with (36, 37 r.e.) their relatives and others. Meetings and face to face conversations are conducted in appropriate cells within the view of penitentiary officers, however in a form that does not enable auditory monitoring (71 r.e.). Special treatment and opportunities are reserved to conversations with relatives.

Phone correspondence with relatives and with third persons in particular cases may be allowed as long as it is in line with conditions and provisions that are indicated by regulations. This is regulated by administrative dispositions of the Department of Prisons.[4] These state that because of the need to listen in to all telephone conversations in order to understand and be aware of their content, conversations in foreign languages that no prison officers understand can lawfully and properly be denied. The Central Direction of the Department of Prisons is conscious of this situation and has ordered prison governors to find and provide reliable interpreters who will simultaneously translate phone conversations in order to make the calls comprehensible for the officers in charge of monitoring them. Officers are authorised to interrupt telephone conversations if they suspect or can circumstantially prove the planning of illicit activities or activities that may be a threat to the order and safety of the establishment.

This also means that other questions such as for instance communication with families and consular representations are partly regulated by the Procedural Criminal Code and partly by the Immigration Law, as stated before.

2.7.1 Foreign prisoners detained under criminal law and who will remain in the country of detention after release

According to Italian law, not all foreign prisoners are forced to return to their country because of the kind and/or length of their sentence. This means first of all that foreigners have the right to be admitted to measures that are alternatives to prison, and to cultural,

---

[2] Art. 26 law n. 354 of 1975; DPR n. 230/2000 artt. 58 and 116.
    Circolare D.A.P. 6 May 1997, n. 535554. *Assistenza religiosa ai detenuti ed internati ex art. 5 DPR 431/76*, referred to the possibility of professing the Muslim faith.
[3] Circolare D.A.P. 12 June 1987. *Art. 36 Convenzione di Vienna. Comunicazioni relative ai detenuti stranieri.*
[4] Circolare D.A.P. 26 Oct. 1988, n. 3254/5704, *Corrispondenza telefonica dei detenuti ed internati. Conversazioni telefoniche in lingua straniera.*
    Circolare D.A.P. 3 Jan. 1990, n. 698564.1/3. *Conversazioni telefoniche in lingua straniera.*

training or working opportunities inside and outside the institutions. Treatment during the sentence is to be individualised based on each individual inmate, but with opportunities offered to everyone without discriminations. The cases in which expulsion for sentenced foreigners can be applied regardless of whether they are regular or irregular before their sentence - are clearly defined by law.

A further element introduced in 2003 is the opportunity for foreign prisoners to obtain the conditional suspension of serving the final part of a sentence to detention (so called *indultino*), unless they are in one of the situations indicated in Article 13, sec. 2 of the Immigration Law, D. lgs. 25 July 1998, n. 286 on illegal entry. It is obvious that the conditional suspension of a sentence is not admissible for foreign prisoners as well as for Italian inmates in such well defined cases as:

- when the sentence is the result of conviction for offences against individuals such as slavery, prostitution of women and children, pornography and similar, trafficking of human beings, harassment and sexual abuse of children, sexual abuses by a group[5];
- when a person has been declared habitually or professionally criminal, or as having a tendency or inclination towards criminal behaviour (Articles. 102, 105 and 108 CP);
- towards those put under a regime of particular control (Article 14-bis L. 26 July 1975, n. 354), apart from cases indicated by art. 14ter or the same law which prescribe the way to appeal the particular regime adopted according to art. 14 bis.
- when the convict has been admitted to measures that are alternatives to prison;
- when the interested person has renounced.

A sentence can be conditionally suspended when at least half of a sentence has already been served, and the remaining period is no longer than two years.

The conditional suspension of a sentence (in the sense of serving sentence) can be decided and applied just once, having taken into consideration the punishment as prescribed by art. 663 cpp. The part of the sanction on which the measure of anticipated liberty has been granted has to be subtracted from the length of sentence upon which conditional suspension is applied (Article 54 L. 26 July 1975, n. 354). Upon request of the individual in question or of his/her legal defence, the magistrate of surveillance provides an order about the suspension (Article 69-bis, sec. 1, 3 and 4, L. 26 July 1975, n. 354). As well as in all other cases, including those in which expulsion is imposed as an alternative or substitutive measure, the magistrate of surveillance can request all the documents and information he needs from the competent authorities.

Within five years of its adoption without having committed any offence, the sentence is extinguished.

2.7.2 Foreign prisoners detained under criminal law who will be expelled to their home country or a third country

The Department of Prisons has adopted administrative dispositions in order to be able to respect national rules referring to the expulsion of foreign prisoners.

---

[5]   It. Criminal Code, book II, Title XII, head III, sec. I, and art. 609-bis, 609-quarter and 609-octies. Art.4-bis L. 26 July 1975, n. 375 and successive modifications.
Immigration law has introduced more severe sanctions against those citizens or foreigners sentenced for offences such as illegal immigration, prostitution and traffic of human beings and adopted in those cases the maximum security regime inside prison prescribed by art . 4 bis of penitentiary law.

If general rules concerning expulsion derive from Immigration law, in 1993 the problem of the costs of expelling a person and which administration should cover the arising expenses were brought into consideration. The Ministry of Justice has formulated the opinion that if deportation and – in particular – accompanying irregular migrants to the border are a responsibility of the bailiffs and thus represent part of the jurisdictional decision of expulsion, as a consequences the costs have to be covered by judicial administration. However, if we divide the procedure of expulsion into two separate parts, the first one represented by accompanying the foreigner to the border which is specifically executed by bailiffs, and the second part represented by sending foreigners back to their state of origin by the police – the costs have to be divided between the Ministry of Justice and the Ministry of Interior[6].

The situation is different for prisoners who have to be extradited from Italy or are sent to Italy from other countries.[7]. In 1996 the penitentiary police were given the responsibility to transfer prisoners who have to be extradited from the penal institution to the border (so called *estradandi*) and from the border to prisons (so called *estradati*). In particular, in the case of extradition abroad, there are three hypotheses of procedures. According to the first one, when the *estradandi* inmate is in one of the seven regions mentioned by authority, he/she is taken from the prison he/she is in to the one the competent bureau of the Ministry has indicated, and the transfer is a duty of penitentiary officers. This duty is also assigned to them when the temporary institution to which the person is taken is in one of the regions, and in this case the penitentiary police have to take the inmates to the border, too. In the second case, if the institution for temporary permanence is in one of the regions where the competence for the transfer lies with the Carabinieri or the State Police, penitentiary officers take the inmates from the prison they are in to the institution of temporary permanence and from there to the border. The third case is given by the regions where the service of transfer is not yet a duty of the penitentiary police, in which cases the responsibility lies with the Carabinieri and the State Police.

In cases of extradition from abroad, inmates are handed over to penitentiary officers by the foreign judicial authority in one of the regions where the penitentiary is competent for the transfer of inmates from the border to the prison to which he/she has been assigned. Otherwise, the extradited inmate is handed over to the police who have been charged to do this.

Direction of the Department of Prisons gave in the past dispositions in order to send foreign prisoners who had been released and who returned to their country the money gained during their serving sentence[8]. In particular, it was ordered that before their release foreign prisoners who are entitled to an amount that is in fact not payable at the moment of their removal can leave an address to which the sums will be sent, or to consent to the payment being sent to the consular representation of their state of origin, which is then in turn responsible for seeing to it that the inmate receives his/her money.

---

[6] Circolare M.G.G. AFF. CIV. 9 Sept. 1993, prot. n. 5/36/U/-1588. *Legge 12 agosto 1993, n. 296. Spese per l'espulsione dei detenuti stranieri.*
Circolare M.G.G. AFF. CIV. 15 Nov. 1993, n. U 1905-S/36. *Legge 12 agosto 1993, n. 296. Spese per l'espulsione dei detenuti stranieri.*

[7] Circolare D.A.P. 21 MAy 1996, n. 3428/5878. *Detenuti estradandi e/o estradati. Estradizioni per l'estero ed estradizioni dall'estero. Competenze e modalità di esecuzione delle tradizioni.*

[8] Circolare D.A.P. 20 July 1999, n. 552569/13. *Corresponsione di somme pertinenti a detenuti stranieri.*

3. ADMINISTRATIVE DETENTION OF FOREIGN PRISONERS

3.1 Institution and capacity

In 1999 regulations were adopted that referred to Centres of Temporary Permanence and Assistance[9]. First of all, the chief constable communicates to foreigners kept in a centre of temporary permanence not only the order referring to his/her delay, but also the one referring to his/her expulsion. In the same order he/she has to be informed of the right to defence and that the defence council can either be a lawyer of his/her own choice or who is chosen and appointed by the court. Also, a foreigner has to be advised of the fact that he/she can request free legal aid that is covered by the State. When he/she is admitted to a centre of temporary permanence, a foreigner has to be advised of the rules that he/she has to respect. One of the most important rules is the prohibition to leave the institution without permission, because in that case he/she will be kept back by public officers. The length of his/her detention must be limited to the time necessary to execute the expulsion or repelling, and must cease if the judge of peace does not confirm the measure of expulsion.

According to regulations, the following ought to be safeguarded inside centres of temporary permanence and assistance: freedom of conversation inside and with visitors from outside; conversations with lawyers and ministries of faith; freedom of correspondence, even phone conversations; fundamental rights of the person; basic health service.

Judges must authorise foreigners kept in one of the centres to go to hospitals while advising consular representations in the meanwhile, in order to prepare the documents valid for returning home. It is always the judge who authorises a person who is being detained in a centre of temporary permanence to go away from the centre for the time necessary to visit a relative or a cohabitee who is in serious danger of life or for other exceptional reasons.

3.2 Decision Procedure

3.2.1 Judicial expulsion

Expulsion has been adopted towards non European foreigners in the cases described by Article 235 and 312 c.p. and on the basis of Article 686 of procedural criminal code, as briefly indicated below.

Expulsion from the national territory of Italy is decided by the judge in a number of cases:

- Foreigner sentenced to at least ten years of detention.

---

[9] DPR 29 Jan. 1999. *Regolamento di attuazione del testo unico delle disposizioni concernenti la disciplina dell'immigrazione e norme sulla condizione dello straniero*, artt. 19 a 23.
  Direttiva generale del Ministro dell'interno 30 agosto 2000 in materia di Centri di Permanenza temporanea ed Assistenza ai sensi dell'art. 22, comma 1, DPR 31 agosto 1999, n. 394, in *Gli stranieri, Rassegna di studi, giurisprudenza e legislazione*, n. 3, settembre-dicembre 2000, p. 360.
  O. DI MAURO, *I centri di permanenza temporanea per immigrati. Aspetti legali e funzionali*, in www.dexl.tsd.unifi.it/l'altrodiritto/migranti.

- Foreign convicts sentenced for one of the offences on traffic, abuse or possession of drugs (Article 3, 74, 79, 82 and 86 DPR 9 Oct. 1990, n. 309). In this case it is an obligatory measure.
- Foreign convicts sentenced for one of the other offences indicated in the same DPR 9 Oct. 1990, n. 309 and in this case it is a facultative measure.
- Expulsion as a safety measure (Article 15 of D.lgs 25 July 1989, n. 286).
- In all cases in which a foreigner is sentenced for one of the offences against the personality of the state (title I, artt. 241 – 313 cp).

It is also prescribed that every time the foreigner violates the order of expulsion that has been decided by the judge, the sanctions established for cases of misdemeanours to the order of an administrative authority as prescribed in the law on public safety are applied (Article 235 cp).

3.2.2 Expulsion as safety measure

According to Article 200 C.P., safety measures can be applied to a foreigner but their application does not prevent a person from being expelling in the cases indicated by Article 235 cp.

Here we can also include the dispositions of Article 15 of D. lgs. n. 286 of 1998 regarding expulsion as a safety measure. Article 15 states that, out of the cases indicated by the Criminal Code, a judge can issue the expulsion of a foreigner who has been sentenced for some of the offences described in Articles 380 and 382 of the Procedural Criminal Code, provided that he/she is socially dangerous.

With regards to the procedure of expulsion it is said that the chief constable is immediately advised of the ruling of pre-trial detention or of the final sentence of conviction to detention against an alien[10], and the same communication is sent to the respective consular authority in order to initiate the procedure of identifying the subject and to permit the execution of expulsion immediately at the end of preventive custody or detention.

3.2.3 Administrative expulsion

This definition includes all the possible forms of expulsion that can be adopted by the Minister of the Interior, by prefect or by the chief constable. Article 13 of the Immigration Law (Decreto legislativo n. 286/1998) introduces a first possibility that applies when there are public order or state safety reasons. In this case the Ministry of the Interior can decide on the expulsion of an alien even if he or she is not resident in the territory of Italy, advising the Prime Minister and the Minister for Foreign Affairs.

Administrative expulsion is decided by the prefect when the alien:

- has entered the national territory of Italy by means of dodging border controls and he/she has been repelled in concordance with Article 10;
- has remained in Italy without having acquired a visa in the time fixed by law, unless delay depends on circumstances beyond the alien's control, or when visa has been revoked or cancelled, or it has expired for more than 60 days without a request of renewal;

---

[10] In this context 'alien' specifically refers to those foreigners who come from States outside of the European Union and to those it is referred to Italian Immigration Law.

- belongs to one of the categories indicated in Article 1 of law 27 Dec. 1956, n. 1423, as substituted with Article 2 of law 3 Aug. 1988, n. 327; or in Article 1 of the law 31 May 1965, n. 575, as substituted with Article 13 of the law 13 Sept. 1982, n. 646.

3.2.4 Expulsion as a substitutive or alternative measure to prison

A further possibility of expulsion is applied after conviction (Article 16 of D. lgs n. 286/1998). If a judge passes a sentence for an unpremeditated offence, applies the sanction asked ex art 444 Procedural Criminal Code towards a foreigner in one of the situations described in Article 13, section 2, the sentence is for a maximum of two years in prison and conditions for conditional suspension of the sentence (Article 163 It. C.P) are not present nor the forbidding causes stated in Article 14, section 1 of the Immigration Law, he can substitute the same sanction with the expulsion for a period of at least five years. In these cases, as well as any other administrative expulsion to which the Constitutional Court has assimilated this one, expulsion is executed by the chief constable, even if the sentence is not definitive and the procedure is the same as that of administrative expulsion (Article 13 of D. lgs. n. 286/1998).

Expulsion can not be applied when a person is convicted of one or more of the crimes indicated in Article 407, sec. 2, litt. a) of the Procedural Criminal Code, or for those indicated in this law and punished with an edictal sanction of more than two years.

If a foreigner who has been expelled because of a sentence that was passed for an unpremeditated offence or as a means of serving sentence ex Article 444 CPP enters the country again illegally before the time fixed by law has passed, the substitutive measure is revoked by the competent judge.

The expulsion is ordered against an identified or imprisoned alien who is in one of the situations described in Article 13, sec. 2, and who has to serve a measure privative of liberty, even if less than two years of the sentence remain. It can not be ordered in cases of convictions for one of the crimes of Article 407, sec. 2, litt. a) of the Procedural Criminal Code, or for one of the offences indicated by immigration law.

Responsibility for ordering the expulsion of a convict lies with the magistrate of surveillance, who decides with a justified decree once he/she has received information about the identity and nationality of the foreigner from the bureaux of police. The decree of expulsion is communicated to the alien who can lodge an appeal within 10 days to the tribunal of surveillance. The court then decides within 20 days.

3.2.5 Procedures to execute administrative or judicial expulsion

In any case, expulsion is ordered with a justified decree which is immediately executable, even if submitted to burden or appeal from the concerned individual. When an alien is submitted to a criminal proceeding and he/she is not in preventive custody, the chief constable, before the expulsion can be carried out, has to request authorisation to do so from the judicial authority. Authorisation can only be denied if there are binding trial needs connected to an assessment of the responsibility of persons who have participated in the crime or who are accused in proceedings for connected offences, as well as regarding the issues of the victims. In such a situation the execution of the measure is deferred until the judicial authority confirms that procedural needs have ceased to exist. Once authorisation has been granted, the chief constable executes the expulsion according to the manner provided for by Immigration law. Authorisation is considered granted if the judicial authority does not reach a decision within fifteen days after the request had been filed. While waiting for authorisation, the chief constable can adopt the measure of keeping the person in a centre for temporary permanence.

The judge authorizes an expulsion when he/she confirms the issue unless one of the causes such as arrest in flagrance or stop occurs, and preventive custody in prison has been adopted ex art. 391, sec. 5, CPP, or if one of the reasons apply for which authorisation can be denied because the person corresponds to one of the categories according to which removal is required. Also, the same procedure is adopted towards foreigners who have been subjected to a criminal proceeding, after the measure of preventive custody has been revoked or declared extinguished for some reason.

The judge, with the same measure of revocation or extinction, decides about the issue of authorisation to expulsion. The measure is immediately communicated to the chief constable.

In the cases in which the judge has the proof that expulsion has been issued, if the measure has not been pronounced yet, he/she enters a so-called non-suit ("way not to proceed"; non luogo a procedure). The things indicated in section two of Article 240 Criminal Code are always confiscated. In such a case the dispositions referring to prohibition of entry after expulsion are applicable as are the sanctions in cases of violations of this order.

If an expelled foreigner (illegally) returns to the territory of Italy before the fixed time period (10 years as general rule; five years if after release; or depending on whether the sentence indicates a period of less than ten years) has passed, or – if the time is longer than that – before the end of the prescribed term for the most serious offence for which there has been proceedings against him/her, Article 345 of the Procedural Criminal Code applies. In accordance with Article 307 of the Procedural Criminal Code, if the alien had been released because the time limit for pre-trial detention had passed, preventive custody can be imposed.

Expulsion is always executed by the chief constable in the form of accompanying the individual to the border by the police, except if the foreigner has been staying in Italy because his permit of stay has expired and a renewal thereof has not been requested. In that case the expulsion order also contains an injunction to leave Italy within fifteen days. The chief constable issues the immediate transportation of the alien to the border just in cases in which the prefect points out that there is a real danger of the foreigner escaping from the execution of the measure.

In the two hypotheses mentioned above, the chief constable communicates to the judge of peace immediately and, however, within 48 hours from its adoption the measure with which it has been decided to accompany the foreigner to the border. Execution of the measure of removal from the territory is deferred until the decision confirming it has been reached. The confirmation-hearing is held in the Council Chamber and the presence of a lawyer, announced in good time, is necessary. Furthermore, the concerned party must also be informed in good time and be present at the hearing.

3.3 Appeal procedure

According to Prisons' Regulations[11] in each prison there is a list of the lawyers of the district, which has to be displayed in a fashion so that it is visible for all prisoners and detainees to see. In order to guarantee a person's freedom of choice, prison operators are strictly not allowed to directly or indirectly influence choices of legal defence counsel.

Generally speaking, however, the right to defence in cases of expulsion or repelling is not as well safeguarded as it ought to be. There has been an evolution since 2002. Immigration law has been amended also because of the sentences of the Italian Constitutional Court, and there is no doubt that knowledge of the rights and right to an interpreter and/or translator are not fully achieved.

A person can file an appeal against an expulsion order only to the judge of peace of the locality where the order was passed, within 60 days. The competence to decide on appeals against administrative expulsion mainly lies in the hands of judges of peace. Their decisions are made within 20 days of the date on which the appeal was lodged by the directly interested person. Regarding the procedure of appeal, it has to be said that this kind of appeal can be subscribed even personally, and it can also be presented through the Italian diplomatic or consular delegation in the State of destination. Subscription of the appeal from the interested person is authenticated by the officials of diplomatic or consular delegations who certify authenticity and take care of its forwarding to the judicial authority. A foreigner is entitled to legal assistance from a lawyer by trust with a special proxy issued in front of the consular authority. Furthermore, he/she can also be granted legal defence that is paid for by the state and, in case of absence of a defence counsel, he/she is assisted by a lawyer who is chosen by the judge among those enrolled in the table of Article 29 of dispositions on application, coordination and temporary of the Procedural Criminal Code, decreto legislativo 28 July 1989, n. 271, as well as by an interpreter if necessary.

The issue of expulsion has to be confirmed by the judge within 48 hours, and this confirmation has to be justified. Before reaching a decision, he/she has to check whether terms and time-limits have been accorded with, that the requirements of the mentioned article are present and that the person has been heard, so long as he/she was present on the day of the decision. While he/she is waiting for the definition of the proceeding for confirming the measure, the foreigner who is to be expelled is detained in one of the centres of temporary permanence and assistance. There is also the possibility that the measure of expulsion is defined before the concerned person is transferred to a centre. Once confirmation has been achieved, the measure of accompanying the foreigner to the border becomes executive. If the measure is not confirmed or if the time limit for reaching the decision elapses, the measure of chief constable loses every effect. The decree of confirmation can be appealed to the Court of Cassazione. However, this appeal does not defer the execution of removal from Italy. The term of 48 hours within which the judge of peace has to confirm the measure starts from the moment of its communication to the chancery.

---

[11] DPR 30 June 2000, n. 230, art. 24.

Due to the short amount of time that judges of peace have to make a decision on whether or not to expel a foreigner[12], the police headquarters provide them with the necessary support and the availability of a proper area in order to facilitate the decision.

Nowadays, one very important change is given by Article 3 of *Decreto legge* 27 July 2005, n. 144 converted, with modifications, in the law 30 July 2005, n. 155 concerning new dispositions about the expulsion of aliens for reasons of preventing terrorism. For terror-suspects, the appeal procedure of Article 13 sec 5-bis of the Immigration Law – that had previously been declared unconstitutional and was consequentially abrogated by the Constitutional Court in sentence n.222 of 2004[13] because it was a violation of the right to defence – has been reintroduced. In fact, in Article 3 that is under examination here it is established that against the decree of section 1 an appeal can be lodged with the administrative tribunal that is competent for the territory. However, a jurisdictional appeal can never suspend the execution of the measure.

Article 3 introduces a new possibility of expulsion apart from the administrative one indicated in Articles 9, section 5, and 13, sec. 1, of the decreto legislativo n. 286 of 1998. The Minister of the Interior or the prefect can dispose the expulsion of a) an alien belonging to one of the categories of Article 16 of law 22 May 1975, n. 152, or b) a foreigner in regard of whom there are founded reasons to suppose his/her stay in Italy can in some way facilitate (even international) terrorist activities. Persons suspected of terrorist activities are expelled immediately, except if they are in prison, in which case the rules for the execution of expulsion of a foreigner under a criminal proceeding are adopted (sec. 3, Article 13 decreto lgs. 25 July 1998, n. 286), and those referring to suspension of executing deportation in cases of appeal (of sec. 5-bis of the same Article 13). The prefect can also omit, suspend or revoke the measure of expulsion ex Article 13, sec. 2, of D. lgs. n. 286 of 1998 when there are the conditions to concede permission of entry as described in the decree on the fight against terrorism, or when it is necessary to do so to obtain information for the prevention of terrorist activities, or to continue investigations of informative

---

[12] Decreto legislative (D. lgs.) n. 286/1998, as indicated in sections 4 and 5, and in art. 14, section 1.

[13] Constitutional Court sentence n. 222 of 2004 (abstract): "The order regulated by art. 13, sec. 5-bis, contravenes principles affirmed by this Court in the sentence mentioned above: the order of accompanying to the border is executed before the confirmation from judicial authority. The foreigner is sent off in a coercive way from the national territory without a judge having pronounced himself on the restrictive order of his/her personal freedom. It is so frustrate the safeguard indicated in the third sec. of art. 13 Const. and that is the loss of effects of the order in hypothesis of denial or lacking confirming from a judicial authority within the successive 48 hours. And with freedom it is violated the right to defence the foreigner has in its unsuppressible nucleus. The censured disposition does not make provision for, indeed, the alien has to be heard by a judge, with the help of a lawyer. It in not under discussion the discretion of the legislator in shaping a proceeding scheme characterized by swiftness and articulated on the sequence police's order – judge ratification.. However, whatever the scheme chosen is, in it the principles of jurisdictional defence have to be realised; the actual control on the order *de libertate* can not be eliminated, nor can it be bereave the party concerned of any defensive safeguard.

Censures proposed by remitting parties cannot finally be over resorting to the thesis of the so-called "double line" of defence for the alien: ratification only 'papery' of the order of accompanying to the border and successive appeal against the decree of expulsion with proper defensive safeguards. It should be in fact eluded the prescriptive significance of art. 13 Const., as appeal on the decree of expulsion (art. 13, sec. 8) does not guarantee immediately and directly the good of personal freedom on which accompanying to the border engraves".

activities directed to single out or to capture the perpetrators of terrorist-motivated offences.

The execution of measures of expulsion in cases of terror suspects can not be suspended during jurisdictional proceedings in application of Article 21 of law 6 Dec. 1971, n. 1037 and successive modifications or of Article 3 of royal decree 17 Aug. 1907, n. 42. An exception to the procedure of appeal after expulsion is contemplated in just one case. In cases of appeals against expulsion orders as described in sec. 4 of the cited article and of appeals as defined in Article 13, sec. 11, of decreto legislative 25 July 1998, n. 286, some information could be covered by State secret. In that case, if a decision depends on knowledge of acts for which there is the secret of investigation or of State, the proceeding is deferred until the moment the act or its main contents can not be communicated to the administrative tribunal. If suspension goes on for a period longer than two years, the administrative tribunal can fix a term within which administration is forced to produce new elements to decide or to revoke the appealed measure. After the term mentioned above has elapsed, the administrative tribunal decides on the basis of what it has.

3.4 Procedures to communicate the order of expulsion and consequences of its violation

The decree of expulsion and the consequent measures indicated in section 1 of Article 14, such as every other act referring to entry, stay and expulsion, are communicated to the concerned person with the indication of the ways in which he/she can lodge an appeal. Furthermore, they are translated in a language he/she understands or, if this is not possible, into French, English or Spanish. Decrees of expulsion as fixed by Immigration Law can be appealed against at the administrative tribunal of Lazio, in Rome.

Except in cases concerning asylum seekers, pregnant women and persons under the age of 18 (Article 19, D. lgs. n. 286/1998), expelled foreigners are returned to the country of which they are citizens or – if this is not possible – to the country from which they crossed the border into Italy.

Expelled persons can not return to Italy without a special authorisation from the Minister of the Interior. Should a foreigner nonetheless violate this prohibition of entry, he/she can be sentenced to between one and four years of imprisonment, and is then expelled again immediately after being accompanied to the border.

In case of expulsion disposed by judge, the transgressor of the prohibition of re-entering the country is sentenced to prison for between one and four years. Foreigners who are accused of the offence of section 13, who are expelled, and who then return to Italy can be imprisoned for a term between one and five years..

In case of unauthorised re-entry (sections 13 and 13-bis, D. lgs. n. 286/1998), the arrest of the offender even out of the cases of flagrancy is obligatory and decision is taken during a proceeding with direct rite.

Unless stated otherwise in the ruling, in general the prohibition of returning to Italy after having been expelled lasts for ten years. Orders can indicate a shorter period, however no shorter than five years, but the person's behaviour while he or she was in Italy has to be taken into account. The described dispositions are not applicable to foreigners who can objectively show that they entered the national territory before the date on which the law n. 40 came into force (6 March 1998). In such cases the chief constable can adopt the same measures indicated in cases of expulsion of persons who have to be identified or for whom means of transportation have to be found.

3.5 Minors

Decreto legislativo of 25 July 1998, n. 286 (Articles 13, 15, 16, 19, 31, 33) specifies that minors below 18 years old can not be expelled, unless their expulsion depends on their right to stay with their parents or tutor should they be expelled. In case an issue of expulsion has been decided against a minor foreigner, the same procedures as those adopted for adults apply. The rules are those referred to illegal entry and to judicial, administrative or as alternative to detention measures. The Tribunal for Minors is responsible for decisions on whether the chief constable can expel a minor foreigner from the country.

In case of illegal entry and of the consequent administrative expulsion, the eventual presence of minors in centres of temporary permanence seems out of real control. Formally, Italy ratified the International Convention on the Rights of children but in practice the situation is quite far from one that safeguards the rights of children[14].

3 NATIONALS DETAINED ABROAD

The matter of Italian nationals detained abroad is briefly concentrated in the numbers given by the Italian Minister for Foreign Affairs[15] in terms of what forms of assistance Consulates and Embassies can provide.

The arrest of nationals abroad, according to declarations from the Minister for Foreign Affairs, can cause very complicated situations. Sometimes a very unusual discrepancy between the committed offence and the resulting sanction can be registered. In this context, there is an example concerning two Italians who were sentenced in the Maldives. They received life sentences for the unlawful possession of light drugs. In such cases it is possible to adopt extraordinary interventions in order to provide help and to effect the liberation of a prisoner. If a national is arrested in a foreign country, the Consulate can:
- visit the detainee, if it has been formally requested;
- provide assitance in finding a lawyer;
- assist in maintaining contacts with the relatives in Italy;
- provide – when it is necessary and admitted by local disposals – health assistance, food, books and newspapers;
- intervene with the aim of transferring a prisoner to Italy, if the national has been detained in one of the countries which signed the Strasbourg Agreement on the transfer of prisoners, or bilateral agreements ad hoc;
- intervene, in particular cases, to support a request of pardon based on humanitarian reasons.

Consulates can not:
- participate in trial as for the national;

---

[14] We remand to Amnesty International report on detention of minors in Italy, published by Association Antogone, http://www.associazioneantigone.it/cpta/cpt.htm

[15] http://www.esteri.it/ita/5_32.asp#9

- cover the legal costs of detained persons;
- effect better treatment in the prison where the national is detained.

The official statistics of 2002, 2003 and 2004 about the distribution of Italian nationals detained abroad with a distinction between sentenced prisoners, persons awaiting their trial and the country in which they are detained are published in the MAE (cp. 2).

Table 2.41 – Italian prisoners abroad according to their judicial situation and geographic area (year 2004)

Geogrpahic Area	2003			2004		
	Awaiting Trial	Convicts	Total	Awaiting trial or extradition	Convicts	Total
Europe	843	1.829	2.672	1.042	1.757	2.799
American continent	72	323	395	100	321	421
Mediterranian and Medio Oriente	2	10	12	8	10	18
Africa Sub-Sahara	5	1	6	10	2	12
Asia and Oceania	21	64	85	15	14	29
Total	943	2.227	3.170	1.175	2.104	3.279

Source: DGIT

Table 2.41.1 – Italian Prisoners abroad according to their judicial situation and country of detention (year 2004)

Country	Prisoners		
	Awaiting trial or extradition	Convicts	Total
Albania	3	2	5
Austria	-	37	37
Belgium	123	150	273
Bulgaria	1	-	1
Croatia	3	1	4
France	103	205	308
Germany	520	830	1.350
Greece	3	5	8
Ireland	-	2	2
Luxemburg	7	8	15
Malta	1	4	5
Norway	1	-	1
Netherlands	30	30	60
Poland	3	1	4
Portugal	19	18	37
United Kingdom	59	83	142
Czech Republic	1	4	5
Former Rep. Yugosl. Macedonia	-	3	3
Romania	5	5	10
Serbia & Montenegro	1	2	3

Country	Prisoners		
	Awaiting trial or extradition	Convicts	Total
Slovakia	5	-	5
Slovenia	1	3	4
Spain	111	141	252
Sweden	-	1	1
Switzerland	41	215	256
Hungary	1	7	8
Total	1.042	1.757	2.799

Source: DGIT

Table 2.21.2 – Italians detained abroad according to judicial situation and country of detention – American Continent (year 2004)

Country	Prisoners		
	Awaiting Trial or ex-tradition	Convicts	Total
Argentina	19	8	27
Bolivia	-	2	2
Brazil	15	23	38
Canada	-	7	7
Chile	-	1	1
Columbia	9	7	16
Costa Rica	7	8	15
Cuba	2	5	7
Ecuador	7	5	12
Mexico	-	2	2
Panama	1	2	3
Paraguay	2	-	2
Peru	5	9	14
Dominican Republic	1	3	4
United States	25	199	224
Venezuela	7	40	47
Total	100	321	421

Source: DGIT

Table 2.41.3 – Italian detained abroad according to their judicial condition and country of detention – Mediteranian and Middle Eastern Countries (year 2004)

Country	Prisoners		
	Awaiting trial or extradition	Convicts	Total
Algeria	-	3	3
Egypt	-	1	1
United Arad Emirates	1	-	1
Jordan	1	-	1
Marokka	4	6	10
Tunisia	1	-	1
Yemen	1	-	1
Total	8	10	18

Source: DGIT

Table 2.41.4 – Italians detained abroad according to judicial situation and country of detention – Sub-saharian Africa (year 2004)

Country	Prisoners		
	Awaiting trial or extradition	Convicts	Total
Cameroon	2	-	2
Cape Verde	1	-	1
Ivory Coast	4	-	4
Eritrea	1	-	1
Kenya	2	1	3
Mauritius	-	1	1
Total	10	2	12

Source: DGIT

Table 2.41.5 – Italians detained abroad according to judicial condition and country of detention – Asia and Oceania (year 2004)

Country	Prisoners		
	Awaiting trial or extradition	Convicts	Total
Afghanistan	-	-	-
Australia	3	2	5
Cambodia	-	1	1
Japan	-	3	3
India	5	3	8
Indonesia	-	1	1
Myanmar	-	1	1
Thailand	7	3	10
Total	15	14	29

Source: DGIT[16]

5 EVALUATION

When focussing on foreign prisoners, central thought has to be aimed at the fact that there are three potential elements that can be correlated or at least be put in connection with each other: conditions of detention; the legal position of convicts or accused persons; the status of foreigners. Each of these three elements represents a component of the sentence or of detention conditions taking into consideration that they influence the decision on the kind of sentence to be served or the regime of detention also according to the seriousness of the crime committed and to the risk of evasion and/or absconding of the persons (i.e. pre-trial detention instead of home detention, bail instead of freedom under supervision, detention in the regime indicated by the court with regard to the offence instead of admission to alternative measures to prison).

Recent Italian legislations[17] represent an example of how European framework decisions and disposals may be applied, but in a sense that sometimes reduce the defence of human rights, or at least the possibility of a true and complete defence thereof. Each country has to be very careful and, moreover, to work with the aim of improving the system of serving sentence towards a more adequate regime that is able to respect a multiracial and multicultural prison population, and that is trained in a way to avoid macroscopic mistakes[18].

---

[16] http://www.esteri.it/ita/6_40_222.asp

[17] I refer mainly to: 1) law 22 aprile 2005, n. 69 – Disposizioni per conformare il diritto interno alla decisione quadro 2002/584/GAI del Consiglio, del 13 giugno 2002, relative al mandato d'arresto europeo e alle procedure di consegna tra Stati membri; 2) Decreto legge 27 luglio 2005, n. 144 convertito con legge 31 luglio 2005, n. 155 (on terrorism).

[18] I mention here an episode that occurred on January 2006 during a proceeding at a Tribunal of surveillance in Italy. A black man in prison serving his sentence appealed against the order of expulsion against him according to art. 16 of D. lgs. n. 286/1998. He denied the legitimacy of his expulsion and the Court had difficulties in determining his citizenship, because the prison was not able to provide any documentary support in order to clarify this. In the end the black man said that he was from the Netherlands and that he was a Dutch citizen. The prison staff had not asked and, even

Under the profile of serving sentences it is more and more desirable to transfer prisoners to their state of origin. However, preliminary to this there is the need of basic conditions: a homogeneous minimum level of execution, first of all inside prison, and then outside of the institutions; stopping treatment that is inhuman or in any way harmful of dignity[19]; prohibition of torture; improvements in the provision of interpreters and translators.

The right to translation is guaranteed by law, but it is violated in practice. By law alternative measures have to be admitted but the lack of opportunities outside quite often makes this impossible. Improving true bilateral agreements has to be considered. The execution of sentences in the country of origin is rarely admitted because:

- there is very shallow knowledge of penitentiary systems;
- very few agreements have been signed between EU Member States in order to make it admissible,
- there is a misunderstanding of what the alternative measures are and what they aim to achieve, and of the role that judging and administrative States have to play.

---

more seriously, nobody had even thought of the possibility of him being a European Union citizen. The colour of his skin and language difficulties could be adduced as inadmissible reasons.

[19] Just to mention an example, the prohibition of private and intimate relations within partners that some States still hold on to is absolutely useless with regard to what the sanction represents, and increases violence inside prisons as well as cases of sexual abuse.
See P. BALBO, *Sesso e carcere*, in '*Sessualità Diritto e Processo*', (a c. di) G. Gulotta e S. Pezzati (2002) Giuffrè ed., Milano, p. 86 sgg

STATISTICS FROM MINISTRY OF JUSTICE DEPARTMENT OF PRISONS
(situation on 31 December 2005)[20]

CITIZENSHIP			

Foreign detainees according to their nationality			On 31 Dec 2005

Country	WOMEN	MEN	SUM
Afghanistan	1	1	2
Albania	64	2907	2971
Algeria	8	1300	1308
Andorra		1	1
Angola	1	6	7
Argentina	8	47	55
Atol NaurNAURU		2	2
Australia	1	6	7
Austria	2	14	16
Bangladesh	1	34	35
Belgium	5	25	30
Benin	1	6	7
Bielorussia		9	9
Bolivia	20	39	59
Bosnia-Herzegovina	25	109	134
Brazil	58	126	184
Bulgaria	12	92	104
Burkina Faso	1	3	4
Burundi	1	12	13
Cameroon	4	14	18
Canada	1		1
Chad		1	1
Chile	17	142	159
Cina Popolare	25	254	279
Columbia	43	155	198
Congo		14	14
Costa Rica	1	5	6
Croatia	39	181	220
Cyprus		1	1
Czech Republic		4	4
Czech Republic	4	20	24
Dominican Republic	55	127	182
Ecuador	17	122	139

---

[20] All statistics can be consulted on website of Italian Ministry of Justice:
http://www.giustizia.it/statistiche/statistiche_dap/det/detg00_organigramma.htm

**Foreign detainees according
to their nationality**

On 31 Dec 2005

Country	WOMEN	MEN	SUM
Egypt	1	197	198
El Salvador	1	5	6
Eritrea	1	14	15
Estonia		2	2
Etheopia	1	14	15
Finland	1		1
Formosa	1		1
France	10	148	158
Gabon		26	26
Gambia	1	72	73
Georgia		3	3
Germany	14	98	112
Ghana	11	129	140
Great Britain	5	25	30
Greece	2	44	46
Guatemala	2	9	11
Guinea		9	9
Guinea Bissao		3	3
Guinea Equatoriale		1	1
Honduras	1	3	4
Hungary	3	48	51
India		68	68
Iran		21	21
Iraq		115	115
Ireland		1	1
Isola Di Cuba	5	6	11
Isola Di Dominica	3	3	6
Isole Bahama		2	2
Isole Del Capo Verde	1	6	7
Isole Maldive		1	1
Israel	2	35	37
Ivory Coast	3	53	56
Jamaica		7	7
Japan		2	2
Jordan		10	10
Kazakhstan	1		1
Kenya		4	4
Kirgyszstan		1	1
Kuwait		1	1
Laos		2	2
Lettonia	1	2	3

Foreign detainees according
to their nationality

On 31 Dec 2005

Country	WOMEN	MEN	SUM
Libano		42	42
Liberia		64	64
Libya		44	44
Lithuania	2	59	61
Macao		1	1
Macedonia	6	125	131
Madagascar		2	2
Malaysia		8	8
Mali		14	14
Malta		2	2
Marocco	38	4170	4208
Mauritania		17	17
Mauritius		4	4
Mexico	2	19	21
Moldavia	27	263	290
Mongolia	4	2	6
Mozambique	1	2	3
Netherlands	14	54	68
Nicaragua		1	1
Niger		5	5
Nigeria	204	568	772
North Yemen		2	2
Norway		1	1
Pakistan		60	60
Palestine		154	154
Panama	1		1
Paraguay	4	5	9
Peru	21	145	166
Phillipines	10	40	50
Poland	20	177	197
Portugal	1	22	23
Romania	185	1602	1787
Russian Federation	15	53	68
Rwanda		14	14
Senegal	2	264	266
Sierra Leone	2	41	43
Singapore		3	3
Slovakia	4	12	16
Slovenia	2	56	58
Somalia	3	21	24
South Africa	2	8	10

Foreign detainees according to their nationality

On 31 Dec 2005

Country	WOMEN	MEN	SUM
Spain	12	115	127
Sri Lanka	1	48	49
Sudan	1	32	33
Surinam		1	1
Sweden		3	3
Switzerland	2	21	23
Syria		19	19
Tanzania	1	30	31
Thailand		1	1
Togo	1	14	15
Trinidad and Tobago		1	1
Tunisia	19	2057	2076
Turkey	3	81	84
Uganda	2	3	5
Ukraine	23	129	152
United States	4	5	9
Unknown Nationality	3	20	23
Uruguay	5	28	33
Venezuela	29	88	117
Vietnam		2	2
Yugoslavia	140	719	859
Zaire		2	2
Total	**1.302**	**18.534**	**19.836**

JUDICIAL CONDITION

Situation on 31 December 2005

DETAINED POPULATION ACCORDING TO REGION OF
DETENTION AND LEGAL POSITION

Region of detention	Legal position					Total
	Awaiting first judgement	Appellant	Clai-mant	Final	Interned	
Abruzzo	218	224	104	1.284	63	1.893
Basilicata	50	40	19	337	-	446
Calabria	440	247	92	1567	1	2.347
Campania	1.877	807	377	3.912	337	7.310
Emilia Romagna	838	521	262	1.976	255	3.852
Friuli Venezia Giulia	159	72	41	558	-	830
Lazio	1.133	757	234	3.768	3	5.895
Liguria	307	155	117	880	1	1.460

Lombardia	1.835	1.141	379	5.113	185	8.653
Marche	192	85	49	624	1	951
Molise	43	23	13	332	-	411
Piemonte	848	571	227	3.077	4	4.727
Puglia	905	260	191	2.480	2	3.838
Sardegna	214	201	124	1.427	23	1.989
Sicilia	1.375	708	289	3.862	178	6.412
Toscana	836	421	100	2.565	129	4.051
Trentino Alto Adige	83	53	6	280	-	422
Umbria	177	94	35	717	-	1.023
Valle D'aosta	36	33	18	193	-	280
Veneto	638	269	99	1.724	3	2.733
National Total	12.204	6.682	2.776	36.676	1.185	59.523

Situation on 31 December 2005

FEMALE DETAINED POPULATION ACCORDING TO REGION OF DETENTION AND LEGAL POSITION

Region of detention	Legal Position					**Total**
	Awaiting 1st judgement	Appellant	Claimant	Final	Interned	
Abruzzo	16	3	2	7	-	28
Basilicata	-	-	-	22	-	22
Calabria	12	4	-	22	-	38
Campania	66	46	7	157	-	276
Emilia Romagna	46	20	11	84	-	161
Friuli Venezia Giulia	8	3	-	14	-	25
Lazio	97	47	37	287	-	468
Liguria	12	11	3	39	-	65
Lombardia	128	89	28	299	63	607
Marche	11	3	1	11	-	26
Molise	4	3	-	8	-	15
Piemonte	57	26	4	104	1	192
Puglia	47	16	12	129	-	204
Sardegna	18	8	4	22	-	52
Sicilia	39	8	9	77	-	133
Toscana	54	27	3	109	4	197
Trentino Alto Adige	5	3	1	15	-	24
Umbria	10	5	1	41	-	57

Valle D'aosta	-	-	-	-	-	-
Veneto	43	28	10	131	2	214
National Total	673	350	133	1.578	70	2.804

SEX

Situation to 31 Dec. 2005

DETAINED POPULATION ACCORDING TO REGION OF DETENTION AND SEX

Region Of Detention	Male	Male %	Female	Female %	Total
Abruzzo	1.865	98,5	28	1,5	1.893
Basilicata	424	95,1	22	4,9	446
Calabria	2.309	98,4	38	1,6	2.347
Campania	7.034	96,2	276	3,8	7.310
Emilia Romagna	3.691	95,8	161	4,2	3.852
Friuli Venezia Giulia	805	97,0	25	3,0	830
Lazio	5.427	92,1	468	7,9	5.895
Liguria	1.395	95,5	65	4,5	1.460
Lombardia	8.046	93,0	607	7,0	8.653
Marche	925	97,3	26	2,7	951
Molise	396	96,4	15	3,6	411
Piemonte	4.535	95,9	192	4,1	4.727
Puglia	3.634	94,7	204	5,3	3.838
Sardegna	1.937	97,4	52	2,6	1.989
Sicilia	6.279	97,9	133	2,1	6.412
Toscana	3.854	95,1	197	4,9	4.051
Trentino Alto Adige	398	94,3	24	5,7	422
Umbria	966	94,4	57	5,6	1.023
Valle D'aosta	280	100,0	0	0,0	280
Veneto	2.519	92,2	214	7,8	2.733
National Total	56.719	95,3	2.804	4,7	59.523

Year 2005

Region Of Detention	Total of entries			of which foreign		
	WOMEN	MEN	TOTAL	WOMEN	MEN	TOTAL
Abruzzo	241	1438	1.679	86	397	483
Basilicata	33	574	607	14	108	122
Calabria	109	2170	2.279	37	344	381
Campania	866	9065	9.931	291	1356	1.647
Emilia Romagna	520	5344	5.864	332	3248	3.580
Friuli V. Giulia	204	1681	1.885	112	971	1.083
Lazio	973	7547	8.520	611	3742	4.353
Liguria	249	2438	2.687	121	1317	1.438
Lombardia	1469	12828	14.297	998	7947	8.945
Marche	192	1549	1.741	140	871	1.011
Molise	39	369	408	9	66	75
Piemonte	1544	7918	9.462	1292	4804	6.096
Puglia	468	6997	7.465	207	1207	1.414
Sardegna	123	1653	1.776	46	160	206
Sicilia	289	6671	6.960	78	1041	1.119
Toscana	553	4991	5.544	294	2802	3.096
Trentino Alto Adige	117	1259	1.376	61	749	810
Umbria	98	1120	1.218	51	616	667
V.Aosta	16	160	176	6	71	77
Veneto	827	5185	6.012	618	3385	4.003
National Total	8.930	80.957	89.887	5.404	35.202	40.606

SEMI-LIBERTY

Situation on 30 June 2005

Region Of Detention	Italians	Foreigners	Total
Abruzzo	16	2	18
Basilicata	15	0	15
Calabria	64	1	65
Campania	203	2	205
Emilia Romagna	110	22	132
Friuli Venezia Giulia	51	3	54
Lazio	104	11	115
Liguria	97	19	116
Lombardia	169	12	181
Marche	14	2	16
Molise	4	0	4
Piemonte	84	14	98
Puglia	215	3	218
Sardegna	43	1	44
Sicilia	132	4	136
Toscana	143	29	172
Trentino Alto Adige	17	8	25
Umbria	12	9	21
Valle D'aosta	1	0	1
Veneto	101	33	134
National Total	1.595	175	1.770

AGE

Figures as recorded on 31 December 2005
PRISON POPOLATION ACCORDING TO THE COUNTY
(REGIONE) OF DETENTION AND AGE

Age groups

Region Of Detention	18 to 20	21 to 24	25 to 29	30 to 34	35 to 39	40 to 44	45 to 49	50 to 59	60 to 69	> 70	??	Total
Abruzzo	34	136	270	384	325	256	216	219	49	4	-	1.893
Basilicata	9	23	77	67	89	73	38	54	12	3	1	446
Calabria	31	137	370	466	413	334	265	263	54	13	1	2.347
Campania	125	531	1.202	1.379	1.288	1.006	718	779	205	77	-	7.310
Emilia Romagna	129	379	676	722	630	487	346	350	107	18	8	3.852
Friuli Venezia Giulia	18	74	138	150	146	109	76	78	37	3	1	830
Lazio	132	439	789	1048	1048	864	611	707	215	40	2	5.895
Liguria	47	162	199	287	258	186	137	137	40	6	1	1.460
Lombardia	244	718	1.371	1.532	1.505	1.141	821	974	286	52	9	8.653
Marche	14	74	138	174	191	134	90	104	27	4	1	951
Molise	1	21	51	92	81	66	46	42	8	3	-	411
Piemonte	125	348	780	964	859	596	418	465	132	16	24	4.727
Puglia	63	383	703	795	680	456	329	321	85	20	3	3.838
Sardegna	29	140	317	407	391	275	183	175	56	16	-	1.989
Sicilia	135	546	1.046	1.207	1.090	884	589	658	216	40	1	6.412
Toscana	118	351	633	686	730	559	393	422	135	18	6	4.051
Trentino Alto Adige	17	56	68	78	72	59	30	31	11	-	-	422
Umbria	13	76	143	183	190	144	109	115	41	8	1	1.023
Valle D'aosta	14	38	48	53	42	43	14	21	6	-	1	280
Veneto	72	288	463	531	478	345	242	239	64	9	2	2.733
National Total	1.370	4.920	9.482	11.205	10.506	8.017	5.671	6.154	1.786	350	62	59.523

Situation to 31 Dec. 2005

FEMALE DETAINED POPOLATION ACCORDING TO THE COUNTY (REGIONE) OF DETENTION AND AGE

Region Of Detention	18 to 20	21 to 24	25 to 29	30 to 34	35 to 39	40 to 44	45 to 49	50 to 59	60 to 69	> 70	??	Total
Abruzzo	1	3	4	6	3	5	3	2	1	-	-	28
Basilicata	3	1	3	3	2	2	5	2	1	-	-	22
Calabria	1	3	8	3	8	3	5	6	1	-	-	38
Campania	5	21	33	37	47	49	38	32	11	3	-	276
Emilia Romagna	6	16	29	25	39	22	12	8	4	-	-	161
Friuli Venezia Giulia	-	3	3	3	4	4	4	3	1	-	-	25
Lazio	23	52	56	73	72	63	56	59	11	3	-	468
Liguria	-	8	10	15	12	8	4	7	-	1	-	65
Lombardia	21	46	83	101	97	92	68	74	24	1	-	607
Marche	1	3	3	4	8	5	1	1	-	-	-	26
Molise	-	-	3	5	2	1	2	2	-	-	-	15
Piemonte	10	19	42	36	37	26	9	7	5	-	1	192
Puglia	2	20	32	33	34	27	28	20	4	3	1	204
Sardegna	-	3	7	17	10	5	6	4	-	-	-	52
Sicilia	1	7	16	25	25	19	17	17	4	2	-	133
Toscana	5	24	29	37	38	27	14	15	7	-	1	197
Trentino Alto Adige	2	4	4	3	6	4	-	1	-	-	-	24
Umbria	1	3	9	12	9	11	4	3	3	2	-	57
Valle D'aosta	-	-	-	-	-	-	-	-	-	-	-	-
Veneto	8	21	49	34	35	27	19	17	3	1	-	214
National Total	90	257	423	472	488	400	295	280	80	16	3	2.804

LENGTH OF SENTENCES

Situation on 31 December 2005

FINAL CONVICTS ACCORDING TO REGION OF DETENTION AND LENGTH OF SENTENCE

Length of sentence

Region Of Detention	Up to 1 year	1 to 2 years	2 to 3	3 to 4	4 to 5	5 to 6	6 to 7	7 to 8	8 to 9	9 to 10	10 to 20	> 20	Life sentence	Total
Abruzzo	102	119	117	162	105	75	53	53	56	37	211	110	84	1.284
Basilicat	20	35	25	41	36	21	23	12	14	8	65	28	9	337
Calabria	89	130	161	185	162	113	95	68	72	73	280	88	51	1.567
Campania	274	385	560	568	436	317	232	181	134	92	382	218	133	3.912
Emilia Romagna	174	191	168	274	202	150	89	66	74	49	331	130	78	1.976
Friuli Venezia Giulia	94	101	93	85	61	27	15	10	8	5	38	9	12	558
Lazio	314	365	411	564	377	284	236	167	118	94	480	228	130	3.768
Liguria	132	120	125	166	95	54	37	25	18	19	65	19	5	880
Lombar Dia	561	483	523	608	512	336	249	233	191	158	793	329	137	5.113
Marche	47	52	45	69	62	43	37	26	23	14	92	67	47	624
Molise	22	31	34	38	33	18	18	11	15	14	59	27	12	332
Piemonte	267	312	351	409	318	245	155	132	118	79	402	170	119	3.077
Puglia	225	277	317	400	252	206	146	115	94	62	270	88	28	2.480
Sardegna	150	197	181	220	122	102	63	45	27	30	177	77	36	1.427
Sicilia	347	400	486	506	377	327	207	175	151	97	504	209	76	3.862
Toscana	222	221	189	267	197	133	105	105	89	67	517	321	132	2.565
Trentino Alto Adige	65	67	48	51	14	17	2	2	-	3	8	3	-	280
Umbria	51	38	55	67	54	41	34	24	14	16	118	97	108	717
Valle D'aosta	26	25	37	36	14	20	8	6	4	2	10	3	2	193
Veneto	174	209	233	254	166	115	86	68	48	39	224	83	25	1.724
National Total	3.356	3.758	4.159	4.970	3.595	2.644	1.890	1.524	1.268	958	5.026	2.304	1224	36.676

FEMALE FINAL CONVICTS ACCORDING TO REGION OF DETENTION AND LENGTH OF SENTENCE

Region Of Detention	Up to 1 year	1 to 2	2 to 3	3 to 4	4 to 5	5 to 6	6 to 7	7 to 8	8 to 9	9 to 10	10 to 20	> 20	Life sentence	Total
Abruzzo	3	2	-	1	-	-	-	1	-	-	-	-	-	7
Basilicata	4	2	-	3	5	1	2	-	-	1	3	1	-	22
Calabria	-	3	3	5	4	2	-	1	1	-	3	-	-	22
Campania	13	11	23	37	20	14	6	9	6	3	13	1	1	157
Emilia Romagna	8	11	7	20	11	8	4	3	-	2	9	1	-	84
Friuli Venezia Giulia	3	2	5	1	2	-	1	-	-	-	-	-	-	14
Lazio	24	24	26	63	24	29	24	16	5	6	27	8	11	287
Liguria	6	1	5	9	6	2	3	-	3	2	2	-	-	39
Lombardia	32	31	23	34	38	25	12	14	12	13	42	15	8	299
Marche	3	2	2	2	1	-	1	-	-	-	-	-	-	11
Molise	3	1	2	1	-	-	-	-	-	1	-	-	-	8
Piemonte	14	12	15	22	10	6	2	4	6	3	7	3	-	104
Puglia	9	8	20	20	17	9	8	6	8	4	13	3	4	129
Sardegna	2	2	3	5	3	-	-	-	-	1	5	1	-	22
Sicilia	5	5	5	17	6	10	7	5	-	2	12	2	1	77
Toscana	15	8	11	23	13	10	5	7	6	-	8	2	1	109
Trentino Alto Adige	7	2	3	2	-	-	-	-	-	-	1	-	-	15
Umbria	1	1	3	3	2	5	6	2	-	1	14	2	1	41
Valle D'aosta	-	-	-	-	-	-	-	-	-	-	-	-	-	-
Veneto	14	14	17	25	15	11	7	3	3	4	16	2	-	131
National Total	166	142	173	293	177	132	88	71	50	43	175	41	27	1.578

OFFENCES

Data for 31 December 2005	Italian				Foreigners					
Kind of offences	Women	Men	Sum	%	Women	Men	Sum	%	Total	%
ASSOCIAZ. DI STAMPO MAFIOSO (art. 416bis c.p.) (Mafia association)	45	5.514	5.559	3,1	8	117	125	0,3	5.684	2,5
LEGGE DROGA Drugs)	853	20.413	21.266	12,0	689	10.974	11.663	24,2	32.929	14,6
LEGGE ARMI (Firearms and explosives)	407	33.368	33.775	19,1	41	2.096	2.137	4,4	35.912	16,0
ORDINE PUBBLICO (Public order)	47	2.664	2.711	1,5	69	665	734	1,5	3.445	1,5
CONTRO IL PATRIMONIO (Against estate)	1.391	53.790	55.181	31,2	877	12.112	12.989	27,0	68.170	30,3
PROSTITUZIONE (Prostitution)	29	297	326	0,2	168	910	1.078	2,2	1.404	0,6
CONTRO LA PUBBLICA AMMINISTRAZIONE (Against public administration)	153	5.290	5.443	3,1	42	2.489	2.531	5,3	7.974	3,5
INCOLUMITA' PUBBLICA (Public safety)	32	1.858	1.890	1,1	7	167	174	0,4	2.064	0,9
FEDE PUBBLICA (Social belief)	290	6.625	6.915	3,9	224	2.920	3.144	6,5	10.059	4,5
MORALITA' PUBBLICA (Public morality)	6	209	215	0,1		60	60	0,1	275	0,1
CONTRO LA FAMIGLIA (Against family)	40	1.076	1.116	0,6	11	144	155	0,3	1.271	0,6
CONTRO LA PERSONA (Against person)	710	24.031	24.741	14,0	350	8.130	8.480	17,6	33.221	14,8
CONTRO LA PERSONALITA' DELLO STATO (Against the personality of the State)	126	391	517	0,3	1	57	58	0,1	575	0,3
CONTRO AMM.NE DELLA GIUSTIZIA (Against admninistration of justice)	244	6.233	6.477	3,7	58	610	668	1,4	7.145	3,2

ECONOMIA PUBBLICA (Public economy)	8	610	618	0,3		6	6	0,0	624	0,3
LIBRO TERZO DELLE CONTRAVVENZIONI (Infringement)	86	4.691	4.777	2,7	28	626	654	1,4	5.431	2,4
LEGGE STRANIERI (Law on aliens)	4	201	205	0,1	216	3.002	3.218	6,7	3.423	1,5
CONTRO IL SENTIM. RELIGIOSO E LA PIETA' DEI DEF. (Against religious feelings and pity for the dead)	27	1.171	1.198	0,7	5	46	51	0,1	1.249	0,6
ALTRI REATI (Other offences)	62	3.968	4.030	2,3	10	211	221	0,5	4.251	1,9
TOTAL OFFENCES	4.560	172.400	176.960	100,0	2.804	45.342	48.146	100,0	225.106	100,0

Fonte: D.A.P - Ufficio per lo Sviluppo e la Gestione del Sistema Informativo Automatizzato – SEZIONE STATISTICA

Note: In case of more and of different categories offences ascribed to a person, he/she will be counted more times, one for each crime. So, general result is higher than the number of persons.

Chapter 15

Latvia

Leine Zeibote

1 INTRODUCTION

1.1 Overview of penalties and measures

Deprivation of liberty as a measure or penalty is foreseen in criminal laws, administrative laws and immigration laws. The table below describes different measures according to which a person can be kept in custody in Latvia.

Measure or penalty	Responsible for execution	Place of execution	Application
Detention before charges in Criminal Procedure	State Police; Ministry of Interior	Cells in Police Units, Isolation units	- Short term detention, not more than 8 hours - Decision of investigator in criminal case - Law on Short Term Detention Order[1]
Administrative Arrest	State Police Ministry of Interior	Cells in Police Units, Isolators	- 1- 15 days - Administrative sentence under Administrative Offence Code - Imposed according to decision of judge
Detention as a security measure in criminal procedure: - pre trial -during trial of first instance -during appeal process	Prison Administration Ministry of Justice	Investigation prisons, Investigation units in prisons	- According to decision of investigation judge or judge - The total amount of time spent in detention cannot be longer than deprivation of liberty term provided in the sanction of Criminal Law - For criminal violations the term of detention before first instance judgment cannot exceed 3 months, for less serious crimes – 9 months, for serious crime – 12 months, for especially serious crime – 24 months.[2]
Deprivation of liberty – criminal sentence	Prison Administration; Ministry of Justice	Open, semi-open, closed prisons, correctional institution for juveniles	- Imposed by decision of judge according to decision of judge - Term of deprivation of liberty from 6 months to 20 years

---

[1] Aizturēšanas kārtība likums (Law on Short-term Detention Order), adopted 12 October 2005.
[2] Kriminālprocesa likums (Code of Criminal Procedure), Section 277.

Measure or penalty	Responsible for execution	Place of execution	Application
Detention of Illegal immigrants and asylum seekers before identification	State Border Guard; Ministry of interior	Cells in Police Units, Isolation units Detention centre for illegal immigrants	- Detention according to immigration Law - 10 days according to decision of State Border Guard up to 20 months according to decision of court
Detention as a compulsory medical measure	Ministry of Health	Closed units in Psychoneurological hospitals	- According to decision of court in criminal matters - Term is not set in Criminal Law

Each year, according to sanctions of state, more than 40 000 persons are deprived of their liberty. There are around 100 closed institutions in Latvia, among them – 15 prisons, 28 Police Detentions / Isolation units, nine psycho-neurological hospitals, 30 social care centres and a centre for illegal immigrants and other institutions.[3]

Types of Criminal offences and Criminal Sentences
According to the Criminal Law, criminal offences are divided into criminal violations and crimes. Crimes are sub-divided as follows: less serious crimes, serious crimes and very serious crimes:
- a criminal violation: deprivation of liberty for a term not exceeding two years;
- a less serious crime: deprivation of liberty for a term exceeding two years but not exceeding five years;
- a serious crime: deprivation of liberty for a term exceeding five years but not exceeding ten years;
- an especially serious crime: deprivation of liberty for a term exceeding ten years, life imprisonment or the death penalty.

Article 36 of the Criminal Law sets the forms of sentences. One of the following basic sentences may be adjudged against a person who has committed a criminal offence:
- the death penalty;
- deprivation of liberty;
- custodial arrest;
- community service;
- fine.

In addition to a basic sentence, the following additional sentences may be adjudged:
- confiscation of property;

---

[3] Latvian Centre for Human Rights and Etnic Studies, *Handbook for Monitoring Closed Institutions*, Riga 2003.

518

- expulsion from the Republic of Latvia;
- fine;
- limitation of rights;
- police supervision.

The death penalty – death by shooting – may be adjudged only for murder in especially ag-gravated circumstances. The death penalty may only be applied where a crime has been committed in times of war.

Deprivation of liberty can be determined for a term of not less than six months and not ex-ceeding fifteen years; for especially serious crimes for a term not exceeding twenty years. In cases specifically provided for in this Law, deprivation of liberty may be determined for life (life sentence). Deprivation of liberty can be imposed in closed custody, semi-closed custody, open custody, as well as in the correctional facility for juveniles. When ruling in a case, the adjudging court determines in which type of correctional facility it will impose the deprivation of liberty.

Custodial arrest shall be determined for a term of not less than three days and not exceed-ing six months. Custodial arrest in practice is applied only to soldiers since there are no places of execution for this sentence. Soldiers serve their sentence in the guardhouse. Custodial arrest may not be applied to pregnant women and mothers caring for an infant under the age of one.

Figure 1 Persons sentenced in 2004: 13 222

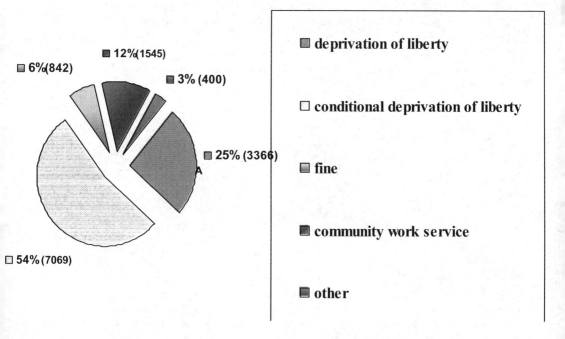

1.2 Overview of Prison System

a) There are 15 prisons and one juvenile correctional institution under the Prison Administration. There can be a mixture of different regimes within individual prisons. Overall, there are five open, eight semi-closed and eight closed departments. According to data from the Prison Administration, the Latvian prison system has an overall capacity of 9,166 places, of which 6,537 are filled. The majority of these places are in closed and semi-closed departments (4,073 and 1,273 respectively), while the open wings had a capacity of 255. The remaining places are in pre-trial-detention wings (3,052 for adults, 209 for juveniles), hospitals (200 places) and juvenile prisons (134). In the administration of prisons in 2000 the responsibility was shifted from the Ministry of the Interior to the Ministry of Justice. The number of employees on in the Latvian Prison Administration and prisons 1 January 2006 was 3,126. The ratio of prison staff to prisoners was 1 to 5[4]. On the same date there were 171 vacant posts (or 5,5%). Fluidity of employees in 2005 reached 15%. Prison staff is under Specialised Civil Service, similar to police staff. 23,7 % of staff have a university degree, 73.6 % have a secondary school degree, and 2,7% have not finished secondary school. There is a training centre for prison staff which organizes all in-service training for prison personnel under the Prison Administration. The Centre runs the professional education courses "Prison inspector" and "Prison guard". 404 persons attended this training in 2005.

Supervision of prisons regarding violations of human rights is performed by the State Human Rights Office. Representatives of this institution regularly visited prisons during 2005, reviewed complaints of prisoners and consulted prison staff. A Draft Law from the Ombudsman is pending in Saeima. In 2005 the budget of the Prison Administration was 21 953 673 Lats. The financing of the prison system has been insufficient in recent years and this has had an effect on all fields of operation of the prison system. The daily expenses per prisoner were 7,55 Lats. In 2005, the Prison Administration received 5,044 complaints from prisoners, of which 2,148 concerned the imprisonment regime and unsatisfactory prison conditions.[5] During 2005 a concept paper on the development of the prison estate and a concept on prisoners' health care were accepted by the cabinet of ministers.

---

[4] Concept of Development of the Prison System, accepted by the Cabinet 2 May 2005, Order No 280.

[5] 2005 Prison Administration Annual Report, available in Latvian on www.ievp.gov.lv

Table 1 Composition of Prisoners[6]

	01.01.2002	01.01.2003	01.01.2004	01.01.2005	01.01.2006
Total number of prisoners	8,426	8,215	8,169	7,632	6,949
a) Number of sentenced persons	4,750	4,639	4,900	4,970	4,750
Citizens of Latvia	3,054 *64%*	3,121 *67%*	3,319 *68%*	3,408 *69%*	3,229 *68%*
Non-citizens and permanent residents	1,172 *25%*	1,114 *24%*	1,358 *28%*	1,374 *28%*	1,425 *30%*
Citizens of other countries	39 *0.8%*	40 *0.9%*	39 *0.8%*	41 *0.8%*	29 *0.6%*
Without any citizenship	485 *10%*	364 *8%*	184 *4%*	147 *3%*	67 *1.4%*
b) Number of persons in pre-trial detention	3676	3576	3269	2662	2199
% of persons in pre-trial detention of all prisoners	*44%*	*43%*	*40%*	*34.8%*	*31.6%*

b) Foreigners can be detained in all institutions described in the first part of this report (see table on page 1 and 2). So far the issue of foreign prisoners has not become a live issue in Latvia. The number of foreigners in the prison system is small and the detention of non-Russian speaking foreigners is a very rare occasion for prison staff. On 1 February 2006 there were only three non-Russian speaking foreigners in Latvian prisons. Most of the time foreigners are successfully integrated in the prison population since the majority of the prison population is Russian speaking.

Table 2 Nationalities of sentenced foreigners in prisons on 1 February 2006

Russia	Lithuania	Belarus	Ukraine	Estonia	Armenia	Moldova	Azerbaijan	Uzbekistan	Sweden	Finland	USA
24	12	6	4	3	3	3	2	1	1	1	1

There is no special training for prison staff and there are no special rules for the detention of foreigners. Data of foreigners in pre-trial detention is not collected and analysed, and thus not available. The issue of persons without any legal status and documents has been challenging for the Prison administration during the past years. Many prisoners were not registered in the Register of Inhabitants and did not receive a personal code in the nineties. This situation has been improved - in 2005 there were only 67 persons without citizenship compared to 485 in 2002.

---

6   Data from the Prison Administration.

1.3 Overview of involvement of Consulates, Embassies, Ministries home country, Probation service home country, NGO's etc.

Consulates and embassies assist foreign prisoners in the communication with institutions in their home country. Mostly consulates are involved in helping to obtain the legal status in the home country and the necessary documentation. There have been some cases when embassies delivered interpreter services to nationals of their country. The Prosecutor General Office is involved in the transfer of sentenced persons to their home countries. The number of transferred sentenced persons is 42. The State Human Rights office is an independent state institution and its competence is to review complaints on violations of human rights. Employees of the centre regularly visit places of detention, prisons and detention centres for illegal immigrants. In 2005 the office received about 500 complaints from prisoners. There are no data about the number of complaints from foreign prisoners, but employees of the office referred to two complaints concerning language barriers. One of them related to problems in communicating with the prison doctor. The Latvian Centre for Human Rights and Ethnic Studies (LCHRES) is the NGO that is most active in the field of human rights and ethnic relations. The centre's activities include monitoring, research and policy analysis, advocacy, human rights education and training, organization of seminars and the provision of legal consultations to victims of human rights violations. LCHRES experts regularly monitor prisons and detention centres for illegal immigrants. In 2004 LCHRES printed the leaflet "Information for immigration detainees" in Latvian, Russian, English, French, Spanish and Arabic. The leaflet is available in Olaine Detention Centre for Illegal Immigrants.

1.4 Overview of trends

62,173 criminal offences were registered in the territory of Latvia during the year 2004, an increase of 19,1% compared to 2003. In the past five years the crime level has not changed. Around 60% of the registered criminal offences are thefts.[7]

Table 3

year	1990	1991	1992	1993	1994	1995	1996	1997
Sentenced persons	7,159	7,372	9,097	11,280	10,877	9,797	10,428	12,772
Sentenced to deprivation of liberty	N/d	N/d	N/d	4,162	3,225	2,839	2,195	3,238
% of deprivation of liberty among all sentenced persons	36.6	35.2	36.1	36.9	29.6	29.0	21.1	25.4
year	1998	1999	2000	2001	2002	2003	2004	2005*
Sentenced persons	12,952	12,862	12,689	12,679	12,615	13,586	13,222	11,240
Sentenced to deprivation of liberty	2,930	2,865	3,305	2,886	3,551	3,260	3,366	2,680
% of deprivation of liberty among all sentenced persons	22.6	22.2	26.0	22.7	28.1	24.0	25.5	23,8

*Data on sentenced persons in 2005 is not available at the time of preparation of this report.

---

[7]   State Police Report on Crime and Operation of Police in 2004, available onlineat www.vp.gov.lv

In 2004 there was a decrease in the overall number of prisoners and the share of adult pre-trial detainees. At the same time the incarceration rate remained high – 326 prisoners per 100,000 inhabitants. The average length of imprisonment increased to 4,5 years in 2005.[8] The number of serious crimes in Latvia has grown which has in turn resulted in an increased in the number of prisoners in closed prisons.[9] Analyses of sentencing trends show that the number of persons sentenced to less than one year has been relatively stable. The number of persons sentenced to five to ten years is growing (from 281 in 2002 to 566 in 2004). The total number of inhabitants in Latvia on 1 January 2006 were 2 290 765, of which 1 834 282 (80 %) were citizens, 418 432 (18.3%) were non –citizens, 37 843(1.7%) were foreigners, and 198 were persons without any citizenship.[10] "Non-citizen" is a special status granted to former citizens of the Soviet Union and their children that have entered Latvia to live after 17 June 1940. These persons have the right to attain citizenship through a naturalization procedure. On 1 January 2006, 0,6% of the total prison population were foreigners, while a further 1,4% were persons without any citizenship. The latter category can include persons belonging to Latvia or to another foreign country. In comparison, foreigners have rather long sentences and most of them have been sentenced for violent crimes.

Figure 2 Length of sentence of foreign prisoners on 1 February 2006

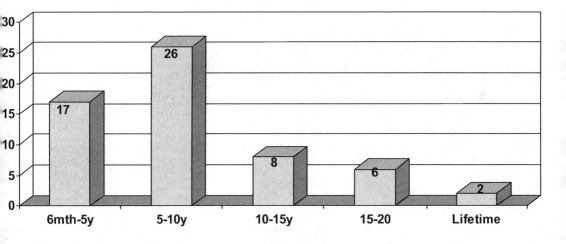

---

8   Latvian Centre for Human Rights and Ethnic Studies (LCHRES), *Human Rights in Latvia in 2004*, Riga   2005.
9   Concept of Development of Prison System, accepted by the Cabinet 2 May 2005, Order No 280
10 Data from the Board of Citizenship and Migration Affairs, www.pmlp.gov.lv

1.5 Overview of national legislation

1.5.1 The legal framework of the criminal justice system and detention of persons is included in the following legislative acts:
- Criminal Code, adopted on 17 June 1998, entered into force on 1 April 1999
- Code of Criminal Procedure, adopted on 21 April 2005, entered into force on 1 October 2005.
- Legal acts concerning the execution of criminal sentences– deprivation of liberty and detention under Criminal Law:
- Law on Detention Order, entered into force on 11 April 2006;[11]
- Law on Short-term Detention Order, adopted 12 October 2005, entered into force 21 October 2005;[12]
- Code on the Execution of Sentences, adopted on 23 December 1970, entered into force on 11 November 1971;
- Regulations on the internal order in prisons, adopted by the Cabinet of Ministers on 19 February 2002, No. 73;
- Regulations on nourishment and household needs for sentenced persons, adopted by the Cabinet of Ministers on 19 April 2002, No. 155;
- Regulations on the material assistance to persons released from prisons, adopted by the Cabinet of Ministers on 12 October 1999, No 351;
- Regulations on medical assistance to detained and sentenced persons, adopted by the Cabinet of Ministers 19 October 1999, No 150;
- Regulations on norms of nourishment, washing means and means of personal hygiene for persons detained under Administrative law and Criminal law and persons under Administrative arrest, adopted by the cabinet of ministers on 12 October 1999, No 351.

Other regulations issued by the Cabinet of Ministers stipulate the order of employment, wages for employed prisoners, the accommodation of children whose mothers are sentenced, inspection of the use of alcohol and drugs.

Regulations concerning the illegal immigrants, their detention and expulsion are contained in the Immigration Law, adopted on 31 October 2002 and entered into force on 1 May 2003. Procedures for the forcible expulsion of foreigners; the form of the document for exit and the procedures of issue of such documents were adopted by the Cabinet of Ministers on 29 April 2003, No 212.

Regulations concerning the detention and deportation of asylum seekers are contained in the Asylum Law, adopted on 7 March 2002 and entered into force on 1 September 2002. The procedure for the deportation of persons from the Republic of Latvia in relation to whom a decision has been made that refuses the granting of refugee status or "alternative status" was adopted by the Cabinet of Ministers on 20 January 2003, No 29.

---

[11] Apcietinājumā turēšanas kārtības likums. This law stipulates detention as a measure of safety in criminal procedure in investigation prisons

[12] Aizturēto personu turēšanas kārtības likums, This law stipulates short-term detention under criminal law in Police establishments

1.5.2 Criminal Procedure Law sets the principle of equal treatment for all persons regardless of their race, nationality, citizenship, social status, religion, gender, education, language and other possible characteristics.[13] Foreign prisoners have the same legal position and the same rights and obligations as national prisoners. Chapters 69 and 70 of the Code of Criminal Procedure provide procedures for the transfer of sentenced persons abroad and for receiving sentenced persons from foreign countries. Latvia recognizes the principle of reciprocity; therefore transfers are also possible in cases where there is no mutual agreement between countries. Latvia has ratified the Convention of the Council of Europe on the Transfer of Sentenced Persons – adopted on 21 March 1983 – and has concluded bilateral agreements with several countries (Russia, Estonia, Lithuania, Ukraine, Belarus, Kyrgyz Republic, Poland, Moldova, and Uzbekistan) on judicial cooperation in civil and criminal matters. The central authority for the organization of transfers is the Prosecutor's General Office. Since 2000 Latvia has received 26 sentenced persons from abroad. In 2005 Latvia received two persons from Lithuania, one from Russia, Germany, Austria, and Estonia. Since the year 2000, Latvia has transferred 42 persons to foreign countries. In 2005 Latvia transferred five persons to Lithuania, three to Estonia, one to Belarus, one to Azerbaijan and one to Sweden.[14]

2 TREATMENT OF PRISONERS

2.1 General remarks

The treatment of prisoners in Latvia has been the focus of attention of human rights experts. The first periodic visit to Latvia by the CPT took place in 1999, the second in 2002. The committee expressed its concerns regarding the treatment of prisoners in Latvia, as well as the lack of progress in numerous fields. Overcrowding, inter-prisoner violence, material conditions in prisons, and the regime for prisoners serving life sentences were areas mentioned by the CPT in its report to the Latvian government in 2003. In 2004, there was another visit to Latvia, but the corresponding report had not been published at the time of writing. The stagnation of the prison system is obvious and it is recognized by the Prison administration and the Ministry of Justice. A permanent lack of funding has resulted in numerous problems such as a lack of rehabilitation possibilities and poor material conditions for prisoners and prison staff. The Ministry of Justice has elaborated several concept papers that are aimed at resolving the situation concerning poor conditions of the prison's estate (including hospitals), as well the employment and education of prisoners. To examine the situation of foreign prisoners I have visited Jelgava Prison and have interviewed several representatives of the Prison Administration, representatives of the State Human Right Office and the State Probation Service. According to the existing legislation there is no difference in the treatment of foreign prisoners. Laws do not contain special rules on living conditions, reception and admission, work, education, training, food, religion or any other aspect described in this report. However, the lack of special regulations sometimes generate unequal opportunities for

---

[13] Criminal Procedure Law, Section 8.
[14] Data from Prosecutor's General Office www.lrp.gov.lv

foreign prisoners, taking into account the distance from relatives, differences in culture, religion and communication barriers. So far there have been no major problems with the unequal treatment of foreigners and the issue of foreign prisoners has not become a problem in Latvia. The number of foreigners is very small and there are mostly no language and cultural barriers.

2.2 Living conditions

Prisoners held in penitentiary establishments in Latvia are separated according to gender, and in terms of whether they are adults or juveniles. Those convicts whose personal peculiarities and criminal histories have negative effects on other convicts or those who might oppress and use others are also kept separately. Pre-trial detainees should be kept separately from convicted prisoners except in cases in which the convicts as well as the court or investigator agree to common accommodation.[15] In detention facilities a strict daily routine is established through ordinance of the governor. A list of things and belongings that are allowed to be possessed by prisoners, the quantity allowed to be kept at places of imprisonment, and procedures of money seizure are governed by the Regulations of Internal Order in Prisons. In Jelgava prison, in the lowest regime level there are two to eight persons per cell. Prisoners live in a dormitory type living area where they can move freely in the medium and highest regime level. The legal standards provide 2,5 m² of living space for male prisoners and 3 m² for female and juvenile prisoners. According to Section 8 of the Regulations of Internal Order in Prisons, foreign nationals will be accommodated together so that persons who speak the same language can communicate. This aspect was taken into account in Riga Central Prison where Finnish and Swedish nationals were placed in the same cell. If there are several prisoners from one country, prison authorities accommodate them together. Foreign prisoners have access to the same prison facilities and they can, however, be accommodated together with nationals and non-nationals of Latvia.

2.3 Reception and admission

Upon arrival, a person goes through the reception area where he/she is registered. Money, jewellery and documents are entrusted to the administration of the prison. Persons fill out a notification document that is to be sent to their family or close relatives with assistance of prison administration. It contains information on their rights to receive letters, the number and length of visits, the number of phone calls, their right to receive newspapers and magazines subscribed to by other persons in their names, their right to have money transferred to their account and the number of parcels they can receive per year. Additionally, during the admission process prisoners are given time to write a letter to supplement the above mentioned notification, the postage of which is paid for by the prison administration. Notification by phone is not foreseen in the legal regulations and is also not performed in practice. Prison staff explains the rules of the internal order upon arrival of the sentenced person, but there is no legal obligation to provide him / her with a copy of these rules.

---

[15] Sodu izpildes kodekss (Code of Execution of Sentences), Section 18.

In practice prisoners receive extracts from "Regulations on the Internal Order in Prisons". These extracts are also available in Latvian and Russian, and are on the walls in the living areas of the prison. The full text is available from the head of the unit upon request of the prisoner. Translations in other languages are not provided by the state. In Riga Central prison embassies made translations of the rules for the inmates.[16] According to the Law on the Detention Order, detained persons must be informed about their rights and obligations in a language that he/she without any delay, as well as of the authorities to which he/she can submit complaints. If necessary an interpreter will be invited.

2.4 Work – Education – Training – Sport – Recreation

Work and education in prisons is one of the main problems faced by the Latvian Prison administration. In 2005 only 1,286 of all sentenced persons with the capacity to work were actually employed (17.6 % of all sentenced persons). The majority of employed prisoners (63.04%) were employed in prison maintenance activities such as kitchens, warehouse workers, janitors, stokers, hair-dressers, bathhouse attendants, cobblers and motor engineers. Only 29% of the employed prisoners worked in production such as wood-processing, tailoring, metal work and agriculture.[17] Access to work for foreign prisoners is the same as for national prisoners, according to the relevant law. It is not possible to evaluate whether foreigners have less possibilities to be employed as the overall rate of employment in prisons is very low. Prison staff have acknowledged that nationality does not have an impact on the employment of prisoners but some authorities mentioned that the language barrier may be an obstacle in employing foreigners. This does not apply to Russian speaking prisoners.

In 2004 nine out of 15 prisons offered some education, but only eight percent of the prisoners took part in general educational programs, and less that five percent participated in accredited vocational training programs. The majority of detainees who were involved in the educational activities were juveniles.[18] 171 adult prisoners were involved in programs of general education in 2004, and it should also be mentioned that adult remand prisoners are not involved in educational activities. 364 prisoners were involved in professional education programs in 2004.[19] Possibilities and opportunities to be involved in educational activities are low for both national and foreign prisoners. There are also equal opportunities to be involved in sporting activities and recreation for national and foreign prisoners. They can use gym, and play basketball or other outdoor games. In the lowest level of regime the activities are limited as the regime provides only one hour of walking per day. In the medium and highest level of regime there is more time for activities. Libraries are equipped with literature in the Latvian and Russian languages. Russian speaking foreigners therefore have better access to literature than other foreigners, who are dependent on the help of relatives and consulates.

---

[16] Data from the administration of Riga Central Prison.
[17] Data from the Prison Administration.
[18] Latvian Centre for Human Rights and Ethnic Studies (LCHRES), *Human Rights in Latvia in 2004*, Riga   2005.
[19] Pētījums „Ieslodzīto un no ieslodzījuma atbrīvoto personu izglītības, nodarbinātības un sociālās rehabilitācijas pakalpojumu pieejamība". P.93.

2.5 Food – Religion - Personal hygiene - Medical care

Legal rules concerning religion, food, personal hygiene or medical care are applicable to both national as foreign prisoners. Religious activities for sentenced persons and persons on remand are organized by the chaplain service and can be performed by the representatives of nine religious confessions (Lutheran, Roman Catholic, Russian Orthodox, Baptist, Old Believer, Methodist, Judaist, Seventh-day Adventist, and Pentecostal). Prisoners in the highest and medium regime level can freely access the special room for religious activities, but for those in the lowest regime meetings with religious representatives are available in cells. For example, in Jelgava prison there are services in Latvian and Russian every morning. If a prisoner wants to meet a religious representative of his/her confession, the chaplain communicates with the representative of the confession and organizes a meeting for the prisoner. The chaplain plays a major role in the organization of the social life in prison, for example by providing English language courses, musical concerts and lectures. When asked about possibilities to meet prisoners' dietary requirements, the prison authorities informed that there are no possibilities to offer special diets. However, prisoners can use products bought in the prison store. The list of products available for purchase is limited by the regulations of the Cabinet of Ministers. There are limited possibilities to carry different religious accessories (e.g. scented oils) as these articles are not on the list of items permitted to be carried in prison. According to the internal rules of order in prisons, sentenced persons shall wear shortly-cut hair, beards and moustaches. Exceptions apply only to persons who have scars on their face or head and have permission from the chief of medical service.[20] The use of baths or showers and changes of underwear and bedclothes shall be guaranteed at least once a week. Sentenced women have access to washrooms every day. Remand prisoners and sentenced persons have the right to wear personal clothes. These items can be sent by relatives or other persons. Equal medical care is guaranteed to foreign and national prisoners. However, overall evaluation of the heath care services in Latvian prisons by the CPT in 2002 pointed out serious shortcomings, most prominently the fact that the buildings and equipment were vastly out of date. A new prison hospital is currently under construction as is expected to be taken into operation in 2007..

2.6 Consular and legal help

Foreigners can correspond and meet with representatives of diplomatic and consular missions. Expenses of such correspondence are covered by the state and letters are not subject to censorship. Furthermore, meetings with representatives from their home country are not deducted from the total number of visits to which inmates are entitled (see 2.7 below). In some prisons regular consultation hours with consular representatives are organized. Prison authorities pointed out that consulates are mainly involved in helping foreign prisoners attain legal status and documentation. There are cases in which they help to establish contacts with state authorities in the foreigner's home country. There is a different level of involvement of embassies – some are more active than others. For example, the Finnish embassy helped with translations as their national could not understand the language and the prison did not have the resources to provide this service. Legal aid during

---

[20] Rules of Internal Order in Prisons, section 24.

criminal proceedings is guaranteed by the Code of Criminal Procedure. If the person cannot afford an advocate, the state ensures participation of an advocate in the procedure and fully or partly covers the expenses. If a person does not master the state language, he has the right to use the services of an interpreter free of charge.[21] According to the State Ensured Legal Aid Law, the categories of persons entitled to receive legal aid funded by the state are Latvian citizens, Latvian non-citizens, stateless persons, EU nationals legally residing in Latvia, third country nationals legally residing in Latvia, asylum seekers, refugees, and persons under subsidiary protection.[22]

2.7 Contacts with the outside world

Prisoners and remand prisoners can communicate with persons via mail, phone calls and meetings. Communication of remand prisoners can be restricted only according to a decision of an investigation judge[23]. Correspondence of a sentenced person is subject to censorship, and postal mails and parcels are subject to check-ups. In 2004 amendments to the Sentence Enforcement Code provided that correspondence of sentenced persons with UN bodies, parliament, prosecutors` offices, courts, sworn advocates, the National Human Rights Office, and, in the case of a foreign prisoner, the relevant diplomatic or consular mission, may not be subjected to censorship and, with the exception of a sworn advocate, the postal expenses are to be borne by the prison authorities. Remand prisoners also have unlimited possibilities to contact diplomatic authorities and their correspondence with diplomatic authorities, human rights bodies, prosecutors` offices and courts may not me subjected to censorship.[24] Prisoners in closed prisons have the right to three to six long term visits and four to six short term visits (each up to two hours) per year depending on the regime in which they are being detained. Additionally they have the right to one to three phone calls per month. The duration of long term visits varies from six to 24 hours.[25] Prisoners in semi-closed prisons are entitled to more meetings – up to eight long term meetings of 48 hours and eight short term meetings. Likewise they can make up to four telephone calls per month depending on their regime. Short meetings are allowed with relatives or other persons in the presence of a prison representative. Persons eligible to make long-term visits to prisoners are immediate relatives such as parents, children, brothers and sisters, grandparents, grandchildren, as well as spouses. Should a convict have no immediate relatives or should they not visit him/her, long-term visits from other relatives or other persons may be allowed, dependent on a decision by the respective prison administration. Short term and long term meetings can be organized at equal time intervals. For example, if there are six short term visits per year, they can be held every two months. There are no special exceptions for foreign prisoners or national prisoners with families abroad concerning the organization of visits. Short as well as long meetings may be substituted by telephone calls at the cost of the convict or the person to whom the call is made. This possibility is frequently used by foreigners as visits from relatives are rare. Remand prisoners have the right to one short term meeting per month and at least one five minutes phone call per week.

---

21 Code of Criminal Procedure, Section 11.
22 English text of State Ensured Legal Aid Law is available at http:// www.ttc..lv
23 Code of Criminal Procedure, section 12.
24 Apcietinājumā turēšanas likums (Law on detention Order), Section 23.
25 Sentence Execution Act. Art. 50.

Telephone calls, including long-distance calls and postal expenses shall be covered by prisoners themselves and prisons have no means to cover these expenses for prisoners who have no access to work. Prisoners in semi-closed prisons in the highest regime have the right to short term leave in the case of death or serious illness of a close relative. In these cases, the involved prisoners receive a temporary identification document. Practically they can attend a funeral in Latvia (yet not abroad) since this temporary card is not a valid travel document. Prisoners have the right to use their personal television set or a TV from the prison. Latvian and Russian channels are available in all prisons, while some institutions have cable TV with programs in English. According to data from the prison administration all prisoners who do not master Russian have access to TV channels in English.

2.8 Re-integration activities

Reintegration work in prisons in Latvia is connected with the arrangement of necessary documents. Many prisoners do not have passports or personal codes. Six months prior to their release, a probation officer meets with the prisoners and finds out about his societal needs like work, a place of residence, family, etc. The person is informed about the services provided by probation service and receives assistance from a probation officer in setting-up a plan for living and possibilities to stay in a half-way house. If a person wants he/she can conclude a voluntary agreement and access assistance of probation regardless of his/her citizenship. The State Probation Service began supervising released offenders in society since 2006. On 1 April 2006 there were five foreign nationals under supervision, one of whom was on parole. All of them had lived in Latvia for a long time and had families there.

Both in theory and in practice equal assistance is granted to both national and foreign prisoners. There are better opportunities for the communication with foreign prisoners (English speaking) since many of the probation officers master the English language. Parole is granted to persons regardless their citizenship. Applications of sentenced prisoners are reviewed by the administrative commission of the prison (representatives from prison, probation, prosecutors office) and then by the judge. In interviews representatives of the commissions mentioned cases in which foreigners had been granted parole. Usually, foreigners are expelled after release according to the judgment of a court or a decision by the Board of Citizenship and Migration Affairs. An example in a research paper of the Latvian Police Academy on parole[26] describes a case where a judge had not granted a person parole because his belonging to a certain country could not be legally established.

2.9 Release –Expulsion

Expulsion from Latvia is either a criminal penalty or an administrative measure under Immigration Law. A citizen of another state or a person who has a permanent residence permit of another state may be expelled from the Republic of Latvia if a court finds that, considering the circumstances of the matter and the personality of the offender, it is not permissible for him or her to remain in the Republic of Latvia. Expulsion from Latvia is

---

[26] Latvijas Policijas akadēmija (Latvian Police academy), *'Nosacīta pirmstermiņa atbrīvošana no kriminālsoda"*, Rīga 2004, p. 22.

adjudged as an additional penalty and execution thereof takes place only after the basic penalty has been served. Temporary and permanent residence permits and expulsion orders under Immigration Law are issued by the Office of Citizenship and Migration Affairs. A temporary residence permit is cancelled if a foreigner by judgment of a court has been found guilty of committing such a criminal offence in or outside the Republic of Latvia for which the law provides a sentence of imprisonment for a time not less than two years. A permanent residence permit is cancelled if a court finds a foreigner guilty of having committed a serious or especially serious crime in the Republic of Latvia. If a foreigner is married to a Latvian citizen or non-citizen a permit can only be voided in cases when it is needed for the safety of the state and society. If an alien does not have a lawful basis to reside in the Republic of Latvia after having served a sentence for criminal offences committed in the Republic of Latvia, the Head of the Office shall make a decision regarding the forcible expulsion of the irregular migrant.[27] According to data from Prison Administration on 1 February 2006 there were 35 persons on the expulsion list. 15 from them did not have personal documents (passports) in their prison files.

2.10 Aftercare-Probation

In the case in which foreign offenders stay in the country after their release they are allowed to make use of aftercare facilities and support from the probation service. There are no special provisions for foreign offenders. Ex-offenders can stay in one of eight half-way houses financed by the Probation Service. The Probation Service covers six months of stay in the program, and in some cases this support can be prolonged to nine months. So far there have been no foreign nationals in the half-way houses, but there have been a few in voluntary aftercare. Further aftercare provisions include assistance in developing a plan to resolve problems, participation in programmes to combat substance abuse and anger management courses, which are free of charge.

2.11 Staff

The staff of the prison service does not receive special training to deal with foreigners. Since there have been few non-Russian speaking foreigners in Latvian prisons, training concerning foreigners has not been organized. However, language training is necessary now because only few staff members master the English language.

2.12 Projects

According to information from the Prison Administration there are no special projects for foreign prisoners organized by the Prison Service or NGOs.

3 ADMINISTRATIVE DETENTION OF FOREIGN PRISONERS

The first Immigration Law in Latvia dates from 1992. The issue of asylum seekers did not become a live topic until the independence of Latvia. The first law on asylum seekers and

---

27 Immigration Law, Section 48.

refugees was enacted in 1998. Prior to this, persons who came to Latvia were detained in the detention centre "Olaine". In the mid-nineties there was quite an active movement of refugees that passed Latvia on their way to Scandinavia. In the literature we can find a description of a group of 120 asylum seekers who were kept in "Olaine" for one year. They were eventually granted refugee status in Scandinavia. In that time the state was not materially prepared to receive asylum seekers, so the help from other countries (Sweden, USA) and the UNHCR[28] played an important role. The reception centre for asylum seekers "Mucenieki" was opened in 1999. According to the data from the Office of Citizenship Affairs and Migration 68 asylum seekers have been accommodated there since the opening of the centre. Conditions are good and persons have the right to move freely outside the centres. In 2005 seven persons were accommodated here. Since 1998 Latvia reviewed 161 applications from asylum seekers:

- eight persons have received a refugee status (five men, one woman and two juveniles) from 1998 to 2001. One of these persons became a Latvian citizen through naturalization in 2004.
- nine persons received alternative status from 2002 to 2005 (three from Belarus and six from Russia). Five lost it in 2004 as they returned to their countries of origin.

Until 2002 all questions related to immigrants and asylum seekers (detention, interviewing, identification and housing) were the responsibility of the Immigration Police of the State Police. The Office of Citizenship and Migration Affairs was responsible for decision making on the status of a person. Since reorganization in 2002 the responsibilities have been with the State Border Guard and the Office of Citizenship and Migration Affairs. According to Section 51 of the Immigration Law the State Border Guard has the right to detain a foreigner who has illegally crossed the state border of the Republic of Latvia or otherwise violated the procedures prescribed by regulatory enactments for the entry and residence of irregular migrants into the Republic of Latvia. In the cases referred to in Section 51 of the Immigration Law the State Police officials have the right to detain an irregular for three hours until handing her/him over to the State Border Guard. An official of the State Border Guard has the right to detain a foreigner for a period not exceeding ten days. Such an official also has the right to detain a foreigner for more than ten days, however only pursuant to the decision of a judge of the District Court. Based on an application from the State Border Guard, a judge then decides whether to detain the foreigner for up to two months or to refuse his/her detention.. The State Border Guard may apply repeatedly for an extension of the term of detention, but the total period may not exceed 20 months. The decision may be revoked by the judge himself pursuant to a protest of the prosecutor. Furthermore, the chairperson of the Regional Court can also revoke such a judgement. In this case, no objection from the prosecutor is necessary.

The actual period of detention of illegal foreign nationals was rather long before 2003 and there was no time limit for detention pending their removal from Latvia. This problem was noted by the CPT after its visit to Latvia in 2002.[29] The situation has improved since the adoption of the Immigration Law in 2003 that set the maximum limit of 20

---

[28] European Community initiative EQUAL project: Soli pa solim (Step by Step), research paper, *"Latvijas iedzīvotāju, valts amatpersonu un NVO attieksme prêt patvēruma meklētājiem (Attitude of inhabitants, state authorities and NGO`s towards asylum seekers")*, 2005.

[29] Report of CPT from visit to Latvia in 2002, Section 43.

months. Amendments to the Immigration Law in 2005 have resulted in a shortening of the intervals in which a foreigner's administrative detention should be reviewed by a judge. According to data from the State Border Guard, 307 foreigners have been detained under Article 51 of the Immigration Law. Forcible expulsion has been applied to 190 foreigners.

Illegal foreigners are detained in detention premises at border posts and police short term detention isolators. These detention places are used for detention that does not exceed ten days. Foreigners detained for periods longer than ten days are placed in detention centre "Olaine". The majority of persons detained are persons who have illegally crossed Latvia's border and who have otherwise violated the formal legal procedure of entry or stay of foreigners in the country. This category includes persons who have entered Latvia legally in the past and who have long established links with the country including a fixed residence and a family, but who have for various reasons failed to apply for or renew the necessary documents. Some of them were persons who had requested asylum but whose identity had not been confirmed yet, or whose asylum request had been rejected and were waiting expulsion.[30] In those cases in which it has been impossible to establish a detainee's link with any country or impossible to expel him/her or to give any legal status to stay in Latvia, the Board of Citizenship and Migration Affairs issues a departure document.

Detention Centre "Olaine"

Detention Centre Olaine is an institution under the State Border Guard, with a capacity of 80 places. There are plans to extend the premises of the centre so that it can accommodate 200 persons. The staff of the centre consists of 30 persons. On any given day the detention centre accommodates around 10 -20 persons. In 2005, 153 people were accommodated in the detention centre, of which 22 were staying in the centre on 13 January 2006.[31] In 2004 the detention centre accommodated 146 persons, while in 2003 174 persons were admitted to the institution. The figure for 2002 was 214.. The average length of stay in the centre is three weeks up to two months. There were several cases in which the length of stay was over a year due to difficulties with providing documentation or the course of appeal procedures.

One of them is the case of six asylum seekers from Somalia. Experts of the State Human Rights Office and Latvian Centre for Human Rights and Ethnic Studies have regularly visited Olaine Detention Centre and expressed their opinion during interviews that the psychological atmosphere in the centre is relaxed and that the staff has a good relationship with the detainees. Similar observations were made by the CPT in 2002 (atsauce uz zi□ojuma 46.punktu)[32] The State Human Rights Office has not received complaints concerning conditions in the centre in the past years. However, the Centre for Human Rights and Ethnic Studies has received several complaints concerning the detention regime. Main concerns of Latvian human rights experts are laid down in the Report on the Situation of Fundamental Rights in Latvia in 2005.[33] Experts expressed the opinion that

---

[30] Latvian Centre for Human Rights and Ethnic Studies (LCHRES), *Human Rights in Latvia in 2004*, Riga 2005.
[31] Data from the State Border Guard.
[32] Report of CPT from its visit to Latvia in 2002, Section 43.
[33] http://cridho.cpdr.ucl.ac.be/DownloadRep/rapports2005/NationalReport/CFRLatvia2005.pdf

in some areas the rules concerning detention of illegal immigrants are more restricting than those applied to persons kept in custody for criminal offences.

The detention regime in the detention centre "Olaine" is governed by the order issued by the State Border Guard and they have not been made public. Regulations include such fundamental rights as meetings with relatives and other persons and the rights to education. These regulations are not available on a public data base of legal acts as they are internal regulations of the State Border Guard. Amendments to laws are being prepared to change the situation. Similar regulations concerning prisoners sentenced under Criminal Law are included in the Sentence Execution Act and "Regulations of the internal order in prisons" issued by the Cabinet of Ministers. Regulations concerning daily norms of food and means of personal hygiene are contained in the Regulations of the Cabinet of Ministers No 339 of 6 August 2002, and these regulations are applicable to all categories of detained persons (criminal and administrative). The possibility to carry out activities of work and education in the centre is limited. The only place where detained foreigners can spend time outside the premises irrespective of the season is a small asphalt backyard.[34]

Amendments to the Asylum law provide that the minor children of an asylum seeker or minor asylum seekers can be ensured that the acquisition of education is in conformity with the laws in force. The Cabinet of Ministers shall determine the procedures according to which education shall be ensured. Such an obligation does not exist in the case of illegal immigrants.

In the beginning of 2005 the project for renovation of detention centres was approved by the Cabinet of Ministers (Data from the State Border Guard), but financing has not yet been allocated. Renovation will ensure better conditions for living, more space for activities and meetings.

Language issues have not been a major problem for communication on a daily basis as the majority of detainees and staff of the centres speaks Russian or English. Problems arise if persons do not communicate in these languages. In the case with the asylum seekers from Somalia only one of them could speak some English and there is no interpreter of the Somali language in Latvia. However, language barriers can impact the execution of the legal rights of detained foreigners, for example their right to appeal. The law provides the obligation to explain a decision in an understandable language but does not provide the obligation to issue written translation, therefore preparation of an appeal in due time can be difficult. According to the Immigration Law illegal immigrants have the right to receive assistance from a lawyer but this right is limited if persons do not have financial means as there is no state guaranteed legal aid for illegal immigrants. According to the Law on State provided legal aid, the categories of persons entitled to receive legal aid funded by the state are Latvian citizens, Latvian non-citizens, stateless persons, EU nationals legally residing in Latvia, third country nationals legally residing in Latvia, asylum seekers, refugees and persons under subsidiary protection. Asylum seekers can receive legal aid for appeal procedures within the process of granting asylum.

There is a room for religious activities in the centre, but there is no religious representative. Since the majority of persons stay in the centre for a short term, there is no practical need to employ a chaplain. The staff of the centre will organize a meeting with a religious representative if one would ask. To improve the capacity of the staff, the State

---

[34] *Ibidem.*

Border Guard is involved in an exchange project of staff to foreign countries and improvement of English language skills of personnel of Olaine detention centre.

4 NATIONALS DETAINED ABROAD

Information on Latvian nationals sentenced abroad is kept by the information centre under the Ministry of Interior. It was not possible to gather information during the preparation of this report. Information is stored on statistical cards and it is processed manually. So far statistics on Latvian nationals detained abroad has not been gathered. According to the 1959 Council of Europe Convention on Mutual Assistance in Criminal Matters, states will exchange information on nationals sentenced abroad. The central authority is the Ministry of Justice. Data available from the Ministry of Justice of Latvia shows that Latvia has received information from the following countries: Portugal, Norway, Sweden, France, Germany, Lithuania, Italy, Finland, and Denmark.

5 EVALUATION AND RECOMMENDATIONS

This report gives an incomplete overview of the questions regarding foreign prisoners in Latvia. There are several reasons for that:
- data for some categories of foreigners has not been collected (persons in pre-trial detention, number of foreigners among sentenced persons);
- data is collected but is not summarized (data about Latvian nationals detained abroad);
- within this given time period deeper research of legislation and practice was not possible.

More accurate data collection would be desirable to attain a better understanding of the situation of sentenced foreigners in Latvia. However, some conclusions and recommendations can be made. The Latvian prison administration is working successfully with Russian-speaking foreigners but is not materially prepared to receive non-Russian speaking foreign prisoners. Only a limited share of prison staff can communicate in foreign languages other than Russian. Translation of all the main legal acts concerning detention must be done in Russian and English and should be available for prisoners. Language training of prison staff would improve their skills in communicating with foreign inmates. That would also provide the opportunity to conduct educational visits abroad and learn from the experience of other countries. More flexible visiting rules would foster the socialization of foreign prisoners. Financial assistance for foreigners who do not have financial means and cannot be granted work in prison would be desirable to cover long-distance phone calls and postal expenses.

Generally the situation of treatment of illegal immigrants does not differ from the situation of prisoners under criminal law. There are some exceptions. For example, rules of internal order in prisons were adopted by the Cabinet of Ministers, but in the detention centre for illegal immigrants the rules are set by an internal order of the State Border Guard. Adopting the new regulations of the Cabinet of Ministers on the order of detention of illegal immigrants would generate a better legal situation for illegal immigrants.

Chapter 16

Lithuania

Sonata Malisauskaite – Simanaitiene

1 INTRODUCTION

1.1 Overview of penalties and measures

A foreign national may be detained on various grounds in the Republic of Lithuania in accordance with both criminal and administrative laws. Primarily, if he is suspected of committing a criminal offence, he may be *detained[1]*, when he is caught red-handed or immediately afterwards. With the grounded suspicions existing that an illegal resident has committed a criminal offence, he or she may be placed in *pre-trial detention.*[2]. If a foreign national is found guilty of having committed a criminal offence; he or she may be imprisoned under the measures of *arrest, deprivation of liberty* or *life imprisonment.*[3]

In addition to the grounds under the criminal laws, a foreign person may be also detained administratively. Primarily, *administrative detention[4]* may be imposed on him or her as a measure for ensuring proceedings of administrative law violations. It is granted in seeking to prevent violations of administrative law, to draw up law infringement records, to ensure timely and fair hearings and the enforcement of orders, or is in other cases foreseen directly under the laws. Subject to the general rule, administrative detention may last not longer than five hours, however, under exclusive necessity, the laws foresee different time limits of administrative detention. Detention may last the same time-limit of up to 48 hours where the person is subjected to administrative liability for petty hooliganism or infringements of the rules of meetings and other mass gatherings. Administrative detention is most often applied and carried out by the police, but it may also be carried out by other institutions authorized to do so by the law when handling the cases of administrative law violations under their competence. For example, administrative detention may be applied by the officers of the State Border Guard Service for violations of the regulations of the frontier, the rules of border crossing point operations or customs rules.

An illegal resident may also be held in custody if the administrative penalty of *administrative arrest* is imposed on him or her for committing an administrative offence.[5]

Detainees are most often kept in police custody; where persons are also accommodated for violations of administrative law. Persons for whom such detention is granted shall be kept in investigatory isolation wards, while persons on whom arrest is imposed as a penalty for crimes are kept in the police custody facilities. A custodial penalty is executed in correctional colonies, correctional houses or prison; while the latter institution is also used for persons sentenced to life imprisonment.

---

[1] Law on the Approval, Enforcement and Implementation of the Code of Criminal Procedure of the Republic of Lithuania. Code of Criminal Procedure. Official Gazette. – 2002, No. 37-1341 (Art. 140).

[2] Law on the Approval, Enforcement and Implementation of the Code of Criminal Procedure of the Republic of Lithuania. Code of Criminal Procedure. Official Gazette. – 2002, No. 37-1341 (Art. 122 - 131).

[3] Law on the Approval, Enforcement and Implementation of the Code of Criminal Procedure of the Republic of Lithuania. Code of Criminal Procedure. Official Gazette. – 2000, No. 89-274 (Art. 42).

[4] The Code of Administrative Violations of the Republic of Lithuania, adopted by the Supreme Council of the Lithuanian Soviet Socialist Republic on 13 December 1984 (Art. 265 – 267).

[5] The Code of Administrative Violations of the Republic of Lithuania, adopted by the Supreme Council of the Lithuanian Soviet Socialist Republic on 13 December 1984 (Art. 21).

An illegal resident / irregular foreigner may be detained under the Law on the Legal Status of Aliens on the following grounds.[6]

- if the he or she has illegally entered or is illegally residing in Lithuania;
- when it is attempted to return the illegal resident, who has been refused entry to the Republic of Lithuania;
- if a decision on expulsion from the Republic of Lithuania has been made;
- in order to stop the spread of dangerous and especially dangerous communicable diseases;
- when the illegal resident's stay in the Republic of Lithuania constitutes a threat to the State security, public order or public health.

An illegal or irregular resident may be detained by the police or any other law enforcement institution officer for a period not exceeding 48 hours. When a longer period of detention is necessary, the respective officer must apply to the court for his detention or for a measure alternative to detention within the said period. The term of detention shall be indicated on court order. A juvenile irregular foreigner (below the age of 18 years) may be detained only in an extreme case when his or her best interests are the main consideration.

It is necessary to focus attention on the fact that at present – subject to the law of the Republic of Lithuania – detention and accommodation of an illegal migrant at the Foreigners' Registration Centre and thus his or her freedom and movement shall be applied only in extreme cases. In view of the fact that the he or she poses no threat to public security and public order, the person's identity has been established or he or she provides assistance in determining his identity – the court may impose measures that are alternatives to detention, for instance: requiring that the foreigner in question regularly reports to the appropriate territorial police agency at a fixed time; requiring that he or she communicates his or her whereabouts to the appropriate territorial police agency at a fixed time; entrusting the care of the illegal migrant to a citizen of the Republic of Lithuania or a foreign family member who is legally residing in Lithuania, provided that the person undertakes to take care of and to support him/her; entrusting the care of an unaccompanied illegally residing minor to a relevant social agency; directly accommodating an foreigner in the Foreigners' Registration Centre without subjecting him or her to restriction of freedom. When imposing a measure alternative to detention, the term of its application shall also be determined. If such an alternative measure is not applied, the police can apply to the court that detention be imposed.

Foreigners that are detained under the Law on the Legal Status of Aliens shall be accommodated at the Foreigners' Registration Centre.

1.2 Overview of the Prison System

1.2.1 Organisational Structure

Prior to the year 2000, the process of execution of penalties as well as the application of all other coercive measures was administered by the institutions under the Ministry of

---

[6] Law on the Legal Status of Aliens in Lithuania of the Republic of Lithuania. Official Gazette. – 2004 No. 73-2539 (Art. 112-119).

the Interior. The institution with the key responsibility in this field was the Department of Correctional Affairs. In carrying out the legal system reform, on 1 September 2000 responsibility for the execution of punishments was transferred from the Ministry of the Interior to the Ministry of Justice. The Prison Department that was then established under the Ministry of Justice became responsible for the administration of the execution of punishment. This department is not only responsible for the execution of all penalties but also for the execution of remand detention.

The internal structure of the Prison Department is of interest since it is organized not according to the execution of separate penalties, but rather according to individual aspects of ensuring the execution of the punishment process, like the social rehabilitation division, the protection and supervision division, the record division, and so on. The Prison Department is constituted of 18 divisions, like the law division, the office, the personnel division, the information division, etc., which are all responsible for ensuring the smooth operation of the Prison Department. Work of other divisions is intended for ensuring the execution of deprivation of freedom, arrest penalties and remand detention measures. Only one division –the correctional inspection division – is responsible for ensuring the execution of penalties that are not related to the deprivation of liberty.

The Prison Department is headed by the director, assisted by his three deputies for work organization who are in charge of the work in the separate divisions. As of 1 January 2006 the Prison Department had 78 employees (they accounted for only 2 percent of the total number of the persons employed in the system of the execution of penalties), of which 58 (74 percent) are officers.[7]

The institutions under the subordination of the Prison Department are involved in executing penalties and arrest. There are five regional inspectorates who perform the administration of the 15 institutions and carry out the measures relating to the deprivation of liberty (pre-trial detention, imprisonment), and 48 territorial correctional inspectorates that are responsible for the execution of non-custodial penalties. The major part (85 percent) of the total number of persons involved the system of the execution of penalties are employed in the prison establishments – on 1 January 2006, the number of employees in these establishments totalled 3,224 of 3,798 employees, whereas the correctional inspectorates had just 218 employees (i.e. six percent of the total number).[8] Attention should be focused on the fact that as of 1 January 2006 the imprisonment establishments had 8,137 inmates (of which deprivation of liberty is imposed on 6,899 persons), and 9,339 persons were under the record of correctional inspectorates.[9]

In the Republic of Lithuania there are three types of penitentiary institutions where convicts serve custodial penalties. The most lenient prison regime can be found in the so called "open colony" where persons are detained who have been convicted of negligent and minor intentional offences. Since there is only one such open institution in Lithuania, it is designed to accommodate both females and males. "Correctional houses" are the main type of penitentiary institutions where the custodial penalties are served by the majority of convicts. Therefore they are most numerous in number in Lithuania, with 11

---

[7]   Report of the Prison Department "Basic Data of the 2005 Activities of the Prison Department and Establishments and State Enterprises under Its Subordination ". Vilnius, 2006, p. 12.

[8]   Report of the Prison Department "Basic Data of the 2005 Activities of the Prison Department and Establishments and State Enterprises under Its Subordination ". Vilnius, 2006, p. 12.

[9]   Report of the Prison Department "Basic Data of the 2005 Activities of the Prison Department and Establishments and State Enterprises under Its Subordination ". Vilnius, 2006, p. 15.

such establishments in operation. Prison is the penal institution with the most stringent regime with more guards, increased supervision of the sentenced persons and their maximum isolation. Persons convicted of particularly serious crimes and convicts who are sentenced to life imprisonment serve their time in such institutions, [10]of which there is only one in Lithuania.

Punishment by arrest is carried out in the remand custody wards. Taking into account that the new criminal code was only enforced in 2003, and that until that time the appropriate separate establishments had not been timely built or installed, four remand custody wards were established in the already operating correctional establishments: two in correctional houses, one in the prison (only for males), and in the correctional house where only females serve their custodial penalty-This remand custody ward is also only for females.[11]

The total number of places in all imprisonment institutions on 1 January 2006 amounted to 9,476, and in 2005 there were 7,939 inmates on average.[12] Thus, for the moment the primary existing problem of the system of execution of penalties in the Republic of Lithuania – the overcrowding of the imprisonment institutions – has been resolved. However, the issue of there being more prisoners than places in penal institutions has not been fully overcome due to the uneven distribution of convicts in the separate penitentiary establishments. The reorganization of these institutions was an attempt to tackle this problem. Therefore, in nearly all correctional houses the problem of overcrowding does not exist – it persisted only in the interrogation isolation wards and the prison. The Šiauliai interrogation isolation ward is overcrowded by 68 percent, the Lukiškės interrogation ward/prison by 22 percent. Also, the problem of overcrowding remained in the hospital ward of imprisonment institutions – it is overcrowded by 35 percent.[13]

Correctional inspectorates execute the following non-custodial penalties: deprivation of public rights, deprivation of the right to perform a certain profession or to be involved in certain activities, community service, restriction of liberty, and probation. On 1 January 2006, the average workload per correctional institution officer was 50.5 convicts, but due to the uneven distribution of the convicts and officers in different territorial correctional inspectorates the work load varied from 21 to 68 convicts per officer.[14]

When describing the organizational structure of the system of execution of penalties it is necessary to mention the Training Department, which is responsible for the proper preparation of the officers working in this system and the improvement of their qualifications.

In 2005, even though quite a considerable part of the staff in the system had received a higher education (32 percent - 30 percent of the total number of the staff had higher

---

[10] Law on the Approval of the Code of Execution of Penalties of the Republic of Lithuania. Code of Execution of Penalties. Official Gazette - 2002, No. 73-3084 (Art. 83 -87).

[11] Report of the Prison Department "Basic Data of the 2005 activities of the Prison Department and Establishments and State Enterprises under Its Subordination". Vilnius, 2006, p. 5-7.

[12] Report of the Prison Department "Basic Data of the 2005 activities of the Prison Department and Establishments and State Enterprises under Its Subordination". Vilnius, 2006, p. 15.

[13] Report of the Prison Department "Basic Data of the 2005 activities of the Prison Department and Establishments and State Enterprises under Its Subordination". Vilnius, 2006, p. 16.

[14] Report of the Prison Department "Basic Data of the 2005 Activities of the Prison Department and Establishments under Its Subordination and State Enterprises". Vilnius, 2006, p. 28.

university and two percent higher non-university education). However, the largest share of the employees had only completed secondary education (42 percent of all the employees). In 2005, 11.2 percent of the employees studied at institutions of higher education, and 26.6 percent of the employees took part in the improvement courses organized by the Training Centre.[15]

Supervision of the system is performed by different public institutions and establishments of the Republic of Lithuania as well as international organizations within the limits of their competence, and the type of this control varies greatly – supervision of lawfulness, being manifest that the institution superior as to its competence may abrogate legal acts adopted by the institution or establishments under its subordination, budgetary control, and disciplinary supervision. Among the more traditional measures of supervision, inspections should be mentioned. The officers from the Ministry of Justice and the Prison Department are entitled to carry out periodical and individual inspections of the establishments under the subordination of the Prison Department, and – upon detecting shortcomings – to give mandatory instructions for the elimination thereof, to perform follow-up control checks of the elimination of the detected shortcomings, and applying various measures (most often the imposition of disciplinary sanctions against the responsible officers).

Another exclusive form of supervision is the surveillance of the lawfulness of the system of execution of penalties that is carried out on the basis of the complaints received from convicts. In addition to the officers from the Prison Department or the heads of the establishments under its subordination, this supervision is carried out by the courts, prosecutors, the Seimas Ombudsman (concerning abuse or bureaucratism of public or municipal officers), Equal Opportunities Ombudsman (if the principle of equal opportunities is infringed by legal acts, orders or actions), Childrens' Rights Protection Ombudsman (if the rights of children are violated), and other institutions responsible for human rights protection. Attention should be focused on the importance of the prosecutor in the system of supervision, who has a number of responsibilities: practising control of the execution of penalties, which he performs primarily by checking whether the enforced judgement is submitted on the defined terms to the competent public institution or establishment; participating in court sessions, where various issues relating to the execution of penalties are considered (e.g., when solving issues concerning probation, early parole, etc.); inspecting the activities of institutions, establishments, officers or persons authorized by the state according to the complaints of convicts.

1.2.2 Foreign Prisoners

Analyzing the prison system for foreign prisoners briefly, it can be concluded that foreign prisoners are generally treated equally to and in the same ways as Lithuanian prisoners.
- There is no special institution or division that is especially concerned with the execution of punishments imposed on foreign prisoners.
- There is no specialized institution or division that is responsible for coordinating the

---

[15] Report of the Prison Department "Basic Data of the 2005 Activities of the Prison Department and Establishments under Its Subordination and State Enterprises". Vilnius, 2006, p. 13-14.

execution of penalties imposed on foreign nationals – the arising problems would be solved by the specialists of the appropriate field of general competence in accordance with the corresponding powers. It is necessary to note that the official specializing in the issues of the execution of penalties to foreign nationals is located in each individual correctional establishment.

- The Republic of Lithuania does not have any special establishments for the imprisonment of convicted foreign nationals, and this is understandable because of their small number. Nor are foreign nationals separated from Lithuanian prisoners in the correctional establishments. However, at their request, they may be accommodated in general wards with their countrymen or in separate premises. But it is important to note that even though there is no special interrogation isolation ward where only foreign nationals are detained; those who are held here are kept in isolation from other convicts.

- Except for the general forms of supervision of the system, no special institution is responsible for the supervision of the protection of the rights of convicted foreign nationals. Therefore, control of the execution of punishment of convicted foreign nationals is carried out in the same way and to the same degree as with native prisoners.

Regarding the training of prison system staff it must be stated that both the programmes for preparing officers at the institutions of higher education and the qualification improvement programmes do not contain a programme aimed at providing special knowledge or skills for dealing with foreign prisoners. In addition, survey of the staff employed in the system showed that such special knowledge or skills were not much needed, except for some officers who wished to learn more foreign languages.

1.3 Involvement of Embassies and Consulates

Information on the involvement of Embassies and Consulates is provided under sections 2.5 and 2.6 of this article.

1.4 Overview of trends

1.4.1 Sentencing Trends

From 1998 to 2002, deprivation of liberty was predominant among the penalties imposed. Other penalties such as for instance fines and correctional works[16] accounted for five to 13 percent of all imposed sanctions. The share of these penalties did not exceed eight percent, and increased only after 2002, when the size of the fine to be imposed was corrected. The size of the minimum fine was reduced from 100 minimum living standards (approximately EUR 3,600) to one minimum living standard (approximately EUR 36). However, the proportion of actually served custodial penalties was considerably lower – it fluctuated from 37.9 percent to 44.4 percent of all imposed penalties, since the execution of the major part of custodial penalties was suspended on parole.[17] This situa-

---

[16] "Correctional works" were a special form of punishment that was popular in Soviet Union States. It was only applicable to employed suspects. The content of this measure mainly consisted of obligatory payments into the state budget from the salary of the accused person.

[17] Report, prepared by the Administration of the National Judiciary "Report on Handling of Criminal Cases at the Court of the First Instance" (including the summary process)" 1998 – 2002.

tion was predetermined by the fact that pursuant to the then valid Criminal Code of the Republic of Lithuania the judges did not have a wide choice of penalties to impose. Correctional works could be imposed only on persons who had jobs – they constituted the majority of those convicted. Also, the levels of fines were unproportionally high, so that in actual fact it was a penalty which was hardly implementable. Simultaneously, sanctions in the special part of the Criminal Code were construed in such a way that deprivation of liberty was the most frequently imposed response to offending. Therefore, in the new Criminal Code it was primarily sought to reduce a share of imposed custodial penalties: new sentences of medium severity were foreseen (community services, restriction of liberty, arrest), the size of a fine was corrected downwards, and sanctions in the special part were construed so that they allowed the opportunities for the imposition the greater number of alternative penalties to the deprivation of an offender's liberty. Amendments to criminal laws had an essential effect on the distribution of the sanctions to be imposed – the penalties that were brought into being in 2003 accounted for 11-17 percent of all penalties imposed. In 2004, the share of imposed fines increased to approximately 20 percent, and the proportion of actually served custodial penalties among all sentences decreased to 29.7.[18]

The primary problem in the Lithuanian system of the execution of penalties was in fact the high share of actually served custodial sanctions, which was manifested in the very high number of criminal prisoners and resulting overcrowding in the institutions in which the sentences were actually being served. In 1998 – 1999, for example, an average of 12,000 convicted persons were serving their custodial penalties in penal institutions, a number that was very high for a country with a total population of 3 million. In 1998, the number of inmates in the prison system per 100,000 of the population was 383[19], one of the highest in Europe (only Belarus, Russia and Ukraine had even higher rates[20]), and worldwide Lithuania was nineteenth.[21] After the new criminal laws were enforced the position changed greatly. On average, 6,800 convicted persons on whom a custodial penalty was imposed served their terms in penitentiary institutions, and in 2005 the number of prisoners per 100,000 of the population was 235[22], a reduction that saw Lithuania in 46th place worldwide.[23] On the 1 January 2006 there were 8,137 persons in penal institutions, of which 310 were female prisoners. At the European level, Lithuania still remains one of the countries with the highest number of imprisoned persons. The number of persons

---

18 Report, prepared by the Administration of the National Judiciary "Report on Handling of Cases. Types of Penalties and Granting Amnesty (in courts of the first instance)" 2003 – 2005.

19 Data provided on the basis of the data of World Prison Brief. International Centre for Prison Studies. University of London, Internet access at the address
http://www.kcl.ac.uk/depsta/rel/icps/worldbrief/europe.html .

20 House Office Research, Development and Statistics Directorate. Research Findings/ World Prison Population List (Second Edition). No 116, Internet access at the address
http://www.houseoffice.gov.uk/rds/pdfs/r116.pdf .

21 House Office Research, Development and Statistics Directorate. Research Findings/ World Prison Population List (Second Edition). No 116, Internet access at the address
http://www.houseoffice.gov.uk/rds/pdfs/r116.pdf .

22 In 1998, the number of persons detained accounted for 17 percent, in 2005 – 13.6 percent of the total number of the imprisoned persons.

23 Data provided on the basis of the data of World Prison Brief. International Centre for Prison Studies. University of London, Internet access at the address
http://www.kcl.ac.uk/depsta/rel/icps/worldbrief/europe.html .

serving custodial penalties has declined very significantly due to the fact that the number of persons convicted to an actual custodial penalty is still lower. While in 1998 – 2002 the detention facilities had the average annual inflow of 6,500 convicts, in 2004- 2005 this number dropped to 4,300 on average.[24] Taking into consideration the still broader application of new penalties and fines, it would be possible to predict that the share of custodial penalties among all imposed sanctions would drop even further, or at least would not rise again.

The large prison population in Lithuania could not only be attributed to the frequency with which persons were sentenced to serve custodial sanctions, but also to the great length of the sentences to be served. From 1998-2002, the average term of a custodial sentence was four years and eight months, and the actually served average penalty in 1998-2000 was two years and two months. After the enforcement of the new criminal laws, the duration of custodial penalties did not decrease, but even increased. In 2003-2004 the average custodial sentence imposed by the courts increased to four years and 11 months, and the actually served average penalty to two years and six months. Nevertheless, it is necessary to mention that tendencies in the distribution of convicts sentenced to custodial penalties according to the duration of their prison terms are changing in the positive direction. While in 1998-2000 the share of offenders who were sentenced to three to five years (32 percent on average) and to five to 10 years (30 percent on average) were the largest, in 2004-2005 these figures had decreased to an average of each 22 percent. Also, the more recent figures show that the largest proportion of custodial sentences was prison terms of one to three years (33.5 percent, on average).[25]

In the criminal structure of the Republic of Lithuania, offences against property are most represented. On average, roughly half of all committed offences are thefts (in 1998-2005, about 60 percent). In the same period, robberies accounted for about five percent of all crimes, and three percent were fraud. Offences against public order in the period from 1998 to 2005 accounted for five percent of all offences. No other offence categories exceeded the one percent mark.[26]

Since the most frequently imposed sanction in Lithuania is the deprivation of liberty, the distribution of prisoners in imprisonment institutions according to the offences that they have committed somewhat corresponds to the overall structure of crime. From 1998 to 2002 the largest proportion of prisoners were convicted of offences against property. 33 to 44 percent of them had committed a theft, while 16 to 25 percent had committed a robbery. A rather large share of prisoners in Lithuania had been convicted of violent crimes in 1998 – 2002. In this period, 13 to 17 percent of all convictions resulting in im-

---

[24] These and further data on the individuals serving custodial penalties are provided based on 1998 – 2005 consolidated reports on the number of convicts, their composition (by offence committed, age, penalty term, etc.) and their change by the Administrative Division of the Prison Department under the Ministry of Justice of the Republic of Lithuania.

[25] Increase in the average custodial penalty imposed by the court order and actually served may be explained by the fact that after the enforcement of a new criminal code a percentage part of the persons convicted for serious offences of violence (e.g., homicides, serious bodily harm, rape, etc.) increased in the detention facilities of the Republic of Lithuania, a percentage part of the prisoners sentenced to the custodial penalty of over 10 years increased conditionally, for example, in 2002-2005, a share of the persons sentenced to custodial penalty from 10 to 15 years increased from 8 to 10 percent.

[26] Report "Data on Criminality in the Republic of Lithuania/Form11Ž" 1998-2005, prepared by the Information Technology and Communications Department under the Ministry of the Interior.

prisonment were for homicides, three percent were in response to serious bodily harm and 4.4 to six percent of sentences to deprivation of liberty were for rape. The composition of the offences for which persons are serving custodial sanctions has in fact changed in recent years, which could also be attributed to the enforcement of the new criminal legislation. The percentage of imprisoned persons convicted of thefts decreased from 33 percent in 2002 to 25 percent in 2004, even though the number of registered thefts as well as the number of persons convicted for them rose. Accordingly, the share of offenders sentenced for committing violent crimes increased. For example, in 2002-2005 the percentage of persons convicted of homicide increased from 17 to 22.5 percent of the total number of the persons serving custodial penalties, even though the number of registered homicides and of the respective offenders remained stable. The share of prisoners who had caused serious bodily harm increased over the period of 2002 to 2005, from 2,6 to 4,3 percent, while the figures for rape saw an increase of 1,5 percent, from four in 2002 to 5,5 in 2005. Finally, a quite significant increase in the representation of robberies in the total of all offences that resulted in a custodial sanction can be observed, rising from 15,7 percent in 2002 to 25 percent in 2005. Thus, in 2003 the majority of the prison population consisted of persons who had been convicted of serious offences of violence. One can observe the tendency that their representation among the persons in penitentiary institutions is increasing.

Taking a closer look at the composition of the prison population, first of all it should be pointed out that the vast majority of the persons in Lithuanian prisons are males. From 1998 to 2005, females accounted for only three to four percent of all prisoners on average. Regarding age, persons of the age groups most capable of working predominated. On average, from 1998 to 2005 roughly 42 percent of all prisoners fell within the age group of 21 to 30 years, while a further 25 percent were between 31 and 40 years of age. In the stated time period, on average persons up to the age of 21 as well as 41 to 50 year olds each constituted around 14 percent of all prisoners. From 2000 to 2005, 41 percent of all prisoners had secondary education, while a further 36 percent had completed basic education. Attention should be focused on the fact that a relatively large share of the prisoners were only primarily educated (15 percent on average), and that one percent of the prisoners had completed no form of education at all. At the other end of the educational scale, persons with special secondary and higher education constituted only seven percent of the total number of persons serving a custodial penalty.[27]

Regarding the trends in the characteristics of the prison population, it should be noted that the prisoners are getting older while their level of education is steadily becoming lower on average. Primarily, the positive tendency of reductions in the number of prisoners under the age of 21 should be maintained, a trend that began with the enforcement of the new criminal laws in 2003, which brought with them new, more humane provisions concerning juvenile criminal responsibility. Increases in the share of 40 to 50 year olds in the overall prison population of Lithuania could be attributed to the increasing percentage of persons who are being sentenced to prison terms of 10 years or more. These tendencies, however, are not very prominent, since the mentioned groups of persons constitute only 13–14 percent of the total number of persons serving custodial penalties,

---

[27] "1999 – 2005 Consolidated Report of the Activity of the Social Rehabilitation Services" of the Administrative Division of the Prison Department under the Ministry of Justice of the Republic of Lithuania.

while the percentage of persons forming the largest from 21 to 40 has changed unevenly and only insignificantly. Meanwhile, the tendency of a decreasing average level of education among the prisoners is quite significant. While the share of prisoners with secondary education has been steadily decreasing, persons whose level of formal education is below secondary have been becoming more and more numerous. On 1 January 2005, the number of persons with basic education was greater (2,331 persons) than the number of persons with secondary education (2,323 persons).

1.4.2 Characteristics of the Foreign Prison Population

Changes in penal policy have also had an impact on the number of foreign nationals who are imprisoned in the Republic of Lithuania. The absolute number of foreign nationals suspected or accused of having committed a crime has been increasing (see table 1.). In 2003, 189 foreigners were suspected or accused of committing a crime, while in 2004 the figure increased to 302. In 2005, 290 persons with foreign citizenship were accused of having committed an offence. However, contrary to this development, the number of foreign nationals serving a custodial penalty decreased considerably.[28] According to the official statistics provided by the Migration Department, in 2006 migrants holding valid residence permits in the Republic of Lithuania accounted for 1,04 percent of the total population (2005 – 0,95). So, bearing in mind that the total number of foreigners is higher (for example if one includes illegal residents, tourists and so on), it can be concluded that they are not overrepresented in the prison population in comparison to their share in the general population[29].

---

[28] Report "Data on the Persons who Committed Crimes in the Republic of Lithuania/Form14Ž" 1998-2005, prepared by the Information Technology and Communications Department under the Ministry of the Interior.

[29] Migration Yearbook 2005, Migration Departament. p. 13.

Table 1: Number of prisoners, suspected or accused persons, pre-trial detainees in Lithuania from 1999 – 2006 [30].

Prisoners								
	1999. 01.01	2000. 01.01	2001. 01.01	2002. 01.01	2003. 01.01	2004. 01.01	2005. 01.01	2006. 01.01
The total number of all prisoners	11,983	12,205	7,601	9,755	9,414	6,701	6,727	6,899
Foreigners	138	144	122	107	111	97	44	43
Percentage of foreigners	1.15	1.18	1.61	1.10	1.18	1.45	0.65	0.62

The suspected or accused persons								
	1999	2000	2001	2002	2003	2004	2005	2006
The total number of all suspected or accused persons	25,373	25,160	25,046	26,662	25,754	20,595	27,343	26,070
Foreigners	348	446	255	223	189	227	302	290
Percentage of foreigners	1.37	1.77	1.02	0.84	0.73	1.10	1.10	1.11

The pre-trial detainees								
	1999. 01.01	2000. 01.01	2001. 01.01	2002. 01.01	2003. 01.01	2004. 01.01	2005. 01.01	2006. 01.01
The total number of pre-trial detainees	2,601	2,207	1,915	1,811	1,656	1,362	1,284	1,127
Foreigners	-	-	-	-	-	34	33	29
Percentage of foreigners	-	-	-	-	-	2.5	2.57	2.57

Even though in 2005[31] the average term of custodial penalties imposed on foreign nationals by the courts is very extensive (seven years and seven months in 2004-2005, compared to an overall average sentence of four years and four months), the amount of time actually served was much shorter (foreigners: nine months; overall average term served:

---

[30] Data povided by "Data on the Persons who Committed Crimes in the Republic of Lithuania/Form14Ž" 1998-2005, prepared by the Information Technology and Communications Department under the Ministry of the Interior and consolidated reports on the Number of Convicts, Composition (by Offence Committed, Age, Penalty Term, etc.) and Their Change 1998 – 2005 by the Administrative Division of the Prison Department under the Ministry of Justice of the Republic of Lithuania.

[31] Formerly the statistical information about the foreign nationals imprisoned in the Republic of Lithuania was almost not collected, therefore here and further statistics about the imprisoned foreign nationals is presented on the basis of the data available from the Prison Department on 1 January 2006, if not indicated otherwise.

two years and nine months[32]). These differences could be explained if one looks more closely at the crimes that were committed by the foreign nationals who have been released from detention facilities.

On 1 January 2006 the majority of foreigners (43 percent) serving custodial penalties were convicted of homicide, for which the average term of imprisonment imposed by the courts was 12 years and five months. Other larger groups are foreign nationals had committed robberies and thefts, accounting for 14 percent of all imprisoned foreign nationals, whereas only one or several persons were simultaneously imprisoned for committing other types of crimes. However, it is not possible to state that the most frequent offence committed by foreign nationals in the Republic of Lithuania is homicide. After an analysis of the distribution of foreign nationals released from the imprisonment institutions in 2005 according to the committed offence, it may be noted that the major part of those persons are those who were convicted of illegally crossing the border, who constituted 58 percent of the total number of foreign nationals released from imprisonment institutions. Furthermore, forging documents (most often travel documents / visas) accounted for 17 percent of the total number of foreign nationals released from imprisonment institutions. Other somewhat larger groups were the individuals who served the custodial penalty for committing thefts or robberies, who accounted for five and seven percent respectively, whereas one or several persons had committed other offences. The same tendencies could be observed when analysing the distribution of the crimes committed that resulted in foreign nationals being delivered to penitentiary institutions in 2005. The predominant groups were persons convicted of illegally crossing the border and of forgery of documents (32 and nine percent respectively). Other offence types that were rather highly represented were thefts and robberies (six and seven percent respectively).

Due to the fact that the most frequently committed offences were illegal entry and the forgery of travel documents (crimes for which very short penalties may be imposed), the resulting terms of imprisonment to be served are relatively short.[33] Meanwhile, predominance of foreign nationals imprisoned for homicide in the imprisonment institutions predetermines the appropriate tendencies of the distribution of those persons by the terms of the custodial penalty granted by court order. The most numerous group consists of foreign nationals imprisoned for ten to 15 years (about 27 percent of all foreigners sentenced to actual imprisonment), whereas the most numerous group in general (persons sentenced to the custodial penalty from one to three years, who accounted for 34 percent in 2005) among the imprisoned foreign nationals makes only 22 percent. Persons sentenced to imprisonment from three to five years and from five to ten years) accounted for 15.5 percent each. Therefore, seeking to evaluate the rigidity of the penal policy in respect of foreign nationals, one has to compare the custodial penalty terms granted by court order and those actually served with the general tendencies for separate crime types. For example,

---

[32] In evaluating the conclusions presented here and further, it is necessary to take into account that the number of foreign nationals imprisoned in the imprisonment institutions of the Republic of Lithuania is very small, therefore separate cases have a significant effect on the general statistics.

[33] The actually served terms of the custodial penalty are calculated according to the served terms of the custodial penalty of the persons released from the imprisonment institutions. Therefore if many persons are released that served the shorter custodial penalties, the actually served custodial penalty term is very low. It is to be mentioned that persons convicted of the illegal crossing of the border are released very often directly from the court session, including the term of remand detention –arrest applied.

the average term of the custodial penalty imposed by court order on foreign nationals for homicide was 12 years and five months, whereas in respect of all prisoners convicted of homicide in 2005 it was ten years and six months. The actually served average term of imprisonment was four years and nine months for foreigners and five years and seven months for all prisoners. Thus, even though stricter penalties are imposed on foreign nationals for homicide, they actually serve shorter terms in detention facilities.[34] Data about foreign nationals convicted of thefts are still more interesting. They are sentenced to the shorter term of custodial penalty (one year and four months on average, whereas the general average is two years and three months). Also, foreigners actually serve a shorter term in detention facilities (the average term of the actually served custodial penalty is six months for foreigners, whereas the general average is one year). Thus it is not possible to state that crimes committed by foreigners are assessed stricter than those committed by Lithuanian citizens.

The majority of the foreign nationals who are imprisoned in detention facilities came from states of the former USSR. In 1998-2005 they accounted for 94 percent of all imprisoned foreign nationals on average. Their number has been declining since 2003 when Lithuania became a member of the EU. From 2003 to 2005 such persons constituted 89 percent of all imprisoned foreigner, but this change is very insignificant and does not change the general situation in the essence. In the group under analysis, from 1998 to 2005 the predominant countries of origin were Russia and Belarus, accounting for 40 and 20 percent of all foreign prisoners respectively. However, irrespective of the decrease in the number of citizens from the former USSR states in the imprisonment institutions of the Republic of Lithuania, the percentage of Russian foreign prisoners has in fact been on the increase – since 2001 their share has risen from 31 to 48 percent. Thus, the decrease in the total number of prisoners from the former USSR states is determined by the significant reduction in the number of imprisoned persons from states like Estonia, Georgia, Uzbekistan and Ukraine.[35] However, there has also been a drop in the number of imprisoned citizens from Belarus. This may be attributable to the fact that after Lithuania attained membership in the EU, shortages emerged in the Lithuanian labour force, which resulted in the active invitation of workers from Belarus, resulting in turn in reduced involvement in illegal activities. Another somewhat larger group of prisoners are the Ukrainian citizens, who in 1998-2004 accounted for seven percent of the total number of the imprisoned foreign nationals. Attention should be drawn to the fact that the number of imprisoned Latvian citizens has decreased considerably. In 2001-2002 they accounted for 18 to 19 percent of all foreigners in penitentiary establishment, while in 2004 this figure had dropped to only six percent, and to merely two percent in 2005 (one person).

---

[34] Release on parole is granted to foreign nationals in significantly fewer cases than for the citizens of the Republic of Lithuania, therefore while interpreting these data it is necessary to bear in mind that a number of foreign nationals sentenced to the custodial penalty is very small, therefore due to several cases when the custodial term actually served by foreigners was very short, statistical data may not reflect the real situation.

[35] Attention should be focused on the fact that the decrease in the absolute number of the imprisoned foreign nationals from all the states is predetermined by the changes in the penal policy of the Republic of Lithuania, due to which the number of the imprisoned and to be imprisoned persons declined significantly.

Lithuania's membership in the EU has not resulted in increases in the number of prisoners from other EU Member States. From 1998 to 2005, one or two individuals from Holland, Germany, Poland, Norway, Greece, Italy, Spain and France were imprisoned periodically. There have also been periodical cases of Asian and American citizens in Lithuanian prisons.

The majority of the foreign prisoners in Lithuania are able-bodied individuals, who account for roughly 73 percent of the total number of the imprisoned foreign nationals. However, when compared with total number of prisoners, the group of imprisoned foreign nationals is older on average. The largest share was constituted of the persons from 31 to 40 years (almost 41 percent), and the persons from 21 to 30 years only accounted for roughly 32 percent. In comparison to the general age distribution among all prisoners, a very small number of imprisoned foreigners are under the age of 21 (there is only one person, accounting for two percent), and larger shares of prisoners are of senior age: persons from 41 to 50 years and persons from 51 to 60 years, respectively, accounted for 16 and nine percent.

On average, foreign prisoners have a higher level of education than Lithuanian inmates. While the largest share have secondary education (about one third), there is also a large number of foreign prisoners with special secondary and higher education (roughly 14 and 25 percent respectively). Furthermore, there is a low rate of foreign prisoners with a level of formal education below secondary education in comparison to the general state of affairs. Persons with basic and/or primary education accounted for 11 and 16 percent respectively. There was not one foreign prisoner without any form of formal education.

Attention should be drawn to the fact that 93 percent of imprisoned foreign nationals were unemployed at the time of committing the offence. The other three imprisoned foreign nationals were hired employees. With the account taken of the distribution of the imprisoned foreign nationals by citizenship it is possible to assume that the largest part of the foreigners committing crimes in Lithuania are individuals who are in search for a better – though often illegal – source of living in Lithuania, or who are crossing Lithuania in order to reach other states.

1.5 Overview of National Legislation

1.5.1 Penitentiary Legislation

In 2003, alongside the new Criminal Code, the new Code on the Execution of Penalties was also enforced which substituted the previously effective Code of Correctional Labour that had been adopted in Soviet times. Reform of the legal system governing the execution of penalties was performed on the basis of the provisions of the Code on the Execution of Penalties, and secondary legislation was adopted in order to implement them. Primarily, it was deemed necessary to adopt new legal acts or to amend those already in place accordingly, with the aim of regulating the execution of new penalties. The legal bases regulating the execution of custodial penalties were somewhat changed. The convicted persons in the custodial penalty institutions were subdivided into several groups that differed in terms of the regimes that were applied to them.[36] Furthermore, more op-

---

[36] The persons in the custodial establishment at first are placed in the ordinary group, afterwards, depending on their conduct, they are transferred into a light group with a more lenient regime, or to

portunities were created for the inmates to establish and remain in contact with the outside world (the right for short-term home visits, a higher number of permitted short-term or long-term visits) and more humane conditions of imprisonment were established.

Important acts of secondary legislation that should be mentioned are the Internal Rules of the Correctional Establishments and the Internal Rules of the Remand Custody Wards, which detail the provisions of the execution of custodial and arrest penalties. They regulate the order and conditions under which persons sentenced to imprisonment or arrest are to be held in custodial establishments, as well as the procedure for ensuring and implementing the rights, freedoms and duties of these persons. The operating instructions of the correctional inspectorates regulate the operation of the correctional inspectorates in executing penalties that are not related to imprisonment, suspension of the sentence and release on parole (probation).

In addition to secondary legislation that implements the provisions of the Code of the Execution of Penalties, there are a significant number of programmes that foresee the prospects for a more humane execution of penalties. The 2004–2009 Programme of Renovation of Prison Establishments and Humanization of the Custodial Conditions can be distinguished in this respect. It aims at reconstructing and renovating the custodial establishments by 2010 so that they are in compliance with the requirements established by the Lithuanian Hygiene Norms and the European Prison Rules, thus improving the living environment and healthcare of the prisoners, and supplying the custodial institutions with long-term tangible assets.[37]

Besides national legislation, Lithuania is a signatory to a lot of international agreements concerning human rights. Furthermore, there are some bi-lateral transfer agreements (among them with Russia and Belarus) for the transfer of sentenced persons.

1.5.2 Penitentiary Legislation & Foreigners

In addition to the general legal act regulating the execution of penalties, the legal status of convicted foreign nationals is also regulated by the Law on the Legal Status of Aliens of the Republic of Lithuania.

The legal status of sentenced irregular migrants is the same as that of the citizens of the Republic of Lithuania, except for a number of certain rights (for instance the right to participate in elections, referendum or public poll (plebiscite), which is not directly or primarily related to imprisonment). Foreign prisoners also have special rights that only they are entitled to, most importantly the right to maintain relations with the representatives of their states. Foreigners may realize this right only by applying through the Ministry of Foreign Affairs of the Republic of Lithuania. Also, such contact is limited to certain institutions: the diplomatic representations of their states, and consular institutions.

---

the disciplinary group as a penalty for systematic or especially persistent violation of the disciplinary requirements.

[37] It is to be mentioned that after solving the problem of overcrowding of the prisons, another most important problem of the Execution of Penalties in the Republic of Lithuania is the poor condition of the buildings of prison establishments. Therefore problems arise in seeking to create the proper humane and everyday conditions for the prisoners in the prison establishment that are in compliance with the requirements of international standards.

2 TREATMENT OF FOREIGN PRISONERS

2.1 General information

In specifying the conditions for the imprisonment of foreign nationals in the Republic of Lithuania, it is of primary importance that – subject to the laws of the Republic of Lithuania – their legal status is analogous to the legal status of the imprisoned citizens of Lithuania, save certain exceptions. The number of foreigners imprisoned in Lithuania is very small, and the majority of them (about 94 percent) are citizens of the former Soviet Union states. Thus, they may communicate perfectly both with other prisoners and the personnel of the correctional institution in the Russian language.[38] Imprisonment conditions and the procedure of implementing custody are similar to the conditions to be faced by the Lithuanian prisoners, sometimes even better. The citizens of former Soviet Union states also know very well the social and cultural living conditions in Lithuania. The imprisonment of citizens of other countries is rare; therefore it is difficult to present exhaustively justified and generalized information. Rare exclusions in the procedure for the execution of the custodial penalty that apply only to foreigners as well as a lack of attention on the part of the personnel to foreign prisoners may be explained by the small overall number of foreign prisoners.

Since the majority of foreign nationals are not an exclusive minority in the Lithuanian prison establishments in terms of their origins (there are quite a number of Lithuanian citizens who originated from the former Soviet Union states), they do not distinguish from the general number of the prisoners, and there are no significant problems related to cultural isolation or discrimination. Certain discriminatory aspects arise in the non-formal internal organization of the prisoners. Prisoners living in the same groups and using the same premises tend to divide into non-formal groups according to the cities where they live, for example, the Vilnius group, the Kaunas group, or the Panevėžys group. Meanwhile, the foreign prisoners lose such informal protectorate. As a matter of fact, an interview of experts showed that the citizens of the Republic of Lithuania of the corresponding origin often took care of their countrymen, therefore the discrimination felt was insignificant. Stronger cultural isolation is felt by the citizens of other states (not of the former Soviet Union), especially from such distant states like for instance China and Morocco,), and most frequently because only one or several such persons are confined simultaneously.

Comparing penalties and incentives granted to foreign and Lithuanian citizens, it is possible to presume certain preconditions for discrimination. Even though the foreign prisoners break the established rules considerably more rarely than the Lithuanian citizens (in 2005, foreigners who broke discipline accounted for 16 percent[39], whereas of the total number of the prisoners 49 percent infringed discipline)[40], there are more offences

---

[38] The major part of the prisoners in the prison establishment is Russian-speaking, and the other part of the prisoners knows Russian well, therefore the prison staff can also speak an adequate level of Russian.

[39] As mentioned previously, statistics should be evaluated carefully not only because of the small number of foreign prisoners, but also due to the fact that such information about foreign nationals in the prison establishments of the Republic of Lithuania was collected for the first time.

[40] In 1998-2005, the percentage of offenders fluctuated from 42 percent to 55 percent, the average was approximately 47 percent.

per foreign offender – on the average seven offences. In 2005, 19 foreigners were punished for 146 disciplinary offences. Meanwhile, in general there were less than three offences per offender. In 2005, 5,385 offenders were punished for 14,688 disciplinary offences.[41] Thus, as compared to the whole number of offenders, there were twice as many offences per foreign offender. This state of affairs is explained by the officers of the prison establishments, who state that a considerable part of the foreign prisoners are Russian and Belarusian citizens who are imprisoned for very serious crimes. They seek to dominate and in doing so break the rules quite often. The major part of the citizens of other states does not get involved in any conflicts and they have no problems as regards adherence to the internal regulations. Foreigners who do breach disciplinary requirements often consume alcoholic beverages and narcotic and psychotropic substances. During 2005, 1.09 percent of the total number of offenders consumed alcoholic beverages, and seven percent took narcotic or psychotropic substances, whereas among foreign offenders these persons constituted 1.37 and 9 percent respectively. Analysis of the imposed disciplinary penalties shows that during 2005 the strictest penalties (disciplinary isolation, solitary confinement (in the prison), and transfer to the cell-type premises for two to six months (the strictest punishment that can be applied to persons who have already been transferred to the disciplinary group regime for disciplinary offences)) were more often applied to citizens of the Republic of Lithuania than to foreign prisoners. On a general scale, these penalties were applied to 40 percent of the disciplinary breaches. Regarding foreigners who had not behaved in according to the disciplinary requirements, solitary confinement and disciplinary isolation were only imposed in 31 percent of the cases. However, placement in the cell-type premises) is more often applied to foreigners (11.6 percent) than to Lithuanian prisoners (two percent).

In the year 2005, there were 0.65 incentives per prisoner in Lithuanian prison establishments,[42] whereas the figure for foreign prisoners lay at only 0.39 per prisoner. Partly, this difference may be explained by the fact that the majority of incentives are granted for active participation in the social rehabilitation programmes, diligent work and training. However, for a foreign national it is rather difficult to actively and willingly participate in these activities on his or her own initiative, especially in the event where the actually served term of the custodial penalty for foreigners is quite short. This also indicates a certain degree of indifference among the personnel of correctional establishments, since incentives may also be granted for irreproachable conduct and initiative, and since the majority of foreign prisoners in fact adhere to disciplinary requirements. The presumption may be made that the officers of the prison establishments do not notice foreign nationals who serve their term peacefully and obediently, and that they do not care enough for the involvement of those persons in the common activities during the serving of their prison sentences.

---

[41] These and further data about penalties applied to the prisoners are provided on the basis of the reports by the administrative division of the Prison department under the Ministry of Justice of the Republic of Lithuania "Discipline of the Persons in the Prison Establishments and Disciplinary measures Applied in Their Respect" 2005.

[42] "The Consolidated Report of the Performance of the Social Rehabilitation Services" 2005 by the administrative division of the Prison Department under the Ministry of Justice of the Republic of Lithuania.

2.2 Living conditions and facilities

Imprisoned and detained foreign nationals are accommodated in the prison establishments together with the citizens of the Republic of Lithuania, and are thus not separated. As expert interviews have shown, foreigners may be accommodated together or separately from other convicts,[43] if they themselves have this desire and the material conditions exist for this purpose. Thus, they live under the same everyday, material and technical custodial conditions as all other prisoners.

2.3 Reception and admission

A sentenced offender who is delivered to the correction facilities is accepted by the record service official. The record service is the administrative structural division of the correctional establishment, which is responsible for the collection, updating and storage of all of the information accumulated about the convict in his or her personal file. The record service official checks and verifies the personal identity of the convict. Afterwards, the arriving prisoner is searched and any prohibited possessions are confiscated. He or she then undergoes a medical examination and sanitary treatment, and is then placed in the quarantine section until he or she is then appointed to the corresponding crew.[44] When the convict is placed in the quarantine section, the officers of the institution implement a "programme of adaptation" of the convicted newcomers to the correctional institution.[45] During the programme, the officers of the corresponding prison establishments become acquainted with the file of the newcomer, his or her social demographic characteristics (information about education, specialisation, labour track history, the level of working capacity, social relations, contacts with the relatives, material position, etc. are collected), they conduct psychological diagnostics in the course of which the personal abilities, interests, inclinations, approach to crime and the impact of deviant culture on the individual are clarified, and information on substance abuse and dependency is collected. On the basis of all of this information, the individual correctional programme for the convicted person is prepared. Another part of the adaptation programme is the familiarization of the convict with the conditions of imprisonment. One of the fundamental rights of a convict punished with any penalty is the right to receive written information about the procedures and conditions of serving the penalty, his rights and duties in his native language

---

43 The Code of the Execution of Penalties establishes that the convicted foreigners shall be held in segregation from other convicts, but in practice this provision is not being implemented. However, it is necessary to draw attention to the fact that convicts who request with justification to be kept in isolation from other convicts is transferred to the cell-type premises, which are usually used as disciplinary accommodation.

44 The procedure of admission of the convict to the correctional facility is regulated by Chapter VIII of the Internal Regulations of the Correctional Institutions *(Order of the Minister of Justice of the Republic of Lithuania "On the Approval of the Internal Regulations of the Correctional Institutions". Official Gazette – 2003 No. 76-3498).*

45 Order of the Director of the Prison Department under the Ministry of Justice of the Republic of Lithuania "On the Model Adaptation Programme of the Newcoming Convicts in the Correction Institution and the Approval of the Model Programme of the Integration into Society of the Convicts". Official Gazette – 2004 No.87-3192.

or the language he or she understands.[46] In practice, the implementation of this right is guaranteed by handing him/her the handbook in which all relevant and important information on serving a prison sentence is provided. The convict shall have it during the entire period of imprisonment.[47] The officer while acquainting the convicted person with the handbook must clarify whether the convict has properly understood the information provided, whether he or she has perceived the perspectives of the change in his or her legal status and the factors determining this change. In addition to the said information, the convict shall also be acquainted with the general information about the correctional institution, with the legal acts regulating the conditions for serving the penalty, the possibilities and procedure for satisfying everyday, material, medical, social, spiritual and cultural needs. It is also worth mentioning that the officers of the correctional institutions must inform a prisoner's spouse or other close relatives of the place of accommodation within three working days.

The primary problem that foreign nationals face lies in language issues, but the majority of the foreigners imprisoned in Lithuania know the Russian or English languages, which are also spoken by the staff of custodial establishments. In rare cases in which a foreign national speaks little or no Russian or English, the employees and representatives of the consulates of the appropriate states and interpreters are called to help. Instead of the handbook, they are given the extracts from the main legal acts, regulating the procedure and conditions of the execution of penalty, which are prepared in three foreign languages (English, Russian and German). The Prison Department is preparing handbooks in the Russian and English languages for foreign nationals.

Thus, the rights of the convicted foreigners have been guaranteed quite sufficiently so far, but with the changing situation in mind (the increase in the number of imprisoned persons from European Union or Asian states) the guarantee of these rights may face new obstacles.

2.4 Work - Education – Training – Sports - Recreation

Most problems arise when organizing the training of foreign nationals in the general secondary and vocational education schools of the prison establishments, since instruction here is conducted only in the Lithuanian language. It is necessary to mention that foreign citizens have the opportunity to learn the Lithuanian language. Only seven foreigners are studying at the prison establishments (17 percent of all imprisoned foreigners).

This is quite a prominent problem provided that 11.4 percent of the imprisoned foreigners have only basic education, and 16 percent are only primarily educated, and that 17 foreigners are currently serving custodial sentences of 10 or more years (even though the actually served term by foreign nationals does not exceed one year). There is the need to find ways and means to organize training in prisons in a language that the foreigner can understand, for example by contacting the educational institutions of the correspond-

---

[46]　Law on the Approval of the Code of the Execution of Penalties of the Republic of Lithuania. Code of the Execution of Penalties. Official Gazette - 2002, No. 73-3084 (Item 1 Pt 1 Art 11).

[47]　Pt 17 of Chapter V of the Model Adaptation Programme of the Newcoming Convicts in the Correction Institution (*Order of the Director of the Prison Department under the Ministry of Justice of the Republic of Lithuania "On the Approval of the Model Adaptation Programme of the Newcoming Convicts in the Correction Institution and the Approval of the Model Programme of the Integration into Society of the Convicts". Official Gazette – 2004 No.87-3192*).

ing states through the foreign diplomatic missions and consulates, which could offer distance learning or learning through mail, if it could be organized taking into consideration the security and isolation conditions of the convicted person. There should at least be training available in Russian, especially in the light of the high number of prisoners from the former Soviet Union states. Also, there are quite considerable real opportunities to organize and provide of such training in Lithuania due to the considerable number of educational institutions that organize training in the Russian language.

The situation is somewhat better concerning the employment of foreign prisoners. Ten (24.4 percent) of them currently have jobs in the prison enterprises or on the farms, and a further three foreign inmates are involved in individual, labour, creative or other activities.[48] In the period from 2003 to 2005, the overall rate of prisoners' employment lay at roughly 31 to 32 percent on average. The current employment situation of foreigners in Lithuanian prison establishments may be partly explained by the low general employment level, the limited possibilities of the imprisonment institutions for involving the convicts in work that corresponds to their fields of specialization[49] and the unwillingness of some convicts to work. The language and cultural differences should not be the key employment problems, since the majority of the prisoners speak Russian and English. However, employing the citizens from the individual states like Jordan, Israel, China, Somalia, Iraq, and so on is more problematic.

In making analysis of the participation of the prisoners in recreational occupations, it is possible to state that they participate successfully in various sport and cultural events. The main problem here also lies in language issues because all cultural events are organized in the Lithuanian language, thus limiting the benefit of such events to persons who speak the national language, which can in turn be seen as excluding a large number of foreigners from them..

In summary, it should be stated that even though the situation is not bad, more considerable attention should be devoted to the specialized measures, and the staff of the correctional institutions should encourage the foreign prisoners to participate more actively in the organized resocialization activities. The opportunities to grant incentives to foreign prisoners should be discussed more often.

2.5 Food – Religion – Personal hygiene – Medical care

Convicts serving their custodial sentence are entitled to perform religious rites during the leisure time that is foreseen in the daily routine of the correctional institutions, so long as it does not hinder the recreation of other inmates. In order to practice their religion, a re-

---

[48] Convicted scientists, artists, or persons of other rare specialities or professions, as well as high-quality and qualified specialists, may be allowed to get engaged in scientific, artistic or creative activity instead of work. However, involvement in such activities is most frequently allowed only outsideworking hours, even though the director of the correctional institution may allow one to undertake the said activity instead of work.

[49] Opportunities of the administration of the prison establishments for employment of the convicts are limited also due to the problems of selling of the manufactured products.

ligious representative of all confessions can be invited to correctional institutions, and the appropriate premises can be provided[50].

The composition of the foreigners serving custodial sentences predetermines that the specific features related to the life of foreigners as regards differences in food habits, religious rites and other cultural and belief-related issues are almost non-existent in the prison establishments. In the Republic of Lithuania, there are quite a number of persons and churches that propagate the Orthodox Church, therefore religious needs of the major part of foreigners are satisfied in the prison establishments. Efforts are also made to satisfy the needs of those foreigners whose religions are not very popular in Lithuania. Meetings are organized with the ministers of those religions on the initiative both of the convicts and ministers of religion themselves. Sometimes the employees of the appropriate consulates also help to organize such meetings. A couple of times there were requests for exclusions in the time table as regards food or time for prayers, but since they were very seldom not any problems were met in satisfying them.

The convicts also have the right to wear watches made of precious metals and to wear their own clothes and footwear – thus no problems are faced as regards wearing special clothes.[51]

An analogous situation exists as regards the organization of medical care – there are no special needs or requests from the convicts, also there are no specific problems, characteristic exclusively of the foreigners. Like all prisoners the foreigners have the right to medical care. The medical provision is for free, according to the needs they have access to emergency treatment, visits to doctors and so on. The situation is the same with hygiene services and articles– the state has to assure that the prisoners are provided with and have access to proper hygiene services according to their needs. Hygiene services and articles are free of charge and thus covered by the institutions. Health care and hygiene services in general are satisfactory and in accordance with the needs of prisoners, except for the main problem that much of the equipment is outdated.

2.6 Consular and legal help

Foreigners sentenced to a custodial penalty have the right to maintain contacts with the diplomatic representations and consular institutions of their own states, as well as with international organizations.[52] These relations are maintained through the Ministry of foreign Affairs of the Republic of Lithuania. The convicts from the countries other than the former Soviet Union most often wish to communicate with the diplomatic representations and consular institutions of their states, therefore due to solitary cases, these contacts are rare and there are no problems organizing them. It is also complicated to evaluate their compliance with the needs of the convicted persons. It is interesting to note that more often the prison establishments themselves show the initiative to contact the diplomatic representations and consular institutions as regards various problems that may

---

[50] Chapter XXX of the Internal Regulations of the Correctional Institutions *(Order "On the Approval of the Internal Regulations of the Correctional Institutions" by the Minister of Justice of the Republic of Lithuania. Official Gazette – 2003 No. 76-3498).*

[51] Law on the Approval of the Code of the Execution of Penalties of the Republic of Lithuania. Code of the Execution of Penalties. Official Gazette - 2002, No. 73-3084 (Art. 97).

[52] Law on the Approval of the Code of the Execution of Penalties of the Republic of Lithuania. Code of the Execution of Penalties. Official Gazette - 2002, No. 73-3084 (Art. 109).

arise during a person's imprisonment – applying for interpretation services, assistance in contacting the relatives of the convicted person or organizing the specific satisfaction of the needs of those persons (for example, concerning the arrival of the priest).

Prisoners also have the right to meet their attorneys-at-law, and these meetings are not restricted and are not included in the total number of visits to which a prisoner is entitled.[53] All the citizens of the Republic of Lithuania, citizens of other European Union Member States, as well as other natural persons legally residing in the Republic of Lithuania and other European Union Member States, and other individuals indicated in the international treaties of the Republic of Lithuania shall be entitled to the State-guaranteed legal aid.[54] Other foreigners, if they are not asylum-seekers or they are not granted temporary security,[55] shall have the right to the State-guaranteed legal aid only in criminal cases (this aid is provided also during the process of the execution of penalty), whereas such aid is not provided for in civil or administrative cases.

2.7 Contact with the outside world

The convicted persons shall be entitled to receive visits from relatives or other persons.[56] Visits may be short-term – lasting up to four hours – and long-term, which may last up to two days, and are allow for the prisoner to stay together only with his/her spouse, co-habitee or a close relative. The number of visits to which a prisoner is entitled depends on the type of the correctional institution and the regime in which he or she is serving his/her sentence. Persons in the ordinary group of the correctional house are entitled to four short-term and four long-term visits per year. Prisoners who have been allocated to the light group receive six short-term and six long-term visits. Persons in the ordinary group in the prison are entitled to 16 short-term visits, while persons in the disciplinary group can receive no visits at all.[57] Prisoners also have the right to make telephone calls and to receive parcels, but their quantity is limited: from six to 12 calls by phone annually[58] and between three to 12 parcels per year.[59]

---

[53] Law on the Approval of the Code of the Execution of Penalties of the Republic of Lithuania. Code of the Execution of Penalties. Official Gazette - 2002, No. 73-3084 (Art. 101).

[54] Law on Amendment of the Law on the State-guaranteed Legal Aid of the Republic of Lithuania. Official Gazette - 2004 No. 73-2539 (Art.11).

[55] Temporary security is granted to foreigners by the resolution of the Government, when the Council of the European Union adopts a resolution that there is a mass flow of foreigners to the European Union. The right of illegal immigrants to the State-guaranteed aid is described in the chapter on the detention of foreign nationals under administrative laws below.

[56] Those other persons may be any persons wishing to visit the convict. A visit may be granted after receiving the written application of the convict or the person that wishes to visit the convict. During one visit, the convict may be visited by not more than three persons at a time, excluding minor children of the convict.

[57] Law on the Approval of the Code of the Execution of Penalties of the Republic of Lithuania. Code of the Execution of Penalties. Official Gazette - 2002, No. 73-3084 (Art. 73, 74, 79, 80, 91, 94 and 152).

[58] For persons in the light group of the correction houses, the right to call by phone is not limited.

[59] Law on the Approval of the Code of the Execution of Penalties of the Republic of Lithuania. Code of the Execution of Penalties. Official Gazette - 2002, No. 73-3084 (Art. 73, 74, 75, 79, 80, 85, 91, 95 and 102).

These entitlements to contacts apply equally to foreigner.. However, due to the geographical position of Lithuania and other states[60] and the complex procedure of entry for foreigners (for coming to Lithuania from the most of the former Soviet Union states a visa is needed), the opportunities of foreign nationals to implement the right to visits are rather limited, since they are rarely visited by their relatives. Therefore the most popular form of communication is telephone communication and letters.

All libraries in the prison establishments have a sufficient stock of books in the Russian, Polish and various West European languages (books in English, German, French and Spanish languages are available), even though books in the Asian and African national languages are practically unavailable (some books are in Chinese). The convicts are given the right for money in their personal accounts to acquire an unlimited amount of literature, to subscribe to newspapers and magazines (except for publications propagating violence and cruelty or pornographic publications).[61] Due to the low rate of employment among foreign prisoners and the poor remuneration received in the correctional establishments, the possibility to implement this right is limited, but it may be compensated by the relatives of the convicts or other natural and legal persons, who also have the right to subscribe to periodicals on behalf of the prisoners or to send literature. In addition, the prison establishments themselves subscribe to some periodicals in Russian and Polish. The prison establishments have cable TV, every convict has the right to use his/her own television and radio sets[62], thus providing access to various broadcasts in languages other than Lithuanian.. There is an especially wide choice of various channels in the Russian language, and some channels are broadcast in Polish, German or English.[63]

2.8 Re-integration activities - Prison leave

Aiming at making the system of penalty-execution in Lithuanian prison establishments more humane, the programme of adaptation of new convicts, societal reintegration programmes and in the individual correctional programme were initiated[64]. In 2005, only 46 percent of all prisoners participated in the resocialisation programmes[65], and among foreign prisoners this figure was only around 23 percent. This situation may be partly explained by the short term of imprisonment that foreigners in Lithuanian prison establishments actually serve. The situation is explained by the staff of the correction establishments as being due to the passiveness of the convicts. However, language differ-

---

[60] Even though Russia and Belarus are neigbours, they are large countries, other former Soviet Union states are still farther, and citizens from Poland, Estonia or Latvia, which are located closer, at the present moment are rarely imprisoned in the Lithuanian prison establishments.

[61] Law on the Approval of the Code of the Execution of Penalties of the Republic of Lithuania. Code of the Execution of Penalties. Official Gazette - 2002, No. 73-3084 (Art. 93).

[62] Law on the Approval of the Code of the Execution of Penalties of the Republic of Lithuania. Code of the Execution of Penalties. Official Gazette - 2002, No. 73-3084 (Art. 96).

[63] Even though some foreign prisoners do not have their own TV or radio sets, they may use those of other prisoners, since TV sets are almost in each premise where prisoners are accommodated.

[64] Order "On the Approval of the Social Rehabilitation Programmes" by the Director of the Prison Department under the Ministry of Justice of the Republic of Lithuania. Official Gazette – 2004 No.7-167

[65] "The Consolidated Report of the Performance of the Social Rehabilitation Services" 2005 by the administrative division of the Prison Department under the Ministry of Justice of the Republic of Lithuania.

ences are of importance – the English-speaking inmates find it complicated to participate in the resocialization programmes, especially in the studies on the moral, legal and economic issues. Thus, the Prison Department should prepare special resocialization programmes for foreign citizens in the English language as well in order to encourage them to take a more active part in the resocialization programmes.

Prisoners may be allowed a short home leave four times per year for three days at a time.[66] Furthermore, a prisoner may be granted the right to leave the institution in cases of death or serious life-threatening illness of a close relative, as well as in cases in which natural calamities have caused considerable material damage to his/her the close relatives. Also, during the holidays leave is allowed for working convicts who are serving their sentence in the light regime of a correction house. The short-term home visit may also be granted as an incentive measure.[67]. Foreigners also have the same rights to short home leaves, but in 2005, foreigners sentenced to custodial penalties were not granted the right to leave for home even once.

Foreign nationals also are eligible for release on parole from correctional institutions or early parole and substitution of the not served custodial sentence by a milder penalty.

Persons who have served the custodial penalty term established by the law may be released on parole if it is possible to further correct them without the segregation from the society but under supervision, and if they commit themselves by their honest conduct and diligent labour to prove their correction. Release on parole cannot be applied in respect of certain groups of persons, for example: persons convicted of crimes against the independence, territorial integrity and constitutional order of the State of Lithuania, for intentional crimes committed in the correctional institutions, persons held in the prison or a correctional house under the conditions of the disciplinary group, or persons sentenced to life imprisonment.[68]

Grounds for applying early parole are similar, only additionally it is required that property damage committed due to the crime should be at least partly compensated, this somewhat limiting the possibilities for application of this measure to foreigners.[69] Nevertheless, in 2005, early parole was applied more often for foreigners than the citizens of the Republic of Lithuania – among the foreigners released in 2005 (there were 75 such persons) those on early parole accounted for eight percent, whereas in 1998-2005 in general persons released on early parole accounted for only three percent on average of all released persons. In 2004-2005 those released on early parole did not account even for one percent or all releases of that period.[70]

---

[66] Law on the Approval of the Code of Execution of Penalties of the Republic of Lithuania. Code of Execution of Penalties. Official Gazette - 2002, No. 73-3084 (Art. 105 and 130).

[67] Law on the Approval of the Code of Execution of Penalties of the Republic of Lithuania. Code of Execution of Penalties. Official Gazette - 2002, No. 73-3084 (Art. 104).

[68] Law on the Approval of the Code of Execution of Penalties of the Republic of Lithuania. Code of Execution of Penalties. Official Gazette - 2002, No. 73-3084 (Art. 157 - 158.).

[69] Law on the Approval and Enforcement of the Criminal Code of the Republic of Lithuania. Criminal Code. Official Gazette - 2000, No. 89-274 (Art. 42).

[70] Situation may be explained by the fact after substituting the part of the not served custodial sentence by another more lenient penalty, not any additional obligations are established in respect of the convict as in the case of release on parole, therefore the application of this measure does not obligate to solve the issues on the execution of the placed obligations. Meanwhile, when applying release on parole, most often in respect of foreigners without the right of permanent residence in Lithuania, the placed obligations are not fulfilled (supervision), since these persons are expelled from the Republic

Foreigners are considerably more rarely eligible for release on parole than the citizens of the Republic of Lithuania. Persons released on parole from custodial institutions in 1998-2005 overall were 54 percent of the total number of all releases, and among the released foreigners, this group of persons constituted merely eight percent. The remaining 84 percent of the foreigners sentenced to a custodial penalty served their full custodial sentence, whereas when looking at all prisoners, such persons accounted for just 38 percent. In explaining the application of early release on parole, the officers of the system of the execution of penalties indicated that the main reason was that in the case of foreign prisoners, it was often not clear how further supervision of such persons should be carried out (control of obligations imposed by the court).[71] Such release on parole is most often applied in respect of foreigners entitled to permanent residence in Lithuania.

Both the persons released on parole and those who have fully served their sentence are prepared for release. Special resocialization programmes are carried out, various sessions are organized during which the prisoners receive legal and social information about their rights to social support, the public organizations that can provide help, etc.[72] However, the applicable custodial regime does not change because there are no special places of detention with semi-liberty in the Republic of Lithuania where the regime should be significantly more lenient. Persons from the closed institutions are not sent to the existing open colony as a measure of preparing them for release.

2.9 Release - Expulsion

The staff of the detention facilities have the duty to ensure that the person to be released are provided with the necessary documents (as well as with a personal identity document), clothes corresponding to the climatic and seasonal requirements, compensation of travel expenses, help in finding the proper premises for living (in the form of sending reports to the hostel facilities about the persons to be released), as well as make settlements with the convict if he/she worked in the prison establishment, and remunerate him/her accordingly with the funds that have been accumulated in the prisoner's personal account throughout his/her stay in the institution.[73] A one-time allowance may be granted to the convict. The same procedure is applied in respect of foreigners, except for the cases when a decision on expulsion is adopted. After a decision on the expulsion of an irregular migrant who has served the custodial sentence is made, he/she shall acquire the rights and duties of an illegal immigrant. Most often such persons are detained at the Foreigners' Registration Centre under the Law on the Legal Status of Aliens of the Republic of Lithuania. They are transported to the Foreigners' Registration Centre at the State's ex-

---

of Lithuania. Certainly, it is not to be rejected that such data could be predetermined by a small number of foreigners and also because only the statistical data about the imprisoned foreigners covering one year were analyzed.

[71] Both in the case of release on parole and on early parole, the courts establish certain obligations to the convicts that they should fulfil, and the supervision of their fulfillment is performed by the correctional inspectorates.

[72] Order "On the Approval of the Instruction on the Preparation Work for Release of Prisoners from Prison Establishments" by the Director of the Prison Department under the Ministry of Justice of the Republic of Lithuania. Official Gazette – 2006 No. 36-1302

[73] Chapter L of the Internal Regulations of the Correctional Institutions *(Order "On the Approval of the Internal Regulations of the Correctional Institutions" by the Minister of Justice of the Republic of Lithuania. Official Gazette – 2003 No. 76-3498).*

pense, whereas deportation is carried out at the foreigner's expense, at the expense of the natural or legal persons who invited him/her to the Republic of Lithuania, or, in the absence of the above-mentioned resources, the irregular migrant shall be expelled at the expense of the State.[74] Practically, the removal of foreigners who have served their sentence is carried out at the expense of the State.

In 2005, of 44 foreigners in the custodial establishments of Lithuania, only 13 were legally in Lithuania, and all of them had the right of permanent residence in the Republic. The remaining foreign prisoners were in Lithuania illegally: ten of them came to Lithuania illegally (for example, not through the border control posts, having presented forged visas and other travel documents, etc.), and the remaining 21 persons were illegally residing in the country as they had no valid visa or other appropriate travel documents. These data explain why of 75 released persons 48 persons were transferred to the Foreigners' Registration Centre. A foreigner's stay in Lithuania is illegal if he/she came to Lithuania illegally or if he/she has no valid visas or any other travel documents. This is one of the grounds for expulsion from the Republic of Lithuania. A decision on expulsion shall be adopted by the Migration Department under the Ministry of the Interior of the Republic of Lithuania. An irregular migrant shall have the right to lodge a complaint to the district administrative court against the decision adopted by the Migration Department, and the decision of the said court may be appealed to the Lithuanian Supreme Administrative Court. Submission of the complaint of the person who is to be expelled suspends the implementation of the appealed decision.[75] After adopting a decision on expulsion from Lithuania, the issue relating to the detention of such person is resolved[76] (the application of administrative detention of illegal residents is more broadly presented in the analysis of the legal status of the illegal immigrants in Lithuania, under section three below.).

2.10 Aftercare – Probation

Like release on parole, probation is actually applied only in respect of those foreigners who are entitled to permanent residence in Lithuania. Probation is not applied to other foreigners due to the objective problems of its implementation (how can supervision be conducted effectively?), even though all of the foreseen criminal responsibility measures – and thus also probation – (may) formally equally be applied to all persons. Analogously, foreigners, having no right to permanent residence in Lithuania, cannot apply for social support, which is usually provided for persons who have served their custodial sentence.

Foreigners who are entitled to permanent residence in Lithuania after having served their custodial penalty are eligible for a single social allowance (paid by the social support units of the local municipalities) and all social services granted in the Republic of Lithuania. Of social services important for the former prisoners, mention should be made of the provision of information and consultations, accommodation in the temporary hostel fa-

---

[74] Law on the Legal Status of Aliens in Lithuania of the Republic of Lithuania. Official Gazette. – 2004 No. 73-2539 (Art. 131).

[75] Law on the Legal Status of Aliens in Lithuania of the Republic of Lithuania. Official Gazette. – 2004 No. 73-2539 (Chapters IX and X).

[76] Under Article 113 of the Law on the Illegal Stay of Aliens in Lithuania of the Republic of Lithuania, adoption of the decision on expulsion from the Republic of Lithuania is one of the grounds where detention of Aliens may be applied.

cilities for up to six months, the fixed-term free catering, assistance in handling and organizing personal documents,[77] etc.[78]

2.11 Staff

The officers of the system of the execution of penalties do not receive any special education, knowledge or skills for working with imprisoned foreigners. The survey of the administration of the correctional facilities showed that there is not even any need for such special knowledge or skills, except for the foreign language course. This, probably, may be explained by the fact that due to the specificities of the foreign prisoner population in the Republic of Lithuania, the majority of the officers do not face special problems. Moreover, no measures especially adapted for foreigners or penalty execution procedures which could enhance the need for specialized knowledge are organized or applied.

2.12 Projects

There are no known projects that have been organized with the specific target group of foreign prisoners in mind. However, they can take part in various resocialization programmes that are organized for all prisoners in the prison establishments. The existing situation may be again explained by the low number of foreign prisoners and by the absence of need.

3 ADMINISTRATIVE DETENTION OF FOREIGN PRISONERS

3.1 Institutions for administrative detention

There is only one institution in Lithuania that is designed for the detention of illegal immigrants, the Foreigners' Registration Centre. Illegal immigrants are placed together with the persons who have committed criminal offences in the police custody facilities until they can be and are accommodated in the Foreigners' Registration Centre. The period of detention in police custody should not exceed 48 hours. Should the material circumstances allow it, foreigners awaiting transfer to the centre for administrative detention are accommodated separately.

3.2 Ministry responsible & legislation

The Foreigners' Registration Centre is under the competence of the State Border Guard Service, which is turn under the Ministry of the Interior. The grounds and procedure for

---

[77] One of the most important social problems of the persons released from the custodial establishments is the absence of personal documents, and the custodial establishments are most often not able to resolve that problem Therefore this provision is to be undertaken by institutions providing social assistance.

[78] Resolution of the Government of the Republic of Lithuania "On the Provision of the Social Support to the Persons, who Returned from the Custodial, Remand Detention Places, Social and Psychological Rehabilitation Establishments, and Employment of Those Persons". Official Gazette. – 1996, No. 119-2796.

detention are regulated by the Law on the Legal Status of Aliens of the Republic of Lithuania, and the order and conditions of their accommodation and living in the centre are regulated by other secondary legislation, adopted by the appropriate institutions (for instance resolutions of the Government, the resolution of the Government on the approval of the order and conditions of temporary accommodation of foreigners at the Foreigners' Registration Centre; orders of the Commander of the State Border Guard Service; orders of the Ministry of Health, etc.).

3.3 Capacity of institutions

The Foreigners' Registration Centre is designed to accommodate up to 300 illegal immigrants.[79] Juvenile illegal immigrants who are not accompanied by their adult guardians are accommodated in the specialized Juvenile Citizens' and Unaccompanied Minor Foreigners' Centre in Kaunas.

3.4 Length of stay

The term for which a person can be administratively detained is not foreseen by the laws. There is merely the provision that a foreigner is to be immediately released from the institution[80] once the grounds for his/her detention as stated in the enforced court order no longer exist.. Thus, the amount of time for which a person can be held in administrative detention is determined only by the court imposing it.[81] Due to the complexity of such procedures and the indefiniteness of the situation, especially when the majority of the European states foresee the maximum term of detention of up to 12 months, very often the term becomes prolonged and, according to expert evaluation, foreigners in the centre are kept somewhat longer than necessary. Even though the average term of detention is 63 days (in 1999-2005, the average fluctuated from 49 to 77 days), however, there are many cases in which foreigners spent one or even two years in the centre (in 2005, maximum detention lasted for 274 days).

3.5 Decisions procedure

As already mentioned, a foreigner may be detained for a period of over 48 hours on court order on the delegation of the officer of the law enforcement institution. The irregular's presence at the court hearing is mandatory, and he/she is entitled to legal aid guaranteed by the State of Lithuania. The court decision to detain an irregular foreigner or to grant

---

[79] In addition to the illegal immigrants, up to 200 asylum seekers that came to Lithuania legally may be also accommodated. Asylum seekers that are legally in Lithuania shall be accommodated separately and their residential premises are not fit for accommodating illegal immigrants, since for these two groups different security regimes are applied – for voluntary asylum seekers the freedom of movement is not restricted. It is necessary to note that persons who were granted asylum may also be accommodated in the Refugee Reception Centre in Rukla.

[80] After disappearance of the grounds for detention the foreigner has the right and the institution that initiated the detention of the foreigner must apply immediately to the court on the consideration of the justification of the detention of the foreigner.

[81] Law on the Legal Status of Aliens in Lithuania of the Republic of Lithuania. Official Gazette. – 2004 No. 73-2539 (Art. 119).

him/her a measure alternative to detention must be forthwith announced in a language that the foreigner in question understands, indicating the reasons for his/her detention, the time period of detention and other rights and duties of the foreign person while in detention.

3.6 Appeal procedure

The court decision may be appealed to the Supreme Administrative Court of Lithuania within ten days from the adoption of the decision by submitting the appeal through the Foreigners' Registration Centre.[82]

3.7 Irregular stay

Illegal presence in the Republic of Lithuania[83] alone is not a crime. However, violations of the formal procedures of entering or living in Lithuania can constitute an administrative offence. Violation of order related to the entry of foreigners into the Republic of Lithuania, living here, passing through it in transit and departure from it is an administrative offence, punished by a warning or a fine from two hundred fifty to one thousand Litas.[84]

3.8 Numbers

The number of foreigners accommodated at the Foreigners' Registration Centre has shown great variation in recent years. The largest number of persons to be detained in the course of one year was 962 persons in 1997[85]. Currently, 100 foreigners are detained in the centre on average.. The total annual number of newly admitted illegal immigrants fluctuated from 203 to 259 between 1999 and 2004. In 2005 only 160 newly admitted illegal immigrants were accommodated during the year. According to the experts of migration processes, even though the issues of migration in Lithuania are becoming more important, the influx of immigrants is not yet deemed threatening.

---

[82] Law on the Legal Status of Aliens in Lithuania of the Republic of Lithuania. Official Gazette. – 2004 No. 73-2539 (Chapter VII).

[83] Subject to Article 23 of the Law on the Unlawful Stay of Aliens of the Republic of Lithuania, an alien's stay in Lithuania shall be deemed illegal if he/she has been staying in the Republic of Lithuania for a period exceeding the period of visa-less stay set by an international treaty of the Republic of Lithuania, a European Union legal act or the Government of the Republic of Lithuania; is staying in the Republic of Lithuania after the expiry of the visa; is staying in the Republic of Lithuania holding an expired visa after the deadline for meeting the obligation to depart from the Republic of Lithuania; is in possession of a forged travel document; is in possession of a forged visa; is staying in the Republic of Lithuania without a visa if it is required; or is staying in the Republic of Lithuania without a valid travel document, save for asylum applicants.

[84] The Code of Administrative Violations of the Republic of Lithuania, adopted by the Supreme Council of the Lithuanian Soviet Socialist Republic on 13 December 1984 (Art. 206).

[85] Here and further data about the Aliens are provided in accordance with the statistical information supplied by the Foreigners' Registration Centre employees.

3.9 Expulsion

In the opinion of the experts, the majority of persons who are administratively detained are expelled from Lithuania. In the years 1997 to 2004, the share of the persons accommodated in centre who were expelled lay fluctuated between 69 and 94 percent. In 2005, 54 percent of all illegal immigrants were expelled. According to the statistics provided by the Migration department, in 2001 342 foreigners were expelled. In 2002 the figure dropped to 312, while in the years 2003, 2004 and 2005 the numbers were 376, 206 and 189 respectively.[86].

3.10 Not-expelled prisoners

However, there are persons who are not expelled (as stated above, in 1997-2004 from 69 to 94 percent of all registered illegal immigrants were expelled), most often because they are granted a permanent permit for residence in Lithuania.

3.11 Detention irregulars under criminal law

Subject to the laws of the Republic of Lithuania, it is a crime to illegally cross of the border into Lithuania if it was committed by a person not seeking asylum in the Republic of Lithuania. This is punishable with a fine, arrest or with a custodial penalty of up to two years. An alien shall be released of criminal responsibility if he/she crossed the border illegally with the aim of crossing illegally from the Republic of Lithuania into a third country; if he/she is expelled in the established procedure into the country from the territory of which he entered Lithuania, or to the state of which he/she is a citizen; if he was permitted to cross the border in the simplified procedure; or the illegal trafficking of people through the State border.[87] Illegal presence in the Republic of Lithuania[88] alone is not a crime.

3.12 Minors

The worse situation is with unaccompanied minor illegal immigrants. It is stated that the Foreigners' Registration Centre in which illegal immigrants are accommodated is incapable – both materially and in terms of staffing – of accommodating unaccompanied minors. They are accommodated in the Centre in Kaunas which is primarily designed for the accommodation of juveniles who have committed criminal offences.

---

[86] Migration Yearbook 2005, Migration Departament. p. 83.

[87] Law on the Approval and Enforcement of the Criminal Code of the Republic of Lithuania. Criminal Code. Official Gazette - 2000, No. 89-274 (Art. 291-292).

[88] Subject to Article 23 of the Law on the Unlawful Stay of Aliens of the Republic of Lithuania, an alien's stay in Lithuania shall be deemed illegal if the alien has been staying in the Republic of Lithuania for a period exceeding the period of visa-less stay set by an international treaty of the Republic of Lithuania, a European Union legal act or the Government of the Republic of Lithuania; is staying in the Republic of Lithuania after the expiry of the visa; is staying in the Republic of Lithuania holding an expired visa after the deadline for meeting the obligation to depart from the Republic of Lithuania; is in possession of a forged travel document; is in possession of a forged visa; is staying in the Republic of Lithuania without a visa if it is required; or is staying in the Republic of Lithuania without a valid travel document, save for asylum applicants.

4 NATIONALS DETAINED ABROAD

4.1 Numbers and composition of group

Information on this issue is very limited and insufficient in Lithuania. Only some un-official data on the number of Lithuanians who are detained or who have been convicted of a crime abroad could be gathered. According to data from 2005, about 1,100 nationals of the Republic of Lithuania were detained in other states, predominantly in the states of the European Union, including 660 in Germany, 132 in the United Kingdom, 69 in Spain, 65 in Sweden and 53 in France. In some other states the number of detained nationals from the Republic of Lithuania fluctuated from three to 28 persons. It should also be mentioned that there was a large number of Lithuanian pre-trial detainees in Spain in 2005 (113 persons). Such high figures can possibly only be explained by the poor conditions in the prisons of Lithuania. Many nationals detained abroad do not want to be expelled to Lithuania because of the severe prison conditions here, so they choose to serve their sentence in the country where they were detained.

4.2 Countries of detention

As stated under 4.1, the majority of nationals of the Republic of Lithuania who have been detained in other states were detained in the European Union states, especially in countries where there is a large number of immigrants in search of better paid employment (for instance Germany, the United Kingdom and Spain).

4.3 Reasons for detention & sentencing

According to the unofficial data at our disposal, the grounds for the detention of Lithuanian nationals vary from country to country. In Spain and the United Kingdom there are very many persons who went there in search of better sources for living and who committed minor offences. Germany and Sweden are among the main countries into which transit of trafficking in people is directed. In Germany, many nationals are also arrested for committing various offences related to organized crime. Lithuanians imprisoned and/or sentenced in Poland had most commonly committed smuggling offences or other financial and economic crimes

4.4 Involved organisations – tasks and activities

The involvement of governmental institutions of the Republic of Lithuania (mostly the Ministry of Justice and the Ministry of the Interior) in the cases of Lithuanians detained abroad is limited only to the extent of the obligations taken under the signed international treaties and bilateral agreements. The majority of them are related to carrying out the criminal prosecution of Lithuanian nationals suspected of committing crimes in the territory of another contract party, legal assistance relating to the execution of procedural actions or writs of execution, extradition of persons, the provision of data on previous convictions or other criminal prosecution results. There are only few provisions in some bilateral agreements on the transfer of the persons on which the custodial penalty has been imposed for serving the remaining penalty. Even though all international treaties on cooperation in criminal cases foresee the obligations for exchange of data on previous convictions or other outcomes of criminal prosecutions, in Lithuania the communications on arrest, conviction or the implementation of other procedural actions sent by other states are merely stored in the database of the IT and Communications Department of the Ministry of the Interior by simply entering the name and surname of the person arrested or on trial. This information is neither systematized nor processed more broadly.

4.5 Release and reception in the home country

Lithuania does not have any State institution that is responsible for receiving persons who have served their penalties in other states. In the opinion of the officers, a person who has served his/her sentence is free, and when he/she is deported and released at the border of the Republic of Lithuania he/she is entitled to use the freedom of movement according to his/her needs.

4.6 Aftercare

Nationals of Lithuania who have served sentences in other countries are guaranteed the same rights of access to social support as persons convicted in the Republic of Lithuania, so long as such support is applied for within two months to the social support division of the municipality where he lived prior to entering the institution executing the custodial penalty or where his family lives. The application therefore requires the submission of the document confirming his/her citizenship or a permit for permanent residence in Lithuania as well as a certificate of the previous conviction.[89]

4.7 Public opinion and the media

Prevailing public opinion about criminal offenders in Lithuania is rather negative. This can be concluded from public polls from which it becomes clear that the majority of citizens wished for the reintroduction of the death penalty, or at least for stricter sanctioning. Crimes committed by Lithuanians abroad are evaluated rather indifferently, in terms of these people spoiling the image of Lithuania.

5 EVALUATION AND RECOMMENDATIONS

In generalization of the analysis conducted on the legal status of foreigners sentenced to a custodial penalty in Lithuania, the following recommendations are to be proposed:
- It needs to be acknowledged that it was indeed complicated to carry out analysis and to formulate the precise conclusions due to the lack of information on the foreign convicts in Lithuania. Therefore, primarily it is necessary to tackle issues concerning the organization of such information collection.
- The area that requires the most attention is the employment of convicted prisoners in

---

[89] In fact, due to important reasons, social support may be provided also without documents, but the monetary allowance in that case is not paid.

the prison establishments as well as the implementation of social integration programmes. The possibility to learn the Lithuanian language is praiseworthy, but taking into consideration the level of education of the imprisoned foreigners and the fact that the majority thereof are sentenced to prison terms exceeding 10 years , and also taking into consideration the fact that the majority of imprisoned foreigners perfectly understand and speak Russian, first of all it may be proposed to provide prisoners' education in the Russian language. Also, means and ways are to be sought to give the possibility for the prisoners to learn in other foreign languages as well, for example, in English.

- Taking into account the fact that under the laws of the Republic of Lithuania a convict by his actions may change his/her legal status in the prison establishment, it may be proposed to draw more considerable attention to the stimulation of the activity of the aliens sentenced to imprisonment. That activity could be oriented in several directions: development of special rehabilitation programmes for foreigners, organization of sessions in most popular languages in the prison establishments (Russian and English) and more attention on the part of the employees themselves devoted to that group of the prisoners' contingent: encouraging more active participation in various types of activities and granting more incentives.

- In cooperation with other states and various organizations functioning in the Republic of Lithuania, it would be a welcome approach to search for various measures of leisure organization that would be available at least in Russian (for example, organization of various cultural events in the Russian language in cooperation with the organizations representing the Russian-speaking national minority in Lithuania).

- Another central group of proposals is related to the protection of the legal status of imprisoned foreigners and the mechanisms for ensuring this protection. First of all, it is proposed that foreigners imprisoned in Lithuania be recognized as a socially disadvantaged group which may face huge problems when it comes to paying for legal assistance expenses, and thus to grant them the right to State-guaranteed legal aid. Also, taking into account the vulnerability of persons who have been sentenced to a custodial penalty – especially foreigners – and the sufficiently complicated and cumbersome mechanism of the protection of rights in Lithuania (the requirement to report and file applications to different institutions and officers depending on which law has been violated), it is recommended to form a special unit (or appoint several persons) with the function of ensuring the legal protection of convicted foreigners in Lithuania. This unit simultaneously within the framework of the system of the execution of penalties could coordinate the main aspects of the execution of penalties imposed on aliens. This in turn would make it possible to optimize both the collection of information and tackle the problems of imprisonment that these persons face.

Chapter 17

Luxembourg

Stefan Braum

1 INTRODUCTION

1.1 Overview of penalties and measures

1.1.1 Legal Framework

The Luxembourg Criminal Code (Code pénal luxembourgeois du 16 juin 1879) is based on a tripartite system that divides infringements into three categories, in order of gravity: crimes, offences and contraventions (administrative offences). Crimes are punished with criminal sanctions (Article 7 CP), including life imprisonment and prison sentences ranging from 5-10 years, 10-15 years, 15-20 years and 20-30 years (Article 8 CP). Offences are punished with prison sentences differing from 8 days up to 5 years (Art.14, Art.15 CP). Contraventions are punished with a fine, which is to be paid to the State (Article 25 CP). Rules relating to the legal status of foreign prisoners in Luxembourg are set out in the following Laws and Regulations:

- law on the execution of sentences (Loi du 26 juillet 1986 relative à certains modes d'exécution des peines privatives de liberté)[1];
- law on the detention of foreigners awaiting trial (Loi du 18 décembre 1855 sur la prévention détention préventive des étrangers).[2] This Law was abrogated by the Law on the modification of different articles of the Criminal Procedure Code from March 6th 2006 (Loi du 6 Mars portant 1. introduction notamment de l'instruction simplifiée, du contrôle judiciaire et réglementant les nullities de la procedure d'enquête, 2.modification de différents articles du Code d'instruction criminelle et 3.abrogation de différents lois spéciales)[3];
- law on the modification of the regime of detention awaiting trial with Article 94 Criminal Procedure Code as applicable rule. (Loi du 28 juillet 1973 portant modification du régime de la détention préventive)[4];
- law on the reorganisation of penitentiary institutions (Loi du 27 juillet 1997 portant réorganisation des établissements pénitentiaires)[5];
- regulation on the administration and the internal regime of penitentiary institutions (Règlement grand-ducal du 24 mars 1989 concernant l'administration et le régime interne des établissements pénitentiaires)[6];
- regulation setting up a centre of provisional stay for foreigners in irregular situations and modifying the Regulation on the administration and the internal regime of penitentiary institutions of 24 March 1989 (Règlement grand-ducal du 20 septembre 2002, créant un Centre de Séjour Provisiore pour Etrangers en Situations Irrégulière, et modifiant le règlement grand-ducal du 24 mars 1989).[7]

---

[1] See Mémorial, *Journal Officiel du Grand-Duché de Luxembourg*, A – N° 70, 11 Septembre 1986, p. 1940.

[2] Mémorial du Grand-Duché de Luxembourg, 29 Décembre 1855, p.31.

[3] Mémorial du Grand-Duché de Luxembourg, A – N° 47, 15 mars 2006, p. 1074.

[4] Mémorial du Grand-Duché de Luxembourg, A – N° 48, 21 août 1973, p. 1104.

[5] Mémorial du Grand-Duché de Luxembourg, A – N° 62, 28 août 1997, p. 1942.

[6] Mémorial du Grand-Duché de Luxembourg, A – N° 17, 3 avril 1989, p. 195.

[7] Mémorial du Grand-Duché de Luxembourg, A – N° 116, 15 octobre 2002, p. 2836.

1.1.2 Legal status of foreign prisoners in Luxembourg

The Laws and Regulations set out above contain provisions that apply to prisoners in Luxembourg. As will be seen, in some respects, foreign prisoners have a different legal status from that of national Luxembourg prisoners.

1. The State prosecutor ('procureur général d'Etat') is the competent authority in the fields of the execution of sentences, the surveillance of institutions, and the educational and medical treatment of prisoners in Luxembourg. In accordance with *Article 100 CP*, the State prosecutor can decide to release a prisoner on parole, if a prisoner has served a certain part of his sentence (specified below) or if the prisoner has shown evidence of good behaviour or social re-adaptation. If the prisoner is sentenced to less than six month he can be released on parole after three months and a prisoner that is sentenced to more than six months can be released on probation if he has served half of his time. Special rules apply to repeat offenders, the so-called recidivists. If convicted for less than nine months, they can be released on parole after six months and those sentenced to more than nine months can be released after having served two thirds of their prison sentence. Prisoners sentenced to life imprisonment can also be released on parole, after having served fifteen years of their time. *Article 100 CP*, however, is only applicable to prisoners residing in Luxembourg and thus does not apply to foreign prisoners. Article 11 of the Law on the execution of sentences fills this gap. This Article provides that foreigners awaiting expulsion or who are to be banned from the territory of Luxembourg can bene-fit from an early release if they satisfy the conditions provided for in *Article 100*, paragraphs 1, 2, or 3 CP. They can thus enjoy an early release after having served at least the specified prison sentence provided for in *Article 100 CP*. In the case of early release, foreign prisoners are banned from the territory of Luxembourg. Violation of this banish-ment entails that the remaining sentence may be executed without any prior trial. The other provisions of the Law on the execution of sentences - for example on the execution of sentences in several stages (Article 2), a regime of partial release (Article 3), release and probation (Article 6-10) - are also only applicable to prisoners having their home or resi-dence in Luxembourg.

2. Article 1 of the Law on the detention of foreigners awaiting trial (dating from the year 1855) also stipulated a difference in the treatment between residents and non-residents. Foreigners not residing in Luxembourg could be arrested and detained in the case that they are suspected to have committed a crime or a contravention. In the case of a contra-vention, this provisional detention ends when the foreigner pays the fine prescribed by the police (Article 2, paragraph 2). However, in the case where the foreigner is unable to pay, he is condemned to a subsidiary prison sentence (Article 5) and will be released when he has served this time. In the case where a foreigner is suspected of having committed an offence, the foreigner could be detained for ten days in order for a judge to decide whether or not to detain the suspect any longer. If these ten days have passed, and no judgement has been given, the prisoner should be released. This law from the 19th cen-tury was abrogated only two months ago. A new legal framework modifying the rules of pre-trial detention has replaced it. In a general sense, the distinction between residents and non-residents has basically been withdrawn. The new version of the criminal proce-dure code now provides several instruments that can serve as substitutes for the detention of a person charged with a crime: In accordance with the new article Art. 107 CPP, this

person can be subject to different obligations, for example: the injunction to leave a certain area, a periodical obligation to register or the making of a deposit.

3. Nevertheless, a different legal status remains for foreign prisoners in some aspects. In accordance with the still applicable Art.94 CPP, a foreigner can be detained if serious indications of guilt exist, and the act can lead to a criminal sanction or imprisonment for reintegrative reasons of two years or over. This also holds true if a danger exists that the suspect will flee, that proof will be obscured or if it is feared that when released, the prisoner will commit other offences.

4. The regime of detention for prisoners in Luxembourg is set out in the Regulation on the administration and the internal regime of penitentiary institutions (Articles 137-325). It contains provisions on the transfer of prisoners, discipline and the contact of prisoners with the outside world through correspondence and visits, the maintenance (care) of prisoners, work and the education of prisoners. Article 331 of the same Regulation stipulates that foreign prisoners are to be subject to the same rules as national prisoners. Consequently, they have for instance, the same right to work, the same right to medical and social services as well as the same right to education and access to the prison library. In addition, some special rules, applicable to foreigners, are set out in Article 331. In the case of absolute necessity, if a prisoner doesn't speak or doesn't understand one of the official languages of Luxembourg, and there is no one around capable of translating, the prison director can call in the help of an interpreter. Prisoners are allowed to communicate in their own language during meetings and correspondence. Letters written by foreigners may, however, be translated for purposes of control and security. According to Article 332, prisoners that are subject to an application for extradition by a foreign government are subject to the regime of suspects. In these cases, the State prosecutor is the competent authority with regard to permission to allow visitors and the right to control their correspondence.

1.2 Overview of the Prison System

1.2.1 General deficiencies

The strong emphasis on security issues causes deficits within the penitentiary system. We find these deficiencies in general, but also as characteristic elements of Luxembourg's penitentiary institutions. The typical situation in many penitentiary institutions is especially characterized by:

- an extreme overcrowding;
- a high percentage of foreign prisoners;
- a lack of qualified personal staff;
- insufficient continued training of penitentiary staff;
- a lack of implementation of modern concepts concerning the special methods of reintegration in view of sensitive groups of prisoners;
- budgetary problems.

1.2.2 The situation in Luxembourg

The situation in Luxembourg's penitentiary institutions expresses the present relationship between modern re-integrative penitentiary concepts and the maximum of security: In February 2006 the situation in Luxembourg's penitentiary institutions was in the media spotlight as some prisoners caused an intentional fire in one of the blocks of the central prison in *Schrassig*. Thus, politicians and the public became temporarily aware of the problematic situation of Luxembourg's penitentiary institutions. Many foreign prisoners were concerned, particularly those foreigners being kept in administrative detention.

Luxembourg has two penitentiary institutions. On the one hand, there is the penitentiary centre in *Schrassig* and on the other hand, there is the penitentiary centre in *Givenich*, which is the smaller one, serving as an institution for lighter punishment and supporting an open execution of a prison sentence. The institution in *Schrassig* was founded in the seventies as a model for the humane execution of prison sentences. The person formerly responsible for the penitentiary institutions, the general public prosecutor *Alphonse Spielmann*, was absolutely engaged in humanitarian issues. He believed that criminal law should have a more preventive and a less repressive character. A traditional prison sentence should be concomitant with alternative sanctions. The idea was to substitute its execution through the use of instruments outside of prison such as social work, driving bans or diversions in general. Therefore, from its beginning, the penitentiary institution in Schrassig was set up for a small group of prisoners (around 350), following the idea that criminal law should be primarily orientated to those alternative sanctions. For this reason a regression to repressive strategies in Europe's criminal policy will necessarily impose problems upon a penitentiary system that was actually intended for criminal law of a liberal character. This discrepancy between old-but-modern concepts of humanitarian criminal law and, new-but-old-fashioned concepts of a more repressive criminal policy, is one of the main causes for the situation of a permanent overcrowding of the penitentiary institutions in *Schrassig*. As Luxembourg is not an isolated entity, it depends on the European political climate, which is dominated by the maxim of security. Of course, this situation has consequences that concern the whole internal organization of a penitentiary institution and contributes to the general deficiencies mentioned above.

Considering the prison of Schrassig, we have to take into account some specific problems. Schrassig combines all kinds of detention. The difference between a prison sentence and an administrative detention, often automatically stipulated, does not really exist. On the contrary, you find all relevant groups of prisoners in Schrassig. These groups are only separated within different blocks of the prison. Thus within Schrassig, there exists:
- foreign prisoners in detention awaiting trial;
- foreign prisoners detained under criminal law;
- juvenile foreign prisoners;
- foreign prisoners under measures other than punishment (like e.g. preventive detention and psychiatric hospital);
- foreign prisoners under administrative detention.

The bringing together of these disparate groups under one roof – of course – raises serious problems. The penitentiary institution has to take care of different groups of prisoners with their totally different needs and their totally different social and psychological situations. The situation of overcrowding and the common confinement of different groups of detainees cause tremendous tension within the prison of Schrassig. As long as this tension exists, so does the possibility of it being unleashed in such dramatic incidences as described above.

1.3 Consulates, Embassies, Ministries of Home country, Probation Services, NGO's, etc.

1.4 Overview of the National Penitentiary System and its trends

Hereinafter we give an overview on the most important trends of the national penitentiary system. The data we use have been taken from statistics collected by the penitentiary institutions and the office of the public prosecutor. It must be emphasised that these figures were not empirically reliable in any case. Nevertheless, they are appropriate to give a very basic analysis of general conditions in Luxembourg's penitentiary institutions. It is important to note however that this analysis has to be careful and must avoid a too extensive interpretation. Considering the general numbers, this framework will contain:
- the total number of prisoners in Luxembourg, differentiated by Luxembourg and foreign nationality;
- the number of prisoners in relation to the whole population over the age of criminal responsibility;
- the relationship of foreigners/foreign prisoners – national residents/national prisoners, in comparison to Germany;
- data concerning the non-confinement enforcement of sentence.

Considering the general reasons for arrest, we offer information concerning:
- the total number of pre-trial detentions, regular detentions and administrative detentions;
- the percentage rates of the nationalities of pre-trial detainees;
- the percentage rates of the nationalities of foreign pre-trial detainees;
- typical background offences committed by foreigners or offences that foreigners are suspected of committing (in percentages);
- different offences of sentenced prisoners (in percentages);
- lengths of sentencing.

1.4.1 Trends in Numbers

Looking at the absolute numbers of prisoners in Luxembourg in the last couple of years, we can see that it has enormously grown. Comparing the evolution between the years 2000 and 2006, we assess a total increase of 66.3 % in the population of *Schrassig* prisoners from 401 to 667. The major problem of this increase is that the penal institution of *Schrassig* was only built for a maximum number of around 350 prisoners. This discrepancy already underlines the situation of a nearly radical overcrowding of the penitentiary institution in Schrassig.

In this context it is remarkable that the number of detainees coming from Luxembourg almost remained at the same level whereas the number of foreign prisoners has disproportionately augmented to 105.6 %. In order to anticipate the false impression that this evolution is due to a higher rate of criminal offences among the foreign population, we try to convey an empirically more differentiated background hereinafter.

Table 1

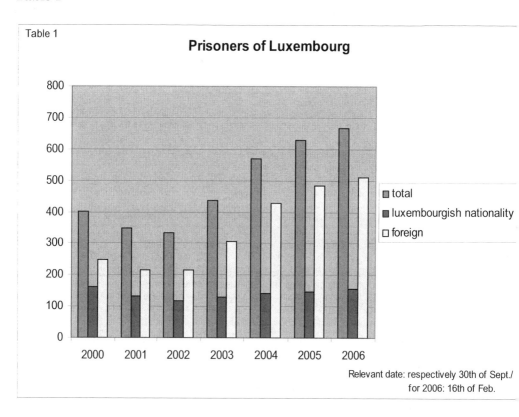

Table 1

Prisoners of Luxembourg

- total
- luxembourgish nationality
- foreign

Relevant date: respectively 30th of Sept./ for 2006: 16th of Feb.

First these statistics have to be analysed in view of the whole population of Luxembourg. Only this relationship can build a reasonable background to interpret these figures. In the period between the year of 2000 and 2006, the vital statistics show that the whole population has modified from 433.600 (2000) to 459.500 (2006)[8]. This is a percentage increase of 5.97 %. This percentage is extremely high when compared to the European average – for example in comparison to Germany (0, 38% in the same period). The increasing numbers of detainees might be explained by an over average increase of the whole population.

Investigating the relationship between all prisoners and the whole population, you can obviously involve only the part of the population that has already achieved the beginning of criminal responsibility. Here we can notice an increase from 0. 098 % (percentage of the population, which was arrested) in 2001 to 0.17 % in 2005 and the tendency is even ascending. In comparison to Luxembourg, this value persists in Germany around 0.086 % in the last couple of years.

---

[8] See STATEC, statnews n° 22/2006, informations statistiques récentes.

Table 2

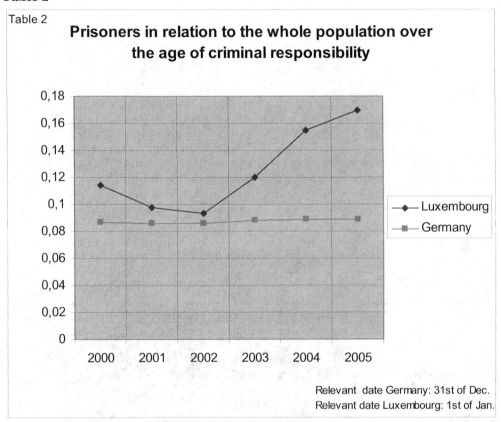

Table 2

Prisoners in relation to the whole population over the age of criminal responsibility

Relevant date Germany: 31st of Dec.
Relevant date Luxembourg: 1st of Jan.

Of course, if the increase in absolute numbers is expressed as a percentage, this causes a much greater effect for small numbers. Thus, regarding the situation in a small country, every augmentation seems to indicate a dramatic change. In fact the real consequences are not that serious. This means on the one hand that Luxembourg has not become a "centre of crime". Looking at the percentage rates, the figures concerning the national rate of crime remain extremely low. Nevertheless, this means on the other hand, that a penitentiary institution that has been built for a small number of detainees might be even more concerning, if it is so far foreseeable working conditions are continuously changed by an increase of the figures. Two consequences can be drawn from this evolution. First, it seems extremely urgent that the capacity of the penitentiary institution be enhanced. But second – bearing in mind the problematic relationship between a liberal criminal policy and the maxim of security – it seems even more important – and effective – to separate the criminal justice system from the premise of security. Otherwise it will be impossible to guarantee an effective re-integration for detainees in the future.

The increase of the total number of prisoners also coincides with the increase in the number of foreign prisoners in the last years. The proportion of foreigners to the whole population of Luxembourg has significantly increased from 36.28 % in the year of 2000 to 38.99 % in 2005.

Table 3

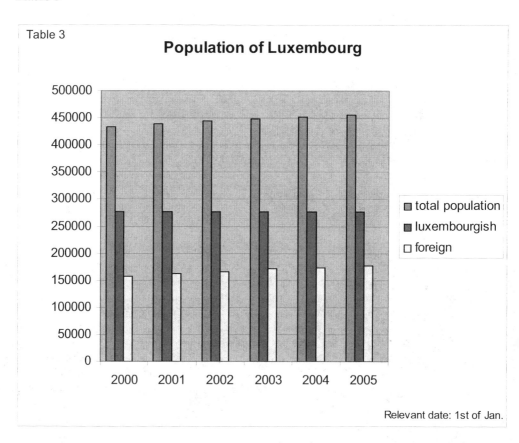

Table 3

Population of Luxembourg

Relevant date: 1st of Jan.

In this context it is very interesting to follow the development of the delinquent portions of each group. In 2000 only 0.06 % of Luxembourg's residents were arrested and this quotient has not changed very much until 2006, where we have a value of 0.05 %. Contrarily, of the foreign portion of the population, 0.16 % was imprisoned in the year 2000. This number has escalated up to 0.27 % in 2006. In comparison with Germany[9] the evolution of national detainees on the one hand and foreign detainees on the other hand has just about stagnated in recent years. The percentage rate of foreign prisoners in Luxembourg also stagnated from 2000 – 2002, and essentially increased from 2003 up to the present.

---

[9] See, P.A. Albrecht, *Kriminologie*, 3rd edition, 2005, pp. 337.

Table 4

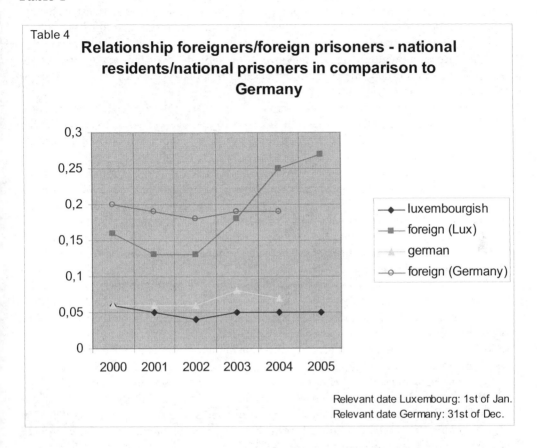

Table 4

Relationship foreigners/foreign prisoners - national residents/national prisoners in comparison to Germany

Relevant date Luxembourg: 1st of Jan.
Relevant date Germany: 31st of Dec.

But as already indicated, this does not allow one to draw the conclusion that the increasing number of foreigners in Luxembourg causes the increase of foreigners in the penitentiary institution. First, uncertain factors concerning the figure itself must be taken into consideration (like e.g. different reference dates). Apart from these inescapable uncertainties we have to recognise that there are several offences that can only be committed by foreigners as for example the legislation acts concerning the entry and residence of foreigners.[10] Also, all immigrants should be registered in the demography but for different reasons (e.g. demanding fluctuation) they are often not, so in some cases detainees only appear in the prison statistics but not in the demography. This is another aspect where guessing at the final result of the statistics leads to the disadvantage of foreigners.

Further items hindering a simple comparison between the deviance of domestic people and the deviance of foreigners consist in the existing socio-demographic and social-cultural factors.[11] Frequently, foreigners belong to social groups, which are over average

---

[10] See art. 31 de la loi du 28 mars 1972 concernant l'entrée et séjour des étrangers (Law concerning the entry and residence of foreigners). Mémorial, *Journal Officiel du Grand-Duché de Luxembourg*, A – N°6, 1er février 1996, p. 76 (version modifiée).

[11] Compare P.A. Albrecht, *Kriminologie*, 3rd edition, 2005, p. 338.

represented in the criminal milieu. Also the school education is – in general – even worse when compared to the domestic population. Unequal education and housing facilities lead to the general effect that the social standards of foreigners are oftentimes not comparable to the standards of the domestic population. Finally, the demographical variables burden foreign individuals: mostly they live in the city of Luxembourg. Also, the rate of male foreigners is usually higher than the number of females. Both aspects are indicators for a higher rate of incrimination.[12]

In general: Due to a basically different etiological structure the deviant behaviour of foreign and domestic offenders cannot be compared. The higher increase of foreign prison population thus may not be interpreted as a scenario of threat for public security. Such an interpretation of the figures being presented here will mean a populist abuse of empirical data. Similar analyses in Germany have shown that the incrimination of foreigners was significantly reduced, if social groups with a sociological similar structure were compared.[13] So, the accurate conclusion should be that it is necessary to purge the falsified factors in order to prevent any discrimination of foreigners.[14]

In addition to the high number of foreign prisoners in the penitentiary institution of *Schrassig*, it is also interesting to consider certain numbers from the institution of *Givenich*. Here we have only those prisoners, either living in non-confinement facilities or joining activities in order to facilitate their re-integration. In this institution the relationship between Luxembourg national prisoners and foreign prisoners is reversed. In the year 2003 there were 26 national and only 11 foreign detainees who were arrested in *Givenich*. This value has developed over the past years: For example, 43 Luxembourg national prisoners and 25 foreign prisoners are registered in this penitentiary in 2006. It is remarkable that the great number of domestic prisoners in *Givenich* contradicts the trend that can be seen in the penitentiary institution of *Schrassig*. That can be explained by the fact that foreign detainees are only allowed to receive preferential treatment when they hold a Luxembourg residency permit. As many foreign prisoners do not have a residence in Luxembourg, they forcibly removed from the institution of *Givenich* already at an early stage of the execution of their prison sentence. Even if we do not have information concerning the total number of prisoners, we can assume that it is relatively high. Another reason for the different population in *Givenich* could be the attitude of the authorities towards foreign prisoners. In some criminological research studies it has been proven that foreigners are more often, and much easier, criminalized than Luxembourg nationals. This concerns both the criminal investigation and the execution of a sentence. Having less communicative capacities, and less social privileges, foreigners are more severely subjected to the labelling process disseminated by the institutions of the criminal justice system.[15] They are more often accused, more often sentenced and finally less often released. This already leads us to the reasons for arrest.

---

[12] Compare Mansel/G. Albrecht, *Migration und das kriminalpolitische Handeln staatlicher Strafverfolgungsorgane – Ausländer als polizeiliche Tatverdächtige und gerichtlich Abgeurteilte*, KZSoziol 2003, pp. 679 ff.

[13] Compare P.-A. Albrecht, *Kriminologie*, 3rd edition, 2005, p. 342.

[14] Compare Akpinar, *Die Entkategorisierung des Begriffs der Ausländerkriminalität*, ZJJ 2003, 258 pp. (p. 264).

[15] Compare Ludwig-Mayerhofer, *Das Strafrecht und seine administrative Rationalisierung*, 1998, p. 239.

Table 5

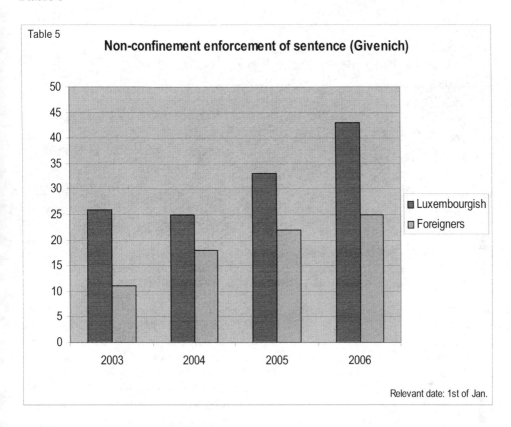

Table 5

Non-confinement enforcement of sentence (Givenich)

Relevant date: 1st of Jan.

1.4.2 Reasons for arrest

First, it is necessary to distinguish between regular detention and pre-trial detention. In 2000, 180 from a total number of 401 total prisoners were kept in pre-trial detention. That means a proportion of 44.89 %. In the following years, the percentage figure steadily moved from 45 % to 53 %. In the year of 2006 we enumerated 320 people, who were regularly arrested and 347 persons (52.02 %), being kept in pre-trial detention. Moreover, we established a significant increase of administrative detainees during the same period. In 2000, only 6 prisoners were listed in the statistics of the administrative detention. In 2006, we have already recorded 35.

Table 6

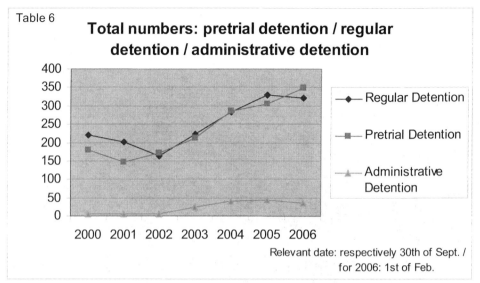

Table 6

Total numbers: pretrial detention / regular detention / administrative detention

- ◆ Regular Detention
- ■ Pretrial Detention
- ▲ Administrative Detention

Relevant date: respectively 30th of Sept. / for 2006: 1st of Feb.

Most of the pre-trial detainees are foreigners. In 2005, 347 prisoners were kept in pretrial detention in Schrassig. No less than 285 of them were of foreign origin, mostly Portuguese (44), but also French (32). Most prisoners come from different states of the African continent (86). As already described above, there could be several reasons for these big numbers of foreign prisoners in the whole penitentiary institution. The reasons mentioned above are all the more applicable to the situation of foreigners being kept in pre-trial detention. For the Portuguese we have to consider that they are highly represented in Luxembourg. They are the largest group of migrant workers. The same applies for the African group. So it is not astonishing that many of the prisoners come from these groups.

Table 7

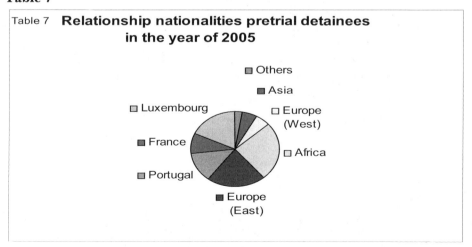

Table 7 **Relationship nationalities pretrial detainees in the year of 2005**

- ▨ Others
- ■ Asia
- □ Luxembourg
- □ Europe (West)
- ■ France
- □ Africa
- ■ Portugal
- ■ Europe (East)

Similar to the situation in pre-trial detention, the proportion of Portuguese, French, Eastern European and African prisoners being kept in regular detention remains at a high level. In particular, the number of sentenced persons from Eastern Europe and Africa has doubled within the last seven years.

Table 8

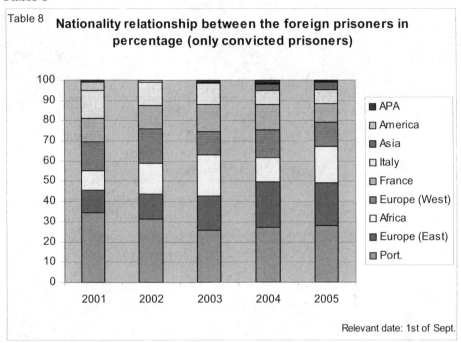

Table 8 **Nationality relationship between the foreign prisoners in percentage (only convicted prisoners)**

Relevant date: 1st of Sept.

In general, the proportion of foreign prisoners being kept in pre-trial detention is even bigger than in regular detention (in 2005 82.13 % foreigners in pre-trial detention compared with 76.7 % in regular detention). This can be explained by the reasons already mentioned. Not only can socio-demographical and socio-cultural variables cause the significant overrepresentation of foreign prisoners, but also the labelling process governed by the institutions of the criminal justice system. The experiences of other European countries have identified that criminal acts are frequently imputed to foreigners. This more frequent imputation is facilitated by the social conditions foreigners are submitted to, always attracting a certain social mistrust. As well, they are facilitated by the lack of communicative capacities, which are expressed in the fact that most foreigners don't have the support of a defence lawyer during the investigation procedure.[16]

Social conditions and the mechanisms of the labelling process they cause, lead to the typical offences like theft, robbery and narcotic offences. Thus the proportion of foreign prisoners, being arrested for narcotic offences, increased from 55.17 % in 2000 to 90.91 % in the year 2006. In 2005 more than 80% of pre-trial detainees were suspected of doing narcotic offences.

---

[16] Compare e.g. Sessar, *Rechtliche und soziale Prozesse einer Definition der Tötungskriminalität*, 1981, p. 178.

Table 9

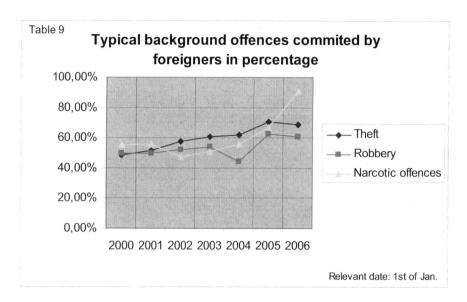

Table 9

Typical background offences commited by foreigners in percentage

Relevant date: 1st of Jan.

Considering all the offences that prisoners are convicted for, one can notice that narcotic crimes (24 % in 2002, 31.23 % in 2006) as well as theft (10.45 % in 2001, 25.26 % in 2005) have increased in the last years. Due to the phenomenon of deviant behaviour undertaken to furnish money for drugs, these two criminal offences are closely linked. At the same time, the proportion of killing crimes, robberies and bodily injury offences has decreased in the last few years.

Table 10

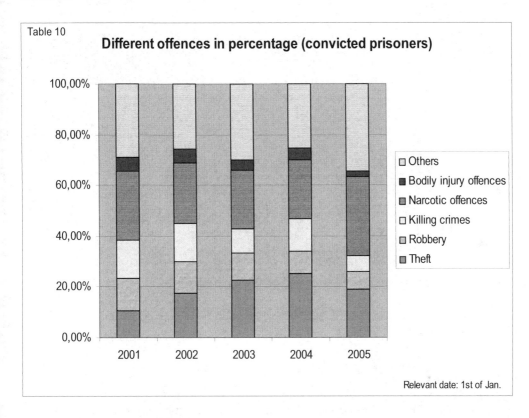

Table 10
Different offences in percentage (convicted prisoners)

Legend:
- □ Others
- ■ Bodily injury offences
- ■ Narcotic offences
- □ Killing crimes
- □ Robbery
- ■ Theft

Relevant date: 1st of Jan.

1.4.3 Length of Sentencing

The increase of detainees in a penitentiary system could as well be caused by a more severe practice of sentencing. Thus, the length of sentencing becomes an important figure with regard to the evaluation of a penitentiary institution. In view of that aspect the proportion of prison sentences between one and three years has increased from 33.57 % (2001) to 46.57 % (2006). However, the proportion of prison sentences of less than one year decreased from 15.73 % (2001) to 9.39 % in the year 2006. Also, the proportion of administrative penalties diminished by around 4% between 2001 and 2006. This trend shows that the penitentiary institutions in Luxembourg could be significantly affected by a change of sentencing practice influenced by security issues. With regard to the development in other EU Member States, the maxim of security is expressed in a more restrictive practice of sentencing and releasing criminal offenders. The most important example of this change of paradigms is the policy of "zero tolerance" that has become an essential element of criminal policy in Europe. This brings us to the conclusion that these paradigms are slowly but steadily implemented within the criminal justice system. We are facing general external conditions caused by the criminal justice system as such which enormously burden the penitentiary institutions. This general trend might just have arrived as well in Luxembourg.

Table 11

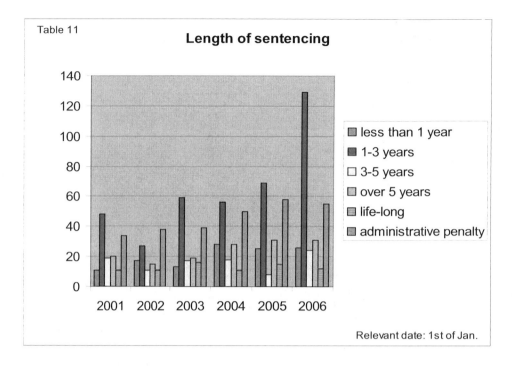

Table 11 — Length of sentencing

Legend: less than 1 year; 1-3 years; 3-5 years; over 5 years; life-long; administrative penalty

Relevant date: 1st of Jan.

To summarize:
- the numbers of foreign prisoners has generally and significantly increased in the last few years. This is due to etiological conditions that are quite different when compared to domestic offenders and are caused by the paradigms of the labelling process: In general, foreigners are more often accused, more often sentenced and less often released;
- in particular the number of foreign prisoners being kept in pre-trial detention has significantly increased during the last years. This underlines and proves the mechanisms of the labelling process. The lack of social and communicative capacities facilitates the imputation of deviance to foreigners;
- narcotic offences linked with other typical offences to furnish money for drugs are the main reasons why foreigners are arrested (pre-trial detention and execution of sentence). This might indicate the fact that public authorities have reinforced the investigation activities in the field of drugs;
- the length of sentencing reveals a more repressive practice of sentencing within the criminal justice system. This might be due to a certain domination of security issues being steadily implemented within the Luxembourg criminal justice system.

If these external conditions on the penitentiary institutions of Luxembourg do not change, the permanent situation of overcrowding will remain and will get dramatically worse. Thus, principally demanded claims of a humane and re-integrative execution of sentence stipulated by the Council of Europe can be hardly fulfilled.

2 TREATMENT OF FOREIGN PRISONERS

2.1 General

The social situation depends on issues of the internal organization of a penitentiary institution. In this field security becomes an important topic. Security as a part of the internal organization has to respect the principles laid down by the Council of Europe concerning the execution of sentence. Only by respecting these principles can security issues be legitimated. Such a legitimated concept of security is not restricted to high walls, modern technical surveillance and impermeable bars. As an enlightened concept security means a combination of different elements[17]:

- first, an instrumental security concerning technical and constructional provisions like walls, bars, video surveillance, alarm systems and last but not least the technical staff who has the duty to implement and to apply all those measures;
- cooperative security concerning the collaboration and partnership between all officials and authorities who are involved in the penitentiary system;
- administrative security concerning the formal and reliable fundament of rules developed by the head of a penitentiary institution and its political background governing the daily life in prison and finally;
- social security concerning the relationship between all the people living and working together within the structure of a penitentiary system, especially the mode of cooperation between the members of the staff and the detainees.

The implementation of this complex understanding of security is relatively frustrated by the typical situation within the penitentiary institutions in Luxembourg. This can put foreign prisoners at a disadvantage as the most sensitive and most represented group of detainees. The general deficiencies described above already characterize the basic conditions of the social situation in the Schrassig penitentiary institution. There may be fewer differences, particularly concerning the social status of foreign prisoners. Rather, we are confronted with problems that every detainee in this institution is subjected to, independent of his or her nationality. The two main issues that remain in the daily life of the Schrassig prison are:

- the situation of dramatic overcrowding;
- the common housing of different groups of detainees.

The group of administrative detainees especially creates an obstacle for the implementation of modern re-integrative concepts. They need the intensified attention of the technical and social staff. The high rate of fluctuation demands nearly all of the attention of the administrative stuff. We can basically note certain absorption of energy caused by the sensitive technical, administrative and social issues of foreign detainees who are held in administrative detention. The group of detainees being kept in pre-trial detention intensifies this process of absorption. Due to the different legal situation (presumption of innocence), this group cannot be integrated into the standardised course of the execution of prison sentence. Not only has the legal status, but as well the psychological and social

---

[17] See P.-A. Albrecht, *Kriminologie*, 3rd edition, 2005, p. 278.

situation of foreign pre-trial detainees demanded a high intensity of preoccupation that might be withdrawn for those "normal prisoners" who have been already sentenced.

This necessarily differing approach to each single group of detainees destabilizes the described balanced concept of security within the structures of the penitentiary system. Considering these conditions, a modern concept of security cannot occur. This deficit can hardly be overcome by one-sided means of instrumental security. In order to protect the rights of (foreign) prisoners we need political and public effort to take care that an enlightened model of security is established within the national penitentiary institutions.

2.2 Living conditions, facilities, work and re-integration activities

Despite this misbalanced situation in Luxembourg's penitentiary institutions, there are positive elements in the internal organization that can facilitate a human and re-integrative execution of a prison sentence. These positive structures are leftovers from the former reform initiatives and are personally safeguarded by the governor of the penitentiary institution in Schrassig.

The working facilities are basically well developed. The penitentiary institution in Schrassig has a modern high-tech laundry, where around twenty prisoners can work. Moreover, the institution in Schrassig has a garage and a workshop for carpentry where many foreign prisoners work. Other working facilities are the kitchen of the institution and its library. This library contains books in most of the important languages represented in the prison of Schrassig. Most prisoners are allowed to participate in a sports program. The psychological service does its very best to look after foreign prisoners and to assure re-integration activities.

But all of those initiatives end at the limits of the described structural problems. The situation of overcrowding does not allow really effective re-integrative work. The lack of qualified social and technical staff does not allow an extended use of working and professionally qualifying facilities. As long as the necessities of instrumental security dominate the practice of the penitentiary system, foreign prisoners keep on suffering from insufficient participation in re-integrative concepts. Then prisoner's rights only exist theoretically

2.3 Prisoner's rights

As mentioned above, the Regulation on the administration and the internal regime of penitentiary institutions sets out the regime of detention in Luxembourg. As regards legal advice, Article 240 provides that in the prison complex, the members of the Luxembourg bar have the right to communicate freely with the prisoners they defend and with prisoners who are about to be extradited. According to Article 218, a prisoner has the right to write (daily) and without any limitations to any person of their choice and receive letters from any person, except if the prisoner is deprived from this right by a judge or as a result of a disciplinary measure. Correspondence between the prisoner and his lawyer is permissible at any time, even in a case where the prisoner has been deprived of the right to correspondence (Article 226). Furthermore, on the basis of Article 275, every prisoner is permitted to practice his religion in prison. In this respect, the prisoner may also receive a visit from a representative of his religious community. If not religious, moral support and moral advisors are also admissible.

3 ADMINISTRATIVE DETENTION OF FOREIGN PRISONERS

On the basis of the Regulation of 20 September 2002, a special section for provisional stay for foreigners in irregular situations was created at the Luxembourg penitentiary centre. This special section was set up for foreigners who are detained on the basis of Article 15 of the Law on the entry and stay of foreigners, the medical control of foreigners and foreign labour. During their stay at the centre, prisoners are kept separate from other prisoners (Article 3) and are subject to a special regime (Article 4) which contains the following particularities:

First of all, they are informed about their administrative situation and rights and duties - at the very latest - the day after their admission to the centre. Secondly, within 24 hours the prisoners will be submitted to a medical examination at the centre and as frequently to medical examinations as are deemed necessary. Thirdly, the prisoners are under no obligation to work at the prison whatsoever. In addition, upon written submission, the prisoner can be authorised by the prison director to participate in activities with prisoners if it is considered to be in the interest of the prisoner. Furthermore, the prisoners enjoy an unlimited right of correspondence; they have the right to follow radio and television broadcasts and a limited right to use the phone. To conclude, with exception to married couples, men and women stay in separate wings of the prison.

4 NATIONALS DETAINED ABROAD

Unfortunately there is no further information concerning this topic.

5 EVALUATION AND RECOMMENDATIONS

The report attempts to give an overview concerning the very special situation of foreign prisoners in Luxembourg. Like all the other reports collected and analysed in this study of the "Tilburg University" and "Prison Watch", it contains a lot of statistical material, figures and graphics. We learned something about the percentage rates of foreign detainees in pre-trial or administrative detention, we gained information about the relationship between foreign prisoners and the foreign population and we might have learned something about the distribution of offences among foreign detainees, the length of their sentences and the different nationalities being kept in custody. Such statistical information does not convey the impression that the prisoners themselves, or the employees of a penitentiary institution, derive from their daily experiences during the execution of a prison sentence. The real meaning of a prison sentence for the citizen concerned often remains rather unknown. Instead of giving an abstract analysis of a system, we should always be aware of the concrete conditions ruling the daily life in a prison and its deep problems.

Already, an inspection of a penitentiary institution allows us to understand the living conditions in prison in an extended sense. Thus, you learn about the often-spoilt smell of the prison kitchen and of the air on the floors. We cannot help but be astonished by how many people can live in a cell and you can feel how movement is made inconvenient by barred doors and windows. Nevertheless, the long-term loss of a social lifetime, the long-term interruption of social relations and finally the renunciation of every claim, every plan, every hope and every perspective in a life are aspects that can hardly be understood by third parties. In short: The execution of a prison sentence results in the "social death" of the concerned citizen, it causes social isolation but it can also represent the loss of human dignity.[18]

The situation of a detainee is even worse when foreigners are concerned. They are a very sensitive group within the penitentiary institutions. Considering the dangers for their rights, a human penitentiary system presupposes judicial safeguards in order to protect the life of detainees in prison and makes it possible for them to develop their own perspective of life in accordance with the social rules, after a prison sentence has been served. We find the essential principles relating to the safeguard of detained citizens in the International legal framework applicable to penitentiary institutions. The recommendations of the Council of Europe provide that all persons deprived of their freedom shall be treated with respect for their human rights.[19] Furthermore, all detention shall be managed so as to facilitate reintegration into free society. Respect for human rights and the facilitation of reintegration are the two basic principles that are essential parts of the restricted legitimacy of a prison sentence. This is at least the general idea of a legal framework related to penitentiary institutions in Europe. Unfortunately, the reality largely deviates from that idea.

The public and its political representatives expect quite another effect that should be guaranteed by a penitentiary system: it is the maximum of security. Prisons – in accordance with this maximum – shall protect "normal" citizens from deviant people and shall, besides that, act as deterrents for those who might become deviant. This maximum of security remains in the daily perception of European societies and thus becomes the predominant political guideline. Spectacular events in a penitentiary institution, such as kidnapping or violent outbreaks, always attract the attention of the media and can decide the future of political careers and even the outcome of an election. In that perspective, penitentiary institutions are instruments that provide social security. This security perspective is increasingly overwhelming the more differentiated perspectives of the safeguarding of human rights and the necessity for re-integration. In recent years the European Union Member States mainly followed a criminal policy guided by the maximum of security. In every case where individual rights are confronted with a maximum of security, the maximum governs judicial argument and gains the upper hand in the balancing of public interests and individual rights. Consequently, in the Member States we have some general trends influencing the penitentiary system. As the criminalization of deviant behaviour is getting stricter, the institutions of the national criminal justice systems are tending towards the detention of persons even for minor reasons, and extending the deprivation of freedom for longer periods. On the political, social, administrative and organizational level the original notions of modern penitentiary systems are being withdrawn.[20]

The tension between the main principles of a human and re-integrative execution of a sentence on the one hand and the maximum of security on the other hand creates enormous disadvantages for the penitentiary institutions. A European political background

---

[18] Compare P. A. Albrecht, *Kriminologie*, 3rd edition 2005, p. 276.

[19] Look for example at *Council of Europe*, Committee of Ministers to member states on the European Prison Rules, Recommendation Rec(2006)2, Adopted by the Committee of Ministers on 11 January 2006 at the 952nd meeting of the Ministers' Deputies.

[20] See also Zoummeroff/Guibert, *La Prison ça n'arrive pas qu'aux autres*, 2006, p. 89.

that is characterized by a relatively repressive criminal policy burdens the penitentiary system in Luxembourg. Nevertheless, there are also home made problems to be overcome. There are three essential points that have to be taken into consideration, if the situation of the penitentiary institutions in Luxembourg as such and the situation of foreign prisoners in particular are to be improved:

- first, the penitentiary institution must gain the central interest of European and domestic politics. The political system has to be aware of the fact that security should not be a one-sided concept of technical security, but it should mean a differentiated system of administrative, cooperative and social security. Such a concept might be much more effective in avoiding problems of internal organization of a penitentiary institution;
- secondly, this security concept demands a reform of the internal structure of the penitentiary institution in Luxembourg. In order to build up a well-structured hierarchy it will be necessary to get new qualified staff and to further qualify the existing staff. Thus, the existing social facilities can be more effectively used for practical concepts of re-integration;
- finally the penitentiary institution has to be freed from the repressive demands of the criminal justice system. We have to strengthen the concepts of alternatives to detention. This concerns both the execution of a sentence and pre-trial detention. Implementing alternative measures to pre-trial detention, as provided in the Law of March 6th 2006, is a step in the right direction. It must now be efficiently implemented in judicial practice with advantages given to domestic people and foreigners.

Chapter 18

Malta

Tonio Cachia
Mark F. Montebello

1 INTRODUCTION

1.1 Overview of Penalties and Measures

The main criminal law statute in Malta, the 'Criminal Code',[1] prescribes both criminal offences, distinguishing between crimes and minor offences,[2] as well as the relative penalties and sanctions. In the case of deprivation of liberty as punishment, the *Prisons Act*[3] and its subsidiary *Prisons Regulations*[4] regulate the conditions of detention. According to the Criminal Code and the Prisons Act, a person may be deprived of liberty in criminal matters in three specified circumstances. These are imprisonment as punishment for crimes (serious offences), detention for minor offences as well as arrest, whether as pre-trial detention or pending extradition proceedings. Pre-trial detention in prison entails the deprivation of liberty after a person has been arraigned in Court, in accordance with Article 5 ECHR.[5] The maximum punishment that may be handed in Malta is 'imprisonment for life',[6] literally translated into imprisonment for one's natural life, until death. The highest definite punishment of imprisonment is for a maximum of 35 years.[7] In the serious drug trafficking cases, a sentence of imprisonment may be accompanied with a fine, which if not fully paid, is converted into a further period of imprisonment of not more than two years. In the case of foreigners, a removal order,[8] effective at the end of the term in prison is usually also handed down. Moreover, whilst still in prison, the punishment of solitary confinement is awardable both as an internal disciplinary measure,[9] as well as by the Criminal Court as a further punishment.[10] The only form of 'early release' available is remission of one-third of the sentence for good behaviour, and this is not applicable for lifers.[11] Hence, in the absence of parole, the only possible exception for lifers to be ever released is the prerogative of mercy (pardon) that may be awarded by the Head of State,[12] on the 'advice' of the Government.

All prisoners deprived of their liberty under criminal law are detained in a single complex, the Corradino Prison, or as it is better known by perhaps the misnomer, Corradino Correctional Facility. Originally built in the mid-nineteenth century, its 150-year old divisions still host the majority of inmates. The addition of a new block in 2003 has taken the full capacity to over 400 cells.[13] The strict one prisoner per cell policy makes Corradino Prison one of the few, if there are any other, prisons in Europe where overcrowding is not an issue. Foreign prisoners are detained in the same prison with Maltese

---

[1] *Criminal Code*, Chapter 9 of the Laws of Malta.
[2] In Maltese Law defined as 'contraventions.' Art.2 Criminal Code.
[3] *Prisons Act* 1976, Chapter 260 of the Laws of Malta.
[4] *Prisons Regulations* 1995, S.L.260.03, L.N. 118 of 1995.
[5] Art. 355AJ(3) Criminal Code; A person cannot be detained for more than 48 hours in police custody without being arraigned in court.
[6] Art. 17 & 31 Criminal Code.
[7] A grade lower than life imprisonment is 30 years (Art.31 Criminal Code), but 35 years is applicable in case of concurrency of offences and 'temporary' punishments. (Art.17 Criminal Code).
[8] Art.5(2d), *Immigration Act*, Chapter 217 of the Laws of Malta.
[9] Reg.71 *Prisons Regulations*.
[10] Art.9 Criminal Code.
[11] Reg. 61 Prisons Regulations.
[12] The President of the Republic, under Art. 93 of the Constitution of Malta.
[13] CPT Report to the Maltese Government 2001, (CPT/Inf (2002-16) 27 August 2002, p.20.

inmates. There is no distinction or difference in treatment whatsoever. Apart from this facility, there are another three institutions still considered part of the prison, but are kept separate due to their nature.[14] These are a ward at the general hospital, a Forensic Unit for prisoners with psychiatric problems at the mental health hospital, and a drug and alcohol addiction rehabilitation facility. The mental health facility is the most commonly used by prisoners, irrespective of sex, status or nationality.

One of the major deficiencies is that, with the exception of the absolute segregation of men from women,[15] there is still no comprehensive classification policy. Young men under the age of 21 should be held in a separate part of the prison.[16] In practice even young men up to the age of 26 are held in this special section. This is quite a doubtful practice when considering that at times this same section hosts children under the age of 16.[17] Meanwhile, it is not so uncommon to encounter 20 year olds detained with adult males. In the case of females it is theoretically worse, as the existence of only one division entails that young women, even under the age of 18, are to be imprisoned with the rest. The only other form of classification exists for security considerations, including two special security divisions segregated from the other parts of the prison. Unfortunately, there is no formal distinction between pre-trial and convicted inmates, or between first time offenders and hardened criminals. It is very likely that one finds a person who has never been in prison before, probably detained for just a few days for some minor offence held in the same division with prisoners convicted of serious crimes, and having been in prison for years.

1.2 Overview of the Prison System

1.2.1. Organisational Structure

The Ministry for Justice and Home Affairs is responsible for 'correctional services', including the prisons. Until 2003, when Justice and Home Affairs were separate ministries, the prisons were part of the 'Home Affairs' portfolio. In fact, they are highly deemed as such as the prominent police influence in prison demonstrates. The Department of Correctional Services is run by a core group of high-ranking police officers, officially on leave of service. The ground personnel are made up of around 300 prison officers and a few police officers on secondment duty. In addition there is the Special Response Team (SRT), a small team of prison and police officers responsible for the maintenance of security and risk management. It is clear that the role and influence of the police in the Maltese prison is moulded in the dynamics of the system. The prison officers, trained and prepared to work appropriately in prison, are administered and controlled by police officers who have been trained otherwise. It is worthwhile to note that in all its visits to Malta the CPT reiterated the importance of entrusting the custody of prisoners to a single team of 'professionally trained prison staff.'[18]

---

[14] *Designation of Places As Prisons Order*, S.L.260.02, L.N. 29 of 2000.
[15] Art.4(3) Prisons Act, Reg. 12 Prisons Regulations, Female Division still part of Corradino Prison.
[16] Reg.12(1) Prisons Regulations, Young Offenders Unit Rehabilitation Services (YOURS).
[17] PQ 9582, 10 Dec 2004 (Leg X S207). Dec 2004 - 4 under 16; Feb 2005 - 1 under 16.
[18] CPT Report 2001 (n 13) p.26.

The Prison Board[19] is vested with the responsibility of acting as the primary supervisory mechanism for the treatment of prisoners. It is obliged to tackle and redress complaints of prisoners. Its role is both of a watchdog as well as an advisory board to the Minister. Any prisoner may request to be interviewed by the Board or the Director in absolute confidentiality. Prisoners may also make a request or complaint to the Minister, petition the President of Malta, or an internationally recognised human rights body, under 'confidential cover'.[20] This list does not include the Parliamentary Ombudsman. Notwithstanding this exclusion, whenever complaints or requests to the Director or the Board prove futile, prisoners resort regularly to the Ombudsman.[21] One of the most important reports of the Office regarded a complaint by four foreign prisoners about the way they were treated during disciplinary proceedings after absconding from prison.[22] The most authoritative and reliable monitoring mechanism is performed by the *Committee Against Torture* (CPT)[23] of the Council of Europe. The CPT visited the Maltese prison and detention facilities in 1990, 1995 and 2001.[24] The Council of Europe's Commissioner for Human Rights has also visited the prison in 2003. Nevertheless, these monitoring mechanisms are not very effective in that, following the so-called dialogue model with the State, they neither have the power of implementing, nor of redressing individual petitions. However, their reports enjoy considerable authority and moral conviction.

1.2.2 Foreign Prisoners

There are no proper statistics available on prisoners in Malta. Information emanates exclusively from parliamentary questions (PQs) and is delivered randomly varying in data provided. This is compiled by the prison authorities themselves, thus it is not scientifically collected or assessed, but nevertheless may provide several interesting indicators. The number of prisoners in Malta has been increasing gradually over the last decade, with a considerable increase in 1997. Whereas in 1992 the number of prisoners was 169, on 18 November 2005 the number was 308. [25] The average prison population per annum from 2001 to 2004 was as follows: 2001 (255), 2002 (277), 2003 (281), 2004 (277). [26] The rate of prisoners has gone up from 47 per 100,000 of the national population [27] in 1992 to 75 (per 100,000) in 2005, [28] and is increasing again in 2006.

The latest statistics on the number of foreign prisoners show 89 out of 292, or 31%, on 14 December 2005. The average number of foreign prisoners stood, at least since the

---

19   Reg.104-116, Part IV Prisons Regulations.
20   Reg. 17-18 Prisons Regulations.
21   Ombudsman Act 1995, Chapter 385 of the Laws of Malta.
22   Report on '*Corradino Correctional Facility Alleged Inhuman Treatment and Violation of Human Rights*', Ombudsman Annual Report 2000.
23   Malta ratified the 'European Convention For The Prevention Of Torture And Inhuman Or Degrading Treatment or Punishment' on 07/03/1988, In Force 01/02/1989.
24   In its last visits in 2003 & 2004 the CPT focused on the treatment of detained asylum seekers.
25   PQ 15778, 17 Jan 2006 (Leg X, S341).
26   PQ 13190, 15/06/2005 (Leg X, S282).
27   Population 404,000, National Statistics Office (Malta), *Census of Population & Housing 2005*, Preliminary Report 26 April 2006, p.xviii.
28   International Standard to Calculate Rate of Imprisonment is Rate per 100,000 of national population year/Rate per 100,000: 1992 (47); 1995 (53); 1998 (69); 2001(65); Source ICPS; 2005 (Rate fluctuating between 70-75).

early nineties, at around 30% of the prison population. In the case of males 29% are foreign, whilst 53% of female prisoners are not Maltese.[29] These figures must be compared with the 2.8% of foreigners residing in Malta.[30] From nine inmates imprisoned for life, two are Tunisian. It also remains to be seen whether EU membership (1 May 2004), and eventually Schengen membership will have any effect on the foreign prisoner population in Malta, such as an increase the proportion of foreign prisoners coming from the EU. There is no official distinction between foreigners who are resident in Malta and others. More than half are Libyan (51%), whereas 28% are European (18% EU).[31] The overrepresentation of Libyans is due to the geographical proximity of Libya and Malta, and the close ties between the two countries in the late seventies and early eighties. Moreover, during the UN sanctions, Malta was the first possible port of call for Libyans travelling to the West. The main indication is that the ratio of European to non-European inmates is 1:3, thus around three quarters of foreign prisoners in Malta are non-European. The nationality is determined based on the official citizenship of the prisoners, and not essentially their country of origin. It is quite common to encounter prisoners of non-European origin who have acquired a *European* passport, i.e. an Italian, Spanish, British, or Dutch passport, amongst others. It is also interesting to compare the number of pre-trial prisoners to those convicted.[32] In April 2005, the ratio stood at around 1:3. One of every four is awaiting trial. This result is not so straightforward, as there are an undisclosed number of convicted prisoners awaiting trial for other offences.[33] Data up to August 2004 illustrates that whereas a 1:2 – 1:3 ratio may stand for Maltese prisoners, in the case of foreigners this is close to 1:1.[34] The main reason is that the Courts are not ready to grant bail to foreigners, in fear that they will flee the island.

1.3 Overview Involvement Consulates, Embassies, Ministries Home Country, Probation Service Home Country and NGO's.

The involvement of the diplomatic channels is satisfactory for those prisoners whose country is represented in Malta. However, one should not expect too much involvement at this level, given that consular representation has other priorities. Yet, given the relatively high number of Libyan prisoners in Malta, the Libyan consular presence is very prominent in Corradino Prison. Embassy representatives regularly visit prisoners, at times even assisting other Arab inmates. This presence is also due to the bilateral transfer agreement between the two countries for the transfer of sentenced persons.[35]

Several missions responsible for relations with Malta are based in Rome, thus creating particular barriers such as the difficulty to encounter the prisoners personally. The situation is less clear for those inmates whose country is not represented in Malta. This is mainly affecting Sub-Saharan inmates, but not just them. It is only in the case of EU citi-

---

[29]   Source MDD (Daritama), December 2005.
[30]   11,000 (or 2.8%) of the Maltese population are foreigners Source: National Statistics Office (NSO), Malta, December 2004.
[31]   Source MDD (Daritama), December 2005.
[32]   PQ 11648, 02 May 2005 (Leg X, S261).
[33]   PQ 35711, 08 Oct 2002 (Leg IX S795).
[34]   PQ 18791, 18 Sep 2000 (Leg IX S363) & PQ 6997, 28 Sep 2004 (Leg X, S165).
[35]   Agreement between the Government of Malta and the Great Socialist People's Libyan Arab Jamahariya on the Transfer of Sentenced Persons' Libya 14th October 1994, in force 1995. vide p.8.

zens that the home Probation Service or its equivalent is actively involved. There is a continuous monitoring and exchange of information where necessary. However, this is more a measure of keeping in touch rather than effectively improving the situation of foreign prisoners in Malta. The main deficiency is the lack of knowledge, even by the home country organs, of the Maltese legal system and its application in penal matters.

There is a felt need for a joint and combined effort involving the home country organs and local institutions in enhancing the effectiveness of such initiatives. The primary drawback is that the local Probation is not entrusted with any official function nor does it offer any services in prison. This service is exclusively offered at NGO level, focused on exchange of information, pressure on the authorities and moral and material assistance to foreign prisoners. The only NGO that operates at this level and is working with prisoners in Malta is *Mid-Dlam Ghad-Dawl* (MDD).[36] It is a lay non-profit organisation, run on a voluntary basis, monitoring the treatment of prisoners in Malta, at least on a weekly basis, seeking to promote the welfare and well being of all prisoners. It is also a point of reference for embassies and foreign Probation Services, dealing with their nationals imprisoned in Malta. On ground level it is approached by a large number of destitute prisoners, most of who are foreign, for the procurement of basic needs. A large number of other groups and NGO's present in the Maltese prison, such as Prison Fellowship Malta, tend to profess a more religious ministry.

1.4. Overview of Trends

1.4.1. Sentencing Trends

An analysis of data showing how long prisoners have been deprived of their freedom reflects the average length of sentences effectively being handed down. In September 2005,[37] this stood at:

Table 1

32%	Less than 6 months
13%	6 months – 1 year
20%	1 – 2 years
17%	2-4 years
8%	4-6 years
6%	6-10 years
3%	Over 10 years

The trend is likely to shift higher in the next decade, with the ever-increasing number of long term and life prisoners. Moreover in 1996 the maximum term of definite imprisonment increased from 25 to 35 years.[38] This has triggered harsher sentences, whilst at the same time pardons are hardly given. The punishment for drug trafficking has been in-

---

36   *Mid-Dlam Ghad-Dawl* (From Darkness to Light), Note: author represents this NGO.
37   PQ 14580, 28 Sep 2005 (LegX. Papers Laid).
38   Amendment to Art. 17 & 31 Criminal Code, by Act XVI of 1996.

creased to a maximum of life imprisonment[39]; so longer sentences are being handed down in these cases as well. One must bear in mind the restrictive interpretation of trafficking in Maltese criminal law, whereby the simple act of 'sharing' is not acknowledged and qualifies as trafficking. Although this will be amended in the near future it is very much instigating severe prison sentences. Moreover, unpaid fines and court expenses are being more commonly converted into imprisonment of up to two years. In 2005, the highest three types of offences for which persons were convicted or detained pending trial, were drugs-related offences, theft, and conversion of fines and court expenses into terms of imprisonment.[40]

1.4.2 Characteristics Foreign Prison Population

The only available data in respect of foreign prisoners is that dealing with 94 foreign convictions between January 2003 and May 2004. These shifted more towards drug related offences, with 30%, followed by 15% on theft, and 14% on fines and expenses, amongst others.[41] Although this data is not scientifically collected one may observe a higher incidence of drug related trafficking offences, especially of importation, in the case of foreigners. This is very much so in the case of female prisoners generally used as mules in drug importation schemes.

Furthermore, once convicted, foreign prisoners are generally handed much longer prison sentences and heftier fines than their Maltese counterparts, even for identical offences. This is also caused by the general lack of understanding of proceedings by foreigners in the Maltese criminal justice system, especially where they do not understand English properly, or are provided inadequate interpretation. This occurs at all levels, from the early stages of investigation involving self-incriminating statements, and all the way to the actual trial, where the quality of legal aid available is unacceptable, prejudicing the right to defend oneself properly. Moreover, before 2002, the period of arrest spent by foreigners was rarely deducted from the sentence handed on conviction. This means that most, if not all, foreign prisoners held in Malta, sentenced before 2002,[42] are actually serving a longer time in prison than that for which they were actually convicted. In this respect one must take into consideration that the only possible early release system in Malta is the remission of one-third of the sentence for good behaviour, which is inapplicable for lifers. [43] There is no parole system, which would not only offer a better incentive for prisoners to be released early, but would abet more properly the social rehabilitation of inmates. The plea to introduce parole in Malta, for all prisoners, including lifers has been made by a number of lawyers and MPs over the last few years. In 2006, a national conference organised by the NGO *Mid-Dlam Ghad-Dawl*, witnessed a general compromise between the stakeholders, including the politicians and the prison service, amongst others, to start seriously considering the introduction of a form of conditional release in Malta. However, it seems that pressure and impetus from the EU would be highly effective in this respect to overcome the lethargy of Maltese policy makers.

---

[39] Art. 120A, *Medical and Kindred Professions Ordinance*, Chapter 31 of the Laws of Malta.
[40] PQ 15778, 17 Jan 2006 (LegX S341).
[41] PQ 5601, 18 May 2004 (LegX S131).
[42] Article 22 of the Criminal Code amended in 2002 after being challenged under Art.5 of the ECHR.
[43] Reg. 14(4) Prisons Regulations.

1.5 Overview of National Legislation

1.5.1. Penitentiary legislation

The Criminal Code, being the main criminal law statute in Malta, includes both substance (crimes and punishments) as well as procedure. It is supplemented by other acts of legislation appropriate for particular circumstances. Therefore, in the case of drug offences, the special 'Dangerous Drugs Ordinance'[44] and 'Medical and Kindred Professions Ordinance'[45], supplement the Criminal Code in determining the crime and the relative punishments. The ancient 'Punishments (Interpretation) Ordinance'[46] abets the interpretation and application of all punishments, whether derivative of the Code or otherwise. The 'Probation Act'[47]deals exclusively with alternative sanctions including, not only as the title denotes, probation orders, but also community service orders or a combination of both as well as conditional discharge. These measures are still very much not resorted to by the Courts in the case of foreigners, even those who are residing in Malta and/or not subject to a removal order. Alternative sentencing in Malta appears to be deemed as tailored more appropriately for the reintegration of the Maltese in their own community.

The general and enabling 'Prisons Act' and its subsidiary 'Regulations' regulate detention in prison whether after conviction or still awaiting trial. The latter are substantially based on the old 'European Prison Rules' (1987), and the now abrogated 'Prison Rules for England & Wales' (1964) as amended up till 1992. Notwithstanding the great detail of the Regulations, they still vest too much discretion in the hands of the Minister and the Director of Prisons. This is permitting the use of a plethora of Ministerial directives and internal rules, more of policy rather than detail. Strangely enough, these 'internal rules' on the interpretation and proper application of the Regulations are not publicly available. They are not even disseminated to the prisoners in their exact form but transposed by word of mouth. This very much reaffirms the notion of prison regulations as being nothing more than *'rubber-tamp'*

1.5.2 Penitentiary Legislation and Foreigners

As legislation, neither the 'Prisons Act' nor the 'Regulations' sufficiently affect the status of foreign prisoners. The 'Immigration Act' empowers the Criminal Court to declare the convicted foreigner as a 'prohibited immigrant' authorising the issue of a 'removal order' from Malta[48] taking effect immediately upon having served the punishment of imprisonment. The problem is that the removal order is being given at sentencing stage thus conditioning the whole span of one's stay in prison. It would appear more appropriate if the removal order is considered closer to the date of release. This would enable a fairer assessment of whether the foreigner is still a threat to public health, order or security. The removal order means nothing less than a label that the convicted foreigner will remain a danger to Maltese society and may never be rehabilitated. This policy should be at least

---

44 Dangerous Drugs Ordinance, Chapter 101 of the Laws of Malta.
45 Medical and Kindred Professions Ordinance, Chapter 31 of the Laws of Malta.
46 Punishments (Interpretation) Ordinance, Chapter 23 of the Laws of Malta.
47 Probation Act 2003, Chapter 446 of the Laws of Malta.
48 Art.5(2) & 15 Immigration Act.

reappraised at EU level, bearing in mind the all-embracing notion of EU citizenship and free movement rights.

The 'Prisons Regulations' refer minimally to foreign prisoners. Regulation 57, entitled 'foreign prisoners', emphasises the importance of and defines the relationship with the consular representatives. They also have the right of being informed of any transfer possibilities between Malta and the home country.[49] Foreign prisoners whose country have a 'treaty or arrangement' with Malta regarding the transfer of sentenced persons, are informed of this possibility on admission to prison.[50] Malta ratified the *European Convention on the Transfer of Sentenced Persons* (1983) in 1991 and the additional Protocol (1998) in 2003. It has also concluded bilateral agreements on the same lines with Libya (1994)[51] and Egypt (2001),[52] whilst a similar agreement with Morocco is still pending.

Although there have been various foreign prisoners detained in Malta who have formally lodged an application to benefit from the 1983 Convention, it was only in May 2006 that it was resorted to successfully for the first time when an Italian prisoner was transferred to serve the rest of the sentence in Italy. Meanwhile, in 1994 a Maltese citizen sentenced and imprisoned in Sweden was brought to serve the remainder of his sentence in Malta.[53] The difficulty for foreigners imprisoned in Malta is that the Maltese authorities insist that the prisoner, once transferred must spend the rest of the minimum time possible before release in Malta, in the state where he is transferred. The position taken by the Maltese Government in principle consents to the transfer provided that Article 10 of the Convention (continued enforcement of the sentence) is executed. The prisoner should serve the minimum term remaining in Malta in the country of destination as well. For this reason rendering transfers from Malta to other European countries, are very difficult to conclude. Prison sentences in Malta by far exceed the maximum sentences for such offences in these countries and the absence of parole in Malta or of any other form of early release renders it less likely to happen.

The most useful prisoner transfer treaty is proving to be the bilateral agreement concluded with Libya in 1994. In view of the significantly high number of Libyan prisoners it was a priority to transfer as many prisoners as possible. Transfers to Libya have occurred gradually over the past years, but still have not reached the desired levels, mostly due to bureaucratic reasons. The most recent group of transfers occurred towards the end of 2005.

---

[49] Reg.16 Prisons Regulations.

[50] Reg. 16(2) Prisons Regulations.

[51] *'Agreement between the Government of Malta and the Great Socialist People's Libyan Arab Jamahariya on the Transfer of Sentenced Persons'* Libya 14th October 1994, in force 1995.

[52] Agreement between the Government of Malta and the Government of the Arab Republic of Egypt on the Transfer of Sentenced Persons (2001).

[56] Prisons Amendment Bill (Second Reading Leg IX, S63 15th February 1999) p.123.

2 TREATMENT OF FOREIGN PRISONERS

2.1 General

In the last report commissioned by the government on prisons in Malta, in 1993, the now retired judge Caruana Curran had called for a serious study on foreign prisoners, highly concerned that they made up one-third of the prison population.[54] More than a decade later, there is still not enough awareness of the severe drawbacks faced by these persons, deprived of their liberty outside their home country. The treatment of foreign prisoners in Malta does not, at face value, vary from that of their local counterparts. They are not generally discriminated against or victimised by the prison service. However, more often than not, they have to submit to diverse and at times disadvantaged treatment solely due to their status. The fewer their numbers are, the more isolated they tend to become. The strong Libyan (and Arab) presence in the Maltese prison decreases the possibility that these groups of prisoners feel marginalized. This is not the case with other foreigners, who have just a few other compatriots, or are completely alone in prison. They find it much harder to integrate and their sense of loneliness and isolation is evident. Nevertheless, the most negative and undoubtedly discriminatory treatment against foreigners is the denial of rehabilitation opportunities for those subject to a removal order.

2.2 Living Conditions and Facilities

Maltese and foreign prisoners, without any distinction, share the same facilities and enjoy the same living conditions. Although on the whole, there is always room for improvement; the material conditions of the prison in Malta are on the whole acceptable. The detention of prisoners in some 'better' parts rather than in others is solely based on security considerations. Moreover, certain foreign prisoners are grouped together in certain divisions to facilitate their integration and decrease the risk of isolation.

Each person admitted in prison in Malta is supposed to be given a so-called kit of personal requirements, including hygiene necessities and, if necessary, clothes. Unfortunately this is neither provided to Maltese nor to foreign prisoners. However, whilst Maltese prisoners may receive such personal belongings from their families, this is not the case for foreigners. They are forced to borrow such basic necessities from other prisoners, or receive them from NGOs and other groups that provide material and financial assistance to a considerable number of destitute prisoners.

2.3 Reception and Admission

Reception is considered as one of the most delicate phases of imprisonment. Therefore, it is essential that there is a proper understanding by all prisoners of what is actually happening. All prisoners, including foreigners, have the right to inform their families or close relatives, but they may also refuse to do so. Prisoners who are not yet sentenced are assisted in contacting a lawyer or in applying for legal aid, if they so wish.[55] Foreigners are

---

[57] Caruana Curran M, *Report on Corradino Prison*, Commissioner for Prisons and Treatment of Offenders, June 1993, pp.5-6.
[55] Reg.5 Prisons Regulations.

informed of their right to get in touch with their embassies or consular representatives.[56] Problems arise in the case of prisoners who are nationals of States having no diplomatic relationship with Malta, or come from countries without proper governments.

2.4 Work – Education – Training – Sports – Recreation

Theoretically, foreign prisoners are to follow the same regime as all other prisoners. Thus, they should be able to work and participate in educational and vocational training, classes, sports and recreational activities. In practice, the situation is much different. It should be noted that in this respect there is no work, education or other activities for all prisoners, including Maltese. In case of activities these are organised unprofessionally for all prisoners, but all inmates can use what is available indiscriminately. The education system is not up to standard but it is accessible for all foreign prisoners knowing the English language. However, there is the problem of Maltese not knowing English. In fact, the Arabs due to proximity of the two languages as easily comprehend most lessons in Maltese. The library books are quite outdated, and so is the computer room. The education system is more successful with those Maltese wanting to pursue further studies in the national education system. In the case of work, it is a known fact that there is not sufficient work for all inmates.[57] In April 2005, 191 out of 279, or 68% of prisoners did some form of work.[58] It appears that a large number of foreigners benefit from work given by the prison as well as work provided by private entities. A case in point is that of a private entrepreneur who procures work for Arabs only, discriminating against all the rest.

2.5 Food – Religion – Personal Hygiene – Medical Care

The prison environment in itself facilitates the spread of certain health risks. In 2001 the CPT reported that 65% of inmates in Corradino Prison suffered from hepatitis C whilst 60% had drug related problems.[59] These bring about particularly serious health challenges that require constant monitoring and attention. Apart from the prison medical service, prisoners have full access to the services provided by health centres and the general hospital. Although health care in Malta is free for Maltese citizens and foreigners generally have to pay, this is not the case with foreign prisoners, who are treated equally like Maltese citizens in receiving health care for free. In the case of particular health requisites not provided efficiently by the health service, foreign prisoners, generally with the help of NGOs, make up for these expenses themselves.

On admission every prisoner must declare his religion, and 'as far as practicable', is to be allowed to satisfy his religious needs, by attending services and meetings provided in prison, and is also permitted to have in possession any necessary books or literature.[60] The population in Corradino Prison may be considered to be about 70% 'officially' Christian, mostly Roman Catholic and 30% Muslim. Therefore, the respect for ethnic minorities is paramount in Corradino Prison, especially in the presence of a strong Arab community. Occasionally there are inmates from other denominations. There is both a

---

[56]   Reg.57 Prisons Regulations.
[57]   PQ 8428, 17 Dec 2004 (Leg X S215).
[58]   PQ 11838, 03 May 2005 (Leg X S262).
[59]   CPT Report 2001 (n 13) pp.23-24.
[60]   Reg. 40-41, Prisons Regulations.

Chapel as well as Mosque. The presence of the Imam as religious representative is playing an important role in the case of Muslim foreign prisoners. He is allowed to hold regular services and activities and pay pastoral visits in private to prisoners of his religion, at times fixed and agreed with the Director.[61] Arrangements are also made so as not to require prisoners to do unnecessary work on their recognised days of religious observance.[62] Muslims also have the full opportunity of fulfilling their special dietary requirements, even during the Ramadan period. The only criticism in this respect is that prisoners, of all religious denominations, detained in special security divisions are not permitted to attend religious services.

2.6 Legal Help

It is fundamental that prisoners know the 'rules' governing this new environment. Although there is a prison information book in Maltese and English this is not appropriate for the large numbers of Arab prisoners and other foreign prisoners unable to understand these languages. A few years ago, a copy of the prison information booklet and the health and drug awareness booklet,[63] were translated into Arabic, though they presently seem to be unavailable. It is a serious deficiency that prisoners, especially foreigners, are put in the impossible situation of being obliged to observe rules and perform duties they are not informed of. Likewise, they have little knowledge or awareness of their rights. The right for legal assistance, where applicable, in the form of legal aid, also has a very high relevance in the case of foreign prisoners awaiting trial. The problem in this respect appears to be one of quality. Whether paid legal assistance, or state provided legal aid, there is a general feeling amongst foreign prisoners that they are not getting enough information about their case. Lawyers fail to appreciate that unlike most Maltese prisoners, these persons do not have any relatives outside prison to follow up and monitor their case. NGOs are sometimes involved in establishing contact between the foreign prisoners and their lawyers and in obtaining some basic information.

2.7 Contact with the outside world

Communication in prison is fundamental at two levels: internal communication with other prisoners and staff as well as communication with the outside world. As already remarked, the language barrier may prove to be a very difficult hurdle in prison life. The case of a female Chinese prisoner demonstrates this point. The supervisor of the female section stated in open Court that 'there is a problem with communication and this prisoner 'cannot voice her needs.[64] Forced isolation due to the inability to communicate is a very serious concern in an environment when the person is totally dependent on others for almost everything. A prisoner can never be socially rehabilitated, if he does not experience a proper 'social life' inside. This is very much tied to the importance of communication with the outside world. Usually families of foreign prisoners are not resident in Malta and thus telephone communication is essential. They have ample time to call

---

[61] Reg. 43, Prisons Regulations.
[62] Reg. 44, Prisons Regulations.
[63] Interim Reply CPT 2001 (n 58) p.15-16.
[64] Times of Malta; (Allied Newspapers Ltd. www.timesofmalta.com)14th April 2005.

home, even more than once daily, as long as they have the financial means to do so. In the case of written correspondence there is the problem of delays due to the systematic reading of all prisoner correspondence. The CPT in 1995, and again in 2001 recommended to the authorities that 'it would be preferable to provide that, save in exceptional cases letters, may only be examined (rather than read) by prison staff.'[65] In the case of visits by families of foreigners in Malta, the normal visitation rules are not applied rigidly. Whilst Maltese prisoners enjoy a contact visit once or twice a week, in these circumstances foreign prisoners are given a daily contact visit with their relatives.

2.8 Reintegration Activities – Prison Leave

Pre-release work in the form of prison leave is available 'during the period commencing three months before the date on which a prisoner may be finally released in order to enable the prisoner to engage in employment, or receive instruction or training or to otherwise assist him in the transition from prison life.'[66] According to the Minister for Justice and Home Affairs, this is restricted to prisoners serving a sentence of not less than two years. The policy of the Government is that, 'in principle' foreign prisoners do have the same opportunities as Maltese prisoners in attending drug rehabilitation programmes. However, such requests by foreign inmates are 'treated cautiously since in reality the risk of escape is higher so as to avoid expulsion at the termination of their sentence.' It must be noted that 'foreign inmates married to Maltese citizens, or those not to be deported upon termination of their sentence,' can benefit from all opportunities.[67] Yet, in practice, as in the case of rehabilitation, even foreigners not subject to an expulsion order are being denied this facility. It demonstrates that the simple fact of being a foreigner it invokes an automatic discrimination, even against those who may qualify for a work permit in Malta. This is a form of indirect discrimination surely not in the spirit of the CPT, EPR and ECHR. Whilst the conditions of imprisonment are more or less equal to everyone, most foreigners have diluted opportunities in aspiring for a better future.

2.9 Release – Expulsion

The release procedure depends on whether the foreign prisoner is subject to a removal order or not. If the prisoner is not subject to a removal order, he is treated like any other Maltese inmate, by simply being accompanied to the prison gates, where hopefully someone will be ready to receive him. The responsibility of the prison service ends at the prison gates. In case of a removal order, on the termination of the sentence, the foreign prisoner is taken to the embassy pending return to the home country. If removal from Malta is not possible on the termination of sentence, the prisoner may have to stay further in prison until the removal can be executed. It must also be noted that a removal order may in any case after release be issued by the Chief Immigration Officer, who is also the Commissioner of Police, for irregular stay in Malta. Although this possibility is taken into consideration, it is nevertheless a possibility and does not hinder the inmate in as much the removal order handed with the sentence. The problem with the sentencing re-

---

[65] CPT Report 2001 (n 13) pp.30-31.
[66] Reg. 62(1f) Prisons Regulations.
[67] Interim Reply CPT 2001(n 58) p.16.

moval order is that it is unjustly depriving foreigners in Malta of benefiting from opportunities such as prison leave, pre-release work, drug-rehabilitation programmes and all other opportunities that entail taking the inmate outside prison, the only exception being on medical grounds.

2.10 Aftercare – Probation

The 'Prisons Regulations'[68] specify that, from the beginning of a prisoner's sentence, consideration shall be given in consultation with the social welfare service authorities, and any 'appropriate aftercare organisation approved by the Minister, to the prisoner's future and the assistance to be given on and after his release. The representatives of these welfare services and organisations are afforded 'reasonable' access to the prison and the prisoners in preparation for the release and aftercare of prisoners. Whilst this is wholly unavailable for foreign prisoners subject to an expulsion order, there are no alternatives for them in this respect. Hence, the inherent contradiction that imprisonment should be immediately geared towards release in community, with foreign prisoners deemed not part of this community, and not thus geared towards release as such.

Prisoners following a drug rehabilitation programme are offered the facility to benefit from follow-up sessions, but this is hardly resorted to.[69] Any prisoner may also avail to continue receiving any medical care that was taken in prison, 'through the medical services available without charge to the community outside prison.'[70] This is obviously unavailable for foreign prisoners subject to an expulsion order. However, it is not known what kind of treatment, assistance or aftercare these inmates are given on their return to their home country. If they had been receiving any kind of medical treatment, including against drug addiction, it would be a pity if this were simply discontinued once the inmate returns to the home country. At least the EU should take this matter into consideration, and ensure that removal orders exercised within EU territory would not deny any EU citizen proper treatment and opportunities to ensure social rehabilitation.

2.11 – 2.12 Staff/Projects

The prison officers do not receive specialised training to foresee the special requirements of foreign prisoners. They are naturally conversant in Maltese, and most of them in English. Otherwise, foreign prisoners not understanding these languages have to rely on makeshift translations even through other prisoners. This dilutes considerably the level of communication required reflecting the lack of any foreign prisoner policy. The large numbers of Arab inmates led to the appointment of an Egyptian assistant manager in order to understand the needs of these foreign inmates better. For this same reason, at the request of the CPT in 2001, a member of the Prison Board practising the Muslim religion was appointed in 2002.[71] Without any explanation they were not confirmed or reappointed in subsequent years. There are no specific projects or courses aimed at this considerable part of the prison population, neither inside nor outside penitentiary

---

[68] Ibidem
[69] PQ 10182, 27 Jan 2005 (Leg X S226).
[70] Reg. 62 Prisons Regulations.
[71] Interim Reply by the government to CPT 2001 ((CPT/Inf (2002-17) – 27 Aug 2002, p.18.

institutions. Unfortunately, it must be noted that the prison bureaucracy is proving to be a serious barrier for NGOs at the forefront of improving the well being of prisoners, including foreign prisoners.

3 ADMINISTRATIVE DETENTION OF FOREIGN PRISONERS

3.1 – 3.3 Institutions, Responsible Ministry, Capacity, Numbers[72]

In Malta, foreign persons detained under immigration legislation are considered to be illegal, irregular or clandestine immigrants rather than prisoners. Legally, and also administratively, asylum seekers and other migrants are distinguished from prisoners detained under criminal law. Yet the term prisoners would not be so out of place given that they are detained in a 'prison-like environment'.[73] They are not detained with prisoners subject to criminal law, but in detention centres under the co-responsibility of the army and the police. The army falls under the portfolio of the Office of the Prime Minister, whilst the Police are part of the Ministry of Justice and Home Affairs. In order to overcome this inter-ministerial responsibility, it was deemed more appropriate to have a single authority, headed by an army colonel administering the six closed centres.

The situation of these immigrants in Malta is very particular if not unique. Since the turn of the millennium the island has witnessed a considerable influx of asylum seekers coming mostly from the sub-Saharan region, mainly from Sudan, Eritrea, Côte d'Ivoire, Ethiopia, Nigeria and Somalia.[74] Whereas at the end of 2004 the number of persons in the closed detention centres was 620,[75] towards the end of 2005, an average of 1500 asylum seekers were detained daily, pending the outcome of their asylum application, or else repatriation.[76] Towards the end of March 2006 the number had gone down to 1017 people in detention.[77] This one-third decrease, when compared to a few weeks before is due to the fact that most 'trips of hope' peak in Spring-Summer due to the favourable weather conditions. This is quite an unusual situation where at its peak there are five times more people detained under immigration law than under criminal law in Malta. Moreover, it is 16 times more the number of foreigners detained in prison under criminal law. In the Maltese context it is a very complex issue requiring a serious study at all levels on its own. It is a deeply concerning problem, bearing in mind that Malta, with 404,000 people[78] already has a population density of 1,282 residents per square kilometre, which is by far the

---

[72] For a detailed discussion on the situation of asylum seekers in Malta, see: Mifsud Stefania, *Detention of Asylum Seekers in Malta*, University of Malta (unpublished) LL.D 2005.

[73] CPT Report to the Maltese Government 2004, (CPT/Inf (2005-15) 25 August 2005, p.13

[74] European Parliament, Civil Liberties, Justice & Home Affairs Committee (LIBE), *Report by the LIBE Committee Delegation on its visit to the administrative detention centres in Malta*, 30 March 2006, Adopted 27 April 2006;p.5.

[75] PQ 10253, 31/01/2005 (Leg X S229).

[76] 26 Sep 2005 – 1437 (PQ 14374, 26/09/2005, Leg X S295,), 3 Oct 2005 – 1617 (PQ 14555, Leg X S298, 3/10/2005)

[77] EP LIBE Report 2006 (n 77), p.5.

[78] National Statistics Office (Malta), *Census of Population & Housing 2005*, Preliminary Report 26 April 2006, p.xviii.

highest in the EU.[79] It is also recognised that such a small island state lacks the financial and infrastructure resources to deal with this considerable amount of asylum seekers. Nevertheless, this does not in any way justify the precarious and inhuman conditions in which these persons are detained in Malta. This has also been pointed out by the CPT (2004), the Commissioner for Human Rights (2003/5) and by a delegation from the Civil Liberties Committee[80] of the European Parliament in 2006. In the words of the Commissioner for Human Rights, the very difficult conditions of detention result from three main factors: the policy of detaining all migrants, the absence of an adequate infrastructure and the length of the outcome of asylum proceedings.[81]

3.4-3.8 Length & Irregularity of Stay, Decisions & Appeal Procedure

Although a few years ago Malta decriminalised illegal entry it still practices a strong detention policy. Detention is automatic and indiscriminate both to irregular immigrants and asylum seekers. The 'Immigration Act' prescribes that any person caught on Maltese territory without the right of entry, transit or residence, is considered a prohibited migrant and is detained until expulsion.[82] However, it must be noted that in practice those who overstay or remain without a valid visa are not detained. The main criticism is that this policy is based on racial discrimination in detaining African asylum seekers, whilst being more lenient with the hundreds of Eastern Europeans who overstay in Malta. The CPT criticised the Maltese government's justification of such a strong detention policy, as to serve as a 'powerful deterrent' to discourage the arrival of more immigrants.[83] These persons are detained on the basis of an administrative decision lacking any proper form of judicial review.

The length of detention and the legality of the detention itself have been challenged, strangely enough, before the Criminal Courts, in seeking a habeas corpus remedy. Although in the case of Karim Barboush[84] the court of first instance decided that detention was unlawful, the Superior Criminal Court reversed the decision. It stated that detention of asylum seekers is deemed to be lawful according to the 'Immigration Act' and that it is not the competence of such court to see if such detention is unlawful according to any other law. It neither could evaluate detention under the Constitution nor the ECHR. In fact, the only way an asylum seeker can challenge the lawfulness of detention is to have it examined under Article 5(4) of the ECHR, before the Constitutional Court. However, it is very difficult for an asylum seeker to take a case before the Constitutional Court due to the limited resources of asylum seekers and the lack of effective access to legal assistance.

The 'Immigration Act' now provides for an Immigration Appeals Board to rule on excessive length of detention of asylum seekers and people awaiting expulsion. Since 1 February 2005 the Board has been able to grant release from custody, but only where the continued detention of such person is, 'taking into account all the circumstances of the

---

79   National Statistics Office (Malta), *Census of Population & Housing 2005*, Preliminary Report 26 April 2006, p.xxiii. (The Netherlands is far second with 480 residents per km².)

80   Ibidem (n 77).

81   Commissioner for Human Rights of the COE, Malta Report 2004 (CommDH(2004)4, 12 February 2004), Part I.

82   Articles 5(1), 10, 14(2) & 22(5) Immigration Act.

83   CPT Report 2004 (n 76) p.8.

84   *Karim Barboush vs Commissioner of Police*, Court of Magistrates (Malta) 4 November 2004.

case, unreasonable as regards duration or because there is no reasonable prospect of expulsion within a reasonable time'. The Act severely restricts the cases where the Board can authorise release.[85] This is a relatively new remedy whose effectiveness remains to be assessed. What is undoubtedly concerning is that the Immigration Appeals Board has been set up under the 'Immigration Act', and does not form part of the Maltese judicial system.

Until 2005, administrative detention in Malta was for an indefinite period. The average length of detention was 22-24 months. In 2005 the maximum duration of detention was set at 18 months. For asylum seekers awaiting the results of an appeal the limit is 12 months. The authorities and the NGOs admitted that, because of limited resources, it can take between seven and nine months for an asylum seeker to be called for interview at the Maltese Commission for Refugees, even in the case of particularly sensitive groups.[86] The EP delegation remarked that release after 18 months is not automatic and some have been held for extra months even if this is against the Maltese Government's official policy. No appeals can be made against the length of detention period. At the end of the 18 months' detention, the immigrants and asylum seekers are transferred to 'open' centres. The government runs four open centres, whilst the Roman Catholic Church and a number of NGOs run another 14. These fall under the responsibility of the Ministry for Solidarity and the Family.[87]

3.9 – 3.12 Detention Irregulars under Criminal Law, Minors, Non-Expulsion

The institutions used for detention pose very serious human rights concerns. Asylum seekers and other migrants are held in six different centres. The three larger ones are run by the army, whilst the three smaller ones by the police. At the entrance of one of the centres there is a prison for migrants guilty of some petty offence.[88] They are overtly overcrowded and undoubtedly inappropriate for human beings. In the army barracks 450 people are detained outdoors in tents subject to all weather conditions. Others are kept in an army warehouse.[89] The remarks of the CPT in 2004, and more recently the EP delegation, in 2006 on the material conditions of these detention centres demonstrate clearly the precarious conditions in which asylum seekers are being 'welcomed' in Malta. The CPT referred to the 'prison-like environment, a climate of tension, a quasi-total absence of activities, a lack of regular outdoor exercise, inadequate medical/psychiatric care, a lack of information for foreign nationals concerning their situation, leading to uncertainty about their future', thus rendering detention unbearable.[90] In the same vein the EP delegation observed that the migrants appear to be 'exhausted by the living conditions of the centre', the length of time of detention, boredom and idleness. Men and women are not separated given that there are couples amongst them. However, they live together 'in extremely tight spaces.' The delegation witnessed that in one room 'there are two married couples living together, each couple sleeping in a single bed, as well as two single

---

[85] Art. 25A Immigration Act.
[86] EP LIBE Report 2006 (n 77), p.1.
[87] Ibidem, p.2.
[88] EP LIBE Report 2006 (n 77), p.8.
[89] Leg X, PQ 14375, Sed 303, 12 Oct 2005.
[90] CPT Report 2004 (n 76), p.13.

girls.' Women four months pregnant were also detained in these closed centres.[91] One of the centres is described as being 'like a cage' and the external area is surrounded 'by barbed wire'. The building is 'dilapidated', many windowpanes are missing and there is no heating. The hygiene conditions are 'intolerable', the showers 'broken' with no hot water available. The toilets 'have no doors' and are 'in a state of total disrepair. There is dirt everywhere.'[92] This general state of neglect and despair is evident in most detention centres and is aggravated by the intense overcrowding. This environment triggers acute health problems and risks of developing infectious and contagious diseases. Medical care offered in the centres themselves is unsatisfactory. According to the authorities a doctor visits the migrants three times a week.[93] In the present circumstances and bearing in mind the detention conditions, this is not enough, if not futile. The impossibility, or at least difficulty, of quickly seeing a doctor is clearly harmful to detainees' health and increases the risk of sickness spreading to healthy detainees. The situation also makes it completely impossible to take preventive measures.[94] The EP delegation alarmingly observed that, many of the migrants 'are suffering from scabies, TB or are HIV positive. They are not released for fear that they may infect the Maltese population.'[95]

For treatment of the most serious conditions migrants are taken to the hospital emergency service, where they are given priority over the Maltese population. However, that preferential treatment in hospital cases does not make up for the poor care arrangements at the detention centres.[96] Moreover, access to medical care in health centres and the general hospital is deemed conditional upon the availability of escorts and means of transport, which at times are quite problematic.[97] These have to be provided by the police and military officers performing custodial duties in the closed centres. Although most of these are 'committed to treating foreign nationals fairly and to meeting their needs to the extent possible,' they have never received any specific training for these duties.[98] The CPT in 2004 had also pointed out allegations of 'deliberate physical ill-treatment' by members of the police and or the armed forces, including kicks, punches and blows with batons.[99] It was also concerned with the practice of calling migrants by their file or tag numbers, and of referring to them similarly in all official documents. Many asylum seekers met by the delegation felt that they did not benefit from a real opportunity to present their case. Secondly, many asylum seekers did not speak Maltese or English and language barriers represented a significant problem.[100] When there is a massive influx, they often do not manage to guarantee the services of interpreters at this stage either.[101]

As the Commissioner for Human Rights pointed out, asylum seekers and migrants have not committed any offence or been tried by any court, yet their systematic arrest

---

[91]   EP LIBE Report 2006 (n 77), p.6.
[92]   Ibidem pp.5-6.
[93]   Ibidem pp.5.
[94]   Commissioner for Human Rights, COE, Follow Up Report 2006 (CommDH(2006) 29 March 2006), Part I.
[95]   EP LIBE Report 2006 (n 77), p.5.
[96]   Commissioner for Human Rights 2006 (n 99) Part I.
[97]   CPT Report 2004 (n 76) p.20.
[98]   Ibidem p.23.
[99]   Ibidem p.11.
[100] Ibidem pp.13-14.
[101] EP LIBE Report 2006 (n 77), p.3.

and detention for as long as 18 months resembles a prison sentence in all but name.[102] Furthermore, he added that the overall situation in the detention centres is all the more shocking 'if compared to the entirely acceptable conditions to be found in the Corradino prison.' Easing the overpopulation and significantly increasing access to outdoors should improve the situation. The aim should be, at the very least to treat migrants 'in a similar manner to ordinary prisoners.'[103] According to the EP rapporteur Giusto Catania, 'the situation in Malta's administrative detention centres is unacceptable for a civilised country and untenable in Europe, which claims to be the home of human rights.'[104]

4 NATIONALS DETAINED ABROAD

4.1 - 4.2 Numbers & Composition Group, Detention Countries

The issue of Maltese prisoners detained abroad is one of the areas where there is an alarming lack of information. After an official request to the Ministry of Foreign Affairs for the purpose of this report, the following information has been provided. As on the 20 April 2006, the number of Maltese detained abroad is 12. Eight are in the EU (Italy, France and the Netherlands), whilst another four are in Turkey, Switzerland and Australia.[105] No information has been provided as to the method used to compile of this data. The only other recent official information of this type was delivered in a PQ of 3 June 2003, whereby there were 12 Maltese prisoners held abroad. Seven were sentenced: three in Italy, two in France and one in Egypt. The other five were awaiting trial, two in Italy, two in Tunisia and one in Turkey.[106] In our opinion there is a possibility that the data provided is incomplete. It appears that whosoever does not get in touch with the Maltese diplomatic channels is not considered. We believe that it is the duty of each and every government to seek if there are any of its nationals detained in other countries.

4.3 – 4.7 Reasons for Detention & Sentencing, Involved Organisatons, Release & Reception Home Country, Aftercare, Public opinion and media

The main reason for detention should in most cases relate to drug offences, bearing in mind that this is the most common crime amongst foreign prisoners. However, this may not necessarily be so as there is no more information about these persons. The Ministry of Foreign Affairs added that 'there is the consular service offered by the Maltese embassies and consulates in the above mentioned countries.'[107] If this is the case, it is still not enough. Hopefully, in as much local NGOs are involved with foreign prisoners in Malta, this should be the situation in other countries, at least in the EU. Nevertheless, when a Maltese NGO [108] has regularly requested further information regarding the exact whereabouts of these persons, or at least invited the authorities to give these prisoners sufficient

---

[102] Commissioner for Human Rights 2006 (n 99) Part I.
[103] Commissioner for Human Rights 2004 (n 85) Part I.
[104] EP LIBE Report 2006 (n 77), p.8.
[105] Electronic Reply by the Ministry of Foreign Affairs (Consular Services), 20 April 2006.
[106] PQ 199, 27 May 2003, LegX S5.
[107] Electronic Reply by the Ministry of Foreign Affairs (Consular Services), 20 April 2006.
[108] MDD in 2004/2005/2006.

information to get in touch with the NGO in Malta, the authorities declined on grounds of data protection. This highly contrasts the role of NGOs in various EU countries that, at least, are afforded this possibility. The families are left to their own resources both during detention as well as after. The Maltese authorities do not assume any responsibility once these persons are released from prison and return back home. As the prison service does not offer any aftercare facilities for foreign prisoners detained in Malta, it can neither offer it to Maltese nationals that had been detained abroad. Unfortunately, there is a complete lack of awareness about this issue in the media. The only information provided about arrested persons is through the Maltese lawyers involved, otherwise, there is absolutely no concern what happens to these persons once the media hype is over. The Maltese Parliament does not show much interest either. The fact that they are just 12 is not an acceptable excuse. More effort and attention must be afforded at consular level to assist these persons. NGOs must be drawn into the picture, maybe in collaboration with others in the country of detention to ensure that these prisoners are treated fairly and with humanity.

5 EVALUATION AND RECOMMENDATIONS

Foreign prisoners and detained asylum seekers in any given country are by their nature in a disadvantaged position. They suffer from double isolation in that not only are they deprived of their liberty, but they are also detained in a foreign country. In the Maltese context, a clear distinction is made between prisoners detained under criminal law, and migrants and asylum seekers held under immigration laws. They are two worlds apart, with completely differing conditions of detention. Although the 'Immigration Act' has considerable influence in both cases, in practice they just cannot be compared. Foreign prisoners are undoubtedly treated much better than migrants and asylum seekers.

5.1 Migrants & Asylum Seekers

It is ironic that those foreigners who have committed serious crimes are treated much better than those who have simply attempted to enter Malta 'irregularly.' The very particular circumstances of the influx of illegal immigration in Malta have to be taken in consideration. Without any hesitation, the Maltese government is detaining migrants and asylum seekers in these conditions, as it cannot do otherwise. Hopefully, the EU Member States will, sooner than later appreciate this state of emergency and relieve the suffering of asylum seekers detained in Malta. It must be clear that any EU assistance should not be given just to assist Malta, but rather to improve the miserable lives of migrants and asylum seekers. It would be too easy, and maybe futile, to propose that their conditions of detention should be improved and that they should not be detained for too long. Everyone, including the government agrees with this, but in the present circumstances this is highly impracticable if not impossible. The assistance of the EU in this field is fundamental. The EP delegation visit should serve to get things going after an initial reluctance by the EU to take cognisance of the situation.

5.2 Foreign Prisoners

Whilst in the case of migrants and asylum seekers the government cannot do much by itself, this does not seem to be the case when dealing with prisoners. A foreign prisoner policy is absolutely essential in addressing a plethora of disadvantages and social exclusions these persons are suffering from. Foreign prisoners are more likely to end up completely excluded and marginalized. Those who do not speak Maltese, Arabic or English suffer from severe communication problems. Fortunately for Arab and Libyan prisoners this may not be the case given that they form a considerably large group and are able to live in a community where their religious and cultural needs can be met. In many cases the 'removal order' prejudices the status of most foreign prisoners by denying them rehabilitation and re-integration opportunities. A serious reappraisal of this practice is essential. It would be much fairer if the 'Immigration Act' were amended in the sense that the evaluation on whether a foreigner should be given a removal order or not is carried out in the last few weeks before release. This would eliminate the inherent discrimination against foreign prisoners in the present situation whereby the 'removal order' has become nothing more than an excuse in depriving most of them of their basic rights.

There are also other issues that must be evaluated and if possible addressed to decrease the negative implications of imprisonment for foreigners in Malta. These commence from the pre-trial proceedings where they are hardly, if ever, given bail. Although this according to the letter of the law, because there is a higher fear that they may abscond the island, there should be a greater effort in keeping the pre-trial detention period as short as possible in accordance with Article 5 ECHR. Furthermore, there is a general lack of understanding of criminal proceedings at levels, before and after conviction. The quality of legal assistance, whether free legal aid or not is not always satisfactory and certain foreign prisoners feel 'abandoned' by their lawyers in being given scant or unsatisfactory information about the case. Finally, foreign prisoners are being given much longer prison sentences and heftier fines when compared to Maltese offenders. Overall Maltese prison sentences are in practice much higher than in most European countries. When considering the length of sentences and the absence of parole, prisoners spend much longer time in Malta than elsewhere in the EU. The interpretation of a life sentence as meaning imprisonment until death illustrates the situation clearly. A prison sentence of considerable length means that the foreign prisoner will be detained away from his home country for a long number of years. The 1983 Council of Europe 'Convention on the Transfer of Sentenced Persons' has sought to afford the opportunity to foreign prisoners to spend part of their prison sentence in their home country. In the case of Malta this has not proved very effective, and in any case proceedings and discussions between the countries involved are taking an excessively long time. A plausible solution would be to have a single authority at European, or at least EU level, to coordinate the transfer of sentenced persons. This should be applicable for intra-European and third country transfers. This authority could also assist countries in identifying nationals detained abroad in order to give them appropriate consular assistance. The lack of information about Maltese citizens detained abroad shows how much more awareness is needed in this respect. Facilitating contact of Maltese nationals detained abroad with Maltese NGOs would guarantee a more far-reaching assistance than that provided at consular level. The same applies to foreign prisoners detained in Malta.

Awareness of the status and problems of social exclusion of foreign prisoners in Malta and elsewhere is the key to improve their situation. If prisoners are usually the marginalized group in society then foreign prisoners may be considered to have been long forgotten. The first and maybe the hardest step, to start tackling the social exclusion and discrimination of foreign prisoners are to acknowledge the existence of the problem. The principle that those who are imprisoned retain all rights with the exception of those rights that are lost as a specific consequence to deprivation of liberty cannot be further than the truth in practice. It seems that in Malta, and especially in the case of foreign prisoners, imprisonment is resulting in the total segregation and isolation of these persons, both from society as well as in the prison itself. Foreign prisoners in Malta, making up one-third of the prison population are not being given due attention and concern. This is not surprising. In a situation where there is a seeming disinterest in Maltese nationals detained abroad, one cannot expect much better treatment for foreign prisoners in Malta.

Chapter 19

Netherlands

Anton van Kalmthout
Femke Hofstee – van der Meulen

1 INTRODUCTION

1.1 Overview penalties and measures

1.1.1 Penalties and measures

The Dutch sanction system differs from sanction systems of many other countries by the large discretionary power and the wide range of options that it offers to public prosecutors and judges in determining the type, degree and modality of the sanction that fits the crime and the offender. With the term sanction is meant all forced or compulsory interventions that can be applied to an offender as reaction to his offence. In the pre-trial phase the public prosecutor and in some cases even the police can decide to waive the prosecution with or without conditions or to settle the case by means of transaction. The law does not specify the conditions that can be attached to a conditional waiver, but leaves it to the discretion of the public prosecutor. Settlement of the case by a transaction is possible for all offences carrying a statutory prison sentence not exceeding six years. Transaction means that the offender accepts the offer by the public prosecutor to fulfil one or more conditions.

Most applied conditions are: 1) payment of an amount of money to the treasury, 2) full or partial compensation to the victim and 3) the performance of unpaid labour or taking part in a training course during 120 hours. The sanctions that can be imposed by a judge can be distinguished in penalties and measures and the penalties in principal penalties and accessory penalties. A particular principal penalty is laid down for every criminal offence. The types of principal penalty are set out in order of severity in section 9 of the Penal Code as follows:
- imprisonment (sects. 10-14 PC);
- detention (sects. 18-20 PC);
- task penalty (sects. 22c-23 PC);
- fine (sects. 23-24b PC).

Only a limited number of crimes can be sentenced with life imprisonment. The fixed term prison sentence is the most frequently applied form of imprisonment. The duration is at least one day up to a maximum of fifteen years. Under certain circumstances however, the maximum may be increased to twenty years or even thirty years. Detention is the custodial penalty for less serious offences and its maximum term is fixed at one year. In special cases the maximum can be increased to one year and four months. Both custodial penalties can also be totally or partly suspended if they do not exceed one year. If the length of imprisonment is more than one year but not exceeding three years, only one third of the total sentence may be suspended. The suspended sentence is always subject to the general condition that the convicted person must not commit another offence before the end of the probationary period, which is normally two years or less (sect. 14 PC). In addition to the general condition, the judge may impose one or more special conditions (sect. 14 PC) such as compensation to the victim and other conditions relating to the convicted person's behaviour.

In 1987 the system of conditional release was replaced by the system of unconditional release. In principle every person convicted to an unconditional prison sentence exceeding six months is entitled, after having served part of his sentence,) to automatic, unconditional and irrevocable release after having served part of his sentence. Those sentenced to one year or less are released after having served six months plus a third of the remaining sentence. Those sentenced to more than a year are released after they have served two-thirds of their sentence. Life prisoners are only considered for early release if their sentence is commuted to a fixed term sentence via a pardon.

The task penalty is a non-custodial (community) punishment, introduced as alternative to imprisonment or detention. This penalty can consist of the obligation to perform unpaid labour (community service), to take part in a training course or a combination of both penalties. The maximum length of this task penalty is fixed at 480 hours, of which up to 240 hours can consist of unpaid labour. A suspended sentence and a task penalty can be combined with electronic monitoring. This is a recently developed new community sanction that is lacking a statutory basis but is still regulated by a Circular of March 2005. According to this Circular, prison sentences not exceeding three months can be replaced by electronic monitoring. Also some categories of offenders who will be released within three months can be granted the possibility to serve the remaining sentence outside prison under electronic surveillance. Electronic monitoring can also be used as a part of a penitentiary programme during the last phase of the execution of the prison sentence.

The fine is the least severe of the principal penalties. The Dutch Penal Code has retained the traditional system of fixed sum fines. Each offence can be punished with a fine. The general minimum for all offences is € 2; the maximum depends on the fine category into which each offence is placed. There are six fine categories with maximal of € 225, € 2,250, € 4,500, € 11,250, € 45,000 and € 450,000 (sect. 23 PC).

Originally, accessory penalties could only be imposed in combination with a principal penalty. Since 1983 they can also be imposed as principal penalty, but only for offences and in circumstances prescribed by law. The accessory penalties listed in section 9 PC are:
- *deprivation of certain rights and disqualification from practicing professions*, such as the right to practice a public office, the right to serve in the army, the right to vote and to be elected, the right to serve as an official administrator and the right to practice specific professions (*sect. 28PC*),
- *confiscation of objects* that are obtained by means of the criminal offence, or in relation to which the offence was committed, or which are manufactured or intended for committing the crime (*sect. 33 PC*),
- *publication of the judicial verdict (sect. 36 PC)*. This is only possible in the case of a small number of offences.

The second category of penal sanctions is the penal measures. They differ from penalties in that - with some exceptions - they can also be imposed where there is no question of culpability, in the sense that the person cannot be blamed for what he has done. This means that a judge may impose certain measures even when a person is acquitted or a case is dismissed. With exception of the measure of internment of persistent offenders and the placement in a psychiatric hospital, all other measures can be imposed without a penalty or in combination with a penalty. The measures, as laid down in the Penal Code are the following:
- *withdrawal from circulation of goods* which are confiscated because they are dangerous or whose possession is undesirable, such as objects obtained entirely or largely by means of or derived from the offence, objects that are related to the offence, objects used to

commit or to prepare the offence, objects used to obstruct the investigation of the offence and objects manufactured or intended for committing the offence *(sect. 36b-36 d PC);*

- *confiscation of the profits of crime (sect. 36e PC).* This measure means that a judge can order a convicted person to pay a sum of money to the State that has the effect of taking away the estimated financial rewards he has obtained from the crime he has committed. Like the withdrawal from circulation this measure can be imposed in conjunction with penalties and other measures;

- *obligation to pay compensation to the victim (sect. 36f PC).* The measure means that the court can oblige the sentenced person to pay to the State Treasure an amount of money for the benefit of the victim of the offence. The Treasury has the duty to collect this amount from the offender and remit it to the victim. If the offender fails to comply with this obligation the court may order default detention of no more than 1 year;

- *psychiatric hospital order (sect. 37 PC).* This measure can be imposed for up to one year by the court upon defendants who cannot be held responsible for their offence because of retarded development or mental illness, provided 1) that the person is a danger to himself, to others, to the general public or to property in general and 2) that the court has consulted a signed and dated recommendation from at least two behavioural experts, including one psychiatrist, who have examined the defendant;

- *inpatient hospital (Entrustment) order (sect. 37a PC).* This measure can be imposed upon offenders who were suffering from retarded development or mental illness when they committed the offence. If the judge considers that, despite the illness, the person can be deemed culpable; the measure can be combined with a penalty. The measure can only be imposed for crimes carrying a statutory penalty of at least four years imprisonment and for a number of other crimes explicitly stated in the Penal Code. According to section 37a, subsection 1 PC the measure cannot be imposed, except where it is considered necessary to protect other people or society. The order lasts for two years, but may be prolonged by one or two years. For certain violent crimes, the duration of this measure may be prolonged more times, provided that the safety of others require this prolongation;

- *outpatient hospital order (sect. 38 CC PC).* If the requirements for an entrustment order are met but hospital care is not considered necessary, the defendant can be obliged to undergo outpatient treatment. If the conditions attached to this measure are not complied with, the measure can be commuted to in an in-patient hospital order.

- *internment of persistent offenders order (sect. 38m-38u PC).* In order to tackle the nuisance and criminal activities of persistent offenders, the Dutch legislature recently introduced a new penal measure. This can be imposed by a court upon offenders who in the previous five years have been sentenced at least three times to a custodial penalty or measure, or to a task penalty, provided that the offender is likely to re-offend and the safety of persons or property is at stake. The order may last two years and can be partly executed under a half-open or open regime in free society.

1.1.2 Daily practice

The most frequently used sanction is the financial sanction (transaction by the public prosecutor or fine imposed by the court). In 2004 the transaction was applied 78,613 times. The courts imposed 54,774 fines in that year. In 48,378 cases a prison sentence was pronounced, of which 23,649 full or partial conditional. In 5 cases the sentence was life imprisonment. The number of task penalties amounted to 33,533. Most frequently imposed accessory penalties in 2004 were the disqualification from driving (18,430 times) and confiscation (3,877 times). Compensation to the victim was the most imposed penal measure (17,272 times), followed by withdrawal from circulation of goods (3,316 times) and the in-patient and outpatient hospital order (321 times).

1.1.3 Foreign nationals and the sanction system

The Dutch sanction system as laid down in the Penal Code does not differentiate between Dutch and foreign offenders. This means that in principle foreign nationals can be sentenced to the same penalties and measures as Dutch nationals. However, the sentencing practice is not only based on the Penal Code but also on prosecutorial sentencing guidelines. These guidelines are meant to establish more equality in sentencing practice and contain detailed criteria for the public prosecutor in determining which intervention and which sanction would fit the crime and the offender. Although the courts are not bound by these guidelines, they do have a great impact on the sentencing process. In some of the guidelines is laid down that special categories of foreign offenders in principle should be excluded from certain sanctions, such as a task penalty, electronic monitoring, in-patient and outpatient hospital order and internment of persistent offenders order. Foreign nationals are excluded from these sanctions if they belong to one of the following categories: 1) irregular migrants, 2) foreign nationals who are expected to lose their residence permit because of the crime committed, 3) foreign nationals who officially are or probably will be considered 'persona non grata'. Only exceptionally do the public prosecutor and the courts not follow these guidelines.

1.2 Overview of the Prison System

1.2.1 Organisational Structure

The National Agency of Correctional Institutions (DJI) is an agency of the Dutch Ministry of Justice. It is responsible for enforcing custodial sentences and measures in the Netherlands. The agency is divided into four divisions, the Prison Service, Juvenile Correctional Institutions, Custodial Clinics and forensic psychiatric hospitals (TBS) and the Temporary Unit Special Provisions. The headquarters of DJI is located in The Hague, next to the Ministry of Justice. The aim of the agency is to ensure public safety by depriving individuals of their liberty when they pose a threat to the legal order or the safety of others. Further it strives to assist and prepare prisoners for a successful reintegration into society.

Around 100 penitentiary institutions (prisons, detention centres, juvenile institutions, custodial clinics and special detention centres for irregular migrants) are scattered throughout the country. The total number of detention places has seen an increase over the last years (see Table 1) and the official total capacity in 2005 was 22.356 places.[1] The expected capacity for December 31st 2006 is 26,304.

---

[1] *Waar vrijheid ophoudt en weer kan beginnen, 1995-2005 Tien jaar Dienst Justitiële Inrichtingen,* Jos J.L.M. Verhagen 2005 page 45.

Table 1 Penitentiary capacity 2001-2005

Year	Total capacity	Percentage of increase
2001	16,500	-
2002	17,871	8%
2003	20,038	12%
2004	22,087	10%
2005	22,356	1%
2006		

Source: DJI, 2005 and 2006

On an annual basis around 75,000 people are being detained for a longer or shorter period. Most of these people are men (93.5%) and the large majority are detained in penitentiary institutions run by the Prison Service[2].

Table 2 Capacity per type of institution

Year	2002	2003	2004	2005	2006
Penitentiary Institutions	13,478	14,771	16,255	16,499	15,472
Juvenile institutions	2,346	2,399	2,566	2,571	2,680
Custodial Clinics	1,264	1,303	1,401	1,637	1,690
Detention irregulars	783	1,565	1,865	1,258	2,170
Total official capacity	17,871	20,038	22,087	21,965	22,012

Source: DJI, 2006

Around 75% of all sentences are being served in one of the 50 penitentiary institutions under the responsibility of the Prison Service. There are various types of institutions and the placement depends on the type of prisoner (male, female, juvenile, mentally ill, irregular migrant), the level of security and the kind of regime. The security level can range from low in (half) open institutions to normal (medium) and to high (maximum). Penitentiary institutions are in general divided in prisons and pre-trial prisons. Pre-trial prisons hold individuals who are suspected of having committed a serious criminal offence and who have not yet been tried. Sometimes pre-trial prisons also hold convicted prisoners with very short sentences or those who are awaiting transfer to a prison or a custodial clinic. In penitentiary institutions the total percentage of the prison population awaiting trial is around 40%. In 2004 the prison population serving a sentence of less than 1 year was 42.3%, compared to 38.3% in 2003 and 32% in 2002.

The total budget of the Ministry of Justice for 2006 is €5,4 billion. The Dutch National Agency of Correctional Institutions receives more than a third of the total budget, namely €1,86 billion. Half of the total costs of the Dutch National Agency of Correctional

---

[2]   Ibidem.

Institutions are being spent on salary and training of staff.[3] Around 17,000 people are working at the National Agency for Correctional Institutions. The average cost to take care of a person in a penitentiary institution is €189, in a juvenile institution € 341 and in a custodial clinic € 500.

Each penitentiary institution in the Netherlands has an independent supervisory committee ('Commissie van Toezicht') that monitors the treatment of prisoners. These committees were introduced in 1953 and consist of lay people from various backgrounds that visit their institution at least once every two weeks to speak to detainees and staff and to handle detainees' grievances. The members of the committees play an intermediary role between prisoners and the penal institutions. Grievances of importance are discussed during the monthly meetings, which are attended by the prison director. A special section of the supervisory committee acts as an independent Complaints Committee, to which a detainee may file a complaint concerning a decision taken by or on behalf of the prison director.

The Dutch National Agency of Correctional Institutions (DJI) has been under pressure over the recent years due to shortages in prison capacity, structural reduced budget and a more complex prison population. Consequently DJI is in a transforming process to make their service more functional and as a result a new target-group oriented structure will be introduced[4]. Prisoners will be divided in three basic target groups; pre-trial prisoners, prisoners with a sentence shorter than 4 months and prisoners with a sentence longer than 4 months. Besides this division there will be special institutions for groups that need more basic care or those who need special safety precautions. All groups will be detained in special targeted facilities that will be more geared towards the aim of the detention, the length (or expected length) of the detention and the risk profile. As a result of this new structure provisions for work, education and re-integration activities will be only be available on a limited scale and only for a selective group.

For foreign prisoners this new structure is likely to have important consequences. Foreigners who have been sentenced to less than 4 months, or who have only 4 months of their sentence left to serve, and who are likely to be extradited to their country of origin, will be put together in a special institution for foreigners. This institution will be located in the centre of the Netherlands, in the vicinity of The Hague where embassies and consulates are based and which is close to Schiphol airport. The idea behind it is to prepare the repatriation papers with embassies and to make foreigners more 'available' to the Dutch Immigration and Naturalisation Service (IND). At this moment foreigners who are no longer allowed to stay in the Netherlands after having served their prison sentence are being arrested upon release by the IND at the prison gate and brought to a special detention centre for irregular migrants. Foreigners with a prison sentence of more than 4 months are transferred to a special institution outside the centre of The Netherlands. Prison regime for foreign prisoners will be similar to other prisoners; they will be excluded from re-integration activities and aftercare. Foreigners serving a sentence longer than 4 months are obliged to work; for those serving less than 4 months there is no work

---

[3] Annual report DJI 2002, page 12.

[4] Information is based on conversation with Ton Daans, National Agency of Correctional Institutions (DJI) and memo by Ton Daans, August 2006. The new structure is called 'Detentie en Behandeling op Maat voor Volwassenen' (Tailer-made Detention and Treatment for Adults).

available. Staff working with foreigners will receive professional training, prison rules will be translated in various languages and the visiting facilities will be extended.

The new structure for the Dutch Prison Service will be discussed in the National Parliament in September 2006. It is expected to be introduced in 2007 and implemented during the coming years.

1.2.2 Detention of Foreign Prisoners

Prisoners who do not have citizenship of the Netherlands can be detained in all kinds of penitentiary institutions and they are not segregated from other prisoners. Institutions can be closed, half-open or open. Women, men and young persons are held separately. Foreign prisoners who have been accused of committing a criminal offence or who have been sentenced are being detained in penitentiary institutions run by the Dutch Prison Service. However, foreigners who are staying irregularly in The Netherlands and who are not sentenced for any offence are detained separately from sentenced prisoners in separate units of the normal penitentiary institutions or are detained in special detention centres where their removal from Dutch territory will be prepared.

Detention centres and these special units for irregular migrants fall under a separate unit of the National Agency of Correctional Institutions, the so-called Temporary Unit Special Provisions that was created in 2003. Although this unit falls under the responsibility of the Ministry of Justice, a special Minister is responsible for the removal of irregular migrants and rejected asylum seekers. This is the Minister for Immigration and Integration at the Ministry of Justice. In 2005 the total capacity for detaining irregular migrants in the detention centres and the special units in the penitentiary institutions was 2,177. In 2006 this capacity will increase to 3,021 places. The 7 detention centres (one for women, five detention boats and one airport detention centre) will provide 2,144 places, the remaining 877 places are situated in special units of 2 penitentiary institutions for pre-trial detainees and 1 institution where men, women as well as children can be detained. With some exceptions, the legal position of these detained irregular migrants does not differ from pre-trial and sentenced detainees because the rules of the Penitentiary Principles Act and the Penitentiary Order also include the administrative detention of irregular migrants. Chapter 3 will provide more information about administrative detention of foreign prisoners.

1.3. Overview involvement Consulates, Embassies, Ministries home country, Probation service home country, NGO's etc.

There are over 100 different nationalities detained in Dutch penitentiary institutions. In general there is very little attention or support from authorities for foreign prisoners by authorities like Consulates and Embassies. Officially, upon arrival in a penitentiary institution all prisoners are asked if they would like to contact a family member or a friend to inform them about their detention. Most Dutch penitentiary institutions work with a telephone card that has a limited amount that they can use to notify relatives. Normally prisoners who are not citizens of The Netherlands are also asked if they would, besides family, like to contact the diplomatic mission of the state of their country of origin. This is according to article 36 of the Vienna Convention on Consular Relations (1963) which states that foreign prisoners should be advised of their right to contact consular officials of their country. Presuming that a prisoner does not object, prison authorities should inform foreign officials about the detention 'without delay'. In practice not all foreign prisoners are willing to inform their consulates. In interviews with foreign prisoners it became clear that this reluctance had various reasons. Most foreign prisoners were not keen on having the embassy know about their detention, some felt that the embassy could not provide any help and lastly some prisoners indicated that they were not given the opportunity to contact their embassy.

In practice consular officials are visiting quite a number of foreign prisoners. Visits take place inside the penitentiary institutions in separate rooms without direct control of prison staff. Consular officials usually inform the prisoners about their rights and criminal procedures in the Netherlands and assist them in obtaining a legal representative. Any communication addressed to the consular post is private and is not seen by prison staff.

Regularly visits to embassies or consulates are organised for foreign nationals who are detained because they don't have a residence permit (irregular migrants), those who have lost or will loose their residence permit because of the crime they committed and those who have to leave the country after having served their sentence. Sometimes these visits take place in the penitentiary institution itself. The visits are organised by the Dutch Immigration and Naturalisation Service (IND) in order to get the travel documents (laissez-passer) that are needed from the embassy or consulate to remove undocumented foreign nationals from the country. A large number of consulates also maintain relationships with the International Organisation for Migration (IOM). IOM plays an important mediating role between the consulates and the foreign national who is willing to return to his country of origin and for that reason needs the required travel documents. Since recent years IOM offers their advice and support also to foreign nationals who are detained in a penitentiary institution or a detention centre. In a few institutions, pilot projects have been set up to promote and support the return programmes among these foreigners.

1.4 Overview of trends

1.4.1 Sentencing trends

Traditionally, the Dutch imprisonment rate has been one of the lowest in Europe. In the 1970s the imprisonment rate, per 100,000 national population, was 20. Over the years this has changed and the number is now above the EU average. The imprisonment rate in Dutch penal institutions (per 100,000 national population) has more than tripled over the last three decades and in 2005 the rate was 127. Over 80% of the Prison Service buildings have been built after 1975 and the total capacity of cells has tripled. Due to a constant shortage of prison cells and for budgetary reasons the Prison Service introduced (in 2004) 'sharing of cells' in 2004. Although most prisons still have single cells there are some cells that can be shared with 2 or 3 persons. In detention centres for irregular migrants cells are normally shared with 4-8 persons.

During the last 25 years the prison population has changed and increased considerably. The two main trends are that the judiciary is imposing more and longer prison sentences and the prison population has a more varied background (nationality, religion, mental state of health). Although the general crime rate doesn't fluctuate very much, one can observe an increase in violent offences and organised crime. Although prison sentences are imposed more frequently, the usage of custodial sentences is still being considered a last resort. The Judiciary's preferred sentence is a fine as well as task penalties, especially the unpaid labour penalty that is frequently used. These task penalties are an alternative sanction for a prison sentence up to 12 months.

A reason behind the trend of imposing more and longer prison sentences by the judiciary can be seen against the background of a different political climate in the Netherlands since 11 September 2001 and the parliamentary elections in May 2002. From a society that could be described as fairly open and liberal, the Netherlands changed into a less tolerant and more restrictive society. Public opinion demanded a more strict approach and punishment towards criminality. People felt less safe and the integration of immigrants in society was not seen as being successful, especially because norms and values of society were not commonly shared and accepted. As a consequence the government provided more capacity for law enforcement organisations like the police in order to contribute to the idea of more public safety. For the National Agency of Correctional Institutions it resulted in coping with a growing and more diverse prison population without a substantial additional budget. This had its effects on the treatment of prisoners and facilities for prisoners. The accent has been placed more on the punitive character of detention like cell sharing, a more sober regime, less opportunities to work, less facilities to follow training and educational courses, less probation service involvement, less provisions for special categories of prisoners and more services (like food) contracted out.

Not only has the criminal and sentencing policy become less tolerant and more repressive. The same tendency can be observed with respect to the Immigration Policy. During recent years, a lot of measures have been taken to reduce the number of asylum seekers and refugees and to increase the forced or compulsory removals of irregular migrants and other immigrants whose residence permit has been withdrawn. The legal possibilities to withdraw a residence permit or to declare a person 'persona non grata' because of the committing of an offence have extended enormously. As a consequence an increasing number of foreign nationals are being detained in order to get them removed from the country. Illegal stay in the country is not a criminal offence in itself, but the Immigration Act makes it possible to detain these foreigners as long as they are not removed. Foreigners who are officially qualified as 'persona non grata' are committing a crime when they do not leave the country and they can be punished with a prison sentence of 6 months maximum. After having served this sentence in a penitentiary institution they can be transferred to a detention centre, where they have to stay until their removal or release. The increase in prison capacity is partly due to the high priority in governments' policy to deter foreign nationals to enter or to stay irregularly in the country.

1.4.2 Composition of Prison Populations

Over the last decades besides a considerable growth of the prison population, the composition has changed significantly as well. From a rather homogeneous population it became a prison population characterised by a wide variation of nationalities, religions and cultural backgrounds.

In August 2005 Dutch penitentiary institutions (including detention centres for irregular migrants) were detaining persons from in total 106 nations. From this group, between 35-40% are being detained in pre-trial institutions, around 45% are detained in prisons and around 10% in detention centres. Another significant shift in the prison population is the fact that prisoners have become more vulnerable because more prisoners suffer from mental illness and addictions to drugs, medication and/or alcohol. As a result prisoners require more individual treatment and care.

In general half of the prison population is addicted to drugs (alcohol, tobacco, soft and/or hard drugs) and around a tenth is mentally ill. Around one third has a violent history. Nearly half of the prisoners have debts and only one fifth earns a living via a job. Most prisoners are male but the percentage of women is increasing. On 1 January 2003 there were 888 female prisoners (6.5%) and 12,412 male prisoners (93.5%) in Dutch penitentiary institutions. Nearly three quarters of the prison population is under 40 years.

Table 3 Prisoner's age

Age	Number	Percentage
Unknown	11	0.1 %
< 18 years	97	0.6 %
18-19	732	4.2 %
20-24	3,265	18.9 %
25-29	3,005	17.4 %
30-34	3,087	17.9 %
35-39	2,696	15.6 %
40-44	1,960	11.4 %
45-49	1,234	7.1 %
50-59	954	5.5 %
60>	219	1.3 %
Total	17,260	100%

Source: DJI, 1 January 2005

There is a wide variety in the type of offences that are being punished. Around 44% of all offences are related to the use of violence. Offences in connection to drugs are around a quarter and crime against property is around 20%. Disruption of the public order is around 4% and traffic offences just above 1%. These percentages have been rather stable through the years. In 1997 and 1998 most offenders received a sentence with duration between 1 to 2 years.

From 1999 onwards the most applied sentence length has been between 2 to 4 years. Despite the trend of longer sentences the usage of very short sentences (less than 3 months) has gone up. In 2004 the short sentence length was used in nearly 20% compared to less than 10% in 1997. Around three quarters of all prisoners have a sentence length of less than 4 years. In the Netherlands early conditional release has been abolished in 1986. It has been replaced by a system in which every prisoner is, without a single condition imposed, automatically released after having served two thirds of the prison sentence. This system is being reviewed and might be changed in the future (see for more information section 2.9).

In 1 January 2005, over 44% of prisoners detained in Dutch penitentiary institutions (including detention centres for irregular migrants) were born in The Netherlands. When the population in detention centres are excluded this number is exactly 50%. The high percentage of people born in Suriname and the Dutch Antilles can be linked to the former colonial relationships.

Table 4 Country of birth of foreign prisoners

Country of Birth	Number including detention centres	Percentage	Number excluding detention centres	Percentage
Netherlands	7,654	44.3 %	7,650	50.0 %
Suriname	1,470	8.5 %	1,415	9.2 %
Dutch Antilles	1,406	8.1 %	1,406	9.2 %
Rest of Africa	1,312	7.6 %	1,011	6.6 %
Morocco	1,167	6.8 %	702	4.6 %
Rest of Asia	1,167	6.8 %	668	4.4 %
Eastern Europe	786	4.6 %	640	4.2 %
Turkey	692	4.0 %	620	4.1 %
Rest of Europe	604	3.5 %	566	3.7 %
Rest of America's	474	2.7 %	438	2.9 %
Unknown	528	3.1 %	192	1.3 %
Total	17,260	100 %	15,308	100 %

Source: DJI, 1 January 2005

The percentage of prisoners with the Dutch nationality is much higher than the 44% of prisoners who have been born in The Netherlands. The total number of prisoners with a Dutch passport is 65% and when the population in detention centres are excluded this number is 73.8%.

Table 5 Percentage of foreign prisoners compared with Dutch prisoners

Nationality	Number including detention centres	Percentage	Number excluding detention centres	Percentage
Netherlands + Dutch Antilles	11,301	65.5 %	11,298	73.8 %
Rest of Africa	1,214	7.0 %	758	5.0 %
Rest of Asia	992	5.7 %	521	3.4 %
Morocco	937	5.4 %	501	3.3 %
Eastern Europe	675	3.9 %	481	3.1 %
Rest of Europe	527	3.1 %	434	2.8 %
Turkey	464	2.7 %	407	2.7 %
Suriname	422	2.4 %	364	2.4 %
Rest of America's	304	1.8 %	267	1.7 %
Unknown	424	2.5 %	277	1.8 %
Total	17,260	100 %	15,308	100 %

Source: DJI, 1 January 2005

The nationality of foreigners in detention centres is also very varied. On 1 January 2005 a fifth of the population was a citizen of an African country and 13% of an Asian country.

Around 10% was citizen of Algeria and also 10% of China. For Morocco and Eastern Europe the percentages were around 9% and for India nearly 6%. The percentage for Sierra Leone and Nigeria were 2.7% and 2.5%.

The numbers point out that around a quarter of the prisoners is citizen of another country. This seems rather low but since over half of the prison population has not been born in the Netherlands, many do not share the Dutch language, culture and customs and it makes the prison population multicultural and full of foreign influences.

1.5 Overview of national legislation

1.5.1 Penitentiary legislation

The Dutch Penal Code contains only a small number of penitentiary rules. Main provisions are the provisions on early release (sect. 15) and the transfer of mentally ill detainees to forensic psychiatric institutions (sect. 13). Most of the penitentiary rules are set down in the Penitentiary Principles Act, the Penitentiary Order and the House Rules, that prescribe the same minimum standards and rules for all penitentiary institutions. There is very little room for a penitentiary institution to go beyond these prescriptions. In many of the penitentiary rules, as laid down in these documents, the various numbers of departmental circulars and guidelines are worked out in more detail. Important are also the various decisions of the National Complaints Appeals Committee to whom the governor and the detainee can issue an appeal against the decision of the Complaints Committee. The decisions of this Appeals Committee are an indispensable source for the understanding and interpretation of the penitentiary rules.

For detainees in forensic psychiatric clinics the penitentiary rules are laid down in a special Principles Act for detainees under a hospital order. This act is worked out in special Rules for the treatment of these detainees as well as in various departmental circulars and guidelines.

1.5.2 Reference to special legislation

1.5.2.1 General remarks

As mentioned already in paragraph 1.1.3, the Dutch legislation in principle does not make any distinction between foreign prisoners and Dutch national prisoners. However, some prosecutorial guidelines explicitly prescribe that some sanctions should not be applied on foreign nationals who have no legal residence permit or who will loose that because of the crime they committed. The penitentiary regulations are also based on the principle that foreign prisoners have the same legal position as other prisoners and have the same legal rights and obligations as Dutch national prisoners. However, this is not always the case. As will be worked out in more detail in the following chapters, there are some legal provisions that are not applicable to all foreign prisoners such as prison leave, the right to participate in a penitentiary programme, access to an open regime and access to the support of a probation service. On the other hand, penitentiary regulations can sometimes contain special provisions for foreigners, such as the right to contact consulates and embassies, the right to an interpreter and the right to have important documents translated in a language he understands, the right to practice their religion and to get food in accordance with their religion,

1.5.2. 2 International or bilateral transfer agreements for foreign prisoners

The Netherlands signed the Council of Europe Convention on the transfer of sentenced Persons (VOGP) in 1983. This Convention is necessary in order to take over the execution of a sentence that was enforced abroad. According to the Enforcement of the Council of Europe's Criminal Judgements Transfer Act (Wet Overdracht tenuitvoerlegging Strafvonnissen) (WOTS) such a take-over cannot be carried out without a convention. Although the Netherlands' point of view is that the transfer of detainees should take place preferably within the framework of the VOGP, it has made some individual agreements with some countries that have not signed the convention by means of a bilateral treaty. In 1999 such an agreement was made with Morocco and in 2004 with Thailand. Also, in 2004, the European arrest warrant came into effect, which substitutes the extradition procedure between the member states of the European Union with a simplified transfer procedure.

Requests from Dutch foreign nationals to undergo a sentence in the Netherlands are considered by the International Legal Aid Agency for Criminal Cases (Bureau Internationale Rechtshulp in Strafzaken) (BIRS). Depending on what has been agreed upon with the respective country, a sentence will be taken over by the Netherlands (the extra judicial continued procedure) or converted into a new sentence, according to Dutch law. As shown in the next table, annually around 5-9 % of all Dutch prisoners detained abroad make use of the possibility to have the sentence or part of it executed in the Netherlands. For more details see chapter 4.

Table 6 Number of Transfer requests between 1995-2004

year	1995	1996	1997	1998	1999	2000	2001	2002	2003	2004
number	124	194	212	231	200	236	264	340	402	465

Table 7 Number of Transfers to the Netherlands between 1995-2004

year	2001	2002	2003	2004
number	98	118	120	231

Source: Parliamentary Papers, 2nd Chamber, 2004-2005, 30010, nrs.1-2. p. 23.

2 TREATMENT OF FOREIGN PRISONERS

2.1 General

This chapter will look into the treatment of prisoners and in particular of foreign prisoners in Dutch penitentiary institutions. For this study 49 people have been interviewed in 5 Dutch penitentiary institutions (3 pre-trial prisons, 1 prison and 1 detention centre for irregular migrants) in early 2006[5]. Of this group 29 people were foreign prisoners, 9 were irregular migrants and 11 were members of staff. The treatment of irregular migrants detained in special detention centres for administrative reasons is being addressed in chapter 3.

The aim of the National Agency of Correctional Institutions is to prepare prisoners to re-enter society and to live a law-abiding and self-supporting life after release. One essential condition to achieve this is to treat all prisoners with humanity and with respect for the inherent dignity of the human person. The purpose of treatment is to sustain the prisoners' health and self-respect and to develop their sense of responsibility.

Differentiation of treatment is only allowed when it is intended to address individual needs of prisoners like age, sex, and mental and physical state. In order to address these needs there are extra care units for vulnerable prisoners, special care units for mentally disturbed prisoners and addiction rehabilitation centres. Young offenders can be placed in custodial institutions or treatment institutions. Treatment institutions are for juveniles who are put either under an institutional placement order or under a supervision order (removal from parental care) by the juvenile court.

Prisoners cannot be subjected to compulsory medical treatment unless the prison governor orders it and only if the opinion of a medical doctor states that this intervention is necessary to avert serious risk to the health or safety of the prisoner or of others (sect. 32 Penitentiary Principles Act). If a court considers a person to be in need of treatment for psychiatric problems or a development or personality disorder during detention, the court will impose a 'hospital order' (TBS) for adults and 'custodial treatment order' (PIJ) for juveniles. But also under these orders, medical treatment is only allowed with the consent of the patient, unless this treatment is considered necessary to avert serious risk to the health or safety of the prisoner or of others.

Treatment of prisoners depends in general on the type of institution and level of security. In practice not all (pre-trial) prisons are run in the same way and there are many differences. People held in pre-trial prisons are suspected of having committed a serious criminal offence, are waiting to be tried or to be transferred, or are serving a short sentence (less than 3 months). People held in prison are serving a sentence. Pre-trail prisons have in principle a medium level of security and a sober regime with restricted 'association' (time spent outside cell). This means that prisoners stay in their cell nearly all day. The court or examining judge 'rechter commissaris' can even restrict the regime further if that is seen necessary for the legal proceedings of the case. The most common restriction is no or restricted communication with other prisoners or/and with the outside world (so no visits, no telephone calls or mail). In prisons we find in general a less sober regime, a medium level of security and more association.

Despite the variation of prison regimes, programmes and facilities in the Netherlands, all prisoners are entitled to one hour of fresh air per day and, when there are no restrictions, at least six hours of exercise or recreation per week, at least one hour per week to receive visitors and a telephone call of 10 minutes. The possibility of participation in work, educational courses and a so-called 'penitentiary programme' depends on the type of institution and the facilities as well as on the behaviour and motivation of the prisoner

---

[5]   Interviews were held by Femke Hofstee-van der Meulen and Saskia Pubben. Permission to conduct interviews was kindly given by Mr. Peter van der Sande, director of the Dutch Prison Service, and logistical assistance was provided by Mr. Geert Mol of the Dutch Prison Service.

himself or herself. All institutions have in-house medical services, psychologists, psychiatrists, general practitioners, dentists, social workers and religious persons.

In 2003 and 2004 the National Agency of Correctional Institutions (DJI) has carried out a survey into the perception of detention by individual prisoners[6]. Around 7,000 prisoners participated in this survey in which foreign prisoners were underrepresented. In the survey of 2004 into the general prison population the major outcomes were that 71% of prisoners feel relatively safe, a majority is bored and unhappy with the long hours behind closed doors. However, although there are limited provisions for activities, the quality is good. Prisoners regard contact with staff as positive and they are in general satisfied with lawyers. More privacy during visiting hour is desirable. In 2005 a survey was carried out especially for foreign prisoners. Although the survey had been carried out and the report was ready in October 2005, DJI has decided not to make the results public yet.

A vast majority of foreign prisoners that were interviewed for this study indicated that they are being treated in the same way as national prisoners. There were no indications that they feel discriminated or isolated from other prisoners. However, most foreign prisoners mentioned that there are several disadvantages related to their foreign status that makes their position more vulnerable in comparison to other prisoners. One of the most common felt disadvantages is language. Due to the fact that prisoners do not understand, speak or read the Dutch language they are less able to communicate with others, they are less aware of the rules and procedures, they have less understanding of the legal proceedings of their criminal case and they are less able to participate in training courses. A second major disadvantage is the physical distance from family and friends and as a result foreign prisoners often feel lonely, uncertain and helpless. In the following sections these differences between foreign prisoners and national prisoners are being highlighted in more detail per topic.

2.2 Living conditions and facilities

The Netherlands was famous for confining of prisoners in a single cell. An exception was made for irregular migrants, who were detained in former military barracks with 'rooms' for 8 people. Mainly due to budgetary reasons, the Dutch Prison started an experiment in 2003 with two prisoners in one cell by replacing a bed by a bunk bed. Although staff and prison directors were not in favour it turned out to be successful and in 2005 many cells were transformed into double occupancy. Even now an experiment takes place with 6 people in one dormitory. Prisoners are not placed randomly together in one cell; a Selection Officer that checks whether prisoners are suitable and willing to share a cell is making a careful selection.

Despite the introduction of 'multiple cell occupancy' most prisoners occupy a single cell. They are required to keep their cell, which has a standard size of around 10m2, clean and in good condition. All cells contain a bed, a desk and chair, a wardrobe and a toilet. Some cells have washing facilities (shower) and are heated centrally. The prison services provide bedding, towels, soap, sugar, coffee and, if necessary, clothing. Prisoners can rent a television and a refrigerator, they may keep a radio, a 'play station', and a bird in a cage or a fish in a bowl or aquarium.

---

[6]   'Gedetineerd in Nederland 2004', DJI 2004.

Apart from the majority of irregular migrants, who are detained in separate penitentiary institutions (detention centres, prison boats), foreign prisoners are detained in the same cells as Dutch nationals and are not separated from other prisoners. In cases where cells for double occupancy are available, prisoners can request to share a cell with other prisoners. In practice, foreign prisoners like to share cells with fellow countrymen or people who speak the same or similar language and who have the same cultural or religious background. In principle these requests are being granted, unless they pose a risk for the internal order and security. For prisoners sharing one cell, prison staff tries to reschedule activity programmes so both prisoners can have some private time in their cell.

Most prisoners like to have television in their room for distraction and it is a way to be informed with news. Besides various Dutch channels a wide variety of foreign channels are available. This is especially important for foreign prisoners. Prisoners have to pay for watching their own television and the weekly rent is high in comparison with the weekly payment for work (maximum €12 a week). Prisoners without financial support from outside the prison are less likely able to afford a television, as they prefer to buy tobacco or purchase telephone cards to stay in contact with their family abroad. In most penitentiary institutions prisoners are allowed to make coffee and tea in their cell with a coffee machine and/or a water cooker. These facilities were also being used creatively to prepare simple meals with ingredients bought in the prison shop. Since a tragic fire broke out in a detention centre at Schiphol airport in October 2005, where 11 people lost their lives, these cooking facilities have been restricted. Especially foreign prisoners deplore this decision because this was a way to prepare food in their traditional way.

2.3 Reception and admission

The Dutch Ministry of Justice has special 'Selection Officials' in charge of coordinating the admission process of prisoners to penal institutions and the transfer process to different wards or institutions. People who receive a prison sentence can be sent directly to a penal institution or the person can be requested to announce/report oneself at a penal institution at a later stage. The 'Selection Officials' are authorised to select for each prisoner individually which institution is most suitable to be detained in. The transport of (pre-trial) prisoners to and from court and between penitentiary institutions is organised by the Prison Service's 'Dienst vervoer en ondersteuning' (Transport and Support Service). Prisoners are transported in little white vans under supervision of at least two uniformed staff members and males, females and juveniles are separated from each other.

Upon admission, prisoners are obliged to co-operate when prison authorities are registering the person and take a picture and/or ask for a hand scan (fingerprints). Prisoners are entitled to inform relatives about their detention and foreign prisoners are allowed to call their diplomatic mission. In practice many foreign prisoners are not informed about their rights to inform a representative of their country about their detention or they are not willing to do so (see section 2.6). Normally one telephone card is provided upon arrival to make necessary calls. In practice the amount on these cards is not sufficient to make long distance calls. Newly arrived prisoners are informed about the prison rules. In practice these rules tend to be only available in Dutch and this is a major disadvantage for foreign prisoners who do not understand the Dutch language. Another disadvantage is that there is not always staff available in reception areas that speak more than one language. As a result newly arrived prisoners feel even more isolated and lost. In practice these cases are 'solved' by seeking a prisoner who can serve the role of interpreter.

All prisoners are strip-searched by a member of staff of the same sex and receive a medical check-up within 24 hours. Prisoners who do not have suitable clothing will be provided accordingly. Some foreign prisoners make use of this provision because they do not have additional clothing with them. Prisoners are allowed to bring one box with personal items to the penitentiary institution. At reception the box will be checked and some items might be put into a safety box that will be kept by the institution until the prisoner is released or transferred. Foreign prisoners are especially vulnerable during the first hours and days of detention. It is important that prison authorities are made more aware of this and provide suitable solutions to reduce this feeling of isolation and helplessness. Some foreign prisoners mentioned that they had to gain the respect of the other prisoners in order to be treated fairly by others and that this process can take some time.

2.4 Work - Education – Training – Sports – Recreation

The majority of prisoners are placed in a standard prison programme where the daily activities do not include many provisions for education, vocational and re-integration training. Motivated prisoners can be selected for 'Penitentiary programmes' (see section 2.4 and 2.8). Most penitentiary institutions offer limited opportunities to work, to follow education and vocational training, to participate in sports and recreation and to visit the library.

2.4.1 Work

(Untried) pre-trial prisoners are not obliged to work in the Netherlands, but most do work because not working means remaining in one's cell during working hours. Prisoners who are sentenced are obliged to work. The hourly rate is €0.64 and prisoners can earn a maximum salary of €12.80 (20 hours) per week. Work is seen as a substantial part of the activity programme of prisoners but due to budgetary reasons there is less work available in Dutch penitentiary institutions. Prisoners who are engaged in work can receive 80% of their wages when there is not enough work for them or when they are sick. Misbehaviour during work or (false sickness) malingering can lead to disciplinary punishment. There used to be a wide variation of work available; simple jobs like wrapping products for transport but also more sophisticated work like making wooden toys. A number of penitentiary institutions have their own steel, wood, paper and textile workshops. Both prison staff and prisoners regret the fact that there are fewer opportunities for work. Involving prisoners in a range of useful work activities is seen as a way to spend less time behind a closed door, to escape boredom, to earn money and to become equipped with professional skills that can be used after release. Sometimes prisoners were even offered an opportunity to take a vocational training in relation to the work they were doing. Each penitentiary institution has also work related to the domestic work inside the prison like cleaning the corridors, common rooms and kitchens. This work is remunerated the same way as other work and cleaners often occupy the most convenient and spacious cells available on the wing.

In the Dutch Penitentiary Principle Act is stated in article 47 that all prisoners are entitled to participate in work available in the institution. Foreign prisoners are not excluded from work and often they are keen to be involved in order to receive money to pay for telephone cards, tobacco, television and food from the prison shop. Without financial support from family and friends many foreigners depend on their prison earnings. Most work is rather simple and can also be understood by prisoners who do not speak the Dutch language. In the future plans of DJI it is very likely that foreign prisoners serving a sentence longer than 4 months will be obliged to work but for those serving a sentence of less than 4 months there will be no work available.

2.4.2 Education and training

Prisoners are entitled to follow educational courses and to participate in vocational training offered by the prison authorities. In practice only motivated prisoners take part in educational activities and the waiting lists are long. The provisions of educational courses and vocational trainings are rather limited and vary per institution. Some institutions provide re-integration and social rehabilitation courses, skills trainings (like reading and writing) and vocational training related to work. Specialised prison staff or regional educational institutes provide the courses and prisoners can obtain certificates which can be used in society or they can continue their training with a regional institute after release. The level of courses varies but is mostly rather low since most prisoners tend to have a limited educational background.

Sometimes Dutch language courses are available for foreign prisoners. In interviews foreign prisoners indicated that they found these courses very helpful but that they were not or too late aware or were informed too late of the existence of these courses or that there were long waiting lists. Since the introduction of the Penitentiary Institutions Act in 1999, the so-called 'Penitentiary programmes' were introduced to motivate prisoners who have served at least five sixths of a sentence of at least 6 months. The minimum length of this programme is four weeks; the maximum is one year. Prisoners participating in these programmes attend training courses outside the institution and/or on-the-job projects with an employer. During the programme, that precedes the early release, participants are no longer detained and belong only administratively to the prison. Participants of these 'Penitentiary programmes' are under strict supervision by the Probation Service.

Penitentiary programmes can be combined with electronic monitoring which replaces cell detention with a programme of assistance and supervision. Electronic monitoring was introduced in 1985 and participants wear an anklet that can be monitored electronically by the prison/or probation service and participants may only leave their home during pre-determined hours to participate in mandatory activities like work and training. One of the conditions to be accepted for a penitentiary programme and electronic monitoring is that the prisoner has a secure home address and there is no risk of escaping. Another condition is that the prisoner is not obliged to leave the country after having served the sentence or will be extradited. The majority of the foreign prisoners cannot meet these conditions, which means that they are excluded and have to spend more time in prison than Dutch nationals.

2.4.3 Sports & Recreation

Prisoners have at least six hours of exercise and/or recreation per week. Each penitentiary institution has provisions and facilities for prisoners to participate in sports and to recreate. If prisoners are healthy they can practice sports twice a week for 45 minutes on a sports field or in the fitness gym. Many prisons have an indoor and an outdoor sports field. Prison staff also makes use of these sport facilities and in particular the fitness gym.

Recreation is an opportunity for prisoners to meet in the communal area on their wing or cellblock. Facilities vary from institution to institution but most of them have communal areas with facilities to sit together or to play cards, games, chess, and table football or to watch television. Some institutions have facilities to cook a meal. During these hours of recreation people can make use of the telephone. In case a prisoner does not want to participate there is no alternative programme.

Foreign prisoners participate in sports and recreational activities as much as other prisoners. Although there are communication difficulties sometimes, foreign prisoners tend to manage with non-verbal communication. Especially the recreation hours are important for foreign prisoners because they can seek assistance from other prisoners or staff for a better understanding about how the institution and its procedures function. Furthermore, foreign prisoners tend to have fewer visitors and for them this is a way to socialise.

2.4.4 Library

Almost every Dutch penitentiary institution has a library with books, music, magazines and newspapers. These libraries offer literature in a wide variety of languages and some foreign newspapers and magazines are available. Prisoners are entitled to read in the library and to borrow books and magazines once a week. Foreign prisoners tend to be very positive about the supply of books and magazines available in so many foreign languages.

2.5 Food – Religion – Personal hygiene – Medical care

All penitentiary institutions in The Netherlands provide prisoners with meals. Medical, cultural and religious dietary requirements of individual prisoners are taken into account. Each institution has provisions for prisoners to practice their religion, to attend religious services and to have personal contact with religious representatives. Furthermore, prisoners are entitled to wear their own clothes and facilities are available to take proper care of their appearance and physical hygiene. All prisoners are entitled to medical care and treatment and most services are provided inside the institution.

2.5.1 Food

The penitentiary institution provides for food and prisoners receive three meals per day. Prisoners are asked upon admission about their dietary requirements for medical, cultural or religious reasons. For prisoners who are Muslim, Jewish or vegetarian the institutions prepare special food. For breakfast (around 7 am) and for dinner (around 5.30 pm) bread is served and for lunch a hot meal. Although there is not much variation in the menu, prisoners are asked regularly to indicate their preferences for lunch (potatoes, rice, vegetables, meat or fish). Some institutions have their own kitchen but due to budgetary restrictions more and more institutions are receiving food from outside and prisoners have to heat the food that is presented in a plastic box, in a microwave. This is not beneficial for the quality of the food. Some institutions provide kitchen facilities where prisoners can cook for themselves during recreation hours. Prisoners are allowed to buy additional food (like fruits) as well as sweets, toiletry, telephone cards, stamps etc directly or via order forms from the prison shop or shops outside the prison, but prisoners generally complain about the high prices. Foreign prisoners indicated in interviews that they were pleased that religious and cultural dietary requirements were taken into account by the institution but that the quality of food was very low, monotonous and not very nutritious. As a result, many foreign prisoners prepare their own meals and cook for each other when there are facilities. If there are no facilities, this is seen as a major disadvantage.

2.5.2 Religion

Prisoners have the right to profess and practice their religion or ideology individually or in association with others. All penal institutions have a room that can be used for church services and other religious or spiritual services or meetings. On a regular basis religious representatives like Catholic priests, Protestant preachers, Rabbi's, Imam's and humanist counsellors for meetings visit penal institutions with prisoners. These meetings can be on an individual basis or in groups. Upon arrival, prisoners are asked about their religious beliefs. It is the responsibility of the prison director to give prisoners the opportunity to have personal contact with a representative of their religion or ideology connected with the institution. In theory, institutions should therefore have a variety of religious representatives available but in practice there is often a lack of representatives especially of Imams. Since there are many Muslim prisoners, the Minister of Justice organised a special Imam training in order to fill this gap.

During Ramadan, the holiest month on the lunar Islamic calendar, Muslim prisoners are allowed to fast from sunrise to sunset. Traditional Muslim food is provided between sunset and sunrise.

Prisoners who are under any form of segregation or punishment can have access to services but are separated from other prisoners. In interviews with foreign prisoners it became clear that practicing their religion was seen as a very important element in their lives. In some cases these religious feelings became more apparent during detention. In general prisoners were satisfied with the opportunities to attend religious services and to meet religious representatives personally. It is also seen as a way to escape the daily routine. One major disadvantage mentioned by foreign prisoners however is those religious representatives tend not to speak another language besides Dutch, Turkish or Arabic.

2.5.3 Personal Hygiene

Prisoners are entitled to wear their own clothes and footwear unless these pose a possible risk to the order or safety in the institution. In case prisoners do not have sufficient or suitable clothing and or shoes, the institution must provide these. All institutions have facilities for prisoners so they can take care of their appearance and physical hygiene properly. Some institutions have communal shower facilities on each wing and other institutions have cells with individual shower facilities. Prisoners are obliged to have a shower at least once a week and after playing sports. Prisoners who work or play sports with specially adapted clothes and footwear are obliged to wear these. Facilities for washing clothes are mostly available per wing on a regular basis. Normally prisoners are allowed to keep soap, toothpaste, toothbrush, shaving and sanitary materials, comb and shampoo in their cell. On a regular basis, normally every 6 weeks, prisoners are allowed to have a hair cut. Foreign prisoners mentioned in interviews that they were able to take proper care of their appearance and physical hygiene. They were not obliged to shave or cut their hair or change their clothing.

2.5.4 Medical Care

All penitentiary institutions offer a number of healthcare provisions as a standard service to all prisoners. Care is available from an in-house medical centre, psychologist, psychiatrist, general practitioner, dentist and social worker. There is a special prison hospital in The Hague and, if prisoners cannot be treated there, they can be transferred to a local hospital. However, operations that are not strictly urgent are normally postponed until after release. Prisoners are provided with treatment, drugs and diets prescribed by the in-house medical centre. They are entitled to consult, at their own expense, a medical doctor of their choice. To cope with the rising numbers of mentally disturbed prisoners, special individual treatment wards have been set up. For prisoners with severe mental disorders who require a high degree of security, there are a number of secure individual treatment wards. The Forensic Observation and Treatment Ward in Amsterdam (FOBA) serves as a crisis centre for incarcerated psychiatric patients with severe reality and contact disorders. In interviews with foreign prisoners it became clear that in general they received similar medical treatment as national prisoners. Foreign prisoners were satisfied with the quality of staff but were unhappy with the long waiting lists and the time spent with medical staff. Another commonly heard comment was that language difficulties are seen as a hampering factor in indicating the medical problem and understanding why and what kind of medicines and treatment were prescribed.

2.6 Consular and legal help

2.6.1 Consular help

Under article 5 of the Vienna Convention on Consular Relations (1963) embassies and consulates are entitled to serve the interests of their citizens. In case a person is arrested or detained outside their own country, persons are allowed to have access to their consular representative in order to seek assistance. In Dutch penitentiary institutions all foreign prisoners are formally entitled to notify their consular representative upon admission to inform about their detention. In practice not all foreigners make use of this provision because they are not informed about this possibility or because they are unwilling or embarrassed to inform their national authorities or to receive their assistance. The kind of assistance provided by consulates or embassies to their national citizens detained in Dutch penitentiary institutions varies from country to country. Some foreign prisoners receive regular visits from consular representatives; they are kept informed about Dutch legal procedures and are put in touch with local lawyers, interpreters or medical doctors. Some consulates and embassies are in contact with prison authorities and keep relatives at home informed about the situation of the prisoners and the legal process. It is difficult to generalise but especially consulates and embassies from other EU member states tend to be active in supporting their citizens detained in Dutch institutions. The foreign prisoners interviewed that received assistance from their embassies or consulates were positive about the help they received.

2.6.2 Legal help

If the police on suspicion of having committed an offence arrests a person he or she will be brought to the police station for questioning. People can be held for 6 hours in police custody. In case the police needs more time for questioning, an assistant public prosecutor ('hulpofficier van justitie') can decide to issue a remand order in police custody for a further 3 days. After these three days the person is brought before the examining magistrate ('rechter commissaris') in the court. The examining magistrate decides whether the remand in custody can be justified and if it should be extended. Once a person has been remanded in a police station the police notify the 'piket' service. This 'piket' service assigns an independent lawyer who happens to be on duty at that moment and who will provide free legal assistance to the remanded person. It is also possible to have a lawyer of his or her own choice but this is often not free of charge. In principle 'piket' lawyers visit their remanded clients in the police station. In case the remanded person does not speak Dutch there is a so-called 'Interpreters hotline' available via intercom in the meeting rooms. The 'piket' lawyer will accompany their client when brought to court after 3 days and if necessary an interpreter will be present in person. In case the examining magistrate considers the remand lawful and that it should be prolonged, the 'piket' lawyer will be assigned to assist the client. The remand in custody can take place in a police station (so called 'preventive detention') or in a pre-trial prison. This remand order takes up to fourteen days and cannot be renewed. During these fourteen days lawyers can visit clients to discuss the case file including the official report from the police with obtained evidence and statements by witnesses. In case the public prosecutor feels that a person should remain in pre-trial detention, a detention order should be obtained from the court. The suspect will be summoned to appear before court together with the lawyer for another opportunity to express their views before the court takes a decision. A detention order is valid for up to 90 days but can also be given for a period of 30 or 60 days, in which case it can be renewed, up to 90 days in total. The person can remain in pre-trial detention for this period until the public prosecutor brings the case to court or decides to drop the charges. If the case is brought to court the defendant remains in pre-trial detention until the judgement is final. If the case ends without a conviction a person held in pre-trial detention may apply for compensation.

All people in remand and in pre-trial detention are entitled to free legal assistance. This legal assistance is paid for by a grant of the state provided via the Legal Aid Council ('Raad van Rechtsbijstand'). Assigned lawyers receive (from the Legal Aid Council) around € 1,000 for each case from the Legal Aid Council. This is a modest legal fee especially since lawyers have to spend an average of 10 hours in each case (including visits, study of the case, appearance in court, travel time). Lawyers have access to their clients at all times and can meet in private meeting rooms inside the institution.

Some foreign prisoners mentioned in interviews that they were not satisfied with the legal assistance provided to them. The main reason was that they had the feeling that lawyers did not spend enough time in their case. A reason for this can be that (foreign) prisoners have a different set of expectations and very often they do not understand that the examining magistrate only considers the remand lawful and that the magistrate does not examine the criminal case.

2.7 Contact with the outside world

There are several ways for prisoners to remain in contact with the outside world. The most important instruments to maintain contact are visits, communication via telephone and letters and access to news via newspapers, magazine, television and radio.

2.7.1 Visits

Prisoners in Dutch penitentiary institutions are entitled to receive visits from friends and/or family for at least 1 hour per week. The duration of these visits is around 1 hour and they take place under the supervision of prison staff. Visits are arranged beforehand and the institution knows which visitors (normally not more than 3) are expected to come. Before and after the visiting hour, the prisoners' clothing can be searched or the prisoner can be forced to undergo a complete body search. Visitors are searched before and after the visit. They are not allowed to bring in valuables, mobile telephones and drugs. Lawyers can visit their clients at all times in private meeting rooms. Consulate officials, probation officers, members of the supervisory board and religious representatives are also allowed to pay visits to prisoners. Foreign prisoners expressed their unhappiness with the strict visiting procedures in Dutch penitentiary institutions. Most foreign prisoners hardly receive visits from relatives because these visits are very expensive and time-consuming due to long distances. In the rare case that foreign prisoners receive visitors from abroad they are not allowed to stay longer than one hour a week. There are no exceptions to the rules. In plans for the new prison structure the visiting arrangements are extended.

2.7.2 Communication

Once a week prisoners are allowed to make a telephone call at their own expense for 10 minutes. In case prison staff is listening to the call, the prisoner is notified beforehand. Prisoners have the right to receive and send letters by mail at their own expense. Telephone cards and stamps can be bought in the prison shop. Incoming and outgoing mail can be opened and only correspondence with the Royal Family, Members of the national and European parliament, National Ombudsman, lawyers, members of the supervisory board and probation officers are exempted from this rule. In order to protect certain persons, for example a victim, the prison director can restrict the prisoner to contact specific numbers. Pre-trial prisoners may also be restricted in their rights by the examining magistrate ('rechter commissaris') to use the phone or to post.
Foreign prisoners indicated that calling abroad is very expensive and that prison staff do not take into account different time zones. As a result it is difficult to stay in contact. Another hampering factor is that there are very often not enough telephones available so people are unable to make a call. In order to afford expensive telephone cards prisoners sometimes have to receive financial help from relatives. In case this financial support is not provided in Euros there are no opportunities to change the money inside the institution.

2.7.3 News

Every institution has a library and the prisoners are entitled to read magazines and newspapers there and borrow books once a week. On each wing a television and radio is available and prisoners can, at their own expense, rent a television for their cell (see also section 2.2 and 2.4).

2.8 Re-integration activities - Prison leave

2.8.1 Re-integration activities

Around one third of the prison population can be selected for 'Penitentiary programmes'. A condition is that participants are motivated and that they have served at least five sixths of a sentence of at least 6 months (see also section 2.4). Participants are allowed to work or follow educational classes outside the institution and stay home overnight and during weekends. The idea behind these programmes is to facilitate the smooth transition from prison to society. Participants are allowed to stay at home and they wear an anklet that functions as a transmitter to a monitor that permits only a pre-determined day schedule. For reasons mentioned in section 2.4 foreign prisoners generally are excluded from participation.

Apart from these 'penitentiary programmes' there are also other training courses available that aim to smoothen the return into society. Each institution provides a limited range of activities from anger-management courses and social-skills courses to skills trainings to teach prisoners a trade, like painting, bricklaying, wood crafting, welding. In practice these courses are very limited and they tend to be very popular. Foreign prisoners are not excluded from participation but in practice there are not a lot of courses and due to the long waiting lists only a few prisoners can participate. In the plans of the new structure of the prison service there are no re-integration facilities available for foreigners.

2.8.2 Prison leave

Prisoners in Dutch penitentiary institutions can be granted special leave (in the event of illness, funerals etc.), fixed leave (weekend leave in open institutions) and general leave (six periods of leave for prisoners with long sentences who will be released within a year). Leave is granted to prisoners by the prison director or - with respect to certain categories of prisoners - by the Minister of Justice. The prison director is allowed to restrict or withdraw the leave. Special leave is granted in the event of serious illnesses, funerals of family relatives, job interviews or to stand trial. Fixed leave is granted to prisoners in open or semi-open institutions when they approach their release date. In semi-open institutions weekend leave is granted every month and in open institutions every week. Participants of 'penitentiary programmes' are allowed to leave prison all days and nights to participate in mandatory activities like work and or training in combination with electronic monitoring. Before a prisoner is granted leave the prison authorities carefully check the home address and Prison leave in its different modalities is not granted for example to: 1) prisoners without an acceptable home address in the Netherlands, 2) prisoners who are suspected of trying to escape, 3) prisoners who will be extradited after their detention or are subject to an extradition procedure, 4) prisoners who are declared 'persona non grata' or who are subject to such a procedure or who will be expelled from the Netherlands after having served the sentence. Because of these strict criteria foreign prisoners are also less likely to be transferred to more open institutions.

2.9 Release – Expulsion

Once prisoners have served their prison sentence they are released from the penitentiary institution. There is no parole or conditional release in the Netherlands. It was abolished in 1986 and replaced by early release. Early release is a system in which prisoners are automatically released after serving a large part of their sentence. Prisoners serving a sentence up to a maximum of one year must be released after having served six months plus one third of the remaining term and prisoners serving a sentence of more than one year must be released after having served two-thirds. Foreign prisoners are not excluded from this right and are also released early. Early release can be refused or postponed only when very serious objections are present. The power to refuse or postpone early release rests with the penitentiary division of the Court of Appeal in Arnhem. The decision is taken in a public trial at which the prisoner, assisted by his or her counsel, is heard. At this moment a Bill is presented to parliament to re-introduce parole in the Netherlands. One of the reasons for this is that the condition of supervision, by for example the Netherlands Probation and Aftercare Service, can be beneficial for the successful social re-integration of prisoners.

Before leaving the institution, prisoners receive their personal belongings that were kept in a safety box at reception. In some cases prisoners receive some pocket money to take a train or bus to go home, but only if their home is in the Netherlands. Foreign prisoners with valid papers and a permission to stay in the Netherlands are given money to travel to the location where they were arrested. Foreign prisoners who do not hold papers (irregular migrants), who have lost their residence permit because of the offence they have committed or who are declared 'persona non grata' are brought to the Aliens Police ('Vreemdelingendienst'). The normal procedure is that these foreigners will stay up to 14 days in a cell in a police station and thereafter will be detained in a detention centre, a detention boat or a prison. They have to stay there as long as there is a prospect that the Dutch Immigration and Naturalisation Service ('Immigratie en Naturalisatie Dienst') can expel them. During recent years the legal possibilities to deprive a foreigner of his residence permit or to declare him 'persona non grata' have extended sharply. Even a small offence can already result in the loss of a residence permit and/or result in the qualification 'persona non grata'. Whether or not this happens depends also on the length of stay in the Netherlands and the severity of the penalty imposed. The decision to withdraw or not to prolong a residence permit or to declare a foreigner 'persona non grata' is taken by the Minister for Immigration and Integration at the Ministry of Justice on the basis of the provisions in the Immigration Law. The foreigner can lodge an (administrative) appeal against this decision with the court (section: migration chamber) and with that decision he can appeal to the Section Administrative jurisdiction of the Council of State. A foreigner who is declared 'persona non grata' automatically looses his residence permit. Without a residence permit a foreigner is not allowed to stay in the Netherlands and is obliged to leave the Netherlands immediately. If he does not leave he can be detained as long as it is considered necessary to expel him. A special expulsion order is not needed. Irregular stay is not a criminal offence, unless it concerns foreigners who are declared 'persona non grata'. By not leaving the country they commit a crime that can be punished by a prison sentence up to six months.

Expulsion and the expulsion procedure belong to administrative law. Criminal Courts have no competence in this. Looking at the figures in the table below one can observe an increasing trend to declare more foreigners 'persona non grata' in order to force them to leave the Netherlands freely or by expulsion. The number of foreigners that left the country for that reason added up to 900 in 2005.

Table 8 Number of foreigners declared 'persona non grata'

year	number
2000	974
2001	1055
2002	1405
2003	1684
2004	1461
2005	2177

Source: IND/NOVA TV 2006

2.10 Aftercare – Probation

The Netherlands Probation and Aftercare Service (Probation Service) is an independent association that consists of three sub-organisations: the Netherlands Probation and After-Care Foundation, the Salvation Army and the Netherlands Institute for Psychological Care. The Probation Service, which is mainly subsidised by the Ministry of Justice, defines its core business through three key tasks: social enquiry and advice to the judicial authorities, counselling and development and organisation and supervision of community sanctions. The Probation Service used to provide support for ex-prisoners in the field of housing, employment and counselling services. Due to severe budgetary cuts in 2004 and 2005 the Probation Service is not able to be very active in this field anymore. With the exception of the activities for Dutch prisoners, who are detained in other countries, foreign prisoners generally are not considered for interventions by the Probation Service, because, as mentioned before, they are not eligible for community sanctions, open prisons, electronic monitoring, penitentiary programmes etc. The probation Service is also rather reserved towards foreign offenders as far as it concerns pre-sentence and social enquiry reports. The Probation Service is neither very involved in information when released foreign prisoners seek assistance from their national probation services upon return. In the plans for the new structure of the prison service there are no facilities of aftercare for foreigners.

2.11 Staff

The National Agency for Correctional Institutions (DJI) has a 'Training Institute" that is the country's largest specialist training centre. The 'Training Institute' is based in The Hague and is over 40 years old. The institute provides training for executive staff. The most common training is the 'Basic Professional Training for Prison Officers' which takes

42 days and includes modules like *prison law, prison organisation, communication skills, intercultural work, disaster management, handling suicide, handling violence, psychiatrically disturbed behaviour, drug dependency problems, reporting* etc. There is one module about cultural diversity in order to make staff more aware of how to deal with prisoners from various cultural backgrounds. Some institutions prefer to hire staff members who are knowledgeable in other languages than Dutch.

Foreign prisoners mentioned in interviews that staff in general was qualified, helpful and respectful. The fact that staff could not always communicate properly with prisoners was seen as a fact that could not be changed easily. The situation in some detention centres and detention boats for irregular migrants is less positive than in the penitentiary institutions, because more and more employees are hired from private security companies. Generally speaking these employees are unqualified and unskilled to work with prisoners.

2.12 Projects

There were no specific projects organised for foreign prisoners inside or outside the penitentiary institutions.

3 ADMINISTRATIVE DETENTION OF FOREIGN PRISONERS

3.1 Legal basis

Foreign nationals can be detained for two reasons. First of all they may have committed a penal offence for which they can be sentenced with a custodial penal sanction (prison sentence, detention, internment or in-patient hospital order). Often this will be preceded by police custody and pre-trail detention. All these cases are a matter of custodial sanction or a measure under the terms of criminal law.

The second reason why foreign nationals can be deprived of their freedom is the fact that their stay in the Netherlands is not legitimate. This group adds up to approximately 150,000 to 200,000 persons. Among them, foreigners who have gained access to the Netherlands without valid papers and asylum seekers whose appeal have been rejected and who have not left the Netherlands within the legal term. This group of irregular migrants also consists of foreigners whose residence permits have not been extended or whose residence permits have been revoked and tourists who have overstayed their welcome in the Netherlands.

Contrary to many other countries, a stay in the Netherlands without a valid residence permit is not a penal offence. This is only the case with foreigners who have been declared 'persona non grata', as described in chapter 1.4.1. If they don't leave the Netherlands they commit a criminal offence of section 197 PC. This offence can lead to imprisonment up to six months.

With the exception of this last category, foreigners who stay in the Netherlands without a valid residence permit and have not committed a penal offence cannot be detained on a criminal basis. Nevertheless, yearly over 20,000 irregular migrants are being confined to a police station, a penitentiary institution or a detention centre for a short or long period of time, not on the basis of the Penal Code but on the basis of the Immigration Law.

The Immigration Law contains two regulations on the basis of which a foreigner without a residence permit (from here on called irregular migrants) can be detained. Section 6 of the Immigration Law offers this possibility with regard to foreign nationals who have been barred from the Netherlands and who are often being held at the border but who cannot leave the country immediately. They can be put in a police cell for a maximum of 10 days after which they must be transferred to an institution with a lighter regime than normally present in an ordinary penitentiary institution. That can be a special institution, like the 'grenshospitium' in Amsterdam, which is a border hostel, but often a few divisions in a normal prison are being reserved for this purpose.

The second article in the Immigration Law that offers the possibility to detain irregular migrants is article 59. This article applies to most of the foreign nationals who have entered the Netherlands, whether legitimate or not, but whose stay is no longer valid. If their irregular status is detected by the proper authorities, for instance by means of a traffic surveillance, an inspection of a workplace, a suspicion of a penal offence, a report by a civilian or any other reason, they are generally handed over to the aliens police. If after interrogation a reasonable suspicion exist that a foreigner indeed has no valid residence permit, he/she is usually confinement to a police cell (for a maximum of 10 days), followed by transferral to a detention centre of a penitentiary institution.

According to the regulations of section 59, confinement must be called for by the public order or national security. However, practice shows that these regulations have lost nearly all its purpose of guarantee. A stay without valid documents and without registration by the proper authorities is enough to comply with the criteria of public order. Rejected asylum seekers, whose repatriation travel documents are either on hand or are soon expected to be on hand, can be detained without question. Deprivation of freedom of these irregular migrants is based on the Immigration Law that can be seen as a special part of the Administrative Law. The term used for this deprivation of freedom is 'Vreemdelingenbewaring' (Aliens Detention). Confinement only has one ground and one goal: expulsion of the foreign national.

Legally, this detention has no fixed duration. In principle, it can last until the expulsion is actually realised or as long as expulsion is still a possibility. When expulsion has not been realised within 6 months, the courts generally rule that the interest of the foreigner who has to be released weighs more than the interest of expulsion of the government. However, this does not apply when the expulsion is to be expected shortly or when the foreigner himself can be blamed for not being able to realise the expulsion. Practice shows that long-term detention from 15 up to 18 months is no exception.

Contrary to the penal detention, the aliens' detention is not checked by a judge within a few days. The Migration Law gives the detainee the right to have his or her detention examined by the special 'Migration Chamber' at the administrative districts court. As soon as the foreigner lodges an appeal, the court must handle this appeal within the timeframe of 14 days. When the appeal has been concluded, judgement must be passed within seven days. If the foreigner does not appeal, the Immigration and Naturalisation Service will inform the court no later than 28 days after the deprivation of freedom. This report will be seen as the appeal of the foreigner.

The foreigner as well as the Immigration and Naturalisation Service, which is acting on behalf of the Minister for Immigration and Integration, can appeal against the sentence to the Section Administrative jurisdiction of the Council of State. As long as detention continues, the foreigner can lodge an appeal against the continuance of the detention with the 'Migration Chamber'. Contrary to the first appeal, with these renewed appeals the foreigner is usually not heard in person en there is no need for a court session.

During the first appeal, the court examines the suitability and the legitimacy of the detention. During the appeal to higher court as well as the following appeals, only the legitimacy is being examined and in particular two questions: is application of the aliens detention in breach of the law or is it not (or no longer) justified by balancing the interests of the state on the one hand and the interests of the foreigner on the other hand. If the answers to these questions are negative, the detention should be withdrawn, either with or without allowing compensation.

Although the aliens detention is an administrative measure based on the Migration Law and enforced by the responsibility of the Minister for Immigration and Integration, the ways of enforcement are not being determined by the Migration Law but by the same law that goes for the criminal detainees: the Penitentiary Principles Act. The Minister for Immigration and Integration is not accountable for the enforcement; it is the responsibility of the Minister of Justice and of The National Agency of Correctional Institutions (DJI) of the Ministry of Justice.

3.2 Aliens detention in practice

3.2.1. Some figures

Twenty-five years ago it was still an exception to confine irregular migrants to a penitentiary institution when they had a view to expulsion. For example, in 1980 the prison capacity for aliens' detention consisted of no more than 45 places. During that year, the measure was carried out no more than 500 times. The following ten years showed a gradual increase up to 200 in 1989. Since 1990 this has changed considerably. In 1994 the first institution, specially intended for this category of detainees, was taken into use with a capacity of 656 places divided over private cells and cells designed for 8 persons. From then on, the number of institutions grew rapidly. At the end of 2006 the total capacity of aliens detention will be over 3000, divided over 10 institutions. Five of these will be boats specially converted for this purpose (detention boats) with a capacity of 1,732 places in total. In the majority of these institutions, the cells are designed for more persons in one cell. Six institutions are exclusively for males and one institution is meant for women only. The remaining three are meant for men, women as well as children, although in separate buildings.

The latest figures regarding the origin of detained irregular migrants date from 2004. At the end of that year, the capacity for aliens' detention in detention centres was over 2,000 places. As shown in the figure below, 1,952 irregular migrants were detained in detention centres for aliens on 31 December of that year. By far the most came from Africa (46 %) and Asia (over 31 %).

Table 9 Nationality of irregular migrants in detention centres at December 31 2004

Nationality	Number of detained irregular migrants	Percentage
Rest of Africa	375	19.2 %
Rest of Asia	257	13.2%
Algeria	218	11.2%
China	187	9.6%
Morocco	179	9.2%
Eastern Europe	174	8.9%
India	114	5.8%
Surinam	58	3.0%
Turkey	57	2.9%
Sierra Leone	52	2.7%
Nigeria	48	2.5%
Rest of Europe	46	2.4%
Rest of America's	37	1.9%
Unknown or Stateless	150	7.7%
Total	1952	100%

Source: DJI, www.dji.nl, Capaciteit en bezetting

The length of stay varies from less than 14 days up to over 1 year to 18 months. The average length of stay in most institutions adds up from 60 to 80 days. A representative sample of 400 irregular migrants from 2004 shows that in 56 % of the cases the detention ended within three months. In 22 % of the cases we see that the detention lasted three to six months. The remaining 22 % were detained for more than six months of whom 4 % for more than ten months.[7]

The length of stay is primarily determined by the fact that many foreigners do not have identification papers or travel documents. Issuing either of these papers, the Dutch Immigration and Naturalisation Service are dependent on the cooperation of foreigners as well as the cooperation of the concerned embassy or consulate. Practice shows that in over 60 % of the cases it is not possible to get a 'laissez-passer' within the timeframe determined by the court. This means that the foundation on which the detention is based, which is being in sight of expulsion, is no longer present and the aliens' detention must be withdrawn. Subsequently, the foreigner will be released with the order to leave the Netherlands. Many of them will not or can not do that en will continue their illegal stay in the Netherlands at the risk of being picked up (again) after some time to be detained yet again.

Due to a special law "De koppelingswet", Irregular migrants are, excluded from all social services, provisions and benefits from the government with the exception of medical necessities, the right to education for children and the right to legal aid.

---

[7] Cfr. A.M. van Kalmthout et. al., Terugkeermogelijkheden van vreemdelingen in vreemdelingenbewaring, Nijmegen 2004, p. 95-98.

3.2.2 Treatment

Aliens detention is an administrative measure and not a criminal sanction. In spite of that, the legislator has not developed a separate regime for the aliens' detention but has included in the Aliens Act the definition that execution will be carried out in the same way as in the criminal detention. That was understandable because at that time irregular migrants were seldom locked up and there were no separate institutions for the detention of irregular migrants. Furthermore, they were under the assumption that the irregular migrant would be expelled soon after her/his confinement making her/his stay in these regular penitentiary institutions of short duration.

Despite the strong increase in the number of irregular migrants in detention and despite the fact that they are being detained in different locations now, the legislator has not changed the legislation itself. That means that the irregular migrants are subject to the same penitentiary rules and regulations as a remand prisoner or a sentenced prisoner.

The Penitentiary Principles Act and the Decrees and Circulars based on that do contain separate regulations for foreign prisoners but these are never in favour of the foreigner and always relate to the exclusion of facilities that apply to Dutch nationals. Examples of that are the exclusion from the right to prison leaves, the right to be transferred to half-open and open prisons and the right to participate in a penitentiary programme. A significant difference in the position of criminal detainees is that the staff in penitentiary institutions also has the task to support the detainee with her/his reintegration process. Irregular migrants, on the other hand, are supposed to leave the Netherlands and therefore hardly any attention is being paid to life after detention in detention centres. In most institutions, staff is mainly assigned to security tasks and, contrary to the staff in penitentiary institutions, is often employed by private security services. Their specific preparatory training is limited to a 7-day course followed by 7 days of 'training on the job'. [8]

Regarding the living conditions, most institutions have an extreme austere regime taking into account that in many of them the detainee is allowed only a few hours per day outside his/her cell. All in all, per week the irregular migrant has the right to 1 hour of visits, 1, 5 hour of sports/physical exercise, 6 hours of recreational activities and 7 hours of airing (1 hour per day). At this moment, in some detention centres detainees are offered the possibility to work. However, on detention boats this facility is not available and from 2007 no detention centre will offer work any more. To compensate the loss of labour, the detainees will receive an allowance of 7,50 Euro per week which is by no means sufficient for expenses like supplementary food, toiletry, smoking materials, phone cards, stamps etc. What weighs heavily though, is the fact that with the loss of labour, the amount of hours the detainee spends in her/his cell has increased enormously.

If one compares the position and treatment of irregular migrants with those of the criminal detainees, we can establish that the foreign prisoners, who are being detained as irregular migrants, are considerably worse of than the Dutch or the foreign nationals who are detained on a criminal basis. Several investigations into the position of foreign nationals in aliens detention show that particularly the uncertainty about the duration of detention to many foreigners is a source of tension and suspense which frequently reveals

---

[8] Cfr. Inspectie voor de sanctietoepassing, detentieboten Zuid-Holland, lokatie Merwehaven, 's-Gravenhage, mei 2006.

itself in rebellious or, on the contrary, in indifferent and disturbed behaviour, fights, suicide attempts, hunger strikes etcetera.[9]

In addition to this, facilities such as legal aid, the use of a library, medical and psychosocial care, education and recreation are often below the standard of regular penitentiary
institutions. This goes especially for the detention boats.

In fact, they are not suitable for a detention longer than a few months, but nevertheless
over 13 % of the detainees remain there for more than six months. Foreigners stay detained for three-quarters of the time in cells for 2, 4 or 6 persons of 11, 22 and 25-29
square metres respectively.

Inquiries into the living conditions on these boats show, among other things, a lack of
a decent airing space, reliable sports- and recreational facilities and air-conditioning systems. Furthermore, the facilities regarding medical and psychosocial aid, legal aid and
privacy are more restricted than in regular penitentiary institutions. Finally, the detention
centres are not equipped for the stay of children who reside there on their own or with
their parent.

4 NATIONALS DETAINED ABROAD

In 2005 a total of 2,645 Dutch nationals were detained in penitentiary institutions in 81
countries around the world. The number of Dutch nationals detained abroad is increasing; in 1992 the number was around 1,000 and in 10 years time it has more than doubled
to 2,330. In the table below information is given about the period 1997 to 2005.

Table 10 Number of Dutch Nationals Detained Abroad

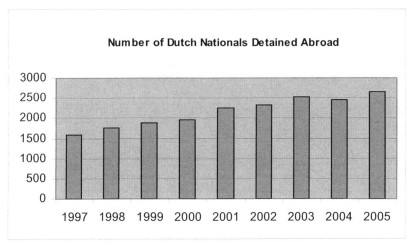

Source: Foreign Liaison Office, Dutch Probation Service, 2006

---

[9] Cfr. A.M. van Kalmthout et. al, . A.M. van Kalmthout et. al., Terugkeermogelijkheden van vreemdelingen in vreemdelingenbewaring, Nijmegen 2004;. Inspectie voor de sanctietoepassing, detentieboten Zuid-Holland, lokatie Merwehaven, 's-Gravenhage, mei 2006; Raad voor strafrechtstoepassing en jeugdbescherming, detentiecentra Rotterdam, locatie Merwehaven, detentieboten
Reno en Stockholm (h.v.b.), 's-Gravenhage juli 2005.

Although Dutch prisoners are scattered around the world, around 60% are detained in EU member states. From this group 75% are detained in only seven European countries, namely Germany (479), France (232), Spain (213), United Kingdom (155), Italy (133) and Belgium (93). Information on numbers per European countries can be found in the table below.

Table 11 Number of Dutch Nationals detained in EU countries

Number of Dutch Nationals detained in EU countries, April 2006	
Country	Number
Germany	479
France	232
Spain	213
United Kingdom	155
Italy	133
Belgium	93
Portugal	74
Sweden	39
Austria	30
Greece	16
Denmark	14
Ireland	13
Hungary	12
Luxembourg	7
Poland	5
Czech Republic	5
Finland	4
Slovakia	1
Other EU countries	-
Total:	1525

Source: Foreign Liaison Office, Dutch Probation Service, 2006

Other countries where Dutch nationals are frequently detained are the United States of America, Surinam, Dominican Republic and Morocco. A majority of the Dutch prisoners do not originally come from the Netherlands; many of them are born in Surinam, Netherlands Antilles/Aruba, Morocco, Turkey or the Dominican Republic. A quarter of the Dutch prisoners do not or barely speak Dutch. Other general observations are that 60% do not have a vocational education or diploma, 60% do not have a job, income or allowance prior to detention and 16% are female. More than 80% of all Dutch prisoners detained are arrested or convicted for possession or smuggling of (mainly hard) drugs. The turnover rate is very high; in 2005 1,241 Dutch nationals were arrested abroad and 1,135 were released. Nearly half of all sentences are longer than one year.

In the Netherlands, the Ministry of Foreign Affairs and the Ministry of Justice promote the interest of detained citizens abroad. Around the world, The Ministry of Foreign Affairs provides care and counselling via their Consular posts as a first point of contact. The Ministry of Justice is mainly involved when Dutch detainees are transferred to the Netherlands within the framework of a bi-lateral transfer agreement. Annually around 6% of all Dutch prisoners detained abroad make use of this agreement called 'Wet Overdracht Tenuitvoerlegging Strafvonnissen' (WOTS). The fact that the Netherlands a relatively mild sentencing regime towards drug crimes makes other countries more hesitant to agree to a transfer.

Besides the two ministries the Dutch Probation Service plays an important role in the care of Dutch nationals detained abroad. The 'Liaison Office for Dutch Prisoners Abroad and International Contacts' (Liaison Office) of the Dutch Probation Service has been established 30 years ago for this purpose. The Liaison Office operates from the Probation Service headquarters in Utrecht with a team of nine regional coordinators, one coordinator international contacts and two administrative staff. Besides staff in Utrecht the Liaison Office coordinates the work of 275 visiting volunteers and 15 corresponding volunteers. The Liaison Office also offers study facilities through a separate foundation, the Foundation Education behind Bars. The visiting volunteers are Dutch nationals who live and work abroad and who voluntarily visit Dutch nationals in detention every four to six weeks. These visits are carried out in close cooperation with the Consular Department of the Ministry of Foreign Affairs and the various Dutch consulates and embassies around the world. The Liaison Office receives financial assistance from both the Ministry of Foreign Affairs and the Ministry of Justice. More information on the work of the Liaison Office can be found in a separate chapter in this book.

For this study a questionnaire has been developed which was sent to Dutch consulates in all EU Member States by the Ministry of Foreign Affairs. Fourteen consulates[10] participated in this survey that has been developed to obtain more insight into consular activities in relation to Dutch nationals in detention. The aim of Dutch consulates is to provide care and assistance to the detainee and to inform their family. The legal basis for having contact with nationals in detention is the Vienna Convention on Consular Relations (1963) that has been ratified by all 25 EU Member States. According to article 36 of the Vienna Convention on Consular Relations it is required that foreign nationals who are arrested or detained should be given notice "without delay" of their right to inform their embassy or consulate of that arrest. If the person so requests (it is not obligatory), the police or prison authority informs their embassy or consulate with information about the person's name, the place of detention and sometimes with the reasons of their arrest. In practice consulates are not always informed or with a long delay.

Dutch consulates indicate in the survey that as soon as they are informed about detention of a Dutch national they start organising a visit to this person and inform the consular department at the Ministry of Foreign Affairs through an information programme called 'PRISON". In case the person wants his/her family to be informed, the department will do so and remains in contact with one designated (Dutch speaking) contact person, mostly a family member or a relative. During this visit the consular official will give information orally and in writing about imprisonment, how to obtain legal assistance and

---

[10] Dutch consulates in Denmark, France, Germany (4 consulates), Ireland, Italy, Luxembourg, Malta, Portugal, Slovakia, Spain and the United Kingdom.

other practicalities. In exceptional cases items like specific medicines will be brought or the consular official will ask to see the Prison Director for assistance in order to request proper medical care. The written information is normally a little booklet that has been developed by the Dutch Ministry of Foreign Affairs. The booklet is called 'Arrested in.... (name country)' and is available in Dutch for a large number of countries. It contains information about the Dutch authorities involved, how to obtain legal assistance, information on the criminal procedure and legal provisions (appeal, early release), imprisonment (visits, correspondence, religion, and medical care), transfer, contact details of authorities and vocabulary (translation of legal terms, abbreviations and useful sentences).

After the first initial visit, a Dutch national will be visited a few times during the year. In general consulates try to visit Dutch nationals four times a year but this frequency depends also on the size of the country, the number of consular staff available and type of individual cases. Contact about transfer agreements is normally between the Dutch Ministry of Justice and the designated authority in the country where the person is detained. Normally there is no interference from the consulate. Some consulates send Dutch newspapers, magazines and books to prisons with Dutch nationals. Once a Dutch national is eligible for release or transfer to the Netherlands, the Dutch consulates provides if necessary travel documents or a laissez-passer.

Besides visits from consular officials many Dutch national prisoners receive social visits by visiting volunteers from the Liaison Office of the Dutch Probation Service. The Liaison Office has a network of 275 volunteers of which 153 are active in the 24 EU Member States. These visits are coordinated by the country coordinator of the Liaison Office and take place around every four to six weeks. From each visit a report is being made and shared by Liaison Office with the consulate.

Occasionally Dutch nationals also receive visits from visiting reverends from the Epafras Foundation. This foundation, which was initiated by Reverend Joop Spoor in 1984, provides pastoral and material assistance for Dutch nationals detained abroad. Epafras is incorporated in the associated churches of the Netherlands and receives funding from the Dutch Ministry of Foreign Affairs and Ministry of Justice.

An important section of the survey is about the observations of the consulates about stimulating or hampering effects for Dutch nationals detained in EU Member Countries. Although a majority of consulates indicated that Dutch nationals are in general not being treated differently compared to national prisoners, there are quite a number of differences, mainly disadvantages. Dutch prisoners consider visits by consular staff as a 'break' in daily (boring) prison routine and an opportunity to speak Dutch. Dutch nationals use the consulate as a 'soundboard' for their problems and although the consulates are not allowed to interfere in individual legal cases their attention and assistance is appreciated. Consulates considered the following issues as hampering for Dutch nationals detained in the EU Member States:
- Apparently not all prisoners are informed about their right to contact their consulate;
- consulates are often not informed (on time) about new legislation, provisions of pardon, illness of detainees;
- legal procedures are often slow and complicated, prisoners receive limited information about their case, and in case free legal aid is provided the quality is often below standard;
- language difficulties contribute to feelings of isolation and disorientation;

- no opportunities for temporary leave (not even for exceptional cases like illness/death family member);
- long periods in pre-trial detention;
- no preparations for release (no placement in open prisons because of the risk of escape);
- long delays in medical care;
- expensive money transfers;
- in some countries it is difficult to get involved in work and educational activities;
- difficulties to maintain contact with family (expensive phone calls, rare visits, rigid and bureaucratic visit arrangements);
- communication difficulties due to no or limited knowledge of national language;
- no aftercare facilities.

For consulates it is often difficult to see that, for a large part of the observed obstacles, they are not able to change anything for the better. Also for Dutch prisoners and their families it is sometimes disappointing that in practice consulates are limited in their activities. Opportunities for consulates to provide care and counselling depend heavily on the willingness of the national authorities. Also in one country there can be differences between penitentiary institutions. The national prison authority is in principle responsible for the care of prisoners, including foreign prisoners. In countries where prisoners are held in relatively good conditions with appropriate care and treatment the role for Dutch consulates can be rather limited. However, often there is a discrepancy between formal rules and provisions and daily practice.

In order to improve consular services some consulates indicated that it would be good to receive professional training. This training should also be open for visiting volunteers from the Liaison Office. In some countries, like the UK, visiting volunteers have monthly meetings with one person from the consulate present. Another suggestion was to have regular (twice a year) conferences organised by the Ministry of Foreign Affairs. Some consulates would like to provide language courses for Dutch nationals in detention.

In the survey, two interesting national initiatives in Spain and UK were mentioned as beneficial to foreign prisoners. Spain has a non-governmental organisation that provides places to stay overnight for foreign prisoners during short leave. In many countries foreign prisoners are not allowed to go on leave because in most cases no permanent address is available in the country of detention. By providing a secure place to stay for foreign offenders Spanish prison authorities are more lenient to grant permission for prison leave. Prison leave is being regarded as a successful way of preparing prisoners for re-entry into society. In England and Wales some prisons are using so called 'Foreign National Orderlies' (FNO). These Foreign National Orderlies' are prisoners who are carefully recruited and trained to provide a range of services for foreign national prisoners. These posts were initiated in HMP Wandsworth, a large London prison with a high proportion of foreigners. The FNO's have a trustee position. They are allowed to move between wings and they are being paid. Their role is to distribute information to foreign nationals (translate information, give useful addresses of organisations and embassies), to visit new arrivals and to help communication with staff and to identify whether foreign nationals are in need of particular help. More information on FNO's can be found in the chapter about the UK.

Once a Dutch national is released and/or transferred back to the Netherlands the contact with the consulate will stop. In practice only the Liaison office of the Dutch Probation remains in contact in case aftercare is facilitated upon return to the Netherlands. Aftercare is limited to offering advice and referral to other professional social workers. There is in general no media attention for prisoners returning from EU Member Countries. However, in the last years there was quite some press coverage about a few Dutch nationals who were detained under harsh conditions in South-East Asia. Also the miserable prison conditions in Morocco and in the Dutch former colony Surinam, where many Dutch nationals are held in custody, were criticised by the press and members of parliament.

5 EVALUATION AND RECOMMENDATIONS

The Dutch sanction system does not differentiate between Dutch and foreign offenders. However, there are prosecutorial sentencing guidelines that indicate that foreign prisoners should be excluded from certain sanctions like task penalty and electronic monitoring. Although these guidelines are non-binding they have a great impact on the sentencing process. Prisoners who do not have citizenship of the Netherlands can in principle be detained in all kinds of penitentiary institutions and they are not segregated from other prisoners. However, irregular migrants are detained in special detention centres that are run by a separate unit of National Agency of Correctional Institutions (DJI). At this moment DJI is going trough a transition process and in the future it is likely that foreigners who have been sentenced will be placed separated from national prisoners with a slightly different regime, like no provisions for work for those sentenced shorter than 4 months.

There are over 100 different nationalities detained in Dutch penitentiary institutions. Although prisoners are entitled to contact consular officials of their country there is in principle not a lot of attention and support. In interviews with foreign prisoners it also became clear that often they are not keen to inform their consulate. Irregular migrants in detention have more regular visits by their embassies in order to prepare return documents. These visits are organised by the Dutch Immigration and Naturalisation Service (IND). The International Organisation for Migration (IOM) plays an important mediating role between consulates and foreign nationals who are willing to return to their country of origin.

The Dutch imprisonment rate has increased considerably and the prison population has become less homogenous. Over 63% of the prison population have been born outside the Netherlands. If the population of detention centres for irregular migrants is excluded, this number is exactly 50%. The percentage of prisoners with a Dutch passport is considerably higher, namely 65%. Although a relatively large percentage of the prison population is Dutch citizen, it does not imply that this group understands the Dutch language and shares the Dutch culture and customs.

The vast majority of foreign prisoners who were interviewed for this study indicated that they are being treated in the same way as national prisoners. There are no indications that they feel discriminated upon or isolated from other prisoners. The fact that religious, cultural and dietary requirements were taken into consideration was seen as positive. However, most foreign prisoners mentioned that there are several disadvantages related to their foreign status, which makes their position more vulnerable in comparison to other prisoners. One of the most common felt disadvantages is language. Due to the fact that prisoners do not understand, speak or read the Dutch language they are less able to communicate with others, they are less aware of the rules and procedures, they have less understanding of the legal proceedings of their criminal case and they are less able to participate in training courses. A second major disadvantage is the physical distance from family and friends and as a result foreign prisoners often feel lonely, uncertain and help-less. A third disadvantage is the fact that foreign prisoners are often uncertain about their legal case and status. Although free legal help and interpreters services are normally be-ing provided it is hard to understand Dutch legal proceedings and implications concern-ing their personal case. Many interviewed prisoners were not aware of whether or not they were being expelled from the Netherlands upon release. This uncertainty has a negative effect on their perception of detention.

A fourth major disadvantage is that most foreign prisoners are excluded from provi-sions like transfer to a more open-institution, weekend leave, electronic monitoring and participation in penitentiary programmes. At this moment it is unclear what kind of effect the proposed new structure in the Dutch National Agency for Correctional Institutions will have on foreign prisoners.

It is clear that, although foreign prisoners are in general treated in the same way as national prisoners, there are several elementary disadvantages that make this group more vulnerable than national prisoners. In order to reduce their vulnerable position and to stimulate their successful return into society the following is recommended: it would be advisable to make translations of prison rules and information about prison life available in all penitentiary institutions in various languages; to allow more flexible visiting schemes and facilities for visitors from abroad; to provide information about legal proceedings and make professional help from lawyers more standard; to provide opportunities for foreign prisoners to make use of open institution, early release and other programmes to facilitate their successful return into society. The group of foreign prisoners is too important to ne-glect and too substantial to delay.

Chapter 20

Poland

Barbara Stando-Kawecka

1 INTRODUCTION

Poland is a relatively large European country. The total national territory of Poland - including internal waters and territorial sea - amounts to 322,600 km², of which 312,000 km² are actual land area. According to recent statistics, Poland's population numbers more than 38 million. In comparison with other European Union countries, Poland is highly homogeneous. Polish citizens constitute 98,2 % of the population, including 1,2 % people who hold the Polish and another countries' citizenship. The percentage of foreigners amounts to 1,8 %, including 0,1 % people having foreign citizenship and 1,7 % without any stated citizenship. Ethnic minorities - mainly Ukrainians, Belarusians and Germans - constitute about 2 % of the whole population. A large majority of residents (about 90 %) are Roman Catholics. There are over one hundred other churches and religious associations as well, the largest of which are the Orthodox Church, the Greek Catholic Church, the Jehovah's Witness Association and several Protestant and Protestant-traditional Churches.[1] According to European Union statistics the net migration indicator in Poland during the last years has been negative; therefore the number of emigrants from the country has exceeded the number of immigrants.[2] In 1991 Poland joined the Council of Europe, and two years later the country ratified the ECHR. In 1994 Poland ratified the European Convention for the Prevention of Torture. Since 1991 Poland has been party to the 1951 Geneva Convention on the Status of Refuges and the 1967 New York Protocol on Refugees.

1.1 Overview penalties and measures

After the collapse of the totalitarian state in 1989 in Poland, a thorough reform of criminal law became a matter of the utmost urgency. Independently of the work done on drafts of the new criminal codification, after 1989 numerous changes to the codes of 1969 were passed in order to adjust the criminal law to international standards as well as to make it more humane, liberal and rational. In 1997 three new codes were issued by Parliament: the Criminal Code, the Code of Criminal Procedure and the Code on the Execution of Penalties. Currently, the criminal sanction system in Poland is regulated by the 1997 Criminal Code. This Code introduced the division of sanctions between penalties and penal measures. The catalogue of penalties includes:
- a fine;
- liberty limitation for one month up to one year;
- imprisonment for one month up to 15 years;
- 25 years of imprisonment;
- life imprisonment.

As for fines, the 1997 Criminal Code introduced a system of day fines. However, in some cases provided by law, fixed sum fines could be imposed as well.

The penalty of liberty limitation is partly similar to the community service order known in West-European countries. According to Article 58.1 of the Code, the imposition of un-

---

[1] Main Statistical Office of the Republic of Poland 2005, Maly Rocznik Statystyczny Polski 2005 (Small Statistical Yearbook of Poland of 2005), available online: http://www.stat.gov.pl.
[2] European Commission 2005, Eurostat Yearbook 2005, available online: htpp://epp.eurostat.cec.eu.int.

suspended imprisonment should be based on the principle of *ultima ratio*; if the act provides for the choice of the type of penalty, the court may impose unsuspended imprisonment only if another penalty or penal measure cannot serve the purposes of punishment. The conditional suspension of the execution of penalty is possible not only for imprisonment but also for liberty limitation and fines. As regards imprisonment, provisions of the 1997 Code provide for the possibility to conditionally suspend the execution of imprisonment terms not exceeding two years for a trial period of two to five years. The death penalty had not been carried out in Poland since 1988, although the statutory moratorium on the execution of this penalty was passed only in 1995. At the same time, life imprisonment – first known in the 1932 Criminal Code - was re-introduced. The catalogue of penalties in the 1997 Criminal Code does not include the death penalty, while life imprisonment was retained in it. Pursuant to Article 78.3 of this Code, in the case of a life imprisonment conditional release is only possible after having served 25 years; the court imposing the prison sentence may state, however, that the offender has to serve a longer period than 25 years before he or she is allowed to bring a motion concerning earlier release.

The catalogue of penal measures covers such measures as the deprivation of civic rights, a ban on holding certain offices, performing a certain profession or certain activities, a ban on driving, a ban on maintaining contacts with certain persons or leaving certain places of stay without the permission of the court, forfeiture of goods, the obligation to redress the damage and making the sentence publicly known. Except for penalties and penal measures the 1997 Criminal Code also provides for preventive or security measures (*sichernde Maßnahmen*). They can be imposed on offenders, regardless whether they can be criminally responsible for having committed an offence, since these measures are not aimed at punishment but at the protection of the safety and security of persons or property. Some of these measures, for example placing the offender in a psychiatric institution, are of a custodial character.

It should be noted that in Poland criminal responsibility for petty offences is not regulated by the Criminal Code but by the Code of Petty Offences. Generally, petty offences are similar to *Übertretungen* under the German law; however, they comprise not only petty traffic and public order offences, but also petty thefts and some other property offences. For a long time those charged with petty offences had been tried outside the judiciary system. Since 2001, however, they have been dealt with by ordinary courts. Currently, the most severe penalty provided for by the Code of Petty Offences is the penalty of confinement from five up to 30 days.

As a rule, juveniles - persons who have committed an offence after having reached 13 but before 17 years of age - are not criminally responsible. Only in very exceptional cases can penalties provided for by the Criminal Code (including imprisonment) be imposed on a juvenile who has committed one of the most serious offences while being 15 or 16 years of age. As for the structure of penalties imposed on offenders, after 1989 the criminal policy in Poland has been liberalized. In the 1990s a steady decrease in the percentage of unsuspended imprisonment could be observed.[3] In 1990 the percentage of unsuspended imprisonment among all imposed penalties amounted to 27 % while in 2002 it dropped to 10 %. At the same time the percentage of suspended imprisonment had been

---

[3] A. Siemaszko, B. Gruszczynska, and M. Marczewski, 'Facts & Figures', in: A Siemaszko, (ed.), *Crime and Law Enforcement in Poland on the threshold of the 21st Century*, Oficyna Naukowa, Warsaw 2000, p. 49.

growing from 49 % in 1990 up to 59 % in 2002. The proportion of fines among all penalties imposed by courts fluctuated between 18 % and 26 % while the proportion of liberty limitation was on the decrease in the early-1990s, mainly due to economic changes that resulted in increased unemployment and a gradual diminishing of the state sector. However, the proportion of sentences to liberty limitation has recently been on the increase, and in 2003 it amounted to 12,7%.[4]

1.2 Overview of the Prison System

1.2.1. Organisational Structure

According to the 1997 Code of Criminal Procedure, a person suspected of having committed an offence can be arrested by the police. He or she should be immediately released if there are no further grounds for detention and also if no motion concerning the warrant of 'temporary arrest' was brought by the court within 48 hours. In any case, persons arrested by the police can not be held in police custody for longer than 72 hours. Suspects detained on remand are then transferred from the police detention facility to a remand prison. Police detention facilities are subordinated to the Ministry of Internal Affairs and Administration while remand prisons as well as prisons for sentenced prisoners are under the supervision of the Ministry of Justice. Prisons in Poland are established by the Minister of Justice; no private prisons are allowed by the law. The prison system has been the responsibility of the Minister of Justice since 1956. The prison staff consists mainly of officers of the Prison Service but civil servants are also employed. The Prison Service is paramilitary. In terms of Article 1.2 of the 1996 Prison Service Act it is a non-political, uniformed and armed corps. The organisational unit which administers the Prison Service is the Central Administration of the Prison Service, headed by the Director General of the Ministry of Justice.

In 2003 about 24,500 persons were employed in prisons including approximately 22,500 officers of the Prison Service and 2,000 civil employees working mainly as psychologists, teachers or members of the prison health service. At the same time, over one in four prison officers (27,6 %) had a tertiary education - this means that they had graduated from a high school or university- and nearly three in four (70,8 %) had the secondary school certificate (*Arbitur*). The average monthly cost of detention per prisoner in 2003 amounted to 1,5 thousand PLN, which is equivalent to about 400 euros.[5]

The prison population in Poland consists of three categories of persons deprived of liberty:
- suspects detained on remand before and pending trial,
- prisoners sentenced to imprisonment under the Criminal Code,

---

[4] Central Statistical Office (2004) Statistical Yearbook of the Republic of Poland, available online: www.ms.gov.pl; see also B. Stando-Kawecka, '*Community Sanctions in Polish Penal Law*", in: Albrecht, H.-J. and van Kalmthout, A. (eds), *Community Sanctions and Measures in Europe and North America*, Max-Planck-Institut für Ausländisches und Internationales Strafrecht, Freiburg/ Breisgau 2002, pp. 448-449; T. Szymanowski,, *Polityka karna i penitencjarna w Polsce w okresie przemian prawa karnego* (The Criminal and Penitentiary Policy in Poland in the Period of Transformation of the Criminal Law), Wydawnictwa Uniwersytetu Warszawskiego, Warsaw 2004, p. 62.

[5] Central Administration of the Prison Service 2004, Podstawowe problemy wieziennictwa (Basic Problems of the Prison System), available online: htpp://www.czsw.gov.pl.

- persons on whom the penalty of arrest has been imposed for petty offences under the Code of Petty Offences.

1.2.2. Foreign Prisoners

According to prison statistics, there was a sharp increase in the absolute number of foreigners deprived of their liberty in the early 1990s, followed by a decrease in the late 1990s. In 2000 the population of imprisoned foreigners - including both pre-trial detainees as well as foreigners serving prison sentences - started to rise again. In the peak year 2001 it amounted to 1,550. Since 2001 the number of foreigners in prisons has been diminishing significantly. The percentage of foreigners in the whole prison population rose in the early 1990s from 0,1 % in 1990 to 2,4 % in 1995. In the late 1990s it fluctuated between 2,4 % in 1996 and 1,9 % in 1999 and then started to decline (Table 1).

Table 1 **Foreigners in the prison population in the years 1989-2005 (as of 31 December)**

Year	Prison population total	Number of foreigners	Percentage of foreigners
1989	40,321	26	0,1
1990	50,165	56	0,1
1991	58,619	209	0,4
1992	61,409	742	1,2
1993	61,562	1,109	1,8
1994	62,719	1,161	1,9
1995	61,136	1,496	2,4
1996	55,487	1,307	2,4
1997	57,382	1,296	2,3
1998	54,373	1,058	1,9
1999	56,765	1,065	1,9
2000	70,544	1,327	1,9
2001	79,634	1,550	1,9
2002	80,467	1,349	1,7
2003	79,281	1,173	1,5
2004	80,368	1,041	1,3
2005	82,955	655	0,8

Source: Central Administration of the Prison Service, http://www.czsw.gov.pl.

In comparison with other EU countries, the proportion of foreigners among prisoners in Poland has been and still is low. It is not surprising, however, given the fact that the proportion of foreigners among all persons suspected by the police has also been relatively low in the whole period after 1989.

It remains to be added that there is no special section within the Prison Service is solely responsible for dealing with foreign prisoners. Additionally, prison staff receive no special training in order to facilitate their treatment.

1.3. Overview involvement Consulates, Embassies, Ministries home country, Probation service home country, NGO's etc.

Under the Code of Criminal Procedure (Article 612) a foreigner arrested by the police is entitled to have contact with the appropriate consular or diplomatic office. Additionally, it is obligatory for the court rendering the decision on pre-trial detention of a foreigner to inform without delay the local consular office – or, in the absence of such an office, the diplomatic representation of the country concerned. Several provisions of the Code of Execution of Penalties provide foreign prisoners with the right to maintain contacts with the appropriate consular or diplomatic office. Research on foreigners in Polish prisons initiated by the Commissioner for Civil Rights Protection in 1992 showed that a large number of complaints made by foreigners related to the fact that they were not able to maintain contacts with the appropriate consular or diplomatic services, because the offices concerned did not answer their letters. According to prison governors, citizens of West-European countries usually had good contacts with consular representatives who visited them and brought them food, books and newspapers. The situation was quite different with respect to nationals of East-European countries.[6]

In the mid-1990s most nationals from Ukraine, Belarus, Russia and Caucasus were still deprived of consular care and of family support. It so happened that some of them sold items of their clothing in prisons in order to obtain money for cigarettes and other goods. Despite their efforts to receive financial support from NGOs they did not succeed in it because of lack of resources.[7] It seems that the situation has not changed significantly since the mid-1990s; according to prison staff members of the remand prison in Cracow, in August 2006 there were 14 foreigners detained before trial, but only two of them were visited by consular officials during the last six months. Nationals of the United States as well as West-European countries were usually visited by consular officials on a regular basis but it was not the case for foreigners coming from East-European countries. In the light of information obtained from the German General Consulate Office in Cracow it happens exceptionally that a German national is deprived of liberty in the area of this office. Frequency of visits paid by consular officials depends on the circumstances of a particular case; some German nationals do not wish for meetings with consular officials while others are visited one or two times per year, or, if it is necessary, almost every day.

Under the 1997 Code of Execution of Penalties the supervision of prisons forms an integral part of the functions of the penitentiary judge. Penitentiary judges are allowed to visit prisons at any time, to talk to prisoners and to move freely within the establishments in order to examine living conditions, health care and so forth. Article 7 of the Code provides for judicial review of the prison administration. Under these provisions a prisoner may lodge an appeal against the decision of prison authorities to the penitentiary court within seven days of being informed of the decision. The correspondence of prisoners with defence counsellors, courts, public prosecutors, government authorities, the Commissioner for Civil Rights Protection (ombudsman) as well as international bodies acting

---

[6] T. Bulenda, and M. Dabrowiecki, 'Cudzoziemcy w polskich aresztach sledczych i zakladach karnych' (Foreigners in Polish Prisons), in: Biuletyn RPO. Materialy (Bulletin of the Commissioner for Civil Rights Protection), 1993 nr 18, pp. 53-54.

[7] J. Malec, 'Cudzoziemcy w polskich jednostkach penitencjarnych' (Foreigners in Polish Penitentiary Institutions), in: Biuletyn RPO. Materialy (Bulletin of the Commissioner for Civil Rights Protection), 1995, nr 28, p. 303.

in the field of protecting human rights may not be censored. Prisoners having no money should be provided by the prison administration with paper, envelopes and stamps enabling them to post complaints. Prisons are also visited by the staff of the Office of the Commissioner for Civil Rights Protection and, upon authorisation, by certain NGOs. In recent years the situation of foreign prisoners in Poland has been thoroughly monitored by the Commissioner for Civil Rights Protection as well as the Helsinki Foundation of Human Rights. The activity of the probation service is generally very limited in prisons; it is mainly the task of the prison administration to prepare the prisoner for his or her release.

1.4 Overview of Trends

1.4.1 Sentencing Trends

Changes to the political system in Poland in 1989 brought with them a growing number of foreigners arriving in Poland as students, tourists and business travellers as well as economic migrants, illegal residents, persons applying for refugee status or asylum-seekers. According to police statistics the number of foreigners suspected of having committed offences was also rising in the early and mid-1990s. The greatest number of suspected foreigners was recorded in 1997, amounting to 8,306. Since 2001 there has been a significant decrease in this figure; in 2001 there were 7,061 foreigners suspected by the police of having committed an offence while in 2005 the number dropped to 3,146. The main reason for this seems to be the strengthening of border control at the east border of Poland. It should be noted, however, that the proportion of foreigners among all persons suspected by the police has been relatively low in the whole period after 1989. As can be seen in table 2, it fluctuated between 0,3 % in 1990 and 2 % in 1997.

Table 2 Foreigners suspected of having committed offences in the years 1989-2005

Year	Suspects in total*	Suspects-foreigners	Percentage of suspects- foreigners
1989	214,513	957	0,4
1990	273,375	719	0,3
1991	305,031	2,402	0,8
1992	307,575	3,575	1,2
1993	299,499	3,010	1,0
1994	388,855	3,983	1,0
1995	423,896	6,349	1,5
1996	381,911	6,956	1,8
1997	410,844	8,306	2,0
1998	396,055	6,390	1,6
1999	364,272	6,017	1,7
2000	405,275	5,106	1,3
2001	533,943	7,061	1,3
2002	552,301	6,815	1,2

Year	Suspects in total*	Suspects-foreigners	Percentage of suspects- foreigners
2003	557,224	5,591	1,0
2004	578,059	3,870	0,7
2005	594,088	3,146	0,5

* *Police statistics of offences cover crimes and misdemeanours; they do not cover petty offences.*
Source: Headquarter of the Police, http://www.kgp.gov.pl.

Among those 3,146 foreigners suspected of committing offences in 2005 there were citizens of many different countries. However, a vast majority of them (73 %) came from six countries: Ukraine, Belarus, Germany, Armenia, Russia and Lithuania. Nearly one out of three foreigners suspected by the police of committing an offence (29 %) was a citizen of Ukraine and two out of three (63 %) were citizens of previous Soviet republics: Ukraine, Belarus, Armenia, Russia and Lithuania (Table 3). According to research carried out by Irena Rzeplinska, the situation has not changed significantly since the early 1990s, when the majority of foreign suspects also came from neighbouring states: Lithuania, Belarus, Ukraine and Russia.[8]

Table 3 Foreign suspects according to their country of origin in 2005

Country of origin	Number of suspects	Percentage
Ukraine	914	29,0
Belarus	419	13,3
Germany	298	9,5
Armenia	287	9,1
Russia	184	5,8
Lithuania	182	5,8
Other	862	27,4
Total	3,146	100

Source: Headquarter of the Police, http://www.kgp.gov.pl.

In most cases foreigners who committed offences in Poland came to the country for a short period of time, and in many cases the committed offence(s) could be seen as the primary motivation for even entering the country, especially regarding offences relating to illegal trade. Data on the crimes that have been committed by foreigners as well as on the composition of the foreign prison population (age, social background, gender) are at most very limited. However, as regards the structure of offences committed by foreigners, research carried out in the late 1990s showed that almost 50 % of recorded offences

---

[8] I. Rzeplinska, *Przestepczosc cudzoziemcow w Polsce* (Offences by Foreigners in Poland), Instytut Nauk Prawnych Polskiej Akademii Nauk, Warsaw 2000, p. 28-29.

committed by them pertained to trade in or the possession of alcohol, cigarettes or compact discs without paying customs duty. The second-ranking category was traffic offences (about 13 %). Eight percent of suspected foreigners were persons suspected of property offences; the percentage of those using false documents (7 %) was much the same. The proportion of foreigners suspected of offences against health and life amounted to 8 % while the percentage of those suspected of homicide was at about 3 %. Citizens of former Soviet republics (Ukraine, Belarus, Lithuania and Russia) constituted nearly 90 % of those suspected of trade in or the possession of commodities without paying customs duties while in the group of foreigners suspected of traffic offences a large number of Germans was observed.[9]

As for the structure of penalties imposed on foreigners by the courts, research carried out by Boguslaw Janiszewski (Table 4) revealed that the percentage of foreigners sentenced to unsuspended imprisonment had been rising during the 1990s from 9 % in 1991 up to 38 % in 1995. At the same time a similar trend could be observed with respect to suspended imprisonment while the proportion of fines imposed as a stand-alone penalty decreased from 51% to 19,2 %.[10] Unfortunately, no further statistical data on sentences imposed on foreigners are available. It seems that the changing structure of penalties imposed on foreigners – which is particularly visible when comparing the years 1991 and 1993 - could be explained by the changing structure of offences committed; those sentenced in 1991 had committed crimes before or just after the changes to the social and political system in Poland.

Table 4   Sentenced foreigners according to the penalty imposed

	1991		1993		1995	
	N.	*%*	*N.*	*%*	*N.*	*%*
Foreigners sentenced by courts total incl. sentenced to:	249	100	396	100	976	100
Unsuspended imprisonment	22	8,8	134	33,8	367	37,6
suspended imprisonment	61	24,5	186	47,0	409	41,9
fine (imposed as a self-standing penalty)	127	51,0	71	17,9	187	19,2

Source: Janiszewski, B. (2000), 'Orzekanie kar i innych srodkow wobec cudzoziemcow' (Imposing Penalties and Other Measures on Foreigners), in: Szwarc, A. (ed.), Przestepczosc przygraniczna. Postepowanie karne przeciwko cudzoziemcom w Polsce (Offences Close to Borders. Criminal Proceedings against Foreigners in Poland), Wydawnictwo Poznanskie, Poznan, p. 175.

---

[9]   I. Rzeplinska, '*Offences by Foreigners*', in: Siemaszko, A. (ed.), Crime and Law Enforcement in Poland on the threshold of the 21st Century, Oficyna Naukowa, Warsaw 2000, pp. 152-153.

[10]   B. Janiszewski, 'Orzekanie kar i innych srodkow wobec cudzoziemcow' (Imposing Penalties and Other Measures on Foreigners), in: Szwarc, A. (ed.), Przestepczosc przygraniczna. Postepowanie karne przeciwko cudzoziemcom w Polsce (Offences Close to Borders. Criminal Proceedings against Foreigners in Poland), Wydawnictwo Poznanskie, Poznan 2000, p. 175.

1.4.2. Characteristics Foreign Prison Population

Recently the majority of imprisoned foreigners have been pre-trial prisoners. According to prison statistics, as of 31 December 2005 there were 336 foreigners detained before trial in Poland while the number of foreigners sentenced for crimes and misdemeanours amounted to 316. At the same time, three foreigners were serving the penalty of confinement imposed for petty offences. Among all foreign prisoners there were nationals from 52 different countries; five prisoners did not have any stated citizenship. The percentage of Ukrainians was particularly high; one in three foreign prisoners was Ukrainian. There were also relatively many citizens of Belarus (54), Armenia (53), Russia (50), Germany (39), Moldova (25), Bulgaria (22) as well as Lithuania, Romania and Vietnam (21 nationals of each nationality).[11]

1.5. Overview of national legislation

1.5.1. Penitentiary Legislation

Issues relating the execution of both the pre-trial detention as well as prison sentences are regulated by the 1997 Code on the Execution of Penalties. Generally, foreign offenders are deprived of their liberty in prisons under the same rules as Polish citizens. The 1997 Code of Execution of Penalties introduced a clear division of prisons into types and regimes. Under Article 69 of the Code there are four types of prisons for sentenced prisoners:
- prisons for young adults (aged up to 21),
- prisons for adult offenders (over 21 years of age) serving terms for the first time,
- prisons for recidivists,
- prisons for soldiers serving terms of military detention.

Article 70.1 of this Code provides that each type of prison may be organized as institutions with closed, semi-open or open regimes. Remand prisons are closed institutions. The conditions in semi-open and open prisons differ significantly from the conditions of closed institutions. In comparison with the latter institutions the semi-open and open prisons have fewer security arrangements and are characterized by a lower degree of isolation of inmates.[12] According to Article 81 of the Code of Execution of Penalties, prison sentences may be executed under the regular, therapeutic or programmed treatment system. The latter can be defined as a system of resocialization. The execution of imprisonment under this system is based on a differentiated treatment plan, which is drawn up by a so-called 'penitentiary commission' appointed by the prison governor, in co-operation with the prisoner. As a rule, it is necessary to obtain the prisoner's consent to the treatment programme. However, young adults serve their terms under this system irrespective of their wishes unless they are placed in the therapeutic system orientated towards prisoners who are mentally ill, addicted or disabled. Prisoners who do not serve their terms un-

---

[11] Central Administration of the Prison Service (2005), Informacja statystyczna za rok 2005 (Statistical data for the year 2005), available online: http://www.czsw.gov.pl.

[12] B. Stando-Kawecka, '*Poland*', in: van Zyl Smit, D. and Dünkel, F. (eds.), Imprisonment Today and Tomorrow. Second Edition, Kluwer Law International, The Hague/ London/ Boston 2001, p. 519.

der a therapeutic or programmed treatment system are placed in a regular one. They should work and be offered vocational training as well as the educational, recreational and therapeutic opportunities that are possible in a prison.

1.5.2. Penitentiary Legislation & Foreigners

There are only few provisions of the Code of Execution of Penalties which apply exclusively or particularly to foreign prisoners:

- a sentenced foreigner who does not speak Polish must have a defence counsellor in the course of court proceedings (Article 8.2 of the Code);
- a foreigner detained before trial has the right to inform the appropriate consular office - or, in the absence of such an office, the diplomatic representation of the country concerned - about his or her place of stay (Article 211.2 of the Code);
- foreigners serving their prison terms have the right to correspondence with the appropriate consular or diplomatic office as well as to meetings with a consular official (Article 105.2 of the Code);
- in terms of Article 109 of the Code meals received by prisoners should meet the norms of their religion and culture as far as possible.

Additionally, the 1997 Code of Criminal Procedure provides for a number of rights for foreigners suspected or accused of having committed an offence in the course of the criminal proceedings. According to Article 79.1 of this Code, foreigners suspected or accused of having committed an offence who do not speak Polish must have a defence counsellor. Under Article 72 of the Code they have the right to receive a translated version - along with the original - of the decision to bring charges, the charges themselves as well as decisions ending prosecution or other decisions against which it is possible to bring an appeal. A foreigner arrested by the police is entitled to have contact with the appropriate consular or diplomatic office. In every case when a foreigner is detained on remand, the local consular office – or, in the absence of such an office, the diplomatic representation of the country concerned – is to be informed without delay (Article 612 of the Code). Pursuant to Article 610 of this Code, if a foreigner has been definitively sentenced by a Polish court to imprisonment, the Minister of Justice can approach the relevant department of the state of which the convicted person is a citizen and attempt to effect that the prisoner be transferred to that state in order to serve the penalty imposed. Such a transfer is only possible if the foreigner consents to it.

2 TREATMENT OF FOREIGN PRISONERS

2.1. General

In Poland there are currently a number of problems that are negatively affecting the situation of both foreign and Polish nationals in prisons; the most important of them seems to be the level of overcrowding. Since September 2000, the currently binding norm of 3 m^2 being the minimum area per prisoner has been violated. In some prisons the number of prisoners amounts to 140 % of the official prison capacity.[13] What is more, the average number of offenders sentenced to imprisonment whose sentence has been postponed primarily due to the lack of places in prisons has recently amounted to roughly 30 thousand. Violation of the binding norm of the minimum area per prisoner contributes to growing tensions between inmates as well as between prisoners and the prison staff. What makes the situation of prisoners worse is the lack of sufficient opportunities to work and participate in other socially useful activities or treatment. Due to overcrowding as well as a lack of sufficient financial resources many prisoners serving terms in closed institutions spend almost 23 hours a day confined to their cells. For several years this state of affairs has been perceived as a matter of a great concern by the prison administration, the Commissioner for the Protection of Civil Rights as well as some academics and members of internal institutions.[14]

2.2. Living conditions and facilities

There are no special prisons or units for foreigners in Poland. An idea to set up such prisons or units was considered in the 1990s. It was, however, criticized both by the prison administration as well as by the foreigners concerned. In the mid-1990s members of the Office of the Commissioner for the Protection of Civil Rights recommended that - as far as possible - foreigners should be placed in cells with other foreigners who speak the same language. To some extent this recommendation was implemented in practice, however, in some cases the prison governors preferred to place foreigners separately in different cells, particularly with respect to perpetrators of serious crimes who were veterans of the Afghanistan war.[15] According to research carried out by Irena Rzeplinska in 1999, in the opinion of prison governors, foreigners:

- were willing to serve their terms in Polish prisons; they did not want to be transferred to the country of their origin;
- nationals of East-European countries were placed as far as possible in prisons situated close to the east border;
- foreigners wishing to be placed in the same cell were serving their terms together, however, some nationalities, for example Russians and Chechens, were placed separately.[16]

Currently the overwhelming majority of foreigners are placed in multi-occupancy cells with Polish nationals and other foreigners. As for living conditions, the major problem is the degree of overcrowding in Polish prisons. After its second periodic visit to Poland carried out in May 2000, the CPT recommended that the Polish authorities should take

---

[13] Central Administration of the Prison Service 2004 ibidem.

[14] T. Bulenda and R. Musidlowski, *Postepowanie z wiezniami w latach 1989-2002* (*Treatment of Prisoners in the years 1989-2002*), Instytut Spraw Publicznych, Warsaw 2003, pp. 20-32; Commissioner for Civil Rights Protection, '*Wykonywanie kar i srodkow karnych*'(Execution of Penalties and Penal Measures), in: Biuletyn RPO Materialy (Bulletin of the Commissioner for Civil Rights Protection), 2004 nr 48, p. 269-289.

[15] J. Malec, ibidem, p. 304.

[16] I. Rzeplinska, 'Wykonywanie kar i srodkow karnych wobec cudzoziemcow w Polsce' (Executing of Penalties and Penal Measures Imposed on Foreigners in Poland), in: Szwarc, A. (ed.), Przestepczosc przygraniczna. Postepowanie karne przeciwko cudzoziemcom w Polsce (Offences Close to Borders. Criminal Proceedings against Foreigners in Poland), Wydawnictwo Poznanskie, Poznan 2000 pp. 192-193.

steps in order to apply a range of measures designed to combat prison overcrowding, including policies to limit or modulate the number of persons sent to prison. The CPT also reiterated the recommendation made after its first visit to Poland in 1996 that the standard for prisoners should be raised to 4 m^2 per prisoner. In the opinion of the CPT the existing standard 3 m^2 per prisoner did not offer a satisfactory amount of living space, in particular in cells of a relatively small size.[17] After its last visit to Poland in 2004 the CPT called upon the Polish authorities to redouble their efforts to combat prison overcrowding.[18]

2.3. Reception and admission

According to the Office of the Commissioner for the Protection of Civil Rights, in the early 1990s the prison administration was - to a large extent - not prepared for non-Polish prisoners. First of all, considerable problems arose from the fact that in most prisons only a few members of the prison staff spoke foreign languages. A large number of foreigners spoke Polish moderately or fluently, but some of them did not and they had very limited opportunities to communicate with the prison staff. In some prisons other prisoners who were able to speak foreign languages were used as translators. Furthermore, laws regulating the execution of pre-trial detention and prison sentences were not available in the languages that foreigners spoke.[19] Since the early 1990s the situation has changed slightly. In the mid-1990s basic provisions regulating the execution of pre-trial detention and prison sentences were translated into English, German, French and Russian.[20] Foreigners are provided with such regulations when they are admitted to prisons.

According to the Article 612 of the Code of Criminal Procedure it is obligatory to inform the local consular office – or, in the absence of such an office, the diplomatic representation of the country concerned – in every case when a foreigner is detained on remand. As for foreigners sentenced to imprisonment, under the Article 105 of the Code on the Execution of Penalties they are entitled to maintain contacts with consular offices, diplomatic representation and their families.

2.4. Work-Education-Training-Sports-Recreation

Prisoners' access to work, education and other activities is limited for both Polish nationals and foreigners. In most of the prison establishments visited, during its second periodic visit to Poland the CPT registered unsatisfactory employment conditions as well as a poor programme of educational, recreational and other purposeful activities. What the CPT particularly emphasized was the recommendation that the Polish authorities should strive to provide young adult prisoners with a full programme of educational, recreational and

---

[17] Council of Europe, Report to the Polish Government on the visit to Poland carried out by the European Committee for the Prevention of Torture and Inhuman or Degrading Treatment or Punishment from 8 to 19 May 2000, Council of Europe, Strasbourg 2002.

[18] Council of Europe, Report to the Polish Government on the visit to Poland carried out by the European Committee for the Prevention of Torture and Inhuman or Degrading Treatment or Punishment from 4 to 15 October 2004, Council of Europe, Strasbourg 2006.

[19] T. Bulenda, and M. Dabrowiecki, ibidem pp. 35-36.

[20] J. Malec, J. ibidem., p. 302.

other purposeful activities that is tailored to their specific needs.[21] In the early 1990s the situation of foreigners was even worse than that of Polish nationals; only seven percent of foreigners were employed, including those employed without remuneration, although most of them were willing to work.[22] On 31 October 2006, the total number of prisoners (both sentenced prisoners and those detained on remand) amounted to 88,494, of which 19,184 were active in remunerated employment. At the same time, 6,810 prisoners were working without remuneration for penitentiary institutions, local government or charity organisations[23]. In 2000 the situation of almost 50 % of foreigners deprived of their liberty in Polish prisons (near 600 persons) was examined once again by members of the Office of the Commissioner for Civil Rights Protection. According to this analysis, foreigners were performing remunerated work only exceptionally (2 %).[24] At the same time they had limited access to other purposeful activities. Despite efforts made by prison governors to provide newspapers and books, the consular offices of East-European countries were not willing to comply with the requests.

2.5. Food-Religion-Personal hygiene-Medical care

The 1997 Code on the Execution of Penalties provides prisoners with the right to free medical and sanitary care at the state's expense. Prisoners are also provided with the right to fulfil the requirements of their religion, including meals that should meet the norms of their religion and culture as far as possible. In the early 1990s most foreigners received the same food as Polish nationals. Some of them, however, asked for a special diet meeting the needs of their religion, but it happened that the prison administration refused to satisfy such demands. At the same time, nearly one in four foreigners made critical remarks concerning the sanitary conditions, such as a lack of toothpaste or a lack of the possibility to take a shower more frequently than once a week[25]. In 1999 in the opinion of prison governors there also were some problems concerning the provision of special diets for foreigners or maintaining contacts with representatives of religions that are not very widespread in Poland.[26] Under Article 106 of the Code on the Execution of Penalties prisoners have the right to practice their religions. They have the right among others to individual meetings with religious representatives and can be visited by religious representatives in their cells. However, the use of the right to freedom of religion must not interfere with the principle of tolerance as well as overall order in a prison. Detailed provisions are included in the order of the Minister of Justice of 2 September 2003 on rules concerning religious practices in prisons. Generally, it is the task of the prison governor to state detailed house rules related to religious practices in co-operation with religious representatives. In 2000 in some institutions foreigners had problems that arose

---

21 Council of Europe ibidem
22 T Bulenda, and M. Dabrowiecki, ibidem, pp. 46-47.
23 Central Administration of the Prison Service 2006, *Informacja o wykonywaniu kary pozbawienia wolnosci i tymczasowego aresztowania za pazdziernik 2006 (Information on the execution of imprisonment and detention on remand in October 2006)*, available online: http://www.czsw.gov.pl
24 Commissioner for Civil Rights Protection Ochrona praw osob pozbawionych wolnosci (Protection of Rights of Persons Deprived of Liberty), in: Biuletyn RPO. Materialy (Bulletin of the Commissioner for Civil Rights Protection), 2001 nr 43, pp. 268-270.
25 T. Bulenda,and M. Dabrowiecki, ibidem, pp. 41-46.
26 Rzeplinska, I. ibidem., pp. 192-193.

from the fact that they were not able to communicate with the prison health-care service because of language barriers.[27]

2.6. Consular and legal help

Under the provisions of the 1997 Code on the Execution of Penalties, foreigners detained before their trial have the right to inform the appropriate consular office or the diplomatic representation of the country concerned about where they are being held. As for foreigners serving prison terms, they have the right to correspondence with the appropriate consular or diplomatic office as well as to meetings with consular officials. In practice, contacts between foreign prisoners and consulate or diplomatic officials are rather limited as far as nationals of East-European countries are concerned. Many of them made complaints related to the lack of contacts with the appropriate consular or diplomatic services because the offices concerned did not respond to their letters. Pursuant to provisions of the Code of Criminal Procedure as well as the Code on the Execution of Penalties, foreigners who do not speak Polish must have a defence counsellor. Consular and legal help can, for instance, be in the form of providing of prisoners with food, books and newspapers, or assisting them in finding or choosing a defence lawyer.

2.7 Contact with the outside world

Under Article 102 of the Code on the Execution of Penalties, sentenced prisoners have the right to maintain contacts with their families and close friends. Article 105 of this Code states that prison administration should enable inmates to maintain contacts with such persons through visits, written correspondence, telephone calls and packages. The frequency of visits depends mainly on the type of prisons. Prisoners serving their sentences in closed prisons are entitled to two visits per month and those in semi-open prisons to three visits per month, while inmates placed in open prisons have the right to receive an unlimited number of visits. In Poland, no long-term family visits are provided for by law; each visit lasts for up to 60 minutes and it is up to the prison governor to allow the prisoner to make use of two or three visits to which he or she is entitled every month on the same day. Such a possibility is of particular importance for foreigners serving their terms far from their family homes. The Code on the Execution of Penalties does not provide for conjugal visits *expressis verbis*. However, the frequency as well as conditions of visits could be modified by means of rewards granted to prisoners for good behaviour or in order to motivate them to improve their behaviour. Pursuant to Article 138 of this Code, rewards include:
-   the permission to receive an additional or longer visit,
-   the permission to receive an unsupervised visit in a common room,
-   the permission to receive an unsupervised visit in a separate room.

As far as the latter visits are concerned, they enable prisoners to consolidate their personal relations with members of their families. Sexual contacts during such visits are not prohibited; however, they are not mentioned directly in provisions regulating the execution of prison sentences. Provisions concerning visits received by pre-trial prisoners are much more restrictive. They could receive visits with the prior consent of the authority at

---

[27] Commissioner for Civil Rights Protection ibidem, pp. 268-270.

whose disposal they remain. This authority can be the public prosecutor or, after bringing the accusation to the court, the competent court. During its periodical visits to Poland the CPT noticed that certain pre-trial prisoners had alleged that they had been denied visits for several months. Generally, the rules and practice applicable to visits, correspondence and access to a telephone for sentenced prisoners were considered as adequate. However, the CPT was concerned by the lack of improvement in the arrangements for pre-trial prisoners.[28]

As regards foreign prisoners' contacts with the outside world in practice, research carried out in the early 1990s revealed that 63 % foreigners sent and received private letters, but only 29 % of foreigners were visited in prison by family members. Generally, they did not make complaints about written correspondence and visits. However, some of those detained before trial pointed that their written correspondence was sent and received with delay.[29] In the opinion of prison governors, in the late 1990s family members of foreign prisoners only seldom visited their imprisoned relatives.[30] At the same time some foreigners made complaints about internal rules according to which they should speak the Polish language while being visited by family members.[31]

Most prisoners have television sets in their cells, and in some prisons it is even possible for them to receive cable television, which in turn makes it possible to access television in foreign languages to a certain extent. Access to written foreign media and books is dependent on the involvement of consular offices, as stated above, or the prisoners' families.

2.8. Reintegration activities – Prison leave

Prison leaves are available for foreigners under the same rules as for Polish nationals. Under Article 141a of the Code on the Execution of Penalties, a prisoner could be granted prison leave for up to five days in cases of particular importance for him or her. If necessary, the prisoner could be granted an escorted prison leave; in such a case he or she can leave the prison under the supervision of prison officers or another trustworthy person. In practice, prison leaves in cases of particular importance for prisoners are granted for periods not exceeding 24 hours. The Code also provides for other kinds of prison leave. A prisoner may be rewarded with a short period of leave not exceeding 30 hours in order to meet relatives, close friends or another trustworthy persons outside the prison; the total number of such rewards is limited to 28 per year. Another leave granted as a reward could last up to 14 days each time, but the whole period of such leaves may not exceed 28 days per year. When granting prison leave as a reward, various factors are taken into consideration, such as behaviour in prison, whether the prisoner will return to prison and a positive prognosis concerning his or her behaviour outside the prison. The formal premise of granting a prisoner such a reward is the completion of at least half of the term that required to have elapsed before the prisoner could apply for conditional release. According to Articles 91 and 92 of the Code, inmates serving their terms in semi-open prisons may be granted prison leave for up to 14 days per year. For inmates of open prisons, the total number of days per year is 28, irrespective of prison leave granted as a

---

28   Council of Europe ibidem.
29   T Bulenda, and M. Dabrowiecki, ibidem, pp. 52-53.
30   I. Rzeplinska, ibidem, pp. 192-193.
31   Commissioner for Civil Rights Protection ibidem, pp. 268-270.

reward. In addition, prison leave for up to 14 days may be granted to a prisoner in the six months before release in order to enable him or her to look for a job or for accommodation. No statistical data concerning prison leaves granted to foreigners are available. Prison governors asked by Irena Rzeplinska in 1999 stated that prison leaves were available for foreigners under the same rules as for Polish nationals.[32] There are no special programmes aiming at the reintegration of foreign prisoners.

2.9. Release-Expulsion

Pursuant to Article 88 of the 2003 Act on Illegal Residents that enumerates grounds for expulsion, a foreigner is to be expelled from the territory of Poland if he or she has crossed or has attempted to cross the border contrary to the laws as well as in cases in which he or she has finished serving the penalty of imprisonment imposed for committing an intentional criminal or tax offence. Under Article 264 of the Criminal Code, illegally crossing or attempting to cross the border is an offence punishable with a fine, liberty limitation or imprisonment for up to two years; under some circumstances, for example related to the use of violence, the maximum term of imprisonment is three years. Foreign prisoners who are to be expelled from Poland after serving their sentences could be released on parole according to the general rules. In Poland there is a discretionary system of conditional release. Prisoners could be granted conditional release after having served half of their sentence, provided that they had been imprisoned for the first time. Recidivists are eligible for release on parole after two thirds or even three quarters of the sentence. The material premise for release on parole is a positive prognosis. According to prison staff with whom I spoke, while releasing a foreigner conditionally the penitentiary court usually imposes an obligation for him / her to leave the country if there are grounds for expulsion as stated in the 2003 Act on Illegal Residents. The expulsion order is imposed by the provincial administrative body – the *voivod*. An appeal against such an order can be filed before the President of the Office for Repatriation and Illegal Residents.

2.10-2.12 Aftercare-Probation, Staff and Projects

Due to the small number of foreign prisoners there are no special projects oriented towards them. The staff working with both Polish nationals and foreigners has the same qualifications. Foreigners released from prisons are placed under the supervision of a probation officer according to the same rules as Polish nationals provided that they are not to be expelled from the territory of Poland. In general, while releasing prisoners conditionally the penitentiary court can – and in some cases is obliged to – place them under the supervision of a probation officer. Additionally, the court can impose several obligations, for example to work, attend school, to undergo treatment, or to abstain from drugs and/or alcohol, to name but a few. The task of the probation officer is to monitor the prisoner while providing him/her with support.

---

[32] I. Rzeplinska, ibidem, pp. 192-193.

3 ADMINISTRATIVE DETENTION OF FOREIGN PRISONERS

3.1. Institution

Foreigners are detained on a basis of administrative provisions in guarded centres for foreigners or detention centres for the purpose of expulsion. Under Article 102 of the 2003 Act on Illegal Residents the following grounds justify the placement of a foreigner in the guarded centre for foreigners:
- it is necessary to ensure the effectiveness of the proceedings on expulsion or on withdrawal of the permit to settle or of the long-term resident's EC resident permit;
- there is a well-founded fear that the foreigner will attempt to evade the execution of the decision on expulsion or on withdrawal of the permit to settle or of the long-term resident's EC resident permit;
- he or she crossed or has attempted to cross the border contrary to the laws, if he or she was not escorted to the border immediately.

As a rule, foreigners detained should be placed in the guarded centre for foreigners. It is possible to place them expulsion detention centres only if there is a risk that they could violate the rules of stay in the guarded centre. Exceptionally, if there are obstacles that make it impossible to escort or admit a foreigner to the guarded centre or to the detention centre for the purpose of expulsion, he or she may be temporarily placed in the separate facilities for detainees of the police or the border guard. The competent court is obliged to notify the appropriate diplomatic mission or consular office of the decision, so long as it has the consent of the foreigner concerned.

3.2. Ministry responsible & legislation

Guarded centres for foreigners as well as detention centres for the purpose of expulsion are subordinated to the Ministry of Interior Affairs and Administration. Basic provisions concerning the legal status of foreigners detained in such institutions are included in the 2003 Act on Illegal Residents. Under Article 117 of the Act, foreigners placed in the guarded centre or expulsion detention centres have the right to:
- contact the state authorities of the Republic of Poland and the diplomatic or consular office of the foreign country in personal and official cases;
- contact the non-governmental or international organizations dealing with granting assistance to foreigners, especially legal aid;
- correspond and use the means of communication at their own cost; in events of emergencies a foreigner may be allowed to use the means of communication and to send correspondence at the cost of the institution;
- submit petitions, complaints and requests to the officer responsible for the functioning of the institution or to the head of the police or the border guard units,
- meet close persons at the consent of the police or the border guard authority supervising the institution.

In a guarded centre foreigners of different genders should be separated , however, if it is possible, foreigners who are the closest members of the family should be placed in the same room if they request it. Foreigners placed in a guarded centre also have the right to move within the area of the centre as well as to use the recreational and sport equipment in the time and place indicated by the head of the institution. Detailed provisions concerning the conditions that the guarded centres and the detention centres for the purpose of expulsion should meet, as well as rules and regulations governing the stay in these institutions, are specified by the ordinances of the Minister of Interior Affairs and Administration.

3.3. Capacity institutions

In practice there is one guarded centre for foreigners in Lesznowola (further guarded centres for foreigners in Bialystok and Przemysl are planned to be taken into operation in the near future) and over 20 expulsion-detention centres. The official capacity of the guarded centre for foreigners in Lesznowola amounts to 131 persons. Detention centres for the purpose of expulsion usually have capacities of between 20 and 50 persons. The guarded center for foreigners in Lesznowola was visited by the CPT's delegation in 2000. At the time of the CPT's delegation visit there were 123 foreigners, of whom 91 were men, 17 were women and 15 were children. Twenty-six different nationalities were represented. The residents were awaiting expulsion; however, 65 % of them had applied for refugee status. Pending the examination of their applications, the execution of the expulsion orders had been suspended.

According to the CPT's report a few complaints were heard of verbal abuse and rough treatment on the part of security staff. Material conditions as well as medical care were acceptable on the whole. The delegation heard hardly any complaints concerning the quality and quantity of the meals. The specific dietary requirements of foreign nationals were taken into account in the provision of food. As regards the regime, the CPT's delegation noticed that residents could circulate freely within the blocks in which they were placed between 6 a.m. and 10 p.m. They were allowed to take outdoor exercise for up to three hours a day. They could watch TV (exclusively Polish cannels), read newspapers, magazines and books (also mostly in Polish language). They had unlimited access to pay-phones and could send and receive as much correspondence as they wished. As for visits, each visit had to receive prior approval from the provincial police commander. The delegation was told that obtaining such an approval could take as long as a month. Additionally, the same procedure applied to visits by lawyers.

In the centre internal regulations were available in a wide range of languages: Arabic, Armenian, Bengali, Bulgarian, English, French, German, Hindi, Punjabi, Romanian, Russian, Serb-Croat, Tamil, Turkish and Vietnamese. Some complaints made by detained foreigners to the delegation related to the absence of information on their legal status and the procedure concerning them. The centre's staff was composed of uniformed police officers serving as security guards and civilian staff employed as educators or contact persons for the residents. The police staff received no special training before taking up their duties. Contacts between staff and residents were difficult because of language barriers. Although several staff members spoke Russian, English or German, the communication difficulties with many of the residents were a source of tension and mutual frustration. The recommendations formulated by the CPT after its visit in the centre mainly related to:

- exploring the possibility of offering foreign nationals held at the centre a wider range of purposeful activities;

- giving particular attention to the educational needs of young children and juveniles;
- taking steps in order to provide residents with psychological and psychiatric support;
- reviewing the procedure concerning receiving visits by residents in order to enable them to receive visits without undue delay as well as to receive visits by lawyers without restrictions;
- reviewing the selection and training of the centre's staff.

Additionally, after its visit in 2000 the CPT recommended that more guarded centres comparable to the one in Lesznowola should be established.[33] In 2004 the situation of foreigners detained in the guarded centre was monitored by members of the Human Rights Association.[34] House rules were available in several languages. However, according to foreigners spoken to during the monitoring mission, some of them were not informed about such rights as to make telephone calls to a lawyer at the expenses of the institution if they had no money. Other complaints made by foreigners related to such issues as, for instance, receiving official documents without translation, receiving visits in the presence of the staff, and the lack of the possibility to receive vegetarian meals.

As for police and border guard facilities for detained foreigners, some were visited by the CPT's delegation during its visits in 1996, 2000 and 2004. In the report on the 1996 visit the CPT made a number of critical remarks concerning the border guard detention facilities at Warsaw International Airport, used for persons to whom entry to the country is refused.[35]

During its second visit to Poland the CPT's delegation visited the detention centre for expulsion located at the district police station in Gdynia as well as some border guard detention facilities usually used to accommodate foreigners for the period of detention of up to 72 hours. As far as the first institution is concerned, the material conditions were on the whole adequate. Cells were unlocked from 6 a.m. to 10 p.m., and foreign detainees could associate in a common room equipped with a TV set, some books, newspapers and games, as well as go to the outdoor exercise yard. In the opinion of the CPT's delegation, however, no possibility to use a telephone was a matter of concern. As regards the border guard establishments, some of them were of a good standard, while conditions in others were less satisfactory.[36]

In 2004 the CPT's delegation visited three expulsion centres (referred to in the CPT's report as 'deportation jails'). Two of them in Suwalki and Wroclaw were managed by the police; the third facility was run by the border guard at Warsaw International Airport. With official capacities of 21 (Suwalki), 22 (Wroclaw) and 49 places (Warsaw), at the time

---

[33] Council of Europe ibidem.

[34] Monitoring the situation of foreigners detained in the guarded center was a part of broader activities aiming at monitoring institutions for foreigners detained under administrative law undertaken by several NGOs: Caritas, Helsinki Foundation of Human Rights, Human Rights Center of the Jagiellonian University, Polish Humanitarian Action, Human Rights Association and university legal clinics in co-operation with the Office of the UNHCR. The results of this action were published in: Helsinki Foundation of Human Rights (2004), Prawa cudzoziemcom umieszczonych w aresztach w celu wydalenia i strzezonym osrodku. Raport (Rights of Foreigners Placed in Arrests for the Purpose of Expulsion and the Guarded Centre), Helsinki Foundation of Human Rights, Warsaw.

[35] Council of Europe, Report to the Polish Government on the visit to Poland carried out by the European Committee for the Prevention of Torture and Inhuman or Degrading Treatment or Punishment from 30 June to 12 July 1996, Council of Europe, Strasbourg 1998.

[36] Council of Europe ibidem.

of the visit, the expulsion centres were accommodating 16, 21 and 49 foreign nationals respectively. The best material conditions of detention were observed at Border Guard arrest that was opened in 2003, located at Warsaw International Airport. However, the CPT recommended that the living space envisaged per male detainee (3 m²) was not sufficient and should be aligned with the standard for female detainees (4 m²).

Material conditions at the expulsion centre located at the Municipal Police Command in Suwalki were also adequate. However, at the time of the visit, the central heating was out of order and the whole detention area was rather cold. The worst conditions were observed at the expulsion centre at the provincial police station in Wroclaw which had already been visited by the CPT in 1996. The delegation was concerned to note that, if anything, the situation had deteriorated. None of the visited expulsion centres offered a regime of activities appropriate to the detainees' legal status and adapted to the length of time they could spend in custody (this is up to a year).

The provision of health care as well as psychological and psychiatric support in the establishments visited could also not be considered as adequate. Staff assigned to work with foreign nationals in the establishments visited had received little specialised training for the job. The delegation observed that there was little communication between staff and detainees, not least because of language barriers. As for contact with the outside world, the CPT was pleased to note that the restrictive rules on visits for detained foreign nationals had been amended; as a result the procedure of visit authorisation took much less time. Foreign detainees were formally entitled to make telephone calls and send letters. However, the delegation observed that in practice the existing provisions were not always respected. The provision of information to foreign detainees varied from one institution to another. At Suwalki and Warsaw International Airport, general information on the internal rules and relevant procedures was available in a range of languages. This was not the case at Wroclaw, where the internal rules existed only in Polish. The major complaint of foreign nationals detained within the visited establishments was the lack of knowledge of what was happening in their case and how long they would spend in custody.[37]

3.4. Length of stay

The court making the decision on placing a foreigner in the guarded centre or in the expulsion centre should specify a period of detention not exceeding 90 days. This period of stay may be prolonged for a specified period necessary to execute the decision on expulsion, if the decision was not executed due to the foreigner's fault. In any case the period of stay in the guarded centre or in the arrest for the purpose of expulsion may not exceed one year.

3.5-3.6. Decisions procedure and appeal procedure

According to the 2003 Act on Illegal Residents (Article 101), a foreigner in relation to whom any circumstances apply that justify an expulsion, or a foreigner who evades carrying out obligations specified in the decision on expulsion, may be detained for a period not exceeding 48 hours. The detention of the foreigner is carried out by the border guard or the police. The authority that has detained the foreigner should, if so required by the

---

[37] Council of Europe ibidem.

circumstances, file a request to the court without delay for placing him or her in the guarded centre for foreigners or in the expulsion centre. The detained foreigner shall be released from detention by order of the court or if:

- within 48 hours of initially being detained, he or she has not been handed over to the court together with the request for placement in the guarded centre or in the expulsion centre;
- within 24 hours from being handed over to the court, he or she has not been delivered a decision on placement in the guarded centre or in the expulsion centre;
- the reason for detention has ceased to exist.

The decision on placing a foreigner in the guarded centre or in the expulsion centre is made by the local district court at the request of the voivod (provincial administrative body), the border guard or the police. The proceedings for placing a foreigner in the guarded centre or in the expulsion centre as well as appeal procedures are carried out according to the provisions of the Code of Criminal Procedure. According to article 105 of the 2003 Act on Illegal Residents, in rendering its decision on placing a foreigner in the guarded centre or in an expulsion centre the local district court shall undertake the necessary precautions to protect his/her property. Furthermore, the court shall notify the following of the decision: the appropriate diplomatic mission or consular office (if the foreigner in question consents to this); the guardianship court when there is a need to provide care for the foreigner's children; an agency for social assistance if there is a need to care for an infirm or ill person who had been in the care of the foreigner in question; a person specified by the foreigner. An appeal against the decision to place a foreigner in the guarded centre or in an expulsion centre can be filed before the regional court within seven days of said decision. Foreigners concerned should be informed by the court, in a language they understand, of undertaken activities and rendered decisions as well as the rights to which they are entitled during the procedures before the courts.

3.7. Irregular stay

Irregular stay in itself does not constitute a criminal offence. According to the 2003 Act on granting protection to illegal residents within the territory of the Republic of Poland, foreigners may be granted protection in one of the following forms:

- the refugee status;
- asylum;
- the permit for tolerated stay;
- temporary protection.

Under Article 19 of this Act a foreigner who is not authorized to enter the territory of the Republic of Poland may submit an application for refugee status during the border control upon entry to Poland, through the commanding officer of the border guard checkpoint. Article 40 of the Act states that a foreigner applying for the granting of refugee status shall not be detained unless:

- he or she submits an application for refugee status while staying within the territory of the Republic of Poland illegally or during the border control while not having the right of entry to Poland;

- prior to submission of an application he or she crossed or attempted to cross the border contrary to laws or obtained the decision on obligation to leave the territory of the Republic of Poland or the decision on expulsion;
- the circumstances justifying rendering of the decision on expulsion referred to in the Act of 13 June 2003 on Illegal Residents apply and this fact has occurred after submission of an application for granting the refugee status.

3.8-3.11 Other aspects

According to the Office for Repatriation and Illegal Residents, in the years 2003 to 2005 8,419, 6,696 and 4,898 persons were expelled from the territory of Poland respectively.[38] No statistical data on the number of foreigners detained in the guarded centre for foreigners or expulsion centres are available. Under Article 107 of the 2003 Act on Illegal Residents a foreigner placed in the guarded centre or in an expulsion centre is to be released if the period specified in of the Act (maximum one year) and in the decision issued by the court referred to in article 106.1 and 106.2 has expired. Expulsion proceedings can be continued but the foreigner in question can no longer be held in custody.

3.12 Minors

The court may place minor foreigners stopped while staying in the territory of the Republic of Poland without care in tutelary–educational institutions at the expenses of the state budget (Article 101a of the Act on Illegal Residents). Minors remaining in care of adults who are placed in the guarded centre for foreigners should, if possible, be accommodated in the same room. Pursuant to Article 94 of the Act on Illegal Residents the expulsion of a minor foreigner to his or her country of origin or to another country shall be executed only when care will be provided in that country by parents, other adults or by competent care institutions in accordance with the standards provided for in the Convention on children's rights. A minor may be expelled only under the care of the legal representative. That provision may not apply if the manner of executing the decision on expulsion provides that the minor shall be handed over to the legal representative or to the representative of the competent agencies of the country to which the expulsion is carried out.

4 NATIONALS DETAINED ABROAD

4.1 Numbers and composition group

According to the Ministry of Foreign Affairs in 2004 Polish consular offices were informed about 5,659 Polish citizens arrested abroad. At the same time there were 1,787 Poles serving sentences outside of Poland.

---

[38] Office for Repatriation and Aliens. Bureau for Informatics, Documentation & Statistics 2005, Quantitative data of procedures concerning foreigners in the years 2003-2005, available online: http://www.uric.gov.pl.

4.2. Detention countries

About 80 per cent (4,401) of the Polish citizens who were arrested abroad in 2004 were confined in countries of the European Union. As regards Poles serving their terms abroad, much the same tendency could be observed. Among those 1,787 imprisoned abroad, 1,403 persons were deprived of their liberty in the European Union. At the same time, the number of Polish citizens arrested abroad within the European Union was particularly high in Germany, Spain, Austria and Great Britain. Most of these sentenced prisoners were serving their terms in Germany, Italy, Spain and France (Table 5).

Table 5   Polish citizens deprived of their liberty in EU countries in 2004.

Country	Number of Polish citizens arrested during 2004	Number of Polish citizens serving prison terms as of December 2004
Germany	1,651	735
Spain	531	122
Austria	517	60
Great Britain	473	24
Italy	178	136
Czech Republic	162	31
France	127	118
Greece	120	17
Finland	115	4
Belgium	105	74
Sweden	101	61
Netherlands	96	34
Cyprus	64	7
Hungary	56	8
Denmark	46	6
Ireland	11	2
Slovak Republic	11	4
Portugal	9	10
Lithuania	7	-
Slovenia	5	-
Estonia	3	-
Latvia	3	-
Total	4,401	1,453

Source: Ministry of Foreign Affairs, http://www.msz.gov.pl.

4.3. Reasons for detention & sentencing

Only very general data are available on the reasons for which Polish nationals are currently detained abroad. In 2004, a vast majority of Polish nationals were serving short prison sentences abroad for misdemeanours and petty offences. Some of them, however, were convicted of serious crimes, such as the possession or smuggling of drugs.

4.4. Involved organizations – tasks and activities

As reported by the Ministry of Foreign Affairs, Polish consular officials maintained contacts with Polish citizens deprived of their liberty abroad. In all known cases of Poles arrested abroad they took steps in order to enable those persons to have a defence counsellor or an interpreter as well as to provide them with the necessary financial support. Another activity of consular offices in this field related to providing Polish prisoners with newspapers or sanitary items. A matter of great concern was the situation of Polish prisoners in Latin America. In 2004 there were total 65 Polish nationals imprisoned in this region in Brazil (19), Venezuela (17), Ecuador (14), Argentina (5), Peru (4), Chile (3) and Columbia (3). Generally, in 2004 consular representatives made 727 visits to remand prisons as well as prisons for convicted offenders in order to meet 616 Polish nationals arrested or serving prison terms abroad.[39]

4.5 – 4.7 Other aspects

Influenced by media coverage public opinion has recently been particularly concerned by the situation of Polish nationals deprived of their liberty in Latin American countries. The Ministry of Justice has taken steps aiming at the transfer of some prisoners from those countries back to Poland. However, this is a rather difficult task due to a lack of bilateral agreements.

It remains to be stated that there are no provisions that concern the reception of Polish nationals once they have been released from detention in foreign countries. Furthermore, there are no legal regulations that aim to provide them with aftercare or re-integrative support once they have returned to Poland.

5 EVALUATION AND RECOMMENDATIONS

Foreigners detained before trial and serving prison terms constitute a relatively small proportion of the prison population in Poland. Generally, they are subordinated to the same provisions as Polish prisoners and are negatively affected by the same factors, such as overcrowding of prisons, and a lack of opportunities to work and to take part in purposeful activities. In comparison with Polish nationals the situation of foreigners is worsened by the fact that most of them have no family support. What is more, consular offices of East-European countries do not to be interested in maintaining contacts with their citizens imprisoned in Poland. Irrespective of steps aiming at combating prison overcrowding in order to improve the situation of foreign prisoners, it is necessary to continue the special training of prison staff working with such prisoners, to widen the access of foreigners to books and newspapers in their own languages as well as the possibility to take part in useful activities. Given the fact that most prisoners in Poland perform no remunerated work and the situation of foreigners is particularly difficult in this respect, efforts should be made in order to involve charity organizations in providing assistance for them. Addi-

---

[39] Ministry of Foreign Affairs 2005, Informacja o dzialalnosci polskiej sluzby konsularnej w 2004 r. (Information on the Polish Consular Service in 2004), http://www.msz.gov.pl.

tionally, more attention should be paid to providing foreign prisoners with detailed information concerning their legal status in prisons.

As for foreigners detained under administrative provisions, as a rule they should be placed in guarded centres for foreigners. Placing a foreigner in an arrest for the purpose of expulsion should be a last resort. Efforts should be made to provide foreigners awaiting expulsion with an environment that meets the needs of persons detained for prolonged periods of time. Particularly, attention should be paid to reducing language barriers, providing foreigners with complete information on their legal status as well as with psychological and psychiatric support. Improving material conditions and widening the possibilities to take part in useful activities are also of great important.

Chapter 21

Portugal

Rui Abrunhosa Gonçalves

1 INTRODUCTION[(*)]

First of all it must be pointed out that historically Portugal has been a country of emigration and since the fifteenth century we have been "discovering the world"; due to that fact we can find Portuguese descendents in every continent and almost every corner of the world[1]. During the first half of the twentieth century our migration was mostly directed to Brazil or other South American countries but during the sixties our people turned to Europe – mostly France and Germany – where nowadays they represent an important and considerable community that is fully mixed and integrated with the native populations. It was only after democracy was consolidated that Portugal became an attractive country for foreign people, initially from Brazil and the former colonies in Africa, and later for people from Northern Europe, especially from the former Soviet Republics (e.g, Ukraine, Moldavia, Lithuania, Russia, among others). The data that we are going to present reflect this change that has occurred not only in the general population but also within the prisons. As an example, in 1980 only four persons from Romania were legally residing in Portugal. This number went up to 81 in 1993. But at that time, no prisoners from Romania where traced. After ten years, in 2003, 55 Romanians were in Portuguese prisons. Official data show that we went from a total of 50,750 foreign residents in Portugal in 1980 to a total of 276,480 in 2005[2]. Through this project we will try to present the features that characterize foreign prisoners in Portugal. We will briefly address our penal code and the penitentiary rules that are applicable to all persons who commit a crime, whether they are foreigners or not. Secondly we will present data concerning the various nationalities involved and the types of crimes that are more relevant in these cases. We will also address the question of correctional treatment of foreign prisoners in Portuguese prisons and finally we will try to enlighten some of the future implications that a probable increase of this population in our prison system may provoke.

1.1 Overview of Penalties and Measures

A prison sentence is the toughest penalty that can be imposed in Portugal. The maximum sentence is 30 years but usually release is granted after 5/6 of the sentence has been served. In general, courts are striving to apply less severe penalties thus trying to avoid the deleterious impact of incarceration and social isolation. However, alternative measures such as probation or working in the community are seldom applied. Fines and the suspension of prison sentences still remain the preferred substitutes for prison sentences that judges impose.

On the other hand, prisoners are sometimes granted the possibility of spending several days (temporary leaves) with their families after having served at least 1/4 of their prison sentence without disciplinary problems. Afterwards prisoners can enter a "softer" prison regime, the Open Regime Turned In or Turned Out (Regime Aberto Voltado para o Interior ou para o Exterior) which is basically a form of preparing the inmate to further attain conditional release by letting him/her work all day in the community and return to

---

[(*)] Rui Abrunhosa Gonçalves works for University of Minho, Braga, Portugal.
  E-mail: rabrunhosa@iep.uminho.pt
[1] See Arroteia, 1983.
[2] See http://www.sef.pt

the prison for dinner and sleeping. Conditional release may be granted after having served half to 2/3 of the prison sentence, depending on the seriousness of the crime committed and the length of the sentence.

Portugal introduced electronic monitoring in 2002. The result and effect of this alternative measure could be interesting but it is mostly applied to younger people. Its application with foreigners has not yet been documented[3].

1.2 Overview of the Prison System

1.2.1. Organizational structure

The Portuguese prison system has 57 prisons, 54 in full operation and the remaining three are either under construction or are undergoing important restoration and adaptations. There are 35 small local prisons, 18 bigger central prisons and four special prisons where certain types of services are provided, such as hospital units or training units for younger prisoners. There is also a classification according to levels of security considering the specific design of the prison and the precautions and measures that the building has in order to prevent escapes. There are no maximum-security prisons in Portugal but some central prisons have special security units. In 2004 the Portuguese prison system had a capacity of 12.435 places of which only 11.413 were able to be used due to their actual physical conditions. Portuguese prisons have been overcrowded since the eighties but the rates have been decreasing in the last ten years (43% in 1996, 34% in 1998, 14,9% in 2002, 12,6% in 2003 and 1,3% in 2004). This decline resulted from an increase in the overall capacity of penal institutions and also from a wider implementation and application of electronic monitoring[4].

All prisons – except for the womens' prison of St^a Cruz do Bispo – are run, fully supported and funded by the General Direction of Prison Services within the Ministry of Justice. In this (so far) exceptional case, there is partnership with a private entity but the state still holds the sectors of security and correctional treatment.

The budget of the General Direction of Prison Services is directly linked with the budget allocated to the Ministry of Justice by the government. In 2003, this budget was 219.049.828 Euros and in 2004 it was 207.053.821 Euros. This difference is in line with the general reduction of state funds imposed by the government in the light of the recommendations of the EU on general deficit reduction. More than half (136.1 millions of Euros) of this budget is allocated to payments to the personnel and – based on data from the General Direction of Prison Services 2004 annual report (see http://www.dgsp.mj.pt) – a total daily amount of 41.30 Euros expenses was calculated for each prisoner.

There is an internal branch within the General Direction of Prison Services – the Inspection Service – which is responsible for conducting inquiries and processes in cases of unusual occurrences (such as for instance deaths, suicides, escapes, etc.). Also the Ombudsman Service (Provedoria da Justiça) conducts regular research on the functioning of prisons (reports were published in 1993, 1996 and 2003 – see http://www.provedor-jus.pt).

---

[3] See for instance Caiado, 2004.

[4] See Caiado, 2004.

1.2.2. Foreign prisoners

The data in table 1 show both the absolute number of foreign prisoners in Portugal as well as their respective share of the overall prison population from 1983 to 2004. Although these figures cover a period of more than twenty years, we will later on focus on more recent periods, because the data for these years are more complete and reliable.

Table 1 – Foreign prisoners in Portugal from 1983 to 2004

YEAR	N	% of the total prison population
1983	322	5.0
1984	510	6.4
1985	585	6.4
1986*	666	8.4
1987	740	9.3
1988	753	9.5
1989	746	8.9
1990	753	8.5
1991*	644	8.2
1992	786	8.3
1993	919	8.3
1994*	991	9.8
1995	1344	11.1
1996	1659	11.9
1997	1602	11.1
1998	1560	10.6
1999*	1387	10.8
2000	1547	12.2
2001	1582	13.7
2002	2095	15.2
2003	2145	15.7
2004	2275	17.3

* - Years where amnesties have been declared.

As we can see, the proportion of foreign prisoners in Portugal has increased more than three fold over the last 20 years, particularly since the beginning of the 21st century. In 1986, data from the European Council published in the "Bulletin d'Information Pénologique" showed that in the Western European countries the percentages ranged from zero in Scotland to 40 in Luxembourg. However, results from the S.PACE inquiry in the year 2000 showed a general increase of foreign prisoners in all western countries, particularly in Switzerland (62,6%), Luxembourg (59,1%), Greece (48,4%), Belgium (40,4%), Austria (30.1%), Italy (28,3%), France (21,6%) and Sweden (21,3%)[5]. Our data are in line with this general tendency but to a lesser degree, possibly because Portugal has a peripheral geographical position that is not so attractive for foreigners. The same seems to apply

---

[5] See Tournier, 2002.

to Spain who had 12.1% in 1986 and 18,8% in 2000. It should be noted that foreigners are greatly overrepresented in the prison population in comparison to their share of the overall population of Portugal. In 2003, 2.3% (276.480) of the total population (10.407.500) were not Portuguese, in comparison to a share of currently 17% of the prison population.

1.3. Overview of Involvement of Consulates, Embassies, Ministries and NGOs

The Service of Illegal Residents and Frontiers (Serviço de Estrangeiros e Fronteiras – SEF; http://www.sef.pt) is the main body responsible for conducting the processes that concern foreign citizens either for administrative purposes or to assure their expulsion is carried out after serving prison sentences. The SEF services can also provide for interpreters whenever necessary, but embassies or consulates might be directly contacted by the respective prison administration to provide this support. The Ministry of Foreign Affairs is responsible for conducting the general politics of Portugal regarding its relationships with other countries, especially those with whom we have more cultural affinities and historical ties such as Brazil and our former African colonies. On the other hand, it is the Ministry of Internal Affairs – in which the SEF is located – that has responsibilities for maintaining national cohesion and provides tools for the integration of newcomers. In general, embassies and consulates fully cooperate either with the SEF or with the central or local administration of the prison service, delivering additional information about their naturals or providing the latter with some support or contact with their home country. This support ranges from helping to cover the prisoners' basic needs (e.g., toilet and hygiene articles) to legal advice and the facilitation of family contacts. In more difficult situations (e.g, the death of a prisoner) they can also arrange for the transportation of the body to the home country. To our knowledge, there is no available information of NGO's working with foreign prisoners in Portugal.

1.4. Overview of Trends

Until 1975 Portugal had several colonies in Africa. After these gained independence, many people in these colonies already had family living in Portugal, which gave them the possibility to migrate to Portugal in search of a better life. Additionally, there is a particular agreement with Brazil, which provides their naturals with the possibility of staying in Portugal for a longer period of time in comparison to other nationalities. Thus, we have to consider that the proportion of naturals from these countries living in Portugal will be far more extensive than from other countries. Another important issue is the fact that Portugal was included into the European Community in 1986 and the creation of the Union Market in 1993 added a considerable growth in the circulation of goods and people. So there have been two major changes in the Portuguese population, one as a result of the ending of our colonial empire (1974-1976), and the other as a result of our entrance into the European Union in 1986. More recently, the end of the former Soviet Union – which affected all of Europe – produced new waves of immigration that have also reached Portugal.

1.4.1. Sentencing Trends

We will now consider a shorter time period (1993-2004) from which more specific information is available, and have a closer look at the figures. In table 2 we present data concerning the most important countries that are represented in the foreign prison population in Portugal. The fact that our criminal statistics were not that complete in the past prevents us from giving a full detailed account of this specific prison population over a long period of time. Therefore, a lot of the data presented hereafter is focused on the last six years. All of our former colonies in Africa are comprised under the acronym ACPOL (African Countries of Portuguese Official Language): Angola, Cape Verde, Guiné-Bissau, Mozambique and S. Tomé. As mentioned above, even prior to their independence, many naturals from these countries were already living in Portugal. Moreover, the subsequent periods of instability, from which the majority of them suffered after independence, impelled most of their residents to seek a better life in the former colonial potency.

Table 2 Foreign prisoners in Portugal according to the most relevant countries of origin (1993 to 2004).

Countries Years	ACPOL	Br	Co	Ve	Fr	It	Sp	UK	Li	Mo	Ro	Ru	Uk	OE	OC	TOTAL
1993	495	49	43	-	-	-	80	33	-	-	-	-	-	101	118	919
...	...	...	...	...	...	...	...	...	...	...	...	...	...	...	...	...
1998	914	68	33	-	36	22	106	24	-	-	-	-	-	98	259	1560
1999	782	68	37	-	37	25	82	18	-	-	-	-	-	76	262	1387
2000	860	79	29	-	37	24	92	11	-	-	-	-	-	165	250	1547
2001	880	109	29	30	41	15	101	11	9	-	9	25	80	94	149	1582
2002	1126	156	30	33	25	20	122	11	12	-	59	44	130	123	204	2095
2003	1122	146	27	38	34	36	125	9	4	89	55	36	125	100	199	2145
2004	1165	183	29	52	31	36	124	8	14	71	80	27	100	117	238	2275

ACPOL - African Countries of Portuguese Official Language; Br – Brazil; Co – Colombia; Ve – Venezuela; Fr – France; It – Italy; SP –Spain; UK – United Kingdom; Li – Lithuania; Mo – Moldavia; Ro – Romania; Ru – Russia; Uk – Ukraine; OE –Others Europe; OC – Other Countries

Considering the data presented in table 2 we can see that persons from the former Portuguese colonies have always been in the majority, in a similar proportion over time; however they seem to have been diminishing during the last years (53,9% in 1993; 55,6% in 2000; 51,2% in 2004). Among them, the naturals from Cape Verde, who were for many years the most important group of foreigners living in our country[6], are the ones who also contribute more to the criminal statistics[7]. Moving to South America we can see that Brazil is a leading country, but countries like Venezuela – who did not present a problem in the nineties – entered the 21st century with an increasing proportion. Colombia – with a longer tradition – presents a similar proportion in the years in focus. Also, almost self-evidently, the direct proximity to Spain leads to a greater representation of

---

6   See Costa, 1996.
7   See for instance Ferreira, 1999.

their naturals in comparison with other western European countries, although these figures appear to have stabilized during the last years. However, in pursuing the changes that occurred in the political geography of Europe at the end of the century, Portugal has been progressively "invaded" by people from the former "communist countries" which in turn brought new and sometimes more violent forms of criminality. In 2004 the majority of convicted prisoners (57,6%) served sentences between three and nine years, while 13,5% were sentenced to prison terms between nine and 15 years in length. 7,5% had sentences longer than 15 years. The foreign prisoners are predominantly represented in the gap between three and nine years (more than 70% of the cases).

1.4.2. Characteristics of the Foreign Prison Population

Apart from the geographical origin of the foreign inmates we also have to consider the differences in terms of age, gender, academic status and other variables. Regarding the age issue, it is difficult to trace differences or similarities between locals and foreigners because we have no statistics at our disposal that indicate this. Figures are grouped in a non-homogeneous way which means that the intervals covered by the groups are not the same which prevents us from making adequate comparisons. In any case, official analyses show that the foreigner prisoners have a tendency of being slightly older than locals as far as men are concerned, while the opposite seems to be the case for women[8]. Consulting the available data regarding gender over the past five years we can see that the proportion of men and women between locals and foreigners present some differences (table 3). In fact, as mentioned earlier, the proportion of foreigners in Portuguese prisons has been consistently increasing in recent years, but the relative increase for women has been much greater than that for men.

Table 3 Gender percentages of locals and foreigners in Portuguese prisons

	2000	2001	2002	2003	2004
Portuguese Men	87,8	88,1	85,1	84,7	83,3
Foreign Men	12,2	11,9	14,9	15,3	16,7
Portuguese Women	88,6	85,7	81,8	78,0	75,5
Foreign Women	11,4	14,3	18,2	22,0	24,5

Concerning the distribution of inmates according to their academic status, we have to point out that the data may not be reliable, especially the information about foreign prisoners, due to the existence of different educational systems and the impossibility of checking their assertions in detail. However, as expected from the literature, they represent very low grades, especially on the Portuguese side. Official data show that in 2004, of the 9,027 Portuguese men with some formal education only 0.5 % had a university degree and the vast majority (65,6%) had only completed the 6th grade or less. This is in sharp contrast to their fellow inmates from abroad of whom 4,5% had a completed a university degree and only 46% had completed 6th grade or less. The same tendency is observed

---

8   See for instance Moreira, 2000, 2001, 2002, 2003, 2005.

among the women, with even more discrepancy (7,8% of foreign female inmates have a university degree compared to 1,0% of the imprisoned Portuguese women).

Table 4 presents data concerning the type of crimes committed by locals and foreigners (men and women) in 2003 and 2004. The figures relating to gender show that – as expected – men and women tend to commit different types of offences.

Table 4 Types of crimes committed by foreigners and locals (percentages)

	Years	Against Persons	Against Society	Against Property	Drug Related	Other Crimes
Men Nationals	2003	21,8	3,1	41,7	30,4	2,9
	2004	25,9	6,7	35,7	23,4	8,3
Men Foreigners	2003	19,1	3,3	25,6	50,1	2
	2004	18,0	8,9	19,4	48,1	5,6
Women Nationals	2003	13,2	1	12,6	67,4	5,9
	2004	16,6	6,2	16,2	58,4	2,7
Women Foreigners	2003	3,3	0	4,4	89	3,3
	2004	4,4	1,8	6,2	87,6	0,0

Nevertheless, it seems that foreign women are more prone to be involved in drug related crimes (mostly trafficking) which is no surprise, bearing in mind the number of them coming from South America. They seldom commit crimes against persons while on the other hand, males show a proportional value, very similar to the ones obtained by their Portuguese colleagues.

1.5. Overview of National Legislation

The execution of penal sentences is regulated in Law # 265/79 of 1 August 1979 in combination with the amendments stated in Law # 49/80 of 22 March 1980 and # 414/85 of 18 October 1985. The Portuguese Penal Code emphasizes the necessity of equal treatment of national and foreign prisoners and makes no distinction in terms of the penalties that are applicable to any person, either Portuguese born or foreigners. However, in this last case an expulsion sentence may be applicable after the prison sentence has been served or in case the inmate is conditionally released. In fact, what happens is that most foreigners in prison are put on conditional release as soon as they have served half of their prison sentence after which they are sent back to their countries of origin[9]. Portuguese legislation also stresses the importance of satisfying specific needs concerning religious and cultural habits and communication with family and relatives to ensure the prisoner's support. Law also allows the individual the request to serve his/her sentence in his/her country of origin; in this case, the two countries are then obliged to make the necessary arrangements to attain the prisoner's demands. Concerning the allocation of foreign prisoners there are no special guidelines for placing them in special prisons or units unless there are specific reasons (e.g., health problems, security problems etc) that indicate that differential treatment is necessary[10]. The only thing that could prevent a prisoner from working or attending training or a professional course in prison is health

---

[9] See Albuquerque, 2006.
[10] See for instance Provedoria da Justiça, 2003.

problems. Of course, foreign inmates may experience some difficulties relating to language differences, but that is by no means a criterion of exclusion. Only health problems can interfere with a job assignment. In some prisons occupational problems are more frequent because of overcrowding, but these affect both Portuguese nationals and foreigners.

A bilateral transfer agreement between Portugal and Brazil has been in place since 2003 that can be applied if the behaviour in question is considered criminal in both countries and the resulting sentence is longer than six months. More elaborate information and documentation on this subject can be accessed at http://www.gddc.pt/siii/docs/rar45-2003.pdf.

2   TREATMENT OF FOREIGN PRISONERS

The Portuguese Penal Code emphasises the importance of rehabilitation and re-socialization being the main objectives of prison sentences. Therefore, all efforts should be made to assure that inmates can serve their sentence in a productive manner, either by studying, working or engaging in professional training courses provided by the administration. Prisoners maintain their fundamental rights as persons and are also entitled to the essential social and cultural rights, that is, the right to have a paying job, the social security benefits, and as far as possible, the right to have access to culture and to the full development of their personality. The exercise of these rights is, however, subordinated by the restrictions that the sentence imposes and also by the internal regulations of the prison and orders from its director or medical constraints. Nevertheless, this subordination must attend criteria of reasonability, normality and non-abusiveness of the prisoner's rights. Finally, it is important to note that there is a great difference between the means and facilities that a central prison can offer compared to local prisons, particularly those that are quite small. In fact, while a more personal and individual approach is more possible in these smaller institutions, there are much more opportunities for problems to occur in the larger prisons where 1,000 prisoners or more can be held[11].

2.1 General

Overall, there is no difference in treatment, prison allocation or prison work assignment between Portuguese prisoners and foreigners. In fact, more restrictive measures are only applied when the security of the institution or special security issues related to the type of crime committed and the type of prison sentence make this necessary. That is mainly the case with criminals who have been convicted for crimes against the state (e.g., terrorism, organized crime) or those who pose a serious threat to other prisoners or themselves. The separation of prisoners who have the same nationality or ethnic background is only implemented if there is solid evidence of planning activities that could threaten the security of the institution or of other inmates or staff. Otherwise no effort is made to impede the more or less spontaneous reunion of prisoners who share affinities or socio-cultural backgrounds.

---

[11]   Nevertheless it should be pointed out that the average number of prisoners in central facilities was 431 in 2004 while in local facilities it was 99; see Moreira, 2005.

Language might be a complicated matter for prisoners from countries that have no affinity with Portugal in terms of culture and language. This is particularly the case for prisoners whose home countries are in the north of Europe such as the former Republic of the USSR or even Russia itself. These prisoners may have more difficulty in making themselves understandable to our personnel; when they refuse to make an effort to understand anything, they may even use their apparent inability to speak our language to cause problems for the Portuguese Prison Administration. In more difficult cases an interpreter is contacted. However, efforts are being made to translate basic materials (for instance the rules of the institution) related to prison that are handed out to the foreign prisoners. At a later point of their sentence, these prisoners can be enrolled in language courses. These courses already exist within the prison system for illiterate prisoners, and with some adaptations they could also be adequate for foreign prisoners. It is necessary to make some adjustments to them because most foreign prisoners from the eastern European countries are not illiterate but simply lack the basic comprehension of the Portuguese language.

2.2 Living conditions and facilities

The allocation of prisoners is initially effected on the grounds of the place where the crime was committed and where the court decision is made. After sentence is pronounced, prisoners can request to be transferred to a prison that is closer to their family in order to facilitate visits. This is generally granted depending solely on the capacity of the requested prison and its rate of occupation. Foreign prisoners are not generally allocated to a specific institution but those who have no potential visitors or family bonds in Portugal are more prone to be transferred to the Funchal Prison on the Island of Madeira, which is one of the newest prisons in Portugal (built in 1994) and generally has more places available, or Izeda (inner north of Portugal). Although the Portuguese prison law specifies that prisoners should be entitled to a single cell, overcrowding has long time ago eluded this "rule" and other typologies of allocating prisoners have emerged. The most common disposition is the allocation of two prisoners to one cell, provided that they accept the presence of each other and no incompatibilities are evident. As the rate of overcrowding is declining it is possible that in a few years all prisoners can have single cells.

2.3 Reception and admission

Reception procedures are the same for Portuguese nationals and for foreigners. Difficulties may arise due to language barriers, but this seems to be more and more exceptional. First of all, prisoners have the right to inform their family and legal representatives, and in the case of foreigners to call their diplomatic mission immediately after their entry into the prison. It is expected that prison staff fulfil their duties and inform foreign prisoners about the legal dispositions and rules of the prison and proceed to allocate the individuals on grounds of reasonability considering the prison's conditions. There is no internal indication or "rule" to constitute "ethnical units" although by reasons of cultural, religious, language or ethnic affinity, prisoners can be put together on the grounds of choices or preferences that they may further enunciate.

2.4 Work – Education – Training – Sports – Recreation

Data concerning professional occupation in prisons show that, proportionally, foreign prisoners have more work assignments than national prisoners, especially the female foreigners. This may be explained by the fact that most of them have no family support and therefore the prison administration will provide them with work more rapidly, so that they can acquire the money they need to cover their basic needs. One aspect that supports this assumption is the fact that most of these prison jobs do not require special skills or procedures that may cause difficulties for the inmate, especially those in which language problems could arise. Concerning the level of education, data show that on average foreign prisoners from European countries and female prisoners from South American countries have higher degrees of formal education than Portuguese prisoners. This can be a feature that may foster future social reintegration. Nevertheless, many foreign prisoners attend school classes in order to improve their knowledge of the Portuguese language. Professional training is also promoted in prisons and foreigners can access it provided they fulfil the minimum requirements and pass selection tests. Professional training is mainly on jobs for constructions and building, mechanics, electricity, gardening and computers. Women are mostly assigned to hairdressing, embroidery and nursing. Sports and recreation are promoted in every institution, but the central prisons naturally have better conditions and facilities for practicing. Gymnasiums and outdoor sports pitches represent one of the latest improvements by the Portuguese Prison Administration. Prisoners can have regular access to these spaces but they use them mostly on weekends when they are not working. Often, prison educators, teachers and social workers organize championships and meetings with teams from the community to foster interaction with the outside world and promote social reintegration. Leisure rooms for the prisoners have also been created lately in some prisons but their number is still small[12]. Following European legislation – Resolution (73) 5 and Recommendation (87) 3 of the European Council – prisoners are entitled to two hours of recreation in open space per day, which is applies even to those who choose to remain inactive during prison time.

2.5 Food – Religion – Personal Hygiene – Medical care

The problems arise with those religious and cultural dress requirements that should be respected and preserved as long as they are feasible and do not collide with prison security. In doing so, the prison administration avoids conflicts and prevents any feeling of hostility or inequality among the prison population. Nowadays, prison uniforms are not so important but they still exist and prisoners should wear trousers, shirts/t-shirts and jackets. Dressing in long robes or wearing turbans is not permitted by the prison administration. Since Portugal is a country with a catholic tradition, prisons were generally built with a chapel but no other religious groupings were expected. In fact, the majorities and minorities that are found within the different ethnic groups in society are the same as in prison. Religious groups can in fact congregate and practice their religious beliefs so long as they are permitted to do so by the prison warden. Also, religious representatives can access the prison institutions and visit the prisoners so long as they are granted access by the warden. Such meetings and visits are only rarely turned down. Food habits can reflect this

---

[12] See Provedoria da Justiça, 2003.

cultural diversity. It may prove difficult for the prison administration to produce a 'menu a la carte' for each preference but, if no family support is present, it should be possible to meet those needs related to cultural background, if only through supplying the prison canteens with the desired product. However, the prison administration must acknowledge the problem and they should be aware of the differences and needs of the prisoners. Over the last ten years efforts have been made to provide WC facilities and showers in all cells. However, some of the oldest prisons still maintain common showers and WC facilities that represent interventions into the privacy and security of inmates[13].

The Portuguese Prison Administration has one central hospital located near Lisbon for situations that require longer medical interventions. Every central prison has an infirmary to which prisoners are moved when their state of health requires it. When more severe health problems require it they are transferred to the prison hospital or to a central prison where they can receive proper care. In matters of urgency transport is provided to the nearest central hospital. Medical assistance is totally free for the prisoners, in a vast number of cases, namely: 1) for the female prisoners during pregnancy, child birth and further assistance to the newborn; 2) female prisoners can have their children living with them until they are three years old; 3) while in prison, all medical care given to the children is also free of charge; 4) if the prisoner had an accident while working[14]; 5) all sorts of dental treatment except prosthesis; 6) and in the cases of sexually transmitted diseases (including AIDS), for which first screening is mandatory, and subsequent treatment and monitoring follow. No distinction between nationals and foreigners is made regarding the provision of medical assistance.

2. 6 Consular and legal help

Prisoners are allowed to contact their legal representatives and receive visits from them in an adequate and appropriate office, where standards of confidentiality and privacy must be granted. He or she is also legally entitled to receive any documents or papers related to the resolution of their legal problems. In the case of the foreigners these rights are also extended to the accredited diplomatic or consular authorities of their home countries, but the visits need to be authorized by the Ministry of Justice. Data show that the number of these visits has been increasing along the years with visits of Spanish representatives predominating, followed by the other European Union countries and South Americans in the case of women. The forms of assistance that Embassies and Consulates generally provide concerns the provision of essential goods, legal representation, the facilitation of making and maintaining contact with the family, and sometimes monetary support.

2.7 Contact with the outside world

Normally, the criteria regarding a prisoners' allocation is to place them in the proximity of their family. However, this is not applicable to most foreign prisoners, especially not to those from Northern Europe, because most of them have no relatives living in Portugal to visit them. Contact by regular mail is common and phone calls using a card phone are

---

[13] Provedoria da Justiça, 2003
[14] The prisoner is also entitled to an insurance allowance the same way as if he was working in the community.

permitted after previous authorization by the prison director. According to the rules existing in every prison, visits to the inmates are permitted on certain days; normally one day is for relatives and the other for friends. The visit period is normally two hours and the number of persons that can enter the prison each time is restricted to avoid confusion and threats to security. In the case of pre-trial detainees, visits from the family are allowed every day of the week. Although newspapers, books and magazines in foreign language can be available, prison directors only rarely authorize them, especially when they are written in languages that are not understandable for the officers whose job is to screen them. Radio and TV sets are allowed with only few limitations (e.g., larger sizes are forbidden) but there is no limit in the number of channels broadcasted. So, foreign prisoners theoretically have access to their home channels and channels in foreign languages so long as these can technically be received in the institution.

2.8 Re-integration activities – Prison leave

No agency or authority is specifically concerned with the foreign prisoners after they have left prison. The Institute of Social Reinsertion is the state institution that provides help when prisoners have completed their sentences, or supervises those who are on probation or conditional release. This institution is also responsible for providing some monetary help at the beginning and their technical staff includes psychologists and social workers who provide contacts with relatives of the prisoner when they face monetary problems and controls for the existence of false declarations regarding professional places that the prisoners allege. This happens mostly when individuals remain under supervision (probation, conditional release), but for those who complete their full prison sentences, rarely any support is given, regardless of their nationality. There is no official data on the number of foreigners who are discharged on conditional release but it is assumed that when an expulsion sentence is annexed to the prison sentence the conditional release is automatically granted at the mid-point of the sentence[15], which means that a foreign prisoner benefits from a less severe regime in the concession of conditional release[16].

2.9 Release- Expulsion

Having committed a crime and to be considered „personna non grata" is sufficient reason for expulsion procedures. According to the 2004 report of the Service of Illegal Residents and Frontiers (Serviço de Estrangeiros e Fronteiras: SEF), available at http://www.sef.pt, a total of 162 expulsions on judicial grounds were executed, with people from Brazil (32 cases), Cape Verde (29 cases), Ukraine (18 cases) and Moldavia (15 cases) accounting for more than 50% of the decisions. The most frequently committed crimes were drug trafficking (102 cases), extortion (20 cases) theft and robbery (7 cases each). Only one homicide and one rape were observed. When individuals are under the measure of expulsion they are escorted under supervision of the SEF authorities from prison to their countries and handed over to their national authorities. In fact, and as of that moment, they become completely free because it is not possible to supervise their conditional release outside the borders of Portugal. According to the Convention on the

---

[15] See Moreira, 2005.
[16] See Albuquerque, 2006.

Transference of Condemned Persons approved by the European Council, the foreign individual has the right to require serving his sentence, either in his country of origin or in the country where he lives at the moment. It should be noted that persons who are also Portuguese nationals due to being married to a Portuguese citizen cannot be expelled.

2.10 Aftercare – Probation

Those foreign offenders who can or will stay in the host country after being released from prison may use the facilities provided by the Instituto de Reinserção Social and Social Welfare Services to foster their reintegration (for instance access to programmes for housing, free meals in Social Welfare canteens, actual financial support, help in finding employment and in accessing the facilities of the Health National System). However, they can only benefit from these services if they have a valid stay permit and are not under a removal or expulsion measure. Additionally, they must hold a regular job to cover their needs and be fully integrated into the social system.

2.11 Staff

Table 5 and figure 1 show the evolution of the various "prison populations" over 16 years. It is quite evident that the main effort has been in reinforcing the number of prison guards compared to the other professional groups, especially the technical staff which is mainly composed of psychologists, social service workers and sociologists.

Table 5 "Prison populations" (1987-2003)

Years	1987	1988	1990	1997	1998	1999	2000	2001	2003
Prisoners	7965	7958	8874	14361	14598	12808	12683	13112	12109
Technical	238	160	222	357	320	342	256	308	478
Guards	2446	2495	2700	3379	3667	3723	4167	4121	4575
Administrat.	268	387	536	439	482	522	677	654	636

Source: Extracted from Gonçalves (2005)

Figure 1 "Prison populations" comparative evolution (1987-2003

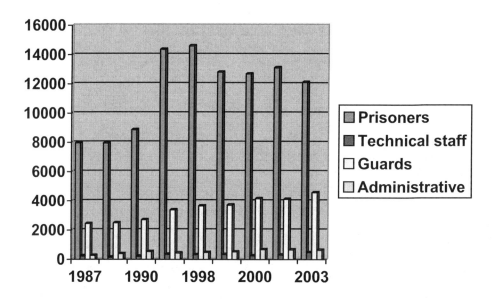

Source: Extracted from Gonçalves (2005).

This indeed shows that the main concern of Portuguese prison authorities relies heavily on security issues and almost forgets the need for the implementation of specific programs and interventions directed to changing attitudes, acquiring social competences and dealing with emotional problems, among others. This is valid for foreigners as well as for nationals. Prison staff receive no special training for dealing with foreign prisoners. However, they are made aware of some special issues that they may face when dealing with these offenders, especially their physical training and their higher degree of school education. In most cases staff learns through experience while performing their jobs in the prison.

2.12 Projects

There are no specific projects for foreign prisoners related to their specific nature and no research has been conducted to acknowledge for their specificity. However, they can benefit from and are indeed included in those other dimensions that prisons provide, for instance drug treatment and cultural manifestations (drama and comedy representation, music, painting and ceramics …).

3 ADMINISTRATIVE DETENTION OF FOREIGN PRISONERS

3.1 Institution

The SEF is responsible for granting permanent residence visas and they manage the processes of removals and expulsions, regardless of criminal procedures. Administrative detention of foreigners is generally executed at four locations in Portugal. These facilities are "transit zones" because they are located in the airports of Lisbon, Porto, Faro and Ponta Delgada (Açores). The creation of new detention centres is not a priority in the short term for the government, even if the Law No. 34/94 of 14 September 1994 allows the creation of such centres[17].

3.2 Ministry responsible and Legislation

The Ministry of Internal Affairs is the highest responsible entity and supervises the SEF. Law 60/93 of 3 March 1993established the special regime of entering permanence and leave of foreign citizens and their relatives, born in EU countries. Law no. 15/98 of 26 March 1998 establishes a new regime for asylum seekers and refugees. This regime basically states that anyone who comes from a country where he/she might be submitted to torture or other reproachable actions because he fought for the ideals of democracy, freedom of speech or where he was socially excluded on the basis of his skin colour, political opinions or religious convictions, can be granted asylum and then become a legally recognized refugee.

3.3 Capacity institutions

Most of the foreigners in administrative detention in Portugal are detained in the transit zone of Lisbon airport, which has a capacity of 40 people. On average, there are 10 to 15 persons being detained at any one time. The building is divided into two wings, one for asylum seekers and one for irregular migrants, each with 20 places.

3.4 Length of stay

The administrative detention of foreigners in Portugal may be imposed for a period not exceeding 60 days as stipulated in Law no. 15/98 of 26 March 1998. There are no known problems concerning delays in the application of the decisions, which are generally in adherence with the deadlines as stated in law.

3.5 Decisions procedure

The persons who may be detained in these centres are:
- People requesting asylum until the SEF decides whether these persons have legitimate grounds for such an application. On average, they are detained for three days. If the SEF decides that they are not entitled to ask for asylum in Portugal, they are expelled to where they came from within a period of time not exceeding 60 days. If

---

[17] The Law refers to "centres of temporary set-up".

an application for asylum is initially approved, they are transferred to reception centres.

- Irregular migrants facing removal. Even though this practice remains seldom, irregular migrants may be arrested by police forces when they have no permit to reside in the country. In such cases, they appear before a judge who may decide to place them in custody for the period of time that is necessary in order to remove them. They may be detained either in prisons with convicted criminals or in one of the transit zones mentioned above.

3.6 Appeal procedure

Appeal procedures must be done through regular administrative courts with legal assistance. Such a procedure should be accompanied with professional legal advice. Courts may provide legal assistance free of charge by designating a lawyer for the petitioner.

3.7 Irregular stay

Unless the person has committed a crime, illegal entrance in Portugal only accounts for administrative procedures that will end in an administrative process of expulsion. Irregular stay in itself is not a criminal offence.

3.8 Numbers

In 2004 the prison system registered 5,670 newcomers of whom 1,180 (20,8%) were foreigners. It should be noted that these figures were 2,5% lower compared to the previous year (2003).

3.9. Expulsion

Data from the 2004 SEF report shows that out of a total of 2.909 individuals who were notified to leave the country voluntarily in that year, Brazil stood ahead (37%), followed by Romania (20%), Ukraine (11,7%), Angola (3,6%) and Cape Verde (3,3%). A total of 1,382 procedures of administrative expulsion were initiated in the same period and decisions were reached in 558. Of these, a total of 445 administrative expulsions were implemented, mostly concerning citizens from Romania (85 cases), Ukraine (83 cases) and Brazil (75 cases), while the 113 remaining cases were authorized to stay in Portugal and cleared of all charges.

3.10 Not-expelled prisoners

There is unfortunately no precise information available on what happens with those administrative prisoners who are not expelled from the country.

3.11 Detention irregulars under criminal law

Foreign nationals under a measure or procedure of removal or expulsion can be detained in regular prisons with other inmates who face criminal charges should the transit zones be overcrowded. Distinctions are made in the case of minors, who can be sent to different institutions, but in most cases they remain with their parents. No actual figures have been disposed regarding this issue.

3.12 Minors

Foreign minors living in Portugal with residence visas are not allowed to leave the country unless they are accompanied by their parents or legally certified and authorized guardians. When irregularities are detected and unless these minors are at risk they stay with their parents or accompany them to the institutions.

4 NATIONALS DETAINED ABROAD

No regular or official information exists on this topic but since Portugal has historically been a country of emigration it is somehow self-evident that its nationals should face problems with justice abroad.

4.1 Numbers and composition group

According to recent information portrayed by the State Secretary of the Communities, a total of 1,900 Portuguese citizens are being held in foreign prisons. This number represents roughly 1/6 of the actual prison population within Portugal.

4.2 Detention countries

Predominantly in South America, but no figures are available.

4.3 Reasons for detention and sentencing

According to the State Secretary of the Communities, 80% of the prisoners are in custody for drug related offences. Others are former workers who become unemployed and commit crimes in order to cover their basic needs. Types of sentences are not documented but in certain countries drug possession can result in a sentence to death.

4.4 Involved organisations

Consular protection is the principal and most effective entity in helping Portuguese prisoners abroad, providing help at various levels by giving basic goods, medication and other goods. In exceptional cases repatriation is also provided.

4.5 Release and reception

When the prisoner is released it is again the Consulate that can provide help for their return to Portugal, but the individual must be aware of the different types of legislation and penalties that each country presents. Cases handled within the European Union are simpler than outside of it. Usually, relatives support reception in the home country.

4.6 Aftercare

Concerning the type of measure given (release or expulsion) the responsibility is upon the individual or the expulsing state. When the person has been released in the foreign state he or she has to pay for his/her own transportation back to Portugal. In cases of expulsion, the foreign state has to cover the expenses of returning the Portuguese prisoner to Portugal.

4.7 Public opinion and the media

This is not a subject that attracts the public opinion, unless a public person is involved. Some months ago a case was particularly covered by the media because a Portuguese film-maker was caught in possession of a certain amount of drugs (which he claimed was for private use) in a Middle-Eastern country where possession is severely punished. It was only through diplomatic channels that this matter came to a good ending. But ultimately no one is aware of the number of Portuguese prisoners abroad.

5 EVALUATION AND RECOMMENDATIONS

As mentioned above, Portuguese prisons are predominantly occupied by Portuguese nationals. The second group of inmates are Africans who were born in our former colonies. The third major group are the Brazilians. However, recent years have seen the emergence of new groups from other countries, especially Europeans. They pose different problems to prison administrations and prison staff contrary to the former groups who have a similitude to Portugal in terms of language and cultural habits. Prison statistics have shown a continuous growth in foreigners among our prison population, especially on the part of women. They tend to be predominantly South American born and are imprisoned for offences related to drug trafficking. On the other hand, there has been an increase in the number of male foreign prisoners from the North European former communist countries, with Ukraine and Romania leading the group, who are detained either for expulsion on behalf of administrative problems or who are serving prison sentences. Although related to drug trafficking as well, their involvement in violent crimes against other persons is considerable. Also, the fact that most of them have had good military training contributes to a portrait of aggressiveness and dangerousness that was not common before. Our data also show that in proportion, foreigner prisoners in general had higher levels of previous school achievement than the Portuguese prisoners, and this is particularly due to the fact that recently most of them have been coming from North European countries such as Ukraine and Moldavia. We wish to particularly emphasize the need to provide prison staff with more skills and training in order to deal with these new groups of prisoners.

The Portuguese Prison Administration is making an effort to provide these new categories of inmates with the same opportunities of social reinsertion and reintegration that are offered to Portuguese nationals. However, since our legislation in these cases frequently imposes expulsion after the prison sentence has been (partially) served, issues of re-integration tend to be overlooked. There is no reliable information about the problems that foreign prisoners state to the prison administration. In fact, the information gathered by the staff only accounts for isolated problems concerning specific individuals in the same way as it occurs with national prisoners. However, foreign prisoners could face problems in the following areas: language, cultural habits, religious habits and diets. The lack of family support, psychiatric problems (morbidity) and proneness to suicide are also grounds for concern. Based on a more impressionistic point of view, we might say that the foreign prisoners in Portugal, although increasing in numbers, are being integrated in the main cultural trend. In prisons as well as in society they are generally treated with tolerance unless their behaviour and attitude indicate the need for a more repressive and secure policy. But that does not appear to be the case.

Contact with inmates originating from South European countries like Spain or Italy and the French-speaking countries do not present problems. Also, the Portuguese people in general are quite familiar with the English language so this should not present a serious problem. Furthermore, as can be taken from the statistics, the great majority of our foreign prisoners either come from former Portuguese colonies in Africa or Brazil who all have Portuguese as their mother-language.

Electronic surveillance appears to be a valuable contribution to solve the overcrowding problems in prisons and can be applied in the cases of persons who have to wait several months before going trial (pre-trial detainees). Using it on individuals who might have communication problems or problems in making themselves understood – like the foreign population – could turn out to be more of a problem than a solution, but it may be worth trying.

Finally, we want to address the gipsy community in our prisons. There is no reliable data concerning the prevalence of the gipsy population in our country. However, in the prison system they represent on average between 5 and 6% of the total inmate population[18]. In recent years their criminal activities have shifted from crimes against property (thefts, robbery, and smuggling) to drug trafficking. Also, several of them were seriously involved in organized crime. Their illiteracy problems put them in a position that makes accessing training and professional courses difficult, which in return influences the prospects of their future re-integration. Their traditional activities (e.g., selling things in the streets or in local fairgrounds) are declining and no other employment possibilities are available. Although they are not foreign prisoners – they are Portuguese – they represent a problem due to the limited qualifications they have and the negative stereotype they carry.

It is clear from our work that, despite the effort made, information is lacking in several domains in which there is no research available. Although foreign prisoners do not currently represent a major issue in our prison system, they unequivocally require our attention now in order to prevent problems from arising in the future.

---

[18]   See for instance Moreira, 1998.

Chapter 22

Slovakia

Martin Skamla

1 INTRODUCTION

Foreigners and persons without nationality are, as probably in almost every country in the world, an inherent part of the prison population in Slovakia. These persons are criminally liable according to Articles 4 to 6 of the Act No. 300/2005 (hereinafter Criminal Code) where principles of personal scope and criminal liability are set.

1.1 Overview penalties and measures

According to the Criminal Code, a criminal offence is an unlawful act, attributes of which are provided in this Code if not provided otherwise. There are two different kinds of criminal offences namely misdemeanour and crime. Tort is a criminal offence committed by negligence or committed intentionally for which the Code stipulates a prison sentence with the upper level of the criminal tariff not exceeding five years. Crime is an intentional criminal offence for which the Code stipulates a prison sentence with the upper level of the criminal tariff exceeding five years.

The most severe punishment for a criminal offence is the prison sentence, which can be imposed as a sentence for a definite period of time, mostly for twenty-five years, or as a life imprisonment sentence.

Pre-trial detention is regulated by the Act No. 301/2005 (Code of Criminal Procedure), which provides that the accused may be detained in pre-trial detention only when:

the facts ascertained so far indicate that the act that initiated prosecution was perpetrated;

- the act has attributes of a criminal offence;
- there are grounds for suspicion that the act was perpetrated by the accused;
- because of his/her conduct and other particular facts there are reasonable grounds to believe that: (a) he/she would escape or go into hiding to avoid prosecution or punishment, in particular if his/her identity cannot be immediately established and if he/she does not have a permanent residence, or if there is a threat of a high penalty; (b) he/she will influence the witnesses, experts, co-accused or otherwise frustrate the investigation of facts relevant for criminal prosecution; or (c) he/she will continue in his/her criminal activity, accomplish the attempted crime or commit the crime he/she had prepared or had threatened to commit.

Administrative detention is another type of measure that results in the deprivation of liberty of foreigners. This measure is specific for foreigners, as only they can be detained under administrative provisions, in particular the Act No. 48/2002 on residence of foreigners. Reasons for administrative detention are cited in the chapter devoted to this issue.

1.2 Overview of the Prison System

The Prison system in Slovakia is represented by the Corps of Prison and Justice Guards (hereinafter Prison Corps) and its operation is governed by the Act No. 4/2001 on Corps of Prison and Justice Guards as amended.

The Prison Corps are security corps who fulfil their tasks in the sector of pre-trial detention, serving of imprisonment sentences, protection and patrol of Prison corps facilities and in the sector of the protection of order and security in judicial facilities and in the facilities of prosecution. The Prison Corps consist of the Directorate General – governing, supervisory and methodical body; pre-trial detention institutions; institutions for serving imprisonment sentences; institutions for serving imprisonment sentences for juveniles; a hospital for the accused and sentenced (hereinafter Institutions) and members of Prison Corps.

The Directorate General and the Institutions are established and recalled by the Ministry of Justice of the Slovak Republic and they are budgetary organisations. The number of members of the Prison Corps is set by the Government of the Slovak Republic. The Prison Corps are subordinated to the Minister of Justice of the Slovak Republic. The head of the Prison Corps is a Director General, who is appointed and recalled by the Minister of Justice of the Slovak Republic. The head of an Institution is a director who is appointed and recalled by the Director General.

Pre-trial detention and the serving of imprisonment sentences are provided for in 18 Institutions; six of them are designed for pre-trial detention only and four of them are a combination of both pre-trial detention and the serving of imprisonment sentences. The total capacity of institutions for pre-trial detention is 3 649 persons. On 1 June 2006, 2 472 persons were in pre-trial detention of which 129 were foreigners. The total capacity of institutions for serving imprisonment sentences is 6 854 persons, including open departments. On 1 June 2006, 6 470 persons were serving a sentence of imprisonment, of which 92 were foreigners. In 2005, on average 3 042 persons were in pre-trial detention, and 6 285 persons were serving imprisonment sentences, which makes it a total average of 9 327 in 2005.

1.3 Overview involvement Consulates, Embassies, Ministries home country, Probation service home country, NGO's etc

No systematic statistics are held on contacts of foreign detainees with consulates or embassies of their countries of origin. Whenever a foreigner in pre-trial detention or a foreigner serving a prison sentence wants to contact the embassy or consulate, he always receives assistance. Some of the embassies (e.g. Czech Republic and Ukraine) are provided monthly with information on the numbers of their citizens serving imprisonment sentences or citizens in pre-trial detention.

Several non-governmental organisations as the Slovak Helsinki Committee, the Citizen and Democracy and the Open Society Foundation are interested in the issues related to pre-trial detention and serving imprisonment sentences. These organisations are provided with their requested information and they are allowed to visit pre-trial detention institutions or institutions for serving imprisonment sentences.

1.4 Overview of trends

In general, the number of imprisoned persons has an increasing tendency. There were 5 405 persons serving imprisonment sentences in 2001, whereas in 2005 the number increased to 6 285. As far as foreigners are concerned, the following numbers are available of foreigners imprisoned from 2001 to 2005:

Table 1 Foreigners in detention

year	Total Number	Pre-trial detention	Imprisonment
2001	194	111	83
2002	192	121	71
2003	209	125	84
2004	225	141	84
2005	237	164	73

1.5 Overview of national legislation

Pre-trial detention is regulated by the Act No. 221/2006 on pre-trial detention (zákon 221/2006 o výkone väzby)[1]. Article 49 of this Act provides that provisions of the Act No. 221/2006 apply to pre-trial detention of foreigners and stateless persons if not provided otherwise. There is also an implementary regulation, the Ordinance of the Ministry of Justice of Slovak Republic No. 437/2006, by means of which Rules for pre-trial detention are issued (vyhláška 437/2006, ktorou sa vydáva Poriadok výkonu väzby)[2]. It comprises also several provisions specifically designated for foreign prisoners, in particular regarding placement in cells and the establishment of contacts with diplomatic missions.

The enforcement of the prison sentence is regulated by the Act No. 475/2005 on serving of the prison sentence and on amendments of some acts (zákon 475/2005 o výkone trestu odňatia slobody a o zmene a doplnení niektorých zákonov)[3]. The ordinance of the Ministry of Justice of Slovak Republic No. 664/2005, by means of which Rules for serving imprisonment are issued (vyhláška 664/2005, ktorou sa vydáva Poriadok výkonu trestu odňatia slobody)[4], is an implementary regulation for the Act No 475/2005.

The Act No. 4/2001 on the Corps of Prison and Justice Guards (zákon 4/2001 o Zbore väzenskej a justičnej stráže)[5] as amended regulates the operation of the Corps of Prison and Justice Guards. While securing pre-trial detention and serving imprisonment sentences, the Prison Corps cooperate also with the probation and mediation officers to the extent provided in Act No. 550/2003 on probation and mediation officers and on amendments of some acts (zákon 550/2003 o probačných a mediačných úradníkoch a o zmene a doplnení niektorých zákonov)[6].

The Act 300/2005 Criminal code (Trestný zákon)[7] regulates principles of criminal liability, types of punishments, types of protective measures, their imposition and bodies of criminal offences.

The Act No. 301/2005 Code of Criminal Procedure (zákon 301/2005 Trestný poriadok)[8] regulates, among other issues, pre-trial detention of substantive and procedural issues, as well as cooperation with foreign justice authorities.

---

[1] Collection of Laws (Zbierka zákonov), Vol. No. 78 (2006).
[2] Collection of Laws (Zbierka zákonov), Vol. No. 160 (2006).
[3] Collection of Laws (Zbierka zákonov), Vol. No. 191 (2005).
[4] Collection of Laws (Zbierka zákonov), Vol. No. 264 (2005).
[5] Collection of Laws (Zbierka zákonov), Vol. No. 2 (2001).
[6] Collection of Laws (Zbierka zákonov), Vol. No. 225 (2003).
[7] Collection of Laws (Zbierka zákonov), Vol. No. 129 (2005).

The Act No. 48/2002 on residence of foreigners and on amendments of some acts (zákon 48/2002 o pobyte cudzincov a o zmene a doplnení niektorých zákonov)[9] as amended regulates administrative detention of foreigners.

2 TREATMENT OF FOREIGN OFFENDERS

2.1 General

As a general rule, provisions of general legislation regarding prison sentence and pre-trial detention applied to Slovak offenders apply to foreigners as well if not provided otherwise. Specific provisions regarding foreigners are dealt with in the following subsections of this chapter below.

According to Article 69 (1) of the Act No. 475/2005 on the execution of the prison sentences and on amendments of some acts (Prison Sentence Act) foreigners are a special category of prisoners and their psychic, physiological, ethnical and national particularities are taken into consideration.

2.2 Living conditions and facilities

According to the law, foreign prisoners have access to the same living conditions and facilities as Slovak prisoners. In regard to placement of foreigners in cells, Article 54 of the Ordinance of the Ministry of Justice of Slovak Republic No. 437/2006, by means of which Rules for pre-trial detention are issued (Pre-trial Detention Rules), provides that when foreigners are placed in cells, capabilities of foreigners to communicate in the same language are taken into consideration. A similar provision is to be found also in Article 75 (7) of the Prison Sentence Act. According to this provision, when foreigners are placed in cells, capabilities of foreigners to communicate in the same or similar language are taken into consideration, with a view to enable them to communicate with each other. Religious and cultural specifications or diversity are according to Slovak legislation not taken into consideration when placing prisoners in cells.

2.3 Reception and admission

In both relevant legislative norms, Prison Sentence Act and Act No. 221/2006 on pre-trial detention (Pre-trial Detention Act), provisions regarding information of foreigners on the prison rules are not missing. Article 50 (5) of the Pre-trial Detention Act and Article 75 (4) of the Prison Sentence Act identically provide that the facility is obliged to inform a foreigner about rights, obligations and conditions of serving of a prison sentence (pre-trial detention) in a language that the foreigner understands. Foreigners are also informed about their right to contact the diplomatic mission of their country of origin. Persons without a nationality are informed about their right to contact a diplomatic mission or international bodies, whose mission it is to protect their interests (Article 50 (1) of the Pre-trial Detention Act and Article 75 (1) of the Prison Sentence Act).

---

8   Collection of Laws (Zbierka zákonov), Vol. No. 129 (2005).
9   Collection of Laws (Zbierka zákonov), Vol. No. 23 (2002).

Article 52 of the Act No. 48/2002 on the residence of foreigners and on the amendments of some acts (the Foreigners Act) constitutes an obligation for Institutions to inform the competent police authority without delay about commencement of pre-trial detention and of serving of prison sentence of a foreigner.

Foreign prisoners can call their family under the same conditions as Slovak citizens. All prisoners pay the cost of their phone calls (Article 21 (3) of the Pre-trial Detention Act and Article 27 (3) of the Prison Sentence Act).

2.4 Work - Education – Training – Sports – Recreation

Foreign prisoners serving prison sentences are able to work. According to Article 42 (2) of the Prison Sentence Act, engagement of a prisoner in work is a specific relationship between an Institution and a condemned person, which does not constitute a creation of a working relationship according to labour law. Therefore, a work permit is not necessary for a foreigner. When serving a prison sentence, prisoners are engaged in work in accordance with the objective of the prison sentence. Their health state, qualifications and fulfilment of the objectives of the treatment programme are taken into consideration (Article 42 (1) of the Prison Sentence Act).

According to Article 32 (1) of the Pre-trial Detention Act, an accused may be, after his/her health state was considered, engaged in work, if a court or authority acting in criminal procedure and the accused agree.

In regard to vocational training, sports and recreational activities the same legal framework for Slovak citizens applies to foreigners.

In libraries in Institutions are also books in foreign languages, e.g. Czech, Russian, and Hungarian. According to Article 77 of the Ordinance of the Ministry of Justice of Slovak Republic No. 664/2005, by means of which Rules for serving imprisonment are issued (Rules for Serving Imprisonment), an Institution will organise a Slovak language course for foreigners if it is expedient and foreigners are interested. According to the Prison Corps, Slovak a language course is organised in one of the Institutions.

2.5 Food – Religion – Personal hygiene – Medical care

Article 19 of the Prison Sentence Act (Article 13 of the Pre-trial Detention Act) provides that by boarding, the cultural and religious traditions of persons condemned (accused) are to be considered. Composition and nutrition value of food by extraordinary requirements according to cultural and religious tradition is generally set by the nutrition assistant (Article 14 (4) of the Rules for Pre-trial Detention and Article 29 (3) of the Rules for serving imprisonment). Prisoners can choose from several types of food, e.g. vegetarian, vegan, without pork, etc.

Provision of religious assistance is regulated by both the Prison Sentence Act and the Pre-trial Detention Act (Article 68 of the Prison Sentence Act and Article 44 of the Pre-trial Detention Act). According to relevant provisions in these acts, the condemned (accused) has a right to provisions of religious assistance. The rules for the operation of religious acts are agreed between churches and religious communities and Institutions in accordance with the Act No. 308/1991 on freedom of religious belief and on the status of churches and religious communities as amended. Religious assistance can be provided only by persons executing religious activity by virtue of assignment by a church or religious community recognized by the government (to this date different Christian churches and a Jewish community is recognized in Slovakia). Individual practice of the religion of prisoners is not regulated in Slovak legislation.

Accused are allowed to wear their own clothes as long as a regular change of clothes is secured. Persons serving prison sentences are allowed to wear their own clothes if they are placed in open prisons or in exit divisions.

In regard to medical care, foreigners are provided with an urgent health care (Article 50 (6) of the Pre-trial Detention Act and Article 75 (5) of the Prison Sentence Act). Urgent health care is specified in Article 2 (3) of the Act No. 576/2004 on the health care, services linked to provision of health care and on amendments of some acts as amended. According to this provision, an urgent health care is a health care provided when the health condition of a person has changed suddenly and the life of the person concerned, or one of his/her basic life functions are threatened, when without a prompt provision of health care the health of the person concerned can be seriously threatened, when the sudden change of the health condition is causing sudden and unbearable pain or sudden changes of behaviour and conduct, if under influence of these changes of behaviour and conduct, he/she or his/her surroundings are imminently threatened. Urgent health care is also health care provided in giving birth.

2.6   Consular and legal help

When a foreigner is taken into pre-trial detention or into serving prison sentences, the Institution shall inform without delay the consular authority of the country of which the foreigner is a citizen (Article 50 (2) of the Pre-trial Detention Act and Article 75 (6) of the Prison Sentence Act).

Article 54 (2) of the Pre-trial Detention Rules provides that the diplomatic mission of a consular authority shall be informed about the transfer of a foreigner, who is a citizen of the country concerned.

According to Article 50 (3) of the Pre-trial Detention Act and Article 75 (2) of the Prison Sentence Act, the Institution shall inform a foreigner about the right to receive a visit of representatives of consular authorities and the visit is generally carried out with direct contact, in pre-trial detention in presence of a member of Prison Corps. If the foreigner is in collusive detention, prior consent of authority acting in criminal procedure or a court is required.

Representatives of diplomatic missions and consular authorities may give newspapers, magazines or books to the foreigner during a visit (Article 50 (4) of the Pre-trial Detention Act and Article 75 (3) of the Prison Sentence Act).

Foreigners have access to legal aid under the same conditions as Slovak citizens. Articles 37, 38, and 40 of the Code of Criminal Procedure deal with the issue. If an accused has no attorney in a case, while he/she should have one, and he/she does not choose one in the time limit set by the court, the court has to appoint an attorney without delay. An accused also has to have an attorney in the preliminary procedure, if he/she is in pre-trial detention, if he/she is serving prison sentence, if he/she is examined in a medical institution, if he/she is incapable for legal acts, if his/her capability is restricted, if there is a procedure regarding particularly serious crime or if there is a procedure against a minor of against an escaped. An accused also has to have an attorney in the case where there is doubt that the accused can defend himself or herself. And an accused has to have an attorney in an extradition procedure as well and in a procedure, where protecting treatment save alcoholism treatment is under consideration.

For an accused, who has not enough means to pay for the defence and who requests an attorney, the court is obliged to appoint one without delay even in the case when there are no reasons for a compulsory defence. The accused has to prove the fact that he/she has not enough means. If during the criminal procedure it is ascertained that the accused has enough means to cover the defence, the appointed attorney will be recalled.

2.7 Contact with the outside world

Foreign prisoners can stay in contact with their relatives and receive their visits under the same conditions as Slovak prisoners. Visits to foreign prisoners are not very frequent; the contact with relatives is mostly maintained in the form of correspondence.

While in pre-trial detention, an accused has the right to make phone calls twice a month for 15 minutes each time in the presence of a member of the Prison Corps. If the foreigner is in collusive detention, prior consent of the authority acting in criminal procedure or a court is required. The cost of the phone call is at the expense of the accused (Article 21 of the Pre-trial Detention Act).

According to Article 27 of the Prison Sentence Act, a person serving a prison sentence has the right to make phone calls once in a month with the duration of ten minutes and in the presence of a member of Prison Corps. The director of the Institution or a member of the Prison Corps may allow the use of a phone more often, if there are urgent family or personal reasons or for the purpose of securing of the fulfilment of the treatment program. The cost of the phone call is for the person serving the sentence. It is possible to send and receive correspondence without any limitation at the expense of the prisoner. If a prisoner has no financial means, two pieces of correspondence can be sent at the expense of the Institution.

An accused has the right to receive visits once in three weeks with duration of at least one hour; in well-founded cases, the director of the Institution may allow visits more often. If the foreigner is in collusive detention, prior consent of the authority acting in criminal procedure or a court is required (Article 19 (1) (2) of the Pre-trial Detention Act). According to Article 24 of the Prison Sentence Act, a person serving a prison sentence has the right to receive visits of close persons once in a month with the duration of two hours. Close persons are according to Article 2 (d) of the Prison Sentence Act the husband, wife and their parents, an unmarried partner, parent, child, grandparent, guardian, sibling and his/her husband or wife, and a person, who takes care of the child of the person condemned while serving prison sentence. In well-founded cases, the director of the Institution may allow visits more often and for other persons.

With the consent of a director of an Institution, visits of representatives of churches, religious communities, civic organisations, foundations, governmental institution and other legal persons or individuals are possible in prisons where prison sentences are served (Article 66 of the Prison Sentence Act).

Foreign prisoners may subscribe to foreign magazines and newspapers at their own expense. In regard to television, prisoners are able to watch channels available through a cable TV.

2.8   Re-integration activities - Prison leave

Provisions of the Prison Sentence Act apply to foreigners if not provided otherwise. Provisions regulating re-integration activities and prison leave do not provide in any different treatment regarding foreigners in comparison with Slovak citizens.

The director of an Institution may grant, as a disciplinary award, an extraordinary leave to a person serving prison sentence. The only legal obstacle is, when the person serving the prison sentence is in an Institution with a maximum degree of guarding. No specific provisions regarding foreigners are in the law.

Accordingly, no specific provisions excluding foreigners are to be found in the provisions regulating the so-called exit divisions. Exit divisions may be established in Institutions and persons serving prison sentence are placed there in appropriate time before release, when they are serving prison sentence for more than three years, or when it is necessary to help them to create appropriate conditions for an independent life. Placement in an exit division should help with the preparation of persons serving prison sentences for a continuous changeover into civil life and an independent way of life after serving prison sentence.

The right to parole is also legally not restricted to Slovak citizens. However, there are decisions of courts dismissing conditional release in case of foreigners, who should be expelled after release, on the grounds that it is not possible to apply the educational effect of a conditional release.

2.9   Release - Expulsion

Article 52 of the Foreigners Act constitutes an obligation for Institutions to inform the competent police authority without delay about release from pre-trial detention and about termination of serving of prison sentence of a foreigner. All other provisions are identical for both Slovak citizens and foreigners.

There are two different possibilities for expulsion in the Slovak legal order. There is the punishment of expulsion, which can be imposed in criminal procedure. This punishment can be challenged in an ordinary criminal procedure on a court of higher instance. Administrative expulsion according to the Foreigners Act is also possible. One of the reasons for administrative expulsion is, according to Article 57 (1) (a) (2) of the Foreigners Act, when a foreigner was validly sentenced for a deliberate criminal act and he/she was not sentenced to punishment of expulsion. In this case, the Foreigners Police is obliged to expel a foreigner. If this foreigner had a permanent residence in Slovakia, private and family life of the foreigner, his/her length of a stay in Slovakia, his/her age, and his/her links to country of origin have to be considered before issuing an administrative decision on expulsion. EEA citizens can be expelled only, if they constitute a threat to the security of the country, public order or public health.

The appeal against the decision on expulsion has a suspensive effect, save the cases where the reason for expulsion is an illegal entry or presence at the territory of Slovak Republic. This does not apply for the rejected asylum applicants (Article 57 (3) of the Foreigners Act). In the administrative expulsion procedure, the appeal body is the regional headquarters of Foreigners and Border Police Bureau of the Presidium of the Police Corps.

The decision of that body can be challenged by a complaint to be lodged at the Supreme Court (Article 244 and 246 (2) of the Code of Civil Procedure). The complaint can be lodged within 2 months from the service of the decision challenged (Article 250b (1) of the Code of Civil Procedure). It has not the suspensive effect. However, the execution of the decision in question can by suspended on the request of the party if the immediate execution could cause a serious damage (Article 250c of the Code of Civil Procedure).

When the decision of the appeal body is issued and the foreigner does not leave the territory of Slovak Republic within the time limit stipulated by the Foreigners and Border Police, the Foreigners and Border Police do not wait for the ruling of the Supreme Court with the execution of the decision on expulsion, not even for its decision on suspension of the execution of the decision. If the execution of the expulsion decision is technically possible, the foreigner is expelled.

When the suspension of the execution of the decision on expulsion is granted, the foreigner can remain at the territory of Slovak Republic until the final ruling of the Supreme Court.

It is difficult to state, whether the said suspension is generally granted. It depends on the assessment of the judge who deals with the particular case. From the praxis of the Supreme Court, we can see both cases where the suspensions were granted on one hand and cases where the suspensions were not granted on the other hand.

2.10 Aftercare – Probation

There are no special provisions applied to foreigners regarding probation service. Moreover, the probation service regulated by the Act No. 550/2003 on probation and mediation officers is not legally restricted to Slovak citizens. Therefore, general provisions on probation service apply also to foreigners remaining legally in the country without any restrictions.

2.11 Staff

There is no legal basis for training regarding language or cultural trainings for members of the Prison Corps. However, the Prison Corps have developed their own conception of education of members of Prison Corps for the years 2004 – 2015. This conception puts an emphasis on educational programs developing five different types of skills. One of them is communication skills, where creation and the processing of information in foreign languages are explicitly mentioned. However, it is questionable if the foreign language courses are focused to members of the Prison Corps with direct contact with foreign prisoners. From the wording of the conception and the languages mentioned (English, French and German) it is more likely that the foreign language courses are intended for officials who are in contact with colleagues from other countries.

According to the Prison Corps, their members are being prepared partly for work with foreigners in basic and special courses after joining Prison Corps. For the selected Prison Corps members' social and psychological courses, one part of the courses is "intercultural communication". Language barriers are addressed on an individual basis.

2.12 Projects

There are no specific projects regarding foreign prisoners at the time being.

3 ADMINISTRATIVE DETENTION OF FOREIGN PRISONERS

The administrative detention of foreigners in Slovakia is regulated by the Foreigners Act. There are two special detention facilities for foreign administrative detainees in Slovakia, one in the eastern part of the country and the other one in the western part. These detention centres are administered by the Bureau of Border and Foreigners Police of the Police Corps in Slovakia (Foreigners Police). The Ministry of Interior is responsible for the Foreigners Police. It is also the Foreigners Police, who decides on administrative detention. According to Article 62 (3) of the Foreigners Act, they may detain a foreigner for the time inevitably needed, with a maximum of 180 days. Unaccompanied minors are not detained.

There is a possibility to lodge an appeal against the decision on detention at the regional court, within 15 days following the delivery of the decision on detention. Lodging an appeal does not have a suspensive effect. One can only once lodge an appeal in the time limit already mentioned. There is no possibility for that afterwards, not even if the circumstances of the case have been changed.

There is an obligation of the Foreigners Police to prove whether the grounds for detention still exist during the entire time of detention. However, it will be quite difficult to enforce them to do so, if they do not. There is no time limit for a court to decide on the appeal. In practice, courts decide in two or three months from the date of detention. In some cases court decisions were issued while the person concerned was already released.

Illegal stay itself is not a criminal offence, but if someone has been issued with a decision on expulsion and he or she does not leave the country despite of this fact, he or she can be charged of a criminal offence of not respecting an official decision. Not only foreigners who have been issued an expulsion decision and are awaiting expulsion are placed in these detention centres. The reasons for administrative detention are provided in Article 62 (1) of the Foreigners Act, which says that a policeman is entitled to detain a foreigner

- who unlawfully enters the territory of the Slovak Republic;
- who unlawfully stays on the territory of the Slovak Republic;
- if it is necessary for the execution of his/her administrative expulsion or for executing the punishment of expulsion;
- who was, after his/her unlawful departure, returned by the authorities of a neighbouring country;
- who attempted to enter unlawfully the territory of another country from the Slovak Republic;
- who filed a statement according to separate law after being sentenced with the punishment of expulsion or after a decision on administrative expulsion was issued, (here, a statement according to separate law means application for asylum);
- if it is necessary in the view of execution of his/her transfer according to a separate Regulation (Dublin Regulation).

Several of these reasons are very controversial and administrative detention of foreigners on these grounds may result in violation of Article 5 (1) of the ECHR. Those foreigners, who are not expelled within 180 days after being detained, are just released. This however means that they are in the country illegally and that they can be detained again at any time. In regard to the figures, up to 500 foreigners can be detained at one time in total. As the Foreigners Law says that a policeman is entitled to detain a foreigner, it means that it is on the discretion of the policeman concerned, if he or she will detain a foreigner in a particular case. What happened in practice was that more foreigners were being detained when the asylum centres were overcrowded, and foreigners in the same situation were not detained when the asylum centres were empty or when the detention facilities were full and were sent to asylum centres instead.

Upon arrival, foreign administrative detainees receive basic information on detention rules. This information is available in Arabic, Chinese, English, Russian, and Slovak. Further information is available at notice boards in the centres.

Foreign administrative detainees are not allowed to work. There is also no possibility to participate in educational and vocational training classes. In regard to sports and recreation, these issues are not regulated in the law. According to Article 70 of the Foreigners Act, a foreigner has the right to a one-hour daily walk in a designated area.

In regard to dietary restrictions, Article 63a (1) of the Foreigners Act provides that the food of a detained foreigner will be secured according to the local conditions and at the respective time in accordance with the principles of healthy alimentation and with regard to the age, health condition and religion of the foreigner.

Practicing religion itself is not regulated in the Foreigners Act. According to officials from detention facilities, no obstacles would be made if there were to be a request with regard to any aspect related to the practice of a religion. Detainees are also allowed to wear their own clothes.

Health care is provided for in the detention centre, where a medical doctor comes several times a week. This is not regulated by the law. However, Article 68 (2) of the Foreigners Act provides that if a foreigner's health state requires health care that cannot be secured in the detention centre, a police department shall secure such health care in a medical establishment outside the centre. Paragraph 3 of the same Article provides that if a foreigner causes damage to his/her health deliberately, he/she shall be obliged to reimburse the costs of the treatment and the actually incurred costs of supervision and transportation to a medical establishment.

Contact with the outside world is possible through several channels. In regard to visits, detainees are entitled to accept a visit of maximum two persons once in three weeks with the duration of 30 minutes. The director of the centre may grant an exception in justified cases. Persons who provide detainees with legal aid can visit them without limitations. Detainees may send written notices at their own expenses and may receive, once in two weeks, a parcel with items of personal use of up to five kilograms. The limitation does not apply to a parcel with clothes; financial means may be received without limitations. A police department will secure their depositing (Articles 71 to 73 of the Foreigners Act).

There are public phones at each floor of the detention centre with free access for all detainees. However, detainees need to have their own resources in order to buy a phone card. Sometimes NGOs provide detainees with phone cards. According to Article 71 (3) of the Foreigners Act, a detainee may order, at his/her own expense, books, daily press and magazines including international magazines, provided that they are distributed in the Slovak Republic. A library was established recently in one of the centres. The amount and variety of books and magazines is not very extensive but the authorities together with NGOs will work on this in the future. On each floor of the centres you will find a satellite TV with free access for all detainees.

There is a project of social counselling and legal aid in the centres. Both social and legal aid is provided by NGO's. Legal aid to detainees is financed by the Open Society Foundation, legal aid for asylum seekers detained in detention centres is financed by European Refugee Fund and social aid is financed by United Nations High Commissioner for Refugees and European Refugee Fund, and is restricted to detained asylum seekers.

4 NATIONALS DETAINED ABROAD

Slovak diplomatic missions have records regarding criminal activities of Slovak citizens abroad. However, not all competent authorities around the world notify Slovak diplomatic missions about activities concerned. Some countries report about cases of detention and pre-trial detention of Slovak citizens to a competent diplomatic mission, but some countries inform about such cases only if the person concerned asks for it or agrees with it, referring to laws on protection of personal data. In many cases, the Slovak diplomatic missions find out about criminal activities of Slovak citizens e.g. from media. Slovak citizens are committing mostly proprietary criminal offences; they breach laws regarding residence of foreigners, work illegally, smuggle and commit criminal offences through car accidents. The most extensive is the criminal activity of Slovak citizens abroad in Czech Republic, where 965 cases were recorded in 2005. In Hungary they had 170 cases, in Poland 121, in Austria 88, and in Germany 84 cases. The total number of registered criminal activities of Slovak citizens abroad is increasing every year and in 2005 there were 1 809 cases registered. In cases where a prison sentence is served abroad, the persons concerned return to Slovakia after serving their prison sentence without any assistance of the government.

5 EVALUATION AND RECOMMENDATIONS

As the numbers of foreigners in pre-trial detention and of those who are serving a prison sentence is not very high, there was probably no imminent need to institutionalise very precisely their specific position in the prison community. Moreover, significant numbers of the foreign prison population comes from neighbouring countries with Slavic population. For this group of people, the language and cultural barriers should not play any role in general. However, as there is still a possible group of people with cultural and religious diversities, it would be appropriate to elaborate the legal provisions more precisely in order to avoid any unnecessary clashes on one hand and easier adaptation of prison life on the other hand.

In regard to foreign administrative detainees, the main problem for them while being in the detention is how to spend their time there. They can spend just one hour out of the barracks and there is not much to do for them while being detained inside. No free time activities are regularly organised. These foreigners are often without any financial means and it is extremely difficult for them to contact their relatives or anyone else outside the detention centre. Another issue is the legal basis for administrative detention and the possibilities of effective legal remedies where the provisions of Slovak legislation seem to be in breach with the ECHR.

Chapter 23

Slovenia

Dragan Petrovec

1 INTRODUCTION

Slovenia gained independence in 1991 and is now a parliamentary democracy. The population numbers two million in an area of roughly 20.000 sq. km. Slovenia borders Italy to the west, Austria to the north, Hungary to the northeast and Croatia to the southeast, with a 47 km Adriatic Sea coastline. In 2004, the GDP was estimated at 13.103 Euros. The country's ethnic composition is as follows: Slovene: 87,8%; Croat: 2,8%; Serb: 2,4%; Bosnian: 1,4%; Magyar: 0,4 %; Albanian: 0,2%; Italian: 0,2%; Macedonian: 0,2%. The majority of people are Roman Catholics (almost 70%), although there are small communities of other Christian denominations (in particular Protestants in the eastern parts of the country), Orthodox, and of Muslims and Jews. There are Slovenian indigenous minorities in Italy, Austria and in Hungary. Ethnic Slovenes living outside the national borders number between 250,000 and 400,000 (depending on the inclusion of second and other generations) with the vast majority of them living overseas and in the countries of the EU. The ethnic composition of Slovenia reflects the historical development of recent decades. Most of the Serbs, Croats and Bosnians moved from their republics (within the former Yugoslavia) to Slovenia for economic reasons. The prison population shows the same picture. The Slovenian majority is followed by Bosnians, Serbs and Croats, while the rest of the prison population is very much dispersed.

Regarding Slovenian criminal policy, it should be emphasized that Slovenia abolished *de facto* capital punishment in 1957, the year in which it was last carried out. It was substituted by twenty years of imprisonment as the maximum penalty. Abolition *de iure* was adopted in 1989 by constitutional law, when Slovenia was still a part of Yugoslavia. Until the end of Yugoslavia, all other republics were still maintaining and carrying out the death penalty. In 1995, Slovenia adopted a new Penal Code that introduced some new principles of punishment (alternative sanctions, omission of aims of punishment), retaining 20 years as the highest sentence. In 1998 it was changed to thirty years and up to now has been imposed in ten cases, thus indicating an increasing severity in our response to crime.

1.1 Overview of penalties and measures

In general, criminal sanctions are:
- sentences;
- admonitory sanctions;
- safety measures;
- educational measures.

If the perpetrator has been convicted of a criminal offence or if any criminal sanction has been imposed on him, he may be subject to confiscation of the property gained by committing the criminal offence and to publication of the judgment.

1.1.1 Sentences

Sentences are divided into the following categories:
- imprisonment;
- fines;
- withdrawal of driving license;

- expulsion from Slovenia.

A prison sentence may be imposed for a period no shorter than fifteen days and no longer than fifteen years. However, the sentence of thirty years imprisonment may alternatively be given for the premeditated commission of the most serious types of crime. A fine can be imposed based on daily rates or as a fixed amount, the lowest being one sixtieth of the offender's last officially published net salary in the Republic of Slovenia, the highest being one third of that salary. The court can withdraw the driving license of perpetrators who have committed a criminal offence against the security of public traffic. Finally, the court can remove a foreign citizen from the Republic of Slovenia for a period ranging from one to ten years. The period of banishment starts on the day on which the judgment is passed. Time spent in prison shall not be credited to such a sentence.

1.1.2 Admonitory sanctions

In Slovenia, the court can suspend the execution of a sentence. This implies that the sentence shall not be carried out unless the offender commits another criminal offence within a period of not less than one and not more than five years (the term of suspension), depending on the court's decision.

Overall, since 1991 the composition of sentencing has not changed significantly. Roughly 17% are sentences to imprisonment, 7% are fines, and 74% of all sentences are suspended.

1.1.3 Safety Measures

There are a number of safety measures that can be imposed by the courts:
- compulsory psychiatric treatment and custody in an appropriate institution;
- compulsory psychiatric treatment in the community;
- compulsory treatment of persons addicted to alcohol and drugs;
- a banning order that prohibits a person from carrying out his/her occupation
- withdrawal of the driving license;
- confiscation.

1.1.4 Educational Measures (for minors)

- reprimands;
- instructions and prohibitions;
- supervision by social services;
- committal to an educational institution, a juvenile detention centre or an institution for physically or mentally handicapped youth. The precise type of institution to which a minor is sent depends on the gravity of the committed offence.

1.2 Overview of the Prison System

1.2.1 Organizational Structure

The Ministry of Justice is responsible for the prison system in Slovenia, while the National Prison Administration performs administrative and professional tasks referring to:
- the enforcement of penal sanctions and detention;
- the organisation and management of prisons and penitentiary institutions;
- providing for staff and financial, material, technical or other conditions for the operation of prisons and penitentiary institutions;
- training of staff concerning the enforcement of penal sanctions;
- exercising the rights and obligations of imprisoned persons.

The Administration is headed and represented by its director-general who has to give account to the Minister. Each prison is headed by a prison governor, who is a senior administrative officer with a university degree and who has to provide the Director-General with an account of his work and the prison's performance.

STRUCTURE OF ORGANISATION

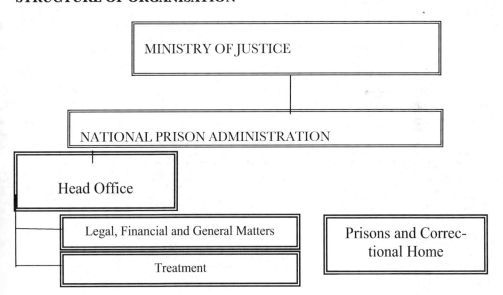

1.2.1.1. Type, size and number of penal institutions

In Slovenia, prison sentences are executed in six prisons, in 13 locations. The fact that the number of locations exceeds the number of actual penitentiary institutions can be attributed to the fact that the main prison institutions have units that are usually within the immediate proximity of the main buildings, while some are separated to more distant locations. The largest is the central Dob Prison, where male prisoners serve prison sentences of between one-and-a half and 30 years in total length. In the regional prisons, sentenced persons serve prison terms of up to one-and-a-half years. Every prison facility has an open, a semi-open and a closed department. They differ in their level of security and freedom of movement. The Juvenile Correctional Home also operates within the Administration. Inside penitentiary institutions, prisoners are separated from those imprisoned for misdemeanours; juveniles are separated from adults and men are separated from women. Prisoners are sent to individual institutions in accordance with the Instructions on the Allocation and Imprisonment of Convicts prescribed by the Minister of Justice. Prisoners are sent to the appropriate prison by the court order, but under certain circumstances they can be relocated by the administration later. The Director-General may allow prisoners who have been sentenced to a prison term of up to six months for a criminal act committed out of negligence to continue work while serving the sentence and to reside at home, with the exception of non-work days - and as a rule at the weekend - when they must reside in prison. However, they must be orderly and have regular employment or attend school. This applies only when they are serving a prison sentence for the first time. The court can decide that a prison sentence of less than three months is to be replaced by performing community work for humanitarian organisations or for the local community.

Table 1   Capacity– average number of inmates in 2005[1]

Capacity	Average no. of inmates	Occupancy (%)
1,103	1,137	103

Categories of inmates: prisoners, remand prisoners (or pre-trial detainees), persons imprisoned for a misdemeanour, juveniles sentenced to juvenile detention, and juveniles in the correctional home.

Table 2 Average structure (categories) of inmates in 2005

No.	Structure	Average	%
1	Convicted prisoners	773	68
2	Persons imprisoned for a misdemeanour	5	0.4
3	Remand prisoners	324	28.5
4	Juveniles	8	0.7
5	Juveniles in the Correctional Home	27	2.4
	TOTAL	1137	100

The total budget for the year 2004 was 6.063.663.324.- SIT which is approx. 25 million Euros.

---

[1]   Annual report 2005; (Ministry of Justice; National Prison Administration).

Figure 1 Development of the prison population:[2]

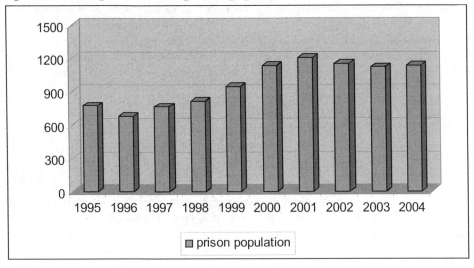

Figure 2 Prisoners per 100.000 of the population:

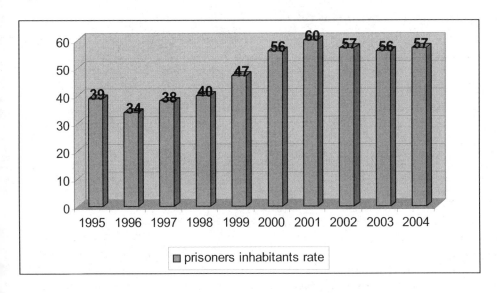

---

2   All graphs are based on statistics presented in: Brinc, Franc: 'Crime Statistics and Crime Policy in Slovenia (Gibanje kriminalitete in kaznovalna politika v Sloveniji v zadnjem desetletju)' in: *Criminality, Social Control and Post-Modernity*. Ed. Kanduč, Zoran; Institute of Criminology, University of Ljubljana, Ljubljana 2005.

1.2.1.2. Bodies outside the prison administration responsible for inspecting or monitoring the operation of the prison system and individual institutions

The monitoring of how prisoners are treated is carried out by the Ministry of Justice and the President of the competent district court. Prisons are also visited by the Human Rights Ombudsman and the bodies that are responsible for the protection of human rights, in accordance with international acts,

1.2.1.3. Prison staff

On 31 December 2004, 798 persons were employed in Slovenian penitentiary institutions. Of whom over 50% (453) were guards. The remainder included – among others - 45 educators, 8 psychologists and 12 social workers. Up to the mid eighties, the prison guards received two years of training. For this purpose, a special school had been established within the Ministry of Justice. However, the term of training has since been reduced to two months at present, for the school was abandoned again twenty years ago. Nowadays, the main emphasis of training is on martial arts, while in the past they had lectures in the fields of psychology, education, penology and criminology.

1.2.2. Foreign Prisoners

The percentage of foreign prisoners is more or less stable and has varied only from 13,5% to 16,1% in the last six years.

Year	Percentage
2000	14,4
2001	15,1
2002	15,6
2003	13,5
2004	14,9
2005	16,1

On 31 December 2005 the number of foreign prisoners was 74. This figure remained approximately the same within the time period mentioned above. The majority of foreign prisoners belong to the former republics of Yugoslavia (65 – 70%). They are allocated to all penitentiary institutions in Slovenia, according to the Code on the Execution of Penal Sanctions. The basic criteria for the allocation of prisoners are the length of the sentence, gender, and security reasons. Approximately 70% of all foreign prisoners are serving their sentence in the largest penitentiary institution in Slovenia (Dob), and all but a few are placed in a closed regime. The formal status of foreign prisoners does not differ much with respect to other prisoners. Yet the differences in status that do exist might be vital in terms of (non) reintegration into society. The situation is described more thoroughly below in the chapter on "treatment of foreign prisoners".

1.3. Overview: involvement of Consulates, Embassies, Ministries in the home country, Probation service in the home country, NGO's etc

According to the most recent data (16 August 2006) from the largest prison institution in Slovenia (Dob), there are 53 foreign prisoners serving sentences who amount to approximately 70% of all foreign prisoners in Slovenia. The composition of the prison population of foreign prisoners in Dob is as follows:

15	Bosnia and Herzegovina
12	Croatia
12	Serbia, Montenegro
2	Lithuania
12	prisoners – each from a different country (Austria, Slovakia, Germany and others)

Foreign prisoners receive visits, but only from representatives of their Embassies or Consulates. The most regular visits are from the Italian, German and Serbian Embassies, while there are almost no contacts with the Croatian and Lithuanian Embassies. The last two visits were on 16 March (Serbian Embassy) and on 11 April 2006(German Embassy). Unfortunately, no detailed information is available on the precise activities of the Embassies and Consulates or on the specific forms of help and support that they provide. In general, their duty lies in taking care of their citizens who are detained abroad and in the provision of financial support where necessary.

The last CPT report to the Slovenian Government on visits to Slovenia was published in 2002 (CPT/Inf. (2002)36-18.12.2002). As to the visits to the penitentiary institutions, the delegation of the CPT did not make any remarks concerning foreign prisoners. As was already the case in 1995, the CPT delegation formed a generally positive impression in 2001 as well, with the exception of measures designed to combat the problem of prison overcrowding (Report, p.25).

On the other hand, the situation in the Detention Centre for Irregular Residents (Postojna) failed to be worthy of praise. Living conditions in the reception area were not acceptable, contacts with the outside world were not sufficiently frequent, food was occasionally poor, and there was a lack of psychiatric and psychological assistance as well as of medical care. In contrast to the engagement in penitentiary institutions, NGO's were quite active in improving conditions in detention centres (primarily and very noticeably regarding detained asylum seekers), providing for a range of additional activities for detainees. The most recent visit of the CPT delegation was carried out in 2006; however the report has not been published yet.

1.4 Overview of Trends

Different statistics show rather different trends. Therefore, we should hesitate, for instance, before taking police recorded crime as a true picture of crime. A more thorough insight can be attained by combining different approaches (police recorded crime, victimisation studies, sentencing etc.).

1.4.1. Sentencing trends

Figure 3 Police recorded crime

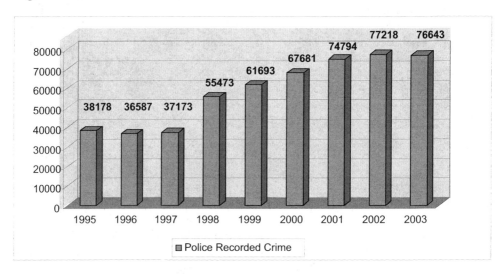

Crime as recorded by the police requires careful interpretation. It does not represent "real crime" in its full extent. To illustrate this, an additional presentation is necessary. The index of reported crime from 1980 varies from 100 (1980) to 264 (2003), while the prisoners/inhabitants rate does not follow the same trend.

Reported crime:

	Crime report rate	Inhabitants Rate
1980	100	100
1985	147	118
1990	132	87
1991	146	75
1992	186	70
1993	153	64
1994	150	59
1995	132	32
1996	126	36
1997	128	45
1998	191	51
1999	213	52
2000	233	55
2001	259	61
2002	266	67
2003	264	59

Figure 4 Trend in the report rate

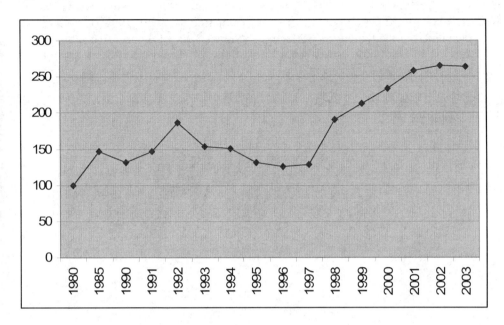

The trend in reported crime shows a clear increase from 1980 to 1992. It slowly decreases up to 1997 when a dramatic change occurs, reaching its peak level in 2002 where it then remained stable.

Figure 5:   Prisoners/inhabitants rate

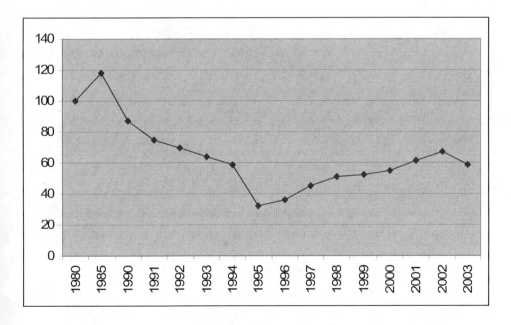

This trend is different from the previous one. Since 1985 it has been constantly decreasing, reaching its lowest point in 1995. Since then we have witnessed an increase that has resulted in a doubled prison population today compared to that of 1995. There are various possibilities for explaining this difference in trends. One of them is that many reports do not result in convictions. Another is that within a certain period of time the courts have started to impose milder sentences.

Figure 6 Structure of sentences (excluding conditional sentences as admonitory sanctions

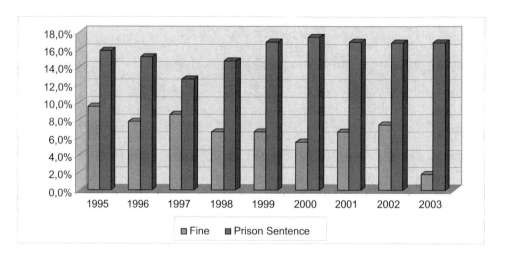

Figure 7 The structure of criminal offences in 2004

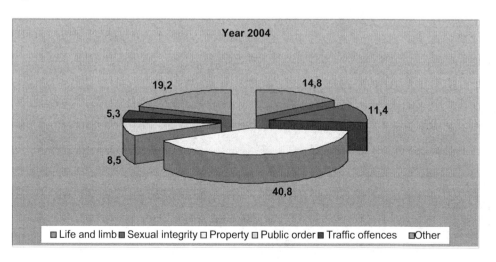

The structure has more or less remained the same over the years. Criminal offences against property have always comprised the greatest proportion of crime in general.

Figure 8 The structure of prison sentences in 1990, 2000 and 2003

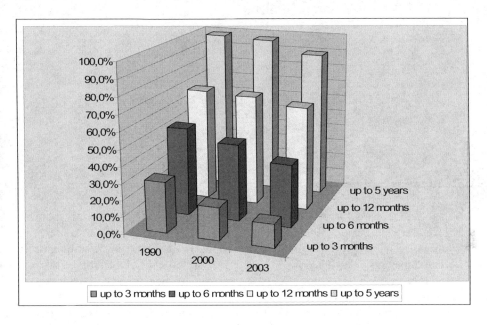

The number of sentences to up to three months imprisonment decreased from 30% in 1990 to 14% in 2003. There has also been a significant change regarding the most severe degree of punishment. In 1990 only 1,4% of all prison sentences exceeded five years, while in 2003 this percentage increased to 9,3% which is almost seven times higher.

1.4.2. Characteristics of the Foreign Prison Population[3]

The structure of crime committed by foreigners is as follows:

Criminal offences against life and limb	14%
Sexual integrity	10%
Unlawful production and trade of narcotic drugs	36%
Property	30%
Public safety	10%

The average length of prison sentences imposed upon foreign prisoners is six years. Female prisoners account for roughly four to five percent of the overall prison population. This share does not change if one compares the Slovenian prison population to detained foreign prisoners.

The origin of foreign prisoners:

Bosnia and Herzegovina	25%
Serbia and Montenegro	19%
Croatia	17%

---

[3] Annual Report 2005.

Not clear	10%
Macedonia	5%
Romania	4%
Germany	4%
Lithuania	4%
Other countries	12%

It is obvious that the majority of foreign prisoners come from the republics of former Yugoslavia – 66%.

1.5 Overview of National legislation

1.5.1. Penitentiary Legislation

A new Penal Sanctions Enforcement Act was adopted in the year 2000, thus following the first Slovenian Penal Code (1995). General provisions have not changed so much, yet a new philosophy has emerged. There is no emphasis on the re-socialization or re-integration of prisoners. Furthermore, the role of psychologists, educators and social workers is minimized while the importance of security is overstressed, thus giving the guards a leading position in the penitentiary institution.

The new legislation still corresponds to the demands of European standards, but compared to the previous Slovenian legislation (followed by very good practice in opening prisons) it is a huge step back towards more repressive concepts of dealing with prisoners.

1.5.2. Penitentiary Legislation and Foreigners

With regard to the basic principles, the Penal Code of the Republic of Slovenia does not differentiate between foreigners and Slovenian nationals. The only specific provisions are as follows:

1. Expulsion of foreign citizens from the country: The court may expel a foreign citizen from the territory of the Republic of Slovenia for a period ranging from one to ten years. The period of banishment starts on the day that judgement is passed. Time spent in prison shall not be credited to such a sentence;[4]
2. Free leaves from prison. Foreign prisoners who have been banished from the territory of the Republic of Slovenia are only exceptionally granted a free leave;[5]
3. House rules and guidelines in each of the six prison institutions regulate the accommodation and living arrangements of inmates with no discrimination between Slovenian and foreign prisoners.

---

[4] The Penal Code of the Republic of Slovenia, Art. 40.
[5] The Penal Sanctions Enforcement Act (2000), 78/2.

2 TREATMENT OF FOREIGN PRISONERS

2.1 General

Activities and programmes organised in penal institutions

Socio-therapeutic forms of professional work. Professional work in penal institutions is directed towards socio-therapeutic activities, treatment for groups and individuals, elements of therapeutic community and the encouragement of cooperation within the community in the broadest possible sense. In this process it is important to include professional institutions and organisations outside the prison system that can implement various programmes with the aim of resolving the problems that the inmates may have. Programmes and activities in penal institutions are focused on providing the necessary training to inmates so they can be successfully reintegrated into the living and working environment. Various programmes conducted in prisons address the education of inmates, work, leisure activities, help for inmates addicted to drugs or alcohol, preparation for release and special programmes connected with the specific needs of inmates. Healthcare is organized within the healthcare department in prisons and in public healthcare institutions outside the prisons. All inmates have health insurance. Their contribution is covered by the state budget. The difference in the treatment of foreign prisoners lies mostly in the lack of cooperation with institutions that would take care of a prisoner after having served a sentence; also, free leaves are more the exception than the rule.

2.2. Living conditions and facilities

As a rule each prisoner is to be allocated to a single room. Dormitories shall have a maximum of eight beds (Art. 42, The Penal Sanctions Enforcement Act). Due to the increasing number of prisoners (100% in the last ten years) these standards are can not be met in many penitentiary institutions. Foreign prisoners share the same facilities with Slovenian prisoners. Since they are mostly from former Yugoslavia there are next to no problems in their ability to communicate with Slovenian prisoners.

2.3. Reception and admission

On arriving, a prisoner's identity is verified and he undergoes a medical examination. He is informed of the prison rules, disciplinary sanctions and benefits. During the reception stage all activities and procedures in order to enable adequate integration of the prisoner into prison life are carried out and a framework individual treatment programme is formulated. Activities for the re-integration of foreign prisoners are minimal as regards the prisoner's social environment (being in a foreign country).

2.4. Work - Education – Training – Sports – Recreation

Prison work is not obligatory. A prisoner who works full time during his time in prison is guaranteed all of the rights that are associated with employment (e.g. payment, holiday for 18 to 30 days a year). Prisons must ensure the provision of education and vocational training for prisoners. This is organized both inside and outside of the prison (Art. 102).

In practice, foreign prisoners do not leave prison institutions for outside education or vocational training. Every prison has facilities for sports and recreation, although standards do differ. Yet there is no difference as to foreign prisoners' access to these facilities. Prisoners are allowed to spend at least two hours outdoors every day (Art.42).

2.5. Food - Religion – Personal Hygiene – Medical Care

There are sometimes complaints about food that actually reflect dissatisfaction with the regime in general. However, prisoners in general - foreigners included - receive food that is deemed sufficient and adequate for the preservation of health and physical well-being. The religious dietary norms of Muslims are respected.

Religious groups are permitted to practice their beliefs freely, and thus far there have been no complaints from inmates stating the contrary. Prisoners regularly receive visits from their respective religious representatives

There are practically no complaints concerning hygiene conditions, while there are some concerning medical care. These reservations are attributable to the lack of medical personnel that should be permanently employed inside the institution. In most cases, prisoners are visited by a doctor once or twice a week, while in emergencies, they are temporarily transferred to the nearest hospital. A full time general practitioner and a part time dentist are employed in the largest penal institution (Dob). The CPT recommended that a qualified nurse should be present at the establishment, also at night, given the location of the institution and the number of inmates that it accommodates[6].

2.6. Consular and legal help

The prison administration is obliged to immediately inform the state in question that one of its nationals is serving a sentence in Slovenia. As already mentioned in Par.1.3, foreign prisoners receive visits from their Embassies or Consulates. The most regular visits are by the Italian, German and Serbian Embassies, while there are almost no contacts with representatives of Croatia and Lithuania. In some cases, when possible and reasonable, Embassies provide legal assistance. The form of assistance depends on the Embassy in question and its rules and guidelines of practice. Legal aid is established by the Vienna Convention which is designed to ensure that foreign nationals who are accused of having committed a criminal offence are provided access to legal counsel by a representative from their home country.

2.7. Contacts with the outside world

Foreign prisoners may always contact the consular bodies of their country. Furthermore, they are provided (as every prisoner) with the opportunity for an unlimited exchange of letters with immediate family members. A prisoner may exchange letters with others if this is in keeping with his treatment programme (Art. 71). A prisoner is entitled to visits from immediate family members at least twice a week. A visit may not be restricted to less than one hour (Art.73). In practice, visits for foreign prisoners are extremely rare. The same goes for free leaves which are quite exceptional for foreign prisoners. Prisoners have

---

6   CPT report, p.32.

the right to conduct telephone conversations with close family members (or another person who the prison administration has authorized to be contacted by the prisoner), the Human Rights Ombudsman, a consular representative or a representative of an official organisation for the protection of refugees. Calls to these authorized persons are free of charge. Telephone conversations with close family members can be prohibited for reasons of security in order to protect order and discipline within the prison. Foreign prisoners can obtain newspapers and magazines in a number of different languages, which are however limited to Serbian, Croatian, Bosnian, Italian, Hungarian and English. Additionally, prisoners have access to cable television which in turn provides them with the opportunity to view a large number of foreign channels.

2.8. Re-integration activities – Prison leave

Reintegration activities are limited to education or vocational training organized inside prison. Prison leave is - like other privileges - granted by the Prison Governor providing the prisoner actively cooperates in the treatment process, is making an effort, is successful in his/her work and respects the prison's rules of conduct. Prison leave can be granted up to four times per month and may last for up to 48 hours. Other privileges include: prolonged and unmonitored visits, unmonitored visits outside the institution, prison leave accompanied by an authorised prison officer, prison leave without permission to return to the environment in which the inmate committed the offence for which he/she is imprisoned, an annual vacation period outside the institution and up to seven days a year. Foreign prisoners are very seldom granted a free leave from prison, firstly because it is feared that they could attempt to abuse it in order to escape from the country. Additionally, the majority of foreign prisoners do not have friends or relatives in Slovenia whom they could actually visit.

2.9. Release – Expulsion

Prisoners have the possibility of conditional release after having served half of their full sentence. This decision is made by the conditional release committee at the Ministry of Justice at the request of the prisoner or his family members, or at the proposal of the governor. In exceptional cases a prisoner may be conditionally released after having served one third of the sentence. A prisoner sentenced to over 15 years in prison may be conditionally released after serving three quarters of his/her sentence. The court may order the inmate to be supervised by a social care body during his/her period of conditional release. The prison governor has the right to release inmates up to one month prior to having completed their sentence if the inmate has served at least three quarters of his sentence. Approximately 65 percent of foreign prisoners are expelled.

2.10. Aftercare – Probation

As regards foreign prisoners there are no such provisions.

2.11. Staff

Staff members are not specially trained for dealing with foreign prisoners. However, they all are familiar with the cultural and social background of most of the prisoners since the majority comes from the countries of former Yugoslavia. Nearly all staff members speak Serbian and Croatian, and the majority are also able to speak English. In institutions close to Italy, most of the prison staff can speak Italian.

2.12. Projects

No special projects that are geared specifically towards foreign prisoners are planned.

3 ADMINISTRATIVE DETENTION OF FOREIGN PRISONERS[7]

Foreign prisoners in administrative detention are foreigners who are kept in custody because they have not been issued a permanent or temporary residence permit by the country in which they are detained, and *not* because they have committed a criminal offence. To fully understand this category of prisoners it is important to note that detained foreigners are, according to national legislation, categorized into two groups: 1. foreigners who have illegally entered the territory of Slovenia or have been detected within the territory without any personal documents that verify their identity and/or without a residence permit; 2. asylum seekers who have been detained as asylum seekers, or as foreigners who have applied for asylum in the course of their detention. Asylum seekers, detained on the four grounds mentioned below under 3.5, are detained in the Asylum Home. However, those illegal residents who have already been detained and who apply for asylum later on remain in the Illegal Residents Centre. Instead of "foreigners" the term "illegal residents" shall be used.

3.1 Institutions for administrative detention

Administrative detention can be imposed either on detained illegal residents or detained asylum seekers, both of whom are classed as non-citizens of Slovenia. The difference between these groups is the legal basis for the imposition of such an order, the authority/ facilities/institutions which implement such orders, and the competent body. Detained illegal residents are accommodated in so-called Illegal Residents Centres, which are located in Postojna (SW part of Slovenia) and in Prosenjakovci (NE part of Slovenia, close to the border to Hungary). The detention measures used for illegal residents differ by the degree of security applied and the restrictions placed on the freedom of movement. Illegal residents can be placed in an Illegal Residents Centre, in a social-care facility or in the rigorous police supervision division within the Illegal Residents Centre. They can be accommodated at a specific address in cases of being issued an order for the delay of expulsion, and they can be accommodated outside the Illegal Residents Centre (a lenient measure). The Illegal Residents Centre only has a closed unit, which means the detainees are detained 24 hours a day, but can be allowed to leave the institution in some cases (to

---

7   Chapter 3 was written by Vita Habjan, Legal Information Centre for NGOs, Ljubljana, Slovenia.

visit a legal advisor, a doctor, etc.). Illegal residents under rigorous police supervision cannot leave the centre. Detained asylum seekers are accommodated in the detention unit of the Asylum Home, which is also a closed unit, allowing them only to have a one - hour walk and exercise period every day.

3.2. Ministry responsible and relevant Legislation

According to the Illegal Residents Act (adopted in 1999 and last amended in 2005) the Slovene Police - a body within the Ministry of the Interior - are a competent body for detained illegal residents. Other laws/regulations applicable to this category are the following:

- Regulations on the implementation of the Illegal Residents Act (adopted in 1991),
- Regulations on special conditions for the accommodation and movement of illegal residents in the Illegal Residents Centre, and on grounds and the procedure for the use of lenient measures (adopted in 2000).

According to the Asylum Act (adopted in 1999 and last amended in 2006) the Asylum Section is a competent authority body for detained asylum seekers which is a body within the Directorate for Administrative Internal Affairs within the Ministry of the Interior. The following laws/regulations are also applicable to this category:

- Instruction on the procedure with and treatment of illegal residents who enter the territory of the Republic of Slovenia who wish to file an application for asylum, and on the acceptance of, content of and the procedure of dealing with filed asylum applications or statements, (adopted in 2000).

This legal document defines procedures that concern migrants who illegally enter the Slovene national territory. It also defines the obligation of illegal migrants to file an application for asylum as soon as possible. When this obligation is not adhered to, their movement can be limited on the suspicion that they are abusing the asylum procedure. The document in question also defines which documents should be completed by the police when they apprehend an illegal migrant, which personal data need to be recorded, where to send the asylum application and within which time-period, since the illegal migrant may show the intent to file an asylum application with the Police. In such cases the Police are only allowed to obtain his statement, but have to immediately send him to the Asylum Section, the competent authority body for asylum seekers.

3.3. Capacity of the institutions for administrative detention

There are two Illegal residents Centres, one each in Postojna and Prosenjakovci. The capacity facility in Postojna's is designed for 120 illegal residents, while Prosenjakovci has a capacity of up to 40 places. The Asylum Centre is located in Ljubljana and the detention unit has a maximum capacity of 20 asylum seekers. However, asylum seekers are also accommodated in the Illegal Residents Centres (see the explanation given above) and the capacity varies with the numbers of asylum seekers detained. There is no special unit intended for their accommodation because this institution is used as a last resort, but they are accommodated separately from 'regular' detained illegal residents. At the moment, due to the lack of facilities, women are accommodated together with men.

3.4. Length of stay

According to Article 56 of the Illegal Residents Act (), the legal and maximum length of stay in an Illegal Residents Centre is six months, but this can be extended by a further six month period as stated in Article 58. Information on the average length of stay could not be obtained from the Centre in Postojna, but according to the information available on the centre in Prosenjakovci the average length is three to four months. Sometimes this period can vary by up to ten months, but this information could not be corroborated by other sources. According to Article 27 of the Asylum Act, the legal maximum length of the detention of asylum seekers is three months, but this can be extended by a further month if the grounds for detention still exist (see 3.5 below on decision procedures). Indefinite limitation of movement is only allowed on the grounds of preventing the spread of contagious diseases. Information on the average length of stay could not be obtained.

3.5. Decisions procedure

An administrative detention order is issued to an illegal resident by the border police. The legal basis for this detention is defined in the Illegal Residents Act (Articles 47, 50 and 56) which defines that illegal residents should leave the national territory of Slovenia either immediately or within a given period (Art. 47). An illegal resident is a person who has illegally entered the Slovene national territory or whose visa has expired or been invalidated, or who has no residence permit or whose permit has expired (Art. 47). An illegal resident who has not left the territory immediately or within the given period is expelled, but only when an expulsion order has an executable effect (Art. 50). An illegal resident who has not left the country immediately or within the given period and who cannot be removed immediately for any reason, is placed in the Illegal Residents Centre or in another facility (social-care facility) by the police (Art. 56). The period of such detention can not exceed six months. An illegal resident can also be detained while his identity is being established (Art. 56). In the case of an asylum seeker, an administrative detention order is issued by the Ministry of the Interior (Asylum Section, the competent body for all asylum seekers). There are four grounds for issuing a detention order: to establish a persons identity, to prevent the spreading of contagious diseases, on the grounds of suspicion of misleading or abusing the asylum procedure, or on the grounds of posing a threat to the life or property of others. The order can be pronounced orally, but within 48 hours after oral pronouncement it must also be issued in writing (Art. 27).

3.6. Appeal procedure

When a detention order has been issued by the police, an illegal resident can file an appeal against that order within eight days. It has to be decided upon by the Minister of the Interior within eight days, but the appeal does not stand in the way of executing the order. The illegal resident can file a lawsuit against this decision which is then decided on by the Administrative Court (Illegal Residents Act, Art. 58). An asylum seeker can appeal against a detention order within three days by filing such a suit. The competent body is the Administrative Court, which has to deliver a judgement within three days after it has heard the case (Asylum Act, Art. 27, Par. 6).

3.7. Irregular stay

Article 96 of the Illegal Residents Act determines violations as follows: when an illegal resident lacks a valid passport, when an illegal resident has no permission to enter the territory of Slovenia, when an illegal resident remains in Slovenia for a longer period than allowed (for example, in case of expiry of a temporary residence permit), when an illegal resident does not leave Slovenia in a period for which a residence was permitted, etc. An illegal resident can be fined between 10.000,00 and 50.000,00 SIT (roughly 40 and 200 euros). A fine of 20.000,00 SIT (roughly 85 euros) will be issued if he/she enters or leaves the territory thus violating the transit visa, if he/she does not leave the territory as soon as his/her visa is invalidated, if he/she does not show his/her permit when requested to do so by a police officer, which allows him/her to lawfully enter and remain in the territory or if he/she does not show his identity card upon a police officer's request (art. 97). An illegal resident can be fined between 20.000,00 and 100.000,00 SIT (between 85 and 420 euros) for illegally entering the territory, for residing in Slovenia without actually having the ground for which the residence permit has been issued, or for residing in Slovenia illegally (Art. 98). It is important to note that these are all violations and do not constitute criminal offences: an illegal migrant will be fined by the Police (by a judge in cases of illegal minors) and deported from Slovenia immediately or as soon as possible.

3.8. Numbers

In 1992, 1,178 illegal residents were detained in the Illegal Residents Centre. The figure for 1993 was 2.797, and 3.048 in 1994. The number dropped to 2.403 in 1995 and further still in 1996 to 2.095. In 1997, 3.747 illegal residents were detained in the centre in total, in 1998 it was 8.869, 12.559 in 1999, 14.576 in 2000, 10.034 in 2001 and 3.272 in 2002. According to the statistical data, 1,908 illegal residents were detained in 2003, the majority of whom were men (1.505). 231 women were detained, while 90 were minors under the age of 18, and 82 were unaccompanied minors. Most of the detainees in 2003 came from Serbia and Montenegro (610), Moldavia (210), Turkey (202), Macedonia (164) and Iraq (100).

The number of detained asylum seekers in the Asylum Home during the period of November 2005 till April 2006 was eight, since a further detention unit was being built. At the moment, only two asylum-seekers are detained in the Asylum Home, while seven asylum-seekers are being detained in the Illegal Residents Centre in Postojna and four in Prosenjakovci.

3.9. Expulsion

In 2003, 648 illegal residents were expelled from the Illegal residents Centre and 661 from police stations, totalling 1.309 (68,6%). Most of illegal migrant were returned according to the Readmission agreements, especially to Croatia. Most illegal migrant were citizens of Serbia and Montenegro, Macedonia, Croatia and Bosnia and Herzegovina.

3.10. Administrative prisoners not expelled after release

Some non-expelled illegal residents gained passports for their return; others applied for asylum or were granted permission to remain in Slovenia. According to Article 52 of the Illegal Residents Act, illegal residents are issued a decision allowing them to remain in Slovenia when expulsion back to their home country may endanger their life or freedom of race, religion, nationality, participation in a particular social group or political opinion, or when they could be subjected to torture or other inhumane and degrading treatment or punishment in that country. Such a decision can also be issued when expulsion is not possible for other reasons.

3.11. Detention of irregulars under criminal law

Administratively detained prisoners cannot be placed together with prisoners who are detained under criminal law, because institutions for detaining these groups are different and under the jurisdiction of two different bodies (the Police and the Prison Administration of the Republic of Slovenia).

3.12. Minors

Detained illegal residents and minors are placed in a separate unit within the Illegal Residents Centre. According to established practice, asylum seekers and minors are never detained, although the Asylum Act does not contain any provision that prohibits the detention of minors.

4 NATIONALS DETAINED ABROAD

4.1 Numbers and composition of the group

Only recently has the Ministry of Foreign Affairs begun to collect some information on Slovenian citizens detained abroad. Thus, data and information on this group are still very sparse. In general, in May 2006, the number of known Slovenian prisoners detained abroad was 103 in total.

4.2 Countries of detention

Most of the detained Slovenian citizens are being held in Germany (51), Austria (21) and Italy (19). Other countries of detention are Croatia, Lichtenstein, Venezuela and Peru.

4.3. Reasons for detention and sentencing

In Germany, Slovenian citizens are mostly detained for traffic offences, while in other countries the main reason for detention and sentencing is drug trafficking or the possession of drugs.

4.4. Involved organizations

In every case Consulates or Embassies contact Slovenian citizens and provide help within the jurisdiction and authorization that they have in foreign countries according to the relevant international conventions. According to the Vienna Convention on Consular Relations, representatives of Consulates shall have the right to visit imprisoned and detained nationals of the country that they represent, as well as those persons remanded to custody or in pre-trial detention. The purpose of such visits lies in conversation and correspondence as well as the arrangement of legal representation. Nevertheless, a Consulate or Embassy can only take such action if the detainee or prisoner in question opposes such support.

4.5 - 4.6 Release and reception in the home country, Aftercare

No special provision is made for released prisoners in either case.

4.7 Public opinion and the media

Only exceptionally does the media report on Slovenian citizens detained and sentenced abroad, mostly when serious crimes have been committed (on average once a decade). At the moment, we are witnessing the trial against Tomo Križnar in Sudan, an internationally recognized humanitarian activist and an envoy of the Slovenian President Drnovšek to Sudan. Tomo Križnar was sentenced to two years of imprisonment for espionage. Many international organizations have supported the liberation or pardon of Tomo Križnar. President Drnovšek and the Ministry for Foreign Affairs are doing their best to resolve the situation which is unclear due to the political situation in Sudan. Public opinion in this case is in favour of Tomo Križnar and all of the efforts that are being made to effect his release from prison.

5 EVALUATIONS AND RECOMMENDATIONS

Two different issues were discussed within this project focused on foreign prisoners. On the one hand we are dealing with delinquents, or at least with detained suspects or accused persons, while on the other hand we have focussed on asylum seekers - even illegal residents - who are mostly non-delinquent persons. Yet we have the tendency of joining up these two categories. Is it a virtual construction made by ourselves, by public opinion or state bureaucracy, or is it an inevitable necessity of perceiving these two groups as an undividable entity of social margin? Or is it perhaps inadmissible to treat all those different people as a homogeneous group, even though only within a theoretical study? What impact might such a concept have on the general perception of their (confused) differences?

What are the differences we should be aware of when we are discussing "foreign prisoners" as defined in the guidelines of this study? First of all, asylum seekers or persons kept under surveillance in detention centres for illegal residents are mostly innocent persons with no criminal intent of committing any offence. In the worst case they may be blamed for illegally crossing the border. Among asylum seekers you will find children, minors and families. None of these groups are to be found in prison institutions (with a few exceptions regarding minors or children in countries with extremely severe criminal policy as, for instance, the United Kingdom). Their motivation lies not in illegal or criminal activities, but is rather focused mostly on surviving. They are trying to avoid social and physical exploitation, poverty or even war. In most cases, protecting those people means establishing and supporting the fundamental rights to which every person is entitled. What are the similarities between the treatment of suspected criminals and refugees seeking asylum? During the first period, they all fall under the jurisdiction of the police. The level of state discretion on what should be done with these people is rather high. Living conditions are poor in each case whether they are sent to a penal institution (with special departments for detainees) or an asylum centre. The public perception - fostered by media reports - is clearly negative towards either group.

The situation in Slovenian prisons has worsened during the last twenty years. However, it is still much more favourable compared to many Western-European countries. Prisoners' rights are less frequently violated, and the number of prisoners is small. The percentage of foreign prisoners does not change much and is low when speaking in absolute numbers. Foreign prisoners do not benefit from free leaves, even though the conditions under which they are detained are almost the same as those of the rest of the inmates. Free leaves are supposed to be the most important link to the outside world and to social rehabilitation. Whatever the substitute may be, it is still not good enough. To overcome this shortage, the prison system in general should encourage and, above all, financially support the number of visits a prisoner can receive in prison. Visits from abroad should not be strictly limited to visits of just one day. Prison institutions should provide for adequate facilities, so that visitors can spend a night with the prisoner. The activities of NGOs should also be focused on the specific needs of foreign prisoners bearing in mind that - compared to other prisoners - they lack contact with the public. We are hesitant to discuss the possible arrangement of transferring prisoners to their native country within bilateral agreements. Many foreign prisoners find the Slovenian prison institution much more "user friendly" than those in other countries. So, not many of them are likely to request a transfer. The fact that most prisoners would surely wish to remain in conditions they find more tolerant and humane reflects well on the Slovenian system and should be taken into account.

Chapter 24

Spain

José Luis de la Cuesta

1 INTRODUCTION[1]

1.1 Overview of Penalties and Measures

Deprivation of freedom in a penitentiary establishment can be imposed in response to a conviction for committing a penal offence, as a security measure, or in the form of pre-trial detention. Apart from the penal and penitentiary system, foreigners awaiting the execution of an administrative expulsion can also be confined in special facilities or detention centres (see below). The internment of minor delinquents also takes place outside the penitentiary system. Although minors between 14 and 18 years of age can be responsible according to the Act of Penal Responsibility of Minors (OA5/2000), they are to be sent to specific institutions if the sanction imposed is an internment measure.

The new Penal Code (OA10/1995; hereinafter PC)[2], as reformed in 2003, establishes three penalties that result in the deprivation of liberty in Spain:
- prison;
- permanent localization (which has substituted the weekend arrest introduced in 1995 but which has nowadays disappeared);
- subsidiary personal responsibility for the non-payment of a fine.

The length of imprisonment is established between three months and 20 years, although it can be raised exceptionally to 25 or even 30 years for certain crimes and in cases of concurrence of certain serious offences; in very exceptional cases (concurrence of crimes of terrorism or organized crime), prison sentences up to 40 years can be imposed. A security period for prison sentences of more than five years is to be observed, and there are further restrictions to the access to the third degree, penitentiary benefits, and conditional release (particularly Article 78).

Although scarce, some alternatives or substitutes to short prison sentences are foreseen. The conditional suspension of a custodial penalty, including subsidiary personal responsibility for not paying a fine (Article 80-97 PC) and the substitution of the prison sentence by a fine or by community service (Article 88 PC) are alternatives for short sentences of up to two years (and five years in cases of drug dependency). In the case of non-legal residents in Spain, expulsion is also generally foreseen as a substitute (see below under B.3). Deprivation of freedom in a penitentiary establishment can also be the result of a security measure imposed by the penal judge. In fact, an internment into a psychiatric, detoxification or a special educative centre can be imposed upon a person having committed a penal offence if the risk of re-offending is appreciated but only within strict limits (Article 101 ff. PC).

According to the Spanish Criminal Procedural Act (Article 503) (hereinafter CPA), pre-trial detention can be adopted if someone:
- has been previously convicted; is reputed to have intentionally committed a new penal infraction or, having no previous penal records, is reputed to have intentionally committed an act of domestic violence; has committed an offence related to organized

---

[1] José Luis de la Cuesta is the Director of the Basque Institute of Criminology. University of the Basque Country (San Sebastian, Spain) and President of the International Association of Penal Law.

[2] De la Cuesta, J.L., 'Le nouveau Code pénal espagnol de 1995', *Revue Internationale de Droit Pénal 1996*, 67, 3-4, pp.715-724.

crime or a penal offence; is punished in this case by imprisonment of at least two years; or
- presents a risk to abscond or of hiding, tampering or destroying evidence or of aggression against the victim's goods or values.

Pre-trial detention can be applied (Article 504 CPA) as long as the mentioned risks subsist and within certain temporal limits: six months, one year, or two years (extendible to two and four years). If an appeal is pending after the conviction, the time limit for pre-trial detention is half of the imposed punishment.

1.2. Overview of the Prison System

1.2.1. Organisational Structure

According to Article 7 of the Penitentiary Act (OA 1/1979, hereinafter PA), the Spanish penitentiary system is composed of different kinds of centres[3]: establishments for prisoners on remand, establishments for the execution of custodial penalties (closed, open, and ordinary prisons), and special establishments such as hospitals, psychiatric establishments, and centres for social rehabilitation. There are also polyvalent centres that integrate different departments, modules, or separate units (Article 12 of the Penitentiary Regulation (R.D.190/1996; hereinafter, PR). The collaboration between the penitentiary administration and other public or even private entities is only authorized in certain fields: in the third degree -dependent units (Article 166 PR) and units for treatment of addicts (Article 182 PR)-, in order to execute measures involving deprivation of freedom (Article 182.3 PR), and for post-penitentiary social assistance.

Along with the (constitutionally recognized) rehabilitative aim, the main principles of penitentiary intervention in Spain are to avoid discrimination, to respect all legal guarantees and the personality and rights[4] of prisoners, as well as the principle of legality, the presumption of innocence of the prisoners on remand, and the prohibition of all forms of torture or mistreatment. Cellular principles and the separation of inmates are also considered fundamental but, due to overcrowding, most of the individual cells in the ordinary establishments are, in practice, collective ones and house three prisoners. Article 16 PA orders different modalities of separation: separation of men and women (mixed departments are exceptionally admitted by the PR), separation of convicted prisoners and prisoners on remand, separation of recidivists and first time offenders, separation of juveniles and adults, separation of sick or disabled and healthy or the able, and separation of prisoners sentenced for intentional offences and those convicted because of recklessness or negligence.

The external control of the Spanish penitentiary system lies with the *Juez de Vigilancia*, a specialized jurisdiction devoted to the control and follow-up of the execution of prison penalties and to safeguarding prisoners' rights (Article 76 & 77 PA). The Spanish Parliament (and the Parliaments or Legislative Assemblies of the Autonomous Communities

---

[3]   There are 77 establishments in the Spanish penitentiary system.
     http://www.mir.es/instpeni/centros/penitenciarios.htm
[4]   See a list in Article 4 PR. See also de la Cuesta, J.L., 'Les droits des prisonniers en Espagne', in Céré, J.P. (Dir.), *Panorama européen de la prison*, Paris 2002, pp.185-214.

with competence in the penitentiary execution) exerts the political control over the prison system. Also the *Defensor del Pueblo* (Ombudsman) and the regional ombudsman are frequently required by the prisoners in order to solve their petitions and claims, and their general and specific reports constitute valuable tools in order to attain a better and more accurate picture of the actual situation in the prisons.

1.2.2. Foreign Prisoners

Foreign prisoners are distributed among the different Spanish prisons. A higher concentration can be observed in some penitentiary centres: Madrid V, Topas (Salamanca), La Moraleja (Palencia), Madrid III, and Alama (Pontevedra)[5]. Outside the prison system, there are, however, specific "Centres for the internment of foreigners", where those foreigners who are awaiting (the decision of) expulsion or to be returned are provisionally kept (not more than 40 days) by order of the judge of instruction.

1.3. Overview: Involvement of Consulates, Embassies, Ministries – home country, Probation Service – home country, NGOs etc.

According to Spanish legislation, foreign *Consulates and Embassies* can be very useful instruments in helping foreign prisoners, and, with this aim, prison authorities are obliged to notify them of the interment of foreign prisoners either in a penitentiary establishment or in a centre for the internment of foreigners. Participation of foreign consulates and embassies is also essential in order to apply the provisions of those conventions established to allow the transfer of prisoners to their country in order to execute the sentence or parole. Often, judges ask the embassies to report either on the modalities of execution or on the mechanisms of control to be applied in their countries to the transferred prisoners.

The real involvement of consulates and embassies is, however, very unequal. Some of them (like the Dutch Embassy) are quite active and even ask periodically for reports. However, most of them remain passive and mainly concentrate their activities around Christmas time, which they use to assure some support to their nationals by distributing telephone cards and providing some money. They are also quite useful in certain cases in order to search for foreign prisoners' relatives or to facilitate the contacts between foreign prisoners and their families in their respective countries.

The participation of different *NGOs* in the penitentiary field is foreseen by Article 62 PR[6], which orders the Penitentiary Administration to especially encourage the collaboration of those organizations devoted to the prisoners' re-socialization and aid, and to open up possibilities of collaboration of the social entities of their countries through the consular authorities. This general frame is particularly complemented in certain aspects by other regulatory provisions. Furthermore, Instruction 5/2000 develops the procedure to be respected by those NGOs willing to make proposals of intervention in the penitentia-

---

[5] Rodríguez Yagüe, C 'Los derechos de los extranjeros en las prisiones españolas: legalidad y realidad', *Revista General de Derecho Penal Iustel* (http://www.iustel.com) 2 November 2004, (II.2.2).

[6] It is the task of the Autonomous Organism "Trabajo Penitenciario y Formación para el Empleo", regulated by RD 868/2005, to coordinate the intervention programs of the NGOs and other institutions in the Penitentiary Centres.

ries, and establishes – among the different programs of assistance to specific collectives – those concerning the assistance of foreigners (III.1).

Different NGOs are active concerning foreign prisoners: some of have general aims, like the Spanish Red Cross or Caritas, while others - particularly in Madrid or in the southern Spanish regions (see, for instance, *Horizontes abiertos*[7] or the network "ACOGE"[8]) - more specifically concentrate in the areas of assistance to immigrants and imprisoned foreigners. Inside the prisons their involvement is dependent on the programs proposed and approved by the Penitentiary Administration. They are, however, essential in practice in order to allow foreign prisoners to enjoy ordinary prison leaves.

1.4. Overview of Trends

1.4.1. Sentencing Trends

According to the information periodically offered by the mass media[9], the Spanish penitentiary population – which is mainly composed of males between 21 and 30 years of age (90% are under 40 years), who are responsible for or accused of property crimes and drug trafficking offences- presents three principal features today:
- a growing percentage of prisoners of a foreign ethnical and cultural origin;
- an increasing population of women, who are present in a higher percentage than that perceived in most of other European countries; and
- the important incidence of drug dependencies and other health problems.

Certainly, dependencies and health problems constitute relevant problems for the present penitentiary systems, more and more characterized by the difficulties of treatment and the conflictive prison population that appears to be "always growing"[10].
In many Western European countries, the permanent increase of penitentiary figures is accompanied by a progressively higher presence of foreigners. Due to their frequently problematic legal and social position penitentiary intervention towards foreigners has always appeared to be an important challenge for those penitentiary systems desirous to respect fundamental rights of prisoners and to promote re-education and re-socialization, as established by Article 25.2 of the Spanish Constitution.

During recent years, the penitentiary population growth in Spain has been very impressive. Although Spain traditionally had a low detention rate (for instance 36.9/100.000 in 1979), the country has rapidly climbed upwards in the European rankings in the last decade. In 2001, with a rate of 117, it occupied the third position in Western Europe, behind Portugal (132) and England and Wales (126). In 2003, the Spanish rate was close to Portugal (135.8 Spain / 136.7 Portugal) and in October 2004, Spain had in fact reached the level of England and Wales (140.3 Spain / 140.04 England and

---

[7] http://www.horizontesabiertos.org/
[8] http://www.acoge.org
[9] In fact, the Spanish Penitentiary Administration Official Reports relay information too generally, and, usually, by this way, it is difficult to generate a realistic image of the Spanish prisons. García España, E. 'Datos oficiales de delincuencia en España', *Revista de Derecho Penal y Criminología* 2004, 13, p.618.
[10] De la Cuesta Arzamendi, J.L. (2005), 'Retos principales del sistema penitenciario hoy', in *Jornadas en Homenaje al XXV Aniversario de la Ley Orgánica General Penitenciaria*, Madrid, pp.119-137.

Wales)[11]. M.Gallizo, the Director General of the Spanish Penitentiary System, already admitted in 2004 that there was a deficit of 12.000 penitentiary places[12].

1.4.2 Characteristics of the Foreign Prison Population

Regarding foreign prisoners, a comparative analysis of the development of this category of inmates in the Spanish Penitentiary System over the last 25 years shows a significant increase (in the last decade). According to the Penitentiary Administration, today foreign prisoners constitute 30% of the overall prison population, which is far above the European average (although foreigners are seven percent of the total population)[13]. Furthermore, in 2005, 38% of all newly admitted prisoners in Spain were not Spanish.[14].

Table 1

EVOLUTION OF THE REPRESENTATION OF FOREIGNERS IN THE PENITENTIARY POPULATION IN SPAIN			

1975-1982		*1998-2005*	
TOTAL	*FOREIGNERS*	*TOTAL*	*FOREIGNERS*
1975 8.440	11'63%	1998 44.747	17'6%
1976 9.937	11'99%	1999 45.384	17'6%
1977 9.392	14'07%	2000 45.104	19'93%
1978 10.463	13'17%	2001 47.571	23'32%
1979 13.627	13'69%	2002 51.882	25'85%
1980 18.253	12'40%	2003 56.096	27'10%
1981 21.185	11'02%	2004 59.375	29'10%
1982 21.942	10'59%	2005 61.054	30'49%

(Elaborated by the author with the information provided by the Dirección General de Instituciones Penitenciarias. Ministerio de Interior)

The common profile of a foreign prisoner is that of a young man (less than 40 years old), who does not consume drugs[15] and who has scarce resources, a low level of formal educa-

---

11   Conseil de l'Europe, 'SPACE I. Enquête 2004 (by M.F.Aebi), Strasbourg, 2005, p.22.
12   *La razón*, 31 October 2004.
13   García España, E, Pérez Jiménez, F. *Evolución de la delincuencia en España y Andalucía: Análisis e interpretación de las estadísticas oficiales*, Málaga 2004, p. 103.
14   García García, J. 'Extranjeros en prisión: aspectos normativos y de intervención penitenciaria', http://penitenciari.meetingcongress.com/ponencies/Julian_Garcia_Garcia.pdf , 2006, p. 2.
15   According to the information provided by J.García García, 15.2% are drug consumers, while a 60% of the total population manifests having used illegal drugs in month prior to entering prison; ibidem, p. 9.

tion, and little knowledge of the Spanish language[16]. Foreigners are most commonly in prison for an offence of drug trafficking (44.6%) or property crimes (28.16%)[17]. Furthermore, they predominantly have no previous criminal convictions (19.5% rate of recidivism; the recidivism rate of Spanish prisoners is around 61.7%) and have been classified in the second degree of treatment[18]. Of the foreign prisoners, the Magrebian population is the most significant one with over 6.000 Muslim inmates; Morocco (5.279), Colombia (1.998), Algeria (1.289), Rumania (1.255), and Ecuador (610) were the most represented nationalities in 2005[19].

The comparison of these figures with those related to the criminality of foreigners in Spain (around 6.30%) fully confirms the overrepresentation of foreigners in prison[20]. The negative incidence of this overrepresentation in the construction of the social image of crime is also well known, particularly because of the automatic link in social perception between immigration and criminality, even though they are fully in contradiction with the results of a reasonable analysis of the statistical data available[21].

The precariousness of the juridical and social situation of the detained foreigners together with a more intensive formal control is to be found at the origin of this overrepresentation. It also results in the more frequent application of pre-trial detention, which is repeatedly confirmed[22]. Many factors contribute to this: the absence of a permanent or stable domicile, the lack of familiar and/or social links, as well as the higher fear of absconding they generate, undoubtedly reduce the possibilities of being placed in provisional freedom. But, leaving aside other criminological factors, the overrepresentation of foreigners in the penitentiary system also has to do with the fact that many of them are serving long-term sentences (partly due to convictions for international drug trafficking): in 2001, 40% of the foreign prisoners had to serve a punishment of more than six years[23]. Furthermore, due to this irregular situation, the absence of coordination between the penitentiary and foreigners' regulations and serious problems of social exclusion at the moment of detention, it becomes nearly impossible for them to have real access to work, permission for leave, and other penitentiary benefits in prison. On the other hand, many difficulties (most of them bureaucratic) have to be faced in order to allow the execution of punishment in their countries of origin. As a result, the time of permanence in prison in

---

[16] Almeida Herrero, C. & Lucena García, M, *Situación de los presos extranjeros en el Centro Penitenciario de Topas*, Salamanca 2002, p.19
http://caritas.caritasalamanca.org/uploads/media/cd0053_Indice_tematico_Situacion_juridico-penitenciaria_Topas_2002.pdf   Fifteen percent does not know any Spanish and nearly 30% can understand it. García García, J. 2006, ibidem, p.8.

[17] The figures in the general population are respectively, 28.8% of inmates because of drug trafficking, and 50.4% because of offences against property. García García, J. 2006, ibidem, pp.5 f.

[18] Almeida Herrero, C. & Lucena García, M. ibidem, pp.24-25.

[19] García García, J. ibidem, p.2.

[20] Varona Martínez, G. 'Extranjería y prisión. ¿Igualdad material en un sistema penitenciario intercultural?', *Eguzkilore* 1994, 8, p.64 ff.

[21] As denounced by García España, E. Inmigración y delincuencia en España: análisis criminológico, Valencia, 2001, pp. 23 ff. See also her article 'Extranjería, delincuencia y legislación penitenciaria', in Derecho migratorio y extranjería, Valencia 2002, pp. 45 ff.

[22] García España, E., ibidem, pp. 444 ff. As J.García García states, 39% of the foreign prisoners are prisoners on remand, while this category constitutes only 23% of the total prison population. On the other hand, 52% of the prisoners on remand are foreigners, but foreigners only represent 24% of all sentenced prisoners, ibidem, p.4.

[23] García España, E., ibidem, p.52.

the case of foreigners is identical or very close to the integral execution; a long period of execution, very often in conditions that can hardly be assimilated to those of an ordinary prisoner[24].

1.5 Overview of National Legislation

The new democratic Spanish Constitution of 1978 generated a deep reform of juridical life and the penal system[25], and the Organic Act of 26 September 1979, i.e., the Penitentiary Act, was the first one to be approved of in execution of it. The enactment of the penitentiary legislation in Spain is an exclusive competence of the State. Nevertheless, some autonomous communities –the Basque Country, Catalonia, Andalusia and Navarre-, according to their respective statutes, are competent in the field of penitentiary execution; to date, however, only Catalonia has received the transfer of prison facilities from the central authority (in 1983).

Following the constitutional trend (Article 25.2), the Penitentiary Act (PA) and the Penitentiary Regulation (PR) establish the primacy of penitentiary treatment, according to the system of "scientific individualization" (Article 72 PA) and divide the execution of imprisonment into four treatment degrees: the closed regime, the ordinary regime, the open regime, and conditional release. The classification is flexible and is decided according to the needs of treatment as manifested by an examination and the study of the inmate's personality. Prisoners have the right to reject collaboration in the accomplishment of any study of their personality, without any disciplinary consequences or regression of the degree under which they are detained (Art.112.3 PR).

2 TREATMENT OF FOREIGN PRISONERS

2.1 General

In principle, the incarceration regime of foreigners does not present many legal differences to the general penitentiary regime.

In fact, the few specific normative provisions related to foreigners[26] are fully justified[27], as they are simply directed to make some of their rights effective (e.g., information, access to consular or diplomatic services, education, freedom of religion, and to be assisted in the disciplinary proceedings) and to facilitate the application of the expulsion measure. Apart from these specific rules, foreign prisoners are submitted in Spain to the general penitentiary regime, according to the rules of separation (mainly, sex, age, previous sentences, pre-trial[28] condition) (Art. 16 PA and 99 PR) and to their classification and treatment needs. According to the system of "scientific individualization" (Art. 72 PA) - a

---

[24] Varona Martínez, G. *La inmigración irregular. Derechos y deberes humanos*, Vitoria-Gasteiz, 1994, pp. 426

[25] De la Cuesta, J.L. & Blanco, I 'Spain', in A.Van Zyl Smit & F.Dünkel (eds.), *Imprisonment Today and Tomorrow. International Perspectives on Prisoners' Rights and Prison Conditions*, 2nd ed, The Hague 2001, pp. 609-633.

[26] See also Instruction 18/2005, 21 December, of the General Direction of Penitentiary Institutions.

[27] Giménez-Salinas i Colomer, E., 'Los extranjeros en prisión', *Eguzkilore*, 7, extra, 1994 p. 136.

[28] Pre-trial prisoners are kept at the disposal of the judicial authority, and the penitentiary regime must guarantee the presumption of their innocence (art. 5 PA).

modality of the progressive system – there are four degrees of treatment in prison: first degree (closed regime), second degree (ordinary regime), third degree (open regime), and fourth degree (conditional freedom). The primacy of treatment (Art. 71 PA) determines that the prisoner's classification (which must be revised every six months) is carried out according to the study of the inmate's personality. The system wants to be flexible, and prisoners have the right to freely reject or not to collaborate in the accomplishment of any study of their personality, without any disciplinary consequences or any regression of the imprisonment degree (Art.112.3 RP). Generally, in the Spanish Penitentiary system, foreign prisoners deserve similar treatment to the Spanish prisoners, with the same net of rights and of reciprocal obligations between the administration and inmates. The difficulties that foreigners experience in every day life are, however, numerous, and the absence of an explicit regulation of certain issues linked to the foreigner's personal reality and the penitentiary conditions result in a sort of "institutional discrimination"[29].

2.2 Living Conditions and Facilities

According to the law, foreign prisoners have access to the same living conditions and facilities as other prisoners. In fact, as already stated above, nationality is not included under the criteria that govern separation of inmates. Nevertheless, in practice, although foreign prisoners are distributed among the different prisons, there is a tendency to concentrate most of them in some certain penitentiary centres: Madrid V, Topas (Salamanca), La Moraleja (Palencia), Madrid III, and Alama (Pontevedra)[30]. In Spain, the existing specific "Centres for the internment of foreigners" do not have a penitentiary nature and do not belong to the prison system. In those facilities, controlled by the Minister of Home Affairs, foreigners who are awaiting (the decision of) expulsion or to be returned can be provisionally detained by order of the judge of instruction and for not more than 40 days (see below, under III).

On the other hand, in certain penitentiary centres, some wings are particularly reserved for foreign prisoners[31]; thus, nationality also becomes a criterion for separation of prisoners. This policy, which could be justified in order to give a particular response (particular programs...) to the particular difficulties encountered by this group of prisoners, should be carefully applied because it can also become the source of even further segregation[32] of a collective whose isolation already constitutes a very important problem – both socially and in the prison life.

In any case, different surveys assure that foreign prisoners are generally satisfied with the material conditions of Spanish prisons[33], although discipline and the absolute routine are very much criticized. But at the same time, they experience important difficulties in the

---

29 García España, E, ibidem, p. 485.
30 Rodríguez Yagüe, C), 'Los derechos de los extranjeros en las prisiones españolas: legalidad y realidad', *Revista General de Derecho Penal Iustel* (http://www.iustel.com) 2 November 2004, (II.2.2)
31 Rodríguez Yagüe reports that, for instance, in Topas (Salamanca) two wings (out of 14) are dedicated to foreign prisoners, ibidem, footnote 28.
32 Rodríguez Yagüe, C., ibidem, (II, 2.2).
33 See, for instance, Sánchez Tarifa, J.A. & Stangeland, P., 'La situación de los extranjeros en cárceles españolas', *Boletín Criminológico*, 25 January 1997, p.1.

enjoyment of visits and communication (particularly, *vis-a-vis* visits and phone calls)[34], as well as in the exercise of many of the penitentiary rights in everyday life.

2.3 Reception and Admission

Foreign prisoners are submitted to general reception procedures[35], and their right to information is fully recognised (art. 15.2 PA; art. 4.2 k PR). Foreign prisoners also have the right to communicate the fact of their incarceration to their consular or diplomatic representatives (Art. 15.5 PR). The Establishment must give them – within 48 hours – the possibility to exert this right (Instruction 18/2005 on the general rules on foreign inmates, 1.1. a), and in the following five days, the address and telephone number of their consular or diplomatic services in Spain must be communicated to them (Art. 52.2 PR and Instruction 18/2005, 1.1. a). The communication to the consular representatives can be essential to obtain the personal documentation (passport/identity or inscription document) of the foreign prisoner, and the Penitentiary Administration is obliged to initiate the necessary procedures to obtain this documentation. However, the prisoner himself can oppose it (for instance, because he believes that expulsion is more difficult then)[36]. Frequently, either because of this legal conflict or due to the delay of the consular or diplomatic offices to identify their citizens, the result is the absence of needed documentation[37]. The lack of personal and regular documentation has, nevertheless, very negative consequences: leaving aside the permission of leave, prisoners without identification documents can be classified in the third degree but, in practice, they can execute the open regime only in a restrictive way (Article 82 PR)[38]. Similar problems arise regarding conditional release (aggravated by the fact that convicted foreign prisoners sentenced to imprisonment of more than one year lose their permission of residence and labour).

On the other hand, practice has shown how often a residence permit that has already been accepted or renewed in favour of a pre-trial inmate finally loses any value because of the obstacles that the prison system poses to the further renewal thereof: due to being detained, the foreigner cannot visit the police office in order to sign the document or to have his/her finger prints taken. However, this could be easily solved by applying in these cases the same procedure followed for the renovation of identity cards of nationals. Here, police officers visit the prison in order to get finger prints and signatures of the inmates. Alternatively, the judge could authorize that foreign prisoner be conducted and escorted to the police office in order to complete these formalities[39].

Returning to the foreign prisoners' right of information, in order to assure this right, the Spanish Prison Administration is obliged to have informative booklets about the prison regime and system in the most popular and common languages. If the booklets are

---

34 Sánchez Tarifa, J.A. & Stangeland, P., ibidem, pp. 1 & 3.
35 In any case, the Establishment must always notify the reception to the Provincial Police Station in order to facilitate the implementation of the regulations concerning foreigners and, in particular, to initiate the expulsion dossier, if legally ordered (Instruction 18/2005, 1.1.d).
36 Almeida Herrero, C. & Lucena García, M. ibidem, p.42.
37 In fact, the percentage of documented foreign prisoners is only 40.2%. Almeida Herrero, C. & Lucena García, M., ibidem, p.41.
38 Hernando Galán, M.B., Los extranjeros en el Derecho penitenciario español, Madrid 1997, p.60.
39 http://www.malaga.acoge.org/prisiones.htm. See also, García España, E. & Rodríguez Candela, J.L. ibidem, p.6.

not in a language that the foreign prisoner can understand[40], an oral translation will be provided by the staff members or by inmates who speak the foreign prisoner's language. If necessary, the Prison Administration will request the help of consular services in order to give the information required by law (Art. 51.3 PR). Nevertheless, this provision is completely insufficient, and it must be said in this respect that the absence of interpreters in the Establishments[41] clearly aggravates the non-communication of certain foreign prisoners. On the other hand, difficulties to communicate obviously have very negative consequences at a personal level and in the penitentiary field. The PR also considers it a foreigner's right to obtain information on their process and penitentiary situation (Article 4.2 k). However, despite the effort to assure that the prisoner is provided with proper information as ordered by the Prison Rules, practice shows that their knowledge of their juridical and penitentiary situation is low[42].

Foreign prisoners must be also informed of the legal possibilities of substitution of the penalty by expulsion, as well as on the application of international treaties or agreements on the transfer of prisoners to other countries in order to execute the sentence or to be conditionally released (Article 52.2 PR; see also Instruction 18/2005, 4). With a view toward facilitating the effective application of this possibility, Article 62.4 PR orders the Penitentiary Administration to accept the collaboration of the social entities of the countries of origin through the consular authorities. This important provision could have a broader field of application in practice: the existence of a valid international instrument is only an initial requirement for this purpose, but the procedure also requires the consent of the parties involved, such as the foreigner him/herself, the representatives of his/her country of origin, and the Spanish authorities. Coordination of foreign administrations is never an easy task and, as practice shows, the possibilities opened by international agreements are often very restrictively applied due to the absence of intermediary intervenors and to the duration of the administrative proceedings (usually more than one year)[43].

2.4 Work - Education – Training – Sports – Recreation

According to the Penitentiary Law, prison labour is a prisoner's duty and a right, as well as a fundamental means of treatment (Art. 26 PA). According to the law, the mandatory characteristics of prison labour are: non-afflictiveness and non-application as a disciplinary sanction; respect for the prisoner's dignity; character, either educational or productive or therapeutic "in order to prepare the inmates to the normal conditions of free work"; non-subjection to the Administration's economic interest; organized in a way directed to satisfy the aptitudes and occupational aspirations of the inmates; and protection by social security. Prison labour also includes professional training, as well as studies, occupational and productive work, personal collaboration in the auxiliary services of the establishment, and crafting, intellectual, and artistic activities (Art. 27.1 PA).

---

[40] There are booklets available in nine languages, including Arab and Rumanian. García García, J., ibidem, 2006, p. 10.

[41] The poor quality of the judicial interpreters is also frequently denounced by foreign prisoners, Sánchez Tarifa, J.A. & Stangeland, P.,ibidem, p. 4.

[42] Rodríguez Yagüe, C.,ibidem, (II.2.1).

[43] García España, E. & Rodríguez Candela, J.L. "Extranjeros en prisión", http://www.icamalaga.es/funcio/extran/doctrina/doc1.pdf, p. 13.

Prison labour must be facilitated by the Administration (Art. 26, II e) and it can be organized directly[44] or in collaboration with external entities or firms (Arts.138 and f. R.), but always trying to get the best assimilation of free work and avoiding any discrimination by reason of nationality, sex, civil status, or age. Article 3 RD 782/2001 establishes the criteria that must govern the adjudication of labour to inmates in the penitentiary workshops, and no reference is included to the inmate's nationality or to the inmate's administrative situation (either regular or irregular). Nevertheless, the lack of work activities in prison is very serious and this affects both national and foreign prisoners, even if sometimes due to their particular situation (they need money and are not drug-addicts) they have a broader access to labour activities than national prisoners[45]. This is an important circumstance, as most penitentiary benefits require working (Art. 204 PR) or the performance of a normal occupational activity that is useful for the prisoner's preparation for life outside (Art. 206 PR).

Completely different is the situation of those foreign prisoners classified in the third degree (open regime) or who are conditionally released (parole). Here the labour activities are submitted to general legislation and, therefore, the (much too usual) lack of personal and regular documentation has very negative consequences for foreigners: the extension of the possibility (sometimes accepted by the Ministry of Labour and Social Security in Spain) of establishing a special administrative labour permission for these cases (limited in time to the duration of third penitentiary degree or parole) appears to be the better solution[46]. In any case, the instructions approved by the government in 2005 in order to authorize labour activities by foreign inmates in the third degree or conditional release[47] are still too restrictive.

Concerning training, education, and the access to culture, Article 118.2 PR goes far beyond the Foreigners' Act and guarantees to foreign prisoners the "same possibilities of access" to educational programs as the national prisoners have. The aim of the Penitentiary Administration is to provide them with adequate means to learn Spanish and the co-official language of the Autonomous Community where the respective establishment is located. Inside the Framework Plan on Educative Intervention with Foreign Inmates, several programs are thus implemented in collaboration with the Autonomous Communities, Consulates, and NGOs (particularly those belonging to the Forum in favour of the Social Integration of Immigrants) to help them to learn Spanish, to attend primary education[48], programs of multicultural education, education in human rights, and programs of education in values and cognitive abilities[49]. Nevertheless, the demand (particularly, Spanish courses) vastly exceeds the supply[50]. Penitentiary libraries are authorized to have publications in the most popular foreign languages, according to the number of foreign inmates (Article 127.3 PR).

---

44 The Autonomous Organism "Trabajo Penitenciario y Formación para el Empleo" (RD 868/2005) is competent to organise prison labour, and also the educational, cultural, and sports activities for prisoners and released persons.

45 Rodríguez Yagüe, C., ibidem, 2004 (II.2.6)

46 García España, E. & Rodríguez Candela, J.L, ibidem, p. 11.

47 García García, J., ibidem, p.17. See also Instruction 18/2005, 5)

48 Article 123.1 PR declares the priority of the basic education offered, among others, to foreign prisoners.

49 García García, J., ibidem, pp.21-23. See also Instruction 18/2005, 6.

50 Rodríguez Yagüe, C. ibidem, (II.2.5).

Foreign prisoners are able to take part in the sports and recreation activities organised in prison, although sometimes language and culture constitute important barriers even for these purposes.

2.5 Food – Religion – Personal Hygiene – Medical Care

Article 21.2 PA and Article 226 clearly establish that the Penitentiary Administration must provide the inmates with nourishment that is controlled and supervised by the physician. It is to be adequately prepared, taking into account (regarding quantity and quality) the dietetic and hygienic requirements, the climate, the age, health situation, the nature of the labour activity developed, habits, and, as far as possible, the personal, philosophical, and religious beliefs of the different inmates[51].

The right to religious freedom is also generally recognized (Art. 54 PA). Inmates have the right to communicate with the ministers of their respective religious confession (Article 51.3 PA) and to request religious assistance according to their will. The Penitentiary Establishments are obliged to organize a place for the practice of religious rites. Article 230.4 PR submits, however, the religious assistance to the content of the agreements established by the Spanish State with the different confessions[52] and, by this way, important differences in the treatment of different religions arise, also at a normative level, in favour of the Catholic Church[53].

Connected to the religious practices, the Penitentiary Administration must also respect and facilitate nourishment rules and rites and religious festivities as long as permitted not only by the budgetary availability, the safety and the ordered life of the establishment, but also by the respect of the other inmates' fundamental rights (Art. 230 PR). Religious dress requirements can be respected in prison as far as the law guarantees to all inmates the right to dress in their own clothes (if they are not indecent), adapted to the weather conditions and free of any element affecting the inmate's dignity (Article 20.1 PA).

Personal hygiene is a general requirement according to the law (Art.19.3 PA), and the Administration is obliged to provide to the inmates (periodically and free of charge) the services and articles of daily hygiene (see also Art.222 PR).

Regarding medical care, all inmates have the same right to pharmaceutical and sanitary services as any other citizens (Art. 208 RP) and deserve the same respect (in particular, the right to an informed consent and to confidentiality) concerning any possible medical research, which must be approved by a Commission of Ethics (Art. 211 RP). They can also request, at their own cost, medical services, detached from the Penitentiary Administration, unless precluded for safety reasons (Art. 36.3 PA). The Penitentiary Administration has to assure integral sanitary assistance (Art. 207.1 PR), either in the penitentiary or in outside facilities.

---

[51] Article 226 PR mentions personal and religious beliefs.
[52] In any case, the Religious Confessions must be registered at the Register of Religious Entities in the Ministry of Justice. See Circular 04/1997 on religious assistance.
[53] Rodríguez Yagüe, C., ibidem, (II.2.3).

2.6 Consular and Legal Assistance

Foreign prisoners have the right to communicate with and to be visited by the representatives of their *consular or diplomatic services* in Spain (Art. 52.2 PR). They can communicate to them the fact of their incarceration (Art. 15.5 PR), and these representatives can help the Administration in giving to the inmate the adequate information (Art. 51.3 PR). They can also be authorized by the Director of the Establishment to visit them, however always in line with the general rules on communication and visits (Art. 49.3 & 4 PR; see also art. 41).

The intervention of foreign Consulates and Embassies can be very useful for many penitentiary purposes and in order to facilitate contact with relatives. Article 62.4 PR also orders the Penitentiary Administration to facilitate the intervention of the social entities of the inmates' respective countries through their consular authorities.

Consulates and Embassies are equally essential in order to make effective the provisions of those conventions established to allow the transfer of prisoners to their home country, where the coordination of the foreign administration is never an easy task, and the practice shows that the possibilities opened by international agreements are often very restrictively applied due to the lack of adequate communication and intermediation, and to the duration of the administrative proceedings (usually more than one year)[54].

However, the real involvement of the representatives of Consulates and Embassies in Spanish Prisons is very unequal, and those particularly active representatives (like the Netherlands') are very much in the minority.

Concerning legal assistance, the situation is very deficient: foreign prisoners generally maintain a scarce[55] relationship with their respective lawyers (they hardly ever meet)[56] and have a very low degree of knowledge of their juridical and penitentiary situation[57]. Here again, the difficulties in communication (which the absence of interpreters in the Establishments[58] clearly aggravates) surely have very negative repercussions in their juridical situation and for the formulation of an adequate legal strategy in the penal process[59]. The same can be said in connection to disciplinary proceedings, where the possibility admitted by Article 242.2 (j) PR (assistance by a member of the prison staff or by another prisoner as an interpreter) is unacceptable. The assurance of sufficient and adequate means to have access to competent interpreters permanently or, at least, to fully guarantee the right to be heard in the penitentiary proceedings should, therefore, be legally recognized as a right of foreign prisoners[60].

2.7 Contact with the Outside World

The Penitentiary Legislation authorizes inmates to be visited and to maintain written communication in their own language (Art. 51.1 PA). These can be restricted only by

---

[54] García España, E. & Rodríguez Candela, J.L. "Extranjeros en prisión", cit., p. 13.

[55] http://www.malaga.acoge.org/prisiones.htm

[56] García España, E., ibidem, p.373.

[57] Rodríguez Yagüe, C, ibidem, (II.2.1).

[58] The poor quality of the judicial interpreters is also frequently denounced by foreign prisoners, Sánchez Tarifa, J.A. & Stangeland, P., ibidem, p. 4.

[59] García España, E. & Rodríguez Candela, J.L, ibidem, p.4.

[60] García España, E. & Rodríguez Candela, J.L, ibidem, pp. 4 f.

reasons of treatment, safety, or for the maintenance good order. Inmates classified in the third degree can have as many visits as permitted by their work schedule. Those classified in the first and second degree have the right to communicate (to receive visits) two times a week (Saturdays and Sundays; exceptionally other days) for at least twenty minutes (cumulative) and with a maximum of four persons simultaneously (Art. 42 PR). The written communications do not find limitations unless subjected to the officers' intervention (Art.46.1 PR)[61]. Family members need only to accredit their relationship to visit the prisoner. Visits of friends or of the representative of organizations of penitentiary cooperation require the Governor's permission. Those who can not obtain permissions of leave are authorized to maintain conjugal (or intimate) visits once a month (from one to three hours). Familiar visits (also once a month and with the same duration) are possible as are visits of those "living together" (up to six hours, once a month). All of these visits are mutually compatible (Art. 45 PR).

In principle, visits and communications are considered a prisoner's right and are not subjected to the officers' intervention, unless by decision duly initiated by the Governor, which must be communicated to the inmate and to the competent judge. Inmates can communicate in their own language. If intervention during visits is required and the prisoners are not going to communicate either in Spanish or in the co-official language of the Autonomous Community, they must notify the Governor. The visits can be suspended in any of the circumstances of Art. 44 RP: undue behaviour, evidence of the preparation of a criminal act, or acts against the order or the safety of the establishment. Neither intervention nor suspension is possible during visits with the attorney or procurator, even in cases of terrorism, unless by application of a previous judicial order (Art. 51.2 PA: Art. 48.3 PR).

Visits and communications with authorities or professionals are also possible: particularly, in the case of foreign prisoners, visits with the consular or diplomatic representatives of their country, or with those persons indicated by their respective Embassy or Consulate. These visits, which need to be authorized by the Director of the Establishment, have to take place in adequate facilities and respect the basic rules concerning the general requirements (Art. 41 PR) and the number of communications (Art. 49 PR).

Telephone calls (Art. 47 PR) are also possible, with the Governor's permission, if the prisoners' relatives live in distant places or cannot visit them. This is also the case if the prisoner must communicate an important matter to his/her family, attorney or to other persons. Prisoners cannot receive telephone calls, but can make five telephone calls per week, the duration of which may not exceed five minutes. The call will take place in the presence of a prison officer. Unless they want to communicate their transfer to another establishment, inmates must bear the cost of their phone calls and, although some consulates and embassies try to give some support to their nationals, mainly at Christmas, the lack of financial means to make telephone calls is quite general among foreign prisoners. Telephone calls and letters between inmates of different establishments can be monitored by a resolution initiated by the Governor.

---

[61] Inmates can also receive two packages a month, unless if they are in the closed regime (first degree: only one package per month). The package cannot exceed 5 kg., but books, publications and clothes are not computed to such effect (Art. 50 PR). Forbidden articles (in addition to those prohibited by the regime rules) are, generally, those which can provoke danger for the safety, order or health as well as drugs, alcohol, food and those items that would be deteriorated by the manipulation needed to control them (Art. 51 PR).

Communications and visits are one of the penitentiary issues where the gap between legal norms and practice is greater: due to the personal situation either of foreign prisoners or of their relatives or friends, to their lack of resources, and even to the administrative situation (irregularity, lack of documentation of their friends and relatives)[62]. Conscious of this reality, the Penitentiary Regulation orders that the Penitentiary Administration organize them in an adequate way in order to cover the special needs of foreign prisoners (Art. 41.7 PR). Furthermore, Instruction 4/2005 allows the Establishment's Governing Board to increase the number of communications or their duration in the case of those relatives living outside Spain. These guidelines, however, can become utterly useless if there is not a sufficient flexibility or if, for purely administrative reasons[63], foreign prisoners are gathered in establishments located at a long distance from the places where they maintain their social relations in Spain or if, as soon as they establish new relations inside the prison, they are transferred to another establishment. On the other hand, the intervention of NGOs in order not only to give some economic support (e.g., to buy stamps or to make phone calls) but also to mediate between prisoners and their relatives and even to give certain guarantees or support concerning the links of the prisoner with the visitor can prove to be highly relevant in helping foreign prisoners benefit from their right to communicate with the outside world.

Concerning access to information from the outside world, the Penitentiary Law allows inmates to have access to books, periodicals, magazines and any other means of social communication – such as radio or TV channels[64]- with certain limitations (Art. 58). Only the publications not registered (unless edited in the centres) or those against the safety and good order of the establishment are forbidden by the Regulation. The withdrawal of a book or a magazine demands, however, an administrative resolution that must be communicated to the inmate and to the penitentiary judge (Art. 128 PR). The use of personal computers can be authorized in exceptional circumstances for educational reasons. The possibility of transmitting tapes or diskettes or the access to communication nets is excluded (Art. 129 PR).

2.8 Re-integration Activities - Prison Leave

As already stated above, in Spain re-education and social re-integration are constitutionally proclaimed as the main orientations of imprisonment. Treatment and, in general, *re-integration activities* should therefore be a fundamental focus of penitentiary intervention. All prisoners have a right to treatment (Art. 4, 2 d) PR) and to take part in its organisation and execution (art. 61 PA and 112 PR). They can equally reject and not collaborate in the treatment without suffering non-favourable consequences (Article 112.3 PR). Penitentiary reclassification every six months is also a prisoner's right (Art. 64.2, 65.4 and 72 PA; art. 100.1 and 105.1 PR): there are four levels of penitentiary classification: first degree (closed regime), second degree (ordinary regime), third regime (open regime), and condi-

---

[62] García España, E. ibidem, pp. 369 ff; Rodríguez Yagüe, C. ibidem, (II.2.7).

[63] Against, Ríos Martín, J., *Manual de Ejecución Penitenciaria. Defenderse en la cárcel*, 2nd. ed, Madrid 2001, p.351.

[64] Inmates can have their own radio or television sets (with certain dimensions and bought through the prison-store). TV channels (also foreign ones) are received through a collective antenna. For security reasons, TV sets with teletext are not authorised.

tional release (parole). All prisoners have the right to be sent to a penitentiary establishment according to the classification degree (Art. 103 and 106 PR).

Different activities are organised inside the prison in order to promote re-integration, all of them accessible to foreign prisoners, but the most important ones are those developed outside prison. In order to take part in them, inmates should, in principle, be classified in the third degree (open regime), and this classification generally requires that inmates have already completed a quarter of their penalty[65]. Even if several life modalities can be found within the open regime (Art. 84 PR), the principles inspiring it are always the confidence in the inmates' capacities and self-responsibility. This confidence authorizes a mitigation of the control measures and a certain degree of normalization and social integration.

For inmates classified in the second degree (ordinary regime), the so called "programmed leaves", regulated by article 114 PR, allow them to be released (for up to two days) in order to take part in re-integration activities outside the prison (Art. 114 PR)[66]. General requirements to be fulfilled in these cases are the same that are foreseen for ordinary leaves. The 1979 PA established a broad system of prison leaves to promote the contacts between inmates and the outside world:

- Ordinary leaves are true penitentiary holidays that are reserved for the prisoners classified in the second or third degree, and who have completed a quarter of their sentence and who have not engaged in bad conduct. The permission is granted by the penitentiary judge who can authorize the inmates to leave the prison for some days (up to seven each leave) for a total amount of 18 days (second degree) or 24 days (third degree) in the semester. Permission is refused if there is a danger of absconding, recidivism, or if enjoyment of the leave can jeopardize its purpose (Art. 47.2 PA; 154 PR).

- Extraordinary leaves are possible in cases of death or serious disease of relatives or of persons intimately linked to the inmates, or on occasion of the birth of his son/daughter. They are authorized for the necessary time, and inmates in the first degree (closed regime) can also benefit from them if the penitentiary judge gives his permission. The judge's permission is equally needed if the extraordinary leave exceeds two days (Art. 155 PR). Extraordinary leaves also include release for up to twelve hours for outpatient treatment in an external institution or release for up to two days in order to enter an external hospital for care (Art. 155 PR).

- Weekend leaves, provided for those classified in the third degree who can leave the prison, as a rule, occur every weekend (Art.87.2 and 101.2 PR).

Being classified in the third degree and thus prison leaves are, of course, legally available to foreign prisoners. Nevertheless, foreign prisoners hardly benefit from them[67]. Although theoretically there is no legal impediment, in practice, concerning prison leaves and third degree detention (but also parole and other favourable opportunities legally

---

[65] This is not, however, a prerequisite for those sentenced to imprisonment for less than one year, for those very seriously sick and prisoners with incurable sufferings (Art. 104.4 PR) and, in cases of specially favorable circumstances, if there has been enough time to obtain an adequate knowledge of the individual (Art. 104.3 PR)

[66] There are also regular leaves (up to eight hours) provided for those inmates classified in second degree who take part in concrete programs of specialized care (Art. 117 PR).

[67] See, for instance, for Catalunya *Justidata* 33, November 2002.

available for both nationals and foreigners), the condition of not being a national is usually considered a variable of higher risk (see Instruction 22/1996) and, as denounced by various prestigious institutions, has very often been used (solely[68] or associated with the absence of familial support) as the justification for the denial of permissions of prison leave for foreign prisoners[69]. Certainly existing rules do not treat all foreigners in the same way and a distinction is made between European and non-European foreigners. Mention of the prisoner's personal and social links has been equally included in the Prison Regulation in order to allow the Director of the Establishment to individualize the decision and to authorize leaves in exceptional cases. But, in reality, the condition of the foreigner has become "a mechanism of nearly automatic denial of the prison leaves due to the presence of the variable of foreignness"[70], a policy severely criticized by the literature and by the jurisprudence itself[71]. The need to establish mechanisms that can broaden the access to prison leaves for foreign prisoners is, thus, urgent. And in this sense, together with the establishment of control measures (including, for instance, different modalities of electronic surveillance), the official recognition of the important work of some NGOs is essential. Furthermore, leaning on the experience of certain entities (like *Horizontes abiertos* or *Caritas*, and others), devoted to assure permanent assistance (by means of shelters or dormitories) and an adequate follow-up on foreign prisoners, new regulations could be adopted, at least in order to effectively assimilate NGOs' support to reliable social or family links with a view to authorise prison leaves for foreign prisoners.

The issue is very relevant and recalls how often (even in the ordinary life) the formal recognition of a right is not sufficient. As Article 9.2 of the Spanish Constitution states, sometimes, in order to give to the citizens the opportunity to profit from their formally proclaimed rights, an intervention (constitutionally endorsed by the public powers) is needed to remove those obstacles that impede or put barriers to their participation in social, cultural, economic, or political life. At the penitentiary level, this is particularly true for many prisoners' rights that cannot be exercised without a positive and effective intervention by the Penitentiary Administration. Also, regarding foreign prisoners, we should not forget that the deficits in the penitentiary conditions always affect much more the less favoured collectives[72], as this is particularly the case.

The problem is quite similar concerning the open regime (and parole), first of all because the condition of foreigners is also a source of significant difficulties to be allocated to the third degree. These difficulties are aggravated if the foreigner is in an irregular situation or lacks personal and regular documentation. working outside prison is one of the most relevant elements for classification to the open regime and, although non-documented prisoners can be classified to this regime, in practice, as they cannot work outside they remain in the second degree but with the benefit of week-end leaves or are classified in third degree but only in the restrictively as foreseen by Article 82 PR[73]. The establishment of special administrative labour permission for these cases, limited in time

---

[68] Critically, because of the extended automatic rejection of the permission for foreigners to go on leave, García España, E. ibidem, p.378; Rodríguez Yagüe, C, ibidem, (II.2.8).

[69] Rodríguez Yagüe, C., ibidem, (II.2.8).

[70] Rodríguez Yagüe, C., ibidem, (II.2.8).

[71] See, for instance, the decisions of the Audiencia Provincial de Madrid, in Rodríguez Yagüe, C. ibidem, (II.2.8).

[72] Rodríguez Yagüe, C., ibidem, (II.2.5).

[73] Hernando Galán, M.B., ibidem, p.60.

to the duration of the third penitentiary degree (or parole) appears to be a good solution[74], and it has sometimes been accepted by the Ministry of Labour and Social Security in Spain. On the other hand, in 2005, the government approved some instructions in order to authorize labour activities by foreign inmates in the third degree or who are on conditional release[75], but they are still too restrictive. As it happened regarding prison leaves, here again the recognition of the NGOs' activities[76] in sheltering those foreign prisoners classified in the third degree and giving them support in order to fulfil a complete program of activities (education, training, other activities of social interest, etc.) would also give more possibilities to the access of foreign prisoners to the open regime (and to parole).

Conditional release (parole) is available in Spain to those convicted persons already in the third degree who present a record of good conduct and a favourable prognosis. The completion of three-quarters of the total penalty (two-thirds in cases of continuous labour or other occupational or cultural activities in prison) is also a general requirement established by the PC, but exceptions are provided for those aged seventy or who will reach this age in the course of their sentence and equally for those who are affected by a very serious disease with incurable sufferings (Art. 91 ff. PC and 205 PR)[77]. Article 197 PR specifically foresees the procedure to be followed in order to authorize serving conditional release by a foreigner in his country of origin[78] and, also with this purpose, Article 62.4 PR orders the Penitentiary Administration to open up possibilities of collaboration of the social entities of the countries of origin through the consular authorities. As already stated above, the execution of conditional release in the country of origin requires not only the inmate's consent but also the consent of the other parties involved: the representatives of his country of origin and the Spanish authorities. Coordination with foreign administrations is never an easy task: as a result, practice shows that possibilities opened by international agreements are often very restrictively applied due to the absence of intermediary interventions and due to the duration of the administrative proceedings (usually more than one year)[79]. In any case, as soon as the judges of surveillance began to receive guarantees for the prisoner's exit from Spain, the system found a broader application, even if due to the absence of control in the country of residence, the decision ultimately had the same effect as a partial discharge or amnesty. The reform introduced in the Penal Code by the OA 11/2003 now generally orders the expulsion of the convicted foreigner (non-resident) in Spain if either sentenced to prison penalties shorter than six years or after the classification to the third degree regime, or after completing three-quarters of the penalty (Article 89 PC)[80].

---

[74] García España, E. & Rodríguez Candela, J.L, ibidem, p. 11.

[75] García García, J. ibidem, p.17.

[76] Rodríguez Yagüe, C. ibidem, (II.2.9).

[77] It is the task of the Autonomous Organism "Trabajo Penitenciario y Formación para el Empleo" to organize activities in order to promote the personality of inmates and parolees and also to provide social assistance to prisoners and their families and the follow-up and control of those conditionally released.

[78] 64 inmates were transferred in 2005. García García, J. ibidem, p.6. See also Instruction 18/2005, 4.2.

[79] García España, E. & Rodríguez Candela, J.L. "Extranjeros en prisión", ibidem, p. 13.

[80] However, only 59 inmates were released in 2005 because of access to the third degree or execution of three-quarters of the sentence; and approximately 400 inmates due to the execution of the conditional release in their country of origin. García García, J. ibidem, p.6.

2.9 Release – Expulsion

One of the most important penitentiary rights of inmates is the right to be released as soon as the penalty has been fully served or if the competent authority orders it. Released prisoners have the right to receive the belongings, values, and effects that belong to them and can also demand a certificate of the time served in deprivation of liberty (or on parole). A medical and therapeutic report can also be delivered to the released prisoner. In any case, according to Article 89 PC, the ordinary legal outcome of a penal sentence imposed upon a non-regular resident in Spain – except for certain crimes and offences (Article 89.4) - is expulsion (with the prohibition of returning to Spain in the next ten years)[81]. In fact, expulsion must be generally applied either as a substitute to imprisonment under six years (see also Art. 27 PR)[82] or, in the case of those prison sentences that equal or are longer than six years, subsequently to access to the third degree (open regime) or to the completion of three quarters of the punishment (see also Art. 26 PR).

Expulsion is also foreseen by Article 108 PC as a substitute to other measures of deprivation of freedom imposed in cases of criminal dangerousness of the foreigner (irregular residents). Furthermore, Article 57 of the Foreigners' Act (hereinafter FA), as well as the possibility of an administrative expulsion of those sentenced in Spain or abroad to an imprisonment sentence of more than one year (n.2), already evoked, allows equally the administrative expulsion in the pre-trial phase in cases of penal prosecution based on the commission of an offence punishable either by deprivation of freedom for up to six years or by any other punishment of a different nature (n.7)[83].

Jurisprudence does not consider any of the modalities of expulsion, including the one adopted after the full completion of the punishment, as a violation of the *ne bis in idem* principle. Nevertheless, literature repeatedly discusses the legitimacy of this kind of expulsion that punishes again the same offence that has already been sanctioned by the penal process[84]. The permanent extension of the possibilities of expulsion has also been deeply criticized, due to its difficult compatibility with constitutional provisions[85], as well as to the contradictions in the official arguments developed in order to defend this measure of penal policy and to the counterproductive effects generated not only in the concerned foreigner[86] and in the penal system itself, but even for the restrictive immigration policy officially maintained[87].

---

[81] Critically, Grupo de Estudios de Política Criminal, *Alternativas al tratamiento jurídico de la discriminación y de la extranjería*, Valencia 1998, p.52.

[82] In 2005, 1.229 inmates were expelled in this way. García García, J. , ibidem, p.6.

[83] In 2005, 140 inmates were expelled in this way. García García, J. , ibidem, p.6.

[84] See Muñoz Lorente, J., 'La expulsión del extranjero como medida sustitutiva de las penas privativas de libertad: el artículo 89 del CP tras su reforma por la Ley Orgánica 11/2003', *Revista de Derecho Penal y Criminología*, extra 2, 2004, p.415 (with a complete bibliography).

[85] Maqueda Abreu, M.L., '¿Es constitucional la expulsión penal del extranjero?, in *Los derechos humanos. Libro homenaje al Excmo.Sr.D.Luis Portero García*, Granada 2001, pp.509-518.

[86] García España, E.ibidem, 2001, p. 472.

[87] Cancio Meliá, M. & Maraver Gómez, in Bacigalupo, S. & Cancio Meliá, M (coord.), *Derecho penal y política transnacional*, Barcelona 2005, pp.385 ff.

After the 2003 reform[88], judges should nearly always pronounce the expulsion of convicted foreigners. Article 89.1 PC provides for only one exception: after having heard the prosecutor, the judge can reject the expulsion if the nature of the offence justifies the execution of the punishment in Spain. More exceptions to the automatic expulsion have, nevertheless, been admitted by jurisprudence, and the Supreme Court (1st July 2004) also deems hearing the convicted persons as necessary in order to consider all personal circumstances as well as the familiar and social links. This is particularly important in certain cases: the existence of minors dependent on the foreigner and resident in Spain; possibilities of victim compensation eventually frustrated by the execution of the expulsion decision; and conflict between the expulsion and the accomplishment of duties and obligations imposed on the convicted person, particularly in cases of domestic violence[89].

According to the Organic Act 19/2003, the expulsion has to be applied without delay and within 30 days. So long as the foreigner has not yet been expelled, the original punishment will be executed[90]. In any case, practice has shown how difficult the effective execution of expulsion is[91] and, although Articles 26 and 27 PR order the Director of the Establishment to notify to the competent authority of the date of leave with an anticipation of three months, few expulsions are really executed[92].

2.10 Aftercare – Probation

According to Article 73.1 PA and 30 PR, released prisoners have a right to rehabilitation, i.e. to the whole integration in the exercise of their citizens' rights. The Act even orders that the penal records should not be a basis for any discrimination, either social or juridical. Released prisoners who do not have enough economic means receive the money that is necessary for them to arrive to their residence and to cover their first expenditures (Art. 17.4 PA). Furthermore, if they worked in prison they can benefit from unemployment subsidies after registering with the unemployment office (Article 35 PA). Finally, every released prisoner can benefit in Spain from post-penitentiary social assistance that is provided by the ordinary social services to those persons without resources (Art. 74 f. PA; art. 229.2 PR). Nevertheless, in practice, specific post-penitentiary assistance is provided through the programs of the different NGOs that are active in this field.

In any case, concerning foreign prisoners, efforts developed at the penitentiary level and in the parole period with a view toward their social reintegration can have a definitive end after their final liberation, when the foreigner usually has only two alternatives:

---

[88]   Encinar del Pozo, M.A. , 'Expulsión de extranjeros: el artículo 89.1 del Código penal. Un ejemplo de infortunio del legislador', *Derecho.com*, March 2005, http://www.derecho.com/boletin /articulos/ articulo0278.htm

[89]   Encinar del Pozo, M.A. , ibidem.

[90]   If the expulsion has not been established according to Instruction 18/2005 (n.2.2), after the execution of half of the punishment (under six years) the penitentiary administration will communicate it to the tribunal to ask if the rest of the punishment can be substituted by the expulsion. If the punishment was equal to or more than six years, this communication will be implemented three months before the fulfilment of three-quarters of the penalty or as soon as the inmate is placed in the open regime.

[91]   García España, E. ibidem, pp. 61 ff. See also Silveira Gorski, H.C. , 'Los Centros de Internamiento de Extranjeros y el futuro del Estado de Derecho', *Mientras Tanto*, 83, 2002, p. 94.

[92]   Defensor del Pueblo, *Informe anual 2004*, Madrid 2005, pp. 477 ff.

expulsion or permanent irregularity[93]: rarely foreigners are exempted from the fulfilment of the general requirement of the absence of penal records in order to ask for a permission of residence or work. Furthermore, Article 57 FA – which is in principle applicable to any foreigner (legally resident or not) - establishes the fact of having been sentenced, in Spain or abroad, to an imprisonment term of more than one year because of an intentional offence as a reason for administrative expulsion, except if the penal records have been already annulled.

The Spanish Ombudsman has repeatedly insisted on the necessity of solving this difficult situation from a juridical and social point of view, or to those foreign citizens affected by non-executable decisions of expulsion: they are supposed to remain in Spain a certain (probably long) time but they cannot have legal access either to work or to the status of a resident. According to the Ombudsman, there are two basic alternatives concerning these persons: increasing the social support and assistance, or (much more appropriate, at least as a proposal to be studied) giving them a legal opportunity to have access (at least temporarily) to certain activities in order to allow them to live with a certain degree of dignity. With the retained payments for social charges, a special fund could be constituted that would be recoverable by the foreigner (through the consular authorities) if the expulsion is finally executed[94].

2.11 Staff

Special training courses, particularly for jurists and social workers are organized by the Prison Administration each year in order to help staff to better deal with issues concerning foreign prisoner. Access to these training programs is always on a voluntary basis. In order to deal with language barriers, special training in different languages is organised in connection with the Spanish Open University (UNED).

3 ADMINISTRATIVE DETENTION OF FOREIGN PRISONERS

Foreign citizens can be subjected to *police arrest*, like any other person. Police arrest is connected by Article 489 ff CPA with the commission of (or intent to commit) a serious or less serious penal offence (not for misdemeanours, if the individual has a known residence or gives enough guarantees).According to Article 17.2 of the Spanish Constitution, within 72 hours the arrested person must be released or put at the disposal of the judicial authority. Nevertheless, in cases of terrorism, the judge can authorize that the period of detention be extended by 48 hours. In addition, in these cases, the judge can place the arrested person in the situation of non-communication (Article 520 bis 1 and 2 CPA). This situation of *incommunicado* entails a restriction of some of the arrested person's rights, and particularly, the right to communicate the arrest (and the place where he/she is being detained) to his family (or to the Consulate, in cases of foreigners) and the right to choose his own lawyer: The lawyer in these cases is officially designated and cannot maintain any reserved communication with the arrested person before or after the declaration. This *incommunicado* status has been repeatedly criticized by the European Committee for the Pre-

---

93 Rodríguez Yagüe, C. ,ibidem, (II.1).
94 Defensor del Pueblo, ibidem, pp.480 ff.

vention of Torture and Inhuman or Degrading Treatment or Punishment (CPT)[95]. The CPT considers that from the very outset of custody, *incommunicado* persons should also be conferred these three rights: the full right of access to a lawyer, the right to have the fact of their detention communicated to a close relative or third party of their choice, and the right to a medical examination by a doctor of their choice (they are examined by the state-appointed doctor)[96].

Internment of irregular foreigners who are susceptible to be sanctioned by expulsion or who are waiting to be expelled or returned is also possible in Spain[97]. Article 61 1 (e) FA regulates preventive internment as a provisional measure (only applicable for the necessary time and never for more than 40 days)[98] adopted by the competent judge of instruction, after having heard the foreigner, and which is susceptible of judicial revision[99]. Such internment must be communicated to the Ministry of Foreign Affairs and to the foreigner's respective embassy or consulate (Article 62.3 FA). Article 62.2 forbids any new internment based on any of the elements of the same dossier. This is also applicable in cases of expulsion decisions adopted by other EU Member States[100].

Foreigners submitted to this administrative detention are confined in the "Centres for the internment of foreigners"[101], first created in 1985[102]. In the case of minors, detention is applied by those services competent in the protection of minors, but the juvenile judge can rule that the minor be detained with his/her parents in a centre for the internment of foreigners if the parents demand it, if the prosecutor has no objections, and the Centre can assure the family's privacy (Article 62.3 FA). In 2004, the existing Centres for the Internment of Foreigners in Spain (and Detention Centres) were:

---

[95] Report to the Spanish Government on the visit to Spain carried out by the European Committee for the Prevention of Torture and Inhuman or Degrading Treatment or Punishment (CPT) from 22 to 26 July 2001, CPT / Inf 2003 22, Strassbourg 2003.

[96] See the official answer of the Spanish Government: Respuesta del Gobierno Español al Informe del Comité Europeo para la Prevención de la Tortura y de las Penas o Tratos Inhumanos o Degradantes (CPT) sobre la visita España llevada a cabo del 22 al 26 de julio de 2001, CPT/Inf (2003)23, Estrasburgo 2003.

[97] See Article 61.1 e), 62, 64 1 & 3, 58.5 & 60 FA.

[98] See also Article 153 FR.

[99] See Defensor del Pueblo, *Informe sobre asistencia jurídica*, Madrid 2005 pp. 247 ff. On the necessity of assuring that the judicial decision comes before the 40 days have elapsed, ibidem, p. 247).

[100] Therefore, the important task of the lawyer in obtaining the necessary information in order to avoid new internments. Defensor del Pueblo , ibidem, p.241.

[101] According to Article 60.2 FA, foreigners waiting to be returned to their countries are only deprived of their freedom of movement and could be interned in other places, determined by the judge of instruction, so far as they are not of a penitentiary nature and provide social, juridical, and assistance services.

[102] Adam Muñoz, M.D. , 'El internamiento preventivo del extranjero durante la tramitación del expediente de expulsión", *La Ley*, 23 December 1991

Table 2

Centre	Capacity	Total internments	Average stay (days)	Daily average occupation
Algeciras	192	1.657	29	58%
Barcelona	111	1.516	19	74%
Fuerteventura(*)	1.070	7.044	31	44%
Gran Canaria	168	1.264	28	56%
Lanzarote(*)	200	616	25	29%
Madrid	75	3.378	27	85%
Málaga	110	2.469	127	92%
Murcia	60	2.981	14	71%
Tenerife	238	511	24	37%
Valencia	60	2.454	13	76%

(*) "Detention Centres"
(Source: Defensor del Pueblo (2005), Informe sobre asistencia jurídica, cit., pp. 228 ff.)

These public establishments do not have a penitentiary nature and thus are not integrated in the Penitentiary Administration. The General Direction of Police is competent to their management under the judicial control. Article 62[103] ff FA (partly introduced by OA14/2003) and Article 153 ff of the Foreigners' Regulation (Royal Decree 2392/2004; hereinafter FR) established the main regulation and provisions of these Centres, whose norms of functioning and internal regulation were approved by the Order of 22 February 1999[104], partially annulled by the Decision of the Supreme Court of 11 May 2005 (due to the restrictions introduced regarding the visits of the families and lawyers, control of mail correspondence, and the use of personal belongings).

Foreigners confined in the Centres maintain all rights not affected by the judicial measure of internment, and particularly those declared by Article 62 bis FA: the right to be informed on the situation; the right to life, physical integrity, and health; the right to dignity and privacy without being submitted to degrading treatments or any other form of mistreatment; the right to see facilitated the exercise of their legally recognized rights; the right to receive adequate medical and health assistance and to be assisted by the social services of the Centre; the right to communicate the internment to certain persons (including a lawyer and the consular authorities); the right to be assisted by a lawyer (officially designated if necessary) and to communicate with him and with their families, the consular authorities, and other persons (this right can be restricted only by a judicial decision); the right to be assisted by an interpreter; and to keep with them their minor children (in the conditions explained above).

---

[103] Reformed by OA 11/2003.
[104] See also the general rules established by the Decision of the Constitutional Tribunal n.115, 7 July 1987.

Confined persons must respect certain duties and obligations (Article 62 ter) and have to be informed of their rights and duties and about the Centre's general rules in a language that they can understand (Article 62 quáter). The Director of the Centre is the only entity competent to adopt the decision of applying physical means of contention whenever needed (except in cases of urgency). In any case, he/she must immediately communicate these incidents to the judge who authorized the internment of the foreigner who is the only competent person to maintain or to put an end to the execution of the measure of preventive separation of the potential aggressor (Article 62 quinquies).

Life inside the Centres is regulated by Chapter V of the 1999 Order, which also establishes the juridical statute of the interned foreigners (Article 27). Whenever possible, administrative detainees are accommodated, if they want, with other foreigners of the same nationality or with a similar language or customs (Article 25). Two hours in the yard and eight hours of sleep are guaranteed daily (Article 29), and they can receive visits and make telephone calls (Article 30). The direction of the Centre has to assure and respect the religious freedom of the detained foreigners and facilitate religious practices (Article 32). The right of petition and complaint before the Director and the Spanish Ombudsman, and the right of appeal (before the judge of instruction) are also guaranteed (Article 33).

Administrative detention is designed to assure the presence of a foreigner during the administrative procedure and the execution of the expulsion order; so it should never last longer than is necessary for those purposes. In this sense, Article 4.3 of the 1999 Order establishes that as soon as the government verifies the impossibility of execution of the expulsion within 40 days, it has to be communicated to the judge in order to put an end to the measure[105]. Criticism of these "hidden prisons"[106], continuously increasing in a number of places, are multiple and very important, due to the overpopulation, the inadequate facilities (where the penitentiary architecture dominates)[107], the hard conditions of life inside, the situation of non-defence of the confined foreigners, secrecy and lack of transparency, the lack of interpreters, and the absence of regular medical service. The Spanish Ombudsman has also repeatedly denounced the unacceptable conditions of these Centres[108].

4 NATIONALS DETAINED ABROAD

In June 2005, the number of Spanish people detained abroad was 1.485 (1.072 because of drug offences: most of them for small trafficking, some of them because of drug use)[109]. The most important countries of detention in recent years have been France (more than 200 in 2003) as well as the USA (143), Portugal (139), Germany (124), Italy (75), and the United Kingdom (74). Leading non-European countries are (apart from the USA) Venezuela (103), Morocco (96), Ecuador (80), Peru (79), Colombia (40).[110]

---

[105] See also Article 39.

[106] http:www.nodo50.org/detensajuridica/article.php3?id_article=13

[107] Defensor del Pueblo, *Informe sobre asistencia jurídica*, ibidem, p.227.

[108] See for instance, *Informe Anual* , ibidem, pp. 441 ff.

[109] http://www.pnsd.msc.es/prensa/2005/nota45.htm

[110] http://www.espamundo.org/informesyestadisticas/estadisticas%202003.htm

Assistance of Spanish people detained abroad is under the competence of the Ministry of Foreign Affairs. According to the norms and instructions applicable thereto[111] the system of assistance and protection falls under the responsibility of the Diplomatic Representatives and Consular Offices in the concerned country. The main aim is to provide Spanish citizens with adequate treatment and respect of their rights from the penitentiary authorities, particularly in those countries where the objective conditions are more deficient. With this purpose, as soon as the detention is known, consulates must get in contact with the local authorities in order to obtain all available information and to assure that the situation will not be prolonged without any evident reason and to make sure that the treatment received by the Spanish detainee is at least similar to the best treatment received by the nationals of the concerned country.

The different modalities of intervention include[112]:

- visits, according to the particular situation and as soon as the citizen demands to be visited in a motivated way. In general, a visit every two months is foreseen if the penitentiary centre is close to the consulate or embassy and in other cases at least twice a year. If it is difficult to visit the detainee, a monthly communication by post should at least be maintained;
- notification of the detention (and eventually of the prison sentence) to the prisoner's family and friends, if the detainee authorizes it. As well as all types of assistance to facilitate the communication between them and with the local authorities in order to attain more information on the case and the bureaucratic procedures;
- assistance finding a lawyer and/or to obtain free legal assistance in case of scarce economic resources; payment of the lawyer's honoraries if this is not possible or if the foreseen sentence could very grave;
- assistance to buy food, clothes, and medicines, if necessary; whenever needed; detainees can receive up to 100 Euros per month in order to allow them to cover their basic needs;
- educational assistance.

On the other hand, either by way of the Convention n° 112 of the Council of Europe, or of the bilateral treaties signed by Spain with the same aim, Spanish citizens sentenced in more than 70 countries have the possibility to be transferred to Spain in order to serve their sentence[113]. In cases where a prisoner desires to be transferred, consular and diplomatic representatives assist him/her in the bureaucratic procedures, which usually take too long (between one and one and a half years) due to the complicated documentation (that must be translated) and to the difficulties to negotiate and establish the exact date of the transfer.

According to the *Defensor del Pueblo*[114], the most frequent claims of Spanish prisoners detained abroad are the delay in the bureaucratic procedures, the bad conditions of the

---

[111] http://www.espamundo.org/Consulares/Indicecirculares.htm

[112] http://www.mac.es/es/MenuPpal/Consulares/Servicios+Consulares/Españoles+en+el+extranjero/ Asistencia+a+detenidos/

[113] In 2004 the Spanish Ministry of Justice received 219 demands and repatriated 175 detainees. http://www.pnsd.msc.es/prensa/2005/nota45.htm

[114] http://www.espamundo.org/informesyestadisticas/informe_del_defensor_del_pueblo%202005. htm. The special difficulties suffered by the drivers of vehicles of transport by road in cases of transport of illicit goods without their knowledge also merit a particular attention.

foreign prisons, and the procedural irregularities. Along with the frequent lack of cooperation of the local authorities, practice shows how often detainees are not informed by
lawyers of the possibilities of assistance. At the same time, the field of discretion of the
consular and diplomatic offices is very important and produces great differences in the intervention even within the same country. Certainly, stricter legal regulation of the assistance of detainees abroad could help to improve the organization of this system. In order
to establish this, in 1999 an interesting and complete proposal was presented to the Senate to approve an Act regulating the assistance and protection of Spanish people deprived
of their freedom abroad[115]. However, regrettably the proposal was not taken into consideration.

In the Senate, in 2000, again a Special Committee was established in order to examine the juridical, personal, and familiar situation of Spanish citizens detained in foreign
prisons. In 2002, the Special Committee presented its proposals and recommendations[116],
of which the following should be specially highlighted:
- to produce an informative booklet to be distributed by the travel agencies;
- to promote a communitarian multilateral action in order to objectify the responsibility
  of the driver of transport vehicles by road, in case of illicit traffic;
- to strengthen the measures of help, particularly legal assistance, in cases that can lead
- to capital punishment, and to consider the possibility of paying fines (totally or in part)
  in special circumstances;
- to promote the action of the consuls in order to gather all the Spanish detainees in
- establishments located near the places where the consulates are located;
- the subscription of agreements with the local NGO and the provision of personnel
  specialized in cooperation and social work in order to assist the consuls;
- the improvement of the mechanisms of transfer of prisoners and the reform of the
  penitentiary legislation in order to better regulate the arrival and internment in Spanish prisons of the Spanish citizens sentenced abroad.

5 EVALUATION AND RECOMMENDATIONS

- The consistent and ongoing increase of the penitentiary population in Spain has
  been accompanied by a progressively higher proportion of foreign prisoners,
  mainly due to the more frequent application of pre-trial detention. Considering
  the nature of the offences generally committed by them as well as their personal
  and social characteristics, more efforts in the search for real alternatives to pre-trial
  detention would be very much advisable.
- Every day life shows the institutional discrimination towards foreign prisoners, due
  to the insufficiency of the specific normative provisions and their personal and social circumstances; both create barriers to their participation in penitentiary life, to
  the enjoyment of permission of leave and visits, and particularly to access to the
  open regime and conditional release.

---

[115] Boletín Oficial de las Cortes Generales. Senado. VI Legislatura, Serie III A: 15 (a), 26 February
1999.
[116] Boletín Oficial de las Cortes Generales. Senado. VII Legislatura, Serie I, 514, 16 October 2002.

- The first purpose of any penitentiary policy concerning foreign prisoners should be to facilitate communication. In this sense, simultaneously to the specific training of staff and the promotion of ways to learn Spanish, the professional collaboration of interpreters in prison should be reinforced in order to cover the specific need of communication and information of foreign prisoners inside the prison (particularly in disciplinary proceedings) and with their lawyers. Making cheaper telephone calls available and sending the prisoners to an establishment located closer to their respective countries' borders could also be considered in order to improve visits and communication.

- It is absolutely necessary to put an end to the extended practice of automatic identification in the absence of regular documentation and a high risk of evasion. A criterion should be developed – also at the penitentiary level – that takes all available information into account (level of knowledge of Spanish, existing social links...). On the other hand, systems of control such as retention of documentation or electronic surveillance could be very useful in order to allow a broader field of application for permissions for leave, access to the open regime or conditional release.

- However, and notwithstanding other interventions than the coordination with consulates and embassies and establishing points of contact with the families, emphasis should be placed in the intensification of the possibilities of collaboration of those NGOs in the penitentiary field that work in favour of foreign prisoners. In fact, they could be the best support in order to fight against non-communication and in the defence of foreign prisoners' rights, as well as in the search for (work) programmes and activities outside. At the same time, these entities could provide the foreign prisoners with the social support that is required in order to have access to leave, the open regime, and conditional release. Furthermore, their collaboration would also be fundamental in the development of those programmes of preparation for re-integration in their own countries, which are becoming increasingly needed as the expulsion's weight in relation to foreign offenders is increasing.

- The combination of provisions of the Foreigners Act and the Penal Code determine a broad field of possibilities to expel imprisoned foreigners, foreigners in the pre-trial phase, as a substitute (totally or partially) for punishment, or even after the sentence has been served. Although often considered purely as an instrument of restrictive immigration policy, this penal policy is also criticized because of its counterproductive effects even in that regard. Among the most important problems generated by the expulsion order, the situation of those foreign citizens affected by non-executable decisions of expulsion, who presumably will remain in Spain a long time, merits special attention in order to search for adequate solutions not only by way of increasing the social support and assistance that they are entitled to, but, preferably, by studying the possibility of providing them with legal access to certain work.

- The "Centres for the internment of foreigners" generate multiple and very important criticism, due to their overcrowding, the inadequate facilities, the hard conditions of life inside, secrecy, lack of transparency, and the lack of interpreters. It is absolutely necessary to improve the conditions of these facilities (which are still too similar to prisons) and services, and to assure better legal assistance of the detained foreigners, admitting visits from lawyers without further restrictions (with an interpreter if the establishment does not provide one). It would also be advisable to have a legal regulation of the foreigner's audience by the judge, respecting the principles of contradiction and defence and the introduction of guarantees in order to avoid delays due to bureaucracy, and to assure the fulfilment of Article 62.2, which forbids any new internment based on any of the elements of the same dossier, a provision that should equally apply if the expulsion's dossier comes from another European Union Member.

- Regarding Spanish prisoners in foreign countries, most of them are concentrated in Europe and the USA. In Morocco and some Latin-American countries the figures are also quite high. Existing programs of assistance try to assure the communication with the prisoners and try to cover their fundamental needs, particularly in those cases in which prisoners have scarce resources and in those countries with deficient penitentiary conditions. The regulation leaves a broad field to the discretion of consular and diplomatic representatives. Better regulation at a higher legal level is to be recommended and, at the same time, the reinforcement of personal means (social workers) in those consulates that have to deal with numerous prisoners in distant establishments. Subscription of agreement in order to gather the Spanish detainees in establishments located near the consulate's location and with local NGOs, as well as the improvement of mechanisms for the transfer of prisoners, would be equally advisable.

Chapter 25

Sweden

Agneta K. Johnson

1 INTRODUCTION[1]

1.1 Overview of sanctions and measures[2]

Detention can be carried out as police detention in police detention centres, as remand in custody in remand prisons, as prison sentences in ordinary prisons and as the detention measures of the Migration Board in its detention centres[3]. Only the punishments provided for under general or special penal legislation can properly be called sanctions. The Swedish Penal Code provides for the main sanctions as follows.

Fines are imposed as day-fines or summary fines. Day-fines are imposed on a scale of from 30 to 150 days, the number of days corresponding to the seriousness of the offence. For each day a sum of money that takes account of the financial situation of the offender shall be paid. A prosecutor where guilt is admitted and a summary fine is accepted may impose summary fines for the less serious offences.

Imprisonment is imposed for a fixed term of from 14 days to ten years or for life. Under certain special circumstances a fixed term may be extended to up to 18 years. Currently, release from a life sentence is possible following commutation by the government of the indeterminate life sentence to one of specified duration, when the normal rules of conditional release apply. It is likely that in the near future a court and not the government will be authorized by legislation to take the decision on commutation. A life sentence usually means 18 – 25 years in prison. Those sentenced to a fixed term of ordinary imprisonment are automatically subject to conditional release when two-thirds of the sentence, but at least one month, has been served. Conditional release may, however, be postponed as a disciplinary punishment. Currently, those sentenced to up to three months' imprisonment may request that the sentence be served in the community under intensive supervision by the probation service and with electronic monitoring. In order to assist the transition from prison to life in the community, those sentenced to more than four years' imprisonment may be provisionally released under intensive supervision with electronic monitoring up to four months before the formal date for conditional release is reached

A court may impose a conditional sentence when a fine is considered an inadequate sanction for the offence. A conditional sentence can be combined with day-fines or, if the offender consents, with community service. During a probationary period of two years the offender must abstain from further offences. A breach of this condition means that the court when sentencing may take account of the original and the new offence. A conditional sentence may be thought of as a serious penal warning.

A court may impose the sanction of probation when a fine is considered an inadequate sanction for the offence. Probation may be combined with day-fines or, if the of-

[1] First and foremost, I would like to thank Norman Bishop for agreeing to edit the final document and thereby allowing me to learn from his wealth of experience. I thank Niclas Åkesson for his ongoing support and assistance and Sophia Tegenfeldt for her help in collecting information. I wish also to express my gratitude to Gunhild Fridh at the Swedish Prison and Probation Administration and Per-Åke Palmquist, Governor of Hall Prison, for recommending me for, and entrusting me with, the present study.

[2] Prison and Probation in Sweden 2005 (Kriminalvård i Sverige 2005) and The Swedish Judicial System-a brief introduction.

[3] These Migration Board detention measures are described in section C of this study

fender consents, with community service. Regular probation means that the offender is under supervision by the probation service, usually for one year. Probation may also be combined with special treatment, usually in cases where alcohol or drug misuse is related to the commission of crime. Probation combined with community service has existed since 1999. The offender undertakes unpaid work of use to the community for from 40 to 240 hours[4].

If the offender is under 18 years of age, or is a substance abuser convicted of a petty offence, or is found to be in need of forensic psychiatric care, the court may decide to surrender the offender to special care. For the young offender such special care could involve being placed in closed juvenile care for a specified period of time. The substance abuser may be committed for care under the Act for the Care of Addicts, and the offender with psychiatric problem may be sentenced to compulsory psychiatric care in accordance with the Act on Forensic Psychiatric Care.

When choosing the sanction, the courts must consider imprisonment to be a more severe sanction than conditional sentence or probation. The Penal Code requires the court to pay special attention to any circumstances that argue for a less severe punishment than imprisonment. In consequence the courts tend to impose the least intrusive sentence possible. By far, the most commonly imposed sanctions are the least severe. Out of 58600 sanctions imposed in 2004, 22000 were fines (38%). In the same year the other sanctions used included 15117 prison sentences (26%), 9000 conditional sentences (15%) and 6000 sentences of probation (10%).

1.2 Overview of the prison system

1.2.1 Organisational structure

The Swedish Prison and Probation Administration, located in Norrköping, is responsible for the management of the prison and probation services throughout the country. Although it is organisationally subordinate to the Ministry of Justice, constitutional law gives it a high degree of independence for the day-to-day management of these services.

The Swedish Prison and Probation Services seek to: ensure that prisoners are always treated with respect for their retained human rights; that prisons are safe and secure places for prisoners, staff and visitors and that more effective ways of influencing offenders to become law-abiding citizens are developed.

Local independent supervision boards take certain local decisions concerning prisoners, probationers and parolees – notably those involving special measures occasioned by breaches of conditions. These boards consist of a chairman, deputy chairman and three ordinary members. The chairman is always a judge.

Administrative decisions concerning prisoners can be appealed first to the central Administration and thereafter, by leave, to an administrative court of appeal. Any offender can also present a complaint to the Parliamentary Justice Ombudsman who may also investigate prison and probation practice on his own initiative. Serious improper practice can lead to prosecution. The Equal Opportunities Ombudsman and the Dis-

---

[4]   A full account of Swedish probation is to be found in: M. Lindholm and N. Bishop Sweden, Probation and Probation Services, ed. A. Van Kalmthout and T.M.J. Derks, 2000 pp. 523-542.

crimination Ombudsman[5] can also exercise an influence on prison and probation practice.

In addition to the central Prison and Probation Administration there are six regional offices with three divisions for remand prisons, ordinary prisons and probation. A separate transportation service transports prisoners within Sweden as well as abroad. In 2004, there were 29 remand prisons, 56 ordinary prisons and 39 probation offices in Sweden. The nominal number of available places in the prisons is 4619 prison places and 1931 in the remand prisons. Prisons are divided into different categories from A (maximum security) to F, (open conditions). Male and female prisoners are housed in separate accommodation. The five prisons in Sweden for female offenders (about 7% of the received prison population) hold approximately 250 prisoners.

In 2004, the total cost of the prison and probation services was approximately € 560 million[6]. In the same year, the daily average cost of a probationer or parolee was approximately € 16[7], while the daily average cost for prisoners in varying security conditions was between € 200 and € 622.

An estimated 60% of the prisoners received during 2004 had a documented drug addiction. The Prison and Probation Services have received special governmental funds to address the problem of drug addiction. This has led to the setting-up of special prison wings or units where emphasis is placed on treating drug misuse. Approximately 27% of available prison places are retained for treatment work with drug misusing prisoners. In 2004 approximately 46% of all drug-misusing prisoners participated in some form of drug misuse treatment programme[8].

1.2.2 Foreign prisoners

Of the 11343 prisoners received into prison during 2004, 8340 (74%) were Swedish citizens, 710 (6%) were other Nordic citizens leaving 2293 prisoners (20%) with citizenship distributed among 66 other countries. There are no routine statistics or special studies that describe the nature and extent of linguistic handicap among foreign prisoners. Nevertheless, it is not unreasonable to suppose that such a handicap exists to a considerable extent and is a contributory factor to social exclusion.

Individual allocation assessments are made on all prisoners prior to prison placement. This assessment, which is more in-depth with prison sentences of over four years, evaluates *inter alia* the risk of escape. Two prisons have special units with a capacity of 96 places for those with expulsion orders in their sentence. Some foreign citizens with expulsion orders may be placed in more open settings (security class E). The prison units housing those with expulsion orders are similar to the kitchen, sports, library facilities, etc. of other ordinary prison units.

---

[5]   R. Höök, et.al., pp..59-60.
[6]   Prison and Probation Statistics (Kriminalvårdens Officiella Statistik) 2004, p. 9
[7]   Ibidem p.42
[8]   Prison and Probation Statistics (Kriminalvårdens Officiella Statistik) 2004, pp.47-48

1.3. Overview of the involvement of consulates, embassies, home-country ministries, home country probation service, non-governmental organisations, etc.

The main objective for diplomatic missions in their work for foreign prisoners is to serve in a supporting capacity. This can include providing guidance to prisoners about national legislative and administrative provisions and practice. However, the extent of contact between foreign prisoners and the diplomatic representatives of their countries varies between the countries involved and is also dependent on the wishes of the individual prisoner. This variation can mean that in addition to social support some diplomatic missions provide the prisoner with financial assistance, for example paying for telephone cards, while others have little or no contact with their prisoners. Variation in the nature of the contact with the prisoner means that some consular representatives may visit the prisoner while others stay in touch by telephone.

Some countries require their embassies to report to a home administration if they learn that a national is suspected of an offence in the host country. This presumably means that the person in question is registered in the home country's criminal records. It is by no means certain that such a registration is annulled if the suspect is subsequently cleared of suspicion.

Several non-governmental organisations are active within the prison setting with some providing volunteer prison visitors and some providing information to prisoners in their own language[9]. Most of these organisations also visit foreign citizens held in Migration Board detention centres.

1.4 Overview of Trends

1.4.1 Sentencing trends

There is a trend towards an increase in the lengths of prison sentences especially for violent crime, sexual offences and drug related crime. The daily average of incarcerated individuals (in the remand prisons and regular prisons) is expected to increase from 6870 in 2006 to 7600 in 2009[10]. So far as lengths of prison sentences are concerned there has been a 25% increase in the number of those sentenced to more than one year and less than four years, from 1431 in the year 2000 to 1802 in 2005. Similarly, the number of those sentenced to prison for four years or more increased by 37%[11]. In 2003 the average length of sentence among those received into prison was 318 days as compared with 278 days in 1988, an increase in average time of 40 days. It is estimated that an average increase of one week in sentence length occurring in the future would necessitate the provision of an additional 200 prison places[12].

The number of offenders within the prison and probation services is influenced to no small extent by the work practices of other sections of the criminal justice system. Thus, a number of changes in other parts of the criminal justice system can be expected to lead to

---

9 An example is KRIS, an ex-prisoner organisation that seeks to help prisoners on release, which has information material available in Lithuanian.

10 Prison and Probation Budget (Kriminalvårdens Budgetunderlag) 2007, p.9-10.

11 Prison and Probation Statistics (Kriminalvårdens Officiella Statistik) 2005 pp.44-63.

12 Prison and Probation Budget (Kriminalvårdens Budgetunderlag) 2006, p.9.

an increase in the prison population. Such changes include the following. There is a proposal to increase the number of police officers from today's number of 16700 to 18400 in 2008. A change is likely in legislation that will provide for the increased use of DNA evidence where serious crime is concerned.

In the year 2002 the daily average number of remanded and sentenced prisoners amounted to 73 per 100000 persons in the national population. By 2004 this number had risen to 82 prisoners per 100000 in the national population[13].

Throughout 2005 the daily average number of cases under supervision by the probation services was 12583. Of this number 4819 were on regular probation, 1268 were probationers with a condition of undergoing treatment and 1179 were probationers performing community service. A further 313 cases concerned offenders sentenced to up to three months' imprisonment who served their sentence in the community under intensive supervision combined with electronic monitoring. Intensive supervision with electronic monitoring was also provided for a small number of prisoners with sentences of more than two years – 74 on average – released for up to four months before the formal date for conditional release. In addition to the foregoing, the probation services also supervised a daily average of 4 930 conditionally released prisoners. Statistics show that the total number of clients under probation or post-release supervision have increased only marginally during the past 10 years - from 12632 in 1995 to 12722 in 2004.

Trends in the number and citizenship of foreign offenders cannot legitimately be inferred from the statistics on the *daily average* numbers under supervision. For this question *annual input* statistics are required. The statistics show that the number of foreign prisoners with expulsion orders has increased – from 397 in 1995 to 447 in 2000 and to 809 in 2005. The following two tables present the statistics in somewhat greater detail. Table 1 shows the absolute numbers and percentage proportions of sentenced Swedish, Nordic and other foreign prisoners received into the prisons during 1995, 2000 and 2005 (rounded percentages in brackets).

Table 1

Year	Swedish	Nordic	Other countries	Total
1995	11,061 (79 %)	975 (7%)	2,005 (14 %)	14,041 (100 %)
2000	6,874 (71 %)	699 (7%)	2,052 (21 %)	9,625 (100 %)
2005	7,680 (72%)	596 (6%)	2,380 (22 %)	10,656 (100 %)

The absolute numbers of foreign prisoners coming from the Nordic countries decreased markedly between 1995 and 2005 while the absolute numbers of foreign prisoners coming from other countries increased somewhat during the same period. Table 2 shows, for the years 1995, 2000 and 2005, the numbers and percentage proportions of sentenced foreign prisoners coming from the Nordic countries and other countries with and without expulsion orders (rounded percentages in brackets).

---

13 Ibidem.

Table 2

Year	Nordic Expulsion	Nordic No expulsion	Other countries Expulsion	Other countries No expulsion	Total
1995	34 (1%)	941 (32 %)	363 (12%)	1,642 (55 %)	2,980
2000	36 (1%)	663 (24%)	411 (15 %)	1,641 (60 %)	2,751
2005	13 (<1%)	583 (20 %)	796 (27%)	1,584 (53%)	2,976

For the years 2000 and 2005 there was a diminution in the absolute numbers of all prisoners coming from the Nordic countries and in the number of expulsion orders made. By contrast, the absolute numbers of expulsion orders for prisoners coming from other countries more than doubled between 1995 and 2005 although the absolute numbers of all prisoners received from those countries remained roughly similar. In year 2005, 1649 foreign citizens began supervision carried out by the probation services. Of this number 58% were conditionally released prisoners[14].

1.4.2 Characteristics of the foreign prisoner population

Few statistics are kept and no studies have been conducted that describe objectively the characteristics of the foreign prisoner population. That this is so is presumably because there it is a general policy to treat the foreign prisoner population as much as possible in the same way as the national prisoner population. This means that discrimination is to be avoided and that foreign prisoners should have the same guarantees of fair and proper prison treatment as national prisoners. A few facts emerge from routinely kept statistics[15].

In 2005, a total of 2976 foreign prisoners were received into the prisons. Of this number, 809 (27%) were subject to expulsion, 95% were men and 5% women. The age distribution of 85% of the total number of foreign prisoners received was as follows: 6% were 18-20, 15% were 21-24, 22% were 25-29, 17% were 30-44 and 25% were 35-44. Sentences of six months or less were being served by 63% of this population whilst just over 16% were serving sentences of two years or more. Of this latter group five persons had been given life sentences.

Thefts and violent offences had been committed by 36% of foreign prisoners and 20% had committed drug or smuggling offences. Only 3% had committed sexual offences and 4% had committed robberies.

Certain perceptions of youthful foreign prisoners suggest that they often are, or feel themselves to be, socially excluded. Thus, in a study conducted by Prison and Probation Administration in 2001[16], staff and prisoners from 22 remand and ordinary prisons were interviewed. Prison staff perceived prisoners with a foreign background as being overrepresented amongst prisoners less than 21 years of age. Prison statistics from 2000 show that these youthful foreign prisoners occupied 61% of the places for young prisoners[17]. However, it should be noted that the term foreign background included second-generation

---

[14] Prison and Probation Statistics (Kriminalvårdens Officiella Statistik) 2005.
[15] Ibidem.
[16] Young men in prison and remand prisons (Unga Män i Anstalt och Häkte Slutrapport) February 2001.
[17] Ibidem p.33.

immigrants. Staff at one of the prisons visited by the writer[18] described their prisoners in these terms: "Many of our youthful prisoners are immigrants... it appears that social exclusion in the community is a problematic situation for many of these [youngsters][19]". Prisoners interviewed in this study spontaneously commented upon the general social welfare situation, saying, for example, "The outside world is significantly harsher than the inside of a prison" and "Many prisoners are scared of life outside [prison][20]". It would seem, therefore, that securing the social integration of young persons of foreign origin is probably an urgent preventive measure and at least as important as securing the social integration of youthful prisoners on release from prison.

1.5 Overview of national legislation

1.5.1 Penitentiary legislation

The Swedish Penal Code regulates *inter alia* the sanction of imprisonment and, to some extent, the way in which it is implemented, notably in providing for mandatory release when two-thirds of a fixed term of imprisonment has been served, the postponement of mandatory release as a disciplinary punishment and the procedure for commuting a life sentence to a fixed term of imprisonment. The Swedish Code of Judicial Procedure regulates *inter alia* decisions on the provisional detention of suspects and court trial procedures.

The Prison Treatment Act and relevant Ordinances provide for the more detailed regulation of prison work. The Act contains provisions on showing respect for prisoners, on the principles for their allocation to prisons varying from those with a high degree of security to open prisons, the conditions under which the imprisonment is to be enforced and the possibilities of appeal against administrative decisions. The Act emphasises the importance of seeking to prepare prisoners to lead law-abiding lives on release and, to that end, provides for work, education and treatment programmes as well as for contact with the outside world through letters, visits, telephone calls and leaves from prison. Since a high proportion of prisoners are dependent on drugs there are provisions on searching and checking for drugs, including urine tests.

The Law on Arrested and Remanded Persons and the relevant Ordinances provide for the imposition of these measures and the juridical safeguards that are to be employed.

1.5.2 Penitentiary legislation and foreign prisoners

The Prison Treatment Act is designed to regulate the treatment of all prisoners. There are, therefore, no provisions in the Act that relate specifically to the treatment of foreign prisoners. There are, however, other national laws and international legal instruments that impinge upon the conditions of carrying out imprisonment and, especially, on the transfer of foreign prisoners to their home countries. Thus, the Law on the Obligation to Transmit Information on Detained Foreigners regulates, and in certain cases limits, the obligation to inform a diplomatic mission when a foreign national is detained. The Aliens

---

[18] Täby Prison.

[19] Young men in prison and remand prisons (Unga Män i Anstalt och Häkte Slutrapport) February 2001, p.21.

[20] Prisoners, Prisons and Society (Fångarna, Fängelset och Samhället), p.14.

Act and relevant Ordinances, *inter alia*, govern immigration and citizenship questions, and, in particular, the conditions under which administrative detention can be used.

Sweden has ratified the European Convention on the International Validity of Criminal Judgements[21] and the European Convention on the Transfer of Sentenced Persons including the additional protocol[22] that regulates the compulsory transfer of foreign prisoners with expulsion orders. The latter Convention has shown itself to be the most useful in practice. The European Convention on the Transfer of Sentenced Persons is primarily based on the notion that a transfer can take place if both the countries concerned and the individual prisoner agree to the transfer. Prisoners are to be informed of their right to apply for transfer when the court's verdict is final. Processing time[23] for such transfers according to data from 2005[24] was 13 months. They should have at least six months remaining to serve when applying and they must be domiciled in a country party to the Convention. As mentioned above, the additional Protocol permits compulsory transfer to take place where an expulsion order has been made.

If a prisoner wishes to apply for transfer to a country not having signed a transfer Convention, such application is sent to the relevant Ministry of Justice for processing. Bilateral agreements have been made with Thailand and Cuba.

The compulsory transfer of prisoners in accordance with the additional Protocol mentioned above took on average 14½ months to process[25]. Transfers between the Nordic countries can take place if the offender is domiciled in, or is a citizen of, a Nordic country and has at least three months remaining to be served of the sentence. These transfers can usually be arranged reasonably swiftly and with minimum formalities.

2 TREATMENT OF FOREIGN PRISONERS

2.1 General

In certain respects the treatment of foreign prisoners is not, and should not be, different from the treatment of national prisoners. They are entitled to the same respect for their individual human value and to be offered the same legal guarantees of just, fair and humane treatment.

If they are not subject to an expulsion order, they should have access to the same forms of assistance as national prisoners. In particular, this means access to vocational, educational and welfare assistance. However, it must be admitted that this ideal is, in practice, subject to limitations arising often from difficulties associated with a poor knowledge of the Swedish language. Thus, a small number of persons interviewed in connection with the recent study[26] did not consider that there was much discrimination based upon race, skin colour or the like. However, they considered that prisoners because of a

---

[21] SÖ 1973:55, 2000:45.

[22] SÖ 1985:1 and 2000:53.

[23] From time of application to the actual time of transfer.

[24] Annual results reported to the government (Kriminalvården, Återrapportering enligt Regleringsbrevet) 2005.

[25] Between initiating and completing transfer.

[26] The number of subjects interviewed was limited to three foreign prisoners and 12 staff (three with foreign backgrounds).

poor understanding of the Swedish language could experience a sense of social exclusion. This appears to be the most prominent difficulty of foreign prisoners

The position of those subject to an expulsion order is clearly different and makes special demands on the way in which they should be treated. Their treatment depends on a number of factors including, for example, their criminal history and the length of the sentence. In general, the courts are empowered to reduce the length of sentence to be imposed taking into account, where appropriate, the fact of expulsion. Any risk assessment made on entry into prison will also strongly influence prison allocation and opportunities to be granted leave.

In 2004, after riots had taken place within three prisons, research was conducted[27] into the possible causes. The research method included interviewing 11 prisoners and 15 staff members, with experience of having been incarcerated in, or working at, a prison where a riot had taken place. One interview question presented to the prisoners was whether they had experienced discrimination – either between staff and prisoners or between prisoners – based on country of origin. Most prisoners felt that staff treated foreign prisoners similarly to national prisoners; they had not experienced discrimination between prisoners based on country of origin. Nevertheless, treating all prisoners alike regardless of nationality, or more precisely regardless of the language they speak, poses great difficulties in some areas that will be described below.

2.2 Living conditions and facilities

The basic living conditions of Swedish prisons must be deemed to be of a high material standard. Furniture, bedding, heating and lighting, living and recreational space are, for example, uniformly of good quality. Most prisoners' single rooms are approximately six square metres in size and equipped with a bed, desk, chair, TV and radio. Prisoners in closed prisons are locked in their rooms between 20.00 and 08.00 hours. There are communication devices that enable them to contact staff during these hours. Prisons vary in size, and are, in comparison with those in many European countries, relatively small, with some holding only about 40 prisoners. A prison that will hold 342 prisoners is currently under construction[28] and on completion will be the largest prison in Sweden.

Foreign prisoners have access to the same living conditions as other prisoners. Even for prisoners with expulsion orders kitchens, sports equipment, libraries, size of rooms, etc are all similar to what is provided in other prison units, something that is agreed upon by prisoners interviewed for this study.

As mentioned above, a sizeable number of prisoners, both national and foreign, are substance abusers. In consequence, prison administrations are compelled to undertake ceaseless control activities to restrict the illicit use of drugs in the prisons. In particular, legislation permits the widespread use of urine tests. The provision of urine samples has to be undertaken under the careful observation of basic grade prison staff. A considerable proportion of basic grade staff in male prisons consists of women prison officers. Foreign prisoners with other cultural values may feel a sense of shame over having to be naked when leaving urine samples or being searched. This feeling of shame is compounded when a male prisoner must be naked in front of a female basic grade prison officer.

---

[27] The Berserkers; a report on prison riots (Bärsärkarna) pp. 39-49.
[28] Salberga Prison.

Prison Regulations[29] state that "If a male prisoner does not wish to leave a urine sample in the presence of female staff, male staff shall be present instead if this can conveniently be arranged". So far as searching is concerned, Rule 54(5) of the recently revised European Prison Rules provides that "persons shall only be searched by staff of the same gender". In practice, prison staffs usually try to meet the prisoner's request for someone of the same gender to perform these duties.

2.3 Reception and admission

The Prison Treatment Act [30] states that when deciding upon the allocation of prisoners to open or closed prisons "a prisoner should be placed in an open prison if no other placement is required for reasons of security or because an opportunity which should be provided for him or her to undertake some form of work, education or training cannot suitably be provided in an open prison. When assessing whether security considerations require placement in a closed prison, consideration shall be given *inter alia* to whether there is a danger that the prisoner will escape or continue in criminal activity. In addition, the prisoner should ordinarily be placed in a closed prison if there is a risk that he or she may misuse drugs or in some other way deal with drugs during the enforcement of the sentence".

For prisoners sentenced to more than four years' imprisonment, a special assessment is made prior to placement. This assessment includes a risk analysis of how escape-prone the prisoner may be. Here, foreign prisoners, at least those with expulsion orders, frequently end up in more secure prison settings than a national with the same length of sentence. This is because it is believed that foreign prisoners serving long prison sentences with subsequent expulsion may well have an increased incitement to escape. However, certain prisoners with expulsion orders and serving shorter sentences may in fact be placed in open (class E) prisons. This can give rise to an anomalous practice that can be illustrated as follows.

A prisoner serving a six-month sentence can be placed in an E class prison for the four months that he must serve, and then he is released and deported. Another prisoner, sentenced to six years' having served 5 ½ years, who wishes to be transferred to a class E prison for his final six months, is most commonly not permitted to do so. Although an expulsion order in itself creates a presumption of a sizeable escape risk this does not prevent certain short-term prisoners with expulsion orders from being allocated from the start to an open prison. Yet, a longer-term prisoner with expulsion orders in a closed prison who has demonstrated a complete absence of escape behaviour is denied re-allocation to an open prison for a short period. Foreign prisoners with longer sentences ask, with some justification, why it is not possible to allow some of them to be given the benefit of a more open placement prior to being deported to their home country.

Prison regulations prohibit the use of clothing other than that supplied by the prison administration on reception but individual exceptions may be made if special reasons exist. The dress code for prisoners is thus uniform in manner, although in the open prisons more lenient dress arrangements are permitted as long as security is not put at risk. In a closed prison a "kippa" may be allowed while a turban may not owing to the search diffi-

---

[29] Prison Regulations, (KVFS 2006:9) Section 3, p.4.
[30] Prison Treatment Act (Lagen om Kriminalvård i anstalt, 1974:203), Section 7.

culties attaching to the latter. Something small and easily searched may be more readily allowed than something that would require more lengthy efforts.

2.4 Work, education, training, sports and recreation

Work is fully provided for in all Swedish prisons. The nature of prison work programmes varies considerably with simpler forms of work being provided in prisons taking relatively short-term prisoners. More skilled production work is undertaken in other prisons. Serious drug misuse may result in prisoners having a reduced capacity to work. In such cases, work periods must be alternated with some other form of activity, for example education. In general, there would not appear to be any serious difficulty in ensuring that foreign prisoners take part in work in the same way as national prisoners.

So far as regular education programmes and programmes aimed to reduce drug addiction or criminal behaviour are concerned language difficulties often limit foreign prisoners' opportunities to participate since these activities usually employ the Swedish language. Linguistic deficiencies are often at the root of the social exclusion of foreign prisoners.

The Prison Treatment Act, Section 10, states: "During working hours a prisoner shall be given the opportunity for work, study, vocational training or other specially arranged form of activity in order to counteract criminality or drug misuse or otherwise facilitate adjustment in society after release[31]". Here, it appears, Swedish Prisons fail to meet their own standards in ensuring that prisoners, regardless of linguistic ability, are treated equally. Educational courses in prisons are held in Swedish and participation in them can therefore only be offered to those speaking the language. Prisons offer courses in "Swedish for Immigrants" for those unable to speak Swedish, but these courses do not compare well with the general educational courses available to Swedish speaking prisoners. If the Swedish system aims to base treatment on making fair distinctions without discrimination, there should also be more and better courses to assist non-Swedish speakers, which is not the case. The Swedish Prison and Probation Services fail to provide equal education opportunities to foreign speaking prisoners as they do native language speakers. This may be an understandable failure due to limited resources, but it is nevertheless a failure.

This failure has, however, been taken up by the Justice Ombudsman. After a local prison authority had initially refused to allow a prisoner with expulsion orders to participate in an educational activity, the Justice Ombudsman issued a statement on 26 September 1995[32] clarifying that not allowing such prisoners to participate in the same activities as those enjoyed by national prisoners is not in accordance with the Prison Treatment Act[33] and that practices excluding a certain sub-group of prisoners from educational activities shall not be allowed.

Virtually all Swedish prisons make provision for outdoor and indoor sporting and athletic activities. Television is widely available. It is not uncommon for theatrical groups to visit prisons and present plays which sometimes are intended to stimulate discussion and thought about achieving a betterment of life.

---

[31] Prison Treatment Act, Section 10 (Lagen (1974:203) om Kriminalvård i anstalt).
[32] Justice Ombudsman statement (JO beslut, no. diarienummer 4588-1994).
[33] Prison Treatment Act, Section 10 (Lagen 1974:203 om Kriminalvård i anstalt).

2.5 Food, religion, personal hygiene, medical care

As a general rule, prison food is well prepared, dietetically balanced and plentiful. Prison Regulations[34] stipulate that those in need of special meals for religious, medical or other reasons shall be accommodated. These accommodations most frequently include preparing meals without pork. Some more specific requests such as wanting halal meat may not be accommodated because such meat may not be readily available in ordinary Swedish food shops.

Section 15 of the Prison Treatment Act[35] provides that foreign prisoners are to be allowed to practice their own religion to the extent that security is not jeopardised. Prisoners may receive visits from their religious representatives. The Prison and Probation Services have a network of representatives of different denominations who are able to visit foreign prisoners. This network, the Council for Spiritual Welfare is made up of about 130 persons. In the larger institutions, representatives often include Catholic and Orthodox priests as well as Muslim Imams. At Kumla Prison there is a special section called the Monastery that provides an opportunity to undertake a meditative retreat. Prisoners, regardless of their religious affiliation, may apply to enter retreats.

As previously mentioned, the provision of basic equipment and services is well catered for in Swedish prisons. Opportunities to shower and maintain healthy standards of personal hygiene are good. Changes of underclothing are regular and frequent. The provision of material and opportunities to maintain personal hygiene is not regulated in the Prison Treatment Act presumably because it is taken for granted as an essential aspect of Swedish life that shall continue in the prisons.

So far as medical care is concerned Section 37 of the Prison Treatment Act prescribes that a prisoner in need of medical attention for the maintenance of health or the treatment of sickness shall be treated in accordance with the instructions of a doctor. Use shall be made of public medical services if any necessary examinations and treatment cannot be conveniently carried out in the prison. In practice, there is considerable reliance on using doctors who are working in the public health services and not specifically attached to particular prisons. State-registered nurses perform important medical screening work in the prisons.

The delivery of the child of a woman prisoner shall as far as possible take place in an external hospital. Special provisions in the Act on Forensic Psychiatric Care govern the admission and treatment of prisoners who may be transferred to psychiatric institutions for voluntary treatment.

So far as healthcare is concerned, the same rules apply for foreign prisoners as national prisoners, with perhaps the difference that, in cases of non-emergency care, the foreign prisoner may have to wait a day or so longer to see a physician if an interpreter's services are to be used.

2.6 Consular and legal help

Please see the overview provided above at section 1.3. It must be emphasised that the provision of consular and legal help is largely dependent on two factors. Firstly, the pris-

---

[34] Prison Regulations (KVFS 2006:20), Chapter 2, Section 3, p.7.
[35] Prison Treatment Act (Lagen om Kriminalvård i Anstalt 1974:20).

oner must usually initiate the contact. Secondly, the consular responses vary from doing nothing or very little to help the prisoner to consistent interest. Dutch prisoners especially are well satisfied with the help they receive – modest financial assistance that helps to pay for telephone calls or buy presents on special occasions and regular visits.

2.7 Contact with the outside world

All prisoners, including foreign prisoners, may write and receive letters. There is no censorship of mail but the Prison Treatment Act contains, however, provisions that allow for the random scrutiny of the mail of prisoners in both closed and open prisons if there is reason to think that it contains drugs or that its content relates to planning criminal activity or escape. Such mail may be withheld but the prisoner must be informed of this and also informed of any harmless content. Depending on a prison's security classification, letters may be read by staff to ensure that they do not contain information concerning criminal activities. In special maximum-security wings all correspondence is monitored which in practice mean that translators are engaged if such correspondence is in a foreign language.

Mail to or from an official Swedish body, the prisoner's lawyer or an international body officially recognised as competent to receive complaints may not be scrutinised unless there is good reason to think that such mail is addressed to, or emanates from, a bogus person or body[36].

Visits are allowed providing that they do not jeopardise prison security, constitute a threat to post-prison adjustment in the community or in some other way are considered damaging to a prisoner. Supervised visits may be ordered if security considerations warrant it. In many prisons visits may be conducted under private circumstances that allow sexual contact to take place. Foreign prisoners who are fortunate enough to have family members or friends in Sweden receive visits under the same circumstances as national prisoners. But foreign prisoners whose family or friends live abroad are frequently unable to receive visits from them and are, to that extent, disadvantaged.

Telephone conversations are permitted to the extent that they can be arranged practically. Telephone conversations may be denied for the same reasons that visits may be denied. However, listening in to any prisoner's telephone conversation may only occur with the prisoner's knowledge. Telephone conversations with a lawyer who represents a prisoner may not be monitored.

In closed prison settings, the prisoner must apply in writing for approval of each telephone number he or she wishes to call. Criminal record checks are then conducted on those persons the prisoner wishes to call. If approved, the telephone number is added to the prison's telephone operating system, and the prisoner, after having purchased a telephone card, can dial this number. However, mobile phone numbers that make use of cash cards and where no physical person is registered on that number rarely get approved in closed prisons. For prisoners with family in countries where such cash cards are used more frequently this poses a significant difficulty. Another difficulty arises for foreign prisoners if the possible criminal records of callers residing abroad are not readily available for prison staff to check In order to obtain approval for visits and telephone calls, those individuals residing abroad must themselves obtain a certificate from the local po-

---

36   Prison Treatment Act (Lagen om Kriminalvård i Anstalt 1974:203) Sections 24-28.

lice proving that they do not appear in criminal records. While in some countries local police are willing to provide certification, it may be more difficult and costly for those residing in other countries. In practice, prison staff takes these difficulties into account and while some calls are denied efforts may be made to try to meet the prisoner's request especially if the person is a close family member.

Most large prisons are able to provide excellent library services for foreign language speaking prisoners. In the two large maximum-security prisons books are available in more than 30 languages[37]. For the more common languages spoken in prison, such as Russian or Arabic, there are hundreds of titles available, whereas the more uncommon languages only have a couple of titles to choose from. Newsmagazines are available in approximately ten different languages (and can be borrowed from the library). Library services sometimes include the librarian printing out the cover page of large daily newspapers that may be found online. Papers are also available in "easy Swedish" for those learning the language.

Kumla Prison, which has a large unit for prisoners with expulsion orders, has prison rules written in 12 foreign languages[38]. The Kumla prison administration also helps prisoners financially so that they may phone family members in the country of residence. If the cost of calling the country exceeds 3 SEK/minute the prisoner receives one telephone card worth 100 SEK (€ 10) per month; if the cost exceeds 6.50 SEK, he receives two cards. This and other forms of financial aid to those with families abroad are not available at all prisons. Prison regulations state "Prisons can pay for telephone calls deemed to be of great importance for the prisoner's preparation for release into society[39]" and adds the later advice "such preparation can include contact with other government agencies, future employers, residence providers, supervision officers and occasionally contact with relatives". As different prisons implement these regulations differently, steps should be taken to secure consistent practice.

Kumla Prison also cooperates with the local church so that visitors who need to stay overnight in Kumla may do so for about €10 per night. Prisoners who have families abroad receive special attention in Kumla. Generally, a visitor to a prisoner is allowed to visit two days in a row. Visitors from abroad, however, may visit for up to ten consecutive days, then, after four days of no visits, return for another ten consecutive day visits. In Kumla Prison's unit for foreign prisoners, four of its 14 staff members were born abroad. The prison also has staff that between them can speak 23 languages. These numbers are similar to those at the maximum security Hall Prison where the staff group speaks 19 languages. Documents such as those concerning prison regulations and concerning repatriation possibilities for foreigners exist in ten languages.

In an explorative study conducted in 1996[40] foreign prisoners are described as being isolated as a result of being incarcerated in a foreign country with no visits from home and perhaps not even in surroundings that allow the use of their native language. Another study[41] states that foreign prisoners may be more scrutinised by other prisoners.

---

[37] Information gathered through interviews with prisoners and staff at Kumla and Hall.

[38] Polish, German, Spanish, Persian, Italian, Estonian, Russian, Czech, Lithuanian, French, Arabic, English.

[39] Prison Regulations (KVFS 2006:20) Chapter 4, Section 5, p.11.

[40] Prison staff on foreigners; an explorative study (Anstaltspersonal om utlänningar, en explorativ intervjustudic) pp.73-76.

[41] Prison, Probation and Ethnicity (Kriminalvård och etnicitet) pp.78-80.

This may lead to a perception of breach of codes of conduct from their fellow prisoners' point of view. On the other hand foreign prisoners may be able to communicate with each other without either other prisoners or staff being able to understand them. And this may in fact strengthen the prisoners' identification with their ethnic origins and thus, to some extent lessen their social exclusion.

2.8 Reintegration activities – prison leave

The Prison Treatment Act[42] provides that prisoners may be granted leave unless there is a manifest risk that they will commit crime or misuse the leave in some other way. The purpose of leave, as stated in the Prison Treatment Act, is to prepare the prisoner for life after release from prison. Such preparation is to begin upon incarceration and continue throughout the prisoner's stay in prison. Leaves are considered a valuable instrument in ensuring that the individual can stay in touch with family and friends as well as ease his or her reintegration into society. Leaves are also viewed as counteracting institutionalisation.

There are different forms of prison leave. A normal leave permits prisoners to spend a certain number of hours away from the prison, often with their families. Special leaves involve a few hours spent outside prison for specific activities related to release preparation, for example to arrange housing or work. Some special leaves can be classified as compassionate leaves granted for important personal reasons, for example to visit a sick close relation, attend a funeral, etc. "Breathing space leaves" may be granted for prisoners serving sentences of two years or more, a category that often includes foreign prisoners. They allow prisoners an annual leave for up to four hours accompanied by a staff member to take part in some normal activity in the outside world, for example, to attend a football match, do some special shopping, etc. The positive effects of leaves must be carefully weighed against any risk to society that may exist[43]. Leaves are to be viewed as a significant means to facilitate the transition from prison life to life in the community, since although it is necessary for prisoners to conform to prison rules it is equally important to avoid institutionalisation as this leads to difficulties in the transition to adjustment in society[44].

Before granting each leave, an individual risk assessment is made. For those prisoners serving more than a four-year sentence, an initial risk analysis is made upon incarceration, which then is valid until either the staff or the prisoner request review. These assessments include stated special conditions and may for instance specify that a prisoner may be granted leave first after having served a certain number of months.

As early as 1974, when a major reform of the Prison and Probation Services was undertaken[45], prison leaves were intended to constitute a major way of counteracting institutionalisation and assisting the adjustment of the released prisoner in the community, Nevertheless prison regulations[46] describe situations when a prisoner may not be granted leave. Chapter 9, which deals with risk assessment, states that "*a prisoner with expulsion or removal orders should generally speaking not be granted normal leaves*". This means that, in addition

---

[42] Prison Treatment Act (Lagen om Kriminalvård i Anstalt 1974:203) Section 32.
[43] Prison and Probation Regulations (Kriminalvårdens Författningssamling KVFS 2006:20).
[44] Prison, Probation and Ethnicity (Kriminalvård och etnicitet) p.79.
[45] Government Bill on the Reform of the Prison and Probation Services (Kriminalvårdsreform prop. 1974:20) p.83.
[46] Prison and Probation Regulations (KVFS 2006:20) p.35.

to the individual risk assessment made prior to each possible leave, foreign prisoners with expulsion orders are subject to a general criterion that limits their possibilities to spend time away from the prison in order to benefit from conditions that facilitate resettlement in the community.

Routine statistics on prison leave[47] do not distinguish between those granted to foreign prisoners and those granted to national prisoners. In consequence it is not possible to make comparisons about the relative frequency of leaves granted. But even in the absence of statistical data about the number and kinds of leave granted to foreign prisoners it seems certain that they are not granted leaves to nearly the same extent as national prisoners. Foreign prisoners who were interviewed for this study expressed their dissatisfaction with the way they are barred from being granted prison leaves. Under certain conditions a significant inequality can exist between the time away from the prison spent by a national and a foreign prisoner with expulsion orders.

In 1999, an investigation[48] was conducted into how decisions to grant leaves were made. The study was occasioned by a much-publicised case in which a prisoner on leave shot and killed two police officers. The study concluded that the decisions to grant special leaves had too often been made on the basis of subjective judgements rather than objective factors. Foreign prisoners were not given any special attention[49] when an analysis of changes in the prison population were taken into account, despite their becoming an increasingly important group in the prison population. The study resulted in new and stricter guidelines that limited the granting of prison leaves. Between 1999 and 2001, special leaves (these are the leaves that foreign prisoners are most likely to be granted rather than regular leaves) decreased from 33 457 to 15 481, that is by almost 50%. The number of regular leaves also declined from 19 934 to 13 657.

In another limited study[50] with only three staff members interviewed, subjects were asked if prisoners with foreign backgrounds reacted differently from national prisoners before, during, or after leaves they were granted. One of the interviewees mentioned that there was increased anxiety among foreigner prisoners, especially young foreign prisoners, when they were to go on leave. This was because they sometimes had not told their families that they were in prison so as to not to bring shame on them. Instead, they may have said that they were away working. However, the truth always comes out since a local prison administration must plan leaves in conjunction with a specific address at which the prisoner would live during the leave.

2.9 Release – expulsion

Prison and probation services work in collaboration with police when time comes to deport the prisoner. Efforts are made in advance to ensure that all legal documents are in order at the time of release. Obtaining such documents is substantially easier when the prisoner is willing to co-operate. There are cases when a deported prisoner has remained in custody due to difficulties in carrying out the expulsion orders (for instance necessary documents have not been obtained or if the airline carrier has made flight changes etc). If

---

[47] Prison and Probation Statistics (Kriminalvårdens Officiella Statistik).
[48] Absconding from leave by long-sentence prisoners (Långtidsdömdas utevistelser) 1999
[49] Ibidem p.97.
[50] Prison, Probation and Ethnicity (Kriminalvård och etnicitet) p.66.

this occurs, the prisoner most often is transferred to a remand prison but may remain in a prison setting. Prisoners who have worked during their incarceration, receive10% of the remuneration[51] which during their prison stay has been held in a separate account. Any sum due is given to the prisoner in cash at time of release and/or expulsion.

2.10 Aftercare

Although foreign prisoners should as much as possible be dealt with in the same way as national prisoners there are formidable difficulties in arranging good aftercare for them as compared with many national prisoners. This is especially true of those who will be subject to expulsion. Contact and communication with the foreign prisoner's home country is often difficult. It is frequently difficult to establish the relevant agencies with which to work, contact and communication draw out in time, language difficulties exist even between the Swedish and foreign professionals concerned and, it has to be said, there is not always a marked interest on the part of the home country's agencies to collaborate in the matter.   Even if those foreign prisoners who will stay in Sweden have the same right to welfare assistance as national prisoners, difficulties over language is often a barrier to securing work. As with national prisoners there are often personal and social problems that need continuing interest, treatment and care, the provision of which is often rendered difficult because of an inadequate understanding of Swedish or other accessible language, for example, English. Social isolation because of linguistic deficiencies easily makes for a return to criminal circles for social acceptance and companionship.

As from January 2006, the probation services are responsible for drawing up an action plan for the implementation of both probation and prison sentences. So far as imprisonment is concerned, the purpose of this policy is to emphasise and enhance the importance of preparation for release. It is too early to say how well the new policy on sentence planning is working. At this stage all that can be said is that the probation services have been given enlarged responsibilities for the provision of aftercare. Little is known about whether existing staff resources are adequate to deal with the problems and difficulties arising and whether suitable forms of organisational collaboration are being developed.

2.11 Staff

In 2004, of the 9014 prison and probation services' employees, 28% were under the age of 35, and 77% under the age of 55. Approximately 43 % were women. 20% of all employees held university degrees and 70% had at least two years of high school education[52].

The Prison and Probation Services provide 19 – 27 weeks of mandatory training that include, unless the employee has studied at university level prior to being hired, 10 college credits in subjects relevant to prison and probation. This training, besides helping employees to further their skills in working within the prison and probation system, also helps the employer to identify any individuals who demonstrate undesirable attributes or attitudes that conflict with the value system of treating all persons in a humanitarian and non-discriminatory manner. Such persons will not be allowed to continue working within

---

[51]   A prisoner collects approximately 1 € per working hour in salary.
[52]   Prison and Probation Budget (Kriminalvårdens Budgetunderlag) 2006, p.18.

the Prison and Probation Services. Some employees working with foreign prisoners have in the past received special training by participating in a university level course in "intercultural understanding". Other prisons have held training opportunities in Diversity and Dialogue[53]. Prison and probation training includes questions of relevance for dealing with foreign prisoners such as human rights, anti-discrimination, ethnic diversity and hate crimes. More practical issues are also considered, such as when an interpreter should be used. Ethical issues are an important part of training and apart from being incorporated in most other subjects taught is also a discussion topic in its own right once a week for all training weeks[54].

The Prison and Probation Services seek to employ staff with diverse ethnic and cultural origins. This can enhance the opportunities to be able to communicate with prisoners in daily activities. However, as noted in one study[55], being able to speak the same language does not necessarily imply a sharing of cultural, religious or other experiences. Thus, it should not be assumed that just because two individuals come from the same country they necessarily share the same cultural values. Sometimes staff speaking the prisoners' language may arouse suspicions amongst other staff since the latter are unable to be sure that the former is not being manipulated by the prisoner. Thus, a staff member communicating with a prisoner in a language his or her colleagues do not comprehend can cause a sense of insecurity within the work force. It is crucial that senior management remains alert to such difficulties, as it is of great importance for both foreign and non-foreign language staffs that such uncertainty can be lessened through open discussion of staff-prisoner communications. Should management fail to create forums for such discussions a critical situation may emerge in that staff loses confidence in each other. This provides prisoners with opportunities to try to exploit or manipulate staff.

Then too, prisoners sharing the same cultural or ethnic background as a staff member sometimes erroneously assume that this staff member should be or will be especially compliant because of a common background. Such misconceptions may lead to the foreign language speaking staff having to clarify their role and position *vis-à-vis* the foreign prisoner in a way that is not necessary for other staff. Immediate clarification is essential to prevent misconceptions about the prisoner-staff relationship leading to false expectations that can threaten safety, security and good order.

2.12 Projects

The major project under way has been described at section 2.10 on Aftercare. The probation services have, as from January 2006, been given the responsibility for planning the implementation of probation and prison sentences. Such an enlargement of responsibility will make considerable demands on co-operation between the prison and probation authorities. Appropriate planning and communication procedures have to be initiated, tried out and improved as necessary. It is too early to report on the progress of this important policy development.

---

[53] Ibidem p.37.
[54] Information from the Training Office of Prison and Probation (KRUT, Stockholm) 31 March 2006.
[55] Prison, Probation and Ethnicity (Kriminalvård och etnicitet) pp.72-80.

3 ADMINISTRATIVE DETENTION OF FOREIGN PRISONERS

3.1 Institution

The Swedish Migration Board describes its responsibilities as follows: "The Migration Board works both with permits for those wishing to migrate to Sweden for one reason or another and with funding to some of those who already have residence permits here but would like to return home. We are also responsible for seeing to it that people refused entry or given expulsion orders leave Sweden..." In a description of migration policy, the Ministry of Foreign Affairs states: "Swedish migration policy is based on a holistic approach which includes refugee, migration and integration policies, voluntary return to the country of origin and support to voluntary returnees. Included in this holistic approach are measures to strengthen respect for human rights, which represent the very basis for the right of asylum, international cooperation and measures to prevent involuntary migration as well as to facilitate cross-border mobility in an organized manner"[56].

3.2 Ministry responsible & legislation

The Swedish Migration Board is subordinate to the Ministry of Foreign Affairs. The government appoints its members. Parliament lays down the guidelines for migration policy on proposition of the government. In addition to the Aliens Act (2005:716) the Migration Board takes account of other regulations specific to its field of operations[57]. These include the Dublin Regulation[58], the Treaty of Amsterdam, the Schengen Agreement, the Vienna Convention (1974:10-12) and certain other international agreements[59].

3.3 Capacity institutions

As of 31 December 2005, the national Swedish population was 9047752[60]. During 2005, 65000 immigrants came to Sweden and joined the approximately half million other foreign citizens already in the country. It is estimated that 1, 8 million persons, that is 20% of the national Swedish population, are first or second generation immigrants. The number of asylum seekers doubled within two years from 16 303 in 2000 to 33016 in 2002, but has since decreased. The decrease is expected to continue and in future years it will be stable at an average of 22000 per year[61]. In 2004, there were 38900[62] registrations in the reception system. There are seven detention centres run by the Migration Board. In connection with the present report, the largest of these detention centres at Märsta, near Stockholm, was visited[63]. It can contain up to 60 detainees. In 2005 a daily average of

---

56 Quotation from the Board's website www.sweden.gov.se (2006-04-29).
57 Swedish Migration Board Regulations, MIGRFS 2003:10 and Regulations (1994:361) concerning reception of asylum seekers etc.
58 See link in bibliography.
59 For further information see website www.migrationsverket.se .
60 Bureau of Statistics, SCB, 2005.
61 Prison and Probation Budget (Kriminalvårdens Budgetunderlag), 2006, pp.14-15.
62 Swedish Migration Board 2004, p.3.
63 Information from Lars Ekblom and Marie Hansson, coordinators at the Märsta detention centre (2006-04-10).

214 individuals were detained in police custody, detention centres, remand prisons and ordinary prisons, as compared with 237 in 2004 and 159 in 2003.

3.4 Length of stay

A person can be detained in a Migration Board detention centre if one of the following applies:
- Detention for up to 48 hours for the purpose of investigating a case. Such detention may not be extended.
- Detention for up to two weeks if there is doubt about the identity of person applying for a residence permit. Such detention may be extended.
- Detention for up to two weeks if it is deemed unlikely that a residence permit will be granted, or for up to two months if a decision to expel has been taken and the person is believed to be an absconding risk or likely to engage in criminal activity. Such detention may also be extended[64].

3.5 Decisions procedure

The Migration Board is the first instance body for examining and deciding on applications for a residence permit and citizenship.

3.6 Appeal procedure

As from 31 March 2006, three Migration Courts and a Migration Court of Appeal hear appeals against Migration Board decisions.

3.7 Irregular stay

Irregular immigration is not a crime but producing false documentation is a fraudulent act punishable by imprisonment.

3.8 Numbers

In 2004 the Migration Board considered 142000 applications for shorter or longer visits to Sweden. The Migration Board and Aliens Appeals Board granted residence permits to a total of 58987 foreign residents (this number includes temporary residence permits as well as quota refugees)[65]. The total cost of the Migration Board's operations in the same year was € 538000. The Board employs approximately 3300 persons.

3.9 Expulsion

The Migration Board provides accommodation in special open reception units for foreign citizens applying for asylum or those awaiting expulsion who are not escape prone. In these units various activities are designed to prepare foreigners for their departure

---

[64] Migration Board information sheet (March 2006).
[65] Swedish Migration Board 2004- and the way forward, pp. 1-2.

from Sweden and reintegration into their home country. Detention centres are similar to the reception units offered asylum seekers. Opportunities to engage in activities, entertain visitors and have time away from the centre exist. Märsta has also a special room for prayer for persons from any denomination.

An individual placed in a detention centre receives € 2,60 per day so that personal items can be purchased. Two to three persons share a room, and men and women are allowed to live together at the same centre. There are, however, units for women only. All meals are provided through external catering services and special arrangements can be made for those with dietary restrictions. Interpreters are used in all relevant conversations with the detainees, even though many staff members are themselves of foreign backgrounds and may be able to communicate with the detainee. Practicalities of completing the expulsion are accommodated in collaboration with police.

3.10 Prisoners not deported

Administrative detention of prisoners who are not deported can take place under certain circumstances. For a description of these circumstances and permitted detention lengths, see section 3.4 above.

3.11 Detention irregulars under criminal law

Under the Aliens Act the Migration Board may detain a person in police custody, in a remand prison or ordinary prison if an expulsion order has been made following conviction for a crime *or* if detention is warranted for national security reasons or if other special circumstances exist[66].

3.12 Minors

Children under the age of 18 may not be placed in such institutions mentioned above. Children should not be separated from parents if one of them is taken into custody. However, if both a child and the person having custody of the child can be detained, they shall be detained together for a maximum period of 72 hours. This period can be extended once for an additional 72 hours. Usually, those detained have shown that they are not prepared to comply with the expulsion order and detention is necessary to prevent evasion.

4 NATIONALS DETAINED ABROAD

4.1 Numbers

Approximately 1000 Swedes are sentenced abroad annually for crime. Most convictions are for minor offences and do not result in a prison sentence. According to the Ministry of Foreign Affairs there were approximately 225 Swedes incarcerated abroad (not counting the Nordic countries) on April 19, 2006.

---

[66]   Aliens Act 2005:716, Chapter 8, Section 8.

4.2 Detention countries

There were Swedish citizens incarcerated in 46 different countries on April 19, 2006. Spain (30), United States (26) and Germany (22) have the largest number of incarcerated Swedes, with 16 serving sentences in Thailand, and 12 in Great Britain and Poland[67].

4.3 Reasons for detention and sentencing

The main reason for the detention of Swedes abroad is that they have committed crime. Of the 225 persons detained abroad, 85 persons or more than one-third had committed offences related to narcotic drugs. The next most common offences are those of completed or attempted homicide and manslaughter (15 persons). Other crimes include the trafficking of persons.

4.4 Involved organisations

For this report, interviews were conducted with representatives from Bridges to Abroad[68], a non-governmental organisation working to helping Swedish citizens imprisoned abroad. These representatives had themselves experienced imprisonment abroad. In consequence their insights into the assistance given – or not given - to them are valuable and relevant. They stated that as foreign prisoners they experienced a high level of social exclusion.

4.5 Release and reception in home country

Those Swedes, who wish to have their foreign sentence transferred to Sweden for enforcement, may apply to have this done through the Swedish diplomatic missions in the country of detention. It is then for the Swedish government to see if such transfers can take place. Whether an individual enforcement can be transferred and carried out in Sweden depends greatly upon the country of incarceration. As mentioned earlier, European Conventions exist for this purpose and some bilateral treaties.

4.6 Aftercare

An interview subject in this study said that some of the greatest difficulties occur on return to Sweden because the municipal authorities give little or no support. For national Swedish prisoners released after serving long sentences there is support from the probation and municipal social services. But for those having served long sentences abroad, perhaps even having experienced traumatic situations during incarceration, no organisation seeks to provide mental or physical assistance. Sweden has a well-established social welfare system to which each individual in need can turn; however, its outreach efforts do not appear to be made for aftercare purposes.

---

[67] Katarina Bjornstad, Ministry of Foreign Affairs, interviewed on April 19, 2006.
[68] See website www.utlandsbryggan.se .

4.7 Public opinion and media

Some cases of Swedes incarcerated abroad receive a high level of media coverage. For instance, a Swedish woman convicted in 1981 of murder in the United States, currently serving 25 years to life, appears in 16200 Google searches on Swedish web sites alone. In some cases such as the above public and official opinion is in favour of transferring enforcement of sentence to Sweden. But in other cases it is, as always, as divided as in any other political matter.

5 EVALUATION AND RECOMMENDATIONS

5.1 General

The limited time available for the present study inevitably means that whilst some questions have been raised and answered, other questions have been raised and left unanswered. But even when answers have been attempted it must be admitted that they often are supported by suppositions rather than firm facts. This means that there is an urgent need for more in-depth studies especially on the topic of administrative detention. A weakness of the present study is that interviews with foreign prisoners and prison staff could only be conducted at two large maximum-security prisons, Kumla Prison and Hall Prison. In any future work to collect facts and illustrate practice it would be desirable for interviews with foreign prisoners and prison staff to be conducted at a number of the smaller Swedish prisons having diverse levels of security. This would make it possible to ascertain to what extent factual and perceived social exclusion is related to type of prison and the numbers of foreign prisoners held in individual establishments.

It must be admitted that the present investigation suggests beyond reasonable doubt that social exclusion is a fact of life among foreign prisoners in Swedish prisons. This is so despite that fact that the Prison and Probation Services have taken steps to minimize exclusion. These measures include the right for foreign prisoners to practise their own religion and receive visits from their religious representatives. Prison libraries provide books, magazines and newspapers in a large number of languages. The prison authorities encourage family contacts and seek to assist such contacts as much as possible. The Prison and Probation Services recruit, train and make use of staff with cultural and ethnic backgrounds that mirror the diversity to be found among foreign prisoners. Interpreter services are provided notably in connection with situations where accuracy of communication is important, for instance, in dealing with illness. Nevertheless, there is some reason to think that many of the positive forms of help exemplified above vary between different prisons in the extent to which they are made available. An important aim for future work should be to investigate unjustified variation in the creation and use of assistance measures and where necessary to secure greater consistency in their application. Some suggestions to this end are presented below.

Following this study of foreign prisoners in Sweden, some matters warrant further examination with a view to improving efforts to reduce their social exclusion. The following are some recommendations.

5.2 Translations

Prison rules and other important information have been translated into different languages at only some prisons or detention centres whilst other prisons have few or no translations available. Much would be gained if the translators of the foreign languages most commonly used by foreign prisoners were to put together information pamphlets in a form that could be easily modified by individual prisons and detention centres. Such information material could leave blank spaces for briefly writing in the local regulations of individual establishments, for example: "Work begins at ___ o'clock". A large number of such rules and regulations, especially those concerning disciplinary procedures and punishments should be translated.

The FAQ form so widely used on the Internet provides a model. In Sweden, the Prison and Probation Services maintain a computer network (Krimnet) that could contain and maintain such translated information for use as and when needed.

5.3 Leaves

As mentioned earlier in this report, a major difference between national and foreign prisoners lies in the granting of leaves from prison. Although there is reason because of escape risks to exclude a number of foreign prisoners with expulsion orders from prison leave possibilities it is desirable to keep this situation under review and enlarge the leave opportunities for foreign prisoners as much as possible. The extent to which the inequalities concerning the numbers of leaves granted between national and foreign prisoners might be lessened is uncertain. There are, however, ways in which, even if the inequalities must be maintained, compensation can be made to foreign prisoners for the less advantageous conditions under which they must serve their sentences. In this connection a relevant provision in the Swedish Penal Code needs to be emphasised.

Chapter 29 of the Penal Code deals with the determination of punishment and exemption from sanction. Section 5 begins by stating that in determining the appropriate punishment, the court shall, besides the penal value of the crime, give reasonable consideration to certain mitigating circumstances. Sub-section 4 then describes one of these mitigating circumstances as "Whether the accused would suffer harm through expulsion from the Realm by reason of the crime". Sub-section 8 adds a further circumstance: "Whether there exists any other circumstance that calls for a lesser punishment than that warranted by the penal value of the crime". These provisions give the courts considerable discretion to take account *inter alia* of the hardships suffered by foreign prisoners with expulsion orders during the serving of a prison sentence. And in practice these mean that courts can and do sentence to shorter periods of imprisonment than would otherwise be the case.

However, Section 1 states "Punishments shall, with due regard to the need for consistency, be determined within the scale of punishments according to penal value of the crime or crimes committed (Author's emphasis). Within the framework for the present study it has not been possible to ascertain to what extent sentences containing expulsion orders are shortened or the degree of consistency in the practice of the different courts. In the interest of fairness and justice these aspects warrant impartial and competent research.

A final point is that there is a humanitarian argument for granting well-behaved prisoners "breathing space" leaves more frequently than once a year in order to counteract institutionalisation.

5.4 Contact with the outside world

Although books, TV, newspapers and magazines are available to foreign prisoners they cannot substitute for talking to, or receiving visits from, family and friends. Here lies the greatest risk for becoming socially excluded while in detention. National prisoners receive regular visits by family members but visits for foreign prisoners are difficult to arrange not least because of the cost of travel. Another obstacle to visiting is the difficulty of securing the screening of potential visitors to ensure that they are not involved in criminal activity as required by prison rules[69]. This difficulty applies even to telephone contact with families and friends living in another country. The relevant diplomatic missions are often unable to certify that a contact has no criminal record whilst telephone numbers often go to mobile telephones and are not therefore easily verifiable.

5.5 Prison allocation

In addition to the two closed prisons[70] taking those with expulsion orders, deported prisoners can also be placed in more open prison settings. A question for further research is whether placements in more open settings are made sufficiently often on the basis of suitability and whether foreign prisoners are sometimes placed unnecessarily in high security prisons as a matter of convenience for the prison services. Presumably it is more cost-efficient to house a large number of foreign prisoners together as staff can become more specialized in meeting their special needs. And it is true that this can be of benefit to the prisoners. Perhaps some concentration of foreign prisoners could be arranged in prisons offering more open conditions than those of Kumla and Mariefred. At a time when new prisons are being built and older ones closed, it might be worthwhile investigating if there are opportunities to create a separate prison, perhaps with an annex where visitors from abroad could rent rooms while visiting foreign prisoners. Such prisons although separating foreigners with expulsion orders from national prisoners, might provide a greater sense of inclusion amongst these foreign prisoners if they were housed with fellow countrymen or at least other foreign citizens.

5.6 Staff

The Prison and Probation Service already seeks to employ staff from diverse ethnic and cultural backgrounds in order to enhance communication with foreign prisoners in daily activities. Staff recruitment and training practice appears already to lead to the employment of a culturally diverse group with awareness of discrimination issues. Here, the recommendation is to continue such recruitment and training and to ensure that the staffs are sufficiently representative and adequate to deal with the numbers of detained foreign prisoners.

---

[69]   See also item 2.7 above.
[70]   Kumla and Mariefred Prisons.

5.7 Transfers

The procedure for using international and bilateral transfer agreements is slow and time consuming. The processing time[71] for voluntary transfers was 13 months in 2005[72]. Involuntary transfers required on average 14 ½ months [73]. It would be desirable to reduce processing time but this can probably only be achieved if increased pressure to speed up transfer routines is exercised by appropriate national and international organisations.

5.8 Visit by the Committee for the Prevention of Torture, etc. (CPT)

The inspections of the CPT constitute an important source for the revelation of a prison administration's difficulties and weaknesses. Accordingly, the report of the last visit to Sweden, which took place between 27 January and 2 February 2003, has been scrutinised for eventual comments on the situation of foreign prisoners. Establishments in which persons were detained were inspected including remand and ordinary prisons, police cells and psychiatric institutions. A report was published one year later. There is nothing in the report, however, that relates specifically to the situation of foreign prisoners.

---

[71] From time of application to the actual time of transfer.
[72] Kriminalvården, Återrapportering enligt Regleringsbrevet 2005.
[73] Between initiating and completing transfer.

Chapter 26

United Kingdom

Nick Hammond

1 INTRODUCTION[1]

Foreign national prisoners (FNPs) represent a significant and growing proportion within prisons in England & Wales. The number of foreign nationals held in prisons in England & Wales rose to 10,265 in February 2006 a 150% increase within a decade. Similarly individuals held in immigration detention in England & Wales have increased significantly.

Foreign national prisoners and immigration detainees held in Scotland and Northern Ireland, while increasing in recent years, are not represent in such numbers or proportions as in England & Wales. These two groups have neither featured in research or Prison Inspection Reports as prominently as in England & Wales. The separate, shorter entries for Scotland and Northern Ireland therefore reflect this situation.

Table 1 Comparative prison statistics in the UK

	England & Wales	Scotland	Northern Ireland
Total prison population	76,678 (02/06)	6,886 (02/06)	1,391 (02/06)
Per 100,000 of national population	143 (02/06)	135 (02/06)	80 (02/06)
Pre-trial detainees	17.8% (01/06)	19.5% (02/06)	37.1% (01/06)
Female prisoners	5.8% (02/06)	4.5% (02/06)	2.8% (01/06)
Juveniles	3.0% (01/06)	2.6% (09/04)	5.2% (09/04)
Foreign national prisoners	13.5% (02/06)	1.3% (09/04)	0.8% (01/06)
Number of institutions	139 (05)	16 (06)	3 (06)

Source: International Centre for Prison Studies, Kings College, London 2006

---

[1] Author Nick Hammond has worked with foreign national offenders since 1990. Firstly as a probation officer in a London prison and then through establishing a specialist probation unit working with foreign nationals arrested at Heathrow Airport. He is currently an Equality & Diversity Officer in London Probation with a lead responsibility for the services work with foreign national offenders. Graduating from Keele University in Applied Social Studies he also has an MA In Refugee Studies at the University of East London. A Council of Europe Pompidou Fellowship in 2000 and a Cropwood Fellowship at the University of Cambridge, Institute of Criminology in 1995 were both used to study foreign national offender issues. He has undertaken and published research on foreign national offenders in the UK and on British prisoners in Europe. At 'Probation 2000' his contribution to international justice was recognised through an individual merit award at the Community Justice Awards and in 2007 he received a Butler Trust Award for his work in this area.

A. England & Wales

A.1.1 Overview penalties and measures

The criminal justice system in England and Wales is going through a major re-organisation with the establishment of the National Offender Management Service, NOMS. Core elements to this are the 'end to end' management of offenders through introducing Offender Managers and commissioning effective interventions through Regional Offender Managers. At the same time, a new sentencing framework is provided through the Criminal Justice Act (CJA) 2003, which amends the Criminal Justice Act 1991. When an offender is convicted following a trial or guilty plea, the court has a range of sentencing options available. These depend on the type, the seriousness and the circumstances of the crime and include custodial and community sentences. The newly established Sentencing Advisory Panel and the Sentencing Guidelines Council work together to ensure that sentencing guidelines are produced which encourage consistency in sentencing. The judge or magistrate giving the sentence must consider punishing the offender, reducing crime, rehabilitating the offender, protecting the public, and ensure the offender makes reparation. The sentence will be a combination of these aims. Magistrates' and Crown Courts have different sentencing powers. The Magistrates' Court Sentencing Guidelines are issued for cases heard in the Magistrates' Courts. These set out the offences that regularly come before magistrates and the aggravating and mitigating factors that ought to be considered when deciding on a sentence. For offences that go before the Crown Court a comprehensive set of guidelines do not exist at present, but this is the future aim of the Sentencing Guidelines Council.

Currently, a limited number of offences attract minimum sentences. These are; an automatic life sentence for a second serious sexual or violent offence (there is a list of qualifying offences, all of which have a maximum penalty of life). There is a minimum 7-year prison sentence for third time trafficking in Class A drugs; this provision applies to the importation, production, supplying and possession with intent to supply Class A drugs. The maximum penalty for these offences is life imprisonment. There is a minimum 3-year prison sentence for third-time domestic burglary; the maximum penalty for burglary is 14 years imprisonment. There is a minimum 5-year prison sentence for possession or distribution of prohibited weapons or ammunition, the maximum penalty is 10 years imprisonment.

The CJA 2003 makes radical changes to the structure of prison and community sentences. Most of its sentences and provisions have been in force since 4 April 2005 with others due for implementation in late 2006. In England & Wales there are four-principle sentencing options, discharges that 8% of sentenced offenders receive, fines, received by 71% of convicted offenders, community sentences 13%, and prison 7% [2].

---

[2] Source: Criminal Statistics, England and Wales, 2003. Also see Sentencing Statistics 2004, England & Wales, HOSB, 15/05 Home Office Research Development Statistics, RDS for detailed analysis and Offender Management Caseload Statistics quarterly brief - July to September 2005, England and Wales.

A.1.2 Overview of the Prison System

A.1.2.1 Organisational Structure

Since 1993, the Prison Service has been an Executive Agency of the Home Office. Since June 2004, the Service is also now part of the National Offender Management Service (NOMS). NOMS spans several organisations with around 69,000 staff to ensure that a range of services, including 'end to end' offender management, custody, community sentences and programmes and interventions, are available to all adult offenders and those on remand in England and Wales. The structure of NOMS is changing in this development stage and as yet concluding legislation is required. The Director General of the Prison Service is responsible to the Chief Executive of NOMS. The Prison Service is the principal provider of Custodial Services in England & Wales. Of the current total of 139 prison establishments and Young Offenders Institutions in England and Wales, 128 establishments are in the public sector. Introduced to the UK in the 1990s, there are currently 11 privately managed prisons.

Prisons are categorised based on the security level of prisoners they can accommodate: All male prisoners are given a security categorisation when they enter prison. These categories are based on the likelihood that they would try to escape and the danger to the public if they did escape. The four categories are: category A - prisoners whose escape would be highly dangerous to the public or national security; category B - prisoners who do not require maximum security, but for whom escape needs to be made very difficult; category C - prisoners who cannot be trusted in open conditions but who are unlikely to try to escape and category D - prisoners who are trusted enough to wander freely but must report for daily roll calls. Prison security categories for women are similar to those for males. Category A is the same, the other two categories are 'closed' for prisoners who cannot be trusted in an open prison, and 'open' for prisoners who are trusted enough to wander freely but must show up for daily roll calls.

When offenders under the age of 17 are sentenced to a custodial sentence (Detention & Training Order) they may be sent, to either: Secure Training Centres (STCs) – privately run, education-focused centres for offenders up to the age of 17; Local Authority Secure Children's Homes (LASCHs) – run by social services and focused on attending to the physical, emotional and behavioural needs of vulnerable young people, or; Young Offender Institutions (YOIs) – run by the prison service.

Prison Service staffing levels in the public sector in 2005 were 1,428 senior operational staff, and 24,440 other officer grades. The State Sector Prison Service accounts for about 60% of the NOMS resources see Government Spending Reviews 2005-2006, 2006-2007, and 2007-2008.

Training of prison staff. Initial training of new main grade staff, is undertaken in one of the Prison Service colleges in England & Wales. On passing basic training and being allocated to a prison, ongoing training is provided through the prison and regional training initiatives. As well as mandatory training, there is a range of optional training opportunities for which staff can apply. Staff training aims to enable prison staff to deal equitably and sensitively with all prisoners taking into account diversity areas such as race, nationality, gender, sexual orientation, faith & religion, age and disability.

Prison Regulation. There are a number of ways in which prisons are regulated. Independent Monitoring Board (formerly Board of Visitors). Every establishment in England and Wales has its own Independent Monitoring Board. These are independent watchdogs drawn from the local community who are appointed by the Home Secretary to monitor the welfare of staff and prisoners and the state of the premises. Members have unrestricted access to all parts of the establishment, with the only exceptions being on grounds of security or personal safety. Board members will raise prisoner and staff concerns with management, the Governor, Area Manager, Headquarters, or even Ministers and the Home Secretary. In the event of a serious incident at an establishment, a Board member must be invited to observe the way it is being handled[3].

Prisons and Probation Ombudsman (PPO). The Home Secretary appoints the Ombudsman. They are an independent point of appeal for prisoners and those supervised by the Probation Service. For the purpose of investigations, the Ombudsman has full access to Prison Service information, documents, establishments and individuals, including classified material and information provided to the Prison Service by other organisations, such as the police. For medical records, the prisoner's consent is required for disclosure[4].

HM Chief Inspector of Prisons (HMCIP) for England and Wales. HM Chief Inspector of Prisons is independent of the Prison Service and reports directly to the Home Secretary on the treatment of prisoners, the conditions of prisons in England and Wales, and such other matters as the Home Secretary may require[5].

International inspections. Committee for the Prevention of Torture (CPT). The Council of Europe's Committee for the prevention of torture and inhuman or degrading treatment or punishment (CPT) visits places of detention which includes prisons, juvenile detention centres, police stations, holding centres for immigration detainees and psychiatric hospitals, to see how persons deprived of their liberty are treated and, if necessary, to recommend improvements to States. In common with other EU countries, the UK receives regular and ad hoc visits from the CPT. Recent reports have commented on foreign national prisoners and those in immigration detention.

During the July 2005 visit, the CPT's delegation examined the treatment of persons detained under the Terrorism Act 2000 and, in this context, visited Paddington Green High Security Police Station and Belmarsh Prison. The practical operation of the Prevention of Terrorism Act 2005 was also examined, and various persons served with control orders under that Act were met by the delegation. In addition, the delegation examined the treatment of persons detained at Campsfield House Immigration Removal Centre.

The November 2005 visit was focused on the treatment of certain persons recently detained under the Immigration Act 1971, with a view to being expelled; for this purpose, the delegation visited Full Sutton and Long Lartin Prisons as well as Broadmoor Special Hospital. Particular attention was given to the mental health of the individuals concerned. The delegation also revisited Paddington Green High Security Police Station and once again met persons served with control orders under the Prevention of Terrorism Act 2005. During this visit, the delegation held an exchange of views with the United Kingdom authorities on the use of diplomatic assurances in the context of deportation proceedings and related Memoranda of Understanding.

---

3   Independent Monitoring Board, formerly Board of Visitors, see http://www.imb.gov.uk/
4   Prisons and Probation Ombudsman (PPO) see http://www.ppo.gov.uk/
5   HM Chief Inspector of Prisons (HMCIP) for England and Wales see
     http://inspectorates.homeoffice.gov.uk/hmiprisons/

The CPT's visit reports and the responses of the United Kingdom Government are available on the Committee's website at http://www.cpt.coe.int

A.1.2.2. Foreign Prisoners

Prison allocation is not determined by nationality as such. Foreign national prisoners on remand are, like any other prisoners, kept in local prisons until trial and sentence. Sentenced foreign nationals, unless serving a short sentence, are risk and security assessed and categorised for transfer to an appropriately secure training prison the same as other prisoner groups[6]. There is no specific Prison Service policy as such, to concentrate foreign national prisoners in certain prisons. However, local circumstances and practise has lead some prisons to have a far higher percentage than the 13.5% average which foreign national prisoners represent in prisons in England and Wales as on February 2006.

Foreign national prisoners are represented in all prisons in England & Wales to varying extents. London prisons, for example, have a particularly high proportion, varying from 48% to 25%. This is due both to the diversity of London and more specifically because these prisons cover the courts where foreign nationals arrested at Heathrow Airport, (principally for drug importation and immigration offences), are remanded[7] In addition, some prisons outside of London have established large proportions of foreign national prisoners due to regional allocation and transfer practises. For example, HMP the Verne in Dorset, (male C Category) 56% and HMP Morton Hall, in Lincolnshire, (female semi-open), 62%.

Table 2 Prison population England & Wales 28/02/06, (public & private prisons)

	males	*female*	*total*
total	72,301	4,416	76,717
UK nationals	62,094 (85%)	3,443 (78%)	65,536 (85.5%)
Foreign nationals	9,388 (13%)	877 (20%)	10,265 (13.5%)
unrecorded	818	96	915 (1%)

Foreign national prisoners – disproportionately represented? While it would appear that foreign national prisoners are disproportionately overrepresented within prisons in England & Wales, accurate analysis is problematic due to the following factors: Accuracy

---

[6]   Security and allocation procedures place prisoners in conditions of security commensurate with the risk they pose to the public and the Prison Service and the likelihood of their trying to escape. They are D – open conditions, C – low risk, B – medium risk and A – high risk.

[7]   The proportion of foreign national prisoners in London prisons, on the 28/02/06 was, HMP Wormwood Scrubs 48% (includes males arrested at Heathrow Airport), HMP Wandsworth 29%, Bronzefield 33% (includes females arrested at Heathrow Airport), HMP Belmarsh 25%, HMP Brixton 36%, HMP Holloway 26%.

of prison statistics: statistics on nationality in prison are primarily obtained by prisoner self-assessment when first received into prison. The liaison between the Prison Service and Immigration service has improved in recent years particularly since the introduction of the Early Release Scheme (PSO 6000) so that there is a greater imperative for the immigration status and nationality of a prisoner to be verified. There remains, however, scope for inaccurate statistical returns. With the nationality of approximately 1% of all prisoners left unrecorded in the official statistics, FNP's could be particularly under-reported.

Inaccuracy of foreign national statistics of the general population: the 2001 National Census recorded 8.3% of the population in the UK as being born abroad though not their present nationality. Being born abroad does not obviously equate to being a foreign national, as nationality can change through obtaining UK citizenship. Also, the Home Office says its best estimate of the number of illegal immigrants in the UK is 430,000, although the number could be between 310,000 and 570,000[8]

Impact of non-UK resident foreign national prisoners; a proportion of foreign national prisoners are those arrested at Ports of Entry, (Airports and Seaports) principally for drug importation and immigration offences, who are not, and have never been, resident in the UK. To accurately comment on whether foreign nationals are disproportionately represented in the general prison population, the group of foreign national prisoners arrested at Ports of Entry who are not UK residents, would need to be removed for the comparison to be meaningful. Without this, it cannot be surmised with accuracy, whether foreign nationals who are resident in this country are over or indeed, under represented within prison. There is no statistical research or analysis on this area in the public domain and comment therefore remains a speculation.

Before the establishment of NOMS, there was a policy section within the Prison Service, the Prisoners Administration Group, (PAG), which held the policy lead for both foreign national prisoners and immigration detainees within prison establishments. In July 2004, PAG organised the first foreign nationals' conference for prison staff in Coventry, an acknowledgement of the needs and concerns of staff in working with this group. In July 2004 PAG started to produce a quarterly 'Foreign National Bulletin' to disseminate relevant information and best practise in different prisons. Since the establishment of NOMS, the policy responsibility for foreign national offenders and immigration detainees is being held by the Offenders Policy & Rights Unit, (OPRU). This group has also taken over the production of the 'Foreign Nationals Bulletin'. The Prison Service has not kept a separate policy lead for foreign national prisoners or immigration detainees. The OPRU of NOMS can issue policy directives and guidance for prisons in the public and private sector, as well as the National Probation Service, on foreign national offenders and immigration detainees.

---

[8] see http://news.bbc.co.uk/1/hi/uk_politics/4637273.stm.

A.1.3 Overview involvement of Consulates, Embassies, Ministries home country, probation service in home country, NGO's etc

Embassies, Consulates and High Commissions The contact and services provided by staff from Embassies, Consulates and High Commissions to their imprisoned nationals varies considerably depending on the priority given to this work by that particular country. Research into foreign national prisoners during the past 15 years has frequently cited widespread dissatisfaction with the services provided by embassies, consulates and High Commissions (Howard League, 1994, Cheney, 1993, Tarzi & Hedges, 1990 & 1993). If the foreign national arrested and detained is a national from a list of countries where there is a bilateral consular agreement in force then the arresting officer is obliged to notify that embassy[9]. The detained national should, if their country has not a bilateral agreement with the UK in force, still be asked whether they wish their embassy to be notified.

Therefore by the time a foreign national enters a prison, their embassy may already be aware of their detention. However, the prison service has, like the Police or Customs & Excise Service, obligations to also notify embassies when they hold their nationals. The UK has ratified 39 bilateral consular conventions[10]. For countries on this list, prisons are obliged to inform embassies on reception of their nationals. For foreign nationals from countries not on this bilateral list, the prisoner should be asked whether they want their embassy informed. Should they decline, their wishes should be respected. Articles 36(1)b and 36 (1)c of the 1963 Vienna Convention sets out the necessary procedures that the Prison Service must undertake in relation to arrested or detained foreign nationals.

Research has suggested that foreign national prisoners are frequently unsure or confused as to whether their embassy has been informed of their imprisonment. Contact with embassy, consular and High Commission staff over a number of years has also revealed that they believe that they are not informed regularly or reliably of the imprisonment of their nationals by prison staff as required[11].

Embassy staff visits to their imprisoned nationals are in the Legal Visits section. Letters from prisoners to their embassies should be at no cost to the prisoner and in addition to their other free letter allowance. Application to use official phones to contact embassies can be granted and calls to embassies can be made at the prisoner's expense at other times.

Foreign national prisoners frequently have unrealistic expectations of what their embassy should and can do to assist them. This often leads to disappointment and criticism from the prisoner creating a pervasive and cynical attitude amongst foreign national pris-

---

[9]   the exception is when the national is applying for asylum.

[10] Armenia, Austria, Azerbaijan, Belgium, Bosnia-Herzegovina, Bulgaria, China, Croatia, Cuba, Czech Republic, Denmark, Eqypt, France, Georgia, Germany, Greece, Hungary, Italy, Japan, Kazakhstan, Macedonia, Mexico, Moldova, Mongolia, Netherlands, Norway, Poland, Romania, Russia, Serbia & Montenegro, Slovakia, Slovenia, Spain, Sweden, Tajikistan, Turkmenistan, Ukraine, USA, Uzbekistan.

[11] Since the early 1990's there have been regular bi-annual training days and liaison meetings organised between London Probation & the Prison Service and more recently by NOMS, to provide Embassy, Consulate and High Commission staff with up to date information to enable them to carry out their role with prisoners effectively and efficiently. These events have proved very useful and valuable by both CJ agencies and the embassies themselves.

oners that 'no embassies are interested in their imprisoned nationals'. The range of services provided by embassies varies from letters, visits to liaison with family back home, to interceding with prison authorities when the prisoner has a concern, to sending in books, money and other items, to facilitating repatriation applications and obtaining travel documents to facilitate deportation/removal. From personal observations, the quality and level of Embassy involvement varies considerably and while the Foreign Ministry and Justice Ministries may set requirements for contact, the attitude of the Head of Consular Affairs/High Commission, is very significant to the priority given to this work.

Good practise. The use of trained embassy volunteers to provide contact, letters and visits to their imprisoned nationals can be an innovative method for embassies to provide contact with their imprisoned citizens. For over 25 years, the Dutch Embassy has used a group of trained Dutch volunteers living in the UK, supported by their consular staff and the Liaison Office of Dutch Prisoners Abroad of the Dutch Probation Service, to visit their imprisoned nationals. This has enabled Dutch prisoners to be offered regular visits and support, a link (through the Dutch Probation Service (with home, and assistance with their resettlement needs. While a number of other, mainly European Embassies also use volunteers, theirs is the most developed. If the prisoner requests it, the Dutch Probation Service will also arrange for a Home Circumstances Report to be provided by the Probation Service in the Netherlands, for the use of the sentencing court in the UK.

Regarding the role of the probation service or similar agency in the prisoner's home country, there is very limited evidence of such agencies having any involvement with this group of prisoners while they are serving sentences in the UK. There is an example of best practise undertaken at a particular prison with a high proportion of foreign national prisoners to establish links with other probation agencies to assist with resettlement – this is highlighted in the 'Treatment of Foreign Prisoners Treatment Section j) – aftercare probation.

NGO's_Prisons, particularly with high numbers of foreign national prisons, often make good use of community support groups and non-governmental agencies. Such groups have credibility, cultural and language skills and specialist knowledge that enables them to provide valuable support and casework for foreign nationals. However, such voluntary groups are small in number, primarily work with female prisoners, are concentrated in the southeast of the UK, and regular funding is a constant problem. In recent years funding has been alleviated to a degree by prisons providing paid contracts for these groups to provide casework, advice 'surgeries' and run groups. Those groups, such as the London based Detention Advice Service, who provide specialist immigration advice, are extremely valued by those prisons with whom they have contracts.

Good Practise. The Detention Advice Service, based in London, is a well-established and respected voluntary group that provides specialist immigration and detention advice to FNP's and immigration detainees. It has a number of contracts with prisons all over the country, such is its reputation, and its caseworkers travel widely. It facilitates FNP groups as well as providing casework support and telephone advice.

A.1.4 Overview of trends

A.1.4.1 Sentencing Trends

The Research Development Statistics Unit of the Home Office produces a wide range of statistics on offender management. They also publish a range of regular statistics on the population in custody and under probation service supervision http://www.homeoffice.gov.uk/rds/index.html. The Sentencing Guideline Council also provides a summary of sentencing trends http://www.sentencing-guidelines.gov.uk.

The UK has highest imprisonment rate in the European Union at 139 per 100,000, averaged between England & Wales, Scotland and Northern Ireland. The prison population in the UK rose by 71% between 1991 and 2001. Home Office predicts a prison population of between 91,400 and 109,600 by end of decade.

National trends in sentencing, England & Wales. Over the decade, 1993-2004, the number of adults sentenced for indictable offences in magistrate's courts has varied around 200,000. The use of custody increased from 6% in 1993 to 16% in 2001 and has subsequently remained at that level. The use of community sentences has also increased slightly while the use of fines has fallen from 46% in 1993 to 30% in 2004.

The average custodial length at Crown Court has increased from 20 months in 1993 to 27 months in 2004. The number of adult offenders sentenced to life imprisonment has more than doubled from 241 in 1993 to 581 in 2004. This reflects in part the change in law in 1997, which made life imprisonment mandatory for a second serious sexual and violence offence. In Crown Court burglary of a dwelling accounted for the highest proportion of prison sentences 12%. There have been increases in robbery, dangerous driving and offences of violence.

Changes in both custody rates and sentence lengths have been reflected in the large increase in the sentenced prison population over the last 10 years. This has grown from 33,046 in 1993 to 62,257 in June 2005. The prison population has grown 2% over the last year, 2004-2005. Remand decisions have also had an impact on the prison population. The remand population grew from 10,623 in June 1993 to 12,864 in June 2005.

A.1.4.2 Characteristics of the Foreign Prisoner Population.

The 2001 National Census recorded that 8.3% (4.9 million) of the total UK population was born overseas. The overseas-born population increased more between 1991 and 2001 than it did in any preceding post-war decades. This was almost double the proportion recorded in the last census of 1991. Compared with the UK-born population, the overseas-born population has a much more diverse mix of ethnic groups. While 96% of the UK-born population was White in 2001, only just over half (53% of 2.6 million) of the overseas-born population was White. The next largest ethnic groups for people born overseas were India (570,000), Pakistan (336,000), Black African (322,000) and Black Caribbean (238,000). Other ethnic groups with significant representation amongst the UK overseas-born population are Chinese (176,000) and Bangladeshi (152,000). The nationality profile of migrants has reflected the UK's historical and colonial history. There have been recent significant numbers of Europeans entering the UK from the new EU Accession countries, particularly Poland, the Czech Republic, Latvia & Lithuania.

Offending trends and foreign nationals. Amongst Criminal Justice agencies at present only the Prison Service routinely record nationality. Other CJ agencies (Police, Crown Prosecution Service and Probation Service) are only required to record race and ethnicity by the Home Office. While the accuracy of Prison Service nationality statistics has been questioned, given the self-reporting of nationality by the prisoner and other issues, they have nevertheless been recorded since the 1980's and provide a valuable indication of changes in profile and composition of this group of prisoners.

Latest available statistics show that there are some 10,265 foreign national prisoners in England & Wales as of the end of February 2006[12]. This total includes approximately 250 immigration detainees held in prison as opposed to an Immigration Removal Centre. Approximately 20% of the female and 13% of the male prison population are foreign nationals. The increase in the foreign national prisoner population is higher than in the British prisoner population for instance, between 2000 and 2005, the foreign national prisoner population increased by 73% from 5,586 to 9,650, in comparison to an increase of 11% in the population of British nationals in prison. While foreign national prisoners comprise of over 168 countries, Jamaica accounts for the largest nationality group for both male and females, followed by Ireland, Nigeria, Pakistan and India. Altogether, these 5 countries account for over half of all foreign national prisoners. Regarding offending trends, Table 3, shows prison population by nationality and offence group.

Table 3 Foreign national prisoners compared with UK national prisoners, by offence group, 2005

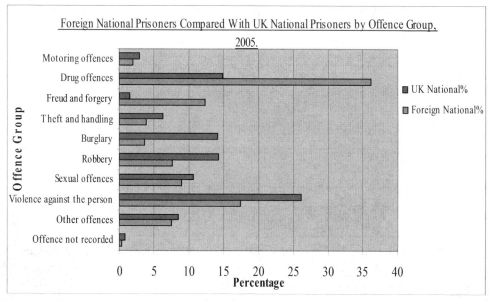

Source RSD Home Office

Table 4 Foreign national prison population by offence type and sentence length, England & Wales, 31st December 2005.

Sentence length	Less than 6 months	6 to 12 months	12 to 48 months	48 months to less than life	Life	total
Violence against the person	75	25	217	462	422	1,202
Sexual offences	15	5	92	470	40	622
Robbery	16	4	189	311	18	536
Burglary	10	6	135	102	1	254
Theft & Handling	77	30	130	30	-	267
Fraud & forgery	122	180	466	84	-	853
Drug offences	9	10	393	2,097	-	2,509
Motoring offences	112	14	15	1	-	142
Other offences	96	46	194	175	10	520
Offence not recorded	4	1	8	6	-	19

As a group, foreign national prisoners are not significantly or disproportionately represented in the above offence categories, compared with UK nationals, except for drug offences and fraud & forgery cases. The largest increases in sentenced foreign national prisoners between 2000 and 2005 were those sentenced for drug offences (from 1,736 to 2,538), followed by fraud and forgery (from 139 to 611). In the case of drug offences, sentenced foreign national prisoners comprise 24% of all prisoners in for drug offences and 51% of those imprisoned for fraud and forgery. Given that foreign national prisoners represent just over 13% of the prison population, they are significantly disproportionately represented in these offence categories.

However, in the case of drug offences, the significant number of foreign nationals who are arrested at Ports of Entry for drug trafficking offences may explain this. 84% of those foreign nationals sentenced for drug offences receive 4 years or more indicating that these are mainly drug importation offences where sentencing usually begins at that point. In the case of fraud and forgery, this disproportionately can be partially explained as the figures covers foreign nationals again arrested at Ports of Entry attempted to leave or enter the country by deception with false/altered travel documents that received between 5 to 18 months imprisonment. Otherwise, foreign national prisoners are either, underrepresented or not significantly overrepresented in other offence categories. The overrepresentation of foreign national prisoners in the drug category has been evident from RDS statistics from at least the late 1980's.

In the early 1990's, the proportion of foreign national prisoners was around 8%, and comprised of mainly Irish and Nigerian nationals. Between 2000 and 2005 the foreign national prisoner population increased by 73% from 5,586 to 9,650, in comparison to an increase of 11%, in the population of British nationals in prison.

Table 5 shows the increase in foreign national prisoners between 2000-2006.

Table 5 Foreign national prisoners in England & Wales 2000-2006

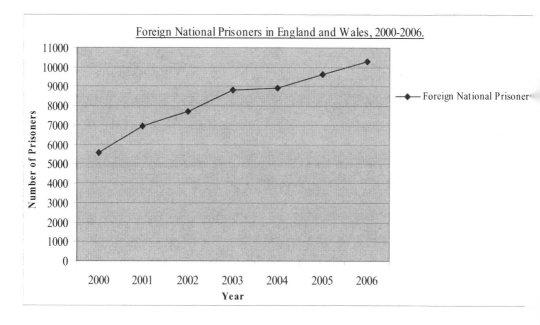

2000	2001	2002	2003	2004	2005	2006
5,58	6,930	7,719	8,799	8,941	9,651	10,265

Table 6 Population in prison by selected nationalities, continents and gender, Engeland and Wales as on 28.02.06

	Males	Females	Total
	72,301	4,416	76,717
UK Nationals	62,094	3,443	65,538
Foreign Nationals	9,388	877	10,265
Unrecorded	818	96	915
Europe	4,878	303	5,181
Albania	120	3	123
Armenia	7	0	7
Austria	8	3	11
Azerbaijan	4	0	4
Belgium	30	4	34
Bosnia-Herzegovina	7	3	10
Bulgaria	11	5	16
Croatia	11	0	11
Cyprus	53	1	54
Czech Republic	25	2	27
Denmark	10	2	12
Estonia	11	0	11
Finland	2	0	2
France	144	16	160
Georgia	23	1	24
Germany	97	21	118
Gibraltar	2	0	2
Greece	16	5	21
Hungary	17	2	19
Iceland	1	0	1
Irish Republic	650	40	691
Italy	108	12	120
Kazakhstan	3	1	4
Kyrgystan	5	0	5
Latvia	41	3	44
Lithuania	160	12	172
Macedonia	6	0	6
Malta	9	0	9
Moldova	34	3	37
Netherlands	111	20	131
Norway	6	0	6
Poland	177	7	184
Portugal	164	9	173

Romania	135	18	153
Russia	99	16	115
Serbia and Montenegro	93	3	96
Slovakia	9	3	12
Slovenia	1	0	1
Spain	71	14	85
Sweden	11	5	16
Switzerland	4	0	4
Turkey	309	5	314
Turkmenistan	1	0	1
Uzbekistan	2	0	2
Asia	1,401	64	1,465
West Indies	1,700	179	1,880
Middle East	580	9	590
North America	95	18	114
Oceania	45	3	48
Africa	7,337	509	7,847
Central or South America	249	37	286
Other	9	0	9

Source RSD Home Office

Jamaica is by far the largest nationality for both males and females, with 1,429 males and 124 females, followed by Nigeria, Ireland and Pakistan. 6,510, or 67%, were serving sentences. A further 2,271 foreign nationals were on remand accounting for 24% of the total foreign national population. The largest increase in the remand population of foreign nationals between 2000 and 2005 was for fraud and forgery (from 73 to 329 for males and from 7 prisoners to 71 prisoners for females.) The largest increases in sentenced foreign nationals between 2000 and 2005 were for those sentenced for drug offences (from 1,736 to 2,538), followed by fraud and forgery (from 139 to 611).

The changes in the profile of foreign national prisoners over the past decade can be explained partly by the changing drug trafficking routes, changes in targeting by the Customs & Excise Service, the impact on visa controls and changes in legislation – particularly with regards immigration offences. Table 7 shows changes over the past 12 years amongst selected nationalities.

Table 7 Foreign national prisoners in England & Wales, 1994-2005, selected nationalities

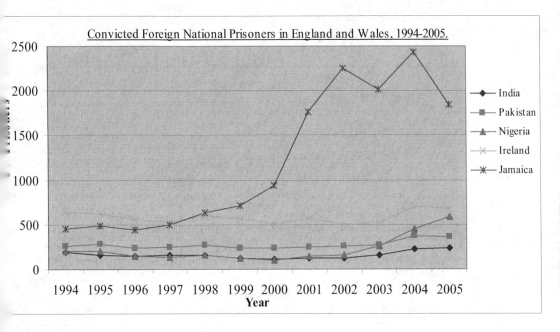

Convicted Foreign National Prisoners in England and Wales, 1994-2005.

The assumption of Jamaican nationals as the largest group of foreign national prisoners (taking over from Irish nationals in 1998) reflected the significant increase in drug importation from Jamaica which itself followed the introduction of visa controls on Colombian nationals in 1997. The recent increase of Nigerian foreign national prisoners is also partly explained by the increase of drug importations from that country. Changes in the numbers and rankings of different foreign national prisoner groups can be partially explained by changes in drug trafficking patterns, law enforcement and targeting changes. Some of the largest recent increases in foreign national groups have been from the EU Accession States. However they are still small numbers compared with the nationals of countries such as Ireland, Jamaica, Pakistan and Nigeria, which in total comprise over a half of all foreign national prisoners. European prisoners represent 20% of foreign nationals in prisons in England & Wales with increases seen in the imprisonment of nationals from the EU Accession countries of Latvia, Lithuania and Poland. Other foreign national groups, which have shown recent significant increases over the past 5 years, are from Somalia, The Netherlands, Portugal, France, China, Algeria, and Iraq. It can be predicted that future significant increases amongst foreign national prisoners in England & Wales will continue to be from amongst these groups.

A.1.5 Overview of legislation

A.1.5.1 Prison Legislation

The Prison Act 1952 consolidates certain enactment's relating to prisons and other institutions for offenders. Prison Rules 1999 and Prison (Amendment) Rules 2000 bring up-to-date legislation on how prisons are managed. Internal instructions from the Prison Service to Prison Governors are issued through Prison Service Instructions (PSI's), Prison Service Orders (PSO's), and Standards.

A.1.5.2 Prison Legislation & Foreigners

Foreign prisoners have the same legal position as other prisoners and have the same legal rights and obligations as UK national prisoners. There is no specific PSI or PSO issued by the Prison Service related to how foreign national prisoners should be managed within prisons. This absence is subject to criticism from various prison campaigning groups (see Section E. Evaluation & Recommendations). The whole catalogue of PSO's and PSI's will impact on the conditions and treatment of foreign national prisoners to some extent. However, there are a number of PSO's that may particularly relate to foreign national prisoners, they are:

PSO 2800 requires that all establishments must be prepared, as far as possible, to provide appropriate interpretation or translation services for communicating with non-English speaking prisoners.
PSI 35/2002 Categorisation & Allocation of Deportees to open Conditions. This PSI allows prisoners recommended for deportation to be considered for open conditions as long as they pass the appropriate risk assessment.
PSI 54/2002 & PSO 4550 on Religion recognises and respects the right of prisoners to practise their religion and these provide guidance on religious observance for staff.
PSI 21/2005 re- Faith Advisors
PSI 70/1999 Religious provision for Shi'a Muslims
PSO 4400 Communications: Telephone calls and Letters
PSO 2800 Race Relations, the primary order to promote good race relations within prison establishments.
PSI 45/2002 Race Relations: Racist Incident Reporting Form & Standardised Log. Instructs staff on how racist incidents should be handled by staff.
PSO 4630 (re-issued 17/07/06) & PSI 53/1998 Immigration and Foreign Nationals in Prison. Guidance on the management of Immigration Act detainees held within prison establishments. Instructions to Prisons on liaison/protocol arrangements with the Immigration Service.
PSO 6000 Parole, early release & recall. Cancelled PSI 27/2004 Early Release & Recall Scheme for Foreign Nationals liable for deportation.
A PSO on the duties and responsibilities of Prisons for contact with Embassies and High Commissions is due for issue in 2006.

The whole range of sentencing options are available for courts to impose on defendants regardless of their nationality. However, a sentencer will take into account whether it is feasible to make a community penalty if the defendant has irregular immigration status. A foreign national with irregular immigration status, such as an overstayer or illegal entrant, with no rights to work or entitlement to benefits may be expelled or removed before they can start or complete a sentence in the community.

A criminal court will be required to consider recommending the deportation of a foreign national defendant if the Crown Prosecution Service, (CPS), informs the court that the defendant has been officially 'served' with a notice that they are liable for deportation[13]. The sentencing court may then recommend deportation as part of the sentence, under Section 3(6), Immigration Act 1971. A court deportation recommendation is not final, as the IND has to confirm the decision, but the IND usually follows a court recommendation. There is a second process leading to deportation following the commission of a criminal offence. This is when, following sentence, the IND decide to expel on the basis that this is "conducive to the public good", 3(5)(a) Immigration Act 1971. In both instances, there is a time limited, appeal right. Whether the court has recommended deportation or the IND has made a decision itself to deport the IND issues a decision notice to the foreign national prisoner usually within a year of their expected release date. Appeal procedures through the criminal courts and the Asylum & Immigration Tribunal appeals system are available.

International and bilateral transfer agreements for foreign prisoners. The UK is a signatory of the Council of Europe Prisoners Transfer Agreement, the Commonwealth Prisoner Transfer Scheme and also has a number of bilateral agreements. Table 8 shows the number of foreign national prisoners who have been returned to serve their sentences in their home countries alongside those British prisoners who similarly returned to serve their prison sentence in the UK.

---

[13] it is the responsibility of the arresting officer to consult the Immigration and Nationality Directorate, (IND), to ascertain the person's immigration status. The IND may then request the police to serve the arrested foreign national, with a warning notice, (an IM3 form), which informs them that 'they are liable for deportation'.

Table 8 Repatriation of prisoners into and out of the UK, 1986 - 200

Year	In	Out
1986	2	10
1987	5	6
1988	7	7
1989	1	12
1990	--	13
1991	6	17
1992	9	18
1993	11	9
1994	17	5
1995	10	12
1996	24	21
1997	34	17
1998	27	42
1999	11	22
2000	20	35
2001	36	39
2002	41	50
2003	46	50
2004	48	100
2005	108	not available

Source; Cross Border Transfer Unit, Home Office

The process is governed by the Repatriation of Prisoners Act 1984. In 2005, 108 foreign national prisoners were repatriated to their country of origin, see table 9

Table 9. Prisoners repatriated from England & Wales 2005, by country

Canada	2
Poland	1
The Netherlands	83
Belgium	12
Cyprus	1
Spain	5
Portugal	1
Denmark	2
Sweden	1
Total Number Transferred	108

Source; Cross Border Transfer Unit, Home Office

Prisoners can start the administrative process to apply for transfer immediately after their sentence is final, the process can take between 6 to 18 months, sometimes longer. While Jamaican prisoners represent the largest single group of foreign national prisoners, the Jamaican Government has decided against signing any repatriation treaty. Given that there is a significant Jamaican prison population in the US and Canada, as well as the UK, the Jamaican Government would presumably be concerned that their prison system could not manage. In 2003, the UK Government agreed that prisoners transferred to the Netherlands could be re-sentenced by the Dutch Courts. This has lead to a significant increase in the number of Dutch nationals repatriated.

A.2 TREATMENT OF FOREIGN PRISONERS

A.2.1 General

A body of research, prison inspection reports and other literature into the treatment, experiences and circumstances of FNP's in England & Wales has emerged during the past 15 years. Their findings and recommendations are generally consistent in reporting that FNP's have distinct needs which, apart from individual examples of good and best practise, are generally not meet adequately or consistently by prison staff or prison management (e.g. see HMIP 2001, 2002a, 2002b, 2003a; Cheney, 1993, Bhui 1995). Literature on foreign national prisoners may be divided into:
- Research from prison reform & campaigning groups; Ellis, (1998); Green, (1991, 1998)Tarzi & Hedges, (1990, 1993), (Cheney (1993), Pourgourides et al, (1996), Bhui, (1995, 2004)
- Reports from Her Majesty's Chief Inspectorate of Prisons (HMPI); see references for recommended reports 1995 - 2005;
- Research from probation staff in prison and outside; ACOP (1990), Abernethy & Hammond (1992, 1999)
- Other literature; Ball, L. and Griffin, S., (2000), Hales, L. (1996)

Research has identified the range of difficulties particularly impacting on FNP's. A range of problems and issues has been identified; some will impact certain FNP's more than others. FNP's who have not lived in this country, with no community ties and who do not speak English face the most problems. Communication/language issues, maintaining family contacts and immigration concerns, usually come out in research as the major issues for FNP's. Some complaints from FNP's overlap with those experienced by Black Minority Ethnic prisoners in general, discriminatory treatment, victimisation and racism. Research into FNP's and HMPI Reports have re-enforced and confirmed the common issues facing this group rather than identifying new areas.
The issue in the context of England & Wales therefore is more whether the Prison Service addresses these issues adequately at a strategic level and how individual establishments perform at a local level.
Prison policy; It has been Prison Service policy regarding FNP's for individual establishments to address the specific needs of their FNP's locally. This is done to allow Governors and staff to best address individual's needs, taking into account the prisoners offending behaviour and other needs. This allows Governors to best use their budget to

address the fluid prison population[14]. The Prison Service has acknowledged that foreign national prisoners present 'many challenges to individual prisons' although they do not acceded to the various requests and recommendations to address these needs through issuing a Prison Service Order (PSO) specifically concerning FNP's. Their position remains that 'the crimes committed by the FNP's population and their security needs are too diverse to be treated as a homogenous group – not all FNPs are from ethnic minorities – and many of the issues they face are similar to those of British citizens'[15]. Prison Service Head Quarters recognise that foreign nationals face specific problems and believe that they can best be address through advising prisons on good practice, providing up to date information and generally promoting the issue of foreign national prisoners.

There are various Prison Service Instructions (PSIs) and Prison Service Orders (PSOs) which are directly or more relevant to FNPs than British National prisoners, i.e. Faith, Contact with Immigration Service, Early Release Scheme & Deportation. There are no specific auditable standards or key performance targets related to FNPs monitored by the Prison Service or external bodies.

The experience of FNPs depends therefore, more on the individual prison management and the priority they give to this group of prisoners. This means that outside the general requirements for managing and treating prisoners, FNPs will experience varying local policies for addressing their particular issues. While the general proportion of FNPs in England & Wales is over 13% there are wide variations with prisons in London and other specific prisons having around 50%. It is not only in metropolitan prisons that there are examples of best practise and innovative work. It is not possible therefore to generalise about the conditions and treatment of FNPs as it varies considerable between individual prisons.

In the absence of a central Prison Service policy on FNPs, however, many prisons have devised a local Foreign National Prisoner Policy or Strategy of their own and created a dedicated Foreign National Co-ordinator (FNLO) post to implement it through a Foreign Nationals Committee (FNC). Where it has been decided that a FNLO or FNC is not required, responsibility for the treatment of FNPs is undertaken by the Race Relation Liaison Officer (RRLO) and the Race Relation Management Team (RRMT). Examples of the most significant progress in establishments are when a prison develops a Foreign Nationals strategy, actively supports and manages the dedicated staff and outside groups implementing it and trains prison staff to understand issues facing FNPs, see HMIP 1999 and 2003d Wandsworth. Other prisons may expect their Diversity Officer or Race Relations Liaison Officer to address the needs of FNPs through their respective management structures with varying degrees of progress usually dependant on the priority given to it by the Governor and Senior Management team. The following section summarises the various issues that research and HMIP Inspections have identified as affecting FNPs to varying degrees.

---

[14] '*The Prisons Handbook* ' 2006 Ed Mark Leech. 2.18 Foreign National Prisoners, Jeanne Steele.

[15] HM Prison Service Prison Administration Group. In Foreign Nationals Bulletin Issue No 1. July 2004. '*A Strategic Approach*'.

A.2.2 Living conditions and facilities

There is no current prison service policy to concentrate FNPs in England and Wales in certain prisons. Prisons however in the Southeast and London hold a significant proportion of FNPs as do a small number of other prisons outside of London. Within prisons, there is no difference in living conditions and facilities between FNPs and other prisoner groupings. Where prisons have a significant proportion of FNPs, there may be local arrangements to place speakers of similar languages together for instance, at the prisoner's request, to alleviate isolation.

A.2.3 Reception and admission

Research in this area has identified language barriers, lack of information (particularly concerning immigration matters) and isolation as issues impacting onto FNPs at the reception and admission stage. FNPs will go through the same reception and admissions procedure as other prisoners. Many prisons have 'First Night' Induction Schemes aimed at alleviating problems experienced by all prisoners newly remanded. These units can build up expertise with regards FNPs, especially those local prisons near Air and Sea Ports who receive a significant proportion of FNPs, using staff and sometimes Foreign National Prisoner Orderlies, with language skills, to inform FNPs and having local prepared translations available. Some reception units, acknowledging that FNPs, especially those arrested at ports of entry with family abroad and no UK contacts, will provide a phone card at the prison expense for family contact to be established as soon as is feasible. This practise varies and is not a mandatory requirement; however, if the prison does not provide a 'free' phone call, an early opportunity for a newly remanded prisoner, including FNPs, to establish contact with home, will be sought. It should be remembered that it is also standard practise for arresting police and customs and excise officers to allow arrested persons, including foreign nationals, a phone call home. Prison Reception staff have a duty, through PSO 4630 (Instructions to Prisons on liaison arrangements with the Immigration Service) to inform the Immigration Service of the remand of all prisoners who state they are foreign nationals or whom they believe may be, to verify their immigration status. Many Induction Units will ask FNPs whether they wish to have contact with their Embassy and facilitate that contact.

Research has identified FNPs as experiencing particular difficulties as a result of lack of information about the prison, the legal process and immigration matters, (PRT 2004, Cheney 1993, Bhui 1995). Initiatives to ameliorate this, by the Prison Service centrally, has seen two editions in the last decade, of a Foreign National Prisoners Information Pack. Such centrally produced information assists FNPs to understand prison rules, their rights, duties and entitlements in prison, how to make a complaint, contact embassies & apply for repatriation etc. The 1994 Foreign Prisoners Resource Pack was produced jointly between Prison Service HQ and the Prison Reform Trust, it came in two sections, one – translated in 20 languages for FNPs and a second section for staff training and education. The latest edition, launched in December 2004, was a joint production between the Prison Service, London Probation and the Prison Reform Trust, is available, in 22 translations, and available on the Prison Services intranet site (so that it can be readily up dated). There are also examples of individual prisons producing local information in translations for prisoners.

To address the range of communication difficulties, isolation and reception problems of FNPs, a significant innovation, pioneered at a large local London prison, HMP Wandsworth, has been the use of Foreign National Orderlies, (FNO). FNO's, carefully recruited, trained and supported by the prisons Foreign Nationals Co-ordinator, have proved they can provide a range of services for FNPs. They contribute in many ways to the assisting FNPs, reducing isolation through support and the provision of information – see below. These posts have been highly praised in prison inspections and adopted by other prisons as an important and effective contribution to assisting FNPs and in producing a healthier prison environment, not just at reception in local prisons, but also at later stages in training prisons. These roles are a core aspect of a wider, comprehensive approach to working effectively with FNPs.

Best Practise. Foreign National Orderlies. *HMP Wandsworth.* These posts were innovative and a central part of a strategic prison policy developed for FNPs in a large, busy London prison. These posts were established to reduce the problems the prison was facing with a high proportion of FNPs and to support and work alongside the Foreign Nationals Co-ordinator and prison staff. They had a place on the Foreign Nationals Committee. The Orderlies are in a trustee position, allowed movement between wings & were paid and either full or part time posts. Training and support was provided. Their roles included; distribution of information to FNPs on the wings (i.e., translated information, addresses of useful organisations and embassies), systematically visiting new arrivals to assist with urgent problems (i.e., immigration referral, language problem), helping to represent the views of FNPs to staff, keeping a list of prisoners willing to interpret and helping to identify FNPs in need of particular help (because of language difficulties, psychological problems etc.) Bhui 2004 p. 42.

There are examples of good practice towards FNPs, reported in prison inspections and in the Foreign Nationals Bulletin initially produced by the Prison Service and now by NOMS. However, research, prison reforming groups and prison inspections continue to report FNPs experiencing particular difficulties in prison not being addressed adequately. Frequent criticisms are that no allowance was made for their lack of English, ignorance of prison rules and expectations and difficulties in establishing and maintaining family contacts abroad[16].

A.2.4 Work - Education – Training – Sports – Recreation

FNPs should be eligible for the same range of work, education, training, sports and recreation opportunities available to all prisoners. All prisoners with a sentence of over 12 months are supposed to go through a sentence planning process conducted by prison staff. This is intended to assess the individual prisoner so that their time in prison can be planned constructively to best reduce their risk of re-offending and begin plan for their resettlement and release. A newly introduced system jointly used by prison and probation, OASys (Offender Assessment System), is being rolled out at present. However, lack of prison staff to undertake this assessment means that a proportion of all prisoners do not undergo this assessment. Unless there are other processes established FNPs, along with British prisoners, would not have a structured needs assessment to ascertain their reset-

---

16 Prison Reform Trust '*Forgotten Prisoners – The Plight of Foreign National Prisoners in England & Wales.* May 2004.

tlement, work, training and education, needs. There is no evidence at present that amongst prisoners, who do not receive an OASys assessment, FNPs are disproportionately represented. However, if FNPs are not represented in the priority groups who receive an OASys assessment, this could occur[17]. The HM Inspectorate of Prisons is preparing a Thematic Inspection on Foreign National prisoners, due for publication in 2006, which may provide evidence in this area.

FNPs with an adequate use of English can more readily find out what resettlement and rehabilitative opportunities the prison can offer but for FNPs with no English, this can be problematic. In general, FNPs are well motivated to make use of the full range of work and education opportunities in prison. For those with language needs, prison education facilities (provided on contract by outside colleges) provide English classes, a wide range of basic, remedial and life skills courses as well as more advanced externally verified certificate courses that cover a wide range of subjects and skills.

It is a common experience that FNP prisoners, especially those who live abroad and have dependants there and those who have no UK contacts or support, are motivated to seek out the best paid work in prison to support themselves and send money back home. Some jobs may be unavailable for a FNP with insufficient use of English to safely work there but otherwise, they have the same opportunities as any other prisoner to obtain paid prison work. Indeed, better-paying (and usually more demanding) prison jobs have a high proportion of FNPs. This is due both to their needs in prison and motivation to support dependants abroad. Work Boards in prison are responsible to ensure that prison jobs are distributed fairly and equitably.

A.2.5 Food – Religion – Personal hygiene – Medical care

The quality and range of food is a contentious area with all prisoner groups including FNPs. The range of food available to prisoners has increased in recent years and Halal meat, for instance, is available widely along with kosher, vegetarian and vegan options. Criticism about the quality of food is widespread throughout the prison estate due to the amount per day available for ingredients. Foreign nationals have commented that prison food is bland without the use of spices and herbs however, there are choices and generally the range is becoming more diverse. Prisoners have access to a canteen to buy items to supplement their diet. There has been criticism over the years that there is limited range of goods and food available for FNPs and BME prisoners. However, this is changing with local prisons being increasingly able to select their own range of items to match different prisoner needs.

The Prison Service recognises and respects the right of prisoners to practice their religion. Guidance on religious observance is found in Prison Service Standard on Religion, PSO 4550 and PSI 54/2002. Prisoners have the right to practise their religion in prison and on reception are asked their religion and/or denomination. Prisoners must have access to the Chaplain of their declared faith. There is a Chaplain General at Prison Service HQ to ensure that the religious needs of prisoners are met. Prisons are required to cater for a range of religions and are required to provide a multi-faith room for the use of different faith groups. The Chaplain in prison is responsible for addressing the needs of all

---

[17] Prisoners who have committed serious violent and sexual offences and who will be released under multi-agency public protection procedures are priority cases for OASys assessments.

faiths and seeking outside faith leaders to lead prison services/worship. Prisoners must be able to follow a diet and be allowed to wear dress and headgear, which accords with the requirements of their religions. In practise, there can be difficulties in obtaining faith leaders to attend some prisons, which are isolated from centres of population and away from diverse congregations. At times of heightened tensions outside prison with regards to terrorism, some Muslim prisoners for instance, reported discriminatory comments towards them from other prisoners. Convicted prisoners are required to where prison clothes although prisoners are allowed to wear religious headdress such as Sikhs - turbans and Muslim women - headscarves.

Medical care. There are specific health care issues for FNPs, particularly focusing on mental health issues due to separation from families abroad and isolation due to cultural and language differences. Isolation leading to depression and general mental health needs would therefore be felt to be greater amongst FNPs than the rest of the prison population. There is no detailed research, which shows that this is the case however. FNPs do not appear to be disproportionately represented amongst suicides in prison. It could be that the established medical services in prisons are not relevant to the mental health needs of FNPs due to expectations and cultural differences in dealing with distress and depression. There was evidence in Pourgourides et al, (1996) of considerable levels of mental health problems amongst immigration detainees particularly within an Immigration Detention facility. Also, amongst foreign nationals held in prison as immigration detainees, after completing their sentence, the uncertainty surrounding deportation decisions and administrative delays has been shown to affect their mental health, (see Paton & Jenkins, (2002), Tarzi & Hedges (1990)).

There is a concern when medical staffs in prisons treat FNPs who speak limited or no English. While medical staffs are able to use a telephone interpreting service, it is not common practise and sometimes other prisoners are used to interpret. Some FNPs, who speak limited or no English bring along fellow prisoners who do speak English as well as their own language for medical consultations. There are obvious concerns as to accuracy and confidentiality in such cases. Complaints by FNPs concerning health care, i.e. delays in seeing a doctor and perceived quality of care, are similar to those from the general prison population.

A.2.6 Consular and legal help

Articles 36(1)(b) and 36(1)(c) of the 1963 Vienna Convention set out the necessary procedures that the prison Service must undertake in relation to detained FN's. The Prison Service has been planning to clarify these obligations through a PSO, which should be issued in 2006. There is evidence that FNPs are frequently unclear whether their embassy or consulate is on the relevant list, which means that they will be informed of their detention by the prison regardless of their personal views due to convention obligations.

Should FNPs request contact themselves with their Embassy, the prison should provide letters, at the prison expense, to do so and facilitate prison visits when requested. Prison staffs have ready access to Embassy addresses. In reality many FNPs either do not want any Embassy contact; it depends significantly on which country. This is for a variety of reasons, sometimes FNPs will believe that contact with their embassy could lead to problems for their family back home or draw unwelcome attention to them when they are eventually expelled and return home. Sometimes, FNPs adopt the attitude perpetuated amongst their fellow countrymen that it is not worth seeking approaching their Embassy, as no services will be provided.

Best Practice. Embassy & High Commission meetings with Prison & Probation. Since 1992, there have been regular meetings hosted by the Prison Service HQ and London Probation. These biannual meetings have been to inform consulate staff about prison regimes and changes to enable them to provide a knowledgeable and professional service to their imprisoned nationals. These well-attended meetings also enable consulate staff to ask questions about prison and probation practice and feedback any problems they are encountering in their work.

Access to legal advice and representation. FNPs have access to free legal advice and representation for both criminal proceedings and for any subsequent appeals. Access is not dependent on their immigration status. Legal Aid Offices within prisons act link FNPs with solicitors.

A.2.7 Contact with the outside world, visits, letters, telephone calls, newspapers

Establishing and maintaining contact with families' abroad is identified in related research, as one of FNPs most important needs. Regular contact can maintain links for successful resettlement, to reassure FNPs of their family's welfare during separation and reduce distress and isolation (Tarzi & Hedge 1990), Cheney 1993).

Regarding visits, FNPs prisoners have the same entitlement to receive prison visitors as other prisoners. FNPs are entitled to receive Prison Visiting Orders (PVO's) that need to be sent out to those visiting. Financial assistance is available for prison visits from family, or in their absence, close friends, who fulfil qualifying conditions. In addition, for those who can receive visitors from either within the UK or from abroad, there is the opportunity, as with all prisoners, to apply for 'accumulated visits' (through saving up PVO's so that a number of visits can be condensed into a short period). Many FNPs, who have been arrested at Ports of Entry and who are not UK residents, will frequently have no UK contacts and do not expect prison visitors. Chaplains and sometimes, NGO's such as the New Bridge organisation, will provide FNPs who approach them, with a prison visitor who can maintain contact with them through letters and visits. Prison chaplains also hold the responsibility within most prisons to organise and provide prison visitors for isolated and vulnerable prisoners. The extent of this service varies between prisons.

Maintaining family ties therefore through letters and telephone calls are very important. Unconvicted FNPs can send out two free letters every week and convicted prisoners, one free weekly letter – the stamps being paid by the prison. Extra letters can be purchased through the prison shop/canteen, including special celebration/birthday cards. There are no specific limitations to the number of letters that may be sent or received. The Prison Service acknowledges the importance of FNPs maintaining family contacts and has sought to obtain the cheapest telephone contract for making telephone calls from abroad. An International Calling Card of varying denominations can be purchased at the prison shop. The card has a scratch pad, which reveals an access number, which prisoners need to use before they are allowed to access the IDD platform. As the call progresses the value of the card reduces. This service is for the exclusive use of prisoners and the cards cannot be purchased outside of the prison system.

Some reception units in local prisons will provide all newly remanded FNPs with a free telephone card so they may inform family of their imprisonment. While it is not a mandatory requirement many prisons will pay for a free monthly 5-minute phone call for a sentenced FNP who has had no prison visitors during the preceding month. This is usually organised from an official prison telephone at public expense or an International Calling Card to the requisite amount will be provided free.

The provision of newspapers and periodicals is a matter for local discretion. Prisons will look to providing a range taking into account the needs of FNPs and prisoners from minority ethnic groups. Subject to security and other considerations, prisoners can receive or buy books, magazines, newspapers etc. of their choice. Prisons can obtain foreign language books and materials from their local authority public library and prisons make efforts to varying degrees to provide non-English language relevant to the background and culture of its population. Some Embassies and High Commissions assist with providing materials to prisons. No examples are available of foreign television channels being available in prisons although there are individual examples in some establishments of foreign films in languages other than English being made available for special showings.

A.2.8 Re-integration activities - Prison leave

Prisoners are expected to go through sentence planning following being sentenced which identifies resettlement needs and offending behaviour issues, see section d). This process should assess what activities the prisoner should undertake which will reduce the prisoner's risk of re-offending on release, i.e. attendance on drug programmes, centrally accredited offending behaviour programmes, substance abuse treatment etc. Where this assessment, (or equivalent process made in the absence of a full OASys assessment), is made and a sentence plan prepared, all prisoners including FNPs, would be required to complete their required targets and referred for attendance on relevant offending behaviour programmes. Compliance and successful completion of a sentence plan can affect early release.

There is evidence that some FNPs are less likely to be assessed for offending behaviour work as they do not meet the criteria for referral – i.e. foreign national drug couriers, usually resident abroad, arrested at airports, with no previous convictions or drug abuse problems (Abernethy & Hammond 1999). In such cases, resettlement plans will concentrate more on a FNP gaining employment and general education skills. There is an example of a prison addressing the offending issues of foreign national drug traffickers through a group work programme. FNPs who are to be considered for early release whether in the UK or expelled abroad, would be expected to show evidence that they have met their sentence plan targets to reduce their risk of re-offending.

Best Practise. Drug Importers Programme. HMP The Verne. FNPs comprise over 50% of this prison's population with many serving sentences for importing cocaine and heroin into the UK. HMP The Verne has therefore established a regionally accredited group work programme to address the offending behaviour aspects of such crime. The sentencing planning process will identify a prisoner as being suitable for such a programme. Over a series of group sessions, the impact on drug abuse on individuals, families and communities, the cost to their own families/communities and choices & options to reduce risk of re-offending, will be examined. Offending rationalisations, minimisation and denial are challenged by prison staff through the group work process.

Prior to the implementation of the Criminal Justice Act 2003, prisoners serving less than 4 years automatically served half before release. In the case of prisoners released into the UK, they were subject to a period of supervision on licence by the probation service following release, the licence period being dependent on the sentence length. For those FNPs being expelled or removed serving prison sentences less than 4 years, there would be no requirement that they would be supervised by a probation service or equivalent, in their home country. For sentences over 4 years, prisoners were eligible to apply for release on parole again after serving half. Those prisoners being released into the UK on parole would be supervised by the probation service. Again, there was no supervision requirement for FNPs gaining parole and being expelled.

The CJA 2003 changed release arrangements considerably for FNPs liable to deportation through PSO 6000. Prison governors are now responsible for making parole decisions in the majority of cases[18]. They also are responsible for taking a decision in respect of the Early Removal Scheme (ERS). The ERS, implemented in April 2004, allows eligible FNPs to be removed up to 4 ½ months before their half way release date, the period dependant on the length of their sentence. For instance, a FNP, serving a 6-year sentence and recommended for deportation could, if granted parole and ERS were expelled after serving 2 years 7½ months. FNPs who appeal against deportation or who have an outstanding asylum claim cannot be considered under the ERS.

The changes to the parole scheme and the introduction of the ERS have meant that an increasing proportion of FNPs are being expelled under these arrangements. By March 2005, over 900 FNPs who had been returned to their country of origin were subject to ERS arrangements. The majority of those removed have been Jamaican nationals but with a significant number of Nigerians, Ghanaians and Dutch nationals. When FNPs are being expelled they are usually escorted straight from the prison to the airport for the flight. If the flight is early, it might necessitate an over night stay in an Immigration Removal Centre or short term holding facility at an airport.

A.2.9 Release – Deportation

The process whereby a foreign national may be considered for deportation following the commission of a criminal offence is detailed in section 5. A defence solicitor may argue against the court making an deportation recommendation. Grounds may be that the foreign national is settled in the UK, has family and community ties here and the impact their deportation will have on them and others and that their risk of re-offending to the community is low. A criminal court has to consider recommending deportation if the prosecution states that the defendant is liable for deportation and has been served with the necessary forms. Sometimes a court may be unaware that the defendant is a foreign national liable for deportation should checks not have been made with the Immigration Service by the prosecution and arresting officer. However, once any prisoner is received into prison, the prison service is required to notify the Criminal Casework Team (CCT) of the Immigration Service (IS) of the remand of all FNPs through PSO 4630. This pro-

---

[18] Governors are now responsible for taking the decision in the majority of parole and early release scheme cases where there is a 'presumption' in favour of early release. Those cases, which are not considered 'presumptive,' are those FNPs serving a sentence of 4 years and over for either a violent or sexual offence. Such cases will require an enhanced risk assessment. Enhanced risk cases whether under the ERS or parole, must be referred to the Release and Recall Section at Prison Service HQ.

tocol for notification between the IS and the Prison Service is to ensure that proper consideration is given to all FNPs as to whether they should be expelled. The CCT undertake checks on the immigration status of referred FNPs. The CCT may then decide to confirm the court recommendation or, should there have been no court recommendation, consider using its own powers to seek the deportation or removal of a FNP on the grounds that their continued residence in the UK is not conducive to the public good.

Recent initiatives have seen Immigration Officers seconded to receptions in London prisons to assist prison staff in identifying FNPs. When a court deportation recommendation has been made the IS review the case and usually confirm the courts view and proceed with deportation. The CCT of IS work to internal guidance lines that they will usually consider for deportation a European Union citizen who receives a prison sentence in excess of two years or a non-EU national receiving a sentence over one year.

For FNPs released into the community in England and Wales, there are no differences in licence or parole requirements compared with British nationals similarly released. Expelled FNPs are not required to be under any supervision arrangements when returned to their country of origin. An deportation order is a formal document, signed by a Minister that requires the named persons to be removed from the UK by the Immigration Service and prohibits them from re-entering the UK. It remains in force indefinitely or until it is revoked on application of the subject. Should a person subject to an deportation order return to the UK they will have committed an offence.

A.2.10 Aftercare – Probation

In case the case of FNPs released on licence or parole within England & Wales, the relevant Offender Manager in the probation area covering their home address will supervise them. They will be managed by the same criteria as other released prisoners dependent on any specific licence requirements imposed to reduce their risk or re-offending and harm to the public. FNPs being expelled on sentence completion are not subject to any mandatory supervision requirements from probation services or equivalent agencies in their home country.

There are a small number of NGO's in England and Wales who provide support and services to FNPs during their sentence. This support usually ends when the FNP is expelled to their home country however. These NGO's are funded through charitable sources and increasingly through contracts with individual prisons to provide specific services. These organisations can be divided between national organisations and local groups visiting their nearest prison. The former groups comprise Vamos Juntos, assisting Spanish, Portuguese and Latin American prisoners, Detention Advice Service, providing specialist immigration advice, New Bridge providing general befriending support and casework and Hibiscus, working with Afro-Caribbean and Latin American Women.

Good Practise. Hibiscus is an example of a specialist NGO working with female foreign national prisoners to alleviate the disadvantages they face imprisoned abroad and assists in their rehabilitation. Hibiscus has been established for over 20 years and currently has paid contracts with several prisons throughout England and Wales, visiting prisons regularly, providing individual casework, holding advise surgeries and running support groups. Foreign nationals in other prisons through letters and phone calls can also contact it. Hibiscus will work with all foreign national women though particularly with Afro-Caribbean and Spanish speaking prisoners. It is unique amongst such NGO's as it has established offices in Jamaica to support the families of Jamaican prisoners and assist in their resettlement on deportation, it is also planning to re-establish links with Nigeria, where it previously had an office, given the recent increase in Nigerian women imprisoned in the UK.

Contact with probation services in England & Wales. The probation and prison services are in the process of establishing 'end to end' offender management. It remains to be seen how this will operate with regards FNPs particularly those arrested at Ports of Entry and those who are expected to be expelled on sentence completion. Residency is the significant factor as opposed to a prisoner's nationality in terms of whether an Offender Manager in the community has been allocated to a FNP. A prisoner who has an address in this country should be allocated an Offender Manager (OM) from the local probation office. The OM will maintain contact with the prisoner; the prison's Offender Supervisor and other prison staff contribute to sentence planning and prepare relevant risk assessments and parole reports when required. This should be the case for any prisoner with an address in this country regardless of the nationality or immigration status of the prisoner. However, in the case of the large number of foreign nationals arrested at a seaport or airport, who has never lived in the UK, different arrangements may be made reflecting resource prioritisation and the risk management of offenders who are likely to be expelled on completion of their sentence. Guidance for NOMS and the National Probation Directorate is required.

The current situation for the group of FNPs arrested at Ports of Entry who have not lived in the UK, is that they will be unlikely to be allocated an outside probation contact or if they are, the extent of this contact will be very limited. For FNPs from this last group, contact with probation staff will usually be limited to those seconded probation staff working in prison who will prepare any parole assessment reports where required, work on addressing offending behaviour identified through sentence planning and other resettlement issues.

There were two specialist probation units, both disbanded in early 2000's, who work with FNPs arrested at Ports of Entry: the London Probation's Foreign National Unit (FNU) covering Heathrow Airport and Kent Probation's European Co-ordinated Resettlement Unit (ECRU) covering EU prisoners in Kent prisons. The former was disbanded due to resource prioritisation, the second due to withdrawal of EU funding. They both provided a range of services and contacts with FNPs and assistance with resettlement. The Foreign Nationals Unit & ECRU developed links with countries abroad to obtain home background information and to contribute to sentencing and resettlement issues. Contacts were established with a number of statutory and voluntary organisations that could assist with resettlement needs in EU countries.

Links abroad have been re-established through an innovative programme initiated by a Resettlement Manager at HMP Morton Hall prompted by the resettlement needs of their large FNP population.

Best Practise .Resettlement of European Nationals. HMP Morton Hall, a female establishment, has the largest proportion of foreign nationals of any prison in England and Wales, 70-80%. With women from over 50 countries they have 2 full time foreign national officers and a Foreign Nationals Co-ordinator. With the desire to ensure the best resettlement provision for FNPs, they have built up contacts with 22 European countries via Embassies, international groups such as the European Group of Prisoners Abroad and the Conference Permanente de la Probation[19]. They have developed contacts with 22 European countries that can assist with the resettlement needs of a European FNP. A European FNP who wants to be put in contact with an agency in her home country will be provided with contact details, it is a voluntary initiative and dependant on the FNP requesting contact

A.2.11 Staff

Prison staffs do not receive specific training for working with FNPs in their initial training. Local or regional training events can be arranged and delivered by NGO's and others involved in this area of work. Prison Service HQ sees its role as promoting and sharing good practise initiatives amongst prisons through the provision of a quarterly Foreign Nationals Bulletin and it held its first National Foreign National Prisoners Conference, at which all prisons were represented, in July 2004.

Prisons manage FNPs who speak little or no English through improving their use of English through the provision of English classes, the availability of translated information and the use of a telephone interpreting service for prison use, Language Line. The Prison Service has had a central contract with a private sector company, Language Line for over 10 years. Each prison has an individual ID code that gains access to a bank of on-line interpreters. Most prisons require agreement of a senior management to authorise LL use, as there is a cost to the individual prison. Language Line has not been used to its full potential and there is evidence, through HMIP Inspections, that prison staff are either unaware of its existence or believe it to be too expensive and not request management authorisation to use them. Everyday reality for staff communicating with FNPs who speak little or no English is through using bi-lingual prisoners.

A.3   ADMINISTRATIVE DETENTION OF FOREIGN NATIONALS UNDER IMMIGRATION LAW IN THE UK

The 1971 Immigration Act (IA 1971) gives wide powers to detain foreign nationals pending examination or pending removal in the UK. Many people held under the IA 1971 are detained near a Port of Entry while the Immigration Service considers their application to enter or while arrangements are made to send them back. It can also include asylum seekers, detained while the Home Office considers their case and those whose asylum claim has been dismissed. Others detained people under IA 1973 are those alleged to have contravened the immigration laws in some way, overstayed their permission to remain or breached visa restrictions. There are no statutory criteria for detention and there is no statutory maximum time limit for detention under Immigration Act powers. There is no upper or lower age for being detained as asylum-seekers or immigrants in UK law. A proportion of immigration detainees will be those who have completed a prison sentence for a criminal matter but who will be kept in detention, either remaining in prison

---

[19]   The European Group of Prisoners Abroad (EGPA) is a grouping of the small number of organisations in Europe who specifically provide services for their nationals when they are serving prison sentences abroad, see http://www.egpa.org.

or being transferred to an Immigration Removal Centre (IRC), while decisions or arrangements are made as to their future in the country[20].

Statistics. The most recent Government figures on immigration detainees are for 2004 and cover those held solely under Immigration Act powers that do not include those who have committed criminal offences who also are subject to an immigration hold. On 25 December 2004 around 78% of those held in detention under IA 1971 powers had sought asylum at some stage. The majority (85%) of immigration detainees were being held in Immigration Removal Centres, with 13% being held in prison establishments and 2% at Immigration Short Term Holding Facilities. The nationalities making up the largest number of detainees were Chinese (205), Jamaican (190), Nigerian (140), Indian (95) and Turkish (90). (89%) of all detainees were male[21].

The snapshot figures for the four quarters of 2004 ranged from 1,105 to 1,515 people who had sought asylum detained on a given day. Based on figures produced by the Home Office, Amnesty International estimates that at least 27,000 people who had sought asylum at some stage were detained in 2003 and 25,000 in 2004. Home Office figures state that, as on the 25 December 2004: 35% of detainees had been in detention for 2 weeks or less, 22% for between 15-29 days, 18% for between one and two months, 11% for between two and four months, and 14% for more than four months. However, because the Home Office only releases 'snapshot' statistics, Amnesty International questions the accuracy of these figures. Amnesty International has concluded that the Home Office quarterly statistics belie the true scale of detention of those who have sought asylum at some stage and believes that thousands of people are being detained each year, some of them for lengthy periods. On the 25 December 2004, 25 people who were detained solely under IA powers were recorded as being under the age of 18 years; the majority (63%) of these persons had been in detention for 14 days or less. These individuals were all detained as part of families whose detention, as a group was considered necessary, and include those minors detained with their families at Oakington Reception Centre.

The number of asylum claims to industrialised countries, including the UK, is declining. In spite of this decline, in recent years, the number of those detained solely under IA 1971 powers in the UK who have claimed asylum at some stage, including families with children, has increased. Currently, capacity in immigration detention facilities, excluding short-term holding facilities (at ports and reporting centres) is 2,672, triple the number of available places when the current government came to power in 1997. Of these places, 370 were for women and 353 for families. The vast majority of those detained under Immigration Act powers have claimed asylum in the UK at some stage[22]

---

20 The Prison Service has been criticised in HMIP Reports for the number of immigration detainees being held in prisons. Government Ministers have agreed that prisons are not appropriate places to hold any but a small minority of immigration detainees – those being mainly on security grounds.

21 'United Kingdom - Seeking asylum is not a crime: detention of people who have sought asylum'. Amnesty International Report 45/015/2005)

22 Annual report of the HM Chief Inspector of Prisons for England & Wales 2004-2005 p 63. Also see 'Control of Immigration: Statistics United Kingdom, 2004.

A.3.1 Institution

Detainees can be held in Immigration Removal Centres (IRC), prisons, police stations and short term holding centres at ports, screening units and appeal hearing centres. Three of the 10 IRC's are fast track centres, where asylum seekers are detained from the time they apply for asylum while their claim is determined. Following determination, they can then remain in detention until they are removed. There is only one centre in Scotland and none in Northern Ireland where prisons are used for immigration detainees. Three of the removal centres are run by the Prison Service, the remained by private security companies contracted by the Immigration and Nationality Directorate.

Prisons also hold a number of foreign national prisoners who have completed their sentence for a criminal offence and are being held solely under Immigration Act powers while the IND is considering decisions or while appeals are pending. While the prison service has made considerable efforts at reducing the number of immigration detainees in prison the numbers have remained between 200-300 at any one time. This is both because the Immigration and Nationality Directorate has insufficient places to accommodate all those they wish to detain in IRC's or due to individual security and risk considerations.

The Detention Centre Rules 2001 provide a comprehensive set of rules and procedures covering the treatment of those held under detention[23]. IRC's are inspected by the HM Inspectorate of Prisons that has a statutory responsibility to do so. Their recent reports have been critical of the conditions found in several IRC and in particular short term holding facilities. In 2005, HM Inspectorate of Prisons published their criteria for assessing the conditions of the treatment of immigration detainees.

A.3.2 Legislative background

1971 Immigration Act gives wide powers of administrative detention, without time limit, pending removal or deportation of non-British citizens from the UK. Immigration detainees can be held on the authority of an official of the Immigration and Nationality Directorate (IND), a Home Office department, for an indefinite period of time. There is no requirement to be produced before an independent judicial authority within any time scale to test the merits of the detention, no presumption in favour of grant of bail, and limited access to legal aid. Since 1999 detainees have been given written reasons for detention, although this is in the form of a checklist with boxes that may be ticked, and is in English only. Schedule 2 of the 1971 Act enables immigration officers to examine people arriving in the UK or embarking. There is no time limit for conclusion of examination. Following examination they can give or refuse leave to enter. They can remove people refused leave to enter or declared to be illegal entrants. Schedule 2 paragraph 16 allows immigration officers to detain pending examination or pending removal.

People can be detained during examination (before a decision has been made about their status) and pending removal even when they cannot immediately be removed – that is, asylum seekers can be detained notwithstanding that they cannot be removed until the asylum claim has been determined.

---

[23] Joint Council for the Welfare of Immigrants. Immigration & Nationality Refugee Law Handbook 2006 edition. p 940.

Detainees can apply for bail to an immigration judge. A chief immigration officer (CIO) can also grant bail, subject to sureties, but CIO bail is rare. A person detained pending examination (that is, while the immigration officer is considering whether to grant or refuse leave to enter) can apply for bail if seven days have passed since arrival in the UK and the immigration officer has not yet made a decision. Where a decision has been made to refuse leave to enter, and removal directions have been issued, a detained person can also apply for bail.

Section 5 of the 1971 Act allows the Secretary of State to make an deportation order against a person who is liable to deportation under Schedule 3 – that is, whose deportation is considered 'conducive to the public good', or following a recommendation for deportation made by a criminal court. Anybody aged 17 or over convicted of an offence, which carries with it a possible term of imprisonment can be recommended for deportation. Dependants of the person recommended for deportation can also be expelled. 1971 Immigration Act gives wide powers of administrative detention, without time limit, pending removal or deportation of non-British citizens from the UK.

The Home Office first issues a notice of decision to make a deportation order specifying the reason for the decision and the destination to which the person is to be expelled. The decision carries a right of appeal. Schedule 3 par. 2 of the 1971 Act allows detention pending deportation where a person is: recommended for deportation by a court, served with notice of a decision to make an deportation order or already the subject of a signed deportation order. A detention order can be made (IA 1971 Schedule 3 paragraph 2(2)) once the notice of intention to expel has been served. If a person is detained and lodges an appeal against the notice of intention to expel, bail can be applied for while the appeal is pending. Once the appeal period lapses or if the appeal is dismissed, the Home Secretary can then sign a deportation order. If the person has not already been detained up till now, s/he can be detained by virtue of the deportation order itself (1971 Act Schedule 3 paragraph 2(3)).

A person who is liable to detention pending deportation proceedings can also be granted temporary release subject to a restriction order, with residential and/or reporting conditions and/or work restrictions, or released unconditionally. A recommendation for deportation is part of sentence, and can be appealed against to a higher criminal court as an appeal against sentence, within the time limit. It is current practice for the Home Office to serve a notice of a decision to expel, which carries its own appeal right to an immigration judge. A person will automatically be detained following a recommendation unless the court directs otherwise; the court can direct release subject to residential and reporting conditions (as can the Home Office), or unconditionally. If a person does appeal against the recommendation to a higher court, that court can grant bail even if the Home Office opposes this or has imposed a restriction order.

Temporary release from Home Office. In the case of people who have been given leave to enter, and against whom the Home Office commences deportation action, there is a power to detain once a notice of a decision to make an deportation order has been served. The Home Office may agree to temporary release from deportation, subject to a restriction order which will include the requirement to live at a specified address and report to a police station/immigration officer at specified intervals.

The stated Immigration and Nationality Directorate policy is to grant temporary admission/release whenever possible, and to authorise detention only where there is no alternative. Likelihood of compliance with restrictions, immigration history, any settled residence/employment/relationship, compassionate circumstances, length of detention, and expectation of removal within a reasonable period are all relevant factors.

Since October 1999 Immigration Act detainees are supposed to have been issued with a monthly progress report, in English, citing reason(s) for detention according to a pro forma checklist. The longer a person has been detained, the higher the decision-making level, with authority to detain beyond two months assigned to Assistant Director level, and beyond six months with the Director (Enforcement). If a person on temporary admission fails to comply with a requirement to report to an immigration officer, his or her examination may be treated as concluded Schedule 2, paragraph 10, of the 1996 Act).

Existing bail provisions under the 1971 Act. There is no automatic right to production before an independent authority to scrutinise the merits of the decision to detain but Immigration detainees can apply for bail under provisions in the 1971 Act. The conditions of bail may include conditions appearing to the judge to be likely to result in the appearance of the person bailed at the required time and place. There is evidence that only a small minority of detainees do in fact make a bail application. There is no automatic right to free legal advice or representation and lack of legal advice is probably a factor in the low level of bail applications.

Conditions for Immigration Act detainees within Immigration Removal Centres, Short Term Holding facilities and prison establishments. Various reports have been produced in recent years critical of the conditions in which Immigration detainees are held. (see Ellis, (1998), Pourgourides (1996), Dunston (1996) and Hales (1996)). In addition, there are regular inspection reports from HM Inspectorate of Prisons on IRC's, see Tinsley House, Haslar, Oakington, Campsfield House and Lindholme an Inspection of five IRCs) 1/Apr/2003 and Five non-residential short-term holding facilities at Queen's Building and Terminals 1-4 Heathrow Airport (10-13 October 2005) Heathrow 10/Oct/2005.

A.4 NATIONALS DETAINED ABROAD

See Chapter 32 Prisoners Abroad

B. Scotland

B.1 INTRODUCTION

Organisation background. The Scottish Prison Service is headed by a Chief Executive supported by a Board of Executive and non-Executive Directors and operates through a series of directorates. Scotland has 16 prison establishments comprising two open prisons, one Young Offender's Institution, one female establishment and one managed privately establishment.

Prison Statistics. On the 24/02/06, the prison population in Scotland was 6,886, representing a prison population rate of 135 per 100,000 of national population.

In 2004/05, the average daily population in Scottish prisons totalled 6,779, an increase of 2 per cent when compared with the 2003/04 figure of 6,621 and the highest annual level ever recorded. In 2004/05, the average daily female prison population increased from 314 in 2003/04 to 332, an increase of 6 per cent. The average daily remand population in 2004/05 was 1,216, down 2 per cent compared with the 2003/04 figures of 1,246. The average population of sentenced young offenders was 560 in 2004/05, a decrease of 2 per cent compared with the 2003/04 figures of 573. The number of long-term adult prisoners, those sentenced to 4 years or more (including life sentences and recalls), increased by 5 per cent from 2,641 in 2003/04 to 2,766 in 2004/05. The number of short-term adult prisoners, those sentenced to less than 4 years (excluding fine defaulters), increased by 4 per cent from 2,100 in 2003/04 to 2,178 in 2004/05.

The prison population could increase by about 4,000 in the next decade to nearly 10,000 - according to recent estimates.

Table 10 Foreign National Prisoners in Scottish Prisons as on 27.02.06

On 27.02.06	Male	Female	Total
British nationals	6481	319	6800
Foreign nationals	76 (1.16%)	2 (0.62%)	78 (1.13%)
totals	6557	321	6878

Source: Scottish Prison Service, unpublished and unverified

The Scottish First Minister, Mr Jack Connell, reported on the 04.05.06, that 'most foreign nationals in Scottish jails were from within the European Union, and about half were from the Republic of Ireland'. He added that out of 188 foreign nationals who finished serving sentences in Scottish jails in 2005, 26 had been transferred to the custody of the Immigration and Nationality Directorate (IND)[24].

B.2 TREATMENT OF FOREIGN PRISONERS

Scotland has one of the lowest proportions of FNPs of any EU country at 1.13%. Foreign national prisoners in Scottish prisons do not therefore appear to be a significant group attracting either internal management attention or external research. Each year, the SPS conducts as part of the Prisoner Survey, an Ethnic Minority Survey, though this does not look at the experience of FNPs specifically.

The SPS Race Relations Policy, (Revised March 2002) in Sections 3.9, and 3.10 in particular, does address however various needs of non-English speaking and foreign national prisoners through their Race Relations guidance to staff. Section 3.9 states that there are translated versions of the Prison Rules and other essential information (i.e. Race Relations Policy, Racial incident Report Form, Mandatory Drug Testing Procedures) available in 6 languages on application to the Operations Directorate.

Section 3.10 requires translations of various local information be made available which includes "Local reception information, arrangements for minority faith worship, the availability of diets to meet religious and cultural preferences".

---

[24] HM Inspectorate of Prisons. Immigration Removal Centre Expectations. Criteria for assessing the conditions for the treatment of immigration detainees. I Jan 2005

It also requires: 'the name, location of the Race Relations Manager' to be made available, 'notification that FMP's be allowed one airmail letter per week',
- 'confirmation that FNPs may contact a diplomatic representative of their choice' and 'information on the availability of approved interpreters, in all situations were confidentiality is important, e.g. health matters, family details, legal advice'.
There is the requirement in Section 3.16 that prison staff record whether a FNP has contact with their consulate.

There is no mention of foreign national prisoners in the annual HM Prisons Inspectorate for Scotland 2004-05. In 1998 there was a Thematic Report from the Inspectorate on "Persons Detained under the Immigration Act 1971 and Ethnic Minority Prisoners".

Immigration detainees are held in Dungavel and these detainees are the responsibility of the Home Office. The Dungavel facility is run by Premier-Serco. Dungavel has been a controversial centre due to holding children, sometimes for considerable periods, sees HMIP Dec 2004[25].

C. Northern Ireland

C.1   INTRODUCTION

The Northern Ireland Prison Service has three operational establishments and has certified accommodation for 1494 prisoners. Hydebank Wood Young Offenders Centre and Prison holds male remands and sentenced young offenders between the ages of 16 and 21 and all female prisoners including young offenders. Maghaberry Prison is a high security prison housing adult male long-term sentenced and remand prisoners, both in separated and integrated conditions. Magilligan Prison is a medium security prison housing shorter term sentenced adult male prisoners that also has low security accommodation for selected prisoners. The total prison population in NI on 20 November 2006 was 1449;

Table 11

Establishments	Sentenced	Remand	Immigration Detainees	Total
Maghaberry (male)	381	412	1	794
Magilligan (male)	426	-	-	426
Hydebank Wood (female)	16	17	-	33
Hydebank Wood (male)	86	110	-	196-
A. Totals	909	539	1	1449

---

[25]   http://news.bbc.co.uk/1/hi/scotland/north_east/4973068.stm

Table 12 Foreign national prisoners in NI, sentenced & remand, by gender on 20 November 2006

	sentenced	remand
male	8	38
female	0	0
Totals	8	38

Northern Ireland has, at 0.8%, one of the lowest proportions of FNPs in Europe. Were prisoners from Eire included this figure would increase though not significantly. Table 13 shows FNPs currently in custody in NI by Nationality and Prison. Of the number currently in custody: 8 are detained at Hydebank Wood, 35 at Maghaberry and 3 at Magilligan. The nationalities of those detained are as follows:

Table 13

Hydebank 8 FNP	Maghaberry 35 FNP				Magilligan 3 FNP
1 Australian	1 Kenyan	7 Polish	1 Afghan		1 French
3 Lithuanian	7 Chinese	3 Portuguese	1 Belgium		1 Canadian
1 Liberian	2 German	1 Italian	1 Egyptian		1 Portuguese
2 Romanian	3 Lithuanian	3 Latvian	2 Slovenian		
1 Estonian	1 Algerian	2 Nigerian			

The offences range from 8 - sexual offences (including 5 charged with rape); 5 - murder, 2 - death by dangerous driving, 4 - drugs, 4 - assault and 4 - motoring and 4 - theft. Other offences include kidnapping, deception, possession of an offensive weapon, disorderly behaviour and others.

A Prison Inspection of Maghaberry in 2004 reported that 'there were very few ethnic minority or foreign national prisoners' although that number has now begun to rise. FNPs reported no instances of deferential treatment other than the fact that they were ineligible for temporary release into the community as they were regarded as 'high risk'. However, there was nothing in place to meet their specific needs; it was usually prisoners who approached staff if they needed to contact their embassy or consulate or the Immigration & nationality Directorate. The recommendation of the inspection was that there should be a policy for dealing with foreign national prisoners and a co-ordinator appointed to look after their needs'[26]. A Service-wide policy is now being developed setting out how the Prison Service meets the specific needs of foreign national prisoners. Already, because of necessity there is a lot of work being done by prison staff. Key issues we are addressing include: language and communication difficulties, lack of information about the prison system and issues such as immigration, cultural and religious needs, as

---

[26] CJINI/HMCIP Inspection Reports Report on an announced inspection of Magilligan Prison by HM Chief Inspector of Prisons and the Chief Inspector of Criminal Justice in Northern Ireland - 20-24.

well as, isolation from friends and family. The policy is to be developed by January 2007 and is to be issued for public consultation.

C.1.1 Immigration Detainees in NI

The Northern Ireland Prison Service no longer routinely holds immigration detainees on behalf of the Immigration Service.

A protocol was signed in August 2006 between Immigration and Nationality Directorate and Her Majesty's Prison Service setting out the requirements of Immigration and Nationality Directorate (IND) on the Northern Ireland Prison Service for the management of Foreign Nationals detained solely under immigration legislation and who are also deemed unsuitable for transfer to an Immigration managed removal centre. On the expiry of their sentence, foreign national prisoners who are outside the criteria detailed in the protocol will be removed from the country (and transferred to a Scottish Prison) or transferred to an Immigration Removal Centre, by the Immigration Service.

Prior to this protocol being signed immigration detainees were held on the authority of an Immigration Detention Order signed by the Chief Immigration Officer. Male detainees were held at a Prisoner Assessment Unit in Belfast, which came under the management of Maghaberry Prison, and females were held at Hydebank Wood Young Offenders Centre and Prison. Immigration detainees were given the option of transferring to a detention centre in England or Scotland.

C.2   ADMINISTRATIVE DETENTION OF FOREIGN NATIONALS UNDER IMMIGRATION DETENTION.

Female Immigration Detainees. Between June 2004 and February 2006, 40 female immigration detainees were held at HMP Hydebank Wood for varying periods.

Table 14 Female detainees in NI by nationality, June 20040-Feb 2006

Nationality	Number
Brazilian	7
Chinese	4
Ghana	1
Jamaican	1
Malaysian	1
Nigerian	13
Other	1
Romanian	2
S. African	8
Zimbabwean	2
TOTAL	40

Male Immigration Detainees. The stated purpose of the detention centre in Belfast is to provide for the 'secure but humane accommodation of detainees in a relaxed regime with as much freedom of movement and association as possible consistent with maintaining a safe and secure environment. To encourage and assist detainees to make the most productive use of their time and to respect in particular their dignity and their rights to individual expression. Due recognition should be given to the need for awareness of particular anxieties to which detainees may be subject and the sensitivity that this will require, especially when handling issues of cultural diversities.'

The data on which this information is based is drawn from Committal and Discharge Books, and committal interviews held in the Unit at this time, and dates back to June 2004 when the Unit opened for the first time having been transferred from Maghaberry Prison on the closure of Mourne House and are current to 21 February 2006. These figures do not include those who may have been held in Maghaberry and released before coming to the detainee unit or those individuals who are being held on other warrants.

Institution Information.
- The maximum number that can be held in the Unit at any one time is 11.
- Total number of detainees processed by the Unit to this date is 147.
- The average length of time an individual spends in the Unit is 14.53 days.
- The minimum period of detention being 1 day or less whilst the maximum period was 204 days.
- Only 2 individuals have spent more than 100 days in the Unit, 204 and 117 respectively.
- The average age of detainees passing through the Unit is 32.5.
- The majority of detainees came from Nigeria.
- By using the Internet and networking with other organisations we are able to translate any documentation produced by the Prison in the language of the detainee (for example, fire orders, tuck shop lists, routine and visits information).

Table 15 Breakdown of male immigration detainees in NI by nationality between June 2004 –February 2006

Nationality	Number	Nationality	Number
Afghanistan	3	Macedonian	1
Algerian	2	Malaysian	2
American	1	Maltese	1
Angolan	1	Moldavian	1
Australian	1	Monrovian	1
Bangladesh	5	Moroccan	1
Brazil	11	Nepal	1
Cameroon	2	Nigerian	51
Chinese	13	Pakistani	5
Ethiopian	1	Palestinian	1
Georgian	1	Romanian	11
Ghana	6	Russian	2
Indian	3	Sierra Leone	1

Nationality	Number	Nationality	Number
Iranian	1	South Africa	3
Iranian Kurd	1	Sudanese	3
Iraq	1	Tunisian	1
Ivory Coast	1	Turkish	1
Japanese	1	*Total*	*144*
Kuwaiti	1		
Kosovo	1		

5 EVALUATIONS AND RECOMMENDATIONS

It can be seen from preceding sections that there are examples of good practise in the treatment and management of FNPs in prisons in the UK. The increasingly common provision of a dedicated post of Foreign Nationals Co-ordinator in many prisons in England & Wales is a positive development. When such posts are established to implement a prisons own foreign nationals strategy, supported and driven through a Foreign Nationals Committee and using, for instance, Foreign National Orderlies from amongst FNPs, real and significant improvements can be achieved in addressing the issues facing this group. However, prison inspections and other research shows that practise in different prisons varies greatly and is often based on uncoordinated, short-term and short-lived initiatives. Recommendations are consistent in calling for:

- The Prison Service to issue guidelines on local policy and practise with FNPs. Auditable standards based on these guidelines should be developed to motivate action in individual prisons and to encourage and enable managers to give foreign national work a higher priority in their business plans, (Bhui 2004).
- It is recommended that the Prison Service should implement a Prison Service Order on work with FNPs that sets out the minimum provisions needed to meet their requirements, standards subject to audit, training requirements and structures of accountability, (PRT May 2004).
- Each prison should produce a FNPs strategy, led by a dedicated member of staff, covering the provision of information, support for prisoners and contact with families. It should be regularly reviewed against clear objectives as part of a wider diversity strategy.
- The Prison Service & the Immigration Service need to improve their liaison so that if FNPs are to be expelled, they do not spend unnecessary time in prison or immigration removal centres awaiting departure.
- Training programmes should be developed, locally, regionally and centrally, for staff working with FNPs.
- The involvement of local and national voluntary organisations/NGO's working with FNPs, especially immigration advice services, should be developed with paid contracts being provided by prisons.
- Embassies should be given every encouragement to provide services for their imprisoned nationals, through for instance, centrally organised seminars to provide up to date information

Since April 2006 the issue of Foreign National Prisoners has attracted unprecedented high levels of media and political attention. This was due to it being revealed that the Immigration Service had released a number of FNPs into the UK on completing their sentence without consideration as to whether they should have been expelled. This led subsequently to the resignation of the Home Secretary and issues surrounding FNPs receiving significant scrutiny. It is difficult to state at present what long term changes there will be to the treatment and management of FNPs. In May 2006 the Home Secretary announced an 8 point Action Plan to improve various aspects of the identification, processing and deportation of FNPs. As part of this review there are major reforms underway at the present time into the liaison between the Prison Service, other Criminal Justice agencies and the Immigration Service to ensure that all FNPs are appropriately assessed as to their immigration status and potential for deportation. It is too early to report on other long term changes that this current review will make to FNPs but it will probably include consideration of enhanced arrangements to facilitate the return of FNPs earlier in their sentence, additional Prisoner Transfer Agreements and signing up to the recent EU proposal on the compulsory transfer of FNPs who are EU citizens. The current political agenda on FNPs in the UK is also affected by the pressure to free up scarce prison places and deport whenever possible.

From a criminal justice perspective, there are initiatives, which should be developed on a European front that would both meet some of the needs of the humanitarian/welfare agenda as well as those of protecting the public and reducing the risk of reoffending, they are not mutually exclusive. These require co-ordination and co-operation between organisations and agencies in the EU. Recommendations could include:

- Provision of information from countries for sentencing, rehabilitation and release purposes. Meeting the needs of justice and public protection, there should be protocols established amongst EU countries so that previous convictions and other relevant information can be obtained for sentencing. Such information will also be important during the prison sentence to work on offending behaviour, rehabilitation and resettlement issues.
- The repatriation of EU prisoners to service their sentence in their own country does have advantages in areas of education, training and general rehabilitation needs. The number of EU prisoners who voluntarily return to serve their sentence in their country is low and while, in the UK context, only about 20% of FNPs are from EU countries, serving their sentence in their own country has distinct advantages. Depending on EU countries prisoner release arrangements, it might also mean that prisoners are released under supervision as opposed to being released with no requirements.
- EU national prisoners, who complete their sentences in the UK and are then expelled, are not under any form of supervision on release. Protocols should be established between EU member countries to facilitate the transfer of supervision licences on expelled prisoners to supervise resettlement and better protect their public against reoffending.
- The ability for community penalties and conditional release to be transferred managed and enforced between EU countries, could also provide courts with sentencing alternatives to imprisonment and thereby reduce the FNP population.

Chapter 27

Aire Centre

Nuala Mole

1 THE HISTORY OF THE AIRE CENTRE

The AIRE Centre was set up in 1993 as a small legal charity specialising in international human rights law, in particular the law of the European Convention on Human Rights (ECHR) and other Council of Europe standards, as well as the rights of individuals under EU law. The Centre gives advice and information across Europe on all aspects of human rights law and represents individuals before the European Court of Human Rights (ECtHR). The ECtHR is the judicial body that oversees the implementation of the Convention and allows for the right of individual petition. In the past 13 years the Centre has been involved in seventy cases against fifteen jurisdictions before the ECHR. A very large proportion of the AIRE Centre's clientele have problems that are related to either immigration or the criminal justice system, and very often, as in the case of most of the Centre's foreign prisoners, they relate to both. Several of the AIRE Centre's cases before the EctHR have involved foreigner prisoners and detainees.

2 THE ACTIVITIES OF THE AIRE CENTRE

2.1 General Remarks

The Centre has provided extensive training on international standards to judges, prosecutors, police, probation services and prison officials as well as other officials involved in the administration of justice across Europe, especially in Central and Eastern Europe and the Former Soviet Union. From the early 1990's the Centre collaborated with Penal Reform International on raising awareness on the international standards applicable to all those deprived of their liberty as well as their affected family members in Central and Eastern Europe and the former Soviet Union. Seminars have been organised in several countries on the international human rights standards applicable to prisons. At the invitation of the Council of Europe (CoE) the AIRE Centre has conducted training on these issues. For example, the Centre was invited to participate at the CoE conference for the Directors of Prison Administrations held in Rome in November 2004, not only for the judiciary and public officials, including prison governors but also for lawyers and NGO's representing prisoner's interests. The Centre has provided speakers for the Irish Commission for Prisoners Overseas conference in Dublin in 2005 and prepared briefing papers on various aspects of prison law and the ECHR as well as on the European Convention on the Transfer of Sentenced Persons and its Additional Protocol. The AIRE Centre has also been working with the UK Prisons Inspectorate and with the London Probation Service Foreign Nationals Unit on these issues.

2.2 The AIRE Centre's work with individual Foreign Prisoners

In addition to our normal varied caseload, the AIRE Centre is currently dealing with more than thirty individual cases involving foreign prisoners' rights. These include persons of different nationalities detained in prisons in the UK and in other European countries, British as well as other foreign nationals including Albanians, Lithuanians, Italians, Nigerians, and Canadians. Many of them contacted the AIRE Centre after being given our details by prisoners who have been helped by the organisation in the past. The Centre's work with individual foreign prisoners often highlights more generic problems. They often complain of a lack of information relating to their rights and discrimination whilst in prison. Problems are compounded by the fact that prisoners often do not speak the language of the country in which they are incarcerated. Furthermore the prison personnel are unable to speak their language or any other language that they understand, all of which leave the prisoners very isolated. The AIRE Centre is fortunate to have many multi-lingual lawyers in its team, and access to others who are able to converse with prisoners in their mother tongue. The AIRE Centre will advise the foreign prisoners on their legal rights (especially under the European Convention on Human Rights and its resulting case law) and will liaise with the prisoners' lawyer (if they have one). The case will often involve written advice being sent to the prisoner and the lawyer. If prisoners have exhausted domestic proceedings and would like to make an application to the ECtHR relating to what they perceive to be a violation of their Convention rights, AIRE Centre lawyers will go through the papers in the case and advise them if they have an arguable case and if so, represent them in Strasbourg at the ECtHR if they so wish.

The AIRE Centre is also contacted by organisations that help their own nationals in prison abroad as well as being directly contacted by prisoners. The Centre is currently working closely with the Irish Commission for Prisoners Overseas (ICPO) on a spate of recent cases where the authorities have suddenly informed Irish nationals imprisoned in Britain that they are to be deported on completion of their sentences. These prisoners have often lived in the UK for many years. The work carried out in relation to them involves advising the prisoner (through the ICPO) on the EU law grounds applicable to their case against deportation. As explained below EU nationals cannot be deported as an automatic consequence of a criminal conviction resulting in a prison sentence. Unfortunately our work with the ICPO has shown that many of these prisoners and their legal representatives are unaware of how the EU law could potentially apply to their benefit.

The AIRE Centre has also taken up several cases in Strasbourg, such as Cooke v Austria and Osu v Italy, Scott v Spain, Worby v Finland, that have come to us through Prisoners Abroad (a charity which looks after British prisoners overseas) over the past ten years.

2.3 The AIRE Centre's work with Foreign Prisoners in Central and Eastern Europe

The AIRE Centre's foreign prisoner project is a collaboration with partner non-governmental organisations (NGOs) in three[1] Central and Eastern European Countries - the Czech Republic, (SOZE – Society of Citizens Assisting Migrants) Albania (Centre for European Law and the Helsinki Committee) and Serbia (Belgrade Centre for Human Rights) and Montenegro (CEDEM – Centre for Human Rights and Democracy for Montenegro). All these countries have either significant numbers of foreign prisoners or significant numbers of their own nationals imprisoned abroad - or both. The project will involve both the situation of foreign prisoners detained in those countries and the situation of nationals of those countries who are held in prison abroad. The AIRE Centre is fortunate in having already secured the necessary support of the authorities for the work to be taken forward in all these countries.

---

[1]   Now four countries since Serbia and Montenegro have separated.

It is anticipated that the Centre's work with the NGO partners will be instrumental in raising awareness on the part of the authorities – both the national prison administrations and the relevant consular authorities - of the particular problems faced by foreign prisoners. It will also fill a vacuum in the legal advice and assistance available to foreign nationals imprisoned in these countries and also to their own nationals imprisoned abroad. There are currently no organisations in these new democracies whose mandate specifically includes problems encountered by their own nationals in prison abroad (similar to Prisoners Abroad in the United Kingdom or the Irish Commission for Overseas Prisoners) or organisations that are dedicated to the problems faced by foreign prisoners in their own countries.

The Centre's work with the NGOs will involve collaboration with national authorities and consular services as well as engaging in direct intervention through both monitoring and litigation. The project will challenge inadequate access to translation of documents or to interpretation facilities that are often a major stumbling block in ensuring that the prisoner is not prevented from effectively participating in the legal process. The project will also aim to provide clear simple briefings including briefings on the disciplinary rules of the establishments where foreign prisoners are held in appropriate languages. This is especially important for foreign prisoners in order to help them integrate into prison life.

2.4 EU Legislation – An Overview

In addition to our European human rights work, the AIRE Centre deals with many requests for assistance relating to the position of EU Citizens and their family members who are third country nationals. Such requests have raised great concerns that the enhanced development of measures adopted to facilitate the prevention of crime and the pursuit of criminals across borders – such as the European Arrest Warrant – has not been accompanied by a commensurate protection for those deprived of their liberty abroad.

European Union Citizens have a privileged protection from expulsion following the commission of criminal offences, particularly under the new Citizens Directive (2004/38/EC) that came into force on 1 May 2006. Expulsion of an individual whose situation is regulated by EU law at the end of a criminal sentence is only ever permitted if the individual represents on grounds of "public policy, public security or public health". . Those who have the right of permanent residence cannot be expelled except on serious grounds of public policy or security and those who have been resident for ten years or more must represent an imperative threat to national security. All these criteria necessarily involve not only an assessment of whether the threat posed reaches the very high threshold needed to justify deportation of persons who have a right to reside in the EU, but also an assessment of whether the rehabilitation measures that they have benefited from whilst in prison have been successful or not.

The AIRE Centre has been able to draw on the extensive experience acquired from our EU law advice service to advise those individuals. The Centre has long sought to question the compatibility of the practice in some Member States of releasing EU citizen prisoners at a certain point during their sentences, and expelling them to their country of origin with EU law. A condition of their release is that they will be returned to prison if they re-enter the territory of that Member State. In many cases this is clearly incompatible with EU law. More recently the UK Government's response to a recent furore that erupted when foreign national prisoners were released without being considered for deportation has been to attempt to remove all foreign nationals at the time of their release, including Irish and French Citizens who have been resident for many years in the UK and whose expulsion was thus not permissible in EU law.

The experience that the AIRE Centre has gained from all these activities, has taught us that foreign prisoners suffer from a double prejudice – they are foreign and they are criminals. For many years the Centre has had a good working relationship with the European Committee for the Prevention of Torture (the CPT) and has listened to their articulated concerns about foreign national prisoners whose problems they see on the visits that they carry out under the Convention for the Prevention of Torture. It was the CPT's concerns (and support for the idea) that prompted the AIRE Centre to embark on a project dedicated to the rights of foreign prisoners in 2004. Seed funding was received from the United Kingdom Foreign and Commonwealth Office (the FCO) whose consular service welcomed the Centre's proposals for providing carefully identified support in this field. We are currently awaiting the outcome of other funding applications to enable us to take the project forward. Meanwhile the AIRE Centre remains in contact with our partners and is building up information each day that the Centre will put to good use if able to progress with the above-mentioned work.

2.5 Third Party Intervention Csoszanski v Sweden, Szabo v Sweden

The Council of Europe's *Transfer of Sentenced Persons Convention* allows foreign prisoners to seek transfer to their home country once the criminal proceedings have reached a final decision. The Additional Protocol (now ratified by twenty-nine countries) allows for non-consensual transfers. The Protocol relates to two categories of sentenced persons: (1) those that have returned to their home state having fled the sentencing state and (2) those that are subject to expulsion or deportation as a consequence of the sentence.

The AIRE Centre's intervention in the above-mentioned case relates only to the second group and examines several aspects of the Protocol and its interplay with the European Convention on Human Rights. This interplay can include such issues as the degree to which the sentencing states who transfer prisoners without their consent remain liable for violations of Article 3 that occur in the administrating state or interferences with the right to respect for family life which may require that the prisoner be allowed to remain in the sentencing state.

The intervention also looks at the position of those whose right to reside in the sentencing state is governed by EU law. As stated above, EU nationals and their designated family members cannot be deported as an automatic consequence of a criminal conviction resulting in a prison sentence. Those offenders whose situation is regulated by EU law include not only EU citizens and their third country national family members who commit offences, but also those whose residence rights are governed by EU law such as Bulgarians and Romanians who are exercising rights under the Europe Agreements or Turkish Citizens whose rights are governed by the EU Turkish Agreement. The terms of the Additional Protocol make it difficult to see how such an assessment of whether or not a prisoner represents a "present threat" under the new Citizen's Directive, can properly be made if the individual is transferred without his consent before the sentence has been completed.

After the AIRE Centre was alerted to the case by the Hungarian lawyer acting for the transferred prisoners, the Centre recently put in a third party intervention in the cases of

Csoszanski v Sweden and Szabo v Sweden before the ECtHR. These cases concerned the non-consensual transfer of Hungarian sentenced persons from Sweden to Hungary in circumstances where the Additional Protocol to the Convention on the Transfer of Sentenced Persons was not in force between the two states at the time of sentence and where the situation of the Hungarian nationals under the EU Hungary Agreement appeared to have been overlooked

3 THE CURRENT SITUATION OF FOREIGN PRISONERS

3.1 Legal representation

Foreign prisoners often have difficulties in accessing legal representation equal to that received by national prisoners. They are often unable to have adequate contact with their lawyers during criminal proceedings, unable to make telephone calls to their lawyers if they do not speak their language and unable to make them if they do because the prison officers cannot monitor the conversations. In some cases they have only the most rudimentary access to legal representation. The AIRE Centre's work in Central and Eastern Europe will seek to challenge discriminatory practices in part by ensuring that such prisoners are made aware of the applicable legal norms so that a lack of access to legal advice does not mean a corresponding lack of information relating to their rights. The AIRE Centre will also seek to negotiate on behalf of the prisoners to eliminate discrimination in access to legal advice.

3.2 The Social Exclusion of Foreign Prisoners

Foreign prisoners are often very isolated and suffer severe social and emotional deprivation. There may be no fellow prisoners with whom they can converse and they are rarely able to access reading materials or to follow television programmes available in the recreation rooms in their own language or a language they understand. This is in addition to the acute isolation felt by prisoners in being away from their families. Many families are unable to visit the prisoner because the cost of travel and accommodation, the difficulties in obtaining the necessary visas and the inevitable bureaucratic hurdles can make maintaining family contacts nearly impossible. Remand prisoners are often unable to make telephone calls because the prisoner's officers cannot monitor what those speaking a foreign language are saying. This form of isolation can be remedied in part by allowing foreign prisoners to accumulate their visiting rights so that several months' entitlement can be enjoyed during the one week when the family is able to visit. But the rules rarely allow this to occur.

The social exclusion of foreign prisoners *inside* the prison can only be remedied if the relevant prison authorities recognise them as a group requiring special attention (a fact reflected in the new European Prison Rules which came into effect on 11 January 2006) – a group whose specific needs cannot be ignored. Tailoring the prison regime to help foreign prisoners could include setting up group meetings where foreign prisoners can talk about their shared experiences. Whilst foreign prisoners are not a homogenous group, they are all likely to be facing similar problems distinct from national prisoners and the ability to talk about this will help them feel less alone.

A further innovation that may be of help to foreign prisoners is one that was first tested in *Wandsworth Prison* in the United Kingdom. The scheme involved having trusted prisoners act as foreign national "orderlies". These orderlies would visit new arrivals, spread information and keep lists of inmates who could interpret. Whilst such a scheme is largely dependant on the support of the prison administration, it provides the foreign prisoner with a level of information and support that they could not obtain on their own. Such a system would be especially useful in countries where there are no dedicated NGOs working on behalf of foreign prisoners or in cases where the foreign national have decided not to avail of consular assistance themselves. They also provide a point of contact for the foreign national inside the prison.

Foreign prisoners in European penitentiary institutions are growing in number. Any scheme aimed at reducing their social exclusion whilst in prison should not be seen as a form of special treatment but a legitimate response to the well-documented problems faced by such prisoners. Problems that the AIRE Centre and other NGOs are striving to eradicate.

Chapter 28

Conférence Permanente Européenne de la Probation (CEP)

Leo Tigges

1 PROBATION FOR FOREIGN PRISONERS IN EUROPE[*]

It is common knowledge in the probation field that most foreign prisoners in the European Prisons have no contact with the probation services, either in the country in which they are detained or from their country of origin. In what way can this be changed? Are there any examples of good practice in Europe? What is the role the CEP (Conférence Permanente Européenne de la Probation) can play in this regard? These are the questions that will be answered in this contribution. First, the position and origin of the CEP will be described. Second, the good practice of the Foreign Liaison unit of the Dutch Probation Service will be dealt with. The third section will discuss EU initiatives to mutually accept the verdicts and probation matters in different European Member States. The fourth and final section will expand upon the stimulating role of the CEP with regard to the foreign offender and the conditions under which this role can be played.

2 CEP

The CEP was founded in 1981[1] by 11 European countries. Today, 26 European countries are members[2]. In 1981, it was the number of foreign prisoners that gave the member countries cause to join forces and to start international cooperation. The first two CEP seminars (in 1981 and 1982) discussed the subject of Probation and Assistance to Offenders of Foreign Origin. They asked how the plight of those being detained in a prison in a foreign country could be eased. How could the ties with the prisoners' country of origin be maintained? In what cases was a pre-sentence report possible and effective? How could the offender be counselled by the probation from the country of origin? How could his release be prepared? The answers to these questions differed from country to country, but one thing was clear: only by cooperation between the nations in question could such questions be addressed. And the cooperation between the probation organisations had to focus mainly on establishing practical possibilities for transferring aftercare as soon the offender had been released and returned to his country of origin after his sentence was complete. Also understood was that the transfer of aftercare could only be realized if the probation organisations in the different countries knew of the existence of probation organisations in the other countries and which persons needed to be contacted. Such understandings meant that both the conferences could be considered successful. It is striking that ever since the abovementioned conferences this subject has not been revisited in CEP seminars. This is perhaps because once the practical contacts between the probation organisations had been established and the possibilities for the transfer of aftercare were being realized, the most pressing needs had been fulfilled. However, the CEP has, in its history since, actively participated in the Council of Europe to achieve European rules on Community Sanctions and Measures (although it should be noted that foreign offenders have not really benefited from these rules).

---

[*] Leo Tigges is secretary-general of CEP.
[1] England, the Netherlands, France, Switzerland, Italy, Denmark, Belgium, Ireland, Northern-Ireland, Luxembourg and Portugal.
[2] It is striking that neither the central Ministry of Justice in Germany is member nor the ministries of justice from the regions or organisations residing under these regions.

Since the founding of the CEP, it has become a very active organization, (but so far not with regard to the question of the foreign offender). It organises at least 3 seminars (mostly bi- or tri-lingual) every year on actual probation issues. Twice a year a bulletin is published with articles on new developments in the several Member States. Reports on the seminars are to be found on its website, together with details of upcoming events. In 2000, it published a book titled "Probation and Probation Services: a European perspective", an account of the status of European probation; it is currently working on an update of this publication. CEP also supports the construction of probation systems in emerging countries in Central and Eastern Europe and CEP experts can be contacted to assist with probation questions from the different Member States. This is a sign that the character of the CEP is changing: from exchanging information, studying together and assisting each other, to influencing governments and European institutions to promote Probation in its widest sense: to bring about effective non-custodial alternatives to prison sentences and to establish programmes in custody which prepare the prisoner for a successful resettlement. In this way prevention of recidivism can be attained. In 2005, the present Board of CEP reformulated its mission:

> *The Conférence Permanente Européenne de la Probation will promote pan-European co-operation in the development and delivery of community sanctions and measures. It is committed to achieving just outcomes, increased public protection and community involvement in the reduction of offending across all the countries of Europe - based on the tenets of human rights, well thought out policies, evidence based practice and the best use of public resources.*

3 GOOD PRACTICE

The overall picture in Europe is that the probation organisations do not pay much attention to the national offenders detained abroad. As far as I know, there are only two European countries that have developed a systematic method for paying attention to their nationals detained in foreign countries. The most extensive is the Foreign Liaisons Office of the Dutch Probation Service; the second is Prisoner's Abroad in England and Wales. (Another chapter in this book will provide more information about these organisations.)

In particular, the work carried out by the Foreign Liaisons Office of the Dutch Probation Service needs to be highlighted. It has the (financial) support of both the Ministry of Justice and the Ministry of Foreign Affairs. The latter sees the Foreign Liaisons Office as an important contribution to its consular work, especially with regard to the high number of Dutch detainees abroad and the great distances in some of the countries where those offenders are detained. In such situations, the number of staff in the consular departments is too small for them to pay enough attention to their fellow countrymen in detention, especially as - quite often - the problems of the detainees require frequent and intensive, or specialized, intervention. The support of the Ministry of Justice stems from the fact that at least some of the offenders will return to The Netherlands and, without a proper preparation for their release, the chances will increase that they might again meet with such difficulties that their life without crime remains no more than a desire.

Another strong advantage of the Dutch Foreign Liaisons Office is the close collaboration with Dutch volunteers who live outside the Netherlands and who are willing to spend time visiting the Dutch detainees on a regular basis. Without such volunteers, who receive guidance and counselling from the Foreign Liaisons Office, prisoners abroad would remain largely deprived of help and support.

At the same time, however, looking with a critical eye at the work of the Dutch Foreign Liaisons Office, one major flaw can be spotted. The differences between the offenders are great: some run a high risk of re-offending because of their high statistic and dynamic (e.g. criminogenic) needs. And those persons are not always detected because there are, at present, no procedures in place or diagnostic instruments at hand that might differentiate between the risks of recidivism. Yet if these risks are recognized, then in some cases a more professional approach will become essential in working with these offenders, a professional level which cannot be expected from the volunteers. Despite the good practice of the Dutch Liaisons Office, however, it must be pointed out that the Dutch Probation Service does not handle foreign offenders in the Netherlands. Although this is not to be glossed over, exactly the same "excuses" are to be heard in the other European countries: lack of resources; problems with the language and cultural difficulties; above all, the impotent feeling of social workers that if their work is not followed up by the country to which the offender will be returned after his release, then all *their* hard work will have gone down the drain. To me it is apparent: in Europe we need to achieve a situation in which imprisoned foreigners in every country receive the same attention as its nationals. A system also needs to be set up to differentiate the risks of re-offending and clear systems of communication must be developed between the probation services in the country in which the foreign offender is detained and the country where he will resettle after his release.

4 NEW EUROPEAN DEVELOPMENTS ON THE TRANSFER OF PENAL MEASURES AND SANCTIONS

Since the founding of the European Union, probation has never been on the agenda of the European Commission or the European Parliament. This, however, should be a logical concern, as the agenda of the EU was from the beginning dominated by the realisation of the free movement of persons, goods, services and capital. And the EU Member States were, and still are, of the opinion that the domain of justice should remain a topic on which the states exercise their autonomy (the so called 'third pillar'). As a result of the increased number of foreign prisoners in all the Member States, at the very least this topic now merits a concerted action. Therefore Austria, the Presidency of the European Council from 1 January 2006 to 1 July 2006, has submitted an initiative for the adoption of a Framework Decision on the transfer of sentenced persons between Member States of the European Union (2005/JHA). The stated background is: "Enforcement of the sentence in the executing Member state should enhance the possibility of social rehabilitation of the sentenced person." Although one might question whether the real reason stems from the desire to remove as quickly as possible sentenced persons to their country of origin, it is nevertheless true that in the majority of cases the possibility of undergoing detention in the country of origin is, indeed, contributing to the resettlement of offenders.

New to this draft framework is the idea that sentenced persons can be transferred without in all cases having his consent. In the words of the draft: "Notwithstanding the necessity of providing the sentenced person with adequate safeguards, his or her involvement in the proceedings should no longer be dominant by requiring in all cases his or her consent to the forwarding of a judgment to another Member State for the purpose of its recognition and enforcement of the sentence imposed." (Recital 5) At the time of this chapter's writing, intensive discussions between the member states over this draft text have taken place and it is remains unclear if and when the final draft will be adopted. But, as the CEP, I believe that we should indeed back the basic principle that undergoing one's detention in one's country of origin will, in the majority of cases, help offenders to resettle in society. At the same time, there are a lot of questions to be solved. I mention here the two most important:

- In some instances, the return of the sentenced person to his country of origin might mean a longer sentence than he would have received had he been imprisoned in the sentencing state, because the rules on conditional release are tighter in the executing state. In addition, in some instances the detention conditions in the country of origin might be much harsher than in the sentencing state.
- If the sentenced offender does not agree with his transfer to his nation state (for instance, because he is of the opinion that his rehabilitation will not be brought about in this way) and the sentencing state nevertheless wants to proceed with the transfer, then in my opinion the probation services in both states should be involved in giving an advice to the sentenced state about the question of whether transfer genuinely serves the interest of the rehabilitation of the offender.[3] This role of the probation services fits in with the "consultations between the competent authorities of the issuing and the executing States. The competent authorities should take into account such elements as, for example, duration of the residence or other links to the executing State." (Recital 6b)

In a wider sense than the transfer of sentenced persons, the EU is trying to foster mutual trust and confidence between the EU Member States and the Commission will shortly present a proposal for a Council Framework Decision on the European supervision order and on the mutual recognition of non-custodial pre-trial supervision measures. The background to this is that EU citizens who are not residents in the territory of the Member State where they are suspected of having committed a criminal offence are often kept in pre-trial detention or subject to a long-term non-custodial supervision order in a foreign environment. This hinders the need to use pre-trial detention as an exceptional measure and it is another area in which the CEP should intervene in future discussions within the EU: in the first place to support these initiatives, but in the second place to formulate - and to implement - these regulations in such a way that Member States make use of them and that they really contribute to the rehabilitation of the offender.

---

3   More detailed questions to be addressed: Which probation service is "leading" in the final report to the authorities? What are the minimum topics that will have to be covered?

5 CONSEQUENCES NATIONAL AND EUROPEAN: A EUROPEAN INSTITUTE

The increased phenomenon of citizens crossing borders and the consequent internationalisation of crime merits debate on the way the probation institutions in the Member States should respond. In the opinion of the CEP and many others it is of the highest importance that:

- Every state should treat prisoners from abroad in the same way as they treat their own nationals in their own prisons. Apart from the fact that I see this as a principle that needs to be adopted by the EU, if it were to be achieved then the costs for every Member State would not be unreasonable, as the bills would be settled on mutually agreed terms. Of course, some Member States would be financially better off, because the number of foreign nationals might be smaller than the number of their country fellowmen abroad or, due to varying sentencing tariffs, the number of "detention years" for the incoming nationals would be less than the number of "outgoing" foreigners.
- When a prisoner from abroad is taken into preventive custody and a pre-sentence report is made, attention should be paid to the possibility of eventual drawbacks to the transfer of the offender once he has been sentenced. This requires:
- Knowledge of the specific rules, regulations, procedures and culturally determined "ways of behaving and addressing the juridical authorities" in the offender's country of origin
- Cooperation with the Probation Service in the country of origin, as they would have to take over - as seamlessly as possible - contact with the offender once he has been transferred.

The foregoing holds true for the situation in which no pre-sentence report has been made, but in which the process of the offender's transfer is prepared after the verdict. The aforementioned situation is easily described, but hard to turn into practice, especially since probation organisations have no real experience in collaborating on individual cases. And it would be undesirable if every country tried to discover on its own the specific situation in the other member states concerning the penal system and probation: this would entail a great number of disconcerted efforts. Therefore, I envisage the founding of a small European Probation Institute that would act as a kind of help desk for the probation services of the Member States, to function as a link between them. This help desk would bring together information about the specific situations in the different states regarding the penal system, the state of probation, and the specific facts to be taken into account when preparing a possible transfer for a sentenced person. But, at the same time, information on which functionaries in which countries are to be contacted when Member States work together would also have to be made available. This Institute might also act as a centre in which new good practices are recorded and disseminated to all the Member States. It could also collect data and statistics and organise training and documentation to educate probation officers working with foreign offenders. It might be helpful to the Member States and the EU to review, after some time has passed, the regulations and common procedures recorded. The establishment of such an institute could give a head start to the process of desirable cooperation regarding the transfer of non-custodial sanctions' supervision measures as well as the transfer of sentenced prisoners.

6 EVALUATIONS AND RECOMMENDATIONS

It was mentioned above that the immediate cause for the founding of the CEP was the increasing number of foreign prisoners. Yet although two conferences on this subject were held 25 years ago, this theme has not been returned to in the years since. But now the issue is back again and the CEP is currently discussing with EGPA (the European Group for Prisoners Abroad) whether the CEP and EGPA could join forces and become a special interest group within the CEP. The CEP would be more than willing to do so, especially in the light of the present developments regarding the transfer of sentenced persons. The CEP is also willing to enter into contact with the EU to participate in preparing the regulations and procedures that are necessary. And, finally, it would very much support the establishment of a European Institute as described above. In summary:

- Probation organisations should pay equal attention to both foreign offenders and national offenders in their national prison systems.
- Probation organisations should monitor whether their nationals detained abroad are receiving adequate assistance from the probation organisations in the countries where they are being detained: if not, the probation organisations should strive for compensating measures (e.g. the involvement of national volunteers living in the country of detention).
- Clear systems of communicating need to be developed between the probation services in the country in which the foreign offender is detained and the country in which he will resettle after his release.
- The EU initiatives to transfer sentenced offenders back to their country of origin as a means of enhancing their rehabilitation are to be supported. The best procedures must then be in place in case the offender does not agree with his transfer to his nation state. In that case, the probation services in the respective states should advise about the desirability of the transfer from the viewpoint of rehabilitation.
- The establishment of a European Probation Institute that would function as centre of knowledge could play an essential supportive role in implementing the proposals for the transfer of sentenced prisoners and the mutual recognition of (non-custodial) supervision measures.

Chapter 29

Foreign Liaison Office of the Dutch Probation Service

Rolf Streng
Raymond Swennenhuis
Hans van Kooten

1.1 Introduction

An increasing number of Dutch citizens are being imprisoned abroad. Whereas in 1992 there were about 1,000 Dutch detainees in foreign countries, by the end of 2000, eight years later, this number had almost doubled. In 2005 there were more than 2,500 Dutch nationals detained abroad. The vast majority of these people have been arrested for the possession or smuggling of drugs. The Dutch Probation Service (Reclassering Nederland) in addition to its tasks in the Netherlands is also involved in dealing with Dutch citizens detained abroad. These people experience particular difficulties; far away from family and friends, they are often forced to survive in a foreign culture, in a foreign area, and facing an unknown legal system.

1.2 History

The Foreign Liaison Office of the Dutch Probation Service in Utrecht has since 1975 been responsible for international probation activities. It started as an experiment with a temporary coordination unit. A few years later the unit was extended and made more permanent. In 1977 there were 305 Dutch nationals detained abroad and the unit had 3 staff members. Slowly the unit grew, as did the number of Dutch nationals imprisoned abroad. In 1994 there were 1236 prisoners abroad. In 1997 the Minister of Foreign Affairs decided –after some incidents regarding the treatment of Dutch national in foreign prisons- to intensify the guidance of Dutch nationals imprisoned abroad. The Foreign Liaison Office of Reclassering Nederland expanded and got financial support for part of its activities from the Ministry of Foreign Affairs. Against this background, the unit has established good working contacts with the Ministries of Foreign Affairs and Justice and with a wide range of aid organisations.

1.3 Activities by the Dutch Probation Service and the Ministry of Foreign Affairs

The Foreign Liaison Office contributes to the general goal of the Dutch Probation Service: reducing the risk of re-offending behaviour in order to strive for a safer society with less crime. With the ultimate goal to reduce recidivism, the Liaison Office aims to prevent unnecessary damage inflicted on Dutch nationals detained abroad and aims to make a proper return into Dutch society possible. The starting point remains that offenders have to take responsibility for their wrongdoings. But social exclusion makes it much more difficult for detainees to prepare their return into Dutch society. That is the reason for the Liaison Office to offer guidance to Dutch nationals imprisoned abroad. The position and working methods of the Liaison Office within the Dutch Probation Service differs from other regular probation units. A team of nine coordinators offer assistance to a total of about 2500 detainees abroad (June 2006). Since the start in 1975, the Foreign Liaison Office has worked together intensively with the Consular Department in the Ministry of Foreign Affairs and the various Dutch consulates and embassies all over the world. The group of 2500 Dutch detainees receive guidance from both the consulates and the Foreign Liaison Office of the Probation Service.

2 PROFILE OF DUTCH NATIONALS DETAINED ABROAD

In the year 2005, there were almost 2,600 Dutch nationals detained abroad. In 1988 this was 579; in 2000 about 2,000. The current population have a number of characteristics[1]:

- 80% are prosecuted or convicted for drug related crimes; usually drug smuggling
- 16% are female
- 60% are detained in another EU member state
- 45% have been detained for more than one year
- 60% do not come originally from the Netherlands
- 20% cannot read or write Dutch
- 65% do not have vocational education or diploma
- 60% did not have a job, income or allowance prior to detention

Table 1: Number of detainees abroad

Year	Average Number of Detainees
1997	1,584
1998	1,755
1999	1,885
2000	1,958
2001	2,250
2002	2,330
2003	2,528
2004	2,444
2005	2,575

The turnover rate is very high. In 2005 1,241 Dutch nationals were arrested abroad and 1,135 were released. In 2004 these figures were 1,688 and 1531. In 2003 the figures were 1,688 and 1419. In 2002 the figures were 1,946 and 1,963.

Table 2: Top 10 countries for Dutch detained abroad in 2005

Country	Number of detainees (average of 2005)
Germany	474
France	239
Spain	216
United Kingdom	160
United States	132
Italy	125
Dominican Republic	107
Belgium	85
Surinam	85
Venezuela	69

---

[1]   Based on a limited random sample survey in 2005.

Table 3: The population of Dutch detainees in the European Union in April 2006.

Country	Number of detainees (April 2006)
Germany	479
France	232
Spain	213
United Kingdom	155
Italy	133
Belgium	93
Portugal	74
Sweden	39
Austria	30
Greece	16
Denmark	14
Ireland	13
Hungary	12
Luxemburg	7
Poland	5
Czech Republic	5
Finland	4
Slovakia	1

In the other EU member states there were no Dutch detainees in April 2006. The majority of the detainees are imprisoned because of crimes related to drug smuggling. In comparison, the sentences for these crimes, which are imposed in other countries including other EU Member States, can be relatively higher than in the Netherlands.

PRODUCTS AND SERVICES OF THE FOREIGN LIAISON OFFICE OF RECLASSERING NEDERLAND

In the first instance, the authorities in the countries where the Dutch citizens are being held bear responsibility for the welfare the detainees. The Dutch Ministry of Foreign Affairs promotes the interests of detained citizens abroad. The leading principle for the work of the Foreign Liaison Office or Reclassering Nederland is the return of the Dutch citizen to the Netherlands. Shortly following the initial contact, the embassy or consulate informs the Dutch national of the possibility of contacting the Dutch probation service. The detainee then can complete a form, indicating what services he or she wishes to request from the probation service. The Foreign Liaison Office subsequently decides whether action can and must be taken regarding the application.

3.1 Services of the Foreign Liaison Offices

The Foreign Liaison Office can provide the following services:

- Counselling and guidance during imprisonment
Where possible and necessary the Foreign Liaison Office prepares a Plan of Action for the individual detainees. Problems in various fields, such as work, housing, debts etc. are assessed. An important goal is to limit the damage that imprisonment inflicts on the detainee. Elements are e.g. informing debtors and landlords and arranging temporary custody over small children. A second goal of the Plan of Action is to prepare for return to the Netherlands. Elements are e.g. participation in long-distance learning and providing practical information about returning to the Netherlands. Regular contact with Dutch nationals in foreign prisons is not always easy. Therefore the Foreign Liaison Office has a network of 275 Dutch volunteers living abroad who visit the detainees on a regular basis. They are so to speak the 'eyes and ears' of the Dutch Probation Service. 153 volunteers are based in EU countries. They make up almost 60% of the total number of volunteers. Similarly (60%) of Dutch nationals detained abroad are imprisoned in Europe.
- Delivering a social enquiry report
In criminal cases abroad, reports sometimes have a role to play in court, or in decisions about whether part of any prison sentence may or may not be served in the Netherlands.
- Preparing for return
Within limits, the Foreign Liaison Office tries to contribute to a proper preparation for release of the inmate. On basis of diagnosis a Plan of Action is drafted. Problems related to work, income, debts, housing, health relations and other matters are assessed and can be part of the Plan of Action. When the date of release of the prisoners comes near, the plan of action is converted into a plan of return and subsequently implemented by the Foreign Liaison Office. Attention is paid to the elements that were diagnosed. On a limited scale, the Foreign Liaison Office tries to offer after-care for the ex-detainee through offering advice and referral to other professional social workers.

3.2 Some figures on products and services of the Foreign Liaison Office

In 2004 the Foreign Liaison Office has produced the following output:

Table 4

Number of detainees visited by volunteers	1,723
Number of completed and received intake/assessment reports	754
Number of visits with visiting report	6,463
Number of advisory reports	826
Number of social inquiry reports	93

3.3 Volunteers

An important aspect of the work of the Foreign Liaison Office is the input from volunteers who visit the detainees. In total the Foreign Liaison Office has about 275 volunteers all over the world. These volunteers are usually Dutch citizens who live and work abroad. To a certain level these volunteers fill in the place of the Dutch Probation Service abroad. The volunteers have intensive contact with the coordinators of the Foreign Liaison Office and receive supervision and coaching from them. A report is produced from each visit. Questions and remarks concerning the detainee are mentioned in the report. The coordinator from the Foreign Liaison Office works on the basis of these questions and reacts to the detainees in writing. The number of visits is recorded electronically. The Liaison Office is responsible for the selection of the volunteers. In cooperation with the local Dutch Embassies candidate-volunteers are recruited. An interview with the candidate is held at the local Embassy after which an advice is offered to the Liaison Office regarding the suitability of the candidate. The Liaison Office then decides to accept the candidate or not. Often candidate volunteers come from the network of other volunteers and social circles around the Embassy. In addition to volunteers who visit detainees abroad, the Foreign Liaison Office also has a number of volunteers who correspond with detainees. The correspondence is always done through the office of the Foreign Liaison Office.

Improvement of expertise of volunteers: Working with, guiding and coaching of volunteers require a structured approach. Strict agreements have been made between the Foreign Liaison Office and the Consular Department of the Ministry of Foreign Affairs concerning the selection of new volunteers. The local Dutch consulates assist in recruitment and selection of volunteers. All volunteers engage in a contract with the Foreign Liaison Office of the Probation Service. In the contract various issues are arranged such as reimbursement of expenses, privacy statements, rules of conduct etc. The coordinators of the Foreign Liaison Office and the volunteers have regular contact through telephone, e-mail and during special conferences. These conferences are organised by the Dutch consulates and the Ministry of Foreign Affairs. Personnel from the Ministry and the consulates take part, as well as coordinators of the Foreign Liaison Office of the Probation Service and the volunteers of the Probation Service. During these conferences the guidance of detainees is coordinated and fine-tuned. If necessary new agreements are made regarding visits and guidance. Depending on the number of Dutch detainees and urgency of matters, these conferences are organised in every country or region once every two or three years. Through lectures and workshops during the conferences, the expertise and knowledge of the volunteers are enhanced. In addition to the conferences, the volunteers take part in specific trainings offered by the Dutch Embassies for their own personnel. These trainings are specifically aimed at social and communicative skills.

Detention damage and reducing recidivism: The aim of the work of the volunteers is reducing the damage caused by detention and preparing the detainees for their return to the Netherlands. The damage of detention has its roots among other things in the social isolation caused by the limited possibilities of family to visit the detainee. Language and cultural differences can also contribute to detention damage. The Foreign Liaison Office tries at the same time to limit the damage in the Netherlands for the detainee. Upon request of a detainee, the Foreign Liaison Office can contact family, landlords, employers, and creditors to seek solutions for the problems the detainee is confronted with because he is in detention abroad. In addition to the contacts with volunteers, the Foreign Liaison Office also offers a possibility to study. The Foreign Liaison Office has close contacts with the Foundation Education behind Bars (EABT). This foundation offers free long-distance courses. For detainees who have no possibility to stay with family or friends after their detention ends, the Foreign Liaison Office tries to arrange a temporary shelter possibility. The coordinators of the Foreign Liaison Office also offer information and advice or can refer to other professional social workers in case detainees have psychiatric, psychosocial or addiction problems. The Foreign Liaison Office works on the principle that its interventions contribute to the reduction of detention damage and that the preparation of return to the Dutch society contributes to the reduction of recidivism.

3.4 'Morse'

The Foreign Liaison Office publishes three times per year a special bulletin 'Morse'. The aim is to inform the volunteers as well as consular employees of the Ministry and other interested partners about various practical matters as well as new developments within the Probation Service and the Foreign Liaison Office.

4 RESULTS INTERVIEWS VOLUNTEERS AND DUTCH DETAINEES ABROAD

4.1 General Remarks

In order to obtain more information about the situation of Dutch detainees in other EU Member States, the Foreign Liaison Office of Reclassering Nederland performed a small-scale research. Two questionnaires were developed. The first questionnaire was directed to the detainees. A list with questions was presented to them through the network of volunteers abroad. The purpose of the questions was to get specific information about the position and treatment of Dutch detainees abroad in relation to the position and treatment of national detainees. The questionnaire was in Dutch. The questions dealt with the following topics: treatment; living conditions and reception; work – schooling – sport – recreations; food – religion – personal hygiene – medical care; consular and legal aid; prison personnel and other prisoners; contacts with the outside world; reintegration activities – leave – release.

The questionnaire was distributed through the volunteers. The Foreign Liaison Office has volunteers in the following EU countries: Austria, Belgium, Czech Republic, Denmark, France, Germany, Hungary, Italy, Luxembourg, Poland, Portugal, Spain, Sweden, and United Kingdom. One or two volunteers per country participated. They distributed the questionnaires amongst the detainees. In some cases the detainees filled in the forms themselves and returned them directly to the Foreign Liaison Office. In other cases, the volunteers interviewed the detainees and filled in the answers for them and then returned the forms. This depended on the possibilities of the individual prison regime per detainee. In total 30 questionnaires were returned. 15 questionnaires came from Dutch detained in Germany; from France there were 4 forms; from the United Kingdom 3; from Spain 3; from Sweden 2; from Italy 2; from Portugal 1. No forms were received from the new Member States from Eastern Europe. In addition to the detainees, the volunteers also received a questionnaire. In total 10 questionnaires were filled in and returned: 4 came from Germany, 4 from the United Kingdom, 1 came from France and 1 came from Italy. The questionnaire for the volunteers dealt with the same issues as the questionnaire for the detainees.

All the questions were open; there were no multiple-choice questions. Therefore it is not possible to present the answers here in detailed manner. We have chosen to present the answers to the questions in summary form. Attention is paid to every item in the questionnaire. Where possible and necessary, striking answers are highlighted. In most cases an overview is presented of the most common answers.

4.2 Special Aspects

4.2.1 Treatment

The question whether the detainee was treated differently than national prisoners was answered in many variations. About half of the group answered that there were no differences at all. Others mentioned that there were huge differences. National prisoners have more privileges and can more easily arrange matters with the guards. Often this is due to the lack of understanding of the local language and cultural habits. Some mentioned specifically that skin colour is a reason for different treatment. Medical treatment was a problem often mentioned. Access to medical treatment was according to the interviewees much more difficult for foreigners than for the national detainees. Different treatment from prison personnel was more often mentioned than different treatment from fellow prisoners. In only a few cases positive different treatment was mentioned because of being a foreigner. Almost all detainees mentioned the lack of proper contacts with family and friends by telephone as a huge problem. Access to telephone is very limited and expensive. In some cases no telephone access is possible at all; e.g. during pre-trial detention. Pre-trial detention can take a very long time in some countries; therefore this is a major problem in relation to social exclusion for foreign prisoners. More possibilities to have contact with family by telephone or though longer visits were the most commonly mentioned advices to the prison warden.

4.2.2 Living conditions and reception

In general, most of the respondents answered that they have the same access to living conditions and facilities as others, at least in theory. However in practice there can be huge differences. It is difficult to indicate under which circumstances these differences exist. It depends largely on the country, the type of detention and the specific prison. Almost all respondents said that they were given no or very little or no instructions on the house rules in the prison. In case they did receive information it was almost always in writing and only in the language of the country. In some cases information was given by guards and in some cases also by a (deputy) governor. Making a telephone call to home or the Embassy was in most cases difficult or impossible. Only a few respondents indicated that they could make the phone call. In some cases making phone calls was explicitly prohibited.

Most respondents mentioned that they felt relatively safe. In some cases they felt very unsafe, referring to aggressive behaviour of other detainees. In a lot of prisons there are other Dutch prisoners present. Often contact is possible, but this depends on the regime and the structure of the prison. Many respondents do not speak the language of the country where they are detained. They indicate that this hinders the proper communication with the guards and other detainees seriously. On average the guards do not speak other languages than their own. The majority of the respondents indicated that they learn at least a little bit of the local language to make communication more easily.

4.2.3 Work-education-sports-recreation

Work is for many of the respondents possible in principle. In some cases there is clear discrimination between national and foreign prisoners. Foreigners get access to work much more difficult than nationals. In other cases however, there seems to be no difference at all. Moreover, sometimes it is necessary to speak and understand the local language; therefore the access to work is limited for many foreign prisoners. Very often there is no work available at all but this affects national and foreign prisoners equally. The type of detention determines often whether work is possible or not. The payment for work is not different for foreign prisoners than for national prisoners. In general the payment is reasonable, in comparison to the Netherlands. In some cases it is higher than in the Netherlands. Payments ranged from 50 to 250 Euros per month. From this amount certain costs are deducted: administration fees, taxes, TV, telephone etc.

It is very often not possible to follow any educational courses. Often courses are not available to all prisoners. Often it depends on the type of detention. Sometimes courses are available but only for those who have sufficient command of the local language. Almost all prisoners have access to books. However books in the Dutch language are very rare. Sometimes books in English are available but mostly in the local language. Access to radio and television is common. Almost everyone can watch television. However it is very rare that radio of television has programmes in Dutch. In only a few cases the respondent indicated that he was able to follow Dutch news events. Access to recreation and sports are mostly the same for national and foreign detainees. In only a few cases there was discrimination in this field.

4.2.4 Food-religion-personal hygiene-medical care

In general religious convictions are respected. Often the house rules of the prison allow special treatment related to food and clothing. This is however not always the case. In general however special needs in relation to food are respected. In most cases, no discrimination is made in this respect between national and foreign prisoners. In most cases it is possible to have contacts with a priest, rabbi or imam. Most detainees mention these contacts as valuable. However many clergymen do not speak any other languages, therefore contacts are difficult. However no discrimination seems to be in order related to the access of clergymen. According to the respondents, access to medical care is usually not much different than with other national detainees. In only a few cases a clear discrimination was mentioned. The level of medical care was rather low according to the respondents. However no discrimination seemed to be the case. Nevertheless, communication is again a big problem. Medical personnel often only speak the local language and translation is not available. Proper access to medical care is thereby hindered.

4.2.5 Consular and legal aid

All respondents said that contact with the consulate was possible. Communication can be either by telephone or post or visits. Mostly the contact with the consulate is a few times per year. Contact with the volunteers of the Foreign Liaison Office is more often, usually once every 4 to 8 weeks. In some cases visits are less frequent because of long travelling distance. Contacts with the Foreign Liaison Office of the Probation Service is usually only by post. In rare cases telephone contact is possible, but this is an exception. Communication by post is usually very slow according to the respondents. In a few cases this is due to the fact that translations are necessary before letters are allowed to be sent. Access to legal aid usually exists in theory. In practice however legal aid is not effective according to respondents. Sometimes there is a pro bono lawyer available, but most respondents mention that their help is very limited, unclear and slow. This however does not seem to differ much between national and foreign detainees. However due to language problems, there are much less possibilities for the foreigner to check on the progress of the legal case and the work of the lawyer. In a few cases no use is made of free legal aid because of mistrust of the system. Complaints can usually be directed at the management of the prison. Sometimes there is a special commission for complaints. All respondents wrote that filing a complaint does not help and in fact can only make your life more difficult. Half of the respondents feel that complaints of foreigners are taken less seriously than those of national prisoners.

4.2.6 About prison personnel and other prisoners

In general the contact with prison personnel is reasonable, according to most respondents. There are some very negative exceptions however, but on average contacts are normal. Most respondents indicate that contact between foreign detainees and guards are not much different than contacts between national prisoners and guards. In some cases, clear mention is made of discrimination of foreign prisoners. It is not always clear whether the discrimination stems from being a foreigner or from having a dark skin. Contacts with other detainees are normal according to most respondents. In only a few cases clear discrimination is mentioned. Here also it is not clear whether the discrimination stems from being a foreigner or from having a dark skin.

4.2.7. Contacts with the outside world

Contacts with the outside world depend strongly on the type of detention, e.g. before or after sentence. Moreover it depends on the type of regime the inmate is staying in. Generally speaking, it is possible to communicate by letters. Although there can be severe restrictions. Sometimes translations are necessary causing delays. This is usually only the case in pre-trial detention. Contact by telephone is not possible is many pre-trial detention houses. Visits are possible, but usually limited to once or twice every one or two months. This is disadvantageous for foreign prisoners, as they have to receive family from abroad, which is costly and difficult to organize. Usually it is not possible to save up unused visiting hours until family from abroad comes for a longer visit with extra hours. In some cases this possibility exists but the guards are not always willing to cooperate. When an inmate is out of pre-trial detention, the possibilities for telephone contact are usually better. Weekly or even more frequent telephone contact is sometimes possible, although in a few cases even telephone contact in detention after the sentence is restricted to once every month. The Dutch consulate or volunteers from the Dutch Probation Service visit the detainees usually once every 6 weeks. In some cases more often, in other cases less. This can depend on the location of the prison and the distance for the visitor. Communication is either by phone or visits. Emails are not possible. In general, the rules for communication are not different for foreign inmates than for national inmates. The same rules apply so there is no discrimination. Often there is flexibility in applying these rules. However because of the fact that family and friends live far away from the prison makes the rules for communication much harsher for foreign inmates than for national inmates which results in poor communication between foreign inmates and their family at home.

4.2.8 Reintegration activities – leave – release

Almost all respondents said that they were not able to participate in reintegration activities. Often the reason is that the inmates will not remain in the country where they are being held. In a few cases it is possible to participate in group sessions under guidance of a social worker, but often there is a problem with the language. In some cases there are no restrictions to participating in these sessions, but sometimes practical problems make it impossible, e.g. the participating of a spouse of partner in group sessions. The availability of the activities heavily depends on the regime and the possibilities of the various prisons. Short leave is often not possible, though in some cases it is. This depends very much on the type of detention (before or after sentence) and the regime of the prison where the inmate is staying. Also it depends on the efforts the of prison managements to make it possible and on the availability of local volunteers who can supervise a day leave of an inmates (e.g. a local priest). If there is a possibility for a leave, it is almost always a leave for one day. Often a permanent address is needed in the country of detention, and that is usually problematic for foreigners. The procedure for release differs greatly between prisons. It also depends on the sentence the inmate is serving. Sometimes expulsion follows the prison sentence. In other cases the inmate is just released outside the prison without guidance. In all cases the guidance and advice for the period after release is minimal or non-existent.

4.2.9 General conclusion and recommendations

In general most of the respondents claimed that they were not deliberately excluded from society and their families more than national prisoners. However all respondents mentioned the lack of proper communication with the home front, both by phone and personal visits. This does have an impact on their social connection with family and home country. Often it seems that there is no clear, formal or open discrimination against foreign inmates. However the house rules of the prisons are not flexible and show no leniency towards special type inmates such as foreigners. A rule regarding visits by family can work well for national inmates but can be extremely disadvantageous for foreign inmates. Although there is no deliberate discrimination or social exclusion the effect of the rules has a harsher impact on the foreigners than on the national prisoners. The possibility to participate in reintegration programmes is almost non-existent. This is mostly due to the fact that it is not expected that the foreign inmates stay in their country of detention after their sentence has finished. In terms of religion, food, work and recreation most of the respondents said that they did not specifically receive a more negative treatment than national inmates, although the lack of proper command of the local language can have negative effects. In terms of treatment and living conditions the answers of the respondents did not give a clear picture either in a positive or negative way. In some cases being a foreigner had a negative effect; in other cases it made no difference. All in all, a careful conclusion might be that the major problems for foreign prisoners can be found in the lack of proper communication with family and friends at home.

One of the best answers to the risks of social exclusion is a speedy return of the inmate to his own country. Therefore a first general recommendation would be that all EU Member States who are party to Council of Europe "Treaty on the transfer of sentenced persons" should step up their efforts in this field. Administrative and legal procedures should be streamlined so that inmates can return swiftly to their home country. Unfortunately a return is not always possible. Therefore it can be recommended that -if a swift return to their own country is not possible- an alternative is proper guidance, information and advice to nationals detained abroad. The aim of these efforts would be to prevent social exclusion and maintain proper communication with family and friends. Social resettlement is a leading principle in the treatment of foreign prisoners. This is also supported by relevant international legal documents and recommendations by organs of the Council of Europe.[2] It is recommended that every Member State make serious efforts to implement this principle. This means that the home-countries of foreign prisoners also should take up their responsibility in guidance of their nationals detained abroad. In the Netherlands we are fortunate that both the Ministry of Foreign Affairs and Justice support the Dutch Probation Service in these tasks. A further recommendation would be that prisons should apply their house rules in a flexible manner that fits the particular needs of the foreigner prisoner. Often house rules are enforced in a consistent manner – which would seem to be fair to all prisoners. However this often does not meet the specific needs of the foreign inmates. One example is that in the absence of a possibility to receive family visits, they often have to rely on telephone contact more than other prisoners. A flexible arrangement in making use of telephone contact is usually not possible. In particular during pre-trial detention this leads to the undesirable situation that foreign inmates hardly can communicate with relatives. This can be even worse in some countries where pre-trial detention can take many months or sometimes even more than one year. In some cases, small changes in prison house rules can mean major improvements for foreign prisoners. All in all many efforts can still be made to improve the situation of foreign prisoners, thus reducing the risk of social exclusion.

---

[2] E.g. Council of Europe, Committee of Ministers, rec. no. R (84) 12 concerning foreign prisoners.

Chapter 30

International Centre for Prison Studies (ICPS)

Andrew Coyle

THE EUROPEAN PRISON RULES 2006

The treatment of foreign national prisoners

1 BACKGROUND [1]

On 11 January 2006 the Committee of Ministers of the Council of Europe adopted their second recommendation of that year to Member States. This recommendation, formally known as Recommendation Rec (2006)2, is known colloquially as the European Prison Rules. The first set of European prison rules, known formally as the European Standard Minimum Rules for the Treatment of Prisoners, was adopted in 1973. These rules were modelled on the United Nations Standard Minimum Rules for the Treatment of Prisoners, which were approved by the UN General Assembly in 1957 as part of a growing consensus about the need for the international regulation of punishment and particularly of the form of judicial punishment that we know as imprisonment.

In 1973 the Council of Europe consisted of only 15 Member States, all from Western Europe. By the beginning of 1987 the Council had expanded to 21 states and in that year the Committee of Ministers adopted a new set of European Prison Rules. In approving this recommendation the Committee of Ministers noted 'that significant social trends and changes in regard to prison treatment and management have made it desirable to reformulate the Standard Minimum Rules for the Treatment of Prisoners, drawn up by the Council of Europe (Resolution (73) 5) so as to support and encourage the best of these developments and offer scope for future progress'.

In the years since 1987 the membership of the Council of Europe has expanded so that it now stretches from Lisbon on the Atlantic to Vladivostok on the Pacific and includes 46 Member States. The countries that now constitute the Council of Europe have a variety of different traditions of imprisonment and different understandings of what constitute the essential elements of imprisonment. The earlier versions of the European Prison Rules (EPRs) were structured within the context of the Western European model of imprisonment. At the beginning of the 21st century the Committee of Ministers recognised the need for a revision that would take account of the different philosophies of imprisonment as practised in the greater European region, while still safeguarding the basic human rights principles relating to deprivation of liberty.

The format of the revised EPRs is different from previous versions. They begin with a set of basic principles that form the bedrock for all the succeeding rules. These principles are worth stating in full:
- All persons deprived of their liberty shall be treated with respect for their human rights.
- Persons deprived of their liberty retain all rights that are not lawfully taken away by the decision sentencing them or remanding them in custody.
- Restrictions placed on persons deprived of their liberty shall be the minimum

---

[1] Andrew Coyle is Professor of Prison Studies in King's College, the University of London. He was one of the experts who drafted the revised European Prison Rules on behalf of the Council of Europe.

necessary and proportionate to the legitimate objective for which they are imposed.
- Prison conditions that infringe prisoners' human rights are not justified by lack of resources.
- Life in prison shall approximate as closely as possible the positive aspects of life in the community.
- All detention shall be managed so as to facilitate the reintegration into free society of persons who have been deprived of their liberty.
- Co-operation with outside social services and as far as possible the involvement of civil society in prison life shall be encouraged.
- Prison staffs carry out an important public service and their recruitment, training and conditions of work shall enable them to maintain high standards in their care of prisoners.
- All prisons shall be subject to regular government inspection and independent monitoring.

The Rules then go on to specify their scope and the persons to whom they apply. In brief, they cover all persons "who have been deprived of their liberty following conviction" (10.1), as well as persons who may be detained for any other reason in a prison, or who have been remanded in custody by a judicial authority or deprived of their liberty following conviction and who may, for any reason, be detained elsewhere (10.3). They go on to confirm that children, that is, those under the age of 18 years, should not be detained in a prison for adults but that if, exceptionally, they are, there must be special regulations that take account of their status and needs (11). Similarly, persons who are suffering from mental illness and whose state of mental health is incompatible with detention in a prison should be detained in an establishment specially designed for the purpose but if, exceptionally, they are held in prison there must be special regulations that take account of their status and needs (12). Finally in this introductory section, there is a stipulation that all the rules must be applied impartially, without discrimination on any ground such as sex, race, colour, language, religion, political or other opinion, national or social origin, association with a national minority, property, birth or other status (13).

The main sections of the rules deal with issues that apply to all prisoners. They include matters such as the conditions of imprisonment (admission arrangements, allocation and accommodation, hygiene, clothing and bedding, nutrition, legal advice, contact with the outside world, the prison regime, work, exercise and recreation, education, freedom of thought, conscience and religion, the information to which they are entitled, personal property, transfer, release); health, including mental health; a wide variety of issues to do with good order; requests and complaints; the management of staff; inspection and monitoring. There are also a number of rules relating to the specific treatment of untried prisoners and convicted prisoners.

While all of these rules are to be applied impartially and without any discrimination, there are also rules referring to specific groups of prisoners. These include women, detained children, infants and foreign prisoners.

2 FOREIGN PRISONERS

In all countries prisons are filled with the marginalized groups in society: the poor, the unemployed, the homeless, the mentally ill, people of ethnic minority. In recent years a new marginalized group has swelled their number: foreign nationals. This has happened in many regions of the world for a variety of reasons. In the greater European region this increased has been more marked in some countries than in others. The reasons for this are explored elsewhere in this report.

In Switzerland over 75% of all prisoners are foreign nationals. In Austria, Belgium, Cyprus and Greece there are over 40%, while in Estonia, Italy, Malta and the Netherlands the proportion is over 30%. In all of 25 European countries nearly one quarter of prisoners are foreign nationals. Many of the prejudices that exist in society against minority groups are reflected in the world of the prison. For these reasons it was felt necessary to strengthen the EPRs as they relate to this group of prisoners.

The revised EPR 37 reflects the growing importance of issues surrounding foreign nationals by incorporating them in a separate rule. The revised rule closely follows Rule 38 of the United Nations Standard Minimum Rules on the Treatment of Prisoners and is in line with the Vienna Convention on Consular Relations. The underlying principle is that foreign nationals may be in particular need of assistance when a state other than their own is exercising the power of imprisoning them. In the first place, assistance should be available from accredited representatives of their countries. It may also be that foreign prisoners can qualify for transfer under the European Convention of the Transfer of Sentenced Prisoners or in terms of bilateral arrangements and should inform such prisoners of the possibility. Rule 37.3 recognises that foreign prisoners may have other special needs. In some countries these prisoners may also receive visits by representatives of organisations concerned with the welfare of foreign prisoners. The commentary on the Rules also makes reference to the Council of Europe Recommendation N° R (84) 12 concerning foreign prisoners.

The increasingly diverse prison population of Europe also led to a new Rule intended to ensure that particular attention is paid to the needs of ethnic and linguistic minorities. Rule 38 states this proposition in general terms and also points out that prison staff need to be given specific training for their specialised work to ensure that they are sensitive to the cultural practices of the various groups in their care.

It seems likely that the proportion of foreign national prisoners in many prison systems will increase in the future. For that reason among others, the final EPR 108, which indicates that the Rules themselves should be regularly updated, is likely to be important as a means of ensuring that the future interpretation of the Rules will be influenced, as the current revision has been, by the expanding case law of the European Court of Human Rights and the recommendations of bodies such as the Committee for the Prevention of Torture in respect of the treatment of foreign national prisoners.

Chapter 31

Jesuit Refugee Service Europe
(JRS-Europe)

Cornelia Bührle RSCJ

Preliminary Remarks[1]

Recently, the legislative decision-making process in the European Union (EU) changed considerably. Until 2004, the European Parliament (EU Parliament), representing the citizens of the EU, only held a consultative role in the legislative process, and the European Council (EU Council), representing the Member States of the European Union (EU Member States), was the only EU institution, which had the right to adopt legislation. Since 1 January 2005, however, co-decision has become the rule in the fields of asylum, immigration[2] and border control issues: The EU Council and the EU Parliament adopt EU legislation jointly. This requires that the two EU institutions have to agree on an identical text proposed by the European Commission (EU Commission). The role of the EU Commission, representing the overall interests of the EU, remains unchanged: The EU Commission has the exclusive right to propose, among EU legislative acts, in particular EU directives.

An EU 'directive' must be transposed into the national law of the EU Member States as follows: 'A directive shall be binding, as to the result to be achieved, upon each Member State to which it is addressed, but shall leave to the national authorities the choice of form and methods.'[3] Insofar an EU directive is also the appropriate legal instrument to define legal notions. Against that background, an 'asylum seeker'[4] or 'applicant for asylum'[5] is legally defined as 'a third country national or a stateless person who has made an application for asylum in respect of which a final decision has not yet been taken'.[6]

An 'illegally staying third-country national' is, as recently proposed by the EU Commission, 'any person who is not a citizen of the (European) Union'[7] and whose 'presence on the territory of a Member State' is regarded as 'illegal stay' because the stay 'does not fulfil, or no longer fulfils the conditions for stay or residence in that Member State'[8]; in the past, the EU Commission had referred to 'illegal immigrants'[9], 'illegal residents'[10], or to 'people residing illegally in the EU'[11].

---

[1] The study considers texts and documents published before 19 April 2006.

[2] except legal immigration.

[3] Art. 249 Treaty of Amsterdam.

[4] Council Directive 2003/9/EC of 27 January 2003 laying down minimum standards for the reception of asylum seekers– below referred to as 'Reception Directive'.

[5] Council Directive 2005/85/EC of 1 December 2005 on minimum standards on procedures in Member States granting and withdrawing refugee status – below referred to as 'Asylum Procedures Directive'.

[6] Art. 2 (c) Reception Directive and Art. 2 (c) Asylum Procedures Directive.

[7] Art. 3 (a) COM (2005) 391 final, Proposal for a Directive of the European Parliament and of the council on common standards and procedures in Member States for returning illegally staying third-country nationals (presented by the Commission) – below referred to as 'Proposal Returns Directive'.

[8] Art. 3 (b) Proposal Returns Directive.

[9] COM (2003) 323 final communication from the Commission to the European Parliament and the Council in view of the European Council of Thessaloniki – below referred to as 'COM (2003) 323 final' –, p. 3.

[10] Cf. COM (2002) 175 final Green Paper on a community return policy on illegal residents (presented by the Commission) – below referred to as 'COM (2002) 175 final'; cf. COM (2003) 323 final

[11] COM (2002) 175, p. 6.

'Administrative detention' is an administrative measure and, consequently, not a measure of the penal system. Thus it is neither pre-trial detention on remand nor imprisonment after criminal court proceedings or a pre- or post-criminal security measure ordered by a court. Still, it is a measure of deprivation of the 'right to liberty'[12] or the right to the 'freedom of movement'[13]. In that sense, 'detention' of asylum seekers is legally defined as the 'confinement (...) by a Member State within a particular place, where (an asylum seeker) is deprived of his or her freedom of movement'[14]; previously, the EU Commission had proposed to define it as 'the confinement of (an applicant for asylum) by a Member State within a restricted area, where his freedom of movement is substantially curtailed'[15].

As far as the notion 'detention' of illegally staying third-country nationals is concerned, the EU Commission is referring to it as 'temporary custody' of a 'third-country national'[16].

1 INTRODUCTION

1.1 Overview on different situations of administrative detention, on justifications and on legal grounds

EU asylum and immigration policy distinguishes three different situations of administrative detention of asylum seekers and illegally staying third-country nationals:
- administrative detention of asylum seekers within the context of reception[17];
- administrative detention of asylum seekers within the context of the asylum procedure[18];
- administrative detention (temporary custody) of illegally staying third-country nationals for the purpose of removal[19].

---

12 Art 3 Universal Declaration of Human Rights; Art. 5 ECHR
13 Article 2 (k) Reception Directive.
14 Article 2 (k) Reception Directive.
15 Article 2 (j) COM (2002) 326 final/2 Amended Proposal for a Council Directive on minimum standards on procedures in Member States for granting and withdrawing refugee status (presented by the Commission – below referred to as 'Amended Proposal Asylum Procedures Directive'.
16 Art. 14 COM Proposal Returns Directive.
17 Cf. Art. 7 Para. 2COM (2001) 181 final, Proposal for a Council Directive laying down minimum standards on the reception of applicants for asylum in Member States (presented by the Commission) – below referred to as 'Proposal Reception Directive'; cf. Article 2 (k) Reception Directive; cf. Art. 33 Asylum Procedures Directive.
18 Cf. Article 2 (j) COM (2002) 326 final/2; cf. Article 2 (k) Reception Directive.
19 Cf. Chapter IV Proposal Returns Directive.

1.1.1 Administrative detention of asylum seekers within the context of reception

1.1.1.1 The 2001 EU Commission Proposal of the EU Commission for a EU Council Directive laying down minimum standards on the reception of applicants for asylum in Member States

Article 7 Paragraph 2 of the 2001 Proposal of the EU Commission for a EU Council Directive laying down minimum standards on the reception of applicants for asylum in Member States [20] (Proposal Reception Directive) had stated that EU Member States 'shall not hold applicants for asylum in detention for the sole reason that their applications for asylum need to be examined. However, Member States may hold an applicant for asylum in detention for the purpose of taking a decision in the cases described in Article [...] of Directive .../.../EC [on minimum standards on procedures in Member States for granting and withdrawing refugee status]'.

1.1.1.2. The 2003 EU Council Directive laying down minimum standards for the reception of asylum seekers

The Council Directive 2003/9/EC of 27 January 2003 laying down minimum standards for the reception of asylum seekers (Reception Directive) itself does not contain the proposal stating that EU Member States 'shall not hold applicants for asylum in detention for the sole reason that their applications for asylum need to be examined'; a similar provision, however, became later part of the Council Directive 2005/85/EC of 1 December 2005 on minimum standards on procedures in Member States granting and withdrawing refugee status[21] (Asylum Procedures Directive). The Reception Directive only states in Article 7 Paragraph 3 that EU Member States 'may confine an applicant to a particular place in accordance with their national law', when 'it proves necessary, for example for legal reasons or reasons of public order'.

1.1.2. Administrative detention of asylum seekers within the context of the asylum procedure

During the preparatory legislative work on an Asylum Procedures Directive, the EU Commission dealt with justifications and legal grounds; the final EU Asylum Procedures Directive itself, however, neither justifies administrative detention of asylum seekers within the context of the asylum procedure nor does the Directive state legal grounds. The development underwent the following major steps.

---

[20] COM (2001) 181.
[21] Asylum Procedures Directive.

1.1.2.1. The 2000 EU Commission Proposal for a Council Directive on minimum standards on procedures in Member States for granting and withdrawing refugee status

In its (first) Proposal for a Council Directive on minimum standards on procedures in Member States for granting and withdrawing refugee status[22] (Proposal Asylum Procedures Directive), presented in 2000, the EU Commission set a 'minimum framework for assessing the legitimacy of cases of detention which are based on the need for an efficient and adequate examination of an asylum application'[23]. Accordingly, administrative detention of an asylum seeker within the context of the asylum procedure was regarded as legitimate in the following cases[24]:

- to ascertain or verify his identity or nationality;
- to determine his identity or nationality when he has destroyed or disposed of his travel and/or identity documents or used fraudulent documents upon arrival in the Member State in order to mislead the authorities;
- to determine the elements on which his application for asylum is based which in other circumstances could be lost;
- in the context of a procedure, to decide on his right to enter the territory.

1.1.2.2 The 2002 EU Commission Amended Proposal for a Council Directive on minimum standards on procedures in Member States for granting and withdrawing refugee status

Later, in 2002, after negotiations with the EU Parliament and the EU Council, the EU Commission's Amended Proposal for a Council Directive on minimum standards on procedures in Member States for granting and withdrawing refugee status[25] (Amended Proposal Asylum Procedures Directive) stated, that 'Member States shall not hold an applicant for asylum in detention for the sole reason that his application for asylum needs to be examined before a decision is taken by the determining authority'[26]; however, Member States may only hold an applicant for asylum in detention:

- where such detention is objectively necessary for an efficient examination of the application[27];
- where, on the basis of the personal conduct of the applicant, there is a strong likelihood of his absconding[28];and may also only hold an applicant for asylum in detention during the examination of his application,
- if there are grounds for believing that the restriction on his freedom of movement is necessary for a quick decision to be made[29] or

---

[22] COM (2000) 578 final Proposal for a Council Directive on minimum standards on procedures in Member States for granting and withdrawing refugee status (presented by the Commission) – below referred to as 'Proposal Asylum Procedures Directive'.

[23] Art. 11 par. 1 Proposal Asylum Procedures Directive.

[24] Cf. Art. 11 par. 1 Proposal Asylum Procedures Directive.

[25] Amended Proposal Asylum Procedures Directive.

[26] Art. 17 par. 1 Amended Proposal Asylum Procedures Directive.

[27] Art. 17 par. 1 Amended Proposal Asylum Procedures Directive.

[28] Art. 17 par. 1 Amended Proposal Asylum Procedures Directive.

- from the moment at which another Member State has agreed to take charge of him or to take him back until the moment the applicant is transferred to the other Member State to prevent him from absconding or effecting an unauthorised stay[30].

The EU Commission's commentary highlighted the difference to the former Article: 'Instead of exhaustively enumerating legitimate grounds for detention, it is proposed to limit the scope of Community law related to first stage harmonisation[31] to laying down guarantees as regards the exceptions to the principle that an applicant should not solely be detained because he is an applicant for asylum'[32], and 'in order to strengthen the mechanism for determining the Member State responsible for examining an application for asylum in the EU, it is proposed that Member States may detain an applicant awaiting his or her transfer to another Member State'.[33]

1.1.2.3 The 2005 EU Council Directive on minimum standards on procedures in Member States for granting and withdrawing refugee status

The final Council Directive 2005/85/EC of 1 December 2005 on minimum standards on procedures in Member States granting and withdrawing refugee status (Asylum Procedures Directive) now only states that EU Member States 'shall not hold a person in detention for the sole reason that he/she is an applicant for asylum'[34]. This Article represents an exclusion clause and mentions neither justifications nor legal grounds for exceptions.

1.1.3. Administrative detention (temporary custody) of illegally staying third-country nationals for the purpose of removal

Concerning administrative detention (temporary custody) of illegally staying third-country nationals for the purpose of removal, the legislative process is presently still going on against the following background.

1.1.3.1 The 2002 EU Commission Green Paper on a community return policy on illegal residents

The EU Commission's Green Paper on a community return policy on illegal residents[35], which was published in 2002, justified 'detention pending removal', which takes place 'in order to safeguard enforcement measures and to facilitate the identification of the illegal resident concerned' and 'in order to obtain return travel documents and to hinder the illegal resident from absconding before removal'.[36]

---

29 Art. 17 par. 2 Amended Proposal Asylum Procedures Directive.
30 Art. 18 par. 1 Amended Proposal Asylum Procedures Directive.
31 Cf. Tampere Programme
32 Art 17 Amended Proposal Asylum Procedures Directive.
33 Art 18 Amended Proposal Asylum Procedures Directive.
34 Art. 18 Asylum Procedures Directive.
35 COM (2002) 175 final.
36 Par. 3.1.3 COM (2002) 175 final.

1.1.3.2 The 2002 EU Commission Communication on a community return policy on illegal residents

The EU Commission Communication on a community return policy on illegal residents[37] specified 'grounds for detention pending removal' covering 'detention of the illegal resident concerned' in order to obtain return travel documents or to prevent the illegal resident from absconding during the removal or during transit.[38]

At the same time, it stated that 'minimum standards on detention pending removal should be set at EU level, defining competencies of responsible authorities and the preconditions for detention in the framework of a future Directive on minimum standards for return procedures'[39]. According to the EU Commission, those minimum standards 'could cover:

- Grounds for detention pending removal. This covers detention of the illegal resident concerned in order to obtain return travel documents or to prevent the illegal resident from absconding during the removal or during transit.
- Identification of the groups of persons who should generally not or only under specific conditions be detained (unaccompanied children and persons under the age of 18; the elderly, especially where supervision is required; pregnant women, unless there is the clear threat of absconding and medical advice approves detention; those suffering from serious medical conditions or the mentally ill; those where there is independent evidence that they have been tortured or mistreated while being detained before they arrived in the EU and people with serious disabilities.)
- Rules concerning the issuing of a detention order. This could include the proportionality of detention and the possibilities of suitable alternatives to detention such as reporting duties, obligatory residence, bail bonds or even electronic monitoring.
- Provisions on the judicial control. A judicial body should be competent to issue or to revise the detention order.
- Time limits for the duration of detention pending removal. Although the grounds for detention (e.g. identification or prevention from absconding) have an inherent limitation of the duration, the Commission considers it necessary to provide for an absolute time limit and time limits for judicial review on the continuation of detention.
- Rules on the conditions of detention, in particular on accommodation standards but also on legal assistance, to ensure humane treatment in all detention facilities in the Member States. The Commission's considered opinion is that for accommodation purposes returnees should as far as possible be separated from convicts in order to avoid any criminalisation.'[40]

---

[37] COM (2002) 564 final Communication from the Commission to the Council and the European Parliament on a Community return policy on illegal residents – below referred to as COM (2002) 564 final.

[38] Par. 2.3.5 COM (2002) 564 final.

[39] Ibidem.

[40] Par. 2.3.5 COM (2002) 564 final.

1.1.3.3 The 2002 EU Council Return Action Programme

The 2002 Danish EU Presidency Proposal for a EU Council Return Action Programme[41], which was adopted by the EU Council[42], mentions 'detention' several times[43], but does not indicate any justifications or legal grounds for detention.

1.1.3.4 The 2005 EU Commission Proposal for a Directive of the European Parliament and the Council on common standards and procedures in Member States for returning illegally staying third-country nationals

Article 14 Paragraph 1 of the EU Commission Proposal for a Directive of the European Parliament and of the Council on common standards and procedures in Member States for returning illegally staying third-country nationals[44] (Returns Proposal) states as legal grounds for detention that Member States shall keep under temporary custody a third-country national, who is or will be subject of a removal order or a return decision', where there are serious grounds to believe that there is a risk of absconding and where it would not be sufficient to apply less coercive measures such as regular reporting to the authorities, the deposit of a financial guarantee, the handing over of documents, an obligation to stay at a designated place or other measures to prevent that risk[45].

The EU Commission comments that 'the use of temporary custody should be limited and bound to the principle of proportionality. Temporary custody should only be used if necessary to prevent the risk of absconding and if the application of less coercive measures would not be sufficient'[46]

A future EU Directive will be adopted according to the rules of the co-decision procedure.

1.2. Overview on the EU system of administrative detention of asylum seekers and illegally staying third-country nationals

The EU detention system distinguishes between 'reception centres'[47] and 'accommodation centres'[48], however, leaving open the exact difference between 'reception centres' and 'accommodation centres' and no name places for 'temporary custody'[49].

---

41 Presidency note, Council of the European Union, Brussels 25 November 2002, 13515/3/02 Rev. 3 migr. 104 front 128 visa 160, proposal for a return action programme.

42 Chapter 9 Council of the European Union Brussels, 19 December 2002, 2469th meeting of the Council of the European Union (Justice, Home Affairs and Civil Protection) held in Brussels on 28/29 November 2002, 14931/02, Limite, PV/CONS, 66 JAI 278.

43 Presidency Note, Council of the European Union, Brussels 25 November 2002, 13515/3/02 Rev 3 migr. 104 front 128 visa 160, Proposal for a return action programme, pp. 22, 29, 32.

44 COM (2005) 391 final Proposal for a Directive of the European Parliament and of the Council on common standards and procedures in Member States for returning illegally staying third-country nationals (presented by the Commission).

45 Art. 14 para. 1 Proposal Returns Directive.

46 Additional information, Chapter IV Proposal Returns Directive; no. (11) Proposal Asylum Procedures Directive.

47 Cf. Commentary on articles 7 (3) Proposal Reception Directive; cf. Art. 33 Asylum Procedures Directive.

As far as the legal language is concerned, it is striking that the 'Reception' Directive does not speak of 'reception' centres, but of 'accommodation' centres[50], and that the 'Procedures' Directive covering the time of the asylum procedure and thus implicitly the accommodation during the asylum procedure, speaks of 'reception' centres[51].

Public authorities running those centres in praxis as well as staff, refer to 'reception centres' in the case of places where the asylum application is made, and to 'accommodation centres' in the case of places where asylum seekers are accommodated while waiting for a decision on their asylum application; but it may occur that 'reception centres' are at the same time 'accommodation centres' in those cases, when asylum seekers are not transferred from one centre to another, remaining in the same facility from the moment of their reception (arrival) until the moment of the final decision on the asylum application.

This does not mean, however, that the respective centres are always explicitly called 'reception centres' or 'accommodation centres', i.e. that those terms established at EU level are literally translated into the various native languages of the EU Member States at national level. Each EU Member State has its own wording, and thus the terminology gets confusing when native terms are translated into English. For example, in the case of Lithuania which, as a very small country, has only one detention centre that consequently serves as the same time as 'reception' and 'accommodation' centre as well as a place for 'temporary custody for the purpose of removal', is called (in English) 'Foreigners Registration Centre'; or, for example, in Italy where those three different kinds of centres are called (in English) either 'centres for temporary stay and assistance' or 'identification centres'.

At EU level, there is neither a common EU institution exercising responsible authority on the system nor a EU institution periodically and publicly reporting about detention centres in the EU or a EU monitoring mechanism[52]. Consequently, official EU information is neither available on the types of institutions and their budgets nor on the capacity of accommodation, the detained population, staff in detention centres, staff training the number etc. or, in particular, the number and location of detention centres in the European Union.[53] Only national authorities run the system, i.e. each EU Member State runs its own system under the terms of the relevant EU Directives.

In March 2005, Mrs. Dr. Silvana Koch-Mehrin, Member of the EU Parliament, submitted a written Parliamentary Question to the EU Commission requiring information on the 'Cost of administrative detention of asylum applicants and of pre-expulsion

48 Cf. Art. 2 (l) Reception Directive.
49 Cf. Additional information Chapter IV Proposal Returns Directive.
50 Art. 2 (l) Reception Directive.
51 Art. 33 Asylum Procedures Directive.
52 The Committee for the Prevention of Torture and Inhuman or Degrading Treatment or Punishment (CPT) of the Council of Europe is not a EU institution.
53 Regarding the numbers of detention centres, a preliminary inventory of detention centres in Europe made by the Jesuit Refugee Service (JRS) – Europe in co-operation with Permanent Representations and Permanent Missions of the EU Member States in Brussels, counted in Belgium and the Czech Republic each six, in Denmark one, in France 20, in Germany 44, in Greece 14, in Hungary eight in Ireland six, in Italy 16, in Lithuania one, in Luxemburg one, in Malta four, in The Netherlands seven, in Poland 24, in Portugal 4, in Spain at least 12, in Slovakia and Slovenia two, in Sweden 5 and in the United Kingdom 12 centres (cf. Jesuit Refugee Service (JRS) – Europe, *Detention in Europe* 17 October 2005, Chapter 5.

custody of illegally resident foreign nationals'[54], and the EU Commission responded that it is unable to answer the questions because at EU level there is no relevant information available at all.

1.3 Overview on the involvement of institutions and organisations external to the EU system

To a very limited extent, several external institutions and organisations deal with issues of detention of asylum seekers and illegally staying third-country nationals:

1.3.1 Committee for the Prevention of Torture and Inhuman or Degrading Treatment or Punishment (CPT)

The only European institution, which is, however, not an institution of the EU, is the Committee for the Prevention of Torture and Inhuman or Degrading Treatment or Punishment (CPT) of the Council of Europe. According to Article 1 of the European Convention for the Prevention of Torture and Inhuman or Degrading Treatment or Punishment its mission is to '(...) by means of visits, examine the treatment of persons deprived of their liberty with a view to strengthening, if necessary, the protection of such persons from torture and from inhuman or degrading treatment or punishment'. However, the work of the CPT is basically strictly confidential.

1.3.2 NGOs operating at EU level

Among NGOs operating at EU or global level[55], there are a few NGOs who can play a role for detainees. Their local representatives may have access to detention centres, such as Caritas-Europa, the Jesuit Refugee Service (JRS) - Europe and Médecins Sans Frontières. Mostly they do social work, occasionally they report publicly about their activities. Rarely do they do legal counselling and hardly ever can they give financial support. The major challenges are two-fold: They are walking a tightrope between their activities and the interests of public authorities being involved, and they desire to assist detainees although the means of assisting them are extremely limited. A special challenge is foreign language knowledge when communicating with detainees.

1.3.3 Churches

The same challenges are faced by representatives of the Catholic Church and of representatives of members of the World Council of Churches who mostly do pastoral care.

---

[54] http://www.europarl.europa.eu/omk/sipade3?PUBREF=-//EP//TEXT+WQ+E-2005-1297+0+DOC+XML+V0//EN&L=EN&LEVEL=2&NAV=S&LSTDOC=Y

[55] other than national NGOs operating at only national level.

1.3.4 Diplomatic and consular missions

As far as asylum seekers are concerned, there is no reliable information available whether or not diplomatic missions[56] and consular missions[57] as well as Ministries in the country of origin are involved when a national of their country is detained as an asylum seeker. In fact, for reasons of safety of the asylum seeker who has fled or otherwise involuntarily left from his country, diplomatic missions and consular missions as well as Ministries in the country of origin should not be involved. As regards detained illegally staying third-country nationals, however, those missions often play an important role in helping national authorities to obtain return travel documents for the person concerned.

1.4.   Overview on EU asylum and immigration policy trends

1.4.1 General retrospective

In the distant past, over hundreds of years, only individual political leaders, empires and countries granted assistance to uprooted people. Only at the beginning of the 20th century, nation-states began to develop a common awareness for the problems of uprooted life, and gradually efforts to help uprooted people turned into a global dimension. In 1921, the League of Nations named the Norwegian Fridtjof Nansen, the famous explorer, scientist and diplomat, as the first (League of Nations) High Commissioner for Refugees and mandated him to assist around 800.000 mostly Russian refugees. After World War II, in 1951, the General Assembly of the United Nations created the position and institution of the United Nations High Commissioner for Refugees (UNHCR), whose initial mission was to look after more than one million of refugees who were, five years after World War II, still in precarious situations. Thus it was due to Europe and European refugees in Europe that international refugee policy and law took a specific shape: In 1951 the General Assembly of the United Nations adopted the Convention relating to the Status of Refugees.

After World War II and until about 40 years ago, 'asylum' and 'immigration' were two distinct concepts in Europe. At the time, it did not constitute a problem to distinguish between 'asylum seekers' and 'immigrants' because the terms of reference were basically clear: An 'asylum seeker' was regarded as a political refugee having been forced to leave his country of origin to save his life. Everybody else was considered as 'immigrant', i.e. a 'voluntary migrant'.

At the time of the Cold war, in Western Europe, the old 15 EU Member States[58] used to offer a relatively generous reception to asylum seekers; many of the asylum seekers came from countries of the Warsaw Pact[59] or from overseas countries at war with those States, which were political adversaries of the old 15 EU Member States[60]. Eastern European governments primarily granted asylum to political leaders whose communist or socialist regimes had been overthrown.

---

[56]   Cf. Art. 3 Vienna Convention on Diplomatic Relations.
[57]   Cf. Art. 5 Vienna Convention on Consular Relations.
[58]   before the 2004 EU enlargement.
[59]   for example from Czechoslovakia, Hungary, Poland.
[60]   for example from Afghanistan during the Russia-Afghanistan war.

As far as immigration was concerned, many of the old 15 EU Member States received large numbers of 'labour immigrants' on a contractual basis because workers were desperately needed to assure economic growth. Countries of the Warsaw Pact invited 'labour immigrants', too, small numbers from ideologically allied countries to express political friendship among the members of the communist world.

But then, communism in Europe collapsed, and a new era began in Europe and elsewhere: the new mobility of humankind and the era of 'irregular migration', i.e. migration movements not fitting existing legal asylum and immigration frames. Since then it is extremely difficult to clearly determine who is an 'asylum seeker' and who is an 'immigrant'.

On the one hand, persons in need of international protection may increasingly take the irregular migration path in order to reach European territory; they often enter the first asylum country illegally and may also remain in the country undocumented, hoping to apply for asylum in another European country at a later stage. Rejected asylum seekers also become irregular migrants when they remain in the country of asylum after the rejection of their asylum application. On the other hand, persons who seek to migrate to Europe but are not in need of protection tend to enter the asylum system, hoping to use this as an alternative means to legal immigration. These two aspects create a number of problems: perilous journeys which put human lives at risk, illegal border crossing, flourishing of criminal acts such as human smuggling and trafficking, obstacles to protection for those in need, human rights violations, 'asylum abuse' and, consequently increasing policy restrictions and the 'securitization' of migration. This overlapping relation between irregular migration and asylum is often referred to as the "asylum-migration nexus."[61] Nevertheless, the EU maintains as distinct policy areas on one hand 'asylum' and on the other hand 'immigration'.

1.4.2. Recent EU asylum and immigration policy trends and selected comparative data of asylum applications (1980 – 2004)

Between 1980 and 2004, 9.9 million applications for asylum were lodged in 39 countries in Europe, North America, Oceania, and Asia[62]:

---

[61] Cf. A. Papadopoulou, 'Exploring the asylum-migration nexus: a case study of transit migrants in Europe', *Global Migration Perpectives*, No. 23, January 2005.

[62] The numbers are provided by http://www.migrationinformation.org/DataTools/asylumresults.cfm (last visit 12 April 2006), the source of the data is the UNHCR Population Data Unit, and the author did the chart.

Figure 1 Number of Asylum applications

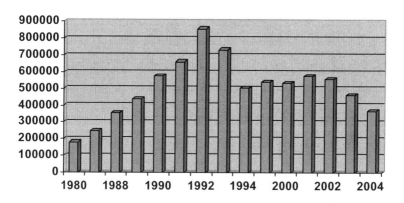

Between 1990 and 2004 the annual number of asylum applications for selected industrialized countries conveys the following figure[63]:

Figure 2

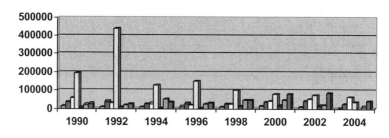

☒ Australia ■ Canada ☐ France ☐ Germany ■ Italy ☒ Netherlands ■ United Kingdom

With growing numbers of asylum applications submitted in Europe, asylum and immigration policies in Europe changed radically. The old 15 EU Member States were no longer aiming at encouraging immigration of 'labour immigrants' and, commencing about 10 years ago[64], political decisions in the old 15 EU Member States began to aim at reducing the number of entries of asylum seekers and discourage new requests for protection because the number of refugees applying for asylum had increased drastically. The old EU Member States tightened their asylum policies. Wealthier receiving countries started to implement increasingly restrictive border control systems.

---

63 The numbers are provided by http://www.migrationinformation.org/GlobalData/charts/3.1.xls (last visit 12 April 2006), the source of the data is the UNHCR Population Data Unit, and the author did the chart.

64 In some EU Member States even earlier.

1.4.3. The Tampere Programme (1999 – 2004)

The 1999 Treaty of Amsterdam had set out a new objective for the EU establishing the EU as an 'area of freedom, security and justice'.[65] The EU Council, held at Tampere in 1999, placed this objective at the head of the EU's political agenda and set a 5 years programme – the 'Tampere Programme'[66]. It provided, inter alia, for 'A Common Asylum and Migration Policy' including the following elements:

- partnership with countries of origin;
- a common European asylum system;
- fair treatment of third-country nationals;
- management of migration flows [67].

According to the EU Council's objectives, a 'Common European Asylum System' should include, in the short term, inter alia, 'common standards for a fair and efficient asylum procedure and common minimum conditions of reception of asylum seekers'[68].

The Tampere Programme and, at the time, the future 2004 EU enlargement were closely interwoven. The old 15 EU Member States, which until then had established only national standards in their asylum and immigration laws, had to make sure that the 10 new EU Member States would meet those general standards, too, because if the standards for asylum procedures and for the reception of asylum seekers in the 10 new EU Member States had been lower than in the 15 old EU Member States, this would have created an EU internal pull factor on the side of the 15 old EU Member States. So it was important to establish common EU legislation, so-called 'Acquis', on asylum procedures and the reception of asylum seekers, as, according to the accession criteria, the new 10 EU Member States had to adopt the 'Acquis' of the old EU Member States. Furthermore, with the accession of the new 10 EU Member States, the old 15 EU Member States would obviously no longer have to receive asylum seekers fleeing from those countries because the new 10 Member States would be considered as democratic and safe countries. Also, the old 15 EU Member States would no longer have an influx of 'irregular immigrants' originating from those countries because their citizens would be EU citizens.

1.4.4 The 2005 – 2010 Hague Programme (2005 – 2010)

In 2004, following-up the Tampere Programme, the EU Council adopted the so-called 'Hague Programme'[69] for the next five years to come. It states, inter alia, that migrants 'who do not or no longer have the right to stay legally in the EU must return on a voluntary or, if necessary, compulsory basis. The European Council calls for the establishment of an effective removal and repatriation policy based on common standards for persons to be returned in a humane manner and with full respect for their human rights and dignity. The European Council considers it essential that the Council begins discussions in early

---

65   Art. 61 Treaty of Amsterdam.
66   Tampere European Council, 15 and 16 October, Presidency Conclusions, Chapter II. A.
67   ibidem, par. 14.
68   ibidem, par. 14.
69   Council of the European Union, Brussels 13 December 2004, 16054/04, JAI 559.

2005 on minimum standards for return procedures including minimum standards to sup
port effective national removal efforts. The proposal should also take into account specia
concerns with regard to safeguarding public order and security. A coherent approach be
tween return policy and all other aspects of the external relations of the Community wit
third countries is necessary as is special emphasis on the problem of nationals of suc
third countries who are not in the possession of passports or other identity documents'[70]
Shortly after, the EU Commission issued an Action Plan referring to the Hague Pro
gramme[71], which lists among action to be taken by the EU Commission a 'Proposal o
return procedures' to be submitted in 2005[72].

1.5 Overview on the legal instruments at the level of EU asylum and immigration legislation and legislation in the making

1.5.1 Detention of asylum seekers in the context of reception and the asylum procedure

Concerning asylum seekers, the EU Council adopted, as set out by the Tampere Pro
gramme, the Council Directive 2003/9/EC of 27 January 2003 laying down minimun
standards for the reception of asylum seekers and the Council Directive 2005/85/EC c
1 December 2005 on minimum standards on procedures in Member States for grantin
and withdrawing refugee status.

1.5.1.1 EU Council Directive laying down minimum standards for the reception of asylum seekers

The Council Directive 2003/9/EC of 27 January 2003 laying down minimum standard
for the reception of asylum seekers (Reception Directive) applies 'to all third country na
tionals and stateless persons who make an application for asylum at the border or in th
territory of a Member State as long as they are allowed to remain on the territory as asy
lum seekers, as well as to family members, if they are covered by such application for asy
lum according to the national law' (scope)[73]. According to Article 4, 'Member States ma
introduce or retain more favourable provisions in the field of reception conditions for asy
lum seekers and other close relatives of the applicant who are present in the same Mem
ber State when they are dependent on him or for humanitarian reasons insofar as thes
provisions are compatible with this Directive.' Article 26 of this Directive provides fo
transposition by 6 February 2005.

---

[70] ibidem, Chapter III par. 1.6.4.
[71] COM (2005) 184 final communication from the Commission to the Council and the European Par
liament, The Hague Programme: Ten priorities for the next five years The Partnership for Euro
pean renewal in the field of Freedom, Security and Justice, Brussels 10 May 2005.
[72] ibidem, Chapter 2.3.3.
[73] Art. 3 par. 1 Reception Directive.

1.5.1.2 EU Council Directive on minimum standards on procedures in Member States for granting and withdrawing refugee status

The Council Directive 2005/85/EC of 1 December 2005 on minimum standards on procedures in Member States for granting and withdrawing refugee status (Asylum Procedures Directive) applies 'to all applications for asylum made in the territory, including at the border or in the transit zones of the Member States, and to the withdrawal of refugee status' (scope)[74]. Under Article 5, 'Member States may introduce or maintain more favourable standards on procedures for granting and withdrawing refugee status, insofar as those standards are compatible with this Directive.' According to Article 43 of this Directive, the Directive shall be transposed by 1 December 2007. However, in February 2006, the EU Parliament decided to challenge the latter one bringing it to the European Court of Justice[75] requiring partial or, on subsidiary grounds, complete annulment.[76] Yet, Article 18 (detention) is not listed among the reasons for that challenge.

1.5.2 Detention of illegally staying third-country nationals for the purpose of removal

Concerning illegally staying third-country nationals, the EU Commission presented, as set out by the Action Plan of the Hague Programme, a Proposal for a Directive of the European Parliament and of the Council on common standards and procedures in Member States for returning illegally staying third-country nationals (Proposal Returns Directive).

Article 2 Paragraph 1 of the Proposal provides that 'this Directive applies to third-country nationals staying illegally in the territory of a Member State, i.e. who do not fulfil or who no longer fulfil the conditions of entry as set out in Article 5 of the Convention Implementing the Schengen Agreement, or who are otherwise illegally staying in the territory of a Member State.'

According to Article 4 Paragraph 3, 'this Directive shall be without prejudice to the right of the Member States to adopt or maintain provisions that are more favourable to persons to whom it applies provided that such provisions are compatible with this Directive.' Article 18 Paragraph 1 of the Proposal states, 'Member States shall bring into force the laws, regulations and administrative provisions necessary to comply with this Directive by, *(24 months from the date of publication in the Official Journal of the European Union)* at the latest.'

---

[74] Art. 3 par. 1 Asylum Procedures Directive.

[75] The European Court of Justice in Luxembourg has, inter alia, jurisdiction over questions of the validity and interpretation of acts of the EU institutions.

[76] Cf. Conseil de l'Union Européenne, Service juridiques au Coreper II, Affaire portée devant la Cour de justice, Affaire C-133/06 (Parlement Européen contre Conseil de l'Union européenne), Requête en annulation de la directive 2005/85/CE, Bruxelles le 27 mars 2006, 7952/06, JUR 156, ASILE 31.

2 TREATMENT OF ADMINISTRATIVE DETAINEES:
Rights of detained asylum seekers and illegally straying third-country nationals as well as obligations of EU Member States according to EU legislation and EU legislation in the making

2.1 Rights of detained asylum seekers and obligations of EU Member States according to the 2003 EU Council Directive laying down minimum standards for the reception of asylum seekers

2.1.1 General

According to the Council Directive 2003/9/EC of 27 January 2003 laying down minimum standards for the reception of asylum seekers (Reception Directive), in general, EU Member States shall ensure that material reception conditions are available to applicants of asylum[77], but Member States may require applicants to cover or contribute to the cost of the material reception conditions[78]; the provisions on material reception conditions shall ensure a standard of living capable of ensuring their subsistence[79].

Specific modalities for material reception conditions are laid down in Article 14. However, according to Article 14 Paragraph 8, 'EU Member States may exceptionally set modalities for material reception conditions different from those provided for in this Article', (…) when, inter alia, 'the asylum seeker is in detention' or 'material reception conditions, as provided for in this Article, are not available in a certain geographical area'; but 'these different conditions shall cover in any case basic needs'[80].

2.1.2 Living conditions and facilities

Facilities are called 'accommodation centres'[81] which means 'any place used for collective housing of asylum seekers'[82]. The Directive does not make a distinction between 'open' and 'closed' accommodation centres. A situation in a closed centre is only referred to as a situation 'in detention'[83] (Article 14 Paragraph 8). The Directive does not mention accommodation separated from prisoners convicted of a crime be those nationals or foreigners. If no exception is made according to Article 14 Paragraph 8, living condition should correspond to the following criteria:

- protection of family life;[84]
- minor children of applicants or applicants who are minors are lodged with their parents or with the adult family member responsible for them whether by law or by custom.[85]

---

77 Art. 13 par. 1 Reception Directive.
78 Art. 13 par. 4 Reception Directive.
79 Art. 13 par. 2 Reception Directive.
80 Art. 14 par. 8 Reception Directive.
81 Art. 14 par. 1 (b) Reception Directive.
82 Article 2 (l) Reception Directive.
83 Art. 6 par. 2 Reception Directive; Art. 13 par. 2 Reception Directive; Art. 14 par. 8 Reception Directive.
84 Art. 14 par. 2 (a) Reception Directive.
85 Art. 14 par. 3 Reception Directive.

Independently from Article 14 Paragraph 8, reception conditions may be reduced or withdrawn, inter alia[86], where an asylum seeker does not comply with reporting duties or with requests to provide information or to appear for personal interviews concerning the asylum procedure during a reasonable period laid down in national law'[87] or 'has failed to demonstrate that the asylum claim was made as soon as reasonably practicable after arrival in that Member State'[88], but EU Member States shall ensure that material reception conditions are not withdrawn or reduced before a negative decision on the asylum application is taken[89]. Additionally, EU Member States 'may determine sanctions applicable to serious breaching of the rules of the accommodation centres as well as to seriously violent behaviour'[90].

2.1.3 Reception and admission

As a general principle, EU Member States shall take into account the specific situation of vulnerable persons such as minors, unaccompanied minors, disabled people, elderly people, pregnant women, single parents with minor children and persons who have been subjected to torture, rape or other serious forms of psychological, physical or sexual violence [91]. 'The best interests of the child shall be a primary consideration' for EU Member States[92]. In particular, EU Member States 'shall ensure access to rehabilitation services for minors who have been victims of any form of abuse, neglect, exploitation, torture or cruel, inhuman and degrading treatment, or who have suffered from armed conflicts, and ensure that appropriate mental health care is developed and qualified counselling is provided when needed'[93]. EU Member States shall as soon as possible take measures to ensure the necessary representation of unaccompanied minors by legal guardianship or, where necessary, representation by an organisation which is responsible for the care and well-being of minors, or by any other appropriate representation.[94] Unaccompanied minors who make an application for asylum shall be placed with adult relatives, with a foster-family, in accommodation centres with special provisions for minors or in other accommodation suitable for minors;[95] but EU Member States may place unaccompanied minors aged 16 or over in accommodation centres for adult asylum seekers.[96] As far as possible, siblings shall be kept together.[97]

---

[86]   Art. 16 par. 1 Reception Directive.
[87]   Art. 16 par. 1 (a) Reception Directive.
[88]   Art. 16 par. 2 Reception Directive.
[89]   Art. 16 par. 5 Reception Directive.
[90]   Art. 16 par. 3 Reception Directive.
[91]   Art. 17 par. 1 Reception Directive.
[92]   Art. 18 par. 1 Reception Directive.
[93]   Art. 18 par. 2 Reception Directive.
[94]   Art. 19 par. 1 Reception Directive.
[95]   ibidem.
[96]   Art. 19 par. 2 Reception Directive.
[97]   ibidem.

2.1.4 Work – Education – Training – Sports - Recreation

In general, adults may have, after a certain time and under particular conditions, access to the labour market[98], and EU Member States 'may allow asylum seekers access to vocational training'[99]. However, the Directive does not indicate, if there shall be a labour market and access to vocational training also in closed accommodation centres.

Schooling and education is accessible only to minors who are defined as 'younger than the age of legal majority in the Member State in which the application for asylum was lodged or is being examined'[100]; but EU Member States 'shall not withdraw secondary education for the sole reason that the minor has reached the age of majority'[101]. To that extent, EU Member States 'shall grant to minor children of asylum seekers and to asylum seekers who are minors, access to the education system under similar conditions as nationals of the host Member State for so long as an expulsion measure against them or their parents is not actually enforced. Such education may be provided in accommodation centres'[102]. The Directive does not indicate if the accommodation centres referred to, are 'open' or 'closed' centres. Possibilities of sports or any other recreation are not mentioned.

2.1.5 Food – Religion – Personal hygiene – Medical care

As far as nutrition is concerned, the Directive only provides for 'a standard of living adequate for the health of applicants' and that the 'standard of living is met in the specific situation of persons who have special needs, in accordance with Article 17' (which takes into account the 'specific situation of vulnerable persons') as well as 'in relation to the situation of persons who are in detention'[103]. Religious practise and special places for worship are not mentioned.

Medical care is, initially, 'medical screening for applicants on public health grounds', which EU Member States may require.[104] Other than that, EU Member States 'shall ensure that applicants receive the necessary health care, which shall include, at least, emergency care and essential treatment of illness'[105] and 'shall provide necessary medical or other assistance to applicants who have special needs'[106] and may require applicants 'to cover or contribute' to 'the health care provided for in this Directive'[107]. There are no provisions on personal hygiene or clothes.

---

98   Cf. Art. 11 Reception Directive.
99   Art. 12 Reception Directive.
100   Art. 10 par. 1 Reception Directive.
101   ibidem.
102   Art. 10 par. 1 Reception Directive.
103   Art. 13 par. 2 Reception Directive.
104   Art. 9 Reception Directive.
105   Art. 15 par. 1 Reception Directive.
106   Art. 15 par. 2 Reception Directive.
107   Art. 13 par. 4 Reception Directive.

2.1.6 Consular and legal help

Due to the specific situation, consular help is not the rule. There is no provision stating a right to legal help. Legal help is only mentioned in the context of contact with the outside world.

2.1.7 Contact with the outside world

EU Member States shall ensure that applicants are assured 'the possibility of communicating with relatives, legal advisers, representatives of the United Nations High Commissioner for Refugees (UNHCR), non-governmental organisations (NGOs) recognised by Member States'[108] and, in cases of transferral from one facility to another 'shall provide for the possibility for applicants to inform their legal advisers of the transfer and of their new address'[109].

'Legal advisors or counsellors of asylum seekers and representatives of the United Nations High Commissioner for Refugees or non-governmental organisations designated by the latter and recognised by the Member State concerned shall be granted access to accommodation centres and other housing facilities in order to assist the said asylum seekers. Limits on such access may be imposed only on grounds relating to the security of the centres and facilities and of the asylum seekers.'[110] Further contact with the outside world is not dealt with, in particular, there are no provisions dealing with pastoral care.

2.1.8 Detention leave

According to Article 7 Paragraph 5, EU Member States 'shall provide for the possibility of granting applicants temporary permission to leave the place of residence mentioned in Paragraphs 2[111] and 4[112] and/or the assigned area mentioned in Paragraph 1. Decisions shall be taken individually, objectively and impartially and reasons shall be given if they are negative'.

2.1.9 Release - Expulsion

The Directive does not state a maximum duration of detention, and no mention is made of legal remedies against the accommodation or detention order. There are no provisions concerning the case of the recognition of an asylum application, i. e. about the situation of release. Aspects of expulsion are normally not relevant in the situation awaiting a decision on the asylum application.

---

[108] Art. 14 par. 2 (b) Reception Directive.
[109] Art. 14 par. 4 Reception Directive.
[110] Art. 14 par. 7 Reception Directive.
[111] 'Member States may decide on the residence of the asylum seeker for reasons of public interest, public order or, when necessary, for the swift processing and effective monitoring of his or her application.'
[112] 'Member States may make provision of the material reception conditions subject to actual residence by the applicants in a specific place, to be determined by the Member States. Such a decision, which may be of a general nature, shall be taken individually and established by national legislation.'

2.1.10 Aftercare

There are no provisions on aftercare, i. e. after having been released because the asylum application was recognised.

2.1.11 Staff

To a certain degree, staff shall receive special training:
- 'Persons working in accommodation centres shall be adequately trained and shall be bound by the confidentiality principle as defined in the national law in relation to any information they obtain in the course of their work'[113].
- 'Those working with unaccompanied minors shall have had or receive appropriate training concerning their needs, and shall be bound by the confidentiality principle as defined in the national law, in relation to any information they obtain in the course of their work'[114].
- 'Member States shall take appropriate measures to ensure that authorities and other organisations implementing this Directive have received the necessary basic training with respect to the needs of both male and female applicants'[115].

2.1.12 Projects

Projects for detained asylum seekers or concerning detention of asylum seekers in general are normally projects implemented at national level.

2.2 Rights of detained asylum seekers and obligations of EU Member States according to the 2005 EU Council Directive on minimum standards on procedures in Member States granting and withdrawing refugee status

2.2.1 General

The EU Council Directive 2005/85/EC of 1 December 2005 on minimum standards on procedures in Member States granting and withdrawing refugee status (Asylum Procedures Directive) basically deals only with the asylum procedure, specifically with procedural rights, and administrative detention does not constitute an explicit element of the procedure, although asylum applicants may be in detention during the whole procedure. Consequently provisions relating to the situation of detention are scarce. Thus, in praxis, public authorities refer to the Reception Directive, although the Asylum Procedures Directive itself does not explicitly refer to the Reception Directive.

---

[113] Art. 14 par. 5.
[114] Art. 19 par. 4.
[115] Art. 24.

2.2.2 Living conditions and facilities

Different from the Reception Directive, the Asylum Procedures Directive does not define the places for detention. It only mentions the notions of 'reception centre'[116] and 'detention facilities'[117]; but those notions are neither defined in the Reception Directive nor in the Asylum Procedures Directive. There are no provisions on general living conditions.

2.2.3 Reception and admission

Article 10 Paragraph 1 states that 'with respect to the procedures provided for in Chapter III', EU Member States shall ensure that all applicants for asylum enjoy the guarantee that 'they shall be informed in a language which they may reasonably be supposed to understand of the procedure to be followed and of their rights and obligations during the procedure and the possible consequences of not complying with their obligations and not cooperating with the authorities'[118] and that 'they shall receive the services of an interpreter'[119].   However, Chapter III refers to 'Procedures at First Instance', which make clear that Article 10 Paragraph 1 (a) is not applicable to information relating to the detention situation. There are no (further) provisions referring to reception and admission.

2.2.4 Work – Education – Training – Sports - Recreation

There are no provisions relating to work, education, training, sports or recreation.

2.2.5 Food – Religion – Personal hygiene – Medical care

Equally, the Asylum Procedures Directive does not mention aspects of food, religion, personal hygiene or medical care.

2.2.6 Consular and legal help

Due to the specific situation, consular help is not the rule. Article 15 Paragraph 1 provides that EU Member States 'shall allow applicants for asylum the opportunity, at their own cost, to consult in an effective manner a legal adviser or other counsellor, admitted or permitted as such under national law, on matters relating to their asylum applications.' This means that issues of detention, which are not related to the asylum application as such, are not covered by this provision. Yet, at least, EU Member States 'shall ensure that the legal adviser or other counsellor who assists or represents an applicant for asylum has access to closed areas, such as detention facilities and transit zones, for the purpose of consulting that applicant'[120].

---

[116] Art. 33 Asylum Procedures Directive.
[117] Art. 16 par. 2 Asylum Procedures Directive.
[118] Art. 10 Par. 1 (a) Asylum Procedures Directive.
[119] Art. 10 par. 1 (b) Asylum Procedures Directive.
[120] Art. 16 par. 2 Asylum Procedures Directive.

2.2.7 Contact with the outside world

Still, EU Member States may 'limit the possibility of visiting applicants in closed areas where such limitation is, by virtue of national legislation, objectively necessary for the security, public order or administrative management of the area, or in order to ensure an efficient examination of the application, provided that access by the legal adviser or other counsellor is not thereby severely limited or rendered impossible'[121].

Except for legal advisors as stated before, EU Member States 'shall allow the UNHCR 'to have access to applicants for asylum, including those in detention'[122] and shall allow, too, access by 'an organisation that is working in the territory of the Member State concerned on behalf of the UNHCR pursuant to an agreement with that Member State'[123]. Asylum seekers 'shall not be denied the opportunity to communicate with the UNHCR or with any other organisation working on behalf of the UNHCR in the territory of the Member State pursuant to an agreement with that Member State'[124] Rights to be visited by family, friends, and pastoral workers or other contacts with the outside world are not mentioned.

2.2.8 Detention leave

No mention is made of possibilities to leave the facility.

2.2.9 Release - Expulsion

The Directive does not state a maximum duration of detention. No mention is made of legal remedies against the accommodation or detention order during the asylum procedure. There are no provisions concerning the case of the recognition of an asylum application, i. e. about the situation of release. Aspects of expulsion are normally not relevant in the situation awaiting a decision on the asylum application.

2.2.10   Aftercare - Probation

There are no provisions on aftercare, i. e. after having been released because the asylum application was recognised.

2.2.11   Staff

Equally, this Directive does not provide for (special) staff training.

2.2.12   Projects

Projects for detained asylum seekers or concerning detention of asylum seekers in general are normally projects implemented at national level.

---

[121] Art. 16 par. 2 Asylum Procedures Directive.
[122] Art. 21 par. 1 Asylum Procedures Directive.
[123] Art. 21 par. 2 Asylum Procedures Directive.
[124] Art. 10 par 1 (c) Asylum Procedures Directive.

2.3. Rights of illegally staying third-country nationals and obligations of EU Member States according to the 2005 EU Commission Proposal for a Directive of the European Parliament and of the Council on common standards and procedures in Member States for returning illegally staying third-country nationals

2.3.1 General

According to Article 15 Paragraph 1 of the EU Commission Proposal for a Directive of the European Parliament and of the Council (Proposal Returns Directive) on common standards and procedures in Member States for returning illegally staying third-country nationals, EU Member States 'shall ensure that third-country nationals under temporary custody are treated in a humane and dignified manner with respect for their fundamental rights and in compliance with international and national law'.

2.3.2 Living conditions and facilities

The Returns Proposal does not define places of 'temporary custody'[125]; but it states that 'temporary custody shall be carried out in specialised temporary custody facilities. Where a Member State cannot provide accommodation in a specialised temporary custody facility and has to resort to prison accommodation, it shall ensure that third country nationals under temporary custody are permanently physically separated from ordinary prisoners'[126] and 'particular attention shall be paid to the situation of vulnerable persons. Member States shall ensure that minors are not kept in temporary custody in common prison accommodation. Unaccompanied minors shall be separated from adults unless it is considered in the child's best interest not to do so'[127].

When implementing this Directive, EU Member States shall take due account of the nature and solidity of the third-country national's family relationships, the duration of his stay in the Member State and of the existence of family, cultural and social ties with his country of origin. They shall also take account of the best interests of the child in accordance with the 1989 United Nations Convention on the Rights of the Child'[128].

2.3.3 Reception and admission

The Proposal does not mention aspects referring to reception and admission conditions.

2.3.4 Work – Education – Training – Sports - Recreation

No mention is made of work, education, training, sports or recreation.

---

[125] Cf. Art. 15 – 16 Proposal Returns Directive.
[126] Art. 15 Para. 2 Proposal Returns Directive.
[127] Art. 15 Para. 3 Proposal Returns Directive.
[128] Art. 5 Proposal Returns Directive.

2.3.5 Food – Religion – Personal hygiene – Medical care

Neither does the Proposal deal with food, religion, personal hygiene or medical care.

2.3.6 Consular and legal help

The Proposal does not explicitly deal with particular consular and legal help for the detainees.

2.3.7 Contact with the outside world

But in the context of contact with the outside world, third-country nationals shall be allowed without delay to establish contact with legal representatives, family members and competent consular authorities as well as with relevant international and non-governmental organisations'[129] and EU Member States 'shall ensure that international and non-governmental organisations have the possibility to visit temporary custody facilities in order to assess the adequacy of the temporary custody conditions. Such visits may be subject to authorisation.'[130] Further kinds of contact are not mentioned.

2.3.8 Leave of temporary custody

The Proposal does not provide for (temporary) leave of temporary custody.

2.3.9 Release - Expulsion

'Temporary custody may be extended by judicial authorities to a maximum of six months'[131]. The Proposal distinguishes between 'return decisions'[132] and 'removal orders'[133].

As far as a return decision is concerned, EU Member States 'shall issue a return decision to any third-country national staying illegally on their territory'[134]; 'the return decision shall provide for an appropriate period for voluntary departure of up to four weeks, unless there are reasons to believe that the person concerned might abscond during such a period. Certain obligations aimed at avoiding the risk of absconding, such as regular reporting to the authorities, deposit of a financial guarantee, submission of documents or the obligation to stay at a certain place may be imposed for the duration of that period'[135]; and 'the return decision shall be issued as a separate act or decision or together with a removal order'[136].

Concerning a removal order, EU Member States 'shall issue a removal order concerning a third-country national who is subject of a return decision, if there is a risk of ab-

---

[129] Art. 15 par. 1 Proposal Returns Directive.
[130] Art. 15 par. 4 Proposal Returns Directive.
[131] Art. 14 par. 4 Proposal Returns Directive.
[132] Art. 6 Proposal Returns Directive.
[133] Art. 7 Proposal Returns Directive.
[134] Art. 6 par. 1 Proposal Returns Directive.
[135] Art. 6 par. 2 Proposal Returns Directive.
[136] Art. 6 par. 3 Proposal Returns Directive.

sconding or if the obligation to return has not been complied with within the period of voluntary departure granted in accordance with Article 6 (2)[137],[138]; 'the removal order shall specify the delay within which the removal will be enforced and the country of return[139]'; 'the removal order shall be issued as a separate act or decision or together with the return decision'[140]. Removal orders 'shall include a re-entry ban of a maximum of 5 years', and 'return decisions may include such a re-entry ban'[141].

'Where Member States use coercive measures to carry out the removal of a third-country national who resists removal, such measures shall be proportional and shall not exceed reasonable force. They shall be implemented in accordance with fundamental rights and with due respect for the dignity of the third-country national concerned'[142].

'Return decisions and removal orders shall be issued in writing. Member States shall ensure that the reasons in fact and in law are stated in the decision and/or order and that the third-country national concerned is informed about the available legal remedies in writing'[143].

EU Member States 'shall provide, upon request, a written or oral translation of the main elements of the return decision and/or removal order in a language the third-country national may reasonably be supposed to understand'[144].

According to Article 12, dealing with 'judicial remedies', EU Member States 'shall ensure that the third-country national concerned has the right to an effective judicial remedy before a court or tribunal to appeal against or to seek review of a return decision and/or removal order'[145]. 'The judicial remedy shall either have suspensive effect or comprise the right of the third-country national to apply for the suspension of the enforcement of the return decision or removal order in which case the return decision or removal order shall be postponed until it is confirmed or is no longer subject to a remedy which has suspensive effects'[146]. Only in the context of those provisions on judicial remedies, the EU Member States 'shall ensure that the third-country national concerned has the possibility to obtain legal advice, representation and, where necessary, linguistic assistance. Legal aid shall be made available to those who lack sufficient resources insofar as such aid is necessary to ensure effective access to justice'[147].

---

[137] 'The return decision shall provide for an appropriate period for voluntary departure of up to four weeks, unless there are reasons to believe that the person concerned might abscond during such a period. Certain obligations aimed at avoiding the risk of absconding, such as regular reporting to the authorities, deposit of a financial guarantee, submission of documents or the obligation to stay at a certain place may be imposed for the duration of that period.'

[138] Art. 7 par. 1 Proposal Returns Directive.

[139] Art. 7 par. 2 Proposal Returns Directive.

[140] Art. 7 par. 3 Proposal Returns Directive.

[141] Art. 9 par. 1 Proposal Returns Directive.

[142] Art. 10 Proposal Returns Directive.

[143] Art. 11 par. 1 Proposal Returns Directive.

[144] Art. 11 par. 2 Proposal Returns Directive.

[145] Art. 12 par. 1 Proposal Returns Directive.

[146] Art. 12 par. 2 Proposal Returns Directive.

[147] Art. 12 par. 3 Proposal Returns Directive.

2.3.10   Aftercare

The International Organization for Migration (IOM), an inter-governmental organisation, may provide 'aftercare' in the sense of accompaniment to the country of return, depending on their programmes, which are called 'assisted voluntary returns'. Organisations such as Amnesty International, Human Rights Watch, the International Catholic Migration Commission, and the World Council of Churches regard the role of IOM critically challenging the 'voluntary' nature of some return programmes.[148]

2.3.11   Staff

The Proposal does not mention special staff training.

2.3.12   Projects

Projects caring favour of illegally staying third-country nationals, who are detained, are normally run at the national level.

3   ADMINISTRATIVE DETENTION OF ASYLUM SEEKERS AND ILLE-GALLY STAYING THIRD-COUNTRY NATIONALS IN EU ACCEEDING AND CANDIDATE COUNTRIES

Bulgaria and Romania, having completed negotiations, signed their Treaty of accession on 25 April 2005. They should normally join the Union on 1 January 2007. Two other candidate countries, Turkey and Croatia, are due to open their membership negotiations in 2005. Initially scheduled for March 2005, the opening date for entry talks with Croatia was put back until the country cooperates fully with the International Criminal Tribunal for former Yugoslavia. Turkey, for its part, is to open negotiations in October 2005. An application for membership, submitted by the former Yugoslav Republic of Macedonia in March 2004, is being examined by the European Commission, which will decide whether it is ready to begin entry negotiations.

A recent CPT report including visits in detention centres in Romania is not available. Concerning Bulgaria, Croatia, Turkey and the former Yugoslav Republic of Macedonia, there are no CPT reports available covering (inter alia) administrative detention of asylum seekers and illegally staying third-country nationals.

4   ADMINISTRATIVE DETENTION OF ASYLUM SEEKERS AND ILLE-GALLY STAYING THIRD-COUNTRY NATIONALS OUTSIDE OF THE EUROPEAN UNION

Administrative detention of asylum seekers and illegally staying third-country nationals is quite common outside of the European Union, too. In 2005, on World Refugee Day,

---

[148]   Cf. for further information: http://www.noborder.org/iom/display.php?id=243 (last visit 18 Apri 2006).

Amnesty International called on governments across the globe to stop detaining asylum seekers and refugees unless it is in full accordance with their obligations under international human rights law.

5 EVALUATION AND RECOMMENDATIONS

In November 2002, Mr. Ruud Lubbers, when he was United Nations High Commissioner for Refugees, declared in a statement at the United Nations, 'while many States have been able to manage their asylum systems without detentions, a more general trend towards increased use of detention – often on a discriminatory basis – is worrying'. In January 2004, in a speech to the Members of the European Parliament, UN Secretary General, Mr. Kofi Annan stated, 'when refugees cannot seek asylum because of offshore barriers, or are detained for excessive periods in unsatisfactory conditions, or are refused entry because of restrictive interpretations of the Convention, the asylum system is broken'. Shortly after, in March 2004, the European Parliament's Committee on Citizens' Freedoms and Rights, Justice and Home Affairs (LIBE Committee) wrote in its 'Report on the Situation as regards Fundamental Rights in the European Union' that it 'is concerned at the plight of foreigners being deprived of their freedom in holding centres despite the fact that they have been charged with no crime or offence; and calls for holding centres, in particular holding centres for asylum seekers, to meet human rights standards'[149].

On 20 February 2006, Mr. Jean-Marie Cavada from France, Chairman of the above-mentioned LIBE Committee, as well as its members Mr. Agustin Diaz de Mera (Spain), Mrs. Martine Roure (France) and Mr. Giusto Catania (Italy) declared[150] that the LIBE Committee has undertaken a series of visits in order to examine the conditions of migrants and asylum seekers in the detention centres in different European States, such as in Lampedusa, Ceuta and Melilla, and that the LIBE Committee would also visit Malta, the Canary Islands, Greece, the United Kingdom and Poland; in the second half of 2006, the EU Parliament would vote on a report on the detention centres in Europe within the frame of a more general reflection on the immigration policy of the European Union.

After a visit of a EU Parliament's Commission to Malta, on 6 April 2006, the EU Parliament adopted with a substantial majority a joint resolution in which various measures to be taken by the Maltese Government, the EU Commission and the EU Member States are proposed. The resolution calls, inter alia, to reduce the length of detention and to allow NGO's and the press to be given access to the closed centres.

5.1 Evaluation

This study follows the Treaty of Amsterdam, stating among the EU's objectives 'the combating of exclusion'[151], and it particularly follows the informal meeting of EU Social

---

[149] European Parliament, Committee on Citizens' Freedoms and Rights, Justice and Home Affairs, *Report on the situation as regards fundamental rights in the European Union (2003)*, 22 March 2004, no. 27

[150] in Paris at the Centre d'Accueil de la Presse Etrangère à Paris
(http://www.capefrance.com/fr/conferences/2006/2/873.html, last visit 5 April 2006).

[151] Art. 136 Treaty of Amsterdam.

Affairs Ministers held on in Lisbon 11 and 12 February 2000, after which the EU Commission issued a Communication 'Building an inclusive Europe'[152]. According to that Communication, 'social exclusion presents one of the major challenges faced by our economies and societies. The challenge is not only to provide a better assistance to those excluded (or at risk of exclusion), but also to actively address the structural barriers to social inclusion thus reducing the incidences of social exclusion'[153]. This Communication identifies as specific challenges of social exclusion, inter alia:

- low income and vulnerability as a phenomenon of exclusion
- exclusion as a multidimensional phenomenon
- exclusion as a structural phenomenon[154]

The legal findings of this study are evaluated against the background of those three criteria.

5.1.1 EU legislation and EU legislation in the making render administative detainees extremely vulnerable and subject to poverty.

Administrative detainees suffer from a basic two-fold exclusion: For various reasons, they are excluded in their countries of origin, and again socially excluded by the deprivation of their liberty of movement in their country of refuge or hope. The protection of their rights in detention, if rights are stated at all, is full of gaps leaving open ranges for interpretation and circumvention and leaving the filling of those gaps to the discretion of the EU Member States and their respective national legislation. This refers, above all, to

- the lack of opportunities for work or any other meaningful activity;
- religious practise;
- legal help;
- contact with the outside world;
- aftercare in case of release.

Generally, asylum seekers and illegally staying third-country nationals are poor persons. Insofar as detained asylum seekers might have some minimum income earned by work in their detention centre, they are obliged to pay for or contribute to their material reception conditions and cost for health care. Among the most vulnerable persons are minors, pregnant women, elderly people or mentally ill persons, who receive, in the case of asylum seekers, for example only emergency health care.

5.1.2 EU legislation and EU legislation in the making perpetuate social exclusion as a multidimensional phenomenon.

Adult administrative detainees are excluded from lifelong learning as promoted by the EU Commission Communication 'Making an European Area of Lifelong Learning a Reality'[155]. Visits by family or friends are not ensured or ensured in an only restrictive manner. When family members are detained, too, family support may be given only by family

---

[152] COM (2000) 79 final communication from the Commission, building an inclusive Europe, Brussels 1.3.2000 – below referred to as 'COM (2000) 79 final'.

[153] Chapter 1.3. COM (2000) 79 final.

[154] Chapter 2. COM (2000) 79 final.

[155] COM (2001) 678 final: Communication from the EU Commission making an European area of life long learning a reality, Brussels 21 November 2001.

needing support themselves. As foreigners, administrative detainees are severely disadvantaged by the lack of language knowledge (language in the host country), and translation in detention situations is not provided for. Equally, as foreigners, they are not familiar with the legal or administrative system of the country where they are detained, and the possibilities of getting, in particular, legal advice are restricted. Being detained in special and closed facilities, administrative detainees easily become subject to aggravation of xenophobia.

5.1.3 EU legislation and EU legislation in the making create social exclusion as a structural phenomenon.

The mere existence of the relevant EU legislation and EU legislation in the making proves that the given effects of administrative detention on detainees are intended. The entire system of detention is placed as a structural element within the EU's efforts to manage migration flows.

5.2 Recommendations for co-ordination and co-operation at a European level

The following recommendations are addressed to political decisions-makers at EU level.
-   The EU should set up a permanent body monitoring administrative detention of asylum seekers and illegally staying third-country nationals in the EU Member States and EU Candidate Countries and report publicly.
-   The EU should elaborate more concrete and comprehensive minimum standards relating to detention of asylum seekers and illegally staying third-nationals in full accordance with their obligations under the ECHR and Public International Law.
-   Non-governmental organisations as well as academic scholars and academic researchers should convince the political EU institutions and their various representatives that the above-mentioned action is necessary in order to make of the EU – for all – 'an area of freedom security and justice' as stated by the Treaty of Amsterdam and should support them in accomplishing that objective.

Chapter 32

Prisoners Abroad

Stephen Nash

1 INTRODUCTION

Prisoners Abroad is a British Non-Governmental Organisation (NGO) that works with British Citizens held outside of the United Kingdom. An independent organisation formed in 1978, Prisoners Abroad is funded through voluntary donations, and works to support British Citizens who are detained overseas, as well as those returning to the UK after a period of imprisonment. Prisoners Abroad employs 16 staff, all based in their office in north London.

2 SOME DATA ON NATIONALS DETAINED ABROAD

2.1 Number and composition of nationals detained abroad

According to the latest figures available from the British Foreign and Commonwealth Office (FCO[1]), there were a total of 2476 British Nationals held in foreign prisons on 31 December 2005. However, they do not record the composition of this group in any significant detail.

Table 1 British Nationals imprisoned overseas on 31 December 2005

	Total	Male	Female
Total	2476	2230	246

Source: FCO[2]

It is possible to gain a better insight into the make-up of this group by using figures published by Prisoners Abroad.

Prisoners Abroad works only with British Citizens who are imprisoned overseas, and its service is provided on an opt-in basis, that is prisoners can choose to contact Prisoners Abroad. Further, it is worth clarifying the difference between a British National and a British Citizen. There are five categories of British National, of which British Citizen is the only group with the right of permanent residence in the UK. This, together with the fact that prisoners must choose to contact Prisoners Abroad, means that the sample size for looking at the composition of prisoners is somewhat reduced when compared to the 2476 Britons we know are held overseas. Furthermore, Prisoners Abroad does not always have access to the relevant information. For example, almost half of prisoners choose not to give details relating to their ethnic origin. However, with those caveats, the data below is the best and most complete available.

---

[1] The foreign ministry of the UK government
[2] FCO data emailed to author, February 2006.

Table 2 Composition of British prisoners held overseas on 1 February 2006

Ethnic Origin	Britons detained overseas (1 February 2006)	Britons in UK prisons (June 2005)
White	76%	82%
Black or Black British	17%	10%
Mixed	3.1%	2.7%
Asian or Asian British	2.3%	4.5%
Chinese or Other ethnic group	1.4%	0.3%

Source: Prisoners Abroad[3], HMPS[4]

Table 3 Age distribution of British prisoners held overseas on 1 February 2006

Ages	
16 or under	-
17-24	8%
25-34	23%
35-44	35%
45-60	30%
61 or over	4.4%

Source: Prisoners Abroad[5]

Note: Where percentages are shown, it is percentage of known.

2.2 Countries of detention

By far the biggest numbers of British prisoners are detained in prisons in the USA. There are a number of factors that could explain this. Firstly, the rate of imprisonment is far higher in the USA than in other countries. According to the International Centre for Prison Studies, the USA has a prison population of 724 per 100,000, compared to, for example, 577 in Russia, 344 in South Africa, 264 for Thailand, 179 for Jamaica, 141 in England & Wales, 140 for Spain, 120 for Australia, 97 for Germany, and 88 in France. Secondly, the USA is a popular destination for those emigrating from the UK. Many of these people have not naturalised and retain their British Citizenship. In particular, it is not unknown for children to emigrate with their parents and live their entire adult life in the USA without gaining American citizenship. These people are then shocked to learn at the end of their sentence that they will be expelled to a country about which they know very little. Thirdly, as an immense country with a large population it is not surprising that

---

[3] See: www.prisonersabroad.org.uk/prison_statistics.html.

[4] Her Majesty's Prison Service, the government organisation responsible for running prisons. Note that not all UK prisons are operated by HMPS. For statistics, see www.homeoffice.gov.uk/rds/pdfs05/prisq205.pdf.

[5] See: www.prisonersabroad.org.uk/prison_statistics.html.

there are many British Citizens living in the USA who have been imprisoned. This also applies to Australia, which is often a magnet for British emigrants attracted by the better climate and more relaxed lifestyle, as well as the benefits of language and cultural similarities.

Table 4 Country of detention of British prisoners held overseas on 31 December 2005

Country	Total	Males	Female	% of total
USA	649	573	76	26%
Australia	337	320	17	14%
Spain	306	278	28	12%
Germany	130	120	10	5.3%
Thailand	118	116	2	4.8%
Jamaica	105	67	38	4.2%
France	94	92	2	3.8%
Ireland	84	82	2	3.4%
Netherlands	45	44	1	1.8%
Japan	43	36	7	1.7%
Brazil	37	27	10	1.5%
Belgium	35	32	3	1.4%
India	26	24	2	1.1%
Other	467	419	48	19%

Source: FCO[6]

2.3 Reasons for detention and types of sentence

Looking at table 5, it is clear that drugs related offences are the most common cause of imprisonment for Britons overseas.

Table 5 Cause of detention for British prisoners held overseas on 1 February 2006.

Offences	Total
Drugs	55%
Murder	13%
Sexual / Rape	8.3%
Violence	8.0%
Fraud	5.4%
Property / Theft	5.3%
Visa overstay	0.9%
Smuggling	0.6%
Other	3.9%

Source: Prisoners Abroad[7]

FCO data emailed to author, February 2006.

However, this masks a wide variation between countries:

Table 6 Cause of detention for British prisoners held in selected countries on 1 February 2006.

Offence	Australia	France	Jamaica	Spain	Thailand	USA
Drugs	38%	82%	98%	49%	57%	24%
Murder	22%	2%	2%	14%	7%	21%
Sexual/Rape	20%	-	-	7%	7%	15%
Violence	15%	5%	-	10%	-	13%
Fraud	-	4%	-	4%	14%	9%
Property/Theft	3%	2%	-	9%	5%	9%
Visa overstay	-	-	-	-	7%	2%
Smuggling	-	5%	-	-	-	-
Other	2%	-	-	6%	2%	6%

Source: Prisoners Abroad[8]

Table 6 shows that the vast majority of British prisoners held overseas are detained under criminal law, rather than being held under administrative or immigration law. In some countries (for instance the USA), prisoners are transferred to immigration detention at the end of their criminal sentence, prior to being expelled back to the UK. This is typically for a short period of time (measured in weeks or a few months), and so does not affect the overall pattern of detention. Although the FCO does not publish a complete breakdown by offence, it does reveal that 34% of British prisoners are held on drugs charges, and 2.4% are detained due to immigration issues.

In all the countries shown above, drugs offences account for the largest number of Britons being detained. However, there is a marked difference between countries. In Jamaica and France, by far the vast majority of imprisoned Britons are being detained on drugs charges. This reflects the transit route of drugs into the United Kingdom. Other countries, particularly the USA and Australia, show a wider spread of offences. This could be due to the factors discussed above, namely that as these two countries are home to Britons who have emigrated; we should expect to see a distribution of offences that more closely matches the native population. The Britons who are imprisoned in these countries have often lived there for a number of years. In contrast, those who are detained in France or Jamaica are often transitory visitors.

Information on sentences is hard to obtain, as neither the FCO nor Prisoners Abroad have detailed statistics on either length of sentence or the actual time served.

---

[7]   See: www.prisonersabroad.org.uk/prison_statistics.html.
[8]   See: www.prisonersabroad.org.uk/prison_statistics.html.

3 RESPONSIBILITIES AND ACTIVITIES OF INVOLVED ORGANISATIONS

3.1 British Foreign and Commonwealth Office

The FCO provides a Consular service, with representatives in most countries in the world. In relation to prisoners, the role of the consular service is to look after the welfare of British nationals whilst they are detained. All Britons will receive a visit when they are detained, and, depending on the country in which they are being held, will receive other visits throughout their time in detention. The Consul can raise, on behalf of the prisoner, any appropriate complaint or serious difficulty that they are experiencing with the local prison authorities.

Relatives or friends of the detainee can use the Consular service to send money to the prisoner. In addition, depending on the country, the Consul may be asked to use this money to buy provisions from outside the prison, and bring these in during a prison visit. Consuls usually have a list of English speaking lawyers, and can help prisoners obtain a lawyer, or change the one they have if they want to.

If the person is held in a country with which the UK has a prisoner transfer agreement, the Consul can explain how the transfer process works, and how to apply for a transfer. In addition, the Consul may be able to help organise prison visits for friends or family to come and see the prisoner.

3.2 Prisoners Abroad

Prisoners Abroad is a UK based charity, which exists, to alleviate the isolation and deprivation of British citizens detained outside the UK. They also offer a resettlement service to those who return to the UK after a period of foreign detention. Its services to prisoners can be broken down into three main areas: survival grants, reduction of isolation, and information.

3.2.1 Survival Grants

Prisoners Abroad can make grant payments to prisoners who do not have other sources of regular money and do not receive money from family or friends. All grant payments are made via local FCO Consular representatives.

Prisoners held in developing countries may not be provided with basic essentials such as food, clothing or toiletries. These prisoners can apply for grants to purchase these vital necessities, varying between £15 and £30 per prisoner per month (depending on the country). Over the year from 1 April 2004, these grants were awarded to 463 prisoners. Prisoners who are detained in developed countries can apply for an annual grant of £50 to purchase essentials that are not provided by the prison. During the financial year 2004 - 2005 Prisoners Abroad provided over 100 such grants.

Medical Fund grants are provided for a wide variety of health issues – operations, asthma inhalers, consultations with specialists, glasses and dental treatment. Over the year from 1 April 2005, more than £7500 was provided to prisoners.

Vitamin Fund grants are provided in 12 countries considered to have extremely low levels of nutrition. This is a vital health-preserving supplement that has, over the year to April 2005, benefited 171 British prisoners.

3.2.2 Reduction of isolation

Prisoners Abroad seeks to reduce the isolation of Britons imprisoned overseas in a number of ways; five main areas of work are described below.

By supplying international freepost envelopes, Prisoners Abroad enables those detained overseas to keep in touch with their relatives and friends, and thus to maintain links to society outside prison. Prisoners have access to as many envelopes as they require, and they can be used to send mail from anywhere to the office of Prisoners Abroad. From there, their letter can be forwarded on to any address at no cost to the detainee. This helps to address the problem of maintaining contact with relatives. According to the British Home Office, "*Maintaining family relationships can help to prevent ex-prisoners re-offending and assist them to resettle into the community. However, 43% of sentenced prisoners [in the UK] say that they have lost contact with their family as a result of going into prison.*"[9] We can assume that the percentage of overseas prisoners losing touch with their family will be higher than the 43% above; therefore anything that can help maintain family ties is vital in aiding the resettlement process.

Prisoners Abroad sends, on request, newspapers and magazines to British Citizens in prison all over the world at a rate of around 9000 per year. Books can also be sent to individual prisoners or, in some cases, prison libraries. This reading material reduces boredom and its consequences on prisoners' mental health. It also stimulates thought and language usage, particularly in prisons where the prisoner is the only English speaker. In addition to the above, Prisoners Abroad produces a thrice-yearly newsletter, which is written largely by British citizens detained overseas. The benefits are two-fold: the newsletter keeps prisoners in touch with the UK and offers an insight into the lives of other Britons in similar circumstances; it also offers prisoners a chance to be creative and to express their thoughts in a constructive manner. As one ex-prisoner puts it: "*For me at the time the newsletters were my lifeline because it was the only contact I had with home. Reading other peoples stories in the newsletter made my situation look like a holiday camp!*"[10]

Prisoners Abroad operates a pen-pal scheme, which is open to all British Citizens imprisoned overseas. In the year 2004 – 2005 over 1200 letters were exchanged between prisoners and volunteer pen-pals. This opportunity to contact somebody unconnected with the situation helps keep prisoners in touch with the UK. As one prisoner puts it, "*I'm looking very much forward to hearing from my pen-pal, to help end some of my isolation from the outside world.*"[11]

Every year, on their birthday, people registered with Prisoners Abroad receive a birthday card signed by all staff members. This personal touch can remind prisoners that they are not forgotten. Furthermore, all prisoners receive, where appropriate, a Christmas card from a supporter of the organisation.

---

[9] British Home Office, 'Reducing Re-offending National Action Plan', p 37.
[10] Ex-prisoner in Jamaica, from interview with the author, February 2006.
[11] Letter from prisoner in The Netherlands to Prisoners Abroad, November 2004.

3.2.3 Information

Prisoners Abroad offers a series of leaflets and handbooks for prisoners, which feature advice and guidance for those in prison. Topics covered include exercise tips, how to protect your mental health, transferring to the UK and preparing for release.

3.3 Reception after release

When prisoners return to the UK after the completion of their sentence, they usually arrive at one of the main London airports, Heathrow or Gatwick. Unless they have been convicted of a major / sexual offence they will not be met at the airport by the police or any statutory agency. If they arrive at Heathrow they can use the services offered by Heathrow Travel-Care, a small British charity that exists to relieve poverty and sickness amongst persons travelling through Heathrow airport. If they arrive at Gatwick airport they can use the services of a similar, but unrelated, charity called Gatwick Travel-Care.

If the person has previously been registered with Prisoners Abroad they are able to use the resettlement service offered by them. To facilitate this they are provided with instructions on how to find the Prisoners Abroad office, as well as enough money to pay for transport to the office. Prisoners Abroad provides this money. If the person has not registered with Prisoners Abroad, both Heathrow Travel-Care and Gatwick Travel-Care can offer a basic range of services. These include the provision of clean clothes and, where required, a suitcase, the use of a shower and toilet facilities. In addition, if the returning prisoner does not have access to money, they can make free phone calls to friends or family members to arrange for money, and transport to a bank to collect funds. Where appropriate, referrals can be made to other agencies to provide further support to the person.

3.4 Aftercare

There are no statutory services for Britons who have been released following a prison sentence overseas, except for general benefits available to all British Citizens.

The only agency in the UK that works specifically with people returning from prison overseas is Prisoners Abroad. There are a number of other NGOs that offer services to people released from prison; however these are designed for people who served a sentence in the UK, and although they are accessible to others may not address all the issues faced by those returning to the UK.

Returning prisoners can be deeply traumatised. Many have served sentences in severe conditions. In addition to this few will have received access to appropriate "preparation for release" programmes, which would be the norm if they were imprisoned in the UK. A great number of returning prisoners have served sentences in the USA, and had lived in the States since they were children; they may have no family or friends to help them once back in the UK. Without many of the things most people take for granted – a roof over your head, proof of ID, access to a bank account, a National Insurance number – it can be a desperate struggle to rebuild your life. According to the British Home Office, "*The transitional points in the system – particularly between custody and the community – often create crises for offenders. Many offenders have poor life and coping skills, which make them particularly ill-equipped to deal with accommodation, benefits, employment and family problems that are faced on immediate release, together with the difficulties in accessing drugs treatment and health care.*"[12] These problems are magnified for those returning from a prison sentence in a foreign country. Prisoners Abroad aims to provide the emergency support and services needed by those returning to the UK, to offer the opportunity of a crime-free future.

British prisoners returning to the UK after serving their sentence overseas will have had no contact with the UK prison or probation services, and these services are under no obligation to provide any form of practical assistance. In many cases, without the help of Prisoners Abroad, the ability of returning prisoners to access welfare systems and obtain emergency accommodation would be severely limited.

Prisoners Abroad offers a limited range of services to released prisoners to help prevent destitution on return to the UK. These services include financial grants, advice, and practical assistance. Prisoners Abroad can only offer financial assistance for the first four weeks after arrival back in the UK. The grants are limited to £58 per week, and cover basic food costs and transport. On top of this Prisoners Abroad can provide funds for emergency accommodation. This is vital in situations where there are no family, or they are unable to help. As one returning prisoner puts it, *"Because my sister was pregnant, and was living in a one bedroom flat, we were practically stepping over each other, there was no room. If Prisoners Abroad wasn't there for me I would have been homeless. "*[13] After four weeks, returned prisoners have no specific financial assistance open to them except the normal welfare benefits which are available to all British Citizens.

Examples of the advice given to returning prisoners includes helping people to claim the welfare benefits (unemployment and housing) to which they are entitled, offering assistance with application forms, advice on long-term housing issues, and referring people to other relevant agencies (e.g. for those needing medical treatment, or those with addiction problems). In the UK, 46% of male prisoners aged 18-49 have a long standing illness or disability[14], and this pattern is likely to be replicated in Britons imprisoned overseas. Specialist advice and treatment is especially important as a large number of prisoners have medical needs. Finally, there is a range of practical assistance that Prisoners Abroad has found is useful to returning prisoners. Examples include the use of a shower and bathroom facilities, provision of clean clothes and toiletries, a London A-Z map, temporary luggage storage, and use of a phone and computer.

In the year to 1 April 2005, Prisoners Abroad supported over 200[15] people returning to the UK from detention overseas. This number is not the same as the number of Britons released from custody in that year, as some will remain in the country of origin, some will move to a third country, and some may choose not to use the services offered. Also, not all Britons in foreign detention choose to register with Prisoners Abroad. Over half of these people (57%[16]) returned from the USA, highlighting the particular difficulties faced when people have few, if any, friends or relatives in the country to which they are expelled.

---

[12] British Home Office (2004), 'Reducing re-offending: National action plan – Reference document', p. 4.

[13] Ex-prisoner in USA, from interview with the author, October 2005.

[14] A Bridgwood and G Malbon, *'Survey of the physical health of prisoners 1994'*, OPCS, London HMSO quoted in Government Office for London, 'London Resettlement Strategy, a commitment to action', 1994, p. 41.

[15] Prisoners Abroad Annual Review 2004/05.

[16] Ibidem.

APPENDIX I

Literature, legislation and websites

Chapter 1 Comparative overview, Conclusions and Recommendations

1.1 Literature

Aebi, M., Stadnic, N. (2007): SPACE I. Council of Europe Annual Penal Statistics. Survey 2005. Internet-publication www.coe.int.

Chapter 5 Human Rights and Arrest, Pre-Trial and Administrative Detention in *Human Rights in the Administration of Justice: A Manual on Human Rights for Judges, Prosecutors and Lawyers.*

Cholewinski, R. (2005), *Irregular migrants: access to minimum social rights,* Strasbourg: Council of Europe Publishing.

Conférenece Permanente Europeénne de la Probation (CEP). *Probation in Europe.* June 2005 No. 33, CEP, Utrecht.

Council of Europe (2006). *European Prison Rules,* Strasbourg: Council of Europe Publishing.

Coyle, Andrew (2002). *A Human Rights Approach to Prison Management. Handbook for prison staff,* London: International Centre for Prison Studies.

Dünkel, J., Vagg, J. (1994): *Waiting for Trial. International Perspectives on the Use of Pre-Trial Detention and the Rights and Living Conditions of Prisoners Waiting for Trial.* Vol. 1 and 2. Freiburg i. Br.: Max-Planck-Institut für ausländisches und internationals Strafrecht.

Gallagher, A.M., Ireland, H., N. Muchopa (2006), *Handbook for visitors and workers in Detention Centres,* Brussels: Jesuit Refugee Service Europe.

HM Prison Service (2004). *Information and Guidance on working with Foreign National Prisoners – Staff Handbook.*

HM Prison Service (2004). *Information and Advice for Foreign National Prisoners*
Morgan, Rod and Malcolm D. Evans (2001). *The Prevention of Torture in Europe. CPT Standards regarding Prisoners.* Brochure No. 6, Association for the Prevention of Torture (APT) and Council of Europe, Geneva 2001.

Lambert, H. (2006), *The position of aliens in relation to the European Convention on Human Rights,* Strasbourg: Council of Europe Publishing.

Macovei, M., *The right to liberty and security of the person. A guide to the implementation of Article 5 of the European Convention on Human Rights (2002)*, Strasbourg: Council of Europe Publishing.

Murdoch, J., *The treatment of prisoners. European Standards* (2006), Strasbourg: Council of Europe Publishing.

National Offender Management Service (NOMS), *Foreign Nationals Bulletin*, Issue No. 5, July 2005, London.

Observation and Position Document: *Detention in Europe. Administrative detention of asylum seekers and irregular migrants* (2004), Jesuit Refugee Service Europe.

Prisoners Abroad, *Prisoners Abroad News* Vol 16, Issue 3 Winter 2005, London.
Singh Bhui, HIndpal (2004), *Going the Distance. Developing Effective Policy and Practice with Foreign National Prisoners*, London: Prison Reform Trust.

Speech by the Deputy Secretary General, Council of Europe. *European Conference on the respect of the rights of foreign minors in Europe and against their detention and forced removal*, Strasbourg, 14 March 2007.

Tapia, S. de (2003), *New patterns of irregular migration in Europe*, Strasbourg: Council of Europe Publishing.

Tomaševski, Katarina (1994). *Foreigners in Prison*. European Institute for Crime Prevention and Control, affiliated with the United Nations (HEUNI), Helsinki.

Undocumented Migrants Have Rights! An overview of the International Human Rights Framework (2007), Brussels: Platform for International Cooperation on Undocumented Migrants.

1.2 Legislation

- Committee of Ministers - Council of Europe, Twenty Guidelines on forced return (2005).

- Council of Europe Convention on Mutual Assistance in Criminal Matters, Strasbourg (1959).

- Council of Europe Convention on the Transfer of Sentenced Persons, Strasbourg (1983).

- Council of Europe, Recommendation No. R (84) 12 concerning foreign prisoners (1984).

- CPT Standards (2002).

- European Convention for the Prevention of Torture and Inhuman or Degrading Treatment or Punishment (1989).

- European Convention for the Protection of Human Rights and Fundamental Freedoms (1953).

- European Prison Rules (2006) – Council of Europe, Recommendation Rec (2006) 2.

- EU Commission Proposal for a Directive of the European Parliament and the Council on common standards and procedures in Member States for returning illegally sttaying third-country nationals (2005).

- Proposal for a Council Framework Decision on the European supervision order in pre-trial procedures between Member States of the European Union (2006).

- Proposal for a Council Framework Decision on the recognition and supervision of suspended sentences and alternative sanctions (2007).

- United Nations Standard Minimum Rules for the Treatment of Prisoners (1955).

- European Parliament: *Report on the situation as regards fundamental rights in the European Union* (2002) by Fodé Sylla, Rapporteur on behalf of the Committee on Citizens' Freedom and Rights, Justice and Home Affairs (A5-0281/2003)

- European Parliament: *Report with a proposal for a European Parliament recommendation to the Council on the rights of Prisoners in the European Union* (2004) by Maurizio Turco, Rapporteur on behalf of the Committee on Citizens' Freedom and Rights, Justice and Home Affairs (A5-0094/2004).

1.3 Websites

Association for the Prevention of Torture (APT), www.apt.ch
Conférenece Permanente Europeénne de la Probation (CEP), www.cep-probation.org
European Committee for the Prevention of Torture (CPT), www.cpt.coe.int
European Group for Prisoners Abroad (EGPA), www.egpa.org
International Centre for Prison Studies (ICPS), www.prisonstudies.org
International Organization for Migration (IOM), www.iom.int
Legislationline, www.legislationline.org
Penal Reform International, www.penalreform.org
Prison Watch, www.prisonwatch.org

Chapter 2 Austria

2.1 Literature

Bundesministerium für Justiz (ed) (2005), Moderner Strafvollzug und Resozialisierung, NWV, Wien .

Fassmann, H. and Stacher, I. (eds) (2003), Österreichischer Migrations- und Integrationsbericht, Drava Verlag, Klagenfurt.

Futo, P. and Jandl, M. (eds)(2005), 2004 Yearbook on Illegal Migration, Human Smuggling and Trafficking in Central and Eastern Europe, Centre for Migration Policy Development, Vienna.

Geyer, W. (2005), ‚Bedingte Entlassung, insbesondere bei integrierten und nicht integrierten Ausländern', in: Bundesministerium für Justiz (ed.), Moderner Strafvollzug und Resozialisierung, NWV, Wien, pp 193-203.

Gratz, W., Held. A. and Pilgram, A. (2001), ‚Austria', in: Smit, D.v.Z. and Dünkel, F. (eds), Imprisonment Today and Tomorrow. International Perspectives On Prisoners' Rights and Prison Conditions. Kluwer Law International, The Hague, pp. 3-31.

Haller, B. and Feistritzer, G. (2001), Wie ist die Haltung der Exekutive zu Fremden in Österreich und wie geht sie damit um? Institut für Konfliktforschung, Wien.

Kravagna, S. (2005), ‚Der Faktor Hautfarbe in der quantitativen Analyse von Gerichtsurteilen gegen weiße und schwarze Straftäter in Wien', Österreichische Zeitschrift für Soziologie, 30, pp. 41-64.

National Contact Point within the European Migration Framework (2005), Illegal Immigration in Austria, Vienna (http://www.emn.at/News-article-folder-104.phtml) .

Pilgram, A. (1999), ‚Austria', in: Smit, D.v.Z. and Dünkel, F. (eds), Prison Labour. Salvation or Slavery? Ashgate, Dartmouth, pp. 1-24.

Pilgram, A. (2003), ‚Migration und Innere Sicherheit', in: Fassmann, H. and Stacher, I. (eds), Österreichischer Migrations- und Integrationsbericht, Drava Verlag, Klagenfurt, pp. 305-339.

Pilgram, A. (2003), ‚Die Entwicklung der Haftzahlen in Österreich. Darstellung und Analyse der Ursachen', in: Bundesministerium für Inneres und Bundesministerium für Justiz (eds), Sicherheitsbericht 2002. Bericht der Bundesregierung über die innere Sicherheit in Österreich, Annex.

Pilgram, A. (2004), Prisoners rates and their background in Austria (1980-2003). Austrian contribution to the international 'Mare Balticum-Projekt: Kriminalitätsentwicklung, gesellschaftliche Veränderungen, Massenmedien, Kriminalpolitik, strafrechtliche Sanktionspraxis und ihre Auswirkungen auf unterschiedliche Gefangenenraten' at the Ernst Moritz Arndt-University, Greifswald, Germany .

Pilgram, A. (2005), ‚Die bedingte Entlassung in Österreich im regionalen Vergleich', in: Bundesministerium für Justiz (ed), Moderner Strafvollzug und Resozialisierung, NWV, Wien pp. 79-104.

Statistik Austria (ed)(2005): Statistisches Jahrbuch Österreichs 2006, Wien.

Zagler, W. (2005), 'Vom Beschwerderecht des Strafgefangenen', Österreichische Juristenzeitung, 56, pp. 948-952.

2.3 Websites

http://www.bmi.gv.at/publikationen/ (Ministry of the Interior)

http://www.bmi.gv.at/kriminalstatistik/ (Police Crime Statistics)

http://www.bmj.gv.at/ (Ministry of Justice)

http://www.emn.at/ (European Migration Network, Austrian Contact Point)

http://www.emn.at/module-Documents-maincat-cid-1-idc-11.phtml (Migration Statistics)

http://www.ris.bka.gv.at/bundesrecht/ (Austrian Law Data Base)

http://www.menschenrechtsbeirat.at (Human Rights Advisory Council, reports, recommendations, evaluations)

http://www.cpt.coe.int/en/states/aut.htm (CTP-reports on Austria)

http://www.asylanwalt.at/ NGO, legal aid information on asylum etc.)

http://www.volksanw.gv.at/ Annual Reports of the Austrian Ombudsman Board)

Chapter 3 Belgium

3.1 Literature

Algemene Politiesteundienst (2000), *Integrated Interpolice Crime Statistics (1994-1999)*, Afdeling Politiebeleidsondersteuning, Brussels, Ministry of Interior.

K. Beyens, S. Snacken & C. Eliaerts, *Barstende muren. Overbevolkte gevangenissen: omvang, oorzaken en mogelijke oplossingen*, Antwerpen-Arnhem: Kluwer-Gouda 1993, Interuniversitaire Reeks Criminologie en Strafwetenschappen nr. 26.

CPT reports on visits to Belgium in 1993, 1997, 2001 and 2005, CPT/Inf (94)15, (98)11, (2002)25, (2006)15.

W. De Pauw, *De afhandeling van drugzaken in Brussel in 1993 en 1994*, BRES, Brussel 1996: IRIS. .

W. De Pauw, *Migranten in de balans*. Brussel 2000: VUBPress. Criminologische Studies.

W. De Pauw, e.a. (2006 forthcoming) De Belgische veroordelingsstatistiek, in: E. Devroe, K. Beyens& E. Enhus (eds.) *Criminografie*, VUBPress, Criminologische studies.

European Union 2002, *Migration and asylum in Europe.*

C. Joppart, *Separated children in Europe. Questionnaire for country assessment: Belgium*, Brussels 2003, Defence for Children International Belgium.

J. Keulen, J., Operatie regularisatie, dissertation in criminology, Brussels 2003, Vrije Universiteit Brussel.

Ministry of Justice 2005 Justitie in cijfers (Justice in numbers).

Office for Foreigners Affairs, Annual report, Ministry of Interior, Brussels 2000.

Office for Foreigners Affairs, Annual Report, Ministry of Interior, Brussels 2004.

A. Raes & S. Snacken, 2005 The application of remand custody and its alternatives in Belgium, *The Howard Journal of Criminal Justice*, Vol. 43, n°5, December 2004: 506-517 .

S. Snacken, S. Deltenre, A. Raes, Ch. Vanneste and P. Paul Verhaeghe, *Kwalitatief onderzoek naar de toepassing van de voorlopige hechtenis en de vrijheid onder voorwaarden*, Onderzoeksrapport VUB/NICC, Brussel 1999.

S. Snacken, S. Belgium. In: *Imprisonment today and tomorrow. International perspectives on prisoners' rights and prison conditions (second edition)*, edited by Dirk van Zyl Smit and Frieder Dünkel, Den Haag, London, Boston 2001: Kluwer Law International: 32-81.

S. Snacken & K. Beyens, Alternatieven voor de vrijheidsberoving: hoop voor de toekomst? In: *Strafrechtelijk beleid in beweging*, edited by Sonja Snacken, Brussel 2002: VUBPress, Criminologische Studies: 271-316.

S Snacken, K. Beyens & H. Tubex, Adult corrections in Belgium. In: *Adult Corrections: International Systems & Perspectives*, edited by John Winterdyk, Monsely, NY 2004: Criminal Justice Press: 21-61.

S. Snacken, J. Keulen, J & L. Winkelmans, *Buitenlanders in de Belgische gevangenissen: knelpunten en mogelijke oplossingen*, Brussel 2004, Koning Boudewijn Stichting.

S. Snacken, J. Keulen & L. Winkelmans, *Détenus étrangers dans les prisons belges: problèmes et solutions possibles*, Bruxelles 2004, Fondation Roi Baudoin.

3.3 Websites

www.reintegration.net/belgium/index.htm

www.dofi.fgov.be

www.kbs-frb.be

www.just.fgov.be/index_nl.htm

www.law.kuleuven.ac.be/lib/databanken/info/**justitie**.htm

Chapter 4 Cyprus

No information available.

Chapter 5 Czech Republic

5.1 Literature

Bernard, J. et al (2005), '*Mediace v rámci výkonu trestu odnětí svobody*', ('*Mediation within Imprisonment*'), Příloha časopisu České vězeňství (Supplement of the Journal of the Czech Prison Service), 1, p.p. 5-14.

The Council of Europe (2004), *Report to the Czech Government on the visit to the Czech Republic carried out by the European Committee for the Prevention of Torture and Inhuman and Degrading Treatment or Punishment (CPT) from 21 to 30 April 2002*, The Council of Europe - CPT/Inf 4, Strasbourg.

The Council of Europe (2004), *Response of the Czech Government to the Report of European Committee for the Prevention of Torture and Inhuman and Degrading Treatment or Punishment (CPT) on its visit to the Czech Republic from 21 to 30 April 2002*, The Council of Europe - CPT/Inf 5, Strasbourg.

Dočekal, M.(2001), '*Koncepce zacházení s vězněnými cizinci*' ('*Conception of treatment of foreign prisoners*'), České vězeňství (Journal of the Czech Prison Service), 1-2.

The General Directorate, Yearbook of the Prison Service (2005), The General Directorate of the Prison Service of the Czech Republic, Prague.

The General Directorate of the Prison Service (2006), Czech Prisons, The General Directorate of the Prison Service of the Czech Republic, Prague.

Generální ředitelství Vězeňské služby ČR (2006), Výroční zpráva Vězeňské služby České republiky za rok 2005, Generální ředitelství Vězeňské služby ČR, Praha.

(The General Directorate of the Prison Service of the Czech Republic (2006), Annual Report of the Activities of the Prison Service of the Czech Republic for 2005), The General Directorate of the Prison Service of the Czech Republic, Prague), bilingual version.

Karabec, Z. et al (2002), *The Criminal Justice System in the Czech Republic*, Institut pro kriminologii a sociální prevenci (The Institute of Criminology and Social Prevention), Praha (Prague).

Kuchta, J., Válková, H. et al (2005), *Základy kriminologie a trestní politiky (Foundations of Criminology and Criminal Policy)*, C. H. Beck, Praha (Prague).

Maguire, M. et al (2002), *The Oxford Handbook of Criminology*, Oxford University Press, Oxford.

Ministerstvo vnitra ČR, Informace o zjištěné trestné činnosti v České republice v roce 2005 ve srovnání s rokem 2004, Ministerstvo Vnitra ČR, Odbor bezpečnostní politiky, Praha.
(The Ministry of the Interior (2006), Information on Crimes detected in the Czech Republic in 2005 in comparison with 2004, The Ministry of the Interior, The Department of Security Policy, Prague).

Ministerstvo spravedlnosti ČR (2005), Statistická ročenka kriminality za rok 2005, Odbor informatiky a statistiky Ministerstva spravedlnosti ČR, Ministerstvo spravedlnosti ČR, Praha. *(The Ministry of Justice of the Czech Republic, Statistical Yearbook of Criminality 2005, Department of statistic, Ministry of Justice of the Czech Republic, Prague 2005).*

Ministerstvo vnitra ČR (2005), Zpráva o situaci v oblasti veřejného pořádku a vnitřní bezpečnosti na území České republiky v roce 2004 ve srovnání s rokem 2003, Ministerstvo Vnitra ČR, Praha. *(The Ministry of the Interior (2005), Report on Public Order and Internal Security in the Czech Republic in 2004 compared with 2003, The Ministry of the Interior, Prague).*

Ministerstvo vnitra ČR (2006), Zpráva o situaci v oblasti veřejného pořádku a vnitřní bezpečnosti na území České republiky v roce 2005 ve srovnání s rokem 2004, Ministerstvo Vnitra ČR, Praha. *(The Ministry of the Interior (2006), Report on Public Order and Internal Security in the Czech Republic in 2005 compared with 2004, The Ministry of the Interior, Prague).*

The Prison Service of the Czech Republic (2005), The Concept for the Development of the Czech Prison System up to 2015, The Prison Service of the Czech Republic, Prague.

Scheinost, M. at al (2004), *Výzkum cizích státních příslušníků v českých věznicích (Research on foreign nationals in the Czech penitentiary institutions)*, Institut pro kriminologii a sociální prevenci *(The Institute of Criminology and Social Prevention)*, Praha (Prague).

Šámal, P., Král, V., Púry F. (2004), *Trestní zákon – komentář (Commentary on the Criminal Code)*, C. H. Beck , Praha (Prague).

Šámal, P., Válková, H., Sotolář, A., Hrušáková, M. (2004) *Zákon o soudnictví ve věcech mládeže – komentář* (Commentary on the Juvenile Justice Act), C. H. Beck , Praha (Prague).

Šámal, P. (2002) *'K úvodním ustanovením připravované rekodifikace trestního zákona'* (*'Commentary to the front provisions of prepared codification of Criminal Code'*), Trestněprávní revue (Criminal Law Revue), 12, pp. 349 ff.

Škvain, P. (2004) *'Nad probíhající kodifikací trestního práva hmotného'* (*'Codification of substantion criminal law in motion'*), Trestněprávní revue (Criminal Law Revue), 10, pp. 304 ff.

Veřejný ochránce práv (2006), Zpráva z návštěv zařízení pro zajištění cizinců, Úřad Veřejného ochránce práv, Brno. *(The Ombudsman (2006) , Report on Visits in Facilities of Detained Foreign Nationals, The Office of the Ombudsman, Brno).*

Vláda České republiky (2006), Zpráva o plnění doporučení Evropského výboru pro zabránění mučení a nelidskému či ponižujícímu zacházení nebo trestnátní (CPT) v roce 2005, vyplývající z návštěvy tohoto výboru v České republice v roce 2002, Vláda České republiky, Praha. *(The Government of the Czech Republic, Report of the Czech Government on measures taken upon CPT visit in 2002 for 2005, The Government of the Czech Republic, Prague.).*

Chapter 6 Denmark

6.1 Literature

Criminal Statistics Yearly Reports 1985, 1990, 1995, 2000, 2001, 2002, 2003, 2004.

Department of Prisons and Probation, Nyt fra Kriminalforsorgen, no. 6, 2005.

Department of Prisons and Probation, Nyt fra Kriminalforsorgen, December 2005.

Department of Prisons and Probation, Yearly Report, 2003, 2004, 2005.

Department of Prisons and Probation, marts 2004: Udmøntningsplan for flerårsaftalen for Kriminalforsorgen 2004-2007.

Engbo, Hans Jørgen, Straffuldbyrdelsesret. (Execution of penalties) (Danish). 2005. Jurist og Økonomforbundet. Copenhagen.

Homann, Gunnar, Kjær, Kim U. and Vedsted-Hansen, Jens in Udlændingeret (Foreign Right) Danish, Copenhagen, 2006.

Holmberg, L. and Kyvsgaard, B. (2003), "Are Immigrants and Their Descendants Discriminated against in the Danish Criminal Justice System?" Journal of Scandinavian Studies in Criminology and Crime Prevention, vol. 4, no. 2 p. 125-142.

Kristeligt Dagblad (Christian Daily) 16 of May 2006, Karitte Lind Bejer is the journalist who interviews Lene Kühle about the anthology "Straffens menneskelige Ansigt?" ("The human face of the penalty") and her PhD on the role of religion in the Danish Prisons.

Rentzmann, William, Esdorf, Annette, Mikkelsen, Jens Kruse, Straffuldbyrdelsesloven (CEP with comments) (Danish). 2003. Jurist og Økonomforbundet. Copenhagen.

Storgaard, Anette: Kontrakten i Ringe Statsfængsel (The contract in the State Prison of Ringe) (Danish) p. 32. Centre for Alcohol and Drug Research, University of Aarhus, Denmark.

Storgaard, Anette: Importmodellen I Vridsløselille (The Import model in the State Prison of Vridsløselille) (Danish), The Department of Prisons and Probation 2003. Copenhagen.

The Ministry of Social Affairs, The Ministry of Justice and The Home Office Psykisk sygdom og kriminalitet. (Psychiatric diseases and crime) (Danish) p. 76. 2006. Copenhagen.

Rigspolitiet. Udlændingeafdelingen. Status på arbejdet med udsendelse af afviste asylansøgere. 2006.

6.2 Legislation

Code on Foreigners, no 826 of 24 August 2005.

Penal Code, no 126 of 15 April 1930. Latest revised edition Consolidate Act no 909 of 27 September 2005.

Supplement to the Penal Code, no. 6 of 3 January 1992.

Code on Execution of Penalties, no 432 of 31 May 2000. Latest revised edition Consolidate Act no 207 of 18 March 2005.

Supplement to Code on Execution of Penalties, no. 367 of 24 May 2005 and Parliamentary instruction no 506 of 17 June 2005.

Procedural Code, no 910 of 27th September 2005

European Prison Rules. Rec(2006)2.

6.3 Websites

http://www.kriminalforsorgen.dk

www.helsinki-komiteen.dk. Engbo, Hans Jørgen .

www.kriminalforsorgen.dk/publikationer/rapporterogundersøgelser/Undersøgelse og anbefalinger vedrørende etniske minoriteter i kriminalforsorgen. 2005 .

http://www.oes-cs.dk/PUBLIKATIONER/LSTATISTIK/2005/Criminal
Statistics. 2004.

www.dst.dk/ Nyt fra Danmarks Statistik, nr. 235, 27 May. 2004

www.jm.dk Notat vedrørende Kriminalitet og national oprindelse. 2002.

http://www.udlst.dk/asyl

http://nyhederne.tv2.dk

http://www.dr.dk/P1

http://drk2.inforce.dk/sw57607.asp?usepf=true

Chapter 7 Estonia

7.1 Literature

Saar, J., Markina, A., Ahven, A. jt. (2002). Crime in Estonia 1991 – 2001. TPÜ Rahvus-vaheliste ja Sotsiaaluuringute Instituut; Ministry of Justice.

Tiit, E.-M. (2006). The main indicators of Estonian population in 2005—2006 in the background of Europe. Office of the Minister for Population and Ethnic Affairs, Tartu University, Statistical Office of Estonia.

7.2 Legislation

Citizenship Act. (1995). */Kodakondsuse seadus/*

Code of Administrative Court Procedure. (1999). */Halduskohtumenetluse seadustik/*

Code of Criminal Procedure. (2003). */Kriminaalmenetluse seadustik/*

Foreigners Act. (1993). */Välismaalaste seadus/*

Imprisonment Act. (2000). */Vangistusseadus/*

Obligation to Leave and Prohibition on Entry Act. (1998). */Väljasõidukohustuse ja sissesõidu-keelu seadus/*

Penal Code. (2001). */Karistusseadustik/*

943

Police Service Act. (1998). */Politseiteenistuse seadus/*

Public Service Act (1995). */Avaliku teenistuse seadus/*

Refugees Act. (1997). */Pagulaste seadus/*

7.3 Websites

The main Social and Economic Indicators of Estonia. 12/06. /2006).Statistical Office of Estonia. www.stat.ee

Citizenship and Migration Board Yearbook. (2006). Tallinn. www.mig.ee

Selection of Rehabilitation Programmes in Prisons 2005. Ministry of Justice. http://www.vangla.ee/19706

Legal acts in English are available on the website of the Estonian Legal Language Centre http://www.legaltext.ee/et/andmebaas/ava.asp?m=022:

Chapter 8 Finland

8.1 Literature

Lappi-Seppälä, Tapio, Penal Policy and Prisoner Rates in Finland. National Research Institute of Legal Policy. Research reports 2007 (forthcoming). Helsinki.

Makkonen, Timo. Racism in Finland 2000. Helsinki: Finnish League for Human Rights, 2001.

Salmenhaara, Perttu. "Immigrants and the Finnish Welfare State: Wasting Human Capital" in Cultural Diversity in the Nordic Welfare States. Helsinki: Svenska Social- och kommunalhögskolan, 2003.

Report to the Finnish Government on the visit to Finland carried out by the European Committee for the Prevention of Torture and Inhuman or Degrading Treatment or Punishment (CPT) from 7 to 17 September 2003.
(http://www.cpt.coe.int/documents/fin/2004-20-inf-eng.htm)

Response of the Government of Finland to the report on the visit carried out by the European Committee for the Prevention of Torture and Inhuman or Degrading Treatment or Punishment (CPT) from 7 to 17 September 2003.

Directorate of Immigration: Applications and Decisions on Asylum 2000-2003.
(http://www.uvi.fi/netcomm/printarticle.asp?path=&article=2102)

ECRI-report (European Commission against Racism and Intolerance) on Finland, adopted on 14 December 2001, and made public on 23 July 2002. (http://www.coe.int/T/E/human%5Frights/Ecri/).

Government's Report on the Implementation of the Integration Act. Government's Reports 5/2002.

8.3 Websites

Ministry of the Interior. Racial Crimes Reported to the Police in the Year 2002. An electronic report published in 12/2003. http://www.poliisi.fi/intermin/biblio.nsf/

Ministry of Labour. Migration Issues and Statistics . http://www.mol.fi/migration/tilastot.html

Statistics of Finland, StatFin http://statfin.stat.fi/StatWeb/start.asp?LA=fi&lp=home

The Criminal Sanctions Agency http://www.rikosseuraamus.fi/17006.htm

European Social Mediation Project "Let's Talk" http://www.iom.fi/letstalk/start.htm

The Refugee Advice Centre: www.pakolaisneuvonta.fi (retrieved 5.7.2006)

Chapter 9 France

9.1 Literature

La criminalisation des migrants (1999), Actes de la recherche en sciences sociales, 129.

Boe, C., Martinez, J. (2004), Prison, rétention : la politique d'enfermement des étrangers, EcoRev´- Revue critique d´écologie politique, 15.

Cimade (2004), Centres et locaux de rétention administrative, Journal Causes communes, hors-série, Paris.

Cimade (2005), Étrangers en France: les textes, Journal Causes communes, hors-série, Paris.

Commission Nationale Consultative des Droits de l´Homme (2004), Étude sur les étrangers détenus, http://www.commission-droits-homme.fr/travauxCncdh/EtudeEtrangerDetenus.html

Gisti (2001), L´enfermement des étrangers, Revue Plein droit, 50.

Gailliègue, G. (2000), La prison des étrangers : clandestins et délinquants, Imago, Paris.

Guillonneau, M., Kensey, A., Portas, C. (1999), Détenus étrangers, Cahiers de démographie pénitentiaire, 6, Ministère de la Justice, Paris.

Herzog-Evans M. (2002), Droit de l'application des peines, Dalloz, Paris.

Kensey, A., Tournier, P. (1997), French prison population, Travaux et documents, Ministère de la Justice, Paris.

Kensey, A., Tournier, P. (2002), Arithmétique de l'exécution des peines, Travaux & documents, Ministère de la Justice, Paris.

Kensey, A., Pitoun, A., Lévy, R., Tournier, P. (2003), Sous surveillance électronique. La mise en place du „bracelet électronique" en France (octobre 2000 – mai 2002), DAP-PMJ1-CESDIP, Travaux & documents, Paris.

Lamy, M., Pitot, S. (2004), La précarité, Institut de Démographie de l'Université de Paris (not published).

Mary, F.L., Tournier, P. (1998), Derrières les chiffres, réalités de la répression pénale de la délinquance des étrangers en France, Information Prison Justice, 84, pp.12-17

Oip (2004), Le guide du prisonnier, La Découverte, Paris.

Oip (2005), Étrangers en prison. Aux confins de l'absurde, Revue Dedans Dehors, 52.

Pinalie, G. (2000), La grande fabrique des étrangers, http://biblioweb.samizdat.net/article16.html

Snacken, S. (2004), Étrangers dans les prisons belges : problèmes et solutions possibles, Fondation Roi Baudoin, Bruxelles.

Tournier, P. (1993), Les étrangers dans les statistiques pénitentiaires, Ausländer, Kriminalität und Strafrechtspflege, 1, Verlag Rüegger, Chur, pp.323-334.

Tournier, P., Robert, P. (1991), Etrangers et délinquances, L'Harmattan, Paris.

Tournier, P., Kensey, A. (2000), Placements à l'extérieur, semi-liberté, libération conditionnelle…Des aménagements d'exception, PMJ1 / CESDIP UA CNRS, Paris.

Trombik, E. (2005), Le vécu carcéral des détenus allemands, Maîtrise de sociologie, Université Marc Bloch, Strasbourg, France (not published).

Tsoukala, A. (2002), Le traitement médiatique de la criminalité étrangère en Europe, Déviance & Société, 26, 1.

Wacquant, L. (1999), Des « ennemis commodes ». Étrangers et immigrés dans les prisons d'Europe, Actes de la Recherche en Sciences Sociales, 129, pp.63-67.

Chapter 10 Germany

10.1 Literature

Albrecht, H.-J., Ethnic Minorities, Crime, and Criminal Justice in Germany, in Tonry, M. (Ed.), Ethnicity, Crime, and Immigration, Chicago: University of Chicago Press (Crime and Justice, Vol. 21), 1997, 31-99.

Albrecht, P.-A., Pfeiffer, C., Die Kriminalisierung junger Ausländer. Befunde und Reaktionen sozialer Kontrollinstanzen, München: Juventa Verlag, 1979.

Bannenberg, B., Migration – Kriminalität – Prävention. Gutachten zum 8. Deutschen Präventionstag, 28./29.4.2003, Teil I, 2003, 1-70 (www.praeventionstag.de/content/8praev/dateien/Gutachten_8_DPT.pdf).

Beauftrage der Bundesregierung für Migration. Flüchtlinge und Integration, („Bericht der Beauftragten der Bundesregierung für Migration, Flüchtlinge und Integration über die Lage der Ausländerinnen und Ausländer in Deutschland Berlin", Juni 2005; available under http://www.bundesregierung.de/Webs/Breg/DE/Bundesregierung/BeauftragtefuerInte gration/Service/service.html; click „Publikationen"; then "Ausländerbericht".

Beichel-Benedetti, St., Gutmann, R., Die Abschiebungshaft in der gerichtlichen Praxis, Neue Juristische Wochenschrift, 2004, 3015-3020.

BMI/BMJ, (Bundesministerium des Innern/Bundesministerium der Justiz), Erster Periodischer Sicherheitsbericht, Berlin, BMI/BMJ, 2001 (see also www.bmi.de).

Boese, S., Ausländer im Strafvollzug. Die Auswirkungen ausländerrechtlicher Maßnahmen auf die Realisierung des Vollzugszieles, Hamburg: Dr. Kovac, 2003.

Brumlik, M., Sutter, H., Rekonstruktion sozial-kognitiver und sozio-moralischer Lernprozesse im Rahmen eines demokratisch geregelten Vollzugs als 'Just Community'. Projektverlängerungsantrag und Zwischenbericht, Heidelberg 1996.

Dittman, J., Wernitznig, B., Strafverfolgung und Sanktionierung bei deutschen und ausländischen Jugendlichen und Heranwachsenden. Eine Untersuchung am Beispiel des Einbruchsdiebstahls. Monatsschrift für Kriminologie und Strafrechtsreform, 86 (2003), 195-205.

Dünkel, F., Youth violence and juvenile justice in Germany, in Dünkel, F., Drenkhahn, K. (Eds.), Youth violence: new patterns and local responses – Experiences in East and West, Mönchengladbach, Forum Verlag Godesberg, 2003, 96-142.

Dünkel, F., Situation und Reform des Jugendstrafvollzugs in Deutschland. Recht der Jugend und des Bildungswesens, 51 (2003a), 318-334.

Dünkel, F., Riskante Freiheiten? – Vollzugslockerungen zwischen Resozialisierung und Sicherheitsrisiko. In: Rehn, G., Nanninga, R., Thiel, A. (Eds.), Freiheit und Unfreiheit. Arbeit mit Straftätern innerhalb und außerhalb des Justizvollzugs. Herbolzheim: Centaurus Verlag 2004, 104-134.

Dünkel, F., Drenckhahn, K.: Strafvollzugskonzepte: Aktuelle Entwicklungen zwischen Reform und Gegenreform. Neue Kriminalpolitik 13 (2001), Heft 2, S. 16-21.

Dünkel, F., Kunkat, A., Zwischen Innovation und Restrauration. 20 Jahre Strafvollzugsgesetz – eine Bestandsaufnahme. Neue Kriminalpolitik 9 (1997), No. 2, 24-33.

Dünkel, F., Scheel, J., Vermeidung von Ersatzfreiheitsstrafen mittels gemeinnütziger Arbeit. Das Projekt „Ausweg" in Mecklenburg-Vorpommern. In: Schöch, H., Jehle, J.-M. (Eds.), Angewandte Kriminologie zwischen Freiheit und Sicherheit. Mönchengladbach: Forum Verlag Godesberg, 2004, 19-37.

Dünkel, F., Scheel, J.: Vermeidung von Ersatzfreiheitsstrafen durch gemeinnützige Arbeit: das Projekt „Ausweg" in Mecklenburg-Vorpommern. Ergebnisse einer empirischen Untersuchung. Mönchengladbach: Forum Verlag Godesberg, 2006.

Dünkel, F., Spiess, G.: Perspektiven der Strafaussetzung zur Bewährung und Bewährungshilfe im zukünftigen deutschen Strafrecht. Bewährungshilfe 39 (1992), 117-138.

Dünkel, F., Walter, J., Young foreigners and members of ethnic minorities in German youth prisons. In: Queloz, N., et al. (Eds.): Youth Crime and Juvenile Justice. The challenge of migration and ethnic diversity. Bern: Staempfli 2005, 517-540.

Engels, D., Martin, M., Typische Lebenslagen und typischer Unterstützungsbedarf von Klientinnen und Klienten der Bewährungshilfe Sekundäranalyse von Befragungsdaten der Arbeitsgemeinschaft Deutscher Bewährungshelferinnen und Bewährungshelfer e.V. Berlin: ISG-Institut für Sozialforschung und Gesellschaftspolitik GmbH, 2002.

Feuerhelm, W., Stellung und Ausgestaltung der gemeinnützigen Arbeit im Strafrecht, Wiesbaden: Kriminologische Zentralstelle, 1997.

Flügge, C., Maelicke, B., Preusker, H. (Eds.): Das Gefängnis als lernende Organisation. Baden-Baden: Nomos Verlag, 2001.

Fluhr, H., Zur Pfändbarkeit der Forderungen des Strafgefangenen. Zeitschrift für Strafvollzug und Straffälligenhilfe 38 (1989), p. 103-108.

Gebauer, M., Kriminalität der Gastarbeiterkinder, Kriminalistik 1981, Vol. 35, 2-8, 83-86.

Geissler, R., Marissen, N., Kriminalität und Kriminalisierung junger Ausländer. Die tickende soziale Zeitbombe, Kölner Zeitschrift für Soziologie und Sozialpsychologie, 42 (1990), 663-687.

Grundies, V, Kriminalitätsbelastung junger Aussiedler. Ein Längsschnittvergleich mit in Deutschland geborenen jungen Menschen anhand polizeilicher Registrierungen. Monatsschrift für Kriminologie und Strafrechtsreform, 83 (2000), 290-305.

Hamburger, F., Seus, L., Wolter, O., Zur Delinquenz ausländischer Jugendlicher – Bedingungen der Entstehung und Prozesse der Verfestigung, Wiesbaden: Bundeskriminalamt (BKA-Schriftenreihe), 1981.

Hagenmeier, M., Seelsorgerische Erfahrungen und Anfragen an das Recht, Neue Kriminalpolitik 2000, issue 1, p. 10-15.

Hailbronner, K., Asyl- und Ausländerrecht, 2006. Interpretation eines gesellschaftlich brisanten Sachverhalts. Informationsdienst zur Ausländerarbeit, 1995, Nr. 3-4, 96-99.

Heinhold, H., Abschiebungshaft in Deutschland. Karlsruhe: van Loeper Literaturverlag, 2nd ed., 2004.

Heinz, W (2004): Das strafrechtliche Sanktionensystem und die Sanktionierungspraxis in Deutschland. Internet-Publikation: www.uni-konstanz.de/rtf/kis/sanks04.htm (Version 1/2006, continously amended).

Horstkotte, H., Realität und notwendige Grenzen der Abschiebehaft, Neue Kriminalpolitik, 1999, issue 4, p. 31-36.

Jescheck, H.-H., Weigend, T., Lehrbuch des Strafrechts: allgemeiner Teil. 5. ed, Berlin: Duncker & Humblot, 1996.

Jehle J.-M., Entwicklung der Untersuchungshaft bei Jugendlichen und Heranwachsenden: vor und nach der Wiedervereinigung, Bonn, Bundesministerium der Justiz, 1995.

Hehle, J.-M., Feuerhelm, W., Block, Gemeinnützige Arbeit statt Ersatzfreiheitsstrafe, Wiesbaden: Kriminologische Zentralstelle, 1990.

Jung, H., Müller-Dietz, H. (Eds.), Langer Freiheitsentzug – wie lange noch? Bonn: Forum-Verlag Godesberg, 1994.

Kaiser, G., Kriminologie. Eine Einführung in die Grundlagen. 10th ed. Heidelberg: C. F. Müller, 1997.

Karger, T., Sutterer, P., Polizeilich registrierte Gewaltdelinquenz bei jungen Ausländern. Befunde der Freiburger Kohortenstudie unter Berücksichtigung von Verzerrungen in der Polizeilichen Kriminalstatistik. Monatsschrift für Kriminologie und Strafrechtsreform, 73 (1990), 369-383.

Kerner, H.-J., et al., Wenn aus Spaß Ernst wird. Untersuchung zum Freizeitverhalten und den sozialen Beziehungen jugendlicher Spätaussiedler. DVJJ-Journal 12 (2001), 370-379.

Kohlberg, L., Moralische Entwicklung und demokratische Erziehung. In: Lind G., Raschert, J. (Eds.), Moralische Urteilsfähigkeit. Eine Auseinandersetzung mit Lawrence Kohlberg über Moral, Erziehung und Demokratie. Weinheim and Basel, Beltz Verlag, 1987, 25-46.

Kubink, M., Verständnis und Bedeutung von Ausländerkriminalität. Eine Analyse der Konstitution sozialer Probleme, Pfaffenweiler: Centaurus Verlag, 1993.

Laubenthal, K., Strafvollzug, Berlin (et al.), 3rd ed., 2003.

Ludwig-Mayerhofer, W., Niemann, H., Gleiches (Straf-)Recht für alle? Zeitschrift für Soziologie, 26 (1997), 35-52.

Mansel, J., Albrecht, G., Migration und das kriminalpolitische Handeln staatlicher Strafverfolgungsorgane. Ausländer als polizeilich Tatverdächtige und gerichtlich Abgeurteilte. Kölner Zeitschrift für Soziologie und Sozialpsychologie, 55 (2003), 679-715.

Melchior, K.: Abschiebungshaft. Kommentar. www.abschiebungshaft.de.(30/07/2006)

Münchener Kommentar zum Strafgesetzbuch §§ 1-51. München: C. H. Beck, 2003. (quoted: Münchener Kommentar-*author*).

Neef, R., Novy, J.: Über die Betreuung deutscher Strafgefangener in Thailand durch die deutsche Botschaft. Zeitschrift für Strafvollzug und Straffälligenhilfe 2004, Vol. 54, 155-160.

Pfeiffer, C. et al., Ausgrenzung, Gewalt und Kriminalität im Leben junger Menschen – Kinder und Jugendliche als Täter und Opfer, Hannover, Eigenverlag der DVJJ (Sonderdruck zum 24. Deutschen Jugendgerichtstag 1998 in Hamburg), 1998.

Pfeiffer, C. et al., Migration und Kriminalität, Baden- Baden, Nomos Verlag, 2005.

Pfeiffer, C., Wetzels, P., Junge Türken als Täter und Opfer von Gewalt, DVJJ-Journal, 2000, Vol. 11, 107-113.

Plachta, M., Transfer of prisoners under international instruments and domestic legislation: a comparative study. Freiburg i. Br.: Max-Planck-Inst. für ausländisches und internationales Strafrecht, 1993.

Reich, K., Delinquent Behaviour: One Possible Response to Migration-related Problems for Young Male Ethnic-Germans, in DÜNKEL F., DRENKHAHN K. (Eds), Youth violence: new patterns and local responses – Experiences in East and West, Mönchengladbach, Forum Verlag Godesberg, 2003, 443-457.

Schöch, H., Gebauer M., Ausländerkriminalität in der Bundesrepublik Deutschland. Kriminologische, rechtliche und soziale Aspekte eines gesellschaftlichen Phänomens, Baden-Baden, Nomos Verlag, 1991.

Schott; T., Ausländer vor Gericht, Zeitschrift für Jugendkriminalrecht und Jugendhilfe, 15 (2004), 385-395.

Schüler-Springorum, H., Ausländerkriminalität – Ursachen, Umfang und Entwicklung, NStZ, 1983, Vol. 3, 529-536.

Schwind, H.-D., Kriminologie, 13th ed., Heidelberg, Kriminalistik Verlag, 2003.

Steffen, W., Problemfall „Ausländerkriminalität", in H.-J. ALBRECHT et al. (Eds), Internationale Perspektiven in Kriminologie und Strafrecht – Festschrift für Günther Kaiser, Berlin, Duncker & Humblot, 1998, 663-680.

Steffen, W., Strukturen der Kriminalität der Nichtdeutschen, in Jehle J.-M. (Ed), Raum und Kriminalität. Sicherheit der Stadt – Migrationsprobleme, Mönchengladbach, Forum Verlag Godesberg, 2001, 231-262.

Suhling, S., Schott T., Ansatzpunkte zur Erklärung der gestiegenen Gefangenenzahlen in Deutschland. In: BERESWILL M., GREVE W., Eds., Forschungsthema Strafvollzug, Baden-Baden, Nomos Verlagsgesellschaft, 2001, 25-83.

Sutter, H.-J., Demokratieerziehung und Moralentwicklung – Kohlbergs Just-Community-Modell unter den Bedingungen des Jugendstrafvollzugs. In: Stark et al., Eds. (Hrsg.): Moralisches Lernen in Schule, Betrieb und Gesellschaft. Bad Boll, Evangelische Akademie (Protokolldienst Nr. 7/96), 1996.

Sutter, H.-J., Baader M., Weyers S., Die „Demokratische Gemeinschaft" als Ort sozialen und moralischen Lernens. Der Modellversuch in der Justizvollzugsanstalt Adelsheim – eine Zwischenbilanz. Neue Praxis, 1998, 383-398.

Tzschaschel, N., Ausländische Gefangene im Strafvollzug. Eine vergleichende Bestandsaufnahme der Vollzugsgestaltung bei ausländischen und deutschen Gefangenen sowie eine Untersuchung zur Anwendung des Paragraphen 456a StPO. Herbolzheim: Centaurus-Verlag, 2002.

Villmow, B., Kriminalität der jungen Ausländer: Ausmaß und Struktur des abweichenden Verhaltens und gesellschaftliche Reaktion, in KERNER H.-J., Göppinger, H., Streng, F. (Eds), Festschrift für Heinz Leferenz, Heidelberg, C. F. Müller, 1983, 323-343.

Walter, M., Über die Bedeutung der Kriminalität junger Ausländer für das Kriminalrechtssystem, DVJJ-Journal, 1993, Vol. 4, 347-359.

Walter, M., Pitsela, A., Ausländerkriminalität in der statistischen (Re-) Konstruktion. *Kriminalpädagogische Praxis*, No. 34, 6-19.

Walter, M., Trautmann, S., Kriminalität junger Migranten und gesellschaftliche (Des-)Integration, in Raitherl J., Mansel J. (Eds), *Kriminalität und Gewalt im Jugendalter*, Weinheim, München, Juventa Verlag, 2003, 64-86.

Weitekamp, E. G. M., Reich K., Bott K, Deutschland als neue Heimat? Jugendliche Aussiedler in Deutschland zwischen Veränderung und Verweigerung. *Neue Praxis*, 2002, 33-52.

Weyers, S., Funktioniert Demokratie(erziehung) im Knast? Demokratische Partizipation und moralisches Lernen im Vollzug. *Neue Kriminalpolitik* 2003, Vol. 15, 106-109.

Wilmers, N. et al., *Jugendliche in Deutschland zur Jahrtausendwende: Gefährlich oder gefährdet?* Baden-Baden, Nomos Verlagsgesellschaft, 2002.

Winkler, S., *Migration – Kriminalität – Prävention. Ausländer und Aussiedler im Strafvollzug. Gutachten zum 8. Deutschen Präventionstag, 28./29.4.2003*, Teil II, 2003, 70-168.

10.3 Websites

www.bundesverfassungsgericht.de (Federal Constitutional Court, all decision from 1999 on are available in a full text version; press releases partly available in English).

http://www.bundesregierung.de/Webs/Breg/DE/Bundesregierung/BeauftragtefuerIntegration/Service/service.html (Federal Commissioner for Migration, Refugees and Immigration).

www.bmi.de (Ministry of the Interior).

www.bamf.de (Federal Agency for Migration, Refugees and Immigration).

www.destatis.de (Federal Bureau of Statistics).

www.praeventionstag.de

www.abschiebungshaft.de (commentary on the relevant provisions for administrative detention for foreigners).

www.gesis.org (Gesellschaft Sozialwissenschaftlicher Infrastruktureinrichtungen e.V.; German Social Science Infrastructure Services e.V.).

www.egpa.de (European Group for prisoners abroad).

www.institut-fuer-menschenrechte.de (German Institute for Human rights).

www.proasyl.de

www.gefaehrdetenhilfe.de

www.sbh-berlin.de

http://www.jesuiten-fluechtlingsdienst.de (with an useful list of further www-links).

www.cpt.coe.int (Council of Europe's Committee for the Prevention of Torture and In-human or Degrading Treatment or Punishment).

Chapter 11 Greece

11.1 Literature

Alexiadis, S. (2001). Corrections, Sakkoulas, Athens, Thessaloniki (in Greek).

Amnesty International (2002). Greece. In the shadow of impunity. Ill-treatment and the misuse of firearms: www.amnesty.org/library/print/ENGEUR2502220

Amnesty International (2005). Greece, out of the Spotlight. The rights of foreigners and minorities are still a grey area: www.amnesty.org/library/print/ENGEUR250162005

Amnesty International (2002). Annual Report 2002.
Anagnostopoulos, I. G. and Magliveras, □.D. (2000). Criminal Law in Greece, Kluwer, Sakkoulas, The Hague et al.

Baldwin-Edwards, M. (2001). Crime and Migrants: Some Myths and Realities, Presenta-tion (in Greek) to the International Police Association. 17th Greek Section Conference, Samos, May, 4th, 2001.

Bakatsulas, M. (1968). The Greek Code of Prison Rules 1967. BritJCrim, 8, pp. 211-213.

Bitzilekis, N. (2001). Regelungen außerhalb des Strafrechts aus griechischer Sicht, in: Hirsch H.J. (ed), Krise des Strafrechts und der Kriminalwissenschaften? Duncker & Humblot, Berlin, pp. 121-123.

Chaidou, A. (1994). Griechenland, in: Dünkel, F. and Vagg J. (eds), Untersuchungshaft und Untersuchungshaftvollzug, International vergleichende Perspektiven zur Untersuchungshaft sowie zu den Rechten und Lebensbedingungen von Untersuchungsgefangenenen - Waiting for Trial. MPI für ausländisches und internationales Strafrecht, Freiburg, pp. 251-269.

Chaidou, A. (2002). Griechenland, in: Albrecht, H.-J. and Kilchling, M. (eds), Jugendstrafrecht in Europa. MPI für ausländisches und internationales Strafrecht, Freiburg, pp. 191-203.

Committee against Torture (CAT) (2002). Fourth periodic report of states parties due in 2001. Addendum, Greece.

Council of Europe (1990). Prison Information Bulletin: www.coe.int

Courakis, N. (1994). Alternative Penal Sanctions in Greece. The Journal of Asset Protection and Financial Crime, 2, pp. 257-264.

Dünkel, F. and Snacken, S. (2001). Strafvollzug im europäischen Vergleich: Probleme, Praxis und Perspektiven. Zeitschrift für Strafvollzug und Straffälligenhilfe, 50, pp. 195-211.

European Committee for the Prevention of Torture and Inhuman or Degrading Treatment or Punishment (CPT). Report to the Government of Greece on the visit to Greece carried out by the CPT, 2001: www.cpt.coe.int

European Council on Refugees and Exile (2003). Greece. Legal and Social Conditions for Asylum Seekers and Refugees. www.ecre.org

Frangoulis, S. (1994). Freiheit durch Arbeit. Die Institution der "wohltätigen" Anrechnung von Arbeitstagen auf die Freiheitsstrafe in Griechenland. Jur. Diss., N.G. Elwert, Marburg.

Hill, G. (2002). The treatment of foreign Prisoners: www.ispac-italy.org

Human Rights Watch Memorandum (2000). Urgent Concerns: Conditions of Detention for foreigners in Greece: www.hrw.org/backgrounder/eca/greece-detention/bck.htm

Ioannou, K. M. (1996). The Application of the European Convention on Human Rights in the Greek Legal Order. Revue Hellénique de Droit International, 16, pp. 223-250.

João Costa, M. (2003). Eurobarometer: Crime & Rising Anxiety. ESC. Criminology in Europe. Newsletter of the European Society of Criminology, 2, pp. 1, 16-18.
Kaiser, G. (1996). Der Europäische Antifolterausschuß und die Vorbeugung kriminellen Machtmissbrauchs, in: Schmoller K. (ed.), Festschrift für Otto Trifterer. Springer, Wien, New York, pp. 777-797.

Karydis, V. (1993). Migrants as a Political Enterprise. The Greek-Albaninan Case. Chronicles, 8, pp. 93-96.

Lambropoulou, E. (1993). Umwandlung der Freiheitsstrafe als kriminalpolitisches Modell? Zur Diskrepanz von Verurteilungen und Inhaftierungen in Griechenland. Monatsschrift für Kriminologie und Strafrechtsreform, 76, pp. 91-100.

Lambropoulou, E. (1997). The Implementation of the CPT☐S Recommendations in Five Southern European Countries. Report on Greece. In: Report. The Prevention of Torture in Southern Europe. Geneva, An Assessment of the Work of the European Committee for the Prevention of Torture in the South of Europe, pp. 49-62.

Lambropoulou, E. (2001). The 'End' of Correctional Policy and the Management of the Correctional 'Problem' in Greece. European Journal of Crime, Criminal Law and Criminal Justice, 9, pp. 33-55.

Lambropoulou, E. (2005). Crime, Criminal Justice and Criminology in Greece. European Journal of Criminology, 2, pp. 211-247.

Manitakis, A. (1989). The Constitutional Rights of Prisoners and their Judicial Protection. Penal Chronicles, 39, pp. 161- 62 (in Greek).

Meurer, D. (1994). Freiheit durch Arbeit nach griechischem Strafrecht, in: Busch, M., Edel, G. and Müller-Dietz H. (eds), Gefängnis und Gesellschaft. Gedächtnisschrift für Albert Krebs. Centaurus, Pfaffenweiler, pp. 78-94.

Neubacher, F., Walter, M. and Pitsela, A. (2003). Jugendstrafvollzug im deutsch-griechischen Vergleich – Ergebnisse einer Befragung. Zeitschrift für Strafvollzug und Straffälligenhilfe, 52, pp. 17-24.

Office of the High Commissioner for Human Rights (1988). Body of Principles for the Protection of All Persons under any form of Detention or Imprisonment: www.unhchr.gr

Pitsela, A.(1988). Greece, in: van Kalmthout, A.K. and Tak P.P. (eds), Sanctions Systems in the Member-States of the Council. Part I. Deprivation of Liberty, Community Service and other Substitutes.Kluwer Law, Deventer et al., pp. 151-170.

Pitsela, A. (1997). Griechenland, in: Dünkel, F., van Kalmthout, A., Schüler-Springorum, H. (eds), Entwicklungstendenzen und Reformstrategien im Jugendstrafrecht im europäischen Vergleich. Forum, Mönchengladbach, pp. 155-191.

Pitsela, A. (1998). Jugendgerichtsbarkeit und Jugenddelinquenz in Griechenland, in: Albrecht H.-J. et al. (eds), Internationale Perspektiven in Kriminologie und Strafrecht. Festschrift für Günther Kaiser. Duncker & Humblot, Berlin, pp. 1085-1107.

Pitsela, A. (2000). Vorschläge für einen rationalen Umgang mit der Jugenddelinquenz, in: Prittwitz, C., Manoledakis, I. (eds.), Strafrechtsprobleme an der Jahrtausendwende. Nomos, Baden-Baden, pp. 131-144.

Pitsela, A. (2003). Jugendstrafvollzugsrecht in Griechenland, in: Bremer Institut für Kriminalpolitik (ed), Quo Vadis III. Innovative Wege zur nachhaltigen Reintegration straffälliger Menschen – Reformmodelle in den EU-Staaten. Bremen (CD).

Pitsela, A. (2004). Greece. Criminal Responsibility of Minors in the National and International Legal Orders. Revue Internationale de Droit Pénal, 75, pp. 355-378.

Pitsela, A. (2006). Das statistische Erscheinungsbild der Gewaltkriminalität in Griechenland. In: M. Lohiniva-Kerkelä (ed.), Violence – Sanctions and Vulnerability. Essays in Honour of Professor Terttu Utriainen. TALENTUM, Helsinki, pp. 479-502.

Spinellis, C.D. (1997). The Brave New World of Ethnic Groups in the Overcrowding Prisons: A Challenge for the Guardians of Human Rights, in: Spinellis, C.D., Crime in Greece in Perspective. A.N. Sakkoulas, Athens, Komotini, pp. 325-344.

Spinellis, C.D. (1997). Crime in Greece in Perspective, A.N. Sakkoulas, Athens, Komotini.

Spinellis, C.D. (1998). Attacking Prison Overcrowding in Greece: A Task of Sisyphus? in: Albrecht, H.-J., et al. (eds), Internationale Perspektiven in Kriminologie und Strafrecht. Festschrift für Günther Kaiser. Vol. □□. Duncker & Humblot, Berlin, pp. 1273-1289.

Spinellis, C.D., Angelopoulou, K., Koulouris, N. (1996). Foreign Detainees in Greek Prisons: A New Challenge to the Guardians of Human Rights, in: Matthews, R. and Francis, P. (eds), Prisons 2000. An International Perspective on the Current State and Future of Imprisonment. Macmillan Press, St. Martin's Press, Houndmills et al., pp. 163-178.

Spinellis, C.D. and Kranidioti, M. (1995). Greek Crime Statistics, in: Jehle, J.-M. and Lewis, Ch. (eds), Improving Criminal Justice Statistics. Kriminologische Zentralstelle e.v. (KrimZ), Wiesbaden, pp. 67-88.

Spinellis, C.D., Spinellis, D. (2002). Sanctions Imposed, Sanctions Executed: Who Benefits from the Discrepancy? Revue Hellénique de Droit International, 55, pp. 311-345.

Spinellis, C.D., Tsitsoura, A. (2004). Juvenile Justice System in Greece. www.esc-eurocrim.org

Spinellis, D.D. (1998). Die Bekämpfung von Folter und unmenschlicher Behandlung in der griechischen Gesetzgebung, Rechtsprechung und Praxis, in: Albrecht, H.-J. et al. (eds), Internationale Perspektiven in Kriminologie und Strafrecht. Festschrift für Günther Kaiser. Duncker & Humblot, Berlin, pp. 1593-1615.

Spinellis, D.D. and Spinellis, C.D. (1999). Criminal Justice System in Greece. Helsinki: HEUNI.

The Greek Ombudsman, www.synigoros.gr

The National Commission for Human Rights, www.nchr.gr

Tsitsoura, □. (2002). Community Sanctions and Measures in Greece, in: Albrecht, H.-J. and van Kalmthout, A. (eds), Community Sanctions and Measures in Europe and North America. MPI für ausländisches und internationales Strafrecht, Freiburg, pp. 271-283.

Winschenbach, K. (1997). Strafvollzug in Griechenland. Zeitschrift für Strafvollzug und Straffälligenhilfe, 46, pp. 275-277.

Chapter 12 Hungary
12.1 Literature

Double Standard: Prison Conditions in Hungary. Hungarian Helsinki Committee, Budapest, 2002.

IHF Report 2006 on Hungary, Events of 2005 in: *Human Rights of the OSCE Region, International Helsinki Federation for Human Rights* (to be published).

András Kádár: *Presumption of Guilt*, Hugarian Helsinki Committee, Budapest, 2004.

Report to the Hungarian Government on the visit to Hungary carried out by the European Committee for the Prevention of Torture and Inhuman or Degrading Treatment or Punishment (CPT) from 30 March to 8 April 2005.

Chapter 13 Ireland

13.1 Literature

Central Statistics Office 2005, *Statistical Yearbook of Ireland, 2004.*

Department of Justice, Equality and Law Reform 2005, *Court Services Report* 2003.

CPT Report, 2003.

CVS Consultants and Migrant and Refugee Communities Forum, 'A Shattered World: The Mental Health Needs of Refugees and Newly Arrived Communities', 1999.

Department of Justice, Equality and Law Reform, *Mental Illness in Irish Prisoners: Psychiatric Morbidity in Sentenced, Remanded and Newly Committed Prisoners.* H.G. Kennedy, S. Monks, K. Curtin, B. Wright, S. Linehan, D.Duffy, D. Teljeur, and A. Kelly, National Forensic Mental Health Service, 2005.

Department of Justice, Equality and Law Reform, *National Prison Chaplains Annual Report 2003.*

Department of Justice, Equality and Law Reform, *Prison Rules,* 2005.

Department of Justice, Equality and Law Reform 2003 *Evaluation of Research and Training Project for Intercultural Awareness Conducted in Wheatfield Prison,* Dublin 2002.

Department of Justice, Equality and Law Reform, *Irish Prison Service Annual Reports,* 2003-5.

Department of Justice, Equality and Law Reform 2005, Annual *Report by the Minister for Justice to the Government on the Operation of The Transfer of Sentenced Persons Act, 1995 & 1997 for the period 1 January 2004- 31 December 2004.*

T. Ellis, C. Tedstone, and D. Curry, *Improving Race Relations in prisons: What Works?' Home Office On line Report,* December 2004

E. Farrell, Working with Non-nationals Detained in Irish prisons: the challenges facing the Probation Service. Unpublished Dissertation. UCD. Dublin 2002.

B. Fanning, A. Veale, D. O'Connor, *Beyond the Pale: Asylum-seeking children and Social Exclusion in Ireland,* Irish Refugee Council, Dublin 2001.

Fitzpatrick Associates, *Evaluation of Research and Training Project for Intercultural Awareness.* Wheatfield Prison, Dublin 2003.

First Annual Report of the Inspector of Prisons and Places of Detention, 2002

HM Inspectorate of Prisons. *Parallel worlds –A thematic review of race relations in prisons,* 2005

Irish Commission for Prisoners Overseas, *Separated Families: Reviewing the needs of Families of Irish Prisoners Overseas.* The Council for Research and Development, IBC, 2005.

M. Kelly, *Immigration – Related Detention in Ireland.* A research report for the Irish Refugee Council, Irish penal Reform Trust and Immigrant Council of Ireland. Human Rights Consultants (HRC) Dublin 2005.

Mountjoy Prison Visiting Committee, *Annual Report,* 2004.

S. Mullally, *Manifestly Unjust: A Report on the Fairness and Sustainability of Accelerated Procedures for Asylum Determinations,* Irish Refugee Council, 2000.

NESF Report No 22, *Re-Integration of Prisoners*, 2002 .

P. O'Mahoney, *Mountjoy Prisoners: A Sociological and Criminological Profile,*' Dublin 1997, Stationary office.

I. O Donnell, 2004, 'Imprisonment and Penal Policy in Ireland', The Howard Submission by Irish Commission for Prisoners Overseas (ICPO) to Joint Committee on Foreign Affairs Sub-Committee on Human Rights 16 June 2005.

Department of Justice, Equality and Law Reform, *Planning for Diversity - The National Action Plan Against Racism,* 2005.

National Training and Development Institute (NDTI) and Fitzpatrick Associates, *Research and Training Project on Multicultural Awareness,* Dublin 2003.

Second Annual Report of the Inspector of Prisons and Places of Detention, 2004.

M. Tonry, (Ed), 'Ethnicity, Crime and Immigration: Comparative and cross national perspectives'. *Crime and Justice, a Review of Research,* Vol.21. University of Chicago Press, Chicago 1997 p.viii.

E. Quinn, G. Hughes, Policy Analysis Report on Asylum and Migration: Ireland 2003 to Mid-2004. European Migration Network. ESRI 2005.

Chapter 14 Italy

14.1 Literature

Amnesty International report on detention of minors in Italy, published by Association Antogone, http://www.associazioneantigone.it/cpta/cpt.htm

[1] P. Balbo, IL detenuto straniero alla luce delle recenti modifiche legislative, in Diritto & Diritti - Rivista giuridica elettronica, pubblicata su Internet all'indirizzo http://www.diritto.it , ISSN 1127-8579, 30 Giugno 2006, http://www.diritto.it/art.php?file=/archivio/21822.html

P.Balbo, Sesso e carcere, in 'Sessualità Diritto e Processo', (a c. di) G. Gulotta e S. Pezzati (2002) Giuffrè ed., Milano, p. 86 sgg.

P. Balbo (2004), Extracomunitari. Profili penali e giurisprudenza interna ed internazionale, Giappichelli ed., Torino.

P. Balbo (2005), Diritto penitenziario internazionale comparato, Laurus Robuffo, Roma.

P. Balbo, Il diritto alla difesa, il ricorso e le modalità di comunicazione dei provvedimenti che riguardano i cittadini extracomunitari, in Diritto & Diritti - Rivista giuridica elettronica, pubblicata su Internet all'indirizzo http://www.diritto.it , ISSN 1127-8579, Marzo 2003,:
http://www.diritto.it/articoli/proc_penale/proc_penale.html 27 marzo 2003) e www.diritto.it/articoli/proc_penale/Balbo.html [Altri risultati su www.diritto.it]

P. Balbo, La giurisprudenza in itinere derivante dall'applicazione della normativa sugli stranieri (D.Lgs. 286/1998)", in Diritto & Diritti - Rivista giuridica elettronica, pubblicata su Internet all'indirizzo http://www.diritto.it , ISSN 1127-8579, Aprile 2003, http://www.diritto.it/articoli/diritto_costituzionale/diritto_costituzionale.html e in http://www.cestim.it/index02lex.html.

P. Bablo, Responses to the Green Paper (16.06.2003, Bruxelles. Procedural safeguards on suspects and defendants rights in criminal proceedings)
eu-
ropa.eu.int/comm/justice_home/fsj/criminal/procedural/wai/fsj_criminal_responses_e
n.htm [Altri risultati su europa.eu.int].

P. Balbo, Elementi costitutivi dell'isolamento giudiziario e criteri interpretativi" pubblicata su: www.dirittoitalia.it - Rivista giuridica interdisciplinare, Registrata presso il Tribunale di Santa Maria C. V. il 16 giugno 2000, al numero 535, URL: http://www.dirittoitalia.it, ISSN: 1590-9654, Anno III,- Numero 4 - 4 aprile 2002.

P. Balbo, L'espulsione a titolo di sanzione sostitutiva o alternativa alla detenzione ovvero come modalità di sospensione della pena (cs. Indultino) nei confronti dello straniero condannato" in Gli stranieri, Rassegna di studi, giurisprudenza e legislazione, anno X, gen-feb., 2003 e in
stranieriinitalia.com/briguglio/immigrazione-e-asilo/2003/aprile/somm-riv-gli-stranieri-1-03.pdf [Altri risultati su stranieriinitalia.com]

P. Balbo, "Cittadino, cittadino europeo e cittadino extracomunitario", in Gli stranieri, Rassegna di studi, giurisprudenza e legislazione, anno X, marzo-aprile 2003
P. BALBO, "Il diritto alla difesa, il ricorso e le modalità di comunicazione dei provvedimenti che riguardano i cittadini extracomunitari", in Diritto & Diritti - Rivista giuridica elettronica, pubblicata su Internet all'indirizzo http://www.diritto.it , ISSN 1127-8579, Marzo 2003, : http://www.diritto.it/articoli/proc_penale/proc_penale.html 27 marzo 2003) e www.diritto.it/articoli/proc_penale/Balbo.html [Altri risultati su www.diritto.it]

P. Balbo (2005), Diritto penitenziario internazionale comparato. Esecuzione penale in carcere e in area esterna, Laurus Robuffo, Roma
Direttiva generale del Ministro dell'interno 30 agosto 2000 in materia di Centri di Permanenza temporanea ed Assistenza ai sensi dell'art. 22, comma 1, DPR 31 agosto 1999, n. 394, in Gli stranieri, Rassegna di studi, giurisprudenza e legislazione, n. 3, settembre-dicembre 2000, p. 360.
O. DI MAURO, I centri di permanenza temporanea per immigrati. Aspetti legali e funzionali, in www.dexl.tsd.unifi.it/l'altrodiritto/migranti.

Chapter 15 Latvia

15.1 Literature

Latvian Centre for Human Rights and Ethnic Studies (LCHRES), Cilvēktiesības Latvijā 2004. gadā (Human Rights in Latvia in 2004), Riga 2005 (on internet: www.humanrights.org.lv)

European Community initiative EQUAL project: Jauni risinājumi bijušo ieslodzīto nodarbinātības veicināšanai (New Solutions for Facilitation of Employment of Ex-prisoners research paper), "Accessibility of education, employment and social rehabilitation services to the prisoners and ex-prisoners", 2005 (on internet in Latvian: www.probacija.lv).

Ilvija Puce, Report on the Situation of Fundamental Rights in Latvia in 2005, http://cridho.cpdr.ucl.ac.be/DownloadRep/rapports2005/NationalReport/CFRLatvia 2005pdf

European Community initiative EQUAL project: Soli pa solim (Step by Step), research paper, "Latvijas iedzīvotāju, valts amatpersonu un NVO attieksme prêt patvēruma meklētājiem ("Attitude of inhabitants, state authorities and NGO`s towards asylum seekers"), 2005.

CPT, Report to the Latvian Government on the visit to Latvia carried out by the European Committee for the Prevention of Torture and Inhuman or Degrating Treatment or Punishment (CPT) from 25 September to 4 October 2002.

Latvian Centre for Human Rights and Ethnic Studies, Rokasgrāmata slēgto iestāžu monitoringa veicējiem (Handbook for Monitoring Closed Institutions), Riga 2003

Ieslodzījuma vietu pārvaldes 2005.gada publiskais pārskats/2005 (Prison Administration Annual Report), (available in Latvian on the internet www.ievp.gov.lv).

Latvijas Valsts Policijas pārskats par noziedzības stāvokli valstī un policijas darbību 2004.gadā (State Police Report on Cime and Oeration of Police in 2004), Rīga 2005 (on the internet in Latvian www.vp.gov.lv).

Latvian Police academy, Nosacīta pirmstermiņa atbrīvošana no kriminālsoda (Conditional release from criminal sentence), Rīga 2004. (available in Latvian on the internet www.probacija.lv).

Andrejs Judins, Nosacīta notiesāšana kā cietumsoda alternatīva (Conditional Sentence as Alternative to Imprisonment), Providus: Riga 2003.

Chapter 16 Lithuania

16.1 Literature

Švedas, G. (2003), Imprisonment: Penal Policy, Penal Legal and Executive Aspects, Vilnius.

Švedas, G. (2003), Law of the Execution of Penalties, Vilnius.

Blaževičius, J., Dermontas, J. , Stalioraitis, P. , Usik, D. (2004), Penitentiary (Execution of Penalties) Law, Vilnius.

Švedas, G. (2002), International documents 2/Treaties on the Legal Cooperation of the Republic of Lithuania, Vilnius.

PHARE Twinning Project of Lithuania and Austria LI2002/IB/JH-01 "The System of Migration and Asylum Management"/Part I. "Migration", Vilnius, 2003.

Prison Department (2006), Prison Department Annual Report "Basic Data of the 2005 Activities of the Prison Department and Establishments and State Enterprises under Its Subordination", Ministry of Justice of the Republic of Lithuania, Vilnius.

Prison Department (2004), Prison Department Annual Report "Basic Data of the 2003 Activities of the Prison Department and Establishments and State Enterprises under Its Subordination" , Ministry of Justice of the Republic of Lithuania, Vilnius..

Prison Department (1998 – 2005), Prison Department Annual Report on the Number of Convicts, Composition (by Offence Committed, Age, Penalty Term, etc.) and Their Change, Ministry of Justice of the Republic of Lithuania, Vilnius.

Prison Department (1999 – 2005), Prison Department Annual Report of the Activity of the Social Rehabilitation Services", the Ministry of Justice of the Republic of Lithuania, Vilnius.

Prison Department (1999 – 2005), Prison Department Annual Report Lithuania "Discipline of Persons in the Offices and Disciplinary Sanctions Imposed on Them", Ministry of Justice of the Republic of Lithuania, Vilnius.

16.3 Legislation

Constitution of the Republic of Lithuania. Official Gazette – 1992, No.33-1014.

Law on the Approval and Enforcement of the Criminal Code of the Republic of Lithuania. Criminal Code. Official Gazette - 2000 No. 89-2741.

Law on the Approval, Enforcement and Implementation of the Code of Criminal Procedure of the Republic of Lithuania. Code of Criminal Procedure. Official Gazette. – 2002 No. 37-1341.
Law on the Approval of the Code of Execution of Penalties of the Republic of Lithuania. Code of Execution of Penalties. Official Gazette - 2002 No. 73-3084.

The Code of Administrative Violations of the Republic of Lithuania, adopted by the Supreme Council of the Lithuanian Soviet Socialist Republic on 13 December 1984.

Law on the Legal Status of Aliens in Lithuania of the Republic of Lithuania. Official Gazette. – 2004 No. 73-2539.

Law on Amendment of the Law on State-Guaranteed Legal Aid of the Republic of Lithuania.
Official Gazette - 2004 No.73-2539

Law on Remand Detention of the Republic of Lithuania. Official Gazette - 1996 No.12-313.

Law on the Approval of the Statute of Service at the Prison Department under the Ministry of Justice of the Republic of Lithuania. Official Gazette - 2000, No. 39-1088

Resolution of the Government of the Republic of Lithuania "On the Approval of the Procedure for Execution of the Decisions Concerning Obligation of the Foreigners to Depart or Their Extradition from the Republic of Lithuania". Official Gazette – 2000 No. 26-693.

Resolution of the Government of the Republic of Lithuania "On the Provision of the Social Support to the Persons, who Returned from the Custodial, Remand Detention Places, Social and Psychological Rehabilitation Establishments, and Employment of Those Persons". Official Gazette. – 1996 No. 119-2796.

Order of the Minister of Justice of the Republic of Lithuania "On the Approval of the Internal Regulations of the Correctional Institutions". Official Gazette – 2003 No. 76-3498.

Order of the Minister of Justice of the Republic of Lithuania "On the Payment of Travel Expenses of Persons Released from the correctional Institutions or the Remand Custody Facilities, Supply with Food, Clothes and Footwear, as well as the Procedure and Conditions for Granting of the Single Non-Repayable Allowance". Official Gazette – 2003 No. 40-1832.
Order of the Director of the Prison Department under the Ministry of Justice of the Republic of Lithuania "On the Model Adaptation Programme of the New coming Convicts in the Correction Institution and the Approval of the Model Programme of the Integration into Society of the Convicts". Official Gazette – 2004 No.87-3192.

Order "On the Approval of the Instruction on the Preparation Work for Release of Prisoners from Prison Establishments" by the Director of the Prison Department under the Ministry of Justice of the Republic of Lithuania. Official Gazette – 2006 No. 36-1302.

Order of the Director of the Prison Department under the Ministry of Justice of the Republic of Lithuania. "On the Approval of the Internal Regulations of the Prison Department under the Ministry of Justice of the Republic of Lithuania". Official Gazette – 2006 No. 14-513.

Order of the Director of the Prison Department under the Ministry of Justice of the Republic of Lithuania. "On the Approval of the Rules for Granting and Payment of Monetary Payments to the Convicts Serving the Penalties of Arrest, Fixed-Term Deprivation of Liberty and Life Imprisonment". Official Gazette – 2005 No.151-5586.

Order of the Director of the Prison Department under the Ministry of Justice of the Republic of Lithuania. "On the Approval of the Instructions for the Protection and Supervision of Detention Facilities". Official Gazette – 2005 No.89-3361.

Order of the Director of the Prison Department under the Ministry of Justice of the Republic of Lithuania. "On the Approval of the Social Rehabilitation Programmes". Official Gazette – 2004 No.7-167.

Order of the Director of the Prison Department under the Ministry of Justice of the Republic of Lithuania. "On the Amendment of Order No. 112 of 27 December 2001 "On the Approval of the Legal and Social Education Programmes for Persons that are Planned to be Released from the Detention Facilities" of the Director of the Prison Department under the Ministry of Justice of the Republic of Lithuania". Official Gazette – 2003 No.92-4182.

16.3 Websites

International Centre for Prison Studies , World Prison Brief, University of London.
http://www.kcl.ac.uk/depsta/rel/icps/worldbrief/europe.html.

European Committee on Crime Problems (2003), European Sourcebook of Crime and Criminal Justice Statistics.
http://www.wodc.nl/onderzoeken/onderzoek_212.asp?loc=/onderwerp.

Seimas Internet database of the legal acts of the Republic of Lithuania at the address
.http://www3.lrs.lt/dokpaieska/forma_e.htm

Internet webpage of the Ministry of Justice at the address
.http://www.tm.lt/default.aspx?lang=3

Internet webpage of the Prison Department under the Ministry of Justice of the Republic of Lithuania at the address .
http://www.kalejimudepartamentas.lt/

Statistical information about crime rate in Lithuania at the address.
www.nplc.lt

Internet webpage of the Migration Department at the address
.http://www.migracija.lt/MDEN/defaulte.htm

Internet webpage of the State Border Guard Service at the address
.http://www.pasienis.lt/english/index.html

Information about migration and asylum in Lithuania at the address
.http://www.asylum-online.lt

Chapter 17 Luxembourg

17.1 Literature

Akpinar, Mine Die Entkategorisierung des Begriffs der Ausländerkriminalität, in: Zeitschrift für Jugendkriminalrecht und Jugendhilfe 2003, p. 258 - 266

Albrecht, Peter-Alexis, Kriminologie – Eine Grundlegung zum Strafrecht, 3rd edition, 2005.

Ludwig-Mayerhofer, Das Strafrecht und seine administrative Rationalisierung. Wolfgang Kritik der informalen Justiz, 2001.

Mansel, Jürgen /Migration und das kriminalpolitische Handeln staatlicher Albrecht, Günther Strafverfolgungsorgane – Ausländer als polizeiliche Tatverdächtige und gerichtliche Abgeurteilte, in: Kölner Zeitschrift für Soziologie 2003, p. 679 – 715

Sessar, Klaus,   Rechtliche und soziale Prozesse einer Definition der Tötungskriminalität, 1981.

Zoummeroff, Philippe /La Prison ça n`arrive pas qu`aux autres, 2006. Guibert, Nathalie

Chapter 18 Malta

18.1 Literature

Agreement between the Government of Malta and the Great Socialist People's Libyan Arab Jamahariya on the Transfer of Sentenced Persons (1995)

Agreement between the Government of Malta and the Government of the Arab Republic of Egypt on the Transfer of Sentenced Persons (2001)

Cachia Tonio, The Treatment of Prisoners in Malta. The Law and Practice, University of Malta (unpublished) LL.D 2005.

Census of Population & Housing 2005, Preliminary Report 26 April 2006

CPT Malta Reports Online - http://www.cpt.coe.int/en/states/mlt.htm 1990 Visit (01 July 1990)

Draft Prison Legislation, June 1993

Follow Up Response of the Maltese Government (CPT/Inf 2003-34) 17 Jul 2003 2001 Visit (13-18 May 2001)

Follow Up Response of the Maltese Government (CPT/Inf 1997-8) – 10 Jul 1997 1995 Visit (16-21 July 1995)

Follow Up Report to Malta CommDH(2006)14, 29 Mar 2006

Interim Reply by the Maltese Government (CPT/Inf 1996-26) – 26 Aug 1996 1995 Visit (16-21 July 1995)

Interim Reply by the Maltese Government (CPT/Inf (2002-17) – 27 Aug 2002 2001 Visit (13-18 May 2001)

Karim Barboush vs Commissioner of Police, Court of Magistrates 4 Nov 2004.

Maltese Cases Online - http://mjha.gov.mt/justice/courtservices.html

Mifsud Stefania, Detention of Asylum Seekers in Malta, University of Malta (unpublished) LL.D 2005.

Police (Inspector Angelo Caruana) v. Anthony Zammit, John Woods u Ahmed Esawi Mohamed Fakri, Constitutional Court 10 Jan 2005.

Report on Corradino Prison, June 1993

Report on Prison Legislation, June 1993

Report by the Civil Liberties, Justice & Home Affairs Committee (LIBE)
Committee Delegation on its visit to the administrative detention centres in Malta
30 March 2006, Adopted 27 Apr 2006.

Report to the Maltese Government (CPT/Inf (2002-16) – 27 Aug 2002 2001 Visit (13-18 May 2001)

Report of the Maltese Goverment (CPT/Inf (2005-15) - 25 Aug 2005. 2003 Visit (18-22 Jan 2004)

Report to the Maltese Government (CPT/Inf 1996-25) – 26 Aug 1996

Report to the Maltese Government (CPT/Inf 1992-5) – 01 Sep 1990 1990 Visit (01 July 1990)

Report on the visit to Malta CommDH(2004)4, 12 Feb 2004

18.2 Legislation

Constitution of Malta

Criminal Code, Chapter 9 of the Laws of Malta

Dangerous Drugs Ordinance, Chapter 101 of the Laws of Malta

European Convention Act, Chapter 319 of the Laws of Malta

Immigration Act, Chapter 217 of the Laws of Malta

Medical and Kindred Professions Ordinance, Chapter 31 of the Laws of Malta

Ombudsman Act 1995, Chapter 385 of the Laws of Malta

Prisons Act, Chapter 260 of the Laws of Malta
- Designation of Places As Prisons Order, S.L. 260.02
- Prisons Regulations, S.L. 260.03

Probation Act 2003, Chapter 446 of the Laws of Malta

Punishments (Interpretation) Ordinance, Chapter 23 of the Laws of Malta

Maltese Legislation Online (English) - *http://www2.justice.gov.mt/lom/home.asp*
- Convention on the Transfer of Sentenced Persons (1983)
- European Convention for the Prevention of Torture and Inhuman or Degrading Treatment of Punishment (CPT) (1987)
- European Convention for the Protection of Human Rights and Fundamental Freedoms (ECHR) (1950)

Mr. Justice Maurice Caruana Curran

Paper Laid 1212 (Leg. VII, Sitting 254) 21April 1994

18.3 Websites

Ministry for Justice & Home Affairs – *www.mjha.gov.mt*

Mid-Dlam Ghad-Dawl (MDD) – Daritama – *www.mddmalta.org*

Jesuit Refugee Service Malta – *www.jrsmalta.org* - *www.jrseurope.org/countries/malta.htm*

http://www.coe.int/T/Commissioner

http://www.europarl.eu.int/meetdocs/2004_2009/documents/pv/609/609597/609597 en.pdf

Chapter 19 Netherlands

Algemene Rekenkamer (2005), *Gedetineerdenbegeleiding buitenland*. SDU Uitgevers, Den Haag

Belangenoverleg Niet-Justitiegebonden Organisaties (BONJO) (2001). *Help ik kom vrij. Informatie en tips voor (ex-)gedetineerden*. BONJO

Bureau Buitenland (2005 – 2006). *Morse*. Reclassering Nederland, Utrecht

Gevangenzorg Nederland (2005). *Informatie Bulletin. Voor gevangenen en hun familie*.

Gevangenzorg Nederland, Zoetermeer

Glastra, Folke, Martha Meerman, Sjiera de Vries (1999). *Allochtonen en detentie*. WODC, Den Haag

Hans van Kooten (2005), *Ogen en Oren, 30 jaar Bureau Buitenland & Buitenlandse Betrekkingen*. Reclassering Nederland, Utrecht

Inspectie voor de sanctietoepassing, detentieboten Zuid-Holland, lokatie Merwehaven, s'-Gravenhage, mei 2006.

Jonge, Gerard de, Rino Verpalen, Hettie Cremers (1999). *Bajesboek. Handboek voor gedetineerden en ter beschikking gestelden*. Papieren Tijger, Breda.

Kalmthout, A.M. van. et. al, . A.M. van Kalmthout et. al., Terugkeermogelijkheden van vreemdelingen in vreemdelingenbewaring, Nijmegen 2004;. Inspectie voor de sanctietoepassing, detentieboten Zuid-Holland, lokatie Merwehaven, s'-Gravenhage, mei 2006; Raad voor strafrechtstoepassing en jeugdbescherming, detentiecentra Rotterdam, locatie Merwehaven, detentieboten Reno en Stockholm (h.v.b.), 's-Gravenhage juli 2005.

Ministerie van Buitenlandse Zaken (2005). *Gearresteerd in … Frankrijk*, Den Haag

Ministerie van Buitenlandse Zaken (2001). *Gedetineerdenbeleid in buitenlands perspectief*. DCZ/CM, Den Haag

Ministerie van Justitie (2006). *Jaarplan 2005 – Fundament voor de nieuwe inrichting*, Dienst Justitiële Inrichtingen, Den Haag

Ministerie van Justitie (2006). *Dienst Justitiële Inrichtingen*. Dienst Justitiële Inrichtingen, Den Haag

Ministerie van Justitie (2004). *Gedetineerd in Nederland 2004*. Dienst Justitiële Inrichtingen, Den Haag

Ministerie van Justitie (2004). *Temporary Special Facilities Directorate (TDBV)*, Dienst Justitiële Inrichtingen, Den Haag

Ministerie van Justitie (2002). *DJI The National Agency of Correctional Institutions. Prisons, Detention Centres, Correctional Institutions for Juvenile Offenders, and Custodial Clinics and Forensic Psychiatric Hospitals in the Netherlands*. Dienst Justitiële Inrichtingen, Den Haag

Muller, E.R. P.C. Vegter (2005). *Detentie. Gevangen in Nederland*. Kluwer, Alphen aan den Rijn

Post, Marieke (2005). *Detentie en culturele diversiteit*. Boom Juridische Uitgevers, Den Haag

Proces. Tijdschrift voor Strafrechtspleging(2005) nr 6. Boom Juridische Uitgevers, Den Haag

Reclassering Nederland (2006*) Vrijwilliger voor de Nederlandse Reclassering*. Bureau Buitenland & Buitenlandse Betrekkingen (B&BB), Utrecht

Reclassering Nederland (2005*). Vrijwilligersbeleid. Bureau Buitenland & Buitenlandse Betrekkingen*. Reclassering Nederland, Utrecht

Tak, P.J.J. (2003). *The Dutch criminal justice system; organization and operation*. WODC, Den Haag

Tweede Kamer der Staten-Generaal (1997). *Nederlanders in buitenlandse gevangenissen en buitenlanders in Nederlandse gevangenissen. Verslag van een schriftelijk overleg*. SDU Uitgevers, Den Haag

Verhagen, Jos J.L.M (2005). *Waar vijheid ophoudt en weer kan beginnen. 1995-2005 Tien Jaar Dienst Justitiële Inrichtingen*. Ministerie van Justitie, Den Haag

19.3 Websites

Penitentiare Beginselenwet (1999) / Dutch Penitentiary Principles Act
Penitentiare Maatregel (1999) / Penitentiary Measure /Huisregels / Dutch House Rules
http://www.legislationline.org/?tid=160&jid=37&ijid=0&less=true

Dienst Justitiële Inrichtingen (DJI)
www.dji.nl

Ministerie van Justitie / Ministry of Justice:
www.justitie.nl

Ministerie van Buitenlandse Zaken / Ministry of Foreign Affairs
www.minbuza.nl

Wetenschappelijk Onderzoek- en Documentatie Centrum (WODC)
www.wodc.nl

Chapter 20 Poland

20.1 Literature

T. Bulenda, and M. Dabrowiecki, 'Cudzoziemcy w polskich aresztach sledczych i zakladach karnych' (Foreigners in Polish prisons), in: Biuletyn RPO. Materialy, Bulletin of the Commissioner for the Civil Rights Protection, 1993 nr 18, pp. 21-62.

T. Bulenda, and R. Musidlowski, Postepowanie z wiezniami w latach 1989-2002 (Treatment of Prisoners in the years 1989-2002), Instytut Spraw Publicznych, Warsaw 2003.

Central Administration of the Prison Service 2004, Podstawowe problemy wieziennictwa (Basic Problems of the Prison System), available online: htpp://www.czsw.gov.pl.

Central Administration of the Prison Service 2005, Informacja statystyczna za rok 2005 (Statistical data for the year 2005), available online: http://www.czsw.gov.pl.

Central Administration of the Prison Service 2006, Informacja o wykonywaniu kary pozbawienia wolnosci i tymczasowego aresztowania za pazdziernik 2006 (Information on the execution of imprisonment and detention on remand in October 2006), available online: http://www.czsw.gov.pl

Commissioner for Civil Rights Protection, 'Ochrona praw osob pozbawionych wolnosci' (Protection of Rights of Persons Deprived of Liberty), in: Biuletyn RPO. Materialy (Bulletin of the Commissioner for Civil Rights Protection), 2001 nr 43, pp. 257-271.

Commissioner for Civil Rights Protection, 'Wykonywanie kar i srodkow karnych' (Execution of Penalties and Penal Measures), in: Biuletyn RPO Materialy (Bulletin of the Commissioner for the Civil Rights Protection), 2004 nr 48, p. 269-289.

Council of Europe, Report to the Polish Government on the visit to Poland carried out by the European Committee for the Prevention of Torture and Inhuman or Degrading Treatment or Punishment from 30 June to 12 July 1996, Council of Europe, Strasbourg 1998.

Council of Europe (2002), Report to the Polish Government on the visit to Poland carried out by the European Committee for the Prevention of Torture and Inhuman or De grading Treatment or Punishment from 8 to 19 May 2000, Council of Europe, Strasbourg.

Council of Europe, Report to the Polish Government on the visit to Poland carried out by the European Committee for the Prevention of Torture and Inhuman or Degrading Treatment or Punishment from 4 to 15 October 2004, Council of Europe, Strasbourg 2006.

European Commission, Eurostat Yearbook 2005, available online: htpp://epp.eurostat.cec.eu.int.

Helsinki Foundation of Human Rights, Prawa cudzoziemcom umieszczonych w aresztach w celu wydalenia i strzezonym osrodku. Raport (Rights of Foreigners Placed in Arrests for the Purpose of Expulsion and the Guarded Centre), Helsinki Foundation of Human Rights, Warsaw 2004.

B. Janiszewski, 'Orzekanie kar i innych srodkow wobec cudzoziemcow' (Imposing Penalties and Other Measures on Foreigners), in: Szwarc, A. (ed.), Przestepczosc przygraniczna. Postepowanie karne przeciwko cudzoziemcom w Polsce (Offences Close to Borders. Criminal Proceedings against Foreigners in Poland), Wydawnictwo Poznanskie, Poznan 2000, p. 172-187.

Main Statistical Office of the Republic of Poland 2005, Maly Rocznik Statystyczny Polski 2005 (Small Statistical Yearbook of Poland of 2005), available online: http://www.stat.gov.pl.

J. Malec, 'Cudzoziemcy w polskich jednostkach penitencjarnych' (Foreigners in Polish Penitentiary Institutions), in: Biuletyn RPO. Materialy (Bulletin of the Commissioner for Civil Rights Protection), 1995 nr 28, pp. 299-305.

Ministry of Foreign Affairs 2005, Informacja o dzialalnosci polskiej sluzby konsularnej w 2004 r. (Information on the Polish Consular Service in 2004), http://www.msz.gov.pl.

Office for Repatriation and Aliens. Bureau for Informatics, Documentation & Statistics (2005), Quantitative data of procedures concerning foreigners in the years 2003-2005, available online: http://www.uric.gov.pl.

I. Rzeplinska, Przestepczosc cudzoziemcow w Polsce (Offences by Foreigners in Poland), Instytut Nauk Prawnych Polskiej Akademii Nauk, Warsaw 2000, p. 28-29.

I. Rzeplinska, 'Offences by Foreigners', in: Siemaszko, A. (ed.), Crime and Law Enforcement in Poland on the threshold of the 21st Century, Oficyna Naukowa, Warsaw 2000, pp. 150-155.

I. Rzeplinska, 'Wykonywanie kar i srodkow karnych wobec cudzoziemcow w Polsce' (Executing of Penalties and Penal Measures Imposed on Foreigners in Poland), in: Szwarc, A. (ed.), Przestepczosc przygraniczna. Postepowanie karne przeciwko cudzoziemcom w

Polsce (Offences Close to Borders. Criminal Proceedings against Foreigners in Poland), Wydawnictwo Poznanskie, Poznan 2000, pp. 188- 195.

A. Siemaszko, B. Gruszczynska, and M. Marczewski, 'Facts & Figures', in: Siemaszko, A. (ed.), Crime and Law Enforcement in Poland on the threshold of the 21st Century, Oficyna Naukowa, Warsaw 2000, p. 29-83.

B. Stando-Kawecka, B., 'Poland', in: van Zyl Smit, D. and Dünkel, F. (eds.), Imprisonment Today and Tomorrow. Second Edition, Kluwer Law International, The Hague/London/Boston 2001, p. 508-550.

B. Stando-Kawecka, B. 'Community Sanctions in Polish Penal Law', in: H.J. Albrecht, and A. van Kalmthout, (eds), Community Sanctions and Measures in Europe and North America, Max-Planck-Institut für Ausländisches und Internationales Strafrecht, Freiburg/ Breisgau 2002, pp. 421-451.

T. Szymanowski, Polityka karna i penitencjarna w Polsce w okresie przemian prawa karnego (The Criminal and Penitentiary Policy in Poland in the Period of Transformation of the Criminal Law), Wydawnictwa Uniwersytetu Warszawskiego, Warsaw 2004.

Chapter 21 Portugal

21.1 Literature

Albuquerque, P. P. (2006). *Direito prisional português e europeu.* Coimbra: Coimbra Editora

Arroteia, J. (1983). *A emigração portuguesa.* Lisboa: Instituto de Cultura e Língua Portuguesa.

Caiado, N. (2004). *Vigilância electrónica, programa experimental 2002-2003, relatório de avaliação.* (Policopiado, 33 págs.). Lisboa: Instituto de Reinserção Social, Estrutura de Missão para o Sistema de Monitorização Electrónica de Arguidos.

Costa, J. M. Barra (1996). *Exílio e asilo (a questão portuguesa 1974-1996).* Lisboa: CEMRI – Universidade Aberta.

Ferreira, V. Peña (1999). Sobrepopulação prisional e sobrelotação em Portugal. *Temas Penitenciários, II Série, 3-4,* 7-38.

Gonçalves, R. A. (2005). Stress e vitimação em meio prisional – O crime e o castigo. In A. Marques Pinto & A. L. Silva (Coords)., *Stress e bem estar* (pp. 135-149). Lisboa: Climepsi.

Moreira, J. J. Semedo (1998). Ciganos na prisão: Um universo diferente? *Temas Penitenciários, II Série, 2,* 5-18.

Moreira, J. J. Semedo (2000). Estatísticas Prisionais – 1999. *Temas Penitenciários, II Série, 5*, 71-80.

Moreira, J. J. Semedo (2001). Estatísticas Prisionais – 2000. *Temas Penitenciários, II Série, 6-7, 85-104.*

Moreira, J. J. Semedo (2002). Estatísticas prisionais – 2001. *Temas Penitenciários, II Série, 8-9, 63-92.*

Moreira, J. J. Semedo (2005). Estatísticas Prisionais. *Temas Penitenciários, III Série, 1-2, 89-122.*

Moreira, J. J. Semedo (2004). *Estatísticas prisionais 2003. Apresentação e análise* (policopiado, 52 págs.). Lisboa: Direcção Geral dos Serviços Prisionais.

Provedoria de Justiça (2003). *Relatório sobre o sistema prisional.* Lisboa: Provedoria de Justiça - Serviços de Documentação.

S.PACE - Statistique sur les populations carcérales dans les états membres du Conseil de l'Europe (Enquête 1997-1998) (2000). *Bulletin d'Information Pénologique, 22*, 20-119.

S.PACE - Statistique sur les populations carcérales dans les états membres du Conseil de l'Europe (Enquête 1999-2001) (2002). *Bulletin d'Information Pénologique, 23 & 24*, 44-158.

Tournier, P. V. (2002). SPACE I : Enquête 2000. *Bulletin d'Information Pénologique, 23/24*, 70-134.

21.2 Websites

www.cpt.coe.int

http://www.sef.pt This is the site of the Service of Foreigners and Frontiers (Serviço de strangeiros e Fronteiras) that provides information and help for foreigners that wish to live in Portugal and also presents all the legislation that regulates this kind of affairs.

www.detention-in

www.min-nestrangeiros.pt This is the site of the Ministry of Foreign Affairs where information can be obtained about relationships between Portugal and other countries and where reference is made to bi-lateral agreements.

www.secomunidades.pt In this site information can be obtained about the situation of Portuguese people living outside Portugal.

http://www.dgsp.mj.pt This is the site of General Direction of Prison Services where information can be found about general trends in criminality, national prisoners and foreign prisoners http://www.provedor-jus.pt This is the site of the Ombusdman Services.

Chapter 22 Slovakia

No information available.

Chapter 23 Slovenia

23.1 Literature

The Illegal residents Act, 1999.

Ministry of Justice, National Prison Administration (2005), Ministry of Justice, National Prison Administration Annual Report 2005. Ljubljana 2006.

Brinc, F. (2005), 'Crime Statistics and Crime Policy in Slovenia' (Gibanje kriminalitete in kaznovalna politika v Sloveniji v zadnjem desetletju), in: Kanduč Z. (ed), Criminality, Social Control and Post-Modernity, Institute of Criminology, University of Ljubljana, Ljubljana, pp.39-59.

Parlamentary Paper No. 36/2002; EU Comission for Prevention of Torture.

The Penal Code of the Republic of Slovenia (1995)

The Penal Sanctions Enforcement Act (2000)

Chapter 24 Spain

24.1 Literature

Adam Muñoz, M.D. (1991), 'El internamiento preventivo del extranjero durante la tramitación del expediente de expulsión", *La Ley*, 23 December.

Almeida Herrero, C. & Lucena García, M. (2002), *Situación de los presos extranjeros en el Centro Penitenciario de Topas (Salamanca)*,

http://caritas.caritasalamanca.org/uploads/media/cd0053_Indice_tematico_Situacion_juridico-penitenciaria_Topas_2002.pdf

Cancio Meliá, M. & Maraver Gómez (2005), in Bacigalupo, S. & Cancio Meliá, M (coord.), *Derecho penal y política transnacional*, Barcelona, pp.343-415.

Conseil de l'Europe (2005), '*SPACE I. Enquête 2004* (by M.F.Aebi), Strasbourg.

De la Cuesta, J.L. (1996), 'Le nouveau Code pénal espagnol de 1995', *Revue Internationale de Droit Pénal*, 67, 3-4, pp.715-724.

De la Cuesta, J.L. (2002), 'Les droits des prisonniers en Espagne', in Céré, J.P. (Dir.), *Panorama européen de la prison*, Paris, pp.185-214.

De la Cuesta Arzamendi, J.L. (2005), 'Retos principales del sistema penitenciario hoy', in *Jornadas en Homenaje al XXV Aniversario de la Ley Orgánica General Penitenciaria*, Madrid, pp.119-137.

De la Cuesta, J.L. & Blanco, I. (2001), 'Spain', in A.Van Zyl Smit & F.Dünkel (eds.), *Imprisonment Today and Tomorrow. International Perspectives on Prisoners' Rights and Prison Conditions*, 2nd ed, The Hage, pp. 609-633.

Defensor del Pueblo (2005), *Informe anual 2004*, Madrid.

Defensor del Pueblo (2005), *Informe sobre asistencia jurídica*, Madrid.

Encinar del Pozo, M.A. (2005), 'Expulsión de extranjeros: el artículo 89.1 del Código penal. Un ejemplo de infortunio del legislador', *Derecho.com*, March.
http://www.derecho.com/boletin/articulos/articulo0278.htm

García España, E, Pérez Jiménez, F. (2004), *Evolución de la delincuencia en España y Andalucía: Análisis e interpretación de las estadísticas oficiales*, Málaga.

García España, E. (2002), 'Extranjería, delincuencia y legislación penitenciaria', in *Derecho migratorio y extranjería*, Valencia, pp. 43-64.

García España, E. & Rodríguez Candela, J.L. "Extranjeros en prisión",
http://www.icamalaga.es/funcio/extran/doctrina/doc1.pdf

García España, E. (2001), *Inmigración y delincuencia en España: análisis criminológico*, Valencia.

García España, E. (2004), 'Datos oficiales de delincuencia en España', *Revista de Derecho Penal y Criminología*, 13.

García García, J. (2006), 'Extranjeros en prisión: aspectos normativos y de intervención penitenciaria',
http://penitenciari.meetingcongress.com/ponencies/Julian_Garcia_Garcia.pdf.

Giménez-Salinas i Colomer, E. (1994), 'Los extranjeros en prisión', *Eguzkilore*, 7, extra, pp.133-145.
Grupo de Estudios de Política Criminal (1998), *Alternativas al tratamiento jurídico de la discriminación y de la extranjería*, Valencia.

Hernando Galán, M.B. (1997), *Los extranjeros en el Derecho penitenciario español*, Madrid.

Justidata 33, November 2002.

La razón, 31 October 2004.

Maqueda Abreu, M.L. (2001), '¿Es constitucional la expulsión penal del extranjero?, in *Los derechos humanos. Libro homenaje al Excmo.Sr.D.Luis Portero García*, Granada, pp.509-518.

Muñoz Lorente, J. (2004), 'La expulsión del extranjero como medida sustitutiva de las penas privativas de libertad: el artículo 89 del CP tras su reforma por la Ley Orgánica 11/2003', *Revista de Derecho Penal y Criminología*, extra 2, pp.401-482.

Ríos Martín, J. (2001), *Manual de Ejecución Penitenciaria. Defenderse en la cárcel*, 2nd. ed, Madrid.

Rodríguez Yagüe, C.(2004), 'Los derechos de los extranjeros en las prisiones españolas: legalidad y realidad', *Revista General de Derecho Penal Iustel* (http://www.iustel.com) 2 November (II.2.2)

Sánchez Tarifa, J.A. & Stangeland, P. (1997), 'La situación de los extranjeros en cárceles españolas', *Boletín Criminológico*, 25 January, p.1 ff.

Silveira Gorski, H.C. (2002), 'Los Centros de Internamiento de Extranjeros y el futuro del Estado de Derecho', *Mientras Tanto*, 83, pp. 93-102.

Varona Martínez, G. (1994), 'Extranjería y prisión. ¿Igualdad material en un sistema penitenciario intercultural?', *Eguzkilore*, 8, pp.63-87.

Varona Martínez, G. (1994), *La inmigración irregular. Derechos y deberes humanos*, Vitoria-Gasteiz.

24.2 Websites

Andalucía Acoge
http://www.acoge.org

Asociación Málaga Acoge
http://www.malaga.acoge.org/

Caritas Española
http://www.caritas.es/

Caritas Salamanca
http://caritas.caritasalamanca.org/58.0.html

Cruz Roja Española
http://www.cruzroja.es

Dirección General de Instituciones Penitenciarias. Ministerio del Interior. España
http://www.mir.es/instpeni/centros/penitenciarios.htm

Fundación Padre Garralda Horizontes Abiertos
http://www.horizontesabiertos.org/

Fundación Ramón Rubial Españoles en el Mundo
http://www.espamundo.org/

Grupo Europeo de Presos en el Extranjero (EGPA)
http://www.egpa.org/spanish/main.html

Ministerio de Asuntos Exteriores. España
http://www.mae.es/es/MenuPpal/Consulares/Servicios+Consulares/Españoles+en+el
+extranjero/Asistencia+a+detenidos/

Chapter 25 Sweden

25.1 Literature

In addition to the listed bibliography, the information in this report has been gathered as follows. Interviews were conducted with prison and remand prison staff at three prisons and one remand prison, all holding foreign prisoners. Discussions were also held with representatives of the Ministry of Foreign Affairs, the Justice Ombudsman's Office, the Migration Board, the central Prison and Probation Administration, three university departments and two non-governmental organisations working with foreign prisoners. In-depth interviews were conducted with three diplomatic missions. Three prisoners with expulsion orders in Hall and Kumla Prisons were interviewed and cursory discussions have been held with an additional number of foreign prisoners. Senior management staff and basic grade staff from Kumla, Hall and Mariefred Prisons have been interviewed, a-long with senior management staff from the Stockholm Remand Prison (Kronoberg) and basic grade coordinators at Migration Board detention centres.

Höök et. al. Law for everyday purposes (2005) (Juridik till Vardags) Wahlström & Widstrand, Sweden

M. Lindholm and N. Bishop, ed. A.van Kalmthout and T.M.J. Derks, *Sweden 2000*. Probation and Probation Services, Wolf Legal Publishers, Nijmegen, The Netherlands.

Swedish Prison and Probation Administration publications:

Absconding from leave by long-sentence prisoners (2000) *Långtidsdömdas utevistelser, 1999 års permissionsutredning Analys och Förslag*

Report 11: Prison, Probation and Ethnicity (2005) *Kriminalvård och etnicitet*

Report 13: Berserkers, a report on prison riots (2005) *Bärsärkarna, En kvalitativ beskrivning och analys av upplevelser från intagna och personal vid incidenter av upploppskaraktär under 2004*

Prison and Probation Services in Sweden 2005 *Kriminalvård i Sverige 2005*

Prisoners, Prisons and Society (Fångarna, Fängelset och Samhället, en jämförelse mellan 1992 och 2002 samt en diskussion om kriminalvårdens framtida inriktning), Gustavsson, J and Kling, B (2004)

Prison staff on Foreigners, an explorative study (1996) *Anstaltspersonal om Utlänningar, en explorativ intervjustudie*

Prison and Probation Statistics 2004 *Kriminalvård och Statistik, 2004*

Prison and Probation Budget (2006 and 2007) *Budgetunderlag.*

Training Manual for staff (2003) *Kursplan, KRUT*

Young Men in Prison and Remand Prisons (2001) *Unga Män i Anstalt och Häkte Slutrapport februari 2001*
Wikrén, G. and Sandesjö, H. (2002), Aliens Act (Utlänningslagen), Norstedts Juridik AB, Stockholm

25.2 legislation

The Aliens Act (Utlänningslagen)
The Law on the Obligation to Transmit Information on Detained Foreigners (Lagen 1989:152 om underrättelseskyldighet)
The Law on Arrested and Remanded Persons (Lag 1976:371 om Behandling av häktade och anhållna) with relevant ordinances
Prison Treatment Act (Lag 1974:203 om Kriminalvård i Anstalt) with relevant ordinances
Swedish Code of Judicial Procedure (Rättegångsbalken)
Swedish Penal Code (Brottsbalken)
Administrative Law (Lag 1986:223 om förvaltningsmyndigheternas handläggning av ärenden – Förvaltningslagen)

25.3 Websites

Swedish Prison and Probation Administration (D*etailed information on prison and probation work*)   http://www.kvv.se/
Swedish government, http://www.sweden.gov.se/sb/d/3083

Court Administration, http://www.dom.se/
Police Administration, http://www.polisen.se/
Bureau of Statistics, www.scb.se
EUROSTAT, http://epp.eurostat.cec.eu.int
Migration Board, http://www.migrationsverket.se/
The Dublin Regulation,
http://europa.eu.int/eur,lex/lex/LexUriServ/LexUriServ.do?uri=CELEX:32003R034
3:EN:NOT)Criminals Return in Society (KRIS), http://www.kris.a.se/

National Association of Voluntary Supervisors (RFS), http://www.rfs.a.se/

Red Cross (Röda korset),http://www.redcross.se/

Bridges to Abroad (Utlandsbryggan), http://www.utlandsbryggan.se

Chapter 26 United Kingdom

26.1 Literature

Abernethy R. & Hammond N. (Middlesex Probation Service) 'Working with Offenders from Abroad: Probation Practice Issues' 1999

Abernethy R. & Hammond N. (Middlesex Probation Service) ' Foreign National Drug Couriers; a role for the Probation Service' 1992

Amnesty International; Cell Culture, The Detention & Imprisonment of Asylum Seekers in the UK. Richard Dunston. London 1996

Association of Chief Officers of Probation, Foreign Prisoners in British Penal Institutions. London: ACPO, 1990

Ball, Lucy and Griffin, Sally Refugee, Asylum Seekers and Foreign National Offenders: Research & Development Project. London: London Offender Employment Network, 2000.

Bhui, Hindpal Singh Developing Effective Policy & Practice with Foreign National Prisoners. Prison Reform Trust & The Butler Trust, 2004.

Bhui, Hindpal Singh 'The Resettlement Needs of Foreign National Offenders" in Criminal Justice Matters 56, 2004 , pp 36-37 and p.44.

Bhui, Hindpal Singh 'Foreign National Prisoner Survey', in Probation Journal 45, 1995 (2)

Cheney, Deborah 'Into The Dark Tunnel: Foreign Prisoners in the British Prison System. London: Prison Reform Trust. 1993

Ellis, Rachel Asylum Seekers and Immigration Act Prisoners – The Practice of Detention. London: Prison Reform Trust. 1998

European Co-ordinated Resettlement Unit Foreign National Prisoners Information Handbook and Good Practise Guide. Kent Probation. (ECRU now disbanded), 2000

Green, Penny Drug Couriers,. London: Howard League of Penal Reform, 1991

Green, Penny Drugs, Trafficking and Criminal Policy –the Scapegoat Policy. Winchester: Waterside Press, 1998

Hammond, Nick The Value of Pre-Sentence Reports on Foreign Nationals. Cropwood Fellowship, Institute of Criminology, University of Cambridge. Published Middlesex Probation Service, 1994

Hales L. 'Refugees and Criminal Justice', Cropwood Occassional Paper No 21 Institute of Criminology, University of Cambridge, 1996.

Harper, Rosalyn and Murphy, Rachel Drug Smuggling: an analysis of the Traffickers 1991-1997. London 1999. Middlesex Probation Service

HM Chief Inspector of Prisons Report of an Announced Short Inspection of HM Holding Centre Haslar. London 1995: Home Office

HM Chief Inspector of Prisons Report of an Unannounced Inspection of HMP Wandsworth. London 1999: Home Office

HM Chief Inspector of Prisons (2003d) Report of an Unannounced Inspection of HMP Wandsworth. London: Home Office

HM Chief Inspector of Prisons Report of an Unannounced Follow-up Inspection of HM Prison The Weare. London 2001: Home Office

HM Chief Inspector of Prisons (2002a) Report of an Unannounced Follop-up Inspection of HMP Birmingham. London: Home Office

HM Chief Inspector of Prisons (2002b) Report of an Unannounced Follow-up Inspection of HMP Blakenhurst. London: Home Office

HM Chief Inspector of Prisons (2003a) Report of an Unannounced Follow-up Inspection of HMP Kingston. London: Home Office

Leech, M. Ed. The Prisons Handbook 2006. 2.18 Foreign National Prisoners, Jeanne Steele.

Paton, J. and Jenkins, R. (eds) Mental Health Primary Care in Prison. London. Royal Society of Medicine, 2002

Prison Reform Trust/Prison Service Foreign Prisoners Resource Pack, 1994.

Prison Reform Trust Forgotten Prisoners – The Plight of Foreign National Prisoners in England & Wales 2004.

Pourgourides C.K., Sashidharan S.P., Braken P.J. 'A Second Exile: The Mental Health Implications of Detention of Asylum Seekers in the UK. The Barlow Cadbury Trust. The University of Birmingham 1996

Richards, M., McWilliams, B., Batten, N., Cameron, C. and Cutler, J. 'Foreign Nationals in English Prisons: 1. Family Ties and Their Maintenance', in Howard Journal 34 (2), 1995 pp. 158-175.

Tarzi A. & Hedge J. 'A Prison Within a Prison- A Study of Foreign National Prisoners'. London 1990: Inner London Probation Service.

Tarzi A. & Hedge J. 'A Prison Within a Prison- Two Years On: An Overview. London 1993: Inner London Probation Service

26.3 Websites

www.homeoffice.gov.uk/rds/index.html
Gives details of Home Office Statistical Bulletins, Statistical Findings, Research Studies, Occasional papers and research Findings, most of which can be viewed on-line.

www.homeoffice.gov.rds/noms.html
RDS NOMS leads of statistics, analysis and research for the national Offender Management Service (NOMS). It provides statistical information on sentencing and offender management caseloads. It has responsibility for producing projections of offender management caseloads. It has responsibility for producing projections of correctional service caseloads and analysis of criminal histories and reconvictions.

www.homeoffice.gov.uk/rds/omcs.html
Information on prison and offender management caseloads statistics.

www.cjsni.gov.uk
Provides access to the main statutory agencies and organisations that make up the CJS together with details of publications

www.scotland.gov.uk
Gives information on all aspects of the Scottish executive together with details of publications and statistics

www.wales.gov.uk
Gives information on all aspects of the Welsh Assembly together with details of publications and statistics

www.hmprisonservice.gov.uk

Gives information about news releases and updates, publications and links to UK government and parliamentary sites, international organisations and prison services around the world.

Chapter 27 Aire Centre

No information available

Chapter 28 Conférence Permanente Européenne de la probation (CEP)

No information available

Chapter 29 Foreign Liaison Office of the Dutch Probation Service

No information available

Chapter 30 International Centre for Prison Studies (ICPS)

No information available

Chapter 31 Jesuit Refugee Service Europe

31.1 Literature

Jesuit Refugee Service (JRS) – Europe, *Detention in Europe: Administrative detention of asylum seekers and irregular migrants*, 17 October 2005

A. Papadopoulou, 'Exploring the asylum-migration nexus: a case study of transit migrants in Europe, *Global migration perspectives*, January 2005, no. 23.

31.3 Websites

EU Commission
- http://europa.eu.int/comm/index_en.htm
- http://europa.eu.int/prelex/apcnet.cfm?CL=en

EU Council
- http://europa.eu.int/scadplus/scad_en.htm
- http://register.consilium.eu.int/

EU Parliament
- http://www.europarl.eu.int/news/public/default_en.htm?redirection
- http://www.europarl.eu.int/parliament/public/staticDisplay.do;jsessionid=81A730084F62E228C46431079E723ABC.node2?language=EN&id=151

- http://www.europarl.eu.int/activities/expert/committees/presentation.do?committee=1248&language=EN
- http://www.europarl.eu.int/members/public/geoSearch/view.do?country=DE&partNumber=1&language=EN&id=28241

Council of Europe
- http://www.coe.int/
- http://www.cpt.coe.int/en/
Other
- Amnesty International: http://www.amnesty.org/
- Caritas Europa: http://www.caritas-europa.org/code/en/hp.asp
- International Organisation for Migration: http://www.iom.int/
- Jesuit Refugee Service (JRS) – Europe: http://www.jrseurope.org/
- Médecins Sans Frontières: http://www.msf.org/
- United Nations: http://www.un.org/
- United Nations Commissioner for Refugees: http://www.unhcr.org/

Administrative detention in Europe
http://www.detention-in-europe.org/

APPENDIX II

Editorial Committee

Anton van Kalmthout

Professor Anton van Kalmthout was born in 1945 in the Hague, the Netherlands. After his studies Latin, Greek and Law he obtained a Doctoral degree at Tilburg University in 2001. Since then he is a full professor Restriction of Freedom and Deprivation of Freedom in Criminal Law and Immigration Law at Tilburg University. He is an editor for several journals and periodicals and has a large number of publications in his name. He has played an active role in several organizations such as the Dutch Probation and Legal Aid agencies and is a member of the Board of the Foundation for Legal Aid Asylum in the Netherlands. In 2005 he was nominated as Dutch representative of the Committee against Torture and Inhuman and Degrading Treatment of the Council of Europe.

Femke Hofstee–van der Meulen

Femke Hofstee-van der Meulen has a degree in History and Post-Graduate International Law from Leiden University and worked in various European organizations like the Council of Europe, the European Commission and the European Parliament. From 2000 until 2002 she worked in London as researcher for Baroness Vivien Stern, Member of the House of Lords, at the International Centre for Prison Studies. In 2003 she set up Prison Watch an independent advisory organization on prison issues. Since August 2005 she is European Director of Altus, a global alliance working across continents and from a multicultural perspective to improve public safety and justice.

Frieder Dünkel

Professor Dr. Frieder Dünkel, born in 1950 in Karlsruhe (Germany) studied law at the universities of Heidelberg and Freiburg. His Ph.D. in 1979 dealt with an empirical research on the effectiveness of therapeutic treatment in prisons. From 1979 until 1992 he worked as a researcher at the Max-Plank-Institute of Foreign and International Penal Law, Criminological Unit, in Freiburg. Since 1992 he teaches criminology, penology, juvenile justice, criminal procedure and criminal law at the University of Greifswald in the north-east of Germany. Since 1989 he is co-editor of the Journal "Neue Kriminalpolitik" and since 2003 co-editor of the "European Journal of Criminology".

Authors and Contributors

Rui Abrunhosa Goncalves
University of Minho
Institut of Education and Psychology
4700 Braga
Portugal
e-mail: rabrunhosa@iep.uminho.pt

Maria Akritidou
Clinical Psychologist
Aristotle University of Thessaloniki
Greece
e-mail: akrita2000@yahoo.de

Paola Balbo
Tribunal of Sourveillance Turin
Via San Lorenzo, 36
10053 Bussoleno (To)
Italy
e-mail: paola-bl@libero.it

Stefan Braum
Luxembourg University
Faculté du Droit, d'Economie et de Finance
162 a, Avenue de la Faïencerie
1511 Luxembourg
Luxembourg
e-mail: stefan.braum@uni.lu

Cornelia Bührle
Jesuit Refugee Service (JRS) – Europe
Rue de Progrès 333
1030 Bruxelles
Belgium
e-mail: cornelia.buehrle@jrs.net

Tonio Cachia
DF Advocates
15, Gerry Zammit Str.
Msida, Malta
e-mail: tonio.cachia@dfadvocates.com

Andrew Coyle
International Centre for Prison Studies (ICPS)
3rd Floor, 26-29 Drury Lane
London WC2B5RL
United Kingdom
e-mail: Andrew.coyle@kcl.ac.uk

Pascal Décarpes
Greifswald University
Department of Criminology
Domstrasse 20
17487 Greifswald
Germany
e-mail: pdecarpes@yahoo.fr

José Luis De la Cuesta
University of the Basque Country
Basque Institute for Criminology
Villa Soroa. Alegerrieta 22
10.013 San Sebastian
Spain
e-mail: joseluis.delacuesta@ehu.es

Frieder Dünkel
Greifswald University
Department of Criminology
Domstrasse 20
17487 Greifswald
Germany
e-mail: duenkel@uni-greifswald.de

Andreas Ellinas
Prison Department
Nicosia
A Giov Paylou 123
2362 Nicosia
Cyprus
e-mail: a.ellinas@yahoo.com

Nick Hammond
London Probation
71-72 Great Peter Street
London SW 1P 2BN
United Kingdom
e-mail: nick.hammond@london.probation.gsi.gov.uk

Veronika Hofinger
Institut für Rechts- und Kriminalsoziologie
Museumstrasse 5/12
1070 Vienna
Austria
e-mail: veronika.hofinger@irks.at

Femke Hofstee-van der Meulen
Prison Watch
Schippersgracht 6a
3603 BC Maarssen
Netherlands
e-mail: femke@prisonwatch.org

Agneta Johnson
Swedish National Prison and Probation System
Prison of Hall
PO Box 631
Södertälje
Sweden
e-mail: Agneta.Johnson@kvv.se

András Kádár
Hungarian Helsinki Committee
Baljcsy-Zsilinszky u. 36-38 – 1/12
1054 Budapest
Hungary
e-mail: andras.kadar@helsinki.hu

Anton van Kalmthout
Tilburg University
Department of Criminal Law
PO Box 90153
5000 LE Tilburg
Netherlands
e-mail: A.M.vKalmthout@uvt.nl

Piret Kasemets
Prison Service
Tõnismägi 5A
15191 Tallinn
Estonia
e-mail: piret.kasemets@just.ee

Tapio Lappi-Seppälä
National Research Institute of Legal Policy
PO Box 444
00531 Helsinki
Finland
e-mail: Tapio.lappi-seppala@om.fi

Sonata Malisauskaite - Simanaitiene
Law Institute
Gedimino pr. 39/Ankstoji g. 1
LT-01109 Vilnius
Lithuania
e-mail: ssimanaitiene@gmail.com

Nuala Mole
Aire Centre
17 Red Lion Square
London WC 7 WC1R 4QH
United Kingdom
e-mail: info@airecentre.org

Mark Montebello
Mid-Dlam Ghad-Dawl
Daritama
Matty Grima Str.
Cospicua, Malta
e-mail: montebellio@gmail.com

Mary Moore
The Probation Service
Mountjoy Prison
North Circular Road
Dublin 7
Ireland
e-mail: MMMoore@probation.ie

Stephen Nash
Prisoners Abroad
83-93 Fonthill Road
London N4 3JH
United Kingdom
e-mail: Stephen@prisonersabroad.org.uk

Dragan Petrovec
University of Ljubljana
Faculty of Law
Institute of Criminology
Poljanski Nasip 2
1000 Ljubljana
Slovenia
e-mail: dragan.petrovec@pf.uni-lj.si

Arno Pilgram
Institut für Rechts- und Kriminalsoziologie
Museumstrasse 5/12
1070 Vienna
Austria
e-mail: arno.pilgram@univie.ac.at

Martin Skamla
Lawyer
Makovického 15
01001 Žilina
Slovakia
e-mail: skamla@gmail.com

Petr Škvain
University of West Bohemia in Plzen (Pilsen)
Faculty of Law
Department of Criminal Law
Sady Petatricatniku 14
306 14 Plzen (Pilsen)
The Czech Republic
e-mail: pskvain@ktr.zcu.cz

Sonja Snacken
Vrije Universiteit Brussel
Pleinlaan 2
1050 Brussels
Belgium
e-mail:ssnacken@vub.ac.be

Barbara Stando Kawecka
Jagiellonian University of Krakow Ul. Olszewskiego 2
Law Faculty
Ul. Olszewskiego 2
31 - 007 Krakow
Poland
e-mail: kawecka@cicero.law.uj.edu.pl

Anett Storgard
Aarhus University
University park
Building 1340 Faculty of Law
8000 Aarhus
Denmark
e-mail: AS@jura.au.dk

Rolf Streng
Foreign Office Dutch Probation Service
Vivaldiplantsoen 100-200
3533 JE Utrecht
Netherlands
e-mail: r.streng@srn.minjus.nl

Raymond Swennenhuis
Foreign Office Dutch Probation Service
Vivaldiplantsoen 100-200
3533 JE Utrecht
Netherlands
e-mail: r.swennenhuis@srn.minjus.nl

Leo Tigges
Conférence Permanente Européenne de la probation (CEP)
Vivaldiplantsoen 100-200
3533 JE Utrecht
Netherlands
e-mail: l.tigges@srn.minjus.nl

Balázs Tóth
Hungarian Helsinki committee
Bajcsy-Zsilinszky u. 36-38 – 1/12
1054 Budapest
Hungary
e-mail: balazs.toth@helsinki.hu

Liene Zeibote
State Probation Service
Dzirnavu Str. 91
Riga
Latvia
e-mail: liene.zeibote@vpdp.gov.lv

13W14543/ T3/ 9789058509758